Choices, Values, and Frames

D1191754

This book presents a selection of the research that grew from the editors' early collaboration on "Prospect Theory," the landmark article that offered the first compelling alternative to the standard "rational agent" model of choice under risk. In the spirit of the highly influential volume *Judgment Under Uncertainty*, first published in 1982, this book collects numerous theoretical and empirical articles that have become classics, important extensions, and applications that range from principles of legal compensation to the behavior of New York cab drivers on busy days. Several surveys prepared especially for this volume illustrate the scope and vigor of the behavioral study of choice.

Theoretically elegant and empirically robust, the research collected in this volume represents an approach to the science of decision making that has influenced numerous fields of study, including decision theory, behavioral economics and behavioral finance, consumer psychology, the study of negotiation and conflict, medical decision making, legal analysis and practice, well-being studies, political science, and philosophical investigations of rationality and ethics. The book provides an accessible introduction to the study of decision-making behavior and is an indispensable reference source for students and specialists.

Daniel Kahneman and the late Amos Tversky have started a new perspective on the traditional economic categories of choice, decision, and value. A series of experimental and empirical studies by them and others have rejected traditional assumptions of rationality. Even more importantly, these scholars have developed alternative generalizations with significant predictive power and have found empirical verification for them. This outstanding collection of studies will make these new results readily accessible.

> Kenneth J. Arrow, Nobel Memorial Laureate in Economic Science,
> Stanford University

Daniel Kahneman is Eugene Higgins Professor of Psychology and Professor of Public Affairs at the Woodrow Wilson School of Public Affairs, Princeton University.

The late Amos Tversky (1937–1996) was Davis–Brack Professor of Behavioral Science at Stanford University.

CHOICES, VALUES, AND FRAMES

Edited by
DANIEL KAHNEMAN
Princeton University

AMOS TVERSKY
Stanford University

Russell Sage Foundation

CAMBRIDGE UNIVERSITY PRESS
Cambridge, New York, Melbourne, Madrid, Cape Town, Singapore, São Paulo

Cambridge University Press
40 West 20th Street, New York, NY 10011–4211, USA
www.cambridge.org
Information on this title:www.cambridge.org/9780521621724

First published 2000
Reprinted 2002, 2003, 2004, 2005

Printed in the United States of America

A catalogue record for this book is available from the British Library.

Library of Congress Cataloguing in Publication Data
Choices, values, and frames / edited by Daniel Kahneman, Amos Tversky.
p.   cm.
ISBN 0-521-62172-0 — ISBN 0-521-62749-4 (pbk.)
1. Decision making.   2. Uncertainty.   3. Risk-taking (Psychology).   4. Value.   I.
Kahneman, Daniel, 1934—   . II. Tversky, Amos.
HD30.23. C469   2000
658.4'03 — dc21   99-059883

ISBN-13 978-0-521-62172-4 hardback
ISBN-10 0-521-62172-0 hardback

ISBN-13 978-0521-62749-8 paperback
ISBN-10 0-521-62749-4 paperback

Contents

Preface

This preface is not the one that Amos Tversky and I intended to write. Soon after Amos learned early in 1996 that he only had a few months to live, we decided to edit a joint book on decision making that would collect much of our work on this topic and congenial research by others. The collection was to be a sequel and companion to a volume on heuristics and biases of judgment that we had edited together with Paul Slovic many years earlier, and a substitute for a book that Amos and I had promised the Russell Sage Foundation.

Most of the editorial task was completed quickly, although some new pieces that Amos wanted to include – notably one that I was to write – were only completed long after he was gone. The problem of writing a preface was more difficult than finding articles we liked. Our initial aspirations for the preface were high; we were going to write a broad essay presenting a view of how the field had changed in the preceding 20 years. But we ran out of time before we had a presentable product. Amos advised me to "trust the model of me that is in your mind" and write for both of us. This was not advice that I was able to follow: the risk of writing in his name statements that he might have rejected proved intimidating to the point of paralysis. I chose to take the smaller risk of writing on my own and in a more personal vein than we would have adopted if we had written jointly. My intent is to provide a perspective on some dominant themes of this book by tracing them to the years that we spent working closely together on the problem of choice.

Amos and I began to collaborate in the study of decision making in 1974, soon after completing a review of our earlier work on judgment, which appeared in *Science* that year. Because I had no expertise in the formal study of choice, in which he was already a star, Amos encouraged me to read the text on mathematical psychology that he had coauthored with his teacher Clyde Coombs and his contemporary Robyn Dawes. The most relevant chapter was concerned with preferences between gambles; it included an introduction to utility theory and an exposition of the Allais paradox. Our discussions of this chapter quickly focused on a remarkable discrepancy: the theoretical analysis implied that the carriers of utility were states of wealth, but the outcomes of gambles were always described as gains and losses. Some extra assumption was clearly required to bridge the gap – either a spontaneous mental activity that transforms gains and losses into states of wealth, or a highly constrained correspondence between the psychophysics of wealth and the psychophysics of gains and losses. Neither hypothesis seemed appealing. This observation eventually led us to develop a theory of choice under risk that we called prospect theory (Chapter 2).

Our method of research in those early Jerusalem days was pure fun. We would meet every afternoon for several hours, which we spent inventing interesting pairs of gambles and observing our own intuitive preferences. If we agreed on the same choice, we provisionally assumed that it was characteristic of humankind and went on to investigate its theoretical implications, leaving serious verification for later. This unusual mode of empirical research enabled us to move quickly. In a few giddy months we raced through more than twenty diverse theoretical formulations. Among others, we considered a treatment of risky choice in terms of regret, but we eventually abandoned this approach because it did not elegantly accommodate the pattern of results that we labeled 'reflection': changing the signs of all outcomes in a gamble almost invariably changed the direction of preferences from risk averse to risk seeking or vice versa.

Prospect theory was nearly complete in the spring of 1975; it was then called value theory. A reader familiar with the final version would find almost all the important ideas in that early draft. However, the three additional years that we spent fine-tuning the theory turned out to be essential to its viability. The idea of editing operations, for example, was our answer to many potential counterexamples; it took three years to get to it. Amos was capable of infinite patience. His frequently repeated exhortation "let's get it right" and the contagious pleasure that he found in the activity of thinking enabled us to persevere in the task of anticipating possible objections – even minor ones – long enough to ensure that they had been resolved, not papered over.

The theory that we constructed was as conservative as possible. We stayed within the decision theoretic framework in which choice between gambles is the model for all decisions. We did not challenge the philosophical analysis of choices in terms of beliefs and desires that underlies utility theory, nor did we question the normative models of rational choice offered by von Neumann and Morgenstern and later by Savage. The goal we set for ourselves was to assemble the minimal set of modifications of expected utility theory that would provide a descriptive account of everything we knew about a severely restricted class of decisions: choices between simple monetary gambles with objectively specified probabilities and at most two nonzero outcomes. Without additional assumptions, prospect theory is not applicable to gambles that have a larger number of outcomes, to gambles on events, or to transactions other than choice; it does not even specify a selling price for monetary gambles. And our hopeful statement that "the extension of equations (1) and (2) to prospects with any number of outcomes is straightforward" (p. 74) turned out to be very optimistic. We got to it some thirteen years later (see Chapter 3), and the extension was not at all straightforward.

It is fair to ask, What is the point of investing so much effort in a theory if its domain of application is so restricted and artificial? The answer is that choice between gambles is the fruit fly of decision theory. It is a very simple case, which contains many essential elements of much larger problems. As with the fruit fly, we study gambles in the hope that the principles that govern the simple case will extend in recognizable form to complex situations. A theory of choice should therefore be evaluated by two distinct criteria, and a successful theory must satisfy both. One requirement is to "get it right" within a precisely specified domain. The theory should be refutable in that domain, and it should be unrefuted. The larger prize, however, lies elsewhere. The principles of the theory should provide a heuristic benefit in the analysis of more complex decisions, by suggesting hypotheses and by providing templates and labels for the identification of phenomena. For example, although it is surely futile to "test" prospect theory against utility theory in the domain of international relations, the concepts of loss aversion and pseudocertainty are useful tools for understanding strategic decisions. No warranty is implied, of course. The scholars who use the tools to explain more complex decisions do so at their own risk.

Many chapters in the present collection explore one or another of four themes that emerged from our attempt to construct a viable theory of our chosen domain. When we published prospect theory we had a clear view of only the first two of these ideas: the nonlinearity of decision weights and the reference-dependent characteristics of the value function. The third theme, the significance of framing effects, was present in rudimentary form in that article and was articulated soon afterward. The fourth idea, the need to distinguish experienced utility from decision utility, came up early in our conversations but was only developed much later.

NONLINEAR DECISION WEIGHTS

The expectation principle of utility theory requires a linear response to variations of probability. As a descriptive generalization, this idea is transparently wrong: intuition suggests, and experiments readily confirm, that raising the probability of an outcome from .39 to .40 has much less impact on preferences than increasing the probability of the same outcome from 0 to .01 or from .99 to 1.00. This observation, which Ward Edwards and others had made before us, was incorporated in the decision weight function of prospect theory. Several chapters of this book document the progress that was subsequently achieved in the understanding of decision weights. These include the rank-dependent formulation that generalizes prospect theory to gambles with any number of outcomes (Chapter 3), Dražen Prelec's novel analysis of the shape of decision weights (Chapter 4), and an important extension to the case of gambles on events, which sheds light on both the Ellsberg and the Allais paradoxes (Chapter 5). I believe that in his last year Amos was close to achieving a major generalization of prospect theory in a unified treatment of risk and uncertainty

(Chapter 6). With characteristic restraint, however, he rejected the suggestion to label this work "extended prospect theory." Chapter 6 also illustrates an important observation that Amos and his students had analyzed in the context of support theory: the large influence of the "packing" or "unpacking" of events on subjective probabilities, and through them, on decision weights. To maintain unity of style Amos chose not to include in the present collection the results of the mathematical explorations of prospect theory to which he devoted a significant effort in the 1990s in a fruitful collaboration with Peter Wakker.

REFERENCE-DEPENDENCE AND LOSS AVERSION

Standard applications of utility theory assume that the outcomes of risky prospects are evaluated as states of wealth. This assumption was the cornerstone of the version of utility theory that Daniel Bernoulli offered in 1738, and it has been retained ever since. The proposition that the carriers of utility are states of wealth is accepted as a matter of course in economic analyses and in the prescriptions of decision analysts. However, casual observation suggests that this assumption must also be modified. In the vernacular of decision making, financial outcomes are almost always described as gains and losses; states of wealth are rarely mentioned unless death or ruin is a possibility. The argument appears to have been closed by Matthew Rabin's demonstration that no utility function for wealth can accommodate the extreme risk aversion that people exhibit when they face gambles with small stakes (Chapter 11).

The isolation effect described in prospect theory was intended as a direct experimental test of the hypothesis that preferences for gambles are determined by the utility of wealth. Respondents were asked to imagine that they had been given an unconditional gift of cash and that they now faced a choice between a sure outcome and a fair gamble. There were two versions of the problem with different combinations of the size of the gift and of the possible outcomes of the choice. The options described in the two versions were strictly identical in terms of possible states of final wealth and their probabilities, but one of the choices was between a sure gain and a positive gamble; the other was between a sure loss and a negative gamble. As expected from the reflection effect, most respondents were risk averse in the first version, and most were risk seeking in the second – much as they would have been if the initial cash gift had not been mentioned at all. This demonstration simultaneously provided a counterexample to the idea that the carriers of utility are states of wealth and positive evidence for the role of gains and losses. It was also the first application of the method that we used later to study framing effects.

The idea that the effective carriers of utility are gains and losses was not new. Markowitz had proposed it much earlier. The distinctive contribution of prospect theory was the S-shaped value function that is reproduced in many articles in this collection. The convex–concave shape contributed to the explanation of the reflection effect, which we then considered our most remarkable experimental result. The value function is also much steeper in the domain of losses than in the domain of gains, a characteristic that we later labeled loss aversion. The assumption of loss aversion helped explain two salient facts of risky choice: the almost universal rejection of gambles that offer equal probabilities to win and lose the same amount, and the increase of this aversion with the size of the stakes. We introduced loss aversion reluctantly. As we well knew, it is hardly elegant for a theory of choice to invoke different explanations of risk aversion for positive prospects and for prospects in which losses are possible, but we found no simpler model that would account for the facts. We realized only much later that loss aversion is the element of prospect theory that has the richest implications beyond its narrow domain.

We had considerable help from a friend in appreciating the broader significance of loss aversion. While we were still working on the final version of prospect theory, a young economist named Richard Thaler sought us out. Dick had begun a career of ironic and deep comments on his discipline while still a graduate student, collecting amusing anecdotal examples of everyday behaviors of consumers that violated basic assumptions of standard economic theory. He realized (Chapter 15) that many of these anomalies could be explained by extending the idea of loss aversion to riskless decisions. The most important application was to the endowment effect, which Thaler illustrated by the memorable example of a bottle of old wine which the owner would refuse to sell for $200 but would not pay as much as $100 to replace. This pattern is odd in the context of standard economic theory in which an individual's buying price and selling price for a good are assumed to differ only because of transaction costs and an income effect. In contrast, the endowment effect is readily explained by two assumptions derived from prospect theory. First, the carriers of utility are not states (owning or not owning the wine), but changes: getting the wine or giving it up. And giving up is weighted more than getting, by loss aversion.

The idea that "losses loom larger than gains" is a major theme of this collection. Loss aversion is invoked to explain phenomena as diverse as indifference curves that cross (Chapter 9), principles of legal compensation (Chapter 24), rules of commercial fairness (Chapter 18), the equity premium puzzle in financial markets (Chapter 17), and the number of hours that New York cab drivers choose to work on busy days (Chapter 20), among many others. There is no reason to suspect that the topic is exhausted. The ramifications of the hypothesis that preferences are reference dependent and loss averse are yet to be fully explored.

FRAMING EFFECTS AND MENTAL ACCOUNTING

Another theme of this collection is the dependence of choices on the description and interpretation of decision problems. Amos and I turned to the study of framing immediately after the completion of prospect theory. Most of our evidence was at hand in 1979 and was first published in 1981. Later essays (Chapters 1 and 3) revisited the same results, reflecting our evolving understanding of their significance as a challenge to the general model of rational choice.

A significant and perhaps unfortunate early decision concerned the naming of the new concept. For reasons of conceptual and terminological economy we chose to apply the label "frame" to descriptions of decision problems at two levels: the formulation to which decision makers are exposed is called a frame and so is the interpretation that they construct for themselves. Thus, framing is a common label for two very different things: an experimental manipulation and a constituent activity of decision making. Our terminological parsimony was helpful in securing the acceptance of the concept of framing, but it also had its costs. The use of a single term blurred the important distinction between what decision makers do and what is done to them: the activities of editing and mental accounting on the one hand and the susceptibility to framing effects on the other.

Prospect theory includes a set of rules of editing for simple gambles. We assumed a preliminary phase of decision making in which specified editing operations transform the problem – usually into a simpler form. The initial motivation for introducing editing operations was defensive: they eliminated some foolish predictions to which prospect theory seemed otherwise committed. For example, the properties of decision weights would imply a preference for the prospect ($100, .01; $100, .01) over ($100, .02). The prediction is wrong because most decision makers will spontaneously edit the former prospect into the latter and treat them as equivalent in subsequent operations of evaluation and choice. Editing operations provided an explicit and psychologically plausible defense against such superficial counterexamples to the core of the theory. Although we did not immediately see it, the conception of editing also led to the more general observation that the true objects of evaluation and choice are neither objects in the real world nor verbal descriptions; they are mental representations. This conceptual move was novel in the context of decision research, but it is entirely natural for cognitive psychologists. Anyone who has taken a course in perception has learned to distinguish objective reality from the proximal stimulus to which the observer is exposed and to distinguish both reality and the stimulus from the mental representation that the observer eventually constructs.

Richard Thaler's early ideas about mental accounting (Chapter 15), which we adopted and elaborated (Chapter 1) offered an informal treatment of how people organize decisions and outcomes by lumping some together and segregating others, in ways that often violate standard assumptions of economic theory. Much of what is known about the psychology of active framing is discussed by Thaler in Chapter 14. A particularly significant feature of the accounting metaphor is that mental accounts are eventually closed and that strong emotions may be experienced at those times of reckoning. An implication of this insight is that people can to some extent control their own rewards and punishments by choosing whether to close an account or keep it open as well as deciding when to evaluate it. Variations on this powerful theme help explain why sunk costs are not ignored (Chapters 14 and 15), why cab drivers stop work too early on busy days (Chapter 20), why investors are more likely to sell "winners" than "losers" when they lighten their portfolio of stocks (Chapter 21), and why financial returns are much higher on stocks than on bonds (Chapter 17).

As is evident in Chapter 1, we were initially more interested in framing effects than in the activity of framing. We were surprised by how easy it was to construct different versions of a decision problem that were transparently equivalent when considered together but evoked different preferences when considered separately. Framing effects are inherently interesting, but the psychological analysis of these effects is awkward because the object of explanation is something that decision makers do *not* do: they do not spontaneously generate a common representation for decision problems that they would judge to be equivalent. Why is this so? The unexciting answer is that decision makers are generally quite passive and therefore inclined to accept any frame to which they are exposed. Framing effects are less significant for their contribution to psychology than for their importance in the real world (a recurrent theme in this book, e.g., in Chapters 13, 16, 19, and 25) and for the challenge they raise to the foundations of a rational model of decision making (Chapter 12).

The isolation effect was our first application of a method in which alternative versions of "the same" decision problem evoked different preferences. We constructed a pair of problems that were identical in the context of a particular interpretation of utility theory and suggested that the observation of different preferences was a counterexample to that theory. However, we eventually adopted a less theory-bound view of what makes two problems the same. It is the decision maker who should determine, after due consideration of both problems, whether the differences between them are sufficiently consequential to justify different choices. Violations of this lenient form of invariance demonstrate incoherence without a need for any judgment from on high about what is truly equivalent. The ubiquity of framing effects demonstrates that the human mind is not designed to achieve coherence. It took us several years to realize that violations of invariance challenge the excessively demanding conception of rationality that prevails in economics and in other sciences of decision (Chapter 12). Violations of invariance provide a compelling reason to separate descriptive from normative models of choice. It is surely rational to treat identical problems identically, but often people do not.

This was as far as Amos and I went together, but over the next decade we each explored aspects of these issues further with various other collaborators. Amos remained fascinated by the idea that the objects of evaluation are descriptions, not their referents. The notion that the carriers of subjective probability are descriptions of events was used to powerful effect in support theory, the model of probabilistic judgment on which he was still working at the end of his life (see Chapter 6). More directly, Amos expanded the concept of violations of invariance from framing effects to diverse types of preference reversals (Chapter 28). In various collaborations with close friends and colleagues, notably Paul Slovic, Eldar Shafir, Itamar Simonson, and Shmuel Sattath (Chapters 28, 29, and 34), he explored other situations in which people's preferences are influenced by variables that they would wish to ignore. My own interest in the area was in framing as an activity, and especially in the notable proclivity of decision makers to frame problems of judgment and choice more narrowly than they should (Chapter 22).

The chapters collected here only provide a glimpse at the evidence for the extreme sensitivity of choices to formulation, context, and procedure. A growing body of findings supports a radical challenge to the assumption, central to much economic theory, that stable preferences exist. The image of a decision maker who makes choices by consulting a preexisting preference order appears increasingly implausible. The alternative image is of a decision maker who chooses reluctantly and with difficulty (Chapter 34) and who constructs preferences in the context and in the format required by a particular situation (Chapters 27–29). Of course, no one wishes to pursue the idea of context dependence to the point of nihilism. Choices are not nearly as coherent as the notion of a preference order would suggest, but they are also far from random. Some explanation of their limited coherence is therefore required. Perhaps people are better described as having attitudes than as having preferences (Chapters 35 and 36).

EXPERIENCED UTILITY

Sometime in the early years of our work on the shape of the value function of prospect theory, I posed to Amos two puzzles that still fascinate me. Consider an individual who faces a course of daily injections that he expects to remain equally painful from day to day. The first injection is due tomorrow. Will the individual be willing to pay the same amount today to eliminate the last injection in a series of 20 daily injections or in a series of 5 injections? And what if a decision must be made today about a series of 5 injections that starts in 15 days? Our intuitive answers to these questions were both definite and clearly unreasonable. They were also widely shared, as we eventually learned from research by Herrnstein, Thaler, Loewenstein, and Prelec. Most people, of course, will pay more to reduce the length of a series of injections from 5 to 4 than they will pay, *ex ante*, to reduce it from 20 to 19. They will also show different patterns of declining willingness to pay to reduce a series of injections that begin tomorrow or in fifteen days. Some investigators, represented here by Loewenstein and Prelec (Chapters 32 and 33), have focused their attention on the remarkable contrast between observed time preferences and the standard economic analyses of discounting. The question that intrigued us was different: What is the justification of *any* departure from linearity in the patient's valuation of injections if the patient believes that the injections will be equally painful from day to day? More generally, what is the normative standing of sharply curved utility functions and of steep discount functions in such cases?

The injection story contains the seeds of several ideas that were only taken up much later and are yet to be fully developed. First, it assumed the possibility of eliciting the "predicted utility" of consequences independently of their "decision utility" by obtaining, in this case, the patient's beliefs about the pain of injections. The task of predicting future tastes and the relation between predicted utility and decision utility are investigated in two chapters in this collection (Chapters 40 and 41). Second, the direct measurement of the patient's pain, his or her "experienced utility," is a potential criterion for evaluating decisions. By this substantive criterion, the standard assumption that people maximize utility is not tautological but false (Chapter 42). Third, considerations of the utility of outcomes as they will actually be experienced highlights an important deficiency in the standard decision-theoretic definition of rationality. The coherence view is not only unreasonably demanding, as was noted in the earlier discussion of framing. When an objective observer considers the consequences actually experienced, the coherence criterion also appears much too permissive. The rule that any utility function is acceptable if only it is applied consistently allows too many foolish decisions to be considered rational. The chapters in the last section of the book indicate some of the progress that has been made in pursuing these ideas.

The concluding section of Chapter 1 briefly mentions the distinction between decision utility and experienced utility and hints that the latter should be the criterion for the former. Amos and I never worked together on this topic, though we often discussed it. Our views sometimes differed, especially when the discussion touched on the role of memory in life, which Amos considered more important than I did – perhaps because his memory was so much better than mine. In his chapter with Dale Griffin (Chapter 39), Amos described life as the gradual accumulation of an endowment of memories, which is not at all the view I take (Chapter 37). One of my enduring regrets is that we never resolved the difference by studying it together. We would have come closer to "doing it right," and it would have been a joy.

Daniel Kahneman
Princeton
August 1999

List of Contributors

Daniel Alder, Department of Social and Decision Sciences, Carnegie Mellon University

Linda Babcock, The Heinz School, Carnegie Mellon University

Ian Bateman, Centre for Social and Economic Research, Department of Environmental Sciences, University of East Anglia, UK

Shlomo Benartzi, John Anderson School of Management, Department of Accounting, University of California, Los Angeles

Colin F. Camerer, Division of Social Sciences, California Institute of Technology

David Cohen, Psychology Department, University of Texas, Austin

Peter Diamond, Department of Economics, Massachusetts Institute of Technology

Baruch Fischoff, Department of Social and Decision Sciences, Carnegie Mellon University

Craig R. Fox, Fuqua School of Business, Duke University

Dale Griffin, School of Cognitive and Computing Sciences, University of Sussex, Brighton, UK

John Hershey, Department of Operations and Information Management, The Wharton School, University of Pennsylvania

Christopher K. Hsee, Graduate School of Business, University of Chicago

Eric J. Johnson, School of Business, Columbia University

Daniel Kahneman, Woodrow Wilson School of Public Affairs and Department of Psychology, Princeton University

Jack L. Knetsch, Department of Economics and Resources Management, Simon Fraser University, Canada

Howard Kunreuther, Department of Operations and Information Management, The Wharton School, University of Pennsylvania

Dan Lovallo,   Australian Graduate School of Management, University of New South Wales, Australia

George Loewenstein,   Department of Social and Decision Sciences, Carnegie Mellon University

Jacqueline Meszaros,   Business Administration Program, University of Washington, Bothell

Alistair Munro,   Department of Economic and Social Studies, University of East Anglia, UK

Terrance Odean,   Graduate School of Management, University of California, Davis

Dražen Prelec,   The Sloan School and Department of Psychology, Massachusetts Institute of Technology

George A. Quattrone,   Department of Psychology, Stanford University

Matthew Rabin,   Department of Economics, University of California, Berkeley

Bruce Rhodes,   Department of Economic and Social Studies, University of East Anglia, UK

Ilana Ritov,   School of Education, Hebrew University, Israel

Shmuel Sattath,   Hebrew University, Israel

David Schkade,   Department of Management, University of Texas, Austin

Eldar Shafir,   Department of Psychology, Princeton University

Itamar Simonson,   Graduate School of Business, Stanford University

Chris Starmer,   School of Economic and Social Studies, University of East Anglia, UK

Robert Sugden,   Department of Economic and Social Studies, University of East Anglia, UK

Richard H. Thaler,   Graduate School of Business, University of Chicago

Amos Tversky (Deceased),   Department of Psychology, Stanford University

1. Choices, Values, and Frames

Daniel Kahneman and Amos Tversky

ABSTRACT. We discuss the cognitive and the psychophysical determinants of choice in risky and riskless contexts. The psychophysics of value induce risk aversion in the domain of gains and risk seeking in the domain of losses. The psychophysics of chance induce overweighting of sure things and of improbable events, relative to events of moderate probability. Decision problems can be described or framed in multiple ways that give rise to different preferences, contrary to the invariance criterion of rational choice. The process of mental accounting, in which people organize the outcomes of transactions, explains some anomalies of consumer behavior. In particular, the acceptability of an option can depend on whether a negative outcome is evaluated as a cost or as an uncompensated loss. The relation between decision values and experience values is discussed.

Making decisions is like speaking prose – people do it all the time, knowingly or unknowingly. It is hardly surprising, then, that the topic of decision making is shared by many disciplines, from mathematics and statistics, through economics and political science, to sociology and psychology. The study of decisions addresses both normative and descriptive questions. The normative analysis is concerned with the nature of rationality and the logic of decision making. The descriptive analysis, in contrast, is concerned with people's beliefs and preferences as they are, not as they should be. The tension between normative and descriptive considerations characterizes much of the study of judgment and choice.

Analyses of decision making commonly distinguish risky and riskless choices. The paradigmatic example of decision under risk is the acceptability of a gamble that yields monetary outcomes with specified probabilities. A typical riskless decision concerns the acceptability of a transaction in which a good or a service is exchanged for money or labor. In the first part of this article

This article was originally presented as a Distinguished Scientific Contributions Award address at the meeting of the American Psychological Association, Anaheim, California, August 1983. This work was supported by grant NR 197-058 from the U.S. Office of Naval Research.

we present an analysis of the cognitive and psychophysical factors that determine the value of risky prospects. In the second part we extend this analysis to transactions and trades.

RISKY CHOICE

Risky choices, such as whether or not to take an umbrella and whether or not to go to war, are made without advance knowledge of their consequences. Because the consequences of such actions depend on uncertain events such as the weather or the opponent's resolve, the choice of an act may be construed as the acceptance of a gamble that can yield various outcomes with different probabilities. It is therefore natural that the study of decision making under risk has focused on choices between simple gambles with monetary outcomes and specified probabilities in the hope that these simple problems will reveal basic attitudes toward risk and value.

We shall sketch an approach to risky choice that derives many of its hypotheses from a psychophysical analysis of responses to money and to probability. The psychophysical approach to decision making can be traced to a remarkable essay that Daniel Bernoulli published in 1738 (Bernoulli 1738/1954) in which he attempted to explain why people are generally averse to risk and why risk aversion decreases with increasing wealth. To illustrate risk aversion and Bernoulli's analysis, consider the choice between a prospect that offers an 85% chance to win $1000 (with a 15% chance to win nothing) and the alternative of receiving $800 for sure. A large majority of people prefer the sure thing over the gamble, although the gamble has higher (mathematical) expectation. The expectation of a monetary gamble is a weighted average, where each possible outcome is weighted by its probability of occurrence. The expectation of the gamble in this example is .85 × $1000 + .15 × $0 = $850, which exceeds the expectation of $800 associated with the sure thing. The preference for the sure gain is an instance of risk aversion. In general, a preference for a sure outcome over a gamble that has higher or equal expectation is called risk aversion, and the rejection of a sure thing in favor of a gamble of lower or equal expectation is called risk seeking.

Bernoulli suggested that people do not evaluate prospects by the expectation of their monetary outcomes, but rather by the expectation of the subjective value of these outcomes. The subjective value of a gamble is again a weighted average, but now it is the subjective value of each outcome that is weighted by its probability. To explain risk aversion within this framework, Bernoulli proposed that subjective value, or utility, is a concave function of money. In such a function, the difference between the utilities of $200 and $100, for example, is greater than the utility difference between $1,200 and $1,100. It follows from concavity that the subjective value attached to a gain of $800 is more than 80% of the value of a gain of $1,000. Consequently, the concavity of the utility function entails a risk averse preference for a sure gain of $800 over an 80% chance to win $1,000, although the two prospects have the same monetary expectation.

It is customary in decision analysis to describe the outcomes of decisions in terms of total wealth. For example, an offer to bet $20 on the toss of a fair coin is represented as a choice between an individual's current wealth W and an even chance to move to W + $20 or to W − $20. This representation appears psychologically unrealistic: People do not normally think of relatively small outcomes in terms of states of wealth but rather in terms of gains, losses,

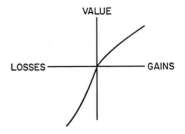

Figure 1.1. A hypothetical value function.

and neutral outcomes (such as the maintenance of the status quo). If the effective carriers of subjective value are changes of wealth rather than ultimate states of wealth, as we propose, the psychophysical analysis of outcomes should be applied to gains and losses rather than to total assets. This assumption plays a central role in a treatment of risky choice that we called prospect theory (Kahneman & Tversky, 1979). Introspection as well as psychophysical measurements suggest that subjective value is a concave function of the size of a gain. The same generalization applies to losses as well. The difference in subjective value between a loss of $200 and a loss of $100 appears greater than the difference in subjective value between a loss of $1,200 and a loss of $1,100. When the value functions for gains and for losses are pieced together, we obtain an S-shaped function of the type displayed in Figure 1.1.

The value function shown in Figure 1.1 is (a) defined on gains and losses rather than on total wealth, (b) concave in the domain of gains and convex in the domain of losses, and (c) considerably steeper for losses than for gains. The last property, which we label *loss aversion*, expresses the intuition that a loss of $X is more aversive than a gain of $X is attractive. Loss aversion explains people's reluctance to bet on a fair coin for equal stakes: The attractiveness of the possible gain is not nearly sufficient to compensate for the aversiveness of the possible loss. For example, most respondents in a sample of undergraduates refused to stake $10 on the toss of a coin if they stood to win less than $30.

The assumption of risk aversion has played a central role in economic theory. However, just as the concavity of the value of gains entails risk aversion, the convexity of the value of losses entails risk seeking. Indeed, risk seeking in losses is a robust effect, particularly when the probabilities of loss are substantial. Consider, for example, a situation in which an individual is forced to choose between an 85% chance to lose $1,000 (with a 15% chance to lose nothing) and a sure loss of $800. A large majority of people express a preference for the gamble over the sure loss. This is a risk seeking choice because the expectation of the gamble (−$850) is inferior to the expectation of the sure loss (−$800). Risk seeking in the domain of losses has been confirmed by several investigators (Fishburn & Kochenberger, 1979; Hershey & Schoemaker, 1980; Payne, Laughhunn, & Crum, 1980; Slovic, Fischhoff, & Lichtenstein, 1982).

It has also been observed with nonmonetary outcomes, such as hours of pain (Eraker & Sox, 1981) and loss of human lives (Fischhoff, 1983; Tversky, 1977; Tversky & Kahneman, 1981). Is it wrong to be risk averse in the domain of gains and risk seeking in the domain of losses? These preferences conform to compelling intuitions about the subjective value of gains and losses, and the presumption is that people should be entitled to their own values. However, we shall see that an S-shaped value function has implications that are normatively unacceptable.

To address the normative issue we turn from psychology to decision theory. Modern decision theory can be said to begin with the pioneering work of von Neumann and Morgenstern (1947), who laid down several qualitative principles, or axioms, that should govern the preferences of a rational decision maker. Their axioms included transitivity (if A is preferred to B and B is preferred to C, then A is preferred to C), and substitution (if A is preferred to B, then an even chance to get A or C is preferred to an even chance to get B or C), along with other conditions of a more technical nature. The normative and the descriptive status of the axioms of rational choice have been the subject of extensive discussions. In particular, there is convincing evidence that people do not always obey the substitution axiom, and considerable disagreement exists about the normative merit of this axiom (e.g., Allais & Hagen, 1979). However, all analyses of rational choice incorporate two principles: *dominance* and *invariance*. Dominance demands that if prospect A is at least as good as prospect B in every respect and better than B in at least one respect, then A should be preferred to B. Invariance requires that the preference order between prospects should not depend on the manner in which they are described. In particular, two versions of a choice problem that are recognized to be equivalent when shown together should elicit the same preference even when shown separately. We now show that the requirement of invariance, however elementary and innocuous it may seem, cannot generally be satisfied.

Framing of Outcomes

Risky prospects are characterized by their possible outcomes and by the probabilities of these outcomes. The same option, however, can be framed or described in different ways (Tversky & Kahneman, 1981). For example, the possible outcomes of a gamble can be framed either as gains and losses relative to the status quo or as asset positions that incorporate initial wealth. Invariance requires that such changes in the description of outcomes should not alter the preference order. The following pair of problems illustrates a violation of this requirement. The total number of respondents in each problem is denoted by N, and the percentage who chose each option is indicated in parentheses.

Problem 1 ($N = 152$): Imagine that the U.S. is preparing for the outbreak of an unusual Asian disease, which is expected to kill 600 people. Two alternative programs to combat the disease have been proposed. Assume that the exact scientific estimates of the consequences of the programs are as follows:

If Program A is adopted, 200 people will be saved. (72%)

If Program B is adopted, there is a one-third probability that 600 people will be saved and a two-thirds probability that no people will be saved. (28%)

Which of the two programs would you favor?

The formulation of Problem 1 implicitly adopts as a reference point a state of affairs in which the disease is allowed to take its toll of 600 lives. The outcomes of the programs include the reference state and two possible gains measured by the number of lives saved. As expected, preferences are risk averse: A clear majority of respondents prefer saving 200 lives for sure over a gamble that offers a one-third chance of saving 600 lives. Now consider another problem in which the same cover story is followed by a different description of the prospects associated with the two programs:

Problem 2 (N = 155): If Program C is adopted, 400 people will die. (22%)

If Program D is adopted, there is a one-third probability that nobody will die and a two-thirds probability that 600 people will die. (78%)

It is easy to verify that options C and D in Problem 2 are undistinguishable in real terms from options A and B in Problem 1, respectively. The second version, however, assumes a reference state in which no one dies of the disease. The best outcome is the maintenance of this state and the alternatives are losses measured by the number of people that will die of the disease. People who evaluate options in these terms are expected to show a risk seeking preference for the gamble (option D) over the sure loss of 400 lives. Indeed, there is more risk seeking in the second version of the problem than there is risk aversion in the first.

The failure of invariance is both pervasive and robust. It is as common among sophisticated respondents as among naive ones, and it is not eliminated even when the same respondents answer both questions within a few minutes. Respondents confronted with their conflicting answers are typically puzzled. Even after rereading the problems, they still wish to be risk averse in the "lives saved" version; they wish to be risk seeking in the "lives lost" version; and they also wish to obey invariance and give consistent answers in the two versions. In their stubborn appeal, framing effects resemble perceptual illusions more than computational errors.

The following pair of problems elicits preferences that violate the dominance requirement of rational choice.

Problem 3 (N = 86): Choose between:
   E. 25% chance to win $240 and 75% chance to lose $760   (0%)
   F. 25% chance to win $250 and 75% chance to lose $750   (100%)

It is easy to see that F dominates E. Indeed, all respondents chose accordingly.

Problem 4 ($N = 150$): Imagine that you face the following pair of concurrent decisions. First examine both decisions, then indicate the options you prefer.

Decision (i) Choose between:
    A. a sure gain of $240   (84%)
    B. 25% chance to gain $1000 and 75% chance to gain nothing   (16%)
Decision (ii) Choose between:
    C. a sure loss of $750   (13%)
    D. 75% chance to lose $1000 and 25% chance to lose nothing   (87%)

As expected from the previous analysis, a large majority of subjects made a risk averse choice for the sure gain over the positive gamble in the first decision, and an even larger majority of subjects made a risk seeking choice for the gamble over the sure loss in the second decision. In fact, 73% of the respondents chose A and D and only 3% chose B and C. The same pattern of results was observed in a modified version of the problem, with reduced stakes, in which undergraduates selected gambles that they would actually play.

Because the subjects considered the two decisions in Problem 4 simultaneously, they expressed in effect a preference for A and D over B and C. The preferred conjunction, however, is actually dominated by the rejected one. Adding the sure gain of $240 (option A) to option D yields 25% chance to win $240 and 75% to lose $760. This is precisely option E in Problem 3. Similarly, adding the sure loss of $750 (option C) to option B yields a 25% chance to win $250 and 75% chance to lose $750. This is precisely option F in Problem 3. Thus, the susceptibility to framing and the S-shaped value function produce a violation of dominance in a set of concurrent decisions.

The moral of these results is disturbing: Invariance is normatively essential, intuitively compelling, and psychologically unfeasible. Indeed, we conceive only two ways of guaranteeing invariance. The first is to adopt a procedure that will transform equivalent versions of any problem into the same canonical representation. This is the rationale for the standard admonition to students of business, that they should consider each decision problem in terms of total assets rather than in terms of gains or losses (Schlaifer, 1959). Such a representation would avoid the violations of invariance illustrated in the previous problems, but the advice is easier to give than to follow. Except in the context of possible ruin, it is more natural to consider financial outcomes as gains and losses rather than as states of wealth. Furthermore, a canonical representation of risky prospects requires a compounding of all outcomes of concurrent decisions (e.g., Problem 4) that exceeds the capabilities of intuitive computation even in simple problems. Achieving a canonical representation is even more difficult in other contexts such as safety, health, or quality of life. Should we advise people to evaluate the consequence of a public health policy (e.g., Problems 1 and 2) in terms of overall mortality, mortality due to diseases, or the number of deaths associated with the particular disease under study?

Another approach that could guarantee invariance is the evaluation of options in terms of their actuarial rather than their psychological consequences. The actuarial criterion has some appeal in the context of human lives, but it is clearly inadequate for financial choices, as has been generally recognized at least since Bernoulli, and it is entirely inapplicable to outcomes that lack an objective metric. We conclude that frame invariance cannot be expected to hold and that a sense of confidence in a particular choice does not ensure that the same choice would be made in another frame. It is therefore good practice to test the robustness of preferences by deliberate attempts to frame a decision problem in more than one way (Fischhoff, Slovic, & Lichtenstein, 1980).

The Psychophysics of Chances

Our discussion so far has assumed a Bernoullian expectation rule according to which the value, or utility, of an uncertain prospect is obtained by adding the utilities of the possible outcomes, each weighted by its probability. To examine this assumption, let us again consult psychophysical intuitions. Setting the value of the status quo at zero, imagine a cash gift, say of $300, and assign it a value of one. Now imagine that you are only given a ticket to a lottery that has a single prize of $300. How does the value of the ticket vary as a function of the probability of winning the prize? Barring utility for gambling, the value of such a prospect must vary between zero (when the chance of winning is nil) and one (when winning $300 is a certainty).

Intuition suggests that the value of the ticket is not a linear function of the probability of winning, as entailed by the expectation rule. In particular, an increase from 0% to 5% appears to have a larger effect than an increase from 30% to 35%, which also appears smaller than an increase from 95% to 100%. These considerations suggest a category-boundary effect: A change from impossibility to possibility or from possibility to certainty has a bigger impact than a comparable change in the middle of the scale. This hypothesis is incorporated into the curve displayed in Figure 1.2, which plots the weight attached to an event as a function of its stated numerical probability. The most salient feature of Figure 1.2 is that decision weights are regressive with respect to stated probabilities. Except near the endpoints, an increase of .05 in the probability of winning increases the value of the prospect by less than 5% of the value of the prize. We next investigate the implications of these psychophysical hypotheses for preferences among risky options.

In Figure 1.2, decision weights are lower than the corresponding probabilities over most of the range. Underweighting of moderate and high probabilities relative to

Figure 1.2. A hypothetical weighting function.

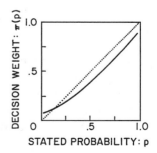

sure things contributes to risk aversion in gains by reducing the attractiveness of positive gambles. The same effect also contributes to risk seeking in losses by attenuating the aversiveness of negative gambles. Low probabilities, however, are overweighted, and very low probabilities are either overweighted quite grossly or neglected altogether, making the decision weights highly unstable in that region. The overweighting of low probabilities reverses the pattern described above: It enhances the value of long shots and amplifies the aversiveness of a small chance of a severe loss. Consequently, people are often risk seeking in dealing with improbable gains and risk averse in dealing with unlikely losses. Thus, the characteristics of decision weights contribute to the attractiveness of both lottery tickets and insurance policies.

The nonlinearity of decision weights inevitably leads to violations of invariance, as illustrated in the following pair of problems:

> **Problem 5 ($N = 85$):** Consider the following two-stage game. In the first stage, there is a 75% chance to end the game without winning anything and a 25% chance to move into the second stage. If you reach the second stage you have a choice between:
>> A. a sure win of $30   (74%)
>> B. 80% chance to win $45   (26%)
>
> Your choice must be made before the game starts, i.e., before the outcome of the first stage is known. Please indicate the option you prefer.

> **Problem 6 ($N = 81$):** Which of the following options do you prefer?
>> C. 25% chance to win $30   (42%)
>> D. 20% chance to win $45   (58%)

Because there is one chance in four to move into the second stage in Problem 5, prospect A offers a .25 probability of winning $30, and prospect B offers .25 × .80 = .20 probability of winning $45. Problems 5 and 6 are therefore identical in terms of probabilities and outcomes. However, the preferences are not the same in the two versions: A clear majority favors the higher chance to win the smaller amount in Problem 5, whereas the majority goes the other way in Problem 6. This violation of invariance has been confirmed with both real and hypothetical monetary payoffs (the present results are with real money), with human lives as outcomes, and with a nonsequential representation of the chance process.

We attribute the failure of invariance to the interaction of two factors: the framing of probabilities and the nonlinearity of decision weights. More specifically, we propose that in Problem 5 people ignore the first phase, which yields the same outcome regardless of the decision that is made, and focus their attention on what happens if they do reach the second stage of the game. In that case, of course, they face a sure gain if they choose option A and an 80% chance of winning if they prefer to gamble. Indeed, people's choices in the sequential version are practically identical to the choices they make between a sure gain of $30 and an 85% chance to win $45. Because a sure thing is overweighted in comparison with events of moderate or high probability (see Figure 1.2) the option that may lead to a gain of $30 is more attractive in the sequential version. We call this phenomenon the *pseudo-certainty* effect because an event that is actually uncertain is weighted as if it were certain.

A closely related phenomenon can be demonstrated at the low end of the probability range. Suppose you are undecided whether or not to purchase earthquake insurance because the premium is quite high. As you hesitate, your friendly insurance agent comes forth with an alternative offer: "For half the regular premium you can be fully covered if the quake occurs on an odd day of the month. This is a good deal because for half the price you are covered for more than half the days." Why do most people find such probabilistic insurance distinctly unattractive? Figure 1.2 suggests an answer. Starting anywhere in the region of low probabilities, the impact on the decision weight of a reduction of probability from p to $p/2$ is considerably smaller than the effect of a reduction from $p/2$ to 0. Reducing the risk by half, then, is not worth half the premium.

The aversion to probabilistic insurance is significant for three reasons. First, it undermines the classical explanation of insurance in terms of a concave utility function. According to expected utility theory, probabilistic insurance should be definitely preferred to normal insurance when the latter is just acceptable (see Kahneman & Tversky, 1979). Second, probabilistic insurance represents many forms of protective action, such as having a medical checkup, buying new tires, or installing a burglar alarm system. Such actions typically reduce the probability of some hazard without eliminating it altogether. Third, the acceptability of insurance can be manipulated by the framing of the contingencies. An insurance policy that covers fire but not flood, for example, could be evaluated either as full protection against a specific risk, (e.g., fire) or as a reduction in the overall probability of property loss. Figure 1.2 suggests that people greatly undervalue a reduction in the probability of a hazard in comparison to the complete elimination of that hazard. Hence, insurance should appear more attractive when it is framed as the elimination of risk than when it is described as a reduction of risk. Indeed, Slovic, Fischhoff, and Lichtenstein (1982) showed that a hypothetical vaccine that reduces the probability of contracting a disease from 20% to 10% is less attractive if it is described as effective in half of the cases than if it is presented as fully effective against one of two exclusive and equally probable virus strains that produce identical symptoms.

Formulation Effects

So far we have discussed framing as a tool to demonstrate failures of invariance. We now turn attention to the processes that control the framing of outcomes and events. The public health problem illustrates a formulation effect in which a change of wording from "lives saved" to "lives lost" induced a marked shift of preference from risk aversion to risk seeking. Evidently, the subjects adopted the descriptions of the outcomes as given in the question and evaluated the outcomes accordingly as gains or losses. Another formulation effect was reported by McNeil, Pauker, Sox, and Tversky (1982). They found that preferences of physicians and patients between hypothetical therapies for lung cancer varied markedly when their probable outcomes were described in terms of mortality or survival. Surgery, unlike radiation therapy, entails a risk of death during treatment. As a consequence, the surgery option was relatively less attractive when the statistics of treatment outcomes were described in terms of mortality rather than in terms of survival.

A physician, and perhaps a presidential advisor as well, could influence the decision made by the patient or by the President, without distorting or suppressing information, merely by the framing of outcomes and contingencies. Formulation effects can occur fortuitously, without anyone being aware of the impact of the frame on the ultimate decision. They can also be exploited deliberately to manipulate the relative attractiveness of options. For example, Thaler (1980) noted that lobbyists for the credit card industry insisted that any price difference between cash and credit purchases be labeled a cash discount rather than a credit card surcharge. The two labels frame the price difference as a gain or as a loss by implicitly designating either the lower or the higher price as normal. Because losses loom larger than gains, consumers are less likely to accept a surcharge than to forego a discount. As is to be expected, attempts to influence framing are common in the marketplace and in the political arena.

The evaluation of outcomes is susceptible to formulation effects because of the nonlinearity of the value function and the tendency of people to evaluate options in relation to the reference point that is suggested or implied by the statement of the problem. It is worthy of note that in other contexts people automatically transform equivalent messages into the same representation. Studies of language comprehension indicate that people quickly recode much of what they hear into an abstract representation that no longer distinguishes whether the idea was expressed in an active or in a passive form and no longer discriminates what was actually said from what was implied, presupposed, or implicated (Clark & Clark, 1977). Unfortunately, the mental machinery that performs these operations silently and effortlessly is not adequate to perform the task of recoding the two versions of the public health problem or the mortality-survival statistics into a common abstract form.

TRANSACTIONS AND TRADES

Our analysis of framing and of value can be extended to choices between multiattribute options, such as the acceptability of a transaction or a trade. We propose that, in order to evaluate a multiattribute option, a person sets up a mental account that specifies the advantages and the disadvantages associated with the option, relative to a multiattribute reference state. The overall value of an option is given by the balance of its advantages and its disadvantages in relation to the reference state. Thus, an option is acceptable if the value of its advantages exceeds the value of its disadvantages. This analysis assumes psychological – but not physical – separability of advantages and disadvantages. The model does not constrain the manner in which separate attributes are combined to form overall measures of advantage and of disadvantage, but it imposes on these measures assumptions of concavity and of loss aversion.

Our analysis of mental accounting owes a large debt to the stimulating work of Richard Thaler (1980, in press), who showed the relevance of this process to consumer behavior. The following problem, based on examples of Savage (1954) and Thaler (1980), introduces some of the rules that govern the construction of mental accounts and illustrates the extension of the concavity of value to the acceptability of transactions.

> **Problem 7:** Imagine that you are about to purchase a jacket for $125 and a calculator for $15. The calculator salesman informs you that the calculator you wish to buy is on sale for $10 at the other branch of the store, located 20 minutes drive away. Would you make a trip to the other store?

This problem is concerned with the acceptability of an option that combines a disadvantage of inconvenience with a financial advantage that can be framed as a *minimal, topical,* or *comprehensive* account. The minimal account includes only the differences between the two options and disregards the features that they share. In the minimal account, the advantage associated with driving to the other store is framed as a gain of $5. A topical account relates the consequences of possible choices to a reference level that is determined by the context within which the decision arises. In the preceding problem, the relevant topic is the purchase of the calculator, and the benefit of the trip is therefore framed as a reduction of the price, from $15 to $10. Because the potential savings is associated only with the calculator, the price of the jacket is not included in the topical account. The price of the jacket, as well as other expenses, could well be included in a more comprehensive account in which the saving would be evaluated in relation to, say, monthly expenses.

The formulation of the preceding problem appears neutral with respect to the adoption of a minimal, topical, or comprehensive account. We suggest, however, that people will spontaneously frame decisions in terms of topical accounts that, in the context of decision making, play a role analogous to that of "good forms" in perception and of basic-level categories in cognition. Topical organization, in conjunction with the concavity of value, entails that the willingness to travel to the other store for a saving of $5 on a calculator should be inversely related to the price of the calculator and should be independent of the price of the jacket. To test this prediction, we constructed another version of the problem in which the prices of the two items were interchanged. The price of the calculator was given as $125 in the first store and $120 in the other branch, and the price of the jacket was set at $15. As predicted, the proportions of respondents who said they would make the trip differed sharply in the two problems. The results showed that 68% of the respondents ($N = 88$) were willing to drive to the other branch to save $5 on a $15 calculator, but only 29% of 93 respondents were willing to make the same trip to save $5 on a $125 calculator. This finding supports the notion of topical organization of accounts, since the two versions are identical both in terms of a minimal and a comprehensive account.

The significance of topical accounts for consumer behavior is confirmed by the observation that the standard deviation of the prices that different stores in a city quote for the same product is roughly proportional to the average price of that product (Pratt, Wise, & Zeckhauser, 1979). Since the dispersion of prices is surely controlled by shoppers' efforts to find the best buy, these results suggest that consumers hardly exert more effort to save $15 on a $150 purchase than to save $5 on a $50 purchase.

The topical organization of mental accounts leads people to evaluate gains and losses in relative rather than in absolute terms, resulting in large variations in the rate at which money is exchanged for other things, such as the number of phone calls made to find a good buy or the willingness to drive a long distance to get one. Most consumers will find it easier to buy a car stereo system or a Persian rug, respectively, in the context of buying a car or a house than separately. These observations, of course, run counter to the standard rational theory of consumer behavior, which assumes invariance and does not recognize the effects of mental accounting.

The following problems illustrate another example of mental accounting in which the posting of a cost to an account is controlled by topical organization:

Problem 8 ($N = 200$): Imagine that you have decided to see a play and paid the admission price of $10 per ticket. As you enter the theater, you discover that you have lost the ticket. The seat was not marked, and the ticket cannot be recovered.

Would you pay $10 for another ticket?
      Yes (46%)   No (54%)

Problem 9 ($N = 183$): Imagine that you have decided to see a play where admission is $10 per ticket. As you enter the theater, you discover that you have lost a $10 bill.

Would you still pay $10 for a ticket for the play?
      Yes (88%)   No (12%)

The difference between the responses to the two problems is intriguing. Why are so many people unwilling to spend $10 after having lost a ticket, if they would readily spend that sum after losing an equivalent amount of cash? We attribute the difference to the topical organization of mental accounts. Going to the theater is normally viewed as a transaction in which the cost of the ticket is exchanged for the experience of seeing the play. Buying a second ticket increases the cost of seeing the play to a level that many respondents apparently find unacceptable. In contrast, the loss of the cash is not posted to the account of the play, and it affects the purchase of a ticket only by making the individual feel slightly less affluent.

An interesting effect was observed when the two versions of the problem were presented to the same subjects. The willingness to replace a lost ticket increased significantly when that problem followed the lost-cash version. In contrast, the willingness to buy a ticket after losing cash was not affected by prior presentation of the other problem. The juxtaposition of the two problems apparently enabled the subjects to realize that it makes sense to think of the lost ticket as lost cash, but not vice versa.

The normative status of the effects of mental accounting is questionable. Unlike earlier examples, such as the public health problem, in which the two versions differed only in form, it can be argued that the alternative versions of the calculator and ticket problems differ also in substance. In particular, it may be more pleasurable to save $5 on a $15 purchase than on a larger purchase, and it may be more annoying to pay twice for the same ticket than to lose $10 in cash. Regret, frustration, and self-satisfaction can also be affected by framing (Kahneman & Tversky, 1982). If such secondary consequences are considered legitimate, then the observed preferences do not violate the criterion of invariance and cannot readily be ruled out as inconsistent or erroneous. On the other hand, secondary consequences may change upon reflection. The satisfaction of saving $5 on a $15 item can be marred if the consumer discovers that she would not have exerted the same effort to save $10 on a $200 purchase. We do not wish to recommend that any two decision problems that have the same primary consequences should be resolved in the same way. We propose, however, that systematic examination of alternative framings offers a useful reflective device that can help decision makers assess the values that should be attached to the primary and secondary consequences of their choices.

Losses and Costs

Many decision problems take the form of a choice between retaining the status quo and accepting an alternative to it, which is advantageous in some respects and disadvantageous in others. The analysis of value that was applied earlier to unidimensional risky prospects can be extended to this case by assuming that the status quo defines the reference level for all attributes. The advantages of alternative options will then be evaluated as gains and their disadvantages as losses. Because losses loom larger than gains, the decision maker will be biased in favor of retaining the status quo.

Thaler (1980) coined the term "endowment effect" to describe the reluctance of people to part from assets that belong to their endowment. When it is more painful to give up an asset than it is pleasurable to obtain it, buying prices will be significantly lower than selling prices. That is, the highest price that an individual will pay to acquire an asset will be smaller than the minimal compensation that would induce the same individual to give up that asset, once acquired. Thaler discussed some examples of the endowment effect in the behavior of consumers and entrepreneurs. Several studies have reported substantial discrepancies between buying and selling prices in both hypothetical and real transactions (Gregory, 1983; Hammack & Brown, 1974; Knetsch & Sinden, in press). These results have been presented as challenges to standard economic theory, in which buying and selling prices coincide except for transaction costs and effects of wealth. We also observed reluctance to trade in a study of choices between hypothetical jobs that differed in weekly salary (S) and in the temperature (T) of the workplace. Our respondents were asked to imagine that they held a particular position (S_1, T_1) and were offered the option of moving to a different position (S_2, T_2), which was better in one respect and worse in another. We found that most subjects who were assigned to (S_1, T_1) did not wish to move to (S_2, T_2), and that most subjects who were assigned to the latter position did not wish to move to the former. Evidently, the same difference in pay or in working conditions looms larger as a disadvantage than as an advantage.

In general, loss aversion favors stability over change. Imagine two hedonically identical twins who find two alternative environments equally attractive. Imagine further that by force of circumstance the twins are separated and placed in the two environments. As soon as they adopt their new states as reference points and evaluate the advantages and disadvantages of each other's environments accordingly, the twins will no longer be indifferent between the two states, and both will prefer to stay where they happen to be. Thus, the instability of preferences produces a preference for stability. In addition to favoring stability over change, the combination of adaptation and loss aversion provides limited protection against regret and envy by reducing the attractiveness of foregone alternatives and of others' endowments.

Loss aversion and the consequent endowment effect are unlikely to play a significant role in routine economic exchanges. The owner of a store, for example, does not experience money paid to suppliers as losses and money received from customers as gains. Instead, the merchant adds costs and revenues over some period of time and only evaluates the balance. Matching debits and credits are effectively canceled prior to evaluation. Payments made by consumers are also not evaluated as losses but as alternative purchases. In accord with standard economic analysis, money is naturally viewed as a proxy for the goods and services that it could buy. This mode of evaluation is made explicit when an individual has in mind a particular alternative, such as "I can either buy a new camera or a new tent." In this analysis, a person will buy a camera if its subjective value exceeds the value of retaining the money it would cost.

There are cases in which a disadvantage can be framed either as a cost or as a loss. In particular, the purchase of insurance can also be framed as a choice between a sure loss and the risk of a greater loss. In such cases the cost–loss discrepancy can lead to failures of invariance. Consider, for example, the choice between a sure loss of $50 and a 25% chance to lose $200. Slovic, Fischhoff, and Lichtenstein (1982) reported that 80% of their subjects expressed a risk-seeking preference for the gamble over the sure loss. However, only 35% of subjects refused to pay $50 for insurance against a 25% risk of losing $200. Similar results were also reported by Schoemaker and Kunreuther (1979) and by Hershey and Schoemaker (1980). We suggest that the same amount of money that was framed as an uncompensated loss in the first problem was framed as the cost of protection in the second. The modal preference was reversed in the two problems because losses are more aversive than costs.

We have observed a similar effect in the positive domain, as illustrated by the following pair of problems:

Problem 10: Would you accept a gamble that offers a 10% chance to win $95 and a 90% chance to lose $5?

Problem 11: Would you pay $5 to participate in a lottery that offers a 10% chance to win $100 and a 90% chance to win nothing?

A total of 132 undergraduates answered the two questions, which were separated by a short filler problem. The order of the questions was reversed for half the respondents. Although it is easily confirmed that the two problems offer objectively identical options, 55 of the respondents expressed different preferences in the two versions. Among them, 42 rejected the gamble in Problem 10 but accepted the equivalent lottery in Problem 11. The effectiveness of this seemingly inconsequential manipulation illustrates both the cost-loss discrepancy and the power of framing. Thinking of the $5 as a payment makes the venture more acceptable than thinking of the same amount as a loss.

The preceding analysis implies that an individual's subjective state can be improved by framing negative outcomes as costs rather than as losses. The possibility of such psychological manipulations may explain a paradoxical form of behavior that could be labeled the *dead-loss effect*. Thaler (1980) discussed the example of a man who develops tennis elbow soon after paying the membership fee in a tennis club and continues to play in agony to avoid wasting his investment. Assuming that the individual would not play if he had not paid the membership fee, the question arises: How can playing in agony improve the individual's lot? Playing in pain, we suggest, maintains the evaluation of the membership fee as a cost. If the individual were to stop playing, he would be forced to recognize the fee as a dead loss, which may be more aversive than playing in pain.

CONCLUDING REMARKS

The concepts of utility and value are commonly used in two distinct senses: (a) *experience value*, the degree of pleasure or pain, satisfaction or anguish in the actual experience of an outcome; and (b) *decision value*, the contribution of an anticipated outcome to the overall attractiveness or aversiveness of an option in a choice. The distinction is rarely explicit in decision theory because it is tacitly assumed that decision values and experience values coincide. This assumption is part of the conception of an idealized decision maker who is able to predict future experiences with perfect accuracy and evaluate options accordingly. For ordinary decision makers, however, the correspondence of decision values between experience values is far from perfect (March, 1978). Some factors that affect experience are not easily anticipated, and some factors that affect decisions do not have a comparable impact on the experience of outcomes.

In contrast to the large amount of research on decision making, there has been relatively little systematic exploration of the psychophysics that relate hedonic experience to objective states. The most basic problem of hedonic psychophysics is the determination of the level of adaptation or aspiration that separates positive from negative outcomes. The hedonic reference point is largely determined by the objective status quo, but it is also affected by expectations and social comparisons. An objective improvement can be experienced as a loss, for example, when an employee receives a smaller raise than everyone else in the office. The experience of pleasure or pain associated with a change of state is also critically dependent on the dynamics of hedonic adaptation. Brickman & Campbell's (1971) concept of the hedonic treadmill suggests the radical hypothesis that rapid adaptation will cause the effects of any objective improvement to be short-lived. The complexity and subtlety of hedonic experience make it difficult for the decision maker to anticipate the actual experience that outcomes will produce. Many a person who ordered a meal when ravenously hungry has admitted to a big mistake when the fifth course arrived on the table. The common mismatch of decision values and experience values introduces an additional element of uncertainty in many decision problems.

The prevalence of framing effects and violations of invariance further complicates the relation between decision values and experience values. The framing of outcomes often induces decision values that have no counterpart in actual experience. For example, the framing of outcomes of therapies for lung cancer in terms of mortality or survival is unlikely to affect experience, although it can have a pronounced influence on choice. In other cases, however, the framing of decisions affects not only decision but experience as well. For example, the framing of an expenditure as an uncompensated loss or as the price of insurance can probably influence the experience of that outcome. In such cases, the evaluation of outcomes in the context of decisions not only anticipates experience but also molds it.

2. Prospect Theory
An Analysis of Decision under Risk

Daniel Kahneman and Amos Tversky

ABSTRACT. This paper presents a critique of expected utility theory as a descriptive model of decision making under risk and develops an alternative model, called prospect theory. Choices among risky prospects exhibit several pervasive effects that are inconsistent with the basic tenets of utility theory. In particular, people underweight outcomes that are merely probable in comparison with outcomes that are obtained with certainty. This tendency, called the certainty effect, contributes to risk aversion in choices involving sure gains and to risk seeking in choices involving sure losses. In addition, people generally discard components that are shared by all prospects under consideration. This tendency, called the isolation effect, leads to inconsistent preferences when the same choice is presented in different forms. An alternative theory of choice is developed, in which value is assigned to gains and losses rather than to final assets and in which probabilities are replaced by decision weights. The value function is normally concave for gains, commonly convex for losses, and is generally steeper for losses than for gains. Decision weights are generally lower than the corresponding probabilities, except in the range of low probabilities. Overweighting of low probabilities may contribute to the attractiveness of both insurance and gambling.

1. INTRODUCTION

Expected utility theory has dominated the analysis of decision making under risk. It has been generally accepted as a normative model of rational choice (Keeney & Raiffa, 1976), and widely applied as a descriptive model of economic behavior, e.g. (Friedman & Savage, 1948; Arrow, 1971). Thus, it is assumed that all reasonable people would wish to obey the axioms of the theory (von Neumann & Morgenstern, 1944; Savage, 1954), and that most people actually do, most of the time.

This work was supported in part by grants from the Harry F. Guggenheim Foundation and from the Advanced Research Projects Agency of the Department of Defense and was monitored by Office of Naval Research under Contract N00014-78-C-0100 (ARPA Order No. 3469) under Subcontract 78-072-0722 from Decisions and Designs, Inc. to Perceptronics, Inc. We also thank the Center for Advanced Study in the Behavioral Sciences at Stanford for its support.

The present paper describes several classes of choice problems in which preferences systematically violate the axioms of expected utility theory. In the light of these observations we argue that utility theory, as it is commonly interpreted and applied, is not an adequate descriptive model, and we propose an alternative account of choice under risk.

2. CRITIQUE

Decision making under risk can be viewed as a choice between prospects or gambles. A prospect $(x_1, p_1; \ldots; x_n, p_n)$ is a contract that yields outcome x_i with probability p_i, where $p_1 + p_2 + \cdots + p_n = 1$. To simplify notation, we omit null outcomes and use (x, p) to denote the prospect $(x, p; 0, 1 - p)$ that yields x with probability p and 0 with probability $1 - p$. The (riskless) prospect that yields x with certainty is denoted by (x). The present discussion is restricted to prospects with so-called objective or standard probabilities.

The application of expected utility theory to choices between prospects is based on the following three tenets.

(i) Expectation: $U(x_1, p_1; \ldots; x_n, p_n) = p_1 u(x) + \cdots + p_n u(x_n)$.

That is, the overall utility of a prospect, denoted by U, is the expected utility of its outcomes.

(ii) Asset Integration: $(x_1, p_1; \ldots; x_n, p_n)$ is acceptable at asset position w iff
$U(w + x_1, p_1; \ldots; w + x_n, p_n) > u(w)$.

That is, a prospect is acceptable if the utility resulting from integrating the prospect with one's assets exceeds the utility of those assets alone. Thus, the domain of the utility function is final states (which include one's asset position) rather than gains or losses.

Although the domain of the utility function is not limited to any particular class of consequences, most applications of the theory have been concerned with monetary outcomes. Furthermore, most economic applications introduce the following additional assumption.

(iii) Risk Aversion: u is concave ($u'' < 0$).

A person is risk averse if he prefers the certain prospect (x) to any risky prospect with expected value x. In expected utility theory, risk aversion is equivalent to the concavity of the utility function. The prevalence of risk aversion is perhaps the best known generalization regarding risky choices. It led the early decision theorists of the eighteenth century to propose that utility is a concave function of money, and this idea has been retained in modern treatments (Pratt, 1964; Arrow, 1971).

In the following sections we demonstrate several phenomena which violate these tenets of expected utility theory. The demonstrations are based on the responses of students and university faculty to hypothetical choice problems. The respondents were presented with problems of the type illustrated below.

Which of the following would you prefer?

A: *50% chance to win 1,000,*   B: *450 for sure.*
  50% chance to win nothing;

The outcomes refer to Israeli currency. To appreciate the significance of the amounts involved, note that the median net monthly income for a family is about 3,000 Israeli pounds. The respondents were asked to imagine that they were actually faced with the choice described in the problem, and to indicate the decision they would have made in such a case. The responses were anonymous, and the instructions specified that there was no 'correct' answer to such problems, and that the aim of the study was to find out how people choose among risky prospects. The problems were presented in questionnaire form, with at most a dozen problems per booklet. Several forms of each questionnaire were constructed so that subjects were exposed to the problems in different orders. In addition, two versions of each problem were used in which the left–right position of the prospects was reversed.

The problems described in this paper are selected illustrations of a series of effects. Every effect has been observed in several problems with different outcomes and probabilities. Some of the problems have also been presented to groups of students and faculty at the University of Stockholm and at the University of Michigan. The pattern of results was essentially identical to the results obtained from Israeli subjects.

The reliance on hypothetical choices raises obvious questions regarding the validity of the method and the generalizability of the results. We are keenly aware of these problems. However, all other methods that have been used to test utility theory also suffer from severe drawbacks. Real choices can be investigated either in the field, by naturalistic or statistical observations of economic behavior, or in the laboratory. Field studies can only provide for rather crude tests of qualitative predictions, because probabilities and utilities cannot be adequately measured in such contexts. Laboratory experiments have been designed to obtain precise measures of utility and probability from actual choices, but these experimental studies typically involve contrived gambles for small stakes, and a large number of repetitions of very similar problems. These features of laboratory gambling complicate the interpretation of the results and restrict their generality.

By default, the method of hypothetical choices emerges as the simplest procedure by which a large number of theoretical questions can be investigated. The use of the method relies on the assumption that people often know how they would behave in actual situations of choice, and on the further assumption that the subjects have no special reason to disguise their true preferences. If people are reasonably accurate in predicting their choices, the presence of common and systematic violations of expected utility theory in hypothetical problems provides presumptive evidence against that theory.

Certainty, Probability, and Possibility

In expected utility theory, the utilities of outcomes are weighted by their probabilities. The present section describes a series of choice problems in which people's preferences systematically violate this principle. We first show that people overweight outcomes that are considered certain, relative to outcomes which are merely probable – a phenomenon which we label the *certainty effect*.

The best known counter-example to expected utility theory which exploits the certainty effect was introduced by the French economist Maurice Allais in 1953. Allais' example has been discussed from both normative and descriptive standpoints by many authors (MacCrimmon and Larsson, forthcoming; Slovic & Tversky, 1974). The following pair of choice problems is a variation of Allais' example, which differs from the original in that it refers to moderate rather than to extremely large gains. The number of respondents who answered each problem is denoted by N, and the percentage who choose each option is given in brackets.

Problem 1: Choose between

A: 2,500 with probability	.33,	B: 2,400 with certainty.
2,400 with probability	.66,	
0 with probability	.01;	
$N = 72$ [18]		[82]*

Problem 2: Choose between

C: 2,500 with probability	.33,	D: 2,400 with probability	.34,
0 with probability	.67;	0 with probability	.66.
$N = 72$ [83]*		[17]	

The data show that 82 percent of the subjects chose B in Problem 1, and 83 percent of the subjects chose C in Problem 2. Each of these preferences is significant at the .01 level, as denoted by the asterisk. Moreover, the analysis of individual patterns of choice indicates that a majority of respondents (61 percent) made the modal choice in both problems. This pattern of preferences violates expected utility theory in the manner originally described by Allais. According to that theory, with $u(0) = 0$, the first preference implies

$$u(2,400) > .33u(2,500) + .66u(2,400)   \text{or}   .34u(2,400) > .33u(2,500)$$

while the second preference implies the reverse inequality. Note that Problem 2 is obtained from Problem 1 by eliminating a .66 chance of winning 2,400 from both prospects under consideration. Evidently, this change produces a greater reduction in desirability when it alters the character of the prospect from a sure gain to a probable one, than when both the original and the reduced prospects are uncertain.

A simpler demonstration of the same phenomenon, involving only two-outcome gambles is given below. This example is also based on Allais (1953).

Problem 3:

    A: (4,000, .80),   or   B: (3,000).
    $N = 95$ [20]   [80]*

Problem 4:

    C: (4,000, .20),   or   D: (3,000, .25).
    $N = 95$ [65]*   [35]

In this pair of problems as well as in all other problem-pairs in this section, over half the respondents violated expected utility theory. To show that the modal pattern of preferences in Problems 3 and 4 is not compatible with the theory, set $u(0) = 0$, and recall that the choice of B implies $u(3,000)/u(4,000) > 4/5$, whereas the choice of C implies the reverse inequality. Note that the prospect $C = (4,000, .20)$ can be expressed as $(A, .25)$, while the prospect $D = (3,000, .25)$ can be rewritten as $(B, .25)$. The substitution axiom of utility theory asserts that if B is preferred to A, then any (probability) mixture (B, p) must be preferred to the mixture (A, p). Our subjects did not obey this axiom. Apparently, reducing the probability of winning from 1.0 to .25 has a greater effect than the reduction from .8 to .2. The following pair of choice problems illustrates the certainty effect with non-monetary outcomes.

Problem 5:

    A: 50% chance to win a three-   B: A one-week tour of
        week tour of England,   England, with certainty.
        France, and Italy;
    $N = 72$ [22]   [78]*

Problem 6:

    C: 5% chance to win a three-   D: 10% chance to win a one-
        week tour of England,   week tour of England.
        France, and Italy;
    $N = 72$ [67]*   [33]

The certainty effect is not the only type of violation of the substitution axiom. Another situation in which this axiom fails is illustrated by the following problems.

Problem 7:

    A: (6,000, .45),   B: (3,000, .90).
    $N = 66$ [14]   [86]*

Problem 8:

C: (6,000, .001),   D: (3,000, .002).
N = 66   [73]*   [27]

Note that in Problem 7 the probabilities of winning are substantial (.90 and .45), and most people choose the prospect where winning is more probable. In Problem 8, there is a *possibility* of winning, although the probabilities of winning are minuscule (.002 and .001) in both prospects. In this situation where winning is possible but not probable, most people choose the prospect that offers the larger gain. Similar results have been reported by MacCrimmon and Larsson (forthcoming).

The above problems illustrate common attitudes toward risk or chance that cannot be captured by the expected utility model. The results suggest the following empirical generalization concerning the manner in which the substitution axiom is violated. If (y, pq) is equivalent to (x, p), then (y, pqr) is preferred to (x, pr), $0 < p, q, r < 1$. This property is incorporated into an alternative theory, developed in the second part of the paper.

The Reflection Effect

The previous section discussed preferences between positive prospects, i.e., prospects that involve no losses. What happens when the signs of the outcomes are reversed so that gains are replaced by losses? The left-hand column of Table 2.1 displays four of the choice problems that were discussed in the previous section, and the right-hand column displays choice problems in which the signs of the outcomes are reversed. We use $-x$ to denote the loss of x, and $>$ to denote the prevalent preference, i.e., the choice made by the majority of subjects.

In each of the four problems in Table 2.1 the preference between negative prospects is the mirror image of the preference between positive prospects. Thus, the reflection of prospects around 0 reverses the preference order. We label this pattern the *reflection effect*.

Let us turn now to the implications of these data. First, note that the reflection effect implies that risk aversion in the positive domain is accompanied by

Table 2.1. Preferences between Positive and Negative Prospects

Positive Prospects		Negative Prospects	
Problem 3: (4,000, .80)	< (3,000).	Problem 3′: (−4,000, .80)	> (−3,000).
N = 95 [20]	[80]*	N = 95 [92]*	[8]
Problem 4: (4,000, .20)	> (3,000, .25).	Problem 4′: (−4,000, .20)	< (−3,000, .25).
N = 95 [65]*	[35]	N = 95 [42]	[58]
Problem 7: (3,000, .90)	> (6,000, .45).	Problem 7′: (−3,000, .90)	< (−6,000, .45).
N = 66 [86]*	[14]	N = 66 [8]	[92]*
Problem 8: (3,000, .002)	< (6,000, .001).	Problem 8′: (−3,000, .002)	> (−6,000, .001).
N = 66 [27]	[73]*	N = 66 [70]*	[30]

risk seeking in the negative domain. In Problem 3', for example, the majority of subjects were willing to accept a risk of .80 to lose 4,000, in preference to a sure loss of 3,000, although the gamble has a lower expected value. The occurrence of risk seeking in choices between negative prospects was noted early by Markowitz (1952). Williams (1966) reported data where a translation of outcomes produces a dramatic shift from risk aversion to risk seeking. For example, his subjects were indifferent between (100, .65; −100, .35) and (0), indicating risk aversion. They were also indifferent between (−200, .80) and (−100), indicating risk seeking. A recent review by Fishburn and Kochenberger (1979) documents the prevalence of risk seeking in choices between negative prospects.

Second, recall that the preferences between the positive prospects in Table 2.1 are inconsistent with expected utility theory. The preferences between the corresponding negative prospects also violate the expectation principle in the same manner. For example, Problems 3' and 4', like Problems 3 and 4, demonstrate that outcomes which are obtained with certainty are overweighted relative to uncertain outcomes. In the positive domain, the certainty effect contributes to a risk averse preference for a sure gain over a larger gain that is merely probable. In the negative domain, the same effect leads to a risk-seeking preference for a loss that is merely probable over a smaller loss that is certain. The same psychological principle – the overweighting of certainty – favors risk aversion in the domain of gains and risk seeking in the domain of losses.

Third, the reflection effect eliminates aversion for uncertainty or variability as an explanation of the certainty effect. Consider, for example, the prevalent preferences for (3,000) over (4,000, .80) and for (4,000, .20) over (3,000, .25). To resolve this apparent inconsistency one could invoke the assumption that people prefer prospects that have high expected value and small variance (see, e.g., Allais (1953); Markowitz (1959); Tobin (1958)). Since (3,000) has no variance while (4,000, .80) has large variance, the former prospect could be chosen despite its lower expected value. When the prospects are reduced, however, the difference in variance between (3,000, .25) and (4,000, .20) may be insufficient to overcome the difference in expected value. Because (−3,000) has both higher expected value and lower variance than (−4,000, .80), this account entails that the sure loss should be preferred, contrary to the data. Thus, our data are incompatible with the notion that certainty is generally desirable. Rather, it appears that certainty increases the aversiveness of losses as well as the desirability of gains.

Probabilistic Insurance

The prevalence of the purchase of insurance against both large and small losses has been regarded by many as strong evidence for the concavity of the utility function for money. Why otherwise would people spend so much money to purchase insurance policies at a price that exceeds the expected actuarial cost? However, an examination of the relative attractiveness of various forms of insurance does not support the notion that the utility function for money is concave everywhere. For example, people often prefer insurance programs that offer limited coverage with low or zero deductible over comparable policies that offer higher maximal coverage with higher deductibles – contrary to risk aversion (see, e.g., Fuchs (1976)). Another type of insurance problem in which people's responses are inconsistent with the concavity hypothesis may be called probabilistic insurance. To illustrate this concept, consider the following problem, which was presented to 95 Stanford University students.

Problem 9: Suppose you consider the possibility of insuring some property against damage, e.g., fire or theft. After examining the risks and the premium you find that you have no clear preference between the options of purchasing insurance or leaving the property uninsured.

It is then called to your attention that the insurance company offers a new program called *probabilistic insurance*. In this program you pay half of the regular premium. In case of damage, there is a 50 percent chance that you pay the other half of the premium and the insurance company covers all the losses, and there is a 50 percent chance that you get back your insurance payment and suffer all the losses. For example, if an accident occurs on an odd day of the month, you pay the other half of the regular premium and your losses are covered, but if the accident occurs on an even day of the month, your insurance payment is refunded and your losses are not covered.

Recall that the premium for full coverage is such that you find this insurance barely worth its cost.

Under these circumstances, would you purchase probabilistic insurance:

	Yes,	No.
$N = 95$	[20]	[80]*

Although Problem 9 may appear contrived, it is worth noting that probabilistic insurance represents many forms of protective action where one pays a certain cost to reduce the probability of an undesirable event – without eliminating it altogether. The installation of a burglar alarm, the replacement of old tires, and the decision to stop smoking can all be viewed as probabilistic insurance.

The responses to Problem 9 and to several other variants of the same question indicate that probabilistic insurance is generally unattractive. Apparently, reducing the probability of a loss from p to $p/2$ is less valuable than reducing the probability of that loss from $p/2$ to 0.

In contrast to these data, expected utility theory (with a concave u) implies that probabilistic insurance is superior to regular insurance. That is, if at asset position w one is just willing to pay a premium y to insure against a probability p of losing x, then one should definitely be willing to pay a smaller premium ry to reduce the probability of losing x from p to $(1-r)p$, $0 < r < 1$. Formally, if one is indifferent between $(w - x, p; w, 1 - p)$ and $(w - y)$, then one should prefer probabilistic insurance $(w - x, (1 - r)p; w - y, rp; w - ry, 1 - p)$ over regular insurance $(w - y)$.

To prove this proposition, we show that

$$pu(w - x) + (1 - p)u(w) = u(w - y)$$

implies

$$(1 - r)pu(w - x) + rpu(w - y) + (1 - p)u(w - ry) > u(w - y).$$

Without loss of generality, we can set $u(w - x) = 0$ and $u(w) = 1$. Hence, $u(w - y) = 1 - p$, and we wish to show that

$$rp(1 - p) + (1 - p)u(w - ry) > 1 - p \quad \text{or} \quad u(w - ry) > 1 - rp$$

which holds if and only if u is concave.

This is a rather puzzling consequence of the risk aversion hypothesis of utility theory, because probabilistic insurance appears intuitively riskier than regular insurance, which entirely eliminates the element of risk. Evidently, the intuitive notion of risk is not adequately captured by the assumed concavity of the utility function for wealth.

The aversion for probabilistic insurance is particularly intriguing because all insurance is, in a sense, probabilistic. The most avid buyer of insurance remains vulnerable to many financial and other risks which his policies do not cover. There appears to be a significant difference between probabilistic insurance and what may be called contingent insurance, which provides the certainty of coverage for a specified type of risk. Compare, for example, probabilistic insurance against all forms of loss or damage to the contents of your home and contingent insurance that eliminates all risk of loss from theft, say, but does not cover other risks, e.g., fire. We conjecture that contingent insurance will be generally more attractive than probabilistic insurance when the probabilities of unprotected loss are equated. Thus, two prospects that are equivalent in probabilities and outcomes could have different values depending on their formulation. Several demonstrations of this general phenomenon are described in the next section.

The Isolation Effect

In order to simplify the choice between alternatives, people often disregard components that the alternatives share and focus on the components that distinguish them (Tversky (1972)). This approach to choice problems may produce inconsistent preferences, because a pair of prospects can be decomposed into common and distinctive components in more than one way, and different decompositions sometimes lead to different preferences. We refer to this phenomenon as the *isolation effect*.

Problem 10: Consider the following two-stage game. In the first stage, there is a probability of .75 to end the game without winning anything, and a probability

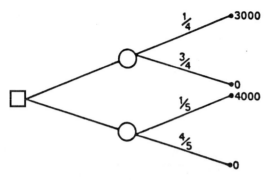

Figure 2.1. The representation of Problem 4 as a decision tree (standard formulation).

of .25 to move into the second stage. If you reach the second stage you have a choice between

(4,000, .80)   and   (3,000).

Your choice must be made before the game starts, i.e., before the outcome of the first stage is known.

Note that in this game, one has a choice between .25 × .80 = .20 chance to win 4,000, and a .2 × 1.0 = .25 chance to win 3,000. Thus, in terms of final outcomes and probabilities one faces a choice between (4,000, .20) and (3,000, .25), as in Problem 4 above. However, the dominant preferences are different in the two problems. Of 141 subjects who answered Problem 10, 78 percent chose the latter prospect, contrary to the modal preference in Problem 4. Evidently, people ignored the first stage of the game, whose outcomes are shared by both prospects, and considered Problem 10 as a choice between (3,000) and (4,000, .80), as in Problem 3 above.

The standard and the sequential formulations of Problem 4 are represented as decision trees in Figures 2.1 and 2.2, respectively. Following the usual convention, squares denote decision nodes and circles denote chance nodes. The essential difference between the two representations is in the location of the

Figure 2.2. The representation of Problem 10 as a decision tree (sequential formulation).

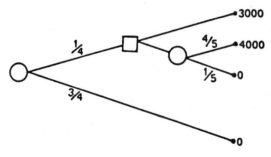

decision node. In the standard form (Figure 2.1), the decision maker faces a choice between two risky prospects, whereas in the sequential form (Figure 2.2) he faces a choice between a risky and a riskless prospect. This is accomplished by introducing a dependency between the prospects without changing either probabilities or outcomes. Specifically, the event 'not winning 3,000' is included in the event 'not winning 4,000' in the sequential formulation, while the two events are independent in the standard formulation. Thus, the outcome of winning 3,000 has a certainty advantage in the sequential formulation, which it does not have in the standard formulation.

The reversal of preferences due to the dependency among events is particularly significant because it violates the basic supposition of a decision-theoretical analysis, that choices between prospects are determined solely by the probabilities of final states.

It is easy to think of decision problems that are most naturally represented in one of the forms above rather than in the other. For example, the choice between two different risky ventures is likely to be viewed in the standard form. On the other hand, the following problem is most likely to be represented in the sequential form. One may invest money in a venture with some probability of losing one's capital if the venture fails, and with a choice between a fixed agreed return and a percentage of earnings if it succeeds. The isolation effect implies that the contingent certainty of the fixed return enhances the attractiveness of this option, relative to a risky venture with the same probabilities and outcomes.

The preceding problem illustrated how preferences may be altered by different representations of probabilities. We now show how choices may be altered by varying the representation of outcomes.

Consider the following problems, which were presented to two different groups of subjects.

Problem 11: In addition to whatever you own, you have been given 1,000. You are now asked to choose between

A: (1,000, .50),   and   B: (500).
N = 70   [16]   [84]*

Problem 12: In addition to whatever you own, you have been given 2,000. You are now asked to choose between

C: (−1,000, .50),   and   D: (−500).
N = 68   [69*]   [31]

The majority of subjects chose B in the first problem and C in the second. These preferences conform to the reflection effect observed in Table 2.1, which exhibits risk aversion for positive prospects and risk seeking for negative ones. Note, however, that when viewed in terms of final states, the two choice problems are identical. Specifically,

A = (2,000, .50; 1,000, .50) = C,   and   B = (1,500) = D.

In fact, Problem 12 is obtained from Problem 11 by adding 1,000 to the initial bonus, and subtracting 1,000 from all outcomes. Evidently, the subjects did not integrate the bonus with the prospects. The bonus did not enter into the comparison of prospects because it was common to both options in each problem.

The pattern of results observed in Problems 11 and 12 is clearly inconsistent with utility theory. In that theory, for example, the same utility is assigned to a wealth of $100,000, regardless of whether it was reached from a prior wealth of $95,000 or $105,000. Consequently, the choice between a total wealth of $100,000 and even chances to own $95,000 or $105,000 should be independent of whether one currently owns the smaller or the larger of these two amounts. With the added assumption of risk aversion, the theory entails that the certainty of owning $100,000 should always be preferred to the gamble. However, the responses to Problem 12 and to several of the previous questions suggest that this pattern will be obtained if the individual owns the smaller amount, but not if he owns the larger amount.

The apparent neglect of a bonus that was common to both options in Problems 11 and 12 implies that the carriers of value or utility are changes of wealth, rather than final asset positions that include current wealth. This conclusion is the cornerstone of an alternative theory of risky choice, which is described in the following sections.

3. THEORY

The preceding discussion reviewed several empirical effects which appear to invalidate expected utility theory as a descriptive model. The remainder of the paper presents an alternative account of individual decision making under risk, called prospect theory. The theory is developed for simple prospects with monetary outcomes and stated probabilities, but it can be extended to more involved choices. Prospect theory distinguishes two phases in the choice process: an early phase of editing and a subsequent phase of evaluation. The editing phase consists of a preliminary analysis of the offered prospects, which often yields a simpler representation of these prospects. In the second phase, the edited prospects are evaluated and the prospect of highest value is chosen. We next outline the editing phase and develop a formal model of the evaluation phase.

The function of the editing phase is to organize and reformulate the options so as to simplify subsequent evaluation and choice. Editing consists of the application of several operations that transform the outcomes and probabilities associated with the offered prospects. The major operations of the editing phase are described below.

> *Coding:* The evidence discussed in the previous section shows that people normally perceive outcomes as gains and losses, rather than as final states of wealth or welfare. Gains and losses, of course, are defined relative to some neutral reference point. The reference point usually corresponds to

the current asset position, in which case gains and losses coincide with the actual amounts that are received or paid. However, the location of the reference point, and the consequent coding of outcomes as gains or losses, can be affected by the formulation of the offered prospects and by the expectations of the decision maker.

Combination: Prospects can sometimes be simplified by combining the probabilities associated with identical outcomes. For example, the prospect (200, .25; 200, .25) will be reduced to (200, .50), and evaluated in this form.

Segregation: Some prospects contain a riskless component that is segregated from the risky component in the editing phase. For example, the prospect (300, .80; 200, .20) is naturally decomposed into a sure gain of 200 and the risky prospect (100, .80). Similarly, the prospect (−400, .40; −100, .60) is readily seen to consist of a sure loss of 100 and of the prospect (−300, .40).

The preceding operations are applied to each prospect separately. The following operation is applied to a set of two or more prospects.

Cancellation: The essence of the isolation effects described earlier is the discarding of components that are shared by the offered prospects. Thus, our respondents apparently ignored the first stage of the sequential game presented in Problem 10, because this stage was common to both options, and they evaluated the prospects with respect to the results of the second stage (see Figure 2.2). Similarly, they neglected the common bonus that was added to the prospects in Problems 11 and 12. Another type of cancellation involves the discarding of common constituents, i.e., outcome-probability pairs. For example, the choice between (200, .20; 100, .50; −50, .30) and (200, .20; 150, .50; −100, .30) can be reduced by cancellation to a choice between (100, .50; −50, .30) and (150, .50; −100, .30).

Two additional operations that should be mentioned are simplification and the detection of dominance. The first refers to the simplification of prospects by rounding probabilities or outcomes. For example, the prospect (101, .49) is likely to be recoded as an even chance to win 100. A particularly important form of simplification involves the discarding of extremely unlikely outcomes. The second operation involves the scanning of offered prospects to detect dominated alternatives, which are rejected without further evaluation.

Because the editing operations facilitate the task of decision, it is assumed that they are performed whenever possible. However, some editing operations either permit or prevent the application of others. For example, (500, .20; 101, .49) will appear to dominate (500, .15; 99, .51) if the second constituents of both prospects are simplified to (100, .50). The final edited prospects could, therefore, depend on the sequence of editing operations, which is likely to vary with the structure of the offered set and with the format of the display. A detailed study of this problem is beyond the scope of the present treatment. In this paper we discuss choice problems where it is reasonable to assume either that the original formulation of the prospects leaves no room for further editing, or that the edited prospects can be specified without ambiguity.

Many anomalies of preference result from the editing of prospects. For example, the inconsistencies associated with the isolation effect result from the cancellation of common components. Some intransitivities of choice are explained by a simplification that eliminates small differences between prospects (see Tversky (1969)). More generally, the preference order between prospects need not be invariant across contexts, because the same offered prospect could be edited in different ways depending on the context in which it appears.

Following the editing phase, the decision maker is assumed to evaluate each of the edited prospects, and to choose the prospect of highest value. The overall value of an edited prospect, denoted V, is expressed in terms of two scales, π and v.

The first scale, π, associates with each probability p a decision weight $\pi(p)$, which reflects the impact of p on the overall value of the prospect. However, π is not a probability measure, and it will be shown later that $\pi(p) + \pi(1 - p)$ is typically less than unity. The second scale, v, assigns to each outcome x a number $v(x)$, which reflects the subjective value of that outcome. Recall that outcomes are defined relative to a reference point, which serves as the zero point of the value scale. Hence, v measures the value of deviations from that reference point, i.e., gains and losses.

The present formulation is concerned with simple prospects of the form $(x, p; y, q)$, which have at most two non-zero outcomes. In such a prospect, one receives x with probability p, y with probability q, and nothing with probability $1 - p - q$, where $p + q \leq 1$. An offered prospect is strictly positive if its outcomes are all positive, i.e., if $x, y > 0$ and $p + q = 1$; it is strictly negative if its outcomes are all negative. A prospect is regular if it is neither strictly positive nor strictly negative.

The basic equation of the theory describes the manner in which π and v are combined to determine the overall value of regular prospects.

If $(x, p; y, q)$ is a regular prospect (i.e., either $p + q < 1$, or $x \geq 0 \geq y$, or $x \leq 0 \leq y$), then

$$V(x, p; y, q) = \pi(p)v(x) + \pi(q)v(y), \tag{1}$$

where $v(0) = 0$, $\pi(0) = 0$, and $\pi(1) = 1$. As in utility theory, V is defined on prospects, while v is defined on outcomes. The two scales coincide for sure prospects, where $V(x, 1.0) = V(x) = v(x)$.

Equation (1) generalizes expected utility theory by relaxing the expectation principle. An axiomatic analysis of this representation is sketched in the Appendix (not printed here), which describes conditions that ensure the existence of a unique π and a ratio-scale v satisfying equation (1).

The evaluation of strictly positive and strictly negative prospects follows a different rule. In the editing phase such prospects are segregated into two components: (i) the riskless component, i.e., the minimum gain or loss which is certain to be obtained or paid; (ii) the risky component, i.e., the additional gain or loss which is actually at stake. The evaluation of such prospects is described in the next equation.

If $p + q = 1$ and either $x > y > 0$ or $x < y < 0$, then

$$V(x, p; y, q) = v(y) + \pi(p)[v(x) - v(y)]. \tag{2}$$

That is, the value of a strictly positive or strictly negative prospect equals the value of the riskless component plus the value-difference between the outcomes, multiplied by the weight associated with the more extreme outcome. For example, $V(400, .25; 100, .75) = v(100) + \pi(.25)[v(400) - v(100)]$. The essential feature of equation (2) is that a decision weight is applied to the value-difference $v(x) - v(y)$, which represents the risky component of the prospect, but not to $v(y)$, which represents the riskless component. Note that the right-hand side of equation (2) equals $\pi(p)v(x) + [1 - \pi(p)]v(y)$. Hence, equation (2) reduces to equation (1) if $\pi(p) + \pi(1 - p) = 1$. As will be shown later, this condition is not generally satisfied.

Many elements of the evaluation model have appeared in previous attempts to modify expected utility theory. Markowitz (1952) was the first to propose that utility be defined on gains and losses rather than on final asset positions, an assumption which has been implicitly accepted in most experimental measurements of utility (see, e.g., (Davidson, Suppes & Siegel, 1957; Mosteller & Nogee, 1951)). Markowitz also noted the presence of risk seeking in preferences among positive as well as among negative prospects, and he proposed a utility function which has convex and concave regions in both the positive and the negative domains. His treatment, however, retains the expectation principle; hence it cannot account for the many violations of this principle; see, e.g., Table 2.1.

The replacement of probabilities by more general weights was proposed by Edwards (1962), and this model was investigated in several empirical studies (e.g., (Anderson and Shanteau, 1970; Tversky, 1967)). Similar models were developed by Fellner (1965), who introduced the concept of decision weight to explain aversion for ambiguity, and by van Dam (1975) who attempted to scale decision weights. For other critical analyses of expected utility theory and alternative choice models, see Allais (1953), Coombs (1975), Fishburn (1977), and Hansson (1975).

The equations of prospect theory retain the general bilinear form that underlies expected utility theory. However, in order to accommodate the effects described in the first part of the paper, we are compelled to assume that values are attached to changes rather than to final states, and that decision weights do not coincide with stated probabilities. These departures from expected utility theory must lead to normatively unacceptable consequences, such as inconsistencies, intransitivities, and violations of dominance. Such anomalies of preference are normally corrected by the decision maker when he realizes that his preferences are inconsistent, intransitive, or inadmissible. In many situations, however, the decision maker does not have the opportunity to discover that his preferences could violate decision rules that he wishes to obey. In these circumstances the anomalies implied by prospect theory are expected to occur.

The Value Function

An essential feature of the present theory is that the carriers of value are changes in wealth or welfare, rather than final states. This assumption is compatible with basic principles of perception and judgment. Our perceptual apparatus is attuned to the evaluation of changes or differences rather than to the evaluation of absolute magnitudes. When we respond to attributes such as brightness, loudness, or temperature, the past and present context of experience defines an adaptation level, or reference point, and stimuli are perceived in relation to this reference point (Helson, 1964). Thus, an object at a given temperature may be experienced as hot or cold to the touch depending on the temperature to which one has adapted. The same principle applies to non-sensory attributes such as health, prestige, and wealth. The same level of wealth, for example, may imply abject poverty for one person and great riches for another – depending on their current assets.

The emphasis on changes as the carriers of value should not be taken to imply that the value of a particular change is independent of initial position. Strictly speaking, value should be treated as a function in two arguments: the asset position that serves as reference point, and the magnitude of the change (positive or negative) from that reference point. An individual's attitude to money, say, could be described by a book, where each page presents the value function for changes at a particular asset position. Clearly, the value functions described on different pages are not identical: they are likely to become more linear with increases in assets. However, the preference order of prospects is not greatly altered by small or even moderate variations in asset position. The certainty equivalent of the prospect (1,000, .50), for example, lies between 300 and 400 for most people, in a wide range of asset positions. Consequently, the representation of value as a function in one argument generally provides a satisfactory approximation.

Many sensory and perceptual dimensions share the property that the psychological response is a concave function of the magnitude of physical change. For example, it is easier to discriminate between a change of 3° and a change of 6° in room temperature, than it is to discriminate between a change of 13° and a change of 16°. We propose that this principle applies in particular to the evaluation of monetary changes. Thus, the difference in value between a gain of 100 and a gain of 200 appears to be greater than the difference between a gain of 1,100 and a gain of 1,200. Similarly, the difference between a loss of 100 and a loss of 200 appears greater than the difference between a loss of 1,100 and a loss of 1,200, unless the larger loss is intolerable. Thus, we hypothesize that the value function for changes of wealth is normally concave above the reference point ($v''(x) < 0$, for $x > 0$) and often convex below it ($v''(x) > 0$, for $x < 0$). That is, the marginal value of both gains and losses generally decreases with their magnitude. Some support for this hypothesis has been reported by Galanter and Pliner (1974), who scaled the perceived magnitude of monetary and non-monetary gains and losses.

The above hypothesis regarding the shape of the value function was based on responses to gains and losses in a riskless context. We propose that the value function which is derived from risky choices shares the same characteristics, as illustrated in the following problems.

Problem 13:

	(6,000, .25),	or	(4,000, .25; 2,000, .25).
N = 68	[18]		[82]*

Problem 13':

	(−6,000, .25),	or	(−4,000, .25; −2,000, .25).
N = 64	[70]*		[30]

Applying equation 1 to the modal preference in these problems yields

$$\pi(.25)v(6,000) < \pi(.25)[v(4,000) + v(2,000)] \quad \text{and}$$
$$\pi(.25)v(-6,000) > \pi(.25)[v(-4,000) + v(-2,000)].$$

Hence, $v(6,000) < v(4,000) + v(2,000)$ and $v(-6,000) > v(-4,000) + v(-2,000)$. These preferences are in accord with the hypothesis that the value function is concave for gains and convex for losses.

Any discussion of the utility function for money must leave room for the effect of special circumstances on preferences. For example, the utility function of an individual who needs $60,000 to purchase a house may reveal an exceptionally steep rise near the critical value. Similarly, an individual's aversion to losses may increase sharply near the loss that would compel him to sell his house and move to a less desirable neighborhood. Hence, the derived value (utility) function of an individual does not always reflect "pure" attitudes to money, since it could be affected by additional consequences associated with specific amounts. Such perturbations can readily produce convex regions in the value function for gains and concave regions in the value function for losses. The latter case may be more common since large losses often necessitate changes in life style.

A salient characteristic of attitudes to changes in welfare is that losses loom larger than gains. The aggravation that one experiences in losing a sum of money appears to be greater than the pleasure associated with gaining the same amount (Galanter & Pliner, 1974). Indeed, most people find symmetric bets of the form $(x, .50; -x, .50)$ distinctly unattractive. Moreover, the aversiveness of symmetric fair bets generally increases with the size of the stake. That is, if $x > y \geq 0$, then $(y, .50; -y, .50)$ is preferred to $(x, .50; -x, .50)$. According to equation (1), therefore,

$$v(y) + v(-y) > v(x) + v(-x) \quad \text{and} \quad v(-y) - v(-x) > v(x) - v(y).$$

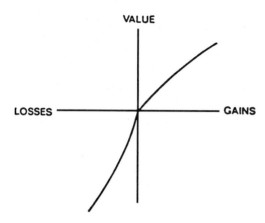

Figure 2.3. A hypothetical value function.

Setting $y=0$ yields $v(x) < -v(-x)$, and letting y approach x yields $v'(x) < v'(-x)$, provided v', the derivative of v, exists. Thus, the value function for losses is steeper than the value function for gains.

In summary, we have proposed that the value function is (i) defined on deviations from the reference point; (ii) generally concave for gains and commonly convex for losses; (iii) steeper for losses than for gains. A value function which satisfies these properties is displayed in Figure 2.3. Note that the proposed S-shaped value function is steepest at the reference point, in marked contrast to the utility function postulated by Markowitz (1952) which is relatively shallow in that region.

Although the present theory can be applied to derive the value function from preferences between prospects, the actual scaling is considerably more complicated than in utility theory because of the introduction of decision weights. For example, decision weights could produce risk aversion and risk seeking even with a linear value function. Nevertheless, it is of interest that the main properties ascribed to the value function have been observed in a detailed analysis of von Neumann–Morgenstern utility functions for changes of wealth (Fishburn and Kochenberger (1979)). The functions had been obtained from thirty decision makers in various fields of business, in five independent studies (Barnes & Reinmuth, 1976; Grayson, 1960; Green, 1963; Halter & Dean, 1971; Swalm, 1966). Most utility functions for gains were concave, most functions for losses were convex, and only three individuals exhibited risk aversion for both gains and losses. With a single exception, utility functions were considerably steeper for losses than for gains.

The Weighting Function

In prospect theory, the value of each outcome is multiplied by a decision weight. Decision weights are inferred from choices between prospects much as subjective probabilities are inferred from preferences in the Ramsey–Savage approach. However, decision weights are not probabilities: they do not obey the probability axioms and they should not be interpreted as measures of degree or belief.

Consider a gamble in which one can win 1,000 or nothing, depending on the toss of a fair coin. For any reasonable person, the probability of winning is .50 in this situation. This can be verified in a variety of ways, e.g., by showing that the subject is indifferent between betting on heads or tails, or by his verbal report that he considers the two events equiprobable. As will be shown below, however, the decision weight $\pi(.50)$ which is derived from choices is likely to be smaller than .50. Decision weights measure the impact of events on the desirability of prospects, and not merely the perceived likelihood of these events. The two scales coincide (i.e., $\pi(p) = p$) if the expectation principle holds, but not otherwise.

The choice problems discussed in the present paper were formulated in terms of explicit numerical probabilities, and our analysis assumes that the respondents adopted the stated values of p. Furthermore, since the events were identified only by their stated probabilities, it is possible in this context to express decision weights as a function of stated probability. In general, however, the decision weight attached to an event could be influenced by other factors, e.g., ambiguity (Ellsberg, 1961; Fellner, 1961).

We turn now to discuss the salient properties of the weighting function π, which relates decision weights to stated probabilities. Naturally, π is an increasing function of p, with $\pi(0) = 0$ and $\pi(1) = 1$. That is, outcomes contingent on an impossible event are ignored, and the scale is normalized so that $\pi(p)$ is the ratio of the weight associated with the probability p to the weight associated with the certain event.

We first discuss some properties of the weighting function for small probabilities. The preferences in Problems 8 and 8′ suggest that for small values of p, π is a subadditive function of p, i.e., $(rp) > r\pi(p)$ for $0 < r < 1$. Recall that in Problem 8, (6,000, .001) is preferred to (3,000, .002). Hence

$$\frac{\pi(.001)}{\pi(.002)} > \frac{v(3,000)}{v(6,000)} > \frac{1}{2} \quad \text{by the concavity of } v.$$

The reflected preferences in Problem 8′ yield the same conclusion. The pattern of preferences in Problems 7 and 7′, however, suggests that subadditivity need not hold for large values of p.

Furthermore, we propose that very low probabilities are generally overweighted, that is, $\pi(p) > p$ for small p. Consider the following choice problems.

Problem 14:

	(5,000, .001),	or	(5).
$N = 72$	[72]*		[28]

Problem 14′:

	(−5,000, .001),	or	(−5).
$N = 72$	[17]		[83]*

Note that in Problem 14, people prefer what is in effect a lottery ticket over the expected value of that ticket. In Problem 14′, on the other hand, they prefer a small loss, which can be viewed as the payment of an insurance premium, over a small probability of a large loss. Similar observations have been reported by Markowitz (1952). In the present theory, the preference for the lottery in Problem 14 implies $\pi(.001)v(5,000) > v(5)$, hence $\pi(.001) > v(5)/v(5,000) > .001$, assuming the value function for gains is concave. The readiness to pay for insurance in Problem 14′ implies the same conclusion, assuming the value function for losses is convex.

It is important to distinguish overweighting, which refers to a property of decision weights, from the overestimation that is commonly found in the assessment of the probability of rare events. Note that the issue of overestimation does not arise in the present context, where the subject is assumed to adopt the stated value of p. In many real-life situations, overestimation and overweighting may both operate to increase the impact of rare events.

Although $\pi(p) > p$ for low probabilities, there is evidence to suggest that, for all $0 < p < 1$, $\pi(p) + \pi(1 - p) < 1$. We label this property subcertainty. It is readily seen that the typical preferences in any version of Allias' example (see, e.g., Problems 1 and 2) imply subcertainty for the relevant value of p. Applying equation (1) to the prevalent preferences in Problems 1 and 2 yields, respectively,

$$v(2,400) > \pi(.66)v(2,400) + \pi(.33)v(2,500), \quad \text{i.e.,}$$
$$[1 - \pi(.66)]v(2,400) > \pi(.33)v(2,500) \quad \text{and}$$
$$\pi(.33)v(2,500) > \pi(.34)v(2,400); \quad \text{hence,}$$
$$1 - \pi(.66) > \pi(.34), \quad \text{or} \quad \pi(.66) + \pi(.34) < 1.$$

Applying the same analysis to Allais' original example yields $\pi(.89) + \pi(.11) < 1$, and some data reported by MacCrimmon and Larsson (forthcoming) imply subcertainty for additional values of p.

The slope of π in the interval (0, 1) can be viewed as a measure of the sensitivity of preferences to changes in probability. Subcertainty entails that π is regressive with respect to p, i.e., that preferences are generally less sensitive to variations of probability than the expectation principle would dictate. Thus, subcertainty captures an essential element of people's attitudes to uncertain events, namely that the sum of the weights associated with complementary events is typically less than the weight associated with the certain event.

Recall that the violations of the substitution axiom discussed earlier in this paper conform to the following rule: If (x, p) is equivalent to (y, pq) then (x, pr) is not preferred to (y, pqr), $0 < p, q, r \leq 1$. By equation (1),

$$\pi(p)v(x) = \pi(pq)v(y) \quad \text{implies} \quad \pi(pr)v(x) \leq \pi(pqr)v(y); \quad \text{hence,}$$
$$\frac{\pi(pq)}{\pi(p)} \leq \frac{\pi(pqr)}{\pi(pr)}.$$

Thus, for a fixed ratio of probabilities, the ratio of the corresponding decision weights is closer to unity when the probabilities are low than when they are high.

This property of π, called subproportionality, imposes considerable constraints on the shape of π: it holds if
and only if $\log \pi$ is a convex function
of $\log p$.

It is of interest to note that subproportionality together with the overweighting of small probabilities imply that π is subadditive over that
range. Formally, it can be shown that
if $\pi(p) > p$ and subproportionality
holds, then $\pi(rp) > r\pi(p)$, $0 < r < 1$,
provided π is monotone and continuous over $(0, 1)$.

Figure 2.4 presents a hypothetical
weighting function which satisfies

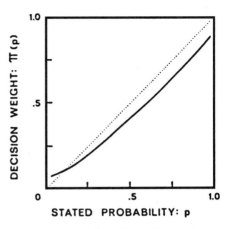

Figure 2.4. A hypothetical weighting function.

overweighting and subadditivity for small values of p, as well as subcertainty
and subproportionality. These properties entail that π is relatively shallow in
the open interval and changes abruptly near the end-points where $\pi(0) = 0$ and
$\pi(1) = 1$. The sharp drops or apparent discontinuities of π at the endpoints are
consistent with the notion that there is a limit to how small a decision weight
can be attached to an event, if it is given any weight at all. A similar quantum
of doubt could impose an upper limit on any decision weight that is less than
unity. This quantal effect may reflect the categorical distinction between certainty and uncertainty. On the other hand, the simplification of prospects in the
editing phase can lead the individual to discard events of extremely low probability and to treat events of extremely high probability as if they were certain.
Because people are limited in their ability to comprehend and evaluate extreme
probabilities, highly unlikely events are either ignored or overweighted, and
the difference between high probability and certainty is either neglected or
exaggerated. Consequently, π is not well-behaved near the end-points.

The following example, due to Zeckhauser, illustrates the hypothesized nonlinearity of π. Suppose you are compelled to play Russian roulette, but are given
the opportunity to purchase the removal of one bullet from the loaded gun.
Would you pay as much to reduce the number of bullets from four to three as
you would to reduce the number of bullets from one to zero? Most people feel
that they would be willing to pay much more for a reduction of the probability of death from 1/6 to zero than for a reduction from 4/6 to 3/6. Economic
considerations would lead one to pay more in the latter case, where the value
of money is presumably reduced by the considerable probability that one will
not live to enjoy it.

An obvious objection to the assumption that $\pi(p) \neq p$ involves comparisons between prospects of the form $(x, p; x, q)$ and $(x, p'; x, q')$, where
$p + q = p' + q' < 1$. Since any individual will surely be indifferent between
the two prospects, it could be argued that this observation entails $\pi(p) +$

$\pi(q) = \pi(p') + \pi(q')$, which in turn implies that π is the identity function. This argument is invalid in the present theory, which assumes that the probabilities of identical outcomes are combined in the editing of prospects. A more serious objection to the nonlinearity of π involves potential violations of dominance. Suppose $x > y > 0$, $p > p'$, and $p + q = p' + q' < 1$; hence, $(x, p; y, q)$ dominates $(x, p'; y, q')$. If preference obeys dominance, then

$$\pi(p)v(x) + \pi(q)v(y) > \pi(p')v(x) + \pi(q')v(y).$$

or

$$\frac{\pi(p) - \pi(p')}{\pi(q') - \pi(q)} > \frac{v(y)}{v(x)}.$$

Hence, as y approaches x, $\pi(p) - \pi(p')$ approaches $\pi(q') - \pi(q)$. Since $p - p' = q' - q$, π must be essentially linear, or else dominance must be violated.

Direct violations of dominance are prevented, in the present theory, by the assumption that dominated alternatives are detected and eliminated prior to the evaluation of prospects. However, the theory permits indirect violations of dominance, e.g., triples of prospects so that A is preferred to B, B is preferred to C, and C dominates A. For an example, see Raiffa [1968, p. 75].

Finally, it should be noted that the present treatment concerns the simplest decision task in which a person chooses between two available prospects. We have not treated in detail the more complicated production task (e.g., bidding) where the decision maker generates an alternative that is equal in value to a given prospect. The asymmetry between the two options in this situation could introduce systematic biases. Indeed, Lichtenstein and Slovic [1971] have constructed pairs of prospect A and B, such that people generally prefer A over B, but bid more for B than A. This phenomenon has been confirmed in several studies, with both hypothetical and real gambles, e.g., Grether and Plott (forthcoming). Thus, it cannot be generally assumed that the preference order of prospects can be recovered by a bidding procedure.

Because prospect theory has been proposed as a model of choice, the inconsistency of bids and choices implies that the measurement of values and decision weights should be based on choices between specified prospects rather than on bids or other production tasks. This restriction makes the assessment of v and π more difficult because production tasks are more convenient for scaling than pair comparisons.

4. DISCUSSION

In the final section we show how prospect theory accounts for observed attitudes toward risk, discuss alternative representations of choice problems induced by shifts of reference point, and sketch several extensions of the present treatment.

Risk Attitudes

The dominant pattern of preferences observed in Allais' example (Problems 1 and 2) follows from the present theory iff

$$\frac{\pi(.33)}{\pi(.34)} > \frac{v(2,400)}{v(2,500)} > \frac{\pi(.33)}{1 - \pi(.66)}.$$

Hence, the violation of the independence axiom is attributed in this case to subcertainty, and more specifically to the inequality $\pi(.34) < 1 - \pi(.66)$. This analysis shows that an Allais-type violation will occur whenever the v-ratio of the two non-zero outcomes is bounded by the corresponding π-ratios.

Problems 3 through 8 share the same structure, hence it suffices to consider one pair, say Problems 7 and 8. The observed choices in these problems are implied by the theory iff

$$\frac{\pi(.001)}{\pi(.002)} > \frac{v(3,000)}{v(6,000)} > \frac{\pi(.45)}{\pi(.90)}.$$

The violation of the substitution axiom is attributed in this case to the subproportionality of π. Expected utility theory is violated in the above manner, therefore, whenever the v-ratio of the two outcomes is bounded by the respective π-ratios. The same analysis applies to other violations of the substitution axiom, both in the positive and in the negative domain.

We next prove that the preference for regular insurance over probabilistic insurance, observed in Problem 9, follows from prospect theory – provided the probability of loss is overweighted. That is, if $(-x, p)$ is indifferent to $(-y)$, then $(-y)$ is preferred to $(-x, p/2; -y, p/2; -y/2, 1 - p)$. For simplicity, we define for $x \geq 0$, $f(x) = -v(-x)$. Since the value function for losses is convex, f is a concave function of x. Applying prospect theory, with the natural extension of equation 2, we wish to show that

$$\pi(p)f(x) = f(y) \quad \text{implies}$$
$$f(y) \leq f(y/2) + \pi(p/2)[f(y) - f(y/2)] + \pi(p/2)[f(x) - f(y/2)]$$
$$= \pi(p/2)f(x) + \pi(p/2)f(y) + [1 - 2\pi(p/2)]f(y/2).$$

Substituting for $f(x)$ and using the concavity of f, it suffices to show that

$$f(y) \leq \frac{\pi(p/2)}{\pi(p)}f(y) + \pi(p/2)f(y) + f(y)/2 - \pi(p/2)f(y)$$

or

$$\pi(p)/2 \leq \pi(p/2), \quad \text{which follows from the subadditivity of } \pi.$$

According to the present theory, attitudes toward risk are determined jointly by v and π, and not solely by the utility function. It is therefore instructive to examine the conditions under which risk aversion or risk seeking are expected to occur. Consider the choice between the gamble (x, p) and its expected value (px). If $x > 0$, risk seeking is implied whenever $\pi(p) > v(px)/v(x)$, which is greater than p if the value function for gains is concave. Hence, overweighting ($\pi(p) > p$) is necessary but not sufficient for risk seeking in the domain of gains. Precisely the same condition is necessary but not sufficient for risk aversion when $x < 0$. This analysis restricts risk seeking in the domain of gains and risk aversion in the domain of losses to small probabilities, where overweighting is expected to hold. Indeed these are the typical conditions under which lottery tickets and insurance policies are sold. In prospect theory, the overweighting of small probabilities favors both gambling and insurance, while the S-shaped value function tends to inhibit both behaviors.

Although prospect theory predicts both insurance and gambling for small probabilities, we feel that the present analysis falls far short of a fully adequate account of these complex phenomena. Indeed, there is evidence from both experimental studies (Slovic, Fischhoff, Lichtenstein, Corrigan, & Coombs 1977), survey research (Kunreuther et al., 1978), and observations of economic behavior, e.g., service and medical insurance, that the purchase of insurance often extends to the medium range of probabilities, and that small probabilities of disaster are sometimes entirely ignored. Furthermore, the evidence suggests that minor changes in the formulation of the decision problem can have marked effects on the attractiveness of insurance (Slovic, Fischhoff, Lichtenstein, Corrigan and Coombs, 1977). A comprehensive theory of insurance behavior should consider, in addition to pure attitudes toward uncertainty and money, such factors as the value of security, social norms of prudence, the aversiveness of a large number of small payments spread over time, information and misinformation regarding probabilities and outcomes, and many others. Some effects of these variables could be described within the present framework, e.g., as changes of reference point, transformations of the value function, or manipulations of probabilities or decision weights. Other effects may require the introduction of variables or concepts which have not been considered in this treatment.

Shifts of Reference

So far in this paper, gains and losses were defined by the amounts of money that are obtained or paid when a prospect is played, and the reference point was taken to be the status quo, or one's current assets. Although this is probably true for most choice problems, there are situations in which gains and losses are coded relative to an expectation or aspiration level that differs from the status quo. For example, an unexpected tax withdrawal from a monthly pay check is experienced as a loss, not as a reduced gain. Similarly, an entrepreneur who is weathering a slump with greater success than his competitors may interpret a small loss as a gain, relative to the larger loss he had reason to expect.

The reference point in the preceding examples corresponded to an asset position that one had expected to attain. A discrepancy between the reference point and the current asset position may also arise because of recent changes in wealth to which one has not yet adapted (Markowitz, 1952). Imagine a person who is involved in a business venture, has already lost 2,000 and is now facing a choice between a sure gain of 1,000 and an even chance to win 2,000 or nothing. If he has not yet adapted to his losses, he is likely to code the problem as a choice between $(-2,000, .50)$ and $(-1,000)$ rather than as a choice between $(2,000, .50)$ and $(1,000)$. As we have seen, the former representation induces more adventurous choices than the latter.

A change of reference point alters the preference order for prospects. In particular, the present theory implies that a negative translation of a choice problem, such as arises from incomplete adaptation to recent losses, increases risk seeking in some situations. Specifically, if a risky prospect $(x, p; -y, 1 - p)$ is just acceptable, then $(x - z, p; -y - z, 1 - p)$ is preferred over $(-z)$ for $x, y, z > 0$, with $x > z$.

To prove this proposition, note that

$$V(x, p; y, 1 - p) = 0 \quad \text{iff} \quad \pi(p)v(x) = -\pi(1 - p)v(-y).$$

Furthermore,

$$
\begin{aligned}
V(x &- z, p; -y - z, 1 - p) \\
&= \pi(p)v(x - z) + \pi(1 - p)v(-y - z) \\
&> \pi(p)v(x) - \pi(p)v(z) + \pi(1 - p)v(-y) \\
&\quad + \pi(1 - p)v(-z) \quad \text{by the properties of } v, \\
&= -\pi(1 - p)v(-y) - \pi(p)v(z) + \pi(1 - p)v(-y) \\
&\quad + \pi(1 - p)v(-z) \quad \text{by substitution,} \\
&= -\pi(p)v(z) + \pi(1 - p)v(-z) \\
&> v(-z)[\pi(p) + \pi(1 - p)]] \quad \text{since } v(-z) < -v(z), \\
&> v(-z) \quad \text{by subcertainty.}
\end{aligned}
$$

This analysis suggests that a person who has not made peace with his losses is likely to accept gambles that would be unacceptable to him otherwise. The well known observation (McGlothlin, 1956) that the tendency to bet on long shots increases in the course of the betting day provides some support for the hypothesis that a failure to adapt to losses or to attain an expected gain induces risk seeking. For another example, consider an individual who expects to purchase insurance, perhaps because he has owned it in the past or because his friends do. This individual may code the decision to pay a premium y to protect against a loss x as a choice between $(-x + y, p; y, 1 - p)$ and (0) rather than as a choice between $(-x, p)$ and $(-y)$. The preceding argument entails that insurance is likely to be more attractive in the former representation than in the latter.

Another important case of a shift of reference point arises when a person formulates his decision problem in terms of final assets, as advocated in decision analysis, rather than in terms of gains and losses, as people usually do. In this case, the reference point is set to zero on the scale of wealth and the value function is likely to be concave everywhere (Spetzler, 1968). According to the present analysis, this formulation essentially eliminates risk seeking, except for gambling with low probabilities. The explicit formulation of decision problems in terms of final assets is perhaps the most effective procedure for eliminating risk seeking in the domain of losses.

Many economic decisions involve transactions in which one pays money in exchange for a desirable prospect. Current decision theories analyze such problems as comparisons between the status quo and an alternative state which includes the acquired prospect minus its cost. For example, the decision whether to pay 10 for the gamble $(1,000, .01)$ is treated as a choice between $(990, .01; -10, .99)$ and (0). In this analysis, readiness to purchase the positive prospect is equated to willingness to accept the corresponding mixed prospect.

The prevalent failure to integrate riskless and risky prospects, dramatized in the isolation effect, suggests that people are unlikely to perform the operation of subtracting the cost from the outcomes in deciding whether to buy a gamble. Instead, we suggest that people usually evaluate the gamble and its cost separately, and decide to purchase the gamble if the combined value is positive. Thus, the gamble $(1,000, .01)$ will be purchased for a price of 10 if $\pi(.01)v(1,000) + v(-10) > 0$.

If this hypothesis is correct, the decision to pay 10 for $(1,000, .01)$, for example, is no longer equivalent to the decision to accept the gamble $(990, .01; -10, .99)$. Furthermore, prospect theory implies that if one is indifferent between $(x(1 - p), p; -px, 1 - p)$ and (0) then one will not pay px to purchase the prospect (x, p). Thus, people are expected to exhibit more risk seeking in deciding whether to accept a fair gamble than in deciding whether to purchase a gamble for a fair price. The location of the reference point, and the manner in which choice problems are coded and edited emerge as critical factors in the analysis of decisions.

Extensions

In order to encompass a wider range of decision problems, prospect theory should be extended in several directions. Some generalizations are immediate; others require further development. The extension of equations (1) and (2) to prospects with any number of outcomes is straightforward. When the number of outcomes is large, however, additional editing operations may be invoked to simplify evaluation. The manner in which complex options, e.g., compound prospects, are reduced to simpler ones is yet to be investigated.

Although the present paper has been concerned mainly with monetary outcomes, the theory is readily applicable to choices involving other attributes, e.g., quality of life or the number of lives that could be lost or saved as a consequence of a policy decision. The main properties of the proposed value function for money should apply to other attributes as well. In particular, we expect outcomes to be coded as gains or losses relative to a neutral reference point, and losses to loom larger than gains.

The theory can also be extended to the typical situation of choice, where the probabilities of outcomes are not explicitly given. In such situations, decision weights must be attached to particular events rather than to stated probabilities, but they are expected to exhibit the essential properties that were ascribed to the weighting function. For example, if A and B are complementary events and neither is certain, $\pi(A) + \pi(B)$ should be less than unity – a natural analogue to subcertainty.

The decision weight associated with an event will depend primarily on the perceived likelihood of that event, which could be subject to major biases (Tversky & Kahneman, 1974). In addition, decision weights may be affected by other considerations, such as ambiguity or vagueness. Indeed, the work of Ellsberg (1961) and Fellner (1965) implies that vagueness reduces decision weights. Consequently, subcertainty should be more pronounced for vague than for clear probabilities.

The present analysis of preference between risky options has developed two themes. The first theme concerns editing operations that determine how prospects are perceived. The second theme involves the judgmental principles that govern the evaluation of gains and losses and the weighting of uncertain outcomes. Although both themes should be developed further, they appear to provide a useful framework for the descriptive analysis of choice under risk.

3. Advances in Prospect Theory
Cumulative Representation of Uncertainty

Amos Tversky and Daniel Kahneman

ABSTRACT. We develop a new version of prospect theory that employs cumulative rather than separable decision weights and extends the theory in several respects. This version, called cumulative prospect theory, applies to uncertain as well as to risky prospects with any number of outcomes, and it allows different weighting functions for gains and for losses. Two principles, diminishing sensitivity and loss aversion, are invoked to explain the characteristic curvature of the value function and the weighting functions. A review of the experimental evidence and the results of a new experiment confirm a distinctive fourfold pattern of risk attitudes: risk aversion for gains and risk seeking for losses of high probability; risk seeking for gains and risk aversion for losses of low probability.

KEY WORDS   cumulative prospect theory

Expected utility theory reigned for several decades as the dominant normative and descriptive model of decision making under uncertainty, but it has come under serious question in recent years. There is now general agreement that the theory does not provide an adequate description of individual choice: a substantial body of evidence shows that decision makers systematically violate its basic tenets. Many alternative models have been proposed in response to this empirical challenge (for reviews, see Camerer, 1989; Fishburn, 1988; Machina, 1987). Some time ago we presented a model of choice, called prospect theory, which explained the major violations of expected utility theory in choices between risky prospects with a small number of outcomes (Kahneman and Tversky, 1979;

An earlier version of this article was entitled "Cumulative Prospect Theory: An Analysis of Decision under Uncertainty."

This article has benefited from discussions with Colin Camerer, Chew Soo-Hong, David Freedman, and David H. Krantz. We are especially grateful to Peter P. Wakker for his invaluable input and contribution to the axiomatic analysis. We are indebted to Richard Gonzalez and Amy Hayes for running the experiment and analyzing the data. This work was supported by Grants 89-0064 and 88-0206 from the Air Force Office of Scientific Research, by Grant SES-9109535 from the National Science Foundation, and by the Sloan Foundation.

Originally published in the *Journal of Risk and Uncertainty*, 5, 297–323. Copyright © 1992 Kluwer Academic Publishers. Reprinted with permission.

Tversky and Kahneman, 1986). The key elements of this theory are 1) a value function that is concave for gains, convex for losses, and steeper for losses than for gains, and 2) a nonlinear transformation of the probability scale, which overweights small probabilities and underweights moderate and high probabilities. In an important later development, several authors (Quiggin, 1982; Schmeidler, 1989; Yaari, 1987; Weymark, 1981) have advanced a new representation, called the rank-dependent or the cumulative functional, that transforms cumulative rather than individual probabilities. This article presents a new version of prospect theory that incorporates the cumulative functional and extends the theory to uncertain as well to risky prospects with any number of outcomes. The resulting model, called cumulative prospect theory, combines some of the attractive features of both developments (see also Luce and Fishburn, 1991). It gives rise to different evaluations of gains and losses, which are not distinguished in the standard cumulative model, and it provides a unified treatment of both risk and uncertainty.

To set the stage for the present development, we first list five major phenomena of choice, which violate the standard model and set a minimal challenge that must be met by any adequate descriptive theory of choice. All these findings have been confirmed in a number of experiments, with both real and hypothetical payoffs.

Framing effects. The rational theory of choice assumes description invariance: equivalent formulations of a choice problem should give rise to the same preference order (Arrow, 1982). Contrary to this assumption, there is much evidence that variations in the framing of options (e.g., in terms of gains or losses) yield systematically different preferences (Tversky and Kahneman, 1986).

Nonlinear preferences. According to the expectation principle, the utility of a risky prospect is linear in outcome probabilities. Allais's (1953) famous example challenged this principle by showing that the difference between probabilities of .99 and 1.00 has more impact on preferences than the difference between 0.10 and 0.11. More recent studies observed nonlinear preferences in choices that do not involve sure things (Camerer and Ho, 1991).

Source dependence. People's willingness to bet on an uncertain event depends not only on the degree of uncertainty but also on its source. Ellsberg (1961) observed that people prefer to bet on an urn containing equal numbers of red and green balls, rather than on an urn that contains red and green balls in unknown proportions. More recent evidence indicates that people often prefer a bet on an event in their area of competence over a bet on a matched chance event, although the former probability is vague and the latter is clear (Heath and Tversky, 1991).

Risk seeking. Risk aversion is generally assumed in economic analyses of decision under uncertainty. However, risk-seeking choices are consistently observed in two classes of decision problems. First, people often prefer a small probability of winning a large prize over the expected value of that prospect. Second, risk seeking is prevalent when people must choose between a sure loss and a substantial probability of a larger loss.

Loss aversion. One of the basic phenomena of choice under both risk and uncertainty is that losses loom larger than gains (Kahneman and Tversky, 1984; Tversky and Kahneman, 1991). The observed asymmetry between gains and losses is far too extreme to be explained by income effects or by decreasing risk aversion.

The present development explains loss aversion, risk seeking, and nonlinear preferences in terms of the value and the weighting functions. It incorporates a framing process, and it can accommodate source preferences. Additional phenomena that lie beyond the scope of the theory – and of its alternatives – are discussed later.

The present article is organized as follows. Section 1.1 introduces the (two-part) cumulative functional; section 1.2 discusses relations to previous work; and section 1.3 describes the qualitative properties of the value and the weighting functions. These properties are tested in an extensive study of individual choice, described in section 2, which also addresses the question of monetary incentives. Implications and limitations of the theory are discussed in section 3.

1. THEORY

Prospect theory distinguishes two phases in the choice process: framing and valuation. In the framing phase, the decision maker constructs a representation of the acts, contingencies, and outcomes that are relevant to the decision. In the valuation phase, the decision maker assesses the value of each prospect and chooses accordingly. Although no formal theory of framing is available, we have learned a fair amount about the rules that govern the representation of acts, outcomes, and contingencies (Tversky and Kahneman, 1986). The valuation process discussed in subsequent sections is applied to framed prospects.

1.1. Cumulative Prospect Theory

In the classical theory, the utility of an uncertain prospect is the sum of the utilities of the outcomes, each weighted by its probability. The empirical evidence reviewed above suggests two major modifications of this theory: 1) the carriers of value are gains and losses, not final assets; and 2) the value of each outcome is multiplied by a decision weight, not by an additive probability. The weighting scheme used in the original version of prospect theory and in other models is a monotonic transformation of outcome probabilities. This scheme encounters two problems. First, it does not always satisfy stochastic dominance, an assumption that many theorists are reluctant to give up. Second, it is not readily extended to prospects with a large number of outcomes. These problems can be handled by assuming that transparently dominated prospects are eliminated in the editing phase, and by normalizing the weights so that they add to unity. Alternatively, both problems can be solved by the rank-dependent or cumulative functional, first proposed by Quiggin (1982) for decision under risk and by Schmeidler (1989) for decision under uncertainty. Instead of transforming each probability separately, this model transforms the entire cumulative distribution function. The present theory applies the cumulative functional separately to gains and to losses. This development extends prospect theory to uncertain as well as to risky prospects with any number of outcomes while preserving most of its essential features. The differences between the cumulative and the original versions of the theory are discussed in section 1.2.

Let S be a finite set of states of nature; subsets of S are called events. It is assumed that exactly one state obtains, which is unknown to the decision maker. Let X be a set of consequences, also called outcomes. For simplicity, we confine the present dicussion to monetary outcomes. We assume that X includes a neutral outcome, denoted 0, and we interpret all other elements of X as gains or losses, denoted by positive or negative numbers, respectively.

An uncertain prospect f is a function from S into X that assigns to each state $s \in S$ a consequence $f(s) = x$ in X. To define the cumulative functional, we arrange the outcomes of each prospect in increasing order. A prospect f is then represented as a sequence of pairs (x_i, A_i), which yields x_i if A_i occurs, where $x_i > x_j$ iff $i > j$, and (A_i) is a partition of S. We use positive subscripts to denote positive outcomes, negative subscripts to denote negative outcomes, and the zero subscript to index the neutral outcome. A prospect is called strictly positive or positive, respectively, if its outcomes are all positive or nonnegative. Strictly negative and negative prospects are defined similarly; all other prospects are called mixed. The positive part of f, denoted f^+, is obtained by letting $f^+(s) = f(s)$ if $f(s) > 0$, and $f^+(s) = 0$ if $f(s) \leq 0$. The negative part of f, denoted f^-, is defined similarly.

As in expected utility theory, we assign to each prospect f a number $V(f)$ such that f is preferred to or indifferent to g iff $V(f) \geq V(g)$. The following representation is defined in terms of the concept of *capacity* (Choquet, 1955), a nonadditive set function that generalizes the standard notion of probability. A capacity W is a function that assigns to each $A \subset S$ a number $W(A)$ satisfying $W(\phi) = 0$, $W(S) = 1$, and $W(A) \geq W(B)$ whenever $A \supset B$.

Cumulative prospect theory asserts that there exist a strictly increasing value function $v: X \rightarrow \mathrm{Re}$, satisfying $v(x_0) = v(0) = 0$, and capacities W^+ and W^-, such that for $f = (x_i, A_i)$, $-m \leq i \leq n$,

$$V(f) = V(f^+) + V(f^-),$$

$$V(f^+) = \sum_{i=0}^{n} \pi_i^+ v(x_i), \quad V(f^-) = \sum_{i=-m}^{0} \pi_i^- v(x_i), \tag{1}$$

where the decision weights $\pi^+(f^+) = (\pi_0^+, \ldots, \pi_n^+)$ and $\pi^-(f^-) = (\pi_{-m}^-, \ldots, \pi_0^-)$ are defined by:

$$\pi_n^+ = W^+(A_n), \quad \pi_{-m}^- = W^-(A_{-m}),$$

$$\pi_i^+ = W^+(A_i \cup \cdots \cup A_n) - W^+(A_{i+1} \cup \cdots \cup A_n), \quad 0 \leq i \leq n-1,$$

$$\pi_i^- = W^-(A_{-m} \cup \cdots \cup A_i) - W^-(A_{-m} \cup \cdots \cup A_{i-1}), \quad 1 - m \leq i \leq 0.$$

Letting $\pi_i = \pi_i^+$ if $i \geq 0$ and $\pi_i = \pi_i^-$ if $i < 0$, equation (1) reduces to

$$V(f) = \sum_{i=-m}^{n} \pi_i v(x_i). \tag{2}$$

The decision weight π_i^+, associated with a positive outcome, is the difference between the capacities of the events "the outcome is at least as good as x_i" and "the outcome is strictly better than x_i." The decision weight π_i^-, associated with a negative outcome, is the difference between the capacities of the events "the outcome is at least as bad as x_i" and "the outcome is strictly worse than x_i." Thus, the decision weight associated with an outcome can be interpreted as the marginal contribution of the respective event,[1] defined in terms of the capacities W^+ and W^-. If each W is additive, and hence a probability measure, then π_i is simply the probability of A_i. It follows readily from the definitions of π and W that for both positive and negative prospects, the decision weights add to 1. For mixed prospects, however, the sum can be either smaller or greater than 1, because the decision weights for gains and for losses are defined by separate capacities.

If the prospect $f = (x_i, A_i)$ is given by a probability distribution $p(A_i) = p_i$, it can be viewed as a probabilistic or risky prospect (x_i, p_i). In this case, decision weights are defined by:

$$\pi_n^+ = w^+(p_n), \quad \pi_{-m}^- = w^-(p_{-m}),$$

$$\pi_i^+ = w^+(p_i + \cdots + p_n) - w^+(p_{i+1} + \cdots + p_n), \quad 0 \leq i \leq n-1,$$

$$\pi_i^- = w^-(p_{-m} + \cdots + p_i) - w^-(p_{-m} + \cdots + p_{i-1}), \quad 1 - m \leq i \leq 0,$$

where w^+ and w^- are strictly increasing functions from the unit interval into itself satisfying $w^+(0) = w^-(0) = 0$, and $w^+(1) = w^-(1) = 1$.

To illustrate the model, consider the following game of chance. You roll a die once and observe the result $x = 1, \ldots, 6$. If x is even, you receive $\$x$; if x is odd, you pay $\$x$. Viewed as a probabilistic prospect with equiprobable outcomes, f yields the consequences $(-5, -3, -1, 2, 4, 6)$, each with probability $1/6$.

---

[1] In keeping with the spirit of prospect theory, we use the decumulative form for gains and the cumulative form for losses. This notation is vindicated by the experimental findings described in section 2.

Thus, $f^+ = (0, 1/2; 2, 1/6; 4, 1/6; 6, 1/6)$, and $f^- = (-5, 1/6; -3, 1/6; -1, 1/6; 0, 1/2)$. By equation (1), therefore,

$$V(f) = V(f^+) + V(f^-)$$
$$= v(2)[w^+(1/2) - w^+(1/3)] + v(4)[w^+(1/3) - w^+(1/6)]$$
$$+ v(6)[w^+(1/6) - w^+(0)] + v(-5)[w^-(1/6) - w^-(0)]$$
$$+ v(-3)[w^-(1/3) - w^-(1/6)] + v(-1)[w^-(1/2) - w^-(1/3)].$$

1.2. Relation to Previous Work

Luce and Fishburn (1991) derived essentially the same representation from a more elaborate theory involving an operation $\circ$ of joint receipt or multiple play. Thus, $f \circ g$ is the composite prospect obtained by playing both f and g, separately. The key feature of their theory is that the utility function U is additive with respect to $\circ$, that is, $U(f \circ g) = U(f) + U(g)$ provided one prospect is acceptable (i.e., preferred to the status quo) and the other is not. This condition seems too restrictive both normatively and descriptively. As noted by the authors, it implies that the utility of money is a linear function of money if for all sums of money x, y, $U(x \circ y) = U(x + y)$. This assumption appears to us inescapable because the joint receipt of x and y is tantamount to receiving their sum. Thus, we expect the decision maker to be indifferent between receiving a \$10 bill or receiving a \$20 bill and returning \$10 in change. The Luce–Fishburn theory, therefore, differs from ours in two essential respects. First, it extends to composite prospects that are not treated in the present theory. Second, it practically forces utility to be proportional to money.

The present representation encompasses several previous theories that employ the same decision weights for all outcomes. Starmer and Sugden (1989) considered a model in which $w^-(p) = w^+(p)$, as in the original version of prospect theory. In contrast, the rank-dependent models assume $w^-(p) = 1 - w^+(1 - p)$ or $W^-(A) = 1 - W^+(S - A)$. If we apply the latter condition to choice between uncertain assets, we obtain the choice model established by Schmeidler (1989), which is based on the Choquet integral.[2] Other axiomatizations of this model were developed by Gilboa (1987), Nakamura (1990), and Wakker (1989a, 1989b). For probabilistic (rather than uncertain) prospects, this model was first established by Quiggin (1982) and Yaari (1987), and was further analyzed by Chew (1989), Segal (1989), and Wakker (1990). An earlier axiomatization of this model in the context of income inequality was presented by Weymark (1981). Note that in the present theory, the overall value $V(f)$ of a mixed prospect is not a Choquet integral but rather a sum $V(f^+) + V(f^-)$ of two such integrals.

---

[2] This model appears under different names. We use *cumulative utility theory* to describe the application of a Choquet integral to a standard utility function, and *cumulative prospect theory* to describe the application of two separate Choquet integrals to the value of gains and losses.

The present treatment extends the original version of prospect theory in several respects. First, it applies to any finite prospect and it can be extended to continuous distributions. Second, it applies to both probabilistic and uncertain prospects and can, therefore, accommodate some form of source dependence. Third, the present theory allows different decision weights for gains and losses, thereby generalizing the original version that assumes $w^+ = w^-$. Under this assumption, the present theory coincides with the original version for all two-outcome prospects and for all mixed three-outcome prospects. It is noteworthy that for prospects of the form $(x, p; y, 1 - p)$, where either $x > y > 0$ or $x < y < 0$, the original theory is in fact rank dependent. Although the two models yield similar predictions in general, the cumulative version – unlike the original one – satisfies stochastic dominance. Thus, it is no longer necessary to assume that transparently dominated prospects are eliminated in the editing phase – an assumption that was criticized by some authors. On the other hand, the present version can no longer explain violations of stochastic dominance in nontransparent contexts (e.g., Tversky and Kahneman, 1986).

1.3. Values and Weights

In expected utility theory, risk aversion and risk seeking are determined solely by the utility function. In the present theory, as in other cumulative models, risk aversion and risk seeking are determined jointly by the value function and by the capacities, which in the present context are called cumulative weighting functions, or weighting functions for short. As in the original version of prospect theory, we assume that v is concave above the reference point $(v''(x) \leq 0, x \geq 0)$ and convex below the reference point $(v''(x) \geq 0, x \leq 0)$. We also assume that v is steeper for losses than for gains $v'(x) < v'(-x)$ for $x \geq 0$. The first two conditions reflect the principle of diminishing sensitivity: the impact of a change diminishes with the distance from the reference point. The last condition is implied by the principle of loss aversion according to which losses loom larger than corresponding gains (Tversky and Kahneman, 1991).

The principle of diminishing sensitivity applies to the weighting functions as well. In the evaluation of outcomes, the reference point serves as a boundary that distinguishes gains from losses. In the evaluation of uncertainty, there are two natural boundaries – certainty and impossibility – that correspond to the endpoints of the certainty scale. Diminishing sensitivity entails that the impact of a given change in probability diminishes with its distance from the boundary. For example, an increase of .1 in the probability of winning a given prize has more impact when it changes the probability of winning from .9 to 1.0 or from 0 to .1, than when it changes the probability of winning from .3 to .4 or from .6 to .7. Diminishing sensitivity, therefore, gives rise to a weighting function that is concave near 0 and convex near 1. For uncertain prospects, this principle yields subadditivity for very unlikely events and superadditivity near certainty. However, the function is not well-behaved near the endpoints, and very small probabilities can be either greatly overweighted or neglected altogether.

Table 3.1. A Test of Independence (Dow-Jones)

		A	B	C	
		if $d < 30$	if $30 \leq d \leq 35$	if $35 < d$	
Problem I:	f	$25,000	$25,000	$25,000	[68]
	g	$25,000	0	$75,000	[32]
Problem II:	f'	0	$25,000	$25,000	[23]
	g'	0	0	$75,000	[77]

Note: Outcomes are contingent on the difference d between the closing values of the Dow-Jones today and tomorrow. The percentage of respondents ($N = 156$) who selected each prospect is given in brackets.

Before we turn to the main experiment, we wish to relate the observed non-linearity of preferences to the shape of the weighting function. For this purpose, we devised a new demonstration of the common consequence effect in decisions involving uncertainty rather than risk. Table 3.1 displays a pair of decision problems (I and II) presented in that order to a group of 156 money managers during a workshop. The participants chose between prospects whose outcomes were contingent on the difference d between the closing values of the Dow-Jones today and tomorrow. For example, f' pays $25,000 if d exceeds 30 and nothing otherwise. The percentage of respondents who chose each prospect is given in brackets. The independence axiom of expected utility theory implies that f is preferred to g iff f' is preferred to g'. Table 3.1 shows that the modal choice was f in problem I and g' in problem II. This pattern, which violates independence, was chosen by 53% of the respondents.

Essentially the same pattern was observed in a second study following the same design. A group of 98 Stanford students chose between prospects whose outcomes were contingent on the point-spread d in the forthcoming Stanford–Berkeley football game. Table 3.2 presents the prospects in question. For example, g pays $10 if Stanford does not win, $30 if it wins by 10 points or less, and nothing if it wins by more than 10 points. Ten percent of the participants, selected at random, were actually paid according to one of their choices. The

Table 3.2. A Test of Independence (Stanford-Berkeley football game)

		A	B	C	
		if $d < 0$	if $0 \leq d \leq 10$	if $10 < d$	
Problem I:	f	$10	$10	$10	[64]
	g	$10	$30	0	[36]
Problem II:	f'	0	$10	$10	[34]
	g'	0	$30	0	[66]

Note: Outcomes are contingent on the point-spread d in a Stanford–Berkeley football game. The percentage of respondents ($N = 98$) who selected each prospect is given in brackets.

modal choice, selected by 46% of the subjects, was f and g', again in direct violation of the independence axiom.

To explore the constraints imposed by this pattern, let us apply the present theory to the modal choices in Table 3.1, using $1,000 as a unit. Since f is preferred to g in problem I,

$$v(25) > v(75)W^+(C) + v(25)[W^+(A \cup C) - W^+(C)]$$

or

$$v(25)[1 - W^+(A \cup C) + W^+(C)] > v(75)W^+(C).$$

The preference for g' over f' in problem II, however, implies

$$v(75)W^+(C) > v(25)W^+(C \cup B);$$

hence,

$$W^+(S) - W^+(S - B) > W^+(C \cup B) - W^+(C). \tag{3}$$

Thus, "subtracting" B from certainty has more impact than "subtracting" B from $C \cup B$. Let $W_+(D) = 1 - W^+(S - D)$, and $w_+(p) = 1 - w^+(1 - p)$. It follows readily that equation (3) is equivalent to the subadditivity of W_+, that is, $W_+(B) + W_+(D) \geq W_+(B \cup D)$. For probabilistic prospects, equation (3) reduces to

$$1 - w^+(1 - q) > w^+(p + q) - w^+(p),$$

or

$$w_+(q) + w_+(r) \geq w_+(q + r), \quad q + r < 1.$$

Allais's example corresponds to the case where $p(C) = .10$, $p(B) = .89$, and $p(A) = .01$.

It is noteworthy that the violations of independence reported in Tables 3.1 and 3.2 are also inconsistent with regret theory, advanced by Loomes and Sugden (1982, 1987), and with Fishburn's (1988) SSA model. Regret theory explains Allais's example by assuming that the decision maker evaluates the consequences as if the two prospects in each choice are statistically independent. When the prospects in question are defined by the same set of events, as in Tables 3.1 and 3.2, regret theory (like Fishburn's SSA model) implies independence, since it is additive over states. The finding that the common consequence effect is very much in evidence in the present problems undermines the interpretation of Allais's example in terms of regret theory.

The common consequence effect implies the subadditivity of W_+ and of w_+. Other violations of expected utility theory imply the subadditivity of W^+ and of w^+ for small and moderate probabilities. For example, Prelec (1990) observed that most respondents prefer 2% to win $20,000 over 1% to win $30,000; they also prefer 1% to win $30,000 and 32% to win $20,000 over

34% to win \$20,000. In terms of the present theory, these data imply that $w^+(.02) - w^+(.01) \geq w^+(.34) - w^+(.33)$. More generally, we hypothesize

$$w^+(p+q) - w^+(q) \geq w^+(p+q+r) - w^+(q+r), \tag{4}$$

provided $p + q + r$ is sufficiently small. Equation (4) states that w^+ is concave near the origin; and the conjunction of the above inequalities implies that, in accord with diminishing sensitivity, w^+ has an inverted S-shape: it is steepest near the endpoints and shallower in the middle of the range. For other treatments of decision weights, see Hogarth and Einhorn (1990), Prelec (1989), Viscusi (1989), and Wakker (1990). Experimental evidence is presented in the next section.

2. EXPERIMENT

An experiment was carried out to obtain detailed information about the value and weighting functions. We made a special effort to obtain high-quality data. To this end, we recruited 25 graduate students from Berkeley and Stanford (12 men and 13 women) with no special training in decision theory. Each subject participated in three separate one-hour sessions that were several days apart. Each subject was paid \$25 for participation.

2.1. Procedure

The experiment was conducted on a computer. On a typical trial, the computer displayed a prospect (e.g., 25% chance to win \$150 and 75% chance to win \$50) and its expected value. The display also included a descending series of seven sure outcomes (gains or losses) logarithmically spaced between the extreme outcomes of the prospect. The subject indicated a preference between each of the seven sure outcomes and the risky prospect. To obtain a more refined estimate of the certainty equivalent, a new set of seven sure outcomes was then shown, linearly spaced between a value 25% higher than the lowest amount accepted in the first set and a value 25% lower than the highest amount rejected. The certainty equivalent of a prospect was estimated by the midpoint between the lowest accepted value and the highest rejected value in the second set of choices. We wish to emphasize that although the analysis is based on certainty equivalents, the data consisted of a series of choices between a given prospect and several sure outcomes. Thus, the cash equivalent of a prospect was derived from observed choices, rather than assessed by the subject. The computer monitored the internal consistency of the responses to each prospect and rejected errors, such as the acceptance of a cash amount lower than one previously rejected. Errors caused the original statement of the problem to reappear on the screen.

The present analysis focuses on a set of two-outcome prospects with monetary outcomes and numerical probabilities. Other data involving more complicated prospects, including prospects defined by uncertain events, will be reported elsewhere. There were 28 positive and 28 negative prospects. Six of the prospects (three nonnegative and three nonpositive) were repeated on

Table 3.3. Median Cash Equivalents (in dollars) for All Nonmixed Prospects

Outcomes	Probability								
	.01	.05	.10	.25	.50	.75	.90	.95	.99
(0, 50)			9		21		37		
(0, −50)			−8		−21		−39		
(0, 100)		14		25	36	52		78	
(0, −100)		−8		−23.5	−42	−63		−84	
(0, 200)	10		20		76		131		188
(0, −200)	−3		−23		−89		−155		−190
(0, 400)	12								377
(0, −400)	−14								−380
(50, 100)			59		71		83		
(−50, −100)			−59		−71		−85		
(50, 150)		64		72.5	86	102		128	
(−50, −150)		−60		−71	−92	−113		−132	
(100, 200)		118		130	141	162		178	
(−100, −200)		−112		−121	−142	−158		−179	

Note: The two outcomes of each prospect are given in the left-hand side of each row; the probability of the second (i.e., more extreme) outcome is given by the corresponding column. For example, the value of $9 in the upper left corner is the median cash equivalent of the prospect (0, 9; $50, .1).

different sessions to obtain the estimate of the consistency of choice. Table 3.3 displays the prospects and the median cash equivalents of the 25 subjects.

A modified procedure was used in eight additional problems. In four of these problems, the subjects made choices regarding the acceptability of a set of mixed prospects (e.g., 50% chance to lose $100 and 50% chance to win x) in which x was systematically varied. In four other problems, the subjects compared a fixed prospect (e.g., 50% chance to lose $20 and 50% chance to win $50) to a set of prospects (e.g., 50% chance to lose $50 and 50% chance to win x) in which x was systematically varied. (These prospects are presented in Table 3.6.)

2.2. Results

The most distinctive implication of prospect theory is the fourfold pattern of risk attitudes. For the nonmixed prospects used in the present study, the shapes of the value and the weighting functions imply risk-averse and risk-seeking preferences, respectively, for gains and for losses of moderate or high probability. Furthermore, the shape of the weighting functions favors risk seeking for small probabilities of gains and risk aversion for small probabilities of loss, provided the outcomes are not extreme. Note, however, that prospect theory does not imply perfect reflection in the sense that the preference between any two positive prospects is reversed when gains are replaced by losses. Table 3.4 presents, for each subject, the percentage of risk-seeking choices (where the certainty equivalent exceeded expected value) for gains and for losses with low

Table 3.4. Percentage of Risk-Seeking Choices

Subject	Gain		Loss	
	$p \leq .1$	$p \geq .5$	$p \leq .1$	$p \geq .5$
1	100	38	30	100
2	85	33	20	75
3	100	10	0	93
4	71	0	30	58
5	83	0	20	100
6	100	5	0	100
7	100	10	30	86
8	87	0	10	100
9	16	0	80	100
10	83	0	0	93
11	100	26	0	100
12	100	16	10	100
13	87	0	10	94
14	100	21	30	100
15	66	0	30	100
16	60	5	10	100
17	100	15	20	100
18	100	22	10	93
19	60	10	60	63
20	100	5	0	81
21	100	0	0	100
22	100	0	0	92
23	100	31	0	100
24	71	0	80	100
25	100	0	10	87
Risk seeking	78[a]	10	20	87[a]
Risk neutral	12	2	0	7
Risk averse	10	88[a]	80[a]	6

[a] Values that correspond to the fourfold pattern.
Note: The percentage of risk-seeking choices is given for low ($p \leq .1$) and high ($p \geq .5$) probabilities of gain and loss for each subject (risk-neutral choices were excluded). The overall percentage of risk-seeking, risk-neutral, and risk-averse choices for each type of prospect appears at the bottom of the table.

($p \leq .1$) and with high ($p \geq .5$) probabilities. Table 3.4 shows that for $p \geq .5$, all 25 subjects are predominantly risk averse for positive prospects and risk seeking for negative ones. Moreover, the entire fourfold pattern is observed for 22 of the 25 subjects, with some variability at the level of individual choices.

Although the overall pattern of preferences is clear, the individual data, of course, reveal both noise and individual differences. The correlations, across subjects, between the cash equivalents for the same prospects on successive sessions averaged .55 over six different prospects. Table 3.5 presents means

Table 3.5. Average Correlations between Certainty Equivalents in Four Types of Prospects

	L$^+$	H$^+$	L$^-$	H$^-$
L$^+$	.41	.17	−.23	.05
H$^+$		.39	.05	−.18
L$^-$			.40	.06
H$^-$				.44

Note: Low probability of gain = L$^+$; high probability of gain = H$^+$; low probability of loss = L$^-$; high probability of loss = H$^-$.

(after transformation to Fisher's z) of the correlations between the different types of prospects. For example, there were 19 and 17 prospects, respectively, with high probability of gain and high probability of loss. The value of .06 in Table 3.5 is the mean of the $17 \times 19 = 323$ correlations between the cash equivalents of these prospects.

The correlations between responses within each of the four types of prospects average .41, slightly lower than the correlations between separate responses to the same problems. The two negative values in Table 3.5 indicate that those subjects who were more risk averse in one domain tended to be more risk seeking in the other. Although the individual correlations are fairly low, the trend is consistent: 78% of the 403 correlations in these two cells are negative. There is also a tendency for subjects who are more risk averse for high-probability gains to be less risk seeking for gains of low probability. This trend, which is absent in the negative domain, could reflect individual differences either in the elevation of the weighting function or in the curvature of the value function for gains. The very low correlations in the two remaining cells of Table 3.5, averaging .05, indicate that there is no general trait of risk aversion or risk seeking. Because individual choices are quite noisy, aggregation of problems is necessary for the analysis of individual differences.

The fourfold pattern of risk attitudes emerges as a major empirical generalization about choice under risk. It has been observed in several experiments (see, e.g., Cohen, Jaffray, and Said, 1987), including a study of experienced oil executives involving significant, albeit hypothetical, gains and losses (Wehrung, 1989). It should be noted that prospect theory implies the pattern demonstrated in Table 3.4 within the data of individual subjects, but it does not imply high correlations across subjects because the values of gains and of losses can vary independently. The failure to appreciate this point and the limited reliability of individual responses has led some previous authors (e.g., Hershey and Schoemaker, 1980) to underestimate the robustness of the fourfold pattern.

2.3. Scaling

Having established the fourfold pattern in ordinal and correlational analyses, we now turn to a quantitative description of the data. For each prospect of the form $(x, p; 0, 1 - p)$, let c/x be the ratio of the certainty equivalent of the prospect to the nonzero outcome x. Figures 3.1 and 3.2 plot the median value of c/x as a function of p, for positive and for negative prospects, respectively. We denote c/x by a circle if $|x| < 200$, and by a triangle if $|x| \geq 200$. The only exceptions are the two extreme probabilities (.01 and .99) where a circle is used for $|x| = 200$. To

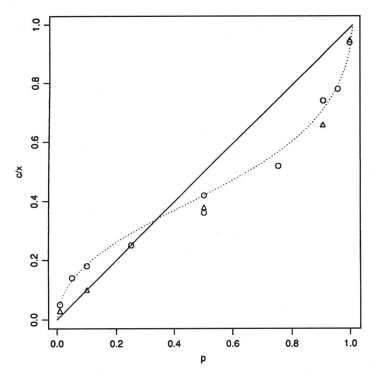

Figure 3.1. Median c/x for all positive prospects of the form $(x, p;$ $0, 1 - p)$. Triangles and circles, respectively, correspond to values of x that lie above or below 200.

interpret Figures 3.1 and 3.2, note that if subjects are risk neutral, the points will lie on the diagonal; if subjects are risk averse, all points will lie below the diagonal in Figure 3.1 and above the diagonal in Figure 3.2. Finally, the triangles and the circles will lie on top of each other if preferences are homogeneous, so that multiplying the outcomes of a prospect f by a constant $k > 0$ multiplies its cash equivalent $c(kf)$ by the same constant, that is, $c(kf) = kc(f)$. In expected utility theory, preference homogeneity gives rise to constant relative risk aversion. Under the present theory, assuming $X = \text{Re}$, preference homogeneity is both necessary and sufficient to represent v as a two-part power function of the form

$$v(x) = \begin{cases} x^\alpha & \text{if } x \geq 0 \\ -\lambda(-x)^\beta & \text{if } x < 0. \end{cases} \tag{5}$$

Figures 3.1 and 3.2 exhibit the characteristic pattern of risk aversion and risk seeking observed in Table 3.4. They also indicate that preference homogeneity holds as a good approximation. The slight departures from homogeneity in Figure 3.1 suggest that the cash equivalents of positive prospects increase more slowly than the stakes (triangles tend to lie below the circles), but no such tendency is evident in Figure 3.2. Overall, it appears that the present data can be

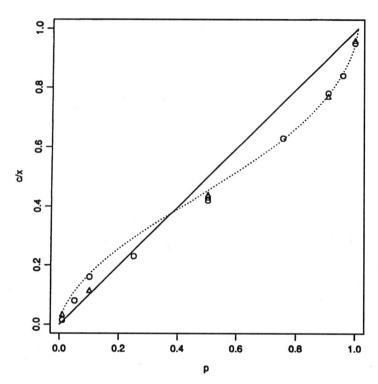

Figure 3.2. Median c/x for all negative prospects of the form $(x, p;$
$0, 1 - p$. Triangles and circles, respectively, correspond to values of x
that lie below or above -200.

approximated by a two-part power function. The smooth curves in Figures 3.1
and 3.2 can be interpreted as weighting functions, assuming a linear value
function. They were fitted using the following functional form:

$$w^+(p) = \frac{p^\gamma}{(p^\gamma + (1 - p)^\gamma)^{1/\gamma}}, \qquad w^-(p) = \frac{p^\delta}{(p^\delta + (1 - p)^\delta)^{1/\delta}}. \tag{6}$$

This form has several useful features: it has only one parameter; it encompasses weighting functions with both concave and convex regions; it does not
require $w(.5) = .5$; and most important, it provides a reasonably good approximation to both the aggregate and the individual data for probabilities in the
range between .05 and .95.

Further information about the properties of the value function can be derived from the data presented in Table 3.6. The adjustments of mixed prospects
to acceptability (problems 1–4) indicate that, for even chances to win and
lose, a prospect will only be acceptable if the gain is at least twice as large
as the loss. This observation is compatible with a value function that changes
slope abruptly, at zero, with a loss-aversion coefficient of about 2 (Tversky and
Kahneman, 1991). The median matches in problems 5 and 6 are also consistent
with this estimate: when the possible loss is increased by k the compensating

Table 3.6. A Test of Loss Aversion

Problem	a	b	c	x	θ
1	0	0	−25	61	2.44
2	0	0	−50	101	2.02
3	0	0	−100	202	2.02
4	0	0	−150	280	1.87
5	−20	50	−50	112	2.07
6	−50	150	−125	301	2.01
7	50	120	20	149	0.97
8	100	300	25	401	1.35

Note: In each problem, subjects determined the value of x that makes the prospect ($a, $\frac{1}{2}$; $b, $\frac{1}{2}$) as attractive as ($c, $\frac{1}{2}$; $x, $\frac{1}{2}$). The median values of x are presented for all problems along with the fixed values a, b, c. The statistic $\theta = (x - b)/(c - a)$ is the ratio of the "slopes" at a higher and a lower region of the value function.

gain must be increased by about $2k$. Problems 7 and 8 are obtained from problems 5 and 6, respectively, by positive translations that turn mixed prospects into strictly positive ones. In contrast to the large values of θ observed in problems 1–6, the responses in problems 7 and 8 indicate that the curvature of the value function for gains is slight. A decrease in the smallest gain of a strictly positive prospect is fully compensated by a slightly larger increase in the largest gain. The standard rank-dependent model, which lacks the notion of a reference point, cannot account for the dramatic effects of small translations of prospects illustrated in Table 3.6.

The estimation of a complex choice model, such as cumulative prospect theory, is problematic. If the functions associated with the theory are not constrained, the number of estimated parameters for each subject is too large. To reduce this number, it is common to assume a parametric form (e.g., a power utility function), but this approach confounds the general test of the theory with that of the specific parametric form. For this reason, we focused here on the qualitative properties of the data rather than on parameter estimates and measures of fit. However, in order to obtain a parsimonious description of the present data, we used a nonlinear regression procedure to estimate the parameters of equations (5) and (6), separately for each subject. The median exponent of the value function was 0.88 for both gains and losses, in accord with diminishing sensitivity. The median λ was 2.25, indicating pronounced loss aversion, and the median values of γ and δ, respectively, were 0.61 and 0.69, in agreement with equations (3) and (4) above.[3] The parameters estimated from the median data were essentially the same. Figure 3 plots w^+ and w^- using the median estimates of γ and δ.

[3] Camerer and Ho (1991) applied equation (6) to several studies of risky choice and estimated γ from aggregate choice probabilities using a logistic distribution function. Their mean estimate (.56) was quite close to ours.

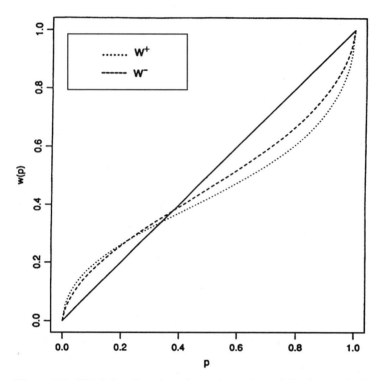

Figure 3.3. Weighting functions for gains (w^+) and for losses (w^-) based on median estimates of γ and δ in equation (12).

Figure 3.3 shows that, for both positive and negative prospects, people over-weight low probabilities and underweight moderate and high probabilities. As a consequence, people are relatively insensitive to probability difference in the middle of the range. Figure 3.3 also shows that the weighting functions for gains and for losses are quite close, although the former is slightly more curved than the latter (i.e., $\gamma < \delta$). Accordingly, risk aversion for gains is more pro-nounced than risk seeking for losses, for moderate and high probabilities (see Table 3.3). It is noteworthy that the condition $w^+(p) = w^-(p)$, assumed in the original version of prospect theory, accounts for the present data better than the assumption $w^+(p) = 1 - w^-(1 - p)$, implied by the standard rank-dependent or cumulative functional. For example, our estimates of w^+ and w^- show that all 25 subjects satisfied the conditions $w^+(.5) < .5$ and $w^-(.5) < .5$, implied by the former model, and no one satisfied the condition $w^+(.5) < .5$ iff $w^-(.5) > .5$, implied by the latter model.

Much research on choice between risky prospects has utilized the triangle diagram (Marschak, 1950; Machina, 1987) that represents the set of all prospects of the form (x_1, p_1; x_2, p_2; x_3, p_3), with fixed outcomes $x_1 < x_2 < x_3$. Each point in the triangle represents a prospect that yields the lowest outcome (x_1) with probability p_1, the highest outcome (x_3) with probability p_3, and the intermediate outcome (x_2) with probability $p_2 = 1 - p_1 - p_3$. An indifference curve is a set of prospects (i.e., points) that the decision maker finds equally attractive. Alternative choice theories are characterized by the shapes of their indifference curves. In particular, the indifference curves of expected utility theory are parallel straight lines. Figures 3.4a and 3.4b illustrate the indifference curves of cumulative prospect theory for nonnegative and nonpositive prospects, respectively. The shapes of the curves are determined by the weighting functions of Figure 3.3; the values of the outcomes (x_1, x_2, x_3) merely control the slope.

Figures 3.4a and 3.4b are in general agreement with the main empirical generalizations that have emerged from the studies of the triangle diagram; see Camerer (1992), and Camerer and Ho (1991) for reviews. First, departures from linearity, which violate expected utility theory, are most pronounced near the edges of the triangle. Second, the indifference curves exhibit both fanning in and fanning out. Third, the curves are concave in the upper part of the triangle and convex in the lower right. Finally, the indifference curves for nonpositive prospects resemble the curves for nonnegative prospects reflected around the 45° line, which represents risk neutrality. For example, a sure gain of $100 is equally as attractive as a 71% chance to win $200 or nothing (see Figure 3.4a), and a sure loss of $100 is equally as aversive as a 64% chance to lose $200 or nothing (see Figure 3.4b). The approximate reflection of the curves is of special interest because it distinguishes the present theory from the standard rank-dependent model in which the two sets of curves are essentially the same.

2.4. Incentives

We conclude this section with a brief discussion of the role of monetary incentives. In the present study we did not pay subjects on the basis of their choices because in our experience with choice between prospects of the type used in the present study, we did not find much difference between subjects who were paid a flat fee and subjects whose payoffs were contingent on their decisions. The same conclusion was obtained by Camerer (1989), who investigated the effects of incentives using several hundred subjects. He found that subjects who actually played the gamble gave essentially the same responses as subjects who did not play; he also found no differences in reliability and roughly the same decision time. Although some studies found differences between paid and unpaid subjects in choice between simple prospects, these differences were not large enough to change any significant qualitative conclusions. Indeed, all major violations of expected utility theory (e.g. the common consequence effect, the common ratio effect, source dependence, loss aversion, and preference reversals) were obtained both with and without monetary incentives.

As noted by several authors, however, the financial incentives provided in choice experiments are generally small relative to people's incomes. What

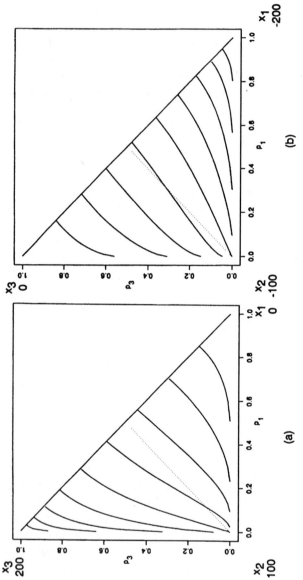

Figure 3.4. Indifference curves of cumulative prospect theory (a) for nonnegative prospects ($x_1 = 0$, $x_2 = 100$, $x_3 = 200$), and (b) for nonpositive prospects ($x_1 = -200$, $x_2 = -100$, $x_3 = 0$). The curves are based on the respective weighting functions of Figure 3.3, ($\gamma = .61$, $\delta = .69$) and on the median estimates of the exponents of the value function ($\alpha = \beta = .88$). The broken line through the origin represents the prospects whose expected value is x_2.

happens when the stakes correspond to three- or four-digit rather than one- or two-digit figures? To answer this question, Kachelmeier and Shehata (1991) conducted a series of experiments using Masters students at Beijing University, most of whom had taken at least one course in economics or business. Due to the economic conditions in China, the investigators were able to offer subjects very large rewards. In the high payoff condition, subjects earned about three times their normal monthly income in the course of one experimental session! On each trial, subjects were presented with a simple bet that offered a specified probability to win a given prize, and nothing otherwise. Subjects were instructed to state their cash equivalent for each bet. An incentive-compatible procedure (the BDM scheme) was used to determine, on each trial, whether the subject would play the bet or receive the "official" selling price. If departures from the standard theory are due to the mental cost associated with decision making and the absence of proper incentives, as suggested by Smith and Walker (1992), then the highly paid Chinese subjects should not exhibit the characteristic nonlinearity observed in hypothetical choices, or in choices with small payoffs.

However, the main finding of Kachelmeier and Shehata (1991) is massive risk seeking for small probabilities. Risk seeking was slightly more pronounced for lower payoffs, but even in the highest payoff condition, the cash equivalent for a 5% bet (their lowest probability level) was, on average, three times larger than its expected value. Note that in the present study the median cash equivalent of a 5% chance to win $100 (see Table 3.3) was $14, almost three times the expected value of the bet. In general, the cash equivalents obtained by Kachelmeier and Shehata were higher than those observed in the present study. This is consistent with the finding that minimal selling prices are generally higher than certainty equivalents derived from choice (see, e.g., Tversky, Slovic, and Kahneman, 1990). As a consequence, they found little risk aversion for moderate and high probability of winning. This was true for the Chinese subjects, at both high and low payoffs, as well as for Canadian subjects, who either played for low stakes or did not receive any payoff. The most striking result in all groups was the marked overweighting of small probabilities, in accord with the present analysis.

Evidently, high incentives do not always dominate noneconomic considerations, and the observed departures from expected utility theory cannot be rationalized in terms of the cost of thinking. We agree with Smith and Walker (1992) that monetary incentives could improve performance under certain conditions by eliminating careless errors. However, we maintain that monetary incentives are neither necessary nor sufficient to ensure subjects' cooperativeness, thoughtfulness, or truthfulness. The similarity between the results obtained with and without monetary incentives in choice between simple prospects provides no special reason for skepticism about experiments without contingent payment.

3. DISCUSSION

Theories of choice under uncertainty commonly specify 1) the objects of choice, 2) a valuation rule, and 3) the characteristics of the functions that map uncertain events and possible outcomes into their subjective counterparts. In standard applications of expected utility theory, the objects of choice are probability distributions over wealth, the valuation rule is expected utility, and utility is a concave function of wealth. The empirical evidence reported here and elsewhere requires major revisions of all three elements. We have proposed an alternative descriptive theory in which 1) the objects of choice are prospects framed in terms of gains and losses, 2) the valuation rule is a two-part cumulative functional, and 3) the value function is S-shaped and the weighting functions are inverse S-shaped. The experimental findings confirmed the qualitative properties of these scales, which can be approximated by a (two-part) power value function and by identical weighting functions for gains and losses.

The curvature of the weighting function explains the characteristic reflection pattern of attitudes to risky prospects. Overweighting of small probabilities contributes to the popularity of both lotteries and insurance. Underweighting of high probabilities contributes both to the prevalence of risk aversion in choices between probable gains and sure things, and to the prevalence of risk seeking in choices between probable and sure losses. Risk aversion for gains and risk seeking for losses are further enhanced by the curvature of the value function in the two domains. The pronounced asymmetry of the value function, which we have labeled loss aversion, explains the extreme reluctance to accept mixed prospects. The shape of the weighting function explains the certainty effect and violations of quasi-convexity. It also explains why these phenomena are most readily observed at the two ends of the probability scale, where the curvature of the weighting function is most pronounced (Camerer, 1992).

The new demonstrations of the common consequence effect, described in Tables 3.1 and 3.2, show that choice under uncertainty exhibits some of the main characteristics observed in choice under risk. On the other hand, there are indications that the decision weights associated with uncertain and with risky prospects differ in important ways. First, there is abundant evidence that subjective judgments of probability do not conform to the rules of probability theory (Kahneman, Slovic and Tversky, 1982). Second, Ellsberg's example and more recent studies of choice under uncertainty indicate that people prefer some sources of uncertainty over others. For example, Heath and Tversky (1991) found that individuals consistently preferred bets on uncertain events in their area of expertise over matched bets on chance devices, although the former are ambiguous and the latter are not. The presence of systematic preferences for some sources of uncertainty calls for different weighting functions for different domains, and suggests that some of these functions lie entirely above others. The investigation of decision weights for uncertain events emerges as a promising domain for future research.

The present theory retains the major features of the original version of prospect theory and introduces a (two-part) cumulative functional, which provides a convenient mathematical representation of decision weights. It also relaxes some descriptively inappropriate constraints of expected utility theory. Despite its greater generality, the cumulative functional is unlikely to be accurate in detail. We suspect that decision weights may be sensitive to the formulation of the prospects, as well as to the number, the spacing and the level of outcomes. In particular, there is some evidence to suggest that the curvature of the weighting function is more pronounced when the outcomes are widely spaced (Camerer, 1992). The present theory can be generalized to accommodate such effects, but it is questionable whether the gain in descriptive validity, achieved by giving up the separability of values and weights, would justify the loss of predictive power and the cost of increased complexity.

Theories of choice are at best approximate and incomplete. One reason for this pessimistic assessment is that choice is a constructive and contingent process. When faced with a complex problem, people employ a variety of heuristic procedures in order to simplify the representation and the evaluation of prospects. These procedures include computational shortcuts and editing operations, such as eliminating common components and discarding nonessential differences (Tversky, 1969). The heuristics of choice do not readily lend themselves to formal analysis because their application depends on the formulation of the problem, the method of elicitation, and the context of choice.

Prospect theory departs from the tradition that assumes the rationality of economic agents; it is proposed as a descriptive, not a normative, theory. The idealized assumption of rationality in economic theory is commonly justified on two grounds: the conviction that only rational behavior can survive in a competitive environment, and the fear that any treatment that abandons rationality will be chaotic and intractable. Both arguments are questionable. First, the evidence indicates that people can spend a lifetime in a competitive environment without acquiring a general ability to avoid framing effects or to apply linear decision weights. Second, and perhaps more important, the evidence indicates that human choices are orderly, although not always rational in the traditional sense of this word.

4. Compound Invariant Weighting Functions in Prospect Theory[1]

Dražen Prelec

1. INTRODUCTION

In their article on Prospect Theory, Kahneman and Tversky (1979) introduced a nonlinear transformation of probabilities, $p \to w(p)$ (or $\pi(p)$ in the 1979 notation), which is also called a *probability weighting function*. The purpose of the transformation was to explain several key expected utility violations, including the classical paradoxes of Allais (1953). Taking each violation as an independent constraint on $w(p)$, they composed a conjecture about its shape – a conjecture that has been refined but not substantially altered by later work (Camerer and Ho 1994, Wu and Gonzalez 1996a).

Although its empirical picture has come into focus, the weighting function has remained a somewhat tricky object to analyze – at least in comparison with utility functions. A glance at Figure 4.1, displaying some recent estimates, reveals the nature of the problem. In the figure, the x-axis represents probability of an outcome, and the y-axis the weight associated with that probability. Unlike utility functions, in which the deviation from linearity has an essentially one-dimensional character (i.e., concavity), here we see both concavity and convexity. Curiously, the function is asymmetrical, with the convex region being about twice as large as the concave region. Overall, it does not look like a shape that one would draw unless compelled by strong empirical evidence.

This paper is a nontechnical exposition of some recent attempts to explain this particular shape from underlying axioms. I will begin by describing three main properties of an empirical weighting function. Then I will introduce an axiomatic functional form that fulfills these requirements (Prelec 1998). This *compound-invariant* form (shown in Figure 4.3) has two variants, a two-parameter: $w(p) = \exp[-\beta(-\ln p)^{\alpha}]$ and a one-parameter: $w(p) \exp[-(-\ln p)^{\alpha}]$ ($\alpha, \beta > 0$). The main theoretical advantage of compound-invariant weighting functions is that they order different classes of expected utility violations in the same way. A secondary advantage is tractability. For example, by combining the one-parameter variant with a power function for money value, one gets a

[1] The paper was written while the author was a Fellow at the Center for Advanced Study in the Behavioral Sciences. I am grateful for financial support by NSF Grants # SBR-9511131 and # SBR-960123 (to the Center).

67

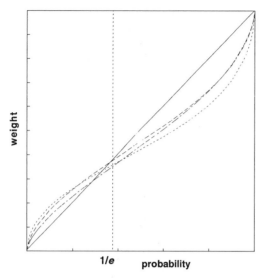

Figure 4.1. Parametric estimates of $w(p)$. The dotted lines are estimates of the function of $w(p) = p^\delta / (p^\delta + (1-p)^\delta)^{1/\delta}$ (by Tversky and Kahneman 1992, Camerer and Ho 1994, and Gonzalez 1996a). The solid line is Tversky and Fox's (1995) estimate of the two-parameter form $w(p) = \alpha p^\delta / (\alpha p^\delta + (1-p)^\delta)$.

linearizable model that seems to hold up well even at probabilities as small as one chance in a million.

2. CUMULATED PROSPECT THEORY

A nonlinear probability transformation arises in several related models, including prospect theory. Although each model creates a slightly different theoretical environment for the function, these differences are on the whole not critical. In this paper, the background model is cumulated prospect theory (CPT) specialized for the domain of risk, that is, for probability distributions over positive (gains) and negative (losses) money outcomes (Tversky and Kahneman 1992). Appendix A discusses briefly some of the advantages of CPT over other models.

A CPT representation requires three continuously increasing scaling functions: a value function, $v(x)$, which gives the value or utility of a money outcome, and two probability weighting functions, one applied to gain probabilities, $w^-(p)$, and one to loss probabilities, $w^+(p)$. The value function is a ratio scale unique up to multiplication by a positive constant (hence $v(0) = 0$); the weighting functions are unique under the standard normalization, $w^+(1) = w^-(1) = 1$.

A *prospect* is a finite distribution over outcomes: $(x, p; y, q; z, r; \ldots)$ assigning probabilities $p, q, r, \ldots$ to outcomes $x, y, z, \ldots$. This paper deals with the two types of prospects: *simple prospects* with one nonzero outcome, (x, p); and *binary prospects* with two nonzero outcomes, $(x, p; y, q)$ (the zero outcome is not explicitly listed in the prospects). Restricted to this subset of prospects, CPT represents preferences by the following formulas:

$$\text{CPT valuation of } (x, p) = \begin{cases} w^+(p)v(x), & x > 0, & (2.1a) \\ w^-(p)v(x), & x < 0, & (2.1b) \end{cases}$$

CPT valuation of $(x, p; y, q)$

$$= \begin{cases} w^+(p+q)v(x) + w^+(q)(v(y) - v(x)), & 0 < x < y, & (2.2a) \\ w^-(p+q)v(x) + w^-(q)(v(y) - v(x)), & y < x < 0, & (2.2a) \\ w^-(p)v(x) + w^+(q)v(y), & x < 0 < y. & (2.3) \end{cases}$$

Equation 2.1 is not controversial. Equations 2.2 and 2.3, on the other hand, assume a "rank- and sign-dependent" framing of outcomes.[2] If x and y have opposite sign, as in Eq. 2.3, then the prospect is framed as a p-chance of losing x and a q-chance of gaining y. If, however, both x, y are gains, or both are losses, as in Eqs. 2.2a or 2.2b, then the prospect $(x, p; y, q)$ is framed as a '$p + q$' chance of gaining [i.e., losing] *at least* the value of the middle outcome, $v(x)$, and a 'q' chance of gaining [i.e., losing] *an extra* $v(y) - v(x)$. In CPT, the argument of the weighting function is not the probability of obtaining outcome x but the cumulated probability of obtaining an outcome *at least as good as* x, if x is positive, or *at least as bad as* x, if x is negative.

3. EMPIRICAL PROPERTIES OF THE WEIGHTING FUNCTION

3.1. Over/Underweighting: Empirical Intuition
The first, and perhaps most important empirical property of probability weighting is that $w(p)$ intersects the diagonal from above. Small probabilities receive "too much" weight, whereas large probabilities receive "too little" weight. This leads to the *fourfold pattern of risk attitudes*, as described and documented by Tversky and Kahneman (1992). The overweighting of small probabilities increases the appeal of low-probability lottery tickets but also increases the aversion to low-probability risks. Hence, the same departure from linearity (overweighting of small p) works in favor of risk seeking in the domain of gains and in favor of risk aversion in the domain of losses. The underweighting of large probabilities has dual implications, too. With gains, the underweighting of a large win probability decreases the attraction of the gamble relative to a

---

[2] Here is a short history of rank and sign dependence before Tversky and Kahneman (1992); see also Camerer (1992), Wakker (1994), and Starmer (1998). Original prospect theory (1979) assumed sign dependence, with $w^+(p) = w^-(p)$, and a restricted form of rank dependence (restricted to binary prospects with two nonzero outcomes of same sign). Quiggin (1982) invented the rank-dependent representation but did not make room for sign dependence. Starmer and Sugden (1989) were the first to combine Quiggin's model with sign dependence. Luce (1991) and Luce and Fishburn (1991) provided an axiomatic derivation of a rank- and sign-dependent representation with linear utility.

sure thing; that is, it promotes risk aversion. With losses, the underweighting of a large loss probability increases the attraction of the gamble relative to a certain, smaller loss; that is, it promotes risk seeking.

3.2. Over/Underweighting: Preference Conditions

Even though over/underweighting is so important for risk attitudes, we still do not have a clean translation of the property into the language of preferences.[3] If value is linear in money, then "simple" risk attitude (i.e., as revealed by preferences between simple prospects and their expected values) is entirely determined by the shape of $w(p)$. In this special case, over/underweighting of probabilities is equivalent to the fourfold pattern of risk attitudes. But value is not linear in money. To sustain the fourfold pattern in the general case, probability weighting must override the curvature of the value function, which sometimes works in favor and sometimes against the pattern.

As Kahneman and Tversky observed in 1979, risk seeking with small-p gains is sufficient evidence for overweighting on the reasonable assumption that $v(x)$ is concave for gains. Indeed, in the real world, there are altogether three factors working against the purchase of a sweepstakes ticket: first there is the concavity of the value function, which diminishes the value of the prize relative to the value of the ticket price; second, there is loss aversion (spending the money for the ticket is a "loss," whereas the prize is a "gain"); third, the price of the ticket is typically much greater than the actuarial expected value of the lottery. That people purchase lottery tickets indicates probability overweighting is strong enough to compensate for all three factors.

3.3. Decreasing Relative Sensitivity (Subproportionality): Empirical Intuition

A second requirement on $w(p)$ derives from a famous Allais paradox called the "common-ratio violation" (Allais 1953). Here, in Table 4.1, is the original demonstration that Allais presented to Leonard Savage, Paul Samuelson, and other members of the "American School" of expected utility theorists in Paris in 1952 (Allais and Hagen 1979).

The top choice in the table is between a 98% chance of 500 million (1952 Francs) and a sure 100 million; the bottom choice is between a 0.98% chance of 500 million and a 1% chance of 100 million. Expected utility theory implies that a sure 100 million will be preferred to the 98% chance of 500 million if and only if the utility of a 100-million gain is more than 98% of the utility of a 500 million gain, which in turn will hold if and only if a 1% chance of

---

[3] In (Prelec 1998; Proposition 6), I have identified an axiom equivalent to the weighting function being concave and underweighting, or convex and overweighting, on an interval. In principle, this lets us characterize over/underweighting for functions that have a finite number of concave or convex intervals. However, the preference conditions that are reached by this path are not easily testable.

Table 4.1. The Allais Common-Ratio Schema

	Riskier Prospect	Allais' Preferences	Safer Prospect
Top-choice pair	$P_1 = 98\%$ chance of 500M	$<$	$P_2 = 100M$
Bottom-choice pair	$P_1' = 0.98\%$ chance of 500M	$>$	$P_2' = 1\%$ chance of 500M

100 million is preferred to a 0.98% chance of 500 million. Hence, the expected utility maximizer should prefer either the riskier or the safer prospect in both cases. Allais' defense of his contrary preferences deserves quoting in full:

The author of this memoir, *who is perfectly familiar with Samuelson's arguments* [for the EU axioms], unhesitatingly prefers prospect (P$_2$) to prospect (P$_1$) and prospect (P$_1'$) to prospect (P$_2'$) and he thinks that most of his readers will share his preference; yet, to the best of his knowledge, he believes that he is not irrational. He is perfectly aware that 2 chances in 100,000 is a nonnegligible quantity, but his view is that this quantity does not offset for him the reduction in the possible gain from 500 to 100 million, whereas for him by contrast, the achievement of *certainty* by raising the chance of winning from 98% to 100% is well worth this reduction. (Allais and Hagen 1979, p. 102).

Prospect theory interprets these intuitions in a specific and entirely plausible way. According to Eq. 2.1, a preference for P_1' over P_2' holds if $v(100\,\mathrm{M})/v(500\,\mathrm{M}) < w^+(.0098)/w^+(.01)$; a preference for P_2 over P_1 holds if $v(100\,\mathrm{M})/v(500\,\mathrm{M}) > w^+(.98)/w^+(1)$. The entire pattern can be reconciled on the assumption that: $w^+(.98)/w^+(1) < w^+(.0098)/w^+(.01)$, which is to say that "raising the chance of winning from 98 to 100%" has a greater impact on relative weight than raising the chance of winning from 0.98 to 1%.

The principle behind the inequality, $w^+(.98)/w^+(1) < w^+(.0098)/w^+(.01)$, can be extended to other probabilities; for example,

$$\frac{w^+(.98)}{w^+(1)} < \frac{w^+(.098)}{w^+(.1)} < \frac{w^+(.0098)}{w^+(.01)} < \frac{w^+(.00098)}{w^+(.001)} < \cdots < 1.$$

or, following Kahneman and Tversky, to the general claim that

for a fixed ratio of probabilities, the ratio of the corresponding decision weights is closer to unity when the probabilities are low than when they are high. This property, called sub-proportionality, imposes considerable constraints on the shape of π [i.e., w]: it holds if and only if log π is a [strictly] convex function of log p. (Kahneman and Tversky 1979, p. 282).

For example, the graphs in Figure 4.1 show that the weight of $p = 1/2$ is about .40, or 40% of the weight of certainty, whereas the weight of $p = 1/4$ is about .30, or 75% of the weight of $p = 1/2$. Hence, the graphs satisfy subproportionality – at least for this particular set of probabilities.

3.4. Decreasing Relative Sensitivity (Subproportionality): Preference Conditions

The preference conditions for subproportionality are a simple generalization of the common-ratio pattern observed by Allais.

SUBPROPORTIONALITY. *For any* $0 < \lambda < 1$, $y > x$, $(x, p) \sim (y, q)$ *implies:* $(y, \lambda q) > (x, \lambda p)$.

In words, indifference between two simple prospects shifts to preference for the prospect with the better nonzero outcome as the probability of the nonzero outcome is reduced by equal proportion in both prospects.

3.5. Increasing Absolute Sensitivity Near $p = 0$ and $p = 1$ (Subadditivity): Empirical Intuition

The third property of probability weighting is that its slope of $w(p)$ increases towards the endpoints of the probability interval. An example by Richard Zeckhauser (cited by Kahneman and Tversky 1979) provides a convincing demonstration. Consider a person forced to play Russian roulette but who is granted the privilege to remove one bullet from the gun before it is fired. How does the value of removing that single bullet depend on the total number of bullets in the gun? Plainly, removing one bullet out of four is a less significant improvement than removing the only bullet from the gun, or, at the other extreme, removing one bullet when all six chambers are loaded. Changing the probability from 1/2 to 2/3 has smaller impact on the value of the prospect than changing them from 0 to 1/6, or from 5/6 to certainty. This kind of non-linearity is exhibited by the functions in Figure 4.1, which are concave near zero and convex near one.

3.6. Increasing Absolute Sensitivity Near $p = 0$ and $p = 1$ (Subadditivity): Preference Conditions

The preference conditions behind increasing absolute sensitivity derive from a second paradox of Allais called the *common-consequence effect*. Table 4.2 gives the exact numbers in Allais' original demonstration.

Allais observed that most people would prefer the riskier prospect in the top pair and the safer prospect in the bottom pair. Yet, in going from the top pair to the bottom one, all that we have done is replace an 89% chance at zero with an 89% chance of $1 M. According to the additive expected utility formula, the expected utility of both the safer and the riskier prospect should improve by

Table 4.2. The Allais Common-Consequence Schema

	Safer Prospect	Allais' Preferences	Riskier Prospect
Top-choice pair	11% chance of 100M	>	10% chance of 500M
Bottom-choice pair	100 M for sure	<	10% chance of 500M
			89% chance of 100M

the same amount, that is, .89 times the utility of a $1 M gain. Hence, expected utility implies that whatever preferences hold for the top pair should also hold for the bottom pair.

Let us see what Allais' preferences imply about the weighting function. In the CPT representation, the top preference shows: $w^+(.11)v(100) < w^+(.10)$ $v(500)$ (applying Eq. 2.1a), whereas the bottom shows $v(1) > w^+(.99)v(100) + w^+(.10)(v(500) - v(100))$ (applying Eq. 2.2a). Eliminating the ratio $v(1)/v(5)$ gives us an inequality: $1 - w^+(.99) > w^+(.11) - w^+(.10)$, which shows that the differential weight placed on the worst centile of the positive outcome distribution $1 - w^+(.99)$ is greater than the differential weight placed on the tenth-best centile of the distribution $w^+(.11) - w^+(.10)$. The CPT model thus fosters a particular interpretation of Allais' example, namely, that the essential difference between adding an 89% chance for 100 M to the safer and to the riskier prospects resides in the safer prospect's modification covering centiles 11 through 100 and thus delivering a sure gain, whereas for the riskier prospect the modification covers centiles 10 through 99, leaving "exposed" the worst centile of the distribution, which corresponds to no gain at all.

There is nothing special about these probabilities, of course. The general property of the weighting function that supports the Allais example is *subadditivity* (Tversky and Wakker 1995). It has two parts. The first part states that an increase in weight produced by adding probability Δ to p is greater when $p + \Delta = 1$, and certainty is clinched, than when $p + \Delta < 1$. This corresponds to the first part of the Russian roulette example, where the impact of removing the single bullet from the gun is perceived to be greater than the impact of removing one of four bullets. At the other end of the probability interval, the increase in weight produced by adding Δ to p is greater when $p = 0$ than when $p > 0$. This corresponds to the second part of the example in which the impact of removing one bullet out of six is greater than the impact of removing one bullet out of four.

Notice that we have said nothing so far about comparisons involving the two endpoints of the probability interval (e.g., between the impact of removing one bullet out of six and removing the only bullet from the gun). Subadditivity only compares the middle of the interval with one or the other endpoint and maintains an agnostic position on whether the slope at one or the other endpoint is greater (indeed, the slope might very well be infinite at both endpoints). For this reason, Tversky and Wakker's formal definition restricts subadditivity by "small" boundary constants c and $c' \geq 0$:

$$w(p + \Delta) - w(p) \leq w(1) - w(1 - \Delta), \quad p \geq c' \geq 0,$$

$$w(\Delta) - w(0) \geq w(p + \Delta) - w(p), \quad p + \Delta \leq 1 - c \leq 1.$$

The corresponding preference conditions (formulated by Tversky and Wakker 1995) are a special case of conditions equivalent to convexity or concavity of the weighting function (Wu and Gonzalez 1996b). Because concavity and convexity have interest in their own right, it is worth the effort

Table 4.3. The Concavity/Convexity (C/C) Schema (Gains)

	Safer Prospect	Concavity Preferences	Convexity Preferences	Riskier Prospect
Top-choice pair	$p + \delta$ chance of x	$\geq$	$\leq$	ε chance of $\$y > \$x$ $p - \varepsilon$ chance of $\$x$
Bottom-choice pair	$p + q + \delta$ chance of x	$<$	$>$	ε chance of $\$y > \$x$ $p + q - \varepsilon$ chance of $\$x$

to develop the more general formulation. The idea is to start with a simple prospect – a $(p + \delta)$ chance at prize x – and compare that with a prospect that offers an ε chance of a higher prize y but only a p chance of winning anything at all (x or y). This choice is shown in the top line of the concavity/convexity schema in Table 4.3 (adapted from Wu and Gonzalez 1996b). The bottom pair then repeats the same question but with the overall probability of winning now shifted upward by q.

Two preference patterns are inconsistent with expected utility, and they are shown in the concavity and convexity columns of the table. Let us examine the convexity pattern. Choosing the riskier prospect in the top pair demonstrates that $w^+(p + \delta)v(x) < w^+(p - \varepsilon)v(x) + w^+(\varepsilon)(v(y) - v(x))$; choosing the safer prospect in the bottom pair demonstrates that $w^+(p + q + \delta)v(x) < w^+(p + q - \varepsilon)v(x) + w^+(\varepsilon)(v(y) - v(x))$. Combining the two inequalities shows that the slope near p is smaller than the slope near $p + q$: $w^+(p + \delta) - w^+(p - \varepsilon) < w^+(p + q + \delta) - w^+(p + q - \varepsilon)$. If this holds for all such constructions, then the weighting function is convex on the interval $[p - \varepsilon, p + q + \delta]$. A similar argument applies to the concavity condition. In summary,

Convexity preferences in C/C Schema
$$\Longrightarrow w^+(p + q + \delta) - w^+(p + q - \varepsilon) > w^+(p + \delta) - w^+(p - \varepsilon),$$

Concavity preferences in C/C Schema
$$\Longrightarrow w^+(p + q + \delta) - w^+(p + q - \varepsilon) < w^+(p + \delta) - w^+(p - \varepsilon).$$

Subadditivity is equivalent to boundary concavity at $p = 0$ and boundary convexity at $p = 1$ ("boundary" means that one of the prospects must fall on the boundary of the three-outcome probability simplex).

SUBADDITIVITY (GAINS). *There exist constants c, c' such that for any probabilities p, q, δ, ε, if $p - \varepsilon \geq c' \geq 0$ and $p + q + \delta = 1$, then we cannot find outcomes $0 < x < y$ producing concavity preferences in the concavity and convexity schema, and if $p + q + \delta \leq 1 - c \leq 1$ and $p - \varepsilon = 0$, then we cannot find outcomes $0 < x < y$ producing convexity preferences in the schema.*

Subadditivity is a conservative interpretation of the Allais common-consequence effect – it does not claim anything about the slope of the function away from the endpoints. For example, a linear weighting function (Bell 1985), discontinuous at the endpoints, satisfies subadditivity. There is good evidence, however, that common-consequence violations of expected utility arise even in the interior of the probability simplex and that the weighting function is nonlinear even away from the endpoints. Wu and Gonzalez (1996b), who have collected some of the most convincing data on this point (see Figure 4.4), propose the more stringent criterion that the function is concave on an initial interval and convex beyond that:

CONCAVITY/CONVEXITY (GAINS). *There exists an inflection probability p^* such that for any p, q, δ, ε: (1) if $p - \varepsilon \geq p^*$, then we cannot find outcomes $0 < x < y$ producing concavity preferences in the concavity/convexity schema, and (2) if $p + q + \delta \leq p^*$, then we cannot find outcomes $0 < x < y$ producing convexity preferences in the concavity/convexity schema.*

4. COMPOUND INVARIANCE

Here, then, we have, as an embarrassment of riches, three separate but closely related requirements on the shape of the weighting function. Logically, the requirements are distinct: one can draw functions that satisfy any single requirement but not the other two (see Figure 4.2); empirically, however, it does not

Figure 4.2. Examples of continuous weighting functions satisfying exactly one of the three target properties. The top function is subproportional, but neither over/underweighting, nor subadditive. The middle function is over/underweighting but neither subproportional and nor subadditive. The bottom function is subadditive but neither subproportional nor over/underweighting.

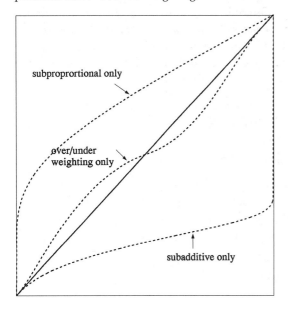

seem that we need the distinctions. Individuals who satisfy one but not the other two of our criteria are probably rare.

In this section I introduce an axiom, *compound invariance*, that aligns all three criteria. Given the axiom, the ordering of weighting functions by over/under-weighting, subproportionality, and subadditivity coincides. Let us start with an example. Consider the following pair of indifference judgments:

($10,000 for sure) $\sim$ (1/2 chance of $30,000),

(1/2 chance of $10,000) $\sim$ (1/6 chance of $30,000).   (Schema A)

The first judgment implies that $v(10\,\mathrm{K}) = w^+(1/2)v(30\,\mathrm{K})$, whereas the second implies that $w^+(1/2)v(10\,\mathrm{K}) = w^+(1/6)v(30\,\mathrm{K})$. Jointly, they show that the weight of a coin toss ($p = 1/2$) relative to a sure thing is the same as the weight of a die roll ($p = 1/6$) to a coin toss, which is to say that $w^+(1)/w^+(1/2) = w^+(1/2)/w^+(1/6)$. This violates expected utility of course. The question now is, What does this imply about other common-ratio violations, or, how do common-ratio violations propagate from one set of probabilities (p, q, r, s) to another set (p', q', r', s')?

Compound invariance gives one possible answer to this question: It claims that common-ratio violations such as in Schema A are preserved when all probabilities are compounded (squared, cubed, etc.). In particular, if Schema A holds, then whatever dollar values (e.g., $6,000 and $30,000) create indifference between the squared probabilities in the top pair will also create indifference between squared probabilities in the bottom pair:

($6,000 for sure) $\sim$ (1/4 chance of $30,000),

(1/4 chance of $6,000) $\sim$ (1/36 chance of $30,000).   (Schema B)

The person in Schema A is indifferent between $10,000 and tossing a coin for $30,000 and is also indifferent between tossing a coin for $10,000 and rolling a die for $30,000. The compound invariance assumption states that requiring N successive wins, either on coin toss or die roll, will preserve the common-ratio violation structure after the dollar outcomes are adjusted.

COMPOUND INVARIANCE. *For any outcomes* x, y, x', $y' \in X$, *probabilities* $q, p, r, s \in [0, 1]$, *and compounding integer* $N \geq 1$:

If: $(x, p) \sim (y, q)$ *and* $(x, r) \sim (y, s)$
then: $(x', p^N) \sim (y', q^N)$ *implies*: $(x', r^N) \sim (y', s^N)$.

At the level of the weighting function, compound invariance claims that if the weight of certainty to a coin toss is just as the weight of a coin toss to a dice roll, then the weights of the compound events, defined by 2 or N independent coin tosses or dice rolls, stand in the exact same relation:

$$\frac{w^+(1)}{w^+(1/2)} = \frac{w^+(1/2)}{w^+(1/6)} \implies \frac{w^+(1^N)}{w^+((1/2)^N)} = \frac{w^+((1/2)^N)}{w^+((1/6)^N)}$$

The intuition behind the axiom can also be expressed in reverse direction, going from Schema B to Schema A. Imagine that Schema B holds for you, so that you are indifferent between a 1/4 chance at 30 K and 6 K for sure and also indifferent between a 1/36 chance at 30 K and a 1/4 chance at 6 K. Because you are willing to pay the same price (i.e., 24 K = 30 K − 6 K) to replace $p = 1/36$ with $p = 1/4$ and to replace $p = 1/4$ with certainty, the value $p = 1/4$ is a *relative midpoint* between $p = 1/36$ and certainty. Now, suppose that exactly one-half of the uncertainty has been resolved favorably in each prospect so that success no longer requires two independent events but only one event, that is, one coin toss instead of two and one die roll instead of two. The axiom states that this uniform resolution of one-half of the uncertainty should preserve the midpoint position of the coin-toss prospect relative to the sure prospect and the die-roll prospect.

The compound invariance axiom is an implication of expected utility, but it is a much weaker condition.[4] Expected utility preserves relative midpoints under compounding but also constrains the location of the midpoint: If p is a relative midpoint between certainty and q, then expected utility implies $q = p^2$. After compounding, q^2 remains a relative midpoint between 1 and p^4, and so on. Under compound invariance the location of the relative midpoint is not constrained in this way, but, as in expected utility, the location is subsequently preserved by compounding.

4.1. Implications of Compound Invariance

Proposition 1 defines the functions consistent with compound invariance. Although the proposition presupposes the full structure of cumulated prospect theory, the axiom and proof only use simple prospects; hence, some version of the proposition would hold in context of any model that represents preferences over (x, p) by the multiplicative formula, $w(p)v(x)$.

PROPOSITION 1 (PRELEC 1998). *In the context of CPT, compound invariance implies that the weighting functions for losses and gains are jointly characterized by three positive parameters, α, β^+, $\beta^- > 0$:*

$$w^+(p) = \exp\{-\beta^+(-\ln p)^\alpha\},$$
$$w^-(p) = \exp\{-\beta^-(-\ln p)^\alpha\}.$$

What do these functions look like? If $\alpha = \beta^+ = \beta^- = 1$, they are linear; this is the expected utility case. If $\alpha = 1$, then they are power functions p^β, which are non-linear but satisfy none of our three properties. If $\alpha \neq 1$, then the case $\alpha > 1$ gives s-shaped functions, initially convex and then concave. Finally, the case $\alpha < 1$ gives inverted s-shaped functions that meet all three empirical requirements

---

[4] See Luce (1998) for an alternative derivation of the CI function in the context of compound lotteries. Luce also shows that we can set $p = 1$ in the statement of the compound invariance axiom.

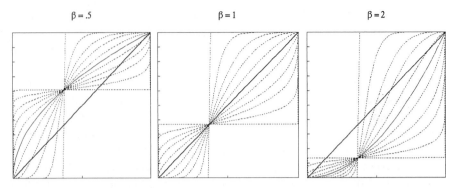

Figure 4.3. The compound-invariant function. Each panel holds the β-value constant ($\beta = .5$, $\beta = 1$, $\beta = 2$) and plots the function for 11 different α-values ($\alpha = .001$, $\alpha = .143$, $\alpha = .33$, $\alpha = .5$, $\alpha = .75$, $\alpha = 1$, $\alpha = 1.33$, $\alpha = 2$, $\alpha = 3$, $\alpha = 7$, $\alpha = 1000$).

from Section 3: they intersect the diagonal from above, are concave–convex (therefore also subadditive), and are subproportional.[5] Figure 4.3 displays the full menu of options. Each panel holds fixed the β value and graphs the function for eleven different α values. The solid line in each panel is the $\beta = 1$ case.

4.2. The α-Parameter as an "Allais Paradox Index"

According to Proposition 1, compound invariance assigns to each person two β-values, one for losses and one for gains, and a single α-value. It turns out that α-values say a great deal about individuals' propensities to commit different sorts of expected utility violations:

PROPOSITION 2. *Consider Person 1 and Person 2, both satisfying compound invariance, with weighting functions parametrized by $(\alpha_1, \beta_1^+, \beta_1^-)$ and $(\alpha_2, \beta_2^+, \beta_2^-)$, respectively. Then the following five statements are equivalent:*

(A) $\alpha_1 < \alpha_2$
(B) w_1^+ and w_1^- are more over/underweighting than w_2^+ and w_2^-
(C) w_1^+ and w_1^- are more subproportional than w_2^+ and w_2^-
(D) w_1^+ and w_1^- are more subadditive than w_2^+ and w_2^-
(E) w_1^+ and w_1^- are more concave/convex than w_2^+ and w_2^-.

Formally, w_1 is more over/underweighting (subproportional, etc.) than w_2 if the composition of w_1 with the inverse of w_2, or $w_1(w_2^{-1})$, is itself an over/underweighting (subproportional, etc.) function. This means that w_1 can "override" the nonlinearity of w_2. For example, $w_1(w_2^{-1})$ is over/underweighting if and only if w_1 intersects w_2 from above. A nice property of compound

---

[5] Although (3.2) is not defined for $p = 0$, it approaches 0 as $p \to 0$, hence, the functions are continuous on the entire probability interval.

invariant functions is that the composition $w_1(w_2^{-1})$, is itself a compound invariant function with an α-parameter equal to α_1/α_2. Therefore, if $\alpha_1 < \alpha_2$, then the α-coefficient for $w_1(w_2^{-1})$, or α_1/α_2, is smaller than 1. This implies that $w_1(w_2^{-1})$ is over/underweighting (subproportional, etc.), which is to say that w_1 is more over/underweighting (subproportional, etc.) than w_2.

In the compound-invariant universe, the ranking of individuals on our three main nonlinearity criteria is consistent and determined entirely their α-values. For example, if one person has a weighting function that intersects another person's function from above, then that person will commit more Allais common-ratio violations *and* more Allais common-consequence violations. For this reason, I will refer to α as the "Allais violation index" of nonlinear probability weighting.

4.3. Behavior near Zero

In many applications domains, such as insurance, lotteries, or health risks, we are especially interested in attitudes to extremely small probabilities. What should probability weights look like as p is drawn down to zero? Three intuitions are in play here. First, the weight of small chances should smoothly decline to zero. Second, the transition from impossibility to possibility has a qualitative character, as if the function has infinite slope at zero. Third, small chances become relatively indistinguishable near zero in the sense that one chance in a million has about the same weight as two chances in a million. This is especially plausible if the weights of small chances are measured independently without drawing attention to their ratios.

The compound-invariant function reconciles these three intuitions, provided $\alpha < 1$. Near $p = 0$, it approximates a continuous step function in the sense that for any p, q, the limit as $\lambda \to 0$ of the ratio $w(\lambda p)/w(\lambda q)$ equals 1. The step function shape means that the *absolute* slope of the function goes to infinity while the *relative* slope goes to zero as $p \to 0$. Figure 4.4 tries to capture visually the contrast between the behavior of the absolute and relative slopes by tracing the function simultaneously over several orders of magnitudes of small chances. The top part of the curve plots the weight of probabilities between one chance in a thousand and one chance in ten thousand. When the probability reaches one chance in ten thousand, the graph jumps to the right, recycling the x-axis again, this time for chances between one in ten thousand and one in a hundred thousand. As we go down by orders of magnitude, we see that each segment becomes flatter and flatter: the relative weight of small chances tends to 1. However, the absolute slope, as measured by $w(p)/p$, increases without bound as $p \to 0$.

The picture at the other endpoint, near $p = 1$, is similar but not idential. It is similar in that the slope of $w(p)$ tends to infinity as $p \to 1$, as does the Pratt–Arrow measure of convexity. However, the limit as $\lambda \to 0$ of $(1 - w(\lambda p))/(1 - w(\lambda q))$, $p \neq q$, does not equal 1.

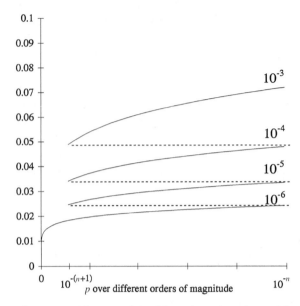

Figure 4.4. The compound-invariant function with $\alpha = .65$ graphed for very small probabilities (explanation in text).

4.4. Diagonal Concavity

The second parameter, β, is a measure of convexity and underweighting, "net" of Allais violations. If we look again at the three panels in Figure 4.3, we see that there is a special symmetry to the middle $\beta = 1$ panel – it is the only panel that includes the diagonal as a special case. Making note of this, we can construct the following informal argument in favor of $\beta = 1$: Imagine a person who obeys the compound invariance axiom but has a very slight tendency to commit Allais common-ratio and common-consequence violations (hence, $\alpha \approx 1$). If these Allais violations are *the* diagnostic of departures from expected utility, so that "few" Allais violations implies "few" violations of any kind, then the weighting function for that person should be approximately linear, with $\beta \approx 1$.

This is admittedly an informal argument. There is an axiomatic argument in favor of $\beta = 1$, which is easier to state at the level of the weighting function than at the level of preferences. Returning again to Figure 4.3, we note that a second distinguishing characteristic of functions in the middle panel is that they are locally concave whenever $w(p) > p$ and locally convex whenever $w(p) < p$. Weighting functions that satisfy this property are *diagonally concave* (Prelec 1998). The preference axiom equivalent to this condition is given in Appendix B. Among compound invariant functions, only those with $\beta = 1$ are diagonally concave.

PROPOSITION 3 (PRELEC 1998). *In the context of CPT, if preferences satisfy subproportionality, compound invariance, and diagonal concavity, then there exists a unique* *value α, $0 < \alpha < 1$ that determines the weighting function for losses and gains:*

$$w^+(p) = w^-(p) = \exp\{-(-\ln p)^\alpha\}.$$

4.5. Empirical Evidence about the $1/e$ Value

Proposition 3 shows that when the structural assumptions of cumulated prospect theory are supplemented by the three conditions: subproportionality, compound invariance, and diagonal concavity, we get a highly constrained theory, which adds only a single parameter (α) to expected utility. An interesting implication of the one-parameter model is the invariant location of the inflection and fixed points. At first pass, the $p = 1/e = .368$ value squares well with the observed asymmetry of the weighting function. Parametric estimates of functional forms that do not constrain the fixed point, such as $w(p) = p^\delta/(p^\delta + (1 - p)^\delta)^{1/\delta}$, (Tversky and Kahneman 1992, Camerer and Ho 1994, Wu and Gonzalez 1996a) or $w(p) = \alpha p^\delta/(\alpha p^\delta + (1 - p)^\delta)$, (Tversky and Fox 1994), generally yield functions with fixed points in the range of .3 to .4. However, these parametric estimates could be wrong if either the value function or the weighting function is misspecified.

More convincing evidence comes from a recent nonparametric experiment by Wu and Gonzalez (1996a). Using prospects like those in the concavity/convexity schema, they constructed ladders of "risky" and "safe" choice pairs spanning the entire probability interval. With these ladders, they could interpret preference for the safe prospect in each pair as an ordinal index of the local slope of the weighting function. This exercise was repeated five times, yielding five independent tracings of the slope of the weighting function.

Figure 4.5 displays the percentages of subjects choosing the safe prospect, which is an ordinal index of the slope of the function. To make the data from the five ladders visually comparable, I express each percentage as a deviation from the mean percentage preference for safe prospects in a given ladder. The slope estimates are quite constant across the different ladders. The probability at which each curve attains a minimum corresponds to the inflection point of the weighting function. In four out of five cases, that value is at the closest possible location to $1/e$. It is evident that $p = .5$ is *not* the location of the inflection point.

Granting that $1/e$ is a good approximation to the inflection or fixed-point location, what are we to make of this? Even though the axioms listed in Proposition 3 do select this unique value, I suspect that the diagonal concavity condition is empirically insubstantial. Under compound invariance, the slope of the weighting function is quite flat near the inflection point. Hence, the requirement that the inflection point coincide with the fixed point will be approximately satisfied even away from the $1/e$ value (though it will be exactly satisfied only at $1/e$). Possibly, the $1/e$ prediction is a lucky coincidence. It is also possible that there is an alternative axiomatization that replaces diagonal concavity with something more robust. In any case, there are data estimation advantages to a one-parameter weighting function, as we shall see in Section 5.

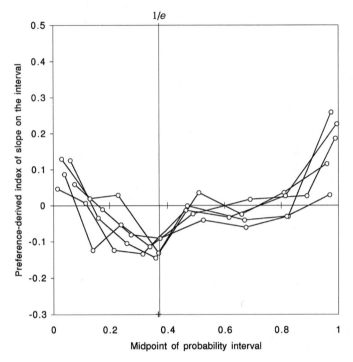

Figure 4.5. Nonparametric local estimates of the slope of the weighting function (adapted from Wu and Gonzalez 1996a).

4.6. Indifference Curves in the Triangle

Because the diagonally concave function has an invariant inflection point, analysis of more complex prospects is simplified. I illustrate this for the case of three-outcome prospects involving two positive outcomes and zero. Preferences over such prospects are usually represented by indifference lines in the probability triangle, where the x axis is the probability of zero and the y axis the probability of the high gain (the residual, $1 - x - y$, is the probability of the middle "consolation prize"). The slope of an indifference curve is a local measure of risk attitude. Steeper slopes indicate more local risk aversion because a greater increase in the high-gain probability is needed to compensate for an increased chance of zero.

Two properties of these curves have attracted theoretical attention, namely, whether they fan out from the origin, as proposed by Machina (1982), and whether they are quasi-convex.[6] Fanning-out means that indifference curves become steeper as one moves from the right, zero-outcome corner to the top,

---

[6] See, for example, Machina (1987), Camerer (1989), Prelec (1990), Camerer and Ho (1994), Wu and Gonzalez (1996b).

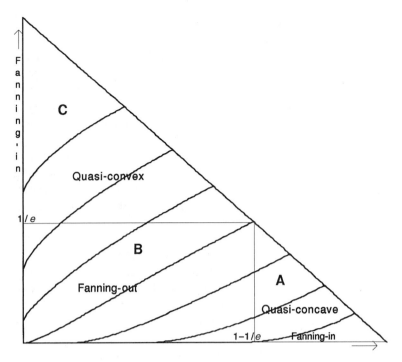

Figure 4.6. Indifference curves in the probability triangle generated by the compound-invariant function.

high-outcome corner. The intuition behind fanning-out is that a person holding a more favorable probability distribution over the three outcomes should be locally more risk averse, that is, should be more eager to exchange some probability of the high prize for a larger probability of the consolation prize. The other conjectured property, quasi-convexity, states that indifference curves are convex with respect to the top corner. The intuition here is that one should not prefer a coin toss between two equally valued prospects to having either prospect for sure. Another term for this is *probabilistic risk-aversion* (Wakker 1994).

Figure 4.6 shows the indifference lines generated by compound invariance with $\alpha = .7$. Their general shape is common to any concave–convex weighting function (e.g., they look like Figure 4.4 of Tversky and Kahneman 1992). The qualitative partitioning of the triangle into the three different regions is likewise generic (see Wu and Gonzalez 1996b for a complete analysis of the triangle). What is new here is that location of the three regions is fixed by the axioms and is independent of the degree of nonlinearity.

In the bottom-right "status quo" region (A), the probability of the zero outcome is at least $1 - 1/e = .63$. Here, indifference curves are quasi-convex for gains (and quasi-concave for losses). With lotteries one should therefore observe probabilistic risk seeking, which is to say, a net preference for multiple prizes over a consolidated chance at a single intermediate prize (with small-p losses, the opposite pattern prevails, and one should find a preference of consolidating small-p losses into a single intermediate loss). In the top-left region (C), the probability of the extreme outcome is greater than $1/e$, and the predictions in region A are exactly reversed. Probabilistic risk is now unattractive for gains and attractive for losses. Finally, in the middle region (B), where the probability of the status quo is less than $1 - 1/e$ and the probability of the extreme outcome less than $1/e$, indifference curves become steeper as the probability distribution that defines the prospect improves, that is, as it moves in the northwest direction within the triangle. This is fanning-out. Regarding the issue of fanning outside of region B, in region A fanning-out will hold for vertical improvements and fanning-in for horizontal ones, whereas in region C the opposite pattern prevails (Roell 1987, Wu and Gonzalez 1996b).

We know now that all four possibilities – fanning-out, fanning-in, quasi-convexity, and quasi-concavity – arise empirically but that fanning-out is more common than fanning-in and quasi-convexity perhaps somewhat more common than quasi-concavity (Camerer and Ho 1994). The greater availability of fanning-out over fanning-in is consistent with the picture in Figure 4.6, which shows that fanning-out is possible for some directions throughout the triangle and is certain (holding for all directions) within region B, whereas fanning-in is only possible in regions A and C and is nowhere certain. Machina's conjecture is a good approximation, counterexamples notwithstanding.[7] The prevalence of quasi-convexity over quasi-concavity is likewise consistent with Figure 4.6, where the former region is larger.

5. COMPOUND INVARIANCE AND POWER VALUE FUNCTIONS (CI+CRRA)

5.1. The Fourfold Pattern of Risk Attitudes

The fully parameterized CPT model requires a parametric form for the value functions as well. In this section, I describe what happens when compound invariant weighting is "married with" power functions for money value:

$$v(x) = \begin{cases} x^\sigma & \text{for } x > 0, \\ -\lambda(-x)^\sigma & \text{for } x < 0. \end{cases}$$

The power value function is the "constant-relative risk-aversion" or "CRRA" case; it is by far the most popular form for estimating money value (see Wakker and Zank 1997 for an elegant axiomatization of power value CPT with different exponents for losses and gains). I will refer to the combination as the CI+CRRA model.

---

[7] Examples of horizontal fanning-in in region C are given in Prelec (1990). Examples of vertical fanning-in in region A are given in Camerer (1989) and Starmer (1992).

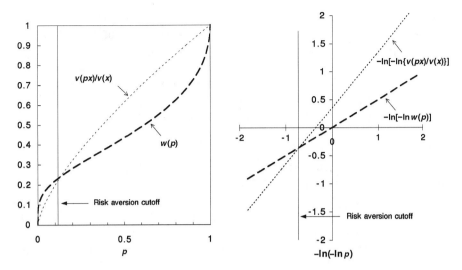

Figure 4.7. The risk-aversion cutoff for a power-value function (dotted line) and a compound-invariant weighting function (dashes) plotted in regular (left panel) and doubly logged (right panel) coordinates.

Consider the choice between a risky simple prospect (y, p) and the sure receipt of its expectation $(py, 1)$. If value is a power function of dollar amount, then the risky prospect will be preferred if $y^\sigma w(p) > (py)^\sigma$, which is to say, if $w(p) > p^\sigma$. With power value functions, therefore, risk seeking in the domain of gains holds for those probabilities at which $w(p)$ lies below the power function with exponent σ, whereas risk aversion holds whenever $w(p)$ lies below the power function. For losses, this implication is reversed: risk seeking holds whenever $w(p)$ lies below the power function, whereas risk aversion holds whenever $w(p)$ lies above the power function. All of this is displayed in the left panel of Figure 4.7.

To obtain the fourfold pattern of risk attitudes with power value functions, it is only necessary for the weighting function to intersect these same power functions from above. This is certainly true for the particular parametrization in Figure 4.7, but what about other parameter values? We can calculate the following:

Risk seeking holds for gains: iff $(y, p) > (yp, 1)$,

iff $y^\sigma w^+(p) > (py)^\sigma$,

iff $w(p) > p^\sigma$,

iff $\exp\{-\beta^+(-\ln p)^\alpha\} > p^\alpha$,

iff $\exp\{-\beta^+/\sigma)(-\ln p)^\alpha\} > p$.

The expression in the bottom line (left side) is a reparametrized compound-invariant function with the β-parameter shifted from β^+ to β^+/σ. Because every subproportional compound invariant function intersects the diagonal from above, there will be an initial region of smaller probabilities where the person exhibits risk seeking as well as a complementary region of larger probabilities where he or she exhibits risk aversion. The argument for losses is identical. Therefore, the fourfold pattern holds irrespective of the power function exponents, that is, it does not at all matter if the value functions are concave or convex. The curvature of the value functions affects not the existence but only the location of the cutoff between the risk-seeking and risk-aversion regions.[8]

We have just proven, in effect, that the compound invariant function ($\alpha < 1$) intersects from above any increasing power function, whether concave or convex. It is difficult to visualize this property in regular probability coordinates. However, if the graphs in Figure 4.7 are replotted in double-log coordinates, as $-\ln(-\ln w(p))$ versus $-\ln(-\ln p)$, then the property becomes more self-evident. In double-log coordinates, the graph of a power function, p^σ, is a straight line with slope 1 and intercept $(-\ln \sigma)$, whereas the graph of the compound-invariant form, $\exp\{-\beta(-\ln p)^\alpha\}$, is a straight line with slope α intercept $(-\ln \beta)$.[9] Because $\alpha < 1$, this latter graph will intersect from above all straight lines of slope one (right panel of Figure 4.7).

5.2. Linear Estimation of Parameters

The approximation, $\beta = 1$, proposed in Section 4.4, yields a CI+CRRA model in which nonlinearity on each dimension is captured by one parameter. These parameters, α for probability and σ for money, can be estimated with Ordinary Least Squares regression in the following way. We start by collecting certainty equivalents for simple gambles, $(x, 1) \sim (y, p)$. If we measure the relative certainty equivalent by the ratio x/y, it follows from $x^\sigma = y^\sigma \exp(-(-\ln p)^\alpha)$ that $-\ln[-\ln(x/y)] = \ln(\sigma) + \alpha[-\ln(-\ln p)]$. Therefore, in double-log coordinates the plot of the elicited relative certainty equivalent, $-\ln[-\ln(x/y)]$, is a linear function of gamble probability, $-\ln(-\ln p)$. The slope of the best-fitting straight line in these coordinates will estimate the α-parameter for the weighting function; the intercept will estimate the exponent for the power-value function.

Table 4.4 gives an example of such an estimate using median certainty equivalents for different chances at a $10,000 prize. There is nothing authoritative about these estimates – they were collected from 39 MIT students through a

---

[8] This implication holds also for the choice between a zero status quo and a prospect combining a sure loss $(-x)$ with a p-chance at gain $+y$. The prospect is prefered to the status quo if $w(p)v(y) + \lambda v(-x) > 0$, that is, if $w(p) > \lambda(-v(-x)) = \lambda x^\sigma$. For the CI weighting function, this translates into $\exp\{-(\beta^+/\sigma)(-\ln p)^\alpha\} > \lambda^{1/\sigma} p$, which holds for sufficiently small p.

[9] The graph of $w(p)$ in double-log coordinates is given by the function ψ defined as

$$\psi[-\ln(-\ln p)] \equiv -\ln[-\ln w(p)].$$

If $t = -\ln(-\ln p)$ is the doubly log-transformed x-coordinate in the right panel of Figure 4.7, then $\psi(t) = -\ln[-\ln\{w(\exp(-(\exp(-t)))\}]$. For, the power function, $w(p) = p^\sigma$, the corresponding $\psi(t) = -\ln \sigma + t$. For the compound invariant, $w(p) = \exp\{-\beta(-\ln p)^\alpha\}$, the corresponding $\psi(t) = -\ln \beta + \alpha t$.

Table 4.4. Median Certainty Equivalents for Different Chances at $10,000

Probability of Winning $y = \$10,000$	Expected Value	Median Certainty Equivalent (x)	Inferred Risk Attitude	Predicted CE $\alpha = .65, \sigma = .60$
1 in 1,000,000	$.01	$1	risk seeking	$1
1 in 10,000	$1	$10	risk seeking	$8
1 in 200	$50	$50	risk neutral	$71
5%	$500	$500	risk neutral	$331
20%	$2,000	$1,000	risk averse	$1,028
50%	$5,000	$2,500	risk averse	$2,685
80%	$8,000	$5,000	risk averse	$5,331
95%	$9,500	$8,000	risk averse	$7,853

questionnaire and are merely presented here as a sample of the kind of data that the model ought to handle.

Consistent with the fourfold pattern, the smallest probability levels induce risk seeking, whereas the larger ones induce risk aversion. Figure 4.8 plots these same relative certainty equivalents against probability with both coordinates doubly logged. The slope and intercept of the estimated line are $+60$ and $-.51$, yielding estimates of $\alpha = .65$, and $\sigma = +.60$.

Figure 4.8. Doubly logged plot of the relative certainty equivalent as a function of gamble probability.

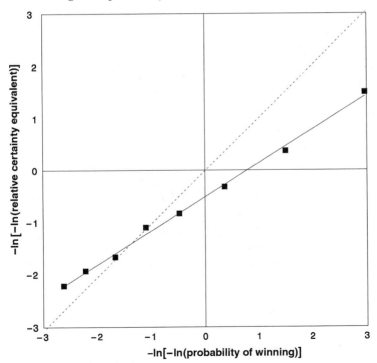

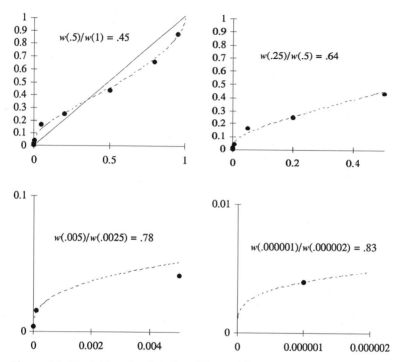

Figure 4.9. Replotting the data from Figure 4.7 in nontransformed coordinates.

These same data were then graphed in nonlogged coordinates (Figure 4.9) across four separate panels to achieve better resolution for small probabilities. The x-axis here is probability, and the dotted line plots the weighting function, $w(p) = \exp[-(-\ln p)^\alpha]$, for $\alpha = .65$. The y-axis plots the relative certainty equivalent raised to the estimated power of the value function, or $(x/y)^\sigma$, with $\sigma = .60$. In the top left panel, the function is traced out over the full probability range. The next three panels plot that same function but over a progressively smaller interval near zero. Specifically, the top-right panel zooms in on the range $(0, .5)$; the bottom left on the range $(0, .005)$, and the bottom right on $(0, .000002)$.

The finding that the strongest violations of expected utility theory, including the original Allais paradoxes, involve prospects with different support (Conlisk 1989, Camerer 1992, Harless 1992) is sometimes interpreted as evidence for the discontinuity of the weighting function near $p=0$ and $p=1$. However, this finding would be also compatible with the CI function which, as Figures 4.4 and 4.9 illustrate, approximates a continuous step function at zero. In general, the conjecture that the weighting function is discontinuous at zero has the same empirical status as the conjecture that the value function for money outcomes is asymptotically bounded. In both cases, we cannot test the conjecture directly (i.e., by measuring $v(x)$ at infinity or $w(p)$ infinitesimally close to zero), but we can assess whether functional forms with asymptotes or discontinuities provide a better fit at measured levels. Looking at Figure 4.8, we see that if the weighting function were indeed discontinuous at $p = 0$ and $p = 1$, then its graph in the coordinates of the figure would have an s-shape bounded above and below by two horizontal asymptotes.

A separate issue is whether the function becomes relatively unstable near zero. It is possible that there exists a decision-weight threshold such that extremely unlikely consequences are either ignored or receive something like the threshold weight. Granting this, one can still study whether a person is equally likely to ignore a probability $p = .01$ as a $p = .00001$ or as a $p = .000000001$. The weighting function is really a description of how the central tendency of decision weights varies with probability, and that central tendency could remain well defined even as the stability of an individual's response to a given probability deteriorates. Intuition, in any case, may not be a reliable guide here. It is difficult to tell introspectively whether a probability or any other attribute is truly ignored or merely overridden by the other attributes in the choice situation.

6. THE DOMINANCE OF THE PROBABILITY DIMENSION

A striking feature of the CI+CRRA model is that simple risk attitudes – the four-fold pattern – are unaffected by the curvature of value function, whose only impact is to modulate the cutoff between risk seeking and risk aversion. In other words, simple risk attitudes are first a matter of nonlinear probability weight and only then a matter of nonlinear money value. Is this an anomalous consequence of these particular functional forms or is there something more general at work here?

I believe, indeed, that probability nonlinearity will eventually be recognized as a more important determinant of risk attitudes than money nonlinearity – at least in situations in which one is comparing only among gain prospects or only among loss prospects (for mixed prospects involving losses and gains, loss aversion of course becomes a critical additional factor). It is difficult to prove such a general claim, but the core intuition is simple enough, namely, that the value or utility dimension has no transitions of a qualitative nature like the transition from impossibility to possibility in the probability domain. An ε-chance can excite hope or worry, provided the stakes are high enough. An ε-gain (or loss) does not feel like much, even if the outcome is certain. Hence, the nonlinearities on the probability side are potentially stronger than those on the money side. In this concluding part of the paper, I will sketch one formal version of this argument without claiming that it is the only one.

Let us return to Allais' original demonstration of the common-ratio effect, recalling that it compared a choice between a sure 100 million and a 98% chance of 500 million and a second choice between a 1% chance of 100 million and a 0.98% chance of 500 million. What Allais exploited is the intuition that "the achievement of *certainty*" creates a qualitative change in one's circumstances.

This exaggerated weighting of certainty is partially captured by subproportion-ality (viz. Sections 3.3 and 3.4). Subproportionality, however, does not grant a special status to certainty per se, nor, as we see from Figure 4.2, does it ensure the right shape for the weighting function.

One can enhance subproportionality by a preference condition, very much in the spirit of the Allais example, that creates the same type of strong end-point nonlinearity we have seen characterize compound invariance. The con-dition addresses certainty overweighting directly. It states that in the special case in which one of the prospects is a sure outcome $(x, 1)$ there exists a posi-tive lower bound ε such that $(x, 1) \approx (y, p)$ implies $(x, p) < (y, p^{2+\varepsilon})$ (whereas "plain" subproportionality only implies $(x, p) < (y, p^2)$). If we add this ε-bound on subproportionality, then it follows that the weighting function will not just only intersect the diagonal from above, but, like the compound-invariant form, it will also interesect from above all increasing power functions, whether concave and convex.[10] This, we know from Section 5.1, guarantees the fourfold pattern of risk aversion irrespective of the exponents on the power functions for money value. The overweighting of small probabilities and underweighting of large ones will, in the limit, overshadow the impact of the value function for power and for all similarly "well-behaved" value functions.[11]

APPENDIX A: THE FRAMING ASSUMPTIONS OF CPT

Equations 2.2 and 2.3, which define the CPT representation for two-outcome prospects, may look complicated. However, simpler alternatives have serious draw-backs. Let us consider first the separable representation for the multioutcome prospect $(x_1, p_1, \ldots, x_n, p_n)$:

$$\sum_{i=1}^{n} w(p_i)v(x_i),$$

which is a direct generalization of Eq. 2.1a. Unfortunately, this representation vio-lates stochastic dominance. Assume that $w(p) + w(q) < w(p + q)$, for some p, q. Then a $p + q$ chance at \$100 would be preferred to a p-chance at \$100 and a q-chance at $100 + \varepsilon$ because $w(p)v(\$100) + w(q)v(\$100 + \varepsilon) < w(p + q)v(\$100)$, for sufficiently small ε.

---

[10] Proposition 2 in Prelec (1998) proves that this condition (called ε-subproportionality) implies that $\forall c > 0$, $\exists pc^* \in (0, 1)$ such that $p \in (0, pc^*) \Rightarrow w(p) > p^c$, and $p \in (pc^*, 1) \Rightarrow w(p) < p^c$.

[11] A sufficient definition of "well-behaved" would be that the value function is bounded above and below by two power functions. A "not well-behaved" function would be one that ap-proximated a step function at zero (like the compound-invariant weighting function). The argument hinges on the claim that the step function shape at zero *is* appropriate for the probability domain but *is not* appropriate for the money domain.

The rank-dependent representation (RDU), first developed by Quiggin (1982), avoids the problem of stochastic dominance. In RDU, outcomes are ordered from worst to best, $x_1 \leq x_2 \leq \cdots \leq x_n$, and then evaluated as

$$\sum_{i=1}^{n} w \left(\sum_{j \geq i}^{n} p_j \right) (v(x_i) - v(x_{i-1})).$$

The critical drawback of the model can be diagnosed at the level of simple prospects. If x is positive, RDU evaluates (x, p) as

$$w(1)v(0) + w(p)(v(x) - v(0)) = w(p)v(x).$$

If x is negative, then RDU evaluates (x, p) as

$$w(1)v(x) + w(1 - p)(v(0) - v(x)) = (1 - w(1 - p))v(x).$$

Consequently, the weight of x will be $w(p)$ for positive x and $(1 - w(1 - p))$ for negative x. This implies, contrary to empirical evidence, that a person cannot simultaneously underweight relative to a sure thing a 50% chance of a gain *and* a 50% chance (Tversky and Kahneman 1992). The RDU language is fundamentally incomplete because it does not let us refer to over/underweighting of uncertain relative to certain outcomes; the language only lets us refer to over/underweighting of superior relative to inferior outcomes.

The CPT formulas (Eqs. 2.2 and 2.3) restore the framing of outcomes relative to the status quo, and thus we can talk about losses and gains, but it also preserves stochastic dominance. Essentially, CPT applies the RDU representation twice, once to the positive part of a prospect and once, in reverse order, to the negative part (Starmer and Sugden 1989 were the first to suggest this splicing of the positive and negative representations). The resulting formula is straightforward conceptually but notationally somewhat complex. The CPT evaluation of a general, finite-outcome prospect, $P = (x_1, p_1; \cdots; x_n, p_n)$, $x_1 \leq \cdots \leq x_k \leq 0 \leq x_{k+1} \leq \cdots \leq x_n$, is

$$V(P) = \sum_{i=1}^{k} \left(w^- \left(\sum_{j=1}^{i} p_j \right) - w^- \left(\sum_{j=1}^{i-1} p_j \right) \right) v(x_i)$$

$$+ \sum_{i=k+1}^{n} \left(w^+ \left(\sum_{j=1}^{n} p_j \right) - w^+ \left(\sum_{j=i+1}^{n} p_j \right) \right) v(x_i).$$

CPT reduces to RDU if $w^-(p) = 1 - w^+(1 - p)$. Empirically, however, one observes $w^+(p) = w^-(p)$.

APPENDIX B: PREFERENCE CONDITIONS BEHIND DIAGONAL CONCAVITY

Here are the notation and definitions needed to state the diagonal concavity axiom. Let $\Delta^+[s, r] = \{(x, p; y, q) \mid 0 < x < y, s \leq q, p + q \leq r\}$ and $\Delta^-[s, r] = \{(x, p; y, q) \mid y < x < 0, s \leq q, p + q \leq r\}$, that is, the sets of binary prospects for which the probability of the extreme outcome is at least s and the probability of the zero outcome at least $1 - r$. Preferences are *quasi-convex* [resp. *quasi-concave*] on $\Delta^+[s, r]$ if $P \approx Q$, implies $Q \gtrsim \mu P + (1 - \mu)Q$ [resp. $Q \lesssim \mu P + (1 - \mu)Q$] for any three P, Q, and $\mu P + (1 - \mu)Q$ in $\Delta^+[s, r]$, and similarly for $\Delta^-[s, r]$. Preferences are *certainty-equivalent (or CE)-quasi-convex* [resp. *CE-quasi-concave*] on $\Delta^+[s, r]$ if $P \approx Q$ implies $Q \gtrsim \mu P + (1 - \mu)Q$ [resp. $Q \lesssim \mu P + (1 - \mu)Q)$] for any certain outcome Q and for any P and $\mu P + (1 - \mu)Q$ in $\Delta^+[s, r]$, and similarly for $\Delta^-[s, r]$. (Note that $Q \notin \Delta^+[s, r]$, $\Delta^-[s, r]$, unless $s = 0$, $r = 1$. In that case, however, CE-quasi-convexity is subsumed by quasi-convexity). *Strict* means strict preference unless $P = Q$. In Prelec (1998) I show (Proposition 6) that the following preference axiom is equivalent to the diagonal concavity of the probability weighting function:

There is no nondegenerate interval $[s, r]$ such that $\gtrsim$ is quasi-convex and strictly CE-quasi-concave on $\Delta^+[s, r]$ or $\Delta^-[s, r]$, nor quasi-concave and strictly CE-quasi-convex on $\Delta^+[s, r]$ or $\Delta^-[s, r]$.

5. Weighing Risk and Uncertainty

Amos Tversky and Craig R. Fox

ABSTRACT. Decision theory distinguishes between risky prospects, where the probabilities associated with the possible outcomes are assumed to be known, and uncertain prospects, where these probabilities are not assumed to be known. Studies of choice between risky prospects have suggested a nonlinear transformation of the probability scale that overweights low probabilities and underweights moderate and high probabilities. The present article extends this notion from risk to uncertainty by invoking the principle of bounded subadditivity: An event has greater impact when it turns impossibility into possibility, or possibility into certainty, than when it merely makes a possibility more or less likely. A series of studies provides support for this principle in decision under both risk and uncertainty and shows that people are less sensitive to uncertainty than to risk. Finally, the article discusses the relationship between probability judgments and decision weights and distinguishes relative sensitivity from ambiguity aversion.

Decisions are generally made without definite knowledge of their consequences. The decisions to invest in the stock market, to undergo a medical operation, or to go to court are generally made without knowing in advance whether the market will go up, the operation will be successful, or the court will decide in one's favor. Decision under uncertainty, therefore, calls for an evaluation of two attributes: the desirability of possible outcomes and their likelihood of occurrence. Indeed, much of the study of decision making is concerned with the assessment of these values and the manner in which they are – or should be – combined.

In the classical theory of decision under risk, the utility of each outcome is weighted by its probability of occurrence. Consider a simple prospect of the form (x, p) that offers a probability p to win \$$x$ and a probability $1 - p$ to win nothing. The expected utility of this prospect is given by $pu(x) + (1 - p)u(0)$, where u is the utility function for money. Expected utility theory has been

This research was supported by National Science Foundation Grants SES-9109535 and SBR-9408684. The article benefited from discussions with Daniel Kahneman and Peter Wakker.
Originally published in *Psychological Review*, 102:2, 269–83.

Table 5.1. The Fourfold Pattern of Risk Attitudes

Probability	Gain	Loss
Low	C($100, .05) = $14 (risk seeking)	C(−$100, .05) = −$8 (risk aversion)
High	C($100, .95) = $78 (risk aversion)	C(−$100, .95) = −$84 (risk seeking)

Note: C is the median certainty equivalent of the prospect in question.

developed to explain attitudes toward risk, namely, risk aversion and risk seeking. Risk aversion is defined as a preference for a sure outcome over a prospect with an equal or greater expected value. Thus, choosing a sure $100 over an even chance to win $200 or nothing is an expression of risk aversion. Risk seeking is exhibited if a prospect is preferred to a sure outcome with equal or greater expected value. It is commonly assumed that people are risk averse, which is explained in expected utility theory by a concave utility function.

The experimental study of decision under risk has shown that people often violate both the expected utility model and the principle of risk aversion that underlie much economic analysis. Table 5.1 illustrates a common pattern of risk seeking and risk aversion observed in choice between simple prospects (adapted from Tversky & Kahneman, 1992), where C(x, p) is the median certainty equivalent of the prospect (x, p). Thus, the upper left-hand entry in the table shows that the median participant is indifferent between receiving $14 for sure and a 5% chance of receiving $100. Because the expected value of this prospect is only $5, this observation reflects risk seeking.

Table 5.1 illustrates a fourfold pattern of risk attitudes: risk seeking for gains and risk aversion for losses of low probability, coupled with risk aversion for gains and risk seeking for losses of high probability. Choices consistent with this pattern have been observed in several studies, with and without monetary incentives[1] (Cohen, Jaffray, & Said, 1987; Fishburn & Kochenberger, 1979; Hershey & Schoemaker, 1980; Kahneman & Tversky, 1979; Payne, Laughhunn, & Crum, 1981; Wehrung, 1989). Risk seeking for low-probability gains may contribute to the popularity of gambling, whereas risk seeking for high-probability losses is consistent with the tendency to undertake risk in order to avoid a sure loss.

Because the fourfold pattern is observed for a wide range of payoffs, it cannot be explained by the shape of the utility function as proposed earlier by Friedman and Savage (1948) and by Markowitz (1952). Instead, it suggests a nonlinear transformation of the probability scale, first proposed by Preston and Baratta (1948) and further discussed by Edwards (1962) and others. This notion is one of the cornerstones of prospect theory (Kahneman & Tversky,

---

[1] Risk seeking for long shots was reported by Kachelmeier and Shehata (1992) in an experiment conducted in China with real payoffs that were considerably higher than the normal monthly incomes of the participants.

1979; Tversky & Kahneman, 1992), which provides the theoretical framework used in the present article. According to this theory, the value of a simple prospect that offers a probability p to win \$$x$ (and probability $1 - p$ to win nothing) is given by $w(p)v(x)$, where v measures the subjective value of the outcome x, and w measures the impact of p on the desirability of the prospect. The values of w are called decision weights; they are normalized so that $w(0) = 0$, and $w(1) = 1$. It is important to note that w should not be interpreted as a measure of degree of belief. A decision maker may believe that the probability of heads on a toss of a coin is one-half but give this event a lower weight in the evaluation of a prospect.

According to prospect theory, the value function v and the weighting function w exhibit diminishing sensitivity: marginal impact diminishes with distance from a reference point. For monetary outcomes, the status quo generally serves as the reference point that distinguishes gains from losses. Thus, diminishing sensitivity gives rise to an S-shaped value function, with $v(0) = 0$, that is concave for gains and convex for losses. For probability, there are two natural reference points – certainty and impossibility – that correspond to the endpoints of the scale. Therefore, diminishing sensitivity implies that increasing the probability of winning a prize by .1 has more impact when it changes the probability of winning from .9 to 1.0 or from 0 to .1 than when it changes the probability from, say, .3 to .4 or from .6 to .7. This gives rise to a weighting function that is concave near zero and convex near one. Figure 5.1 depicts the weighting functions for gains and for losses, estimated from the median data

Figure 5.1. Weighting functions for gains ($w+$) and losses ($w-$).

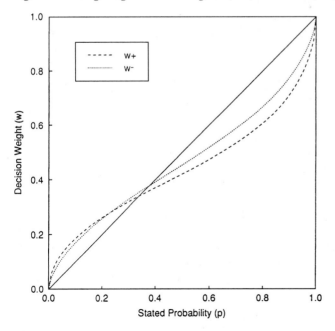

of Tversky and Kahneman (1992).[2] Such a function overweights small probabilities and underweights moderate and high probabilities, which explains the
fourfold pattern of risk attitudes illustrated in Table 5.1. It also accounts for the
well-known certainty effect discovered by Allais (1953). For example, whereas
most people prefer a sure $30 to an 80% chance of winning $45, most people also
prefer a 20% chance of winning $45 to a 25% chance of winning $30, contrary to
the substitution axiom of expected utility theory (Tversky & Kahneman, 1986).
This observation is consistent with an S-shaped weighting function satisfying $w(.20)/w(.25) \geq w(.80)/w(1.0)$. Such a function appears to provide a unified
account of a wide range of empirical findings (see Camerer & Ho, 1994).

A choice model that is based on a nonlinear transformation of the probability
scale assumes that the decision maker knows the probabilities associated with
the possible outcomes. With the notable exception of games of chance, however,
these probabilities are unknown, or at least not specified in advance. People
generally do not know the probabilities associated with events such as the guilt
of a defendant, the outcome of a football game, or the future price of oil. Following Knight (1921), decision theorists distinguish between risky (or chance)
prospects where the probabilities associated with outcomes are assumed to be
known, and uncertain prospects where these probabilities are not assumed to be
known. To describe individual choice between uncertain prospects, we need to
generalize the weighting function from risk to uncertainty. When the probabilities are unknown, however, we cannot describe decision weights as a simple
transformation of the probability scale. Thus, we cannot plot the weighting
function as we did in Figure 5.1, nor can we speak about the overweighting of
low probabilities and underweighting of high probabilities.

This article extends the preceding analysis from risk to uncertainty. To accomplish this, we first generalize the weighting function and introduce the
principle of bounded subadditivity. We next describe a series of studies that
demonstrates this principle for both risk and uncertainty, and we show that it
is more pronounced for uncertainty than for risk. Finally, we discuss the relationship between decision weights and judged probabilities, and the role of
ambiguity in choice under uncertainty. An axiomatic treatment of these concepts is presented in Tversky and Wakker (in press).

THEORY

Let S be a set whose elements are interpreted as states of the world. Subsets of
S are called *events*. Thus, S corresponds to the certain event, and ϕ is the null
event. A weighting function W (on S) is a mapping that assigns to each event
in S a number between 0 and 1 such that $W(\phi) = 0$, $W(S) = 1$, and $W(A) \geq W(B)$
if $A \supset B$. Such a function is also called a *capacity*, or a *nonadditive probability*.

As in the case of risk, we focus on simple prospects of the form (x, A),
which offer $x if an uncertain event A occurs and nothing if A does not occur.

---

[2] Figure 5.1 corrects a minor error in the original drawing.

According to prospect theory, the value of such a prospect is $W(A)v(x)$, where W is the decision weight associated with the uncertain event A. (We use W for uncertainty and w for risk.) Because the present treatment is confined to simple prospects with a single positive outcome, it is consistent with both the original and the cumulative versions of prospect theory (Tversky & Kahneman, 1992). It is consistent with expected utility theory if and only if W is additive, that is, $W(A \cup B) = W(A) + W(B)$ whenever $A \cap B = \phi$.[3]

Prospect theory assumes that W satisfies two conditions.

    (i) Lower subadditivity: $W(A) \geq W(A \cup B) - W(B)$, provided A and B are disjoint and $W(A \cup B)$ is bounded away from one.[4] This inequality captures the possibility effect: The impact of an event A is greater when it is added to the null event than when it is added to some nonnull event B.

    (ii) Upper subadditivity: $W(S) - W(S - A) \geq W(A \cup B) - W(B)$, provided A and B are disjoint and $W(B)$ is bounded away from zero.[5] This inequality captures the certainty effect: The impact of an event A is greater when it is subtracted from the certain event S than when it is subtracted from some uncertain event $A \cup B$.

A weighting function W satisfies bounded subadditivity, or subadditivity (SA) for short, if it satisfies both (i) and (ii) above. According to such a weighting function, an event has greater impact when it turns impossibility into possibility or possibility into certainty than when it merely makes a possibility more or less likely. To illustrate, consider the possible outcome of a football game. Let H denote the event that the home team wins the game, V denote the event that the visiting team wins, and T denote a tie. Hence, $S = H \cup V \cup T$. Lower SA implies that $W(T)$ exceeds $W(H \cup T) - W(H)$, whereas upper SA implies that $W(H \cup V \cup T) - W(H \cup V)$ exceeds $W(H \cup T) - W(H)$. Thus, adding the event T (a tie) to ϕ has more impact than adding T to H, and subtracting T from S has more impact than subtracting T from $H \cup T$. These conditions extend to uncertainty the principle that increasing the probability of winning a prize from 0 to p has more impact than increasing the probability of winning from q to $q + p$, and decreasing the probability of winning from 1 to $1 - p$ has more impact than decreasing the probability of winning from $q + p$ to q. To investigate these properties empirically, consider four simple prospects, each of which offers a fixed prize if a particular event (H, T, $H \cup V$, or $H \cup T$) occurs and nothing if it does not. By asking people to price these prospects, we can estimate the decision weights associated with the respective events and

---

[3] For other discussions of decision weights for uncertain events, see Hogarth and Einhorn (1990), Viscusi (1989), and Wakker (1994).

[4] The boundary conditions are needed to ensure that we always compare an interval that includes an endpoint to an interval that is bounded away from the other endpoint (see Tversky & Wakker, in press, for a more rigorous formulation).

[5] The upper subadditivity of W is equivalent to the lower subadditivity of the dual function $W'(A) = 1 - W(S - A)$.

test both lower and upper SA, provided the value function is scaled independently.

Several comments concerning this analysis are in order. First, risk can be viewed as a special case of uncertainty where probability is defined through a standard chance device so that the probabilities of outcomes are known. Under this interpretation, the S-shaped weighting function of Figure 5.1 satisfies both lower and upper SA. Second, we have defined these properties in terms of the weighting function W that is not directly observable but can be derived from preferences (see Wakker & Tversky, 1993). Necessary and sufficient conditions for bounded SA in terms of the observed preference order are presented by Tversky and Wakker (in press) in the context of cumulative prospect theory. Third, the concept of bounded SA is more general than the property of diminishing sensitivity, which gives rise to a weighting function that is concave for relatively unlikely events and convex for relatively likely events. Finally, there is evidence to suggest that the decision weights for complementary events typically sum to less than one, that is, $W(A) + W(S - A) \leq 1$ or equivalently, $W(A) \leq W(S) - W(S - A)$. This property, called *subcertainty* (Kahneman & Tversky, 1979), can also be interpreted as evidence that upper SA has more impact than lower SA; in other words, the certainty effect is more pronounced than the possibility effect. Some data consistent with this property are presented below.

An Illustration

We next present an illustration of SA that yields a new violation of expected utility theory. We asked 112 Stanford students to choose between prospects defined by the outcome of an upcoming football game between Stanford and the University of California at Berkeley. Each participant was presented with three pairs of prospects, displayed in Table 5.2. The percentage of respondents who chose each prospect appears on the right. Half of the participants received the problems in the order presented in the table; the other half received the problems in the opposite order. Because we found no significant order effects,

Table 5.2. A Demonstration of Subadditivity in Betting on the Outcome of a Stanford–Berkeley Football Game

Problem	Option	Events				Preference (%)
		A	**B**	**C**	**D**	
1	f_1	$25	0	0	0	61
	g_1	0	0	$10	$10	39
2	f_2	0	0	0	$25	66
	g_2	$10	$10	0	0	34
3	f_3	$25	0	0	$25	29
	g_3	$10	$10	$10	$10	71

Note: A = Stanford wins by 7 or more points; B = Stanford wins by less than 7 points; C = Berkeley ties or wins by less than 7 points; D = Berkeley wins by 7 or more points. Preference = percentage of respondents ($N = 112$) that chose each option.

the data were pooled. Participants were promised that 10% of all respondents, selected at random, would be paid according to one of their choices.

Table 5.2 shows that, overall, f_1 was chosen over g_1, f_2 over g_2, and g_3 over f_3. Furthermore, the triple (f_1, f_2, g_3) was the single most common pattern, selected by 36% of the respondents. This pattern violates expected utility theory, which implies that a person who chooses f_1 over g_1 and f_2 over g_2 should also choose f_3 over g_3. However, 64% of the 55 participants who chose f_1 and f_2 in Problems 1 and 2 chose g_3 in Problem 3, contrary to expected utility theory. This pattern, however, is consistent with the present account. To demonstrate, we apply prospect theory to the modal choices in Table 5.2. The choice of f_1 over g_1 in Problem 1 implies that

$$v(25)W(A) > v(10)W(C \cup D).$$

Similarly, the choice of f_2 over g_2 in Problem 2 implies that

$$v(25)W(D) > v(10)W(A \cup B).$$

Adding the two inequalities and rearranging terms yields

$$\frac{W(A) + W(D)}{W(A \cup B) + W(C \cup D)} > \frac{v(10)}{v(25)}.$$

On the other hand, the choice of g_3 over f_3 in Problem 3 implies that

$$v(10)W(A \cup B \cup C \cup D) > v(25)W(A \cup D), \quad \text{or}$$

$$\frac{v(10)}{v(25)} > \frac{W(A \cup D)}{W(A \cup B \cup C \cup D)}.$$

Consequently, the modal choices imply

$$\frac{W(A) + W(D)}{W(A \cup B) + W(C \cup D)} > \frac{W(A \cup D)}{W(A \cup B \cup C \cup D)}.$$

It can be shown that this inequality is consistent with a subadditive weighting function. Moreover, the inequality follows from such a weighting function, provided that subcertainty holds. To demonstrate, note that according to lower SA, $W(A) + W(D) \geq W(A \cup D)$. Furthermore, it follows from subcertainty that

$$W(A \cup B) + W(C \cup D) \leq W(A \cup B \cup C \cup D) = 1.$$

Thus, the left-hand ratio exceeds the right-hand ratio, in accord with the modal choices. Note that under expected utility theory W is an additive probability measure, hence the left-hand ratio and the right-hand ratio must be equal.

Relative Sensitivity

As noted earlier, prospect theory assumes SA for both risk and uncertainty. We next propose that this effect is stronger for uncertainty than for risk. In other words, both lower and upper SA are amplified when outcome probabilities are not specified.

To test this hypothesis, we need a method for comparing different domains or sources of uncertainty (e.g., the outcome of a football game or the spin of a roulette wheel). Consider two sources, **A** and **B**, and suppose that the decision weights for both sources satisfy bounded subadditivity. We say that the decision maker is less sensitive to **B** than to **A** if the following two conditions hold for all disjoint events A_1, A_2 in **A**, and B_1, B_2 in **B**, provided all values of W are bounded away from 0 and 1.

If $W(B_1) = W(A_1)$ and $W(B_2) = W(A_2)$

then $W(B_1 \cup B_2) \leq W(A_1 \cup A_2)$. $\qquad\qquad$ (1)

If $W(S - B_1) = W(S - A_1)$ and $W(S - B_2) = W(S - A_2)$,

then $W(S - [B_1 \cup B_2]) \geq W(S - [A_1 \cup A_2])$. $\qquad\qquad$ (2)

The first condition says that the union of disjoint events from **B** "loses" more than the union of matched events from **A**. The second condition imposes the analogous requirement on the dual function. Thus, a person is less sensitive[6] to **B** than to **A** if **B** produces more lower SA and more upper SA than does **A**.

This definition can be readily stated in terms of preferences. To illustrate, consider a comparison between uncertainty and chance.[7] Suppose B_1 and B_2 are disjoint uncertain events (e.g., the home team wins or the home team ties a particular football game). Let A_1 and A_2 denote disjoint chance events (e.g., a roulette wheel landing red or landing green). The hypothesis that people are less sensitive to the uncertain source **B** than to the chance source **A** implies the following preference condition. If one is indifferent between receiving $50 if the home team wins the game or if a roulette wheel lands red ($p = 18/38$), and if one is also indifferent between receiving $50 if the home team ties the game or if a roulette wheel lands green (i.e., zero or double zero, $p = 2/38$), then one should prefer receiving $50 if a roulette wheel lands either green or red ($p = 20/38$) to receiving $50 if the home team either wins or ties the game.

The following studies test the two hypotheses discussed above. First, decision makers exhibit bounded subadditivity under both risk and uncertainty. Second, decision makers are generally less sensitive to uncertainty than to risk.

EXPERIMENTAL TESTS

We conducted three studies using a common experimental paradigm. On each trial, participants chose between an uncertain (or risky) prospect and various cash amounts. These data were used to estimate the certainty equivalents of

---

[6] Relative sensitivity is closely related to the concept of relative curvature for subjective dimensions introduced by Krantz and Tversky (1975).

[7] Although probabilities could be generated by various chance devices, we do not distinguish between them here, and treat risk or chance as a single source of uncertainty.

Table 5.3. Outline of Studies

	Study 1	Study 2	Study 3
Participants	NBA fans	NFL fans	Psychology students
	($N = 27$)	($N = 40$)	($N = 45$)
Sources	Chance	Chance	Chance
	NBA playoffs	Super Bowl	San Francisco temperature
	San Francisco temperature	Dow–Jones	Beijing temperature

Note: NBA = National Basketball Association; NFL = National Football League.

each prospect (i.e., the sure amount that the participant considers as attractive as the prospect) and to derive decision weights. The basic features of the studies are outlined in Table 5.3.

Method

Participants. The participants in the first study were 27 male Stanford students (median age = 21) who responded to advertisements calling for basketball fans to take part in a study of decision making. Participants received $15 for participating in two 1-hour sessions, spaced a few days apart. The participants in the second study were 40 male football fans (median age = 21), recruited in a similar manner. They were promised that in addition to receiving $15 for their participation in two 1-hour sessions, some of them would be selected at random to play one of their choices for real money. The participants in the third study were 45 Stanford students enrolled in an introductory psychology course (28 men, 17 women, median age = 20) who took part in a 1-hour session for course credit. The responses of a few additional participants (one from Study 1, four from Study 2, and three from Study 3) were excluded from the analysis because they exhibited a great deal of internal inconsistency. We also excluded a very small number of responses that were completely out of line with an individual's other responses.

Procedure. The experiment was run using a computer. Each trial involved a series of choices between a prospect that offered a prize contingent on chance or an uncertain event (e.g., a 25% chance to win a prize of $150) and a descending series of sure payments (e.g., receive $40 for sure). In Study 1, the prize was always $75 for half the respondents and $150 for the other half; in Studies 2 and 3, the prize for all respondents was $150. Certainty equivalents were inferred from two rounds of such choices. The first round consisted of six choices between the prospect and sure payments, spaced roughly evenly between $0 and the prize amount. After completing the first round of choices, a new set of seven sure payments was presented, spanning the narrower range between the lowest payment that the respondent had accepted and highest payment that the respondent had rejected. The program enforced internal consistency. For example, no respondent was allowed to prefer $30 for sure over a prospect and also prefer the same prospect over a sure $40. The program allowed respondents to backtrack if they felt they had made a mistake in the previous round of choices.

The certainty equivalent of each prospect was determined by a linear interpolation between the lowest value accepted and the highest value rejected in the second round of choices. This interpolation yielded a margin of error of ±$2.50 for the $150 prospects and ±$1.25 for the $75 prospects. We wish to emphasize that although our analysis is based on certainty equivalents, the data consisted of a series of choices between a given prospect and sure outcomes. Thus, respondents were not asked to generate certainty equivalents; instead, these values were inferred from choices.

Each session began with detailed instructions and practice. In Study 1, the first session consisted of chance prospects followed by basketball prospects; the second session replicated the chance prospects followed by prospects defined by a future temperature in San Francisco. In Study 2, the first session consisted of chance prospects followed by Super Bowl prospects; the second session replicated the chance prospects followed by prospects defined by a future value of the Dow–Jones index. Study 3 consisted of a single session in which the chance prospects were followed by prospects defined by a future temperature in San Francisco and Beijing; the order of the latter two sources was counterbalanced. The order of the prospects within each source was randomized.

Sources of Uncertainty. Chance prospects were described in terms of a random draw of a single poker chip from an urn containing 100 chips numbered consecutively from 1 to 100. Nineteen prospects of the form (x, p) were constructed where p varied from .05 to .95 in multiples of .05. For example, a typical chance prospect would pay $150 if the number of the poker chip is between 1 and 25, and nothing otherwise. This design yields 90 tests of lower SA and 90 tests of upper SA for each participant.

Basketball prospects were defined by the result of the first game of the 1991 National Basketball Association (NBA) quarter final series between the Portland Trailblazers and the Utah Jazz. For example, a typical prospect would pay $150 if Portland beats Utah by more than 6 points. The event space is depicted in Figure 5.2. Each of the 32 rows in the figure represents a target event A that defines an uncertain prospect (x, A). For example, the top row in Figure 5.2, which consists of two segments, represents the event "the margin of victory exceeds 6 points." This design yields 28 tests of lower SA and 12 tests of upper SA. For example, one test of lower SA is obtained by comparing the decision weight for the event "Utah wins" to the sum of the decision weights for the two events "Utah wins by up to 12 points" and "Utah wins by more than 12 points."

Super Bowl prospects were defined by the result of the 1992 Super Bowl game between the Buffalo Bills and the Washington Redskins. The event space is depicted in Figure 5.3. It includes 28 target events yielding 30 tests of lower SA and 17 tests of upper SA

Dow–Jones prospects were defined by the change in the Dow–Jones Industrial Average over the subsequent week. For example, a typical prospect would

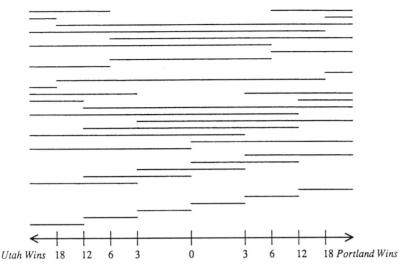

Utah Wins   18   12   6   3   0   3   6   12   18 Portland Wins

Figure 5.2. Event space for prospects defined by the result of the Utah–Portland basketball game. The horizontal axis refers to the point spread in that game. Each row denotes a target event that defines a prospect used in Study 1. Segments that extend up to the arrowhead represent unbounded intervals. Each interval includes the more extreme endpoint relative to 0, but not the less extreme endpoint.

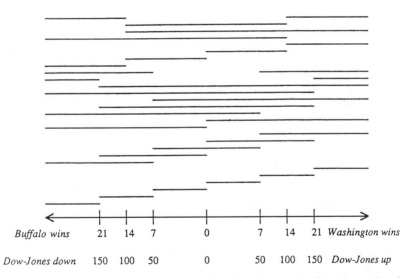

Buffalo wins   21   14   7   0   7   14   21 Washington wins

Dow-Jones down   150 100 50   0   50 100 150 Dow-Jones up

Figure 5.3. Event space for prospects defined by the result of the Super Bowl game between Washington and Buffalo (and for the Dow-Jones prospects). The horizontal axis refers to the point spread in the Super Bowl (and the change in the Dow-Jones in the next week). Each row denotes a target event that defines a prospect used in Study 2. Segments that extend up to the arrowhead represent unbounded intervals. Each interval includes the more extreme endpoint relative to 0, but not the less extreme endpoint.

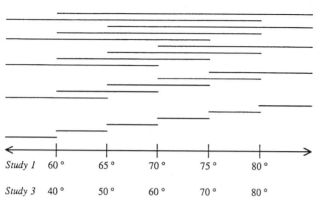

Figure 5.4. Event space for prospects defined by future temperatures in San Francisco and Beijing. The horizontal axis refers to the daytime high temperature on a given date. Each row denotes a target event that defines a prospect used in Studies 1 and 3. Segments that extend up to the arrowhead represent unbounded intervals. Each interval includes the left endpoint but not the right endpoint.

pay $150 if the Dow–Jones goes up by more than 50 points over the next seven days. The event space has the same structure as that of the Super Bowl (Figure 5.3).

San Francisco temperature prospects were defined by the daytime high temperature in San Francisco on a given future date. The 20 target events used in Studies 1 and 3 are depicted in Figure 5.4. This design yields 30 tests of lower SA and 10 tests of upper SA. For example, a typical prospect would pay $75 if the daytime high temperature in downtown San Francisco on April 1, 1992, is between 65° and 80°. Similarly, Beijing temperature prospects were defined by the daytime high temperature in Beijing on a given future day. The event space is identical to the San Francisco temperature in Study 3, as depicted in Figure 5.4.

Results

To test lower and upper SA, the decision weights for each respondent were derived as follows. Using the choice data, we first estimated the certainty equivalent C of each prospect by linear interpolation, as described earlier. According to prospect theory, if $C(x, A) = y$, then $v(y) = W(A)v(x)$ and $W(A) = v(y)/v(x)$. The decision weight associated with an uncertain event A, therefore, can be computed if the value function v for gains is known. Previous studies (e.g., Tversky, 1967) have indicated that the value function for gains can be approximated by a power function of the form $v(x) = x^\alpha$, $0 \leq \alpha \leq 1$. This form is characterized by the assumption that multiplying the prize of a prospect by a positive constant multiplies its certainty equivalent by the same constant.[8]

---

[8] This follows from the fact that for $t > 0$, the value of the prospect (tx, A) is $W(A)(tx)^\alpha$; hence, $C(tx, A) = W(A)^{1/\alpha}tx$, which equals $tC(x, A)$.

This prediction was tested using the data from Study 1 in which each event was paired both with a prize of $75 and with a prize of $150. Consistent with a power value function, we found no significant difference between $C(150, A)$ and $2C(75, A)$ for any of the sources.

Although the present data are consistent with a power function, the value of the exponent cannot be estimated from simple prospects because the exponent α can be absorbed into W. To estimate the exponent for gains, we need prospects with two positive outcomes. Such prospects were investigated by Tversky and Kahneman (1992), using the same experimental procedure and a similar subject population. They found that estimates of the exponent did not vary markedly across respondents and the median estimate of the exponent was .88. In the analysis that follows, we first assume a power value function with an exponent of .88 and test lower and upper SA using this function. We then show that the test of SA is robust with respect to substantial variations in the exponent. Further analyses are based on an ordinal method that makes no assumption about the functional form of v.

Using the estimated W for each source of uncertainty, we define measures of the degree of lower and upper SA as follows. Recall that lower SA requires that $W(A) \geq W(A \cup B) - W(B)$, for $A \cap B = \phi$. Hence, the difference between the two sides of the inequality,

$$D(A, B) \equiv W(A) + W(B) - W(A \cup B),$$

provides a measure of the degree of lower SA. Similarly, recall that upper SA requires that $1 - W(S - A) \geq W(A \cup B) - W(B)$, for $A \cap B = \phi$. Hence, the difference between the two sides of the inequality,

$$D'(A, B) \equiv 1 - W(S - A) - W(A \cup B) + W(B),$$

provides a measure of the degree of upper SA.

Table 5.4 presents the overall proportion of tests, across participants, that strictly satisfy lower and upper SA (i.e., $D > 0$, $D' > 0$) for each source of uncertainty. Note that if W were additive (as implied by expected utility theory), then

Table 5.4. Proportion of Tests That Strictly Satisfy Lower and Upper Subadditivity (SA)

Source	Study 1		Study 2		Study 3	
	Lower SA	Upper SA	Lower SA	Upper SA	Lower SA	Upper SA
Chance	.80	.81	.77	.83	.81	.79
Basketball	.88	.83				
Super Bowl			.86	.87		
Dow–Jones			.77	.87		
S.F. temp.	.83	.89			.85	.89
Beijing temp.					.89	.91

Note: S.F. = San Francisco; temp. = temperature.

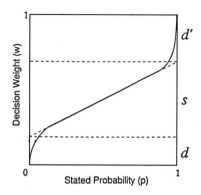

Figure 5.5. A weighting function that is linear except near the endpoints (d = "lower" intercept of the weighting function; d' = "upper" intercept of the weighting function; s = slope).

both D and D' are expected to be zero; hence, all entries in Table 5.4 should be close to one-half. However, each entry in Table 5.4 is significantly greater than one-half ($p < .01$, by a binomial test), as implied by SA.

To obtain global measures of lower and upper SA, let d and d', respectively, be the mean values of D and D' for a given respondent. Besides serving as summary statistics, these indexes have a simple geometric interpretation if the risky weighting function is roughly linear except near the endpoints. It is easy to verify that within the linear portion of the graph, D and D' do not depend on A and B, and the summary measures d and d' correspond to the "lower" and "upper" intercepts of the weighting function (see Figure 5.5). Its slope, $s = 1 - d - d'$, can then be interpreted as a measure of sensitivity to probability changes. For uncertainty, we cannot plot d and d' as in Figure 5.5. However, d and d' have an analogous interpretation as a "possibility gap" and "certainty gap," respectively, if W is roughly linear except near the endpoints.[9] Note that under expected utility theory, $d = d' = 0$ and $s = 1$, whereas prospect theory implies $d \geq 0, d' \geq 0$, and $s \leq 1$. Thus, prospect theory implies less sensitivity to changes in uncertainty than is required by expected utility theory. To test these predictions, we computed the values of d, d', and s, separately for each respondent. Table 5.5 presents the median values of these indexes, across respondent for each source of uncertainty.

In accord with SA, each value of d and d' in Table 5.5 is significantly greater than zero ($p < .05$). Furthermore, both indexes are larger for uncertainty than for chance: The mean values of d and of d' for the uncertain sources are significantly greater than each of the corresponding indexes for chance ($p < .01$, separately for each study). Finally, consistent with subcertainty, d' tends to exceed d, though this difference is statistically significant only in Studies 2 and 3 ($p < .05$).

Recall that all participants evaluated the same set of risky prospects, and that respondents in each of the three studies evaluated two different types of uncertain prospects (see Table 5.3). Figure 5.6 plots, for each respondent, the average sensitivity measure s for the two uncertain sources against s for the risky source. (One respondent who produced a negative s was excluded from this analysis.) These data may be summarized as follows. First, all values of s

---

[9] More formally, this holds when $W(A \cup B) - W(A)$ does not depend on A, for all $A \cap B = \phi$, provided $W(A)$ is not too close to zero and $W(A \cup B)$ is not too close to 1.

Table 5.5. Median Values of d, d', and s, across Respondents, Measuring the Degree of Lower and Upper Subadditivity (SA) and Global Sensitivity, Respectively

Source	Study 1			Study 2			Study 3		
	d	d'	s	d	d'	s	d	d'	s
Chance	.06	.10	.81	.05	.19	.75	.11	.14	.72
Basketball	.21	.19	.61						
Super Bowl				.15	.23	.57			
Dow–Jones				.12	.22	.67			
S.F. temp.	.20	.26	.51				.27	.23	.50
Beijing temp.							.28	.32	.42

Note: S.F. = San Francisco; temp. = temperature.

for the uncertain prospects and all but two values of s for the risky prospects were less than or equal to one as implied by SA. Second, the values of s are considerably higher for risk (mean $s = .74$) than for uncertainty (mean $s = .53$), as demonstrated by the fact that 94 out of 111 points lie below the identity line ($p < .01$ by a sign test). Third, the data reveal a significant correlation between the sensitivity measures for risk and for uncertainty ($r = .37$, $p < .01$). The average correlation between the uncertain sources is .40. If we restrict the analysis to Studies 1 and 2 that yielded more stable data (in part because the

Figure 5.6. Joint distribution for all respondents of the sensitivity measure s for risk and uncertainty.

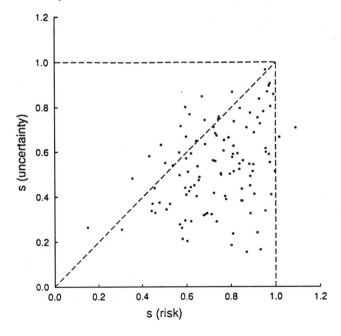

risky prospects were replicated), the correlation between sensitivity for risk and for uncertainty increases to .51, and the mean correlation between the uncertain sources increases to .54. These correlations indicate the presence of consistent individual differences in SA and suggest that sensitivity to uncertainty is an important attribute that distinguishes among decision makers. An axiomatic analysis of the conditions under which one individual is consistently more SA than another is presented in Tversky and Wakker (in press).

Robustness. The preceding analysis summarized in Table 5.5 assumes a power value function with an exponent $\alpha = .88$. To investigate whether the above conclusions depend on the particular choice of the exponent, we rean-alyzed the data using different values of α varying from one-half to one. To appreciate the impact of this difference, consider the prospect that offers a one-third chance to win $100. [We choose one-third because, according to Figure 5.1, $w(1/3)$ is approximately one-third.] The certainty equivalent of this prospect is $33.33 if $\alpha = 1$, but it is only $11.11 if $\alpha = .5$. Table 5.6 shows that as α decreases (indicating greater curvature), d increases and d' decreases. More important, however, both d and d' are positive throughout the range for all sources, and the values of s are significantly smaller than one ($p < .01$) in all cases. SA, there-fore, holds for a fairly wide range of variation in the curvature of the value function.

Ordinal Analysis. The preceding analysis confirmed our hypothesis that people are less sensitive to uncertainty than to chance using the sensitivity measure s. We next turn to an ordinal test of this hypothesis that makes no as-sumptions about the value function. Let B_1, B_2 denote disjoint uncertain events, and let A_1, A_2 denote disjoint chance events. We searched among the responses of each participant for patterns satisfying

$$C(x, B_1) \geq C(x, A_1) \quad \text{and} \quad C(x, B_2) \geq C(x, A_2)$$
$$\text{but } C(x, B_1 \cup B_2) < C(x, A_1 \cup A_2), \tag{3}$$

or

$$C(x, S - B_1) \leq C(x, S - A_1) \quad \text{and} \quad C(x, S - B_2) \leq C(x, S - A_2)$$
$$\text{but } C(x, S - [B_1 \cup B_2]) > C(x, S - [A_1 \cup A_2]). \tag{4}$$

A response pattern that satisfies either condition 3 or 4 provides support for the hypothesis that the respondent is less sensitive to uncertainty (**B**) than to chance (**A**).

Several comments regarding this test are in order. First, note that if we replace the weak inequalities in conditions 3 and 4 with equalities, then these condi-tions reduce to the definition of relative sensitivity (see Equations 1 and 2). The above conditions are better suited for the present experimental design because

Table 5.6. Median Values of *d*, *d′*, and *s* across Respondents, Measuring the Degree of Lower Subadditivity, Upper Subadditivity, and Global Sensitivity, Respectively, for Several Values of α between .5 and 1

Source and Index	α				
	0.500	0.625	0.750	0.875	1.00
Chance (Study 1)					
d	.29	.19	.12	.06	.01
d′	.02	.05	.07	.10	.12
s	.66	.73	.77	.81	.83
Chance (Study 2)					
d	.28	.18	.11	.05	.003
d′	.09	.12	.15	.19	.23
s	.66	.70	.74	.75	.75
Chance (Study 3)					
d	.33	.24	.17	.11	.06
d′	.05	.08	.11	.14	.17
s	.59	.65	.69	.72	.75
Basketball					
d	.40	.33	.26	.21	.16
d′	.10	.14	.17	.19	.22
s	.50	.56	.58	.61	.63
Super Bowl					
d	.36	.28	.20	.15	.11
d′	.15	.18	.20	.23	.25
s	.49	.54	.55	.57	.60
Dow–Jones					
d	.34	.25	.17	.11	.07
d′	.12	.15	.19	.22	.25
s	.54	.61	.64	.67	.70
SF temp (Study 1)					
d	.40	.32	.26	.20	.15
d′	.15	.18	.22	.26	.30
s	.42	.48	.49	.51	.52
SF temp (Study 3)					
d	.47	.39	.33	.27	.22
d′	.15	.18.	.20	.23	.26
s	.39	.43	.48	.50	.52
Beijing temp					
d	.48	.40	.34	.28	.23
d′	.21	.25	.29	.32	.35
s	.33	.38	.42	.42	.43

Note: SF = San Francisco; temp = temperature.

participants were not asked to "match" intervals from different sources. Second, the present analysis is confined to contiguous intervals; conditions 3 and 4 may not hold when comparing contiguous to noncontiguous intervals (see Tversky & Koehler, 1994). Third, because of measurement error, the above conditions are not expected to hold for all comparisons; however, the conditions indicating less sensitivity to uncertainty than to chance are expected to be satisfied more frequently than the opposite conditions.

Let $M(\mathbf{B}, \mathbf{A})$ be the number of response patterns that satisfy condition 3 above (i.e., less sensitivity to uncertainty than to chance). Let $M(\mathbf{A}, \mathbf{B})$ be the number of response patterns that satisfy 3 with the As and Bs interchanged (i.e., less sensitivity to chance than to uncertainty). The ratio $m(\mathbf{B}, \mathbf{A}) = M(\mathbf{B}, \mathbf{A})/(M(\mathbf{B}, \mathbf{A}) + M(\mathbf{A}, \mathbf{B}))$ provides a measure of the degree to which a respondent is less sensitive to uncertainty than to chance, in the sense of condition 3. We define $M'(\mathbf{B}, \mathbf{A})$, $M'(\mathbf{A}, \mathbf{B})$, and $m'(\mathbf{B}, \mathbf{A})$ similarly for preference patterns that satisfy condition 4. If the respondent is invariably less sensitive to $\mathbf{B}$ than to $\mathbf{A}$, then the ratios $m(\mathbf{B}, \mathbf{A})$ and $m'(\mathbf{B}, \mathbf{A})$ should be close to one. On the other hand, if the respondent is not more sensitive to one source than to another, these ratios should be close to one-half. Table 5.7 presents the median ratios, across respondent, comparing each of the five uncertain sources to chance. As predicted, all entries in the table are significantly greater than one-half ($p < .05$, by t tests), indicating that people are generally less sensitive to uncertainty than to chance.

We conclude this section with a brief methodological discussion. We have attributed the findings of bounded subadditivity and lower sensitivity for uncertainty than for risk to basic psychological attitudes toward risk and uncertainty captured by the weighting function. Alternatively, one might be tempted to account for these findings by a statistical model that assumes that the assessment of certainty equivalents, and hence the estimation of decision weights, is subject to random error that is bounded by the endpoints of the outcome scale, because $C(x, A)$ must lie between 0 and x. Although bounded error could

Table 5.7. Ordinal Analysis of Differential Sensitivity

	Study 1		Study 2		Study 3	
Source Comparison	m	m'	m	m'	m	m'
Basketball vs. chance	.85	.64				
Super Bowl vs. chance			.91	.89		
Dow–Jones vs. chance			.79	.76		
S.F. temp. vs. chance	.76	.93			.87	.87
Beijing temp. vs. chance					.83	.94

Note: Each entry corresponds to the median value, across respondents, of m and m' measuring the degree to which respondents are less sensitive to uncertainty than to chance. S.F. = San Francisco; temp. = temperature.

contribute to SA, this model cannot adequately account for the observed pattern of results. First, it cannot explain the subadditivity observed in simple choice experiments that do not involve (direct or indirect) assessment of certainty equivalents, such as the Stanford–Berkeley problem presented in Table 5.2. More extensive evidence for both lower and upper SA in simple choices between risky prospects is reported by Wu and Gonzalez (1994), who also found some support for the stronger hypothesis that w is concave for low probabilities and convex for moderate and high probabilities. Second, a statistical model cannot readily account for the result of the ordinal analysis reported above that respondents were less sensitive to uncertainty than to chance. Third, because a random error model implies a bias toward one-half, it cannot explain the observation that the decision weight of an event that is as likely as not to occur is generally less than one-half (see Figures 5.7, 5.8, and 5.9 below). Finally, it should be noted that subadditivity and differential sensitivity play an important role in the pricing of risky and uncertain prospects, regardless of whether these phenomena are driven primarily by psychological or by statistical factors.

Figure 5.7. Median decision weights for chance prospects, from Study 2, plotted as a function of stated (objective) probabilities.

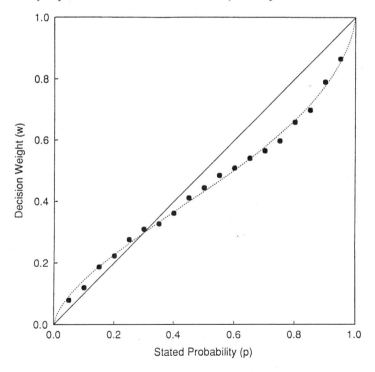

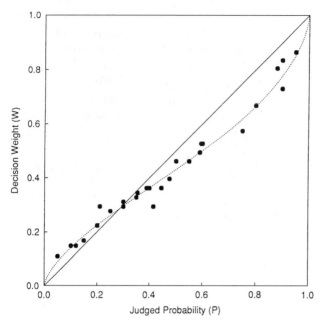

Figure 5.8. Median decision weights for Super Bowl prospects, from Study 2, plotted as a function of median judged probabilities.

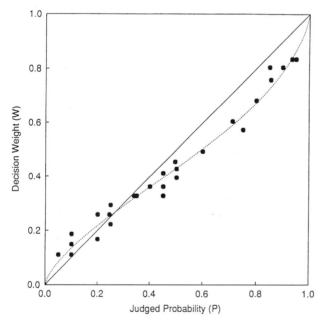

Figure 5.9. Median decision weights for Dow–Jones prospects, from Study 2, plotted as a function of median judged probability.

DISCUSSION

The final section of this article addresses three topics. First, we explore the relationship between decision weights and judged probabilities. Second, we investigate the presence of preferences for betting on particular sources of uncertainty. Finally, we discuss descriptive and normative implications of the present results.

Preference and Belief

The present account distinguishes between decision weights derived from preferences and degree of belief expressed by probability judgments. What is the relation between the judged probability, $P(A)$, of an uncertain event, A, and its associated decision weight $W(A)$? To investigate this problem, we asked respondents, after they completed the choice task, to assess the probabilities of all target events. Following the analysis of decision weights, we define measures of the degree of lower and upper SA in probability judgments as follows:

$$D(A, B) \equiv P(A) + P(B) - P(A \cup B),$$
$$D'(A, B) \equiv 1 - P(S - A) + P(B) - P(A \cup B),$$

provided $A \cap B = \phi$. Clearly, P is additive if and only if $D = D' = 0$ for all disjoint A, B in S. As before, let d and d' be the mean values of D and D', respectively, and let $s = 1 - d - d'$. Table 5.8, which is the analog of Table 5.5, presents the median values of d, d', and s, across respondents, for each of the five uncertain sources.

All values of d and d' in Table 5.8 are significantly greater than zero ($p < .05$), demonstrating both lower and upper SA for probability judgments. Comparing Table 5.8 and Table 5.5 reveals that the values of s for judged probabilities (overall mean .70) are greater than the corresponding uncertain decision weights (overall mean .55). Thus, probability judgments exhibit less SA than do uncertain decision weights. This finding is consistent with a two-stage process in

Table 5.8. Median Values of d, d', and s, across Respondents, That Measure the Degree of Lower and Upper Subadditivity, SA, and Global Sensitivity, Respectively, for Judged Probability

	Study 1			Study 2			Study 3		
Source	d	d'	s	d	d'	s	d	d'	s
Basketball	.08	.11	.74						
Super Bowl				.11	.08	.81			
Dow–Jones				.07	.08	.84			
S.F. temp.	.13	.16	.70				.29	.21	.51
Beijing temp.							.24	.25	.53

Note: SA = Subadditivity; S.F. = San Francisco; temp. = temperature; s = degree of global sensitivity.

which the decision maker first assesses the probability P of an uncertain event A, then transforms this value by the risky weighting function w. Thus, $W(A)$ may be approximated by $w[P(A)]$.

We illustrate this model using the median risky and uncertain decision weights derived from Study 2 (assuming $\alpha = .88$). In Figure 5.7 we plot decision weights for chance prospects as a function of stated (objective) probabilities. In Figures 5.8 and 5.9, respectively, we plot decision weights for Super Bowl prospects and for Dow–Jones prospects as functions of (median) judged probabilities. The comparison of these figures reveals that the data in Figures 5.8 and 5.9 are less orderly than those in Figure 5.7. This is not surprising because judged probability (unlike stated probability) is measured with error, and because the uncertain decision weights exhibit greater variability (both within and between subjects) than risky decision weights. However, the underlying relation between probability and decision weights is nearly identical in the three figures.[10] This is exactly what we would expect if the uncertain weighting function W is obtained by applying the risky weighting function w to judged probabilities.

The subadditivity of probability judgments reported in Table 5.8 is consistent with support theory[11] (Tversky & Koehler, 1994), according to which $P(A) + P(B) \geq P(A \cup B)$. The combination of the two-stage model (which is based on prospect theory) with an analysis of probability judgments (which is based on support theory) can therefore explain our main finding that decision weights are more subadditive for uncertainty than for chance. This model also implies that the decision weight associated with an uncertain event (e.g., an airplane accident) increases when its description is unpacked into its constituents (e.g., an airplane accident caused by mechanical failure, terrorism, human error, or acts of God; see Johnson, Hershey, Meszaros, & Kunreuther, 1993). Furthermore, this model predicts greater subadditivity, ceteris paribus, when $A \cup B$ is a contiguous interval (e.g., future temperature between 60° and 80°) than when $A \cup B$ is not a contiguous interval (e.g., future temperature less than 60° or more than 80°). A more detailed treatment of this model will be presented elsewhere.

Source Preference

The finding that people are less sensitive to uncertainty than to risk should be distinguished from the observation of ambiguity aversion: People often prefer to bet on known rather than unknown probabilities (Ellsberg, 1961). For example, people generally prefer to bet on either side of a fair coin than on either side of a coin with an unknown bias. These preferences violate expected utility

---

[10] The smooth curves in Figures 5.5 and 5.6 were obtained by fitting the parametric form $w(p) = \delta p^{\gamma} / (\delta p^{\gamma} + [1 - p]^{\gamma})$, used by Lattimore, Baker, and Witte (1992). It assumes that the relation between w and p is linear in a log odds metric. The estimated values of the parameters in Figures 5.7, 5.8, and 5.9, respectively, are .69, .69, and .72 for γ, and .77, .76, and .76 for δ.

[11] In this theory, $P(A) + P(S - A) = 1$; hence, the equations for lower and upper SA coincide.

theory because they imply that the sum of the subjective probabilities of heads and of tails is higher for the unbiased coin than for the coin with the unknown bias.

Recent research has documented some significant exceptions to ambiguity aversion. Heath and Tversky (1991) showed that people who were knowledgeable about sports but not about politics preferred to bet on sports events rather than on chance events that these people had judged equally probable. However, the same people preferred to bet on chance events rather than on political events that they had judged equally probable. Likewise, people who were knowledgeable about politics but not about sports exhibited the reverse pattern. These data support what Heath and Tversky call the competence hypothesis: People prefer to bet on their beliefs in situations where they feel competent or knowledgeable, and they prefer to bet on chance when they feel incompetent or ignorant. This account is consistent with the preference to bet on the fair rather than the biased coin, but it predicts additional preferences that are at odds with ambiguity aversion.

The preceding studies allow us to test the competence hypothesis against ambiguity aversion. Recall that the participants in Studies 1 and 2 were recruited for their knowledge of basketball and football, respectively. Ambiguity aversion implies a preference for chance over uncertainty because the probabilities associated with the sports events (e.g., Utah beating Portland) are necessarily vague or imprecise. In contrast, the competence hypothesis predicts that the sports fans will prefer to bet on the game than on chance.

To establish source preference, let A and B be two different sources of uncertainty. A decision maker is said to prefer source A to source B if for any events A in A and B in B. $W(A) = W(B)$ implies $W(S - A) > W(S - B)$, or equivalently, $C(x, A) = C(x, B)$ implies $C(x, S - A) > C(x, S - B)$, $x > 0$. To test for source preference we searched among the responses of each participant for patterns that satisfy $C(x, A) \geq C(x, B)$ and $C(x, S - A) > C(x, S - B)$. Thus, a decision maker who prefers to bet on event A than to bet on event B, and also prefers to bet against A than to bet against B exhibits a preference for source A over source B. The preference to bet on either side of a fair coin rather than on either side of a coin with an unknown bias illustrates such a preference for chance over uncertainty.

Let $K(A, B)$ be the number of response patterns indicating a preference for source A over source B, as defined above, and let $K(B, A)$ be the number of response patterns indicating the opposite preference. For each pair of sources, we computed the ratio $k(A, B) = K(A, B)/(K(A, B) + K(B, A))$, separately for each respondent. This ratio provides a comparative index of source preference; it should equal one-half if neither source is preferred to the other, and it should be substantially greater than one-half if source A is generally preferred to source B.

The present data reveal significant source preferences that are consistent with the competence hypothesis but not with ambiguity aversion. In all three studies, participants preferred to bet on their uncertain beliefs in their area of competence rather than on known chance events. The basketball fans in Study 1 preferred betting on basketball than on chance (median $k = .76$, $p < .05$ by t test); the football fans in Study 2 preferred betting on the Super Bowl than on chance (median $k = .59$, though this effect is not statistically significant); and the students in Study 3 (who live near San Francisco) preferred betting on San Francisco temperature than on chance (median $k = .76$, $p < .01$). Two other comparisons consistent with the competence hypothesis are the preference for basketball over San Francisco temperature in Study 1 (median $k = .76$, $p < .05$), and the preference for San Francisco temperature over Beijing temperature in Study 3 (median $k = .86$, $p < .01$). For further discussions of ambiguity aversion and source preference, see Camerer and Weber (1992), Fox and Tversky (in press), and Frisch and Baron (1988).

Concluding Comments

Several authors (e.g., Ellsberg, 1961; Fellner, 1961; Keynes, 1921; Knight, 1921), critical of expected utility theory, distinguished among uncertain prospects according to the degree to which the uncertainty can be quantified. At one extreme, uncertainty is characterized by a known probability distribution; this is the domain of decision under risk. At the other extreme, decision makers are unable to quantify their uncertainty; this is the domain of decision under ignorance. Most decisions under uncertainty lie somewhere between these two extremes: People typically do not know the exact probabilities associated with the relevant outcomes, but they have some vague notion about their likelihood. The role of vagueness or ambiguity in decision under uncertainty has been the subject of much experimental and theoretical research.

In the present article we have investigated this issue using the conceptual framework of prospect theory. According to this theory, uncertainty is represented by a weighting function that satisfies bounded subadditivity. Thus, an event has more impact when it turns impossibility into possibility, or possibility into certainty, than when it merely makes a possibility more likely. This principle explains Allais's examples (i.e., the certainty effect) as well as the fourfold pattern of risk attitudes illustrated in Table 5.1. The experiments reported in this article demonstrate SA for both risk and uncertainty. They also show that this effect is more pronounced for uncertainty than for risk. The latter finding suggests the more general hypothesis that SA, and hence the departure from expected utility theory, is amplified by vagueness or ambiguity. Consequently, studies of decision under risk are likely to underestimate the degree of SA that characterizes decisions involving real-world uncertainty.[12] Subadditivity, therefore, emerges as a unifying principle of choice that is manifested to varying degrees in decisions under risk, uncertainty, and ignorance.

---

[12] Evidence for substantial SA in the decisions of professional options traders is reported by Fox, Rogers, and Tversky (1995).

The psychological basis of bounded subadditivity includes both judgmental and preferential elements. As noted earlier, SA holds for judgments of probability (see Table 5.8), but it is more pronounced for decision weights (see Table 5.5). This amplification may reflect people's affective responses to positive and negative outcomes. Imagine owning a lottery ticket that offers some hope of winning a great fortune. Receiving a second ticket to the same lottery, we suggest, will increase one's hope of becoming rich but will not quite double it. The same pattern appears to hold for negative outcomes. Imagine waiting for the results of a biopsy. Receiving a preliminary indication that reduces the probability of malignancy by one-half, we suggest, will reduce fear by less than one-half. Thus, hope and fear seem to be subadditive in outcome probability. To the extent that the experience of hope and fear is treated as a consequence of an action, subadditivity may have some normative basis. If lottery tickets are purchased primarily for entertaining a fantasy, and protective action is undertaken largely to achieve peace of mind, then it is not unreasonable to value the first lottery ticket more than the second, and to value the elimination of a hazard more than a comparable reduction in its likelihood.

6. A Belief-Based Account of Decision under Uncertainty

Craig R. Fox and Amos Tversky

ABSTRACT. We develop a belief-based account of decision under uncertainty. This model predicts decisions under uncertainty from (i) judgments of probability, which are assumed to satisfy support theory; and (ii) decisions under risk, which are assumed to satisfy prospect theory. In two experiments, subjects evaluated uncertain prospects and assessed the probability of the respective events. Study 1 involved the 1995 professional basketball playoffs; Study 2 involved the movement of economic indicators in a simulated economy. The results of both studies are consistent with the belief-based account, but violate the partition inequality implied by the classical theory of decision under uncertainty.

KEY WORDS decision making; risk; uncertainty; expected utility; prospect theory; support theory; decision weights; judgment; probability

1. INTRODUCTION

It seems obvious that the decisions to invest in the stock market, undergo a medical treatment, or settle out of court depend on the strength of people's beliefs that the market will go up, that the treatment will be successful, or that the court will decide in their favor. It is less obvious how to elicit and measure such beliefs. The classical theory of decision under uncertainty derives beliefs about the likelihood of uncertain events from people's choices between prospects whose consequences are contingent on these events. This approach, first advanced by Ramsey (1931),[1] gives rise to an elegant axiomatic theory that yields simultaneous measurement of utility and subjective probability, thereby bypassing the thorny problem of how to interpret direct expressions of belief.

From a psychological (descriptive) perspective, the classical theory can be questioned on several counts. First, it does not correspond to the common

---

[1] The notion that beliefs can be measuredbased on preferences was anticipated by Borel (1924).

intuition that belief precedes preference. People typically choose to bet $50 on team *A* rather than team *B* because they believe that *A* is more likely to win; they do not infer this belief from the observation that the former bet is more attractive than the latter. Second and perhaps more important, the classical theory does not consider probability judgments that could be useful in explaining and predicting decisions under uncertainty. Third, and most important, the empirical evidence indicates that the major assumptions of the classical theory that underlie the derivation of belief from preference are not descriptively valid.

This article develops a belief-based account in which probability judgments are used to predict decisions under uncertainty. We first review recent work on probability judgment and on the weighting function of prospect theory that serves as the basis for the present development. We next formulate a two-stage model of decision under uncertainty and explore its testable implications. This model is tested against the classical theory in two experiments. Finally, we address some empirical, methodological, theoretical, and practical issues raised by the present development.

2. THEORETICAL BACKGROUND

There is an extensive body of research indicating that people's choices between risky prospects depart systematically from expected utility theory (for a review, see Camerer 1995). Many of these violations can be explained by a nonlinear weighting function (see Figure 6.1) that overweights low probabilities and underweights moderate to high probabilities (Kahneman and Tversky 1979, Tversky and Kahneman 1992, Prelec 1998). Such a function accounts for violations of the independence axiom (the common consequence effect) and the substitution axiom (the common ratio effect), first demonstrated by Allais (1953). It also accommodates the commonly observed fourfold pattern of risk attitudes: risk seeking for gains and risk aversion for losses of low probability, together with risk aversion for gains and risk seeking for losses of high probability (Tversky and Kahneman 1992). Finally, it is consistent with the observed pattern of fanning in and fanning out in the probability triangle (Camerer and Ho 1994, Wu and Gonzalez 1998a).

Although most empirical studies have employed risky prospects, where probabilities are assumed to be known, virtually all real-world decisions (with the notable exception of games of chance) involve uncertain prospects (e.g., investments, litigation, insurance) where this assumption does not hold. In order to model such decisions we need to extend the key features of the risky weighting function to the domain of uncertainty. Tversky and Wakker (1995) established such a generalization, within the framework of cumulative prospect theory, by assuming that an event has more impact on choice when it turns an impossibility into a possibility or a possibility into a certainty than when it merely makes a possibility more or less likely.

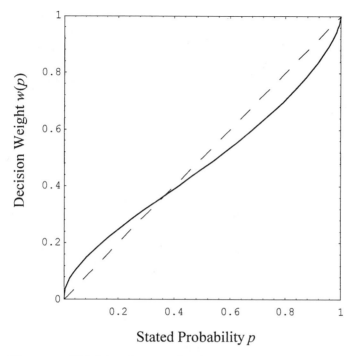

Decision Weight $w(p)$

Stated Probability p

Figure 6.1. Weighting function for decision under risk, $w(p) = \exp(-\beta(-\ln p)^\alpha)$, with $\alpha = 0.7$, $\beta = 1$ (Prelec 1998).

Formally, let W denote the weighting function defined on subsets of a sample space S, where $W(\phi) = 0$ and $W(S) = 1$. W satisfies *bounded subadditivity* if:

(i) $W(A) \geq W(A \cup B) - W(B)$, and
(ii) $W(S) - W(S - A) \geq W(A \cup B) - W(B)$,

provided A and B are disjoint and $W(B)$ and $W(A \cup B)$ are bounded away from 0 and 1, respectively.[2] Condition (i) generalizes the notion that increasing the probability of winning a prize from 0 to p has more impact than increasing the probability of winning from q to $q + p$, provided $q + p < 1$. This condition reflects the *possibility effect*. Condition (ii) generalizes the notion that decreasing the probability of winning from 1 to $1 - p$ has more impact than decreasing the probability of winning from $q + p$ to q, provided $q > 0$. This condition reflects the *certainty effect*. Note that risk can be viewed as a special case of uncertainty where probability is defined via a standard chance device so that the probabilities of outcomes are known.

[2] The boundary conditions are needed to ensure that we always compare an interval that includes an endpoint to an interval that is bounded away from the other endpoint (see Tversky and Wakker 1995 for a more rigorous formulation).

Tversky and Fox (1995) tested bounded subadditivity in a series of studies using both risky prospects and uncertain prospects whose outcomes were contingent on upcoming sporting events, future temperature in various cities, and changes in the Dow–Jones index. The data satisfied bounded subadditivity for both risk and uncertainty. Furthermore, this effect was more pronounced for uncertainty than for risk, indicating greater departures from expected utility theory when probabilities are not known. The results of these experiments are consistent with a two-stage model in which the decision maker first assesses the probability P of an uncertain event A, then transforms this value using the risky weighting function,[3] w.

In the present article we elaborate this two-stage model and investigate its consequences. To simplify matters, we confine the present treatment to simple prospects of the form (x, A) that pay \$$x$ if the target event A obtains, and nothing otherwise.[4] We assume that the overall value V of such prospects is given by

$$V(x, A) = v(x)W(A) = v(x)w[P(A)], \tag{1}$$

where v is the value function for monetary gains, w is the risky weighting function, and $P(A)$ is the judged probability of A. The key feature of this model, which distinguishes it from other theories of decision under uncertainty, is the inclusion of probability judgments. Note that if $W(A)$ can be expressed as $w[P(A)]$, as implied by Equation (1), we can predict decisions under uncertainty from decisions under risk and judgments of probability. We further assume that risky choices satisfy prospect theory[5] (Kahneman and Tversky 1979, Tversky and Kahneman 1992) and that judged probabilities satisfy support theory (Tversky and Koehler 1994, Rottenstreich and Tversky 1997), a psychological model of degree of belief to which we now turn.

There is ample evidence that people's intuitive probability judgments are often inconsistent with the laws of chance. In particular, different descriptions of the same event often give rise to systematically different responses (e.g., Fischhoff et al. 1978), and the judged probability of the union of disjoint events is generally smaller than the sum of judged probabilities of these events (e.g., Teigen 1974). To accommodate such findings, support theory assumes that (subjective) probability is not attached to events, as in other models, but rather to descriptions of events, called *hypotheses*; hence, two descriptions of the same event may be assigned different probabilities. Support theory assumes that each hypothesis A has a nonnegative support value $s(A)$ corresponding to the strength of the evidence for this hypothesis. The judged probability $P(A, B)$,

---

[3] We use the lower case w to denote the weighting function for risk and the upper case W to denote the weighting function for uncertainty.

[4] The two-stage model has not yet been extensively tested for multiple nonzero outcomes; however, see Wu and Gonzalez (1998c) for a preliminary investigation.

[5] For the simple prospects considered here, the separable and cumulative versions of the theory are identical.

that hypothesis A rather than B holds, assuming that one and only one of them obtains, is given by:

$$P(A, B) = \frac{s(A)}{s(A) + s(B)},$$ (2)

where

$$s(A) \leq s(A_1 \vee A_2) \leq s(A_1) + s(A_2),$$ (3)

provided (A_1, A_2) is recognized as a partition of A.

In this theory, judged probability is interpreted as the support of the focal hypothesis A relative to the alternative hypothesis B (equation 2). The theory further assumes that (i) unpacking a description of an event A (e.g., homicide) into disjoint components $A_1 \vee A_2$ (e.g., homicide by an acquaintance, A_1, or homicide by a stranger, A_2) generally increases its support, and (ii) the sum of the support of the component hypotheses is at least as large as the support of their disjunction (Equation (3)). The rationale for these assumptions is that (i) unpacking may remind people of possibilities that they have overlooked, and (ii) the separate evaluation of hypotheses tends to increase their salience and enhance their support.

Equation (2) implies *binary complementarity*: $P(A, B) + P(B, A) = 1$. For finer partitions, however, Equations (2) and (3) imply *subadditivity*: the judged probability of A is less than or equal to the sum of judged probabilities of its disjoint components. These predictions have been confirmed in several studies reviewed by Tversky and Koehler (1994). For example, experienced physicians were provided with medical data regarding the condition of a particular patient who was admitted to the emergency ward, and asked to evaluate the probabilities of four mutually exclusive and exhaustive prognoses. The judged probability of a prognosis (e.g., that the patient will survive the hospitalization) against its complement, evaluated by different groups of physicians, summed to one, in accord with binary complementarity. However, the sum of the judged probabilities for the four prognoses was substantially greater than one, in accord with subadditivity (Redelmeier et al. 1995).

Implications

Perhaps the most striking contrast between the two-stage model and the classical theory (i.e., expected utility theory with risk aversion) concerns the effect of partitioning. Suppose $(A_1, \ldots, A_n)$ is a partition of A, and $C(x, A)$ is the certainty equivalent of the prospect that pays $\$x$ if A occurs, and nothing otherwise. The classical theory implies the following *partition inequality*:

$$C(x, A_1) + \cdots + C(x, A_n) \leq C(x, A),$$ (4)

for all real x and $A \subset S$. That is, the certainty equivalent of an uncertain prospect exceeds the sum of certainty equivalents of the subprospects (evaluated independently) obtained by partitioning the target event. In the context of expected utility theory, the partition inequality is implied by risk aversion.[6] However, if people follow the two-stage model, defined in Equation (1), and if the judged probabilities are subadditive, as implied by support theory, then the partition inequality is not expected to hold. Such failures are especially likely when the curvature of the value function (between 0 and $x) is not very pronounced and the target event (A) is partitioned into many components. Thus, the partition inequality provides a simple method for testing the classical theory and contrasting it to the two-stage model.

To test the two-stage model, we predict the certainty equivalent of an uncertain prospect, $C(x, A)$, from two independent responses: the judged probability of the target event, $P(A)$, and the certainty equivalent of the risky prospect, $C(x, P(A))$. It follows readily from Equation (1) that

$$\text{if } P(A) = p, \quad \text{then } C(x, A) = C(x, p). \tag{5}$$

This condition provides a method for testing the two-stage model that does not require an estimation of the value function. The following two studies test the partition inequality and compare the predictions derived from Equation (5) to those of the classical theory.

3. EXPERIMENTS

STUDY 1: BASKETBALL PLAYOFFS METHOD

Participants. The participants in this study were 50 students at Northwestern University (46 men, 4 women; median age $= 20$) who responded to fliers calling for fans of professional basketball to take part in a study of decision making. Subjects indicated that they had watched several games of the National Basketball Association (NBA) during the regular season (median $= 25$). They received $10 for completing a one-hour session and were told that some participants would be selected at random to play one of their choices for real money and that they could win up to $160.

Procedure. The experiment was run using a computer. All subjects were run on the same day, during the beginning of the NBA quarterfinals. Subjects were given detailed instructions and an opportunity for supervised practice. The study consisted of four tasks.

The first task was designed to estimate subjects' certainty equivalents (abbreviated C) for risky prospects. These prospects were described in terms of a random draw of a single poker chip from an urn containing 100 chips numbered consecutively from 1 to 100. Nineteen prospects of the form ($160, p$) were constructed where p varied from 0.05 to 0.95 in multiples of .05. For example, the

---

[6] To demonstrate, set $u(0)=0$. Hence, $C(x, A_1) + \cdots + C(x, A_n) = u^{-1}(u(x)\mathcal{P}(A_1)) + \cdots + u^{-1}(u(x)\mathcal{P}(A_n)) \leq u^{-1}(u(x)\mathcal{P}(A)) = C(x, A)$ if u is concave. We use $\mathcal{P}$ to denote an additive probability measure, to be distinguished from P, that denotes judged probability.

($160, .25) prospect would pay $160 if the number of the poker chip is between 1 and 25, and nothing otherwise.

Each trial involved a series of choices between a prospect and an ascending series of sure payments (e.g., receive $40 for sure). The order of the 19 risky prospects was randomized separately for each subject. Certainty equivalents were inferred from two rounds of such choices. The first round consisted of nine choices between the prospect and sure payments that were spaced evenly from $0 to $160. After completing the first round of choices, a new set of nine sure payments was presented, spanning the narrower range between the lowest payment that the subject had accepted and the highest payment that the subject had rejected (excluding the endpoints). The program enforced dominance and internal consistency within a given trial. For example, the program did not allow a respondent to prefer $30 over a prospect and also prefer the same prospect over $40. The program allowed subjects to backtrack if they felt they had made a mistake in the previous round of choices.

For each risky prospect, C was determined by linear interpolation between the lowest value accepted and the highest value rejected in the second round of choices, yielding a margin of error of $\pm\$1.00$. Note that although our analysis is based on C, the data consisted of a series of choices between a given prospect and sure outcomes. Thus, respondents were not asked to generate C; it was inferred from their choices.

The second task was designed to estimate certainty equivalents for uncertain prospects. Each prospect offered to pay $160 if a particular team, division, or conference would win the 1995 NBA championship. At the time of the study, eight teams remained (Chicago, Indiana, Orlando, New York, Los Angeles, Phoenix, San Antonio, Houston) representing four divisions (Central, Atlantic, Pacific, Midwestern) and two conferences (Eastern, Western). Fourteen prospects of the form ($160, A) were constructed that offered to pay $160 if a particular team, division, or conference were to win the 1995 NBA championship. For example, a typical prospect would pay $160 if the Chicago Bulls won the championship. The elicitation method was identical to that of the first task.

The third task was designed to provide an independent test of risk aversion under expected utility theory. Subjects were presented with a "fixed" prospect of the form (a, 0.25; b, 0.25; 0, 0.50) and a "variable" prospect of the form (c, 0.25; x, 0.25; 0, 0.50). These prospects were displayed as "spinner games" that would pay the designated amount depending on the particular region on which the spinner would land. In each trial, the values of a, b, and c were fixed, while the value of x varied. The initial value of x was set equal to b. Eight such pairs of prospects were constructed (see Table 6.1) presented in an order that was randomized separately for each subject. On each trial, participants were asked to indicate their preference between the prospects. When a subject preferred the fixed prospect, the value of x increased by $16; when a subject preferred the

Table 6.1. Values of *a*, *b*, and *c* Used in the Spinner Games of Study 1 and Median Value of Subjects' Responses (*x*)

	Fixed Prospect			Variable Prospect		
Probability	0.25	0.25	0.50	0.25	0.25	0.50
Outcome	$a	$b	$0	$c	$x (Median)	$0
1)	50	100		25	131	
2)	30	60		10	86.5	
3)	20	90		40	70	
4)	10	110		35	82	
5)	85	55		120	31	
6)	50	45		75	29	
7)	95	25		70	42	
8)	115	15		80	43	

variable prospect, the value of *x* decreased by $16. When a subject's preference switched from the fixed prospect to the variable prospect or from variable to fixed, the change in *x* reversed direction and the increment was cut in half (i.e., from $16 to $8, from $8 to $4, and so forth) until the increment was $1. This process was repeated until the subject indicated that the two prospects were equally attractive. The program did not allow subjects to violate dominance.

The fourth task required participants to estimate the probability of each target event (i.e., that a particular team, division, or conference would win the NBA playoffs). The fourteen events were presented in an order that was randomized separately for each subject. On each trial, subjects could respond by either typing a number between 0 and 100, or by clicking and dragging a "slider" on a visual scale.

Subjects performed two additional tasks. They judged the probability that one team rather than another would win the NBA championship assuming that two particular teams reached the finals, and they rated the "strength" of each team. These data are discussed in Fox (1998).

Results

Judged Probability. The median judged probability for each target event is listed in Figure 6.2. The figure shows that the sum of these probabilities is close to one for the two conferences, nearly one and a half for the four divisions, and more than two for the eight teams. This pattern is consistent with the predictions of support theory that

$$\sum_{\text{teams}} P \geq \sum_{\text{divisions}} P \geq \sum_{\text{conferences}} P, \tag{6}$$

and the sum over the two conferences equals one. Moreover, in every case the sum of the probabilities for the individual teams is greater than the probability

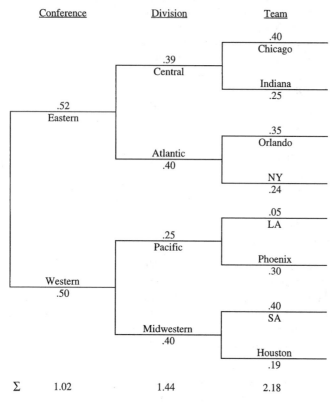

Figure 6.2. Median judged probabilities for all target events in Study 1.

of the respective division, and the sum of the probabilities for the divisions is greater than the probability of the respective conference, consistent with support theory.[7]

The same pattern holds in the analysis of individual subjects. The median sum of probabilities for the eight teams was 2.40, the median sum for the four divisions was 1.44, and the median sum of probabilities for the two conferences was 1.00. Moreover, 41 of 50 respondents satisfied Equation (6) with strict inequalities, and 49 of 50 respondents reported probabilities for the eight teams that summed to more than one ($p < 0.001$ by sign test in both cases).

Certainty Equivalents. Figure 6.3 presents the median normalized C for each prospect; that is, the median certainty equivalent divided by $160. The choice data in Figure 6.3 echo the judgment data in Figure 6.2. In every case, the sum of Cs for the individual teams is greater than C for the respective division, and the sum of Cs for the divisions is greater than C for the respective

---

[7] In every case this also holds for a significant majority of subjects ($p < 0.01$ by sign tests).

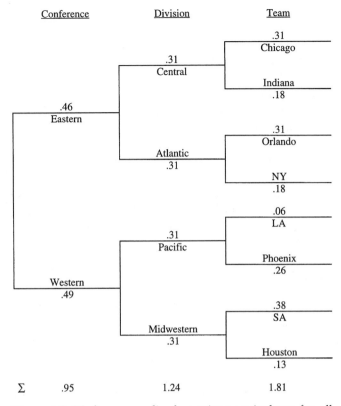

Figure 6.3. Median normalized certainty equivalents for all prospects in Study 1.

conference[8]. Furthermore, the sum of Cs for the 8 teams exceeds $160; that is, the sum of the normalized Cs is greater than one.

Again, the same pattern holds in the analysis of individual subjects. The median sum of normalized Cs for the 8 teams was 2.08, the median sum for the 4 divisions was 1.38, and the median sum for the 2 conferences was 0.93. Moreover, the pattern implied by the partition inequality (Equation (4)):

$$\sum_{teams} C \le \sum_{divisions} C \le \sum_{conferences} C,$$

was satisfied by only one respondent, whereas 41 of the 50 respondents satisfied the reverse pattern that is consistent with the two-stage model ($p < 0.001$):

$$\sum_{teams} C > \sum_{divisions} C > \sum_{conferences} C.$$

[8] In every case this also holds for a significant majority of subjects ($p < 0.01$).

Furthermore, only 5 subjects produced Cs for the 8 teams that summed to less than \$160, whereas 44 subjects produced Cs that summed to more than \$160 ($p < 0.001$). This pattern violates the partition inequality, with $A = S$.

Comparing Models. We next compare the fit of the classical theory to that of the two-stage model. For each event A, we observed the median judged probability $P(A)$, then searched for the median C of the risky prospect (x, p) where $p = P(A)$. For example, the median judged probability that the San Antonio Spurs (SAS) would win the NBA championship was 0.40, and the median value of $C(\$160, .40)$, was \$59. According to Equation (5), therefore, $C(\$160, SAS)$ should equal \$59; the actual value was \$60. In cases where the $P(A)$ is not a multiple of 5 percent, we determined the certainty equivalent by linear interpolation.

To fit the classical theory, let C_A be the certainty equivalent of the prospect (\$160, A). Setting $u(0) = 0$, the classical theory yields $u(C_A) = u(160)P(A)$, where u is concave and $P(A)$ is an additive (subjective) probability measure. Hence, $P(A) = u(C_A)/u(160)$. Previous studies (e.g., Tversky 1967, Tversky and Kahneman 1992) have indicated that the value function for small to moderate gains can be approximated by a power function of the form $u(x) = x^\alpha$, $\alpha > 0$. To estimate the exponent, we used data from the "spinner games" described above. If a subject is indifferent between the fixed prospect (\$a, 0.25; \$b, 0.25; \$0, 0.5) and the variable prospect (\$c, 0.25; \$x, 0.25; \$0, 0.5) then assuming a power utility function, $a^\alpha + b^\alpha = c^\alpha + x^\alpha$. Because a, b, and c are given and the value of x is determined by the subject, one can solve for $\alpha > 0$. The exponent for each subject was estimated using the median value of α over the eight problems listed in Table 6.1. This analysis showed that participants were generally risk-averse: 32 subjects exhibited $\alpha < 1.00$ (risk aversion); 14 exhibited $\alpha = 1.00$ (risk neutrality); and 4 exhibited $\alpha > 1.00$ (risk seeking) ($p < 0.001$ by sign test). The median response to each of the eight trials yielded $\alpha = 0.80$. The finding that the majority of subjects exhibited risk aversion in this task shows that the violations of the partition inequality described earlier cannot be explained by a convex utility function.

Subjective probabilities were estimated as follows. For each elementary target event A, we computed $(C_A/160)^\alpha$ and divided these values by their sum to ensure additivity. Figure 6.4 displays the median C for each of the eight teams along with the predictions of the two-stage model and the standard theory (assuming $\alpha = 0.80$, based on the median response to each item). It is evident from the figure that the two-stage model fits the data (mean absolute error $= \$5.83$) substantially better than does the standard theory (mean absolute error $= \$23.71$).[9] The same pattern is evident in the responses of individual subjects. The two-stage model fits the data better than does the classical theory for 45 of the 50 subjects ($p < 0.001$).

Note that the predictions of the two-stage model were derived from two independent tasks; no parameters were estimated from the fitted data. In contrast,

---

[9] A more conservative test of the standard theory assuming $\alpha = 1.00$ yields a mean absolute error of \$13.29.

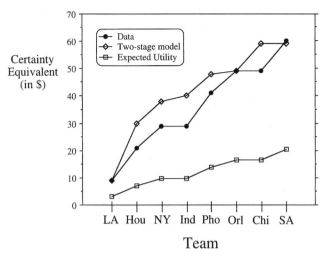

Figure 6.4. Median certainty equivalents of bets for all eight teams and predictions of two-stage model and classical theory (with $\alpha = 0.80$).

the predictions of the classical theory were derived by estimating a parameter for each of the fitted data points; these estimates were constrained only by the requirement that the subjective probabilities sum to unity. In light of the substantial advantage conferred to the classical theory in this comparison, its inferior fit provides compelling evidence against the additivity of subjective probabilities that are inferred from choice.

Studies of Unpacking. We have attributed the failure of the partition inequality to the subadditivity of judged probability that is implied by support theory. A more radical departure from the classical theory is suggested by the *unpacking principle* of support theory, according to which unpacking the description of an event into an explicit disjunction of constituent events generally increases its judged probability. Under the two-stage model, therefore, unpacking the description of an event is also expected to increase the attractiveness of a prospect whose outcome depends on this event. Furthermore, if this effect is sufficiently pronounced, it can give rise to violations of monotonicity where $C(x, A) < C(x, A_1 \vee \cdots \vee A_n)$ even when $A_1 \vee \cdots \vee A_n$ is a proper subset of A.

To explore this possibility, we presented a brief questionnaire to 58 business students at Northwestern University shortly before the beginning of the 1996 NBA playoffs. The survey was administered in a classroom setting. Prior to the survey, respondents were presented with the records of all NBA teams listed by their division and conference. Subjects were randomly assigned to one of two groups. Subjects in the first group ($N = 28$) stated their certainty equivalent for two prospects: a prospect that offered \$75 if the winner of the 1996 playoffs belongs to the Eastern conference, and a prospect that offered \$75 if one of the four leading Western conference teams (Seattle, Utah, San Antonio, or Los Angeles) would win the 1996 playoffs. Subjects in the second group ($N = 30$)

Table 6.2. Median Judged Probability and Certainty Equivalent
for the Two Conferences and Respective Leading Teams for the
1996 NBA Playoffs

	Judged Probability	Certainty Equivalents
Eastern Conference	0.78	$50
Chi ∨ Orl ∨ Ind ∨ NY	0.90	$60
Western Conference	0.18	$15
Seattle ∨ Utah ∨ SA ∨ LA	0.20	$15

stated their certainty equivalent for the two parallel prospects: a prospect that
offered $75 if the winner of the 1996 playoffs belongs to the Western conference,
and a prospect that offered $75 if one of the four leading Eastern conference
teams (Chicago, Orlando, Indiana, or New York) would win the 1996 playoffs.[10]
Each group also assessed the probability of the two target events that defined
the prospects evaluated by the other group. For example, the group that evaluated the prospect that would pay if an Eastern team will win assessed the
probability that a Western team will win, and vice versa.

Table 6.2 presents the median judged probability and certainty equivalent for
the two conferences, and the four leading teams in each conference. Although
these teams had the best record in their respective conferences, some strong
teams (e.g., the defending champion Houston Rockets) were not included in the
list. Monotonicity requires, therefore, that the judged probability and certainty
equivalent assigned to each conference should exceed those assigned to their
leading teams. The unpacking principle, on the other hand, suggests that a nontransparent comparison (e.g., a between-subjects test) may produce violations
of monotonicity. Indeed, the data of Table 6.2 do not satisfy the monotonicity
requirement. There is essentially no difference in either judged probability or
the certainty equivalent between the Western conference and its four leading
teams, whereas the judged probability and the certainty equivalent assigned to
the Eastern conference are significantly smaller than those assigned to its four
leading teams ($p < 0.05$, by a t-test in each case).[11]

Violations of monotonicity (or dominance) induced by unpacking have been
observed by several investigators. Johnson et al. (1993), for example, reported
that subjects were willing to pay more for a health insurance policy that covers
hospitalization for all diseases and accidents than for a policy that covers hospitalization for any reason. Wu and Gonzalez (1998b) found similar effects in

[10] Eight teams qualified for the playoffs from each conference.

[11] Violations of monotonicity are also evident in the certainty equivalent data for Study 1 reported
in Figure 6.3. Note that the median certainty equivalent for San Antonio is higher than the
median certainty equivalent for the Midwestern Division; Chicago and Orlando are priced as
high as their respective divisions. While these results are consistent with the present account,
none of these differences is statistically significant.

the evaluation of prospects contingent on diverse events such as the winner of the World Series, the outcomes of the 1996 elections, and future temperature in Boston. Although the effects observed in the above studies are not very pronounced, they indicate that unpacking can give rise to nonmonotonicity in judgments of probability as well as the pricing of uncertain prospects.

STUDY 2: ECONOMIC INDICATORS

The study above, like previous tests of bounded subadditivity, relied on subjects' beliefs regarding the occurrence of various real-world events. In the following study, subjects were given an opportunity to learn the probability of target events by observing changes in inflation and interest rates in a simulated economy. This design allows us to test both the classical theory and the two-stage model in a controlled environment in which all subjects are exposed to identical information. It also allows us to compare subjects' judged probabilities to the actual probabilities of the target events.

Method

Participants. Subjects were students ($N = 92$) enrolled in an introductory class in judgment and decision making at Stanford University. Students were asked to download a computer program from a world wide web page, run the program, and e-mail their output to a class account. At the time of the study, the students had been exposed to discussions of probability theory and judgmental biases, but they were unfamiliar with decision theory. We received 86 complete responses. Four subjects were dropped because they apparently did not understand the instructions. The 82 remaining subjects included 49 men and 33 women (median age $= 21.5$). Most of them completed the study in less than an hour (median $= 47$ minutes).

Procedure. Subjects were first given an opportunity to learn the movement of two indicators (inflation and interest rates) in a simulated economy. Each indicator could move either up or down relative to the previous quarter. In this economy both indicators went up 60 percent of the time, inflation went up and interest went down 25 percent of the time, inflation went down and interest went up 10 percent of the time, and both indicators went down 5 percent of the time. The order of these events was randomized over 60 quarters of learning, separately for each subject. Participants were informed that the probabilities of the target events were the same for each quarter.

The learning procedure was divided into two parts. During the first 20 quarters, subjects merely clicked the mouse to advance to the next quarter and observed what happened. During the remaining 40 quarters, subjects also played a game in which they predicted the direction that each indicator would move in the subsequent quarter, and they made (hypothetical) bets on their predictions. After each prediction, subjects were given feedback and the computer adjusted their "bank balance" according to whether they had predicted correctly.

The second task was designed to estimate C for risky prospects. We constructed eleven prospects of the form ($1600, p) that offered to pay $1600 with probability (0.01, 0.05, 0.10, 0.15, 0.25, 0.50, 0.75, 0.85, 0.90, 0.95, 0.99). The elicitation procedure was identical to that used in the basketball study, except that all dollar amounts were multiplied by 10. Using this method we could estimate C for $1600 prospects within $\pm$$10.

The third task was designed to estimate C for uncertain prospects. Subjects were first given an opportunity to review up to three times a 35-second "film" that very briefly displayed changes in the two indicators over each of the 60 quarters that subjects had previously observed. They were then presented with prospects that offered $1600 contingent on the movement of the indicators in the next (i.e., 61st) quarter. The first four trials involved movement of a single indicator (e.g., win $1600 if inflation up). The next four trials involved movement of both indicators (e.g., win $1600 if inflation up and interest down). The final four trials involved negations of the previous four events (e.g., win $1600 *unless* inflation up and interest down). The order of prospects within each set of trials was randomized separately for each subject. C was elicited through a series of choices between uncertain prospects and sure payments, as in the previous task.

The fourth task was designed to obtain an independent test of risk aversion. The procedure was essentially identical to the third task of the basketball study, except that the dollar amounts were multiplied by 10, and the initial value of x for the variable prospect was set so that the expected value of the two spinner games was equal (see Table 6.7).

In the fifth task, subjects judged the probability of each target event. Subjects were first given an opportunity to review again up to three times a "film" of the 60 quarters they had previously observed. The first eight trials involved the movement of a single economic indicator (e.g., what is the probability that the following happens: inflation up) or combination of indicators (e.g., inflation up and interest down). The last four trials involved complementary events (e.g., what is the probability that the following does *not* happen: inflation up and interest down). The order of these events within each set was randomized separately for each subject, and responses were elicited as in the basketball study.

Subjects performed one additional task involving the acceptability of mixed prospects. The results of this task will not be discussed here.

Results

Judged Probabilities. Figure 6.5 plots for each target event the median judged probability against the actual probability. The figure shows that participants had learned the probabilities of the target events with impressive accuracy ($r = 0.995$). The mean absolute difference (MAD) between median judged probability and actual probability was 0.048. The median correlation for individual subjects was 0.89 (median MAD $= 0.14$). Subjects also exhibited a tendency to overestimate low probabilities and underestimate high probabilities. Of the 82 subjects, 60 both overestimated, on average, events with true probabilities less

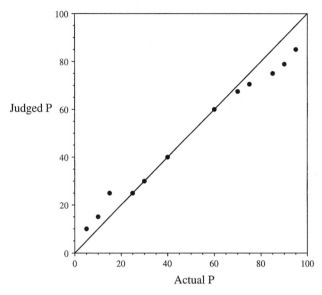

Figure 6.5. Median judged probability as a function of actual probabilities for all target events in Study 2.

than 50 percent, and underestimated, on average, events with true probabilities greater than 50 percent ($p < 0.001$ by sign test).

The median judged probability for each target event is listed in Table 6.3. Each cell displays the probability that the two indicators move as specified. The median judged probabilities of the complementary events are given in brackets. For example, the median judged probability that both indicators go up is 0.60, the probability that it is not the case that both indicators go down is 0.85, and the probability that inflation goes up is 0.75.

Recall that support theory predicts that the judged probability of an event and its complement will sum to unity (binary complementarity), but in all other cases the sum of the judged probabilities of disjoint events will be greater than or equal to the judged probability of their union (subadditivity). Table 6.4a

Table 6.3. Median Judged Probability of All Target Events in Study 2 (data for complementary events are given in brackets)

		Interest		
		Up	Down	
Inflation	Up	0.60 [0.40]	0.25 [0.71]	0.75
	Down	0.15 [0.79]	0.10 [0.85]	0.25
		0.68	0.30	

Table 6.4a. Tests of Binary Complementarity for Median Judged Probabilities in Study 2

Partition	ΣP_i	$\Delta = \Sigma P_i - 1$
$U\bullet, D\bullet$	1.00	0.00
$\bullet U, \bullet D$	0.98	−0.02
$UU, \overline{UU}$	1.00	0.00
$UD, \overline{UD}$	0.96	−0.04
$DU, \overline{DU}$	0.94	−0.06
$DD, \overline{DD}$	0.95	−0.05
MEAN	0.97	−0.03

Note: The first column presents binary partitions of S, the second column (ΣP_i) presents the sum of median judged probabilities for this partition, and the third column (Δ) presents the difference between this sum and one.

presents six tests of binary complementarity, based on the median response to each item. Each row presents a binary partition of the sample space, along with the sum of median judged probabilities for this partition. The column labeled Δ lists the difference between this sum and one. For each event, the first letter corresponds to inflation (U for up, D for down) and the second to interest. For example, UD is the event "inflation up and interest down," $U\bullet$ is the event "inflation up," and $\bullet D$ is the event "interest down." Complements are denoted by a bar. For example, $\overline{UU}$ is the event "it is not the case that interest up and inflation up." As expected, the sum of median judged probabilities for complementary events is close to unity (mean $= 0.97$). However, these values were systematically smaller than one: the median value of the mean of these tests for each subject is 0.98; 48 subjects exhibited a mean less than 1.00, 10 exhibited a mean equal to 1.00, and 24 exhibited a mean greater than 1.00 ($p < 0.01$).

Table 6.4b presents eight tests of subadditivity based on median judged probabilities. Each row presents the sum of judged probabilities of disjoint events, the judged probability of their union, and the difference between them (Δ). For example, the first row shows that $P(\textit{inflation Up and interest Up}) + P(\textit{inflation Up and interest Down}) = 0.85$, and $P(\textit{inflation Up}) = 0.75$, so that $\Delta = 0.10$. As expect d, Table 6.4b shows that in every case the sum of judged probabilities of

Table 6.4b. Tests of Subadditivity for Median Judged Probabilities in Study 2

Event	Partition	ΣP_i	P	$\Delta = \Sigma P_i - P$
$U\bullet$	UU, UD	0.85	0.75	0.10
$D\bullet$	DU, DD	0.25	0.25	0.00
$\bullet U$	UU, DU	0.75	0.68	0.07
$\bullet D$	UD, DD	0.35	0.30	0.05
$\overline{UU}$	UD, DU, DD	0.50	0.40	0.10
$\overline{UD}$	UU, DU, DD	0.85	0.71	0.14
$\overline{DU}$	UU, UD, DD	0.95	0.79	0.16
$\overline{DD}$	UU, UD, DU	1.00	0.85	0.15
MEAN		0.69	0.59	0.10

Note: The first column presents a target event, the second column presents a partition of that event, the third column (ΣP_i) presents the sum of median judged probabilities over the partition, the fourth column (P) presents the median judged probability of the target event, and the fifth column (Δ) presents the difference between these two values.

Table 6.5. Median Normalized Certainty Equivalents of all Target Events in Study 2 (data for complementary events are given in brackets)

		Interest		
		Up	**Down**	
Inflation	Up	0.43 [0.29]	0.22 [0.48]	0.62
	Down	0.13 [0.59]	0.10 [0.76]	0.18
		0.49	0.28	

disjoint events is greater than or equal to the judged probability of their union,[12] and the mean difference between them is 0.10. Furthermore, 60 of 82 subjects exhibited this pattern (i.e., mean $\Delta > 0$) on average ($p < 0.001$ by sign test).

Certainty Equivalents. The median normalized C_A for each target event A is presented in Table 6.5. The corresponding medians for the complementary events are given in brackets. For example, the median normalized C for the event that both indicators go up is 0.43 and the median for the complementary event is 0.29. It can be shown that whenever $w(p) + w(1 - p) \leq 1$ and the value function is concave, the two-stage model implies the partition inequality for binary partitions of the sample space[13] (i.e., $C(x, A) + C(x, S - A) \leq C(x, S) = x$), but it does not imply the partition inequality for finer partitions of S or for binary partitions of other events.

Table 6.6a presents six tests of the partition inequality for binary partitions of the sample space. Analogous to Table 6.4a, each row presents a binary partition of S along with the sum of median normalized Cs for this partition and the difference (Δ) between this sum and one. As predicted by both the classical theory and the present account, the partition inequality holds for all comparisons listed in Table 6.6a (mean $\Delta = -0.24$). It also holds on average for 68 of 82 subjects ($p < 0.001$).

Table 6.6b presents eight additional tests of the partition inequality based on proper subsets of S. Analogous to Table 6.4b, each entry presents the sum of median normalized Cs of disjoint events, the normalized C of their union, and the difference between them. Table 6.6b shows that the partition inequality fails in all cases (mean $\Delta = 0.09$).[14] Furthermore, 51 of 82 subjects exhibited this pattern on average (i.e., $\Delta > 0$, $p < 0.05$ by sign test).

---

[12] In every case $\Delta > 0$ for a significant majority of subjects ($p < 0.05$).

[13] The condition $w(p) + w(1 - p) \leq 1$, called *subcertainty*, is generally supported by empirical data (see e.g., Tversky and Kahneman 1992). It says that the certainty effect is more pronounced than the possibility effect, and it implies the common finding that $w(0.5) < 0.5$ (see Figure 6.1).

[14] In every case $\Delta > 0$ for a majority of subjects; this majority is statistically significant ($p < 0.05$ by sign test) for all tests but the first and fourth listed in the table.

Table 6.6a. Tests of the Partition Inequality for Binary Partitions of S in Study 2

Partition	ΣC_i	$\Delta = \Sigma C_i - 1$
$U\bullet, D\bullet$	0.79	−0.21
$\bullet U, \bullet D$	0.78	−0.22
$UU, \overline{UU}$	0.73	−0.27
$UD, \overline{UD}$	0.70	−0.30
$DU, \overline{DU}$	0.72	−0.28
$DD, \overline{DD}$	0.86	−0.14
MEAN	0.76	−0.24

Note: The first column presents a partition of S, the second column (ΣC_i) presents the sum of median normalized certainty equivalents for this partition, and the third column (Δ) presents the difference between this sum and one.

The preceding results can be summarized as follows. For binary partitions of the sample space S, judged probabilities (nearly) satisfy binary complementarity (Table 6.4a), and certainty equivalents satisfy the partition inequality (Table 6.6a). This pattern is consistent with both the classical theory and the present account. For finer partitions, however, the data yield subadditivity for judged probabilities (Table 6.4b) and reversal of the partition inequality for certainty equivalents (Table 6.6b). This pattern is consistent with the two-stage model but not with the classical theory.

Comparing Models. We next compare the fit of the classical theory to that of the two-stage model using the same method as in the previous study. To fit the classical theory, the exponent α of the utility function was estimated from the spinner games and the exponent for each subject was estimated using the median value of α derived from that subject's responses to the eight problems listed in Table 6.7. Subjects were generally risk-averse: 48 subjects exhibited $\alpha < 1.00$ (risk aversion); 32 exhibited $\alpha = 1.00$ (risk neutrality); and 2 exhibited $\alpha > 1.00$ (risk seeking) ($p < 0.001$). Applying the same analysis to the median response to each of the eight trials yields $\alpha = 0.80$.

Table 6.6b. Tests of the Partition Inequality in Study 2 for Proper Subsets of S

Event	Partition	ΣC_i	C	$\Delta = \Sigma C_i - C$
$U\bullet$	UU, UD	0.65	0.62	0.03
$D\bullet$	DU, DD	0.23	0.18	0.05
$\bullet U$	UU, DU	0.56	0.49	0.07
$\bullet D$	UD, DD	0.32	0.28	0.04
$\overline{UU}$	UD, DU, DD	0.45	0.29	0.16
$\overline{UD}$	UU, DU, DD	0.66	0.48	0.18
$\overline{DU}$	UU, UD, DD	0.75	0.59	0.16
$\overline{DD}$	UU, UD, DU	0.78	0.76	0.02
MEAN		0.55	0.46	0.09

Note: The first column presents a target event, the second column presents a partition of that event, the third column (ΣC_i) presents the sum of median normalized certainty equivalents over the partition, the fourth column (C) presents the median normalized certainty equivalent of the target event, and the fifth column (Δ) presents the difference between these two values.

Table 6.7. Values of *a*, *b*, and *c* Used in Spinner Games of Study 2 and Median Value of Subjects' Responses (*x*)

	Fixed Prospect			Variable Prospect		
Probability	0.25	0.25	0.50	0.25	0.25	0.50
Outcome	$a	$b	$0	$c	$x (Median)	$0
1)	500	1000		250	1330	
2)	500	700		250	990	
3)	200	1200		400	985	
4)	200	800		400	600	
5)	650	550		800	400	
6)	650	350		800	210	
7)	1100	100		750	360	
8)	1100	250		750	520	

According to the classical theory with a power utility function, $C_A^\alpha = 1600^\alpha P(A)$. Recall that in this study subjects learned probabilities by observing the frequencies of the four elementary events (e.g., inflation up and interest up). For each elementary target event A, we computed $(C_A/1600)^\alpha$, and divided these values by their sum to ensure additivity. The subjective probabilities of all other events were derived from these estimates, assuming additivity.

The two-stage model was estimated using Equation (5) as in the previous study. The data show that this model fits the median certainty equivalents (mean absolute error $= \$69$) better than the classical theory (mean absolute error $= \$128$).[15] The same holds within the data of individual subjects. Using individual estimates of the parameters, the two-stage model fits the data better than the standard theory for 50 of the 82 participants ($p < 0.05$).

4. DISCUSSION

The two preceding studies indicate that to a reasonable first approximation, the certainty equivalents of uncertain prospects can be predicted from independent judgments of probability and certainty equivalents for risky prospects, without estimating any parameters from the fitted data. Moreover, this model can account for the observed violations of the partition inequality. We conclude this article with a review of related studies, a comment regarding response bias, a discussion of the problem of source preference, and some closing thoughts concerning practical implications of the two-stage model.

Previous Studies

In the basketball study reported above, the event space has a hierarchical structure (conferences, divisions, teams). In the economic indicators study, the

---

[15] A least-square procedure for estimating all subjective probabilities simultaneously subject to the additivity constraint did not improve the fit of the classical theory.

Table 6.8. Summary of Previous Studies

Study/Population	N^*	Sources of Uncertainty	Judged Probabilities		Certainty Equivalents	
			$(A, S - A)$	$(A_1, \ldots, A_n)$	ΣC	$\%V$
a. NBA Fans	27	Playoff Game	0.99	1.40	1.40	93
		SF Temperature	0.98	1.47	1.27	77
b. NFL Fans	40	Super Bowl	1.01	1.48	1.31	78
		Dow Jones	0.99	1.25	1.16	65
c. Stanford	45	SF Temperature	1.03	2.16	1.98	88
Students		Beijing Temperature	1.01	1.88	1.75	82
d. Options Traders	32	Microsoft	1.00	1.40	1.53	89
(San Francisco)		General Electric	0.96	1.43	1.50	89
e. Options Traders	28	IBM	1.00	1.27	1.47	82
(Chicago)		Gannett Co.	0.99	1.20	1.13	64
		Median	1.00	1.42	1.44	82

Note: The first three columns identify the subject population, sample sizes, and sources of uncertainty. Studies a, b, and c are reported in Tversky and Fox (1995) and are based on a sixfold partition. Studies d, and e are reported in Fox et al. (1996), and are based on a fourfold partition. The next two columns present the median sum of judged probabilities for a binary partition $(A, S - A)$ and for n-fold partitions $(A_1, \ldots, A_n)$ of S. The next column, labeled ΣC, presents the median sum of normalized certainty equivalents over an n-fold partition of S. The final column, labelled $\%V$, presents the percentage of subjects who violated the partition inequality. A few table entries are based on smaller samples than indicated because of missing data.

event space has a product structure (inflation up/down $\times$ interest up/down). Previous tests of bounded subadditivity employed a dimensional structure in which a numerical variable (e.g., the closing price per share of Microsoft stock two weeks in the future) was partitioned into intervals (e.g., less than \$88, \$88 to \$94, more than \$94). Subjects priced prospects contingent on these events and assessed their probabilities.

The results of these studies, summarized in Table 6.8, are consistent with the present account. First, consider probability judgments. The column labeled $(A, S - A)$ presents the median sum of judged probabilities for binary partitions of S, and the column labeled $(A_1, \ldots, A_n)$ presents the median sum of judged probabilities for finer partitions of S. The results conform to support theory: sums for binary partitions of S are close to one, whereas sums for n-fold partitions are consistently greater than one. Next, consider certainty equivalents. The column labeled ΣC presents the median sum of normalized certainty equivalents for the finest partition of S in each study, and the column labeled $\%V$ presents the corresponding percentage of subjects who violated the partition inequality. In accord with the present findings, the majority of subjects in every study violated the partition inequality, and the sum of certainty equivalents was often substantially greater than the prize. This pattern holds for a wide range of sources, with and without monetary incentives, and for both naive and expert subjects. Taken together, these findings suggest that subadditivity of judged probability is a major cause of violations of the partition inequality.

The studies of Fox et al. (1996) are particularly interesting in this respect. Participants were professional options traders who priced prospects contingent on the closing price of various stocks. Unlike typical subjects, the options traders priced risky prospects by their expected value, yielding $v(x) = x$ and $w(p) = p$. Like most other subjects, however, their judged probabilities were subadditive (i.e., $P(A_1) + \cdots + P(A_n) > P(A)$). Under these circumstances, the two-stage model predicts

$$C(x, A_1) + \cdots + C(x, A_n) = P(A_1)x + \cdots + P(A_n)x > P(A)x = C(x, A),$$

whereas the classical theory requires equality throughout. The data for the options traders, summarized in Table 6.8, confirms the prediction of the two-stage model.

Response Bias

We have attributed the subadditivity of judged probabilities and of decision weights to basic psychological principles advanced in support theory and prospect theory. Alternatively, one might be tempted to account for these findings by a bias toward the midpoint of the response scale. This bias could be induced by anchoring on the midpoint of the scale, or by a symmetric error component that is bounded by the endpoints of the response scale. Although such response bias may contribute to subadditivity in some studies, it cannot provide a satisfactory account of this phenomenon. First, there is compelling evidence for bounded subadditivity in simple choices between uncertain prospects (see e.g., Tversky and Kahneman 1992, Tables 6.1 and 6.2; Wu and Gonzalez 1996) that cannot be explained as a response bias.[16] Second, response bias cannot account for the observation that unpacking the description of a target event can increase the attractiveness of the corresponding prospect, nor can it account for the resulting nonmonotonicities described above. Third, a symmetric bias toward the midpoint of the response scale cannot explain the observation that both cash equivalents and decision weights for complementary prospects generally sum to less than one. Finally, it should be noted that the significance of subadditivity to the prediction of judgment and choice is not affected by whether it is interpreted as a feature of the evaluation process, as a response bias, or as a combination of the two.

Source Preference

There is evidence that people's willingness to bet on an uncertain event depends not only on the degree of uncertainty but also on its source. We

---

[16] The studies of Wu and Gonzalez (1996) provide evidence of concavity for low probabilities and convexity for moderate to high probabilities, which are stronger than lower and upper subadditivity, respectively.

next review this phenomenon and discuss its relation to the belief-based account.

A person exhibits source preference if he or she prefers to bet on a proposition drawn from one source rather than on a proposition drawn from another source, and also prefers to bet against the first proposition rather than against the second. Source preference was first illustrated by Ellsberg (1961) using the following example. Consider an urn containing 50 red and 50 black balls and a second urn containing 100 red and black balls in an unknown proportion. Suppose you are offered a cash prize if you correctly guess the color of a ball drawn blindly from one of the urns. Ellsberg argued that most people would rather bet on a red ball from the first urn than on a red ball from the second, and they also would rather bet on a black ball from the first urn than on a black ball from the second. This pattern has been observed in several studies (see Camerer and Weber 1992 for a review). The preference to bet on clear or known probabilities rather than vague or unknown probabilities has been called *ambiguity aversion*.

More recent research has shown that although people exhibit ambiguity aversion in situations of complete ignorance (e.g., Ellsberg's urn), they often prefer betting on their vague beliefs than on matched chance events. Indeed, the evidence is consistent with a more general account, called the *competence hypothesis*: people prefer to bet on their vague beliefs in situations in which they feel particularly competent or knowledgeable, and they prefer to bet on chance when they do not (Heath and Tversky 1991). For example, subjects who were knowledgeable about football but not about politics preferred to bet on the outcome of professional football games than on matched chance events, but they preferred to bet on chance than on the results of a national election. Analogously, subjects who were knowledgeable about politics but not about football preferred to bet on the results of an election than on matched chance events, but they preferred to bet on chance than on football.[17]

The present studies provide some evidence for source preference that is consistent with the competence hypothesis. Recall that subjects in Study 1 were recruited for their interest in professional basketball. Indeed, these subjects preferred betting on basketball to betting on matched chance events: the median certainty equivalent for the Eastern Conference ($79) and the Western Conference ($74) were both greater than the median certainty equivalent for the 50-percent chance prospect ($69). In contrast, subjects in Study 2 did not have special expertise regarding the simulated economy. Indeed, these subjects generally preferred betting on chance to betting on the economic indicators. For example, the median certainty equivalent for both inflation and interest going

---

[17] To complicate matters further, Fox and Tversky (1995) have shown that ambiguity aversion, which has been commonly observed when people evaluate both clear and vague propositions jointly, seems to diminish or disappear when people evaluate only one of these propositions in isolation.

up ($690) was the same as the median certainty equivalent for the 50-percent chance prospect, but the median certainty equivalent for the complementary event ($470) was considerably lower.

It is evident that source preference cannot be explained by the present model, though it can be accommodated by a more general belief-based account. For example, we can generalize equation (1) by letting $W(A) = F[P(A)]$ so that the transformation F of judged probability depends on the source of uncertainty. One convenient parameterization may be defined by $W(A) = (w[P(A)])^{\theta}$, where $\theta > 0$ is inversely related to the attractiveness of the source.[18] These generalizations no longer satisfy Equation (5), but they maintain the decomposition of W into two components: P, which reflects a person's belief in the likelihood of the target event; and F (or w^{θ}), which reflects a person's preference to bet on that belief.

Practical Implications

The two-stage model may have important implications for the management sciences and related fields. First, the unpacking principle implies that the particular descriptions of events on which outcomes depend may affect a person's willingness to act. Hence, the attractiveness of an opportunity such an investment might be increased by unpacking the ways in which the investment could be profitable; willingness to take protective action such as the purchase of insurance might be increased by unpacking the ways in which a relevant mishap might occur.

Second, violations of the partition inequality suggest that people are willing to pay more for a prospect when components are evaluated separately; thus, they are willing to pay a premium, on average, for specificity. When such decisions are aggregated over time or across individuals within an organization, this pattern can lead to certain losses. To illustrate, the first author ran a classroom exercise in which MBA students were divided into six "firms" of eight students each, and each student was asked to decide their firm's maximum willingness to pay for an "investment" that would yield $100,000 depending on future movement of indicators in the U.S. economy. The state space was partitioned into eight events (one for each student) so that each firm's portfolio of investments resulted in a certain return of exactly $100,000. Nevertheless, the six firms reported willingness-to-pay for the eight investments that summed to between $107,000 and $210,000.

---

[18] Alternatively, one might accommodate source preference by varying a parameter of the risky weighting function that increases or decreases weights throughout the unit interval. For example, one can vary β of Prelec's (1998) two-parameter risky weighting function, $w(p) = \exp(-\beta(-\ln p)^{\alpha})$, where $\beta > 0$ is inversely related to the attractiveness of the source. This has the advantage of manipulating the "elevation" of the function somewhat independently of its degree of "curvature." For more on elevation and curvature of the weighting function, see Gonzalez and Wu (1998).

5. CONCLUDING REMARKS

We have provided evidence that decision weights under uncertainty can be predicted from judged probabilities of events and risky decision weights. To the extent that the two-stage model reflects the psychological process underlying decision under uncertainty, this model suggests two independent sources of departure from the classical theory: a belief-based source (subadditivity of judged probability) and a preference-based source (nonlinear weighting of chance events). While the development of effective prescriptions for correcting such bias awaits future investigation, this decomposition of the weighting function offers a new approach to the modeling of decision under uncertainty that integrates probability judgment into the analysis of choice.[19]

[19] This research was conducted while the first author was visiting at Northwestern University. It was supported in part by grant SBR-9408684 from the National Science Foundation to the second author. The authors thank George Wu and Peter Wakker for helpful discussions and suggestions.

7. Loss Aversion in Riskless Choice
A Reference-Dependent Model

Amos Tversky and Daniel Kahneman

ABSTRACT. Much experimental evidence indicates that choice depends on the status quo or reference level: changes of reference point often lead to reversals of preference. We present a reference-dependent theory of consumer choice, which explains such effects by a deformation of indifference curves about the reference point. The central assumption of the theory is that losses and disadvantages have greater impact on preferences than gains and advantages. Implications of loss aversion for economic behavior are considered.

The standard models of decision making assume that preferences do not depend on current assets. This assumption greatly simplifies the analysis of individual choice and the prediction of trades: indifference curves are drawn without reference to current holdings, and the Coase theorem asserts that, except for transaction costs, initial entitlements do not affect final allocations. The facts of the matter are more complex. There is substantial evidence that initial entitlements do matter and that the rate of exchange between goods can be quite different depending on which is acquired and which is given up, even in the absence of transaction costs or income effects. In accord with a psychological analysis of value, reference levels play a large role in determining preferences. In the present paper we review the evidence for this proposition and offer a theory that generalizes the standard model by introducing a reference state.

The present analysis of riskless choice extends our treatment of choice under uncertainty [Kahneman and Tversky, 1979, 1984; Tversky and Kahneman, 1991], in which the outcomes of risky prospects are evaluated by a value function that has three essential characteristics. *Reference dependence:* the carriers of value are gains and losses defined relative to a reference point. *Loss aversion:* the function

This paper has benefited from the comments of Kenneth Arrow, Peter Diamond, David Krantz, Matthew Rabin, and Richard Zeckhauser. We are especially grateful to Shmuel Sattath and Peter Wakker for their helpful suggestions. This work was supported by Grants No. 89-0064 and 88-0206 from the Air Force Office of Scientific Research, and by the Sloan Foundation.

143

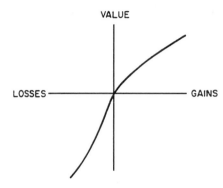

Figure 7.1. An illustration of a value function.

is steeper in the negative than in the positive domain; losses loom larger than corresponding gains. *Diminishing sensitivity:* the marginal value of both gains and losses decreases with their size. These properties give rise to an asymmetric S-shaped value function, concave above the reference point and convex below it, as illustrated in Figure 7.1.

In this article we apply reference dependence, loss aversion, and diminishing sensitivity to the analysis of riskless choice. To motivate this analysis, we begin with a review of selected experimental demonstrations.

I. EMPIRICAL EVIDENCE

The examples discussed in this section are analyzed by reference to Figure 7.2. In every case we consider two options x and y that differ on two valued dimensions and show how the choice between them is affected by the reference point from which they are evaluated. The common reason for these reversals of preference

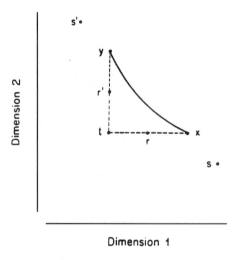

Figure 7.2. Multiple reference points for the choice between x and y.

is that the relative weight of the differences between x and y on dimensions 1 and 2 varies with the location of the reference value on these attributes. Loss aversion implies that the impact of a difference on a dimension is generally greater when that difference is evaluated as a loss than when the same difference is evaluated as a gain. Diminishing sensitivity implies that the impact of a difference is attenuated when both options are remote from the reference point for the relevant dimension. This simple scheme serves to organize a large set of observations. Although isolated findings may be subject to alternative interpretations, the entire body of evidence provides strong support for the phenomenon of loss aversion.

a. *Instant Endowment.* An immediate consequence of loss aversion is that the loss of utility associated with giving up a valued good is greater than the utility gain associated with receiving it. Thaler [1980] labeled this discrepancy the endowment effect, because value appears to change when a good is incorporated into one's endowment. Kahneman, Knetsch, and Thaler [1990] tested the endowment effect in a series of experiments, conducted in a classroom setting. In one of these experiments a decorated mug (retail value of about $5) was placed in front of one third of the seats after students had chosen their places. All participants received a questionnaire. The form given to the recipients of a mug (the "sellers") indicated that "You now own the object in your possession. You have the option of selling it if a price, which will be determined later, is acceptable to you. For each of the possible prices below indicate whether you wish to (x) Sell your object and receive this price; (y) Keep your object and take it home with you. . . . " The subjects indicated their decision for prices ranging from $0.50 to $9.50 in steps of 50 cents. Some of the students who had not received a mug (the "choosers") were given a similar questionnaire, informing them that they would have the option of receiving either a mug or a sum of money to be determined later. They indicated their preferences between a mug and sums of money ranging from $0.50 to $9.50.

The choosers and the sellers face precisely the same decision problem, but their reference states differ. As shown in Figure 7.2, the choosers' reference state is t, and they face a positive choice between two options that dominate t; receiving a mug or receiving a sum in cash. The sellers evaluate the same options from y; they must choose between retaining the status quo (the mug) or giving up the mug in exchange for money. Thus, the mug is evaluated as a gain by the choosers, and as a loss by the sellers. Loss aversion entails that the rate of exchange of the mug against money will be different in the two cases. Indeed, the median value of the mug was $7.12 for the sellers and $3.12 for the choosers in one experiment, $7.00 and $3.50 in another. The difference between these values reflects an endowment effect which is produced, apparently instantaneously, by giving an individual property rights over a consumption good.

The interpretation of the endowment effect may be illuminated by the following thought experiment.

> *Imagine that as a chooser you prefer $4 over a mug. You learn that most sellers prefer the mug to $6, and you believe that if you had the mug you would do the same. In light of this knowledge, would you now prefer the mug over $5?*

If you do, it is presumably because you have changed your assessment of the pleasure associated with owning the mug. If you still prefer $4 over the mug – which we regard as a more likely response – this indicates that you interpret the effect of endowment as an aversion to giving up your mug rather than as an unanticipated increase in the pleasure of owning it.

b. *Status Quo Bias.* The retention of the status quo is an option in many decision problems. As illustrated by the analysis of the sellers' problem in the example of the mugs, loss aversion induces a bias that favors the retention of the status quo over other options. In Figure 7.2, a decision maker who is indifferent between x and y from t will prefer x over y from x, and y over x from y. Samuelson and Zeckhauser [1988] introduced the term "status quo bias" for this effect of reference position.

Knetsch and Sinden [1984] and Knetsch [1989] have offered compelling experimental demonstrations of the status quo bias. In the latter study two undergraduate classes were required to answer a brief questionnaire. Students in one of the classes were immediately given a decorated mug as compensation; students in another class received a large bar of Swiss chocolate. At the end of the session students in both classes were shown the alternative gift and were allowed the option of trading the gift they had received for the other, by raising a card with the word "Trade" written on it. Although the transaction cost associated with the change was surely slight, approximately 90 percent of the participants retained the gift they had received.

Samuelson and Zeckhauser [1988] documented the status quo bias in a wide range of decisions, including hypothetical choices about jobs, automobile color, financial investments, and policy issues. Alternative versions of each problem were presented to different subjects: each option was designated as the status quo in one of these versions; one (neutral) version did not single out any option. The number of options presented for each problem was systematically varied. The results were analyzed by regressing the proportions of subjects choosing an option designated as status quo $P(SQ)$, or an alternative to the status quo $P(ASQ)$, on the choice proportions for the same options in the neutral version $P(N)$. The results were well described by the equations,

$$P(SQ) = 0.17 + 0.83P(N) \quad \text{and} \quad P(ASQ) = 0.83P(N).$$

The difference (0.17) between $P(SQ)$ and $P(ASQ)$ is a measure of the status quo bias in this experiment.

Samuelson and Zeckhauser [1988] also obtained evidence of status quo bias in a field study of the choice of medical plans by Harvard employees. They found that a new medical plan is generally more likely to be chosen by new employees than by employees hired before that plan became available – in spite of the yearly opportunity to review the decision and the minimal cost of changing it. Furthermore, small changes from the status quo were favored over larger changes: enrollees who did transfer from the originally most popular Blue Cross/Blue Shield plan tended to favor a new variant of that plan over other new alternatives. Samuelson and Zeckhauser also observed that the allocations of pension reserves to TIAA and CREF tend to be very stable from year to year, in spite of large variations in rate of return. They invoked the status quo bias as an explanation of brand loyalty and pioneer firm advantage, and noted that rational models that ignore status quo effects "will present excessively radical conclusions, exaggerating individuals' responses to changing economic variables and predicting greater instability than is observed in the world" [p. 47].

Loss aversion implies the status quo bias. As noted by Samuelson and Zeckhauser [1988], however, there are several factors, such as costs of thinking, transaction costs, and psychological commitment to prior choices that can induce a status quo bias even in the absence of loss aversion.

    *c. Improvements versus Tradeoffs.*Consider the evaluation of the options x and y in Figure 7.2 from the reference points r and r'. When evaluated from r, option x is simply a gain (improvement) on dimension 1, whereas y combines a gain in dimension 2 with a loss in dimension 1. These relations are reversed when the same options are evaluated from r'. Considerations of loss aversion suggest that x is more likely to be preferred from r than from r'.

Ninety undergraduates took part in a study designed to test this hypothesis. They received written instructions indicating that some participants, selected at random, would receive a gift package. For half the participants (the dinner group) the gift consisted of "one free dinner at MacArthur Park Restaurant and a monthly Stanford calendar." For the other half (the photo group) the gift was "one 8 × 10 professional photo portrait and a monthly Stanford calendar." All subjects were informed that some of the winners, again selected at random, would be given an opportunity to exchange the original gift for one of the following options:

    x: *two free dinners at MacArthur Park Restaurant*
    y: *one 8 × 10 professional photo portrait plus two 5 × 7 and three wallet*
       size prints.

The subjects were asked to indicate whether they preferred to (i) keep the original gift, (ii) exchange it for x, or (iii) exchange it for y. If people are averse to giving up the reference gift, as implied by loss aversion, then the preference for a dinner-for-two (x) over multiple photos (y) should be more common among the subjects whose reference gift was a dinner-for-one (r) than among subjects whose reference gift was the single photo (r'). The results confirmed this prediction. Only ten participants chose to keep the original gift. Among the remaining subjects, option x was selected by 81 percent of the dinner group and by 52 percent of the photo group ($p < 0.01$).

d. *Advantages and Disadvantages.* In our next demonstration a combination of a small gain and a small loss is compared with a combination of a larger gain and a larger loss. Loss aversion implies that the same difference between two options will be given greater weight if it is viewed as a difference between two disadvantages (relative to a reference state) than if it is viewed as a difference between two advantages. In the representation of Figure 7.2, x is more likely to be preferred over y from s than from s', because the difference between x and y in dimension 1 involves disadvantages relative to s and advantages relative to s'. A similar argument applies to dimension 2. In a test of this prediction subjects answered one of two versions of the following question:

Imagine that as part of your professional training you were assigned to a part-time job. The training is now ending, and you must look for employment. You consider two possibilities. They are like your training job in most respects except for the amount of social contact and the convenience of commuting to and from work. To compare the two jobs to each other and to the present one, you have made up the following table:

	Social Contact	**Daily Travel Time**
Present job	isolated for long stretches	10 min.
Job x	limited contact with others	20 min.
Job y	moderately sociable	60 min.

The second version of this problem included the same options x and y, but a different reference job (s'), described by the following attributes: "much pleasant social interaction and 80 minutes of daily commuting time."

In the first version both options are superior to the current reference job on the dimension of social contact and both are inferior in commuting time. The different amounts of social contact in jobs x and y are evaluated as advantages (gains), whereas the commuting times are evaluated as disadvantages (losses). These relations are reversed in the second version. Loss aversion implies that a given difference between two options will generally have greater impact when it is evaluated as a difference between two losses (disadvantages) than when it is viewed as a difference between two gains (or advantages). This prediction was confirmed: Job x was chosen by 70 percent of the participants in version 1 and by only 33 percent of the participants in version 2 ($N = 106$, $p < 0.01$).

II. REFERENCE DEPENDENCE

In order to interpret the reversals of preference that are induced by shifts of reference, we introduce, as a primitive concept, a preference relation indexed to a given reference state. As in the standard theory, we begin with a choice set $X = \{x, y, z, \ldots\}$ and assume, for simplicity, that it is isomorphic to the positive quadrant of the real plane, including its boundaries. Each option, $x = (x_1, x_2)$ in X, $x_1, x_2 \geq 0$, is interpreted as a bundle that offers x_1 units of good 1 and x_2 units of good 2, or as an activity characterized by its levels on two dimensions of value. The extension to more than two dimensions is straightforward.

A *reference structure* is a family of indexed preference relations, where $x \geq_r y$ is interpreted as x is weakly preferred to y from reference state r. The relations $>_r$ and $=_r$ correspond to strict preference and indifference, respectively. Throughout this article we assume that each $\geq_r$, $r \in X$, satisfies the standard assumptions of the classical theory. Specifically, we assume that $\geq_r$ is complete, transitive, and continuous; that is, $\{x : x \geq_r y\}$ and $\{x : y \geq_r x\}$ are closed for any y. Furthermore, each preference order is strictly monotonic in the sense that $x \geq_r y$ and $x \neq y$ imply that $x >_r y$. Under these assumptions each $\geq_r$ can be represented by a strictly increasing continuous utility function U_r (see, e.g., Varian [1984], Ch. 3).

Because the standard theory does not recognize the special role of the reference state, it implicitly assumes *reference independence*; that is, $x \geq_r y$ iff $x \geq_s y$ for all $x, y, r, s \in X$. This property, however, was consistently violated in the preceding experiments. To accommodate these observations, we describe individual choice not by a single preference order but by a family or a book of indexed preference orders $\{\geq_r : r \in X\}$. For convenience, we use the letters r, s to denote reference states and x, y to denote options, although they are all elements of X.

A treatment of reference-dependent choice raises two questions: what is the reference state, and how does it affect preferences? The present analysis focuses on the second question. We assume that the decision maker has a definite reference state in X, and we investigate its impact on the choice between options. The question of the origin and the determinants of the reference state lies beyond the scope of the present article. Although the reference state usually corresponds to the decision maker's current position, it can also be influenced by aspirations, expectations, norms, and social comparisons [Easterlin, 1974; van Praag, 1971; van de Stadt, Kapteyn, and van de Geer, 1985].

In the present section we first define loss aversion and diminishing sensitivity in terms of the preference orders $\geq_r$, $r \in X$. Next we introduce the notion of a decomposable reference function and characterize the concept of constant loss aversion. Finally, we discuss some empirical estimates of the coefficient of loss aversion.

Loss Aversion

The basic intuition concerning loss aversion is that losses (outcomes below the reference state) loom larger than corresponding gains (outcomes above the reference state). Because a shift of reference can turn gains into losses and vice versa, it can give rise to reversals of preference, as implied by the following definition.

A reference structure satisfies *loss aversion* (LA) if the following condition holds for all x, y, r, s in X. Suppose that $x_1 \geq r_1 > s_1 = y_1$, $y_2 > x_2$ and $r_2 = s_2$; see Figure 7.3. Then $x =_s y$ implies that $x >_r y$; the same holds if the subscripts 1 and 2 are interchanged throughout. (Note that the relations $>$ and $=$ refer to the numerical components of the options; whereas $>_r$ and $=_r$ refer to the preference between options in reference state r.) Loss aversion implies that the slope of the indifference curve through y is steeper when y is evaluated from r than when it is evaluated from s. In other words, $U_r^*(y) > U_s^*(y)$, where $U_r^*(y)$ is the marginal rate of substitution of U_r at y.

To motivate the definition of loss aversion, it is instructive to restate it in terms of advantages and disadvantages, relative to a reference point r. An ordered pair $[x_i, r_i]$, $i = 1, 2$, is called an advantage or a disadvantage, respectively, if $x_i > r_i$, or $x_i < r_i$. We use brackets to distinguish between the pair $[x_i, r_i]$ and the two-dimensional option (x_1, x_2). Suppose that there exist real-valued functions v_1, v_2 such that $U_r(x)$ can be expressed as $U(v_1[x_1, r_1], v_2[x_2, r_2])$. To simplify matters, suppose that $x_1 = r_1$ and $x_2 > r_2$, as in Figure 7.3. Hence, $x =_s y$ implies that the combination of the two advantages, $[x_1, s_1]$ and $[x_2, s_2]$, relative to the reference state s, has the same impact as the combination of the advantage $[y_2, s_2]$ and the null interval $[y_1, y_1]$. Similarly, $x >_r y$ implies that the combination of the advantage $[x_2, r_2]$ and the null interval $[x_1, x_1]$ has greater impact than the combination of the advantage $[y_2, r_2]$ and the disadvantage $[y_1, r_1]$. As the reference state shifts from s to r, therefore, the disadvantage $[y_1, r_1] = [s_1, r_1]$, enters into the evaluation of y, and the advantage $[x_1, s_1] = [r_1, s_1]$ is deleted from the evaluation of x. But since $[s_1, r_1]$ and $[r_1, s_1]$ differ by sign only, loss aversion implies that the introduction of a disadvantage has a bigger effect than the deletion of the corresponding advantage. A similar argument applies to the case where $x_1 > r_1 > s_1$.

The present notion of loss aversion accounts for the endowment effect and the status quo bias described in the preceding section. Consider the effect of

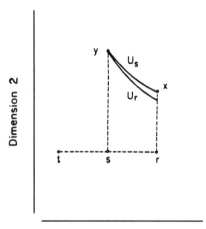

Figure 7.3. A graphic illustration of loss aversion.

different reference points on the preference between x and y, as illustrated in Figure 7.2. Loss aversion entails that a decision maker who is indifferent between x and y from t will prefer x over y from x, and y over x from y. That is, $x =_t y$ implies that $x >_x y$ and $y >_y x$. This explains the different valuations of a good by sellers and choosers and other manifestations of the status quo bias.

Diminishing Sensitivity

Recall that, according to the value function of Figure 7.1, marginal value decreases with the distance from the reference point. For example, the difference between a yearly salary of $60,000 and a yearly salary of $70,000 has a bigger impact when current salary is $50,000 than when it is $40,000. A reference structure satisfies *diminishing sensitivity* (DS) if the following condition holds for all x, y, s, t in X. Suppose that $x_1 > y_1$, $y_2 > x_2$, $s_2 = t_2$, and either $y_1 \geq s_1 \geq t_1$ or $t_1 \geq s_1 \geq x_1$; see Figure 7.3. Then $y =_s x$ implies that $y \geq_t x$; the same holds if the subscripts 1 and 2 are interchanged throughout. *Constant sensitivity* is satisfied if the same hypotheses imply that $y =_t x$. DS states that the sensitivity to a given difference on a dimension is smaller when the reference point is distant than when it is near. It follows from DS that the slope of the indifference curve through x is steeper when evaluated from s than from t, or $U_s^*(x) > U_t^*(x)$. It is important to distinguish between the present notion of diminishing sensitivity, which pertains to the effect of the reference state, and the standard assumption of diminishing marginal utility. Although the two hypotheses are conceptually similar, they are logically independent. In particular, diminishing sensitivity does not imply that the indifference curves are concave below the reference point.

Each reference state r partitions X into four quadrants defined by treating r as the origin. A pair of options, x and y, belong to the same quadrant with respect to r whenever $x_i \geq r_i$ iff $y_i \geq r_i$, $i = 1, 2$. A reference structure satisfies *sign dependence* if for all x, y, r, s in X $x \geq_r y$ iff $x \geq_s y$ whenever (i) x and y belong to the same quadrant with respect to r and with respect to s, and (ii) r and s belong to the same quadrant with respect to x and with respect to y. This condition implies that reference independence can be violated only when a change in reference turns a gain into a loss or vice versa. It is easy to verify that sign dependence is equivalent to constant sensitivity. Although sign dependence may not hold in general, it serves as a useful approximation whenever the curvature induced by the reference state is not very pronounced.

The assumption of diminishing (or constant) sensitivity allows us to extend the implications of loss aversion to reference states that do not coincide with x or y on either dimension. Consider the choice between x and y in Figure 7.4. Note that r is dominated by x but not by y, whereas s is dominated by y but not by x. Let t be the meet of r and s; that is, $t_i = \min(r_i, s_i)$, $i = 1, 2$. It follows from loss aversion and diminishing sensitivity that if $x =_t y$, then $x >_r y$ and $y >_s x$. Thus, x is more likely to be chosen over y when

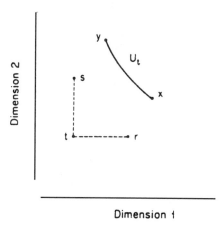

Figure 7.4. An illustration of reference-dependent preferences.

evaluated from r than when evaluated from s. This proposition is illustrated by our earlier observation that a gift was more attractive when evaluated as a moderate improvement on one attribute than when evaluated as a combination of a large improvement and a loss (see example c above).

Consider two exchangeable individuals (i.e., hedonic twins), each of whom holds position t, with low status and low pay; see Figure 7.4. Suppose that both are indifferent between position x (very high status, moderate pay) and position y (very high pay, moderate status). Imagine now that both individuals move to new positions, which become their respective reference points; one individual moves to r (high status, low pay), and the other moves to s (high pay, low status). LA and DS imply that the person who moved to r now prefers x, whereas the person who moved to s now prefers y, because they are reluctant to give up either salary or status.

Constant Loss Aversion

The present section introduces additional assumptions that constrain the relation among preference orders evaluated from different reference points. A reference structure $(X, \geq_r), r \in X$, is *decomposable* if there exists a real-valued function U, increasing in each argument, such that for each $r \in X$, there exist increasing functions $R_i : X_i \to$ Reals, $i = 1, 2$ satisfying

$$U_r(x_1, x_2) = U(R_1(x_1), R_2(x_2)).$$

The functions R_i are called the reference functions associated with reference state r. In this model the effect of the reference point is captured by separate monotonic transformations of the two axes. Decomposability has testable implications. For example, suppose that U_r is additive; that is, $U_r(x_1, x_2) = R_1(x_1) + R_2(x_2)$. It follows then that, for any $s \in X$, U_s is also additive although the respective scales may not be linearly related.

In this section we focus on a special case of decomposability in which the reference functions assume an especially simple form. A reference structure $(X, \geq_r)$ satisfies *constant loss aversion* if there exist functions $u_i : X_i \to$ Reals, constants $\lambda_i > 0$, $i = 1, 2$, and a function U such that $U_r(x_1, x_2) = U(R_1(x_1), R_2(x_2))$, where

$$R_i(x_i) = \begin{cases} u_i(x_i) - u_i(r_i) & \text{if } x_i \geq r_i \\ (u_i(x_i) - u_i(r_i))/\lambda_i & \text{if } x_i < r_i. \end{cases}$$

Thus, the change in the preference order induced by a shift of reference is described in terms of two constants, λ_1 and λ_2, which can be interpreted as the coefficients of loss aversion for dimensions 1 and 2, respectively. Figure 7.5 illustrates constant loss aversion, with $\lambda_1 = 2$ and $\lambda_2 = 3$. For simplicity, we selected a linear utility function, but this is not essential.

Although we do not have an axiomatic characterization of constant loss aversion in general, we characterize below the special case where U is additive, called additive constant loss aversion. This case is important because additivity serves as a good approximation in many contexts. Indeed, some of the commonly used utility functions (e.g., Cobb-Douglas, or CES) are additive. Recall that a family of indifference curves is additive if the axes can be monotonically transformed so that the indifference curves become parallel straight lines. The following cancellation condition, also called the Thomsen condition, is both necessary and sufficient for additivity in the present context [Debreu, 1960; Krantz, Luce, Suppes, and Tversky, 1971].

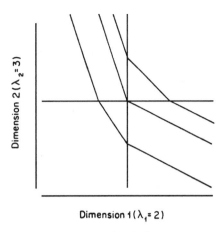

Figure 7.5. A set of indifference curves illustrating constant loss aversion.

> For all $x_1, y_1, z_1, \in X_1, x_2, y_2, z_2, \in X_2$, and $r \in X$,
> if $(x_1, z_2) \geq_r (z_1, y_2)$ and $(z_1, x_2) \geq_r (y_1, z_2)$, then $(x_1, x_2) \geq_r (y_1, y_2)$.

Assuming cancellation for each $\geq_r$, we obtain an additive representation for each reference state. In order to relate the separate additive representations to each other, we introduce the following axiom. Consider $w, w', x, x', y, y', z, z'$ in X that (i) belong to the same quadrant with respect to r as well as with respect to s, and (ii) satisfy $w_1 = w'_1$, $x_1 = x'_1$, $y_1 = y'_1$, $z_1 = z'_1$ and $x_2 = z_2$, $w_2 = y_2$, $x'_2 = z'_2$, $w'_2 = y'_2$; see Figure 7.6. A reference structure $(X, \geq_r)$, $r \in X$, satisfies *reference interlocking* if, assuming (i) and (ii) above, $w =_r x$, $y =_r z$ and $w' =_s x'$ imply that $y' =_s z'$. Essentially the same condition was invoked by Tversky, Sattah, and Slovic [1988] in the treatment of preference reversals, and by Wakker [1988] and Tversky and Kahneman [1991] in the analysis of decision under uncertainty.

Figure 7.6. A graphic illustration of reference interlocking.

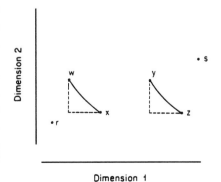

To appreciate the content of reference interlocking, note that, in the presence of additivity, indifference can be interpreted as a matching of an interval on one dimension to an interval on the second dimension. For example, the observation $w =_r x$ indicates that the interval $[x_1, w_1]$ on the first dimension matches the interval $[w_2, x_2]$ on the second dimension. Similarly, $y =_r z$ indicates that $[z_1, y_1]$ matches $[y_2, z_2]$. But since $[w_2, x_2]$ and $[y_2, z_2]$ are identical by construction (see Figure 7.6), we conclude that $[x_1, w_1]$ matches $[z_1, y_1]$. In this manner we can match two intervals on the *same* dimension by matching each of them to an interval on the *other* dimension. Reference interlocking states that if two intradimensional intervals are matched as gains, they are also matched as losses. It is easy to verify that reference interlocking follows from additive constant loss aversion. Furthermore, the following theorem shows that in the presence of cancellation and sign-dependence, reference interlocking is not only necessary but it is also sufficient for additive constant loss aversion.

THEOREM   *A reference structure $(X, \geq_r)$, $r \in X$, satisfies additive constant loss aversion iff it satisfies cancellation, sign-dependence, and reference interlocking.*

An estimate of the coefficients of loss aversion can be derived from an experiment described earlier, in which two groups of subjects assigned a monetary value to the same consumption good: sellers who were given the good and the option of selling it, and choosers who were given the option of receiving the good or a sum of money [Kahneman, Knetsch, and Thaler, 1990]. The median value of the mug for sellers was $7.12 and $7.00 in two separate replications of the experiments; choosers valued the same object at $3.12 and $3.50. According to the present analysis, the sellers and the choosers differ only in that the former evaluate the mug as a loss, the latter as a gain. If the value of money is linear in that range, the coefficient of loss aversion for the mug in these experiments was slightly greater than two.

There is an intriguing convergence between this estimate of the coefficient of loss aversion and estimates derived from decisions under risk. Such estimates can be obtained by observing the ratio G/L that makes an even chance to gain G or lose L just acceptable. We have observed a ratio of just over 2:1 in several experiments. In one gambling experiment with real payoffs, for example, a 50-50 bet to win $25 or lose $10 was barely acceptable, yielding a ratio of 2.5:1. Similar values were obtained from hypothetical choices regarding the acceptability of larger gambles, over a range of several hundred dollars [Tversky and Kahneman, 1990]. Although the convergence of estimates should be interpreted with caution, these findings suggest that a loss aversion coefficient of about two may explain both risky and riskless choices involving monetary outcomes and consumption goods.

Recall that the coefficient of loss aversion could vary across dimensions, as illustrated in Figure 7.5. We surmise that the coefficient of loss aversion associated with different dimensions reflects the importance or prominence of these dimensions [Tversky, Sattath, and Slovic, 1988]. For example, loss aversion appears to be more pronounced for safety than for money [Viscusi, Magat, and Huber, 1987], and more pronounced for income than for leisure.

III. IMPLICATIONS OF LOSS AVERSION

Loss aversion is an important component of a phenomenon that has been much discussed in recent years: the large disparity often observed between the minimal amount that people are willing to accept (WTA) to give up a good they own and the maximal amount they would be willing to pay (WTP) to acquire it. Other potential sources of this discrepancy include income effect, strategic behavior, and the legitimacy of transactions. The buying–selling discrepancy was initially observed in hypothetical questions involving public goods (see Cummings, Brookshire, and Schulze [1986], for a review), but it has also been confirmed in real exchanges [Heberlein and Bishop, 1985; Kahneman, Knetsch, and Thaler, 1990; Loewenstein, 1988]. It also survived, albeit reduced, in experiments that attempted to eliminate it by the discipline of market experience [Brookshire and Coursey, 1987; Coursey, Hovis, and Schulze, 1987]; see also Knetsch and Sinden [1984, 1987]. Kahneman, Knetsch, and Thaler [1990] showed that the disparate valuations of consumption goods by owners and by potential buyers inhibits trade. They endowed half the participants with a consumption good (e.g., a mug) and set up a market for that good. Because the mugs were allocated at random, standard theory predicts that half the sellers should trade their mugs to buyers who value them more. The actual volume of trade was consistently observed to be about half the predicted amount. Control experiments in which subjects traded tokens redeemable for cash produced nearly perfect efficiency and no disparity between the values assigned by buyers and sellers.

A trade involves two dimensions, and loss aversion may operate on one or both. Thus, the present analysis suggests two ways in which loss aversion could contribute to the disparity between WTA and WTP. The individual who states WTA for a good considers giving it up; the individual who states WTP for that good considers acquiring it. If there is loss aversion for the good, the owner will be reluctant to sell. If the buyer views the money spent on the purchase as a loss, there will be reluctance to buy. The relative magnitude of the two effects can be estimated by comparing sellers and buyers to choosers, who are given a choice between the good and cash, and are therefore not susceptible to loss aversion. Results of several comparisons indicated that the reluctance to sell is much greater than the reluctance to buy [Kahneman, Knetsch, and Thaler, 1990]. The buyers in these markets do not appear to value the money they give up in a transaction as a loss. These observations are consistent with the standard theory of consumer choice, in which the decision of whether or not to purchase a good is treated as a choice between it and other goods that could be purchased instead.

Loss aversion is certainly not involved in the exchange of a $5 bill for $5, because the transaction is evaluated by its net outcome. Similarly, reluctance to sell is surely absent in routine commercial transactions, in which goods held for sale have the status of tokens for money. However, the present analysis implies that asymmetric evaluations of gains and losses will affect the responses of both buyers and sellers to changes of price or profit, relative to the reference levels established in prior transactions [Kahneman, Knetsch, and Thaler, 1986; Winer, 1986]. The response to changes is expected to be more intense when the changes are unfavorable (losses) than when they are for the better. Putler [1988] developed an analysis of demand that incorporates an asymmetric effect of price increases and decreases. He tested the model by estimating separate demand elasticities for increases and for decreases in the retail price of shell eggs, relative to a reference price estimated from the series of earlier prices. The estimated elasticities were -1.10 for price increases and -0.45 for price decreases, indicating that price increases have a significantly greater impact on consumer decisions. (This analysis assumes that the availability of substitutes eliminates loss aversion in the response to the reduced consumption of eggs.) A similar result was observed in scanner-panel data in the coffee market [Kalwani, Yim, Rinne, and Sugita, 1990]. The reluctance to accept losses may also affect sellers: a study of the stock market indicated that the volume of trade tends to be higher when prices are rising than when prices are falling [Shefrin and Statman, 1985].

Loss aversion can complicate negotiations. Experimental evidence indicates that negotiators are less likely to achieve agreement when the attributes over which they bargain are framed as losses than when they are framed as gains [Bazerman and Carroll, 1987]. This result is expected if people are more sensitive to marginal changes in the negative domain. Furthermore, there is a natural asymmetry between the evaluations of the concessions that one makes and the concessions offered by the other party; the latter are normally evaluated as gains, whereas the former are evaluated as losses. The discrepant evaluations of concessions significantly reduces the region of agreement in multi-issue bargaining.

A marked asymmetry in the responses to favorable or unfavorable changes of prices or profits was noted in a study of the rules that govern judgments of the fairness of actions that set prices or wages [Kahneman, Knetsch, and Thaler, 1986]. In particular, most people reject as highly unfair price increases that are not justified by increased costs and cuts in wages that are not justified by a threat of bankruptcy. On the other hand, the customary norms of economic fairness do not absolutely require the firm to share the benefits of reduced costs or increased profits with its customers or its employees. In contrast to economic analysis, which does not distinguish losses from forgone gains, the standards of fairness draw a sharp distinction between actions that impose losses on others and actions (or failures to act) that do not share benefits. A study of court decisions documented a similar distinction in the treatment of losses and forgone gains; in cases of negligence, for example, compensation is more likely to be awarded for out-of-pocket costs than for unrealized profits [Cohen and Knetsch, 1990].

Because actions that are perceived as unfair are often resisted and punished, considerations of fairness have been invoked as one of the explanations of wage stickiness and of other cases in which markets clear only sluggishly [Kahneman, Knetsch, and Thaler, 1986; Okun, 1981; Olmstead and Rhode, 1985]. For example, the difference in the evaluation of losses and of forgone gains implies a corresponding difference in the reactions to a wage cut and to a failure to increase wages when such an increase would be feasible. The terms of previous contracts define the reference levels for collective as well as for individual bargaining; in the bargaining context the aversion to losses takes the form of an aversion to concessions. The rigidity induced by loss aversion may result in inefficient labor contracts that fail to respond adequately to changing economic circumstances and technological developments. As a consequence, new firms that bargain with their workers without the burden of previous agreements may gain a competitive advantage.

Is loss aversion irrational? This question raises a number of difficult normative issues. Questioning the values that decision makers assign to outcomes requires a criterion for the evaluation of preferences. The actual experience of consequences provides such a criterion: the value assigned to a consequence in a decision context can be justified as a prediction of the quality of the experience of that consequence [Kahneman and Snell, 1990]. Adopting this predictive stance, the value function of Figure 7.1, which was initially drawn to account for the pattern of risky choices, can be interpreted as a prediction of the psychophysics of hedonic experience. The value function appropriately reflects three basic facts: organisms habituate to steady states, the marginal response to changes is diminishing, and pain is more urgent than pleasure. The asymmetry of pain and pleasure is the ultimate justification of loss aversion in choice. Because of this asymmetry a decision maker who seeks to maximize the experienced utility of outcomes is well advised to assign greater weight to negative than to positive consequences.

The demonstrations discussed in the first part of this paper compared choices between the same two objective states, evaluated from different reference points. The effects of reference levels on decisions can only be justified by corresponding effects of these reference levels on the experience of consequences. For example, a bias in favor of the status quo can be justified if the disadvantages of any change will be experienced more keenly than its advantages. However, some reference levels that are naturally adopted in the context of decision are irrelevant to the subsequent experience of outcomes, and the impact of such reference levels on decisions is normatively dubious. In evaluating a decision that has long-term consequences, for example, the initial response to these consequences may be relatively unimportant, if adaptation eventually induces a shift of reference. Another case involves principal-agent relations: the principal may not wish the agent's decisions to reflect the agent's aversion to losses, because the agent's reference level has no bearing on the principal's experience of outcomes. We conclude that there is no general answer to the question about the normative status of loss aversion or of other reference effects, but there is a principled way of examining the normative status of these effects in particular cases.

8. Anomalies

The Endowment Effect, Loss Aversion, and Status Quo Bias

Daniel Kahneman, Jack L. Knetsch, and Richard H. Thaler

Economics can be distinguished from other social sciences by the belief that most (all?) behavior can be explained by assuming that agents have stable, well-defined preferences and make rational choices consistent with those preferences in markets that (eventually) clear. An empirical result qualifies as an anomaly if it is difficult to "rationalize," or if implausible assumptions are necessary to explain it within the paradigm. This column presents a series of such anomalies. Readers are invited to suggest topics for future columns by sending a note with some reference to (or better yet copies of) the relevant research. Comments on anomalies printed here are also welcome. The address is Richard Thaler, c/o Journal of Economic Perspectives, Johnson Graduate School of Management, Malott Hall, Cornell University, Ithaca, NY 14853.

After this issue, the "Anomalies" column will no longer appear in every issue and instead will appear occasionally, when a pressing anomaly crosses Dick Thaler's desk. However, suggestions for new columns and comments on old ones are still welcome. Thaler would like to quash one rumor before it gets started, namely that he is cutting back because he has run out of anomalies. *Au contraire*, it is the dilemma of choosing which juicy anomaly to discuss that takes so much time.

INTRODUCTION

A wine-loving economist we know purchased some nice Bordeaux wines years ago at low prices. The wines have greatly appreciated in value, so that a bottle that cost only $10 when purchased would now fetch $200 at auction. This economist now drinks some of this wine occasionally, but would neither be willing to sell the wine at the auction price nor buy an additional bottle at that price.

Thaler (1980) called this pattern – the fact that people often demand much more to give up an object than they would be willing to pay to acquire it – the *endowment effect*. The example also illustrates what Samuelson and Zeckhauser

The authors wish to acknowledge financial support from Fisheries and Oceans Canada, the Ontario Ministry of the Environment, the Russell Sage Foundation, and Concord Capital Management.

(1988) call a *status quo bias*, a preference for the current state that biases the economist against both buying *and* selling his wine. These anomalies are a manifestation of an asymmetry of value that Kahneman and Tversky (1984) call *loss aversion* – the disutility of giving up an object is greater than the utility associated with acquiring it. This column documents the evidence supporting endowment effects and status quo biases, and discusses their relation to loss aversion.

The Endowment Effect

An early laboratory demonstration of the endowment effect was offered by Knetsch and Sinden (1984). The participants in this study were endowed with either a lottery ticket or with $2.00. Some time later, each subject was offered an opportunity to trade the lottery ticket for the money, or vice versa. Very few subjects chose to switch. Those who were given lottery tickets seemed to like them better than those who were given money.

This demonstration and other similar ones (Knetsch, 1989), while striking, did not settle the matter. Some economists felt that the behavior would disappear if subjects were exposed to a market environment with ample learning opportunities. For example, Knez, Smith and Williams (1985) argued that the discrepancy between buying and selling prices might be produced by the thoughtless application of normally sensible bargaining habits, namely understating one's true willingness to pay (WTP) and overstating the minimum acceptable price at which one would sell (willingness to accept or WTA). Coursey, Hovis, and Schultze (1987) reported that the discrepancy between WTP and WTA diminished with experience in a market setting (although it was probably not eliminated, see Knetsch and Sinden, 1987). To clarify the issue, Kahneman, Knetsch, and Thaler (1990) ran a new series of experiments to determine whether the endowment effect survives when subjects face market discipline and have a chance to learn. We will report just two experiments from that series.

In the first experiment, students in an advanced undergraduate economics class at Cornell University participated in a series of markets. The objects traded in the first three markets were 'induced value tokens.' In such markets all subjects are told how much a token is worth to them, with the amounts varying across subjects. Half the subjects were made owners of tokens, the other half were not. In this way, supply and demand curves for tokens are created. Subjects alternated between the buyer and seller role in the three successive markets, and were assigned a different individual redemption value in each trial. Experimenters collected the forms from all participants after each market period, and immediately calculated and announced the market-clearing price and the number of trades. Three buyers and three sellers were selected at random after each of the induced markets and were paid off according to the preferences stated on their forms and the market clearing price for that period.

These markets contained no grist for the anomaly mill. On each trial, the market clearing price was exactly equal to the intersection of the induced supply and demand curves, and the volume of trade was within one unit of the predicted quantity. These results demonstrate that the subjects understood the task, and that the market mechanism used did not impose high transactions costs.

Immediately after the three induced value markets, subjects on alternating seats were given Cornell coffee mugs, which sell for $6.00 each at the bookstore. The experimenter asked all participants to examine a mug, either their own or their neighbor's. The experimenter then informed the subjects that four markets for mugs would be conducted using the same procedures as the prior induced markets with two exceptions: (1) One of the four market trials would subsequently be selected at random and only the trades made on this trial would be executed. (2) On the binding market trial, *all* trades would be implemented, unlike the subset implemented in the induced value markets. The initial assignment of buyer and seller roles was maintained for all four trading periods. The clearing price and the number of trades were announced after each period. The market that "counted" was indicated after the fourth period, and transactions were executed immediately – all sellers who had indicated that they would give up their mug at the market clearing price exchanged their mugs for cash, and successful buyers paid this same price and received their mug. This design was used to permit learning to take place over successive trials and yet make each trial potentially binding. The same procedure was then followed for four more successive markets using boxed ball-point pens with a visible bookstore price tag of $3.98, which were distributed to the subjects who had been buyers in the mug markets.

What does economic theory predict will happen in these markets for mugs and pens? Since transactions costs have been shown to be insignificant in the induced-value markets, and income effects are trivial, a clear prediction is available: When the market clears, the objects will be owned by those subjects who value them most. Call the half of the subjects who like mugs the most "mug lovers" and the half who like mugs least "mug haters." Then, since the mugs were assigned at random, on average half of the mug lovers will be given a mug, and half will not. This implies that in the market, half of the mugs should trade, with mug haters selling to mug lovers.

The 50 percent predicted volume of trade did not materialize. There were 22 mugs and pens distributed so the predicted number of trades was 11. In the four mug markets the number of trades was 4, 1, 2, and 2 respectively. In the pen markets the number of trades was either 4 or 5. In neither market was there any evidence of a trend over the four trials. The reason for the low volume of trade is revealed by the reservation prices of buyers and sellers. For mugs, the median owner was unwilling to sell for less than $5.25, while the median buyer was unwilling to pay more than $2.25-$2.75. The market price varied between $4.25 and $4.75. In the market for pens the ratio of selling to buying prices was also about 2. The experiment was replicated several times, always with similar results: median selling prices are about twice median buying prices and volume is less than half of that expected.

Another experiment from this series allows us to investigate whether the low volume of trading is produced by a reluctance to buy or a reluctance to sell. In this experiment, 77 students at Simon Fraser University were randomly assigned to three conditions. One group, the Sellers, were given SFU coffee mugs and were asked whether they would be willing to sell the mugs at each of a series of prices ranging from $0.25 to $9.25. A second group of Buyers were asked whether they would be willing to buy a mug at the same set of prices. The third group, called Choosers, were not given a mug but were asked to choose, for each of the prices, between receiving a mug or that amount of money.

Notice that the Sellers and the Choosers are in objectively identical situations, deciding at each price between the mug and that amount of money. Nevertheless, the Choosers behaved more like Buyers than like Sellers. The median reservation prices were: Sellers, $7.12; Choosers, $3.12; Buyers, $2.87. This suggests that the low volume of trade is produced mainly by owner's reluctance to part with their endowment, rather than by buyers' unwillingness to part with their cash. This experiment also eliminates the trivial income effect present in the first experiment, since the Sellers and Choosers are in the same economic situation.

One of the first lessons in microeconomics is that two indifference curves can never intersect. This result depends on the implicit assumption that indifference curves are reversible. That is, if an individual owns x and is indifferent between keeping it and trading it for y, then when owning y the individual should be indifferent about trading it for x. If loss aversion is present, however, this reversibility will no longer hold. Knetsch (1990) has demonstrated this point experimentally. One group of subjects received 5 medium priced ball point pens, while another group of subjects received $4.50. They were then made a series of offers which they could accept or reject. The offers were designed to identify an indifference curve. For example, someone who had been given the pens would be asked if she would give up one of the pens for a dollar. One of the accepted offers (including the original endowment) was selected at random at the end of the experiment to determine the subject's payment. By plotting the line between accepted and rejected offers, Knetsch was able to infer an indifference curve for each subject. Then he plotted the average indifference curve for each of the two groups (those who started with pens and those who started with money). These plots are shown in Figure 8.1. The curves are quite different: the pens were worth more money to those subjects who started with pens than to those subjects who started with money. As a result, the curves intersect.[1]

What produces these "instant endowment effects"? Do subjects who receive a gift actually value it more than others who do not receive it? A recent study by Loewenstein and Kahneman (1991) investigated this issue. Half the students in

---

[1] These curves were obtained from different individuals. Because subjects were randomly assigned to the two endowment groups, however, it is reasonable to attribute crossing indifference curves to the representative individual.

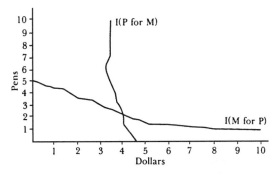

Figure 8.1. Crossing indifference curves.

a class ($N = 63$) were given pens, the others were given a token redeemable for an unspecified gift. All participants were then asked to rank the attractiveness of six gifts under consideration as prizes in subsequent experiments. Finally, all the subjects were then given a choice between a pen and two chocolate bars. As in previous experiments, there was a pronounced endowment effect. The pen was preferred by 56 percent of those endowed with it, but only 24 percent of the other subjects chose a pen. However, when making the attractiveness ratings, the subjects endowed with pens did not rate them as more attractive. This suggests that the main effect of endowment is not to enhance the appeal of the good one owns, only the pain of giving it up.

Status Quo Bias

One implication of loss aversion is that individuals have a strong tendency to remain at the status quo, because the disadvantages of leaving it loom larger than advantages. Samuelson and Zeckhauser (1988) have demonstrated this effect, which they term the *status quo bias*. In one experiment, some subjects were given a hypothetical choice task, such as the following, in a 'neutral' version in which no status quo is defined: "You are a serious reader of the financial pages but until recently have had few funds to invest. That is when you inherited a large sum of money from your great-uncle. You are considering different portfolios. Your choices are to invest in: a moderate-risk company, a high risk company, treasury bills, municipal bonds."

Other subjects were presented with the same problem but with one of the options designated as the status quo. In this case, after the same opening sentence the passage continues: "... That is when you inherited a portfolio of cash and securities from your great-uncle. A significant portion of this portfolio is invested in a moderate risk company ... (The tax and broker commission consequences of any change are insignificant.)"

Many different scenarios were investigated, all using the same basic experimental design. Aggregating across all the different questions, Samuelson and Zeckhauser are then able to estimate the probability that an option will be selected when it is the status quo or when it is competing as an alternative to the status quo as a function of how often it is selected in the neutral setting. Their results implied that an alternative became significantly more popular when it was designated as the status quo. Also, the advantage of the status quo increases with the number of alternatives.

A test of status quo bias in a field setting was performed by Hartman, Doane, and Woo (forthcoming) using a survey of California electric power consumers. The consumers were asked about their preferences regarding service reliability and rates. They were told that their answers would help determine company policy in the future. The respondents fell into two groups, one with much more reliable service than the other. Each group was asked to state a preference among six combinations of service reliabilities and rates, with one of the combinations designated as the status quo. The results demonstrated a pronounced status quo bias. In the high reliability group, 60.2 percent selected their status quo as their first choice, while only 5.7 percent expressed a preference for the low reliability option currently being experienced by the other group, though it came with a 30 percent reduction in rates. The low reliability group, however, quite liked their status quo, 58.3 percent of them ranking it first. Only 5.8 percent of this group selected the high reliability option at a proposed 30 percent increase in rates.[2]

A large-scale experiment on status quo bias is now being conducted (inadvertently) by the states of New Jersey and Pennsylvania. Both states now offer a choice between two types of automobile insurance: a cheaper policy that restricts the right to sue, and a more expensive one that maintains the unrestricted right. Motorists in New Jersey are offered the cheaper policy as the default option, with an opportunity to acquire an unrestricted right to sue at a higher price. Since this option was made available in 1988, 83 percent of the drivers have elected the default option. In Pennsylvania's 1990 law, however, the default option is the expensive policy, with an opportunity to opt for the cheaper kind. The potential effect of this legislative framing manipulation was studied by Hershey, Johnson, Meszaros, and Robinson (1990). They asked two groups to choose between alternative policies. One group was presented with the New Jersey plan while the other was presented with the Pennsylvania plan. Of those subjects offered the New Jersey plan, only 23 percent elected to buy the right to sue whereas 53 percent of the subjects offered the Pennsylvania plan retained that right. On the basis of this research, the authors predict that more Pennsylvanians will elect the right to sue than New Jerseyans. Time will tell.

---

[2] Differences in income and electricity consumption between the two groups were minor and did not appear to significantly influence the results. Could the results be explained by either learning or habituation? That is, might the low reliability group have learned to cope with frequent outages, or found out that candlelight dinners are romantic? This cannot be ruled out, but it should be stressed that no similar explanation can be used for the mug experiments or the surveys conducted by Samuelson and Zeckhauser, so at least some of the effects observed are attributable to a pure status quo bias.

One final example of a presumed status quo bias comes courtesy of the *JEP* staff. Among Carl Shapiro's comments on this column was this gem: "You may be interested to know that when the AEA was considering letting members elect to drop one of the three Association journals and get a credit, prominent economists involved in that decision clearly took the view that fewer members would choose to drop a journal if the default was presented as all three journals (rather than the default being 2 journals with an extra charge for getting all three). We're talking economists here."

Loss Aversion

These observations, and many others, can be explained by a notion of loss aversion. A central conclusion of the study of risky choice has been that such choices are best explained by assuming that the significant carriers of utility are not states of wealth or welfare, but changes relative to a neutral reference point. Another central result is that changes that make things worse (losses) loom larger than improvements or gains. The choice data imply an abrupt change of the slope of the value function at the origin. The existing evidence suggests that the ratio of the slopes of the value function in two domains, for small or moderate gains and losses of money, is about 2:1 (Tversky and Kahneman, 1991). A schematic value function is shown in Figure 8.2.

The natural extension of this idea to riskless choice is that the attributes of options in trades and other transactions are also evaluated as gains and losses relative to a neutral reference point. The approach is illustrated in Figure 8.3. Decision makers have a choice between state A, where they have more of good Y and less of good X, and state D, where they have more of good X and less of good Y. Four different reference points are indicated in the figure. The individual faces a positive choice between two gains if the reference point is C, a negative choice

Figure 8.2. A typical value function.

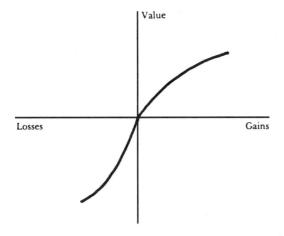

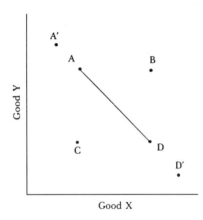

Figure 8.3. Multiple reference points for the choice between A and D.

between two losses if the reference point is B, and two different exchanges if the references are A or D, respectively. For example, if good Y is a mug and good X is money, the reference points for the sellers and the choosers in the mugs experiment are A and C. Loss aversion implies that the difference between the states of having a mug and not having one is larger from A than from C, which explains the different monetary values that subjects attach to the mug in these conditions.[3] For a formal treatment that generalizes consumer theory by introducing the notions of reference and loss aversion, see Tversky and Kahneman (1991).

In general, a given difference between two options will have greater impact if it is viewed as a difference between two disadvantages than if it is viewed as a difference between two advantages. The status quo bias is a natural consequence of this asymmetry: the disadvantages of a change loom larger than its advantages. However, the differential weighting of advantages and disadvantages can be demonstrated even when the retention of the status quo is not an option. For an example, consider the following question (from Tversky and Kahneman, 1991):

Imagine that as part of your professional training you were assigned to a part-time job. The training is now ending and you must look for employment. You consider two possibilities. They are like your training job in most respects except for the amount of social contact and the convenience of commuting to and from work. To compare the two jobs to each other and to the present one you have made up the following table:

Job	*Contact with Others*	*Commute Time*
Present job	*isolated for long stretches*	*10 min.*
Job A	*limited contact with others*	*20 min.*
Job D	*moderately sociable*	*60 min.*

The options A and D are evaluated from a reference job which is better on commute time and worse on personal contact (a point like A' in Figure 8.3). Another version of the problem presented the same options, but the reference job involved "much pleasant social interaction and 80 minutes of daily

---

[3] Loss aversion does not affect all transactions. In a normal commercial transaction, the seller does not suffer a loss when trading a good. Furthermore, the evidence indicates that buyers do not value the money spent on normal purchases as a loss, so long as the price of the good is not thought to be unusually high. Loss aversion is expected to primarily affect owners of goods that had been bought for use rather than for eventual resale.

commuting time," which corresponds to the point D'. The proportion of subjects choosing job A was 70 percent in the first version, 33 percent in the second. Subjects are more sensitive to the dimension in which they are losing relative to their reference point.

Some asymmetries between buying and selling prices are much too large to be explained by garden-variety loss aversion. For example, Thaler (1980) told subjects that they had been exposed to a rare fatal disease and that they now face a .001 chance of painless death within two weeks. They must decide how much they would be willing to pay for a vaccine, to be purchased immediately. The same subjects were also asked for the compensation they would demand to participate in a medical experiment in which they face a .001 chance of a quick and painless death. For most subjects the two prices differed by more than an order of magnitude.

A study by Viscusi, Magat and Huber (1987) documented a similar effect in a more realistic setting. Their respondents were recruited at a shopping mall and hardware store. The respondents were shown a can of fictitious insecticide, and were asked to examine it for their use. The current price of the can was said to be $10. Respondents were informed that all insecticide can cause injuries if misused, including inhalation and skin poisoning (in households with young children, child poisoning replaced skin poisoning). The current risk level was said to be 15 injuries of each type per 10,000 bottles sold. Respondents were asked to state their willingness-to-pay (WTP) to eliminate or reduce the risks. In households without children, the mean WTP to eliminate both risks was $3.78. The respondents were also asked to state the price reduction they would require to accept an increase of 1/10,000 in each of the two risks. The results were dramatic: 77 percent of respondents in this condition said they would refuse to buy the product at any positive price.

The striking difference between WTA and WTP in these studies probably reflects the large difference in the responsibility costs associated with voluntary assumption of additional risk, in contrast to a mere failure to reduce or eliminate existing risk. The asymmetry between omission and commission is familiar in legal doctrine, and its impact on judgments of responsibility has been confirmed by psychological research (Ritov and Baron, forthcoming). The asymmetry affects both blame and regret after a mishap, and the anticipation of blame and regret, in turn, could affect behavior.

A moral attitude is involved in another situation where huge discrepancies between buying and selling prices have been observed, the evaluation of environmental amenities in cost benefit analyses. Suppose some corporation offers to buy the Grand Canyon and make it into a water park complete with the world's largest water slide. How do we know whether the benefits of this idea exceed its costs? As usual there are two ways to ask the question, depending on what is the status quo. If there is no theme park in the status quo, then people can be asked the minimum amount of money they would accept to agree to add one (WTA). Alternatively, if the corporation currently owns the right, people could be asked how much they would be willing to pay to buy it back and prevent the theme park from being built (WTP). Several surveys have been conducted where the researchers asked both types of questions for such things as clean air and well-maintained public parks. Most studies find that the WTA responses greatly exceed the WTP answers (Cummings, Brookshire, and Schulze, 1986). The difference in typical responses actually does not tell the entire story. As two close observers of this literature note (Mitchell and Carson, 1989, p. 34): "Studies using WTA questions have consistently received a large number of protest answers, such as 'I refuse to sell' or 'I want an extremely large or infinite amount of compensation for agreeing to this,' and have frequently experienced protest rates [outright refusals to answer the question] of 50 percent or more." These extreme responses reflect the feelings of outrage often seen when communities are faced with the prospect of accepting a new risk such as a nuclear power plant or waste disposal facility (Kunreuther, Easterling, Desvousges, and Slovic, forthcoming). Offers of compensation to proposed communities often do not help as they are typically perceived as bribes.[4]

Judgments of Fairness and Justice

An implication of the endowment effect is that people treat opportunity costs differently than "out-of-pocket" costs. Foregone gains are less painful than perceived losses. This perception is strongly manifested in people's judgments about fair behavior. Kahneman, Knetsch and Thaler (1986) present survey evidence supporting this proposition. Samples of the residents of Toronto and Vancouver were asked a series of questions over the telephone about whether they thought a particular economic action was "fair." In some cases, alternative versions of the same question were presented to different groups of respondents. For each question, respondents were asked to judge whether the action was completely fair, acceptable, somewhat unfair, or very unfair. In reporting the results the first two categories were combined and called "acceptable" and the last two combined and called "unfair." Perceptions of fairness strongly depended on whether the question was framed as a reduction in a gain or an actual loss. For example:

> Question 1a. A shortage has developed for a popular model of automobile, and customers must now wait two months for delivery. A dealer has been selling these cars at list price. Now the dealer prices this model at $200 above list price.
>
> N = 130   *Acceptable 29 percent*   *Unfair 71 percent*

---

[4] This is a situation in which people loudly say one thing and the theory asserts another. It is of interest that the practitioners of contingent valuation elected to listen to the theory, rather than to the respondents (Cummings, Brookshire and Schulze, 1986). The accepted procedure uses WTP questions to assess value even in a context of compensation, relying on the theoretical argument that WTP and WTA should not be far apart when income effects are small.

Question 1b. A shortage has developed for a popular model of automobile, and customers must now wait two months for delivery. A dealer has been selling these cars at a discount of $200 below list price. Now the dealer sells this model only at list price.

$N = 123$ *Acceptable 58 percent*   *Unfair 42 percent*

Imposing a surcharge (which is likely to be judged a loss) is considered more unfair than eliminating a discount (a reduction of a gain). This distinction explains why firms that charge cash customers one price and credit card customers a higher price always refer to the cash price as a discount rather than to the credit card price as a surcharge (Thaler, 1980).

The different intensity of responses to losses and to foregone gains may help explain why it is easier to cut real wages during inflationary periods:

Question 2a. A company is making a small profit. It is located in a community experiencing a recession with substantial unemployment but no inflation. The company decides to decrease wages and salaries 7 percent this year.

$N = 125$ *Acceptable 37 percent*   *Unfair 63 percent*

Question 2b. A company is making a small profit. It is located in a community experiencing a recession with substantial unemployment and inflation of 12 percent. The company decides to increase salaries only 5 percent this year.

$N = 129$ *Acceptable 78 percent*   *Unfair 22 percent*

In this case a 7 percent cut in real wages is judged reasonably fair when it is framed as a nominal wage increase, but quite unfair when it is posed as a nominal wage cut.

The attitudes of the lay public about fairness, which are represented in their answers to these fairness questions, also pervade the decisions made by judges in many fields of the law. Supreme Court Justice Oliver Wendell Holmes (1897) put the principle this way: "It is in the nature of a man's mind. A thing which you enjoyed and used as your own for a long time, whether property or opinion, takes root in your being and cannot be torn away without your resenting the act and trying to defend yourself, however you came by it. The law can ask no better justification than the deepest instincts of man."

Cohen and Knetsch (1990) showed that this principle, embodied in the old expression that "possession is nine tenths of the law," is reflected in many judicial opinions. For example, in tort law judges make the distinction between "loss by way of expenditure and failure to make gain." In one case, several bales fell from the defendant's truck and hit a utility pole, cutting off power to the plaintiff's plant. The plaintiff was able to recover wages paid to employees which were considered "positive outlays" but could not recover lost profits which were merely "negative losses consisting of a mere deprivation of an opportunity to earn an income" (p. 18). A similar distinction is made in contract law. A party that breaches a contract is more likely to be held to the original terms if the action is taken to make an unforeseen gain than if it is taken to avoid a loss.

COMMENTARY

It is in the nature of economic anomalies that they violate standard theory. The next question is what to do about it. In many cases there is no obvious way to amend the theory to fit the facts, either because too little is known, or because the changes would greatly increase the complexity of the theory and reduce its predictive yield. The anomalies that we have described under the labels of the endowment effect, the status quo bias and loss aversion may be an exceptional case, where the needed amendments in the theory are both obvious and tractable.

The amendments are not trivial: the important notion of a stable preference order must be abandoned in favor of a preference order that depends on the current reference level. A revised version of preference theory would assign a special role to the status quo, giving up some standard assumptions of stability, symmetry and reversibility which the data have shown to be false. But the task is manageable. The generalization of preference theory to indifference curves that are indexed to reference level is straightforward (Tversky and Kahneman, 1991). The factors that determine the reference point in the evaluations of outcomes are reasonably well understood: the role of the status quo, and of entitlements and expectations are sufficiently well established to allow these factors to be used in locating the relevant reference levels for particular analyses.

As Samuelson and Zeckhauser noted, rational models that ignore the status quo tend to predict "greater instability than is observed in the world" (p. 47). We have added the claim that models that ignore loss aversion predict more symmetry and reversibility than are observed in the world, ignoring potentially large differences in the magnitude of responses to gains and to losses. Responses to increases and to decreases in price, for example, might not always be mirror images of each other. The possibility of loss aversion effects suggests, more generally, that treatments of responses to *changes* in economic variables should routinely separate the cases of favorable and unfavorable changes. Introducing such distinctions could improve the precision of predictions at a tolerable price in increased complexity.

After more than a decade of research on this topic we have become convinced that the endowment effect, status quo bias, and the aversion to losses are both robust and important. Then again, we admit that the idea is now part of our endowment, and we are naturally keener to retain it than others might be to acquire it.

9. The Endowment Effect and Evidence of Nonreversible Indifference Curves

Jack L. Knetsch

Indifference curves are normally taken to indicate corresponding trade-offs of goods *A* for *B* or *B* for *A* over the same interval: "the rate of commodity substitution at a point on an indifference curve is the same for movements in either direction" (James Henderson and Richard Quandt, 1971, p. 12). However, recent empirical findings of asymmetric evaluations of gains and losses imply that the presumed reversibility may not accurately reflect preferences, and that people commonly make choices that differ depending on the direction of proposed trades.

The evidence from a wide variety of tests is consistent with the suggestions of Daniel Kahneman and Amos Tversky (1979), and Richard Thaler (1980), that losses from a reference position are systematically valued far more than commensurate gains. The minimum compensation people demand to give up a good has been found to be several times larger than the maximum amount they are willing to pay for a commensurate entitlement. For example, when questioned about the possible destruction of a duck habitat, hunters responded that they would be willing to pay an average of $247 to prevent its loss but would demand $1044 to accept it (Judd Hammack and Gardner Brown, 1974). Respondents in another study demanded payments to accept various levels of visibility degradation that were from 5 to over 16 times higher than their valuations based on payment measures (Robert Rowe, Ralph d'Arge, and David Brookshire, 1980). Similar large differences in valuations of a wide variety of goods and entitlements have been reported in numerous survey studies.[1]

These valuation differences based on responses to hypothetical survey questions prompted further, more severe, tests of the disparity using a variety of real exchange experimental designs. The results have been much the same. Even when exchanges of real goods and actual cash payments motivated the

[1] See, for example, Ronald Cummings et al. (1986) for a summary of many earlier studies.

This research was supported by Fisheries and Oceans Canada and The Ontario Ministry of the Environment; it has benefited from discussions with Curtis Eaton, Daniel Kahneman, Peter Kennedy, and Richard Thaler.

evaluations, the compensation demanded to give up an entitlement has been reported to far exceed the comparable payment measure of value (Knetsch and John Sinden, 1984; Thomas Heberlein and Richard Bishop, 1985).

While some studies have found that the size of an initial disparity may decrease over successive valuation trials for some entitlements, differences between the measures generally remain (Don Coursey, John Hovis, and William Schulze, 1987, and Knetsch and Sinden, 1987). For example, Brookshire and Coursey found that the differences between payment and compensation valuations of trees in a park decreased substantially from initial hypothetical responses, but the ratio of the two measures remained at "approximately five to one" after the last real exchange iteration (1987, p. 563). Other more recent tests of the evaluation disparities, or endowment effects, have shown that the observed disparities between valuations of entitlements are not the result of wealth effects or income constraints, strategic behavior, or transactions costs, and that the differences persist over repeated binding iterations of market trials (Knetsch, Thaler, and Kahneman, 1988).

The purpose here is to report the results of more direct tests of the reversibility of indifference curves. A variety of test designs were used in these exercises, but in each case one-half of a sample of participants were offered one good or money for another good, and the other half were offered a similar trade but in the opposite direction.[2]

I. TEST 1: EXCHANGES OF TWO GOODS

A straightforward preference exercise involving a choice between two goods was conducted with three comparable groups of University of Victoria students.

In one class, 76 participants were given a coffee mug and were then asked to complete a short questionnaire. The students had the mug in their possession while they answered the written questions. After the questionnaires were completed, the experimenter showed the participants a 400-gram Swiss chocolate bar and told them they could have one in exchange for their mug.[3] Participants were informed that they could either keep their mugs, or have a chocolate bar. They were instructed to hold up a colored paper with the word "trade" marked on it if they preferred the candy to their mug and wished to make an exchange. All desired trades were made immediately by one of four experimenters present, there was no uncertainty of receiving the other good and no effort was required beyond raising the paper to indicate a willingness to make an exchange.

The 87 participants in the second group were offered an opportunity to make the opposite trade of giving up a candy bar, which had been given to them

---

[2] Instructions for all of the exercises are available from the author.
[3] Participants were familiar with both the mugs and the candy bars. The mugs were sold in the University bookstore for $4.95 and the candy bars were available in local shops for around $6.

initially, for a mug. All conditions were the same except for the direction of the exchange offer.

The 55 people in the third group were simply offered a choice between receiving a candy bar or mug.

The choices presented to people in each of the first two groups differed only in terms of which good they had to give up to obtain the other – incentives were compatible and there were no income, or wealth, effect possibilities, nor any wealth constraints. However, contrary to the expectation of an equal proportion favoring one good over the other in each group, based on the conventional assertion of economic theory and practice, the different initial entitlements and subsequent direction of potential trades heavily influenced the participants' valuations of the two goods.

The preferences indicated by the choices were:

	Proportion favoring (in percent)		
Group	Mug over candy	Candy over mug	N
1. Give up mug to obtain candy	89	11	76
2. Give up candy to obtain mug	10	90	87
3. No initial entitlement	56	44	55

When given a simple choice without a prior entitlement or reference position, 56 percent of the participants (Group 3) selected a mug in preference to a candy bar. But only 10 percent valued a mug more than a candy bar when they had to give up the candy to obtain a mug (Group 2), while 89 percent of those who initially received a mug (Group 1) declined to give it up for a candy bar. The preferences for a mug over a candy bar varied from 10 to 89 percent depending entirely on the reference position of the endowment at the time of the valuations.

In this simple experiment, participants' preferences were not independent of the direction of the exchanges, as is commonly assumed. They expressed a dramatic asymmetry in valuations by weighing the loss of giving up their initial or reference entitlement far more heavily than the foregone gains of not obtaining the alternative entitlement.

II. TEST 2: MINIMUM ACCEPTABLE EXCHANGES

The symmetry of exchange preferences was further tested in a second experiment involving real goods and actual cash payments. As in the first test, the design of this experiment also precluded the influence of a wealth constraint and the possibility of an income, or wealth, effect. The participants were 80 students in five tutorial groups of an introductory pre-principles economics class at Simon Fraser University. The exercise was repeated in the five tutorial meetings in a single afternoon.

Forty-one individuals in three of the groups were first given two 100-gram Swiss chocolate candy bars.[4] They were then asked to state the smallest amount of money they would accept to give up both of their candy bars.

The 39 members of the other two tutorial groups were each given two single-dollar bills. They were then asked the minimum number of chocolate bars they would require to give up their two dollars. The initial offering of money or candy bars was alternated over the five participating groups.

The method of obtaining the declarations of minimum acceptable trades was designed so that stating the smallest compensation each participant would agree to was in the person's best interest. To ensure that the individuals understood that this was the case, a preliminary instruction and screening test was conducted so that they could demonstrate their understanding before becoming participants in the real exchange exercise. This preliminary test involved a hypothetical, induced, or prescribed, value and the identical bidding mechanism that was used to reveal preferences in the subsequent real good exchange.[5]

All participants were given the same form for the preliminary demonstration and screening test:

THIS FIRST PART OF THIS EXERCISE IS HYPOTHETICAL ONLY; NO ACTUAL PAYMENTS WILL BE MADE. HOWEVER, DEPENDING ON THE RESPONSE OF PARTICIPANTS IN THIS GROUP, A SECOND PART MAY BE CONDUCTED IN WHICH ACTUAL PAYMENTS WILL BE MADE.

IF THE SECOND PART IS CONDUCTED, YOU CAN ONLY WIN; YOU CANNOT LOSE.

Assume that the person conducting this exercise will pay you $2.50 for the ticket attached to this sheet.

Now assume that before you redeem the ticket you are given an opportunity to sell it. The price you will be offered for it will be determined by a random draw of one of six cards with the dollar amounts: $0, $1, $2, $3, $4, or $5 on them.

What is the smallest of these offer prices you would accept to give up your ticket?

$ ——— (use only whole dollars – i.e., no cents). If the offer price on the randomly drawn card is the same or higher than the price you stated above, you will receive the amount of money on the card in exchange for your ticket. If the offer price on the card is lower than your indicated minimum selling price, you will keep the ticket (and turn it in for the $2.50).

---

[4] These candy bars sell for around $2.00 each in most shops.

[5] Real exchange experiments using such prescribed, or induced, values have been widely used to test the efficiency of various types of market institutions (for example, Vernon Smith, 1976).

A comparison of the outcomes of induced value markets with subsequent goods markets carried out with identical trading rules also provides a test for possible transactions costs and strategic behavior as possible sources of valuation disparities (Knetsch, Thaler, and Kahneman, 1988). If no inhibitions to trades are observed in the induced-value markets, none should then be expected from such causes in markets for goods that are valued by the individual participants themselves.

After the participants read the instructions for the preliminary test, the experimenter gave a further explanation and answered questions. Participants then completed the forms. The experimenter checked the forms to ensure that at least 75 percent of the individuals knew how to respond in a way that served their best interest (by stating $3 as the minimum acceptable price). If more than 25 percent failed to answer in this way the experiment was terminated for that whole group.[6]

Of the 80 individuals in the five groups that went on to the second part involving the real exchanges, only 14 (18 percent) failed to answer the first part correctly.[7] Before proceeding with the second part, the experimenter explained the bidding mechanism again, and pointed out the reasons why other answers could work to the disadvantage of the respondent. These further explanations, and the screening of participants by their demonstrated ability to reveal their true minimum values in this market, ensured that individuals participating in the real exchange experiment fully understood the value revealing incentives of the bidding procedure.

Participants in the second, real exchange, part of the experiment were given their endowment of either candy bars or dollar bills and were told that these were theirs to keep. Those with an entitlement of candy bars then received the following second form:

THIS SECOND PART WILL INVOLVE REAL PAYMENTS.
THERE ARE NO RIGHT OR WRONG ANSWERS, YOUR RESPONSE SHOULD REFLECT ONLY YOUR OWN PREFERENCES.

You have been given 2 candy bars. They are yours to keep. However, if you like – and the choice is entirely yours – you may be able to trade the 2 candy bars for money. We want to know about your personal preferences in terms of the smallest number of dollars you would accept to give up the two candy bars.

The amount you will be offered to give up your 2 candy bars will be determined in the same way as it was in Part 1 of this exercise. That is, an offer price, in dollars, will be determined by a random draw of one of the six cards with amounts ranging from $0 to $5.

If you are willing to give up the 2 candy bars for $5 or less, write the smallest of these offer prices that you would accept to give up both of the candy bars in the blank below.

If it would take more than $5 for you to agree to give up your two candy bars, then write a 6 in the blank, and you will then keep your candy bars.

$ ——— (use only whole dollars – i.e., no cents). If the offer amount on the randomly drawn card is the same or higher than the number you have written above, you will receive the amount of money on the card in exchange for your 2 candy bars. If the offer on the card is lower than the number you have written above you will be allowed to keep the candy bars.

---

[6] This occurred in four other groups.

[7] All but 3 of the 14 individuals answering incorrectly specified a selling price *lower* than the most profitable one, an error that would bias the results toward lower evaluations of the initial entitlements and symmetry and away from the much higher values of losses subsequently revealed.

Individuals receiving an initial endowment of money were given a comparable form.

The bid procedure was then explained yet again and questions answered. The random draw of the card was made after the forms were completed, and exchanges were made according to the indicated minimum acceptable trades.

The results again demonstrated a strong aversion to giving up an initial entitlement.

The participants' dollar value of the candy bars is given either by the minimum amount demanded to give them up, or by the number of candy bars required to give up dollars. The proportions of the two samples valuing a candy bar equal to or greater than $1 and $2 are given in the following tabulation.

Group	Proportion of individuals valuing candy bar equal to or more than: (in percent)	
	$1	$2
1. Give up money to get candy bars (N = 39)	33	8
2. Give up candy bars to get money (N = 41)	95	37
Chi-squared value	35.05	9.57

The participants valued the candy or money significantly more when considering the prospect of giving it up than they did when they had the opportunity to acquire either in exchange for their original entitlement.[8] The average evaluations of the candy bars, based on the responses of all of the participants in each original endowment group, were approximately $1.83 with the entitlement and $0.90 without it. That is, the people starting with the candy bars valued them at a little over twice as much as the people did who were given money.[9]

As in the earlier test, the relative preferences of participants in this exercise depended on reference entitlements and the subsequent direction of trade offers.

[8] Based on 1 degree of freedom, both chi-squared values are significant at the 1-percent level.

[9] The differences indicated in the tabulation and the statistical significance of the disparity are, if anything, understated. First, for people stating minimum money demands the recorded numbers are those valuing the money *more than* the candy. Individuals in the other groups stating required candy bar payments include those who value the candy *equal to* as well as more than the various sums.

   Second, the proportions of participants valuing the bars at the stated sums imply that the individuals valued all candy bars and dollars over the relevant range equally. If they in fact valued each successive candy bar or dollar by a decreasing amount – with diminishing marginal utility – then the surplus from the intramarginal units would prompt an even greater demand for the other good, given the all or nothing nature of the choice.

III. TEST 3: SURVEY RESPONSES

While the results from the first two tests were from real exchange experiments, similar indications of large valuation disparities that varied with the direction of proposed exchanges were also obtained from general public reactions recorded in a series of telephone surveys.

These random household telephone interviews were conducted in metropolitan Toronto, with an equal number of adult males and females called during early evening hours. In each case, one subsample of respondents was asked if they would trade one good for another; a second subsample was asked if they would make the opposite exchange.

Two groups of respondents were asked about their preferences between a change of $700 per year in their current income and a 0.5 percent change in the chance of having an accident during the year that would result in some time in the hospital. Among respondents in the group asked if they would accept $700 to have their chance of an accident increased by 0.5 percent (from 0.5 percent to 1.0 percent), 61 percent ($N = 149$) refused, indicating that this proportion valued the negative change in risk more than $700.

In the group asked to trade a decrease of the same accident risk (over the same range of from 1.0 percent to 0.5 percent) for a reduction of $700 in their income, only 27 percent ($N = 146$) indicated a higher valuation of the positive increment of risk change by being willing to make the trade. Again, relative preferences varied greatly depending on the direction of the proposed exchange – 39 percent preferred $700 to the change in risk one way, and 73 percent preferred $700 to the change the other way.[10]

In the same way, two groups of respondents were asked about their preferences between a new job that offered more or less pay and more or less vacation time than their current employment. When asked to trade an increase of $500 annual salary for one week less vacation, 66 percent ($N = 143$) indicated a greater valuation of the holiday time. For respondents offered the opposite exchange of more vacation for less pay, only 29 percent ($N = 147$) indicated a preference for an equal amount of time off.[11]

IV. THE ASYMMETRY OF PREFERENCES

The evidence from these three tests is widely at variance with the conventional strong empirical assertion of completely reversible indifference curves. The tests used three different designs which varied in several dimensions: they included both real exchange experiments and surveys using hypothetical questions; they used student and nonstudent participants; they involved choices between goods and money and between two goods; they included small and

---

[10] The chi-squared value of 35.32 with 1 d.f. is significant at the 0.1 percent level.
[11] With 1 d.f. the chi-squared value of 43.77 is significant at a 0.1 percent level.

large sums; and they included valuations that could be affected by wealth effects and income restraints and others which excluded such possibilities. The results, however, were all the same. In every case, people exhibited valuations and preferences that varied systematically and substantially with the initial reference entitlement and the direction of exchange offers.

Further, the windfall nature of the endowment in the real exchange tests could well lead to these results understating the extent of the disparities that might be expected under nonexperimental conditions. People were given a good or money in these experiments, and their valuations were assessed in terms of what they would demand to give it up. However, individuals have generally been found to give up such windfall gains more easily than assets from their own original endowment (Thaler and Eric Johnson, 1989). The manipulations used in these experiments may therefore be weaker than might be encountered in most actual assessments – and indifference curves may be even less reversible.

The results of the exercises reported here are consistent with other empirical tests of people's evaluations. The greater value ascribed to entitlements that might be lost over ones that might be gained gives rise to the disparity between bid and offer values (Kahneman and Tversky, 1979 and 1984). This appears to be similar to the observed nonreversibility of indifference curves in the data reported here.

Substantial disparities between valuations have now been reported for a number of goods, including an array of environmental assets, lottery tickets, personal safety, and many consumer goods. Except for cases of transparent choices, such as the obvious worth of alternatives presented in induced-value experimental markets where specific values are assigned by experimenters and individuals act on the basis of these valuations, there is yet little indication of the limits to the range of goods and assets where such differences might not be found. This raises the possibility that the significant endowment effects and nonreversible indifference curves found in these exercises may exist in a larger class of cases. Only additional empirical study can determine the extent that this is the case.

If the existence of nonreversible indifference curves is pervasive, then the assumption of reversibility will represent a normative ideal but will not serve as a very useful description of actual economic behavior in most circumstances. Nor will the traditional assumption of symmetry of valuations and complete reversibility of indifference curves seem as useful a basis for predicting economic behavior or as defendable a basis for the common practice of substituting payment measures for compensation measures of welfare losses (Robert Willig, 1976). The common practice of assessing losses in economic well-being by people's willingness to pay to avoid the change may result in significant understatements if indifference curves are not reversible.

The widespread irreversibility of indifference curves would not imply that people will not make any trades, or that consumers will not change future consumption patterns in response to changing relative prices. However, the presence of irreversibilities would imply that fewer trades will be made than predicted by standard assumptions, and they offer little assurance that the shifts in future consumption will be as complete or as prompt as would be expected if indifference curves were reversible.

In a similar way, the presence of irreversibilities also suggests that common presumptions of the potential gains from trade may often be overstated. In terms of an Edgeworth box, the area representing mutually advantageous exchanges may be very much smaller, or may not even exist, if curves showing points of indifference when giving up initial allocations differ from those indicating trades in the other direction. An apparent reluctance to trade may be due to the availability of few real gains to the parties. And the commonly observed aversion to giving up concessions in negotiations may well be due to a similar asymmetry in valuations of gains and losses (Kahneman, Knetsch, and Thaler, 1986).

10. A Test of the Theory of Reference-Dependent Preferences

Ian Bateman, Alistair Munro, Bruce Rhodes, Chris Starmer, and Robert Sugden

ABSTRACT. Eight alternative methods of eliciting preferences between money and a consumption good are identified: two of these are standard willingness-to-accept and willingness-to-pay measures. These methods differ with respect to the reference point used and the dimension in which responses are expressed. The loss aversion hypothesis of Tversky and Kahneman's theory of reference-dependent preferences predicts systematic differences between the preferences elicited by these methods. These predictions are tested by eliciting individuals' preferences for two private consumption goods; the experimental design is incentive-compatible and controls for income and substitution effects. The theory's predictions are broadly confirmed.

In conventional consumer theory each individual's choices are determined by a preference ordering over consumption bundles; this ordering is independent of the individual's endowment. However, a number of recent papers have suggested that preferences may be conditioned on current endowments, and that individuals are typically "loss averse": for example, a person may prefer bundle x to bundle y if she is endowed with x, but prefer y to x if endowed with y. The most fully worked-out general theory of this kind is probably Tversky and Kahneman's [1991] theory of *reference-dependent* preferences. Tversky and Kahneman present their theory as an explanation of a body of preexisting evidence. In this paper we report a systematic experimental test of some of the implications of reference-dependent theory.

One interesting feature of reference-dependent theory is that it offers a possible explanation of the frequently observed divergence between willingness-to-accept (*WTA*) and willingness-to-pay (*WTP*) valuations. We show that the

This paper was written as part of a project, "Identifying and Correcting for Biases in the Contingent Valuation Method," supported by the Economic and Social Research Council of Great Britain, through its Transport and the Environment Programme (award No. W 119 25 1014). We are also grateful to Jan Anderson for help with running the experiment, and to the chocolatiers Digby's of Holt for sponsorship.

theory has implications for a range of valuation measures, of which *WTP* and *WTA* are just two. We test these implications by eliciting individuals' valuations of private goods in an incentive-compatible experimental setting. An important aspect of our design is that it controls for all income and substitution effects that are compatible with conventional theory: thus, we look for certain patterns of behavior that are predicted by reference-dependent theory but which contravene conventional theory. As a consequence of this feature of our design, our tests control for the income and substitution effects that Hanemann [1991] has suggested may explain some of the divergences between *WTA* and *WTP* that have been observed in contingent valuation studies.

I. THEORY

I.A. Four Valuation Measures

Consider an individual who consumes two goods. One of the goods is to be interpreted as a particular consumption good while the other is a composite commodity, quantities of which are measured in money units. We wish to measure the value to the individual, in units of one of these goods j, of a change in her consumption of the other good i from x_i' to x_i'' or vice versa, given some initial endowment, x_j', of good j.

We shall consider four alternative measures. These are defined as follows for any x_i', x_i'', x_j' such that $x_i' < x_i''$.

(1) *Willingness to Pay.* Let the individual be endowed with the quantities x_i', x_j'. $WTP_{ji}(x_i', x_i'', x_j')$ is the maximum amount of good j that she would be willing to give up in return for an increase in her consumption of good i from x_i' to x_i''.

(2) *Willingness to Accept.* Let the individual be endowed with the quantities x_i'', x_j'. $WTA_{ji}(x_i', x_i'', x_j')$ is the minimum amount of good j that she would be willing to accept in return for a decrease in her consumption of good i from x_i'' to x_i'.

(3) *Equivalent Loss (EL).* Let the individual be endowed with the quantities x_i'', x_j'. $EL_{ji}(x_i', x_i'', x_j')$ is the maximum amount of good j that she would be willing to give up in place of a reduction in her consumption of good i from x_i'' to x_i'.

(4) *Equivalent Gain (EG).* Let the individual be endowed with the quantities x_i', x_j'. $EG_{ji}(x_i', x_i'', x_j')$ is the minimum amount of good j that she would be willing to accept in place of an increase in her consumption of good i from x_i' to x_i''.

These definitions do not depend on any theory of preference: the four measures are to be interpreted as independently observable empirical magnitudes. We shall now consider some of the implications of conventional consumer theory and of reference-dependent theory for these measures.

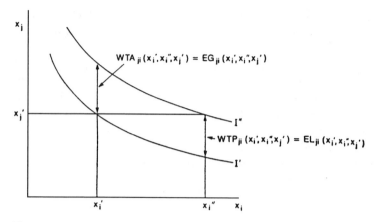

Figure 10.1.

I.B. Hicksian Theory

We shall use the term "Hicksian theory" to refer to the conventional neoclassical theory of consumer choice, as refined by Hicks [1943, 1956]. In this theory the individual has preferences over all nonnegative bundles of consumption goods: these preferences have the properties of transitivity, continuity, increasingness, and convexity, and can be represented by a utility function. In our two-good case this utility function may be written as[1] $u(x_i x_j)$.

For an individual with Hicksian preferences, the four valuation measures considered in subsection I.A can be defined implicitly by the following equations:

$$u(x_i'', x_j' - WTP_{ji}[x_i', x_i'', x_j']) = u(x_i', x_j') \qquad (1)$$

$$u(x_i', x_j' + WTA_{ji}[x_i', x_i'', x_j']) = u(x_i'', x_j') \qquad (2)$$

$$u(x_i'', x_j' - EL_{ji}[x_i', x_i'', x_j']) = u(x_i', x_j') \qquad (3)$$

$$u(x_i', x_j' + EG_{ji}[x_i', x_i'', x_j']) = u(x_i'', x_j'). \qquad (4)$$

This Hicksian case is illustrated in Figure 10.1. I' and I'' are indifference curves corresponding to the utility levels $u(x_i', x_j')$ and $u(x_i'', x_j')$. Notice that Hicksian theory implies $EL_{ji} = WTP_{ji}$ and $EG_{ji} = WTA_{ji}$. Take the case of WTP_{ji} and EL_{ji}. Conceptually, these measures differ with respect to the individual's initial endowment: WTP_{ji} is based on the endowment (x_i', x_j') while EL_{ji} is based on (x_i'', x_j'). But this difference has no significance within the Hicksian framework, in which preferences over consumption bundles are independent of initial endowments.

---

[1] Throughout the paper we use the indices i and j to refer to the two goods, without specifying which of i or j is the composite commodity and which is the specific good. To simplify the notation, however, we always write the utility function so that its first argument is consumption of good i and its second is consumption of good j. Similarly, consumption bundles are written as (x_i, x_j).

However, Hicksian theory does not imply equality between WTA_{ji} and WTP_{ji}. If good i is normal, it can be shown that

$$WTP_{ji}(x_i', x_i'', x_j') < WTA_{ji}(x_i'', x_i', x_j'). \tag{5}$$

It is natural to ask how large a divergence between these two measures is compatible with Hicksian theory. This question has been investigated by Randall and Stoll [1980] and by Hanemann [1991]. Randall and Stoll show that the divergence between WTA and WTP will be no more than a few percentage points, provided that WTP is a small proportion of the individual's total income and that the "price flexibility of income" (that is, the elasticity of the marginal valuation of good i with respect to x_j) is "small." Hanemann shows that the price flexibility of income is equal to the income elasticity of demand for good i divided by the elasticity of substitution between the two goods. He uses this result to argue that "large empirical divergences between WTP and WTA" might be expected when good i is a public good for which private consumption goods are imperfect substitutes [p. 646].

In the absence of a direct measure of the price flexibility of income, or of the elasticity of substitution, it is difficult to decide whether an observed divergence between WTA and WTP is too large to be compatible with Hicksian theory. Because of this problem, there has been considerable controversy over the interpretation of empirical findings about the relative magnitudes of WTA and WTP (see Mitchell and Carson [1989, pp. 30–38] for a survey of the issues involved).

I.C. Reference-Dependent Theory

Tversky and Kahneman [1991] propose reference-dependent theory as an alternative to the Hicksian theory of preferences. The fundamental idea in reference-dependent theory is that individuals understand the options in decision problems as gains or losses relative to a *reference point*. The reference point is normally[2] the "current position" of the individual.

Tversky and Kahneman present their model for the case of two goods. Preferences are defined over the set of all nonnegative consumption bundles; bundles will be denoted by bold lowercase letters, e.g., $\mathbf{x} = (x_i, x_j)$. One such bundle, $\mathbf{r}$, is the individual's reference point. The individual has a preference relation over bundles, *conditional on the reference point*; the relation "is at least as preferred as, evaluated in relation to $\mathbf{r}$" is written as $\geq_r$. The reference-dependent relations of strict preference and indifference are written as $\succ_r$ and $\sim_r$. Tversky and Kahneman assume that each $\geq_r$ is transitive, continuous, and increasing (but not necessarily convex); it can be represented by a reference-dependent utility function[3] $u_r(.\,,.)$.

---

[2] Tversky and Kahneman [1991, pp. 1046–47] allow certain exceptions to this rule, but these are not relevant to this paper.

[3] This function may not be everywhere differentiable: Tversky and Kahneman allow indifference curves to be kinked at reference levels (i.e., where $x_i = r_i$ or $x_j = r_j$).

Given this theory, our four measures can be defined implicitly by the equations:

$$u_y(x_i'', x_j' - WTP_{ji}[x_i', x_i'', x_j']) = u_y(x_i', x_j') \tag{6}$$

$$u_z(x_i', x_j' + WTA_{ji}[x_i', x_i'', x_j']) = u_z(x_i'', x_j') \tag{7}$$

$$u_z(x_i', x_j' - EL_{ji}[x_i', x_i'', x_j']) = u_z(x_i', x_j') \tag{8}$$

$$u_y(x_i', x_j' - EG_{ji}[x_i', x_i'', x_j']) = u_y(x_i'', x_j'), \tag{9}$$

where $y = (x_i', x_j')$ and $z = (x_i'', x_j')$. Notice that in reference-dependent theory, WTP_{ji} and WTA_{ji} are defined in relation to different utility functions. Thus, the methods used by Randall and Stoll and by Hanemann to investigate divergences between WTA and WTP do not apply when preferences are reference-dependent. Notice also that the theory does not imply equality between WTP_{ji} and EL_{ji}, or between WTA_{ji} and EG_{ji}.

The distinctive predictions of reference-dependent theory result from the assumptions that are made about how the preference ranking of a given pair of bundles may change as the reference point changes. It is convenient to use the following definition. Consider preferences over any two bundles **x** and **y** viewed from any two reference points **r** and **s**. We shall say that **s** *favors* **x** if, as the reference point shifts from **r** to **s**, the reference-dependent ranking of **x** and **y** either remains the same or changes in favor of **x**. Formally, **s** favors **x** in relation to **y** and **r** iff (i) $x \sim_r y$ implies that $x \succ_s y$ and (ii) $x \succ_r y$ implies that $x \succ_s y$. Now consider preferences over any two bundles **x**, **y**, such that $x_i > y_i$ and $y_j > x_j$, and any reference points **r**, **s** such that $r_j = s_j$. After some minor revisions,[4] Tversky and Kahneman's assumptions can be summarized as follows:

(1) *Loss Aversion.* If $y_i = r_i < s_i \leq x_i$, then **s** favors **x** in relation to **y** and **r**.
(2) *Diminishing Sensitivity in Gains.* If $r_i < s_i \leq y_i$, then **s** favors **x** in relation to **y** and **r**.
(3) *Diminishing Sensitivity in Losses.* If $x_i \leq r_i < s_i$, then **s** favors **y** in relation to **x** and **r**.

Tversky and Kahneman [1991, p. 1049] introduce the diminishing sensitivity assumptions to "extend the implications of loss aversion to reference states that do not coincide with [**x** and **y**] on either dimension." In the context of our four valuation measures, this extension is not needed, and so we may focus on the assumption of loss aversion.

---

[4] Tversky and Kahneman's [1991] formal statement of the loss aversion condition is if $y_i = r_i < s_i \leq x_i$, then $x \sim_r y$ implies that $x \succ_s y$. We have made two revisions to this condition: (1) we have weakened the original condition to '$x \sim_r y$ implies that $x \succeq_s y$' so as to allow Hicksian theory as a limiting case, and (2) we have added the implication that '$x \succ_r y$ implies $x \succ_s y$', which we believe to be wholly in the spirit of Tversky and Kahneman's analysis. Where appropriate, we have made corresponding revisions to Tversky and Kahneman's conditions of diminishing sensitivity.

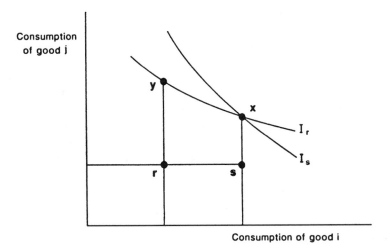

Figure 10.2.

The loss aversion assumption is illustrated in Figure 10.2. Here $y_i = r_i < s_i = x_i$. I_r and I_s are indifference curves based on the reference points **r** and **s**. When the reference point is **r**, **x** and **y** are indifferent, but when the reference point is **s**, **x** is preferred to **y**. Tversky and Kahneman [1991, p. 1047] see this assumption as representing the psychological intuition that, for each good, "losses...loom larger than corresponding gains." When the reference point is **r**, **y** is perceived as offering the reference level of good i, while **x** offers a gain of $x_i - y_i$ on the i-dimension. When the reference point is **s**, **x** is perceived as offering the reference level of good i, while **y** imposes a loss of $x_i - y_i$ on the i-dimension. Because losses have more psychological impact than forgone gains, **x**'s superiority over **y** on the i-dimension has more weight in the determination of preferences when the reference point is **s** than when it is **r**.

Loss aversion has implications for the relative magnitudes of the four valuation measures. Here we will provide an intuitive account of these implications. A more formal analysis will be given in Section III, when we describe the principles of our experimental design. Recall that each of the measures is a valuation, in units of good j, of a given change on the i-dimension. WTP_{ji} measures the individual's willingness to incur *losses* on the j-dimension to bring about a *gain* on the i-dimension. In contrast, WTA_{ji} measures the individual's willingness to accept *gains* on the j-dimension in return for incurring *losses* on the i-dimension. If losses loom larger than gains, then, in the absence of income effects, we should expect WTA_{ji} to be greater than WTP_{ji}. EG_{ji}, which expresses an equivalence between gains on the two dimensions, and EL_{ji}, which expresses an equivalence between losses, should be expected to take values intermediate between WTP_{ji} and WTA_{ji}.

II. EXISTING EVIDENCE

Proponents of theories of reference-dependent preferences are able to point to supporting evidence from a wide range of laboratory experiments and "real" economic decisions. For example, evidence of endowment effects has been found: in a double-auction experimental market for insurance [Myagkov and Plott 1995], in a public goods experiment [Andreoni 1995], and in the decisions of Harvard University employees in relation to health plans [Samuelson and Zeckhauser 1988]. It has been argued that the discrepancy between the long-run returns on stocks and on bonds may be explained by loss aversion [Benartzi and Thaler 1995].

However, the most significant source of relevant evidence concerns observed disparities between WTA and WTP. When contingent valuation surveys elicit both WTP and WTA valuations of the same good, it is quite common for the mean and median values of WTA to be several times higher than the corresponding WTP values (e.g., Bishop and Heberlein [1979]; Rowe, d'Arge, and Brookshire [1980]; Jones-Lee, Hammerton, and Philips [1985]; and Viscusi, Magat, and Huber [1987]). Significant WTA-WTP divergences have also been found in many laboratory experiments. These experiments have typically used incentive-compatible designs, in which subjects report WTP and WTA for low-value private goods (e.g., Knetsch and Sinden [1984] and Kahneman, Knetsch, and Thaler [1990]).

Some commentators have interpreted this evidence as showing that, contrary to the implications of Hicksian theory, individuals are subject to loss aversion [Kahneman, Knetsch, and Thaler 1990]. Others have argued that large WTA-WTP divergences may be the result of low elasticities of substitution between income and the goods being valued [Hanemann 1991]. Relatively few tests for WTA-WTP divergences have controlled for income and substitution effects. Shogren et al. [1994] test for the impact of substitution effects by eliciting WTP and WTA valuations for two kinds of good, "market" (represented by candy bars) and "nonmarket" (stringent screening of food for various pathogens). They find that, after subjects have gained experience of the experiment's incentive mechanism, there are significant WTA-WTP divergences for nonmarket goods, but not for the market good. Hypothesizing that the relevant elasticities of substitution are smaller for nonmarket than for market goods, Shogren et al. interpret their results as evidence that large WTA-WTP divergences can be caused by substitution effects. However, in the absence of any direct measure of elasticities of substitution, this interpretation can only be speculative. Countervailing evidence has come from experiments that have found significant WTA-WTP divergences after controlling for income and substitution effects [Knetsch and Sinden, 1984, p. 512; Knetsch, 1989].

Reference-dependent theory offers one explanation of the observed tendency for WTA to exceed WTP. However, since the discovery of WTA-WTP divergences predates the development of reference-dependent theory, this evidence cannot be regarded as a powerful test of that theory. Our strategy is to derive a range of new predictions from the theory and to test these.

III. EXPERIMENTAL DESIGN: BASIC PRINCIPLES

Our experimental design is built around the following setup. As in Section I, consider an individual who consumes a specific good (good 1) and a composite commodity (good 2). Let x_1', x_1'' be two levels of consumption of good 1, such that $x_1' < x_1''$. Similarly, let x_2', x_2'' be two levels of consumption of good 2, such that $x_2' < x_2''$. Consider four bundles $\mathbf{a}, \mathbf{b}, \mathbf{c}, \mathbf{d}$ defined by $a_1 = c_1 = x_1'$, $b_1 = d_1 = x_1''$, $a_2 = b_2 = x_2''$, $c_2 = d_2 = x_2'$. Now consider the following ways of posing the question, "Is $\mathbf{a}$ preferred to $\mathbf{d}$?"

(1) Is $WTP_{21}(x_1', x_1'', x_2'')$ less than $x_2'' - x_2'$? If preferences are Hicksian, and if the answer to this question is yes, we may infer that $\mathbf{a} \succ \mathbf{d}$. To see why, look at Figure 10.3, in which I' and I'' are Hicksian indifference curves. If preferences are reference-dependent, it becomes relevant that $WTP_{21}(x_1', x_1'', x_2'')$ is based on an initial endowment of $\mathbf{a}$. Thus, if the answer to the question is yes, we may infer that $\mathbf{a} \succ_{\mathbf{a}} \mathbf{d}$. Preferences inferred from valuations in this way will be called *implicit preferences*.

(2) Is $WTA_{21}(x_1', x_1'', x_2')$ less than $x_2'' - x_2'$? If the answer is yes, the implicit Hicksian preference is $\mathbf{a} \succ \mathbf{d}$, and the implicit reference-dependent preference is $\mathbf{a} \succ_{\mathbf{d}} \mathbf{d}$.

(3) Is $EL_{21}(x_1', x_1'', x_2')$ less than $x_2'' - x_2'$? If the answer is yes, the implicit Hicksian preference is $\mathbf{a} \succ \mathbf{d}$, and the implicit reference-dependent preference is $\mathbf{a} \succ_{\mathbf{b}} \mathbf{d}$.

Figure 10.3.

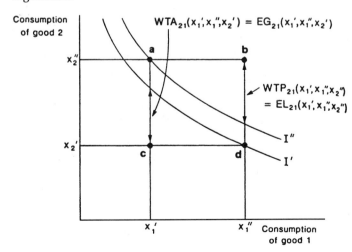

(4) Is $EG_{21}(x_1', x_1'', x_2')$ less than $x_2'' - x_2'$? If the answer is yes, the implicit Hicksian preference is $\mathbf{a} \succ \mathbf{d}$, and the implicit reference-dependent preference is $\mathbf{a} \succ_c \mathbf{d}$.

Hicksian theory implies that the implicit preference between $\mathbf{a}$ and $\mathbf{d}$ should be the same, irrespective of whether it is derived from answers to the questions (1), (2), (3), or (4). In contrast, reference-dependent theory allows the four implicit preferences to differ, because each is based on a different reference point. The loss aversion assumption implies the following propositions about changes in the ranking of $\mathbf{a}$ and $\mathbf{d}$ as the reference point shifts:

(1) Comparing reference points $\mathbf{a}$, $\mathbf{b}$: $\mathbf{b}$ favors $\mathbf{d}$.
(2) Comparing reference points $\mathbf{a}$, $\mathbf{c}$: $\mathbf{c}$ favors $\mathbf{d}$.
(3) Comparing reference points $\mathbf{b}$, $\mathbf{d}$: $\mathbf{d}$ favors $\mathbf{d}$.
(4) Comparing reference points $\mathbf{c}$, $\mathbf{d}$: $\mathbf{d}$ favors $\mathbf{d}$.

Thus, reference-dependent theory makes specific predictions about the directions of any differences between the implicit rankings of $\mathbf{a}$ and $\mathbf{d}$ derived from (1), (2), (3), and (4). So by eliciting the four measures, $WTP_{21}(x_1', x_1'', x_2'')$, $WTA_{21}(x_1', x_1'', x_2')$, $EL_{21}(x_1', x_1'', x_2'')$, and $EG_{21}(x_1', x_1'', x_2')$, we can test whether implicit rankings vary with reference points as reference-dependent theory predicts. Notice that all four implicit rankings are of *the same* bundles $\mathbf{a}$ and $\mathbf{d}$: thus, this test controls for all Hicksian income and substitution effects.

So far in this section, we have considered valuations of good 1 (the specific good) in units of good 2 (the composite commodity). But it is also possible to test reference-dependent theory by eliciting valuations of good 2 in units of good 1. This gives us four more ways of asking whether $\mathbf{a}$ is preferred to $\mathbf{d}$ (see Figure 10.4, which is drawn on the same principles as Figure 10.3):

(5) Is $WTA_{12}(x_2', x_2'', x_1')$ greater than $x_1'' - x_1'$? If the answer is yes, the implicit Hicksian preference is $\mathbf{a} \succ \mathbf{d}$, and the implicit reference-dependent preference is $\mathbf{a} \succ_a \mathbf{d}$.
(6) Is $WTP_{12}(x_2', x_2'', x_1')$ greater than $x_1'' - x_1'$? If the answer is yes, the implicit Hicksian preference is $\mathbf{a} \succ \mathbf{d}$, and the implicit reference-dependent preference is $\mathbf{a} \succ_d \mathbf{d}$.
(7) Is $EL_{12}(x_2', x_2'', x_1')$ greater than $x_1'' - x_1'$? If the answer is yes, the implicit Hicksian preference is $\mathbf{a} \succ \mathbf{d}$, and the implicit reference-dependent preference is $\mathbf{a} \succ_b \mathbf{d}$.
(8) Is $EG_{12}(x_2', x_2'', x_1')$ greater than $x_1'' - x_1'$? If the answer is yes, the implicit Hicksian preference is $\mathbf{a} \succ \mathbf{d}$, and the implicit reference-dependent preference is $\mathbf{a} \succ_c \mathbf{d}$.

By comparing the implicit rankings generated by (5)–(8), we can make further tests of whether preferences vary with reference points in the directions predicted by reference-dependent theory.

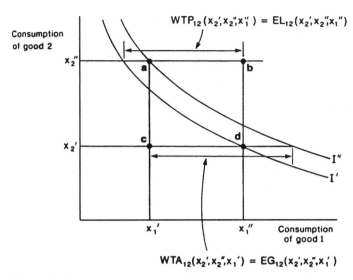

$$WTP_{12}(x_2', x_2'', x_1'') = EL_{12}(x_2', x_2'', x_1'')$$

$$WTA_{12}(x_2', x_2'', x_1') = EG_{12}(x_2', x_2'', x_1')$$

Figure 10.4.

Comparisons between the implicit rankings generated by these elicitation methods can also be used to investigate the effect of changes in the *response mode* (i.e., the units in which valuations are expressed). For example, compare $WTP_{21}(x_1', x_1'', x_2'')$ and $WTA_{12}(x_2', x_2'', x_1')$. Each of these measures generates an implicit ranking of **a** and **d**, conditional on the same reference point **a**. Hicksian theory and reference-dependent theory both imply that these two implicit rankings should be the same. However, there are theories (some of which have been developed by Kahneman and Tversky themselves) which suggest that implicit preferences may differ according to the response mode. The guiding idea behind these theories is that each response mode makes certain information, certain concepts, or certain decision-making heuristics particularly salient to the individual [Tversky and Kahneman 1974; Tversky, Sattath, and Slovic 1988]. For example, observations of preference reversal have been explained by the hypothesis that different decision-making heuristics are used, according to whether tasks require responses in the form of binary choices or in the form of money valuations [Slovic and Lichtenstein 1983; Tversky, Slovic, and Kahneman 1990].

The *contingent weighting* theory of Tversky, Sattath, and Slovic [1988] has the closest application to the decision problems considered in this paper. This theory is designed to apply to "matching tasks" in which subjects compare two options, each of which can be described in two dimensions of desirability (e.g., two candidates for a job are each described by two test scores, one for literacy and one for numeracy). One option is fully described, while the other has one missing piece of information (e.g., the numeracy score for one of the candidates). Subjects are instructed to fill in this missing information so as to make the two options equally desirable. Here, the response mode is the dimension of the missing information (e.g., numeracy). Contingent weighting theory predicts that subjects will give greater implicit weight to any given dimension if it is the response mode than if it is not.

The valuation measures considered in this paper might be interpreted as the products of matching tasks. For example, suppose that an individual is endowed with $\mathbf{a} = (x_1', x_2')$ and is asked to state the value x_2^* at which she would be indifferent about exchanging $\mathbf{a}$ for (x_1'', x_2^*). This is a matching task in which the response mode is good 2. But it can also be understood as a method of eliciting WTP, since $x_2'' - x_2^* = WTP_{21}(x_1', x_1'', x_2'')$: see Figure 10.3. If the decision tasks of our experiment are treated as equivalent to matching tasks, contingent weighting theory implies that changing the response mode from good 2 to good 1 should tend to shift implicit preferences between $\mathbf{a}$ and $\mathbf{d}$ in favor of $\mathbf{d}$ (the option that is better on the dimension of good 1).

IV. EXPERIMENTAL DESIGN: DETAILS

The experiment was designed to elicit preferences between two bundles $\mathbf{a}$ and $\mathbf{d}$, using each of the eight methods described in Section III, for each of two specifications of the bundles $\mathbf{a}$, $\mathbf{b}$, $\mathbf{c}$, $\mathbf{d}$. In one specification the two goods were cans of Coke (good 1) and money (good 2), with $x_1' = 2$ cans, $x_1'' = 6$ cans, $x_2' = £2.20$, $x_2'' = £3.00$. In the other specification the goods were vouchers for chocolates (good 1) and money (good 2), with $x_1' = 2$ chocolates, $x_1'' = 12$ chocolates, $x_2' = £1.50$, $x_2'' £3.50$. The vouchers were redeemable at a local specialist chocolate shop for given numbers of a premium range of Belgian chocolates. These chocolates sell at approximately £0.40 each (they are normally sold by weight).

In choosing these particular values of x_1', x_1'', x_2', x_2'', we recognized that our design would fail as a test of reference-dependent theory if $\mathbf{a}$ was so attractive relative to $\mathbf{d}$ that, for all elicitation methods, almost all subjects reported an implicit preference for $\mathbf{a}$. Equally, it would fail if $\mathbf{d}$ was too attractive relative to $\mathbf{a}$. We used a pilot study to identify specifications of $\mathbf{a}$ and $\mathbf{d}$ such that, aggregating over all eight elicitation methods, we could expect significant proportions of subjects to report each of the implicit preferences $\mathbf{a} \succ \mathbf{d}$ and $\mathbf{d} \succ \mathbf{a}$.

We chose Coke and luxury chocolates to represent two very different types of good. We expected that many of our subjects would buy Coke fairly regularly, while few would have much experience in buying this type of chocolate. There are a number of reasons for thinking that WTA-WTP disparities might be less in the case of the regularly consumed good. First, subjects might be expected to be surer of their own preferences in the case of Coke, and thus their valuations might be less liable to stochastic variation and error. Second, subjects who know the market price of a good might use this as an "anchor" when thinking about their own valuations, with the result that valuations for Coke might tend to cluster around its price. Third, if a subject is a regular Coke buyer, she might think of any cans of Coke received in an experiment as representing money savings (she needs to buy fewer cans) rather than extra consumption. If she does, loss aversion might be expected to have less psychological impact.

The experiment involved 156 subjects, mostly undergraduate and post-graduate students, recruited on the campus of the University of East Anglia. After inspecting samples of the goods, receiving pre-scripted instructions, and carrying out some practice exercises (described later), each subject was given a series of eighteen decision tasks. Each subject knew that one of these tasks, to be picked at random at the end of the experiment, would be for real. Of the eighteen tasks, eight were designed to test the implications of reference-dependent theory; we shall focus on these.[5]

Each such task was described by a display on a VDU screen. At the top of the screen were the words: "If this question is selected, you will be given . . . ," followed by a specification of an endowment of money and of Coke or chocolates (e.g., ". . . £3.50 and 12 chocolates"). The next text on the screen was: "In addition to this, you will be required to accept either K or L" (or some other pair of letters). The letters denoted alternative options, which were then described in terms of transfers of money or the other good or both from the subject to the experimenters ("you give us") or from the experimenters to the subject ("we give you"). The second option was fully described. For the first option one quantity (of money or of the other good) was unspecified. In place of this quantity there was an empty box. If the unspecified quantity was a transfer from the subject to the experimenters, we effectively asked the subject to state the highest value of this quantity at which she would still prefer the first option. If the unspecified quantity was a transfer from the experimenters to the subject, we effectively asked the subject to state the lowest value at which she would still prefer the first option. The precise mechanism used to elicit responses will be described later.

This general format can be used to elicit answers to any of the questions (1)–(8) considered in Section III. For example, one task, based on an endowment of £3.50 and 12 chocolates, involved the options: "You give us. . . in cash" and "You give us 10 chocolates." This elicits EL_{21}(2 chocolates, 12 chocolates, £3.50). Another task, based on an endowment of £3.00 and 2 cans of Coke, involved the options: "We give you . . . cans of Coke and you give us £0.80 in cash" and "Nothing" (i.e., no change from the initial endowment). This elicits WTA_{12}(£2.20, £3.00, 2 cans).

In using this design to test reference-dependent theory, we treat the endowment for each task as the relevant reference point. Notice that, for a subject facing a given task, the relevant endowment is merely conditional: she will be

---

[5] The other ten tasks involved two other goods (bottles of sparkling wine and boxes of teabags) and were of two types. One type of task had the same format as those described in this paper, and elicited *WTP* or *WTA* valuations for the relevant good. The other type of task required a choice between two fully described options. This part of the experiment, which we plan to report in another paper, was designed to test whether implicit preferences elicited by valuation tasks are systematically different from preferences revealed in binary choices.

given it only if that task is later picked to be the one that is for real. This conditionality may weaken the tendency for a subject to integrate her endowment into her mental conception of her "current position." Some relevant evidence is provided by Loewenstein and Adler [1995], who compare WTA valuations reported by subjects who have actually been endowed with a good with corresponding valuations reported by subjects whose endowments are conditional on random events. The former valuations tend to be significantly greater than the latter. This suggests that our design may fail to pick up the full effects of shifts in reference points. In this respect, we are subjecting reference-dependent theory to a particularly severe test.

To ensure incentive compatibility, we used a Becker-DeGroot-Marschak [1964] mechanism. We believe that this mechanism is preferable to the repeated auctions used in some recent investigations of WTA-WTP divergences (e.g., Coursey, Hovis and Schulze [1987]; Kahneman, Knetsch, and Thaler [1990]; and Shogren et al. [1994]). It is well-known that an individual's reported valuation of a good can be influenced by cues which carry suggestions about the good's real value [Mitchell and Carson 1989, pp. 240–46] or which can work as anchors in an anchor-and-adjustment heuristic [Tversky and Kahneman 1974]. If subjects bid against one another in repeated auctions for the same good, and if the market price determined in each auction is then reported to the subjects, later bids may be influenced by earlier prices. A Becker-DeGroot-Marschak mechanism is equivalent to an auction in which the only bidders are the subject herself and a random device. This ensures that subjects' responses cannot contaminate one another.

The incentive mechanism worked in the following way. Recall that the description of the first option in each task included an empty box in place of a quantity. Subjects were told: "The computer will pick an amount at random to write in the box. Please complete the following statement." If the amount in the box referred to a transfer from the subject to the experimenters, the statement had the following form: "If this question is selected, I (i.e., the subject) will take K if the amount in the box is . . . or less. Otherwise, I will take L." If the amount in the box referred to a transfer from the experimenters to the subject, "or more" was substituted for "or less." The subject's task was to fill in the blank in the statement. This was done by using the up and down arrow keys on the keyboard, which increased or decreased the amount in the statement in steps of five pence (for money) or one unit (for cans of Coke or chocolates) from an initial value of zero. When the blank referred to a transfer from the subject to the experimenters, the subject was not allowed to give a response greater than her endowment of the relevant good. It was explained that the maximum permitted response would guarantee that the subject received the second option.

At the end of the experiment, one decision problem was selected at random and displayed on the screen. The specified endowments of money and the other good were then handed to the subject. A random device, represented by a display of a ball spinning around a roulette wheel, picked an amount to write in the box for the first option. This, combined with the statement that the subject had completed, determined which of the two options the subject had to accept, and any necessary exchanges were then carried out.

Clearly, it is essential for this design that subjects understand the incentive compatibility of the Becker–DeGroot–Marschak mechanism. In each session about 30 minutes were spent on instructing subjects by means of four practice exercises. These exercises used the same screen displays as were used in the main experiment, but with a well-known brand of individually packaged biscuits as the nonmoney good in place of Coke or chocolates. The exercises elicited in turn: WTP_{21}, EG_{12}, WTA_{12}, and EL_{21}. In each exercise, after the subject had completed the relevant statement, the "roulette wheel" was used, just as it would be at the end of the experiment, to determine the (in this practice case, hypothetical) outcome for the subject. Subjects were guided through the first two exercises by the experimenters reading from a script. The oral instructions explained in simple terms the incentive compatibility of the Becker-DeGroot-Marschak mechanism. Subjects did the remaining two exercises on their own.

To allow us to check subjects' understanding of the design, each subject had to answer two multiple-choice questions – one as part of the second exercise, the other as part of the fourth exercise. These questions were presented after the subject had completed the statement, but before the roulette wheel was displayed. For example, the two options for the second exercise were "We give you . . . biscuits" and "We give you £2.00." Suppose that the subject's response had been 10. Then the multiple-choice question might be:[6] "If the computer wrote 11 in the box, which of these options would you be required to accept? a: We give you 11 biscuits. b: We give you 10 biscuits. c: We give you £2.00." The other multiple-choice question had the same format. Subjects were not allowed to ask for advice while answering these questions, but if a subject gave the wrong answer, an experimenter provided further explanation to that subject. In most cases, incorrect answers seemed to be the result of carelessness or error rather than of misunderstandings of the principles of the incentive system. Of the 156 subjects, 123 gave correct answers to both test questions, 15 gave the correct answer to the second question but not to the first, 16 gave the correct answer to the first but not to the second, and 2 answered both questions incorrectly. The overall success rate of 89 percent correct answers suggests that most subjects had a clear understanding of the incentive system.

Recall that the experiment was designed to elicit eight distinct valuation measures for each of two specifications of the set {a, b, c, d}. Ideally, we would have liked to use a completely between-subjects design, so as to exclude any possibility that subjects' responses to one task might be influenced by their responses to another, but this would have required a prohibitively large sample size. As a

---

[6] There were two alternative forms of the question, of which one was picked at random. One question was based on the hypothesis that the amount picked by the computer was slightly larger than the subject's response, the other on the hypothesis that it was slightly smaller.

compromise solution, we divided subjects at random into two subgroups (here labeled I and II), and each subgroup faced four of the eight decision tasks for each of the "Coke" and "chocolate" specifications.[7] By spacing out these four related tasks among the eighteen tasks for the whole experiment, we hoped to reduce cross-task contamination as much as possible. In addition, we randomized the order of related tasks, independently for each subject. Thus, if any contamination were to occur, it would not have any systematic effect on our results.

Our statistical tests use the null hypothesis that each subject acts on Hicksian preferences, but with some random variation. We represent this random variation by a *random preference* model [Becker, DeGroot, and Marschak 1963; Loomes and Sugden 1995]. For each individual in such a model, there is a probability distribution over a set of alternative preference orderings, each of which satisfies the restrictions imposed by the relevant theory (in the present case, Hicksian consumer theory). In each decision task the individual acts on one of these orderings, drawn independently and at random from the set.

On the assumption that the null hypothesis is true, we can infer a *strict* implicit preference between **a** and **d** from each response. Recall that in each task, each subject chose one of a set of *discrete* alternative responses (amounts of money in multiples of five pence, numbers of chocolates, or cans of Coke). For example, consider the task that elicits WTP_{21} for Coke. The subject is endowed with **a** (i.e., 2 cans of Coke and £3.00). She is asked to state the highest multiple of five pence that she is willing to pay for four extra cans of Coke. If her response is £x, she is reporting that she is willing to pay £x but not willing to pay £$x + 0.05$; so the true value of WTP_{21} expressed on a continuous scale, is in the range $x \leq WTP_{21} < x + 0.05$. Thus, a response of £0.80 or more reveals the implicit preference **d** > **a** (where **d** is 6 cans of Coke and £2.20); a response of less than £0.80 reveals the implicit preference **a** > **d**. A similar analysis applies to every other task.

Our null hypothesis of stochastic Hicksian preferences implies that, for any given individual in the experiment and for given **a**, **d**, the probability that she will reveal the implicit preference **a** > **d** is constant across decision tasks. Since the two subgroups are random samples from the same population, this implication can be extended to comparisons across subgroups: the probability that a randomly selected individual will reveal the implicit preference **a** > **d** is constant across both decision tasks and subgroups.

V. RESULTS

The results are summarized in Tables 10.1 and 10.2. Table 10.1 refers to the eight tasks that involved Coke. Each row refers to a distinct task. The first

---

[7] In assigning tasks to subgroups, we tried to ensure that the tasks faced by any given subject were as different from one another as possible. Thus, whenever two valuations (e.g., WTP_{21} and EL_{21}) were equivalent to one another according to Hicksian theory, one was elicited from one subgroup and one from the other.

Table 10.1. **Implicit Preferences in Tasks Involving Coke**

Subgroup	Response Mode	Measure	Reference Point	$a \succ d$	$d \succ a$
I	money	WTP_{21}	a	60.0	40.0
II	money	EL_{21}	b	50.0	50.0
I	money	EG_{21}	c	26.3	73.7
II	money	WTA_{21}	d	15.8	84.2
I	Coke	WTA_{12}	a	43.7	56.3
I	Coke	EL_{12}	b	43.7	56.3
II	Coke	EG_{12}	c	35.5	64.5
II	Coke	WTP_{12}	d	15.8	84.2

Note: $n = 80$ for subgroup I; $n = 76$ for subgroup II.

column shows which subgroup faced this task; the next three columns identify the task by response mode, valuation measure, and reference point. The last two columns report the distribution of implicit preferences between **a** and **d** (reported values are percentages, and sample sizes are given below the tables). Table 10.2 is constructed in a similar way, but the data refer to the eight tasks that involved chocolates.

V.A. Reference Point Effects

We begin by examining the effect of changing the reference point, holding the response mode constant. If reference-dependent theory is correct, then the proportion of subjects with an implicit preference for **a** over **d** should be less when the reference point is **b** or **c** than when it is **a**, and less when it is **d** than when it is **b** or **c**.

Inspecting the first four rows of Table 10.1 (the data for Coke when the response mode is money), notice that, as the reference point shifts from **a** (row 1) to **d** (row 4), there is a marked decrease in the proportion of subjects with the implicit preference $a \succ d$ (from 60 percent to 16 percent). Notice also that the proportions revealing an implicit preference for **a** when the reference point is **b** or **c** (50 percent and 26 percent, respectively) are intermediate between the proportions observed for reference points **a** and **d**. A similar pattern is observed in the data for Coke when the response mode is Coke, and for chocolates for both response modes (Table 10.2).[8] Thus, the data appear to follow the pattern implied by reference-dependent theory.

Could these data also be explained in terms of random variation within a stochastic Hicksian preference model? Table 10.3 reports a set of tests of association between the distribution of implicit preferences between **a** and **d** and the

---

[8] With one exception: in the data for Coke when the response mode is Coke, the proportion of subjects with the implicit preference $a \succ d$ when the reference point is **b** is equal to the corresponding proportion when the reference point is **a**. Reference-dependent theory would lead us to expect this proportion to be lower when the reference point is **b**.

Table 10.2. Implicit Preferences in Tasks Involving Chocolates

Subgroup	Response Mode	Measure	Reference Point	$a \succ d$	$d \succ a$
I	money	WTP_{21}	a	92.5	7.5
II	money	EL_{21}	b	92.1	7.9
I	money	EG_{21}	c	70.0	30.0
II	money	WTA_{21}	d	64.5	35.5
I	chocolate	WTA_{12}	a	92.5	7.5
I	chocolate	EL_{12}	b	75.0	25.0
II	chocolate	EG_{12}	c	81.6	18.4
II	chocolate	WTP_{12}	d	56.6	43.4

Note: $n = 80$ for subgroup I; $n = 76$ for subgroup II.

reference points used to elicit them. The extreme left-hand column indicates the reference points being compared. The remaining columns contain chi-square statistics, one column for each combination of good (Coke or chocolates) and response mode. These statistics are based on different combinations of rows from Tables 10.1 and 10.2, though using raw data rather than percentages. One value is recorded for each pairwise comparison between reference points except for that between **b** and **c**, where reference-dependent theory makes no definite prediction. In addition, the final row of the table provides an overall test of association combining data for all four reference points.

The general null hypothesis tested is that of no association between implicit preferences and reference points, as predicted by Hicksian theory. These tests indicate significant violation of that theory: the null is rejected in fourteen out of the twenty pairwise comparisons and hence, unsurprisingly, in the four aggregate tests too.

Two of the pairwise comparisons in which the null is rejected are instances of the well-known divergence between *WTA* and *WTP* (comparisons between

Table 10.3. Tests for Reference Point Effects

Comparison	Good: Coke Response Mode		Good: Chocolates Response Mode	
	Money	Coke	Money	Coke
a, b	1.58	0.0	0.09	9.00**
a, c	18.58**	1.10	13.29**	4.16*
a, d	32.19**	14.47**	18.35**	26.82**
b, d	20.15**	14.47**	17.07**	5.90*
c, d	2.56	7.76**	0.54	11.12**
a, b, c, d	1.62**	17.74**	30.99**	29.45**

*indicates significance at the 5-percent level.
**indicates significance at the 1-percent level.

the reference points **a** and **d** when the response mode is money). These results add to the existing body of evidence of *WTA-WTP* disparities. Since our design has controlled for income and substitution effects, these disparities are clearly contrary to Hicksian theory; and they are in the direction predicted by reference-dependent theory.

The two comparisons between **a** and **d** when the response mode is the consumption good provide a new type of test for a divergence between *WTA* and *WTP*. Here, too, the differences between implicit preferences are highly significant, contrary to Hicksian theory, and in the direction predicted by reference-dependent theory.

Clearly, any theory that predicts a change in implicit preferences as the reference point shifts from **a** to **d** must also predict such a change for at least one of the reference point pairs (**a**, **b**) and (**b**, **d**), and similarly for at least one of the pairs (**a**, **c**) and (**c**, **d**). Thus, we need to be careful before claiming that the evidence from (**a**, **b**), (**b**, **d**), (**a**, **c**) and (**c**, **d**) comparisons provides *additional* support for reference-dependent theory. But if we were to find significant (and correctly signed) changes in implicit preference for both (**a**, **b**) and (**b**, **d**), this *would* be new evidence in favor of reference-dependent theory, and not merely a predictable consequence of *WTA–WTP* disparities. Similarly, significant changes in implicit preferences for both (**a**, **c**) and (**c**, **d**) would be new evidence for that theory. There are eight cases in which such evidence can be looked for (two in each column of chi-square statistics in Table 10.3). It can be found in two of those cases: the combination of (**a**, **c**) and (**c**, **d**) for chocolates with chocolate as the response mode, and the combination of (**a**, **b**) and (**b**, **d**) for chocolates with chocolate as the response mode.

On the basis of pairwise comparisons, then, we cannot draw firm conclusions about the effects of having **b** or **c**, rather than **a** or **d**, as reference points.[9] One way to pursue this question further would be to analyze the data at a more aggregated level. In subsection V.C below we shall present such an analysis.

V.B. Response Mode Effects

Table 10.4 reports a set of eight tests for response mode effects. These are chi-square tests of association between the distribution of implicit preferences over **a**, **d** and the response mode used to elicit them; in each test the reference point is held constant. Recall that contingent weighting theory implies that shifting the

---

[9] One hypothesis that goes some way toward organizing the data is that there are no systematic differences between *WTP* and *EL* responses, or between *WTA* and *EG* responses. This hypothesis would lead us to expect no significant differences in implicit preferences over the reference point pairs (**a**, **b**) or (**c**, **d**) when the response mode is money, and no significant differences over (**a**, **c**) or (**b**, **d**) when the response mode is the consumption good. Five out of the six insignificant chi-square statistics fit this pattern, but there are three significant statistics that do not fit it.

Table 10.4. Tests for Response Mode Effects

Reference Point	Good: Coke	Good: Chocolates
a	4.23*(−)	0.0
b	0.61 (−)	8.21**(−)
c	1.58 (+)	2.84 (+)
d	0.0	0.99 (−)

* indicates significance at the 5-percent level.
** indicates significance at the 1-percent level.

response mode from money to the consumption good should tend to reduce the proportion of subjects with the implicit preference a ≻ d (see Section III). To aid interpretation, we have placed a (−) in cells where switching the response mode from money to the consumption good has reduced the proportion of subjects with the implicit preference a ≻ d and a (+) where there has been the opposite effect. There are significant differences in two cases, and both have changes in the direction predicted by contingent weighting theory. But while this suggests that changes in the response mode can matter, there is no obvious pattern in the data as a whole. Again, it seems that a more aggregated analysis is needed if we are to draw firm conclusions.

V.C. Econometric Analysis

Table 10.5 presents a summary of an econometric analysis of the aggregated data. Two models, one for each of the goods, were estimated using the Probit routine in LIMDEP. The dependent variable was the implicit preference ranking of a and d (coded 0 if a ≺ d; 1 if a ≻ d). Three dummy variables, BREF, CREF, DREF, were introduced to model the impact of changes in the reference point, using reference point a as the benchmark. BREF was coded with a value of 1 when the reference point was b, 0 otherwise; CREF and DREF were constructed in a similar way for reference points c and d, respectively. Finally, a dummy variable RMODE was introduced, with a value of one when the response mode

Table 10.5. Aggregate Probit Analysis

	Good: Coke	Good: Chocolates
Constant	0.073 (0.652)	1.504 (9.425)
Regression coefficient with respect to:		
BREF	−0.111 (−0.785)	−0.466 (−2.455)
CREF	−0.534 (−3.699)	−0.749 (−4.084)
DREF	−1.035 (−6.561)	−1.174 (−6.531)
RMODE	−0.084 (−0.793)	−0.125 (−1.070)
log-likelihood	−380.936	−300.909
log-L (slopes = 0)	−409.072	−327.163
$X^2(4)$	56.271	52.507

t-ratios are in parentheses.
Dependent variable = (0 if d ≻ a; 1 if a ≻ d).

was the consumption good, zero otherwise. The final row of the table reports likelihood ratio statistics for the two models.

A priori expectations based on the Hicksian model suggest $BREF = CREF = DREF = RMODE = 0$. Alternatively, reference-dependent theory suggests that $0 > BREF, CREF > DREF$, and contingent weighting theory implies $RMODE < 0$.

The estimation results may be summarized as follows. The restriction that all slope coefficients are zero (the Hicksian model) is confidently rejected for both goods on the basis of the likelihood ratio test (1 percent). There is little support for a response mode effect: although $RMODE$ is correctly signed in each case, it is never significantly different from zero. The results, however, are largely consistent with the implications of reference-dependent theory: all six reference point dummies are correctly signed, they are strongly significant (1 percent) in all but one case ($BREF$ is not significant in the model for Coke), and $DREF$ has the largest quantitative effect in each case. In both models, each of the hypotheses $BREF = DREF$ and $CREF = DREF$ can be rejected at the 1 percent level in favor of the alternative hypotheses that $BREF > DREF$ and $CREF > DREF$.

V.D. Comparing Coke with Chocolates

As explained in Section IV, when designing the experiment, we thought of Coke and chocolates as representatives of different types of good: we could be fairly confident that many subjects would have experience in buying and consuming Coke, while few would have such experience for the premium brand of chocolates that we used. Our prior hunch was that reference point effects, if they occurred at all, would be stronger for chocolates than for Coke.

In fact, our results show considerable similarity between responses for the two goods. In particular, for each good (and for either response mode), moving the reference point from **a** to **d** is associated with a large and statistically significant reduction in the proportion of subjects with an implicit preference for **a** over **d**. However, the data for chocolates are marginally more supportive of reference-dependent theory than are the data for Coke.[10] Since our experiment was not designed to be a formal test of the hypothesis that the day-to-day experience of buying a good tends to reduce reference point effects, we cannot draw firm conclusions on this issue.

VI. CONCLUSIONS

The principal objective of the research reported in this paper was to test a set of predictions derived from the loss aversion hypothesis of the theory of reference-dependent preferences. We have identified eight alternative methods of eliciting

---

[10] The number of significant pairwise comparisons in Table 10.3 is greater when the good is chocolate than when it is Coke; all three of the reference point dummies are significant in the chocolate equation while only two are in the Coke equation.

an individual's preferences between money and a consumption good; most previous investigations of disparities between valuation measures have focused on just two of these. Hicksian consumer theory implies that these methods will elicit a common system of preferences, while reference-dependent theory predicts systematic divergences between them. Our main result is that significant divergences do occur, and that these divergences are in the directions predicted by reference-dependent theory.

Our experiment elicited valuations for two private consumption goods, one of which is sold in almost every supermarket and would have been extremely familiar to most subjects. The experiment was incentive-compatible and controlled for income and substitution effects. In respect of divergences between willingness-to-accept (WTA) and willingness-to-pay (WTP) valuations, our results are consistent with those of a large number of other experiments and field surveys. In the light of this evidence, it seems that the influence of loss aversion is a robust effect.

If loss aversion is a fundamental property of many people's preferences, then observed divergences between different valuation measures must be attributed, not to biases in elicitation methods, but to the limitations of Hicksian consumer theory. The challenge for economics is then to design measures of welfare change that are compatible with reference-dependent preferences.

However, our results are open to an alternative interpretation. It might be suggested that loss aversion, although resulting from predictable psychological mechanisms of the kind modeled by reference-dependent theory, is a relatively superficial phenomenon which would quickly be eroded by the experience of buying and selling the relevant good. On this view, experienced economic agents in real-world markets might behave according to Hicksian theory, even though laboratory subjects and survey respondents do not. This is an issue that clearly needs to be investigated. We suggest that a precondition for such an investigation is that defenders of Hicksian theory propose testable hypotheses about the precise mechanisms by which market experience induces Hicksian behavior.

If such a hypothesis were to be proposed and to be confirmed by empirical tests, then preferences revealed in market behavior might be interpreted as "true" preferences. However, economists would still be left with the problem of discovering an unbiased method of eliciting individuals' preferences for nontraded goods, and so it would still be important to understand the way loss aversion impacts on survey responses.

There seems to be a consensus in the contingent valuation literature that WTP measures should be preferred to WTA ones (e.g., Arrow et al. [1993]), but the merits and demerits of other measures are rarely discussed. Those economists who argue that divergences between WTA and WTP would disappear with market experience have usually predicted that market-induced convergence would be toward initial WTP valuations (e.g., Coursey, Hovis, and Schulze [1987]). But if reference-dependent theory is accepted as the explanation of those divergences, it is not obvious that *WTP* is the natural point of convergence. For example, suppose that the difference between individuals with and without market experience is that the latter tend to overweight losses. Then we might expect equivalent gain measures, which establish equivalences between gains of the relevant good and gains of money, to be less biased than *WTP* measures, in which losses of money compensate for gains of the good. We hope that our work will lead to further investigation of the possibility of eliciting preferences using welfare measures other than *WTP* and *WTA*.

11. Diminishing Marginal Utility of Wealth Cannot Explain Risk Aversion

Matthew Rabin

1. INTRODUCTION

Economists pervasively explain widespread risk aversion by the realistic assumption that people generally have diminishing marginal utility of wealth. Indeed, diminishing marginal utility of wealth probably explains much of our aversion to large-scale financial risk: We dislike vast uncertainty in lifetime wealth because the marginal value of a dollar when we are poor is higher than when we are rich.

Within the expected-utility framework, the concavity of the utility-of-wealth function is not only sufficient to explain risk aversion – it is also necessary: Diminishing marginal utility of wealth is the *sole* explanation for risk aversion. Unfortunately, it is an utterly implausible explanation for appreciable risk aversion, except when the stakes are very large. Any utility-of-wealth function that does not predict absurdly severe risk aversion over very large stakes predicts negligible risk aversion over modest stakes.

Arrow (1971, p. 100) shows that an expected-utility maximizer with a differentiable utility function will always want to take a sufficiently small stake in any positive-expected-value bet. That is, expected-utility maximizers are arbitrarily close to risk neutral when stakes are arbitrarily small. Although most economists understand this formal limit result, fewer appreciate that the approximate risk-neutrality prediction holds not just for very small stakes but for quite sizable and economically important stakes as well. Diminishing marginal utility of wealth is not a plausible explanation of people's aversion to risk on the scale of $10, $100, $1,000, or even more. After illustrating and providing intuition for these claims, I shall argue that economists often reach misleading conclusions by invoking expected-utility theory to explain substantial risk aversion in contexts in which the theory actually predicts virtual risk neutrality.

2. ILLUSTRATIONS

The inability of expected-utility theory to provide a plausible account of risk aversion over modest stakes has been illustrated in writing in a variety of different contexts using standard utility functions.[1] For instance, Hansson (1988) notes that a person with constant absolute risk aversion who is indifferent between gaining $7 for sure and a 50–50 gamble of gaining either $0 or $21 prefers a sure gain of $7 to *any* lottery in which the chance of gaining positive amounts of money is less than 40% – no matter how large the potential gain.

In Rabin (forthcoming), I provide a theorem showing that such implications are not restricted to particular contexts or to particular functional specifications of the utility function. Within the expected-utility framework, for *any* concave utility function, even very little risk aversion over modest stakes implies an absurd degree of risk aversion over large stakes. The theorem is "nonparametric", and literally nothing is assumed about the utility function except that it is increasing and concave. Without invoking assumptions like constant absolute risk aversion, we can make statements of the form "If an expected-utility maximizer always turns down modest-stakes Gamble X, he or she will always turn down large-stakes Gamble Y."[2]

Suppose that, from any initial wealth level, an expected-utility maximizer turns down gambles in which he or she loses $100 or gains $110, each with 50% probability. Then he or she will turn down 50–50 bets of losing $1,000 or gaining *any* sum of money. An expected-utility maximizer who always turns down 50–50 lose-$1,000-or-gain-$1,050 bets would always turn down 50–50 bets of losing $20,000 or gaining any sum. An expected-utility maximizer who always turns down 50–50 lose-$100-or-gain-$101 bets would always turn down 50–50 bets losing $10,000 or gaining any sum. In each case, the aversion to the small bet realistically describes many people's risk attitudes, whereas the implied large-scale risk attitudes do not. Table 11.1 lists these and many more examples.

The intuition for the implications presented in Table 11.1 is that, within the expected-utility framework, turning down a modest-stakes gamble means that the marginal utility of money must diminish very quickly. Suppose you have initial wealth of W and that you reject a 50–50 lose-$10-or-gain-$11 gamble because of diminishing marginal utility of wealth. Then it must be that $U(W + 11) - U(W) \leq U(W) - U(W - 10)$. Hence, on average you value each of the dollars between W and $W + 11$ by at most 10/11 as much as you on average value each of the dollars between W and $W - 10$. By concavity, this implies that you value the dollar $W + 11$ at most 10/11 as much as you value the dollar $W - 10$. Iterating this observation, if you have the same aversion to the lose-$10-or-gain-$11 bet at wealth level $W + 21$, then you value dollar $W + 21 + 11 = W + 32$ by at most 10/11 as you value

[1] See, for example, Epstein (1992), Epstein and Zin (1990), Kandel and Stambaugh (1991), Loomes and Segal (1994), and Segal and Spivak (1990).

[2] Many of the arguments and examples in this article closely match those in Rabin (forthcoming).

Table 11.1. Examples of Risk Attitudes

If an expected-utility maximizer always turns down the 50/50 bet . . .	then he or she always turns down the 50/50 bet . . .
lose $10/gain $10.10	lose $800/gain $3,494
lose $10/gain $10.10	lose $1,000/gain $∞
lose $10/gain $11	lose $100/gain $∞
lose $100/gain $101	lose $8,000/gain $34,940
lose $100/gain $101	lose $10,000/gain $∞
lose $100/gain $105	lose $1,000/gain $1,570
lose $100/gain $105	lose $2,000/gain $∞
lose $100/gain $110	lose $1,000/gain $∞
lose $1,000/gain $1,010	lose $80,000/gain $349,400
lose $1,000/gain $1,010	lose $100,000/gain $∞
lose $1,000/gain $1,050	lose $20,000/gain $∞
lose $1,000/gain $1,100	lose $10,000/gain $∞
lose $1,000/gain $1,250	lose $6,000/gain $∞
lose $10,000/gain $11,000	lose $100,000/gain $∞
lose $10,000/gain $12,500	lose $60,000/gain $∞

dollar $W + 21 - 10 = W + 11$, which means you value dollar $W + 32$ by at most $10/11 \times 10/11 \approx 5/6$ as much as dollar $W - 10$. You will value the $W + 220$th dollar by at most $3/20$ as much as dollar $W - 10$, and the $W + 880$th dollar by at most $1/2000$ as much as dollar $W - 10$. This is an absurd rate for the value of money to deteriorate, and the rate of deterioration implied by expected-utility theory is actually quicker than this. This algebra shows that any attempt to explain attitudes to modest risk in terms of the utility of lifetime wealth would imply a paralyzing aversion to risks that everyone finds extremely attractive. It appears safe to conclude that aversion to modest-stakes risk has nothing to do with the diminishing marginal utility of wealth.

A similar argument can be developed without invoking the assumption that the person turns down the given gamble for all initial wealth levels. Suppose, for instance, we know a risk-averse person turns down 50–50 lose-$100-or-gain-$105 bets for any lifetime wealth level less than (say) $350,000 but know nothing about his or her utility function for wealth levels above $350,000, except that it is not convex. Then we know that from an initial wealth level of $340,000 the person will turn down a 50–50 bet of losing $4,000 and gaining $635,670. If we only know that a person turns down 50–50 lose-$100-or-gain-$125 bets when his or her lifetime wealth is below $100,000, we also know this person will turn down a 50–50 lose-$600-or-gain-$36 billion bet beginning from a lifetime wealth of $90,000. If an expected-utility maximizer turns down a 50–50 lose-$1,000-or-gain-$1,050 gamble whenever his or her lifetime wealth is below $500,000, then from an initial wealth level of $400,000 this person will turn down a 50–50 lose-$40,000-or-gain-$6,356,700 gamble.

The intuition is that the extreme concavity of the utility function between (say) $290,000 and $300,000 assures that the marginal utility at $300,000 is tiny compared with the marginal utility at wealth levels below $290,000; hence, even if the marginal utility does not diminish at all above $300,000, a person will not care nearly as much about money above $300,000 as he or she does below $290,000.

3. MISLEADING ECONOMICS FROM A MISLEADING EXPLANATION

Expected-utility theory seems to be a useful and adequate model of risk aversion for many purposes such as understanding the motivation for large-stakes insurance. It is attractive more generally in lieu of an equally tractable alternative model. But expected-utility theory is manifestly not close to the right explanation of risk attitudes over modest stakes. Moreover, when the specific structure of expected-utility theory is used to analyze situations involving modest stakes – such as in research that assumes that large-stake and modest-stake risk attitudes derive from the same utility-for-wealth function, it can be very misleading.

Some research methods economists currently employ rely crucially on the expected-utility interpretation of modest-scale risk aversion. One example arises in experimental economics. In recent years, there has been extensive laboratory research in economics in which participants generate payoffs for themselves on the order of $10 to $20. Researchers are often interested in inferring subjects' beliefs from their behavior. Doing so often requires knowing the relative value subjects hold for different money prizes; if a person chooses $5 in event A over $10 in event B, we know that he or she believes A is at least twice as likely as B only if we can assume that the subject likes $10 at least twice as much as $5. Yet economic theory teaches us that, because of diminishing marginal utility of wealth, we should not assume people like $10 twice as much as $5. Experimentalists have developed a clever scheme to avoid this problem. Instead of prizes of $10 and $5, subjects are given prizes such as a 10% chance of winning $100 versus a 5% chance of winning $100. Expected-utility theory says that, irrespective of the utility function, a subject values the 10% chance of a prize exactly twice as much as the 5% chance of winning the same prize.

The problem with this lottery procedure is that it is known to be sufficient for neutralizing risk aversion only when we maintain the expected-utility hypothesis. But then it is not necessary because expected-utility theory tells us that people will be virtually risk neutral in decisions on the scale of laboratory stakes. On the other hand, if we think that subjects in experiments are risk averse, then we know they are not expected-utility maximizers. Hence, the lottery procedure, which is motivated by expected-utility theory's assumptions that preferences are linear in probabilities and that risk attitudes come only from the curvature of the utility-of-wealth function, has little presumptive value in "neutralizing" risk aversion. In a sense, this cumbersome procedure exists because economists have interpreted the expected-utility hypothesis literally – but not seriously.

Indeed, the observation that diminishing marginal utility of wealth is irrelevant in laboratory experiments raises questions about interpreting experimental tests of the adequacy of expected-utility theory. For instance, while demonstrating that existing alternative models fit experimental data better than does expected-utility theory, Harless and Camerer (1994) show that expected-utility theory fits experimental data better than does "expected-value theory" – risk-neutral expected-utility theory. But because expected-utility theory implies that laboratory subjects should be risk neutral, such evidence that expected-utility theory explains behavior better than expected-value theory is evidence *against* expected-utility theory.

Expected-utility theory's presumption that risk aversion over modest-scale and large-scale risks derives from the same utility-of-wealth function relates to a widely discussed implication of the theory: that people have approximately the same risk attitude towards an aggregation of independent, identical gambles as they do towards each of the independent gambles. This observation was introduced in a famous article by Samuelson (1963), who showed that expected-utility theory implies that if (for some sufficiently wide range of initial wealth levels) a person turns down a particular gamble, then he or she should also turn down an offer to play $n > 1$ of those gambles. Hence, in the example Samuelson discussed, if, when close to his current wealth level, his colleague is unwilling to accept a 50–50 lose-$100-or-gain-$200 gamble, then he should also be unwilling to accept 100 of those gambles taken together.

This result seems counterintuitive. Although many people might reject the single 50–50 lose-$100-or-gain-$200 bet, virtually everybody would find the aggregated gamble of 100 50–50 lose-$100-or-gain-$200 bets attractive. It has an expected yield of $5,000 with negligible risk, for there is only a 1/2,300 chance of losing any money and merely a 1/62,000 chance of losing more than $1,000. A good lawyer could have you declared legally insane for turning down this gamble. In fact, the theorem in Rabin (forthcoming) implies that, under exactly the same assumptions invoked by Samuelson, an individual who turns down a 50–50 lose-$100-or-gain-$200 gamble will turn down a 50–50 lose-$200-or-gain-$20,000 gamble. This has an expected return of $9,900 – with zero chance of losing more than $200. Even a *lousy* lawyer could have you declared legally insane for turning down *this* bet.

Although Samuelson's insight 35 years ago might naturally have been used to reach the same conclusion I am reaching here – that people's aversion to modest-scale risks does not derive from diminishing marginal utility of wealth-economists have not used the insight in this way. In fact, Samuelson seemed to hypothesize that the mistake people were making was to treat probabilities on the scale of 1/2,300 or 1/62,000 as negligible. He invents a colorful "virtual quote" from Gertrude Stein – "Epsilon ain't zero" – to argue that the discrepancy between people's attitudes and the predictions of expected-utility theory is due to people's sloppiness in treating probabilities such as these as negligible. In fact, given the limited nature of the risk in this example, 1/2,300 and 1/62,000 plainly *are* negligible.[3] In one sense, Samuelson's intuition was right. The utility-of-wealth function needed to reconcile his colleague's aversion to the 50–50 lose-$100-or-gain-$200 gamble with expected-utility theory would indeed render 1/62,300 far from negligible, because it would imply that the colleague values a dollar 800,000,000,000,000,000,000,000 times as much when $10,000 poorer than at his current wealth. In this case, economists have cleverly identified the logical consequences of applying the expected-utility model to modest-scale risk, but rather than recognize the ludicrousness of those consequences, economists have insisted that we live by them. Expected-utility theory's prescription about how people who are (for whatever reason) risk averse over modest stakes should feel about these risks when amalgamated is not counterintuitive because people have poor intuitions about near-zero probabilities. It is counterintuitive because it is crazy.

4. EXPLAINING MODEST-SCALE RISK AVERSION

Many alternatives to expected-utility theory seem to provide a more plausible account of modest-scale risk attitudes and can reconcile substantial risk aversion over modest stakes and nonridiculous risk aversion over large stakes. Indeed, a direct explanation for modest-scale risk aversion is provided by what is empirically the most firmly established feature of risk preferences. *Loss aversion*, first highlighted by Kahneman and Tversky (1979), says that people are significantly more averse to losses relative to the status quo than they are attracted by gains and, more generally, that people's utilities are determined by changes in wealth rather than absolute levels. Preferences incorporating loss aversion can reconcile significant modest-scale risk aversion with reasonable degrees of large-scale risk aversion. A loss-averse person may, for instance, turn down one 50–50 lose-$100-or-gain-$200 gamble but surely accept 100 such gambles pooled together.

Kahneman and Lovallo (1993), Benartzi and Thaler (1995), and Read, Loewenstein, and Rabin (forthcoming) note that an additional departure from standard assumptions is implicated in many risk attitudes: People tend to assess risky choices in isolation and as a result behave differently than if they assessed these risks jointly. We might reject one 50–50 lose-$100-or-gain-$200 gamble on each of 100 days but accept all of these gambles if they were offered at the same time. Benartzi and Thaler (1995) argue that a related type of myopia is

---

[3] In any event, as indicated by the evidence presented in Thaler, Tversky, Kahneman, and Schwartz (1997) and Gneezy and Potter (1997), the more accurately people see the amalgamated gamble, the *more* apt they are to prefer it.

an explanation for the "equity premium puzzle" – the mystery about the curiously large premium on returns that investors seem to demand as compensation for the riskiness associated with investing in stocks. Such risk aversion can be explained with plausible loss-averse preferences if investors are assumed to assess gains and losses over a short-run (yearly) horizon rather than the longer-term horizon for which they are actually investing. This is but one illustration of how a recognition that the expected-utility model is fundamentally flawed and massively miscalibrated can lead us to consider behaviorally realistic alternatives that permit us to improve economic analysis.

12. Rational Choice and the Framing of Decisions

Amos Tversky and Daniel Kahneman

ABSTRACT. Alternative descriptions of a decision problem often give rise to different preferences, contrary to the principle of invariance that underlies the rational theory of choice. Violations of this theory are traced to the rules that govern the framing of decision and to the psychophysical principles of evaluation embodied in prospect theory. Invariance and dominance are obeyed when their application is transparent and often violated in other situations. Because these rules are normatively essential but descriptively invalid, no theory of choice can be both normatively adequate and descriptively accurate.

The modern theory of decision making under risk emerged from a logical analysis of games of chance rather than from a psychological analysis of risk and value. The theory was conceived as a normative model of an idealized decision maker, not as a description of the behavior of real people. In Schumpeter's words, it "has a much better claim to being called a logic of choice than a psychology of value" (1954, p. 1058).

The use of a normative analysis to predict and explain actual behavior is defended by several arguments. First, people are generally thought to be effective in pursuing their goals, particularly when they have incentives and opportunities to learn from experience. It seems reasonable, then, to describe choice as a maximization process. Second, competition favors rational individuals and organizations. Optimal decisions increase the chances of survival in a competitive environment, and a minority of rational individuals can sometimes impose rationality on the whole market. Third, the intuitive appeal of the axioms of rational choice makes it plausible that the theory derived from these axioms should provide an acceptable account of choice behavior.

This work was supported by contract N00014-84-K-0615 from the Office of Naval Research to Stanford University. The present article reviews our work on decision making under risk from a new perspective, discussed primarily in the first and last sections. Most of the empirical demonstrations have been reported in earlier publications. Problems 1, 2, and 6 are published here for the first time.

The thesis of the present article is that, in spite of these a priori arguments, the logic of choice does not provide an adequate foundation for a descriptive theory of decision making. We argue that the deviations of actual behavior from the normative model are too widespread to be ignored, too systematic to be dismissed as random error, and too fundamental to be accommodated by relaxing the normative system. We first sketch an analysis of the foundations of the theory of rational choice and then show that the most basic rules of the theory are commonly violated by decision makers. We conclude from these findings that the normative and the descriptive analyses cannot be reconciled. A descriptive model of choice is presented, which accounts for preferences that are anomalous in the normative theory.

I. A HIERARCHY OF NORMATIVE RULES

The major achievement of the modern theory of decision under risk is the derivation of the expected utility rule from simple principles of rational choice that make no reference to long-run considerations (von Neumann and Morgenstern 1944). The axiomatic analysis of the foundations of expected utility theory reveals four substantive assumptions – cancellation, transitivity, dominance, and invariance – besides the more technical assumptions of comparability and continuity. The substantive assumptions can be ordered by their normative appeal, from the cancellation condition, which has been challenged by many theorists, to invariance, which has been accepted by all. We briefly discuss these assumptions.

> *Cancellation.* The key qualitative property that gives rise to expected utility theory is the "cancellation" or elimination of any state of the world that yields the same outcome regardless of one's choice. This notion has been captured by different formal properties, such as the substitution axiom of von Neumann and Morgenstern (1944), the extended sure-thing principle of Savage (1954), and the independence condition of Luce and Krantz (1971). Thus, if A is preferred to B, then the prospect of winning A if it rains tomorrow (and nothing otherwise) should be preferred to the prospect of winning B if it rains tomorrow because the two prospects yield the same outcome (nothing) if there is no rain tomorrow. Cancellation is necessary to represent preference between prospects as the maximization of expected utility. The main argument for cancellation is that only one state will actually be realized, which makes it reasonable to evaluate the outcomes of options separately for each state. The choice between options should therefore depend only on states in which they yield different outcomes.
>
> *Transitivity.* A basic assumption in models of both risky and riskless choice is the transitivity of preference. This assumption is necessary and essentially sufficient for the representation of preference by an ordinal utility scale u such that A is preferred to B whenever $u(A) > u(B)$. Thus transitivity

is satisfied if it is possible to assign to each option a value that does not depend on the other available options. Transitivity is likely to hold when the options are evaluated separately but not when the consequences of an option depend on the alternative to which it is compared, as implied, for example, by considerations of regret. A common argument for transitivity is that cyclic preferences can support a "money pump," in which the intransitive person is induced to pay for a series of exchanges that returns to the initial option.

Dominance. This is perhaps the most obvious principle of rational choice: if one option is better than another in one state and at least as good in all other states, the dominant option should be chosen. A slightly stronger condition – called stochastic dominance – asserts that, for unidimensional risky prospects, A is preferred to B if the cumulative distribution of A is to the right of the cumulative distribution of B. Dominance is both simpler and more compelling than cancellation and transitivity, and it serves as the cornerstone of the normative theory of choice.

Invariance. An essential condition for a theory of choice that claims normative status is the principle of invariance: different representations of the same choice problem should yield the same preference. That is, the preference between options should be independent of their description. Two characterizations that the decision maker, on reflection, would view as alternative descriptions of the same problem should lead to the same choice – even without the benefit of such reflection. This principle of invariance (or extensionality [Arrow 1982]), is so basic that it is tacitly assumed in the characterization of options rather than explicitly stated as a testable axiom. For example, decision models that describe the objects of choice as random variables all assume that alternative representations of the same random variables should be treated alike. Invariance captures the normative intuition that variations of form that do not affect the actual outcomes should not affect the choice. A related concept, called consequentialism, has been discussed by Hammond (1985).

The four principles underlying expected utility theory can be ordered by their normative appeal. Invariance and dominance seem essential, transitivity could be questioned, and cancellation has been rejected by many authors. Indeed, the ingenious counterexamples of Allais (1953) and Ellsberg (1961) led several theorists to abandon cancellation and the expectation principle in favor of more general representations. Most of these models assume transitivity, dominance, and invariance (e.g., Hansson 1975; Allais 1979; Hagen 1979; Machina 1982; Quiggin 1982; Weber 1982; Chew 1983; Fishburn 1983; Schmeidler 1984; Segal 1984; Yaari 1984; Luce and Narens 1985). Other developments abandon transitivity but maintain invariance and dominance (e.g., Bell 1982; Fishburn 1982, 1984; Loomes and Sugden 1982). These theorists responded to observed violations of cancellation and transitivity by weakening the normative theory in order to retain its status as a descriptive model. However, this strategy cannot be extended to the failures of dominance and invariance that we shall document. Because invariance and dominance are normatively essential and descriptively invalid, a theory of rational decision cannot provide an adequate description of choice behavior.

We next illustrate failures of invariance and dominance and then review a descriptive analysis that traces these failures to the joint effects of the rules that govern the framing of prospects, the evaluation of outcomes, and the weighting of probabilities. Several phenomena of choice that support the present account are described.

II. THE FRAMING AND WEIGHTING OF CHANCE EVENTS

In expected-utility theory, the utility of each possible outcome is weighted by its probability. In prospect theory, the value of an uncertain outcome is multiplied by a decision weight $\pi(p)$, which is a monotonic function of p but is not a probability. The weighting function π has the following properties. First, impossible events are discarded, that is, $\pi(0) = 0$, and the scale is normalized so that $\pi(1) = 1$, but the function is not well behaved near the end points (Kahneman and Tversky 1979). Second, for low probabilities, $\pi(p) > p$, but $\pi(p) + \pi(1 - p) \leq 1$ (subcertainty). Thus low probabilities are overweighted, moderate and high probabilities are underweighted, and the latter effect is more pronounced than the former. Third, $\pi(pr)/\pi(p) < \pi(pqr)/\pi(pq)$ for all $0 < p, q, r \leq 1$ (subproportionality). That is, for any fixed probability ratio r, the ratio of decision weights is closer to unity when the probabilities are low than when they are high, for example, $\pi(.1)/\pi(.2) > \pi(.4)/\pi(.8)$. A hypothetical weighting function that satisfies these properties is shown in Figure 12.1. Its consequences are discussed in the next section.[1]

Nontransparent Dominance

The major characteristic of the weighting function is the overweighting of probability differences involving certainty and impossibility, for example, $\pi(1.0) - \pi(.9)$ or $\pi(.1) - \pi(0)$, relative to comparable differences in the middle of the scale, for example, $\pi(.3) - \pi(.2)$. In particular, for small p, π is generally subadditive, for example, $\pi(.01) + \pi(.06) > \pi(.07)$. This property can lead to violations of dominance, as illustrated in the following pair of problems.

---

[1] The extension of the present analysis to prospects with many (nonzero) outcomes involves two additional steps. First, we assume that continuous (or multivalued) distributions are approximated, in the framing phase, by discrete distributions with a relatively small number of outcomes. For example, a uniform distribution on the interval (0, 90) may be represented by the discrete prospect (0, .1; 10, .1; ...; 90, .1). Second, in the multiple-outcome case the weighting function, $\pi_p(p_i)$, must depend on the probability vector p, not only on the component $p_i, i = 1, \ldots, n$. For example, Quiggin (1982) uses the function $\pi_p(p_i) = \pi(p_i)/[\pi(p_1) + \cdots + \pi(p_n)]$. As in the two-outcome case, the weighting function is assumed to satisfy subcertainty, $\pi_p(p_1) + \cdots + \pi_p(p_n) \leq 1$, and subproportionality.

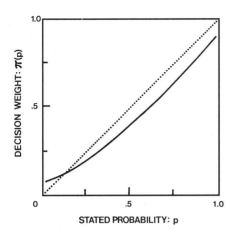

Figure 12.1. A typical weighting function.

Problem 1 ($N = 88$): Consider the following two lotteries, described by the percentage of marbles of different colors in each box and the amount of money you win or lose depending on the color of a randomly drawn marble. Which lottery do you prefer?

Option A

90% white	6% red	1% green	1% blue	2% yellow
$0	win $45	win $30	lose $15	lose $15

Option B

90% white	6% red	1% green	1% blue	2% yellow
$0	win $45	win $45	lose $10	lose $15

It is easy to see that option B dominates option A: for every color the outcome of B is at least as desirable as the outcome of A. Indeed, all respondents chose B over A. This observation is hardly surprising because the relation of dominance is highly transparent, so the dominated prospect is rejected without further processing. The next problem is effectively identical to Problem 1, except that colors yielding identical outcomes (red and green in B and yellow and blue in A) are combined. We have proposed that this operation is commonly performed by the decision maker if no dominated prospect is detected.

Problem 2 ($N = 124$): Which lottery do you prefer?

Option C

90% white	6% red	1% green	3% yellow
$0	win $45	win $30	lose $15

Option D

90% white	7% red	1% green	2% yellow
$0	win $45	lose $10	lose $15

The formulation of problem 2 simplifies the options but masks the relation of dominance. Furthermore, it enhances the attractiveness of C, which has two

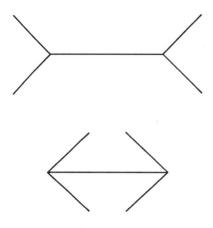

Figure 12.2. The Müller–Lyer illusion.

positive outcomes and one negative, relative to D, which has two negative outcomes and one positive. As an inducement to consider the options carefully, participants were informed that one-tenth of them, selected at random, would actually play the gambles they chose. Although this announcement aroused much excitement, 58% of the participants chose the dominated alternative C. In answer to another question the majority of respondents also assigned a higher cash equivalent to C than to D. These results support the following propositions. (i) Two formulations of the same problem elicit different preferences, in violation of invariance. (ii) The dominance rule is obeyed when its application is transparent. (iii) Dominance is masked by a frame in which the inferior option yields a more favorable outcome in an identified state of the world (e.g., drawing a green marble). (iv) The discrepant preferences are consistent with the subadditivity of decision weights. The role of transparency may be illuminated by a perceptual example. Figure 12.2 presents the well-known Müller-Lyer illusion:

Figure 12.3. A transparent version of the Müller–Lyer illusion.

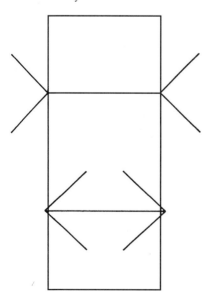

the top line appears longer than the bottom line, although it is in fact shorter. In Figure 12.3, the same patterns are embedded in a rectangular frame, which makes it apparent that the protruding bottom line is longer than the top one. This judgment has the nature of an inference, in contrast to the perceptual impression that mediates judgment in Figure 12.2. Similarly, the finer partition introduced in problem 1 makes it possible to conclude that option D is superior to C, without assessing their values. Whether the relation of dominance is detected depends on framing as well as on the sophistication and experience of the decision maker. The dominance relation in problem 2 could be transparent to a sophisticated decision maker, although it was not transparent to most of our respondents.

Certainty and Pseudocertainty

The overweighting of outcomes that are obtained with certainty relative to outcomes that are merely probable gives rise to violations of the expectation rule, as first noted by Allais (1953). The next series of problems (Tversky and Kahneman 1981, p. 455) illustrates the phenomenon discovered by Allais and its relation to the weighting of probabilities and to the framing of chance events. Chance events were realized by drawing a single marble from a bag containing a specified number of favorable and unfavorable marbles. To encourage thoughtful answers, one-tenth of the participants, selected at random, were given an opportunity to play the gambles they chose. The same respondents answered problems 3–5, in that order.

Problem 3 ($N = 77$): Which of the following options do you prefer?
A. a sure gain of $30 [78%]
B. 80% chance to win $45 and 20% chance to win nothing [22%]

Problem 4 ($N = 81$): Which of the following options do you prefer?
C. 25% chance to win $30 and 75% chance to win nothing [42%]
D. 20% chance to win $45 and 80% chance to win nothing [58%]

Note that problem 4 is obtained from problem 3 by reducing the probabilities of winning by a factor of four. In expected utility theory a preference for A over B in problem 3 implies a preference for C over D in problem 4. Contrary to this prediction, the majority preference switched from the lower prize ($30) to the higher one ($45) when the probabilities of winning were substantially reduced. We called this phenomenon the *certainty effect* because the reduction of the probability of winning from certainty to .25 has a greater effect than the corresponding reduction from .8 to .2. In prospect theory, the modal choice in problem 3 implies $v(45)\pi(.80) < v(30)\pi(1.0)$, whereas the modal choice in problem 4 implies $v(45)\pi(.20) > v(30)\pi(.25)$. The observed violation of expected utility theory, then, is implied by the curvature of π (see Figure 12.1) if

$$\frac{\pi(.20)}{\pi(.25)} > \frac{v(30)}{v(45)} > \frac{\pi(.80)}{\pi(1.0)}.$$

Allais's problem has attracted the attention of numerous theorists, who attempted to provide a normative rationale for the certainty effect by relaxing the cancellation rule (see, e.g., Allais 1979; Fishburn 1982, 1983; Machina 1982; Quiggin 1982; Chew 1983). The following problem illustrates a related phenomenon, called the *pseudocertainty effect*, that cannot be accommodated by relaxing cancellation because it also involves a violation of invariance.

Problem 5 ($N = 85$): Consider the following two stage game. In the first stage, there is a 75% chance to end the game without winning anything, and a 25% chance to move into the second stage. If you reach the second stage you have a choice between:

216 Amos Tversky and Daniel Kahneman

E. a sure win of $30 [74%]

F. 80% chance to win $45 and 20% chance to win nothing [26%]

Your choice must be made before the outcome of the first stage is known.

Because there is one chance in four to move into the second stage, prospect E offers a .25 probability of winning $30, and prospect F offers a .25 × .80 = .20 probability of winning $45. Problem 5 is therefore identical to problem 4 in terms of probabilities and outcomes. However, the preferences in the two problems differ: most subjects made a risk-averse choice in problem 5 but not in problem 4. We call this phenomenon the pseudocertainty effect because an outcome that is actually uncertain is weighted as if it were certain. The framing of problem 5 as a two-stage game encourages respondents to apply cancellation: the event of failing to reach the second stage is discarded prior to evaluation because it yields the same outcomes in both options. In this framing problems 5 and 3 are evaluated alike.

Although problems 4 and 5 are identical in terms of final outcomes and their probabilities, problem 5 has a greater potential for inducing regret. Consider a decision maker who chooses F in problem 5, reaches the second stage, but fails to win the prize. This individual knows that the choice of E would have yielded a gain of $30. In problem 4, on the other hand, an individual who chooses D and fails to win cannot know with certainty what the outcome of the other choice would have been. This difference could suggest an alternative interpretation of the pseudocertainty effect in terms of regret (e.g., Loomes and Sugden 1982). However, the certainty and the pseudocertainty effects were found to be equally strong in a modified version of problems 3–5 in which opportunities for regret were equated across problems. This finding does not imply that considerations of regret play no role in decisions. (For examples, see Kahneman and Tversky [1982, p. 710].) It merely indicates that Allais's example and the pseudocertainty effect are primarily controlled by the nonlinearity of decision weights and the framing of contingencies rather than by the anticipation of regret.[2]

The certainty and pseudocertainty effects are not restricted to monetary outcomes. The following problem illustrates these phenomena in a medical context. The respondents were 72 physicians attending a meeting of the California Medical Association. Essentially the same pattern of responses was obtained from a larger group ($N = 180$) of college students.

---

[2] In the modified version – problems 3'–5' – the probabilities of winning were generated by drawing a number from a bag containing 100 sequentially numbered tickets. In problem 4', the event associated with winning $45 (drawing a number between one and 20) was included in the event associated with winning $30 (drawing a number between one and 25). The sequential setup of problem 5 was replaced by the simultaneous play of two chance devices: the roll of a die (whose outcome determines whether the game is on) and the drawing of a numbered ticket from a bag. The possibility of regret now exists in all three problems, and problems 4' and 5' no longer differ in this respect because a decision maker would always know the outcomes of alternative choices. Consequently, regret theory cannot explain either the certainty effect (3' vs. 5') or the pseudocertainty effect (4' vs. 5') observed in the modified problems.

Problem 6 (N = 72): In the treatment of tumors there is sometimes a choice between two types of therapies: (i) a radical treatment such as extensive surgery, which involves some risk of imminent death, (ii) a moderate treatment, such as limited surgery or radiation therapy. Each of the following problems describes the possible outcome of two alternative treatments, for three different cases. In considering each case, suppose the patient is a 40-year-old male. Assume that without treatment death is imminent (within a month) and that only one of the treatments can be applied. Please indicate the treatment you would prefer in each case.

CASE 1

Treatment A: 20% chance of imminent death and 80% chance of normal life, with an expected longevity of 30 years. [35%]

Treatment B: certainty of a normal life, with an expected longevity of 18 years. [65%]

CASE 2

Treatment C: 80% chance of imminent death and 20% chance of normal life, with an expected longevity of 30 years. [68%]

Treatment D: 75% chance of imminent death and 25% chance of normal life, with an expected longevity of 18 years. [32%]

CASE 3

Consider a new case where there is a 25% chance that the tumor is treatable and a 75% chance that it is not. If the tumor is not treatable, death is imminent. If the tumor is treatable, the outcomes of the treatment are as follows:

Treatment E: 20% chance of imminent death and 80% chance of normal life, with an expected longevity of 30 years. [32%]

Treatment F: certainty of normal life, with an expected longevity of 18 years. [68%]

The three cases of this problem correspond, respectively, to problems 3–5, and the same pattern of preferences is observed. In case 1, most respondents make a risk-averse choice in favor of certain survival with reduced longevity. In case 2, the moderate treatment no longer ensures survival, and most respondents choose the treatment that offers the higher expected longevity. In particular, 64% of the physicians who chose B in case 1 selected C in case 2. This is another example of Allais's certainty effect.

The comparison of cases 2 and 3 provides another illustration of pseudo-certainty. The cases are identical in terms of the relevant outcomes and their probabilities, but the preferences differ. In particular, 56% of the physicians who chose C in case 2 selected F in case 3. The conditional framing induces people to disregard the event of the tumor's not being treatable because the two treatments are equally ineffective in this case. In this frame, treatment F enjoys the advantage of pseudocertainty. It appears to ensure survival, but the assurance is conditional on the treatability of the tumor. In fact, there is only a .25 chance of surviving a month if this option is chosen.

The conjunction of certainty and pseudocertainty effects has significant implications for the relation between normative and descriptive theories of choice. Our results indicate that cancellation is actually obeyed in choices – in those problems that make its application transparent. Specifically, we find that people make the same choices in problems 5 and 3 and in cases 3 and 1 of problem 6. Evidently, people "cancel" an event that yields the same outcomes for all options, in two-stage or nested structures. Note that in these examples cancellation is satisfied in problems that are formally equivalent to those in which it is violated. The empirical validity of cancellation therefore depends on the framing of the problems.

The present concept of framing originated from the analysis of Allais's problems by Savage (1954, pp. 101–4) and Raiffa (1968, pp. 80–86), who reframed these examples in an attempt to make the application of cancellation more compelling. Savage and Raiffa were right: naive respondents indeed obey the cancellation axiom when its application is sufficiently transparent.[3] However, the contrasting preferences in different versions of the same choice (problems 4 and 5 and cases 2 and 3 of problem 6) indicate that people do not follow the same axiom when its application is not transparent. Instead, they apply (nonlinear) decision weights to the probabilities as stated. The status of cancellation is therefore similar to that of dominance: both rules are intuitively compelling as abstract principles of choice, consistently obeyed in transparent problems and frequently violated in nontransparent ones. Attempts to rationalize the preferences in Allais's example by discarding the cancellation axiom face a major difficulty: they do not distinguish transparent formulations in which cancellation is obeyed from nontransparent ones in which it is violated.

III. DISCUSSION

In the preceding sections we challenged the descriptive validity of the major tenets of expected utility theory and outlined an alternative account of risky choice. In this section we discuss alternative theories and argue against the reconciliation of normative and descriptive analyses. Some objections of economists to our analysis and conclusions are addressed.

---

[3] It is noteworthy that the conditional framing used in problems 5 and 6 (case 3) is much more effective in eliminating the common responses to Allais's paradox than the partition framing introduced by Savage (see, e.g., Slovic and Tversky 1974). This is probably due to the fact that the conditional framing makes it clear that the critical options are identical – after eliminating the state whose outcome does not depend on one's choice (i.e., reaching the second stage in problem 5, an untreatable tumor in problem 6, case 3).

Table 12.1. Summary of Empirical Violations and Explanatory Models

Tenet	Empirical Violation	Explanatory Model
Cancellation	Certainty effect (Allais 1953, 1979; Kahneman and Tversky 1979) (problems 3, 4, and 6 [cases 1 and 2])	All models
Transitivity	Lexicographic semiorder (Tversky 1969) Preference reversals (Slovic and Lichtenstein 1983)	Bivariate models
Dominance	Contrasting risk attitudes Subadditive decision weights (problem 2)	Prospect theory
Invariance	Framing effects (problems 1, 2, 4, 5, and 6)	Prospect theory

Descriptive and Normative Considerations

Many alternative models of risky choice, designed to explain the observed violations of expected utility theory, have been developed in the last decade. These models divide into the following four classes. (i) Nonlinear functionals (e.g., Allais 1953, 1979; Machina 1982) are obtained by eliminating the cancellation condition altogether. These models do not have axiomatizations leading to a (cardinal) measurement of utility, but they impose various restrictions (i.e., differentiability) on the utility functional. (ii) The expectations quotient model (axiomatized by Chew and MacCrimmon 1979; Weber 1982; Chew 1983; Fishburn 1983) replaces cancellation by a weaker substitution axiom and represents the value of a prospect by the ratio of two linear functionals. (iii) Bilinear models with nonadditive probabilities (e.g., Kahneman and Tversky 1979; Quiggin 1982; Schmeidler 1984; Segal 1984; Yaari 1984; Luce and Narens 1985) assume various restricted versions of cancellation (or substitution) and construct a bilinear representation in which the utilities of outcomes are weighted by a nonadditive probability measure or by some nonlinear transform of the probability scale. (iv) Nontransitive models represent preferences by a bivariate utility function. Fishburn (1982, 1984) axiomatized such models, while Bell (1982) and Loomes and Sugden (1982) interpreted them in terms of expected regret. For further theoretical developments, see Fishburn (1985).

The relation between models and data is summarized in Table 12.1. The stub column lists the four major tenets of expected utility theory. Column 1 lists the major empirical violations of these tenets and cites a few representative references. Column 2 lists the subset of models discussed above that are consistent with the observed violations.

The conclusions of Table 12.1 may be summarized as follows. First, all the above models (as well as some others) are consistent with the violations of cancellation produced by the certainty effect.[4] Therefore, Allais's "paradox"

---

[4] Because the present article focuses on prospects with known probabilities, we do not discuss the important violations of cancellation due to ambiguity (Ellsberg 1961).

cannot be used to compare or evaluate competing nonexpectation models. Second, bivariate (nontransitive) models are needed to explain observed intransitivities. Third, only prospect theory can accommodate the observed violations of (stochastic) dominance and invariance. Although some models (e.g., Loomes and Sugden 1982; Luce and Narens 1985) permit some limited failures of invariance, they do not account for the range of framing effects described in this article.

Because framing effects and the associated failures of invariance are ubiquitous, no adequate descriptive theory can ignore these phenomena. On the other hand, because invariance (or extensionality) is normatively indispensable, no adequate prescriptive theory should permit its violation. Consequently, the dream of constructing a theory that is acceptable both descriptively and normatively appears unrealizable (see also Tversky and Kahneman 1983).

Prospect theory differs from the other models mentioned above in being unabashedly descriptive and in making no normative claims. It is designed to explain preferences, whether or not they can be rationalized. Machina (1982, p. 292) claimed that prospect theory is "unacceptable as a descriptive model of behavior toward risk" because it implies violations of stochastic dominance. But since the violations of dominance predicted by the theory have actually been observed (see problem 2), Machina's objection appears invalid.

Perhaps the major finding of the present article is that the axioms of rational choice are generally satisfied in transparent situations and often violated in nontransparent ones. For example, when the relation of stochastic dominance is transparent (as in problem 1), practically everyone selects the dominant prospect. However, when these problems are framed so that the relation of dominance is no longer transparent (as in problem 2), most respondents violate dominance, as predicted. These results contradict all theories that imply stochastic dominance as well as others (e.g., Machina 1982) that predict the same choices in transparent and nontransparent contexts. The same conclusion applies to cancellation, as shown in the discussion of pseudocertainty. It appears that both cancellation and dominance have normative appeal, although neither one is descriptively valid.

The present results and analysis – particularly the role of transparency and the significance of framing – are consistent with the conception of bounded rationality originally presented by Herbert Simon (see, e.g., Simon 1955, 1978; March 1978; Nelson and Winter 1982). Indeed, prospect theory is an attempt to articulate some of the principles of perception and judgment that limit the rationality of choice.

The introduction of psychological considerations (e.g., framing) both enriches and complicates the analysis of choice. Because the framing of decisions depends on the language of presentation, on the context of choice, and on the nature of the display, our treatment of the process is necessarily informal and incomplete. We have identified several common rules of framing, and we have demonstrated their effects on choice, but we have not provided a formal theory of framing. Furthermore, the present analysis does not account for all the observed failures of transitivity and invariance. Although some intransitivities (e.g., Tversky 1969) can be explained by discarding small differences in the framing phase, and others (e.g., Raiffa 1968, p. 75) arise from the combination of transparent and nontransparent comparisons, there are examples of cyclic preferences and context effects (see, e.g., Slovic, Fischhoff, and Lichtenstein 1982; Slovic and Lichtenstein 1983) that require additional explanatory mechanisms (e.g., multiple reference points and variable weights). An adequate account of choice cannot ignore these effects of framing and context, even if they are normatively distasteful and mathematically intractable.

Bolstering Assumptions

The assumption of rationality has a favored position in economics. It is accorded all the methodological privileges of a self-evident truth, a reasonable idealization, a tautology, and a null hypothesis. Each of these interpretations either puts the hypothesis of rational action beyond question or places the burden of proof squarely on any alternative analysis of belief and choice. The advantage of the rational model is compounded because no other theory of judgment and decision can ever match it in scope, power, and simplicity.

Furthermore, the assumption of rationality is protected by a formidable set of defenses in the form of bolstering assumptions that restrict the significance of any observed violation of the model. In particular, it is commonly assumed that substantial violations of the standard model are (i) restricted to insignificant choice problems, (ii) quickly eliminated by learning, or (iii) irrelevant to economics because of the corrective function of market forces. Indeed, incentives sometimes improve the quality of decisions, experienced decision makers often do better than novices, and the forces of arbitrage and competition can nullify some effects of error and illusion. Whether these factors ensure rational choices in any particular situation is an empirical issue, to be settled by observation, not by supposition.

It has frequently been claimed (see, e.g., Smith 1985) that the observed failures of rational models are attributable to the cost of thinking and will thus be eliminated by proper incentives. Experimental findings provide little support for this view. Studies reported in the economic and psychological literature have shown that errors that are prevalent in responses to hypothetical questions persist even in the presence of significant monetary payoffs. In particular, elementary blunders of probabilistic reasoning (Grether 1980; Tversky and Kahneman 1983), major inconsistencies of choice (Grether and Plott 1979; Slovic and Lichtenstein 1983), and violations of stochastic dominance in nontransparent problems are hardly reduced by incentives. The evidence that high stakes do not always improve decisions is not restricted to laboratory studies.

Significant errors of judgment and choice can be documented in real world decisions that involve high stakes and serious deliberation. The high rate of failures
of small businesses, for example, is not easily reconciled with the assumptions
of rational expectations and risk aversion.

Incentives do not operate by magic: they work by focusing attention and
by prolonging deliberation. Consequently, they are more likely to prevent errors that arise from insufficient attention and effort than errors that arise from
misperception or faulty intuition. The example of visual illusion is instructive.
There is no obvious mechanism by which the mere introduction of incentives
(without the added opportunity to make measurements) would reduce the illusion observed in Figure 12.2, and the illusion vanishes – even in the absence
of incentives – when the display is altered in Figure 12.3. The corrective power
of incentives depends on the nature of the particular error and cannot be taken
for granted.

The assumption of the rationality of decision making is often defended by
the argument that people will learn to make correct decisions and sometimes
by the evolutionary argument that irrational decision makers will be driven out
by rational ones. There is no doubt that learning and selection do take place and
tend to improve efficiency. As in the case of incentives, however, no magic is involved. Effective learning takes place only under certain conditions: it requires
accurate and immediate feedback about the relation between the situational
conditions and the appropriate response. The necessary feedback is often lacking for the decisions made by managers, entrepreneurs, and politicians because
(i) outcomes are commonly delayed and not easily attributable to a particular
action; (ii) variability in the environment degrades the reliability of the feedback,
especially where outcomes of low probability are involved; (iii) there is often no
information about what the outcome would have been if another decision had
been taken; and (iv) most important decisions are unique and therefore provide
little opportunity for learning (see Einhorn and Hogarth 1978). The conditions
for organizational learning are hardly better. Learning surely occurs, for both
individuals and organizations, but any claim that a particular error will be eliminated by experience must be supported by demonstrating that the conditions
for effective learning are satisfied.

Finally, it is sometimes argued that failures of rationality in individual decision making are inconsequential because of the corrective effects of the market
(Knez, Smith, and Williams 1985). Economic agents are often protected from
their own irrational predilections by the forces of competition and by the action
of arbitrageurs, but there are situations in which this mechanism fails. Hausch,
Ziemba, and Rubenstein (1981) have documented an instructive example: the
market for win bets at the racetrack is efficient, but the market for bets on place
and show is not. Bettors commonly underestimate the probability that the favorite will end up in second or third place, and this effect is sufficiently large
to sustain a contrarian betting strategy with a positive expected value. This
inefficiency is found in spite of the high incentives, of the unquestioned level

of dedication and expertise among participants in racetrack markets, and of obvious opportunities for learning and for arbitrage.

Situations in which errors that are common to many individuals are unlikely to be corrected by the market have been analyzed by Haltiwanger and Waldman (1985) and by Russell and Thaler (1985). Furthermore, Akerlof and Yellen (1985) have presented their near-rationality theory, in which some prevalent errors in responding to economic changes (e.g., inertia or money illusion) will (i) have little effect on the individual (thereby eliminating the possibility of learning), (ii) provide no opportunity for arbitrage, and yet (iii) have large economic effects. The claim that the market can be trusted to correct the effect of individual irrationalities cannot be made without supporting evidence, and the burden of specifying a plausible corrective mechanism should rest on those who make this claim.

The main theme of this article has been that the normative and the descriptive analyses of choice should be viewed as separate enterprises. This conclusion suggests a research agenda. To retain the rational model in its customary descriptive role, the relevant bolstering assumptions must be validated. Where these assumptions fail, it is instructive to trace the implications of the descriptive analysis (e.g., the effects of loss aversion, pseudocertainty, or the money illusion) for public policy, strategic decision making, and macroeconomic phenomena (see Arrow 1982; Akerlof and Yellen 1985).

13. Framing, Probability Distortions, and Insurance Decisions

Eric J. Johnson, John Hershey, Jacqueline Meszaros, and Howard Kunreuther

ABSTRACT. A series of studies examines whether certain biases in probability assessments and perceptions of loss, previously found in experimental
studies, affect consumers' decisions about insurance. Framing manipulations lead the consumers studied here to make hypothetical insurance-
purchase choices that violate basic laws of probability and value. Subjects
exhibit distortions in their perception of risk and framing effects in evaluating premiums and benefits. Illustrations from insurance markets suggest
that the same effects occur when consumers make actual insurance purchases.

KEY WORDS   insurance decisions, biases, probability distortions, framing

Insurance purchases form the basis for an extraordinarily large industry. The industry has assets of $1.6 trillion and employs over 2 million people (Insurance Information Institute, 1990a). Consumers are responsible for a significant proportion of this market, either directly through their own purchase decisions, or indirectly through their choices of employers, mortgages, etc. These investments are sizable and commonplace. For example, the average insured household carries over $100,000 of life insurance, and surveys reveal that 70% of all households report having property insurance. Insurance represents, perhaps, the most significant tool for managing financial risks available to individuals.

The last decade has seen the advent of an "insurance crisis" in the U.S. and several other countries. With respect to liability insurance, for example, there have been large increases in premiums and vanishing coverage for some risks, factors that present major problems for businesses, professionals, and

Presented at the Conference on *Making Decisions about Liability and Insurance*. The Wharton School,
University of Pennsylvania, Philadelphia, PA, 6–7 December, 1991. This research is supported by
National Science Foundation Grant SES88-09299. The authors thank Jon Baron, Colin Camerer,
Neil Doherty, Paul Kleindorfer, Amos Tversky, and two anonymous referees for many helpful
comments. We particularly acknowledge the efforts of Matthew Robinson and Penny Pollister
for their help with data analysis.

consumers (Committee for Economic Development, 1989). For other classes of risk, such as floods, coverage is underpurchased by consumers, even when it is heavily subsidized. Given the solid economic theory underlying the insurance industry, these failures present a puzzle.

Insurance decisions offer a natural test bed for ideas arising from descriptive theories of choice under uncertainty. To buy an insurance policy, the consumer can be seen as assessing the probability of loss distributions for each risk and deciding if the presented policy warrants its premium. Psychologists and economists have documented biases in probability assessments and in perceptions of losses, and it seems fitting to examine insurance decisions for evidence of these biases.

This article reports the results of studies that examine consumers' decisions about insurance. We start by offering a framework for analyzing these decisions, dividing the insurance decision into three components – the risk itself, the policy premium, and the benefit. We then examine evidence that perceptions of each component are potentially distorted or manipulable by well-known psychological mechanisms. In closing, we describe some of the implications of our research.

1. ANALYZING INSURANCE DECISIONS

The economics of insurance is primarily a story of risk shifting. The standard story is that risk-averse individuals confronted with sizable hazards will pay a more diversified insurer to bear the risk (see Dionne and Harrington, 1992, for an introduction to this literature). Insurance companies assume risk because the law of large numbers applies to their portfolios of relatively independent events diversified over different risk categories. Failures of risk sharing occur for three reasons – moral hazard, adverse selection, and transaction costs (Arrow, 1963).

For the consumer, an insurance purchase can be conceptualized as a decision in which he or she is faced with a risk that has some distribution of losses across probabilities. To reduce this risk, the consumer pays a premium and is compensated by a benefit if the loss occurs. A rational, risk-neutral consumer would purchase coverage at an actuarially fair price that is equivalent to the expected loss. Risk aversion raises this reservation price.

In practice, the story is apparently not that simple. There is abundant evidence, although much of it is anecdotal, that consumers do not make these choices rationally. Eisner and Strotz (1961) argue that people pay far more for flight insurance than they should. Kunreuther et al. (1978) have demonstrated that people do not buy flood insurance even when it is greatly subsidized and priced far below its actuarially fair value. The recognition that consumer perceptions and decision processes are imperfect and manipulable could be used to support insurance regulation and prohibition of certain types of insurance.

Consumer errors could be attributed to distortion in any component of the insurance decision. For example, consumers may have distorted perceptions of the size or probability of the risks they face. Alternatively, they may have distorted values of the benefits or cost of the policy. While there are few direct demonstrations of such distortions in insurance decisions, there is now a sizable literature examining similar phenomena elsewhere. Our experimental goal is to demonstrate some cases where such distortions occur in close analogues to insurance decisions. In the next three sections, we review anecdotal evidence that suggests that systematic distortions may exist in insurance-purchase decisions, and we present the results of questionnaire studies that explore these hypotheses.

2. DISTORTIONS IN THE PERCEPTION OF RISK

"All the big money on an accident policy comes from railroad accidents. They found out pretty quick, when they began to write accident insurance, that the apparent danger spots, the spots that people think are danger spots, aren't danger spots at all. I mean, people always think a railroad train is a pretty dangerous place to be, or they did, anyway, before the novelty wore off, but the figures show not many people get killed, or even hurt, on railroad trains. So on accident policies, they put in a feature that sounds pretty good to the man that buys it, because *he's* a little worried about train trips, but it doesn't cost the company much, because it knows he's pretty sure to get there safely. They pay double indemnity for railroad accidents." (From *Double Indemnity*, by James Cain, New York: Random House, 1936)

In 1990, retired business consultant and self-proclaimed climatologist Iben Browning estimated that there was a .5 chance that a severe earthquake would occur on the New Madrid fault during a two-day period centered on December 3, 1990. The New Madrid fault is a known and potentially catastrophic earthquake risk, the site of an earthquake in 1811 that was the most severe North American earthquake on record. However, seismologists did not agree with the magnitude or precision of Browning's assessment. They estimated that the probability was about one in sixty thousand and that there was no reason for the probability to vary widely from day to day, or year to year. Government and academic geologists had been trying for years to improve building standards and increase public awareness of the earthquake hazard in the area. However, there was also significant concern about potential public panic. A special conference was held to discredit Browning's claim.

December 3rd came and went, and with the exception of hordes of reporters descending upon New Madrid, nothing unusual happened. The fault was uncommonly quiet. Largely unreported, however, was perhaps the most interesting phenomenon associated with Browning's prediction: sales of earthquake insurance in the area skyrocketed. To quote one insurer:

More than 650,000 State Farm policyholders in the eight states near the fault added an earthquake endorsement to their homeowners policies, mostly in the two months prior to the Dec. 3 predicted date for the earthquake.

So brisk was demand that Corporate Headquarters had to make an emergency print-ing and distribution of earthquake endorsements in October when the regions ordered 200,000 copies, more than in all of 1989.

The number of earthquake endorsements in the eight states more than tripled from . . . year-end 1989. (State Farm, 1990)

Media reports suggest that these increases in coverage also occurred for many other companies (United Press International, 1990).

There was apparently no reason other than Browning's prediction for con-sumers to markedly increase their probability assessments. Of course, it is pos-sible that increased awareness of a legitimate risk, which had not increased in likelihood, determined these purchases. However, we know that public percep-tions of the frequency of risks can be systematically biased. A series of studies by Lichtenstein et al. (1978) asked people to estimate the frequency of several dozen causes of death in the United States. They found that vivid causes that killed many people during a single occurrence were overestimated, while less vivid causes were systematically underestimated. Combs and Slovic (1979) showed that these biases are highly correlated with the amount of media coverage.

Could such biases affect the desirability of certain kinds of insurance? Do apparent systematic distortions in the probability or size of a risk result in systematic distortions in the prices consumers are willing to pay?

Estimating what an individual should pay for coverage requires information that we lack – specifically, accurate estimates of that individual's perceived risks and risk attitudes. Therefore, we cannot judge whether any single choice or price is reasonable. We test instead for consistency across choices, made by different, randomly assigned groups, employing a simple principle of probability, which we term the inclusion principle.

Our approach is to ask respondents to price incrementally two individual insurance policies that provide coverage against two mutually exclusive risks. We also elicit prices for coverage against a third risk that is a superset of the first two risks. While any price could be justified for the two components, the in-clusion principle states that it is an error for the sum of the prices of the compo-nents to exceed the price of the larger, inclusive risk.[1] This simply reflects the probabilistic principle that two disjoint subsets cannot be more probable than a larger set that includes both.

To illustrate, suppose a concert pianist approaches Lloyds to insure her hands against any injury that would limit her performances. Imagine that she first gives a reservation price for coverage of her right hand, and then gives the reservation price for *incremental* coverage of her left hand. We do not make any statement about how reasonable either price might be. However, we know that

---

[1] In some of our questions, the price for the second component is not conditioned on previous coverage for the first component. In these cases, it might be justified to give a price for the inclusive risk that is smaller than the sum of the prices for the individual risks because of utility considerations. However, the magnitude of the effects we observe would not be expected.

Table 13.1. Flight Insurance Questions

As you know from news reports, both terrorism and mechanical failures are sources of danger to travelers. Suppose that you are planning to fly to London next week. You are offered a flight insurance policy that will provide $100,000 worth of life insurance in case of your death due to

(1) *any act of terrorism*	[mean = $14.12, s.e. = 3.36, $n = 34$]
(2) *any non-terrorism related mechanical failure*	[mean = $10.31, s.e. = 1.99, $n = 36$]
(3) *any reason*	[mean = $12.03, s.e. = 2.83, $n = 34$]

This insurance covers you from the moment you step on the plane until the moment you exit the plane at your desired location. How much would you pay for this coverage?

the sum of these two prices should exactly equal the price that she would be willing to pay for a policy covering both hands. A similar logic is employed by Tversky and Kahneman (1983), Kahneman (1986), and Kahneman and Knetsch (1992).

2.1. Flight Insurance and Availability

Our first question examined the willingness of consumers to pay for different types of hypothetical flight insurance, inspired, in part, by the observations of Eisner and Strotz (1961) and the ubiquity of flight insurance counters in air terminals. The question, which is reproduced in Table 13.1, was answered along with several other unrelated insurance questions by a group consisting mostly of university-hospital employees in return for a $2.00 payment. Each subject received one of the three versions of the questionnaire. The three versions, which differed only by the italicized phrases, were randomly distributed to respondents. We hypothesized that events associated with "terrorism" and "mechanical failure" would be more vivid and available than events suggested by the inclusive phrase "any reason."

The mean prices, standard errors, and sample sizes are shown in square brackets next to the phrase describing the coverage. The stated reservation prices for each form of insurance are all approximately equal, and do not differ from each other by simple t-tests. The sum of the premiums subjects offered for terrorism and mechanical failure (which are disjoint events) is $24.43, more than twice the price subjects were willing to pay for coverage for any reason. This difference is statistically significant ($p < .001$) by a t-test.[2] Thus, the isolation of specific but quite available and vivid causes of death seems to greatly increase the perceived value of insurance. We collected a number of demographic measures for the three randomly assigned subject groups; as expected, there were no significant differences.

---

[2] Because we do not know how between-subject responses covary, our variance estimate for the t-test assumes perfect correlation between the answers to the first two questions, the most conservative assumption we can make.

2.2. Disease-Specific Insurance

Several commonly advertised forms of health insurance have the similar characteristic of providing coverage for only specific causes of illness. These policies usually provide cash payments if the beneficiary is hospitalized due to a particular disease. Such coverage is intriguing because it relates so closely to the research reported above on misperceived causes of death. Would it be possible to make health insurance more attractive by making the cause of hospitalization more specific and available, but less likely?

We constructed an item that parallels these real-world policies, using two causes of death that are usually overestimated according to Lichtenstein et al. (1978) – diseases and accidental death. One group of 30 subjects was first asked how much they would pay for insurance against any disease. Then they were asked how much they would pay for coverage against any accident, assuming they had already bought the disease insurance at their stated price (to control for wealth and risk-attitude effects). Another group of 28 subjects was asked the same two questions in the reverse order – accident then disease. Two other groups of 30 subjects each were asked just a single question: how much would they pay for insurance for "any reason" or "any disease or accident"?

Table 13.2 shows the relevant text for each item, the mean reported price, the standard error, and the sample size. Responses were given using an open-ended format with anchors of $15 for each of the components for the first two questionnaires and $30 for the second two. Note that any anchoring effects work against our hypotheses.

The effect of isolating vivid causes appears to be quite strong. The total price reported for disease and then accident protection is more than twice that reported for protection for "any reason." We compared the answers to each of the first two forms of the question with the third. Both differences are significant by a t-test ($p < .01$) as well as by a Mann–Whitney U-test for rank differences ($p < .006$), a violation of inclusion. The fourth form of the question has an average price that is higher than the third, but it is not significant.

Table 13.2. Disease-Specific Hospitalization Insurance

We are interested in your reaction to a new kind of insurance.

Imagine that you are offered a new kind of health insurance that supplements your major medical insurance. This insurance policy covers you if you are hospitalized for

any disease (followed by *any accident*)	[mean = $89.10, s.e. = 14.60, $n = 30$]
any accident (followed by *any disease*)	[mean = $69.55, s.e. = 8.84, $n = 28$]
any reason	[mean = $41.53, s.e. = 4.51, $n = 30$]
any disease or accident	[mean = $47.12, s.e. = 4.02, $n = 30$]

This policy will pay you $100 a day, which you may apply to your hospital expenses or use in any other way, while you are hospitalized. . . .

2.3. Availability, Vividness, and Inclusion

As the Iben Browning story indicated, distortions in the perception of risk might be exacerbated by vivid and dramatic news. We explored a potentially dramatic increase in perceived risk of terrorism. Many of the respondents, Executive MBA students at the Wharton School, were scheduled to travel to Bangkok, Thailand, as part of their degree program. During the period that this question was administered (late February/early March 1991), the U.S. State Department issued a warning that there was a possibility of terrorist acts aimed at Americans in Bangkok. In fact the students' trip was subsequently canceled.

Our questionnaire examined the role of such vivid information by asking what these students would pay for $100,000 of terrorism insurance. Again we wondered if asking for more limited, but presumably more vivid, coverage would lead subjects to generate higher prices. To exclude various real-world considerations, such as insurance provided by credit cards, the items were somewhat longer than shown here, but the relevant portions are presented in Table 13.3.

The flight-insurance policies covered terrorist acts during flights to and from Bangkok. The first group of subjects provided estimates for each half of the trip, while a second group of subjects reported the price they would be willing to pay for roundtrip coverage. We reasoned that providing estimates for each component of the trip may be more vivid than providing estimates for the entire round trip. Note, of course, that the two legs of the trip are mutually exclusive and exhaustive subsets of the round trip.

As can be seen from Table 13.3, subjects' responses violate inclusion. The mean reported price for the two components, $30.82, is significantly different from the mean price for the equivalent roundtrip coverage, $13.90. These means differ significantly by a t-test ($p < .01$). A Mann-Whitney U-test shows that the

Table 13.3. Insurance Pricing, Availability, and News

Imagine you are about to take a one-week trip to Thailand as part of your Wharton education. You do not have any terrorism insurance for this trip: no insurance is provided by the credit card company through which the tickets were purchased or through Wharton. . . .

This policy pays $100,000 in case of your death due to terrorism during this part of your trip.

Results.

Flight Insurance.

Flight terrorism from the US to Thailand:	[mean = $13.63, s.e. = 2.60, $n = 21$]
Flight terrorism from Thailand to the U.S.:	[mean = $17.19, s.e. = 3.39, $n = 21$]
Round trip terrorism:	[mean = $13.90, s.e. = 2.79, $n = 20$]

Travel Insurance.

Flight terrorism:	[mean = $7.42, s.e. = 1.68, $n = 16$]
Ground terrorism:	[mean = $9.00, s.e. = 1.57, $n = 16$]
Complete terrorism:	[mean = $7.44, s.e. = 1.36, $n = 16$]

rank orders of the sums of the component flight-terrorism results are significantly different from the rank orders of the roundtrip flight ($p < .009$).

The travel-insurance policies covered terrorist acts either in the air or on the ground in Thailand. Again, these two components are mutually exclusive and exhaustive subsets of the inclusive coverage. The sum of the two components, $16.42, exceeded the reported price for the inclusive coverage, $7.44; t-tests show that these violations of inclusion are also significant ($p < .02$). As above, the Mann–Whitney U-test is also significant ($p < .009$).

It is worth noting that coverage for the flight back from Thailand and for ground coverage were judged to be more valuable than inclusive policies, although the difference is not significant. The imagined dangers that could occur in Thailand, or returning from this trip, may seem more vivid, and therefore more important to insure against. What is intriguing, however, is that these dangers may be magnified by segregating them from the entire trip and providing separate insurance protection for each component.

As a whole, this anecdotal and experimental evidence suggests that insurance decisions may be based on distorted beliefs concerning the probability and size of some potential losses. Our results are consistent with other research, most notably in the areas of societal risk perception and contingent valuation (Tversky and Kahneman, 1983; Kahneman and Knetsch, 1992).

3. FRAMING EFFECTS IN EVALUATING PREMIUMS

Insurance premiums, particularly those for coverage over time, can involve complex streams of transactions. Insurers seem, implicitly, to believe that some descriptions of premiums may be more attractive than others: "Coverage for only pennies a day...."

A large psychological literature suggests that consumer preferences may not be invariant over such changes of description. Failures of descriptive invariance are due mainly to two factors. The first, reference dependence, suggests that evaluation is often made relative to some reference point. The second, loss aversion, suggests that decision makers are hurt more by a loss than they are pleased by a gain of the same magnitude (Tversky and Kahneman, 1991).

Many demonstrations of these framing effects exist, and there is some evidence that insurance itself imposes its own frame upon risky choice (Camerer and Kunreuther, 1989). For example, revealed risk attitudes, as assessed by a certainty-equivalence lottery, differ when the lottery is described as a gamble as opposed to an insurance policy (Hershey and Schoemaker, 1980; Hershey, Kunreuther and Schoemaker, 1982). We wondered, therefore, if such manipulations of frames would have significant effects upon revealed preferences.

3.1. Deductibles vs. Rebates
Most insurance policies do not completely shift risk from the insured to the insurer. An important reason for this is moral hazard, a term that recognizes that a complete shift could lead the insured to be irresponsible because he or

she bears no cost of a loss. The most common mechanism for controlling moral hazard is a deductible, in which the insured pays a fixed amount for each loss, although other mechanisms such as copayments are based on the same principle of incentive compatibility.

Consumers appear to dislike deductibles, even though policies with high deductibles can offer considerable savings.[3] When Herbert Denenberg, then the Insurance Commissioner of Pennsylvania, tried to raise the minimum auto insurance deductible from $50 to $100, the resulting consumer outcry forced him to withdraw the request (Cummins and Weisbart, 1978). We attribute this reluctance toward purchasing policies with higher deductibles, in part, to loss aversion. Consumers may frame the deductible as a segregated loss. In essence, the consumer, when faced with the loss, feels both 1) the cost of accumulated insurance premiums, and 2) the additional out-of-pocket cost of the deductible. It is segregated losses – the two separate costs – that are the least attractive (Thaler, 1985).

In principle, other frames could be presented by insurance firms. The deductible could, for example, be incorporated into the cost of insurance simply by raising rates. An inducement for consumers to avoid accidents could be provided by a rebate from which claims are deducted. This integration of losses should be more attractive than the segregated loss, and not easily reframed by consumers (Thaler and Johnson, 1990). Thus, insurance with a rebate should be more attractive than an equivalent but initially less expensive policy with a deductible.

Figure 13.1 illustrates the logic of the argument above using the Prospect Theory value function (Kahneman and Tversky, 1979) with the usual properties – reference dependence (value is measured in terms of changes from the status quo), loss aversion (the impact of a loss is greater than the impact of a gain of the same magnitude) and diminishing sensitivity (the incremental impact of changes in value decreases). (Also see Kahneman and Tversky, 1984; Tversky and Kahneman, 1981, 1991.) The actual monetary magnitudes for rebates, deductibles, and increased premiums are shown on the horizontal axis, and in our example they are all the same, namely, $600. However, the values or psychological impacts of these changes in wealth, indicated by the vertical lines, differ. Note that the deductible, since it is a loss from the status quo, has the greatest impact because of loss aversion. The rebate, on the other hand, is a gain and has less impact. Finally, the additional premium necessary to offset the rebate, while a loss, may have the least impact. This is because it is measured far from the status quo.[4]

---

[3] This reflects the fact that premiums reflect the fixed costs of settling any claim, and that small claims require approximately the same paperwork as large ones (Pashigian et al., 1966).

[4] This analysis also depends upon the probability of a loss occurring, because of possible distortions in probabilities. For example, the attractiveness of rebates will be enhanced if the probability of receiving them is low, because this probability will be overweighted according to prospect theory's probability weighting function.

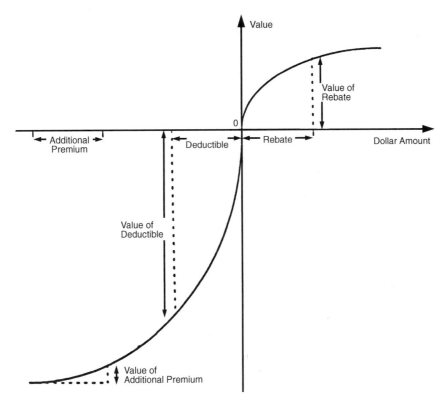

Figure 13.1. Deductible and rebate frames.

The implication of this analysis is that the rebate policy will appear more attractive whether an accident occurs or not. If an accident occurs, the additional premium seems less consequential than the segregated deductible payment the consumer must make. If no accident occurs, the negative value of the additional premium may be more than offset by the positive value of the segregated rebate the consumer receives.

Table 13.4 shows the text of an item we used to test this hypothesis. Note that the policy with the rebate is worse than the policy with a deductible, since the rebate is in essence a $600 interest-free loan to the insurance company. Given any positive discount rate for money, the consumer is worse off choosing the rebate policy. However, respondents were more likely to take the rebate policy than the deductible (chi-square significant at $p < .001$).

3.2. Disability Insurance with Rebates

We wondered if we could create differences in the attractiveness of disability policies based upon the presence of a rebate alone. In other words, we wondered if simply segregating a rebate from the stream of premium payments would make a policy more attractive. Recall that in Figure 13.1 the positive value of the

Table 13.4. Auto Insurance, Deductibles, and Rebates

Imagine that you have just bought a new $12,000 car and are buying insurance for your car. The insurance package described below includes all coverage mandated by the state including comprehensive and collision insurance. Suppose you are offered the policy described below.

[Deductible frame]

This policy has a deductible of $600 which will be subtracted from the total claims against the policy. In other words, if you make any claims against the policy, the company will give you the total amount of the claims minus the deductible. If your claims in one year total less than $600, the company will pay nothing. If your claims exceed $600, the company will pay all of the amount above $600.

Would you pay a premium of $1000 for one year of this coverage?   [44.3% yes]

[Rebate frame]

With this policy, a rebate of $600 minus any claims paid will be given to you at the end of the year. In other words, if you have no claims against the policy, the company will give you $600 back at the end of the year. If you do file one or more claims, you will get back $600 minus the amount the company paid out for your claims. Should your total claims exceed $600, the company will give you no rebate but will pay the claims.

Would you pay a premium of $1600 for one year of this coverage?   [67.8% yes]

[n = 187]

rebate can more than offset the negative value of the additional premium. Thus, we would predict that isolating the rebate would make the policy more attractive, particularly when rebates are small compared to relatively high premiums.

We constructed two policies. One policy is a standard disability contract. The second, which is $20 per month more expensive, offers a rebate equivalent to the sum of these additional premiums ($1200) if no disability claim is filed in five years. Table 13.5 shows the two policies. The policy without the rebate should be preferred, both because of the time value of money and because the rebate would not be paid in the case of a claim.

Our respondents, 100 people, mostly university-hospital employees, first chose between the two policies. Subjects were then prompted with smaller or larger monthly premiums, depending on their preference, until they were

Table 13.5. A Disability Policy with and without a Rebate

Suppose that you have just started a new job. You are considering buying disability insurance. This insurance provides you with an income if you have an injury or sickness that restricts your ability to do your normal work for more than 30 days.

You are considering purchasing one of two policies. Both policies pay 2/3 of your salary for as long as you are disabled.

Policy A will refund $1200 to you if you do not file a claim within five years. The monthly cost of Policy A is $90.

Policy B has no refund. The monthly cost of Policy B is $70.

indifferent between the policies. We randomly varied which of the two policies was held constant and which was adjusted. No differences were found, so the results from the two groups were pooled. We also asked respondents to estimate the chance that in the next five years they would have an injury or sickness that would restrict their ability to do their normal work for more than 30 consecutive days: we found no significant differences as a function of choices.

The rebate policy, which was preferred by 57% of the respondents, had an average premium that was $21.65 higher than the average premium for the no-rebate policy. The standard deviation was 11.1. Even if consumers were sure they would not become disabled, this implies a negative discount rate. At the .05 level, the average premium difference is significantly higher than a premium difference of $19.82 (one-tailed), which implies a return of less than 1%, far less than the rate consumers should demand. Since we found that the average estimated probability of collecting disability payments on the policy, and hence not receiving some or all of the rebate, was 3.6%, this result becomes even more striking.

In sum, the evidence provided by these two examples suggests that the way that premiums are framed can determine the attractiveness of coverage. These findings are consistent with research on framing effects in other domains. Furthermore, policies similar to these do exist in the marketplace. Mutual of Omaha offered a popular disability insurance policy that refunded the entire premium if the insured did not make a claim on the policy from inception to reaching age 65. Maccabees Life Insurance Company offers a disability policy that refunds as much as 80% of premiums paid every 10 years if the insured does not become disabled. The existence of such policies, even when moral-hazard considerations are minimal, suggests that insurers understand the appeal of rebates.

4. FRAMING EFFECTS IN EVALUATING BENEFITS

4.1. Status Quo Effects

A number of states have changed or are considering changing their automobile liability insurance laws to give consumers more choice (Insurance Information Institute, 1990b). One approach to reform that has gained favorable attention in several states is to give motorists a choice between a "full-priced" policy that includes the right to sue for any auto-related injury and a less expensive policy that places certain restrictions on the right to sue. With restricted rights, motorists may sue for pain and suffering when they sustain severe injuries in an accident, but they may not sue for pain and suffering if their injuries are not serious. In all cases, they can still sue for economic damages and medical costs.

The choice between the two options (wealth and budget effects aside) should be the same whether the consumer currently has the full right to sue or the limited right. However, if the status quo serves as a reference point, the right to sue might be valued more when it is given up than when it is being acquired.

Table 13.6. Auto Insurance, the Status Quo, and Limited Right to Sue

There is currently some debate in the U.S. over the causes of the recent rise in auto insurance premiums. One theory places blame on an excessive number of court cases resulting from minor accidents. Another theory blames the profiteering of the insurance industry. A third theory claims the rise is merely a temporary fluctuation inherent in the insurance industry. One method for lowering auto insurance rates that has already been implemented in several states consists of placing restrictions on one's right to sue for pain and suffering. Pain and suffering awards provide monetary compensation to the injured for pain and suffering.

Imagine that you are moving to a new state. In this state, standard auto insurance policies. . . .

[Full Right Group]

. . . do not restrict the bearer's right to sue for pain and suffering resulting from a car accident. Note that you would also be able to recover for all losses other than pain and suffering (e.g., medical bills, lost wages, etc.)

However, you have the option of forgoing your right to sue for pain and suffering in exchange for a reduction in your auto insurance premium. . . . All other features of the two policies' coverage are exactly the same. This option decreases the price of your annual premium by 10%.

[Limited Right Group]

. . . restrict the bearer's right to sue for pain and suffering resulting from a car accident. Note that you would still be able to recover for all losses other than pain and suffering (e.g., medical bills, lost wages, etc.). . . .

However, you have the option of acquiring your right to sue for pain and suffering in exchange for an increase in your auto insurance premium. . . . All other features of the two policies' coverage are exactly the same. This option increases the price of your annual premium by 11%.

[Neutral Group]

. . . come in two different versions. Version 1 restricts the bearer's right to sue for pain and suffering resulting from a car accident. . . .Version 2 does not restrict the bearer's right to sue for pain and suffering. . . . All other features of the two policies' coverage are exactly the same. . . . Version 2 costs 11% more than version 1.

We asked 136 university employees to tell us what the right to sue was worth. They were randomly assigned to three groups and were all asked to imagine that they were moving to a new state. Table 13.6 shows the three versions of the questionnaire. About a third of the respondents, the "Full Right" group, were told that the state's standard auto insurance policies had no restrictions on the bearer's right to sue. They had the option of forgoing their right to sue in exchange for a 10% reduction in their auto insurance premium.[5] If they chose not to exercise the option, they were asked to indicate a percentage decrease in

---

[5] Specifically, subjects were told that they would forgo their right to sue for pain and suffering unless the injury was extreme. Extreme injury was defined as serious impairment of an important body function that prevents the injured from performing substantially all usual and customary activities during at least 90 of the 180 days following the accident. This definition parallels the conditions of several states, laws.

premium that would be just large enough that they would give up the right to sue. If they chose to exercise the option, they were asked to indicate a percentage decrease in the premium that would be just small enough that they would not give up their right to sue.

Another third of the subjects, the "Limited Right" group, were told that the state's standard auto insurance policies restricted the bearer's right to sue. Subjects had the option of *acquiring* the right to sue for pain and suffering in all accidents in exchange for an 11% increase in their auto insurance premium (which is equivalent to the 10% decrease described to the Full Right group). As with the Full Right group, subjects first made a choice and then answered a follow-up question that asked for a premium difference that would make the options equally attractive.

The final third, the "Neutral" group, were given the same choice, but no information was provided about the standard policies in the state. Again, subjects reported both their choice and the premium difference that would make the two options equally attractive.

In the Full Right group, 53% of the respondents ($n = 62$) preferred to retain the right to sue. Only 23% of the Limited Right group ($n = 74$) chose to acquire the full right. On average, the subjects in the Full Right group were willing to pay 32% more for full coverage than for limited coverage. In contrast, the Limited Right subjects would pay no more than an 8% average increase to acquire the right. Both the differences in choices and in premium amounts are statistically significant ($p < .001$).

The results for the Neutral group fell between the other two groups. Forty-eight percent of the subjects ($n = 67$) preferred the full right to sue, and these policies were worth 23% more than a policy with limited rights. Overall, the three distributions differ by a chi-square test ($p < .006$), and the rank-order test (Kruskall-Wallis, three levels) is also significant ($p < .0001$).

In sum, the value of the right to sue was highly dependent on whether that right was presented as the standard option or one that had to be chosen actively. Why is this the case? Many theses from behavioral decision research predict this result. The simplest is a framing explanation: the two versions of the question describe the options relative to a different reference point. Because of loss aversion, framing the limited right as a loss from the full right increases the relative attractiveness of the full right.

More generally, Samuelson and Zeckhauser (1988) describe a "status quo bias" in decision making to summarize the results of their experiments demonstrating that people show a strong and robust tendency to stick with what they have, the status quo, even when it is randomly determined. Ritov and Baron (1992) argue that this preference for the status quo is largely due to different perceptions of errors of omission and errors of commission. In a series of experiments they show that decision makers' aversion to errors of commission is much stronger than any attachment to an original state of affairs. Similar explanations describe differences between the willingness to pay to acquire an object and the amount demanded to sell the same object (Kahneman, Knetsch, and Thaler, 1990).

4.2. Limited Torts and the Status Quo: A Natural Quasi-Experiment

Recent changes in the insurance laws in Pennsylvania and New Jersey provide an opportunity to see if our result carries over to real choices. Both states have recently introduced the option of a reduced right to sue, accompanied by lower insurance rates. The laws in the two states differ in several ways, but one critical difference is that the two states give consumers different default options. New Jersey motorists have to acquire the right to sue actively, at an additional cost. In Pennsylvania, the default is the full right. Our questionnaire study preceded the implementation of the Pennsylvania law. We wondered if the differences we observed in our questionnaire study would be replicated.

When offered the choice, only about 20% of New Jersey drivers chose to acquire the full right to sue, while approximately 75% of Pennsylvanians retained the full right to sue (Insurance Information Institute, 1992). This difference is in fact somewhat larger than that observed in the hypothetical questionnaire study.

This last example illustrates that framing can have sizable economic consequences. Attributing part of the differences in the adoption rate in the two states to differences in frames suggests that the financial repercussions may be in the tens or hundreds of millions of dollars. What may have seemed to some legislators as insignificant changes in wording turned out to have important effects. If we assume that Pennsylvanians would have adopted limited tort at the same frequency as New Jersey residents, if limited tort had been the default, Pennsylvanians would have paid over $200 million dollars less for auto insurance.

5. DISCUSSION AND CONCLUSIONS

5.1. Summary and Limitations

Our central argument is that consumers' decisions about insurance can be affected by distortions in their perceptions of risk and by alternative framing of premiums and benefits. In our survey studies, these effects led subjects to make inconsistent choices and to violate basic principles of probability and value. Real-world observations suggest that these phenomena occur in insurance markets.

Our work has several limitations. First, the studies do not explore systematically the mechanisms that produce these effects. For example, the risk-distortion results could be due to a number of related mechanisms, including availability (Lichtenstein et al., 1978) or distortions in perceptions of small probabilities (Kahneman and Tversky, 1979). To understand how decisions can be improved, researchers, consumers, and policy makers need to understand which of these mechanisms is at work.

A second limitation is that our survey questions did not have real-world consequences for respondents, and are therefore open to doubts about whether the results will generalize to decisions with real financial consequences for consumers. This is an important discussion point in the expanding dialogue between economists and psychologists. We ensured that subjects were real insurance consumers, questions were derived from real insurance products, and many prices quoted for hypothetical policies were based on market prices. Furthermore, we found examples of actual insurance products that have traits that seem to reflect our survey findings. Still, our research was based on responses to hypothetical questions. We encourage more field studies of actual insurance decisions.

5.2. Distortions and Insurance Markets

If consumers exhibit systematic biases, insurance markets may fail to operate efficiently. For example, if consumers perceive deductible policies to be less attractive than more expensive rebate policies, as our subjects did, they may pay more for some insurance than they should. To take another example, the risk of flood losses seems to be underestimated systematically by homeowners in hazard-prone areas. If insurers offer actuarially "fair" coverage, residents will perceive it to be overpriced, and will remain uninsured. Homeowners would have to be sufficiently risk averse so that their concern with losses would be great enough to induce them to purchase a policy.

The surveys reported here suggest that individuals will exhibit judgmental biases and are influenced by how problems are framed. Other studies suggest that insurance firms may behave in ways that are inconsistent with normative models of choice. Surveys of actuaries and underwriters indicate that insurers price policies for ambiguous events, such as earthquakes and leakage of underground storage tanks, higher than would be suggested by expected-utility theory or profit-maximization models. These pricing decisions could be due primarily to biases similar to those exhibited by consumers, or they may be explained by other factors such as imperfect capital markets and capacity constraints due to insurers' limited liability (Kunreuther, Hogarth, and Meszaros, 1993; Winter, 1991).

5.3. Conclusions

Two criticisms of behavioral experiments such as the ones described in this article are often heard. One concern is that the effects are explained primarily by the artificiality of experimental settings. According to this argument, people may behave one way in laboratories and in questionnaire studies, but when their choices really matter to them, they will take more care, reframe the questions in their minds before making any decisions, and behave in a manner that is consistent with normative models. A second argument is that, even if these effects occur in real contexts, market discipline will eliminate any systematic effects except for those that have trivial economic consequences.

The experience with limited torts and automobile insurance provided an opportunity to address both of these concerns. By varying the status-quo or default option for individuals who would be making a choice of whether to accept the limited tort option in the near future, it was possible to show that loss-aversion framing effects affected motorists' choices. A similar effect was found in the real world in the contrasting experiences of New Jersey and Pennsylvania. This suggests that framing makes a difference in a real world as well as experimental setting.

In Pennsylvania, just as in New Jersey, limited-tort policies were offered in order to provide economic relief to many of the consumers who felt overburdened by high automobile insurance rates. The considerably lower premium associated with the limited-tort policy was designed to encourage consumers to take advantage of this option. However, status-quo framing apparently led many drivers to accept the default option, even though it was more expensive than the alternative. Framing thus had a systematic and predictable effect on market behavior that produced significant economic consequences.

14. Mental Accounting Matters

Richard H. Thaler

ABSTRACT. Mental accounting is the set of cognitive operations used by individuals and households to organize, evaluate, and keep track of financial activities. Making use of research on this topic over the past decade, this paper summarizes the current state of our knowledge about how people engage in mental accounting activities. Three components of mental accounting receive the most attention. This first captures how outcomes are perceived and experienced, and how decisions are made and subsequently evaluated. The accounting system provides the inputs to be both *ex ante* and *ex post* cost–benefit analyses. A second component of mental accounting involves the assignment of activities to specific accounts. Both the sources and uses of funds are labeled in real as well as in mental accounting systems. Expenditures are grouped into categories (housing, food, etc.) and spending is sometimes constrained by implicit or explicit budgets. The third component of mental accounting concerns the frequency with which accounts are evaluated and 'choice bracketing'. Accounts can be balanced daily, weekly, yearly, and so on, and can be defined narrowly or broadly. Each of the components of mental accounting violates the economic principle of fungibility. As a result, mental accounting influences choice, that is, it matters.

KEY WORDS   mental accounting; choice bracketing; fungibility; budgeting

- A former colleague of mine, a professor of finance, prides himself on being a thoroughly rational man. Long ago he adopted a clever strategy to deal with life's misfortunes. At the beginning of each year he establishes a target donation to the local United Way charity. Then, if anything untoward happens to him during the year, for example an undeserved speeding ticket, he simply deducts this loss from the United Way account. He thinks of it as an insurance policy against small annoyances.*

---

* This strategy need not reduce his annual contribution to the United Way. If he makes his intended contribution too low he risks having 'uninsured' losses. So far he has not been 'charitable' enough to have this fund cover large losses, such as when a hurricane blew the roof off his beach house.

Originally published in the *Journal of Behavioral Decision Making*, 12:183–206. Copyright © 1999 John Wiley & Sons, Ltd. Reprinted with permission.

- A few years ago I gave a talk to a group of executives in Switzerland. After the conference my wife and I spent a week visiting the area. At that time the Swiss franc was at an all-time high relative to the US dollar, so the usual high prices in Switzerland were astronomical. My wife and I comforted ourselves that I had received a fee for the talk that would easily cover the outrageous prices for hotels and meals. Had I received the same fee a week earlier for a talk in New York though, the vacation would have been much less enjoyable.
- A friend of mine was once shopping for a quilted bedspread. She went to a department store and was pleased to find a model she liked on sale. The spreads came in three sizes: double, queen and king. The usual prices for these quilts were $200, $250 and $300 respectively, but during the sale they were all priced at only $150. My friend bought the king-size quilt and was quite pleased with her purchase, though the quilt did hang a bit over the sides of her double bed.

INTRODUCTION

The preceding anecdotes all illustrate the cognitive processes called mental accounting. What is mental accounting? Perhaps the easiest way to define it is to compare it with financial and managerial accounting as practiced by organizations. According to my dictionary accounting is 'the system of recording and summarizing business and financial transactions in books, and analyzing, verifying, and reporting the results'. Of course, individuals and households also need to record, summarize, analyze, and report the results of transactions and other financial events. They do so for reasons similar to those which motivate organizations to use managerial accounting: to keep trace of where their money is going, and to keep spending under control. Mental accounting is a description of the ways they do these things.

How *do* people perform mental accounting operations? Regular accounting consists of numerous rules and conventions that have been codified over the years. You can look them up in a textbook. Unfortunately, there is no equivalent source for the conventions of mental accounting; we can learn about them only by observing behavior and inferring the rules.

Three components of mental accounting receive the most attention here. The first captures how outcomes are perceived and experienced, and how decisions are made and subsequently evaluated. The accounting system provides the inputs to do both *ex ante* and *ex post* cost–benefit analyses. This component is illustrated by the anecdote above involving the purchase of the quilt. The consumer's choice can be understood by incorporating the value of the 'deal' (termed transaction utility) into the purchase decision calculus.

A second component of mental accounting involves the assignment of activities to specific accounts. Both the sources and uses of funds are labeled in real as well as in mental accounting systems. Expenditures are grouped into categories (housing, food, etc.) and spending is sometimes constrained by implicit or explicit budgets. Funds to spend are also labeled, both as flows (regular income versus windfalls) and as stocks (cash on hand, home equity, pension wealth, etc.). The first two anecdotes illustrate aspects of this categorization process. The vacation in Switzerland was made less painful because of the possibility of setting up a Swiss lecture mental account, from which the expenditures could be deducted. Similarly, the notional United Way mental account is a flexible way of making losses less painful.

The third component of mental accounting concerns the frequency with which accounts are evaluated and what Read, Loewenstein, and Rabin (1998) have labeled 'choice bracketing'. Accounts can be balanced daily, weekly, yearly, and so on, and can be defined narrowly or broadly. A well-known song implores poker players to 'never count your money while you're sitting at the table'. An analysis of dynamic mental accounting shows why this is excellent advice, in poker as well as in other situations involving decision making under uncertainty (such as investing).

The primary reason for studying mental accounting is to enhance our understanding of the psychology of choice. In general, understanding mental accounting processes helps us understand choice because mental accounting rules are not neutral.* That is, accounting decisions such as to which category to assign a purchase, whether to combine an outcome with others in that category, and how often to balance the 'books' can affect the perceived attractiveness of choices. They do so because mental accounting violates the economic notion of fungibility. Money in one mental account is not a perfect substitute for money in another account. Because of violations of fungibility, mental accounting matters.

The goal of this paper is to illustrate how mental accounting matters. To this end I draw upon research conducted over the past two decades. This describes where I think the field is now, having been informed by the research of many others, especially over the past few years.

THE FRAMING OF GAINS AND LOSSES

The Value Function

We wish to understand the decision-making process of an individual or a household interacting in an economic environment. How does a person make economic decisions, such as what to buy, how much to save, and whether to buy or lease an item? And how are the outcomes of these financial transactions evaluated and experienced?

---

* An accounting system is a way of aggregating and summarizing large amounts of data to facilitate good decision making. In an ideal world the accounting system would accomplish this task in such a way that the decision maker would make the same choice when presented with only the accounting data as she would if she had access to all the relevant data. This is what I mean by 'neutral'. In a sense, such an accounting system would provide decision makers with 'sufficient statistics'. Of course, achieving this goal is generally impossible, because something must be sacrificed in order to reduce the information the decision maker has to look at. Thus neither organizational nor mental accounting will achieve neutrality.

Following my earlier treatment of these questions (Thaler, 1980, 1985) I assume that people perceive outcomes in terms of the value function of Kahneman and Tversky's (1979) prospect theory. The value function can be thought of as a representation of some central components of the human perceived pleasure machine.* It has three important features, each of which captures an essential element of mental accounting:

(1) *The value function is defined over gains and losses relative to some reference point.* The focus on changes, rather than wealth levels as in expected utility theory, reflects the piecemeal nature of mental accounting. Transactions are often evaluated one at a time, rather than in conjunction with everything else.

(2) *Both the gain and loss functions display diminishing sensitivity.* That is, the gain function is concave and the loss function is convex. This feature reflects the basic psychophysical principle (the Weber–Fechner law) that the difference between $10 and $20 seems bigger than the difference between $1000 and $1010, irrespective of the sign.

(3) *Loss aversion.* Losing $100 hurts more than gaining $100 yields pleasure: $v(x) < -v(-x)$. The influence of loss aversion on mental accounting is enormous, as will become evident very quickly.

Decision Frames

The role of the value function in mental accounting is to describe how events are perceived and coded in making decisions. To introduce this topic, it is useful to define some terms. Tversky and Kahneman (1981, p. 456) define a mental account† quite narrowly as 'an outcome frame which specifies (i) the set of elementary outcomes that are evaluated jointly and the manner in which they are combined and (ii) a reference outcome that is considered neutral or normal'. (Typically, the reference point is the status quo.) According to this definition, a mental account is a frame for evaluation. I wish to use the term 'mental accounting' to describe the entire process of coding, categorizing, and evaluating events, so this narrow definition of a mental account is a bit confining. Accordingly, I will refer to simply outcome frames as 'entries.'

In a later paper, Kahneman and Tversky (1984, p. 347), propose three ways that outcomes might be framed: in terms of a minimal account, a topical account, or a comprehensive account. Comparing two options using the minimal account entails examining only the differences between the two options, disregarding all their common features. A topical account relates the consequences of possible choices to a reference level that is determined by the context within which the

---

* Prospect theory predates Kahneman's (1994) important distinction between decision utility and experienced utility. In his terms, the prospect theory value function measures decision utility.

† Actually, they use the term psychological account in their 1981 paper, following the terminology I used in my 1980 paper. Later (Kahneman and Tversky, 1984) they suggest the better term 'mental account'.

decision arises. A comprehensive account incorporates all other factors including current wealth, future earnings, possible outcomes of other probabilistic holdings, and so on. (Economic theory generally assumes that people make decisions using the comprehensive account.) The following example* illustrates that mental accounting is topical:

> *Imagine that you are about to purchase a jacket for ($125)[$15] and a calculator for ($15)[$125]. The calculator salesman informs you that the calculator you wish to buy is on sale for ($10)[$120] at the other branch of the store, located 20 minutes drive away. Would you make the trip to the other store? (Tversky and Kahneman, 1981, p. 459)*

When two versions of this problem are given (one with the figures in parentheses, the other with the figures in brackets), most people say that they will travel to save the $5 when the item costs $15 but not when it costs $125. If people were using a minimal account frame they would be just asking themselves whether they are willing to drive 20 minutes to save $5, and would give the same answer in either version.

Interestingly, a similar analysis applies in the comprehensive account frame. Let existing wealth be W, and W^* be existing wealth plus the jacket and calculator minus $140. Then the choice comes down to the utility of W^* plus $5 versus the utility of W^* plus 20 minutes. This example illustrates an important general point – the way a decision is framed will not alter choices if the decision maker is using a comprehensive, wealth-based analysis. Framing does alter choices in the real world because people make decisions piecemeal, influenced by the context of the choice.

Hedonic Framing

The jacket and calculator problem does demonstrate that mental accounting is piecemeal and topical, but there is more to learn from this example. Why are we more willing to drive across town to save money on a small purchase than a large one? Clearly there is some psychophysics at work here. Five dollars seems like a significant saving on a $15 purchase, but not so on a $125 purchase. But this disparity implies that the utility of the saving must be associated with the differences in values rather than the value of the difference. That is, the utility of saving $5 on the purchase of the expensive item must be $(v(-\$125) - v(-\$120))$ (or perhaps the ratio of these values) rather than $v(\$5)$, otherwise there would be no difference between the two versions of the problem.

What else do we know about mental accounting arithmetic? Specifically, how are two or more financial outcomes (within a single account) combined? This is an important question because we would like to be able to construct a model of how consumers evaluate events such as purchases that typically involve combinations of outcomes, good or bad.

One possible place to start in building a model of how people code combinations of events is to assume they do so to make themselves as happy as possible.

---

* This problem was based on similar examples discussed by Savage (1954) and Thaler (1980).

To characterize this process we need to know how someone with a prospect theory value function could wish to have the receipt of multiple outcomes framed.
That is, for two outcomes x and y, when will $v(x + y)$ be greater than $v(x) + v(y)$?
I have previously considered this question (Thaler, 1985). Given the shape of the
value function, it is easy to derive the following principles of hedonic framing,
that is, the way of evaluating joint outcomes to maximize utility.

(1) Segregate gains (because the gain function is concave).
(2) Integrate losses (because the loss function is convex).
(3) Integrate smaller losses with larger gains (to offset loss aversion).
(4) Segregate small gains (silver linings) from larger losses (because the gain
    function is steepest at the origin, the utility of a small gain can exceed the
    utility of slightly reducing a large loss).

As I showed, most people share the intuition that leads to these principles.
That is, if you ask subjects 'Who is happier, someone who wins two lotteries
that pay $50 and $25 respectively, or someone who wins a single lottery paying
$75?' 64% say the two-time winner is happier. A similar majority shared the
intuition of the other three principles.

These principles are quite useful in thinking about marketing issues. In other
words, if one wants to describe the advantages and disadvantages of a particular product in a way that will maximize the perceived attractiveness of the
product to consumers, the principles of hedonic framing are a helpful guide.
For example, framing a sale as a 'rebate' rather than a temporary price reduction
might facilitate the segregation of the gain in line with principle (4).

The Failure of the Hedonic Editing Hypothesis

It would be convenient if these same principles could also serve as a good
descriptive model of mental accounting. Can people be said to edit or parse the
multiple outcomes they consider or experience in a way that could be considered
optimal, that is, hedonic editing.* More formally, if the symbol '&' is used to
denote the cognitive combination of two outcomes, then hedonic editing is the
application of the following rule:

$$v(x \,\&\, y) = \text{Max}[v(x + y), v(x) + v(y)]$$

The hypothesis that people engage in hedonic editing has obvious theoretical
appeal,[†] but some thought reveals that it cannot be descriptively correct. Consider the jacket and calculator problem again. If the $5 saving were coded in a

---

* Johnson and I used the term 'editing' for this process, though on reflection 'parsing' might
  have been better. I will stick with the original term to avoid confusion with the prior literature.
  Note that editing refers to active cognitions undertaken by the decision maker. In contrast, I
  will use 'framing' to refer to the way a problem is posed externally. As we will see, people
  prefer to have outcomes framed hedonically, but fail to edit (or one could say, reframe) them
  accordingly.
[†] Indeed, see Fishburn and Luce (1995) for an axiomatic treatment of hedonic editing.

utility-maximizing way it would be segregated in either case, inconsistent with the data. Furthermore, there must be some limits to our abilities to engage in self-deception. Why stop at segregating the $5 gain? Why not code it as five gains of $1? Nevertheless, hedonic editing represents a nice starting point for the investigation of how people do code multiple events.

Eric Johnson and I have investigated the limits of the hedonic editing hypothesis (Thaler and Johnson, 1990). Our ultimate goal was to explore the influence of prior outcomes on risky choices (see below), but we began with the more basic question of how people choose to code multiple events such as a gain of $30 followed by a loss of $9. One approach we used was to ask people their preferences about temporal spacing. For two specified financial outcomes, we asked subjects who would be happier, someone who had these two events occur on the same day, or a week or two apart? The reasoning for this line of inquiry was that temporal separation would facilitate cognitive segregation. So if a subject wanted to segregate the outcomes x and y, he would prefer to have them occur on different days, whereas if he wanted to integrate them, he would prefer to have them occur together. The hedonic editing hypothesis would be supported if subjects preferred temporal separation for cases where the hypothesis called for segregation, and temporal proximity when integration was preferred. For gains, the hedonic editing hypothesis was supported. A large majority of subjects thought temporal separation of gains produced more happiness. But, in contrast to the hedonic editing hypothesis, subjects thought separating losses was also a good idea. Why?

The intuition for the hypothesis that people would want to combine losses comes from the fact that the loss function displays diminishing sensitivity. Adding one loss to another should diminish its marginal impact. By wishing to spread out losses, subjects seem to be suggesting that they think that a prior loss makes them *more* sensitive towards subsequent losses, rather than the other way around. In other words, subjects are telling us that they are unable to simply add one loss to another (inside the value function parentheses). Instead, they feel that losses must be felt one by one, and that bearing one loss makes one more sensitive to the next.*

To summarize, the evidence suggests that the rules of hedonic framing are good descriptions of the way people would like to have the world organized (many small gains including silver linings; losses avoided if possible but otherwise combined). People will also actively parse outcomes consistent with these rules, with the exception of multiple losses.

There are two important implications of these results for mental accounting. First, we would expect mental accounting to be as hedonically efficient as possible. For example, we should expect that opportunities to combine losses with larger gains will be exploited wherever feasible. Second, loss aversion is even

---

* Linville and Fischer (1991) also investigate the predictive power of hedonic editing, with similar results.

more important than the prospect theory value function would suggest, as it is difficult to combine losses to diminish their impact. This result suggests that we should expect to see that some of the discretion inherent in any accounting system will be used to avoid having to experience losses.

MENTAL ACCOUNTING DECISION MAKING

Transaction Utility

What happens when a consumer decides to buy something, trading money for some object? One possibility would be to code the acquisition of the product as a gain and the forgone money as a loss. But loss aversion makes this frame hedonically inefficient. Consider a thirsty consumer who would rather have a can of soda than one dollar and is standing in front of a vending machine that sells soda for 75 cents. Clearly the purchase makes her better off, but it might be rejected if the payment were cognitively multiplied by 2.25 (an estimate of the coefficient of loss aversion). This thinking has led both Kahneman and Tversky (1984) and me (Thaler, 1985) to reject the idea that costs are generally viewed as losses.

Instead, I proposed that consumers get two kinds of utility from a purchase: *acquisition utility* and *transaction utility*. Acquisition utility is a measure of the value of the good obtained relative to its price, similar to the economic concept of consumer surplus. Conceptually, acquisition utility is the value the consumer would place on receiving the good as a gift, minus the price paid. Transaction utility measures the perceived value of the 'deal'. It is defined as the difference between the amount paid and the 'reference price' for the good, that is, the regular price that the consumer expects to pay for this product. The following example (from Thaler, 1985) illustrates the role of transaction utility.

> You are lying on the beach on a hot day. All you have to drink is ice water. For the last hour you have been thinking about how much you would enjoy a nice cold bottle of your favorite brand of beer. A companion gets up to go make a phone call and offers to bring back a beer from the only nearby place where beer is sold (a fancy resort hotel) [a small, run-down grocery store]. He says that the beer might be expensive and so asks how much you are willing to pay for the beer. He says that he will buy the beer if it costs as much or less than the price you state. But if it costs more than the price you state he will not buy it. You trust your friend, and there is no possibility of bargaining with the (bartender) [store owner]. What price do you tell him?

Two versions of the question were administered, one using the phrases in parentheses, the other the phrases in brackets. The median responses for the two versions were $2.65 (resort) and $1.50 [store] in 1984 dollars. People are willing to pay more for the beer from the resort because the reference price in that context is higher. Note that this effect cannot be accommodated in a standard economic model because the consumption experience is the same in either case; the place of purchase should be irrelevant.

The addition of transaction utility to the purchase calculus leads to two kinds of effects in the marketplace. First, some goods are purchased primarily because they are especially good deals. Most of us have some rarely worn items in our closets that are testimony to this phenomenon. Sellers make use of this penchant by emphasizing the savings relative to the regular retail price (which serves as the suggested reference price). In contrast, some purchases that would seemingly make the consumer better off may be avoided because of substantial negative transaction utility. The thirsty beer drinker who would pay $4 for a beer from a resort but only $2 from a grocery store will miss out on some pleasant drinking when faced with a grocery store charging $2.50.

Opening and Closing Accounts

One of the discretionary components of an accounting system is the decision of when to leave accounts 'open' and when to 'close' them. Consider the example of someone who buys 100 shares of stock at $10 a share. This investment is initially worth $1000, but the value will go up or down with the price of the stock. If the price changes, the investor has a 'paper' gain or loss until the stock is sold, at which point the paper gain or loss becomes a 'realized' gain or loss. The mental accounting of paper gains and losses is tricky (and depends on timing – see below), but one clear intuition is that a realized loss is more painful than a paper loss. When a stock is sold, the gain or loss has to be 'declared' both to the tax authorities and to the investor (and spouse). Because closing an account at a loss is painful, a prediction of mental accounting is that people will be reluctant to sell securities that have declined in value. In particular, suppose an investor needs to raise some cash and must choose between two stocks to sell, one of which has increased in value and one of which has decreased. Mental accounting favors selling the winner (Shefrin and Statman, 1987) whereas a rational analysis favors selling the loser.* Odean (1998) finds strong support for the mental accounting prediction. Using a data set that tracked the trades of investors using a large discount brokerage firm, Odean finds that investors were more likely to sell one of their stocks that had increased in value than one of their stocks that had decreased.[†]

Other evidence of a reluctance to close an account in the 'red' comes from the world of real accounting. Most public corporations make official earnings announcements every quarter. Although earnings are audited, firms retain some discretion in how quickly to count various components of revenues and expenses, leaving them with some control over the actual number they report. Several recent papers (e.g. Burgstahler and Dichev, 1997; Degeorge, Patel and Zeckhauser, forthcoming) show that firms use this discretionary power to avoid

---

* A rational investor will choose to sell the loser because capital gains are taxable and capital losses are deductible.

† Of course, such a strategy could be rational if the losers they kept subsequently increased in value more than the winners they sold, but this outcome was not observed. Indeed, these investors are not particularly savvy. The stocks they sell subsequently outperform the stocks they buy!

announcing earnings decreases and losses. Specifically, a plot of earnings per share (in cents per share) or change in earnings per share (this quarter versus same quarter last year) shows a sharp discontinuity at zero. Firms are much more likely to make a penny a share than to lose a penny a share, and are much more likely to exceed last year's earnings by a penny than to miss by a penny. So small losses are converted into small gains. In contrast, large gains seem to be trimmed down (to increase the chance of an increase again next year) whereas moderate losses are somewhat inflated (a procedure known in accounting circles as 'taking the big bath'). Apparently, firms believe that shareholders (or potential shareholders) react to earnings announcements in a manner consistent with prospect theory.

Advance Purchases, Sunk Costs, and Payment Depreciation

Another situation in which a consumer has to decide when to open and close an account is when a purchase is made well in advance of consumption. Consider paying $100 for two tickets to a basketball game to be held in a month's time. Suppose that the tickets are being sold at the reference price so transaction utility is zero. In this case the consumer can be said to open an account at the point at which the tickets are purchased. At this time the account has a negative balance of $100. Once the date of the game comes and the game is attended, the account can be closed.

What happens if something (a blizzard) prevents the consumer from attending the game? In this case the consumer has to close the account at a loss of $100; in accounting terminology the loss has to be recognized. Notice that this event turns a cost into a loss, which is aversive. Still, why does the prior expenditure (now a sunk cost) make someone more willing to go to the game in a blizzard (as in the example in Thaler, 1980)?

To answer this question we need to consider how transactions are evaluated. For most routine purchases there is no *ex post* evaluation of the purchase when the account is closed. Such evaluations become more likely as the size of the transaction increases or as the purchase or situation becomes more unusual. Failing to attend an event that has been paid for makes the purchase highly salient and an evaluation necessary. By driving through the storm, the consumer can put the game back into the category of normal transactions that are not explicitly evaluated and thus avoid adding up the costs and benefits (barring an accident!). Furthermore, even if an *ex post* evaluation is made, the extra cost of going to the game may not be included in the evaluation. As Heath (1995) suggests, because the costs of driving to the game are not monetary, they may not be included in the analysis.* In Heath's terms they are incidental, that is, in

---

* Of course, although the driving costs may not be included in the basketball game account, they must be compared, at least prospectively, to something when one is deciding whether to go. In this formulation someone would choose to take the drive, not in order to enjoy the game, but to avoid feeling the pain associated with the unamortized ticket expense.

a different mental account. He makes the telling comparison between this case and the Kahneman and Tversky (1984) theater ticket example, in which subjects are *less* willing to buy a ticket to a play after having lost their ticket than after having lost an equivalent sum of money. In the theater ticket example, buying a second ticket is aversive because it *is* included in the mental account for the theater outing, but the loss of the money is not.

Although sunk costs influence subsequent decisions, they do not linger indefinitely. A thought experiment illustrates this point nicely. Suppose you buy a pair of shoes. They feel perfectly comfortable in the store, but the first day you wear them they hurt. A few days later you try them again, but they hurt even more than the first time. What happens now? My predictions are:

(1) The more you paid for the shoes, the more times you will try to wear them. (This choice may be rational, especially if they have to be replaced with another expensive pair.)

(2) Eventually you stop wearing the shoes, *but you do not throw them away.* The more you paid for the shoes, the longer they sit in the back of your closet before you throw them away. (This behavior cannot be rational unless expensive shoes take up less space.)

(3) At some point, you throw the shoes away, regardless of what they cost, the payment having been fully 'depreciated'.

Evidence about the persistence of sunk costs effects is reported by Arkes and Blumer (1985). They ran an experiment in which people who were ready to buy season tickets to a campus theater group were randomly placed into three groups: one group paid full price, one group got a small (13%) discount, and one group received a large (47%) discount. The experimenters then monitored how often the subjects attended plays during the season. In the first half of the season, those who paid full price attended significantly more plays than those who received discounts, but in the second half of the season there was no difference among the groups. People do ignore sunk costs, eventually.

The gradual reduction in the relevance of prior expenditures is dubbed 'payment depreciation' by Gourville and Soman (1998) who have conducted a clever field experiment to illustrate the idea. They obtained usage data from the members of a health club that charges the dues to its members twice a year. Gourville and Soman find that attendance at the health club is highest in the month in which the dues are paid and then declines over the next five months, only to jump again when the next bill comes out.

Similar issues are involved in the mental accounting of wine collectors who often buy wine with the intention of storing it for ten years or more while it matures. When a bottle is later consumed, what happens? Eldar Shafir and I (1998) have investigated this pressing issue by surveying the subscribers to a wine newsletter aimed at serious wine consumers/collectors. We asked the following question:

> *Suppose you bought a case of a good 1982 Bordeaux in the futures market for $20 a bottle. The wine now sells at auction for about $75 a bottle. You have decided to drink a bottle. Which of the following best captures your feeling of the cost to you of drinking this bottle?*

We gave the respondents five answers to choose from: $0, $20, $20 plus interest, $75, and −$55 ('I drink a $75 bottle for which I paid only $20'). The percentages of respondents choosing each answer were 30, 18, 7, 20 and 25. Most of the respondents who selected the economically correct answer ($75) were in fact economists. (The newsletter, *Liquid Assets*, is published by economist Orley Ashenfelter and has many economist subscribers). More than half the respondents report that drinking the bottle either costs nothing or actually saves them money!

The results of this survey prompted us to run a follow-up survey the following year. The question this time was:

> *Suppose you buy a case of Bordeaux futures at $400 a case. The wine will retail at about $500 a case when it is shipped. You do not intend to start drinking this wine for a decade. At the time that you acquire this wine which statement more accurately captures your feelings?*
> *(a) I feel like I just spent $400, much as I would feel if I spent $400 on a weekend getaway.*
> *(b) I feel like I made a $400 investment which I will gradually consume after a period of years.*
> *(c) I feel like I just saved $100, the difference between what the futures cost and what the wine will sell for when delivered.*

Respondents rated each answer on a five-point scale. Most respondents selected answer (b) as their favorite, coding the initial purchase as an investment. Notice that this choice means that the typical wine connoisseur thinks of his initial purchase as an investment and later thinks of the wine as free when he drinks it. We have therefore titled our paper 'Invest Now, Drink Later, Spend Never'. Note that this mental accounting transforms a very expensive hobby into one that is 'free'. The same mental accounting applies to time-share vacation properties. The initial purchase of a week every year at some resort feels like an investment, and the subsequent visits feel free.

Payment Decoupling

In the wine example, the prepayment separates or 'decouples' (Prelec and Loewenstein, 1998; Gourville and Soman, 1998) the purchase from the consumption and in so doing seems to reduce the perceived cost of the activity. Prepayment can often serve this role, but the mental accounting advantages of decoupling are not all associated with prepayment. Consider the case of the pricing policies of the Club Med resorts (Thaler, 1980). At these vacation spots consumers pay a fixed fee for a vacation that includes meals, lodging, and recreation. This plan has two advantages. First, the extra cost of including the meals and recreation in the price will look relatively small when combined with the other costs of the vacation. Second, under the alternative plan each of the small expenditures looks large by itself, and is likely to be accompanied by a substantial dose of negative transaction utility given the prices found at most resorts.

Another disadvantage of the piece-rate pricing policy is that it makes the link between the payment and the specific consumption act very salient, when the opposite is highly desirable. For example, a *prix fixe* dinner, especially an expensive multi-course meal, avoids the unsavory prospect of matching a very high price with the very small quantity of food offered in each course.* Along the same lines, many urban car owners would be financially better off selling their car and using a combination of taxis and car rentals. However, paying $10 to take a taxi to the supermarket or a movie is both salient and linked to the consumption act; it seems to raise the price of groceries and movies in a way that monthly car payments (or even better, a paid-off car) do not.

More generally, consumers don't like the experience of 'having the meter running'. This contributes to what has been called the 'flat rate bias' in telecommunications. Most telephone customers elect a flat rate service even though paying by the call would cost them less.† As Train (1991, p. 211) says, 'consumers seem to value flat-rate service over measured service even when the bill that the consumer would receive under the two services, given the number of calls the consumer places, would be the same . . . The existence of this bias is problematical. Standard theory of consumer behavior does not accommodate it. Similarly, health clubs typically charge members by the month or year rather than of a per-use basis. This strategy decouples usage from fees, making the marginal cost of a visit zero. This plan is attractive because a health club is a service that many consumers feel they should use more often, but fail to do so for self-control reasons (see below). Indeed, the monthly fee, although a sunk cost, encourages use for those who want to reduce their per-visit charges. Compare this system to a pure usage-based pricing system in which Stairmaster users pay 'per step'. This pricing system would be completely incompatible with the psychological needs of the club member who desires usage encouragement rather than discouragement.

Perhaps the best decoupling device is the credit card. We know that credit cards facilitate spending simply by the fact that stores are willing to pay 3% or more of their revenues to the card companies (see also Feinberg, 1986; Prelec

---

* In contrast, the review of one expensive San Francisco restaurant in the Zagat guide includes the following gripe from a customer, $13 for two scallops. Who are they kidding?'

† This example is cited by Prelec and Loewenstein (1998). America Online seems to have learned this lesson the hard way. When they offered a flat rate Internet service in early 1996 they were so overwhelmed with demand that consumers had trouble logging on to the service, causing embarrassing publicity.

and Simester, 1998). A credit card decouples the purchase from the payment in several ways. First, it postpones the payment by a few weeks. This delay creates two distinct effects: (a) the payment is *later* than the purchase; (b) the payment is *separated* from the purchase. The payment delay may be attractive to some consumers who are either highly impatient or liquidity constrained, but as Prelec and Loewenstein (1998) stress, *ceteris paribus*, consumers prefer to pay before rather than after, so this factor is unlikely to be the main appeal of the credit card purchase. Rather, the simple separation of purchase and payment appears to make the payment less salient. Along these lines, Soman (1997) finds that students leaving the campus bookstore were much more accurate in remembering the amount of their purchases if they paid by cash rather than by credit card. As he says, 'Payment by credit card thus reduces the salience and vividness of the outflows, making them harder to recall than payments by cash or check which leave a stronger memory trace' (p. 9).

A second factor contributing to the attractiveness of credit card spending is that once the bill arrives, the purchase is mixed in with many others. Compare the impact of paying $50 in cash at the store to that of adding a $50 item to an $843 bill. Psychophysics implies that the $50 will appear larger by itself than in the context of a much larger bill, and in addition when the bill contains many items each one will lose salience. The effect becomes even stronger if the bill is not paid in full immediately. Although an unpaid balance is aversive in and of itself, it is difficult for the consumer to attribute this balance to any particular purchase.

BUDGETING

So far I have been discussing mental accounting decision making at the level of individual transactions. Another component of mental accounting is categorization or labeling. Money is commonly labeled at three levels: expenditures are grouped into budgets (e.g. food, housing, etc.); wealth is allocated into accounts (e.g. checking, pension, 'rainy day'); and income is divided into categories (e.g. regular or windfall). Such accounts would be inconsequential if they were perfectly fungible (i.e. substitutable) as assumed in economics. But, they are not fungible, and so they 'matter'.

Consumption Categories

Dividing spending into budget categories serves two purposes. First, the budgeting process can facilitate making rational trade-offs between competing uses for funds. Second, the system can act as a self-control device. Just as organizations establish budgets to keep track of and limit divisional spending, the mental accounting system is the household's way of keeping spending within the budget (Thaler and Shefrin, 1981). Of course, there is considerable variation among households in how explicit the budgeting process is.* As a rule, the tighter the budget, the more explicit are the budgeting rules, both in households and organizations. Families living near the poverty level use strict, explicit budgets; in wealthy families budgets are both less binding and less well defined.† Poorer families also tend to have budgets defined over shorter periods (a week or month), whereas wealthier families may use annual budgets. For example, Heath and Soll (1996) report that most of their MBA student subjects had weekly food and entertainment budgets and monthly clothing budgets. It is likely that these rules changed dramatically when the students got jobs at the end of their studies (in violation of the life-cycle hypothesis – see below).

Heath and Soll describe the process by which expenses are tracked against these budgets. They divide the tracking process into two stages:

> (1) Expenses must first be noticed and (2) then assigned to their proper accounts. An expense will not affect a budget if either stage fails. To label these stages we borrow terminology from financial accounting in which the accounting system is also divided into two stages. Expenses must be booked (i.e. recorded in the accounting system) and posted (i.e. assigned to a specific expense account). Each process depends on a different cognitive system. Booking depends on attention and memory. Posting depends on similarity judgments and categorization (p. 42).‡

Many small, routine expenses are not booked. Examples would include lunch or coffee at the workplace cafeteria (unless the norm is to bring these items from home, in which case buying the lunch might be booked). Ignoring such items is equivalent to the organizational practice of assigning small expenditures to a 'petty cash' fund, not subject to the usual accounting scrutiny. The tendency to ignore small items may also explain an apparent contradiction of hedonic framing. As noted by John Gourville (1998), in many situations sellers and fund raisers elect to frame an annual fee as 'pennies-a-day'. Thus a $100 membership for the local public radio station might be described as a 'mere 27 cents a day'. Given the convex shape of the loss function, why should this strategy be effective? One possibility is that 27 cents is clearly in the petty cash category, so when the expense is framed this way it tends to be compared to other items that are not booked. In contrast, a $100 membership is large enough that it will surely be booked and posted, possibly running into binding budget constraints in the charitable giving category. The same idea works in the opposite direction. A

---

* Many of the generalizations here are based on a series of interviews conducted on my behalf in the early 1980s. See also Zelizer (1994) and her references. At one time many households used a very explicit system with envelopes of cash labeled with various spending categories. To some extent, programs such as Quicken serve as a modern replacement for this method.

† Still, budgets can matter even in well-off families. As the discussion of 'decoupling' below will illustrate, spending on vacations may depend on whether a family rents or owns a vacation home.

‡ Regarding the categorization process, see Henderson and Peterson (1992). It should be noted that in a financial accounting system in a firm any expense that is booked is also posted.

firm that markets a drug to help people quit smoking urges smokers to aggre-gate their annual smoking expenditures and think of the vacation they could take with these funds. Again, $2 a day might be ignored but $730 pays for a nice getaway.

Implications of Violations of Fungibility

Whenever budgets are not fungible their existence can influence consump-tion in various ways. One example is the case in which one budget has been spent up to its limit while other accounts have unspent funds remaining. (This situation is common in organizations. It can create extreme distortions espe-cially if funds cannot be carried over from one year to the next. In this case one department can be severely constrained while another is desperately looking for ways to spend down this year's budget to make sure next year's is not cut.) Heath and Soll (1996) provide several experiments to illustrate this effect. In a typical study two groups of subjects were asked whether they would be willing to buy a ticket to a play. One group was told that they had spent $50 earlier in the week going to a basketball game (same budget); the other group was told that they had received a $50 parking ticket (different budget) earlier in the week. Those who had already gone to the basketball game were significantly less likely to go to the play than those who had gotten the parking ticket.*

Using the same logic that implies that money should be fungible (i.e. that money in one account will spend just as well in another), economists have argued that time should also be fungible. A rational person should allo-cate time optimally, which implies 'equating at the margin'. In this case, the marginal value of an extra minute devoted to any activity should be equal.† The jacket and calculator problem reveals that this rule does not describe choices about time. Subjects are willing to spend 20 minutes to save $5 on a small pur-chase but not a large one. Leclerc *et al.* (1995) extend this notion by reversing the problem. They ask people how much they would be willing to pay to avoid waiting in a ticket line for 45 minutes. They find that people are willing to pay twice as much to avoid the wait for a $45 purchase than for a $15 purchase. As in the original version of the problem, we see that the implicit value people put on their time depends on the financial context.

Self-Control and Gift Giving

Another violation of fungibility introduced by the budgeting system occurs because some budgets are intentionally set 'too low' in order to help deal with

---

* One might think this result could be attributed to satiation (one night out is enough in a week). However, another group was asked their willingness to buy the theater ticket after going to the basketball game for free, and they showed no effect.
† I am abstracting from natural discontinuities. If television shows come in increments of one hour, then one may have to choose an integer number of hours of TV watching, which alters the argument slightly.

particularly insidious self-control problems. For example, consider the dilemma of a couple who enjoy drinking a bottle of wine with dinner. They might decide that they can afford to spend only $10 a night on wine and so limit their purchases to wines that cost $10 a bottle on average, with no bottle costing more than $20. This policy might not be optimal in the sense that an occasional $30 bottle of champagne would be worth more than $30 to them, but they don't trust themselves to resist the temptation to increase their wine budget unreasonably if they break the $20 barrier. An implication is that this couple would greatly enjoy gifts of wine that are above their usual budget constraint. This analysis is precisely the opposite of the usual economic advice (which says that a gift in kind can be at best as good as a gift of cash, and then only if it were something that the recipient would have bought anyway). Instead the mental accounting analysis suggests that the best gifts are somewhat more luxurious than the recipient normally buys, consistent with the conventional advice (of non-economists), which is to buy people something they wouldn't buy for themselves.

The idea that luxurious gifts can be better than cash is well known to those who design sales compensation schemes. When sales contests are run, the prize is typically a trip or luxury durable rather than cash. Perhaps the most vivid example of this practice is the experience of the National Football League in getting players to show up at the annual Pro Bowl. This all-star game is held the week after the Super Bowl and for years the league had trouble getting all of the superstar players to come. Monetary incentives were little inducement to players with seven-figure salaries. This problem was largely solved by moving the game to Hawaii and including *two* first-class tickets (one for the player's wife or girlfriend) and accommodations for all the players.

The analysis of gift giving illustrates how self-control problems can influence choices. Because expensive bottles of wine are 'tempting', the couple rules them 'off limits' to help control spending. For other tempting products, consumers may regulate their consumption in part by buying small quantities at a time, thus keeping inventories low. This practice creates the odd situation wherein consumers may be willing to pay a premium for a smaller quantity. This behavior is studied by Wertenbroch (1996), who finds that the price premium for sinful products in small packages is greater than for more mundane goods. His one-sentence abstract succinctly sums up his paper: 'To control their consumption, consumers pay more for less of what they like too much'.

Wealth Accounts

Another way of dealing with self-control problems is to place funds in accounts that are off-limits. Hersh Shefrin and I have proposed (Shefrin and Thaler, 1988) that there is a hierarchy of money locations arranged by how tempting it is for a household to spend the money in each. The most tempting class of accounts is in the 'current assets' category, for example cash on hand and money market or checking accounts. Money in these accounts is routinely spent each period. Less tempting to spend is money in the 'current wealth' category, which includes a range of liquid asset accounts such as savings accounts, stocks and bonds, mutual funds, and so on. These funds are typically designated for saving. Next in the hierarchy is home equity. Even though the advent of home equity loans has made this category of funds somewhat less sacred, still most households aim to pay off their mortgage by the time they retire (and most succeed). Finally, in the least tempting category of funds lies the 'future income' account. These funds include money that will be earned later in life (i.e. human capital) and designated retirement savings accounts such as IRAs and 401(k)s. According to our analysis, the marginal propensity to spend a dollar of wealth in the current income account is nearly 1.0, whereas the propensity to spend a dollar of future income wealth is close to zero.

These predictions are in sharp contrast to standard economic theory of saving: the life-cycle model (Modigliani and Brumberg, 1954; Friedman, 1957). Here is a simplified version that captures the spirit of the life-cycle model. Suppose a person has a certain remaining lifetime of N years, and that the rate of interest is zero. Let W be the person's wealth, equal to the sum of her assets, this year's income, and future (expected) income over the rest of her life. Consumption in this period is then equal to W/N.* Notice that in this model any change in wealth, ΔW, no matter what form it takes (e.g. a bonus at work, an increase in the value of one's home, even an inheritance expected in a decade), produces the same change in current consumption, namely $\Delta W/N$. In other words, the theory assumes that wealth is perfectly fungible.

Shefrin and I proposed a modified version of the life-cycle model, the behavioral life-cycle model, that incorporates the mental accounting temptation hierarchy described above. A powerful prediction of the mental accounting model is that if funds can be transferred to less tempting mental accounts they are more likely to be saved. This insight can be used in designing government programs to stimulate saving. According to the behavioral life-cycle model, if households can be persuaded to move some of their funds from the current income account to future income accounts, long-term savings will increase. In other words, IRAs and 401(k)s are good vehicles to promote savings.[†] My reading of the literature on this topic is that this prediction is borne out. Households who contribute to retirement savings plans display steady increases in the

* More generally, in a world with uncertainty and positive interest rates, the life-cycle theory says that a person will spend the annuity value of his wealth in any period, that is, if he used W to buy a level annuity that paid y in every period, he would set consumption equal to y. Bequests can also be accommodated.

[†] These accounts are especially good because not only are they less tempting 'mental' accounts but they also have a penalty for withdrawal that provides an additional incentive to leave the money in these accounts alone.

funds in these accounts with no apparent reduction in the funds in other accounts. That is, they save more.*

Income Accounting

So far we have considered violations of fungibility produced either by the budgeting process or by the location of funds. A third class of violations can be produced by the source of the income. O'Curry (1997) investigates this phenomenon. She first has one group of subjects judge both sources and uses of funds on a serious–frivolous scale: the winnings of an office football pool are considered frivolous whereas an income tax refund is serious; eating out is frivolous but paying the bills is serious. She then asks other subjects to say what they would do with a particular windfall, such as $30 found in the pocket of a jacket in the back of the closet. She finds that people have a tendency to match the seriousness of the source of some windfall with the use to which it is put. Another example of income non-fungibility is provided by Kooreman (1997). He studies the spending behavior of families that receive child allowance payments from the Dutch government. He finds that spending on children's clothing is much more sensitive to changes in the designated child allowance than to other income sources.†

In the previous example the fact that the child allowance was labeled as such seemed to matter in the way people spent the money. Labeling effects are common. One surprising domain in which this idea can be applied is dividend payments by corporations. Suppose a corporation is earning profits and wishes to return some of these profits to its shareholders. One (traditional) method is to pay a dividend. Another method is simply to repurchase shares. In a world with no taxes, these two methods are equivalent. But, if (as in the United States) dividends are taxed at a higher rate than capital gains, then tax-paying shareholders would prefer share repurchases to dividends (and those who have their shares in non-taxable accounts are indifferent). Under these conditions no firm should ever pay a dividend.

Why do firms pay dividends? Shefrin and Statman (1984) have proposed an explanation based on mental accounting. They argue that investors like dividends because the regular cash payment provides a simple self-control rule: spend the dividends and leave the principal alone. In this way, the dividend

---

* See Poterba, Venti and Wise (1996) for a current summary of the evidence supporting my claim. Their results are hotly disputed by Engen, Gale and Scholz (1996). One reason I side with the first set of authors (aside from the fact that their results support mental accounting) is that the simplest analyses show that the savings plans increase saving. Obtaining the opposite results seems to require a lot more work.

† There is a similar finding in public finance called the 'flypaper effect'. When local governments receive earmarked payments for particular kinds of expenditure (e.g. schools), they tend to increase their spending on that activity by the full amount of the grant. Economic theory predicts that they would increase their spending only by the fraction of their income that they normally spend on this activity. See Hines and Thaler (1995).

acts like an allowance. If, instead, firms simply repurchased their own shares, stockholders would not receive a designated amount to spend, and would have to dip into capital on a period basis. Retirees (who tend to own high-dividend-paying stocks) might then worry that they would spend down the principal too quickly. A similar non-fungibility result is offered by Hatsopoulos, Krugman and Poterba (1989). Although capital gains in the stock market tend to have little effect on consumption, these authors found that when takeovers generate cash to the stockholders, consumption does increase. This is sometimes called the 'mailbox effect'. When the check arrives in the mailbox it tends to get spent. Gains on paper are left alone.

CHOICE BRACKETING AND DYNAMIC MENTAL ACCOUNTING

A recurring theme of this paper is that choices are altered by the introduction of notional (but non-fungible) boundaries. The location of the parentheses matters in mental accounting – a loss hurts less if it can be combined with a larger gain; a purchase is more likely to be made if it can be assigned to an account that is not already in the red; and a prior (sunk) cost is attended to if the current decision is in the same account. This section elaborates on this theme by considering other ways in which boundaries are set, namely whether a series of decisions are made one at a time or grouped together (or 'bracketed' to use the language of Read, Loewenstein and Rabin, 1998).

Prior Outcomes and Risky Choice

In their prospect paper, Kahneman and Tversky mention the empirical finding that betting on long shots increases on the last race of the day,* when the average bettor is (i) losing money on the day, and (ii) anxious to break even. An interesting feature of this sunk cost effect is that it depends completely on the decision to close the betting account daily. If each race were a separate account, prior races would have no effect, and similarly if today's betting were combined with the rest of the bettor's wealth (or even his lifetime of bets), the prior outcome would likely be trivial.

This analysis applies to other gambling decisions. If a series of gambles are bracketed together then the outcome of one gamble can affect the choices made later. Johnson and I investigated how prior outcomes affect risky choice (Thaler and Johnson, 1990). Subjects were MBA students who played for real money. The following three choices illustrate the type of problems studied. The percentage of subjects taking each option appears in brackets.

Problem 1: You have just won $30. Now choose between:
    (a) A 50% chance to gain $9 and a 50% chance to lose $9. [70]
    (b) No further gain or loss. [30]

---

* That is, long shots become even worse bets at the end of the day. They are always bad bets. See Thaler and Ziemba (1988).

Problem 2: You have just lost $30. Now choose between:
(a) A 50% chance to gain $9 and a 50% chance to loose $9. [40]
(b) No further gain or loss. [60]

Problem 3: You have just lost $30. Now choose between:
(a) A 33% chance to gain $30 and a 67% chance to gain nothing. [60]
(b) A sure $10. [40]

These and other problems of this sort were used to investigate how prior outcomes affect risky choices. Two results are worth nothing. First, as illustrated by Problem 1, a prior gain can stimulate risk seeking in the same account. We called this phenomenon the 'house money' effect since gamblers often refer to money they have won from the casino as house money (the casino is known as 'the house'). Indeed, one often sees gamblers who have won some money early in the evening put that money into a different pocket from their 'own' money; this way each pocket is a separate mental account. Second, as illustrated by Problems 2 and 3, prior losses did not stimulate risk seeking unless the gamble offered a chance to break even.

The stakes used in the experiments just described were fairly large in comparison to most laboratory experiments, but small compared to the wealth of the participants. Limited experimental budgets are a fact of life. Gertner (1993) has made clever use of a set of bigger stakes choices over gambles made by contestants on a television game show called 'Card Sharks'.* The choices Gertner studies were the last in a series of bets made by the winner of the show that day. The contestant had to predict whether a card picked at random from a deck would be higher or lower than a card that was showing. Aces are high and ties create no gain or loss. The odds on the bet therefore vary from no risk (when the showing card is a 2 or an Ace) to roughly 50–50 when the up-card is an 8. After making the prediction, the contestant then can make a bet on the outcome, but the bet must be between 50% and 100% of the amount she has won on the day's show (on average, about $3000). Ignoring the sure bets, Gertner estimates a Tobit regression model to predict the size of the contestant's bet as a function of the card showing (the odds), the stake available (that is, today's winnings), and the amount won in previous days on the show. After controlling for the constraint that the bet must lie between 50% and 100% of the stake, Gertner finds that today's winnings strongly influence the amount wagered.† In contrast, prior cash won has virtually no effect. This finding implies that cash won

---

* See also Biswanger (1981), who obtains similar results. He also was able to run high stakes experiments by using subjects in rural villages in India.
† Gertner offers the following example to illustrate this difference. Suppose a first-time contestant has won $5000 so far and has a Jack showing, so a bet of 'lower' offers 3–1 odds. (She loses with an A, K, or Q, ties with a J, and wins otherwise.) The regression predicts a bet of $2800. Compare this contestant to one who has won only $3000 today but won $2000 the previous day. Although their winnings on the show are identical, this player is predicted to bet only $1544.

today is treated in a different mental account from cash won the day before.[*] This behavior is inconsistent with any version of expected utility theory that treats wealth as fungible.

Narrow Framing and Myopic Loss Aversion

In the gambling decisions discussed above, the day of the experiment suggested a natural bracket. Often gambles or investments occur over a period of time, giving the decision-maker considerable flexibility in how often to calculate gains and losses. It will come as no surprise to learn that the choice of how to bracket the gambles influences the attractiveness of the individual bets. An illustration is provided by a famous problem first posed by Paul Samuelson. Samuelson, it seems, was having lunch with an economist colleague and offered his colleague an attractive bet. They would flip a coin, and if the colleague won he would get $200; if he lost he would have to pay only $100. The colleague turned this bet down, but said that if Samuelson would be willing to play the bet 100 times he would be game. Samuelson (1963) declined to offer this parlay, but went home and proved that this pair of choices is irrational.[†]

There are several points of interest in this problem. First, Samuelson quotes his colleague's reasoning for rejecting the single play of the gamble: 'I won't bet because I would feel the $100 loss more than the $200 gain'. Modern translation: 'I am loss averse'. Second, why does he like the series of bets? Specifically, what mental accounting operation can he be using to make the series of bets attractive when the single play is not?

Suppose Samuelson's colleague's preferences are a piecewise linear version of the prospect theory value function with a loss aversion factor of 2.5:

$$U(x) = \begin{matrix} x & x \geq 0 \\ 2.5x & x < 0 \end{matrix}$$

Because the loss aversion coefficient is greater than 2, a single play of Samuelson's bet is obviously unattractive. What about two plays? The attractiveness of two bets depends on the mental accounting rules being used. If each play of the bet is treated as a separate event, then two plays of the gamble are twice as bad as one play. However, if the bets are combined into a portfolio, then the two-bet parlay {$400, 0.25; 100, 0.50; −$200, 0.25} yields positive expected utility with the hypothesized utility function, and as the number of repetitions increases the portfolio becomes even more attractive. So Samuelson's colleague should accept any number of trials of this bet strictly greater than one *as long as he does not have to watch*!

---

[*] This result is all the more striking because 'yesterday's' show was probably taped just an hour before 'today's' (several shows are taped in the same day) and 'yesterday's' winnings have certainly not been collected.

[†] Specifically, he showed that an expected utility maximizer who will not accept a single play of a gamble for any wealth level that could obtain over a series of such bets will not accept the series. For a more general result, see Tversky and Bar Hillel (1983).

More generally, loss-averse people are more willing to take risks if they combine many bets together than if they consider them one at a time. Indeed, although the puzzle to Samuelson was why his colleague was willing to accept the series of bets, the real puzzle is why he was unwilling to play one. Risk aversion cannot be a satisfactory explanation if his colleague has any significant wealth. For example, suppose Samuelson's colleague's utility function is $U(W) = \ln W$ and his wealth is a modest $10, 000. In that case he should be willing to risk a 50% chance of losing $100 if he had a 50% chance to gain a mere $101.01! Similar results obtain for other reasonable utility functions. In fact, Rabin (1998) shows that expected utility theory implies that someone who turns down Samuelson's bet should also turn down a 50% chance to lose $200 and a 50% chance to win $20,000. More generally, he shows that expected utility theory requires people to be virtually risk neutral for 'small' bets. To explain the fact that many people do reject attractive small bets (such as Samuelson's), we need a combination of loss aversion and one-bet-at-a-time mental accounting.

Benartzi and I (1995) use the same analysis to offer a mental accounting explanation for what economists call the equity premium puzzle (Mehra and Prescott, 1985). The equity premium is the difference in the rate of return on equities (stocks) and a safe investment such as treasury bills. The puzzle is that this difference has historically been very large. In the USA the equity premium has been roughly 6% per year over the past 70 years. This means that a dollar invested in stocks on 1 January 1926 was worth more than $1800 on 1 January 1998, whereas a dollar invested in treasury bills was worth only about $15 (half of which was eaten up by inflation). Of course, part of this difference can be attributed to risk, but what Mehra and Prescott show is that the level of risk aversion necessary to explain such a large difference in returns is implausible.*

To explain the puzzle we note that the risk attitude of loss-averse investors depends on the frequency with which they reset their reference point, i.e. how often they 'count their money'. We hypothesize that investors have prospect theory preferences (using parameters estimated by Tversky and Kahneman, 1992).† We then ask how often people would have to evaluate the changes in their portfolios to make them indifferent between the (US) historical distributions of returns on stocks and bonds? The results of our simulations suggest that the answer is about 13 months. This outcome implies that if the most prominent evaluation period for investors is once a year, the equity premium puzzle is 'solved'.

We refer to this behavior as myopic loss aversion. The disparaging term 'myopic' seems appropriate because the frequent evaluations prevent the

---

* They estimate that it would take a coefficient of relative risk aversion of about 40 to explain the history equity premium. In contrast, a log utility function has a coefficient of 1.

† Specifically, the value function is: $v(x) = x^{\alpha}$ if $x \geq 0 - \lambda(-x)^{\beta}$ if $x < 0$ where λ is the coefficient of loss aversion. They have estimated α and β to be 0.88 and λ to be 2.25. We also use their rank-dependent weighting function. For details see Benartzi and Thaler (1995).

investor from adopting a strategy that would be preferred over an appropriately long time horizon. Indeed, experimental evidence supports the view that when a long-term horizon is imposed externally, subjects elect more risk. For example, Gneezy and Potters (1997) and Thaler *et al.* (1997) ran experiments in which subjects make choices between gambles (investments). The manipulations in these experiments are the frequency with which subjects get feedback. For example, in the Thaler *et al.* study, subjects made investment decisions between stocks and bonds at frequencies that simulated either eight times a year, once a year, or once every five years. The subjects in the two long-term conditions invested roughly two-thirds of their funds in stocks while those in the frequent evaluation condition invested 59% of their assets in bonds. Similarly, Benartzi and I (forthcoming) asked staff members at a university how they would invest their retirement money if they had to choose between two investment funds, A and B, one of which was based on stock returns, the other on bonds. In this case the manipulation was the way in which the returns were displayed. One group examined a chart showing the distribution of *one-year* rates of return, and the other group was shown the simulated distribution of *30-year* rates of return. Those who saw the one-year returns said they would invest a majority of their funds in bonds, whereas those shown the 30-year returns invested 90% of their funds in stocks.*

Myopic loss aversion is an example of a more general phenomenon that Kahneman and Lovallo (1993) call narrow framing; projects are evaluated one at a time, rather than as part of an overall portfolio. This tendency can lead to an extreme unwillingness to take risks. I observed an interesting illustration of this phenomenon while teaching a group of executives from one firm, each of whom was responsible for managing a separate division. I asked each whether he would be willing to undertake a project for his division if the payoffs were as follows: 50% chance to gain $2 million, 50% chance to lose $1 million. Of the 25 executives, three accepted the gamble. I then asked the CEO, who was also attending the session, how he would like a portfolio of 25 of these investments. He nodded enthusiastically. This story illustrates that the antidote for excessive risk aversion is aggregation, either across time or across different divisions.

The examples discussed so far show that narrow bracketing can inhibit risk taking. Narrow bracketing can also have other perverse side-effects. For example, Camerer *et al.* (1997) study the daily labor supply decisions of New York City taxi drivers. In New York, as in many cities, the cab drivers typically rent their cars for a 12-hour period for a fixed fee. They are then entitled to keep all the revenues they earn during that half-day. Since 12 hours is a long time to drive a car, especially in New York City, the drivers must decide each day how long to drive; that is, whether to keep the car for the full 12 hours or quit earlier. This

---

* Similar results for gambles are also obtained by Keren and Wagenaar (1987) and Redelmeier and Tversky (1992).

decision is complicated by the fact that there is more demand for their services on some days than others (because of differences in weather or the presence of a big convention, for example). A rational analysis would lead drivers to work longer hours on busy days, as this policy would maximize earnings per hour worked. If, instead, drivers establish a target earnings level *per day*, they will tend to quit earlier on good days. This is precisely what Camerer *et al.* find. The elasticity of hours worked with respect to the daily wage (as measured by the earnings of *other drivers that day*) is strongly negative. The implication is that taxi drivers do their mental accounting one day at a time.*

The Diversification Heuristic

The unit of analysis can also influence how much variety consumers elect. This effect was first demonstrated by Simonson (1990). He gave students the opportunity to select among six snacks (candy bars, chips, etc.) in one of two conditions: (a) sequential choice: they picked one of the six snacks at each of three class meetings held a week apart; (b) simultaneous choice: on the first class meeting they selected three snacks to be consumed one snack per week over the three class meetings. Simonson observed that in the simultaneous choice condition subjects displayed much more variety seeking than in the sequential choice condition. For example, in the simultaneous choice condition 64% of the subjects chose three different snacks whereas in the sequential choice condition only 9% of the subjects made this choice. Simonson suggests that this behavior might be explained by variety seeking serving as a choice heuristic. That is, when asked to make several choices at once, people tend to diversify. This strategy is sensible under some circumstances (such as when eating a meal – we typically do not order three courses of the same food), but can be misapplied to other situations, such as sequential choice. This mistake represents a failure of predicted utility to accurately forecast subsequent experienced utility. Many students who liked Snickers best elected that snack each week when they picked one week at a time, but went for variety when they had to choose in advance.

This result has been called the 'diversification bias' by Read and Loewenstein (1995). They demonstrate the role of choice bracketing in an ingenious experiment conducted on Halloween night. The 'subjects' in the experiment were young trick-or-treaters who approached two adjacent houses. In one condition the children were offered a choice between two candies (Three Musketeers and Milky Way) at each house. In the other condition they were told at the first house they reached to 'choose whichever two candy bars you like'. Large piles of both candies were displayed to assure that the children would not think it rude to take two of the same. The results showed a strong diversification bias in the simultaneous choice condition: every child selected one of each candy. In

---

* Rizzo and Zeckhauser (1998) find a similar result for physicians whose evaluation period appears to be one year rather than one day.

contrast, only 48% of the children in the sequential choice condition picked different candies. This result is striking, since in either case the candies are dumped into a bag and consumed later. It is the portfolio in the bag that matters, not the portfolio selected at each house.

The diversification bias is not limited to young people choosing among snacks. Benartzi and I (1998) have found evidence of the same phenomenon by studying how people allocate their retirement funds across various investment vehicles. In particular, we find some evidence for an extreme version of this bias that we call the $1/n$ heuristic. The idea is that when an employee is offered n funds to choose from in her retirement plan, she divides the money evenly among the funds offered. Use of this heuristic, or others only slightly more sophisticated, implies that the asset allocation an investor chooses will depend strongly on the array of funds offered in the retirement plan. Thus, in a plan that offered one stock fund and one bond fund, the average allocation would be 50% stocks, but if another stock fund were added, the allocation to stocks would jump to two thirds. We find evidence supporting just this behavior. In a sample of pension plans we regress the percentage of the plan assets in stocks on the percentage of the funds that are stock funds and find a very strong relationship.

We also find that employees seem to put stock in the company they work for into a separate mental account. For companies that do not offer their own stock as one of the options in the pension plan the employees invest 49% of their money in bonds and 51% in stocks. When the company stock is included in the plan this investment attracts 42% of the funds. If the employees wanted to attain a 50% equity exposure, they would invest about 8% of the rest of their funds in stocks, the rest in bonds. Instead they invest their non-company stock funds evenly: 29% in stocks, 29% in bonds.

DISCUSSION

My own thinking about mental accounting began with an attempt to understand why people pay attention to sunk costs, why people are lured by bargains into silly expenditures, and why people will drive across town to save $5 on a small purchase but not a large one. I hope this paper has shown that we have learned quite a bit about these questions, and in so doing, the researchers working in this area have extended the scope of mental accounting far beyond the original set of questions I had set out to answer. Consider the range of questions that mental accounting helps us answer:

- Why do firms pay dividends?
- Why do people buy time-share vacation properties?
- Why are flat-rate pricing plans so popular?
- Why do sales contests have luxuries (instead of cash) as prizes?

- Why do 401 (k) plans increase savings?
- Why do stocks earn so much higher a return than bonds?
- Why do people decline small-stakes attractive bets?
- Why can't you get a cab on a rainy day? (hint: cab drivers earn more per hour on rainy days).

A question that has not received much attention is whether mental accounting is good for us. What is the normative status of mental accounting? I see no useful purpose in worrying about whether or not mental accounting is 'rational'. Mental accounting procedures have evolved to economize on time and thinking costs and also to deal with self-control problems. As is to be expected, the procedures do not work perfectly. People pay attention to sunk costs. They buy things they don't need because the deal is too good to pass up. They quit early on a good day. They put their retirement money in a money market account.

It is not possible to say that the system is flawed without knowing how to fix it. Given that optimization is not feasible (too costly), repairing one problem may create another. For example, if we teach people to ignore sunk costs, do they stop abiding by the principle: 'waste not, want not'? If we stop being lured by good deals, do we stop paying attention to price altogether? There are no easy answers.

Those interested in improving individual decision making can do more work on mental accounting as a prescriptive device. How can mental accounting rules be modified to achieve certain goals?* For example, Jonathan Clements, the author of a regular column for new investors in the *Wall Street Journal*† called 'Getting Going' invited readers to submit tips on how to do a better job of saving and investing. Many of the tips he later published had a strong mental accounting flavor. A reader called David Guerini submitted the following advice:

I started a little 'side' savings account eight years ago. During the day, I try to accumulate change. If I spend $4.50 at a store, I give the cashier a $5 bill, even if I have 50 cents in my pocket. At the end of each day, the money is put aside. If I have no change, I put a $1 bill aside. I add income-tax refunds, money from products I purchased and returned for a refund, and all those annoying little mail-in rebates they give you when you purchase batteries, shaving cream, and so on. I end up painlessly saving between $500 and $1000 each year.

An economist might argue that it would be even less painful to just write a check once a year and send it to his mutual fund. But that would miss the point: mental accounting matters.

---

* Along these lines, Read, Loewenstein and Rabin (1998) have a useful discussion of when broad bracketing works better than narrow bracketing. Short answer: usually.
† See his column on 20, 24, and 31 January 1998.

ACKNOWLEDGMENTS

I have been thinking about mental accounting for more than 20 years, so it is not possible to thank everyone who has helped me write this paper. Some who have helped recently include John Gourville, Chip Heath, Daniel Kahneman, France Leclerc, George Loewenstein, Cade Massey, Dražen Prelec, Dilip Soman, and Roman Weil. This paper began as an invited lecture to the SPUDM conference in Aix-en-Provence held in 1993. It was finally completed during my stay at The Center for Advanced Study in the Behavioral Sciences. Their help in reaching closure is gratefully acknowledged.

15. Toward a Positive Theory of Consumer Choice

Richard H. Thaler

ABSTRACT. The economic theory of the consumer is a combination of positive and normative theories. Since it is based on a rational maximizing model it describes how consumers *should* choose, but it is alleged to also describe how they *do* choose. This paper argues that in certain well-defined situations many consumers act in a manner that is inconsistent with economic theory. In these situations economic theory will make systematic errors in predicting behavior. Kahneman and Tversky's prospect theory is proposed as the basis for an alternative descriptive theory. Topics discussed are underweighting of opportunity costs, failure to ignore sunk costs, search behavior, choosing not to choose and regret, and precommitment and self-control.

1. INTRODUCTION

Economists rarely draw the distinction between normative models of consumer choice and descriptive or positive models. Although the theory is normatively based (it describes what rational consumers *should* do), economists argue that it also serves well as a descriptive theory (it predicts what consumers in fact do). This paper argues that exclusive reliance on the normative theory leads economists to make systematic, predictable errors in describing or forecasting consumer choices.

In some situations the normative and positive theories coincide. If a consumer must add two (small) numbers together as part of a decision process, then one would hope that the normative answer would be a good predictor. So

The author wishes to acknowledge the many people who have made this paper possible. Colleagues, too numerous to name individually, at the Center for Naval Analyses, Cornell University. The National Bureau of Economic Research-West, Decision Research, and the University of Rochester have contributed importantly to the final product. Special thanks go to Daniel Kahneman, Amos Tversky, H. M. Shefrin, Thomas Russell, and particularly Victor Fuchs, who has supported the research in every possible way. Of course, responsibility for remaining deficiencies is the author's. He also wishes to acknowledge financial support from the Kaiser Family Foundation, while he was a visiting scholar at NBER-West.

Reprinted from *Journal of Economic Behavior and Organization*, 1, Richard H. Thaler, "Toward a Positive Theory of Consumer Choice," 39–60, 1980 with kind permission from Elsevier Science – NL, Sara Burgerhart Straat 25, 1055 KV Amsterdam, The Netherlands.

if a problem is sufficiently simple the normative theory will be acceptable. Furthermore, the sign of the substitution effect, the most important prediction in economics, has been shown to be negative even if consumers choose at random (Becker, 1962). Recent research has demonstrated that even rats obey the law of demand (Kagel and Battalio, 1975).

How does the normative theory hold up in more complicated situations? Consider the famous birthday problem in statistics: if 25 people are in a room what is the probability that at least one pair will share a birthday? This problem is famous because everyone guesses wrong when he first hears it. Furthermore, the errors are systematic – nearly everyone guesses too low. (The correct answer is greater than 0.5.) For most people the problem is a form of mental illusion. Research on judgment and decision making under uncertainty, especially by Daniel Kahneman and Amos Tversky (1974, 1979), has shown that such mental illusions should be considered the rule rather than the exception.[1] Systematic, predictable differences between normative models of behavior and actual behavior occur because of what Herbert Simson (1957, p. 198) called "bounded rationality":

The capacity of the human mind for formulating and solving complex problems is very small compared with the size of the problems whose solution is required for objectively rational behavior in the real world – or even for a reasonable approximation to such objective rationality.

This paper presents a group of economic mental illusions. These are classes of problems where consumers are particularly likely to deviate from the predictions of the normative model. By highlighting the specific instances in which the normative model fails to predict behavior, I hope to show the kinds of changes in the theory that will be necessary to make it more descriptive. Many of these changes are incorporated in a new descriptive model of choice under uncertainty called prospect theory (Kahneman and Tversky, 1979). Therefore I begin this paper with a brief summary of prospect theory. Then several types of predicted errors in the normative theory are discussed. Each is first illustrated by an anecdotal example. These examples are intended to illustrate the behavior under discussion in a manner that appeals to the reader's intuition and experiences. I have discussed these examples with hundreds of friends, colleagues, and students. Many of the examples have also been used as questionnaires – I can informally report that a large majority of non-economists say they would act in the hypothesized manner. Yet I am keenly aware that more formal tests are necessary. I try to provide as many kinds of evidence as possible for each type of behavior. These kinds of evidence range from questionnaires, to regressions using market data, to laboratory experiments, to market institutions that exist apparently to exploit these actions. I hope

---

[1] Some of these studies have recently been replicated by economists. See Grether and Plott, 1979, and Grether, 1979.

to gather more evidence in future experimental research. For readers who remain unconvinced, I suggest they try out the examples on some non-economist friends.

2. PROSPECT THEORY

Not very long after expected utility theory was formulated by von Neumann and Morgenstern (1944) questions were raised about its value as a descriptive model (Allais, 1953). Recently Kahneman and Tversky (1979) have proposed an alternative descriptive model of economic behavior that they call prospect theory. I believe that many of the elements of prospect theory can be used in developing descriptive choice models in deterministic settings. Therefore, I will present a very brief summary of prospect theory here.

Kahneman and Tversky begin by presenting the results of a series of survey questions designed to highlight discrepancies between behavior and expected utility theory. Some of these results are presented in Table 15.1. A prospect is a gamble (x, p, y, q) that pays x with probability p and y with probability q. If $q = 0$ that outcome is omitted. A certain outcome is denoted (z). N refers to number of subjects who responded, the percentage who chose each option is given in parentheses, and majority preference is denoted by *. Subjects were also given problems such as these:

Problem 11: In addition to whatever you own you have been given 1,000. You are now asked to choose between

    A: (1,000, 0.5) and   B: (500) $N = 70$.
      (16)   (84)

Problem 12: In addition to whatever you own, you have been given 2,000. You are now asked to choose between

    C: (−1,000, 0.5) and   D: (−500) $N = 68$.
      (69)   (31)

Table 15.1. Preferences between Positive and Negative Prospects

	Positive Prospects		Negative Prospects	
Problem 3	(4,000, 0.80)	<(3,000)	Problem 3′	(−4,000, 0.80)	>(−3,000)
$N = 95$	(20)	(80)*	$N = 95$	(92)*	(8)
Problem 4	(4,000, 0.20)	>(3,000, 0.25)	Problem 4′	(−4,000, 0.20)	<(−3,000, 0.25)
$N = 95$	(65)*	(35)	$N = 95$	(42)	(58)
Problem 7	(3,000, 0.90)	>(6,000, 0.45)	Problem 7′	(−3,000, 0.90)	<(−6,000, 0.45)
$N = 66$	(86)*	(14)	$N = 66$	(8)	(92)*
Problem 8	(3,000, 0.002)	<(6,000, 0.001)	Problem 8′	(−3,000, 0.002)	>(−6,000, 0.001)
$N = 66$	(27)	(73)*	$N = 66$	(70)*	(30)

Source: Kahneman and Tversky (1979).

The results of these questionnaires led to the following empirical generalizations.

1. Gains are treated differently than losses. (Notice the reversal in signs
   of preference in the two columns in Table 15.1.) Except for very small
   probabilities, risk seeking is observed for losses while risk aversion is
   observed for gains.
2. Outcomes received with certainty are overweighted relative to uncertain
   outcomes. (Compare 3 and 3' with 4 and 4'.)
3. The structure of the problem may affect choices. Problems 11 and 12 are
   identical if evaluated with respect to final asset positions but are treated
   differently by subjects.

Kahneman and Tversky then offer a theory that can predict individual choices,
even in the cases in which expected utility theory is violated. In expected utility
theory, an individual with initial wealth w will value a prospect $(x, p; y, q)$ as
$EU = pU(w + x) + qU(w + y)$ if $p + q = 1$. In prospect theory the objective probabilities are replaced by subjective decision weights $\pi(p)$. The utility function
is replaced by a value function, v, that is defined over changes in wealth rather
than final asset position. For "regular" prospects (i.e., $p + q < 1$ or $x \geq 0 \geq y$ or
$x \leq 0 \leq y$) then the value of a prospect is given by

$$V(x, p; y, q) = \pi(p)v(x) + \pi(q)v(y). \tag{1}$$

If $p + q = 1$ and either $x > y > 0$ or $x < y < 0$ then

$$V(x, p; y, q) = v(y) + \pi(p)[v(x) - v(y)]. \tag{2}$$

The value function is of particular interest here since I will discuss only
deterministic choice problems. The essential characteristics of the value function
are:

1. It is defined over gains and losses with respect to some natural reference
   point. Changes in the reference point can alter choices as in Problems 11
   and 12.
2. It is concave for gains and convex for losses. The shape of the value function is based on the psychophysical principle that the difference between
   0 and 100 seems greater than the difference between 1,000 and 1,100 irrespective of the sign of the magnitudes. This shape explains the observed
   risk-seeking choices for losses and risks averse choices for gains.[2]
3. It is steeper for losses than for gains. "The aggravation that one experiences in losing a sum of money appears to be greater than the pleasure
   associated with gaining the same amount."[3]

---

[2] The loss function will be mitigated by the threat of ruin or other discontinuities. See Kahneman
and Tversky (1979, p. 279).
[3] Kahneman and Tversky (1979, p. 279).

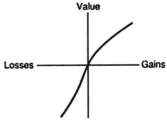

Figure 15.1. A hypothetical value function.

A hypothetical value function with these properties is pictured in Figure 15.1. Insurance purchasing and gambling are explained through the π function, which is regressive with respect to objective probabilities and has discontinuities around 0 and 1. For details, of course, the reader is encouraged to read the original paper.

3. OPPORTUNITY COSTS AND THE ENDOWMENT EFFECT

Example 1. Mr. R bought a case of good wine in the late 50s for about $5 a bottle. A few years later his wine merchant offered to buy the wine back for $100 a bottle. He refused, although he has never paid more than $35 for a bottle of wine.

Example 2. Mr. H mows his own lawn. His neighbor's son would mow it for $8. He wouldn't mow his neighbor's same-sized lawn for $20.

Example 3. Two survey questions: (a) Assume you have been exposed to a disease which if contracted leads to a quick and painless death within a week. The probability you have the disease is 0.001. What is the maximum you would be willing to pay for a cure? (b) Suppose volunteers were needed for research on the above disease. All that would be required is that you expose yourself to a 0.001 chance of contracting the disease. What is the minimum payment you would require to volunteer for this program? (You would not be allowed to purchase the cure.)

   The Results. Many people respond to questions (a) and (b) with answers which differ by an order of magnitude or more! (A typical response is $200 and $10,000.)

These examples have in common sharp differences between buying and selling prices. While such differences *can* be explained using income effects or transactions costs, I will argue that a more parsimonious explanation is available if one distinguishes between the opportunity costs and out-of-pocket costs.

The first lesson of economics is that all costs are (in some sense) opportunity costs. Therefore opportunity costs *should* be treated as equivalent to out-of-pocket costs. How good is this normative advice as a descriptive model? Consider Kahneman and Tversky's Problems 11 and 12. In Problem 11 the gamble is viewed as a chance to gain while in Problem 12 it is viewed as a chance to avert a loss. We know the problems are viewed differently since the majority responses are reversed. Kahneman and Tversky incorporate this in their model by focusing on gains and losses (rather than final asset positions which are identical in these two problems) and by having the loss function steeper than the gains function, $v(x) < -v(x)$. This shape of the value function implies that if out-of-pocket costs are viewed as losses and opportunity costs are viewed as foregone gains, the former will be more heavily weighted. Furthermore, a certain degree of inertia is introduced into the consumer choice process since goods that are included in the individual's endowment will be more highly valued than those not held in the endowment, *ceteris paribus*. This follows because removing a good from the endowment creates a loss while adding the same good (to an endowment without it) generates a gain. Henceforth, I will refer to the underweighting of opportunity costs as the *endowment effect*.

Clearly the endowment effect can explain the behavior in Examples 1–3. In Example 1 it works in two ways. First, as just mentioned, giving up the wine will induce a loss while purchasing the same bottle would create a (less highly weighted) gain. Second, the money paid for a bottle purchased might be viewed as a loss,[4] while the money received for the sale would be viewed as a gain.

The endowment effect is a hypothesis about behavior. What evidence exists (aside from Kahneman and Tversky's survey data) to support this hypothesis? Unfortunately, there is little in the way of formal tests. One recent study by SRI International does provide some supporting evidence. Weiss, Hall, and Dong (1978) studied the schooling decision of participants in the Seattle–Denver Income Maintenance Experiment. They found that variation in the out-of-pocket costs of education had effects which were "stronger and more systematic than that of a controlled change in opportunity costs."[5]

An experimental test was conducted by Becker, Ronen, and Sorter (1974). They asked MBA students to choose between two projects that differed only in that one had an opportunity cost component while the other had only out-of-pocket costs. The students systematically preferred the projects with the opportunity costs. However, some problems with their experimental design make this evidence inconclusive. (See Neumann and Friedman, 1978.)

Other kinds of evidence in support of the endowment effect hypothesis are less direct but perhaps more convincing. I refer to instances in which businesses have used the endowment effect to further their interests.

Credit cards provide a particularly clear example. Until recently, credit card companies banned their affiliated stores from charging higher prices to credit card users. A bill to outlaw such agreements was presented to Congress. When it appeared likely that some kind of bill would pass, the credit card lobby turned its attention to form rather than substance. Specifically, it preferred that any difference between cash and credit card customers take the form of a cash discount rather than a credit card surcharge. The preference makes sense if

---

[4] More about the psychology of spending appears in Section 4.
[5] Weiss, Hall, and Dong (1978).

consumers would view the cash discount as an opportunity cost of using the credit card but the surcharge as an out-of-pocket cost.[6]

The film processing industry seems also to have understood the endowment effect. Some processing companies (notably Fotomat) have a policy whereby they process and print any photographs no matter how badly exposed they are. Customers can ask for refunds (on their next trip if they wish) for any pictures they do not want. The endowment effect helps explain why they are not besieged by refund requests.

Other marketing strategies can be understood with the use of the endowment effect. Consider the case of a two-week trial period with a money-back guarantee. At the first decision point the consumer thinks he can lose at most the transactions costs of taking the good home and back. If the transactions costs are less than the value of the utilization of the good for two weeks, then the maximizing consumer pays for the good and takes it home. The second decision point comes two weeks later. If the consumer has fully adapted to the purchase, he views the cost of keeping the good as an opportunity cost. Once this happens the sale is more likely. Of course, it is entirely possible that were the good to be stolen and the price of the good refunded by his insurance company he would fail to repurchase the good.[7]

A final application of the endowment effect comes from the field of sports economics. Harold Demsetz (1972) argues that the reserve clause (which ties a player to a team for life) does not affect the distribution of players among teams. His argument is as follows. Resources go to their highest valued use. Teams are free to sell or trade players to other teams. Thus, if a player is owned by one team but valued more highly by another, a transaction will take place. Since the transaction costs appear to be low, the argument seems correct, but the facts clearly contradict the conclusion!

Consider first the free agent draft in football. Teams take turns selecting players who have finished their collegiate eligibility. The teams pick in a specified order. Demsetz (and economic theory) would suggest that teams should draft

[6] In his testimony before the Senate Committee on Banking, Housing and Urban Affairs, Jeffrey Bucher of the Federal Reserve Board argued that surcharges and discounts should be treated the same way. However he reported that 'critics argued that a surcharge carries the connotation of a penalty on credit card users while a discount is viewed as a bonus to cash customers. They contended that this difference in psychological impact makes it more likely that surcharge systems will discourage customers from using credit cards . . . ' This passage and other details are in United States Senate (1975).

[7] Suppose your neighbors are going to have a garage sale. They offer to sell any of your household goods for you at one half of the original purchase price. You must only tell them which goods to sell and they will take care of everything else, including returning any unsold items. Try to imagine which goods you would decide to sell and which goods you would decide to keep. Now imagine that some of the goods you decided to keep are stolen, and that your insurance will pay you half the original price. If you could also replace them at half price how many would you replace? (Assume identical quantity.) Many people say that there would be some items which they would not sell in the first case *and* wouldn't buy in the second case, even though transactions costs have been made very low in this example.

at their turn the player with the highest market value and then trade or sell him to the team that values him most. Thus we should expect to see a flurry of trades right after the draft. Instead, while drafting rights (i.e., turns to pick) are frequently traded, players drafted are virtually never traded during the period between the draft and the start of the season. Why? Before offering an answer, consider another empirical observation. In baseball over the last few years the reserve clause has been weakened and many players (starting with "Catfish" Hunter) have become free agents, able to sign with any team. If players are already on the teams where their value is highest these free agents should all re-sign with their former teams (at new higher salaries that give the rents to the player rather than the owner). Yet this has not happened. Instead, virtually all of the players who have become free agents have signed with new teams.

I believe that the endowment effect can explain at least part of these puzzles. When a player is drafted he becomes part of the fans' endowment. If he is sold or traded this will be treated by the fans as a *loss*. However, when a player is declared a free agent he drops out of the endowment, and the fans will recognize that he can only be regained at substantial *out-of-pocket* expense. Similarly, trading the rights to draft a player will be preferred to trading the player since he will never enter the fans' endowment.

4. SUNK COSTS: MODELING PSYCHIC COSTS

Example 4. A family pays $40 for tickets to a basketball game to be played 60 miles from their home. On the day of the game there is a snowstorm. They decide to go anyway, but note in passing that had the tickets been given to them, they would have stayed home.

Example 5. A man joins a tennis club and pays a $300 yearly membership fee. After two weeks of playing he develops a tennis elbow. He continues to play (in pain) saying, "I don't want to waste the $300!"

Economic theory implies that only incremental costs and benefits *should* affect decisions. Historical costs should be irrelevant. But do (non-economist) consumers ignore sunk costs in their everyday decisions? As Examples 4 and 5 suggest, I do not believe that they do. Rather, I suggest the alternative hypothesis that paying for the right to use a good or service will increase the rate at which the good will be utilized, *ceteris paribus*. This hypothesis will be referred to as the *sunk cost effect*.

Gathering evidence to test this hypothesis is complicated by problems of selectivity bias. People who have paid to join a tennis club are likely to enjoy tennis more than those who have not, and thus they are likely to use it more than another group who didn't have to pay the membership fee. This problem makes market tests difficult. Other evidence does exist, however, and it is generally supportive.

First, some of Kahneman and Tversky's survey questions indicate a sunk cost effect. For example, one set of subjects preferred (0) to (−800, 0.2; 200, 0.8), while a different set preferred (−1,000, 0.2) to (−200). This suggests that the 200 subtracted from the first problem to obtain the second is not viewed as sunk by the subjects. Kahneman and Tversky also cite the empirical finding that betting on long shots increases during the course of a racing day, again implying that bettors have not adapted to their losses. Similar behavior is well known to anyone who plays poker.

Second, social psychologists have done experiments on a related concept. Aronson and Mills (1959) tested to see whether people who had to undertake considerable effort to obtain something would like it better. Their procedure was to advertise for students to participate in a discussion group. Subjects were then assigned to one of three groups: severe initiation, mild initiation, and control. Those in the severe initiation group had to read aloud an embarrassing portion of some sexually oriented material. Those in the mild condition read aloud some more timid material. Those in the control group had no initiation. Basically, the results confirmed the hypothesis of the experimenters. Those in the severe initiation group reported enjoying the subsequent group discussion (which, in fact, was deadly dull) more than those in the other group. These results were later replicated by Gerard and Mathewson (1966).[8]

Third, there are many examples of the governmental failing to ignore sunk costs. A dramatic example of this was revealed in a Congressional investigation of the Teton Dam disaster.[9] One part of the hearings was devoted to an analysis of the *theory of momentum* − "that is, the inclination on the part of the Bureau of Reclamation to continue dam construction, once commenced, despite hazards which might emerge during the course of construction."[10] The commissioner of the Bureau of Reclamation denied that such a problem existed. However, when asked to "give an example of any dam whose construction was halted or even paused or interrupted temporarily once the physical construction processes actually began on the dam itself,"[11] the commissioner came up empty-handed.

Finally, perhaps the strongest support for the sunk cost hypothesis can be found in the classroom. Anyone who has ever tried to teach this concept knows that it is not intuitively obvious, even to some experienced businesspeople.

---

[8] I also plan some experiments to test the sunk cost effect. In one pilot study undertaken by one of my students, Lewis Broad, customers at an all-you-can-eat pizza restaurant were randomly given free lunches. They, in fact, ate less than the control group who paid the $2.50 normal bill.

[9] This example was suggested by Paul Slovic.

[10] U.S. Government (1976, p. 14). This issue was raised because the Bureau had in fact received such warnings about the Teton Dam.

[11] *Ibid*, p. 14.

4.1. Modeling Sunk Costs

If the sunk cost effect does exist, it is interesting to speculate on the thought process that produces it. A reasonable explanation can be offered using prospect theory. First, however, we must consider the individual's psychic accounting system. To do this it is necessary to introduce a psychic equivalent to debits and credits which, for lack of better terms, I will call pleasure and pain. In terms of prospect theory, pleasure can be thought of as the value function in the domain of gains while pain corresponds to the value function in the domain of losses. (Henceforth, for expository purposes, I will refer to the value function for losses as $\tilde{v}$.) When will a customer feel pain? Pain will *not* be felt when a purchase is made for immediate consumption (like buying a hamburger for lunch) as long as the price is "reasonable." If the value of the hamburger is g and the cost is c, then the net pleasure will be $v(g) + \tilde{v}(-c)$.[12] Only in the event of a loss will there be actual net pain.

Now, however, consider the case described in Example 4. When the basketball tickets are purchased the consumer just exchanges cash for an asset (the tickets). At this point the consumer *could* experience $40 worth of pain with the expectation of feeling pleasure at the game as if the tickets had been free, but this seems unlikely. A much more plausible story is that no pain or pleasure is felt at this point except perhaps in anticipation of the game. Then when the game is attended the consumer feels net pleasure as in the case of the hamburger. The snowstorm, however, creates a problem. If the tickets aren't used then their value has become zero and the consumer should feel a $40 loss ($\tilde{v}(-40)$). But, the economist would say, how does going to the game help? Let's assume that the cost of going to the game through the snow is c and the value of seeing the game is g. (I will ignore uncertainty about getting to the game as it would add nothing to the analysis.) Further, assume that had the tickets been free, the consumer would have been indifferent about going, i.e., $v(g) = -\tilde{v}(-c)$. In this case the $40 paid for the tickets will induce the consumer to go since $v(g) + \tilde{v}(-(c+40)) > -\tilde{v}(-40)$ due to the convexity of $\tilde{v}$.

4.2. Sunk Costs and Multipart Pricing

Example 5 can be used to illustrate an application of the sunk cost effect in microeconomics. The tennis club uses a two-part pricing scheme. The membership fee is $300 and the court fees are $10 per hour. Suppose the membership fee is raised to $400 keeping the court fees fixed. The standard theory would predict the following effects: (1) some members will drop out, (2) those who remain will use the club slightly less because of the income effect of the increased

---

[12] What if the price is "unreasonable?" In this case the customer will feel pain that is a function of the difference between the price paid and some reference (or just) price. Similarly, if the price is especially low there will be extra pleasure that is related to the difference between the reference price and the price paid. A complete analysis of these issues will be presented in a future paper.

membership fee (assuming tennis playing is normal), and (3) *average* utilization will rise if the change in the mix of members toward higher demanders outweighs the income effect; otherwise, average utilization will fall. Total utilization will certainly fall.

If the sunk cost effect is valid then the analysis of effect (2) must be changed. The sunk cost effect will increase utilization, which is in the opposite direction of the income effect. If the sunk cost effect is large enough in magnitude, then raising the membership fee could increase *total* utilization. Given the wide ranging uses of multipart pricing this analysis could have many important applications.

5. SEARCHING AND THE PSYCHOPHYSICS OF PRICES

Example 6. (a) You set off to buy a clock radio at what you believe to be the cheapest store in your area. When you arrive, you find that the radio costs $25, a price consistent with your priors (the suggested retail price is $35). As you are about to make the purchase, a reliable friend comes by and tells you that the same radio is selling for $20 at another store ten minutes away. Do you go to the other store? What is the minimum price differential which would induce you to go to the other store? (b) Now suppose that instead of a radio you are buying a color television for $500 and your friend tells you it is available at the other store for $495. Same questions.

On the second page of his price theory text, George Stigler (1970) states a traditional theory of consumer search behavior:

> To maximize his utility the buyer searches for additional prices until the expected saving from the purchase equals the cost of visiting one more dealer. Then he stops searching, and buys from the dealer who quotes the lowest price he has encountered.

Example 6 suggests an alternative to Stigler's theory. The alternative theory states that search for any purchase will continue until the expected amount saved as a proportion of the total price equals some critical value.

This hypothesis is a simple application of the Weber–Fechner law of psychophysics.[13] The law states that the just noticeable difference in any stimulus is proportional to the stimulus. If the stimulus is price, then the law implies that

$$\Delta p / p = k,$$

where Δp is the just noticeable difference, p is the mean price, and k is a constant.

Again, this hypothesis is difficult to test empirically. However, a recent paper by Pratt, Wise, and Zeckhauser (1977) studied price dispersions of consumer goods and found nearly a linear relationship between the mean price of a good and its standard deviation. They interpret this result as inconsistent with the standard search theory: "If search costs were constant, we might expect that the expected gains from searching would lead to ratios between standard deviation

---

[13] For more on the Weber-Fechner Law see Stigler (1965).

and price that declined rather rapidly with mean price."[14] While these results are supportive, they are inconclusive because the observed price dispersions represent an equilibrium resulting from both buyer *and* seller behavior. Thus, even if consumers searched optimally, firm behavior could produce this result. A cleaner test may only be possible experimentally.

Because of its psychophysical foundation, prospect theory can be used to model search behavior as observed in Example 6. To see how, reconsider Equation (2) (repeated here for convenience),

$$V(x, p; y, q) = v(y) + \pi(p)[v(x) - v(y)]. \tag{2}$$

Notice that the decision weight given to the chance of winning, $\pi(p)$, is multiplied by the difference in the valuation of the alternative prizes $(v(x) - v(y))$ rather than the value of the monetary differences $(v(x - y))$ because of the concavity of v, $v(x) - v(y) < v(x - y)$. Similarly, the value of obtaining the clock radio at \$20 instead of \$25 would be $\tilde{v}(-25) - \tilde{v}(-20)$ which is greater (in absolute value) than $\tilde{v}(-500) - \tilde{v}(-495)$ because of the convexity of $\tilde{v}$. Put simply, \$5 seems like a lot to save on a \$25 radio but not much on a \$500 TV. Needless to say, it would be virtually unnoticed on a \$5,000 car.

Market behavior consistent with this hypothesis is easy to find. An old selling trick is to quote a low price for a stripped-down model and then coax the consumer into a more expensive version in a series of increments, each of which seems small relative to the entire purchase. (One reason why new cars have whitewall tires and old cars do not is that \$20 seems a small extra to equip a *car* with whitewalls but a large extra for a new set of *tires*.) Funeral parlors, as well as automobile dealers, are said to make a living off this idea.[15]

6. CHOOSING NOT TO CHOOSE: REGRET

Example 7.[16] Members of the Israeli Army display a resistance to trading patrol assignments, even when it would be convenient for both individuals to do so.

Example 8.[17] Mr. A is waiting in line at a movie theater. When he gets to the ticket window he is told that as the 100,000th customer of the theater he has just won \$100.

---

[14] Pratt, Wise, and Zeckhauser (1977, p. 22).

[15] Madison Avenue also seems to understand this principle. An advertisement appeared on television recently for a variable-month car loan (46 months, say, instead of the usual 48). The bank wanted to stress the amount of interest that could be saved by financing the car over two fewer months. In the advertisement an actor had about \$5,000 in bills stacked up on a table to represent the total amount of money repaid. He then took \$37 representing the interest saved, removed it from the pile, and said, "It may not seem like a lot here . . . " (pointing to the pile) ". . . but it will feel like a lot here" (pointing to his wallet).

[16] This example is due to Daniel Kahneman and Amos Tversky.

[17] This example is due to Ronald Howard.

Mr. B is waiting in line at a different theater. The man in front of him wins $1,000 for being the 1,000,000th customer of the theater. Mr. B wins $150.

Would you rather be Mr. A or Mr. B?

This and the following section discuss situations where individuals voluntarily restrict their choices. In Section 5 the motive is self-control. Choices in the future are reduced because the current self doesn't trust the future self. In this section we consider a motive for reducing choice which is a special kind of decision-making cost. Here the act of choosing or even just the knowledge that choice exists induces costs, and these costs can be reduced or eliminated by restricting the choice set in advance. These costs fall into the general category of *regret* which will be defined to include the related concepts of *guilt* and *responsibility*.

That responsibility can cause regret is well illustrated by Example 7. If two men trade assignments and one is killed, the other must live with the knowledge that it could (should?) have been he. By avoiding such trades these costs are reduced. Since the opportunity to exchange assignments must surely be a valued convenience, the observed resistance to trading suggests that the potential responsibility costs are non-trivial.

Sometimes just information can induce psychic costs. This is obvious, since it is always possible to make someone feel terrible just by relating a horror story of sufficient horror. Example 8 illustrates the point in a more interesting way. There seems little doubt that were the prizes won by Mr. A and Mr. B the same, Mr. A would be better off. The knowledge that he just missed winning causes regret to Mr. B, enough to cause some people to prefer Mr. A's position in the Example as stated!

Whenever choice can induce regret consumers have an incentive to eliminate the choice. They will do so whenever the expected increase in utility (pleasure) derived from making their own choices is less than the expected psychic costs which the choices will induce.

Regret, in prospect theory, can be modeled through induced changes in the reference point. In Example 8, Mr. A simply gains $100 or $v(100)$. Mr. B however must deal with the near miss. If, for example, the person in front of him cut into the line he may feel he has gained $150 but lost $1,000 yielding $v(150) + \tilde{v}(-1,000)$.

Two markets seem to have been strongly influenced by this preference for not choosing: the health care industry, and the vacation and recreation industry.

Choosing not to choose is apparent at many levels in the health care industry. It explains, I believe, two major institutional features of the health delivery system. A puzzle for many economists who have studied the industry is the popularity of shallow, first dollar (no deductible or low deductible) coverage which is precisely the opposite pattern which would be predicted by a theoretical analysis of the problem. Many economists have criticized the system because the insurance creates a zero marginal cost situation for most consumers and this, it is argued, helps create the massive inflation we have experienced in this sector in recent years. The analysis may be correct, but an important issue seems ignored. Why do consumers want the first dollar coverage? I believe the reasons involve regret. Most consumers find decisions involving trade-offs between health care and money very distasteful. This is especially true when the decision is made for someone else, like a child. A high deductible policy would force individuals to make many such decisions, at considerable psychic costs. The costs can occur no matter which way the decision is made. Consider a couple who must decide whether to spend X for a diagnostic test for their child. There is some small probability p that the child has a serious disease which could be treated if detected early enough. There will surely be regret if the decision is made not to get the test and the child later is found to have the disease. If the disease can be fatal, then the regret may loom so large that the test will be administered even for very large values of X or very small value of p. Yet once the test is ordered and the likely negative result is obtained, the couple may regret the expenditure, especially if it is large relative to their income. Obviously, these costs are avoided if all health care is prepaid, via either first dollar coverage or a prepaid health organization.

Though many individuals seem averse to explicit trade-offs between money and health, money does not have to be at stake for regret to enter the picture. The health industry has frequently been criticized for failing to involve the patient in the decision-making process, even when no out-of-pocket expenses are involved. Again, regret seems to provide an attractive explanation for this characteristic of the system. Suppose that a patient must have an operation, but two different procedures are possible. Assume that only one of the procedures can ever be attempted on any individual, that each has the same probability of success and (to make the case as clean as possible) that physicians know that if one procedure doesn't work the other would have. Clearly, in this situation a rational consumer would want the physician to make the choice, and furthermore, he would not want to know that a choice existed! In less dramatic examples there will still be an incentive to let the physician choose, particularly if the physician knows the patient well (and thus can do a good job of reflecting the patient's preferences).

Of course, the physician must then bear all the responsibility costs so there may be advantages to further delegation. One method is to obtain a second opinion, which at least divides the responsibility. Another is to utilize rules-of-thumb and standard-operating-procedures which may eliminate the costs altogether.[18]

The other major example of the market yielding to consumer preferences to not choose is the recreation industry. An excellent case in point is Club Med,

---

[18] I should add here that these comments about the health sector are strictly of a *positive* nature. I am simply offering an explanation of why the institutions are structured as they are. Policy implications must be drawn carefully.

which is actually not a club but rather a worldwide chain of resort hotels.[19] One heavily promoted characteristic of the resorts is that they are virtually cashless. Almost all activities including food and drink are prepaid, and extra drinks are paid for via poppit beads which are worn necklace style.[20] This example presents an interesting contrast with the health example. Consumers may feel guilty about not buying health and guilty about spending on their vacation. Having everything prepaid avoids decisions about whether to *spend* to do something, and reduces the psychic costs of engaging in the costly activities. The reduction in psychic costs may be enough so that a consumer would prefer to spend $1,000 for a vacation than to spend $400 on plane fare and another $500 in $20 increments, especially given the hypothesis of the preceding section. Club Med has taken the prepaid concept furthest, but the basic idea is prevalent in the recreation industry. Other examples include ocean cruises, "package travel tours," and one-price amusement parks, such as Marriott's Great America.

7. Precommitment and Self-Control[21]

Example 9. A group of hungry economists is awaiting dinner when a large can of cashews is opened and placed on the coffee table. After half the can is devoured in three minutes, everyone agrees to put the rest of the cashews into the pantry.

Example 10. Professor X agreed to give a paper at the AEA meetings "to ensure that the paper would get written by the end of the year."

A basic axiom of economic theory is that additional choices can only make one better-off (and that an additional constraint can only make one worse-off). An exception is sometimes made due to decision-making costs, a concept that was expanded to include regret in the previous section. This section demonstrates that the axiom is also violated when self-control problems are present.

The question examined now is why individuals impose rules on themselves. This question was brought to economists' attention by Strotz (1955/56) in his now classic paper on dynamic inconsistency. Strotz begins his article with a famous quote from the *Odyssey*:

---

[19] This example was suggested by Paul Joskow.

[20] "Cash is useless at Club Med. You prepay your vacation before leaving home. Included in the price are room accommodations, three fabulous meals each day, all the wine you can drink, lunch and dinner, scores of sports activities, plus expert instruction and use of rent-free sporting equipment. The only extras, if there are any, are totally up to you. Drinks at the bar, boutique purchases, optimal excursions, beauty salon visits – simply sign and then pay for them before leaving the village. And there's no tipping. So it couldn't be easier to stick to your vacation budget" (from a Club Med brochure).

[21] The ideas in this section are explored in detail in Thaler and Shefrin (1979). Details on the formal model appear in Shefrin and Thaler (1979). Others who have written in this area are Ainslee (1975), Schelling (1978), Elster (1977), and Scitovsky (1976).

... but you must bind me hard and fast, so that I cannot stir from the spot where you will stand me ... and if I beg you to release me, you must tighten and add to my bonds.

Strotz described Ulysses' problem as one of *changing tastes*. He now would prefer not to steer his ship upon the rocks, but he knows that once he hears the Sirens he will want to get closer to their source and thus to the rocks. The solution Ulysses adopts is to have his crew tie him to the mast. Strotz refers to this type of solution as *precommitment*.

Strotz's formal model concerns savings behavior. How should an individual allocate a fixed exhaustible resource over his lifetime? The major finding in Strotz's paper is that unless the individual has an exponential discount function, he will not follow his own plan. That is, if at time t the individual reconsiders a plan formulated at time $t' < t$, he will change the plan. Thus people will be *inconsistent* over time. While changing tastes can explain inconsistency, they cannot explain precommitment. Why should the person with changing tastes bind himself to his *current* preferences, knowing that he will wish to break the binds in each succeeding period? Yet there is no denying the popularity of precommitment devices. One such device which has always been an enigma to economists is Christmas clubs which currently attract over one billion dollars a year in deposits from millions of depositors. Other examples of precommitment are discussed below.

The key to understanding precommitment is to recognize that it is a device used to solve problems of *self-control*. While this seems obvious, it has not been incorporated in the formal models of dynamic choice behavior. Yet it is not difficult to do so. The concept of self-control suggests the existence of a controller and a controllee. To capture this, the individual can be modeled as an organization with a *planner* and a series of *doers*, one for every time period. Conflict arises because the current doer's preferences are always myopic relative to the planner's. This conflict creates a *control problem* of the same variety as those present in any organization. Since the planner's preferences are consistent over time it does make sense for him to adopt rules to govern the doers' behavior. These rules are adopted for the same reasons employees are not given complete discretion: the existence of a conflict of interest.

Since the full details of the model are available elsewhere I will limit my discussion here to the predictions of the model regarding market behavior. One immediate implication of the model is that self-control problems will be most important for those consumption activities which have a time dimension. Since the planner maximizes a function that depends on the doers' utilities, if all the costs and benefits of a particular activity occur in the present there will be no conflict. Of course, as long as there is a finite budget constraint, any current consumption will reduce future consumption, but the conflicts are likely to be greatest for saving per se and for those activities which have an explicit time dimension. For lack of a better term, I will refer to such activities as *investment goods*. Further, goods whose benefits accrue later than their costs (such as education and exercise) are termed *positive investment goods*, while those with the opposite time structure (such as tobacco and alcohol) are termed *negative investment goods*.

Since precommitment usually requires external help (Ulysses needed his crew to tie him to the mast), if it is an important phenomenon we should expect to see evidence of market provision of precommitment services in the investment goods industries. Indeed, such evidence is abundant.

Negative investment goods provide the most dramatic examples: Alcoholics Anonymous, drug abuse centers, diet clubs, "fat farms," and smoking clinics. Note that addiction is not the only factor involved in these services. Calling food addictive is stretching the definition somewhat, so the diet clubs and fat farms can be considered pure self-control administrators. Even the drug examples, such as Alcoholics Anonymous, perform most of their activities for individuals who are "on the wagon." The problem is not that they are addicted to alcohol, rather that they would quickly become readdicted. The problem is to avoid the first drink, and AA helps them do that. One extreme technique of precommitment used by alcoholics is taking the drug Antabuse, which makes the individual sick if he ingests any alcohol.

The most obvious positive investment good is saving itself, and here we find an industry dominated by precommitment devices. Christmas clubs, which have already been mentioned, were particularly noteworthy in previous years because they paid no interest and were thus a "pure" self-control device.[22] Another curious savings institution is the passbook loan. A typical example would be of an individual who had $8,000 in a savings account and wanted to buy a $5,000 car. Rather than withdraw the $5,000 and lose the $5^1/2$ percent interest it was earning, the individual uses the money in the account as collateral for a loan at 8 percent. These loans are reasonably popular, in spite of the obvious interest costs, because they guarantee that the money in the savings account will be replaced and not spent. A final example is whole life insurance which is often alleged to be a bad investment but again provides a specific savings *plan*.

Other investment goods, such as education and exercise, evidence self-control considerations in their pricing policies. Virtually all such services are sold via prepaid packages. This device lowers the cost to the doer of engaging in the investment activity on a day-to-day basis. If the sunk cost effect is also present then the membership fee will also act as an actual inducement to go.

8. CONCLUSION

Friedman and Savage (1948) defined economic theory as a positive science using an analogy to a billiard player:

---

[22] The vice president of one savings bank has reported to me the results of a survey his bank completed on Christmas club users. They found that the average savings account balance of Christmas club users was over $3,000. This suggests that Christmas clubs should not be considered as a device for people who can't save but as a tool of people who do!

Consider the problem of predicting, before each shot, the direction of travel of a billiard ball hit by an expert billiard player. It would be possible to construct one or more mathematical formulas that would give the direction of travel that would score points and, among these, would indicate the one (or more) that would leave the balls in the best positions. The formulas might, of course, be extremely complicated, since they would necessarily take account of the location of the balls in relationship to one another and to the cushions and of the complicated phenomena introduced by "english." Nonetheless, it seems not at all unreasonable that excellent predictions would be yielded by the hypothesis that the billiard player made his shots *as if* he knew the formulas, could estimate accurately by eye the angles etc., from the formulas, and could then make the ball travel in the direction indicated by the formulas. It would in no way disprove or contradict the hypothesis or weaken our confidence in it, if it should turn out that the billiard player had never studied any branch of mathematics and was utterly incapable of making the necessary calculations: unless he was capable in some way of reaching approximately the same result as that obtained from the formulas, he would not in fact be likely to be an expert billiard player.[23]

I would like to make two points about this passage and the relationship between Friedman and Savage's position and mine. First, I do not base my critique of the economic theory of the consumer on an attack of the assumptions. I agree with Friedman and Savage that positive theories should be evaluated on the basis of their ability to predict behavior. In my judgment, for the classes of problems discussed in this paper, economic theory fails this test.

Second, Friedman and Savage only claim that their mathematical model would be a good predictor of the behavior of an *expert* billiard player. It is instructive to consider how one might build models of two non-experts.

A novice who has played only a few times will mainly be concerned with the choice of what ball to try to sink, which will depend primarily on the *perceived* degree of difficulty of the shot. (In contrast, an expert can make nearly any open shot and is likely to sink 50 or more in a row. Thus he will be concerned with planning several shots ahead.) The novice will use little or no "english," will pay little attention to where the cue ball goes after the shot, and may be subject to some optical illusions that cause him to systematically mishit some other shots.

An intermediate player who has played an average of two hours a week for twenty years may only average 4 or 5 balls per turn (compared with the expert's 50). He will have much less control of the cue ball after it strikes another ball and will have some shots that he knows cause him trouble (perhaps long bank shots or sharp angles). He will plan ahead, but rarely more than one or two shots.

Clearly, descriptive models for the novice or intermediate will have to be quite different than the model for the expert. If one wanted to model the behavior of the *average* billiard player, the model selected would be for some kind of intermediate player, and would probably resemble the model of the novice

---

[23] Friedman and Savage (1948, p. 298).

more than the model of the expert. Rules-of-thumb and heuristics would have important roles in this model.

It is important to stress that both the novice and intermediate players described above behave rationally. They choose different shots than the expert does because they have different technologies. Nonetheless, the expert model has a distinct normative flavor. The model chooses from all the shots available the *best* shot. Thus the novice and intermediate players choose rationally and yet violate a normative model. The reason, of course, is that the model is not an acceptable normative (or positive) model for *them*. The novice model (aim at the ball that seems easiest to sink – don't worry about much else) is also a normative model. It is the best the novice can do. Clearly the relationship between rationality and normative models is a delicate one.

How does consumer behavior relate to billiard behavior? Again there will be various classes of consumers. Some will be experts (Ph. D.s in economics?), others will be novices (children?). What I have argued in this paper is that the orthodox economic model of consumer behavior is, in essence, a model of robot-like experts. As such, it does a poor job of predicting the behavior of the average consumer.[24] This is not because the average consumer is dumb, but rather that he does not spend all of his time thinking about how to make decisions. A grocery shopper, like the intermediate billiard player, spends a couple of hours a week shopping and devotes a rational amount of (scarce) mental energy to that task. Sensible rules-of-thumb, such as don't waste, may lead to occasional deviations from the expert model, such as the failure to ignore sunk costs, but these shoppers are doing the best they can.

Prospect theory and the planner-doer model attempt to describe *human* decision-makers coping with a very complex and demanding world. Failure to develop positive theories such as these will leave economists wondering why people are frequently aiming at the balls lined up right in front of the pockets rather than at the three-ball carom their computer model has identified as being optimal.

[24] Some related issues have been discussed in the literature on the theory of the firm. See, for example, Winter (1975) and the references cited therein.

16. Prospect Theory in the Wild
Evidence from the Field

Colin F. Camerer

The workhorses of economic analysis are simple formal models that can explain naturally occurring phenomena. Reflecting this taste, economists often say they will incorporate more psychological ideas into economics if those ideas can parsimoniously account for field data better than standard theories do. Taking this statement seriously, this article describes 10 regularities in naturally occurring data that are anomalies for expected utility theory but can all be explained by three simple elements of prospect theory: loss aversion, reflection effects, and nonlinear weighting of probability; moreover, the assumption is made that people isolate decisions (or edit them) from others they might be grouped with (Read, Loewenstein, and Rabin 1999; cf. Thaler, 1999). I hope to show how much success has already been had applying prospect theory to field data and to inspire economists and psychologists to spend more time in the wild.

The 10 patterns are summarized in Table 16.1. To keep the article brief, I sketch expected utility and prospect theory very quickly. (Readers who want to know more should look elsewhere in this volume or in Camerer 1995 or Rabin 1998a). In expected utility, gambles that yield risky outcomes x_i with probabilities p_i are valued according to $\Sigma p_i u(x_i)$, where $u(x)$ is the *utility* of outcome x. In prospect theory they are valued by $\Sigma \pi(p_i)v(x_i - r)$, where $\pi(p)$ is a function that weights probabilities nonlinearly, overweighting probabilities below .3 or so and underweighting larger probabilities.[1] The value function $v(x-r)$ exhibits diminishing marginal sensitivity to deviations from the reference point r, creating a "reflection effect" because $v(x-r)$ is convex for losses and concave for gains (i.e., $v''(x-r) > 0$ for $x < r$ and $v''(x-r) < 0$ for $x > r$). The value function also exhibits *loss aversion* if the value of a loss $-x$ is larger in magnitude than the value of an equal-sized gain (i.e., $-v(-x) > v(x)$ for $x > 0$).

---

[1] In rank-dependent approaches, the weights attached to outcomes are differences in weighted cumulative probabilities. For example, if the outcomes are ordered $x_1 > x_2 > \cdots > x_n$, the weight on outcome x_i is $\pi(p_i + p_2 + \cdots p_i) - \pi(p_1 + p_2 + \cdots p_{i-1})$. (Notice that if $\pi(p) = p$ this weight is just the probability p_i). In cumulative prospect theory, gains and losses are ranked and weighted separately (by magnitude).

The research was supported by NSF grant SBR-9601236 and the hospitality of the Center for Advanced Study in Behavioral Sciences during 1997–98. Linda Babcock and Barbara Mellers gave helpful suggestions.

Table 16.1. Ten Field Phenomena Inconsistent with EU and Consistent with Cumulative Prospect Theory

Domain	Phenomenon	Description	Type of Data	Isolated Decision	Ingredients	References
Stock market	Equity premium	Stock returns are too high relative to bond returns	NYSE stock, bond returns	Single yearly return (not long-run)	Loss aversion	Benartzi and Thaler (1995)
Stock market	Disposition effect	Hold losing stocks too long, sell winners too early	Individual investor trades	Single stock (not portfolio)	Reflection effect	Odean (in press), Genesove and Mayer (in press)
Labor economics	Downward-sloping labor supply	NYC cabdrivers quit around daily income target	Cabdriver hours, earnings	Single day (not week or month)	Loss aversion	Camerer et al. (1997)
Consumer goods	Asymmetric price elasticities	Purchases more sensitive to price increases than to cuts	Product purchases (scanner data)	Single product (not shopping cart)	Loss aversion	Hardie, Johnson, Fader(1993)
Macro-economics	Insensitivity to bad income news	Consumers do not cut consumption after bad income news	Teachers' earnings, savings	Single year	Loss aversion, reflection effect	Shea (1995); Bowman, Minehart and Rabin (1999)
Consumer choice	Status quo bias, Default bias	Consumers do not switch health plans, choose default insurance	Health plan, insurance choices	Single choice	Loss aversion	Samuelson and Zeckhauser (1988), Johnson et al. (1993)
Horse race betting	Favorite-longshot bias	Favorites are underbet, longshots overbet	Track odds	Single race (not day)	Overweight low p(loss)	Jullien and Salánie (1997)
Horse race betting	End-of-the-day effect	Shift to longshots at the end of the day	Track odds	Single day	Reflection effect	McGlothlin (1956)
Insurance	Buying phone wire insurance	Consumers buy overpriced insurance	Phone wire insurance purchases	Single wire risk (not portfolio)	Overweight low p(loss)	Cicchetti and Dubin (1994)
Lottery betting	Demand for Lotto	More tickets sold as top prize rises	State lottery sales	Single lottery	Overweight low p(win)	Cook and Clotfelter (1993)

289

1. FINANCE: THE EQUITY PREMIUM

Two important anomalies in finance can be explained by elements of prospect theory. One anomaly is called the *equity premium*. Stocks – or equities – tend to have more variable annual price changes (or "returns") than bonds do. As a result, the average return to stocks is higher as a way of compensating investors for the additional risk they bear. In most of this century, for example, stock returns were about 8% per year higher than bond returns. This was accepted as a reasonable return premium for equities until Mehra and Prescott (1985) asked how large a degree of risk aversion is implied by this premium. The answer is surprising: under the standard assumptions of economic theory, investors must be absurdly risk averse to demand such a high premium. For example, a person with enough risk aversion to explain the equity premium would be indifferent between a coin flip paying either $50,000 or $100,000 and a sure amount of $51,209.

Explaining why the equity premium is so high has preoccupied financial economists for the last 15 years (see Siegel and Thaler 1997). Benartzi and Thaler (1997) suggested a plausible answer based on prospect theory. In their theory, investors are not averse to the variability of returns; they are averse to loss (the chance that returns are negative). Because annual stock returns are negative much more frequently than annual bond returns are, loss-averse investors will demand a large equity premium to compensate them for the much higher chance of losing money in a year. Keep in mind that the higher average return to stocks means that the cumulative return to stocks over a longer horizon is increasingly likely to be positive as the horizon lengthens. Therefore, to explain the equity premium Benartzi and Thaler must assume that investors take a short horizon over which stocks are more likely to lose money than bonds. They compute the expected prospect values of stock and bond returns over various horizons, using estimates of investor utility functions from Kahneman and Tversky (1992) and including a loss-aversion coefficient of 2.25 (i.e., the disutility of a small loss is 2.25 times as large as the utility of an equal gain). Benartzi and Thaler show that over a 1-year horizon, the prospect values of stock and bond returns are about the same if stocks return 8% more than bonds, which explains the equity premium.

Barberis, Huang, and Santos (1999) include loss-aversion in a standard general equilibrium model of asset pricing. They show that loss-aversion and a strong "house money effect" (an increase in risk-preference after stocks have risen) are both necessary to explain the equity premium.

2. FINANCE: THE DISPOSITION EFFECT

Shefrin and Statman (1985) predicted that because people dislike incurring losses much more than they like incurring gains and are willing to gamble in the domain of losses, investors will hold on to stocks that have lost value (relative to their purchase price) too long and will be eager to sell stocks that have risen in value. They called this the *disposition effect*. The disposition effect is anomalous because the purchase price of a stock should not matter much for whether you decided to sell it. If you think the stock will rise, you should keep it; if you think it will fall, you should sell it. In addition, tax laws encourage people to sell losers rather than winners because such sales generate losses that can be used to reduce the taxes owed on capital gains.

Disposition effects have been found in experiments by Weber and Camerer (1998).[2] On large exchanges, trading volume of stocks that have fallen in price is lower than for stocks that have risen. The best field study was done by Odean (in press). He obtained data from a brokerage firm about all the purchases and sales of a large sample of individual investors. He found that investors held losing stocks a median of 124 days and held winners only 104 days. Investors sometimes say they hold losers because they expect them to "bounce back" (or mean-revert), but in Odean's sample, the unsold losers returned only 5% in the subsequent year, whereas the winners that were sold later returned 11.6%. Interestingly, the winner–loser differences did disappear in December. In this month investors have their last chance to incur a tax advantage from selling losers (and selling winners generates a taxable capital gain), and thus their reluctance to incur losses is temporarily overwhelmed by their last chance to save on taxes.

Genovese and Meyer (in press) report a strong disposition effect in housing sales. Owners who may suffer a nominal loss (selling at a price below what they paid) set prices too high and, as a result, keep their houses too long before selling.

3. LABOR SUPPLY

Camerer, Babcock, Loewenstein, and Thaler (this volume) talked to cab drivers in New York City about when they decide to quit driving each day. Most of the drivers lease their cabs for a fixed fee for up to 12 hours. Many said they set an income target for the day and quit when they reach that target. Although daily income targeting seems sensible, it implies that drivers will work long hours on bad days when the per-hour wage is low and will quit earlier on good high-wage days. The standard theory of the supply of labor predicts the opposite: Drivers will work the hours that are most profitable, quitting early on bad days and making up the shortfall by working longer on good days.

The daily targeting theory and the standard theory of labor supply therefore predict opposite signs of the correlation between hours and the daily wage. To measure the correlation, we collected three samples of data on how many hours drivers worked on different days. The correlation between hours and

---

[2] In the Weber and Camerer experiment, subjects whose shares were automatically sold every period (but could be bought back with no transaction cost) did not buy back the shares of losers more than winners. This shows they are not optimistic about the losers but simply reluctant to sell them and lock in a realized loss.

wages was strongly negative for inexperienced drivers and close to zero for experienced drivers. This suggests that inexperienced drivers began using a daily income targeting heuristic, but those who did so either tended to quit or learned by experience to shift toward driving around the same number of hours every day.

Daily income targeting assumes loss aversion in an indirect way. To explain why the correlation between hours and wages for inexperienced drivers is so strongly negative, one needs to assume that drivers take a 1-day horizon and have a utility function for the day's income that bends sharply at the daily income target. This bend is an aversion to "losing" by falling short of an income reference point.

4. ASYMMETRIC PRICE ELASTICITIES OF CONSUMER GOODS

The price elasticity of a good is the change in quantity demanded, in percentage terms, divided by the percentage change in its price. Hundreds of studies estimate elasticities by looking at how much purchases change after prices change. Loss-averse consumers dislike price increases more than they like the windfall gain from price cuts and will cut back purchases more when prices rise compared with the extra amount they buy when prices fall. Loss aversion therefore implies elasticities will be asymmetric, that is, elasticities will be larger in magnitude after price increases than after price decreases. Putler (1992) first looked for such an asymmetry in price elasticities in consumer purchases of eggs and found it.

Hardie, Johnson, and Fader (1993) replicated the study using a typical model of brand choice in which a consumer's utility for a brand is unobserved but can be estimated by observing purchases. They included the possibility that consumers compare a good's current price to a reference price (the last price they paid) and get more disutility from buying when prices have risen than the extra utility they get when prices have fallen. For orange juice, they estimate a coefficient of loss aversion (the ratio of loss and gain disutilities) around 2.4.

Note that for loss aversion to explain these results, consumers must be narrowly bracketing purchases of a specific good (e.g., eggs or orange juice). Otherwise, the loss from paying more for one good would be integrated with gains or losses from other goods in their shopping cart and would not loom so large.

5. SAVINGS AND CONSUMPTION: INSENSITIVITY TO BAD NEWS

In economic models of lifetime savings and consumption decisions, people are assumed to have separate utilities for consumption in each period, denoted $u[c(t)]$, and discount factors that weight future consumption less than current consumption. These models are used to predict how much rational consumers will consume (or spend) now and how much they will save, depending on their current income, anticipations of future income, and their discount factors. The models make many predictions that seem to be empirically false. The central prediction is that people should plan ahead by anticipating future income to make a guess about their "permanent income" and consume a constant fraction of that total in any one year. Because most workers earn larger and larger incomes throughout their lives, this prediction implies that people will spend more than they earn when they are young – borrowing if they can – and will earn more than they spend when they are older. But in fact, spending on consumption tends to be close to a fixed fraction of current income and does not vary across the life cycle nearly as much as standard theory predicts. Consumption also drops steeply after retirement, which should not be the case if people anticipate retirement and save enough for it.

Shea (1995) pointed out another prediction of the standard life-cycle theory. Think of a group of workers whose wages for the next year are set in advance. In Shea's empirical analysis, these are unionized teachers whose contract is negotiated 1 year ahead. In the standard theory, if next year's wage is surprisingly good, then the teachers should spend more now, and if next year's wage is disappointingly low, the teachers should cut back on their spending now. In fact, the teachers in Shea's study did spend more when their future wages were expected to rise, but they *did not* cut back when their future wages were cut.

Bowman, Minehart, and Rabin (1999) can explain this pattern with a stylized two-period consumption–savings model in which workers have reference-dependent utility, $u(c(t) - r(t))$ (cf. Duesenberry, 1949). The utility they get from consumption in each period exhibits loss aversion (the marginal utility of consuming just enough to reach the reference point is always strictly larger than the marginal utility from exceeding it) and a reflection effect (if people are consuming below their reference point, the marginal utility of consumption rises as they get closer to it). Workers begin with some reference point $r(t)$ and save and consume in the first period. Their reference point in the second period is an average of their initial reference point and their first-period consumption, and thus $r(2) = \alpha r(1) + (1 - \alpha)c(1)$. The pleasure workers get from consuming in the second period depends on how much they consumed in the first period through the effect of previous consumption on the current reference point. If they consumed a lot at first, $r(2)$ will be high and they will be disappointed if their standard of living is cut and $c(2) < r(2)$.

Bowman et al. (1999) show formally how this simple model can explain the behavior of the teachers in Shea's study. Suppose teachers are consuming at their reference point and get bad news about future wages (in the sense that the distribution of possible wages next year shifts downward). Bowman et al. show that the teachers may not cut their current consumption at all. Consumption is "sticky downward" for two reasons: (1) Because they are loss averse, cutting current consumption means they will consume below their reference point this year, which feels awful. (2) Owing to reflection effects, they are willing to gamble that next year's wages might not be so low; thus, they would rather take a gamble in which they either consume far below their reference point or consume right at it than accept consumption that is modestly below the reference point. These two forces make the teachers reluctant to cut their current consumption after receiving bad news about future income prospects, which explains Shea's finding.

6. STATUS QUO BIAS, ENDOWMENT EFFECTS, AND BUYING–SELLING PRICE GAPS

Samuelson and Zeckhauser (1988) coined the term *status quo bias* to refer to an exaggerated preference for the status quo and showed such a bias in a series of experiments. They also reported several observations in field data that are consistent with status quo bias.

When Harvard University added new health-care plan options, older faculty members who were hired previously when the new options were not available were, of course, allowed to switch to the new options. If one assumes that the new and old faculty members have essentially the same preferences for health-care plans, then the distribution of plans elected by new and old faculty should be the same. However, Samuelson and Zeckhauser found that older faculty members tended to stick to their previous plans; compared with the newer faculty members, fewer of the old faculty elected new options.

In cases in which there is no status quo, people may have an exaggerated preference for whichever option is the default choice. Johnson, Hershey, Meszaros, and Kunreuther (1993) observed this phenomenon in decisions involving insurance purchases. At the time of their study, Pennsylvania and New Jersey legislators were considering various kinds of tort reform allowing firms to offer cheaper automobile insurance that limited the rights of the insured person to sue for damages from accidents. Both states adopted very similar forms of limited insurance, but they chose different default options, creating a natural experiment. All insurance companies mailed forms to their customers asking them whether they wanted the cheaper limited-rights insurance or the more expensive unlimited-rights insurance. One state made the limited-rights insurance the default (the insured person would get that if they did not respond), and the other made unlimited-rights the default. In fact, the percentage of people actively electing the limited-rights insurance was higher in the state where that was the default. An experiment replicated the effect.

A closely related body of research on endowment effects established that buying and selling prices for a good are often quite different. The paradigmatic experimental demonstration of this is the "mugs" experiments of Kahneman, Knetsch, and Thaler (1990). In their experiments, some subjects are endowed (randomly) with coffee mugs, and others are not. Those who are given the mugs demand a price about 2–3 times as large as the price that those without mugs are willing to pay, even though in economic theory these prices should be extremely close together. In fact, the mugs experiments were inspired by field observations of large gaps in hypothetical buying and selling prices in "contingent valuations." Contingent valuations are measurements of the economic value of goods that are not normally traded – like clean air, environmental damage, and so forth. These money valuations are used for doing benefit–cost analysis and establishing economic damages in lawsuits. There is a huge literature establishing that selling prices are generally much larger than buying prices, although there is a heated debate among psychologists and economists about what the price gap means and how to measure "true" valuations in the face of such a gap.

All three phenomena (status quo biases, default preference, and endowment effects) are consistent with aversion to losses relative to a reference point. Making one option the status quo or default or endowing a person with a good (even hypothetically) seems to establish a reference point people move away from only reluctantly, or if they are paid a large sum.

7. RACETRACK BETTING: THE FAVORITE-LONGSHOT BIAS

In parimutuel betting on horse races, there is a pronounced bias toward betting on "longshots," which are horses with a relatively small chance of winning. That is, if one groups longshots with the same percentage of money bet on them into a class, the fraction of time horses in that class win is far smaller than the percentage of money bet on them. Longshot horses with 2% of the total money bet on them, for example, win only about 1% of the time (see Thaler and Ziemba 1988, Hausch and Ziemba 1995).

Overbetting longshots implies favorites are underbet. Indeed, some horses are so heavily favored that up to 70% of the win money is wagered on them. For these heavy favorites, the return for a dollar bet is very low if the horse wins. (Because the track keeps about 15% of the money bet for expenses and profit, bettors who bet on such a heavy favorite share only 85% of the money with 70% of the people, which results in a payoff of only about $2.40 for a $2 bet.) People dislike these bets so much that, in fact, if one makes those bets it is possible to earn a small positive profit (even accounting for the track's 15% take).

There are many explanations for the favorite-longshot bias, each of which probably contributes to the phenomenon. Horses that have lost many races in a row tend to be longshots, and thus a gambler's fallacious belief that such horses are due for a win may contribute to overbetting on them. Prospect-theoretic overweighting of low probabilities of winning will also lead to overbetting of longshots.

Within standard expected utility theory, the favorite-longshot bias can only be explained by assuming that people have convex utility functions for money outcomes. The most careful study comparing expected utility and prospect theory was done by Jullien and Salanié (1997). Their study used a huge sample of all the flat races run in England for 10 years (34,443 races). They assumed that bettors value bets on horses by using either expected utility theory, rank-dependent utility theory, or cumulative prospect theory (see Kahneman and Tversky 1992). If the marginal bettor is indifferent among bets on all the horses at the odds established when the race is run, then indifference conditions can be used to infer the parameters of that bettor's utility and probability weighting functions.

Jullien and Salanié found that cumulative prospect theory fits much better than rank-dependent theory and expected utility theory. They estimated that the utility function for small money amounts is convex. Their estimate of the probability weighting function $\pi(p)$ for probabilities of gain is almost linear, but the weighting function for loss probabilities severely overweights low probabilities of loss (e.g., $\pi(.1) = .45$ and $\pi(.3) = .65$). These estimates imply a surprising new explanation for the favorite-longshot bias: Bettors like longshots because they have convex utility and weight their high chances of losing and small chances of winning roughly linearly. They hate favorites, however, because they like to gamble ($u(x)$ is convex) but are disproportionately afraid of the small chance of losing when they bet on a heavy favorite. (In my personal experience as a betting researcher I have found that losing on a heavy favorite is particularly disappointing – an emotional effect the Jullien-Salanié estimates capture.)

8. RACETRACK BETTING: THE END-OF-THE-DAY EFFECT

McGlothlin (1956) and Ali (1977) established another racetrack anomaly that points to the central role of reference points. They found that bettors tend to shift their bets toward longshots, and away from favorites, later in the racing day. Because the track takes a hefty bite out of each dollar, most bettors are behind by the last race of the day. These bettors really prefer longshots because a small longshot bet can generate a large enough profit to cover their earlier losses, enabling them to break even. The movement toward longshots, and away from favorites, is so pronounced that some studies show that conservatively betting on the favorite to show (to finish first, second, or third) in the last race is a profitable bet despite the track's take.

The end-of-the-day effect is consistent with using zero daily profit as a reference point and gambling in the domain of losses to break even. Expected utility theory cannot gracefully explain the shift in risk preferences across the day if bettors integrate their wealth because the last race on a Saturday is not fundamentally different than the first race on the bettor's next outing. Cumulative prospect theory can explain the shift by assuming people open a mental account at the beginning of the day, close it at the end, and hate closing an account in the red.

9. STATE LOTTERIES

Lotto is a special kind of lottery game in which players choose six different numbers from a set of 40–50 numbers. They win a large jackpot if their six choices match six numbers that are randomly drawn in public. If no player picks all six numbers correctly, the jackpot is rolled over and added to the next week's jackpot; several weeks of rollovers can build up jackpots up to $350 million or more. The large jackpots have made lotto very popular.[3] Lotto was introduced in several American states in 1980 and accounted for about half of all state lottery ticket sales by 1989.

Cook and Clotfelter (1993) suggest that the popularity of Lotto results from players' being more sensitive to the large jackpot than to the correspondingly low probability of winning. They write (p. 634):

If players tend to judge the likelihood of winning based on the frequency with which someone wins, then a larger state can offer a game at longer odds but with the same perceived probability of winning as a smaller state. The larger population base in effect conceals the smaller probability of winning the jackpot, while the larger jackpot is highly visible. This interpretation is congruent with prospect theory.

Their regressions show that across states, ticket sales are strongly correlated with the size of a state's population (which is correlated with jackpot size). Within a state, ticket sales each week are strongly correlated with the size of the rollover. In expected utility, this can only be explained by utility functions for money that are convex. Prospect theory easily explains the demand for high jackpots, as Cook and Clotfelter suggest, by overweighting of, and insensitivity toward, very low probabilities.

10. TELEPHONE WIRE REPAIR INSURANCE

Ciccheti and Dubin (1994) conducted an interesting study of whether people purchase insurance against damage to their telephone wiring. The phone companies they studied either required customers to pay for the cost of wiring repair, about $60, or to buy insurance for $.45 per month. Given phone company estimates of the frequency of wire damage, the expected cost of wire damage is only $.26.

Ciccheti and Dubin looked across geographical areas with different probabilities of wire damage rates to see whether cross-area variation in the tendency to buy insurance was related to different probabilities. They did find a relation and exploited this to estimate parameters of an expected utility model. They found some evidence that people were weighting damage probabilities nonlinearly and also some evidence of status quo bias. (People who had previously been uninsured, when a new insurance option was introduced, were less likely to buy it than new customers were.)

More importantly, Ciccheti and Dubin never asked whether it is reasonable to purchase insurance against such a tiny risk. In standard expected utility, a

[3] A similar bet, the "pick six," was introduced at horse racing tracks in the 1980s. In the pick six, bettors must choose the winners of six races. This is extremely hard to do, and thus a large rollover occurs if nobody has picked all six winners several days in a row, just like lotto. Pick-six betting now accounts for a large fraction of overall betting.

person who is averse to very modest risks at all levels of wealth should be more risk averse to large risks. Rabin (in press) was the first to demonstrate how dramatic the implications of local risk aversion are for global risk aversion. He showed formally that a mildly risk-averse expected-utility maximizer who would turn down a coin flip (at all wealth levels) in which he or she is equally likely to win $11 or lose $10 should not accept a coin flip in which $100, could be lost, *regardless of how much he or she could win*. In expected utility terms, turning down the small-stakes flip implies a little bit of curvature in a $21 range of a concave utility function. Turning down the small-stakes flip for all wealth levels implies the utility function is slightly curved at all wealth levels, which mathematically implies a dramatic degree of global curvature.

Rabin's proof suggests a rejection of the joint hypotheses that consumers who buy wire repair insurance are integrating their wealth and valuing the insurance according to expected utility (and know the correct probabilities of damage). A more plausible explanation comes immediately from prospect theory – consumers are overweighting the probability of damage. (Loss aversion and reflection cannot explain their purchases because, if they are loss averse, they should dislike spending the $.45 per month, and reflection implies they will never insure unless they overestimate the probability of loss.) Once again, narrow bracketing is also required: consumers must be focusing only on wire repair risk; otherwise, the tiny probability of a modest loss would be absorbed into a portfolio of life's ups and downs and weighted more reasonably.

11. CONCLUSION

Economists value (1) mathematical formalism and econometric parsimony, and (2) the ability of theory to explain naturally occurring data. I share these tastes. This article has demonstrated that prospect theory is valuable in both ways because it can explain 10 patterns observed in a wide variety of economic domains with a small number of modeling features. Different features of prospect theory help explain different patterns. *Loss aversion* can explain the extra return on stocks compared with bonds (the equity premium), the tendency of cab drivers to work longer hours on low-wage days, asymmetries in consumer reactions to price increases and decreases, the insensitivity of consumption to bad news about income, and status quo and endowment effects. *Reflection effects* – gambling in the domain of a perceived loss – can explain holding losing stocks longer than winners and refusing to sell your house at a loss (disposition effects), insensitivity of consumption to bad income news, and the shift toward longshot betting at the end of a racetrack day. *Nonlinear weighting of probabilities* can explain the favorite-longshot bias in horse race betting, the popularity of lotto lotteries with large jackpots, and the purchase of telephone wire repair insurance. In addition, note that the disposition effect and downward-sloping labor supply of cab drivers were not simply observed but were also predicted in advance based on prospect theory.

In all these examples it is also necessary to assume people are isolating or narrowly bracketing the relevant decisions. Bracketing narrowly focuses attention most dramatically on the possibility of a loss or extreme outcome, or a low probability. With broader bracketing, outcomes are mingled with other gains and losses, diluting the psychological influence of any single outcome and making these phenomena hard to explain as a result of prospect theory valuation.

I have two final comments. First, I have chosen examples in which there are several studies, or one very conclusive one, showing regularities in field data that cannot be easily reconciled with expected utility theory. However, these regularities can be explained by adding extra assumptions. The problem is that these extras are truly ad hoc because each regularity requires a special assumption. Worse, an extra assumption that helps explain one regularity may contradict another. For example, assuming people are risk-preferring (or have convex utility for money) can explain the popularity of longshot horses and lotto, but that assumption predicts stocks should return *less* than bonds, which is wildly false. You can explain why cab drivers drive long hours on bad days by assuming they cannot borrow (they are liquidity constrained), but liquidity constraint implies teachers who get good income news should not be able to spend more, whereas those who get bad news can cut back, which is exactly the opposite of what they do.

Second, prospect theory is a suitable replacement for expected utility because it can explain anomalies like those listed above and can *also* explain the most basic phenomena expected utility is used to explain. A prominent example is pricing of financial assets discussed above in Sections 1 and 2. Another prominent example, which appears in every economics textbook, is the voluntary purchase of insurance by people. The expected utility explanation for why people buy actuarially unfair insurance is that they have concave utility, and thus they hate losing large amounts of money disproportionally compared with spending small amounts on insurance premiums.

In fact, many people *do not* purchase insurance voluntarily (e.g., most states require automobile insurance by law). The failure to purchase is inconsistent with the expected utility explanation and more easy to reconcile with prospect theory (because the disutility of loss is assumed to be convex). When people *do* buy insurance, people are probably avoiding low-probability disasters that they overweight (the prospect theory explanation) rather than avoiding a steep drop in a concave utility function (the expected utility theory explanation).

A crucial kind of evidence that distinguishes the two explanations comes from experiments on probabilistic insurance, which is insurance that does *not* pay a claim, if an accident occurs, with some probability r. According to expected utility theory, if r is small, people should pay approximately $(1 - r)$ times as much for probabilistic insurance as they pay for full insurance (Wakker, Thaler, and Tversky, 1997). But experimental responses show that people hate probabilistic insurance; they pay a multiple much less than $1 - r$ for it (for example, they pay 80% as much when $r = .01$ when they should pay 99% as much). Prospect theory can explain their hatred easily: probabilistic insurance does not reduce the probability of loss all the way toward zero, and the low probability r is still overweighted. Prospect theory can therefore explain why people buy full insurance *and* why they do not buy probabilistic insurance. Expected utility cannot do both.

Because prospect theory can explain the basic phenomena expected utility was most fruitfully applied to, like asset pricing and insurance purchase, and can also explain field anomalies like the 10 listed in Table 16.1 (two of which were predicted), there is no good scientific reason why it should not be used alongside expected utility in current research and be given prominent space in economics textbooks.

17. Myopic Loss Aversion and the Equity Premium Puzzle*

Shlomo Benartzi and Richard H. Thaler

ABSTRACT. The equity premium puzzle refers to the empirical fact that stocks have outperformed bonds over the last century by a surprisingly large margin. We offer a new explanation based on two behavioral concepts. First, investors are assumed to be "loss averse," meaning that they are distinctly more sensitive to losses than to gains. Second, even long-term investors are assumed to evaluate their portfolios frequently. We dub this combination "myopic loss aversion." Using simulations, we find that the size of the equity premium is consistent with the previously estimated parameters of prospect theory if investors evaluate their portfolios annually.

I. INTRODUCTION

There is an enormous discrepancy between the returns on stocks and fixed income securities. Since 1926 the annual real return on stocks has been about 7 percent, while the real return on treasury bills has been less than 1 percent. As demonstrated by Mehra and Prescott [1985], the combination of a high equity premium, a low risk-free rate, and smooth consumption is difficult to explain with plausible levels of investor risk aversion. Mehra and Prescott estimate that investors would have to have coefficients of relative risk aversion in excess of 30 to explain the historical equity premium, whereas previous estimates and theoretical arguments suggest that the actual figure is close to 1.0. We are left with a pair of questions: why is the equity premium so large, or why is anyone willing to hold bonds?

The answer we propose in this paper is based on two concepts from the psychology of decision-making. The first concept is *loss aversion*. Loss aversion

* Some of this research was conducted while Thaler was a visiting scholar at the Russell Sage Foundation. He is grateful for its generous support. While there, he also had numerous helpful conversations on this topic, especially with Colin Camerer and Daniel Kahneman. Olivier Blanchard, Kenneth French, Russell Fuller, Robert Libby, Roni Michaely, Andrei Shleifer, Amos Tversky, Jean-Luc Vila, and the participants in the Russell Sage-NBER behavioral finance work shop have also provided comments. This research has also been supported by the National Science Foundation, Grant # SES-9223358.

refers to the tendency for individuals to be more sensitive to reductions in their levels of well-being than to increases. The concept plays a central role in Kahneman and Tversky's [1979] descriptive theory of decision-making under uncertainty, prospect theory.[1] In this model, utility is defined over gains and losses relative to some neutral reference point, such as the status quo, as opposed to wealth as in expected utility theory. This utility function has a kink at the origin, with the slope of the loss function steeper than the gain function. The ratio of these slopes at the origin is a measure of loss aversion. Empirical estimates of loss aversion are typically in the neighborhood of 2, meaning that the disutility of giving something up is twice as great as the utility of acquiring it [Tversky and Kahneman 1991; Kahneman, Knetsch, and Thaler 1990].

The second behavioral concept we employ is *mental accounting* [Kahneman and Tversky 1984; Thaler 1985]. Mental accounting refers to the implicit methods individuals use to code and evaluate financial outcomes: transactions, investments, gambles, etc. The aspect of mental accounting that plays a particularly important role in this research is the dynamic aggregation rules people follow. Because of the presence of loss aversion, these aggregation rules are not neutral. This point can best be illustrated by example.

Consider the problem first posed by Samuelson [1963]. Samuelson asked a colleague whether he would be willing to accept the following bet: a 50 percent chance to win $200 and a 50 percent chance to lose $100. The colleague turned this bet down, but announced that he was happy to accept 100 such bets. This exchange provoked Samuelson into proving a theorem showing that his colleague was irrational.[2] Of more interest here is what the colleague offered as his rationale for turning down the bet: "I won't bet because I would feel the $100 loss more than the $200 gain." This sentiment is the intuition behind the concept of loss aversion. One simple utility function that would capture this notion is the following:

$$U(x) = \begin{array}{ll} x & x \geq 0 \\ 2.5x & x < 0, \end{array} \tag{1}$$

where x is a *change* in wealth relative to the status quo. The role of mental accounting is illustrated by noting that if Samuelson's colleague had this utility function he would turn down one bet but accept two or more *as long as he did not have to watch the bet being played out*. The distribution of outcomes created by the portfolio of two bets {$400, .25; 100, .50; −$200, .25} yields positive expected utility with the hypothesized utility function, though of course simple repetitions

---

[1] The notion that people treat gains and losses differently has a long tradition. For example, Swalm [1966] noted this phenomenon in a study of managerial decision making. See Libby and Fishburn [1977] for other early references.

[2] Specifically, the theorem says that if someone is unwilling to accept a single play of a bet at any wealth level that could occur over the course of some number of repetitions of the bet (in this case, the relevant range is the colleague's current wealth plus $20,000 to current wealth minus $10,000) then accepting the multiple bet is inconsistent with expected utility theory.

of the single bet are unattractive if evaluated one at a time. As this example illustrates, when decision-makers are loss averse, they will be more willing to take risks if they evaluate their performance (or have their performance evaluated) infrequently.

The relevance of this argument to the equity premium puzzle can be seen by considering the problem facing an investor with the utility function defined above. Suppose that the investor must choose between a risky asset that pays an expected 7 percent per year with a standard deviation of 20 percent (like stocks) and a safe asset that pays a sure 1 percent. By the same logic that applied to Samuelson's colleague, the attractiveness of the risky asset will depend on the time horizon of the investor. The longer the investor intends to hold the asset, the more attractive the risky asset will appear, so long as the investment is not evaluated frequently. Put another way, two factors contribute to an investor being unwilling to bear the risks associated with holding equities, loss aversion and a short evaluation period. We refer to this combination as *myopic loss aversion*.

Can myopic loss aversion explain the equity premium puzzle? Of course, there is no way of demonstrating that one particular explanation is correct, so in this paper we perform various tests to determine whether our hypothesis is plausible. We begin by asking what combination of loss aversion and evaluation period would be necessary to explain the historical pattern of returns. For our model of individual decision making, we use the recent updated version of prospect theory [Tversky and Kahneman 1992] for which the authors have provided parameters that can be considered as describing the representative decision-maker. We then ask, how often would an investor with this set of preferences have to evaluate his portfolio in order to be indifferent between the historical distribution of returns on stocks and bonds? Although we do this several ways (with both real and nominal returns, and comparing stocks with both bonds and treasury bills), the answers we obtain are all in the neighborhood of one year, clearly a plausible result. We then take the one-year evaluation period as given and ask what asset allocation (that is, what combination of stocks and bonds) would be optimal for such an investor. Again we obtain a plausible result: close to a 50-50 split between stocks and bonds.

II. IS THE EQUITY PREMIUM PUZZLE REAL?

Before we set out to provide an answer to an alleged puzzle, we should probably review the evidence about whether there is indeed a puzzle to explain. We address the question in two ways. First, we ask whether the post-1926 time period studied by Mehra and Prescott is special. Then we review the other explanations that have been offered. As any insightful reader might guess from the fact that we have written this paper, we conclude that the puzzle is real and that the existing explanations come up short.

The robustness of the equity premium has been addressed by Siegel [1991, 1992] who examines the returns since 1802. He finds that real equity returns have been remarkably stable. For example, over the three time periods 1802–1870, 1871–1925, and 1926–1990, real compound equity returns were 5.7, 6.6, and 6.4 percent. However, returns on short-term government bonds have fallen dramatically, the figures for the same three time periods being 5.1, 3.1, and 0.5 percent. Thus, there was no equity premium in the first two-thirds of the nineteenth century (because bond returns were high), but over the last 120 years, stocks have had a significant edge. The equity premium does not appear to be a recent phenomenon.

The advantage of investing in stocks over the period 1876 to 1990 is documented in a rather different way by MaCurdy and Shoven [1992]. They look at the historical evidence from the point of view of a faculty member saving for retirement. They assume that 10 percent of the hypothetical faculty member's salary is invested each year, and ask how the faculty members would have done investing in portfolios of all stocks or all bonds over their working lifetimes. They find that faculty who had allocated all of their funds to stocks would have done better in virtually every time period, usually by a large margin. For working lifetimes of only 25 years, all bond portfolios occasionally do better (e.g., for those retiring in a few years during the first half of the decades of the 1930s and 1940s) though never by more than 20 percent. In contrast, those in all-stock portfolios often do better by very large amounts. Also, all 25-year careers since 1942 would have been better off in all stocks. For working lifetimes of 40 years, there is not a single case in which the all-bond portfolio wins (though there is a virtual tie for those retiring in 1942), and for those retiring in the late 1950s and early 1960s, stock accumulators would have more than seven times more than bond accumulators. MaCurdy and Shoven conclude from their analysis that people must be "confused about the relative safety of different investments over long horizons" [p. 12].

Could the large equity premium be consistent with rational expected utility maximization models of economic behavior? Mehra and Prescott's contribution was to show that risk aversion alone is unlikely to yield a satisfactory answer. They found that people would have to have a coefficient of relative risk aversion over 30 to explain the historical pattern of returns. In interpreting this number, it is useful to remember that a logarithmic function has a coefficient of relative risk aversion of 1.0. Also, Mankiw and Zeldes [1991] provide the following useful calculation. Suppose that an individual is offered a gamble with a 50 percent chance of consumption of $100,000 and a 50 percent chance of consumption of $50,000. A person with a coefficient of relative risk aversion of 30 would be indifferent between this gamble and a certain consumption of $51,209. Few people can be this afraid of risk.

Previous efforts to provide alternative explanations for the puzzle have been, at most, only partly successful. For example, Reitz [1988] argued that the equity premium might be the rational response to a time-varying risk of economic catastrophe. While this explanation has the advantage of being untestable, it does not seem plausible. (See Mehra and Prescott's [1988] reply.) First of all, the data since 1926 do contain the crash of 1929, so the catastrophe in question must be of much greater magnitude than that. Second, the hypothetical catastrophe must affect stocks and not bonds. For example, a bout of hyperinflation would presumably hurt bonds more than stocks.

Another line of research has aimed at relaxing the link between the coefficient of relative risk aversion and the elasticity of intertemporal substitution, which are inverses of each other in the standard discounted expected utility framework. For example, Weil [1989] introduces Kreps-Porteus nonexpected utility preferences, but finds that the equity premium puzzle simply becomes transformed into a "risk free rate puzzle." That is, the puzzle is no longer why are stock returns so high, but rather why are T-bill rates so low. Epstein and Zin [1990] also adopt a nonexpected utility framework using Yaari's [1987] "dual" theory of choice. Yaari's theory shares some features with the version of prospect theory that we employ below (namely a rank-dependent approach to probability weights) but does not have loss aversion or short horizons, the two key components of our explanation. Epstein and Zin find that their model can only explain about one-third of the observed equity premium. Similarly, Mankiw and Zeldes [1991] investigate whether the homogeneity assumptions necessary to aggregate across consumers could be the source of the puzzle. They point out that a minority of Americans hold stock, and their consumption patterns differ from nonstockholders. However, they conclude that while these differences can explain a part of the equity premium, a significant puzzle remains.

An alternative type of explanation is suggested by Constantinides [1990]. He proposes a habit-formation model in which the utility of consumption is assumed to depend on past levels of consumption. Specifically, consumers are assumed to be averse to reductions in their level of consumption. Constantinides shows that this type of model can explain the equity premium puzzle. However, Ferson and Constantinides [1991] find that while the habit formation specification improves the ability of the model to explain the intertemporal dynamics of returns, it does not help the model explain the differences in average returns across assets.

While Constantinides is on the right track in stressing an asymmetry between gains and losses, we feel that his model does not quite capture the right behavioral intuitions. The problem is that the link between stock returns and consumption is quite tenuous. The vast majority of Americans hold no stocks outside their pension wealth. Furthermore, most pensions are of the defined benefit variety, meaning that a fall in stock prices is inconsequential to the pension beneficiaries. Indeed, most of the stock market is owned by three groups of investors: pension funds, endowments, and very wealthy individuals. It is hard to see why the habit-formation model should apply to these investors.[3]

---

[3] We stress the word "should" in the previous sentence. Firms may adopt accounting rules with regard to their pension wealth which create a sensitivity to short-run fluctuations in pension fund assets, and foundations may have spending rules that produce a similar effect. An investigation of this issue is presented below.

III. PROSPECT THEORY AND LOSS AVERSION

The problem with the habit-formation explanation is the stress it places on consumption. The way we incorporate Constantinides' intuition about behavior into preferences is to assume that investors have preferences over returns, per se, rather than over the consumption profile that the returns help provide. Specifically, we use Kahneman and Tversky's [1979, 1992] prospect theory in which utility is defined over gains and losses (i.e., returns) rather than levels of wealth. Specifically, they propose a value function of the following form:

$$v(x) = \begin{cases} x^\alpha & \text{if } x \geq 0 \\ -\lambda(-x)^\beta & \text{if } x < 0, \end{cases} \tag{2}$$

where λ is the coefficient of loss aversion.[4] They have estimated α and β to be 0.88 and λ to be 2.25. Notice that the notion of loss aversion captures the same intuition that Constantinides used, namely that reductions are painful.[5]

The "prospective utility" of a gamble, G, which pays off x_i with probability p_i is given by

$$V(G) = \sum \pi_i v(x_i), \tag{3}$$

where π_i is the decision weight associated assigned to outcome i. In the original version of prospect theory [Kahneman and Tversky 1979), π_i is a simple nonlinear transform of p_i. In the cumulative version of the theory [Tversky and Kahneman 1992], as in other rank-dependent models, one transforms cumulative rather than individual probabilities. Consequently, the decision weight π_i depends on the cumulative distribution of the gamble, not only on p_i. More specifically, let w denote the nonlinear transform of the cumulative distribution of G, let P_i be the probability of obtaining an outcome that is at least as good as x_i, and let P_i^* be the probability of obtaining an outcome that is strictly better than x_i. Then the decision weight attached to x_i is $\pi_i = w(P_i) - w(P_i^*)$. (This procedure is applied separately for gains and losses.)

Tversky and Kahneman have suggested the following one-parameter approximation:

$$w(p) = \frac{p^\gamma}{(p^\gamma + (1 - p)^\gamma)^{1/\gamma}} \tag{4}$$

and estimated γ to be 0.61 in the domain of gains and 0.69 in the domain of losses.

---

[4] Note that since x is a change it is measured as the difference in wealth with respect to the last time wealth was measured, so the status quo is moving over time.

[5] This value of λ is consistent with other measures of loss aversion estimated in very different contexts. For example, Kahneman, Knetsch, and Thaler [1990] (KKT) investigate the importance of loss aversion in a purely deterministic context. In one experiment half of a group of Cornell students are given a Cornell insignia coffee mug, while the other half of the subjects are not given a mug. Then, markets are conducted for the mugs in which mug owners can sell their mug while the nonowners can buy one. KKT found that the reservation prices for two groups were significantly different. Specifically, the median reservation price of the sellers was roughly 2.5 times the median reservation price of the buyers.

As discussed in the Introduction, the use of prospect theory must be accompanied by a specification of frequency that returns are evaluated. We refer to the length of time over which an investor aggregates returns as the *evaluation period*. This is not, in any way, to be confused with the planning horizon of the investor. A young investor, for example, might be saving for retirement 30 years off in the future, but nevertheless experience the utility associated with the gains and losses of his investment every quarter when he opens a letter from his mutual fund. In this case his horizon is 30 years but his evaluation period is 3 months.

That said, in terms of the model an investor with an evaluation period of one year behaves very much *as if* he had a planning horizon of one year. To see this, compare two investors. Mr. X receives a bonus every year on January first and invests the money to spend on a Christmas vacation the following year. Both his planning horizon and evaluation period are one year. Ms. Y has received a bonus and wishes to invest it toward her retirement 30 years away. She evaluates her portfolio annually. Thus, she has a planning horizon of 30 years but a one-year evaluation period. Though X and Y have rather different problems, in terms of the model they will behave approximately the same way. The reason for this is that in prospect theory, the carriers of utility are assumed to be changes in wealth, or returns, and the effect of the level of wealth is assumed to be second order. Therefore, every year Y will solve her asset allocation problem by choosing the portfolio that maximizes her prospective utility one year away, just as X does.[6] In this sense, when we estimate the evaluation period of investors below, we are also estimating their implicit time horizons.

Of course, in a model with loss aversion, the more often an investor evaluates his portfolio, or the shorter his horizon, the less attractive he will find a high mean, high risk investment such as stocks. This is in contrast to the well-known results of Merton [1969] and Samuelson [1969]. They investigate the following question. Suppose that an investor has to choose between stocks and bonds over some fixed horizon of length T. How should the allocation change as the horizon increases? There is a strong intuition that a rational risk-averse investor would decrease the proportion of his assets in stocks as he nears retirement and T approaches zero. The intuition comes from the notion that when T is large, the probability that the return on stocks will exceed the return on bonds approaches 1.0, while over short horizons there can be substantial shortfalls from stock investments. However, Merton and Samuelson show that this intuition is wrong. Specifically, they prove that as long as the returns on stocks and bonds are a random walk,[7] a risk-averse investor with a utility function that displays constant relative risk in aversion (e.g., a logarithmic or power function) should

---

[6] An important potential qualification is if recent gains or losses influence subsequent decisions. For example, Thaler and Johnson [1990] find evidence for a "house money effect." Namely, people who have just won some money exhibit less loss aversion toward gambles that do not risk their entire recent winnings.

[7] If stock returns are instead mean reverting, then the intuitive result that stocks are more attractive to investors with long horizons holds.

choose the same allocation for any time horizon. An investor who wants mostly stocks in his portfolio at age 35 should still want the same allocation at age 64. Without questioning the normative validity of Merton and Samuelson's conclusions, we offer a model that can reveal why most investors find this result extremely counterintuitive.

IV. HOW OFTEN ARE PORTFOLIOS EVALUATED?

Mehra and Prescott asked the question, how risk averse would the representative investor have to be to explain the historical equity premium? We ask a different question. If investors have prospect theory preferences, how often would they have to evaluate their portfolios to explain the equity premium? We pose the question two ways. First, what evaluation period would make investors indifferent between holding all their assets in stocks or bonds. We then take this evaluation period and ask a question with more theoretical justification. For an investor with this evaluation period, what combination of stocks and bonds would maximize prospective utility?

We use simulations to answer both questions. The method is to draw samples from the historical (1926–1990) monthly returns on stocks, bonds, and treasury bills provided by CRSP. For the first exercise we then compute the prospective utility of holding stocks, bonds, and T-bills for evaluation periods starting at one month and then increasing one month at a time.

The simulations are conducted as follows. First, distributions of returns are generated for various time horizons by drawing 100,000 n-month returns (with replacement) from the CRSP time series.[8] The returns are then ranked, from best to worst, and the return is computed at twenty intervals along the cumulative distribution.[9] (This is done to accommodate the cumulative or rank-dependent formulation of prospect theory.) Using these data, it is possible to compute the prospective utility of the given asset for the specified holding period.

We have done this simulation four different ways. The CRSP stock index is compared both with treasury bill returns and with five-year bond returns, and these comparisons are done both in real and nominal terms. While we have done all four simulations for the sake of completeness, and to give the reader the opportunity to examine the robustness of the method, we feel that the most weight should be assigned to the comparison between stocks and bonds

---

[8] Our method, by construction, removes any serial correlation in asset price returns. Since some research does find mean reversion in stock prices over long horizons, some readers have worried about whether our results are affected by this. This should not be a concern. The time horizons we investigate in the simulations are relatively short (in the neighborhood of one year) and at short horizons there is only trivial mean reversion. For example, Fama and French [1988] regress returns on the value weighted index in year t on returns in year $t - 1$ and estimate the slope coefficient to be −0.03. The fact that there is substantial mean reversion at longer horizons (the same coefficient at three years is −0.25) only underscores the puzzle of the equity premium since mean reversion reduces the risk to a long-term investor.

[9] We have also tried dividing the outcomes into 100 intervals instead of 20, and the results are substantially the same.

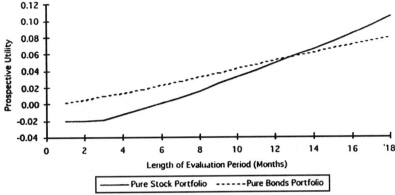

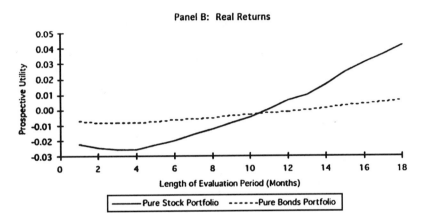

Figure 17.1. Prospective utility as function of the evaluation period.

in nominal terms. We prefer bonds to T-bills because we think that for long-term investors these are the closest substitutes. We prefer nominal to real for two reasons. First, returns are usually reported in nominal dollars. Even when inflation adjusted returns are calculated, it is the nominal returns that are given prominence in most annual reports. Therefore, in a descriptive model, nominal returns should be the assumed units of account. Second, the simulations reveal that if investors were thinking in real dollars they would not be willing to hold treasury bills over any evaluation period as they always yield negative prospective utility.[10]

The results for the stock and bond comparisons are presented in Figure 17.1, panels A and B. The lines show the prospective value of the portfolio at different

---

[10] This suggests a solution to the "risk-free rate puzzle" employing a combination of framing and money illusion. In nominal terms, treasury bills offer the illusion of a sure gain which is very attractive to prospect theory investors, while in real terms treasury bills offer a combination of barely positive mean returns and a substantial risk of a loss – not an attractive combination.

evaluation periods. The point where the curves cross is the evaluation period at which stocks and bonds are equally attractive. For nominal returns, the equilibrium evaluation period is about thirteen months, while for real returns it is between ten and eleven months.[11]

How should these results be interpreted? Obviously, there is no single evaluation period that applies to every investor. Indeed, even a single investor may employ a combination of evaluation periods, with casual evaluations every quarter, a more serious evaluation annually, and evaluations associated with long-term planning every few years. Nevertheless, if one had to pick a single most plausible length for the evaluation period, one year might well be it. Individual investors file taxes annually, receive their most comprehensive reports from their brokers, mutual funds, and retirement accounts once a year, and institutional investors also take the annual reports most seriously. As a possible evaluation period, one year is at least highly plausible.

There are two reasonable questions to ask about these results. Which aspects of prospect theory drive the results, and how sensitive are the results to alternative specifications? The answer to the first question is that loss aversion is the main determinant of the outcomes. The specific functional forms of the value function and weighting functions are not critical. For example, if the weighting function is replaced by actual probabilities, the evaluation period for which bonds have the same prospective utility as stocks falls from eleven–twelve months to ten months. Similarly, if actual probabilities are used and the value function is replaced by a piecewise linear form with a loss aversion factor of 2.25 (that is, $v(x) = x$, $x \geq 0$, $v(x) = 2.25\,x$, $x < 0$), then the equilibrium evaluation period is eight months. With this model (piecewise linear value function and linear probabilities) a twelve-month evaluation period is consistent with a loss aversion factor of 2.77.

The previous results can be criticized on the grounds that investors form portfolios rather than choose between all bonds or all stocks. Therefore, we perform a second simulation exercise that is grounded in an underlying optimization problem. We use this as a reliability check on the previous results. Suppose that an investor is maximizing prospective utility with a one-year horizon. What mix of stocks and bonds would be optimal? We investigate this question as follows. We compute the prospective utility of each portfolio mix between 100 percent bonds and 100 percent stocks, in 10 percent increments. The results are shown in Figure 17.2, using nominal returns. (Again, the results for real returns are similar.) As the figure shows, portfolios between about 30 percent and 55 percent stocks all yield approximately the same prospective value. Once again, this result is roughly consistent with observed behavior. For example, Greenwich Associates reports that institutions (primarily pensions funds and endowments) invest, on average, 47 percent of the assets on bonds and

---

[11] The equilibrium evaluation period between stocks and T-bills is about one month less in both real and nominal dollars.

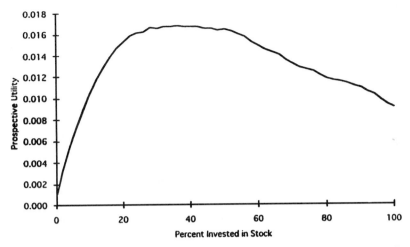

Figure 17.2. Prospective utility as function of asset allocation (one-year evaluation period).

53 percent in stocks. For individuals, consider the participants in TIAA-CREF, the defined contribution retirement plan at many universities, and the largest of its kind in the United States. The most frequent allocation between CREF (stocks) and TIAA (mostly bonds) is 50-50, with the average allocation to stocks below 50 percent.[12]

V. MYOPIA AND THE MAGNITUDE OF THE EQUITY PREMIUM

According to our theory, the equity premium is produced by a combination of loss aversion and frequent evaluations. Loss aversion plays the role of risk aversion in standard models, and can be considered a fact of life (or, perhaps, a fact of preferences). In contrast, the frequency of evaluations is a policy choice that presumably could be altered, at least in principle. Furthermore, as the charts in Figure 17.1 show, stocks become more attractive as the evaluation period increases. This observation leads to the natural question: by how much would the equilibrium equity premium fall if the evaluation period increased?

---

[12] See MaCurdy and Shoven [1992] for illustrative data. It is interesting to note that average allocation of new contributions is now and has always been more than half in TIAA, but the size of the two funds is now about equal because of the higher growth rate of CREF. As Samuelson and Zeckhauser [1988] report, the typical TIAA – CREF participant makes one asset allocation decision and never changes it. This does not seem consistent with any coherent optimization. Consider a contributor who has been dividing his funds equally between TIAA and CREF, and now has two-thirds of his assets in CREF because of higher growth. If he likes the 2–1 ratio of stocks to bonds consistent with his asset holdings, why not change the flow of new funds? But if a 50-50 allocation is optimal, then why not switch some of the existing CREF holdings into TIAA (which can be done costlessly)?

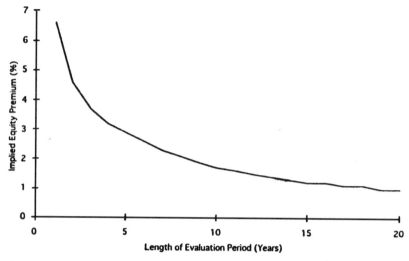

Figure 17.3. Implied equity premium as function of the evaluation period.

Figure 17.3 shows the results of an analysis of this issue using real returns on stocks, and the real returns on five-year bonds as the comparison asset. With the parameters we have been using, the actual equity premium in our data (6.5 percent per year) is consistent with an evaluation period of one year. If the evaluation period were two years, the equity premium would fall to 4.65 percent. For five, ten, and twenty-year evaluation periods, the corresponding figures are 3.0 percent, 2.0 percent, and 1.4 percent. One way to think about these results is that for someone with a twenty-year investment horizon, the psychic costs of evaluating the portfolio annually are 5.1 percent per year! That is, someone with a twenty-year horizon would be indifferent between stocks and bonds if the equity premium were only 1.4 percent, and the remaining 5.1 percent is potential rents payable to those who are able to resist the temptation to count their money often. In a sense, 5.1 percent is the price of excessive vigilance.[13]

VI. DO ORGANIZATIONS DISPLAY MYOPIC LOSS AVERSION?

There is a possible objection to our explanation in that it has been based on a model of *individual* decision making, while the bulk of the assets we are concerned with are held by organizations, in particular pension funds and endowments. This is a reasonable concern, and our response should help indicate the way we interpret our explanation.

[13] Blanchard [1993] has recently argued that the equity premium has fallen. If so, then our interpretation of his result would be that the length of the average evaluation period has increased.

As we stressed above, the key components of our explanation are loss aversion and frequent evaluations. While we have used a specific parameterization of cumulative prospect theory in our simulation tests, we did so because we felt that it provided a helpful discipline. We did not allow ourselves the luxury of selecting the parameters that would fit the data best. That said, it remains true that almost any model with loss aversion and frequent evaluations will go a long way toward explaining the equity premium puzzle, so the right question to ask about organizations is whether they display these traits.

A. Pension Funds

Consider first the important case of defined benefit pension funds. In this, this most common type of pension plan, the firm promises each vested worker a pension benefit that is typically a function of final salary and years of service. For these plans, the firm, not the employees, is the residual claimant. If the assets in the plan earn a high return, the firm can make smaller contributions to the fund in future years, whereas if the assets do not earn a high enough return, the firm's contribution rate will have to increase to satisfy funding regulations.

Although asset allocations vary across firms, a common allocation is about 60 percent stocks and 40 percent bonds and treasury bills. Given the historical equity premium, and the fact that pension funds have essentially an infinite time horizon, it is a bit puzzling why pension funds do not invest a higher proportion in stocks.[14] We argue that myopic loss aversion offers an explanation. In this context the myopic loss aversion is produced by an agency problem.

While the pension *fund* is indeed likely to exist as long as the company remains in business (barring a plan termination), the pension fund *manager* (often the corporate treasurer, chief financial officer (CFO), or staff member who reports to the CFO) does not expect to be in this job forever. He or she will have to make regular reports on the funding level of the pension plan and the returns on the funds assets. This short horizon creates a conflict of interest between the pension fund manager and the stockholders.[15] This view appears

---

[14] See Black [1980] for a different point of view. He argues that pension funds should be invested entirely in bonds because of a tax arbitrage opportunity. However, his position rests on the efficient market premise that there is no equity premium puzzle; that is, the return on stocks is just enough to compensate for the risk.

[15] The importance of short horizons in financial contexts is stressed by Shleifer and Vishny (1990). For a good description of the agency problems in defined-benefit pension plans see Lakonishok, Shleifer, and Vishny [1992]. Our agency explanation of myopic loss aversion is very much in the same spirit of the one they offer to explain a different puzzle: why the portion of the pension fund that *is* invested in equities is invested so poorly. The equity component of pension plans systematically underperforms market benchmarks such as the S&P 500. Although pension fund managers eschew index funds, they often inadvertently achieve an inferior version of an index fund by diversifying across money managers who employ different styles. The portfolio of money managers is worse on two counts: lower performance and higher fees.

to be shared by two prominent Wall Street advisors. In Leibowitz and Langetieg [1989] the authors make numerous calculations regarding the long-term results of various asset allocation decisions. They conclude as follows:

> If we limit our choice to "stocks" and "bonds" as represented by the S&P 500 and the BIG Index, then under virtually any reasonable set of assumptions, stocks will almost surely outperform bonds as the investment horizon is extended to infinity. Unfortunately, most of us do not have an infinite period of time to work out near term losses. Most investors and investment managers set personal investment goals that must be achieved in time frames of 3 to 5 years . . . " [p. 14].

Also, when discussing simulation results for twenty-year horizons under so-called favorable assumptions (e.g., that the historic equity premium and mean reversion in equity returns will continue) they offer the following remarks. "[Our analysis] shows that, under 'favorable' assumptions, the stock/bond [return] ratio will exceed 100% most of the time. *However, for investors who must account for near term losses, these long-run results may have little significance*" [p. 15, emphasis added]. In other words, agency costs produce myopic loss aversion.[16]

B. Foundation and University Endowments

Another important group of institutional investors is endowment funds held by universities and foundations. Once again, an even split between stocks and bonds is common, although the endowment funds are explicitly treated as perpetuities. In this case, however, there appear to be two causes for the myopic loss aversion. First, there are agency problems similar to those for pension plans. Consider a foundation with 50 percent of its assets invested in stocks. Suppose that the president of the foundation wanted to increase the allocation to 100 percent, arguing that with an infinite horizon, stocks are almost certain to outperform bonds. Again the president will face the problem that his horizon is distinctly finite *as are the horizons of his board members*. In fact, there is really no one who represents the interests of the foundation's potential beneficiaries in the twenty-second century. This is an agency problem without a principal!

An equally important source of myopic loss aversion comes from the spending rules used by most universities and foundations. A typical rule specifies that the organization can spend x percent of an n-year moving average of the value of the endowment, where n is typically five or less.[17] Although the purpose of such moving averages is to smooth out the impact of stock market fluctuations,

---

[16] Of course, many observers have accused American firms of myopia. The pension asset allocation decision may be a useful domain for measuring firms' horizons.

[17] Foundations also have minimum spending rules that they have to obey to retain their tax-free status.

a sudden drop or a long bear market can have a pronounced effect on spending. The institution is forced to choose between the competing goals of maximizing the present value of spending over an infinite horizon, and maintaining a steady operating budget. The fact that stocks have outperformed bonds over every twenty-year period in history is cold comfort after a decade of zero nominal returns, an experience most institutions still remember.

There is an important difference between universities (and operating foundations) and individuals saving for retirement. For an individual saving for retirement, it can be argued that the only thing she should care about is the size of the annuity that can be purchased at retirement, i.e., terminal wealth. Transitory fluctuations impose only psychic costs. For universities and operating foundations, however, there is both a psychic cost to seeing the value of the endowment fall and the very real cost of cutting back programs if there is a cash flow reduction for a period of years. This in no way diminishes the force of the myopic loss aversion explanation for the equity premium. If anything, the argument is strengthened by the existence of economic factors contributing to loss aversion. Nevertheless, institutions could probably do better at structuring their spending rules to facilitate a higher exposure to risky assets.

VII. CONCLUSIONS

The equity premium *is* a puzzle within the standard expected utility-maximizing paradigm. As Mehra and Prescott forcefully argue, it seems impossible to reconcile the high rates of return on stocks with the very low risk-free rate. How can investors be extremely unwilling to accept variations in returns, as the equity premium implies, and yet be willing to delay consumption to earn a measly 1 percent per year? Our solution to the puzzle is to combine a high sensitivity to losses with a prudent tendency to frequently monitor one's wealth. The former tendency shifts the domain of the utility function from consumption to returns, and the latter makes people demand a large premium to accept return variability. In our model investors are unwilling to accept return variability even if the short-run returns have no effect on consumption.

In their reply to Reitz, Mehra and Prescott [1988] offer the following guidelines for what they think would constitute a solution to the equity premium puzzle. "Perhaps the introduction of some other preference structure will do the job. . . . For such efforts to be successful, though, they must convince the profession that the proposed alternative preference structure is more useful than the now-standard one for organizing and interpreting not only these observations on average asset returns, but also other observations in growth theory, business cycle theory, labor market behavior, and so on" [p. 134]. While prospect theory has not yet been applied in all the contexts Mehra and Prescott cite, it has been extensively tested and supported in the study of decision-making under uncertainty, and loss aversion appears to offer promise as a component of an explanation for unemployment[18] and for understanding the outcomes in many legal contexts.[19] For this reason, we believe that myopic loss aversion deserves consideration as a possible solution to Mehra and Prescott's fascinating puzzle.

---

[18] For example, Kahneman, Knetsch, and Thaler [1986] find that perceptions of fairness in labor market contexts are strongly influenced by whether actions are framed as imposing losses or reducing gains.

[19] See Hovankamn [1991].

18. Fairness as a Constraint on Profit Seeking
Entitlements in the Market

Daniel Kahneman, Jack L. Knetsch, and Richard H. Thaler

ABSTRACT. Community standards of fairness for the setting of prices and wages were elicited by telephone surveys. In customer or labor markets, it is acceptable for a firm to raise prices (or cut wages) when profits are threatened and to maintain prices when costs diminish. It is unfair to exploit shifts in demand by raising prices or cutting wages. Several market anomalies are explained by assuming that these standards of fairness influence the behavior of firms.

Just as it is often useful to neglect friction in elementary mechanics, there may be good reasons to assume that firms seek their maximal profit as if they were subject only to legal and budgetary constraints. However, the patterns of sluggish or incomplete adjustment often observed in markets suggest that some additional constraints are operative. Several authors have used a notion of fairness to explain why many employers do not cut wages during periods of high unemployment (George Akerlof, 1979; Robert, Solow, 1980). Arthur Okun (1981) went further in arguing that fairness also alters the outcomes in what he called customer markets – characterized by suppliers who are perceived as making their own pricing decisions, have some monopoly power (if only because search is costly), and often have repeat business with their clientele. Like labor markets, customer markets also sometimes fail to clear:

... firms in the sports and entertainment industries offer their customers tickets at standard prices for events that clearly generate excess demand. Popular new models of automobiles may have waiting lists that extend for months. Similarly, manufacturers in a number of industries operate with backlogs in booms and allocate shipments when they obviously could raise prices and reduce the queue. [p. 170]

Okun explained these observations by the hostile reaction of customers to price increases that are not justified by increased costs and are therefore viewed

The research was carried out when Kahneman was at the University of British Columbia. It was supported by the Department of Fisheries and Oceans Canada. Kahneman and Thaler were also supported by the U. S. Office of Naval Research and the Alfred P. Sloan Foundation, respectively. Conversations with J. Brander, R. Frank, and A. Tversky were very helpful.

Originally published in *The American Economic Review*, 76:4, 728–41. Copyright © 1986 American Economic Association. Reprinted with permission.

as unfair. He also noted that customers appear willing to accept "fair" price increases even when demand is slack, and commented that "... in practice, observed pricing behavior is a vast distance from do-it-yourself auctioneering" (p. 170).

The argument used by these authors to account for apparent deviations from the simple model of a profit-maximizing firm is that fair behavior is instrumental to the maximization of long-run profits. In Okun's model, customers who suspect that a supplier treats them unfairly are likely to start searching for alternatives; Akerlof (1980, 1982) suggested that firms invest in their reputation to produce goodwill among their customers and high morale among their employees; and Arrow argued that trusted suppliers may be able to operate in markets that are otherwise devastated by the lemons problem (Akerlof, 1970; Kenneth Arrow, 1973). In these approaches, the rules of fairness define the terms of an enforceable implicit contract: Firms that behave unfairly are punished in the long run. A more radical assumption is that some firms apply fair policies even in situations that preclude enforcement – this is the view of the lay public, as shown in a later section of this paper.

If considerations of fairness do restrict the actions of profit-seeking firms, economic models might be enriched by a more detailed analysis of this constraint. Specifically, the rules that govern public perceptions of fairness should identify situations in which some firms will fail to exploit apparent opportunities to increase their profits. Near-rationality theory (Akerlof and Janet Yellen, 1985) suggests that such failures to maximize by a significant number of firms in a market can have large aggregate effects even in the presence of other firms that seek to take advantage of all available opportunities. Rules of fairness can also have significant economic effects through the medium of regulation. Indeed, Edward Zajac (forthcoming) has inferred general rules of fairness from public reactions to the behavior of regulated utilities.

The present research uses household surveys of public opinions to infer rules of fairness for conduct in the market from evaluations of particular actions by hypothetical firms.[1] The study has two main objectives: (*i*) to identify community standards of fairness that apply to price, rent, and wage setting by firms in varied circumstances; and (*ii*) to consider the possible implications of the rules of fairness for market outcomes.

The study was concerned with scenarios in which a *firm* (merchant, landlord, or employer) makes a pricing or wage-setting decision that affects the outcomes of one or more *transactors* (customers, tenants, or employees). The scenario

---

[1] Data were collected between May 1984 and July 1985 in telephone surveys of randomly selected residents of two Canadian metropolitan areas: Toronto and Vancouver. Equal numbers of adult female and male respondents were interviewed for about ten minutes in calls made during evening hours. No more than five questions concerned with fairness were included in any interview, and contrasting questions that were to be compared were never put to the same respondents.

was read to the participants, who evaluated the fairness of the action as in the following example:

Question 1: A hardware store has been selling snow shovels for $15. The morning after a large snowstorm, the store raises the price to $20. Please rate this action as:

Completely Fair   Acceptable
Unfair   Very Unfair

The two favorable and the two unfavorable categories are grouped in this report to indicate the proportions of respondents who judged the action acceptable or unfair. In this example, 82 percent of respondents ($N = 107$) considered it unfair for the hardware store to take advantage of the short-run increase in demand associated with a blizzard.

The approach of the present study is purely descriptive. Normative status is not claimed for the generalizations that are described as "rules of fairness," and the phrase, "it is fair" is simply an abbreviation for "a substantial majority of the population studied thinks it fair." The paper considers in turn three determinants of fairness judgments: the reference transaction, the outcomes to the firm and to the transactors, and the occasion for the action of the firm. The final sections are concerned with the enforcement of fairness and with economic phenomena that the rules of fairness may help explain.

I. REFERENCE TRANSACTIONS

A central concept in analyzing the fairness of actions in which a firm sets the terms of future exchanges is the *reference transaction*, a relevant precedent that is characterized by a reference price or wage, and by a positive reference profit to the firm. The treatment is restricted to cases in which the fairness of the reference transaction is not itself in question.

The main findings of this research can be summarized by a principle of *dual entitlement*, which governs community standards of fairness: Transactors have an entitlement to the terms of the reference transaction and firms are entitled to their reference profit. A firm is not allowed to increase its profits by arbitrarily violating the entitlement of its transactors to the reference price, rent or wage (Max Bazerman, 1985; Zajac, forthcoming). When the reference profit of a firm is threatened, however, it may set new terms that protect its profit at transactors' expense.

Market prices, posted prices, and the history of previous transactions between a firm and a transactor can serve as reference transactions. When there is a history of similar transactions between firm and transactor, the most recent price, wage, or rent will be adopted for reference unless the terms of the previous transaction were explicitly temporary. For new transactions, prevailing competitive prices or wages provide the natural reference. The role of prior history in wage transactions is illustrated by the following pair of questions:

> **Question 2A:** A small photocopying shop has one employee who has worked in the shop for six months and earns $9 per hour. Business continues to be satisfactory, but a factory in the area has closed and unemployment has increased. Other small shops have now hired reliable workers at $7 an hour to perform jobs similar to those done by the photocopy shop employee. The owner of the photocopying shop reduces the employee's wage to $7.
> ($N = 98$)   Acceptable 17%   Unfair 83%

> **Question 2B:** A small photocopying shop has one employee...[as in Question 2A]... The current employee leaves, and the owner decides to pay a replacement $7 an hour.
> ($N = 125$)   Acceptable 73%   Unfair 27%

The current wage of an employee serves as reference for evaluating the fairness of future adjustments of that employee's wage – but not necessarily for evaluating the fairness of the wage paid to a replacement. The new worker does not have an entitlement to the former worker's wage rate. As the following question shows, the entitlement of an employee to a reference wage does not carry over to a new labor transaction, even with the same employer:

> **Question 3:** A house painter employs two assistants and pays them $9 per hour. The painter decides to quit house painting and go into the business of providing landscape services, where the going wage is lower. He reduces the workers' wages to $7 per hour for the landscaping work.
> ($N = 94$)   Acceptable 63%   Unfair 37%

Note that the same reduction in wages that is judged acceptable by most respondents in Question 3 was judged unfair by 83 percent of the respondents to Question 2A.

Parallel results were obtained in questions concerning residential tenancy. As in the case of wages, many respondents apply different rules to a new tenant and to a tenant renewing a lease. A rent increase that is judged fair for a new lease may be unfair for a renewal. However, the circumstances under which the rules of fairness require landlords to bear such opportunity costs are narrowly defined. Few respondents consider it unfair for the landlord to sell the accommodation to another landlord who intends to raise the rents of sitting tenants, and even fewer believe that a landlord should make price concessions in selling an accommodation to its occupant.

The relevant reference transaction is not always unique. Disagreements about fairness are most likely to arise when alternative reference transactions can be invoked, each leading to a different assessment of the participants' outcomes. Agreement on general principles of fairness therefore does not preclude disputes about specific cases (see also Zajac, forthcoming). When competitors change their price or wage, for example, the current terms set by the firm and the new terms set by competitors define alternative reference transactions. Some people will consider it unfair for a firm not to raise its wages when competitors are increasing theirs. On the other hand, price increases that are not justified by increasing costs are judged less objectionable when competitors have led the way.

It should perhaps be emphasized that the reference transaction provides a basis for fairness judgments because it is normal, not necessarily because it is just. Psychological studies of adaptation suggest that any stable state of affairs tends to become accepted eventually, at least in the sense that alternatives to it no longer readily come to mind. Terms of exchange that are initially seen as unfair may in time acquire the status of a reference transaction. Thus, the gap between the behavior that people consider fair and the behavior that they expect in the marketplace tends to be rather small. This was confirmed in several scenarios, where different samples of respondents answered the two questions: "What does fairness require?" and "What do you think the firm would do?" The similarity of the answers suggests that people expect a substantial level of conformity to community standards – and also that they adapt their views of fairness to the norms of actual behavior.

II. THE CODING OF OUTCOMES

It is a commonplace that the fairness of an action depends in large part on the signs of its outcomes for the agent and for the individuals affected by it. The cardinal rule of fair behavior is surely that one person should not achieve a gain by simply imposing an equivalent loss on another.

In the present framework, the outcomes to the firm and to its transactors are defined as gains and losses in relation to the reference transaction. The transactor's outcome is simply the difference between the new terms set by the firm and the reference price, rent, or wage. The outcome to the firm is evaluated with respect to the reference profit, and incorporates the effect of exogenous shocks (for example, changes in wholesale prices) which alter the profit of the firm on a transaction at the reference terms. According to these definitions, the outcomes in the snow shovel example of Question 1 were a $5 gain to the firm and a $5 loss to the representative customer. However, had the same price increase been induced by a $5 increase in the wholesale price of snow shovels, the outcome to the firm would have been nil.

The issue of how to define relevant outcomes takes a similar form in studies of individuals' preferences and of judgments of fairness. In both domains, a descriptive analysis of people's judgments and choices involves rules of *naive accounting* that diverge in major ways from the standards of rationality assumed in economic analysis. People commonly evaluate outcomes as gains or losses relative to a neutral reference point rather than as endstates (Kahneman and Amos Tversky, 1979). In violation of normative standards, they are more sensitive to out-of-pocket costs than to opportunity costs and more sensitive to losses than to foregone gains (Kahneman and Tversky, 1984; Thaler, 1980). These characteristics of evaluation make preferences vulnerable to framing effects, in which inconsequential variations in the presentation of a choice problem affect the decision (Tversky and Kahneman, 1986).

The entitlements of firms and transactors induce similar asymmetries between gains and losses in fairness judgments. An action by a firm is more likely to be judged unfair if it causes a loss to its transactor than if it cancels or reduces a possible gain. Similarly, an action by a firm is more likely to be judged unfair if it achieves a gain to the firm than if it averts a loss. Different standards are applied to actions that are elicited by the threat of losses or by an opportunity to improve on a positive reference profit – a psychologically important distinction which is usually not represented in economic analysis.

Judgments of fairness are also susceptible to framing effects, in which form appears to overwhelm substance. One of these framing effects will be recognized as the money illusion, illustrated in the following questions:

Question 4A: A company is making a small profit. It is located in a community experiencing a recession with substantial unemployment but no inflation. There are many workers anxious to work at the company. The company decides to decrease wages and salaries 7% this year.
($N = 125$)   Acceptable 38%   Unfair 62%

Question 4B: ... with substantial unemployment and inflation of 12%... The company decides to increase salaries only 5% this year.
($N = 129$)   Acceptable 78%   Unfair 22%

Although the real income change is approximately the same in the two problems, the judgments of fairness are strikingly different. A wage cut is coded as a loss and consequently judged unfair. A nominal raise which does not compensate for inflation is more acceptable because it is coded as a gain to the employee, relative to the reference wage.

Analyses of individual choice suggest that the disutility associated with an outcome that is coded as a loss may be greater than the disutility of the same objective outcome when coded as the elimination of a gain. Thus, there may be less resistance to the cancellation of a discount or bonus than to an equivalent price increase or wage cut. As illustrated by the following questions, the same rule applies as well to fairness judgments.

Question 5A: A shortage has developed for a popular model of automobile, and customers must now wait two months for delivery. A dealer has been selling these cars at list price. Now the dealer prices this model at $200 above list price.
($N = 130$)   Acceptable 29%   Unfair 71%

Question 5B: ... A dealer has been selling these cars at a discount of $200 below list price. Now the dealer sells this model only at list price.
($N = 123$)   Acceptable 58%   Unfair 42%

The significant difference between the responses to Questions 5A and 5B (*chi*-squared = 20.91) indicates that the $200 price increase is not treated identically in the two problems. In Question 5A the increase is clearly coded as a loss relative to the unambiguous reference provided by the list price. In Question 5B the reference price is ambiguous, and the change can be coded either as a loss (if the reference price is the discounted price), or as the elimination of a gain (if the reference price is the list price). The relative leniency of judgments in Question 5B suggests that at least some respondents adopted the latter frame. The following questions illustrate the same effect in the case of wages:

> **Question 6A:** A small company employs several people. The workers' incomes have been about average for the community. In recent months, business for the company has not increased as it had before. The owners reduce the workers' wages by 10 percent for the next year.
> (*N* = 100)   Acceptable 39%   Unfair 61%

> **Question 6B:** A small company employs several people. The workers have been receiving a 10 percent annual bonus each year and their total incomes have been about average for the community. In recent months, business for the company has not increased as it had before. The owners eliminate the workers' bonus for the year.
> (*N* = 98)   Acceptable 80%   Unfair 20%

III. OCCASIONS FOR PRICING DECISIONS

This section examines the rules of fairness that apply to three classes of occasions in which a firm may reconsider the terms that it sets for exchanges. (*i*) *Profit reductions*, for example, by rising costs or decreased demand for the product of the firm. (*ii*) *Profit increases*, for example, by efficiency gains or reduced costs. (*iii*) *Increases in market power*, for example, by temporary excess demand for goods, accommodations or jobs.

A. Protecting Profit

A random sample of adults contains many more customers, tenants, and employees than merchants, landlords, or employers. Nevertheless, most participants in the surveys clearly consider the firm to be entitled to its reference profit: They would allow a firm threatened by a reduction of its profit below a positive reference level to pass on the entire loss to its transactors, without compromising or sharing the pain. By large majorities, respondents endorsed the fairness of passing on increases in wholesale costs, in operating costs, and in the costs associated with a rental accommodation. The following two questions illustrate the range of situations to which this rule was found to apply.

> **Question 7:** Suppose that, due to a transportation mixup, there is a local shortage of lettuce and the wholesale price has increased. A local grocer has bought

the usual quantity of lettuce at a price that is 30 cents per head higher than normal. The grocer raises the price of lettuce to customers by 30 cents per head.

   ($N = 101$)   Acceptable 79%   Unfair 21%

Question 8: A landlord owns and rents out a single small house to a tenant who is living on a fixed income. A higher rent would mean the tenant would have to move. Other small rental houses are available. The landlord's costs have increased substantially over the past year and the landlord raises the rent to cover the cost increases when the tenant's lease is due for renewal.

   ($N = 151$)   Acceptable 75%   Unfair 25%

The answers to the last question, in particular, indicate that it is acceptable for firms to protect themselves from losses even when their transactors suffer substantial inconvenience as a result. The rules of fairness that yield such judgments do not correspond to norms of charity and do not reflect distributional concerns.

The attitude that permits the firm to protect a positive reference profit at the transactors' expense applies to employers as well as to merchants and landlords. When the profit of the employer in the labor transaction falls below the reference level, reductions of even nominal wages become acceptable. The next questions illustrate the strong effect of this variable.

Question 9A: A small company employs several workers and has been paying them average wages. There is severe unemployment in the area and the company could easily replace its current employees with good workers at a lower wage. The company has been making money. The owners reduce the current workers' wages by 5 percent.

   ($N = 195$)   Acceptable 23%   Unfair 77%

Question 9B: ... The company has been losing money. The owners reduce the current workers' wages by 5 percent.

   ($N = 195$)   Acceptable 68%   Unfair 32%

The effect of firm profitability was studied in greater detail in the context of a scenario in which Mr. Green, a gardener who employs two workers at $7 an hour, learns that other equally competent workers are willing to do the same work for $6 an hour. Some respondents were told that Mr. Green's business was doing well; others were told that it was doing poorly. The questions, presented in open format, required respondents to state "what is fair for Mr. Green to do in this situation," or "what is your best guess about what Mr. Green would do...." The information about the current state of the business had a large effect. Replacing the employees or bargaining with them to achieve a lower wage was mentioned as fair by 67 percent of respondents when business was said to be poor, but only by 25 percent of respondents when business was good. The proportion guessing that Mr. Green would try to reduce his labor costs was 75 percent when he was said to be doing poorly, and 49 percent when he was said to be doing well. The differences were statistically reliable in both cases.

A firm is only allowed to protect itself at the transactor's expense against losses that pertain directly to the transaction at hand. Thus, it is unfair for a landlord to raise the rent on an accommodation to make up for the loss of another source of income. On the other hand, 62 percent of the respondents considered it acceptable for a landlord to charge a higher rent for apartments in one of two otherwise identical buildings because a more costly foundation had been required in the construction of that building.

The assignment of costs to specific goods explains why it is generally unfair to raise the price of old stock when the price of new stock increases:

> **Question 10:** A grocery store has several months' supply of peanut butter in stock which it has on the shelves and in the storeroom. The owner hears that the wholesale price of peanut butter has increased and immediately raises the price on the current stock of peanut butter.
> ($N = 147$)   Acceptable 21%   Unfair 79%

The principles of naive accounting apparently include a FIFO method of inventory cost allocation.

B. The Allocation of Gains

The data of the preceding section could be interpreted as evidence for a cost-plus rule of fair pricing, in which the supplier is expected to act as a broker in passing on marked-up costs (Okun). A critical test of this possible rule arises when the supplier's costs diminish: A strict cost-plus rule would require prices to come down accordingly. In contrast, a dual-entitlement view suggests that the firm is only prohibited from increasing its profit by causing a loss to its transactors. Increasing profits by retaining cost reductions does not violate the transactors' entitlement and may therefore be acceptable.

The results of our previous study (1986) indicated that community standards of fairness do not in fact restrict firms to the reference profit when their costs diminish, as a cost-plus rule would require. The questions used in these surveys presented a scenario of a monopolist supplier of a particular kind of table, who faces a $20 reduction of costs on tables that have been selling for $150. The respondents were asked to indicate whether "fairness requires" the supplier to lower the price, and if so, by how much. About one-half of the survey respondents felt that it was acceptable for the supplier to retain the entire benefit, and less than one-third would require the supplier to reduce the price by $20, as a cost-plus rule dictates. Further, and somewhat surprisingly, judgments of fairness did not reliably discriminate between primary producers and middlemen, or between savings due to lower input prices and to improved efficiency.

The conclusion that the rules of fairness permit the seller to keep part or all of any cost reduction was confirmed with the simpler method employed in the present study.

Question 11A: A small factory produces tables and sells all that it can make at $200 each. Because of changes in the price of materials, the cost of making each table has recently decreased by $40. The factory reduces its price for the tables by $20.

(N = 102)   Acceptable 79%   Unfair 21%

Question 11B: ... the cost of making each table has recently decreased by $20. The factory does not change its price for the tables.

(N = 100)   Acceptable 53%   Unfair 47%

The even division of opinions on Question 11B confirms the observations of the previous study. In conjunction with the results of the previous section, the findings support a dual-entitlement view: the rules of fairness permit a firm not to share in the losses that it imposes on its transactors, without imposing on it an unequivocal duty to share its gains with them.

C. Exploitation of Increased Market Power

The market power of a firm reflects the advantage to the transactor of the exchange which the firm offers compared to the transactor's second-best alternative. For example, a blizzard increases the surplus associated with the purchase of a snow shovel at the regular price compared to the alternatives of buying elsewhere or doing without a shovel. The respondents consider it unfair for the hardware store to capture any part of the increased surplus because such an action would violate the customer's entitlement to the reference price. Similarly, it is unfair for a firm to exploit an excess in the supply of labor to cut wages (Question 2A) because this would violate the entitlement of employees to their reference wage.

As shown by the following routine example, the opposition to exploitation of shortages is not restricted to such extreme circumstances:

Question 12: A severe shortage of Red Delicious apples has developed in a community and none of the grocery stores or produce markets have any of this type of apple on their shelves. Other varieties of apples are plentiful in all of the stores. One grocer receives a single shipment of Red Delicious apples at the regular wholesale cost and raises the retail price of these Red Delicious apples by 25% over the regular price.

(N = 102)   Acceptable 37%   Unfair 63%

Raising prices in response to a shortage is unfair even when close substitutes are readily available. A similar aversion to price rationing held as well for luxury items. For example, a majority of respondents thought it unfair for a popular restaurant to impose a $5 surcharge for Saturday night reservations.

Conventional economic analyses assume as a matter of course that excess demand for a good creates an opportunity for suppliers to raise prices, and that such increases will indeed occur. The profit-seeking adjustments that clear the market are in this view as natural as water finding its level – and as ethically neutral. The lay public does not share this indifference. Community standards of fairness effectively require the firm to absorb an opportunity cost in the presence of excess demand by charging less than the clearing price or paying more than the clearing wage.

As might be expected from this analysis, it is unfair for a firm to take advantage of an increase in its monopoly power. Respondents were nearly unanimous in condemning a store that raises prices when its sole competitor in a community is temporarily forced to close. As shown in the next question, even a rather mild exploitation of monopoly power is considered unfair.

> **Question 13:** A grocery chain has stores in many communities. Most of them face competition from other groceries. In one community the chain has no competition. Although its costs and volume of sales are the same there as elsewhere, the chain sets prices that average 5 percent higher than in other communities.
>
> ($N = 101$)   Acceptable 24%   Unfair 76%

Responses to this and two additional versions of this question specifying average price increases of 10 and 15 percent did not differ significantly. The respondents clearly viewed such pricing practices as unfair, but were insensitive to the extent of the unwarranted increase.

A monopolist might attempt to increase profits by charging different customers as much as they are willing to pay. In conventional theory, the constraints that prevent a monopolist from using perfect price discrimination to capture all the consumers' surplus are asymmetric information and difficulties in preventing resale. The survey results suggest the addition of a further restraint: some forms of price discrimination are outrageous.

> **Question 14:** A landlord rents out a small house. When the lease is due for renewal, the landlord learns that the tenant has taken a job very close to the house and is therefore unlikely to move. The landlord raises the rent $40 per month more than he was planning to do.
>
> ($N = 157$)   Acceptable 9%   Unfair 91%

The near unanimity of responses to this and similar questions indicates that an action that deliberately exploits the special dependence of a particular individual is exceptionally offensive.

The introduction of an explicit auction to allocate scarce goods or jobs would also enable the firm to gain at the expense of its transactors, and is consequently judged unfair.

> **Question 15:** A store has been sold out of the popular Cabbage Patch dolls for a month. A week before Christmas a single doll is discovered in a storeroom. The managers know that many customers would like to buy the doll. They announce

over the store's public address system that the doll will be sold by auction to the customer who offers to pay the most.

(N = 101)   Acceptable 26%   Unfair 74%

Question 16: A business in a community with high unemployment needs to hire a new computer operator. Four candidates are judged to be completely qualified for the job. The manager asks the candidates to state the lowest salary they would be willing to accept, and then hires the one who demands the lowest salary.

(N = 154)   Acceptable 36%   Unfair 64%

The auction is opposed in both cases, presumably because the competition among potential buyers or employees benefits the firm. The opposition can in some cases be mitigated by eliminating this benefit. For example, a sentence added to Question 15 indicating that "the proceeds will go to UNICEF" reduced the negative judgments of the doll auction from 74 to 21 percent.

The strong aversion to price rationing in these examples clearly does not extend to all uses of auctions. The individual who sells securities at twice the price paid for them a month ago is an object of admiration and envy – and is certainly not thought to be gouging. Why is it fair to sell a painting or a house at the market-clearing price, but not an apple, dinner reservation, job, or football game ticket? The rule of acceptability appears to be this: Goods for which an active resale market exists, and especially goods that serve as a store of value, can be sold freely by auction or other mechanisms allowing the seller to capture the maximum price. When resale is a realistic possibility, which is not the case for most consumer goods, the potential resale price reflects the higher value of the asset and the purchaser is therefore not perceived as sustaining a loss.

IV. ENFORCEMENT

Several considerations may deter a firm from violating community standards of fairness. First, a history or reputation of unfair dealing may induce potential transactors to take their business elsewhere, because of the element of trust that is present in many transactions. Second, transactors may avoid exchanges with offending firms at some cost to themselves, even when trust is not an issue. Finally, the individuals who make decisions on behalf of firms may have a preference for acting fairly. The role of reputation effects is widely recognized. This section presents some indications that a willingness to resist and to punish unfairness and an intrinsic motivation to be fair could also contribute to fair behavior in the marketplace.

A willingness to pay to resist and to punish unfairness has been demonstrated in incentive compatible laboratory experiments. In the ultimatum game devised by Werner Guth, Rolf Schmittberger, and Bernd Schwarze (1982), the participants are designated as allocators or recipients. Each allocator anonymously proposes a division of a fixed amount of money between himself (herself) and a recipient. The recipient either accepts the offer or rejects it, in which case both players get nothing. The standard game theoretic solution is for the allocator to make a token offer and for the recipient to accept it, but Guth et al. observed that many allocators offer an equal division and that recipients sometimes turn down positive offers. In our more detailed study of resistance to unfairness (1986), recipients were asked to indicate in advance how they wished to respond to a range of possible allocations: A majority of participants were willing to forsake $2 rather than accept an unfair allocation of $10.

Willingness to punish unfair actors was observed in another experiment, in which subjects were given the opportunity to share a sum of money evenly with one of two anonymous strangers, identified only by the allocation they had proposed to someone else in a previous round. About three-quarters of the undergraduate participants in this experiment elected to share $10 evenly with a stranger who had been fair to someone else, when the alternative was to share $12 evenly with an unfair allocator (see our other paper).

A willingness to punish unfairness was also expressed in the telephone surveys. For example, 68 percent of respondents said they would switch their patronage to a drugstore five minutes further away if the one closer to them raised its prices when a competitor was temporarily forced to close; and, in a separate sample, 69 percent indicated they would switch if the more convenient store discriminated against its older workers.

The costs of enforcing fairness are small in these examples – but effective enforcement in the marketplace can often be achieved at little cost to transactors. Retailers will have a substantial incentive to behave fairly if a large number of customers are prepared to drive an extra five minutes to avoid doing business with an unfair firm. The threat of future punishment when competitors enter may also deter a temporary monopolist from fully exploiting short-term profit opportunities.

In traditional economic theory, compliance with contracts depends on enforcement. It is a mild embarrassment to the standard model that experimental studies often produce fair behavior even in the absence of enforcement (Elizabeth Hoffman and Matthew Spitzer, 1982, 1985; our paper, 1986; Arvin Roth, Michael Malouf, and J. Keith Murninghan, 1981; Reinhard Selten, 1978). These observations, however, merely confirm commonsense views of human behavior. Survey results indicate a belief that unenforced compliance to the rules of fairness is common. This belief was examined in two contexts: tipping in restaurants and sharp practice in automobile repairs.

Question 17A: If the service is satisfactory, how much of a tip do you think most people leave after ordering a meal costing $10 in a restaurant that they visit frequently?

($N = 122$)   Mean response $= \$1.28$

Question 17B: . . . in a restaurant on a trip to another city that they do not expect to visit again?

($N = 124$)   Mean response $= \$1.27$

The respondents evidently do not treat the possibility of enforcement as a significant factor in the control of tipping. Their opinion is consistent with the widely observed adherence to a 15 percent tipping rule even by one-time customers who pay and tip by credit card and have little reason to fear embarrassing retaliation by an irate server.

The common belief that tipping is controlled by intrinsic motivation can be accommodated with a standard microeconomic model by extending the utility function of individuals to include guilt and self-esteem. A more difficult question is whether firms, which the theory assumes to maximize profits, also fail to exploit some economic opportunities because of unenforced compliance with rules of fairness. The following questions elicited expectations about the behavior of a garage mechanic dealing with a regular customer or with a tourist.

Question 18A: [A man leaves his car with the mechanic at his regular/A tourist leaves his car at a] service station with instructions to replace an expensive part. After the [customer/tourist] leaves, the mechanic examines the car and discovers that it is not necessary to replace the part; it can be repaired cheaply. The mechanic would make much more money by replacing the part than by repairing it. Assuming the [customer/tourist] cannot be reached, what do you think the mechanic would do in this situation?

Make more money by replacing the part

customer: 60%   tourist: 63%

Save the customer money by repairing the part

customer: 40%   tourist: 37%

Question 18B: Of the mechanics dealing with a [regular customer/tourist], how many would you expect to save the customer money by repairing the part?

Mean response

customer: 3.62   tourist: 3.72

The respondents do not approach garages with wide-eyed naive faith. It is therefore all the more noteworthy that they expect a tourist and a regular customer to be treated alike, in spite of the obvious difference between the two cases in the potential for any kind of enforcement, including reputation effects.[2]

Here again, there is no evidence that the public considers enforcement a significant factor. The respondents believe that most mechanics (usually excluding their own) would be less than saintly in this situation. However, they also appear to believe that the substantial minority of mechanics who would

---

[2] Other respondents were asked to assess the probable behavior of their own garage under similar circumstances: 88 percent expressed a belief that their garage would act fairly toward a regular customer, and 86 percent stated that their garage would treat a tourist and a regular customer similarly.

Robert Frank (1985) found that the individuals in a university who already are the most highly paid in each department are also the most likely targets for raiding. Frank explains the observed behavior in terms of envy and status. An analysis of this phenomenon in terms of fairness is the same as for the seasonal pricing of resort rooms: Just as prices that clear the market at peak demand will be perceived as gouging if the resort can also afford to operate at off-peak rates, a firm that can afford to pay its most valuable employees their market value may appear to grossly underpay their less-valued colleagues. A related prediction is that variations among departments will also be insufficient to clear the market. Although salaries are higher in academic departments that compete with the private sector than in others, the ratio of job openings to applicants is still lower in classics than in accounting.

The present analysis also suggests that firms that frame a portion of their compensation package as bonuses or profit sharing will encounter relatively little resistance to reductions of compensation during slack periods. This is the equivalent of Proposition 4. The relevant psychological principle is that losses are more aversive than objectively equivalent foregone gains. The same mechanism, combined with the money illusion, supports another prediction: Adjustments of real wages will be substantially greater in inflationary periods than in periods of stable prices, because the adjustments can then be achieved without making nominal cuts – which are always perceived as losses and are therefore strongly resisted. An unequal distribution of gains is more likely to appear fair than a reallocation in which there are losers.

This discussion has illustrated several ways in which the informal entitlements of customers or employees to the terms of reference transactions could enter an economic analysis. In cases such as the pricing of resort facilities, the concern of customers for fair pricing may permanently prevent the market from clearing. In other situations, the reluctance of firms to impose terms that can be perceived as unfair acts as a friction-like factor. The process of reaching equilibrium can be slowed down if no firm wants to be seen as a leader in moving to exploit changing market conditions. In some instances an initially unfair practice (for example, charging above list price for a popular car model) may spread slowly until it evolves into a new norm – and is no longer unfair. In all these cases, perceptions of transactors' entitlements affect the substantive outcomes of exchanges, altering or preventing the equilibria predicted by an analysis that omits fairness as a factor. In addition, considerations of fairness can affect the form rather than the substance of price or wage setting. Judgments of fairness are susceptible to substantial framing effects, and the present study gives reason to believe that firms have an incentive to frame the terms of exchanges so as to make them appear "fair."

treat their customers fairly are not motivated in each case by the anticipation of sanctions.

V. ECONOMIC CONSEQUENCES

The findings of this study suggest that many actions that are both profitable in the short run and not obviously dishonest are likely to be perceived as unfair exploitations of market power.[3] Such perceptions can have significant consequences if they find expression in legislation or regulation (Zajac, 1978; forthcoming). Further, even in the absence of government intervention, the actions of firms that wish to avoid a reputation for unfairness will depart in significant ways from the standard model of economic behavior. The survey results suggest four propositions about the effects of fairness considerations on the behavior of firms in customer markets, and a parallel set of hypotheses about labor markets.

A. Fairness in Customer Markets

Proposition 1: *When excess demand in a customer market is unaccompanied by increases in suppliers' costs, the market will fail to clear in the short run.*

Evidence supporting this propositions was described by Phillip Cagan (1979), who concluded from a review of the behavior of prices that, "Empirical studies have long found that short-run shifts in demand have small and often insignificant effects [on prices]" (p. 18). Other consistent evidence comes from studies of disasters, where prices are often maintained at their reference levels although supplies are short (Douglas Dacy and Howard Kunreuther, 1969).

A particularly well-documented illustration of the behavior predicted in proposition 1 is provided by Alan Olmstead and Paul Rhode (1985). During the spring and summer of 1920 there was a severe gasoline shortage in the U.S. West Coast where Standard Oil of California (SOCal) was the dominant supplier. There were no government-imposed price controls, nor was there any threat of such controls, yet SOCal reacted by imposing allocation and rationing schemes while maintaining prices. Prices were actually higher in the East in the absence of any shortage. Significantly, Olmstead and Rhode note that the eastern firms had to purchase crude at higher prices while SOCal, being vertically integrated, had no such excuse for raising price. They conclude from confidential SOCal documents that SOCal officers "... were clearly concerned with their public image and tried to maintain the appearance of being 'fair'" (p. 1053).

---

[3] This conclusion probably holds in social and cultural groups other than the Canadian urban samples studied here, although the detailed rules of fairness for economic transactions may vary.

Proposition 2: *When a single supplier provides a family of goods for which there is differential demand without corresponding variation of input costs, shortages of the most valued items will occur.*

There is considerable support for this proposition in the pricing of sport and entertainment events, which are characterized by marked variation of demand for goods or services for which costs are about the same (Thaler, 1985). The survey responses suggest that charging the market-clearing price for the most popular goods would be judged unfair.

Proposition 2 applies to cases such as those of resort hotels that have in-season and out-of-season rates which correspond to predictable variations of demand. To the extent that constraints of fairness are operating, the price adjustments should be insufficient, with excess demand at the peak. Because naive accounting does not properly distinguish between marginal and average costs, customers and other observers are likely to adopt offpeak prices as a reference in evaluating the fairness of the price charged to peak customers. A revenue-maximizing (low) price in the off-season may suggest that the profits achievable at the peak are unfairly high. In spite of a substantial degree of within-season price variation in resort and ski hotels, it appears to be the rule that most of these establishments face excess demand during the peak weeks. One industry explanation is: "If you gouge them at Christmas, they won't be back in March."

Proposition 3: *Price changes will be more responsive to variations of costs than to variations of demand, and more responsive to cost increases than to cost decreases.*

The high sensitivity of prices to short-run variations of costs is well documented (Cagan). The idea of asymmetric price rigidity has a history of controversy (Timur Kuran, 1983; Solow; George Stigler and James Kindahl, 1970) and the issue is still unsettled. Changes of currency values offer a potential test of the hypothesis that cost increases tend to be passed on quickly and completely, whereas cost decreases can be retained at least in part. When the rate of exchange between two currencies changes after a prolonged period of stability, the prediction from Proposition 3 is that upward adjustments of import prices in one country will occur faster than the downward adjustments expected in the other.

Proposition 4: *Price decreases will often take the form of discounts rather than reductions in the list or posted price.*

This proposition is strongly supported by the data of Stigler and Kindahl. Casual observation confirms that temporary discounts are much more common than temporary surcharges. Discounts have the important advantage that their

subsequent cancellation will elicit less resistance than an increase price. A temporary surcharge is especially aversive because it does the prospect of becoming a reference price and can only be coded as

B. Fairness in Labor Markets

A consistent finding of this study is the similarity of the rules of fairn apply to prices, rents, and wages. The correspondence extends to the ed predictions that may be derived for the behavior of wages in labor n and of prices in customer markets. The first proposition about prices as that resistance to the exploitation of short-term fluctuations of demand prevent markets from clearing. The corresponding prediction for labor ma is that wages will be relatively insensitive to excess supply.

The existence of wage stickiness is not in doubt, and numerous explana have been offered for it. An entitlement model of this effect invokes an imp contract between the worker and the firm. Like other implicit contract theo such a model predicts that wage changes in a firm will be more sensitive recent firm profits than to local labor market conditions. However, unlike implicit contract theories that emphasize risk shifting (Costas Azariadis, 19 Martin Baily, 1974; Donald Gordon, 1974), explanations in terms of fairne (Akerlof, 1979, 1982; Okun; Solow) lead to predictions of wage stickiness eve in occupations that offer no prospects for long-term employment and therefor provide little protection from risk. Okun noted that "Casual empiricism about the casual labor market suggests that the Keynesian wage floor nonetheless operates; the pay of car washers or stock clerks is seldom cut in a recession, even when it is well above any statutory minimum wage" (1981, p. 82), and he concluded that the employment relation is governed by an "invisible hand shake," rather than by the invisible hand (p. 89).

The dual-entitlement model differs from a Keynesian model of sticky wage in which nominal wage changes are always nonnegative. The survey findin suggest that nominal wage cuts by a firm that is losing money or threatened w bankruptcy do not violate community standards of fairness. This modificat of the sticky nominal wage dictum is related to Proposition 3 for custor markets. Just as they may raise prices to do so, firms may also cut wage protect a positive reference profit.

Proposition 2 for customer markets asserted that the dispersion of price similar goods that cost the same to produce but differ in demand will be ficient to clear the market. An analogous case in the labor market in positions that are similar in nominal duties but are occupied by ind als who have different values in the employment market. The predic that differences in income will be insufficient to eliminate the excess d for the individuals considered most valuable, and the excess supply considered most dispensable. This prediction applies both within and occupations.

19. Money Illusion

Eldar Shafir, Peter Diamond, and Amos Tversky

ABSTRACT. The term *money illusion* refers to a tendency to think in terms of nominal rather than real monetary values. Money illusion has significant implications for economic theory, yet it implies a lack of rationality that is alien to economists. This paper reviews survey questions, which are designed to shed light on the psychology that underlies money illusion, regarding people's reactions to variations in inflation and prices. We propose that people often think about economic transactions in both nominal and real terms and that money illusion arises from an interaction between these representations, which results in a bias towards a nominal evaluation.

"A nickel ain't worth a dime anymore."

Yogi Berra

We have standardized every other unit in commerce except the most important and universal unit of all, the unit of purchasing power. What business man would consent for a moment to make a contract in terms of yards of cloth or tons of coal, and leave the size of the yard or the ton to chance? . . . We have standardized even our new units of electricity, the ohm, the kilowatt, the ampere, and the volt. But the dollar is still left to the chances of gold mining.

Irving Fisher, 1913

The term *money illusion* refers to a tendency to be influenced by nominal as well as real monetary values in one's thinking about, and the conduct of, economic transactions. Money illusion has significant implications for economic theory, yet it implies a lack of rationality that is alien to economists. As summarized by Peter Howitt in the *New Palgrave Dictionary of Economics* [Vol. 3, pp. 518–19]:

the attitude of economists to the assumption of money illusion can best be described as equivocal. The assumption is frequently invoked and frequently resisted. The presence of a concept so alien to economists' pervasive belief in rationality indicates a deeper failure to understand the importance of money and of nominal magnitudes in economic life.

This chapter is an abridged version of an article that first appeared in *The Quarterly Journal of Economics*, 112:2, 341–74. Copyright © 1997 by the President and Fellows of Harvard College and the Massachusetts Institute of Technology. Reprinted with permission.

This failure is evident, for example, in the lack of any convincing explanation for why people persist in signing non-indexed debt contracts, or why the objective of reducing the rate of inflation, even at the cost of a major recession, should have such wide popular support in times of high inflation.

There appear to be three classes of anomalous observations related to the assumption of money illusion. One is that prices are "sticky." A second is that indexing does not occur in contracts and laws as theory would predict.[1] The third class manifests itself through conversation rather than behavior: people talk and write in ways that seem to indicate some confusion between money's nominal and real worth.

That changes in the money supply have their impact first on quantities and only later on prices is a widely accepted description of economies in many times and many places.[2] This observation often leads to an examination of the "stickiness" of prices and wages. Stickiness is documented in a variety of ways. At one extreme of aggregation, there are the lags in aggregate price equations.[3] Some studies of individual markets also show large quantity movements and small price movements. The theoretical mold that tries to derive these results from overlapping contracts or costs of price adjustment must recognize the presence of similar phenomena in markets, like housing, where prices are negotiated.

Economists do not find indexed contracts in nearly as many places as theory suggests they should be found. Furthermore, when indexed contracts are found, their form often seems peculiar to economists.[4] Moreover, there is only a slow introduction of indexed contracts when inflation picks up, and, more strikingly, the partial disappearance of indexed contracts when inflation slows down. Frequently, governments also use unindexed contracts and have tax systems that are unindexed or incompletely indexed. Courts do not treat inflation the same as unexpected events that destroy the value of contracts.[5]

Common discourse and newspaper reports often manifest money illusion even in familiar contexts and among people who, at some level, know better.

---

[1] In general, economists do not expect to find the same level of economic rationality in governments as among private agents. However, it is hard to see how a satisfactory theory of government behavior would account for policies incorporating money illusion if none of the citizen-voters or politicians were subject to money illusion.

[2] For a recent test of such lags, see Romer and Romer [1989].

[3] See, e.g., Gordon [1983].

[4] For a discussion of the difficulty of writing indexed contracts and the patterns in actual contracts for the delivery of coal see Joskow [1988]. For a history of COLAs in U.S. labor contracts, see Hendricks and Kahn [1985]. For a history of labor market indexation in Israel, see Kleiman [1986]. For a description of COLAs in Canadian labor contracts, see Card [1983]. For discussion of indexation more generally in Canada, see Howitt [1986]. For a discussion of responses to inflation in the U.S., see Fischer [1982].

[5] The Supreme Court of Canada upheld an unindexed 65-year contract between Quebec and Newfoundland for the delivery of hydro power despite subsequent inflation (Fortin, personal communication, 1995). For an example of the refusal of English courts to revise contracts in response to inflation, see Hirschberg [1976], page 101. For a discussion of the refusal of courts to extend the rewriting of contracts for unexpected events to inflation see Leijonhufvud [1977].

There are frequent newspaper comparisons of unadjusted costs, charitable donations, and salaries across time.[6] There are newspaper accounts of debt-financed projects that add together the initial costs and the interest costs coming from debt financing and report a single sum. Naturally, one would expect to find greater awareness of the difference between nominal and real values when inflation is high than when it is low. Nevertheless, residues of money illusion are observed even in highly inflationary environments. When inflation was high in Israel, it was common to use the U.S. dollar for both analysis and transactions. Yet, this substitution did not seem to preclude the continuation of money illusion relative to the changing value of the dollar.[7] The persistence of money illusion indicates that this phenomenon is not readily eliminated by learning. People may resort to an analysis in real terms when inflation is high, but may then go back to relying on nominal evaluations when the inflation subsides. For example, there is evidence that COLA's disappear from some contracts when inflation rates diminish, indicating that the appeal of a nominal evaluation persists despite extensive experience with evaluation in real terms.[8]

The present article proposes a psychological account of money illusion, which may help economists understand and model this phenomenon rather than ignore it or model its consequences in alternative ways.[9] Section I presents an analysis of money illusion in terms of multiple representations. Section II reports a series of studies that examine people's representations of various economic transactions. Section III provides summary and discussion.

I. MULTIPLE REPRESENTATIONS:
A PSYCHOLOGICAL ACCOUNT

Research in cognitive psychology indicates that alternative representations of the same situation can lead to systematically different responses. For example, choice between risky prospects may be represented either in terms of gains

---

[6] One can also consider the difficulty involved in doing the calculations correctly. Since the posting of unit price information (thus saving the difficulty of dividing) and the listing of prices together (thus saving on memory) both appear to affect purchases [Russo 1977], there may be a relationship between the difficulty of the correct calculation and the extent of systematic error.

[7] Similarly, Fisher [1928, p. 8] tells about a woman with a mortgage debt denominated in marks but thought about in dollars. In discharging her debt, she refused to take advantage of the change in the exchange rate (which altered the value of the debt from $7000 to $250) but did not adjust for the decline in the value of the dollar.

[8] Of the workers covered by major collective bargaining agreements in the U.S., for example, the percentage covered by COLA's was 50.0% in 1958, 20.0% in 1966, 61.2% in 1977, 57.3% in 1984 [Hendricks and Kahn 1985, Table 2-7.]

[9] Several authors have constructed alternative models that produce similar results to those generated by money illusion. Lucas [1972], for example, creates an inference problem that permits rational agents to exhibit similar behavior to that of agents with money illusion. For alternative accounts that assume particular forms of contracting, or of price or wage stickiness, see Barro and Grossman [1971], Fischer [1977], Lucas [1989], Malinvaud [1977], and Taylor [1979].

and losses, which seems natural to most people, or in terms of final assets, as recommended by normative theory. Consider an individual who faces a choice between a total wealth of $250,000, and an even chance at a total wealth of either $240,000 or $265,000. The same situation can also be represented in terms of gains and losses, as a choice between the status quo (here, $250,000) and an even chance to win $15,000 or to lose $10,000. These alternative representations of the same choice problem tend to induce different responses. When the problem is framed in terms of final assets, with no reference to changes in wealth, people tend to prefer the risky prospect, which has a higher expected value. But when the same problem is presented in terms of gains and losses, people prefer the status quo over the risky prospect, presumably because, in accord with the principle of loss aversion, a potential $10,000 loss offsets an equal chance of a $15,000 gain [Kahneman and Tversky 1979; Tversky and Kahneman 1991].

In another demonstration, McNeil, Pauker, Sox, and Tversky [1982] (see also McNeil, Pauker and Tversky [1988]) presented respondents with a choice between two alternative treatments for lung cancer, surgery and radiation therapy, whose outcomes were described either in terms of mortality rates or in terms of survival rates. Although the alternative representations were logically equivalent, they led to markedly different preferences: the percentage of respondents who favored radiation therapy rose from 18 percent in the survival frame to 44 percent in the mortality frame. This result was observed among experienced physicians, statistically sophisticated business students, as well as clinic patients.

In the above examples, as in other demonstrations of framing effects, people tend to adopt the particular frame that is presented (e.g., wealth versus changes in wealth; mortality versus survival), and proceed to evaluate the options in that frame. The reliance on a particular frame is typically guided by what is more salient, simpler, or more natural, not by strategic calculations. Because certain aspects of the options loom larger in one representation than in another, alternative framings of the same options can give rise to different choices.

In other situations, instead of evaluating the options in terms of a single representation, people entertain multiple representations contemporaneously. In such cases, the response is often a mixture of the assessments induced by the different representations, each weighted by its relative salience. This mechanism, we suggest, underlies money illusion. Economic transactions can be represented either in nominal or in real terms. The nominal representation is simpler, more salient, and often suffices for the short run (in the absence of hyperinflation), yet the representation in real terms is the one that captures the true value of transactions. People are generally aware that there is a difference between real and nominal values, but because at a single point in time, or over a short period, money is a salient and natural unit, people often think of transactions in predominantly nominal terms. Consequently, the evaluation of transactions often represents a mixture of nominal and real assessments, which gives rise to money illusion.

As an example, consider a person who receives a 2 percent raise in salary in times of 4 percent inflation. (We assume that the person is aware of inflation and momentarily ignore other factors, such as the possible social significance of a salary raise.[10]) Naturally, this person would be happier with the same raise in times of no inflation. However, because the nominal evaluation is positive (i.e., the person is making more money), we expect the person to find the change less aversive than a 2 percent cut in times of no inflation, in which both the nominal and the real evaluations are negative. Thus, we propose that holding real change constant, people's reactions will be determined by the nominal change. Moreover, in some situations a nominal change may even offset a real change, as will be illustrated below.

Finally, we also expect money illusion to arise in situations where there has been a relative change in prices, even if unaccompanied by a change in the price of money. Consider someone trying to sell his house (say, with the intention of buying another) during noninflationary times when housing prices have gone down by 5 percent relative to other prices. This person, even if aware of the true value of houses, may anchor on the (historical) price that he paid for the house and may be reluctant to sell the house for less than that nominal anchor. Holding real (replacement) value constant, we propose that in times of changing relative prices people's reactions will be determined by the change between an item's current price and its historical, nominal anchor. Loss aversion occurs relative to a reference point, and the reference point can often be nominal, yielding further manifestation of money illusion.

We thus interpret money illusion as a bias in the assessment of the real value of economic transactions, induced by a nominal evaluation. Reliance on a nominal evaluation is not strategic or motivational in nature. Rather, it is due to the ease, universality, and salience of the nominal representation. The strength and persistence of this bias is likely to depend on several factors, notably the relative salience of the nominal and real representations, and the sophistication and experience of the decision maker. Biases induced by multiple representations can be observed also in perception, as is illustrated by the visual illusion in Figure 19.1.

The blocks in Figure 19.1 can be interpreted either as two-dimensional figures or as three-dimensional objects. The illusion that the farthest block is larger than the closer ones – although the three are actually identical – arises because the observer spontaneously adopts the more natural three-dimensional interpretation, in which the farthest block is indeed largest. Consequently, the perception of (two-dimensional) picture size is biased by the simultaneous assessment

[10] With positive interest rates, there is a similar possibility of multiple representations of dollar values at different times without necessarily having inflation.

Figure 19.1. The block illusion.

of (three-dimensional) object size. It is noteworthy that people's perceptions are inconsistent with either the three- or the two-dimensional interpretation of the figure. Rather, they correspond to a mixture of the two (see Tversky and Kahneman [1983, pp. 312–13 for discussion). Similarly, in the case of money illusion, people's judgments do not correspond to either the real or the nominal evaluation but, rather, to a mixture of the two. Thus, a person who receives a 2 percent raise in times of 4 percent inflation does not react as he would to a 2 percent raise, or to a 2 percent cut, in times of no inflation. Rather, this person's reaction to the real loss is tempered by the nominal gain. Just as the natural three-dimensional interpretation of Figure 19.1 interferes with the two-dimensional interpretation, so the familiar nominal evaluation interferes with the real evaluation in the salary example.

We next present a series of studies that investigate the effects of nominal and real changes on people's stated choices and evaluation of economic conditions. The studies are divided into six subsections. Subsection A addresses people's attitudes toward salary raises in times of inflation; subsection B investigates people's evaluation of monetary transactions; subsection C demonstrates the effect of framing transactions in nominal or in real terms on a choice between indexed and unindexed contracts; subsection D describes money illusion in an experimental study of investment; subsection E explores intuitive accounting practices; subsection F considers judgments regarding fairness and morale.

II. EXPERIMENTAL STUDIES

The data presented in this paper come from survey questions presented to people in Newark International Airport, and in two New Jersey shopping malls (Menlo Park Mall in Edison, and Woodbridge Center Mall in Woodbridge). In addition, we have also surveyed undergraduate students at Princeton University. (Unless otherwise specified, all problems presented to undergraduates were posed, embedded among other, unrelated problems, in a questionnaire format. People in the malls and airport received the problems on single sheets of paper.) In most cases, responses from these diverse groups did not differ significantly, and the data are reported in a combined format. Whenever significant differences were observed, we report the data separately. The use of surveys has obvious limitations. First, one may question whether people's intuitions in the context of hypothetical questions extend to actual behavior in real-world settings. Second, one may wonder about the extent to which people interpret the situation as conceived by the experimenter, and do not bring to bear other, unspecified assumptions, such as hypothesized prior savings, unmentioned debts, or presumed interest rates. We are keenly aware of these limitations, but believe that carefully constructed survey questions can provide useful information about the problem under study. In fact, behavioral phenomena first observed in hypothetical contexts have often been replicated in realistic settings involving high stakes and serious deliberation (see, e.g., Benartzi and Thaler [1995]; Johnson, Hershey, Meszaros and Kunreuther [1993]; Kachelmeier and Shehata [1992]; and Lichtenstein and Slovic [1973]). The initial explorations of money illusion reported below will hopefully stimulate further research into the psychological causes and the economic consequences of this phenomenon.

A. Earnings

It has long been argued that people's degree of satisfaction with their income depends not only on its buying power but, among other things, on how it compares with an earlier salary or with the salaries of coworkers (see, e.g., Duesenberry [1949]). We asked subjects, for example, to consider two individuals, Carol and Donna, who graduated from the same college, and upon graduation took similar jobs with publishing firms. Carol was said to have started with a yearly salary of $36,000 in a firm where the average starting salary was $40,000. Donna started with a yearly salary of $34,000 in a firm where the average starting salary was $30,000. Note that Carol has a higher absolute salary whereas Donna has a higher income relative to her coworkers. When we asked subjects who they thought was happier with her job situation, 80 percent of respondents (N = 180) chose Donna, the woman with the lower absolute salary, but with the better relative position. Furthermore, when we asked a second group of respondents (N = 175) who they thought was more likely to leave her position for a job with another firm, 66 percent chose Carol, the one with the higher absolute salary but the lower relative position. A similar discrepancy between an absolute and a comparative job evaluation was reported by Tversky and Griffin [1991], who presented subjects with two hypothetical job offers, one with a higher yearly salary in a company where others with similar training earn more, and the other offering a lower salary in a company where others with similar training earn less. Whereas a majority of subjects chose the job with the higher absolute salary and lower relative position, the majority anticipated higher satisfaction in the job with the higher relative position and lower salary. Even in cases where it is clear that Option A is better than Option B, people sometimes expect to be happier with Option B than with Option A, when it is favored by comparative considerations.

Similar effects in the perception of well-being can be produced from a very different source, namely, the interaction between nominal and real representations. Money illusion is observed when, evaluating a higher income, an individual is content with more money income although a simultaneous rise in prices keeps real income unchanged. What matters when economic conditions change, of course, is a person's buying power (say, the *ratio* between income and costs) rather than how much money the person actually has (the *difference* between income and costs). If everything doubles – you make twice as much, everything costs twice as much, etc. – you will also save twice as much, but it will have the same buying power as before: the set of commodity bundles available for purchase is unchanged. On the other hand, if people's evaluation of their income is based not only on its actual buying power, but also on the sheer number of dollars, then their preferences may correlate with nominal changes even when there is no real change.

The following survey presented three different groups of subjects with a scenario involving two individuals who receive raises in salary. One group was asked to rate the two protagonists' salary raises on purely "economic terms"; a second group was asked to indicate which of the two they thought would be happier; the third group was asked to indicate which of the two was more likely to leave her present job for another position. (The number of respondents is denoted by N. To the right of each option is the percentage of subjects who chose it.)

Problem 1: Consider two individuals, Ann and Barbara, who graduated from the same college a year apart. Upon graduation, both took similar jobs with publishing firms. Ann started with a yearly salary of $30,000. During her first year on the job there was no inflation, and in her second year Ann received a 2% ($600) raise in salary. Barbara also started with a yearly salary of $30,000. During her first year on the job there was a 4% inflation, and in her second year Barbara received a 5% ($1500) raise in salary.

Economic terms (N = 150):
As they entered their second year on the job, who was doing better in economic terms?

　　Ann:　71%　　Barbara:　29%

Happiness (N = 69):
As they entered their second year on the job, who do you think was happier?

　　Ann:　36%　　Barbara:　64%

Job attractiveness (N = 139):
As they entered their second year on the job, each received a job offer from another firm. Who do you think was more likely to leave her present position for another job?

　　Ann:　65%　　Barbara:　35%

When economic terms are emphasized, the majority of respondents correctly evaluate the scenario above in real rather than in nominal terms. (The minority who do not may have interpreted "economic terms" sufficiently broadly to incorporate, e.g., issues of happiness as discussed in what follows. Alternatively, they really may not understand the logic of inflation.) When the emphasis is not purely economic, however, the attribution of well-being is driven primarily by a nominal rather than a real evaluation. The majority of respondents attribute happiness to people based on greater nominal raises, despite lower real raises. Thus, the attribution of happiness incorporates money illusion, even when an analysis in terms of real value is easily accessible. Finally, the majority of respondents thought that a nominal evaluation not only would underlie feelings of well-being, but would also have consequences for action. Thus, the majority predicted that Ann, who is doing better in economic terms but is perceived to be less happy, would be more likely than Barbara to leave her present position. (Note the indistinguishable pattern of responses for the "Happiness" and "Job attractiveness" questions, despite what may initially look like a reversal due to the semantics of the questions.) As the overall pattern of responses makes clear, it is not the case that people simply cannot distinguish between nominal and real representations (any more than they could not distinguish between absolute and comparative considerations in the context of the previous examples.) Rather, it appears that while an evaluation in real terms dominates when the need to think in purely economic terms is made salient, less transparent judgments trigger evaluations that are heavily biased by a nominal representation.

B. Transactions

We turn now from people's assessment of income to their evaluation of specific transactions. As noted earlier, economic transactions can be represented either in nominal or in real terms, which can lead to different evaluations. Clearly, in times of inflation we can make a nominal profit and incur a real loss; in times of deflation we can suffer a nominal loss and enjoy a real gain. (In addition, there is the complexity of inventory-holding costs, including opportunity costs). To the extent that people consider the nominal in addition to the real representation, their perception will be influenced by the number of dollars they earned or lost, not only by their real worth. Consider the following problem.

Problem 2 ($N = 431$): Suppose Adam, Ben, and Carl each received an inheritance of $200,000, and each used it immediately to purchase a house. Suppose that each of them sold the house a year after buying it. Economic conditions, however, were different in each case:

- When Adam owned the house, there was a 25% deflation – the prices of all goods and services decreased by approximately 25%. A year after Adam bought the house, he sold it for $154,000 (23% less than he paid).

- When Ben owned the house, there was no inflation or deflation – prices had not changed significantly during that year. He sold the house for $198,000 (1% less than he paid for it).
- When Carl owned the house, there was a 25% inflation – all prices increased by approximately 25%. A year after he bought the house, Carl sold it for $246,000 (23% more than he paid).

Please rank Adam, Ben, and Carl in terms of the success of their house-transactions. Assign '1' to the person who made the best deal, and 3 to the person who made the worst deal.

Half the subjects saw the problem as it appears above; the other half saw the three cases in reversed order. Because order had no effect on responses, the data were combined and are presented below:

	Adam	Ben	Carl
Nominal transaction:	−23%	−1%	+23%
Real transaction:	+2%	−1%	−2%
Rank:			
1st:	37%	17%	48%
2nd:	10%	73%	16%
3rd:	53%	10%	36%

Clearly, the protagonists' transactions rank differently in nominal and real terms, as shown in the first two rows above. Adam, who sold his house for a 23 percent nominal loss, received for the house approximately 2 percent more than its real purchase value. Ben and Carl, on the other hand, both sold their houses for less than their real purchase value. Ben's 1 percent real loss was also nominal, whereas Carl made a 2 percent real loss but a 23 percent nominal "gain."

It is clear from the data above that subjects' evaluations are influenced by the nominal transactions. The modal ranking, chosen by roughly half the subjects, was Carl first, Ben second, and Adam third. Thus, Carl, the only one to make a nominal gain (but a real loss), was the modal choice for the best deal. Adam, who was the only one to make a real gain (but a nominal loss), was the modal choice for the worst deal. Ben, who suffered a 1 percent real and nominal loss, was ranked above Adam, who had a 2 percent real profit but a large nominal loss, and below Carl, who had a 2 percent real loss but a large nominal gain. We have replicated this pattern in another version of this problem involving 2 percent inflation or deflation.

If people are influenced by nominal changes, then selling a house following times of rising prices should appear more attractive, whereas buying one should be less attractive.[11] To compare people's attitudes to nominal changes in

[11] The psychology of buying has been studied extensively by consumer and marketing researchers (for a review see, e.g., Lea, Tarpy, and Webley [1987]).

sales and acquisitions, we constructed the following simple pair of questions, regarding consumer goods.

Problem 3 ($N = 362$): Changes in the economy often have an effect on people's financial decisions. Imagine that the U.S. experienced unusually high inflation which affected all sectors of the economy. Imagine that within a six-month period all benefits and salaries, as well as the prices of all goods and services, went up by approximately 25%. You now earn and spend 25% more than before.

Six months ago, you were planning to buy a leather armchair whose price during the 6-month period went up from $400 to $500. Would you be more or less likely to buy the armchair now?

More: 7%   Same: 55%   Less: 38%

Six months ago, you were also planning to sell an antique desk you own, whose price during the 6-month period went up from $400 to $500. Would you be more or less likely to sell your desk now?

More: 43%   Same: 42%   Less: 15%

Half the subjects received the above version, in which changes were described in dollar terms (i.e., "up from $400 to $500"); the rest received an identical scenario that differed only in that changes were described in percentages (e.g., "went up by 25%.") Also, the order of the two questions (buy and sell) was counterbalanced across subjects. Both manipulations had no effect on preferences: hence the data were combined. To the right of each response is the percentage of subjects who chose it. The proportions of subjects who were more and less likely to buy and sell differed significantly ($X^2 = 128$, $p < .0001$). The majority of subjects thought they would be more likely to sell for a larger nominal price, and the modal choice also indicated a diminished tendency to buy. Higher nominal prices – although real prices had not changed – were conducive to selling and aversive to buying. It is noteworthy that less than half the subjects chose to answer "Same" in both questions.

The reluctance to buy when nominal prices have increased can explain the buy-now-and-best-inflation psychology that often characterizes times of high inflation. In a Gallup Poll in August 1979, for example, 27 percent of respondents answered yes when asked, "Have you or your family bought anything during the last few months because you thought it would cost more later?" (see Maital [1982]. In fact, advertisers seem to believe that playing on consumers' aversion to increases in nominal prices can be an effective ploy for boosting sales. Consider the following typical advertisement (in Maital and Benjamini [1980]): "...all prices will probably go up including car prices. So if you're thinking about a new car, think about buying a___now. There will probably never be a better time." This argument, of course, ignores the role of interest and the question of whether the nominal interest rate is higher in inflationary times. It is based on the assumption that, in times of inflation, framing purchase decisions in terms of rising nominal prices is likely to boost sales.

C. Contracts

Imagine signing a contract for a future transaction in an inflationary context and having to decide whether to agree upon a specified amount to be paid upon delivery or, instead, agree to pay whatever the price is at the future time. A risk-averse decision maker is likely to prefer an indexed contract since, at a future time, a predetermined nominal amount may be worth more or less than its anticipated real worth. On the other hand, a nominally risk-averse decision maker may perceive indexed contracting as riskier since the indexed amount may end up being greater or smaller in nominal terms than a fixed dollar amount. We next show that alternative framings of a contracting decision lead people to think of a problem in either real or nominal terms, thereby influencing their choices between contracts.[12] The following problem was presented to 139 subjects in the spring of 1991.

> **Problem 4:** Imagine that you are the head of a corporate division located in Singapore that produces office computer systems. You are now about to sign a contract with a local firm for the sale of new systems, to be delivered in January, 1993.
>
> These computer systems are currently priced at $1000 apiece but, due to inflation, all prices, including production costs and computer prices, are expected to increase during the next couple of years. Experts' best estimate is that prices in Singapore two years from now will be about 20% higher, with an equal likelihood that the increase will be higher or lower than 20%. The experts agree that a 10% increase in all prices is just as likely as a 30% increase.
>
> You have to sign the contract for the computer systems now. Full payment will be made only upon delivery in January, 1993. Two contracts are available to you. Indicate your preference between the contracts by checking the appropriate contract below:

One group of subjects (N = 47) chose between contracts A and B below. (The percentage of subjects who chose each contract is indicated in brackets.)

Contracts framed in real terms:
Contract A: You agree to sell the computer systems (in 1993) at $1200 a piece, no matter what the price of computer systems is at that time. Thus, if inflation is below 20% you will be getting more than the 1993-price; whereas, if inflation exceeds 20% you will be getting less than the 1993-price. Because you have agreed on a fixed price, your profit level will depend on the rate of inflation. [19%]
Contract B: You agree to sell the computer systems at 1993's price. Thus, if inflation exceeds 20%, you will be paid more than $1200, and if inflation is

---

[12] For other illustrations and a discussion of framing effects, see Tversky and Kahneman [1986].

below 20%, you will be paid less than $1200. Because both production costs and prices are tied to the rate of inflation, your "real" profit will remain essentially the same regardless of the rate of inflation. [81%]

Contracts A and B are framed in terms of real values. Contract A (agreeing to sell for a fixed nominal amount) is risky: you will get more than the 1993-price if inflation is lower than expected, and you will get less if it is higher. Contract B (agreeing to sell for the indexed price) is riskless: your profit is guaranteed and will not depend on the rate of inflation. As expected, the majority of subjects opt for the riskless option. Another group of subjects (N = 49) chose between contracts C and D:

Contracts framed in nominal terms:
Contract C: You agree to sell the computer systems (in 1993) at $1200 apiece, no matter what the price of computer systems is at that time. [41%]
Contract D: You agree to sell the computer systems at 1993's price. Thus, instead of selling at $1200 for sure, you will be paid more if inflation exceeds 20%, and less if inflation is below 20%. [59%]

Contracts C and D are equivalent to contracts A and B, respectively, except that they are framed in terms of nominal rather than real values. Contract C, in contrast to A, is framed as (nominally) riskless; Contract D, in contrast to B, now appears risky: depending on inflation you may be paid more or less than the fixed nominal price. Thus, the first decision was between a guaranteed real price (contract B) and a nominal price that could be larger or smaller than the real (contract A), whereas the second decision is between a guaranteed nominal price (contract C) and a real price that could be larger or smaller than the nominal (contract D). As expected, subjects are influenced by the frame presented in each problem, and tend to exhibit the risk-averse attitudes triggered by that frame: a larger proportion of subjects now prefer contract C, the seemingly riskless nominal contract, than previously preferred the equivalent contract A ($X^2 = 5.34$, $p = .02$). The disposition to evaluate options in the frame in which they are presented could have significant consequences for bargaining and negotiation. Ratification of union contracts, for example, may partly depend on whether contracts are proposed in nominal or in real terms.

A third group of subjects (N = 43) read Problem 4 and was presented with the following, neutral version of the problem:

Contracts under a neutral frame:
Contract E: You agree to sell the computer systems (in 1993) at $1200 a piece, no matter what the price of computer systems is at that time. [46%]
Contract F: You agree to sell the computer systems at 1993's prices. [54%]

Contracts E and F are economically equivalent to the previous two pairs of contracts, but they are framed in neutral terms. Contract E is to be signed in nominal prices (and is thus riskless in nominal terms), Contract F is to be signed in terms of 1993 prices (and is, therefore, riskless in real terms). A substantial proportion of subjects now opt for the nominally riskless option. Thus, the present pattern of preferences is similar to that observed between contracts C and D, which were framed in nominal terms, and it is significantly different from that observed between contracts A and B, which were framed in real terms ($X^2 = 7.7$, $p < .01$). It appears that people naturally tend to evaluate the contracts in predominantly nominal terms and avoid nominal rather than real risk. This observation is reminiscent of the tendency noted earlier to favor unindexed contracts.

We have run a second version of the above study, this time exploring people's contracting preferences as buyers rather than sellers. The following problem, along with the alternative framings of contract choices, are identical to those of Problem 4 except that the subject is now buying instead of selling.

Problem 5: Imagine that you are the head of a financial services firm located in Singapore, and that you are now about to sign a contract with a local corporation for the purchase of new computer systems, to be delivered to your firm in January, 1993.

These computer systems are currently valued at $1000 apiece but, due to inflation, all prices, including those of computers and financial services, are expected to increase during the next couple of years. Experts' best estimate is that prices in Singapore two years from now will be about 20% higher, with an equal likelihood that the increase will be higher or lower than 20%. The experts agree that a 10% increase in all prices is just as likely as a 30% increase. You have to sign the contract for the computer systems now. Full payment will be made only upon delivery in January, 1993. Two contracts are available to you. Indicate your preference between the contracts by checking the appropriate blank on the scale below:

Contracts framed in real terms: (N = 50)

Contract A': You agree to buy the computer systems (in 1993) at $1200 apiece, no matter what the price of computer systems is at that time. Thus, if inflation exceeds 20%, you will be paying for the computers less than the 1993-price; whereas if inflation is below 20%, you will be paying more than the 1993-price. Because you have agreed on a fixed price, your profit level will depend on the rate of inflation. [36%]

Contract B': You agree to buy the computer systems at 1993's price. Thus, if inflation exceeds 20%, you will pay more than $1200, and if inflation is below 20%, you will pay less than $1200. Because the prices of both computer systems and financial services are tied to the rate of inflation, your "real" profit will remain essentially the same regardless of the rate of inflation. [64%]

Contracts framed in nominal terms: (N = 47)

Contract C': You agree to buy the computer systems (in 1993) at $1200 apiece, no matter what the price of computer systems is at that time. [51%]

Contract D': You agree to buy the computer systems at 1993's price. Thus, instead of buying at $1200 for sure, you will pay more if inflation exceeds 20%, and less if inflation is below 20%. [49%]

Contracts under a neutral frame: (N = 44)
Contract E': You agree to buy the computer systems (in 1993) at $1200 apiece, no
matter what the price of computer systems is at that time. [52%]
Contract F': You agree to buy the computer systems at 1993's price. [48%]

As in the previous problem, subjects exhibit frame-dependent risk aversion: a larger proportion opt for the contract that is nominally riskless when the contracts are framed in nominal terms than when they are framed in real terms. Clearly, by opting for the "sure" nominal value, subjects are in effect taking a real risk. As before, the neutral version yields results remarkably similar to those obtained under the nominal as opposed to the real frame. Finally, in all three versions there is a somewhat smaller tendency to opt for the indexed contracts when buying than when selling, although the differences are not statistically significant. This tendency may be due to the belief – contrary to our explicit instructions – that inflation is more likely to exceed rather than fall below the 20 percent forecast. To the extent that inflation is higher than expected, one is better off signing for a fixed nominal price when buying but not when selling.

D. Investments (Market Experiments)

Experimental evidence for money illusion comes from a study of financial investment by Thaler and Tversky [1996]. The participants in the experiment were asked to imagine that they were a portfolio manager for a small college, and were told that they would be required to allocate a portfolio of 100 shares between two funds. Fund A was drawn from a normal distribution with a mean real return per month of 0.25 percent and a standard deviation of 0.18 percent. Fund B was drawn from a normal distribution with a mean real return of 1 percent and a standard deviation of 3.5 percent. These values correspond approximately to the actual return of bond and stock investment over six weeks. These distributions were not described to the subject; they were learned from experience.

Each subject made 200 decisions, and received immediate feedback. At the conclusion of these trials each subject made a final allocation that would be binding for 400 trials. Subjects' payoffs were proportional to the results of their decisions. Subjects' earnings ranged from $5 to $30.

One group of subjects evaluated the investments in a noninflationary context; whereas the second group evaluated the investment under conditions of a 10 percent yearly inflation. In accord with money illusion, inflation had a profound impact on subjects' allocations. The mean allocation to the risky fund was 42.3 percent in the no-inflation condition and 71.5 percent in the inflation condition. Because of the overwhelmingly positive nominal returns in the inflation condition, people exhibited much less risk aversion in that condition, and consequently earned considerably more money. Loss aversion occurs relative to some reference point, which in the present context is perceived in nominal terms. Evidently, a real loss of 5 percent in the presence of 10 percent inflation, which appears as a 5 percent nominal gain, is much less aversive than a 5 percent loss in a period of no inflation, in which the nominal and the real values coincide.

E. Mental Accounting

With changing relative prices, an effect of past nominal values on purchase or sale decisions is a form of money illusion that could be present even if the inflation rate is zero. Examples would be reluctance to sell a house at a nominal loss, or reluctance to accept a nominal wage cut. In these as well as in standard inventory valuation decisions, money illusion may arise from the use of historic cost, which can differ from replacement cost because of a change in the value of money or because of a change in relative prices.

With nominal and real prices changing, people's assessment of the value of their possessions presents them with some conflicting intuitions, as illustrated by the following problem presented to experienced wine collectors and subscribers to a wine newsletter [Shafir and Thaler 1996]:

> **Problem 6 (N = 76):** Suppose you bought a case of a good 1982 Bordeaux in the futures market for $20 a bottle. The wine now sells at auction for about $75 a bottle. You have decided to drink a bottle of this wine with dinner. Which of the following best captures your feeling of the cost to you of drinking this bottle?

Twenty percent of respondents evaluated the cost of drinking the bottle at $75, its replacement value; 30 percent opted for the option, "drinking the bottle does not feel like it costs me anything. I paid for the bottle already, many years ago, and probably don't remember exactly what I paid for it anyway;" and 25 percent reported that "drinking the bottle feels like I saved $55, because I am able to drink a $75 bottle for which I only paid $20." Other versions, involving breaking the bottle, or giving it as a gift, yielded similar results.[13]

Evidently, people have conflicting intuitions about current value, and do not fully appreciate considerations of replacement cost. As they earn, borrow, spend, save, and invest money, people's intuitive accounting is often based on multiple representations rather than on a single representation of the transaction. Some representations, moreover, even in inflationary times, are grounded in nominal calculations and can lead to erroneous results. To further explore contexts in which profits are estimated on the basis of nominal rather than real changes, we invoked comparisons between sellers who acquired their inventories at different times and sold at the same time.

> **Problem 6 (N = 130):** Two competing bookstores have in stock an identical leather-bound edition of Oscar Wilde's collected writings. Store A bought its copies for $20 each. Tom, who works for Store A, has just sold 100 copies of the

---

[13] A variant of this problem conducted at Princeton University (N = 85) yielded identical results among students with no formal education in economics and students who had at least a one-semester course in economics.

book to a local high school for $44 a copy. Store B bought its copies a year after Store A. Because of a 10% yearly inflation, Store B paid $22 per copy. Joe, who works for Store B, has just sold 100 copies of the book to another school for $45 a copy.

Who do you think made a better deal selling the books, Tom or Joe?[14]

Eighty-seven percent of subjects chose Tom. Apparently, selling at a lower price ($44 versus $45) was perceived as constituting a better deal as long as inventory was acquired at an even lower price ($20 versus $22). Subjects felt justified in ignoring inflation and computed the relevant transaction based solely on nominal differences. This was further confirmed by variations on the problem, in which we asked subjects not only to indicate who they thought made a better deal, but also to estimate by how much. Profit estimates, in these cases, mostly amounted to plain nominal differences.

It is worth pointing out that the mental accounting difficulties exhibited by our subjects arise in a variety of traditional accounting methods. Methods like FIFO (first in, first out) and LIFO (last in, first out) rely on historic prices, not replacement cost. It is also true that U.S. tax laws do not adjust properly for inflation. Churchill [1982] discusses the fact that many businesses continue selling the old stock at old prices, despite the fact that replacement costs have gone up with inflation. This could be fatal for small business that, after having sold the old stock at old prices, cannot afford to pay the replacement costs. Of course, even when businesses are aware of the accounting dangers, there is always the consumers' perception to contend with. To the extent that consumers suffer from money illusion, they may object to higher prices on items sold from old stocks.[15]

F. Fairness and Morale

Community standards of fairness appear to have a significant influence on economic behavior. Kahneman, Knetsch, and Thaler [1986] have presented a number of findings regarding people's perception of fairness, some of which bear directly on money illusion. Respondents in a telephone interview were asked to evaluate the fairness of a grocery store owner who has several months supply of peanut butter in stock, on the shelves and in the storeroom. The owner hears that the wholesale price of peanut butter has increased and immediately raises the price on the current stock of peanut butter. This vignette captures essentially the same accounting requirements as those described in the context of Problem 6, and addressed in Churchill [1982]. Unlike many of our subjects, the store owner in the present vignette sees the importance of selling his goods at their current value rather than their original price (plus markup).

---

[14] Some were asked who they thought "was more successful in selling the books, Tom or Joe?" Responses to the two versions of the question were statistically indistinguishable.

[15] Witness the American public's indignation during the United States–Iraq war at the substantial rise in the price of oil that was reported to be supplied from stocks acquired before the war.

Seventy-nine percent of Kahneman, Knetsch, and Thaler's subjects, however, found this "unfair." To the extent that subjects are estimating profits based on nominal rather than real changes, the store owner's action would bring her an unwarranted higher (nominal) profit. She benefits from having inventories when the price rises, compared with if she had not had them. The fact that her real profit (from selling and replacing, not holding) remains unchanged does not justify her action in the eyes of the majority of subjects.

Another vignette explored by Kahneman, Knetsch, and Thaler [1986] addresses the role of money illusion in judgments of fairness. In this vignette a company that is making a small profit is said to be located in a community experiencing a recession with substantial unemployment. Half the respondents were told that there is no inflation and the company decides to decrease wages and salaries by 7 percent. Other respondents were told that there is a 12 percent inflation and that the company decides to increase salaries by only 5 percent. Although the real income change is practically the same in the two versions, the percentage of respondents who judged the action of the company "unfair" was 62 percent in the case of the nominal cut but only 22 percent in the case of the nominal raise. Evidently, judgments of fairness are based largely on nominal rather than on real changes.[16] Many people, for example, who would strongly object to a 1 percent cut in salary in times of no inflation, are less likely to complain when they get a 5 percent raise in times of 6 percent inflation. Based on extensive interviews, Bewley [1994] reports that businessmen are sensitive to the implications of nominal wage cuts for worker morale.

The perception of fairness is expected to impinge on worker morale and, consequently, may have implications for actual job decisions. To explore this issue, we presented Princeton students with the hypothetical scenario below, followed by one of two questions: half the subjects received the "morale" question, the other half the "job decision" question:

Problem 7 ($N = 72$): Ablex and Booklink are two publishing firms, each employing a dozen editors. Because the firms are small, unequal raises in salary can create morale problems. In a recent year of no inflation, Ablex gave half its editors a 6% raise in salary and the other half a 1% raise. The following year there was a 9% inflation, and Booklink gave half its editors a 15% raise in salary and the other half a 10% raise.

Morale: In which firm do you think there were likely to be more morale problems?

Ablex:	49%
Booklink:	8%
Same in both:	43%

---

[16] Furthermore, similar phenomena are likely to arise in the context of other ethical judgments. Exploring people's perception of distributive justice, for example, Yaari and Bar-Hillel [1984] present numerous studies in which nominally equal distributions are rated as most just, despite the fact that they involve dubious interpersonal comparisons.

Job decision: Suppose that an editor who received the lower raise in each firm was then offered a job with a competing company. Which editor do you think was more likely to leave their present position for another job?

The editor who received the lower raise in Ablex   57%
The editor who received the lower raise in Booklink   5%
The two were equally likely   38%

Problem 7 describes two situations where salary raises were the same in real terms, but proportionally different in nominal terms. The discrepancy between raises of 10 percent and 15 percent (i.e., a 50 percent difference), appears less offensive than the discrepancy between raises of 1 percent and 6 percent (a fivefold difference). As a result, our respondents expected greater morale problems in the latter situation than in the former. Furthermore, most participants thought that the workers who received a 1 percent rather then a 6 percent raise will be more likely to leave their present job than those who got 10 percent instead of 15 percent. We obtained similar data in another version of the problem ($N = 71$) in which the second company, Booklink, gave its (10 percent and 15 percent) raises in a context of 11 percent inflation. Note that here half the workers are getting a real pay cut. Nonetheless, 52 percent of our subjects still expected greater morale problems for Ablex (where raises were 1 percent and 6 percent in no inflation), and 43 percent thought the Ablex workers were more likely to leave their present position.

It appears that money illusion enters into our subjects' perceptions of fairness and worker morale, and then naturally extends to their views regarding workers' propensity to quit their present position. This observation, of course, is not new:

Now ordinary experience tells us, beyond doubt, that a situation where labor stipulates (within limits) for a money-wage rather than a real wage, so far from being a mere possibility, is the normal case ... It is sometimes said that it would be illogical for labour to resist a reduction of money-wages but not to resist a reduction of real wages ... But, whether logical or illogical, experience shows that this is how labour in fact behaves [Keynes 1936, p. 9].

III. DISCUSSION

In this paper we have investigated the effects of variations in nominal values on people's evaluations of monetary transactions and on their economic decisions. The responses of the participants in our surveys departed systematically from standard economic prescription in a manner suggestive of money illusion. We proposed that economic agents often entertain both nominal and real representations of economic transactions, and we interpreted money illusion as a bias in the assessment of the real value of transactions, induced by their nominal representation. We also illustrated the role of money illusion in other decision phenomena, such as framing, anchoring, mental accounting, and loss aversion.

The present research does not tell us to what extent the attitudes documented in our surveys will be observed in the real economy, in people's decisions to quit jobs, sign contracts, etc. However, the consistency of trends observed across diverse subject populations (students, shoppers, airline passengers), and a variety of problem contexts (contracts, acquisitions, fairness perception, judgments about others, trading experiments, etc.), provide strong presumptive evidence. Furthermore, the data are consistent with various observations of anomalous behavior in contracting and legislation.

People attend to nominal value because it is salient, easy to gauge, and in many cases provides a reasonable estimate of real worth. Furthermore, it fits with the general notion that most objects around us, particularly units of measurement, do not regularly change. We rarely encounter constant changes of unit, especially when it is not transparent what it changes relative to.[17] Money illusion, we suggest, arises in large part because it is considerably easier and more natural to think in nominal rather than in real terms. This tendency, we suspect, is likely to persist despite economists' attempts to educate the public (e.g., Fisher [1928]).[18]

Both Fisher [1928] and Fischer and Modigliani [1978] assume, in effect, that individuals would be making the correct decisions if only they were not confused by inflation. On this account, one might think that the elimination of inflation should eliminate money illusion and restore rational behavior. However, because money illusion influences reactions to nominal price and wage cuts per se, the effects of money illusion are likely to extend to noninflationary settings. Moreover, the study of individual decision making has revealed systematic departures from rationality that go beyond reactions to inflation and are likely to interact with money illusion. Common examples include the undue influence of sunk costs, and the underweighting of opportunity costs relative to out of pocket costs (see, e.g., Thaler [1992]). Recognizing that decisions do not always conform to the classical account and that people may be prone to money illusion raises the possibility that different rates of inflation have normative implications different from those assumed in standard rational models. Thus, moderate inflation will affect the allocation of labor and housing insofar as people are particularly averse to nominal wage cuts and to nominal losses resulting from home ownership. Conversely, money illusion may result in a larger

---

[17] Another interesting domain in which nominal–real confusions may arise is in thinking about time. When the Gregorian calendar was adopted in England in 1752, omitting eleven days so that the day ensuing to September 2 was September 14, "much discontent was provoked among uneducated people who imagined that they were being defrauded of the omitted days; and there were riots with the cry 'Give us back our 11 days' " (*The Chambers Encyclopedia*). We thank Philip Johnson-Laird for pointing this out to us.

[18] This is in line with the finding of Tolley [1990] that the price decline anomaly in fantasy baseball auctions is reduced roughly in half in experienced players compared with novices. But the fact that people know that there is a price decline anomaly is not sufficient to make it go away.

contribution of inflation to poverty among the elderly as a result of the choice of nominal annuities along with confusion about the difference between real and nominal interest rates. In addition, money illusion may affect multinational trade and tourism. As Fisher [1928, p. 4] observed, "almost everyone is subject to the 'money illusion' in respect to his own country's currency. This seems to him to be stationary while the money of other countries seems to change." As former Israeli foreign minister Abba Eban remarked (in jest) at a time when Israel was experiencing three-digit inflation, "the dollar is an extremely unstable currency: one month it is worth 100 Israeli pounds, the next month it's worth 200...." It appears that the choice of an optimal inflation target should not overlook the effects of money illusion. Indeed, the implications of money illusion may be the most important factor to consider when contrasting between zero and other low rates of inflation.

More generally, cognitive illusions on the part of individual agents can have important economic consequences. As a number of researchers have argued (see, e.g., Akerlof and Yellen, 1985; Haltiwanger and Waldman, 1985; Russell and Thaler, 1985), small departures from optimality on the part of individual agents can have a significant impact on the characteristics of economic equilibria. It may be interesting to explore the institutions that firms use to reduce some of the effects of money illusion on worker morale. A better understanding of people's view of money, and of the impact it has on their economic systems, may lead to an improved descriptive economic theory.

20. Labor Supply of New York City Cab Drivers
One Day at a Time

Colin F. Camerer, Linda Babcock, George Loewenstein,
and Richard H. Thaler

"It was raining hard in Frisco/I needed one more fare to make my night"

Harry Chapin, "Taxi"

I. INTRODUCTION

Theories of labor supply predict how the number of hours people work will change when their hourly wage or income changes. The standard economic prediction is that a temporary increase in wages should cause people to work longer hours. This prediction is based on the assumption that workers substitute labor and leisure intertemporally, working more when wages are high and consuming more leisure when its price – the forgone wage – is low (e.g., Lucas and Rapping 1969). This straightforward prediction has proven difficult to verify. Studies of many types often find little evidence of intertemporal substitution (e.g., Laisney, Pohlmeier, and Staat 1996). However, the studies are ambiguous because when wages change, the changes are usually not clearly temporary (as the theory requires). The studies also test intertemporal substitution jointly along with auxiliary assumptions about persistence of wage shocks, formation of wage expectations, separability of utility in different time periods, and so forth.

An ideal test of labor supply responses to temporary wage increases requires a setting in which wages are relatively constant within a day but uncorrelated across days, and hours vary every day. In such a situation, all dynamic optimization models predict a positive relationship between wages and hours (e.g., MaCurdy, 1981, p. 1074).

Such data are available for at least one group of workers: New York City cab drivers. Drivers face wages that fluctuate on a daily basis owing to demand shocks caused by weather, subway breakdowns, day-of-the-week effects, holidays, conventions, and so forth. Although rates per mile are set by law, on busy days drivers spend less time searching for customers and thus earn a higher hourly wage. These wages tend to be correlated within days and uncorrelated across days (i.e., transitory).

This paper is a revised and shortened version of one with the same title published in *The Quarterly Journal of Economics*, 112:2, 407–41.

Another advantage of studying cab drivers is that, unlike most workers, they choose the number of hours they work each day because drivers lease their cabs from a fleet for a fixed fee (or own them) and can drive as long as they like during a continuous 12-hour shift. Furthermore, most analyses of labor supply measure hours (and sometimes income) by self-reports. For cab drivers, better measures of hours and income are available from "trip sheets" the drivers fill out and from meters installed in cabs, which automatically record the fares.

Because drivers face wages that fluctuate from day to day and can work flexible hours, the intertemporal substitution hypothesis makes a clear prediction: drivers will work longer hours on high-wage days. Behavioral economics suggests an alternative prediction (which is what motivated our research in the first place): Many drivers told us they set a target for the amount of money they wanted to earn that day and quit when they reached the target. (The target might be a certain amount beyond the lease fee or twice the fee.) Daily targeting makes exactly the opposite prediction of the intertemporal substitution hypothesis. When wages are high, drivers will reach their target more quickly and quit early; on low-wage days they will drive longer hours to reach the target. To test the standard intertemporal substitution hypothesis against the daily targeting alternative, we collected three samples of data on the hours and wages of drivers.

We find little evidence for positive intertemporal substitution because most of the wage elasticities – the ratio of percentage change in hours to percentage change in wages – are estimated to be negative. This means that drivers tend to quit earlier on high-wage days and drive longer on low-wage days. Elasticities for inexperienced drivers are around −1 for two of the three samples of cab drivers we used in our study. The results are robust to outliers and many different specifications. There are several possible explanations for these negative elasticities, other than the daily targeting hypothesis, but most can be comfortably ruled out.

II. EMPIRICAL ANALYSES

In this section, we use data on trip sheets of New York City cab drivers to explore the relationship between hours that drivers choose to work each day and the average daily wage. Many details are omitted here but are included in Camerer et al. (1997).

A trip sheet is a sequential list of trips that a driver took on a given day. For each trip, the driver lists the time the fare was picked up and dropped off and the amount of the fare (excluding tip). Fares are set by the Taxi and Limousine Commission (TLC). For the first period we study (1988), the fares were $1.15 per trip plus $.15 for each 1/5 of a mile or 60 seconds of waiting time. For the second period we study (1990 and 1994) fares were $1.50 per trip plus $.25 each 1/5 of a mile or 75 seconds of waiting time. In both periods, a $.50-per-trip surcharge is added between 8 p.m. and 6 a.m.

Our data consist of three samples of trip sheets. We describe each data set briefly. The first data set, TRIP, came from a set of 192 trip sheets from the spring of 1994. We borrowed and copied these from a fleet company. Fleet companies are organizations that own many cabs (each affixed with a medallion that is required to operate it legally). They rent these cabs for 12-hour shifts to drivers who, in our sample period, typically paid $76 for a day shift and $86 for a night shift. The driver also has to fill the cab up with gas at the end of the shift (costing about $15). Drivers get most of their fares by "cruising" and looking for passengers. (Unlike many cities, trips to the airport are relatively rare – around one trip per day on average). Drivers keep all the fares, including tips. The driver is free to keep the cab out as long as he or she wants up to the 12-hour limit. Drivers who return the cab late are fined. When a driver returns the cab, the trip sheet is stamped with the number of trips that have been recorded on the cab's meter. This can then be used to determine how carefully the driver has filled in the trip sheet.

The measure of hours worked is obtained directly from the trip sheet. It is the difference between the time that the first passenger is picked up and the time that the last passenger is dropped off. Total revenue was calculated by adding up the fares listed on the trip sheet. The average hourly wage is total revenue divided by hours worked.

Many of the trip sheets were incomplete because the number of trips listed by the cab driver was much fewer than the number of trips recorded by the meter. Therefore, we exclude trip sheets that listed a number of trips that deviate by more than two from the metered number. This screen leaves us with 70 trip sheets from 13 drivers (8 of whom drive on more than one day in the sample).

The advantage of the TRIP data set is that we can use the trip sheets to measure the within-day autocorrelation in hourly earnings as well as differences in earning across days. Even though taxi fares are fixed by the TLC, earnings differ from day to day because of differences in how "busy" drivers are; that is, whether they spend most of the day with passengers in their cab or have to spend considerable time searching for passengers.

The second and third data sets of trip sheets were obtained from the TLC. The TLC periodically samples trip sheets to satisfy various demands for information about drivers and earnings (e.g., when rate increases are proposed). In these two data sets, hours and the number of driver-listed trips are obtained from the trip sheets, and the number of recorded trips, fares, and miles driven are obtained from the meter.

The TLC developed a screen to discard incomplete trip sheets. Because the TLC provided us with the summary measures but not the trip sheets themselves, we are unable to create an alternative screening procedure, and thus we use their screened data for our analyses.

The first of the TLC data sets, TLC1, is a summary of 1,723 trip sheets from 1990. This data set includes three types of drivers: daily fleet drivers, lease drivers who lease their cabs by the week or month, and others who own a medallion-bearing cab and drive it. Most owner-drivers rent their cab out to other drivers for some shifts, imposing constraints on when and how long they can drive. Those who do not rent out their cabs can drive whenever they want.

The screened data contain 1,044 trip sheets and 484 drivers (234 of whom drove more than one day in the data). The main advantages of this sample are that it includes several observations for each of many drivers and contains a range of different types of drivers.

The second TLC data set, TLC2, is a summary of 750 trip sheets, mostly from November 1–3, 1988. This data set samples owner-drivers as well as drivers from minifleet companies (minifleets usually lease cabs to drivers weekly or monthly). We discard 38 trip sheets using the TLC screen, leaving us with 712 trip sheets. The main differences between TLC2 and TLC1 are that no drivers appear more than once in the data in TLC2, and the fares in TLC2 are slightly lower.

The analyses reported in the body of the paper use only the screened samples of trip sheets for all three data sets. Including the screened-out data does not make much difference.

To learn about important institutional details we also conducted a phone survey of 14 owners and managers at fleet companies that rent cabs to drivers. The average fleet in New York operates 88 cabs, and thus the responses roughly summarize the behavior of over a thousand drivers. The survey responses help make sense of the results derived from analysis of hours and wages.

Sample Characteristics

Table 20.1 presents means, medians, and standard deviations of the key variables. Cab drivers work about 9.5 hours per day, take between 28 and 30 trips, and collect almost $17 per hour in revenues (excluding tips). In the TRIP data, the average trip duration was 9.5 minutes, and the average fare was $5.13. Average hourly wage is slightly lower in the TLC2 sample because of the lower rates imposed by the TLC during that time period.

In the empirical analyses that follow, we estimate labor supply functions using the daily number of hours as the dependent variable and the average wage the driver earned during that day as the independent variable (both in logarithmic form). The average wage is calculated by dividing daily total revenue by daily hours. This, however, assumes that the decisions drivers make regarding when to stop driving depend on the average wage during the day rather than fluctuations of the wage rate during the day.

Fluctuations within- and across-days are important because testing for substitution requires that wages be different and roughly uncorrelated across days (and they were) and that hourly wages be correlated within a day. We used the trip-by-trip data available in the TRIP sample to construct hour-by-hour measures of wages. One hour's median wage had an autocorrelation of .493 with the previous hour's wage, and thus there is indeed a strong positive

Table 20.1. Summary Statistics

	Mean	Median	Standard Dev
TRIP (n = 70)			
Hours Worked	9.16	9.38	1.39
Average Wage	16.91	16.20	3.21
Total Revenue	152.70	154.00	24.99
No. Trips Counted by Meter	30.70	30.00	5.72
TLC1 (n = 1044)			
Hours Worked	9.62	9.67	2.88
Average Wage	16.64	16.31	4.36
Total Revenue	154.58	154.00	45.83
No. Trips Counted by Meter	27.88	29.00	9.15
TLC2 (n = 712)			
Hours Worked	9.38	9.25	2.96
Average Wage	14.70	14.71	3.20
Total Revenue	133.38	137.23	40.74
No. Trips Counted by Meter	28.62	29.00	9.41

correlation within each day; when a day starts out as a high-wage day, it will probably continue to be a high-wage day. The fleet managers surveyed weakly agreed[1] with these patterns, saying the within-day autocorrelation is positive or zero (none said it was negative). Because wages are different each day, fairly stable within days, but uncorrelated across days, they are ideal for calculating the labor-supply response to temporary changes in wages.

Wage Elasticities

The simple correlations between log hours and log wages are all modestly negative: −.503, −.391, and −. 269. Figure 20.1 shows scatterplots of log hours and log wages in the three samples, which corroborate the negative correlations.

The wage elasticity – the percentage change in hours relative to the percentage change in wage – can be estimated by simply regressing the logarithm of hours against the logarithm of a worker's wage, using ordinary least squares. These regressions yield estimates between −.19 and −.62, which generally are highly significantly different from zero.

However, this standard technique can be misleading because of a potential bias caused by measurement error. Measurement error is a pervasive concern in studies of labor supply, particularly because most data are self-reports of income and hours, which may be subject to memory or recording errors or

---

[1] Fleet managers were asked whether "a driver who made more money than average in the first half of a shift" was likely to have a second half that was better than average (3 agreed), worse than average (0), or about the same as average (6). Expressing the target-income hypothesis, two fleet managers spontaneously said the second-half earnings were irrelevant "because drivers will quit early."

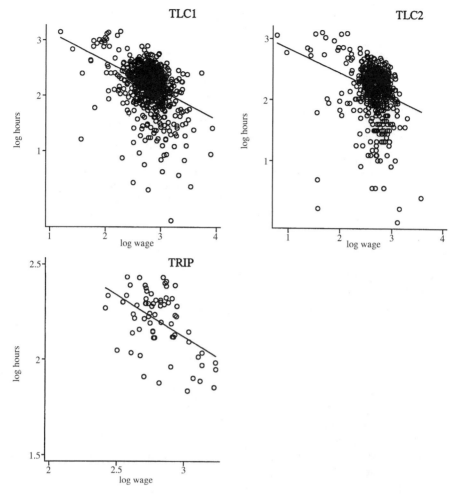

Figure 20.1. Scatter plots of log hours and log wages in the three samples.

self-presentation biases. Though the data on hours come from trip sheets rather than from memory, they may still include recording errors. Unfortunately, even if errors in the measurement of hours are random, they lead to a predictable bias in the wage elasticity: Because the average hourly wage is derived by dividing daily revenue by reported hours, overstated hours will produce hours that are too high *and* wages that are too low. Understated hours will produce hours that are too low and wages that are too high. Measurement error in hours can therefore create spuriously negative elasticities. This bias can be eliminated if we can find a proxy for the drivers' wage that is highly correlated with the wage but uncorrelated with a particular driver's measurement error in hours. (Such a proxy is called an "instrumental variable" (IV) in econometrics.) Fortunately, an excellent proxy for a driver's wage is a measure of the wage of *other* drivers who

Table 20.2. Instrumental Variable (IV) Regression of Log Hours against Log Hourly Wage

Sample	TRIP		TLC1		TLC2
Log Hourly Wage	−.319	.005	−1.313	−.926	−.975
	(.298)	(.273)	(.236)	(.259)	(.478)
Fixed Effects	No	Yes	No	Yes	No
Sample Size	70	65	1044	794	712
Number of Drivers	13	8	484	234	712

Note: Dependent variable is the log of hours worked. Other independent variables (not shown) are high temperature, rain, and dummy variables for during-the-week shift, night shift, and day shift. Standard errors are in parentheses. Instruments for the log hourly wage include the summary statistics of the distribution of hourly (log) wages of other drivers on the same day and shift (the 25th, 50th, and 75th percentiles).

are working on the same day during the same shift.[2] We use these measures of other-driver wages in all the regressions that follow.

Regressions of (log) hours on (log) wages are shown in Table 20.2 for the three data sets. The TRIP and TLC1 data include multiple observations for each driver, and thus either the standard errors are corrected to account for the panel nature of the data or driver fixed effects are included. A driver fixed effect is a dummy variable for each driver that adjusts for the possibility that each driver might systematically drive more or less hours, holding the wage constant, than other drivers. Several other variables controlling for weather conditions and shift dummy variables were also included; their effects were modest and are not shown in Table 20.2.

The IV elasticities in Table 20.2 are negative and significantly different from zero, except in the TRIP sample when fixed effects are included. Indeed, the elasticities in the TLC samples are close to −1, which is the number predicted by daily targeting theory. The results in Table 20.2 are quite robust with respect to various specifications we tried to control for outliers, such as median regression. The difference between the wage elasticities in the two TLC samples and the fixed-effects estimate in the TRIP sample can be explained by a difference in the composition of types of drivers across the three samples.[3]

[2] In fact, we used three summary statistics of the distribution of hourly wages of other drivers who drove on the same day and shift (the 25th, 50th, and 75th percentiles) as instruments for a driver's wage.

[3] TRIP consists entirely of fleet drivers (who pay daily), whereas the TLC samples also include weekly and monthly lease-drivers, and owner-drivers. Lease-drivers and owner-drivers have more flexibility in the number of hours they drive (because fleet drivers are constrained to drive no more than 12 hours). Elasticities for the fleet drivers are substantially smaller in magnitude (less negative) than for lease- and owner-drivers (as we see below). The different results in the TRIP sample, which consists exclusively of fleet drivers, reflects this compositional difference in driver types.

Table 20.3. IV Log Hours Regression by Driver Experience Level

Sample	TRIP		TLC1		TLC2	
Experience Level	Low	High	Low	High	Low	High
Log Hourly Wage	−.841	.613	−.559	−1.243	−1.308	2.220
	(.290)	(.357)	(.406)	(.333)	(.738)	(1.942)
Fixed Effects	Yes	Yes	Yes	Yes	No	No
Sample Size	26	39	319	458	320	375
P-value for Difference in Wage Elasticity	.030		.666		.058	

Note: See note to Table 20.2.

How Do Elasticities Vary with Experience?

Drivers may learn over time that driving more on high-wage days and less on low-wage days provides more income and more leisure. If so, the wage elasticities of experienced drivers should be more positive than for inexperienced drivers. There are good measures of driver experience in these data sets. In the TLC data sets, the TLC separated drivers into experience groups: for TLC1, those with greater or less than 4 years of experience, and in TLC2, those with greater or less than 3 years of experience. These group measures are absent in the TRIP data. However, cab driver licenses are issued with six-digit numbers (called hack numbers), in chronological order, so that lower numbers correspond to drivers who obtained their licenses earlier. On the basis of their license numbers, we use a median split to divide drivers into low- and high-experience subsamples for the TRIP data.

Table 20.3 presents the wage elasticities estimated separately for low- and high-experience drivers. All regressions include fixed effects (except, of course for TLC2). In all three samples, the low-experience elasticity is significantly negative and insignificantly different from −1. The wage elasticity of the high-experience group is significantly larger in magnitude for the TRIP and TLC2 samples ($p = .030$ and .058 respectively), and insignificantly smaller in the TLC1 sample.

How Do Elasticities Vary with Payment Structure?

The way drivers pay for their cabs may affect their responsiveness of hours to wages if, for example, the payment structure affects the horizon over which they plan. Alternatively, the way drivers pay for their cabs may affect the degree to which they can significantly vary hours across days. The TLC1 sample contains data from three types of payment schemes: daily rental (fleet cabs), weekly or monthly rental (lease cabs), or owned. Table 20.4 presents elasticity estimates in the three payment categories from the TLC1 sample. All regressions are estimated using instrumental variables and include driver-fixed effects.

364 Colin F. Camerer, Linda Babcock, George Loewenstein et al.

Table 20.4. IV Log Hours Regressions by Payment Structure (TLC1 Data)

Type of Cab	Fleet	Lease	Owned
Log Hourly Wage	−.197	−.978	−.867
	(.252)	(.365)	(.487)
Fixed Effects	Yes	Yes	Yes
Sample Size	150	339	305

Note: See note to Table 20.2. Fleet cabs are rented daily, leased cabs are rented by the week or month, and owned cabs are owned by the drivers.

All wage elasticities in Table 20.4 are negative. The elasticity that is smallest in magnitude, for fleet drivers, is not significantly different from zero. The lease and owner-driver wage elasticities are approximately −.9 and are significantly different from zero. Part of the explanation for the lower elasticity for fleet drivers is a technical one. Because they are constrained to drive no more than 12 hours, the dependent variable is truncated, biasing the slope coefficient towards zero.

Could Drivers Earn More by Driving Differently?

One can simulate how income would change if drivers changed their driving behavior. Using the TLC1 data, we take the 234 drivers who had two or more days of data in our sample. For a specific driver i, call the hours and hourly wages on a specific day t, h_{it} and W_{it}, respectively, and call driver i's mean hours over all the days in the sample h_i. By construction, the driver's actual total wages earned in our sample is $\Sigma_t h_{it} W_{it}$.

One comparison is to ask how much money that driver would have earned if he had driven h_i hours every day rather than varying the number of hours. Call this answer "fixed-hours earnings" (FHE), $\Sigma_t h_{it} W_{it}$.

Is FHE greater than actual earnings? We know that, on average, h_{it} and W_{it} are negatively correlated, and thus the difference between FHE and actual earnings will be positive in general. In fact, drivers would increase their net earnings by 5.0 percent on average (standard error $= 0.4$ percent) if they drove the same number of hours (h_i) every day rather than varying their hours every day. If we exclude drivers who would earn less by driving fixed hours (because their wage elasticity is positive), the improvement in earnings would average 7.8 percent. And note that if leisure utility is concave, fixed-hours driving will improve overall leisure utility too.

These increases in income arise from following the simplest possible advice: drive a constant number of hours each day. Suppose instead that we hold each driver's average hours fixed but reallocated hours across days as if the wage elasticity were +1. Then the average increase in net income across all drivers is 10 percent. Across drivers who gain, the average increase is 15.6 percent.

III. EXPLAINING NEGATIVE WAGE ELASTICITIES

Wage elasticities estimated with instrumental variables are significantly negative in two out of three samples. Elasticities are also significantly higher for experienced drivers in two of three samples and significantly more negative for lease- and owner-drivers than for fleet drivers. These two empirical regularities, along with other patterns in the data and information gleaned from our telephone survey of fleet managers, allow us to evaluate four alternative explanations for the observed negative elasticities. Ruling out these alternatives is important (see Camerer et al. 1997 for details) because it leaves daily targeting as the most plausible explanation for anomalous negative elasticities.

One hypothesis is that drivers are "liquidity-constrained", that is, they do not have much cash to pay everyday expenses (and cannot borrow), and thus they cannot quit early on low-wage days. But drivers who own their cab medallions are presumably not liquidity-constrained (because medallions are worth $130,000), and their elasticities are negative too. Another possibility is that drivers finish late on low-wage days but take many unrecorded breaks on those days and therefore actually work fewer hours. But we excluded long breaks from the TRIP sample and found no difference in the results. A third possibility is that drivers quit early on high-wage days because carrying a lot of passengers is especially tiring. But the fleet managers we surveyed said the opposite; most of them thought that fruitlessly searching for fares on a low-wage day was more tiring than carrying passengers. A fourth alternative is more subtle. We only have observations of work hours on the days that drivers chose to work at all (or "participate," in labor economics jargon). Omitting non-working days can bias the measured elasticity negatively if the tendency for a driver to work unexpectedly on a certain day is correlated with the tendency to work unusually long hours (Heckman 1979). But drivers usually participate on a fixed schedule of shifts each week (and often must pay their lease fee, or some penalty, if they do not show up for scheduled work), and thus there is little unexpected participation and probably very little bias.

Daily Income Targeting

As explained in the introduction, the prediction we sought to test in our study is based on two assumptions: Cab drivers take a one-day horizon, set a target (or target range), and quit when the target is reached.

Taking a one-day horizon is an example of narrow "bracketing" (Read and Loewenstein 1996), which entails simplifying decisions by isolating them from the stream of decisions they are embedded in. For example, people are risk averse to single plays of small gambles even though they typically face many uncorrelated small risks over time that diversify away the risk of a single play. Bettors at horse tracks seem to record the betting activity for each day in a separate "mental account" (Thaler, this volume). Because the track takes a percentage of each bet, most bettors are behind by the end of the day. Studies show that they tend to shift bets toward longshots in the last race in an attempt to "break even" on that day (McGlothlin 1956). Read and Loewenstein (1995) observed an unusual kind of bracketing among trick-or-treaters on Halloween. Children told to take any two pieces of candy at a single house always chose two different candies. Those who chose one candy at each of two adjacent houses (from the same set of options) typically chose the same candy at each house. Normatively, the children should diversify the portfolio of candy in their bag, but in fact they only diversify the candy from a single house. Isolation of decisions has also been observed in strategic situations: Camerer et al. (1993) found that subjects in a three-stage "shrinking-pie" bargaining experiment often did not bother to look ahead and find out how much the "pie" they bargained over would shrink if their first-stage offers were rejected.

The notion that drivers are averse to falling below a target income is consistent with other evidence that judgments and decisions depend on a comparison of potential outcomes against some aspiration level or reference point (Helson 1964, Kahneman and Tversky 1979, Tversky and Kahneman 1991), and people are disproportionally sensitive to losing, or falling short of a reference point.[4]

Both narrow bracketing and loss aversion are analytically necessary to explain negative wage elasticities. A 1-day horizon is necessary because drivers who take a longer horizon, even 2 days, can intertemporally substitute between the 2 days and will have positive wage elasticities. Therefore, if their elasticities are negative they *must* be taking a 1-day horizon. Aversion to falling short of the target is a necessary ingredient because, if drivers do take a 1-day horizon, elasticities will only be highly negative if the marginal utility of daily income drops sharply around the level of average daily income, which is just a labor-supply way of saying they really dislike falling short of a daily average (compared with how much they like exceeding it).

Furthermore, the daily targeting hypothesis rang true to many of the fleet managers we surveyed. They were asked to choose which one of three sentences "best describes how many hours cab drivers drive each day." Six fleet managers chose "drive until they make a certain amount of money." Five chose the response "fixed hours." Only one chose the intertemporal substitution response "drive a lot when doing well; quit early on a bad day."

Several other studies with field data have used the same ingredients (narrow bracketing and loss aversion) to explain anomalies in stock market behavior and consumer purchases. For example, the "equity premium puzzle" is the tendency for stocks (or "equity") to offer much higher rates of returns than bonds over almost any moderately long time interval, which cannot be reconciled with standard models of rational asset pricing. Benartzi and Thaler (1995) argue that the large premium in equity returns compensates stockholders for the risk of

---

[4] Other applications of loss aversion include Kahneman, Knetsch, and Thaler (1990) on "endowment effects" in consumer choice and contingent valuation of nonmarket goods, Samuelson and Zeckhauser (1988) on "status quo biases," and Bowman et al. (1999) and Shea (1995) on anomalies in savings-consumption patterns.

suffering a loss over a short horizon. They show that if investors evaluate the returns on their portfolios once a year (taking a narrow horizon) and have a piecewise-linear utility function that is twice as steep for losses as for gains, then investors will be roughly indifferent between stocks and bonds, which justifies the large difference in expected returns. If investors took a longer horizon, or cared less about losses, they would demand a smaller equity premium. Two experimental papers have demonstrated the same effect (Thaler et al. 1997, Gneezy and Potters 1997).

Experimental and field studies show that investors who own stocks that have lost value hold them longer than they hold "winning" stocks before selling (Shefrin and Statman 1985; Odean 1996; Weber and Camerer 1998). Purchases of consumer goods like orange juice fall a lot when prices are increased compared with how much purchases rise when prices are cut (Hardie, Johnson, and Fader 1993). These tendencies can only be explained by investors and consumers isolating single decisions about stocks and products from the more general decision about the contents of their stock portfolio or shopping cart and being unusually sensitive to losing money on the isolated stock or paying more for the isolated product.

Various psychological processes could cause drivers to use daily income targeting. For example, targeting is a simple decision rule: It requires drivers to keep track only of the income they have earned. This is computationally easier than tracking the ongoing balance of forgone leisure utility and marginal income utility (that depends on expected future wages), which is required for optimal intertemporal substitution. Targeting may just be a heuristic shortcut that makes deciding when to quit easier.

Daily targets can also help mitigate self-control problems (as many mental accounts do; see Shefrin and Thaler 1992). There are two kinds of self-control problems drivers may face. First, driving a cab is tedious and tiring and, unlike many jobs, work hours are not rigidly set; drivers are free to quit any time they want. A daily income goal, like an author imposing a daily goal of written pages, establishes an output-based guideline of when to quit. A weekly or monthly target would leave open the temptation to quit early today and make up for today's shortfall tomorrow, or next week, and so on, in an endless cycle.

Second, to substitute intertemporally, drivers must save the windfall of cash they earn from driving long hours on a high-wage day so they can afford to quit early on low-wage days. But a drive home through Manhattan with $200–$300 in cash from a good day is an obstacle course of temptations for many drivers, creating a self-control problem that is avoided by daily targeting.

Finally, daily targeting can account for the effect of experience rather naturally: Experienced drivers who have larger elasticities either learn over time to take a longer horizon (and to resist the temptations of quitting early and squandering cash from good days) or to adopt the simple rule of driving a fixed number of hours each day. Alternatively, some drivers may just lack these qualities to begin with, and they quit at higher rates, selecting themselves out of the experienced-driver pool because they have less leisure and income. Either way, experienced drivers will have more positive wage elasticities.

IV. DISCUSSION AND CONCLUSIONS

Dynamic theories of labor supply predict a positive labor supply response to temporary fluctuations in wages. Previous studies have not been able to measure this elasticity precisely, and the measured sign is often negative, contradicting the theory. These analyses, however, have been plagued by a wide variety of estimation problems.

Most estimation problems are avoided by estimating wage elasticities for taxi drivers. Drivers have flexible, self-determined work hours and face wages that are highly correlated within days but only weakly correlated between days, (so fluctuations are transitory). That our analyses yield negative wage elasticities suggests that elasticities of intertemporal substitution around zero (or at least not strongly positive) may represent a real behavioral regularity. Further support for this assertion comes from analyses of the labor supply of farmers (Berg 1961, Orde-Brown 1946) and self-employed proprietors (Wales 1973) who, like cab drivers, set their own hours and often have negative measured wage elasticities. These data suggest that it may be worthwhile to search for negative wage elasticities in other jobs in which workers pay a fixed fee to work, earn variable wages, and set their own work hours – such as fishing, some kinds of sales, and panhandling.

Of course, cab drivers, farmers, and small-business proprietors are not representative of the working population. Besides some demographic differences, all three groups have self-selected into occupations with low variable wages, long hours, and (in the case of farmers and cab drivers) relatively high rates of accidents and fatalities. However, there is no reason to think their planning horizons are uniquely short. Indeed, many cab drivers are recent immigrants who, by immigrating, are effectively making long-term investments in economic and educational opportunity for themselves and their children.

Because evidence of negative labor supply responses to transitory wage changes is so much at odds with conventional economic wisdom, these results should be considered a provocation for further theorizing. It may be that the cab drivers' situation is special. Or it may be that people generally take a short horizon and set income targets but adjust these targets flexibly in ways that can create positive responses to wage increases,[5] and therefore myopic adjustable targeting can explain both positive elasticities observed in some studies and the negative elasticities observed in drivers.

---

[5] For example, suppose the target is adjusted depending on the daily wage (e.g., a driver realizes this will be a good day and raises his target for that day). Then his behavior will be very much like that of a rational driver's intertemporally substituting over time even though the psychological basis for it is different (and does not require any foresight).

We have two ideas for further research. A natural way to model a driver's decision is by using a hazard model that specifies the probability that a driver will quit after driving t hours as a function of different variables observable at t. Daily targeting predicts that quitting will depend on the total wages cumulated at t in a strongly nonlinear way (when the daily total reaches a target the probability of quitting rises sharply). Intertemporal substitution predicts that quitting will depend only on the average wage earned up to time t, and the expected future wage.

Another prediction derived from daily targeting is that drivers who receive an unusually big tip will go home early. Experimenters posing as passengers could actually hand out big tips (say, $50) to some drivers and measure, unobstrusively, whether those drivers quit early compared with a suitable control group. Standard theory predicts that a single large tip produces a tiny wealth effect that should not make any difference to current behavior,[6] and thus a perceptible effect of a big tip would be more evidence in favor of daily targeting and against intertemporal substitution.

Final Comments

As part of a broader project in behavioral economics, work like ours strives to draw discipline and inspiration for economic theorizing from other social sciences, particularly psychology, while respecting the twin aesthetic criteria that characterize postwar economics: models should be formal and make field-testable predictions. The goal is to demonstrate that economic models with better roots in psychology can create interesting challenges for formal modeling and make better predictions.

The ingredients of our project suggest a recipe for doing convincing behavioral economics "in the wild." We derived a simple hypothesis from behavioral economics – daily targeting – that predicts that the *sign* of a regression coefficient would be the opposite of the sign predicted by standard theory, and thus we have a dramatic difference in two theories. We got lucky and found good data. We had an excellent proxy variable (or instrument) for a driver's daily wage, the wage of other drivers working at the same time, which eliminated the bias caused by measuring hours with error. We also obtained variables that enabled us to rule out some alternative explanations (such as liquidity constraint and effects of breaks). And we found an effect of experience consistent with the hypothesis that targeting is a costly heuristic that drivers move away from with experience in the direction of intertemporal substitution. Critics who think our findings of negative elastiticities are an econometric fluke must explain why we did *not* find negative elasticities for experienced drivers.

A crucial assumption is that the tip is seen by the driver as a temporary wage increase rather than an indicator that more large tips may come in the hours ahead (which would cause him or her to drive longer). Controlling for drivers' beliefs and observing their hours are challenges for experimental design.

Finally, a growing number of economists have begun to question the benefits of increasing sophistication in mathematical models. In game theory, theorists and experimenters have shown that simple evolutionary and adaptive models of behavior can often explain behavior better than sophisticated equilibrium concepts (e.g., Camerer and Ho 1999). Experimental economists have noted how "zero-intelligence" programmed agents can approximate the surprising allocative efficiency of human subjects in double auctions (Gode and Sunder 1993) and how demand and choice behavior of animals duplicates patterns seen in empirical studies of humans (Kagel, Battalio, and Green 1995). Our research, too, shows that relatively simple principles and models can often go a long way toward explaining and predicting economic behavior and even outperform more sophisticated models of economic agents.

21. Are Investors Reluctant to Realize Their Losses?

Terrance Odean

ABSTRACT. I test the disposition effect, the tendency of investors to hold losing investments too long and sell winning investments too soon, by analyzing trading records for 10,000 accounts at a large discount brokerage house. These investors demonstrate a strong preference for realizing winners rather than losers. Their behavior does not appear to be motivated by a desire to rebalance portfolios, or to avoid the higher trading costs of low priced stocks. Nor is it justified by subsequent portfolio performance. For taxable investments, it is suboptimal and leads to lower after-tax returns. Tax-motivated selling is most evident in December.

The tendency to hold losers too long and sell winners too soon has been labeled the disposition effect by Shefrin and Statman (1985). For taxable investments the disposition effect predicts that people will behave quite differently than they would if they paid attention to tax consequences. To test the disposition effect, I obtained the trading records from 1987 through 1993 for 10,000 accounts at a large discount brokerage house. An analysis of these records shows that, overall, investors realize their gains more readily than their losses. The analysis also indicates that many investors engage in taxmotivated selling, especially in December. Alternative explanations have been proposed for why investors

University of California, Davis. This paper is based on my dissertation at the University of California, Berkeley. I would like to thank an anonymous referee, Brad Barber, Peter Klein, Hayne Leland, Richard Lyons, David Modest, John Nofsinger, James Poterba, Mark Rubinstein, Paul Ruud, Richard Sansing, Richard Thaler, Brett Trueman, and participants at the Berkeley Program in Finance, the NBER behavioral finance meeting, the Financial Management Association Conference, the American Finance Association meetings, and seminar participants at UC Berkeley, the Yale School of Management, the University of California, Davis, the University of Southern California, the University of North Carolina, Duke University, the Wharton School, Stanford University, the University of Oregon, Harvard University, the Massachusetts Institute of Technology, the Amos Tuck School, The University of Chicago, the University of British Columbia, Northwestern University, the University of Texas, UCLA, the University of Michigan, and Columbia University for helpful comments. I would also like to thank Jeremy Evnine and especially the discount brokerage house that provided the data necessary for this study. Financial support from the Nasdaq Foundation is gratefully acknowledged.

might realize their profitable investments while retaining their losing invest-ments. Investors may rationally, or irrationally, believe that their current losers will in the future outperform their current winners. They may sell winners to rebalance their portfolios. Or they may refrain from selling losers due to the higher transactions costs of trading at lower prices. I find, however, that when the data are controlled for rebalancing and for share price, the disposition ef-fect is still observed. And the winning investments that investors choose to sell continue in subsequent months to outperform the losers they keep.

The next section of the paper discusses the disposition effect and literature related to it. Section II describes the data set, and Section III describes the em-pirical study and its findings. Section IV discusses these findings and Section V concludes.

I. THE DISPOSITION EFFECT

A. Prospect Theory

The disposition effect is one implication of extending Kahneman and Tversky's (1979) prospect theory to investments. Under prospect theory, when faced with choices involving simple two and three outcome lotteries, people behave as if maximizing an "S"-shaped value function (see Figure 21.1). This value function is similar to a standard utility function except that it is defined on gains and losses rather than on levels of wealth. The function is concave in the domain of gains and convex in the domain of losses. It is also steeper for losses than for gains, which implies that people are generally risk-averse. Critical to this value function is the reference point from which gains and losses are mea-sured. Usually the status quo is taken as the reference point; however, "there are situations in which gains and losses are coded relative to an expectation or aspiration level that differs from the sta-tus quo.... A person who has not made peace with his losses is likely to accept gambles that would be unacceptable to him otherwise" (Kahneman and Tversky (1979)).

For example, suppose an investor pur-chases a stock that she believes to have an expected return high enough to jus-tify its risk. If the stock appreciates and the investor continues to use the purchase price as a reference point, the stock price will then be in a more concave, more risk-averse, part of the investor's value func-tion. It may be that the stock's expected return continues to justify its risk. How-ever, if the investor somewhat lowers her expectation of the stock's return, she will

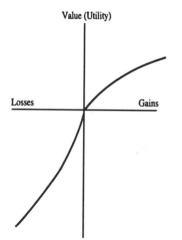

Figure 21.1. Prospect theory value function.

Value (Utility)

Losses

Gains

be likely to sell the stock. What if, instead of appreciating, the stock declines? Then its price is in the convex, risk-seeking part of the value function. Here the investor will continue to hold the stock even if its expected return falls lower than would have been necessary for her to justify its original purchase. Thus the investor's belief about expected return must fall further to motivate the sale of a stock that has already declined than one that has appreciated. Similarly, consider an investor who holds two stocks. One is up; the other is down. If the investor is faced with a liquidity demand, and has no new information about either stock, she is more likely to sell the stock that is up.

Throughout this study, investors' reference points are assumed to be their purchase prices. Though the results presented here appear to vindicate that choice, it is likely that for some investments, particularly those held for a long time over a wide range of prices, the purchase price may be only one determinant of the reference point. The price path may also affect the level of the reference point. For example, a homeowner who bought her home for $100,000 just before a real-estate boom and had the home appraised for $200,000 after the boom may no longer feel she is "breaking even" if she sells her home for $100,000 plus commissions. If purchase price is a major component, though not the sole component, of reference point, it may serve as a noisy proxy for the true reference point. Using the proxy in place of the true reference point will make a case for the disposition effect more difficult to prove. It seems likely that if the true reference point were available the statistical evidence reported here would be even stronger.

B. An Alternative Behavioral Theory

Investors might choose to hold their losers and sell their winners not because they are reluctant to realize losses but because they believe that today's losers will soon outperform today's winners. If future expected returns for the losers are greater than those for the winners, the investors' belief would be justified and rational. If, however, future expected returns for losers are not greater than those for winners, but investors continue to believe they are despite persistent evidence to the contrary, this belief would be irrational. In experimental settings Andreassen (1988) finds that subjects buy and sell stocks as if they expect short-term mean reversion.[1]

Most of the analysis presented here does not distinguish between prospect theory and an irrational belief in mean reversion as possible explanations for why investors hold losers and sell winners. It may be that investors themselves do not always make a clear distinction. For example, an investor who will not sell a stock for a loss might convince himself that the stock is likely to bounce back rather than admit his unwillingness to accept a loss.

---

[1] Subjects' tendencies to trade as if making regressive predictions diminish when their attention is focused on price changes rather than price levels (Andreassen (1988)) and when casual attributions for price trends, such as might normally be provided by the media, are made available (Andreassen (1987, 1990)).

C. Taxes

Investors' reluctance to realize losses is at odds with optimal tax-loss selling for taxable investments. For tax purposes investors should postpone taxable gains by continuing to hold their profitable investments. They should capture tax losses by selling their losing investments, though not necessarily at a constant rate. Constantinides (1984) shows that when there are transactions costs, and no distinction is made between the short-term and long-term tax rates (as is approximately the case from 1987 to 1993 for U.S. federal taxes[2]), investors should gradually increase their tax-loss selling from January to December. Dyl (1977), Lakonishok and Smidt (1986), and Badrinath and Lewellen (1991) report evidence that investors do sell more losing investments near the end of the year.

Shefrin and Statman (1985) propose that investors choose to sell their losers in December as a self-control measure. They reason that investors are reluctant to sell for a loss but recognize the tax benefits of doing so. The end of the year is the deadline for realizing these losses. So each year, investors postpone realizing losses until December when they require themselves to sell losers before the deadline passes.

A sophisticated investor could reconcile tax-loss selling with her aversion to realize losses though a tax-swap. By selling her losing stock and purchasing a stock with similar risk characteristics, she could realize a tax-loss while maintaining the same risk exposure. Thaler (1985) argues that people tend to segregate different gambles into separate mental accounts. These are then evaluated separately for gains and losses. A tax-swap requires closing such an account for a loss, which people are reluctant to do.

D. Previous Studies

Previous research[3] offers some support for the hypothesis that investors sell winners more readily than losers, but this research is generally unable to

---

[2] Prior to 1987 long-term capital gains tax rates were 40 percent of the short-term capital gains tax rates; from 1987 to 1993 long-term and short-term gains were taxed at the same marginal rates for lower income taxpayers. The maximum short-term rate at times exceeded the maximum long-term rate. In 1987 the maximum short-term rate was 38.5 percent and the maximum long-term rate was 28 percent. From 1988 to 1990 the highest income taxpayers paid a marginal rate of 28 percent on both long-term and short-term gains. In 1991 and 1992 the maximum long-term and short term-rates were 28 percent and 31 percent. In 1993 the maximum long-term and short-term rates were 28 percent and 39.6 percent.

[3] Starr-McCluer (1995) finds that 15 percent of the stock-owning households interviewed in the 1989 and 1992 Surveys of Consumer Finances have paper losses of 20 percent or more. She estimates that in the majority of cases the tax advantages of realizing these losses would more than offset the trading costs and time costs of doing so. Heisler (1994) documents loss aversion in a small sample of futures speculators. In a study of individual federal tax returns, Poterba (1987) finds that although many investors do offset their capital gains with losses, more than 60 percent of the investors with gains or losses realized only gains. Weber and Camerer (1995) report experimental evidence of the disposition effect. Lakonishok and Smidt (1986) and Ferris, Haugen, and Makhija (1988) find a positive correlation between price change and volume. Bremer and Kato (1996) find the same correlation for Japanese stocks. Such a correlation could be caused by investors who prefer to sell winners and hold losers, but it could also be the result of buyers' trading preferences.

distinguish among various motivations investors might have for doing so. Investors may be behaviorally motivated to hold losers and sell winners, that is, they may have value functions like those described in prospect theory or they may incorrectly expect mean-reverting prices. There are also rational reasons why investors may choose to hold their losers and sell their winners: (1) Investors who do not hold the market portfolio may respond to large price increases by selling some of the appreciated stock to restore diversification to their portfolios (Lakonishok and Smidt (1986)); (2) Investors who purchase stocks on favorable information may sell if the price goes up, rationally believing that price now reflects this information, and may continue to hold if the price goes down, rationally believing that their information is not yet incorporated into price (Lakonishok and Smidt (1986)); and (3) Because trading costs tend to be higher for lower priced stocks, and because losing investments are more likely to be lower priced than winning investments, investors may refrain from selling losers simply to avoid the higher trading costs of low-priced stocks (Harris (1988)).

The contribution of this paper is to demonstrate, with market data, that a particular class of investors (those with discount brokerage accounts) sell winners more readily than losers. Even when the alternative rational motivations listed above are controlled for, these investors continue to prefer selling winners and holding losers. Their behavior is consistent with prospect theory; it is also consistent with a (mistaken) belief that their winners and losers will mean revert.

II. THE DATA

The data for this study are provided by a nationwide discount brokerage house. From all accounts active in 1987 (those with at least one transaction), 10,000 customer accounts are randomly selected. The data are in three files: a trades file, a security number to CUSIP file, and a positions file. Only the first two files are used in this study. The trades file includes the records of all trades made in the 10,000 accounts from January 1987 through December 1993. This file has 162,948 records, each record is made up of an account identifier, the trade date, the brokerage house's internal number for the security traded, a buy-sell indicator, the quantity traded, the commission paid, and the principal amount. Multiple buys or sells of the same stock, in the same account, on the same day, are aggregated. The security number to CUSIP table translates the brokerage house's internal numbers into CUSIP numbers. The positions file contains monthly position information for the 10,000 accounts from January 1988 through December 1993. Each of its 1,258,135 records is made up of the account identifier, year, month, internal security number, equity, and quantity. Accounts that were closed between January 1987 and December 1993 are not replaced; thus the data set may have some survivorship bias in favor of more successful investors. The data do not distinguish different account types. Therefore it is not possible to separate taxable accounts from tax-free accounts. Given the large sample size, we can expect the sample proportions of different account types to be close to the proportions for all of the brokerage's accounts. At the beginning of the data period, 20 percent of the brokerage's accounts were either IRA or Keogh accounts, and these accounts were responsible for 17.5 percent of all trades. The inclusion of these tax-exempt accounts will reduce tax-motivated trading in the data set, but with 80 percent of the accounts taxable, tax-motivated selling is easily detectable.

There are two data sets similar to this one described in the literature. Schlarbaum et al. (1978) and others analyze trading records for 2500 accounts at a large retail brokerage house for the period January 1964 to December 1970; Badrinath and Lewellen (1991) and others analyze a second data set provided by the same retail broker for 3000 accounts over the period January 1971 to September 1979. The data set studied here differs from these primarily in that it is more recent and comes from a discount broker. By examining discount brokerage records I can rule out the retail broker as an influence on observed trading patterns.

Badrinath and Lewellen (1991) look for evidence of tax-motivated trading and find that the ratio of stocks sold for a loss to those sold for a gain rises as the year progresses. Using a somewhat different measure, I also find evidence that investors increase their tax-motivated selling as the year progresses. However the focus of this paper, unlike that of Badrinath and Lewellen, is to test the disposition effect. As the next section describes, this is done by analyzing the rates at which investors realize gains and losses relative to their opportunities to do so.

III. EMPIRICAL STUDY

A. Methodology

This study tests whether investors sell their winners too soon and hold losers too long. It also investigates tax-motivated trading in December. To determine whether investors sell winners more readily than losers, it is not sufficient to look at the number of securities sold for gains versus the number sold for losses. Suppose investors are indifferent to selling winners or losers. Then in an upward-moving market they will have more winners in their portfolios and will tend to sell more winners than losers even though they had no preference for doing so.[4] To test whether investors are disposed to selling winners and holding losers, we must look at the frequency with which they sell winners and losers relative to their opportunities to sell each.

By going through each account's trading records in chronological order, I construct for each date a portfolio of securities for which the purchase date and

---

[4] In Badrinath and Lewellen (1991) 49 percent of all round-trip sales are for a loss. In my database only 43 percent of such sales are for a loss. The difference could be due to different trading practices by retail and discount investors, but quite likely it simply reflects the greater rise in prices during the period I examine.

price are known. Clearly this portfolio represents only part of each investor's total portfolio. In most accounts there will be securities that were purchased before January 1987 for which the purchase price is not available, and investors may also have other accounts that are not part of the data set. Though the portfolios constructed from the data set are only part of each investor's total portfolio, it is unlikely that the selection process will bias these partial portfolios toward stocks for which investors have unusual preferences for realizing gains or losses.

I obtain information on splits and dividends as well as other price data needed for this study from the 1993 Center for Research in Security Prices daily stock file for NYSE, AMEX, and Nasdaq stocks. The study is limited to stocks for which this information is available. Of the 10,000 accounts, 6,380 trade stocks in the CRSP file for a total of 97,483 transactions.

Each day that a sale takes place in a portfolio of two or more stocks, I compare the selling price for each stock sold to its average purchase price to determine whether that stock is sold for a gain or a loss. Each stock that is in that portfolio at the beginning of that day, but is not sold, is considered to be a paper (unrealized) gain or loss (or neither). Whether it is a paper gain or loss is determined by comparing its high and low price for that day (as obtained from CRSP) to its average purchase price. If both its daily high and low are above its average purchase price it is counted as a paper gain; if they are both below its average purchase price it is counted as a paper loss; if its average purchase price lies between the high and the low, neither a gain or loss is counted. On days when no sales take place in an account, no gains or losses, realized or paper, are counted.

Suppose, for example, that an investor has five stocks in his portfolio, A, B, C, D, and E. A and B are worth more than he paid for them; C, D, and E are worth less. Another investor has three stocks F, G, and H in her portfolio. F and G are worth more than she paid for them; H is worth less. On a particular day the first investor sells shares of A and of C. The next day the other investor sells shares of F. The sales of A and F are counted as realized gains. The sale of C is a realized loss. Since B and G could have been sold for a profit but weren't, they are counted as paper gains. D, E, and G are paper losses. So for these two investors over these two days, two realized gains, one realized loss, two paper gains, and three paper losses are counted. Realized gains, paper gains, realized losses, and paper losses are summed for each account and across accounts. Then two ratios are calculated:

$$\frac{\text{Realized Gains}}{\text{Realized Gains} + \text{Paper Gains}} = \text{Proportion of Gains Realized (PGR)} \qquad (1)$$

$$\frac{\text{Realized Losses}}{\text{Realized Losses} + \text{Paper Losses}} = \text{Proportion of Losses Realized (PLR)} \qquad (2)$$

In the example PGR $= 1/2$ and PLR $= 1/4$. A large difference in the proportion of gains realized (PGR) and the proportion of losses realized (PLR) indicates that investors are more willing to realize either gains or losses.

Any test of the disposition effect is a joint test of the hypothesis that people sell gains more readily than losses and of the specification of the reference point from which gains and losses are determined. Some possible choices of a reference point for stocks are the average purchase price, the highest purchase price, the first purchase price, or the most recent purchase price. The findings of this study are essentially the same for each choice; results are reported for average purchase price. Commissions and dividends may or may not be considered when determining reference points, and profits and losses. Although investors may not consider commissions when they remember what they paid for a stock, commissions do affect capital gains and losses. And because the normative standard to which the disposition effect is being contrasted is optimal tax-motivated selling, commissions are added to the purchase price and deducted from the sales price in this study except where otherwise noted. Dividends are not included when determining which sales are profitable because they do not affect capital gains and losses for tax purposes. The primary finding of the paper, that investors are reluctant to sell their losers and prefer to sell winners, is unaffected by the inclusion or exclusion of commissions or dividends. In determining whether the stocks that are not sold on a particular day could have been sold for a gain or a loss, the commission for the potential sale is assumed to be the average commission per share paid when the stock was purchased.[5] All gains and losses are calculated after adjusting for splits.

There are two hypotheses to be tested. The first is that investors tend to sell their winners and hold their losers. Stated in terms of realization rates for gains and losses this is:

HYPOTHESIS 1: *Proportion of Gains Realized > Proportion of Losses Realized (for the entire year).*

The null hypothesis in this case is that PGR $\leq$ PLR. The second hypothesis is that in December investors are more willing to sell losers and less willing to sell winners than during the rest of the year. That is:

HYPOTHESIS 2: *Proportion of Losses Realized − Proportion of Gains Realized in December > Proportion of Losses Realized − Proportion of Gains Realized in January–November.*

The null hypothesis here is: PLR − PGR in December $\leq$ PLR − PGR in January through November.

B. Results

Table 21.1 reports the PGR realized and the PLR realized for the entire year, for January through November, and for December. We see that for the entire year investors do sell a higher proportion of their winners than of their losers. For both

---

[5] If, for potential sales, the commission is instead assumed to be the same percentage of principal as paid when the stock was purchased, the results do not significantly change.

Table 21.1. PGR and PLR for the Entire Data Set

	Entire Year	December	Jan.–Nov.
PLR	0.098	0.128	0.094
PGR	0.148	0.108	0.152
Difference in proportions	−0.050	0.020	−0.058
t-statistic	−35	4.3	−38

Note: This table compares the aggregate Proportion of Gains Realized (PGR) to the aggregate Proportion of Losses Realized (PLR), where PGR is the number of realized gains divided by the number of realized gains plus the number of paper (unrealized) gains, and PLR is the number of realized losses divided by the number of realized losses plus the number of paper (unrealized) losses. Realized gains, paper gains, losses, and paper losses are aggregated over time (1987–1993) and across all accounts in the data set. PGR and PLR are reported for the entire year, for December only, and for January through November. For the entire year there are 13,883 realized gains, 79,658 paper gains, 11,930 realized losses, and 110,348 paper losses. For December there are 866 realized gains, 7,131 paper gains, 1,555 realized losses, and 10,604 paper losses. The t-statistics test the null hypotheses that the differences in proportions are equal to zero assuming that all realized gains, paper gains, realized losses, and paper losses result from independent decisions.

Hypothesis 1 and Hypothesis 2 the null hypotheses can be rejected with a high degree of statistical significance. A one-tailed test of the first null hypothesis, PGR $\leq$ PLR, is rejected with a t-statistic greater than 35. The second null hypothesis, PLR − PGR in December $\leq$ PLR − PGR in January through November, is also rejected (t equals 16). These tests count each sale for a gain, sale for a loss, paper gain on the day of a sale, and paper loss on the day of a sale as separate independent observations.[6] These observations are aggregated across investors. This independence assumption will not hold perfectly. For example, suppose an investor chooses not to sell the same stock on repeated occasions. It is likely that the decision not to sell on one date is not independent of the decision not to sell on another date. Alternatively, two investors may be motivated to sell the same stock on, or about, the same day because they receive the same information. This lack of independence will inflate the test statistics, though it won't bias the observed proportions. For Hypotheses 1 and 2 the null hypotheses are rejected with such a high degree of statistical significance that some lack of independence is not problematic. In the following discussion, the data are, at times, divided into several partitions (e.g., Figure 21.2 and Table 21.6). Where

---

[6] To calculate the t-statistics in Table 21.1, the standard error for the difference in the proportions PGR and PLR is:

$$\sqrt{\frac{\text{PGR}(1 - \text{PGR})}{n_{rg} + n_{pg}} + \frac{\text{PLR}(1 - \text{PLR})}{n_{rl} + n_{pl}}}$$

where n_{rg}, n_{pg}, n_{rl}, and n_{pl} are the number of realized gains, paper gains, realized losses, and paper losses.

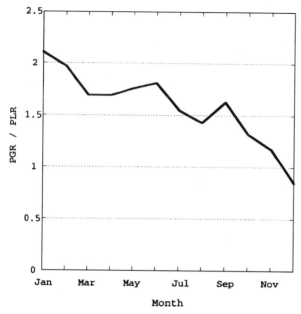

Figure 21.2. Ratio of the proportion of gains realized (PGR) to the proportion of losses realized (PLR) for each month. PGR is the number of realized gains divided by the number of realized gains plus the number of paper (unrealized) gains, and PLR is the number of realized losses divided by the number of realized losses plus the number of paper (unrealized) losses. Realized gains, paper gains, losses, and paper losses are aggregated over time (1987–1993) and across all accounts in the data set.

t-statistics for individual partitions approach the conventional thresholds of statistical significance, they should be viewed with some skepticism.

To gain some perspective into how critical the independence assumptions made above are to the primary finding of this paper – that investors realize gains too soon and hold losers too long – it is instructive to look at an alternative test. Suppose that instead of assuming that independence exists at a transactional level we assume only that it exists at an account level. That is, we assume that the proportions of gains and losses realized in each account are independent of those realized in other accounts. PGR and PLR are then estimated for each account, and their difference, PGR − PLR, is calculated for each account. The average account PGR is 0.57, the average account PLR is 0.36, the average of PGR − PLR is 0.21, and the hypothesis that the mean of PGR − PLR is less than or equal to zero is rejected with a t-statistic of 19.[7] This alternative test also attempts to control for dependence caused by common information. To do this

---

[7] An account is included in this test only if the denominators for both PGR and for PLR are nonzero for that account. There are 1893 such accounts. These same accounts are used to calculate share-based and dollar-based PGR and PLR.

the sale of a stock is only counted if no sale has been previously counted for that stock in any account within a week before or after the sale date. That is, no two sales of the same stock within a week of each other are counted. Similarly, no two unrealized paper losses or gains of the same stock within a week of each other are counted. This test provides an alternative to the one reported in Table 21.1 and throughout the rest of the paper, but it is not without drawbacks. The previous test, in effect, weights each account by the number of realized and paper gains and losses in that account. This alternative test weights each account equally, which means we ignore the fact that accounts with more transactions provide more accurate estimates of their actual PGR and PLR. In other words, by treating each account the same, we assume that the observed account PGRs and PLRs are homoskedastic when they are clearly heteroskedastic. However, to properly weight for this heteroskedasticity we need to know the degree of independence of transactions within accounts, which is exactly the issue this test is intended to circumvent. It is presented here simply to demonstrate that when a different set of independence assumptions is made, the null to Hypothesis 1 is still rejected at a very significant level.

It should be noted that the PGR and the PLR measures are dependent on the average size of the portfolios from which they are calculated. When the portfolio sizes are large, both of these proportions will be smaller. Thus these proportions are smaller for traders who trade frequently and generally have larger portfolios than for those who trade less frequently. When PGR and PLR are calculated for Table 21.1, the accounts with more trades weigh more heavily than those with fewer trades. In the alternative specification described in the last paragraph all accounts are weighted equally. For this reason PGR and PLR are both larger in the alternative specification than in Table 21.1. Of primary interest is not the individual values of PGR and PLR, but their values relative to each other.

Throughout this paper PGR and PLR are calculated in terms of trades and potential trades. An alternative specification is to calculate them in terms of number of shares traded and potential number of shares traded. When gains, losses, paper gains, and paper losses are aggregated across accounts before calculating PGR and PLR, as is done throughout most of this paper, measuring in shares further complicates the question of independence. However, if PGR and PLR are first calculated for each account and then the mean of PGR − PLR is calculated − as in the alternative test described in the previous paragraph − independence is assumed only between accounts. When this alternative test is done for PGR and PLR based on shares rather than trades, the results are virtually unchanged: average PGR is 0.58, average PLR is 0.36, and the null hypothesis that the mean of PGR − PLR is less than or equal to zero is rejected with a t-statistic of 18.[8]

---

[8] As in the previous test no two sales or potential sales of the same stock within a week of each other are counted here. If sales and potential within a week of each other are also counted, share-based PGR is 0.51 and share-based PLR is 0.31.

Suppose investors frequently realize small gains and less frequently take large losses. It is then possible that they are selling similar proportions of the values of their gains and losses, though realizing gains at a higher rate on a trade-counted basis. This is, however, not the case. I calculate the average PGR and PLR per account by measuring losses, gains, potential losses, and potential gains in terms of dollars rather than shares or trades. When, as before, no two sales or potential sales of the same stock within a week of each other are counted, the average dollar-based PGR is 0.58 and the average dollar-based PLR is 0.42. The hypothesis that the mean of PGR − PLR is less than or equal to zero is rejected with a t-statistic of 13.[9]

In Table 21.1 the ratio of PGR to PLR for the entire year is a little over 1.5, indicating that a stock that is up in value is more than 50 percent more likely to be sold from day to day than a stock that is down. In Weber and Camerer's (1995) experimental studies of the disposition effect, a stock that is up is also about 50 percent more likely to be sold than one that is down. Figure 21.2 charts the ratio of PGR to PLR for each month. This ratio declines from 2.1 in January to 0.85 in December. This decline is consistent with Constantinides' tax-loss selling model and suggests that at least some investors pay attention to tax-motivated selling throughout the year. From January through November, however, the observed ratio of PGR to PLR is greater than 1, and the hypothesis that the population ratio is less than or equal to 1 is rejected in each of these months with t-statistics ranging from 3.6 in November to 18 in January.[10]

To test the robustness of these results the data set is partitioned into two time periods and also into two groups of traders. Table 21.2 displays results when the data set is partitioned into stocks sold from 1987 to 1990 and 1990 to 1993 and when it is partitioned into the decile of traders who trade most frequently and the nine deciles of traders who trade least frequently. In the data set, the most active 10 percent of the traders account for 57 percent of all stock trades.

---

[9] To examine this issue from another perspective, I look at each year in each portfolio and tally the total number of years for which both potential gains and potential losses are present in the portfolio and either net gains or net losses are realized. Net dollar gains are realized for 2,116 of these years and net dollar losses for 1,477 years. This indicates that, in most cases, large losses are not offsetting small gains.

[10] In Tables 21.1–21.6, realized and unrealized losses are tabulated on days that sales took place in portfolios of two or more stocks. One objection to this formulation is that for portfolios that hold only winners or only losers an investor cannot choose whether to sell a winner or to sell a loser, but only which winner or loser to sell. Another objection is that if an investor has net capital losses of more than $3,000 for the current year (in non-tax-deferred accounts) it may be normative for that investor to choose to sell a winner rather than a loser. I have repeated the analyses reported in the tables subject to the additional constraints that there be at least one winner and one loser in a portfolio on the day of a sale for that day to be counted and that the net realized capital losses for the year to date in the portfolio be less than $3,000. When these constraints are imposed, the difference in PGR and PLR is, for each analysis, greater. For example, for the entire sample and the entire year (as in Table 21.1) there are 10,111 realized gains, 71,817 paper gains, 5,977 realized losses, and 94,419 paper losses. Thus the PLR is 0.060; the PGR is 0.123; their difference is 0.063; and the t-statistic for the difference in proportions is 47.

Table 21.2. PGR and PLR Partitioned by Period and Trading Activity

	1987–1990	1991–1993	Frequent Traders	Infrequent Traders
Entire year PLR	0.126	0.072	0.079	0.296
Entire year PGR	0.201	0.115	0.119	0.452
Difference in proportions	−0.075	−0.043	−0.040	−0.156
t-statistic	−30	−25	−29	−22
December PLR	0.143	0.110	0.095	0.379
December PGR	0.129	0.097	0.084	0.309
Difference in proportions	0.014	0.013	0.010	0.070
t-statistic	1.9	2.3	2.3	3.5
Jan.–Nov. PLR	0.123	0.069	0.078	0.282
Jan.–Nov. PGR	0.207	0.117	0.123	0.469
Difference in proportions	−0.084	−0.048	−0.045	−0.187
t-statistic	−32	−27	−31	−254

Note: This table compares the aggregate Proportion of Gains Realized (PGR) to the aggregate Proportion of Losses Realized (PLR), where PGR is the number of realized gains divided by the number of realized gains plus the number of paper (unrealized) gains, and PLR is the number of realized losses divided by the number of realized losses plus the number of paper (unrealized) losses. The data are partitioned into the periods 1987–1990 and 1990–1993 and into the 10 percent of the accounts that trade most frequently and the 90 percent that trade least frequently. For 1987–1990 there are 7,280 realized gains, 28,998 paper gains, 7,253 realized losses, and 50,540 paper losses. For 1990–1993 there are 6,603 realized gains, 50,660 paper gains, 4,677 realized losses, and 59,808 paper losses. For frequent traders there are 10,186 realized gains, 75,182 paper gains, 8,886 realized losses, and 103,096 paper. For infrequent traders there are 3,697 realized gains, 4,476 paper gains, 3,042 realized losses, and 7,251 paper losses. The t-statistics test the null hypotheses that the differences in proportions are equal to zero assuming that all realized gains, paper gains, realized losses, and paper losses result from independent decisions.

In both time periods and for both the frequent and the infrequent traders, a significantly greater proportion of all possible gains than of all possible losses is realized throughout the year (t greater than 22, in all cases). In December, losses are realized at a higher rate relative to gains than during the rest of the year, indicating that investors are realizing tax losses in December. Due to how portfolios are reconstructed over time, average portfolio sizes are larger for the later years of the sample. PGR and PLR are therefore smaller for the second temporal partition, just as they are smaller for the partition of frequent traders.

One reason investors might choose to sell winners rather than losers is that they anticipate a change in the tax law under which capital gains rates will rise. The tax law of 1986 made such a change. If investors sold off winners in anticipation of higher tax rates, they might have entered 1987 with a larger percentage of losers in their portfolio than usual. Because such stocks are purchased prior to 1987 they would not show up in the portfolios reconstructed here. It is possible therefore that the rate at which winners are being realized relative to losers is lower in the investors' total portfolio than in the partial reconstructed portfolios. As old stocks are sold and new ones purchased the partial portfolios become more and more representative of the total portfolio.

Table 21.3. Average Returns

	Jan.–Nov.	December	Entire Year
Return on realized gains	0.275	0.316	0.277
Return on paper gains	0.463	0.500	0.466
Return on realized losses	−0.208	−0.366	−0.228
Return on paper losses	−0.391	−0.417	−0.393

Note: This table reports the mean return realized on stocks sold for a gain and on stocks sold for a loss. It also reports mean return that could be realized by stocks that are not sold on days that other stocks in the same portfolio are sold. These stocks are classified as paper gains and paper losses. For all accounts over the entire year, there are 13,883 realized gains, 79,658 paper gains, 11,930 realized losses, and 110,348 paper losses. For all accounts during the month of December, there are 866 realized gains, 7,131 paper gains, 1,555 realized losses, and 10,604 paper losses.

We would expect that if a sell-off of winners in anticipation of the 1986 tax law affects the observed rate at which gains and losses are realized in the partial portfolios, that effect would be greater in the first part of the sample period than in the last part. However the ratio PGR/PLR is virtually the same for the periods 1987 to 1990 and 1991 to 1993.

Table 21.3 reports the average returns since the day of purchase for realized and paper winners and losers. In December the losses that are realized are of much greater magnitude than those realized throughout the rest of the year. This is additional evidence that some investors do engage in tax-motivated selling in December.

Lakonishok and Smidt (1986) suggest that investors might sell winners and hold on to losers in an effort to rebalance their portfolios. We expect that investors who are rebalancing will sell a portion, but not all, of their shares of winning stocks. A sale of the entire holding of a stock is most likely not motivated by the desire to rebalance. So to eliminate trades that may be motivated by a desire to rebalance, I calculate PGR and PLR using only sales that are of an account's entire position in a stock (and using paper gains and losses on the days of those sales). There may be some cases where shares of a stock are already in the portfolio before 1987 and then additional shares are purchased. For these, the sale of all shares purchased after 1987 may not amount to the sale of all shares held. So this removal of sales that could be motivated by diversification is not perfect. Even so, if the preference for selling winners is due to rebalancing, removing most rebalancing-motivated trades will greatly reduce the preference for selling winners.

In Table 21.4, for the entire year, when partial sales are ignored the preference for selling winners rather than losers is not substantially changed. The tendency to sell winners and hold losers does not appear to be the result of rebalancing. When partial sales are ignored, investors realize losses in December at an even higher rate relative to realizing gains. Perhaps this is because investors who are intentionally realizing tax losses choose to sell their entire position in the losing stock.

**Table 21.4. PGR and PLR When the Entire Position in a
Stock Is Sold**

	Entire Year	December
PLR	0.155	0.197
PGR	0.233	0.162
Difference in proportions	−0.078	0.035
t-statistic	−32	4.6

Note: This table compares the aggregate proportion of gains realized (PGR) to the aggregate Proportion of Losses Realized
(PLR), where PGR is the number of realized gains divided by
the number of realized gains plus the number of paper (unrealized) gains, and PLR is the number of realized losses divided
by the number of realized losses plus the number of paper (unrealized) losses. In this table losses and gains are counted only
if a portfolio's total position in a stock was sold that day. Paper (unrealized) gains and losses are counted only if the portfolio's total position in another stock held in the portfolio was
sold that day. Realized gains, paper gains, losses, and paper
losses are aggregated over time (1987–1993) and across all accounts in the data set. PGR and PLR are reported for the entire year and for December only. For the entire year there are
10,967 realized gains, 36,033 paper gains, 9,476 realized losses,
and 51,502 paper losses. For December there are 666 realized
gains, 3,440 paper gains, 1,171 realized losses, and 4,759 paper
losses. The *t*-statistics test the null hypotheses that the differences in proportions are equal to zero assuming that all realized
gains, paper gains, realized losses, and paper losses result from
independent decisions.

Investors who sell winners for the purpose of rebalancing their portfolios
are likely to make new purchases. In an alternative effort to eliminate trades
that may be motivated by a desire to rebalance, I calculate PGR and PLR using
only sales for which there is no new purchase into a portfolio on the sale date
or during the following three weeks (and using paper gains and losses on the
days of those sales). Table 21.5 reports that when sales motivated by a desire to
rebalance are eliminated in this way, investors continue to prefer to sell winners.
Once again, investors realize losses at a higher rate than gains in December.

Another reason investors might sell winners and hold losers is that they
expect the losers to outperform the winners in the future. An investor who
buys a stock because of favorable information may sell that stock when it goes
up because she believes her information is now reflected in the price. On the
other hand, if the stock goes down she may continue to hold it, believing that
the market has not yet come to appreciate her information. Investors could also
choose to sell winners and hold losers simply because they believe prices mean
revert. I test whether such beliefs are justified, ex post.

Table 21.6 reports excess returns for periods following the sale of a winning stock or the observation of a paper loss. Three investment horizons are
examined: 84 trading days, which is the approximate median in sample holding

Table 21.5. PGR and PLR When No New Stock Is Purchased within Three Weeks of Sale

	Entire Year	December
PLR	0.281	0.391
PGR	0.449	0.366
Difference in proportions	−0.168	0.015
t-statistic	−36	1.6

Note: This table compares the aggregate proportion of gains realized (PGR) to the aggregate Proportion of Losses Realized (PLR), where PGR is the number of realized gains divided by the number of realized gains plus the number of paper (unrealized) gains, and PLR is the number of realized losses divided by the number of realized losses plus the number of paper (unrealized) losses. In this table losses and gains are counted only if a no new purchase was made into a portfolio on the day of the sale or within three weeks following the sale. Paper (unrealized) gains and losses are counted for days on which qualifying sales were made. Realized gains, paper gains, losses, and paper losses are aggregated over time (1987–1993) and across all accounts in the data set. PGR and PLR are reported for the entire year and for December only. For the entire year there are 8,336 realized gains, 10,240 paper gains, 7,553 realized losses, and 19,370 paper losses. For December there are 590 realized gains, 1,024 paper gains, 1,194 realized losses, and 1,863 paper losses. The t-statistics test the null hypotheses that the differences in proportions are equal to zero assuming that all realized gains, paper gains, realized losses, and paper losses result from independent decisions.

Table 21.6. Ex Post Returns

	Performance over Next 84 Trading Days	Performance over Next 252 Trading Days	Performance over Next 504 Trading Days
Average excess return on winning stocks sold	0.0047	0.0235	0.0645
Average excess return on paper losses	−0.0056	−0.0106	0.0287
Difference in excess returns (p-values)	0.0103 (0.002)	0.0341 (0.001)	0.0358 (0.014)

Note: This table compares average returns in excess of the CRSP value-weighted index to stocks that are sold for a profit (winning stocks sold) and to stocks that could be, but are not, sold for a loss (paper losses). Returns are measured over the 84, 252, and 504 trading days subsequent to the sale of a realized winner and subsequent to days on which sales of other stocks take place in the portfolio of a paper loser. p-values refer to the frequency with which differences in excess returns over the same periods in the empirical (bootstrapped) distributions exceed the difference in excess returns observed in the data.

period for stocks,[11] 254 trading days (one year), which is Benartzi and Thaler's (1995) estimate of the average investor's investment horizon, and 504 trading days (two years), which is how often, on average, New York Stock Exchange equities turned over during this period. Returns are calculated in excess of the CRSP value-weighted index. For winners that are sold, the average excess return over the following year is 3.4 percent more than it is for losers that are not sold. Investors who sell winners and hold losers because they expect the losers to outperform the winners in the future are, on average, mistaken. The superior returns to former winners noted here are consistent with Jegadeesh and Titman's (1993) finding of price momentum in security returns at horizons of up to eighteen months, though De-Bondt and Thaler (1985, 1987) find price reversals at longer horizons of three to five years.[12]

The average excess returns to winners sold in Table 21.6 are determined by calculating excess buy-and-hold returns over the periods subsequent to each profitable sale of each stock and then taking an average that weighs each observation equally. Many stocks are sold for a profit on more than one date; sometimes the same stock is sold for a profit on the same date by more than one investor. Each of these sales is counted as a separate observation. The same procedure applies to paper losses. The *p*-values in Table 21.6 are estimated by bootstrapping an empirical distribution for the difference in average excess buy-and-hold returns to realized winners and paper losses. This empirical distribution is generated under the null hypothesis that subsequent excess returns to realized winners and paper losers are drawn from the same underlying distribution. The methodology is similar to that of Brock, Lakonishok, and LeBaron (1992) and Ikenberry, Lakonishok, and Vermaelen (1995). Lyon, Barber, and Tsai (1999) test the acceptance and rejection rates for this methodology and find that it performs well in random samples. For each stock in the sample for which CRSP return data are available, a replacement stock is drawn (with replacement) from the set of all CRSP stocks of the same size decile and same book-to-market quintile as the original stock. Using the replacement stocks together with the original observation dates, average excess buy-and-hold returns are calculated for the 84, 252, and 502 trading days following the dates on which sales for a profit or paper losses are observed. These averages, and their differences, constitute one observation from the empirical distribution. One thousand such observations are made. The null hypothesis is rejected at the α percent level if the average subsequent excess return to realized winners minus that to paper losers in the data set is greater than the $(1 - \alpha)$ percentile average excess

---

[11] Note that the in-sample median holding period is a downwardly biased estimate of the true median holding period since stocks held for long periods are more likely to be bought before or sold after the data period and therefore not counted in the sample averages. The average turnover rate for equity in these accounts is 6.5 percent per month, which corresponds to an average holding period of about 15 months.

[12] At the time of this study CRSP data were available through 1994. For this reason two-year subsequent returns are not calculated for sales dates in 1993.

return to realized winners minus that to paper losers observed in the empirical distribution.

We saw in Table 21.3 (column 3) that investors are more likely to realize smaller, rather than larger, gains and losses. It may be that, due to regret aversion, investors are most loath to realize their greatest losses, and, due to tax consequences, they postpone realizing their greatest gains. Lower price ranges are likely to have a greater proportion of large losers and a smaller proportion of large winners than upper price ranges. Investors will therefore have a greater propensity to not sell losers in lower price ranges, and to not sell winners in higher price ranges.

Harris (1988) suggests that investors' reticence to sell losers may be due to their sensitivity to higher trading costs at lower stock prices. Table 21.7 reports PGR and PLR for different price ranges and return ranges for January through November. Stocks with a price less than or equal to $10, with prices greater than $10 and less than or equal to $25, and with prices higher than $25, represent, respectively, 36 percent, 35 percent, and 29 percent of the data set. Partitioning on magnitude of return controls for the disproportionate numbers of large losers in the lower price range and of large winners in the top price range. The ranges

Table 21.7. PGR and PLR Partitioned by Price and Return

	$|R| \leq 0.15$	$0.15 < |R| \leq 0.30$	$0.30 < |R| \leq 0.50$	$0.50 \leq |R|$
Price $\leq$ $10				
PLR	0.141	0.129	0.109	0.030
PGR	0.267	0.257	0.295	0.282
Difference	−0.126	−0.128	−0.186	−0.252
t-statistic	13.0	10.2	11.7	17.5
$10 $\leq$ Price $\leq$ $25				
PLR	0.138	0.105	0.076	0.058
PGR	0.222	0.186	0.172	0.135
Difference	−0.084	−0.081	−0.096	−0.077
t-statistic	16.9	13.1	13.1	11.3
$25 $\leq$ Price				
PLR	0.125	0.104	0.104	0.049
PGR	0.197	0.126	0.081	0.055
Difference	−0.072	−0.022	0.023	−0.006
t-statistic	19.4	4.5	−3.2	0.61

Note: This table compares the aggregate Proportion of Gains Realized (PGR) to the aggregate Proportion of Losses Realized (PLR), where PGR is the number of realized gains divided by the number of realized gains plus the number of paper (unrealized) gains, and PLR is the number of realized losses divided by the number of realized losses plus the number of paper (unrealized) losses. The data are partitioned on stock price and on absolute value of the return to date (R), for all accounts, 1987–1993, January through November only. The t-statistics test the null hypotheses that the differences in proportions are equal to zero assuming that all realized gains, paper gains, realized losses, and paper losses result from independent decisions.

for absolute value of return are: 0 to 0.15, 0.15 to 0.30, 0.30 to 0.50, and greater than 0.50. We see that in fourteen of fifteen partitions winners are realized at a higher rate than losers. This difference is statistically significant in thirteen partitions. When comparing winners and losers of similar magnitude, investors appear to prefer to sell winners and hold losers even when trading costs for both are about the same.

There is another way to contrast the hypothesis that losses are realized more slowly due to the higher transactions costs with the two behavioral hypotheses. We can look at the rates at which investors purchase additional shares of stocks they already own. The proportion of gains purchased again (PGPA) and the proportion of losses purchased again (PLPA) can be calculated in a manner analogous to how PGR and PLR are calculated. When a stock already in the portfolio is purchased again it is counted as a gain purchased again or a loss purchased again. On days when purchases are made, stocks already in the portfolio for which additional shares are not repurchased are counted as gains or losses potentially purchased again. Thus:

$$\frac{\text{Gains Purchased Again}}{\text{Gains Purchased Again} + \text{Gains Potentially Purchased Again}} = \frac{\text{Proportion of Gains Purchased Again}}{} \text{(PGPA)} \quad (3)$$

$$\frac{\text{Losses Purchased Again}}{\text{Losses Purchased Again} + \text{Losses Potentially Purchased Again}} = \frac{\text{Proportion of Losses Purchased Again}}{} \text{(PGPA)} \quad (4)$$

When these proportions are calculated, additional purchases of a particular stock in a particular account are not counted if they take place within one week of a previous purchase of the stock. This is done to avoid the possibility of counting a purchase order filled over more than one day as an additional purchase.

If investors avoid the higher transactions cost of low priced stocks we would expect PLPA to be less than PGPA. If, however, investors are more risk seeking for losing investments (prospect theory) or if they believe prices will revert (as do Andreassen's subjects), then PLPA will be greater than PGPA. This is the case. For the entire sample PLPA = 0.135 and PGPA = 0.094. If we assume that all decisions to purchase or not purchase additional stock are independent, the hypothesis that these two proportions are equal can be rejected with a t-statistic of 19. This supports the two behavioral theories but not the transaction cost hypothesis.[13]

In Table 21.3 we saw that investors tend to sell their larger gains and losses at a slower rate than their smaller gains and losses. Prospect theory does not

---

[13] For the same reasons as discussed in Section III B, these decisions will not always be independent. So the t-statistic of 19 overstates the actual statistical significance.

predict that investors realize their large gains more slowly than their small gains. Nor does a belief in mean reversion predict this. If, however, investors believe that stocks that perform moderately well will revert, but those that perform unusually well will trend,[14] they might sell their small winners and hold their larger ones. These beliefs could then also lead them to buy fewer additional shares of small winners and more additional shares of larger winners. To test this I partition winning investments into large or small winners using the mean unrealized winners' return of 0.47 as a break point (see Table 21.3). Similarly I partition losers into large and small losers using −0.39 as a break point. Small winners are repurchased at a rate of 0.112, large winners are repurchased at a rate of 0.043. Small losers are repurchased at a rate of 0.172 and large losers at 0.067. The difference in the rates at which large and small gains are realized is highly significant (t equals 26, assuming independence); so, too, is the difference in the rate at which large and small losses are realized (t equals 39). These investors do not tend to buy additional shares of big winners. This is not consistent with the hypothesis that they believe small winners will revert but large winners will perform well; however, other factors may be working against the hypothesis. Investors who are in the habit of buying additional shares of stocks they already own may reach their limit of additional purchases before these stocks have an opportunity to make large gains (or losses). Regret aversion may also influence investors to not buy additional shares of big winners. For example, suppose an investor buys 100 shares of stock A at $100 per share. Then stock A appreciates to $150. The investor may believe stock A will continue to appreciate but he may still refrain from buying an additional 100 shares, for if he does purchase more shares, he will more poignantly regret that he didn't buy them at $100 per share to begin with. The greater the difference between the original and additional purchase prices, the greater is this potential regret.

The results presented so far are not able to distinguish between the two behavioral hypotheses. Both prospect theory and a belief in mean reversion predict that investors will hold their losers too long and sell their winners too soon. Both predict that investors will purchase more additional shares of losers than of winners. However a belief in mean reversion should apply to stocks that an investor does not already own as well as those she does, but prospect theory applies only to the stocks she owns. Thus a belief in mean reversion implies that investors will tend to buy stocks that had previously declined even if they don't already own these stocks, and prospect theory makes no prediction in this case. Odean (1997) finds that this same group of investors tends to buy stocks that have, on average, outperformed the CRSP value-weighted index by about 25 percent over the previous two years. This would appear inconsistent with a simple belief in mean reversion. (It is, though, consistent with a belief that big winners will continue to perform well.)

---

[14] In this vein Barberis, Shleifer, and Vishny (1996) develop a model in which investors believe that earnings switch between two regimes, one mean reverting and the other trend following.

IV. DISCUSSION

This paper examines the behavior of individual investors and finds that investors exhibit disposition effects; that is, they realize their profitable stocks investments at a much higher rate than their unprofitable ones, except in December. The extent to which this behavior affects market prices depends on the trading activities of other market participants such as professional traders and institutional investors. If the disposition effect holds in aggregate it may contribute to the positive relationship between price change and volume identified by Lakonishok and Smidt (1986) and by Ferris et al. (1988). The disposition effect could also be a cause of the positive correlation between price changes and volume in other markets such as residential real estate. Case and Shiller (1988) report evidence of disposition effects from interviews with homeowners in boom and post-boom real estate markets.

By affecting supply, the disposition effect may also contribute to market stability near prices at which substantial trading has previously taken place. If many investors buy a stock at a particular price, that price may become their reference point. If the stock falls below this reference point, these investors will be averse to selling for a loss, reducing the supply of potential sellers. A reduced supply of potential sellers could slow further price decreases. On the other hand, if the stock rises above the reference point, these investors will be more willing to sell, increasing the supply of potential sellers, and possibly slowing further price increases. If these investors have private information about the future prospects of a company whose stock they hold, the disposition effect may slow the rate at which this information is incorporated into price. For example, investors with negative information may be unwilling to sell a stock if its price is below their reference point. In not selling the stock, these investors will fail to signal their negative information to the market, and there could be a delay before that information is reflected in prices.

Though the disposition effect may influence market prices, its economic significance is likely to be greatest for individual investors. To get a rough idea of the economic costs of the loss aversion, let us imagine that a hypothetical investor is choosing to sell one of two stocks. The first of these stocks behaves like the average realized winner in this data set and the other like the average paper loser. The investor wishes to sell $1,000 worth of stock after commissions and that happens to be what his position in each stock is currently worth. Suppose he is averse to realizing losses and so sells the winning stock. If his experience is similar to that of the average investor in this data set, his return on the sale will be 0.277 (Table 21.3, third column). Since the stock is currently worth $1000, its purchase price must have been $783, and his capital gain is $217. If he instead chooses to sell $1,000 worth of the losing stock, his return will be −0.393, with a purchase price of $1,647, and a capital loss of $647. One year later the (losing) stock that he held will have, on average, a return 1 percent below the market (Table 21.6); the winning stock that he sold will have, on average, a return 2.4 percent above the market. Marginal tax rates for capital gains for investors in this sample vary from 0 to 28 percent, plus state taxes. Assume that our investor's marginal tax rate is 15 percent and that he has taxable gains against which to offset losses. Then by choosing to sell the winning stock rather than the loser, he gives up an immediate tax savings of $130. Suppose that whichever stock the investor does not sell now, he will sell in one year; then the investor is paying $130 in taxes one year earlier than he otherwise would. If he can expect a return of 8 percent on his money, choosing not to defer these taxes costs him about $10. In addition to this, over the next year the investor's return on the stock he holds (the loser) is $34 less than if he had held the other stock (the winner). Using $1,000 as a basis, and including the value of the immediate tax savings ($10) as well as the anticipated difference in capital gains ($34), the investor's return is about 4.4 percent higher over the next year if he sells the loser rather than the winner. The benefits of deferring taxes may be even higher if the investor chooses to delay realizing his gains for more than one year. On the other hand, a habit of regular loss realizations may reduce the magnitude of available capital losses.

The trading records analyzed in this paper are obtained from a discount brokerage house. This avoids the need to consider agency issues that influence institutional investors or to disentangle the decisions and motivations of individual investors from those of their retail brokers. It would be illuminating to repeat this study with data on institutional trading and with data from a retail brokerage house.

V. CONCLUSION

This paper finds that individual investors demonstrate a significant preference for selling winners and holding losers, except in December when tax-motivated selling prevails. This investor behavior does not appear to be motivated by a desire to rebalance portfolios or by a reluctance to incur the higher trading costs of low priced stocks. Nor is it justified by subsequent portfolio performance. It leads, in fact, to lower returns, particularly so for taxable accounts.

22. Timid Choices and Bold Forecasts
A Cognitive Perspective on Risk Taking

Daniel Kahneman and Dan Lovallo

ABSTRACT. Decision makers have a strong tendency to consider problems as unique. They isolate the current choice from future opportunities and neglect the statistics of the past in evaluating current plans. Overly cautious attitudes to risk result from a failure to appreciate the effects of statistical aggregation in mitigating relative risk. Overly optimistic forecasts result from the adoption of an inside view of the problem, which anchors predictions on plans and scenarios. The conflicting biases are documented in psychological research. Possible implications for decision making in organizations are examined.

KEY WORDS   decision making; risk; forecasting; managerial cognition

The thesis of this essay is that decision makers are excessively prone to treat problems as unique, neglecting both the statistics of the past and the multiple opportunities of the future. In part as a result, they are susceptible to two biases, which we label isolation errors: their forecasts of future outcomes are often anchored on plans and scenarios of success rather than on past results and are therefore overly optimistic; their evaluations of single risky prospects neglect the possibilities of pooling risks and are therefore overly timid. We argue that the balance of the two isolation errors affects the risk-taking propensities of individuals and organizations.

The cognitive analysis of risk taking that we sketch differs from the standard rational model of economics and also from managers' views of their own activities. The rational model describes business decisions as choices among gambles with financial outcomes, and assumes that managers' judgments of the odds are Bayesian, and that their choices maximize expected utility. In this model, uncontrollable risks are acknowledged and accepted because they are compensated by chances of gain. As March and Shapira (1987) reported in a well-known essay, managers reject this interpretation of their role, preferring to view risk

Reprinted by permission, "Timid Choices and Bold Forecasts: A Cognitive Perspective on Risk Taking," Daniel Kahneman and Dan Lovallo, *Management Science*, Vol. 39, No. 1, January 1993. Copyright © 1993, The Institute of Management Sciences (INFORMS), 2 Charles Street, Suite 300, Providence, RI 02904, USA.

as a challenge to be overcome by the exercise of skill and choice as a commitment to a goal. Although managers do not deny the possibility of failure, their idealized self-image is not a gambler but a prudent and determined agent, who is in control of both people and events.

The cognitive analysis accepts choice between gambles as a model of decision making, but does not adopt rationality as a maintained hypothesis. The gambling metaphor is apt because the consequences of most decisions are uncertain, and because each option could in principle be described as a probability distribution over outcomes. However, rather than suppose that decision makers are Bayesian forecasters and optimal gamblers, we shall describe them as subject to the conflicting biases of unjustified optimism and unreasonable risk aversion. It is the optimistic denial of uncontrollable uncertainty that accounts for managers' views of themselves as prudent risk takers, and for their rejection of gambling as a model of what they do.

Our essay develops this analysis of forecasting and choice and explores its implications for organizational decisions. The target domain for applications includes choices about potentially attractive options that decision makers consider significant and to which they are willing to devote forecasting and planning resources. Examples may be capital investment projects, new products, or acquisitions. For reasons that will become obvious, our critique of excessive risk aversion is most likely to apply to decisions of intermediate size: large enough to matter for the organization, but not so large as to be truly unique, or potentially fatal. Of course, such decisions could be perceived as both unique and potentially fatal by the executive who makes them. Two other restrictions on the present treatment should be mentioned at the outset. First, we do not deal with decisions that the organization explicitly treats as routinely repeated. Opportunities for learning and for statistical aggregation exist when closely similar problems are frequently encountered, especially if the outcomes of decisions are quickly known and provide unequivocal feedback; competent management will ensure that these opportunities are exploited. Second, we do not deal with decisions made under severely adverse conditions, when all options are undesirable. These are situations in which high-risk gambles are often preferred to the acceptance of sure losses (Kahneman and Tversky 1979a), and in which commitments often escalate and sunk costs dominate decisions (Staw and Ross 1989). We restrict the treatment to choices among options that can be considered attractive, although risky. For this class of projects we predict that there will be a general tendency to underestimate actual risks, and a general reluctance to accept significant risks once they are acknowledged.

TIMID CHOICES

We begin by reviewing three hypotheses about individual preferences for risky prospects.

Risk Aversion. The first hypothesis is a commonplace: most people are generally risk averse, normally preferring a sure thing to a gamble of equal expected value, and a gamble of low variance over a riskier prospect. There are two important exceptions to risk aversion. First, many people are willing to pay more for lottery tickets than their expected value. Second, studies of individual choice have shown that managers, like other people, are risk-seeking in the domain of losses (Bateman and Zeithaml 1989, Fishburn and Kochenberger 1979, Laughhunn et al. 1980).[1] Except for these cases, and for the behavior of addictive gamblers, risk aversion is prevalent in choices between favorable prospects with known probabilities. This result has been confirmed in numerous studies, including some in which the subjects were executives (MacCrimmon and Wehrung 1986, Swalm 1966).[2]

The standard interpretation of risk aversion is decreasing marginal utility of gains. Prospect theory (Kahneman and Tversky 1979a; Tversky and Kahneman 1986, 1992) introduced two other causes: the certainty effect and loss aversion. The certainty effect is a sharp discrepancy between the weights that are attached to sure gains and to highly probable gains in the evaluation of prospects. In a recent study of preferences for gambles the decision weight for a probability of 0.95 was approximately 0.80 (Tversky and Kahneman 1992). Loss aversion refers to the observation that losses and disadvantages are weighted more than gains and advantages. Loss aversion affects decision making in numerous ways, in riskless as well as in risky contexts. It favors inaction over action and the status quo over any alternatives, because the disadvantages of these alternatives are evaluated as losses and are therefore weighted more than their advantages (Kahneman et al. 1991, Samuelson and Zeckhauser 1988, Tversky and Kahneman 1991). Loss aversion strongly favors the avoidance of risks. The coefficient of loss aversion was estimated as about 2 in the Tversky-Kahneman experiment, and coefficients in the range of 2 to 2.5 have been observed in several studies, with both risky and riskless prospects (for reviews, see Kahneman, Knetsch and Thaler 1991; Tversky and Kahneman 1991).

Near-Proportionality. A second important generalization about risk attitudes is that, to a good first approximation, people are proportionately risk averse: cash equivalents for gambles of increasing size are (not quite) proportional to the stakes. Readers may find it instructive to work out their cash equivalent for a 0.50 chance to win $100, then $1,000, and up to $100,000. Most readers will find that their cash equivalent increases by a

---

[1] Observed correlations between accounting variability and mean return have also been interpreted as evidence of risk-seeking by unsuccessful firms (Bowman 1982, Fiegenbaum 1990, Fiegenbaum and Thomas 1988), but this interpretation is controversial (Ruefli 1990).

[2] A possible exception is a study by Wehrung (1989), which reported risk-neutral preferences for favorable prospects in a sample of executives in oil companies.

factor of less than 1,000 over that range, but most will also find that the factor is more than 700. Exact proportionality for wholly positive prospects would imply that value is a power function, $u(x) = x^a$, where x is the amount of gain (Keeney and Raiffa 1976). In a recent study of preferences for gambles (Tversky and Kahneman 1992), a power function provided a good approximation to the data over almost two orders of magnitude, and the deviations were systematic: cash equivalents increased slightly more slowly than prizes.

Much earlier, Swalm (1966) had compared executives whose planning horizons, defined as twice the maximum amount they might recommend be spent in one year, ranged from $50,000 to $24,000,000. He measured their utility functions by testing the acceptability of mixed gambles, and observed that the functions of managers at different levels were quite similar when expressed relative to their planning horizons. The point on which we focus in this article is that there is almost as much risk aversion when stakes are small as when they are large. This is unreasonable on two grounds: (i) small gambles do not raise issues of survival or ruin, which provide a rationale for aversion to large risks; (ii) small gambles are usually more common, offering more opportunities for the risk-reducing effects of statistical aggregation.

Narrow Decision Frames. The third generalization is that people tend to consider decision problems one at a time, often isolating the current problem from other choices that may be pending, as well as from future opportunities to make similar decisions. The following example (from Tversky and Kahneman 1986) illustrates an extreme form of narrow framing:

Imagine that you face the following pair of concurrent decisions. First examine both decisions, then indicate the options you prefer.

Decision (i) Choose between:
(A) a sure gain of $240 (84%)
(B) 25% chance to gain $1000 and 75% chance to gain nothing (16%)

Decision (ii) Choose between:
(C) a sure loss of $750 (13%)
(D) 75% chance to lose $1000 and 25% chance to lose nothing (87%)

The percentage of respondents choosing each option is shown in parentheses. As many readers may have discovered for themselves, the suggestion that the two problems should be considered concurrently has no effect on preferences, which exhibit the common pattern of risk aversion when options are favorable, and risk seeking when options are aversive. Most respondents prefer the conjunction of options A & D over other combinations of options. These preferences are intuitively compelling, and there is no obvious reason to suspect that they could lead to trouble. However, simple arithmetic shows that the conjunction of preferred options A & D is dominated by the conjunction of rejected options B & C. The combined options are as follows:

A & D: 25% chance to win $240 and 75% chance to lose $760,
B & C: 25% chance to win $250 and 75% chance to lose $750.

A decision maker who is risk averse in some situations and risk seeking in others ends up paying a premium to avoid some risks and a premium to obtain others. Because the outcomes are ultimately combined, these payments may be unsound. For a more realistic example, consider two divisions of a company that face separate decision problems.[3] One is in bad posture and faces a choice between a sure loss and a high probability of a larger loss; the other division faces a favorable choice. The natural bent of intuition will favor a risk-seeking solution for one and a risk-averse choice for the other, but the conjunction could be poor policy. The overall interests of the company are better served by aggregating the problems than by segregating them, and by a policy that is generally more risk-neutral than intuitive preferences.

People often express different preferences when considering a single play or multiple plays of the same gamble. In a well-known problem devised by Samuelson (1963), many respondents state that they would reject a single play of a gamble in which they have equal chances to win $200 or to lose $100, but would accept multiple plays of that gamble, especially when the compound distribution of outcomes is made explicit (Redelmeier and Tversky 1992). The question of whether this pattern of preferences is consistent with utility theory, and with particular utility functions for wealth has been discussed on several occasions (e.g., Lopes 1981, Tversky and Bar-Hillel 1983). The argument that emerges from these discussions can be summarized as "If you wish to obey the axioms of utility theory and would accept multiple plays, then it is logically inconsistent for you to turn down a single play." We focus on another observation: the near-certainty that the individual who is now offered a single play of the Samuelson gamble is not really facing her last opportunity to accept or reject a gamble of positive expected value. This suggests a slightly different argument: "If you would accept multiple plays, then you should accept the single one that is offered now, because it is very probable that other bets of the same kind will be offered to you later." A frame that includes future opportunities reduces the difference between the two versions of Samuelson's problem, because a rational individual who is offered a single gamble will adopt a policy for $m + 1$ such gambles, where m is the number of similar opportunities expected within the planning horizon. Will people spontaneously adopt such a broad frame? A plausible hypothesis, supported by the evidence for narrow framing in concurrent decisions and by the pattern of answers to Samuelson's problems, is that

---

[3] We are endebted to Amos Tversky for this example.

expectations about risky opportunities of the future are simply ignored when decisions are made.

It is generally recognized that a broad view of decision problems is an essential requirement of rational decision making. There are several ways of broadening the decision frame. Thus, decision analysts commonly prescribe that concurrent choices should be aggregated before a decision is made, and that outcomes should be evaluated in terms of final assets (wealth), rather than in terms of the gains and losses associated with each move. The recommended practice is to include estimates of future earnings in the assessment of wealth. Although this point has attracted little attention in the decision literature, the wealth of an agent or organization therefore includes future risky choices, and depends on the decisions that the decision maker anticipates making when these choices arise.[4] The decision frame should be broadened to include these uncertainties: neglect of future risky opportunities will lead to decisions that are not optimal, as evaluated by the agent's own utility function. As we show next, the costs of neglecting future opportunities are especially severe when options are evaluated in terms of gains and losses, which is what people usually do.

The Costs of Isolation

The present section explores some consequences of incorporating future choice opportunities into current decisions. We start from an idealized utility function which explains people's proportional risk preferences for single gambles. We then compute the preferences that this function implies when the horizon expands to include a portfolio of gambles.

Consider an individual who evaluates outcomes as gains and losses, and who maximizes expected utility in these terms. This decision maker is risk-averse in the domain of gains, risk-seeking in the domain of losses, loss-averse, and her risky choices exhibit perfect proportionality. She is indifferent between a 0.50 chance to win $1,000 and a sure gain of $300 (also between 0.50 chance to win $10,000 and $3,000 for sure) and she is also indifferent between the status quo and a gamble that offers equal chances to win $250 or to lose $100. The aversion to risk exhibited by this individual is above the median of respondents in laboratory studies but well within the range of observed values. For the sake of simple exposition we ignore all probability distortions and attribute the risk preferences of the individual entirely to the shape of her utility function for gains and losses. The preferences we have assumed imply that the individual's utility for gains is described by a power function with an exponent of 0.575 and that the function in the domain of losses is the mirror image of the function for gains,

---

[4] Two agents that have the same current holdings and face the same series of risky choices do not have the same wealth if they have different attitudes to risk and expect to make different decisions. For formal discussions of choice in the presence of unresolved uncertainty, see Kreps (1988) and Spence and Zeckhauser (1972).

after expansion of the *X*-axis by a factor of 2.5 (Tversky and Kahneman 1991). The illustrative function was chosen to highlight our main conclusion: with proportional risk attitudes, even the most extreme risk aversion on individual problems quickly vanishes when gambles are considered part of a portfolio.

The power utility function is decreasingly risk averse, and the decrease is quite rapid. Thus, a proportionately risk averse individual who values a 0.50 chance to win $100 at $30 will value a gamble that offers equal chances to win either $1,000 or $1,100 at $1,049. This preference is intuitively acceptable, indicating again that the power function is a good description of the utility of outcomes for single gambles considered in isolation. The power function fits the psychophysical relation of subjective magnitude to physical magnitude in many other contexts (Stevens 1975).

To appreciate the effects of even modest aggregation with this utility function, assume that the individual owns three independent gambles:

one gamble with a 0.50 chance to win $500,
two gambles, each with a 0.50 chance to win $250.

Simple arithmetic yields the compound gamble:

0.125 chance to win $1,000, and 0.25 to win $750, $500, and $250.

If this individual applies the correct probabilities to her utility function, this portfolio will be worth $433 to her. This should be her minimum selling price if she owns the gamble, her cash equivalent if she has to choose between the portfolio of gambles and cash. In contrast, the sum of the cash equivalents of the gambles considered one at a time is only $300. The certainty premium the individual would pay has dropped from 40% to 13% of expected value. By the individual's own utility function, the cost of considering these gambles in isolation is 27% of their expected value, surely more than any rational decision maker should be willing to pay for whatever mental economy this isolation achieves.

The power of aggregation to overcome loss aversion is equally impressive. As already noted, our decision maker is indifferent between accepting or rejecting a gamble that offers a 0.50 chance to win $250 and a 0.50 chance to lose $100. However, she would value the opportunity to play two of these gambles at $45, and six gambles at $304. Note that the average incremental value of adding the third to the sixth gamble is $65, quite close to the EV of $75, although each gamble is worth nothing on its own.

Finally, we note that decisions about single gambles will no longer appear risk-proportional when gambles are evaluated in the context of a portfolio, even if the utility function has that property. Suppose the individual now owns a set of eleven gambles:

one gamble with a 0.50 chance to win $1,000,
ten gambles, each with a 0.50 chance to win $100.

The expected value of the set is $1,000. If the gambles were considered one at a time, the sum of their cash equivalents would be only $600. With proper aggregation, however, the selling price for the package should be $934. Now suppose the decision maker considers trading only one of the gambles. After selling a gamble for an amount X, she retains a reduced compound gamble in which the constant X is added to each outcome. The decision maker, of course, will only sell if the value of the new gamble is at least equal to the value of the original portfolio. The computed selling price for the larger gamble is $440, and the selling price for one of the smaller gambles is $49. Note that the premium given up to avoid the risk is 12% of expected value for the large gamble, but only 2% for the small one. A rational decision maker who applies a proportionately risk averse utility function to aggregate outcomes will set cash equivalents closer to risk neutrality for small gambles than for large ones.

As these elementary examples illustrate, the common attitude of strong (and proportional) aversion to risk and to losses entails a risk policy that quickly approaches neutrality as the portfolio is extended.[5] Because possibilities of aggregation over future decisions always exist for an ongoing concern, and because the chances for aggregation are likely to be inversely correlated with the size of the problem, the near-proportionality of risk attitudes for gambles of varying sizes is logically incoherent, and the extreme risk aversion observed for prospects that are small relative to assets is unreasonable. To rationalize observed preferences one must assume that the decision maker approaches each choice problem as if it were her last – there seems to be no relevant tomorrow. It is somewhat surprising that the debate on the rationality of risky decisions has focused almost exclusively on the curiosities of the Allais and Ellsberg paradoxes, instead of on simpler observations, such as the extraordinary myopia implied by extreme and nearly proportional risk aversion.

Risk Taking in Organizations: Implications and Speculations

The preceding sections discussed evidence that people, when faced with explicitly probabilistic prospects in experimental situations, tend to frame their decision problem narrowly, have near-proportional risk attitudes, and are as a consequence excessively risk averse in small decisions, where they ignore the effects of aggregation. Extending these ideas to business decisions is necessarily speculative, because the attitudes to risk that are implicit in such decisions are not easily measured. One way to approach this problem is by asking whether the

---

[5] The conclusions of the present section do not critically depend on the assumption of expected utility theory, that the decision maker weights outcomes by their probabilities. All the calculations reported above were repeated using cumulative prospect theory (Tversky and Kahneman 1992) with plausible parameters ($a = 0.73; b = c = 0.6$ and a loss aversion coefficient of 2.5). Because extreme outcomes are assigned greater weight in prospect theory than in the expected utility model, the mitigation of risk aversion as the portfolio expands is somewhat slower. Additionally, the risk seeking that prospect theory predicts for single low-probability positive gambles is replaced by risk aversion for repeated gambles.

organizational context in which many business decisions are made is more likely to enhance or to inhibit risk aversion, narrow framing and near-proportionality. We examine this question in the present section.

Risk Aversion. There is little reason to believe that the factors that produce risk aversion in the personal evaluation of explicit gambles are neutralized in the context of managerial decisions. For example, attempts to measure the utility that executives attach to gains and losses of their firm suggest that the principle of decreasing marginal values applies to these outcomes (MacCrimmon and Wehrung 1986, Swalm 1966). The underweighting of probable gains in comparisons with sure ones, known as the certainty effect, is also unlikely to vanish in managerial decisions. The experimental evidence indicates that the certainty effect is not eliminated when probabilities are vague or ambiguous, as they are in most real-life situations, and the effect may even be enhanced (Curley et al. 1986, Hogarth and Einhorn 1990). We suspect that the effect may become even stronger when a choice becomes a subject of debate, as is commonly the case in managerial decisions: the rhetoric of prudent decision making favors the certainty effect, because an argument that rests on mere probability is always open to doubt.

Perhaps the most important cause of risk aversion is loss aversion, the discrepancy between the weights that are attached to losses and to gains in evaluating prospects. Loss aversion is not mitigated when decisions are made in an organizational context. On the contrary, the asymmetry between credit and blame may enhance the asymmetry between gains and losses in the decision maker's utilities. The evidence indicates that the pressures of accountability and personal responsibility increase the status quo bias and other manifestations of loss aversion. Decision makers become more risk averse when they expect their choices to be reviewed by others (Tetlock and Boettger 1991) and they are extremely reluctant to accept responsibility for even a small increase in the probability of a disaster (Viscusi et al. 1987). Swalm (1966) noted that managers appear to have an excessive aversion to any outcome that could yield a net loss, citing the example of a manager in a firm described as "an industrial giant," who would decline to pursue a project that has a 50–50 chance of either making for his company a gain of $300,000 or losing $60,000. Swalm hypothesized that the steep slopes of utility functions in the domain of losses may be due to control procedures that bias managers against choices that might lead to losses. This interpretation seems appropriate since "several respondents stated quite clearly that they were aware that their choices were not in the best interests of the company, but that they felt them to be in their own best interests as aspiring executives."

We conclude that the forces that produce risk aversion in experimental studies of individual choice may be even stronger in the managerial context. Note, however, that we do not claim that an objective observer would describe managerial decisions as generally risk averse. The second part of this essay will argue that decisions are often based on optimistic assessments of the chances of success, and are therefore objectively riskier than the decision makers perceive them to be. Our hypotheses about risk in managerial decisions are: (i) in a generally favorable context, the threshold for accepting risk will be high, and acceptable options will be *subjectively* perceived as carrying low risk, (ii) for problems viewed in isolation the willingness to take risks is likely to be approximately constant for decisions that vary greatly in size, and (iii) decisions will be narrowly framed even when they could be viewed as instances of a category of similar decisions. As a consequence, we predict (iv) an imbalance in the risks that the organization accepts in large and in small problems such that relative risk aversion is lower for the aggregate of small decisions than for the aggregate of large decisions. These hypotheses are restricted to essentially favorable situations, which often yield risk aversion in laboratory studies. We specifically exclude situations in which risk seeking is common, such as choices between essentially negative options, or choices that involve small chances of large gain.

Narrow Framing. We have suggested that people tend to make decisions one at a time, and in particular that they are prone to neglect the relevance of future decision opportunities. For both individuals and organizations, the adoption of a broader frame and of a consistent risk policy depends on two conditions: (i) an ability to group together problems that are superficially different; (ii) an appropriate procedure for evaluating outcomes and the quality of performance.

A consistent risk policy can only be maintained if the recurrent problems to which the policy applies are recognized as such. This is sometimes easy: competent organizations will identify obvious recurring questions – for example, whether or not to purchase insurance for a company vehicle – and will adopt policies for such questions. The task is more complex when each decision problem has many unique features, as might be the case for acquisitions or new product development. The explicit adoption of a broad frame will then require the use of an abstract language that highlights the important common dimensions of diverse decision problems. Formal decision analysis provides such a language, in which outcomes are expressed in money and uncertainty is quantified as probability. Other abstract languages could be used for the same purpose. As practitioners of decision analysis well know, however, the use of an abstract language conflicts with a natural tendency to describe each problem in its own terms. Abstraction necessarily involves a loss of subtlety and specificity, and the summary descriptions that permit projects to be compared almost always appear superficial and inadequate.

From the point of the individual executive who faces a succession of decisions, the maintenance of a broad decision frame also depends on how her performance will be evaluated, and on the frequency of performance reviews. For a schematic illustration, assume that reviews occur at predictable points in the sequence of decisions and outcomes, and that the executive's outcomes are determined by the *value* of the firm's outcomes since the last review. Suppose the evaluation function is identical to the utility function introduced in the preceding numerical examples: the credit for gaining 2.5 units and the blame for losing 1 unit just cancel out. With this utility function, a single gamble that offers equal probabilities to win 2 units or to lose 1 unit will not be acceptable if performance is evaluated on that gamble by itself. The decision will not change even if the manager knows that there will be a second opportunity to play the same gamble. However, if the evaluation of outcomes and the assignment of credit and blame can be deferred until the gamble has been played twice, the probability that the review will be negative drops from 0.50 to 0.25 and the compound gamble will be accepted. As this example illustrates, reducing the frequency of evaluations can mitigate the inhibiting effects of loss aversion on risk taking, as well as other manifestations of myopic discounting.

The attitude that "you win a few and you lose a few" could be recommended as an antidote to narrow framing, because it suggests that the outcomes of a set of separable decisions should be aggregated before evaluation. However, the implied tolerance for "losing a few" may conflict with other managerial imperatives, including the setting of high standards and the maintenance of tight supervision. By the same token, of course, narrow framing and excessive risk aversion may be unintended consequences of excessive insistence on measurable short-term successes. A plausible hypothesis is that the adoption of a broad frame of evaluation is most natural when the expected rate of success is low for each attempt, as in drilling for oil or in pharmaceutical development.[6] The procedures of performance evaluation that have evolved in these industries could provide a useful model for other attempts to maintain consistent risk policies.

Near Proportionality of Risk Attitudes. Many executives in a hierarchical organization have two distinct decision tasks: they make risky choices on behalf of the organization, and they supervise several subordinates who also make decisions. For analytical purposes, the options chosen by subordinates can be treated as independent (or imperfectly correlated) gambles, which usually involve smaller stakes than the decisions made personally by the superior. A problem of risk aggregation inevitably arises, and we conjecture that solving it efficiently may be quite difficult.

To begin, ignore the supervisory function and assume that all decisions are made independently, with narrow framing. If all decision makers apply the same nearly-proportional risk attitudes (as suggested by Swalm 1966), an unbalanced set of choices will be made: The aggregate of the subordinates' decisions will be more risk averse than the supervisor's own decisions on larger problems – which in turn are more risk averse than her global utility for the portfolio, rationally evaluated. As we saw in an earlier section, the costs of such inconsistencies in risk attitudes can be quite high.

---

[6] We owe this hypothesis to Richard Thaler.

Clearly, one of the goals of the executive should be to avoid the potential inefficiency by applying a consistent policy to risky choices and to those she supervises – and the consistent policy is *not* one of proportional risk aversion. As was seen earlier, a rational executive who considers a portfolio consisting of one large gamble (which she chose herself) and ten smaller gambles (presumably chosen by subordinates) should be considerably more risk averse in valuing the large gamble than in valuing any one of the smaller gambles. The counter-intuitive implication of this analysis is that, in a generally favorable context, an executive should encourage subordinates to adopt a higher level of risk-acceptance than the level with which she feels comfortable. This is necessary to overcome the costly effects of the (probable) insensitivity of her intuitive preferences to recurrence and aggregation. We suspect that many executives will resist this recommendation, which contradicts the common belief that accepting risks is both the duty and the prerogative of higher management.

For several reasons, narrow framing and near-proportionality could be difficult to avoid in a hierarchical organization. First, many decisions are both unique and large at the level at which they are initially made. The usual aversion to risk is likely to prevail in such decisions, even if from the point of view of the firm they could be categorized as recurrent and moderately small. Second, it appears unfair for a supervisor to urge acceptance of a risk that a subordinate is inclined to reject – especially because the consequences of failure are likely to be more severe for the subordinate.

In summary, we have drawn on three psychological principles to derive the prediction that the risk attitudes that govern decisions of different sizes may not be coherent. The analysis suggests that there may be too much aversion to risk in problems of small or moderate size. However, the conclusion that greater risk taking should be encouraged could be premature at this point because of the suspicion that agents' view of prospects may be systematically biased in an optimistic direction. The combination of a risk-neutral attitude and an optimistic bias could be worse than the combination of unreasonable risk aversion and unjustified optimism. As the next sections show, there is good reason to believe that such a dilemma indeed exists.

BOLD FORECASTS

Our review of research on individual risk attitudes suggests that the substantial degree of risk to which individuals and organizations willingly expose themselves is unlikely to reflect true acceptance of these risks. The alternative is that people and organizations often expose themselves to risk because they misjudge the odds. We next consider some of the mechanisms that produce the "bold forecasts" that enable cautious decision makers to take large risks.

Inside and Outside Views

We introduce this discussion by a true story, which illustrates an important cognitive quirk that tends to produce extreme optimism in planning.

In 1976 one of us (Daniel Kahneman) was involved in a project designed to develop a curriculum for the study of judgment and decision making under uncertainty for high schools in Israel. The project was conducted by a small team of academics and teachers. When the team had been in operation for about a year, with some significant achievements already to its credit, the discussion at one of the team meetings turned to the question of how long the project would take. To make the debate more useful, I asked everyone to indicate on a slip of paper their best estimate of the number of months that would be needed to bring the project to a well-defined stage of completion: a complete draft ready for submission to the Ministry of education. The estimates, including my own, ranged from 18 to 30 months. At this point I had the idea of turning to one of our members, a distinguished expert in curriculum development, asking him a question phrased about as follows: "We are surely not the only team to have tried to develop a curriculum where none existed before. Please try to recall as many such cases as you can. Think of them as they were in a stage comparable to ours at present. How long did it take them, from that point, to complete their projects?" After a long silence, something much like the following answer was given, with obvious signs of discomfort: "First, I should say that not all teams that I can think of in a comparable stage ever did complete their task. About 40% of them eventually gave up. Of the remaining, I cannot think of any that was completed in less than seven years, nor of any that took more than ten". In response to a further question, he answered: "No, I cannot think of any relevant factor that distinguishes us favorably from the teams I have been thinking about. Indeed, my impression is that we are slightly below average in terms of our resources and potential".

This story illustrates several of the themes that will be developed in this section.

Two distinct modes of forecasting were applied to the same problem in this incident. The *inside view* of the problem is the one that all participants in the meeting spontaneously adopted. An inside view forecast is generated by focusing on the case at hand, by considering the plan and the obstacles to its completion, by constructing scenarios of future progress, and by extrapolating current trends. The *outside view* is the one that the curriculum expert was encouraged to adopt. It essentially ignores the details of the case at hand, and involves no attempt at detailed forecasting of the future history of the project. Instead, it focuses on the statistics of a class of cases chosen to be similar in relevant respects to the present one. The case at hand is also compared to other members of the class, in an attempt to assess its position in the distribution of outcomes for the class (Kahneman and Tversky 1979b). The distinction between inside and outside views in forecasting is closely related to the distinction drawn earlier between narrow and broad framing of decision problems. The critical question in both contexts is whether a particular problem of forecast or decision is treated as unique, or as an instance of an ensemble of similar problems.

The application of the outside view was particularly simple in this example, because the relevant class for the problem was easy to find and to define. Other cases are more ambiguous. What class should be considered, for example, when a firm considers the probable costs of an investment in a new technology in an unfamiliar domain? Is it the class of ventures in new technologies in the recent history of this firm, or the class of developments most similar to the proposed one, carried out in other firms? Neither is perfect, and the recommendation would be to try both (Kahneman and Tversky 1979b). It may also be necessary to choose units of measurement that permit comparisons. The ratio of actual spending to planned expenditure is an example of a convenient unit that permits meaningful comparisons across diverse projects.

The inside and outside views draw on different sources of information, and apply different rules to its use. An inside view forecast draws on knowledge of the specifics of the case, the details of the plan that exists, some ideas about likely obstacles and how they might be overcome. In an extreme form, the inside view involves an attempt to sketch a representative scenario that captures the essential elements of the history of the future. In contrast, the outside view is essentially statistical and comparative, and involves no attempt to divine future history at any level of detail.

It should be obvious that when both methods are applied with equal intelligence and skill, the outside view is much more likely to yield a realistic estimate. In general, the future of a long and complex undertaking is simply not foreseeable in detail. The ensemble of possible future histories cannot be defined. Even if this could be done, the ensemble would in most cases be huge, and the probability of any particular scenario negligible.[7] Although some scenarios are more likely or plausible than others, it is a serious error to assume that the outcomes of the most likely scenarios are also the most likely, and that outcomes for which no plausible scenarios come to mind are impossible. In particular, the scenario of flawless execution of the current plan may be much more probable a priori than any scenario for a specific sequence of events that would cause the project to take four times longer than planned. Nevertheless, the less favorable outcome could be more likely overall, because there are so many different ways for things to go wrong. The main advantage of the outside approach to forecasting is that it avoids the snares of scenario thinking (Dawes 1988). The outside view provides some protection against forecasts that are not even in the ballpark of reasonable possibilities. It is a conservative approach, which will fail to predict extreme and exceptional events, but will do well with common ones. Furthermore, giving up the attempt to predict extraordinary events is not a great sacrifice when uncertainty is high, because the only way to score 'hits' on such events is to predict large numbers of other extraordinary events that do not materialize.

This discussion of the statistical merits of the outside view sets the stage for our main observation, which is psychological: the inside view is overwhelmingly preferred in intuitive forecasting. The natural way to think about a problem is to bring to bear all one knows about it, with special attention to its unique features. The intellectual detour into the statistics of related cases is seldom chosen spontaneously. Indeed, the relevance of the outside view is sometimes

---

[7] For the purposes of this exposition we assume that probabilities exist as a fact about the world. Readers who find this position shocking should transpose the formulation to a more complex one, according to their philosophical taste.

explicitly denied: physicians and lawyers often argue against the application of statistical reasoning to particular cases. In these instances, the preference for the inside view almost bears a moral character. The inside view is valued as a serious attempt to come to grips with the complexities of the unique case at hand, and the outside view is rejected for relying on crude analogy from superficially similar instances. This attitude can be costly in the coin of predictive accuracy.

Three other features of the curriculum story should be mentioned. First, the example illustrates the general rule that consensus on a forecast is not necessarily an indication of its validity: a shared deficiency of reasoning will also yield consensus. Second, we note that the initial intuitive assessment of our curriculum expert was similar to that of other members of the team. This illustrates a more general observation: statistical knowledge that is known to the forecaster will not necessarily be used, or indeed retrieved, when a forecast is made by the inside approach. The literature on the impact of the base rates of outcomes on intuitive predictions supports this conclusion. Many studies have dealt with the task of predicting the profession or the training of an individual on the basis of some personal information and relevant statistical knowledge. For example, most people have some knowledge of the relative sizes of different departments, and could use that knowledge in guessing the field of a student seen at a graduating ceremony. The experimental evidence indicates that base-rate information that is explicitly mentioned in the problem has some effect on predictions, though usually not as much as it should have (Griffin and Tversky 1992, Lynch and Ofir 1989: for an alternative view see Gigerenzer et al. 1988). When only personal information is explicitly offered, relevant statistical information that is known to the respondent is largely ignored (Kahneman and Tversky 1973, Tversky and Kahneman 1983).

The sequel to the story illustrates a third general observation: facing the facts can be intolerably demoralizing. The participants in the meeting had professional expertise in the logic of forecasting, and none even ventured to question the relevance of the forecast implied by our expert's statistics: an even chance of failure, and a completion time of seven to ten years in case of success. Neither of these outcomes was an acceptable basis for continuing the project, but no one was willing to draw the embarrassing conclusion that it should be scrapped. So, the forecast was quietly dropped from active debate, along with any pretense of long-term planning, and the project went on along its predictably unforeseeable path to eventual completion some eight years later.

The contrast between the inside and outside views has been confirmed in systematic research. One relevant set of studies was concerned with the phenomenon of overconfidence. There is massive evidence for the conclusion that people are generally overconfident in their assignments of probability to their beliefs. Overconfidence is measured by recording the proportion of cases in which statements to which an individual assigned a probability p were actually true. In many studies this proportion has been found to be far lower than p

(see Lichtenstein et al. 1982; for a more recent discussion and some instructive exceptions see Griffin and Tversky 1992). Overconfidence is often assessed by presenting general information questions in a multiple-choice format, where the participant chooses the most likely answer and assigns a probability to it. A typical result is that respondents are only correct on about 80% of cases when they describe themselves as "99% sure." People are overconfident in evaluating the accuracy of their beliefs one at a time. It is interesting, however, that there is no evidence of overconfidence bias when respondents are asked after the session to estimate the number of questions for which they picked the correct answer. These global estimates are accurate, or somewhat pessimistic (Gigerenzer et al. 1991, Griffin and Tversky 1992). It is evident that people's assessments of their overall accuracy does not control their confidence in particular beliefs. Academics are familiar with a related example: finishing our papers almost always takes us longer than we expected. We all know this and often say so. Why then do we continue to make the same error? Here again, the outside view does not inform judgments of particular cases.

In a compelling example of the contrast between inside and outside views, Cooper et al. (1988) interviewed new entrepreneurs about their chances of success, and also elicited from them estimates of the base rate of success for enterprises of the same kind. Self-assessed chances of success were uncorrelated to objective predictors of success such as college education, prior supervisory experience and initial capital. They were also wildly off the mark on average. Over 80% of entrepreneurs perceived their chances of success as 70% or better. Fully one-third of them described their success as certain. On the other hand, the mean chance of success that these entrepreneurs attributed to a business like theirs was 59%. Even this estimate is optimistic, though it is closer to the truth: the five-year survival rate for new firms is around 33% (Dun and Bradstreet 1967).

The inside view does not invariably yield optimistic forecasts. Many parents of rebellious teenagers cannot imagine how their offspring would ever become a reasonable adult, and are consequently more worried than they should be, since they also know that almost all teenagers do eventually grow up. The general point is that the inside view is susceptible to the fallacies of scenario thinking and to anchoring of estimates on present values or on extrapolations of current trends. The inside view burdens the worried parents with statistically unjustified premonitions of doom. To decision makers with a goal and a plan, the same way of thinking offers absurdly optimistic forecasts.

The cognitive mechanism we have discussed is not the only source of optimistic errors. Unrealistic optimism also has deep motivational roots (Tiger 1979). A recent literature review (Taylor and Brown 1988) listed three main forms of a pervasive optimistic bias: (i) unrealistically positive self-evaluations, (ii) unrealistic optimism about future events and plans, and (iii) an illusion of control. Thus, for almost every positive trait – including safe driving, a sense of humor, and managerial risk taking (MacCrimmon and Wehrung 1986) – there is a large majority of individuals who believe themselves to be above the median. People also exaggerate their control over events, and the importance of the skills and resources they possess in ensuring desirable outcomes. Most of us underestimate the likelihood of hazards affecting us personally, and entertain the unlikely belief that Taylor and Brown summarize as "The future will be great, especially for me."

Organizational Optimism

There is no reason to believe that entrepreneurs and executives are immune to optimistic bias. The prevalence of delusions of control among managers has been recognized by many authors (among others, Duhaime and Schwenk 1985, March and Shapira 1987, Salancik and Meindl 1984). As we noted earlier, managers commonly view risk as a challenge to be overcome, and believe that risk can be modified by "managerial wisdom and skill" (Donaldson and Lorsch 1983). The common refusal of managers to refuse risk estimates provided to them as "given" (Shapira 1986) is a clear illustration of illusion of control.

Do organizations provide effective controls against the optimistic bias of individual executives? Are organizational decisions founded on impartial and unbiased forecasts of consequences? In answering these questions, we must again distinguish problems that are treated as recurrent, such as forecasts of the sales of existing product lines, from others that are considered unique. We have no reason to doubt the ability of organizations to impose forecasting discipline and to reduce or eliminate obvious biases in recurrent problems. As in the case of risk, however, all significant forecasting problems have features that make them appear unique. It is in these unique problems that biases of judgment and choice are most likely to have their effects, for organizations as well as for individuals. We next discuss some likely causes of optimistic bias in organizational judgments, some observations of this bias, and the costs and benefits of unrealistic optimism.

Causes. Forecasts often develop as part of a case that is made by an individual or group that already has, or is developing a vested interest in the plan, in a context of competition for the control of organizational resources. The debate is often adversarial. The only projects that have a good chance of surviving in this competition are those for which highly favorable outcomes are forecast, and this produces a powerful incentive for would-be promoters to present optimistic numbers. The statistical logic that produces the winner's curse in other contexts (Capen, Clapp and Campbell 1971; Bazerman and Samuelson 1983; Kagel and Levin 1986) applies here as well: the winning project is more likely than others to be associated with optimistic errors (Harrison and March 1984). This is an effect of regression to the mean. Thus, the student who did best in an initial test is also the one for whom the most regression is expected on a subsequent test. Similarly, the projects that are forecast to have the highest returns are the ones most likely to fall short of expectations.

Officially adopted forecasts are also likely to be biased by their secondary functions as demands, commands and commitments (Lowe and Shaw 1968,

Lawler and Rhode 1976, Lawler 1986, Larkey and Smith 1984). A forecast readily becomes a target, which induces loss aversion for performance that does not match expectations, and can also induce satisfying indolence when the target is exceeded. The obvious advantages of setting high goals is an incentive for higher management to adopt and disseminate optimistic assessments of future accomplishments – and possibly to deceive themselves in the process.

In his analysis of "groupthink," Janis (1982) identified other factors that favor organizational optimism. Pessimism about what the organization can do is readily interpreted as disloyalty, and consistent bearers of bad news tend to be shunned. Bad news can be demoralizing. When pessimistic opinions are suppressed in this manner, exchanges of views will fail to perform a critical function. The optimistic biases of individual group members can become mutually reinforcing, as unrealistic views are validated by group approval.

The conclusion of this sketchy analysis is that there is little reason to believe organizations will avoid the optimistic bias – except perhaps when the problems are considered recurrent and subjected to statistical quality control. On the contrary, there are reasons to suspect that many significant decisions made in organizations are guided by unrealistic forecasts of their consequences.

Observations. The optimistic bias of capital investment projects is a familiar fact of life: the typical project finishes late, comes in over budget when it is finally completed, and fails to achieve its initial goals. Grossly optimistic errors appear to be especially likely if the project involves new technology or otherwise places the firm in unfamiliar territory. A Rand Corporation study on pioneer process plants in the energy field demonstrates the magnitude of the problem (Merrow et al. 1981). Almost all project construction costs exceeded initial estimates by over 20%. The norm was for actual construction costs to more than double first estimates. These conclusions are corroborated by PIMS data on start-up ventures in a wide range of industries (cited by Davis 1985). More than 80% of the projects studied fell short of planned market share.

In an interesting discussion of the causes of failure in capital investment projects, Arnold (1986) states:

Most companies support large capital expenditure programs with a worst case analysis that examines the projects' loss potential. But the worst case forecast is almost always too optimistic. . . . When managers look at the downside they generally describe a mildly pessimistic future rather than the worst possible future.

As an antidote against rosy predictions Arnold recommends staying power analysis, a method used by lenders to determine if organizations under severe strain can make payments. In effect, the advice is for managers to adopt an outside view of their own problem.

Mergers and acquisitions provide another illustration of optimism and of illusions of control. On average, bidding firms do not make a significantly positive return. This striking observation raises the question of why so many takeovers and mergers are initiated. Roll (1986) offers a "hubris hypothesis" to explain why decision makers acquiring firms tend to pay too much for their targets. Roll cites optimistic estimates of "economies due to synergy and (any) assessments of weak management" as the primary causes of managerial hubris. The bidding firms are prone to overestimate the control they will have over the merged organization, and to underestimate the "weak" managers who are currently in charge.

Costs and Benefits. Optimism and the illusion of control increase risk taking in several ways. In a discussion of the Challenger disaster, Landau and Chisholm (1990) introduced a "law of increasing optimism" as a form of Russian roulette. Drawing on the same case, Starbuck and Milliken (1988) noted how quickly vigilance dissipates with repeated successes. Optimism in a competitive context may take the form of contempt for the capabilities of opponents (Roll 1986). In a bargaining situation, it will support a hard line that raises the risk of conflict. Neale and Bazerman (1983) observed a related effect in a final-offer arbitration setup, where the arbiter is constrained to choose between the final offers made by the contestants. The participants were asked to state their subjective probability that the final offer they presented would be preferred by the arbiter. The average of these probabilities was approximately 0.70; with a less sanguine view of the strength of their case the contestants would surely have made more concessions. In the context of capital investment decisions, optimism and the illusion of control manifest themselves in unrealistic forecasts and unrealizable plans (Arnold 1986).

Given the high cost of mistakes, it might appear obvious that a rational organization should want to base its decisions on unbiased odds, rather than on predictions painted in shades of rose. However, realism has its costs. In their review of the consequences of optimism and pessimism, Taylor and Brown (1988) reached the deeply disturbing conclusion that optimistic self-delusion is both a diagnostic indication of mental health and well-being, and a positive causal factor that contributes to successful coping with the challenges of life. The benefits of unrealistic optimism in increasing persistence in the face of difficulty have been documented by other investigators (Seligman 1991).

The observation that realism can be pathological and self-defeating raises troubling questions for the management of information and risk in organizations. Surely, no one would want to be governed entirely by wishful fantasies, but is there a point at which truth becomes destructive and doubt self-fulfilling? Should executives allow or even encourage unrealistic optimism among their subordinates? Should they willingly allow themselves to be caught up in productive enthusiasm, and to ignore discouraging portents? Should there be someone in the organization whose function it is to achieve forecasts free of optimistic bias, although such forecasts, if disseminated, would be demoralizing? Should the organization maintain two sets of forecasting books (as some do, see Bromiley 1986)? Some authors in the field of strategy have questioned the value of realism, at least implicitly. Weick's famous story of the lost platoon that finds its way in the Alps by consulting a map of the Pyrenees indicates more respect for confidence and morale than for realistic appraisal. On the other hand, Landau and Chisholm (1990) pour withering scorn on the "arrogance of optimism" in organizations, and recommend a pessimistic failure-avoiding management strategy to control risk. Before further progress can be made on this difficult issue, it is important to recognize the existence of a genuine dilemma that will not yield to any simple rule.

CONCLUDING REMARKS

Our analysis has suggested that many failures originate in the highly optimistic judgments of risks and opportunities that we label bold forecasts. In the words of March and Shapira (1987), "managers accept risks, in part, because they do not expect that they will have to bear them." March and Shapira emphasized the role of illusions of control in this bias. We have focused on another mechanism – the adoption of an inside view of problems, which leads to anchoring on plans and on the most available scenarios. We suggest that errors of intuitive prediction can sometimes be reduced by adopting an outside view, which forecasts the outcome without attempting to forecast its history (Kahneman and Tversky 1979b). This analysis identifies the strong intuitive preference for the inside view as a source of difficulties that are both grave and avoidable.

On the issue of risk we presented evidence that decision makers tend to deal with choices one at a time, and that their attitudes to risk exhibit risk-aversion and near-proportionality. The reluctance to take explicit responsibility for possible losses is powerful and can be very costly in the aggregate (for a discussion of its social costs see Wildavsky 1988). We claimed further that when the stakes are small or moderate relative to assets the aversion to risk is incoherent and substantively unjustified. Here again, the preference for treating decision problems as unique causes errors that could be avoided by a broader view.

Our analysis implies that the adoption of an outside view, in which the problem at hand is treated as an instance of a broader category, will generally reduce the optimistic bias and may facilitate the application of a consistent risk policy. This happens as a matter of course in problems of forecasting or decision that the organization recognizes as obviously recurrent or repetitive. However, we have suggested that people are strongly biased in favor of the inside view, and that they will normally treat significant decision problems as unique even when information that could support an outside view is available. The adoption of an outside view in such cases violates strong intuitions about the relevance of information. Indeed, the deliberate neglect of the features that make the current problem unique can appear irresponsible. A deliberate effort will therefore be required to foster the optimal use of outside and inside views in forecasting, and the maintenance of globally consistent risk attitudes in distributed decision systems.

Bold forecasts and timid attitudes to risk tend to have opposite effects. It would be fortunate if they canceled out precisely to yield optimal behavior in every situation, but there is little reason to expect such a perfect outcome. The conjunction of biases is less disastrous than either one would have been on its own, but there ought to be a better way to control choice under risk than pitting two mistakes against each other. The prescriptive implications of the relation between the biases in forecast and in risk taking is that corrective attempts should deal with these biases simultaneously. Increasing risk taking could easily go too far in the presence of optimistic forecasts, and a successful effort to improve the realism of assessments could do more harm than good in an organization that relies on unfounded optimism to ward off paralysis.[8]

[8] An earlier version of this paper was presented at a conference on Fundamental Issues in Strategy, held at Silverado, CA, in November 1990. The preparation of this article was supported by the Center for Management Research at the University of California, Berkeley, by the Russell Sage Foundation, and by grants from the Sloan Foundation and from AFOSR, under grant number 88-0206. The ideas presented here developed over years of collaboration with Amos Tversky, but he should not be held responsible for our errors. We thank Philip Bromiley, Colin Camerer, George Loewenstein, Richard Thaler, and Amos Tversky for their many helpful comments.

23. Overconfidence and Excess Entry
An Experimental Approach

Colin F. Camerer and Dan Lovallo

INTRODUCTION

Psychological studies demonstrate that most individuals are overconfident about their own abilities, compared with others, as well as unreasonably optimistic about their futures (e.g., Taylor and Brown 1988, Weinstein 1980). When assessing their position in a distribution of peers on almost any positive trait such as driving ability or income prospects, 90% of people say they are in the top half (see Svenson 1981). Few people say they are below average, although half must be.[1]

This paper explores one setting in which optimistic biases could plausibly and predictably influence economic behavior: entry into competitive games or markets. Many empirical studies show that most new businesses fail within a few years. For example, using plant level data from the U.S. Census of Manufacturers spanning 1963–1982, Dunne, Roberts, and Samuelson (1988) estimated that 61.5% of all entrants exited within 5 years and 79.6% exited within 10 years. Most of these exits are failures (see also Dunne, Roberts, and Samuelson 1988, 1989a, Shapiro and Khemani 1987).

There are many possible explanations for the high rate of business failure (reviewed below). In this paper we consider the hypothesis that business failure is a result of managers acting on the optimism about relative skill they exhibit in surveys. This hypothesis is worth exploring because it is consistent with so much psychological evidence, and optimistic overentry will persist if the

[1] There are interesting exceptions. For many traits, women are not optimistic (and even pessimistic; e.g., Maccoby and Jacklin 1974), and clinically depressed patients are not optimistic (e.g., Alloy and Ahrens 1987). The latter finding calls into question the common psychiatric presumption that "realistic" people are well-adjusted and happy and also raises the question of whether optimism might be evolutionarily adaptive (e.g., Tiger 1979). Waldman (1994) shows how such optimism could be evolutionarily stable and also mentions conditions under which gender differences could arise.

This is an abridged version of a paper by the same name in the American Economic Review (1999). Help and comments were received from Daniel Kahneman, Marc Knez, Matthew Rabin, David Teece, Dick Thaler, participants at the MacArthur Foundation Preferences Group, the 1995 J/DM Society, workshops at the Universities of Chicago and Colorado, UCLA, Harvard Business School, and Wharton, and several anonymous referees. Gail Nash provided superb secretarial help and Roberto Weber provided research assistance. The research was funded by NSF SBR 95-11001.

performance feedback necessary to correct it is relatively noisy, infrequent, or slow.

The idea that overconfidence causes business entry mistakes has, of course, been suggested before (e.g., Roll 1986) but has not been tested directly by comparing economic decisions and personal overconfidence simultaneously. To link the two we created an experimental setting with basic features of business entry situations. In the experiments, the success of entering subjects depends on their relative skill (compared with other entrants). Most subjects who enter expect the total profit earned by all entrants to be negative but think their own profit will be positive. The findings are consistent with the prediction that overconfidence leads to excessive business entry.

The experiments also extend a paradigm in which business entry and other skill-based competitions (e.g., labor market tournaments) could be studied further. The paradigm is a useful step because it includes two features that many psychological studies lack: (1) financial incentives for judging one's skill accurately, and (2) a clear definition of the skill one is judging.[2]

Of course, experimental data are hardly conclusive evidence that overconfidence plays a role in actual entry decisions by firms. A bigger scientific payoff comes when experimental observations suggest a new phenomenon that might be studied in the field. Our data suggest a new phenomenon we call "reference group neglect". Excess entry is much larger when subjects volunteered to participate knowing that payoffs would depend on skill. These self-selected subjects seem to neglect the fact that they are competing with a reference group of subjects who all think they are skilled too. (Neglecting the increased level of competition is like the neglect of adverse selection, which leads to the "winner's curse" in bidding.)

Possible Explanations for Entrant Failure

There are three primary explanations for the frequency of entrant failure. The first explanation is that failures are frequent because entrants have only brief opportunities to make money. In this view, failures are actually hit-and-run entries that are profitable but brief.

A second explanation is that business entries are expensive lottery tickets with positively skewed returns; thus, although most firms expect to lose money and fail, entry still maximizes expected profits because the payoffs to success are very large. Two variants of this argument are notable. If small-business owners are risk-preferring or get psychic income from running businesses, the expected utility from entering may be high even if the expected profit is low. In addition, it is well-known from multiarmed bandit problems that, when one samples from distributions of possible payoffs (such as career paths or profitable industries),

---

[2] Earlier studies showed that overconfidence is smaller when traits are defined unambiguously, that is, "driving ability" is more ambiguous than "ability to brake quickly to avoid an accident" (Dunning, Meyerowitz, and Holzberg 1989).

it may pay to sample from "arms" with negative expected payoffs if the possible payoffs from those arms is large (because sampling provides information about which arms to choose or avoid in the future).

The third explanation is that many entry decisions are mistakes made by boundedly rational decision makers. Firms could mistakenly enter too often for two different reasons: they know their own skills but fail to appreciate how many competitors there will be (they have "competitive blind spots"), or they forecast competition accurately but overconfidently think their firm will succeed while most others will fail.

In a natural setting it is very difficult to distinguish between these three explanations for high failure rates. The overconfidence explanation is particularly hard to establish because it predicts that firms will enter even if they expect negative industry profits. But even if cumulative industry profits are actually negative at some point t, it is possible positive returns will roll in after t (or the industry simply made a large unpredictable forecasting mistake). Thus it is hard to imagine how to establish conclusively that expected industry returns were negative.

Although more field research is surely worthwhile, some progress may be made in the laboratory. In an experiment, everything needed to distinguish the three theories – entry decisions, forecasts of industry profits, and forecasts of the number of total entrants – can be measured. If subjects forecast positive industry profits and enter, the rational-entry theories appear correct. If subjects forecast positive industry profits, but they underestimate the amount of entry and industry profit is actually negative, the blind spots story appears correct. If subjects accurately forecast negative industry profits, and enter anyway, then the overconfidence explanation appears correct.

EXPERIMENTAL DESIGN

Our experiments extend a paradigm first used by Kahneman (1988) and Brander and Thaler and then explored more throughly by Rapoport and colleagues. In their game, N players choose simultaneously, and without communicating, whether to enter a market or not. The market "capacity" is a pre-announced number c. If players stay out, they earn a payment K. If the total number of entrants is E, the entrants each earn $K + rK(c - E)$ (with $rK > 0$). The optimal behavior is simple: Players want to enter only if the number of expected entrants (including themselves) is less than the capacity c. If they do enter, players prefer the number of entrants to be as small as possible. The interesting questions are whether the right number of players enter (is E around c?), whether E changes with c, and how players figure out whether to enter or not.

Kahneman (1988) was surprised to see that the number of entrants E was typically in the range $[c - 2, c + 2]$ even though subjects could not communicate or coordinate their decisions in any explicit way. "To a psychologist", he wrote, "it looks like magic". Rapoport (1995) replicated the results using doctoral students playing for much larger stakes. He also found that subjects entered a bit too frequently at first, but gradually E converged very close to c. E and c were highly correlated across trials. Other extensions were conducted by Sundali, Rapoport, and Seale (1995) and Rapoport et al. (1998), who basically duplicated the earlier findings.

Our experiments extend this paradigm in four ways: payoffs in some periods depend on a subject's rank (relative to other entrants); ranks depend on either a chance device or on a subject's skill; subjects in some experiments are told in advance that the experiment depends on skill (and hence, presumably more skilled subjects self-select in); and subjects forecast the number of entrants in each period.

Skill is the crucial new design feature. The early experiments capture an important aspect of entry, tacit coordination among potential entrants to avoid excess entry, but all entrants earned the same amount. In naturally occurring settings, some entrants win and others lose owing at least partly to differences in managerial skill (see MacCrimmon and Wehrung 1986).

Payoffs depend on a subject's rank and on the market capacity c. The top c entrants share \$50 proportionally, and higher-ranking entrants earning more. (The entrant with rank r earns $\$50(c+1-r)/(1+2+\cdots c)$.) All entrants ranking below the top c lose \$10. For example, if the market capacity is $c=2$, then the highest ranked entrant receives \$33, the second highest ranked entrant receives \$17, and any lower-ranked entrant loses \$10. (Subjects are staked \$10 initially.) Notice that if the number of entrants is exactly $c+5$, then the total payoff to all entering subjects ("industry profit") is zero; if there are more than $c+5$ entrants, the average entrant loses money.

Actual ranks are assigned in two different ways. Each subject is ranked by a random drawing and also ranked according to his or her relative performance on a skill or trivia task. Skill ranks are determined by how many questions subjects answer correctly on a sample of 10 "brain teaser" puzzles (sessions 1–2) or trivia questions about sports or current events (sessions 3–8). It is important to stress that subjects' ranks were not determined until the end of the experiment *after* they made all their entry decisions.

In each experimental session, subjects were recruited using either standard recruiting instructions or self-selection instructions explaining that skill in sports or current events trivia would affect their payoff. (They were also reminded during the experiment that other subjects were recruited this way.) After instructions, subjects were shown examples of the skill questions along with sample answers. Subjects then made entry decisions in 2 sequences of 12 rounds for each condition – one sequence for the random rank and another for the skill rank counterbalanced in order across sessions. In each sequence the values of c were 2, 4, 6, or 8; the order of c values varied across sessions.

In each round subjects privately forecast how many entrants they expected would enter (including themselves) in the round and were paid \$.25 for each correct forecast. Subjects then made their entry decisions privately and simultaneously. After each round, they were told how many subjects had entered, but *they were not told their rank*.

At the end of the experimental session, after all of the rounds in both conditions were played, subjects either solved puzzles (sessions 1–2) or took the trivia quiz (sessions 3–8). Then one of the subjects randomly chose a round, and subjects' earnings from that round were computed and paid.

It is important to reiterate that the only feedback subjects got throughout the session of 24 rounds was the total number of entrants per round. This design was chosen to model initial entry behavior by firms that do not learn much about their competitive advantage until after they incur substantial nonsalvageable fixed costs. The question of how postentry feedback about performance impacts subsequent behavior is interesting, of course; it is certainly likely that overconfidence would be diminished if subjects were given a separate skill test and told their ranks after each round. But it is natural to begin by establishing whether overconfidence is present in the first place before turning to the question of what forces make it go away.

The procedures described above were used in eight sessions. Sessions 1–4 used regular recruiting, and sessions 5–8 allowed self-selection. Subjects were undergraduates and MBAs at the Universities of Chicago and Pennsylvania. (There were no significant effects of subject pool.)

Equilibrium Predictions

If risk neutrality is assumed, there are many pure-strategy Nash equilibria in which $c + 4$ or $c + 5$ subjects enter (the fifth subject is indifferent because he or she expects to earn zero from entering). Because the pure-strategy equilibria are necessarily asymmetric, it is hard to see how they might arise without communication or some coordinating device, like history, sequential moves, or public labels distinguishing subjects. There is also a unique symmetric mixed-strategy equilibrium in which (risk-neutral) players enter with a probability close to $(c + 5)/N$.

If we relax the assumption of risk neutrality, there is no way to determine the equilibrium number of entrants without measuring or making specific assumptions about subjects' risk preferences.[3] The random-rank condition gives an empirical estimate of observed equilibrium without having to impose any a priori assumption about risk preferences. Because each subject participates in both random- and skill-rank conditions, their decisions in the random-rank condition act as a within-subject control for risk preferences. Thus, the *difference*

---

[3] An alternative is to try to induce risk neutrality (or some other specific degree of risk aversion) by paying subjects in units of probability using lottery tickets as payoffs instead of money (see Berg et al. 1986). We chose to use the random-rank condition instead because it is simpler and as theoretically valid as the lottery-ticket procedure, and the lottery-ticket procedure does not work reliably (e.g., Selten, Sadrieh, and Abbink 1995).

Table 23.1. Average Industry Profit by Round and Condition

Rank						Rounds							
Condition	1	2	3	4	5	6	7	8	9	10	11	12	Average
					Regular Instructions (Sessions 1–4)								
Random	15	25	15	27.5	12.5	12.5	17.5	27.5	17.5	22.5	20	25	19.79
Skill	15	2.5	15	17.5	7.5	0	17.5	5	10	12.5	10	15	10.83
					Self-Selection Instructions (Sessions 5–8)								
Random	20	15	15	15	12.5	17.5	7.5	20	7.5	10	7.5	20	13.96
Skill	−12.5	−20	−15	−12.5	−22.5	−17.5	−25	−5	−17.5	−2.5	−12.5	−5	−13.96

in the number of entrants in the random and skill conditions will be the primary measure of interest.

RESULTS

Does Overconfidence About Skill Increase Entry?

Table 23.1 lists the average amount of money earned by subjects ("industry profit") per round in each rank condition averaged across groups of experimental sessions. Recall that if c subjects enter, the total profit is $50. If $c + 5$ enter, the total profits are 0.

The main question in this study is whether there is a disparity in entry behavior when people are betting on their own relative skill rather than on a random device. There certainly appears to be. In the majority of the random-rank rounds (75/96 or 77%), industry profit is strictly positive,[4] and total profit is negative only six times (6%). Average total profit across rounds is $16.87. In contrast, in the skill-rank rounds, industry profit is positive in only 38 rounds (40%) and negative in 40 (42%). Average profit in the skill-rank rounds is −$1.56. The difference in average profits between the conditions is $18.43, which is about two extra entrants per round in the skill conditions. The nonparametric rank-sum test for a difference between random and skill conditions, using industry profit totals across all rounds of each experiment – a conservative test – shows a significant difference between the random-and skill-rank conditions ($p < .01$).

A more powerful test exploits the yoked design by comparing industry profit in each pair of skill-rank and random-rank periods in exactly the same periods of experiments t and $t + 1$ (for $t = 1, 3, 5, 7$). In this comparison, each pair of periods has exactly the same location in time and value of c and differ only in whether ranks were due to skill or chance. (Fixed effects of periods, self-selection, and subject pool are controlled for by this comparison.) A matched-pair test using

---

[4] This is also consistent with tacit collusion among risk-neutral players because having exactly c entrants is the collusive solution (but is not a Nash equilibrium) or with some degree of risk aversion or (more likely) loss aversion.

these comparisons yields a t-statistic of -7.43 ($dof = 95$, $p < .0001$); industry profits under skill-based entry are clearly lower.

The next question is whether reference group neglect produces a larger skill-random entry differential in the experiments with self-selected subjects. The answer appears to be yes. In sessions without self-selection (1–4), the average per period industry profit is \$19.79 and \$10.83 for the random and skill conditions, respectively, which is a difference of \$9.14 or about one extra entrant in the skill-based rounds. In sessions with self-selection (5–8) profit is \$13.96 in the random condition and $-\$13.96$ in the skill condition, which results in an entry differential of \$27.92 – about three times as large as in the sessions without self-selection. Furthermore, in the experiments with self-selection, industry profits are positive in only 3 of the 48 skill-rank periods compared with 34 of 48 in the non-self-selected sessions. A matched-pairs test comparing the skill-random profit differentials for matched periods between sessions 1–4 and 5–8 strongly rejects the hypothesis that differentials are the same in sessions with and without self-selection ($dof = 94$, $z = 4.08$, $p < .001$). Thus, self-selection makes the overconfidence effect stronger.

Estimating Overconfidence with Expected Profit Statistics

The matched-pairs tests illustrate the effect of overconfidence on entry and demonstrate that self-selection makes the effect stronger. But these tests do not carefully control for all alternative explanations.[5] For example, the blind spots hypothesis suggests that excessive entry in the skill conditions may be due to players underforecasting how many others will enter.

To test this hypothesis, we use subject j's forecast F_{ijt} to compute the profit that subject j expects the average entrant to earn in round t of experiment i. If the capacity is c_{it} in that particular period, then the "expected average profit" – the amount of profit subject j thinks the average entrant will earn – is $(50 - 10^*(F_{ijt} - c_{it}))/F_{ijt}$, which we denote by $E_j(\Pi_{ijt})$. This method effectively separates the blind spot hypothesis from the overconfidence hypothesis. Suppose, for example, that in skill conditions subjects are more apt to enter because they think fewer people will enter, not because they feel they are more skilled. Then their $E_j(\Pi_{ijt})$ values will be larger in the skill condition, and thus including $E_j(\Pi_{ijt})$ in an entry regression will wipe out the effect spuriously attributed to skill.

If entering subjects are more overconfident in the skill rounds, then their expected average profits $E(\Pi_{ijt})$ will be smaller than in random rounds because the skilled subjects expect to earn more than the average entrant (and hence, are willing to enter even when the expected average profit is low). To test this

---

[5] In Camerer and Lovallo (1999) we also report a logit regression of entry decisions, which effectively controls for all treatment effects at once. We find that a skill dummy variable is highly significant, and the interaction of skill and a dummy variable for self-selection sessions is significant too.

Table 23.2. Average Difference in Expected Profits Per Entrant between Random and Skill Conditions

Measure	Exp. 1	Exp. 2	Exp. 3	Exp. 4	Exp. 5	Exp. 6	Exp. 7	Exp. 8	Total
$\Pi_r - \Pi_s$	1.635	0.477	−1.19	0.24	1.62	2.49	3.16	1.80	1.31
	(1.98)	(1.41)	(1.72)	(2.41)	(1.32)	(1.27)	(1.61)	(1.20)	(2.04)
No. of S's with	10/12	10/13	3/11	7/14	12/13	12/13	13/13	11/12	78/101
$\Pi_r - \Pi_s < 0$	(83%)	(77%)	(27%)	(50%)	(92%)	(92%)	(100%)	(92%)	(77%)
No. of S's with	0/12	0/13	0/12	2/15	12/15	15/16	12/14	11/14	52/111
$\Pi_r < 0$	(0%)	(0%)	(0%)	(13%)	(80%)	(94%)	(86%)	(79%)	(47%)

prediction, Table 23.2 reports the difference between expected average profits in random rounds (denoted Π_r) and the same statistic in skill rounds (Π_s,) using only the rounds in which a subject entered. The table shows three different measures for each session: the mean difference $\Pi_r - \Pi_s$ averaged across entering subjects, the number and percentage of subjects who have a negative mean (i.e., who expect less average profit in skill periods), and the number and percentage of subjects whose expected average profit is negative, on average, across skill periods. In sessions without self-selection (1–4) the mean difference $\Pi_r - \Pi_s$ is generally positive and modestly significant, 60 percent of the subjects expect to earn less in skill periods, but only a few subjects (4 percent) actually expect losses in skill periods. In the sessions with self-selection (4–8) the statistics are more striking. There are large, modestly significant average differences $\Pi_r - \Pi_s$ in all four sessions, almost all subjects expect to earn less in skill periods than in random periods, and 85 percent of the subjects have negative expected average profits in skill periods. The large majority of subjects in the self-selection sessions seem to be saying, "I expect the average entrant to lose money, but not me!."

Additional Analyses: Forecasts and Equilibrium Behavior

Because subjects forecasted the number of entrants in each period, we can test whether their forecasts reflect rational use of available information (see our working paper for details). For most subjects forecasts pass other tests of "rational expectations." Economists judge rationality of expectations by whether those expectations use available information effectively. For example, if forecast errors can be predicted by previous forecast errors (e.g., if people consistently predict more price inflation than actually occurs, quarter after quarter), because the previous forecast errors are observable, agents could improve their forecasts by adjusting them until the autocorrelation between errors is eliminated. For most of our subjects, their forecast errors were not predictable by either previous forecast errors or by the current forecast level; thus, their forecasts pass the rational-expectations tests. Indeed, compared with other economics experiments in which paid forecasts have been gathered (cf. Camerer 1995, pp. 609–12), the informational rationality of these forecasts is quite good. This fact is important because it means subjects are not generally irrational in processing information. They are just overconfident about their relative skill.

The time series of matched-pair, skill-random differentials in entry shows a slight downward trend across periods. This raises the important question of whether sufficient repetition of periods would drive the effect of overconfidence on entry to zero. Statisical methods that forecast the equilibrium skill-random differential by extrapolating from the 12 periods (see Camerer 1987) yield estimated differentials of 1.96, 1.79, and 1.34 (all of which are highly significant; see Lovallo and Camerer 1996 for details).

These numbers imply that if the experiment were repeated for a much longer time, one or two more subjects would enter when their payoffs depend on skill than when payoffs are random. Keep in mind that 5 or 6 subjects on average are predicted to stay out in each period (depending on the design). Two extra entrants means that more than a third of the number predicted to stay out actually enter.

DISCUSSION

Empirical studies show a high rate of business failure. We tried to understand whether overconfidence about relative ability might be part of the explanation for excessive failure by creating experimental entry games in which entrants' payoffs depend on their skill. When subjects' postentry performances are based on their own abilities, individuals tend to overestimate their chances of success in tasks based on relative skill and enter more frequently.

A new dimension of overconfidence emerges when subjects self-select into the experimental sessions knowing their success will depend partly on their skill. In these sessions, there is even more entry – in fact, total subject earnings are negative in 34 of the 48 periods and strictly positive in only four periods. This result suggests a new phenomenon that is specific to competition, *"reference group neglect"*, which is the tendency of people to underweigh the nature of the reference group against which they compete.

Reference group neglect was nicely expressed by Joe Roth, chairman of Walt Disney Studios, when he was asked why so many expensive big-budget movies are released on the same weekends (such as Memorial Day and Independence Day). Roth replied:

Hubris. Hubris. If you only think about your own business, you think, "I've got a good story department, I've got a good marketing department, we're going to go out and do this." *And you don't think that everybody else is thinking the same way.* In a given weekend in a year you'll have five movies open, and there's certainly not enough people [moviegoers] to go around. (emphasis added; *Los Angeles Times* 1996).

Reference group neglect is one byproduct of a psychological phenomenon called the "inside view" (Kahneman and Lovallo 1993). An inside view forecast is generated by focusing on the abilities and resources of a particular group, constructing scenarios of future progress, and by extrapolating current trends. In contrast, an "outside view" ignores the special details of the case at hand, constructs a class of cases similar to the current one, and guesses where the current case lies in that class (cf. Kahneman and Tversky 1977). The inside view tells a story full of hope; the outside view recites drab statistics. In the inside view, anticipating the number of competitors or their abilities is optional. In the outside view, the fact that most entries fail cannot be ignored.

Camerer and Lovallo (1999) discuss several economic implications of over-confidence and reference-group neglect. For example, standard economic theory predicts that in risky businesses (such as sales or farming), as the variance in output, which cannot be controlled, rises, subjecting workers to large fluctuations in income, employers who can bear the risk more easily should offer wage contracts to agents with a larger fixed income component and a smaller bonus. However, overconfident agents might actually *prefer* riskier contracts when output variance is high because they think they can beat the odds. In fact, there is evidence from analysis of sharecropping contracts that crops with larger yield variation are more likely to be farmed with cash leases in which farmers pay a landowner a fixed fee to lease the land and bear all the crop risk themselves (e.g., Allen and Lueck 1995). This result is the opposite of the prediction of the standard theory but is consistent with overconfidence.

Reference group neglect predicts that in hierarchical tournaments, where "winners" at one level advance to the next level, overconfidence will get stronger and stronger if winners neglect the increase in the quality of competition at each level. Perhaps as cream rises to the top, hubris does too.

In addition to reference group neglect and its testable implications, an important implication of our study is methodological. In some settings with uncertainty, it is sensible to characterize economic agents as making decisions about random events and use chance devices in laboratory experiments to mimic such events. However, when agents are betting on their own abilities, assuming that random luck and skill are the same is a mistake (cf. Babcock and Loewenstein 1997).

24. Judicial Choice and Disparities between Measures of Economic Values

David Cohen and Jack L. Knetsch

ABSTRACT. An important idea, which characterizes law in society, is a reluctance to move from the *status quo*. In general, one can argue that legal institutions and legal doctrine are not engaged in the redistribution of wealth from one party to another. This paper explores a possible explanation for that principle. The authors' research suggests that, across a wide range of entitlements and in a variety of contexts, individuals value losses more than forgone gains. The paper argues, as a matter of efficiency, that law and social policy might have developed in a manner consistent with this valuation disparity. Furthermore, this valuation disparity can be transformed into conceptions of fairness, and, as a matter of fairness, legal decisions might have developed in a manner consistent with this fairness norm. In the first part of the paper, the economic and psychological research on the valuation disparity is described in detail. The paper then examines a series of legal doctrines, all of which can be explained by the valuation disparity phenomenon revealed in the experimental data. Cohen and Knetsch conclude that the behaviour of legal institutions and actors can be explained by the valuation disparity.

I. INTRODUCTION

The idea that the legal system should not move wealth from one person to another pervades common law doctrine and reasoning. As Oliver Wendell Holmes stated, "The general principle of our law is that loss from accident must lie where it falls."[1] Common explanations of that position focus on the political power and class bias of those who make legal decisions and create legal rules.

---

[1] *The Common Law* (Boston: Little, Brown, 1881) at 94. As we point out later, it is not as simple as it might first appear to know *where* losses lie, in order to decide where they should fall. As well, it is clear to us that the idea to which Holmes is alluding has application far beyond *accidents*, and may inform our understanding of property rights, contract remedies, and regulatory policy.

The authors acknowledge the support of the Social Sciences and Humanities Research Council of Canada, the Ontario Ministry of the Environment, and the British Columbia Science Council. The authors also wish to thank William Fischel and Stephen Waddams for their helpful comments and further examples.

Originally published in *Osgoode Hall Law Journal*, 30:3, 737–70. Copyright © 1992 Osgoode Hall Law Journal. Reprinted with permission.

We propose an alternative interpretation of the historical truism that "losses should lie where they fall." People value actual losses far more than forgone gains, and thus, it is a matter of efficiency,[2] as well as of fairness, to adopt presumptive legal rules which do not direct nonconsensual transfers of wealth. We explore the extent to which such disparities in valuations between gains and losses have been incorporated in legal doctrines and principles.

The following two puzzles illustrate the issue. They represent examples of apparent *irrationality* in law, which we believe are perfectly understandable in terms of common behaviour and are probably desirable.

Puzzle I: A seller sells an automobile to a buyer (B1), permitting B1 to take possession of the car before payment in full.[3] The seller reserves *ownership* of the car until full payment. Before full payment, B1 enters into an agreement with a sub-buyer (B2) who pays B1 a down payment of $500 for the car, with delivery arranged for the following day. Before delivery to the sub-buyer, the original seller discovers the sub-sale. In a dispute between the original seller claiming ownership of the car and B2, who also claims ownership, the *original seller* will win.[4]

A seller sells an automobile to a buyer (B1), permitting B1 to take possession of the car before payment in full. The seller reserves *ownership* of the car until full payment. Before full payment, B1 enters into an agreement with a sub-buyer (B2) who pays B1 a down payment of $500 for the car, with immediate delivery arranged from B1 to B2. After delivery to the sub-buyer, the original seller discovers the sub-sale. In a dispute between the original seller claiming ownership of the car and B2, who in this case has taken delivery of the car and who also claims ownership, the *sub-buyer* wins![5]

Puzzle II: A seller contracts with a buyer to purchase a piece of jewellery. The buyer pays $100 as a deposit and agrees to pay $200 per month for twelve months

---

[2] The definition of efficiency that we employ in this paper is quite simple. A legal decision or rule is efficient if, after its application, at least one person is better off and no one is worse off than before. We might adopt a Kaldor-Hicks definition of efficiency, which permits hypothetical compensatory wealth transfers between the affected parties; whether we choose a Pareto or such a potential Pareto superiority criterion does not matter to our thesis.

[3] This puzzle is equally apparent in the treatment of sales by *sellers* who remain in possession of goods. Here, sales legislation, which deals with sales by *sellers in possession*, generally expropriates the interest of the first buyer only where the second buyer has received *delivery* of the property.

[4] The original seller wins because at common law the first buyer could not transfer any better *title* than she or he had. Thus, the first sub-buyer could not receive any better ownership claim than *the person selling to this sub-buyer* and would lose to the original owner. See *Cole* v. *North Western Bank* (1875), L.R. 10 C.P. 354 at 362, [1874-80] All E.R. Rep. 486,44 L.J.C.P. 233. See generally, M.D. Chalmers, *The Sale of Goods Act, 1889* (London: William Clowes & Sons, 1905) at 57–66.

[5] The outcome is produced through the operation of section 25(2) of the original English *Sale of Goods Act* (U.K.), 1893, c. 71, which re-enacted with some slight modifications section 9 of the *Factors Act* (U.K.), 1889, c. 45 [hereinafter *Factors Act*]. However, that section only operates where the sub-buyer obtains *delivery of the goods or transfer of documents of title*, and thus does not protect mere contract or ownership expectations.

to pay off the purchase price of $2,500. The buyer also agrees that, on default, the seller will be able to retain any money that has been paid as of the date of default. The buyer defaults after six months. The seller repossesses the jewellery and retains the $1,300, which has been paid. If the buyer seeks to set aside the *forfeiture clause* and recover the amount paid, then the buyer will only be able to do so if it would be "unconscionable for the seller to retain the money."[6] In the vast majority of cases, the courts will leave the money with the seller.

A seller contracts with a buyer for the purchase of a piece of jewellery. The buyer pays nothing down and agrees to pay $200 per month for twelve months to pay off the purchase price of $2,400. The buyer agrees to pay $1,300 on default to the seller as liquidated damages. The buyer defaults, and the seller repossesses the jewellery and sues to recover the $1,300 as liquidated damages. The liquidated damages clause will, however, be held unenforceable where the buyer persuades the court that the clause was *intended as a penalty*. In a large percentage of the cases, the courts will refuse to enforce the clause and leave the money with the buyer.[7]

The *puzzle* in these examples is that the outcome differs depending on the *location* of the object of the dispute. In Puzzle I, the issue of which claimant's ownership interest is expropriated depends on whether the sub-buyer has or has not taken delivery of the car. In Puzzle II, the issue of the enforceability of the private damage assessment term depends on whether the money has or has not been transferred to the seller.

Many writers have seen the similarity between the penalty and forfeiture cases and have argued forcefully for solutions, which would *reconcile*[8] the two

---

We should also point out that this example suggests that Holmes's insight is equally accurate of legislative action, at least where the legislative institution is purporting to create a framework for contract and ownership disputes analogous to the framework established at common law.

Finally, some insight into the reasons we protect the sub-buyer who has possession of the goods may be gained from early decisions, which refused to extend the equivalent section of the *Factors Act*, to lessees, even where the lessee had entered into a lease-option arrangement. See *Helby* v. *Matthews*, [1895] A.C. 471, 64 L.J.Q.B. 465, 60 J.P. 20 (H.L.).

[6] See *Stockloser* v. *Johnson*, [1954] 1 Q.B. 476 at 492, [1954] 2 W.L.R. 439, [1954] 1 All E.R. 630. While there is no empirical data on this point, our impression, and the impression of most commentators, is that judicial discretion to take wealth away from the seller, and thus return monies to the buyer, is only very rarely exercised, compared to judicial willingness to review *penalty clauses*. See S.M. Waddams, *The Law of Contracts*, 2d ed. (Toronto: Canada Law Book, 1984) at 341–45.

[7] The distinction between the treatment of liquidated damages or penalties and forfeiture clauses becomes even more problematic where the defendant has promised to pay a deposit, which is subject to forfeiture on breach, and then fails to pay it. The cases are split on this third situation. Some hold that the buyer must pay, which treats the arrangement as a forfeiture. Others hold that the arrangement represents a penalty clause in which case, as above, the buyer does not have to pay. See *Hinton* v. *Sparkes* (1868), L.R. 3 C.P. 161, 37 L.J.C.P. 81, 17 L.T. 600 (buyer liable for promised amount, even though penal); *Dewar* v. *Mintoft*, [1912] 2 K.B. 373, 81 L.J.K.B. 885, 106 L.T. 763 (amount not recoverable by seller as a penalty). See S.M. Waddams, *The Law of Damages* (Toronto: Canada Law Book, 1991) at para. 8.310.

[8] See Waddams, *ibid.*

doctrines, or which would eliminate the "illogical distinction drawn by the existing law between penalty clauses and the doctrine of forfeiture."[9] It does not matter, of course, whether the proponents of reform would prefer the penalty/liquidated damages solution over the forfeiture clause solution[10] or the converse. The point is that *rationality*, to some reformers, means that the situations should be treated the same way.

While the legal treatment of these cases appears anomalous, the results reflect real and important differences in valuations of losses relative to gains and in their judgments of fairness predicated on this disparity. The differences in valuations of gains and losses appear to go a long way towards explaining the *rationality* of the apparently illogical puzzles presented above, and of many others as well.[11] These puzzles can be explained as manifestations of the idea that *possession*[12] losses are much more important than forgone gains, and the law takes such real differences into account. In each case the legal rule treats economic gains and losses differently, even though nominally commensurate. These doctrines reflect powerful human sentiments:

bare expectations were less important than expectations allied to present rights, especially rights of property. Hume and Adam Smith, for example, both said that expectations arising out of rights of property deserved greater protection than expectations to something which had never been *possessed*. To deprive somebody of something which he merely expects to receive is a less serious wrong, deserving of less protection, than to deprive somebody of the expectation of continuing to hold something which he already *possesses*.[13]

---

[9] Ontario Law Reform Commission, *Report on Sale of Goods* (Toronto: Minister of the Attorney General, 1979) at 425. Law Commission, *Penalty Clauses and Forfeiture of Monies Paid* (Working Paper No. 61) (London: Her Majesty's Stationery Office, 1975) at 51–54.

[10] The Law Commission of England would prefer that both be treated like penalty clauses, while Waddams would prefer that both be treated like forfeiture clauses. See Law Commission, *ibid.*; and Waddams, *supra* note 7.

[11] Common law judges seemingly apply Aristotelian concepts of corrective justice by restoring parties to the position they were in prior to the wrongful act. Law as it has developed in most common law jurisdictions implicates ideas of corrective, rather than distributive justice. Corrective justice is a system for preserving what we have and for minimizing disruptions of feelings of loss, not for bringing about new distributions of wealth.

Maintaining entitlements is implicit in law in three ways. First, compensation will usually be considered in terms of remedying actual losses to plaintiffs rather than in compensating forgone gains. Second, and more important, law will represent itself as a passive, political institution, demanding justification for transfers of wealth from defendants to plaintiffs. Finally, judicial discretion implicit in fact-finding, interpretation rule selection, and rule application may incorporate concepts of fairness, which reflect the idea that losses are much more important than forgone gains.

[12] While we use the word *possession* to denote the critical element in these cases as well as in the empirical studies, which we describe, we are not suggesting that a physical connection or even legal entitlement is a prerequisite to the occurrence of the phenomenon. The reference position from which changes are perceived as gains or losses may well depend on factors other than physical possession.

[13] P.S. Atiyah, *The Rise and Fall of Freedom of Contract* (Oxford: Clarendon Press, 1979) at 428 [emphasis added].

II. THE VALUATION DISPARITY

In each of the cases of judicial choices that we explore in this paper, greater weight is given to actual out-of-pocket losses than to the opportunity cost of forgone gains. Such asymmetries in the valuations of gains and losses are not at all consistent with the assurances of most economists that valuations of gains and losses are equivalent, or with generally accepted principles of analysis based on such assumptions of people's preferences.

There is no dispute that the economic value of both gains and losses is measured by what people are willing to sacrifice. That is, gains are valued by a payment measure, and losses are valued by a compensation measure. For example, Posner suggests, "[T]he economic value of something is how much someone is willing to pay for it or, if he [or she] has it already, how much money he [or she] demands to part with it."[14] Similarly, Michelman suggests, "[B]enefits are measured by the total number of dollars which prospective gainers would be willing to pay to secure adoption, and losses are measured by the total number of dollars which prospective losers would insist on as the price of agreeing to adoption."[15]

Although income effects or limits on ability to pay may cause the two measures to differ, these are normally not a factor of any practical importance and can safely be ignored in most applications. The common view is that, "for many goods, services, and amenities that command a modest fraction of the consumer's budget, the differences between [the] ... measures are trivial."[16] Consequently, the usual advice is that "as a practical matter it usually does not make much difference which of these two approaches ... is adopted."[17]

Common preferences and reactions to actual choices are, however, not consistent with the assertion of equivalence between the measures of loss and gain. Nor, it seems, are judicial reactions and choices.

The traditional assumption of equivalence between the willingness-to-pay and the compensation-demanded measures of value is largely an empirical assertion that is common to both economic and legal analysis. It is based on the behavioural assumption that people assess gains and losses by comparing how well off they would be with more or with less of something – for example, by comparing how they would feel with their present wealth with how they would feel with their present holdings plus $100; or by comparing their level of welfare with an injury and their economic well-being without one.

New empirical evidence indicates that people evaluate gains and losses in terms of changes from some reference position, instead of comparing alternative

[14] R. Posner, *An Economic Analysis of Law*, 3d ed. (Boston: Little, Brown, 1986) at 11.

[15] F.I. Michelman, "Property, Utility, and Fairness: Comments on the Ethical Foundation of 'Just Compensation' Law" (1967) 80 Harv. L. Rev. 1165 at 1214.

[16] A. Randall, *Resource Economics* (New York: Wiley, 1987) at 244.

[17] S.E. Rhoads, *The Economist's View of the World* (Cambridge: Cambridge University Press, 1985) at 125.

end states. This evidence also indicates that they value losses from this neutral point much more than they value gains beyond it: "[T]he aggravation that one experiences in losing a sum of money appears to be greater than the pleasure associated with gaining the same amount."[18]

Virtually all controlled evaluation tests, as well as the commonplace reactions of people to real choices, point to large and persistent differences between the valuation of losses and forgone gains and do not confirm the traditional assumption that these two measures of value are equal. Large differences were first noted in survey studies of people's valuations of various losses of environmental assets or the degradation of environmental quality. For example, a sample of duck hunters said they would be willing to pay an average of $247 to save a marsh area used by ducks but would demand an average of $1044 to accept the identical loss.[19] Similarly, a survey of anglers yielded a payment value of $35 and a compensation value of $100 for the loss of a fishing area.[20] The disparity between the two measures of value was also reported to vary from $43 to $120 for the loss of a fishing pier;[21] from $22 to $93 for the loss of a local postal service;[22] from $21 to $101 for the loss of a goose-hunting permit;[23] from $54 to $143 for the loss of an opportunity to hunt elk;[24] and from $40 to $833 for the loss of the chance to hunt deer.[25] We are not aware of any surveys reporting equivalence between the two measures.

Later studies based on real exchange experiments have provided more stringent tests than the earlier ones, which were based on hypothetical survey questions. The results have been essentially the same. Even when exchanges of real goods and actual cash payments motivated the evaluations, the compensation demanded to give up an entitlement far exceeded the comparable payment measures of value. For example, people required about four times more money to give up a lottery ticket than they would be willing to pay to acquire one.[26] To hunt deer in the northern United States, the values were

---

[18] D. Kahneman & A. Tversky, "Prospect Theory: An Analysis of Decision Under Risk" (1979) 47 Econometrica 263 at 279.

[19] J. Hammack & G.M. Brown, *Waterfowl and Wetlands: Toward Bioeconomic Analysis* (Washington: Resources for the Future, 1974).

[20] W.F. Sinclair, *The Economic and Social Impact of Kemano II Hydroelectric Project on British Columbia's Fisheries Resources* (Vancouver: Fisheries and Marine Service, Department of the Environment, 1976).

[21] N.D. Banford, J.L. Knetsch & G.A. Mauser, "Feasibility Judgements and Alternative Measures of Benefits and Costs" (1980) 11 J. Bus. Admin. 25.

[22] *Ibid.*

[23] R.C. Bishop & T.A. Heberlein, "Measuring Values of Extra-Market Goods: Are Indirect Measures Biased?" (1979) 61 Am. J. Agric. Econ. 926.

[24] D. Brookshire, A. Randall & J.R. Stoll, "Valuing Increments and Decrements in Natural Resource Service Flows" (1980) 62 Am. J. Agric. Econ. 478.

[25] R.C. Bishop & T.A. Heberlein, "Does Contingent Valuation Work?" in R.G. Cummings, D.S. Brookshire & W.D. Schulze, eds., *Valuing Environmental Goods* (Totowa, N.J.: Roman & Allanheld, 1986) 123.

[26] J.L. Knetsch & J.A. Sinden, "Willingness to Pay and Compensation Demanded: Experimental Evidence of an Unexpected Disparity in Measures of Value" (1984) 99 Q. J. Econ. 507.

reported to be $25 for the acquisition of a permit and $172 for the actual loss of a permit.[27]

A more recent series of real exchange experiments has affirmed the persistence of the evaluation disparities over repeated valuations, and has eliminated the possibility that the differences might be attributable to transaction costs or strategic behaviour on the part of participants.[28] The results indicate that, consistent with other evidence and contrary to conventional assertions, people value losses much more than gains. The differences are pervasive and large. They persist over repeated valuations and they are not the result of inhibitions posed by transaction costs.

An indication of the general findings is illustrated by the results of a simple exercise involving people's actual choices between a coffee mug and a large, four-hundred-gram chocolate bar.[29] Each member of one group of seventy-six participants was given a mug and told to keep it. Each was then given a chance to give up the mug to obtain a chocolate bar. A second group of eighty-seven participants was given the opposite choice: to give up chocolate bars to obtain coffee mugs.

Traditional economics predicts that, in the absence of any significant transaction costs, about the same proportion of participants in each of the groups will prefer mugs to chocolate bars and will choose accordingly. The actual results were in sharp contrast to this prediction: 89 per cent indicated a preference for the mug when initially given a mug, and only 10 per cent revealed a similar preference for mugs when they had to give up a chocolate bar to obtain one. The relative value of mugs and chocolate bars varied greatly and depended on whether the evaluation was made in terms of a gain or a loss. The mug was valued more when it had to be given up to obtain a chocolate bar, and was valued less when the chocolate bar had to be given up to obtain a mug. The influence of income constraints and wealth or income effects was entirely eliminated in the exercise, leaving the choices dependent on individual preferences. These choices showed that gains and losses were valued very differently.

A further test for the equivalence or non-equivalence of valuations of gains and losses was modeled on the Coase Theorem, a mainstay of the economic analysis of law and the basis for many legal policy prescriptions. A major conclusion of the Coase proposition is that, in the absence of transaction costs and wealth effects, people are presumed to make mutually advantageous exchanges to ensure that resources are put to their most valued use.[30] "Since a receipt foregone of a given amount is the equivalent of a payment of the same amount,"[31]

---

[27] Bishop & Heberlein, *supra* note 25.

[28] D. Kahneman, J.L. Knetsch & R.H. Thaler, "Experimental Test of the Endowment Effect and the Coase Theorem" (1990) 98 J. Pol. Econ. 1325.

[29] J.L. Knetsch, "The Endowment Effect and Evidence of Non-Reversible Indifference Curves" (1989) 79 Am. Econ. Rev. 1277.

[30] R.H. Coase, "The Problem of Social Cost" (1960) 3 J. L. & Econ. 1.

[31] *Ibid.* at 7.

final allocations of entitlements are assumed to be independent of initial entitlements. "[T]he ultimate result (which maximizes the value of production) is independent of the legal position if the pricing system is assumed to work without cost."[32]

The Coase Theorem test was conducted by randomly giving one member of each of a large number of paired participants a good, a large chocolate bar. Those participants were told it was theirs to take home or to sell, if the person with whom they were paired made a sufficiently attractive offer. The experiment was deliberately arranged so that the potential buyers had been given a larger windfall sum of money than the sellers. Despite this effort to encourage buyers to use their unanticipated gain to make larger offers to acquire the goods, few transactions were concluded.[33] In spite of the entitlements' random distribution, the people holding them demanded much more to give them up than potential buyers were willing to pay to acquire them. The valuations were *not*, contrary to the Coase prediction, independent of the initial assignments of entitlements.[34]

Individuals have now repeatedly been shown to exhibit disparities between gain and loss valuations in experimental settings, as reported by many investigators using a variety of methods to evaluate widely varied assets. As well, people's actual behaviour in making everyday choices increasingly has been observed to be consistent with these findings. For example, the valuation disparity and consequent reluctance to sell at a loss is observed in the greater volume of house sales when prices are rising, over the number when they are falling. This can also be observed in the smaller volume of sales of securities that have declined in price relative to those for which prices have increased.[35] Firms frequently are reluctant to divest themselves of plants and product lines even though they would not consider buying these same assets, and stock prices often rise when they do give them up.

A further illustration of the differing valuations of gains and losses is provided by responses to recent automobile insurance legislation in two American states. In both jurisdictions people are given a choice between cheaper policies, which limit rights to subsequent recovery of further damages, and a more expensive policy permitting such actions. Importantly, the default option differs: the *reduced* rights policy is offered in New Jersey unless it is given up; and *full* rights policy is given in Pennsylvania unless the less expensive option is specified. Given the minimal costs in both states of choosing either option and the large amounts of money at issue, the results have been dramatic. At last count over 70 per cent of New Jersey automobile owners have adopted the

---

[32] *Ibid.* at 8.

[33] *Supra* note 28.

[34] The major efficiency implications of the valuations of gains and losses have been demonstrated in H. Hovenkamp, "Legal Policy and the Endowment Effect" (1991) 20 J. Legal Stud. 225 at 230.

[35] H. Shefrin & M. Statman, "The Disposition to Sell Winners Too Early and Ride Losers Too Long: Theory and Evidence" (1985) 40 J. Fin. 777.

reduced rights policy, but fewer than 25 per cent of Pennsylvanians have done so.[36]

The differing weights attached to gains and losses have also been found to influence the judgment of what people regard as acceptable or unfair behaviour in economic relationships. If an action is seen to impose a loss on one party for the benefit of another, this will nearly always be widely seen to be unfair – quite apart from whatever economic justification might exist. For example, raising prices in response to sudden shifts in demand is seen to benefit the seller, who has not incurred any cost increase, at the expense of the buyer and is, therefore, judged to be unfair. Similarly, cutting wages when unemployment increases is thought to be unfair by the vast majority of people because the employer benefits in direct proportion to the worker's loss. As a less aversive relinquishment of a gain, the reduction of a customary bonus payment to workers is apparently viewed as more acceptable than an equivalent reduction in wages, which is commonly seen as imposing a loss on workers.[37]

Raising rents of a new, as opposed to a sitting, tenant or cutting wages of a new, rather than an old, employee is generally considered to be fair because the benefit to the landlord or the employer is not seen to be gained at the expense of a loss to the other party. The evidence also suggests a willingness of most people to back up their judgments with sacrifices to punish unfair behaviour and reward what they take to be fair dealings.[38] A major motivation for these judgments appears to be that losses matter more to people than do foregone gains.

This strong intuition to value losses more than commensurate gains, and the implications for the resolution of competing claims, was summarized earlier by Holmes in the following terms:

It is in the nature of man's mind. A thing which you have enjoyed and used as your own for a long time, whether property or an opinion, takes root in your being and cannot be torn away without your resenting the act and trying to defend yourself, however you came by it. The law can ask no better justification than the deepest instincts of man.[39]

While there has been very little empirical work investigating this phenomenon among legal actors, Stewart Macaulay's seminal work in the sociology of law almost three decades ago offers some support for the appearance

---

[36] J. Meszarose et al., Framing, Loss Aversion and Insurance Decisions (Working Paper) (Philadelphia: University of Pennsylvania Press, 1991).

[37] D. Kahneman, J.L. Knetsch & R.H. Thaler, "Fairness as a Constraint on Profit Seeking: Entitlements in the Market" (1986) 76 Am. Econ. Rev. 728.

[38] D. Kahneman, J.L. Knetsch & R.H. Thaler, "Fairness and the Assumptions of Economics" (1986) 59 J. Bus. 285.

[39] O.W. Holmes, "The Path of Law" (1897) 10 Harv. L. Rev. 457 at 477. The only difference revealed by the empirical evidence is that the reluctance to give up something does not necessarily only occur after "a long time" but may well set in immediately. Once a reference position is perceived, which leads to a change being viewed as a loss, then the valuation will respond accordingly. See, particularly, supra note 28.

of this phenomenon among members of at least one business community when they confront legal disputes.[40] Macaulay interviewed sixty-eight business people and lawyers representing forty-eight companies and six law firms. All but two of the companies were engaged in manufacturing, with plants in Wisconsin. In his investigation of dispute settlements, Macaulay began with the formal assumption that, on breach of contract, the breaching party, the buyer, for example, would be legally obligated to pay all of the seller's wasted expenses up to the time of breach, plus anticipated lost profits. However, the responses of the purchasing agents and sales personnel revealed attitudes consistent with the experimental data discussed above. That is, they uniformly believed that all they ought to recover or to pay in damages was an amount representing the seller's actual expenses:

[A]ll ten of the purchasing agents [that were] asked about cancellation of orders once placed indicated that they expected to be able to cancel orders freely subject to only an obligation to pay for the seller's major expenses such as scrapped steel. All seventeen sales personnel asked reported that they often had to accept cancellation. One said "You can't ask a man to eat paper [the firm's product] when he has no use for it."[41]

The empirical findings discussed earlier, together with Macaulay's evidence, suggest that people value gains and losses from some neutral reference point or level. Losses from this reference are commonly weighed more than gains beyond it. The reference position, therefore, determines whether an adverse change is regarded as a loss or as a forgone gain, and whether a positive change is treated as a gain or as a reduction of a loss. Given the large disparities between valuations, these differences can have significant practical impact.

III. THE DISPARITY AND JUDICIAL CHOICE

The legitimacy of the common law has largely been based on its decentralized, *ad hoc*, incremental development by judges who have little enforcement power, and who therefore respond to an intuitive, nonempirical interpretation of community mores and individual preferences. If such interpretations underlie individual judgments, then a phenomenon as pervasive as the valuation disparity would be expected to be implicated, either explicitly or implicitly, in the development of legal doctrine. Indeed, as expected, the idea that *losses count more than expected gains* is encountered in an enormous range of ideas in law.[42]

An important way in which the valuation disparity has been incorporated in law is through the widespread recognition of possession as a foundation

---

[40] See "Non-Contractual Relations in Business: A Preliminary Study" (1963) 28 Am. Soc. Rev. 55.

[41] *Ibid.* at 64.

[42] Other, independent, *ad hoc* explanations can be offered for many specific results, but the valuation disparity alone appears uniquely robust as a consistent explanation across a wide range of apparently independent legal issues.

for the declaration or recognition of legal entitlements.[43] The often misused expression that "possession is nine-tenths of the law"[44] is a manifestation of judicial intuition that possession of things is intimately connected to establishing the endowment effect and underlies judicial choices favouring protection against losses over forgone gains.

Both legal writers and the designers of the empirical studies discussed earlier have used the term possession in extremely ambiguous ways. But regardless of one's choice of definition, it is incontrovertible that judicial sensitivity to the notion of possession, or seisin, in English law is deeply rooted and utterly pervasive: "In the history of our law there is no idea more cardinal than that of seisin."[45]

Frederick Pollock,[46] while noting that it was difficult to obtain a consistent doctrine or consistent terminology,[47] offered several theories on why judge-made common law presumes in favour of possession.[48] Utilitarian justifications for the protection of possession range from a concern with reducing the risk of civil disobedience – a response to the risk of personal injuries associated with self-help dispossession – to the protection of ownership interests. But once

---

[43] One of the most articulate writers on the relationship of possession and the human condition is C.B. MacPherson who, in *The Political Theory of Possessive Individualism* (Oxford: Clarendon Press, 1962) at 3, wrote that "[t]he human essence is freedom from dependence on the wills of others, and freedom is a function of possession." See also British Columbia Law Reform Commission, *Wrongful Interference with Goods* (Working Paper No. 67) (Vancouver: British Columbia Law Reform Commission, 1992) at 21.

[44] Historians have traced its development from Roman rather than Germanic Law. See S.S. Peloubet, *A Collection of Legal Maxims in Law and Equity, with English Translations* (Littleton, Colo.: F.B. Rothman, 1985) at 225; Sir F. Pollock & F.W. Maitland, *The History of English Law: Before the Time of Edward I*, vol. 2, 2d ed. (Cambridge: Cambridge University Press, 1968) at 29. In *The Corporation of Kingston-upon-Hull* v. *Horner*, [1774] Lofft. 592, 98 E.R. 807 at 815 (K.B.), Lord Mansfield C.J. said, "Possession is very strong; rather more than nine points of the law." He used the expression in a case concerning prescriptive rights where, in the absence of evidence of a crown grant, one was presumed to exist, thus supporting a possessory title. By 1881 in *Beddal* v. *Maitland* (1881), 17 Ch.D. 174 at 183 (H.C.), Sir Edward Fry was noting that the old saying that possession is nine points of the law was created by a forcible entry statute, which resulted in a man in possession being able to use force to keep out a trespasser. If a trespasser had gained possession, however, the rightful owner could not use force to put him out, but had to appeal to the law for assistance. As late as 1946, *Wharton's Law Lexicon* was expressing the idea as possession constituting "nine points" of the law: A.S. Oppe, ed., *Wharton's Law Lexicon*, 13th ed. (London: Stevens, 1938) at 666. H.C. Black, ed., *Black's Law Dictionary*, 6th ed. (St. Paul, Minn.: West Publishing, 1990) at 1164, currently uses the phrase: "Possession is nine-tenths of the law."

[45] Pollock & Maitland, *ibid.* at 29. See also F. Pollock & R.S. Wright, *An Essay on Possession in the Common Law* (Oxford: Clarendon Press, 1888) at 1.

[46] Both with R.S. Wright (see Pollock & Wright, *ibid.*) and with F.W. Maitland (see Pollock & Maitland, *ibid.*).

[47] Pollock & Maitland, *ibid.* at 44. Pollock and Maitland make the point that "so far as concerns our own English law we make no doubt that at different times and in different measures every conceivable reason for protecting possession has been felt as a weighty argument and has had its influence on rights and remedies." *Ibid.*

[48] *Ibid.* at 40.

again, we find references to the *natural* expectation that a person should and will be allowed to keep what he or she possesses until someone has proved a better title.[49]

A. Adverse Possession

The rule of adverse possession provides a means by which the user of property can successfully assert a claim of ownership over a prior owner. Many of the cases involve mistakes on the location of boundaries.[50] Others, however, reward those who make effective use of an asset over an owner who has effectively abandoned it.[51]

The advantages in efficiency of awarding titles to adverse possessors usually include the reduction of administrative costs of establishing rightful ownership and the encouragement to make productive use of assets that are left unused by their owners.[52] Posner suggests a further advantage in efficiency of the rule of adverse possession turning on possible differences between the valuations of owners and possessors because of differences in the marginal value of their wealth levels:

The adverse possessor would experience the deprivation of property as a diminution in his wealth; the original owner would experience the restoration of the property as an increase in *his* wealth. If they have the same wealth, then probably their combined utility will be greater if the adverse possessor is allowed to keep the property.[53]

Posner chooses to interpret Holmes's views[54] of the disparity between feelings of gains and losses as "a point about diminishing marginal utility of income."[55] The evidence discussed earlier suggests instead that Holmes's notion is a prescient articulation of the endowment effect, that is, the disparity between the valuation of gains and losses. The reference positions are probably such that taking away from a current user would likely be valued as a loss, and giving back to the original owner would likely be valued as a gain. And given the greater valuations of losses over gains, the rule seems consistent with maximizing

---

[49] *Ibid.* at 41–43.

[50] Distinctions in granting variances are commonly made between not requiring destruction of an improvement built too close to a neighbour by mistake and proposing to do so, and between wilfully ignoring a zoning ordinance and doing so by mistake.

[51] While now largely matters of statute in most jurisdictions, the rules grew out of resolutions favouring current users because of the difficulty of establishing old entitlements due to lost records and fading memories. See R. Cooter & T. Ulen, *Law and Economics* (Glenview, Ill.: Scott, Foresman & Company, 1988).

[52] See *ibid.*, W.Z. Hirsch, *Law and Economics: An Introductory Analysis* (New York: Academic Press, 1979).

[53] R. Posner, *An Economic Analysis of Law*, 3d ed. (Boston: Little Brown, 1986) at 70.

[54] See Holmes, *supra* note 39.

[55] *Supra* note 53. This was previously observed by R.C. Ellickson, "Bringing Culture and Human Frailty to Rational Actors: A Critique of Classical Law and Economics" (1989) 65 Chicago-Kent L. Rev. 23 at 38.

joint welfare, quite apart from any concern with the diminishing marginal utility of income or any incentives to encourage investment and use.

The potential gains depend on how well the limitations and restrictions on length of time and behaviour needed to acquire title reflect reference positions of the parties and their consequent views of gains and losses. If a person makes very temporary use of a parcel of land while the owner is absent for a short time, the reference position is unlikely to shift, and an award of title would then be taken as a gain. If the use continues over many years, a reasonable expectation of continued use would probably develop so that any unexpected termination would be viewed as a more important loss. An owner deprived of title after a short absence would surely take this as a loss, and the discovery that ownership extended several metres beyond an old boundary fence would likely be regarded as a less valued gain.

The rules of adverse possession may be consistent with lowering administrative costs and encouraging use. Neither addresses, however, the disparate valuations – and consequent efficiency outcomes – that depend on perceptions of gains and losses, and the specification of requirements in terms of reference positions. A short limitation period might well induce use of *unused* property. If such a specification leaves the original owner in the domain of losses and the possessor feeling that the title is a gain, the result is likely to be an inefficient change in which the gain is outweighed by the loss.

B. Limitations on Recovery of Lost Profits

A second, more specific example of the operation of the valuation disparity on judicial decisions is the reluctance of judges to compensate for *lost profits*, whether the claim is framed in contract or tort. As Adam Smith wrote: "[W]e naturally depend more on what we possess than what is in the hands of others. A man robbed of five pounds thinks himself much more injured than if he had lost five pounds by a contract."[56] When permitting the recovery of economic losses in tort law, this idea is reflected in the consistent distinction that judges draw between loss by way of expenditure and failure to make gain.[57] While recovery of expenditures is sometimes permitted, recovery of forgone gains is not.[58] Several recent decisions have explicitly recognized the distinction. In one,

[56] *Lectures on Justice, Police, Revenue and Arms*, ed. by E. Cannan (Oxford: Clarendon Press, 1896) at 131.

[57] Thus in R.W.M. Dias, ed., *Clerk & Lindsell on Torts*, 15th ed. (Agincourt, Ont.: Carswell, 1982) at 32–33 and at 371–385, the authors typically offer the formal statement that recovery has been extended to economic losses representing expenditures, but "the general rule is that loss of profit *per se* is not actionable: there is a no duty-situation." Similarly, in *Weller & Co.* v. *Foot and Mouth Disease Research Institute* (1965), [1966] 1 Q.B. 569, [1965] 3 All E.R. 560, the Court held that the loss of profit did not constitute a harm of a sort that the law would remedy, and that the rule against recovery is independent both of negligence and foreseeability.

[58] The House of Lords' decision in *Junior Books Ltd.* v. *Veitchi* (1982), [1983] 1 A.C. 520, [1982] 3 W.L.R. 477 [hereinafter *Junior Books*], which might have presented a radical development in compensation law and which permitted recovery of lost profits in a non-contractual setting,

Dominion Tape of Canada Ltd. v. *L.R. McDonald & Sons Ltd.*,[59] several bales fell from a trailer and hit a hydro pole, cutting power to the plaintiff's plant. The plaintiff successfully sued to recover wages paid to employees, which represented *positive outlays*, but could not recover loss of profits, which were only *negative losses*, consisting of a "mere deprivation of an opportunity to earn an income." The latter, while foreseeable, was judged as too remote.[60]

While lost profits are said to be recoverable in contract law, it is difficult to defend the proposition that the *expectation* interest of a non-breaching party is recognized in contract actions in the same fashion as are *actual* losses.[61] As Atiyah argued, the costs of depriving a breaching party of his or her wealth are considered by most to outweigh the expected benefit to the non-breaching party: "[I]t might well be thought by most people that the inconvenience to the promisor of being held to his contract would be enough to outweigh the *prima facie* desirability of not disappointing the promisee."[62] Fuller and Perdue in their seminal article, "The Reliance Interest in Contract Damages,"[63] argued that the public interest in redressing wrongs varies directly with the type of claim that the complainant makes. In their eyes, it is relatively easy to justify claims to compensation where the plaintiff is seeking return of wealth transferred to the defendant, and almost as easy to justify claims to compensation for actual out-of-pocket expenses incurred as a result of the breach of contract. However, while contract law protects expectations of gain: "[I]n passing from compensation for change of position to compensation for loss of expectancy . . . [t]he

has not been widely followed. See J.F. Clerk, *Fifth Cumulative Supplement to the Fifteenth Edition,* ed. by R.W.M. Dias (London: Sweet & Maxwell, 1987) at paras. 10-14, which describes six limiting factors on the *Junior Books* decision.

59 [1971] 3 O.R. 627, 21 D.L.R. (3d) 299 (Co. Ct.). See also *MacMillan Bloedel Ltd.* v. *Foundation Co. of Canada Ltd.* (1977), 75 D.L.R. (3d) 294, [1977] 2 W.W.R. 717 (B.C.S.C.) (employer may be permitted to recover actual wages paid to employees); and *Ontario (A.G.)* v. *Crompton* (1976), 14 O.R. (2d) 659, 74 D.L.R. (3d) 345 (H.C.J.) (specific expenditure incurred in putting out fire recoverable).

60 This approach received some support from Wilson J.A. as an innovative approach in *Ontario (A.G.)* v. *Fatehi* (1981), 34 O.R. (2d) 129 at 140, 127 D.L.R. (3d) 603 at 615 (C.A.), rev'd [1984] 2 S.C.R. 536, 15 D.L.R. (4th) 132.

61 Thus Hugh Collins writes that "[i]n practice . . . the courts rarely countenance the . . . head of damages for anticipated profits." H. Collins, *The Law of Contract* (London: Weidenfeld & Nicolson, 1986) at 181–82. See also L.E. Wolcher, "The Accommodation of Regret in Contract Remedies" (1988) 73 Iowa L. Rev. 797 at 873.

The most vocal proponent of the thesis that contract liability is based on reliance and restoration of benefits, and thus that contract recovery should be similarly defined, is Patrick Atiyah, who has made this point on several occasions. See P.S. Atiyah, *The Rise and Fall of Freedom of Contract* (Oxford: Clarendon Press, 1979) at 763–779. See also P.S. Atiyah, "Contracts, Promises and the Law of Obligations" (1978) 94 L.Q. Rev. 193.

62 "Contracts, Promises and the Law of Obligations," *ibid.* at 216. Professor Scott has more pointedly written of the intuition that "a loss of $100.00 is more unpleasant than a gain of $100.00 is attractive." R.E. Scott, "Error and rationality in Individual Decisionmaking: An Essay on the Relationship Between Cognitive Illusions and the Management of Choices" (1986) 59 S. Cal. L. Rev. 329 at 335.

63 (1936) 46 Yale L.J. 52 at 53–57.

law no longer seeks... to heal a disturbed *status quo*, but... assumes a more active role. *With the transition, the justification for legal relief loses its self-evident quality."*[64] Fuller and Perdue justify the protection of economic expectations by explaining that the promisee's assets are *actually* reduced but only in the sense that this would be understood "according to the modes of thought which enter into our economic system."[65] Moreover, they explain that the reason for the protection of expectations is that the adoption of a rule, which protects forgone opportunities is, in effect, the most effective means of encouraging reliance and thus compensating for actual incurred losses!

In recent years, several judges have reinterpreted the application of *remoteness* limitations on contract damage recovery. Remoteness concepts are employed to place limits on damage awards by requiring that the risk of loss be foreseeable with some degree of probability at the time of contracting.[66] The doctrinal rules support the view that the limiting concepts are not the same in tort as in contract, and that tort law – employed to compensate for actual losses rather than forgone gains – "imposes a much wider liability."[67]

The valuation disparity has been explicitly recognized in *H. Parsons (Livestock) Ltd.* v. *Uttley Ingham & Co.*,[68] where the Court considered the recoverability of losses associated with the sale and installation of a defective feed hopper. Lord Denning reinterpreted earlier remoteness cases as establishing two distinct rules, which could be understood as applying *not* to the doctrinal categories of tort and contract, but rather to the kinds of losses for which compensation was being sought. In the case of physical damage and actual expenses, the injured party should be able to recover losses which are foreseeable as resulting from a breach of contract even if, at the time of contract, there was only an extremely small probability of the loss occurring. However, claims representing loss of profit or loss of opportunities for gain are recoverable only if the risk of loss was contemplated as a serious possibility or a real danger.[69] The

---

[64] *Ibid.* at 56–57 [emphasis added].

[65] *Ibid.*

[66] The common law rules defining remoteness concepts in contract and tort are expressed in *Koufos* v. *C. Czarnikow Ltd.* (1967), [1969] 1 A.C. 350, [1967] 3 W.L.R. 1491, [1967] 3 All E.R. 686 (H.L.), and *Overseas Tankship (U.K.) Ltd.* v. *The Miller Steamship Company* (1966), [1967] 1 A.C. 617, 3 W.L.R. 498 [1966] 2 All E.R. 709 (P.C.) [hereinafter *The Wagon Mound No. 2*], respectively. In the former case, all of the judges attempted to delineate the particular degree of probability with which the parties ought to have foreseen the risk of loss resulting from the breach of contract. *The Wagon Mound No. 2* served similar purposes in the law of torts – the issue being whether the defendant ought to be liable for all reasonably foreseeable risks regardless of their degree of probability or whether some threshold statistical level of probability would trigger liability.

[67] Lord Reid in *The Wagon Mound No. 2, ibid.* at 634.

[68] (1977), [1978] Q.B. 791, [1977] 3 W.L.R. 900, [1978] 1 All E.R. 525 (C.A.).

[69] This idea was articulated by H.L.A. Hart & A.M. Honore in *Causation in the Law* (Oxford: Clarendon Press, 1959) at 281–87. It is also explicitly recognized in some Civilian jurisdictions. For example, the German Civil Code limits contract recovery in certain cases to the "negative" or reliance interest, as discussed in G.E. Clos, *Comparative Law* (Littleton, Colo.:

obvious result, whether or not one supports Lord Denning's re-articulation of the traditional remoteness rules,[70] is that the likelihood of recovery of losses is far greater than the likelihood of recovery of unrealized gains.

The principle reflected in this decision – that physical injuries and property damage should be given greater legal protection than unrealized expected economic gains – is again consistent with the empirical observation that people value losses more than forgone gains.

C. Contract Modifications

A third area where the valuation disparity manifests itself is in the distinctive treatment of performed and unperformed *intracontractual promises*. For example, where a person promises to pay an additional amount of money for a previously arranged contractual performance,[71] the courts have uniformly denied the promisee the right to enforce the promise.[72] Thus, if a construction company agrees to pay an additional $20,000 to ensure delivery of steel, which has already been contracted for, the court will not enforce the promise to pay the additional sum. However, if the construction company agrees to pay the additional $20,000 and actually transfers the money to the steel supplier, the promise is presumptively enforceable. The court will not order the money to be returned unless the construction company can demonstrate that the money was extorted from it under conditions of economic duress.[73]

The situations are indistinguishable except, again, for the location of the money. In the first example, the court will not order the transfer of wealth from the promisor to the promisee, preferring the *status quo*. In the second example, the court will not order the return of the wealth from the promisee to the

---

Fred B. Rothman & Co., 1979) at 226–236. Furthermore, article 252 explicitly limits recovery of losses of particular gains to situations where the risk is foreseeable as a probable consequence of the breach. See Germany, *The German Civil Code*, trans. by I.S. Forrester, S.L. Goren & H.-M. Ilgen (South Hackensack, NJ.: Fred B. Rothman & Co., 1975).

[70] The judgment is important because he confesses that the physical injury/property damage versus economic loss distinction operates *de facto* whatever formal test one accepts. See *supra* note 68 at 533 where he emphasizes a particular set of product liability cases in which personal injury claims were compensated "even though [manufacturers and retailers] had not the faintest suspicion of any trouble."

[71] The same anomaly operates where a creditor promises to accept less than the full amount owing from a debtor. At common law, the creditor could retract the promise even where the debtor had paid the money. See *Foakes* v. *Beer* (1884), 9 App. Cas. 605 (H.L.). However, the *Mercantile Law Amendment Act*, R.S.O. 1980, c. 265, s. 16, provides that *part performance* of the promise will extinguish the obligation. Again, the distinction is simply where the money is *located*.

[72] See *Gilbert Steel Ltd.* v. *University Construction Ltd.* (1976), 12 O.R. (2d) 19, 67 D.L.R. (3d) 606 (C.A.).

[73] See R. Goff & G. Jones, *The Law of Restitution*, 2d ed. (London: Sweet & Maxwell, 1978). See *Peter Kiewet Sons' Co. of Canada* v. *Eakins Construction Ltd.*, [1960] S.C.R. 361, 22 D.L.R. (2d) 465; *Re Municipal Spraying & Contracting Ltd.* (1980) 15 B.L.R. 37, (sub nom. *Municipal Spraying and Contracting Ltd.* v. *Nfld.*) 153 A.P.R. 91 (Nfld. T.D.) (plaintiff entitled to recover $195,000 worth of additional work performed for defendant on ground that performance was rendered in response to threatened legal action and was not voluntary).

promisor, again preferring the *status quo*. There are very persuasive reasons for singling out these *intracontractual* promises for special treatment. They represent very real risks of extortion generated by reliance-based situational monopolies; they introduce uncertainty relating to the authority to make the alleged modification of the agreement; and they generate additional transaction costs to contractual dispute resolution. But those reasons apply with equal force to performed and unperformed promises. The distinction developed in the cases is, once more, consistent with the empirical data, which point to significant welfare losses in the case of coerced transfers of wealth.

D. Gratuitous Promises

Judges have traditionally and consistently drawn a distinction between *giving* a gift to someone and *promising* to do so.[74] Performed gifts are enforceable; unperformed promises to give gifts are not. The undelivered gift cases are consistent with contract doctrines; the courts have not looked kindly on gratuitous promises[75] either at common law or at equity, and normally the rule is that they are not enforceable.[76] The major exception to the bargain theory of consideration is the enforcement of promises that have generated reasonable, detrimental reliance.[77]

Eisenberg classifies donative promises into three groups: informal and not relied-upon, formal but not relied-upon, and relied-upon.[78] Judges have consistently refused to enforce those gift promises that fall into the first and second categories. Several underlying rationales for the non-enforcement have been examined by several authors and various explanations have been offered. For example, Posner argues that the rule perhaps reflects an empirical *hunch* that "gratuitous promises tend to ... [involve] small stakes"[79] and, therefore, that the

---

[74] See M.A. Eisenberg, "The Principles of Consideration" (1982) 67 Cornell L. Rev. 640; M.A. Eisenberg, "Donative Promises" (1979) 47 U. Chi. L. Rev. 1; and *Halsbury's Laws of England*, 4th ed., vol. 20 (London: Butterworths, 1978) para. 62 at 36: "where a gift rests merely in promise, whether written or verbal ... it is incomplete ... and the court will not compel the intending ... to complete and perfect it."

[75] Gratuitous or donative promises are those given without the exchange of something of value, whether it be tangible property or another promise. *Currie* v. *Mesa* (1875), L.R. 10 Ex. 153, 23 W.R. 450; *Spruce Grove* v. *Yellowhead Regional Library Board* (1982), 44 A.R. 48, 143 D.L.R. (3d) 188, 21 M.P.L.R. 62 (C.A.).

[76] See for example, A.G. Guest, *Anson's Law of Contract*, 26th ed. (Oxford: Clarendon Press, 1984) at 82.

[77] R.A. Posner, "Gratuitous Promises in Economics and Law" (1977) 6 J. Leg. Stud. 411; and C. Fried, *Contract as Promise* (Cambridge: Harvard University Press, 1981) at 56.

[78] "Donative Promises," *supra* note 74 at 6–11.

[79] Posner, *supra* note 77 at 417. Posner argues that "[p]romises should not be enforced where the enforcement cost – to the extent not borne by the promisor – exceeds the gains from enforcement," and where the only reason for enforcement would be an increase in net social welfare. *Ibid.* at 414. It would, as Posner puts it at 417, be uneconomical to enforce casual social promises where the increment in utility to the promisor would be small if the promise were enforceable and the legal error costs high.

social costs of enforcing the promise will generally exceed the utility of doing so. Swan and Reiter suggest that we are naturally suspicious of gift promises. Because the law has provided rules for the completion of legally enforceable gifts, we should ask ourselves why those rules were not followed and whether, in fact, the donor really intended to complete the gift.[80]

An alternative explanation points to the small welfare loss associated with not receiving a gift, which is measured by the donee's forgone gain of the opportunity, relative to the welfare loss associated with depriving an existing owner of property of an entitlement, which is measured by the owner's asking price to give it up. This explanation, unlike the others, is consistent with the empirical data described earlier. Thus, Eisenberg argues that "lost expectation – a special form of disappointment – is among the least intense of injuries" and, therefore, is not worthy of legal remedy.[81] Since "lost expectation" is a forgone gain, Eisenberg clearly reveals an intuitive awareness of the valuation disparity and its role in understanding and predicting judicial choice. An unperformed gift promise is not treated as a loss. The "wrench of delivery"[82] has not been experienced by the promisor and no *real* loss has been experienced by the promisee.

A more realistic assessment of gains and losses, taking the valuation disparity into account, would predict that gratuitous promises that are relied upon will often be enforced because in those cases a *real* loss would have been incurred.[83] In *Skidmore* v. *Bradford*,[84] a nephew was promised a gift of a warehouse by his uncle who, in addition to paying one thousand pounds towards the purchase price of five thousand pounds, had asked the owner to amend the agreement by writing in the nephew's name and by preparing the receipt in the nephew's name. Before he died, the uncle paid a further five hundred pounds on the purchase price. Since the nephew had signed the agreement to purchase, he was held liable for it. He paid, sued the uncle's estate to enforce the promise to give the warehouse as a gift, and *won*. There the Court held that the nephew had "incurred that liability on the faith of the representations of the testator that he would give him the warehouse."[85]

Article 90(1) of the *Restatement (Second) of Contracts*[86] represents the modern version of this position. It provides that promises, which can reasonably be

---

[80] J. Swan & B.J. Reiter, *Contracts, Gases, Notes and Materials*, 3d ed. (Toronto: Emond Montgomery, 1985) at 223; and M.D. Bayles, "Legally Enforceable Commitments" (1985) 4 L. & Phil. 312 at 338.

[81] "Donative Promises," *supra* note 74 at 3. See also "The Principles of Consideration," *supra* note 74 at 656 where he says that "[t]his principle can be justified on several grounds, the most important of which is the low level of injury resulting from breach."

[82] P. Mecham, "The Requirement of Delivery in Gifts of Chattels and of Choses in Action Evidenced by Commercial Instruments" (1926) 21 Ill. L. Rev. 341 at 348–49.

[83] This is, in effect, the argument presented by P. Atiyah, *Consideration in Contracts: A Fundamental Restatement* (Canberra: Australian National University Press, 1971).

[84] (1869), L.R. 8 Eq. 134.

[85] *Ibid.* at 137.

[86] *Restatement (Second) of Contracts* §90 (1981).

expected to induce reliance, are binding and should be enforced through remedies "limited as justice requires." While the cases discussing the appropriate remedy under Article 90 are not uniform, a substantial percentage of them award remedies limited by the promisee's reliance losses rather than expected benefits.[87]

E. Opportunistic Conduct

Opportunistic conduct during contract formation and performance may take several forms, including withholding information during contract formation, taking advantage of ambiguities in language, demanding performance in unintended situations, and failing to perform in order to take advantage of unexpected opportunities. Yet contract negotiations and performance will likely take place more effectively if trust is present and is generated by the process.[88] Risks of opportunism can be reduced by questioning the other's motives, honesty, and future plans,[89] but it is inappropriate and probably dysfunctional to do so.

The treatment by the courts of one form of opportunistic behaviour – deliberate contract breaches motivated by attempts to capture unanticipated profitable opportunities – represents another example of the incorporation of the valuation disparity concept into judicial decision making. Here the valuation disparity manifests itself in *fairness* norms, which track those generated by the *fairness* studies discussed earlier.

One model of contract law, employed by Posner, ignores the motives or gains of a person who breaks a contract. Whether the contract breaker fails to perform in order to avoid losses or to generate windfall gains is irrelevant.[90] An alternate model of contract, which reflects the gain–loss valuation disparity, holds that motives for breach are important, and that failing to perform in order to avoid unanticipated expenses will be treated differently from failing to

---

[87] See *supra* note 63 at 64-65. See for example, *Goodman* v. *Dicker*, 169 F.2d 684 (D.C. Cir. 1948); and *Associated Tabulating Services* v. *Olympic Life Insurance Co.*, 414 F.2d 1306 (5th Cir. 1969).

[88] See R. McKean, "Economics of Trust, Altruism, and Corporate Responsibility" in E.S. Phelps, ed., *Altruism, Morality and Economic Theory* (New York: Russell Sage Foundation, 1975) 29; D. Collard, *Altruism and Economy: A Study in Non-Selfish Economics* (Oxford: Martin Robertson, 1978) at 12; and I.R. Macneil, *The New Social Contract* (New Haven: Yale University Press, 1980).

By trust we mean attitudes and behaviour which indicate that each person is willing to rely on the other to act fairly and to take into account the other's welfare. Ian Macneil suggests that he uses solidarity and trust as equivalents, referring to a belief in future harmonious affirmative cooperation. See I.R. Macneil, "Exchange Revisited: Individual Utility and Social Solidarity" (1986) 96 Ethics 567 at 572.

[89] For an example of opportunistic behaviour in long-term supply contracts, see *Fratelli Gardino S.p.A.* v. *Caribbean Lumber Co.*, 587 F.2d 204 (5th Cir. 1979). (The seller claims that it is unable to meet contract commitments due to insufficient shipping facilities. The Court finds that facilities were available, but that the seller had chosen to use them for more profitable engagements.)

[90] See *supra* note 53 and *supra* note 38 at 458–62. See also *Butler* v. *Fairclough* (1917), 23 C.L.R. 78 at 79; and *Asamera Oil Corp.* v. *Sea Oil and General Corp.* (1978), [1979] 1 S.C.R. 633, 89 D.L.R. (3d) 1, (*sub nom. Baud Corp. N.V.* v. *Brook no. 2*) [1979] 3 W.W.R. 93.

perform in order to generate a windfall gain to the breaching party.[91] Kessler, Gilmore, and Kronman describe the "implicitly amoral"[92] contract theory of Posner and Holmes, which ignores the motives for breach. Alternatively, they argue that breaches motivated by a gain to the contract breaker will be treated more severely:

> Many will say that [the] breach ought still to be condemned from an ethical point of view ... The inclination to blame A will be even stronger if he has benefitted from his breach, although B has not been harmed ... The Holmesian view ... seems never to have fully overcome the resistance of common sense, which stubbornly insists that moral blame (unlike legal liability) is not entirely a function of the consequences of an action but depends, as well, upon the motives and intentions of the actor.[93]

This second model appears to operate more consistently in contract damage disputes.[94] Predictions,[95] both as to liability and the extent of recovery by plaintiffs, vary directly with information on the motives for breach. In addition, the rule that "motives don't count" has been subject to a number of decisions in which judges have explicitly recognized that they are treating the two situations differently and have designed damage awards deliberately to deprive the breaching parties of the gains, which motivated their non-performance.[96]

---

[91] See A.S. Burrows, *Remedies for Torts and Breach of Contract* (London: Butterworths, 1987) at 252 and at 273.

[92] *Contracts, Cases and Materials*, 3d ed. (Boston: Little, Brown, 1986) at 1067.

[93] *Ibid.*

[94] It may operate in many other contexts as well. For example, deliberate breach for profit may influence judicial discretion in saying that a breach is *fundamental*, thus triggering judicial review of otherwise enforceable exclusion clauses. Or, wilful breach for profit might influence judicial interpretation of terms as conditions rather than warranties. Both choices would work to the contract breaker's disadvantage. Perhaps the application of the mistake doctrines can be explained by examining the motives of the person who is seeking to enforce agreements against others who misinterpreted the word or the agreement.

[95] What is surprising is that many, if not all, academics interpret the cases as supporting this view without any data except their intuitions. Thus Kessler, Gilmore and Kronman suggest that, in the case of wilful breach, *the inclination to blame [the contract breaker] will be even stronger if he has benefited from the breach. Supra* note 92 at 1067.

[96] For Example, in *Penarth Dock Engineering Co.* v. *Pounds*, [1963] 1 Lloyd's Rep. 359 (Q.B.), a defendant refused to remove its ship from the plaintiff's dock. Even though the plaintiff did not suffer any loss, the Court ordered the defendant to pay money to the plaintiff representing the cost of renting the space, which it saved by not having to rent alternate space.

The cases in which judges have explicitly deprived contract-breakers of the gains generated by breach are characterized, as the valuation disparity data would predict, by behaviour that often represents deliberate interference with possessory or property rights of the plaintiff. Thus, in *Wrotham Park Estate Co.* v. *Parkside Homes Ltd.*, [1974] 1 W.L.R. 798, [1974] 2 All E.R. 321 (Ch.), the defendants entered into a restrictive covenant with the plaintiff, which prohibited the construction of houses on the plaintiff's property. The defendants built several houses, which did not diminish the value of the plaintiff's property, but were ordered to pay 5% of the 50,000 pounds profit which they made on the construction of the houses. The damages were ordered in lieu of an injunction to demolish the houses. The Court referred to several *tort* decisions, which provided for restitutionary awards in the case of interference with plaintiff's property; the case had been deemed analogous to that situation. See *supra* note 91 at 274–75.

But the treatment of opportunism is more subtle than merely awarding damages to deprive contract breakers of windfall gains. It extends to the interpretation of facts and the discretionary application of principles, which permit judges to incorporate *fairness* attitudes in their decision making. These fairness norms, like those reflected in the empirical studies described earlier, are associated with the distinction between gains and losses.

The operation of fairness norms in contract law can be demonstrated by contrasting cases in which judges respond differently, depending on whether the otherwise similar behaviour of contracting parties is motivated by attempts to take advantage of unexpected opportunities or by attempts to respond to unanticipated losses.

One example of such a response might be found in the application of promissory estoppel doctrines in contract performance and modification. Promissory estoppel was developed by the courts in an effort to protect the interests of contracting parties who rely on the promises for which they did not bargain or representations of their contracting parties. It is applied, as most writers admit, to avoid unjust enrichment and the opportunistic manipulation of legal rules and ambiguous contract language.[97]

A recent example of the application of the doctrine, which offers insight into these underlying *fairness* norms, is a recent decision of the British Columbia Court of Appeal in a dispute between a landlord and a tenant regarding the ability of the tenant to exercise an option to renew its tenancy.[98] The facts were straightforward. Dukes Cookies had entered into a three-year contractual tenancy agreement with the Alma Mater Society of the University of British Columbia. The lease included a term which permitted Dukes to extend the lease for two years if it gave written notice to the landlord during a specific two-month period.

During the term of the lease, Dukes and the Alma Mater Society began negotiations for a new five-year lease. The negotiations included discussions relating to profit-sharing arrangements and an expansion of the leased premises. The negotiations were prolonged until after the two-month notice period had ended. Dukes failed to give written notice to extend the existing lease because they assumed, based on statements made by the Alma Mater Society's principals, that they would obtain a new five-year lease. After the expiry of the two-month notice period, the Alma Mater Society notified Dukes that it would terminate the lease according to its terms because Dukes had not given written notice to extend the original lease. Dukes brought the legal action to prevent the

---

[97] See J.A. Manwaring, "Promissory Estoppel in the Supreme Court of Canada" (1987) 10 Dalhousie L.J. 43 at 51. The common law doctrine of promissory estoppel is reflected in *supra* note 96. See also J.M. Feinman, "Promissory Estoppel and Judicial Method" (1984) 97 Harv. L. Rev. 678.

[98] *Re 6781427 Holdings Ltd. and Alma Mater Society of University of British Columbia* (1987), 44 D.L.R. (4th) 257 (B.C.C.A.), aff'g (1987), 36 D.L.R. (4th) 753 [hereinafter *Dukes*].

Alma Mater Society from enforcing the written notice provision in the current lease.

Both the trial judge and the Court of Appeal decided the case in favour of Dukes with the result that it was permitted to exercise its option notwithstanding the expiration of the notice period. The formal justification for the decision was the application of the doctrine of promissory estoppel. Through this doctrine, judges can protect the unbargained for reliance of a party to a contract where it would be inequitable to permit the other party to retract a representation that induced the reliance.[99] However, it is obvious from the decision that the Court could just as easily have decided the case in favour of the landlord on either of two grounds. First, the Court could have found that no representation was made by the landlord to the tenant regarding the likelihood of entering into the new arrangement because the testimony of both parties was in conflict on this ground. Also, there was considerable authority that there must be an unequivocal and explicit representation in order to trigger the doctrine. Second, the Court could have found that it was unreasonable for the tenant to infer that the notice provision would not be enforced even if the representation had been made.

What is missing from *both* judgments, and yet what must have been critical from the perspective of everyone concerned, is any evidence explaining the abrupt reversal by the landlord of its negotiation position. Why, one can ask, did the landlord negotiate for months as if it would enter into an extended new lease, and then, without warning, give the tenant notice to vacate the premises?

That is the first question that comes to the mind of many readers, and yet is left unanswered in the reported reasons for the decisions. Discussions with the lawyer for the defendant landlord, however, reveal a very different picture. The lawyer indicates that the trial judge was extremely interested in the motives for the landlord's behaviour – an irrelevant consideration in formal terms.[100] The motive as described in the evidence was simple. The landlord discovered during negotiations that the profits generated by the tenant's business far exceeded its expectations, *and had terminated negotiations in order to open its own cookie business in the same location!* What is remarkable about the case is that neither the trial nor appellate decisions mentions this fact. That is, the motive for the termination of the negotiations consisted of an attempt to obtain unexpected gains at the expense of the tenant.

The case can be interpreted as an example of judges responding to the valuation disparity. That is, the unilateral decision by the landlord to terminate

---

[99] The American position is not substantially different, although there is considerable debate regarding the extent to which the promisor can be taken to be responsible for the promisee's reliance. See *supra* note 86; and Feinman, *supra* note 97.

[100] That is, the formal doctrine of promissory estoppel, which was applied to justify deciding the case in favour of the tenant, does not include an assessment of the motive of the party who attempts to retract a representation.

the lease without giving the tenant the opportunity to renew for two years generated an expected gain to the landlord *at the expense of the tenant*. The decision can be seen as a reflection of judicial intuition, consistent with the empirical data on the valuation disparity, that the benefit to the landlord, consisting of expected profit, would be substantially less than the harm imposed on the tenant by the eviction. This valuation disparity gives rise to strong perceptions of unfairness consistent with the empirical evidence indicating that when one person gains at the expense of another – a zero-sum game – the transaction is overwhelmingly seen as unfair.[101]

A second example of judges responding to the valuation disparity and the motive for the defendant's action is a decision on the doctrine of commercial impracticability in *Aluminum Company of America* v. *Essex Group, Inc.*[102] That case involved a claim for relief from contractual obligations on the doctrinal grounds of mistake, frustration, and commercial impracticability by the plaintiff Alcoa. Alcoa successfully obtained judicially ordered relief from a long-term obligation to process aluminum ore, which had turned out to be unprofitable because of unanticipated increases in Alcoa's energy costs. The case is generally considered remarkable for two reasons. First, the trial judge was forced to distinguish a long line of cases, which most people interpreted as precluding relief where the plaintiff's expected profits had failed to materialize due to unanticipated cost increases. Second, the trial judge did not simply relieve Alcoa from its smelting obligations, but imposed a loss and risk-sharing modification to the contract by developing new pricing terms to reduce the losses to Alcoa associated with the explicit contract pricing arrangement.[103]

In *Alcoa*, the Court explicitly recognized *fairness* norms as justifying judicial choices.[104] The problem, of course, is identifying or articulating the content of this fairness norm. Again, as in *Dukes*, the interpretation of judicial behaviour is problematic. But the judgment includes a reference to the formally *irrelevant* fact that, when Essex Group had discovered that it was in a position to own substantial amounts of very cheap aluminum, it decided to enter the commodities market. Instead of ordering and using the aluminum in its commercial

---

[101] See *supra* note 37.

[102] 499 F. Supp. 53 (W.D. Pa. 1980) [hereinafter *Alcoa*].

[103] The literature on the case is voluminous, although most writers focus on issues other than the distinction between gain and loss, which we consider in this paper. See V.P. Goldberg, "Price Adjustment in Long-Term Contracts" (1985) Wis. L. Rev. 527; R.E. Speidel, "The New Spirit of Contract" (1982) 2 J.L. & Com. 193; and R.E. Speidel, "Court Imposed Price Adjustments under Long-Term Supply Contracts" (1981) 76 Nw. U.L. Rev. 369.

[104] See *supra* note 102 at 76, where the trial judge alludes to the idea that the contract would not be enforced where it would be "commercially senseless and unjust." See also "The New Spirit of Contract," *ibid.* at 201, referring to the courts' policing transactions "in the interests of fairness"; and S.W. Halpern, "Application of the Doctrine of Commercial Impracticability. Searching for the 'Wisdom of Solomon'" (1987) 135 U. Pa. L. Rev. 1123, referring to an obligation to act in good faith and to agree to contractual adjustments in order to avoid any fortuitous *advantage* at the expense of the other party.

operations, it had sought out and entered into contracts with third parties to sell its aluminum at current market prices and, thus, reap a windfall gain at the expense of Alcoa.[105]

Again, the implication of the judgment is consistent with judicial sensitivity to the valuation disparity which generates perceptions of unfairness. Essex Group was gaining a windfall profit at the direct expense of Alcoa, a transaction consistently seen as unfair.

One cannot, of course, point to two ambiguous cases and conclude that judges are responding to conflict only in terms of fairness and the valuation disparity. Certainly there is little explicit recognition of their doing so. What is required to verify the connection of *law* to the fairness data, and what is obviously impossible, is to identify two populations of cases in which all *facts* are identical but for the relevant variable – the acquisition of an advantage at the direct expense of another party. If judges are acting in this way, the outcomes in the two groups of cases should be different.[106]

F. Repossession

A final example of judges developing principles consistent with the valuation disparity consists of a series of decisions in which judges have restricted creditors' rights to repossess delivered goods on default by buyers prior to full payment of the purchase price. This is evident first, in the presumptive treatment by judges of time-of-payment clauses, where judges have consistently held that "time is not of the essence" in regard to payment for goods.[107] Without an explicit contract term, the result is that sellers cannot terminate the contract and repossess goods simply on default and that buyers are given the opportunity to remedy the defect and retain possession.

Second, even where time-of-payment clauses have been expressly stated as conditions – thus apparently permitting the seller to elect to be discharged from the contract and to repossess the goods – the courts have developed several

---

[105] Apparently, Essex Group was taking advantage of its 36.25 cents per pound price for aluminum by selling 25 per cent of its supply in the open market at the then current market price of 73.13 cents per pound. In fact, Essex Group was underbidding Alcoa and, according to Alcoa, taking Alcoa's customers. See Note, "Court-Imposed Modifications: Supplementing the All-or-Nothing Approach to Discharge Cases" (1983) 44 Ohio St. L.J. 1079 at 1089 n. 107 and n. 108.

[106] The obvious and insurmountable problem with conducting the experiment is that the two populations of cases do not exist. However, we are not alone in suspecting that deliberate breach for profit is influencing the exercise of judicial discretion. For example, Swan and Reiter, in a discussion of the dissent of Irwin J. in *Peevyhouse* v. *Garland Coal and Mining Co.*, 382 P. 2d 109 (Okla. 1963), suggest that he is responding to deliberate decisions to break contracts and thus gain wealth at the expense of another. See *Contracts, Cases, Notes and Materials, supra* note 80 at 10.

[107] M.G. Bridge, *Sale of Goods* (Toronto: Butterworths, 1988) at 409. See also *Mersey Steel and Iron Co.* v. *Naylor Benzon and Co.* (1884), 9 App. Cas. 434, [1881–85] All E.R. 365; and *Decro-Wall International S.A.* v. *Practitioners in Marketing Ltd.*, [1971] 1 W.L.R. 361, [1971] 2 All E.R. 216 (C.A.).

techniques to protect the possessory welfare of the buyer. These include liberal doctrines of waiver[108] and restrictions on the self-help repossession tactics of sellers.[109]

Third, a significant number of jurisdictions have enacted seize-or-sue legislation, which precludes sellers from both repossessing goods and suing for the purchase price.[110] Finally, in many jurisdictions, repossession is permitted only with permission of the court where the buyer has paid more than two-thirds of the purchase price.[111] This array of judicial and legislative activity can be explained by the data on the valuation disparity, which would predict substantial welfare losses associated with repossession of goods from debtors on default.

Schwartz has attacked seize-or-sue legislation as being "without coherent justification."[112] He argues, first, that there is no evidence of systematic underselling of repossessed goods through organized cartels; and second, that repossession does *not* impose greater harms on debtors than it creates gains for creditors. Schwartz does discuss the valuation disparity, but unfortunately, he misses its significance in several ways. First, in discussing the effects of repossession, he admits that the losses associated with repossession may reflect the fact that debtors may value the goods more than the market price. However, he then states that the "harms could not occur if debtors were perfectly informed of the consequences of granting security."[113] That is, if the future welfare loss were known at the time of contracting, then the debtor would either not grant security, or would grant less and pay a higher interest rate. Whether Schwartz is correct or not depends on when the buyer's reference point changes, and thus when the repossession is perceived as a loss rather than a forgone gain. If, as seems reasonable, the shift does not take place until some time after possession of the good, then the buyer's ability to contract *ex ante* is compromised.

---

[108] See *Pantoutsos* v. *Raymond Hadley Corp. of New York*, [1917] 2 K.B. 473, [1916–17] All E.R. Rep. 448 (the failure to object to late payment held to constitute waiver of the right to treat timely payment as a condition).

[109] For example, sellers must give buyers notice of their intention to repossess or take control of property. See *Traders Bank of Canada* v. *G. & J. Brown Manufacturing Co.* (1889), 18 O.R. 430 (Ch.); and *Royal Bank of Canada* v. *Cal Glass Ltd.* (1980), 22 B.C.L.R. 328 (C.A). The restrictions are described in detail in D. Paciocco, "Personal Property Security Act Repossession: The Risk and the Remedy" in M.A. Springman & E. Gertner, eds., *Debtor-Creditor Law: Practice and Doctrine* (Toronto: Butterworths, 1985) at 365. Recent statutory developments have removed the notice requirement. See for example, *The Personal Property Security Act*, C.C.S.M. c. P35, s. 57.

[110] See *Uniform Commercial Code* §5.103; *The Limitation of Civil Rights Act*, R.S.S. 1965, c. 103, s. 18; *Sale of Goods on Condition Act*, R.S.B.C. 1979, c. 373, s. 20; and *Chauel Mortgage Act.*, R.S.B.C. 1979, c. 48, s. 23.

[111] See for example, *Consumer Protection Act*, R.S.O. 1980, c. 87, s. 23(1).

[112] A. Schwartz, "The Enforceability of Security Interests in Consumer Goods" (1983) 26 J. L. Econ. 117 at 161.

[113] *Ibid.* at 140.

Second, even assuming debtor ignorance of the costs of repossession, Schwartz argues that the alleged welfare losses associated with repossession either would not occur or would be trivial. He acknowledges that, if debtors value the goods because they own them and thus, if the amount they would demand to give up their goods exceeds the amount they would pay to obtain the goods in a significant way, then the assignment of legal rights could determine outcomes more frequently than is commonly supposed. However, the valuation disparity may be linked to a kind of relationship connected not to the assignment of legal rights, but to possession. If that is so, then merely shifting *ownership* will not eliminate the valuation disparity.

Third, in assessing whether repossession generates losses, he denies the empirical validity of claims that "creditors necessarily derive less value from repossessed goods than debtors lose."[114] While the empirical studies described above do not support the proposition that the creditors *necessarily* derive less value, they certainly do offer support for the proposition that the loss to the debtor will consistently, and in a very significant way, exceed the expected gain to the creditor.

Finally, Schwartz argues that the gain to the buyer who purchases repossessed goods from the creditor may offset the loss to the original buyer, and thus that repossession does not necessarily destroy value. Again, the empirical studies discussed earlier suggest that the loss of economic welfare measured by the original buyer's reservation price will almost certainly exceed the gain of the second buyer.

Our conclusion, drawn from the empirical evidence described above, is that buyers in possession will consistently value the possessed goods significantly above the value placed on them either by repossessing creditors or hypothetical future buyers, and the purchaser will not generally be able to take the higher valuation into account when contracting. Recognizing this valuation disparity offers considerable support for the judicial restrictions on repossession framed in common law rules and presumptive interpretations of contract language, as well as for the legislative restrictions on repossession adopted in many jurisdictions.

IV. CONCLUSION

Contrary to the assertions of conventional economic practice and the prescriptions of many critics of legal outcomes, people commonly do not value losses the same as they value gains. The greater weight given to losses over objectively commensurate gains appears pervasive and is a major determinant of which actions or changes meet community standards of being fair or acceptable and which are likely to be considered unfair or less acceptable.

---

[114] *Ibid.* at 142–43.

Further, legal institutions appear to reflect the same disparity between valuations. Court decisions over a very broad array of cases seem to take account of these differences in according greater protection of losses over forgone gains.

This greater weight given to losses in legal outcomes is not only consistent with people's judgments of fairness and normal business practices but, to the extent that these different weights reflect actual valuations of welfare changes, this differential treatment in judicial choices may also promote efficiency. Equivalent treatment of gains and losses called for by reform proposals "to reconcile" the differences[115] seems not only unlikely to be adopted, but may also lead to inefficient outcomes and may be contrary to community fairness and equity standards.

[115] Waddams, *supra* note 7 at 540.

25. Contrasting Rational and Psychological Analyses of Political Choice

George A. Quattrone and Amos Tversky

ABSTRACT. We contrast the rational theory of choice in the form of expected utility theory with descriptive psychological analysis in the form of prospect theory, using problems involving the choice between political candidates and public referendum issues. The results showed that the assumptions underlying the classical theory of risky choice are systematically violated in the manner predicted by prospect theory. In particular, our respondents exhibited risk aversion in the domain of gains, risk seeking in the domain of losses, and a greater sensitivity to losses than to gains. This is consistent with the advantage of the incumbent under normal conditions and the potential advantage of the challenger in bad times. The results further show how a shift in the reference point could lead to reversals of preferences in the evaluation of political and economic options, contrary to the assumption of invariance. Finally, we contrast the normative and descriptive analyses of uncertainty in choice and address the rationality of voting.

The assumption of individual rationality plays a central role in the social sciences, especially in economics and political science. Indeed, it is commonly assumed that most if not all economic and political agents obey the maxims of consistency and coherence leading to the maximization of utility. This notion has been captured by several models that constitute the rational theory of choice, including the expected utility model for decision making under risk, the riskless theory of choice among commodity bundles, and the Bayesian theory for the updating of belief. These models employ different assumptions about the nature of the options and the information available to the decision maker, but they all adopt the principles of coherence and invariance that underlie the prevailing notion of rationality.

The research reported in this article was funded by a grant awarded to Quattrone by the National Institute of Health 1 RO1 MH41382-01 and to Tversky by the Office of Naval Research ON00014-84-K-0615. We are indebted to Philip Converse, Robyn Dawes, Alexander George, Robert Jervis, and Scott Plous for their helpful comments on an earlier draft.

The rational theory of choice has been used to prescribe action as well as to describe the behavior of consumers, entrepreneurs, voters, and politicians. The use of the rational theory as a descriptive model has been defended on the grounds that people are generally effective in pursuing their goals, that the axioms underlying the theory are intuitively compelling, and that evolution and competition favor rational individuals over less rational ones. The objections to the rationality assumption were primarily psychological. The human animal, it has been argued, is often controlled by emotions and desires that do not fit the model of calculating rationality. More recent objections to the maximization doctrine have been cognitive rather than motivational. Following the seminal work of Herbert Simon (1955, 1978) and the emergence of cognitive psychology, it has become evident that human rationality is bounded by limitations on memory and computational capabilities. Furthermore, the experimental analysis of inference and choice has revealed that the cognitive machinery underlying human judgment and decision making is often inconsistent with the maxims of rationality. These observations have led to the development of a descriptive analysis of judgment and choice that departs from the rational theory in many significant respects (see, e.g., Abelson and Levi 1985; Dawes 1988; Kahneman, Slovic, and Tversky 1982; Tversky and Kahneman 1986).

We contrast the rational theory of choice with a descriptive psychological analysis, using a series of questions involving political candidates and public referenda. These problems are used to illustrate the differences between rational and descriptive theories of choice and to test their predictions. Some of the questions probed our respondents' views about familiar political issues, such as the Equal Rights Amendment and the prevalence of crime in black neighborhoods compared to white neighborhoods. In other cases involving the test of general hypotheses, such as risk aversion, we introduced hypothetical problems in order to achieve experimental control and eliminate the influence of irrelevant factors. The use of hypothetical problems raises obvious questions regarding the generality and the applicability of the finding. Nevertheless, we believe that the use of carefully worded questions can address key issues regarding people's values and beliefs so long as respondents take the questions seriously and have no particular reason to disguise or misrepresent their true preferences. Under these conditions hypothetical questions can be used to compare alternative theories of political choice that cannot be readily tested using available survey and voting data. Our results, of course, do not provide definitive conclusions about political decision making, but they may shed light on the formation of political judgment and stimulate new hypotheses that can be tested in national election surveys in the years to come.

We focus on expected utility theory, which is the major normative theory of decision making under risk (von Neumann and Morgenstern 1947; Raiffa 1968; Savage 1954). This model is contrasted with prospect theory, a descriptive analysis developed by Kahneman and Tversky (1979, 1984). The first section deals

with the role of the reference point and its impact on the choice between political candidates. In the second section we test the assumption of invariance
and contrast it with a psychophysical analysis of numerical scales. The third
section deals with the perception and the weighting of chance events and the
role of uncertainty in choice. The fourth section addresses the classical issue
of the rationality of voting. It contrasts, again, a rational analysis based on the
probability of casting a decisive vote with a less rational analysis that incorporates an element of self-deception. The implications of the present analysis are
discussed in the fifth and final section.

REFERENCE EFFECTS, RISK ATTITUDES,
AND LOSS AVERSION

The standard utility function, derived from the expected utility model, has two
essential characteristics. First, it is defined on wealth, or final asset position.
Thus, a person with wealth W accepts an even chance to win $1,000 or lose $500 if
the difference between the utility of $W + $1,000 and the utility of W (the upside)
exceeds the difference between the utility of W and the utility of $W - $500 (the
downside). Second, the utility function is concave; that is, the subjective value
of an additional dollar diminishes with the total amount of money one has.
The first assumption (asset integration) is necessitated by basic considerations
of coherence. The second assumption (concavity) was introduced by Bernoulli
(1954) to accommodate the common observations of risk aversion, and it has
played an essential role in economics. A person is risk-averse if he or she prefers
a sure outcome over a risky prospect that has an equal or greater expected value.
For example, most people prefer $100 for sure over an even chance to win $200
or nothing. Risk aversion is implied by the concavity of the utility scale because
the utility of $2x$ is less than twice the utility of x.

Although risk aversion is quite common, particularly for prospects with positive outcomes, risk seeking is also prevalent, particularly for prospects with
negative outcomes. For example, most people find a sure loss of $100 more aver-
sive than an even chance to lose $200 or nothing. To explain the combination of
risk aversion and risk seeking, prospect theory replaces the traditional concave
utility function for wealth by an S-shaped function for changes of wealth. In
this theory, therefore, the carriers of values are positive or negative changes (i.e.,
gains and losses) defined relative to a neutral reference point. Furthermore, the
value function is assumed to be concave above the reference point and convex
below it, giving rise to risk aversion in the domain of gains and risk seeking in
the domain of losses. As in the classical theory, it is assumed that the difference
between $100 and $200 is subjectively larger than the (numerically equivalent)
difference between $1,100 and $1,200. Unlike the classical theory, however, it
is assumed that the difference between a loss of $100 and a loss of $200 is
subjectively larger than the numerically equivalent difference between a loss

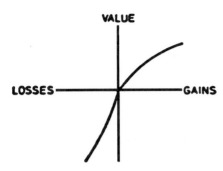

Figure 25.1. A hypothetical value function.

of $1,100 and a loss of $1,200. Thus, the value function of prospect theory is steepest at the origin, and it gets shallower as one moves away from the reference point in either direction. An important property of the value function – called loss aversion – is that the downside is considerably steeper than the upside; that is, losses loom larger than the corresponding gains. A typical value function with these characteristics is given in Figure 25.1.

Attitudes towards Risk

Expected utility theory and prospect theory yield different predictions. The classical theory predicts risk aversion independent of the reference point, whereas prospect theory predicts risk aversion in the domain of gains and risk seeking in the domain of losses (except for small probabilities). Furthermore, prospect theory implies that shifts in the reference point induced by the framing of the problem will have predictable effects on people's risk preferences. These phenomena are illustrated in the following four problems, each involving a choice between alternative political prospects.

The respondents to these and other problems reported in this article were undergraduates at Stanford University or at the University of California at Berkeley. The problems were presented in a questionnaire in a classroom setting. Each problem involved a simple choice between two candidates or positions on a public referendum. The respondents were asked to imagine actually facing the choice described, and they were assured that the responses were anonymous and that there were no correct or incorrect answers. The number of respondents in this and all subsequent problems is denoted by N, and the percentage who chose each outcome is given in parentheses.

Problem 1 ($N = 89$): Suppose there is a continent consisting of five nations, Alpha, Beta, Gamma, Delta, and Epsilon. The nations all have very similar systems of government and economics, are members of a continental common market, and are therefore expected to produce very similar standards of living and rates of inflation. Imagine you are a citizen of Alpha, which is about to hold its presidential election. The two presidential candidates, Brown and Green, differ from each other primarily in the policies they are known to favor and are sure to implement. These policies were studied by Alpha's two leading economists, who are of equal expertise and are impartial as to the result of the election. After studying the policies advocated by Brown and Green and the policies currently being pursued by the other four nations, each economist made a forecast. The forecast consisted of three predictions about the expected standard of living index (SLI). The SLI measures the goods and services consumed (directly or indirectly) by the average citizen yearly. It is expressed in dollars per capita so that the higher the SLI the higher the level of economic prosperity. The three projections concerned

1. the average SLI to be expected among the nations Beta, Gamma, Delta, and Epsilon
2. the SLI to be expected by following Brown's policy
3. the SLI to be expected by following Green's policy

The forecasts made by each economist are summarized in the following table:

	Projected SLI in Dollars per Capita		
	Other Four Nations	**Brown's Policy**	**Green's Policy**
Economist 1	$43,000	$65,000	$51,000
Economist 2	$45,000	$43,000	$53,000

Suppose that as a citizen of Alpha, you were asked to cast your vote for Brown or Green. On the basis of the information provided, whom would you vote for? [Brown, 28%; Green, 72%]

A second group of respondents received the same cover story as in Problem 1, but the economists' forecasts about the other four nations were altered. The forecasts made about the candidates remained the same.

Problem 2 ($N = 96$):

	Projected SLI in Dollars per Capita		
	Other Four Nations	**Brown's Policy**	**Green's Policy**
Economist 1	$63,000	$65,000	$51,000
Economist 2	$65,000	$43,000	$53,000

Suppose that as a citizen of Alpha, you were asked to cast your vote for Brown or Green. On the basis of the information provided, whom would you vote for? [Brown, 50%; Green, 50%]

Comparing the responses to problems 1 and 2 shows that the choice between Brown and Green was influenced by the projected SLI in other countries. This effect can be explained in terms of the value function of prospect theory. Because the two economists were said to be impartial and of equal expertise, we assume that respondents gave equal weight to their projections. Hence, the actuarial expected value of Brown's policy ($54,000) is about the same as that of Green's policy ($52,000). However, Brown is riskier than Green in the sense that the outcomes projected for Brown have greater spread than those projected for Green. Therefore, Brown would profit from risk seeking and Green from risk aversion. According to prospect theory, an individual's attitude towards risk depends on whether the outcomes are perceived as gains or losses, relative to the reference point.

In Problems 1 and 2 it seems reasonable to adopt the average SLI projected for the other nations as a point of reference, because all five nations were said to have comparable standards of living. The reference point then will be about $44,000 in problem 1 and $64,000 in problem 2. Outcomes projected for Brown and Green would, therefore, be treated as gains in the first problem and as losses in the second. As a consequence, the value function entails more risk aversion in problem 1 than in problem 2. In fact, significantly more respondents opted for the relatively risk-free Green in problem 1 (72%) than in problem 2 (50%) ($p < .005$ by chi-square). Another factor that may have contributed to the finding is a tendency for people to discount the highly discrepant projection for the risky candidate, Brown (i.e., the one made by Economist 1 in problem 1 and by Economist 2 in problem 2). Although this consideration may have played a role in the present case, the same shift in attitudes towards risk have been observed in many other problems in which this account does not apply (Tversky and Kahneman 1986).

To address whether the predictions based on the value function apply to other attributes besides money, we included in the same questionnaire one of two problems in which the rate of inflation was the outcome of the choice.

Problem 3 ($N = 76$): Now imagine that several years have passed and that there is another presidential contest between two new candidates, Frank and Carl. The same two economists studied the candidates' preferred policies and made a projection. This time, however, the forecast concerned the projected rate of inflation. The forecasts made by each economist are summarized in the following table:

	Projected Rate of Inflation (%)		
	Other Four Nations	Frank's Policy	Carl's Policy
Economist 1	24	16	4
Economist 2	26	14	26

Suppose that as a citizen of Alpha, you were asked to cast your vote for Frank or Carl. On the basis of the information provided, whom would you vote for? [Frank, 74%; Carl, 26%]

A second group of respondents received the same cover story as in problem 3, but the economists' forecasts about the other four nations were altered. The forecasts made about the candidates remained the same.

Problem 4 ($N = 75$):

	Projected Rate of Inflation (%)		
	Other Four Nations	Frank's Policy	Carl's Policy
Economist 1	4	16	4
Economist 2	6	14	26

Suppose that as a citizen of Alpha, you were asked to cast your vote for Frank or Carl. On the basis of the information provided, whom would you vote for? [Frank, 52%; Carl, 48%]

The analysis of problems 3 and 4 closely follows that of problems 1 and 2. The expected rate of inflation was 15% for both candidates. However, this value was below the expected continental rate of 25% in problem 3 and above the expected continental rate of 5% in problem 4. Because high inflation is undesirable, values below reference are likely to be viewed as gains, whereas values above reference are likely to be viewed as losses. Assuming that the continental rate of inflation was taken as a point of reference, the results confirmed the prediction of prospect theory that the more risky candidate (Carl) would obtain more votes in problem 4 (48%) than in problem 3 (26%) ($p < .01$ by chi-square).

Together, the responses to problems 1–4 confirm the prediction of prospect theory that people are risk-averse in the domain of gains and risk-seeking in the domain of losses, where gains and losses were defined relative to the outcomes projected for other countries. These results may shed light on the so-called incumbency-oriented voting hypothesis. Numerous investigators have shown that the evaluation of an incumbent party is responsive to fluctuations in the national economy. In general, incumbent presidents and congressional candidates of the same party benefit at the polls from improving economic conditions whereas they suffer from deteriorating conditions (Kramer 1971). These results can be understood, in part, as a consequence of the divergent attitudes towards risks for outcomes involving gains and losses. Following Shepsle (1972), we maintain that incumbents are usually regarded by voters as less risky than the challengers, who are often unknowns and whose policies could drastically alter the current trends, for better or for worse. If people are risk-averse for gains and risk-seeking for losses, the less risky incumbent should fare better when conditions are good than when they are bad. This analysis assumes that the reelection of the incumbent is perceived by voters as a continuation of the current trends, which is attractive when times are good. In contrast, the election of the challenger offers a political gamble that is worth taking when "four more years" of the incumbent is viewed as an unsatisfactory state.

It is important to distinguish this analysis of incumbency-oriented voting from the more common explanation that "when times are bad you throw the rascals out." In the latter account, voters are thought to regard a credible challenger as having to be better than the incumbent, who "got us into this mess to begin with." The present account, in contrast, is based on the notion that the challenger is *riskier* than the incumbent, not necessarily better overall. In problems 2 and 4, the risky candidates profit from hard times even though their expected value was no better than that of the relatively riskless candidates. Obviously, however, a challenger whose expected value is substantially below the incumbent's is unlikely to be elected even in the presence of substantial risk seeking.

In light of this discussion, it is interesting to share an unsolicited response given by one of our participants, who received problem 4 in the winter of 1981. This respondent penciled in *Carter* over Frank, the less risky candidate, and *Reagan* over Carl, the riskier candidate. Recall that in this problem the outcomes were less desirable than the reference point. Evidently our respondent – who voted for Carl – believed that the erstwhile incumbent Carter would have guaranteed the continuation of unacceptable economic conditions, while the erstwhile challenger Reagan, with his risky "new" theories, might have made matters twice as bad as they were or might have been able to restore conditions to a satisfactory level. Because economic and global conditions were widely regarded as unacceptable in 1980, the convexity of the value function for losses may have contributed to the election of a risky presidential prospect, namely Reagan.

Loss Aversion

A significant feature of the value function is that losses loom larger than gains. For example, the displeasure associated with losing a sum of money is generally greater than the pleasure associated with winning the same amount. This property, called *loss aversion*, is depicted in Figure 25.1 by the steeper slope for outcomes below the reference point than for those above.

An important consequence of loss aversion is a preference for the status quo over alternatives with the same expected value. For example, most people are reluctant to accept a bet that offers equal odds of winning and losing x number of dollars. This reluctance is consistent with loss aversion, which implies that the pain associated with the loss would exceed the pleasure associated with the gain, or $v(x) < -v(-x)$. This observation, however, is also consistent with the concavity of the utility function, which implies that the status quo (i.e., the prospect yielding one's current level of wealth with certainty) is preferred to any risky prospect with the same expected value. These accounts can be discriminated from each other because in utility theory the greater impact of losses than of gains is tied to the presence of risk. In the present analysis, however, loss aversion also applies to riskless choice. Consider the following example: Let $x = (x_i, x_u)$ and $y = (y_i, y_u)$ denote two economic policies that produce inflation rates of x_i and y_i and unemployment rates of x_u and y_u. Suppose $x_i > y_i$ but $x_u < y_u$; that is, y produces a lower rate of inflation than x but at the price of a higher rate of unemployment. If people evaluate such policies as positive or negative changes relative to a neutral multiattribute reference point and if the (multiattribute) value function exhibits loss aversion, people will exhibit a reluctance to trade; that is, if at position x (the status quo) people are indifferent between x and y, then at position y they would not be willing to switch to x (Kahneman and Tversky 1984). We test this prediction in the following pair of problems.

Problem 5 ($N = 91$): Imagine there were a presidential contest between two candidates, Frank and Carl. Frank wishes to keep the level of inflation and unemployment at its current level. The rate of inflation is currently at 42%, and the rate of unemployment is currently at 15%. Carl proposes a policy that would decrease the rate of inflation by 19% while increasing the rate of unemployment by 7%. Suppose that as a citizen of Alpha, you were asked to cast your vote for either Frank or Carl. Please indicate your vote. [Frank, 65%; Carl, 35%]

Problem 6 ($N = 89$): Imagine there were a presidential contest between two candidates, Frank and Carl. Carl wishes to keep the rate of inflation and unemployment at its current level. The rate of inflation is currently at 23%, and the rate of unemployment is currently at 22%. Frank proposes a policy that would increase the rate of inflation by 19% while decreasing the rate of unemployment by 7%. Suppose that as a citizen of Alpha you were asked to cast your vote for either Frank or Carl. Please indicate your vote. [Frank, 39%; Carl, 61%]

It is easy to see that problems 5 and 6 offer the same choice between Frank's policy (42%, 15%) and Carl's policy (23%, 22%). The problems differ only in the location of the status quo, which coincides with Frank's policy in problem 5 and with Carl's policy in problem 6. As implied by the notion of multiattribute loss aversion, the majority choice in both problems favored the status quo ($p < .001$ by chi-square). The reluctance to trade is in this instance incompatible with standard utility theory in which the preference between two policies should not depend on whether one or the other is designated as the status quo. In terms of a two-dimensional value function, defined on changes in inflation and unemployment, the present results imply that both $v(19, -7)$ and $v(-19, 7)$ are less than $v(0, 0) = 0$.

We have seen that the combination of risk aversion for gains and risk seeking for losses is consistent with incumbency-oriented voting: incumbents profit from good times, and challengers from bad times. We wish to point out that loss aversion is consistent with another widely accepted generalization, namely that the incumbent enjoys a distinct advantage over the challenger. This effect is frequently attributed to such advantages of holding office as that of obtaining free publicity while doing one's job and being perceived by voters as more experienced and effective at raising funds (Kiewiet 1982). To these considerations, the present analysis of choice adds the consequences of the value function. Because it is natural to take the incumbent's policy as the status quo – the reference point to which the challenger's policy is compared – and because losses loom larger than gains, it follows that the incumbent enjoys a distinct advantage. As we argued earlier, the introduction of risk or uncertainty also tends to favor the incumbent under conditions that enhance risk aversion; that is, when the general conditions are good or even acceptable, voters are likely to play it safe and opt for the relatively riskless incumbent. Only when conditions become unacceptable will the risky challenger capture an edge. Hence, the properties of the value function are consistent with the generally observed incumbency effects, as well as with the exceptions that are found during hard times.

Loss aversion may play an important role in bargaining and negotiation. The process of making compromises and concessions may be hindered by loss aversion because each party may view its own concessions as losses that loom larger than the gains achieved by the concessions of the adversary (Bazerman 1983; Tversky and Kahneman 1986). In negotiating over missiles, for example, each superpower may sense a greater loss in security from the dismantling of its own missiles than it senses a gain in security from a comparable reduction made by the other side. This difficulty is further compounded by the fact, noted by several writers (e.g., Lebow and Stein 1987; Ross 1986), that the very willingness of one side to make a particular concession (e.g., eliminate missiles from a particular location) immediately reduces the perceived value of this concession.

An interesting example of the role of the reference point in the formation of public opinion was brought to our attention by the actor Alan Alda. The objective of the Equal Rights Amendment (ERA) can be framed in two essentially equivalent ways. On the one hand, the ERA can be presented as an attempt to eliminate discrimination against women. In this formulation, attention is drawn to the argument that equal rights for women are not currently guaranteed by the constitution, a negative state that the ERA is designed to undo. On the other hand, the ERA can be framed as legislation designed to improve women's status in society. This frame emphasizes what is to be gained from the amendment, namely, better status and equal rights for women. If losses loom larger than gains, then support for the ERA should be greater among those who are exposed to the frame that emphasizes the elimination of discrimination than the improvement of women's rights. To test Alda's hypothesis, we presented two groups of respondents with the following question. The questions presented to the two groups differed only in the statement appearing on either side of the slash within the brackets.

Problem 7 ($N = 149$): As you know, the Equal Rights Amendment to the Constitution is currently being debated across the country. It says, "Equality of rights under law shall not be denied or abridged by the United States or by any state on account of sex." Supporters of the amendment say that it will [help eliminate discrimination against women/improve the rights of women] in job opportunities, salary, and social security benefits. Opponents of the amendment say that it will have a negative effect by denying women protection offered by special laws. Do you favor or oppose the Equal Rights Amendment? (check one)

Not surprisingly, a large majority of our sample of Stanford undergraduates indicated support for the ERA (74%). However, this support was greater when the problem was framed in terms of eliminating discrimination (78%) than in terms of improving women's rights (69%).

Just as the formulation of the issue may affect the attitude of the target audience, so might the prior attitude of the audience have an effect on the preferred formulation of the issue. Another group of respondents first indicated their opinion on the ERA, either pro or con. They then responded to the following question.

> **Problem 8 ($N = 421$):** The status and rights of women have been addressed in two different ways, which have different social and legal implications. Some people view it primarily as a problem of eliminating inequity and discrimination against women in jobs, salary, etc. Other people view it primarily as a problem of improving or strengthening the rights of women in different areas of modern society. How do you see the problem of women's rights? (check one only)

Of those who indicated support of the ERA, 72% chose to frame the issue in terms of eliminating inequity, whereas only 60% of those who opposed the ERA chose this frame. This finding is consistent with the common observation regarding the political significance of how issues are labeled. A familiar example involves abortion, whose opponents call themselves prolife, not antichoice.

INVARIANCE, FRAMING, AND THE RATIO-DIFFERENCE PRINCIPLE

Perhaps the most fundamental principle of rational choice is the assumption of invariance. This assumption, which is rarely stated explicitly, requires that the preference order among prospects should not depend on how their outcomes and probabilities are described and thus that two alternative formulations of the same problem should yield the same choice. The responses to problems 7 and 8 above may be construed as a failure of invariance. In the present section, we present sharper tests of invariance in which the two versions of a given choice problem are unquestionably equivalent. Under these conditions, violations of invariance cannot be justified on normative grounds. To illustrate such failures of invariance and motivate the psychological analysis, consider the following pair of problems.

> **Problem 9 ($N = 126$):** Political decision making often involves a considerable number of trade-offs. A program that benefits one segment of the population may work to the disadvantage of another segment. Policies designed to lead to higher rates of employment frequently have an adverse effect on inflation. Imagine you were faced with the decision of adopting one of two economic policies.
>
> If program J is adopted, 10% of the work force would be unemployed, while the rate of inflation would be 12%. If program K is adopted, 5% of the work force

would be unemployed, while the rate of inflation would be 17%. The following table summarizes the alternative policies and their likely consequences:

Policy	Work Force Unemployed (%)	Rate of Inflation (%)
Program J	10	12
Program K	5	17

Imagine you were faced with the decision of adopting program J or program K. Which would you select? [program J, 36%; program K, 64%]

A second group of respondents received the same cover story about trade-offs with the following description of the alternative policies:

Problem 10 (N = 133):

Policy	Work Force Employed (%)	Rate of Inflation (%)
Program J	90	12
Program K	95	17

Imagine you were faced with the decision of adopting program J or program K. Which would you select? [Program J, 54%; program K, 46%]

The modal response was program K in problem 9 and program J in problem 10. These choices constitute a violation of invariance in that each program produces the same outcomes in both problems. After all, to say that 10% or 5% of the work force will be unemployed is to say, respectively, that 90% or 95% of the work force will be employed. Yet respondents showed more sensitivity to the outcomes when these were described as rates of unemployment than as rates of employment. These results illustrate a "psychophysical" effect that we call the *ratio-difference principle*.

Psychophysics is the study of the functional relation between the physical and the psychological value of attributes such as size, brightness, or loudness. A utility function for money, therefore, can also be viewed as a psychophysical scale relating the objective to the subjective value of money. Recall that a concave value function for gains of the form depicted in Figure 25.1 implies that a difference between $100 and $200 looms larger than the objectively equal difference between $200 and $300. More generally, the ratio-difference principle says that the impact of any fixed positive difference between two amounts increases with their ratio. Thus the difference between $200 and $100 yields a ratio of 2, whereas the difference between $300 and $200 yields a ratio of 1.5. The ratio-difference principle applies to many perceptual attributes. Increasing the illumination of a room by adding one candle has a much larger impact when the initial illumination is poor than when it is good. The same pattern is observed for many sensory attributes, and it appears that the same psychophysical principle is applicable to the perception of numerical differences as well.

Unlike perceptual dimensions, however, numerical scales can be framed in different ways. The labor statistics, for example, can be described in terms of employment or unemployment, yielding the same difference with very different ratios. If the ratio-difference principle applies to such scales, then the change from an unemployment rate of 10% to 5%, yielding a ratio of 2, should have more impact than the objectively equal change from an employment rate of 90% to 95%, yielding a ratio that is very close to unity. As a consequence, program K would be more popular in problem 9 and program J in problem 10. This reversal in preference was obtained, although the only difference between the two problems was the use of unemployment data in problem 9 and employment data in problem 10.

The ratio-difference principle has numerous applications to political behavior. For example, many political choices involve the allocation of limited funds to various sectors of the population. The following two problems demonstrate how the framing of official statistics can affect the perceived need for public assistance.

Problem 11 ($N = 125$): The country of Delta is interested in reducing the crime rate among its immigrant groups. The Department of Justice has been allocated $100 million ($100M) for establishing a crime prevention program aimed at immigrant youths. The program would provide the youths with job opportunities and recreational facilities, inasmuch as criminal acts tend to be committed by unemployed youths who have little to do with their time. A decision must be made between two programs currently being considered. The programs differ from each other primarily in how the $100M would be distributed between Delta's two largest immigrant communities, the Alphans and the Betans. There are roughly the same number of Alphans and Betans in Delta. Statistics have shown that by the age of 25, 3.7% of all Alphans have a criminal record, whereas 1.2% of all Betans have a criminal record.

The following two programs are being considered. Program J would allocate to the Alphan community $55M and to the Betan community $45M. Program K would allocate $65M to the Alphan community and to the Betan community $35M. The following table summarizes these alternative programs:

Program	To Alphan Community	To Betan Community
Program J	$55M	$45M
Program K	$65M	$35M

Imagine you were faced with the decision between program J and program K. In light of the available crime statistics, which would you select? [program J, 41%; program K, 59%]

A second group of respondents received the same cover story and program description as in problem 11, with the criminal statistics framed as follows:

Problem 12 ($N = 126$): Statistics have shown that by the age of 25, 96.3% of all Alphans have no criminal record whereas 98.8% of all Betans have no criminal record.... In light of the available crime statistics, which would you select? [program J, 71%; program K, 29%]

It should be apparent that the crime statistics on which respondents were to base their choice were the same across the two problems. Because of the ratio-difference principle, however, the Alphans are perceived as much more criminal than the Betans in problem 11 – roughly three times as criminal – but they are seen as only slightly less noncriminal than the Betans in problem 12. As hypothesized, respondents selected that program in which differences in allocations between the groups matched as closely as possible differences in perceived criminality, resulting in a large reversal of preference ($p < .001$ by chi-square).

The preceding two problems illustrate an important social problem concerning the perception of crime rates among minority and nonminority segments of the population. It is generally believed that the members of minority groups, such as blacks, have much higher crime rates than do the members of nonminority groups, such as whites (Tursky et al. 1976). Indeed, according to the actual crime statistics compiled by the FBI in 1982, 2.76% of black citizens were arrested for a serious crime compared to .68% of white Americans. The between group difference does appear quite large. Problems 11 and 12 suggest, however, that judgments about the divergent crime rates in the two communities may be altered by how the data are framed. The apparently large difference between crime rates of 2.76% and .68% can be reframed as a relatively small difference between law-obedience rates of 97.24% and 99.32%.

Quattrone and Warren (1985) showed a sample of Stanford undergraduates the 1982 crime statistics framed either in terms of the percentages of blacks and whites who were arrested for crime or the percentages who were not. Other respondents were not exposed to these data. As implied by the ratio-difference principle, the respondents who were exposed to the crime commission statistics considered the crime rate to be substantially higher in black communities than in white communities, whereas those exposed to the law-obedience statistics considered the communities to be more at par in crime. Furthermore, the subjects who were not shown the FBI crime data gave responses that were virtually indistinguishable from those given by subjects exposed to the crime commission statistics. This comparison suggests that people may generally formulate beliefs about the proportions of blacks and whites who commit crime, not the proportions who abide by the law.

In another question the subjects who had consulted the FBI statistics were asked to allocate $100M targeted for the prevention of crime between the two racial communities. It was observed that subjects exposed to the crime commission statistics allocated more money to the black community (mean = $58.4M) than did the subjects exposed to the law obedience statistics (mean = $47.2M). Hence, the basic results of this section were replicated for nonhypothetical groups. Moreover, a second study by Quattrone and Warren demonstrated that the same reversals due to framing are obtained when racial differences in crime must be inferred from a set of photographs rather than being explicitly pointed out in a neat statistical table. Taken as a whole, the results suggest that the decision of how to frame the data can have significant political consequences for individuals as well as for entire social groups. We suspect that the more successful practitioners of the art of persuasion commonly employ such framing effects to their personal advantage.

THE WEIGHTING OF CHANCE EVENTS

A cornerstone of the rational theory of choice is the expectation principle. In the expected utility model, the decision maker selects that option with the highest expected utility that equals the sum of the utilities of the outcomes, each weighted by its probability. The following example of Zeckhauser illustrates a violation of this rule. Consider a game of Russian roulette where you are allowed to purchase the removal of one bullet. Would you be willing to pay the same amount to reduce the number of bullets from four to three as you would to reduce the number from one to zero? Most people say that they would pay more to reduce the probability of death from one-sixth to zero, thereby eliminating the risk altogether, than to reduce the probability of death from four-sixths to three-sixths. This response, however, is incompatible with the expectation principle, according to which the former reduction from a possibility (one bullet) to a certainty (no bullets) cannot be more valuable than the latter reduction (from four to three bullets). To accommodate this and other violations of the expectation principle, the value of each outcome in prospect theory is multiplied by a decision weight that is a monotonic but nonlinear function of its probability.

Consider a simple prospect that yields outcome x with probability p, outcome y with probability q, and the status quo with probability $1 - p - q$. With the reference point set at the status quo, the outcomes are assigned values $v(x)$ and $v(y)$, and the probabilities are assigned *decision weights*, $\pi(p)$ and $\pi(q)$. The overall value of the prospect is

$$\pi(p)v(x) + \pi(q)v(y).$$

As shown in Figure 25.2, π is a monotonic nonlinear function of p with the following properties:

1. Impossible events are discarded, that is, $\pi(0) = 0$, and the scale is normalized so that $\pi(1) = 1$. The function is not well behaved at the endpoints though, for people sometimes treat highly likely events as certain and highly unlikely events as impossible.

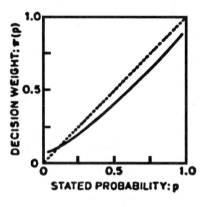

Figure 25.2. A hypothetical weighting function.

2. Low probabilities are overweighted, giving rise to some risk seeking in the domain of gains. For example, many people prefer one chance in a thousand to win $3,000 over $3 for sure. This implies

$$\pi(.001)v(\$3,000) > v(\$3),$$

hence

$$\pi(.001) > v(\$3)/v(\$3,000) > .001,$$

by the concavity of v for gains.

3. Although for low probabilities, $\pi(p) > p$, in general, $\pi(p) + \pi(1-p) < 1$. Thus low probabilities are overweighted, moderate and high probabilities are underweighted, and the latter effect is more pronounced than the former.

4. For all $0 < p, q, r < 1$, $\pi(pq)/\pi(p) < \pi(pqr)/\pi(pr)$; that is, for any ratio of probabilities q, the ratio of decision weights is closer to unity when the probabilities are small than when they are large; for example, $\pi(.4)/\pi(.8) < \pi(.1)/\pi(.2)$. This property implies the common response to the Russian roulette problem because $\pi(1/6) - \pi(0) > \pi(4/6) - \pi(3/6)$.

Although the description of π has involved stated numerical probabilities, it can be extended to events whose probabilities are subjectively assessed or verbally implied. In these situations, however, the decision weights may also be affected by the vagueness or other details of the choice.

CERTAINTY AND PSEUDOCERTAINTY

Many public policies involve the allocation of funds for projects whose outcomes cannot be known with certainty. The following problems illustrate how preferences among risky projects may be affected by the properties of π, and the results are contrasted with those predicted by the expected utility model.

Problem 13 (N = 88): The state of Epsilon is interested in developing clean and safe alternative sources of energy. Its Department of Natural Resources is considering two programs for establishing solar energy within the state. If program X is adopted, then it is virtually certain that over the next four years the state will save $20 million ($20M) in energy expenditures. If program Y is adopted, then there is an 80% chance that the state will save $30M in energy expenditures over the next four years and a 20% chance that because of cost overruns, the program will produce no savings in energy expenditures at all. The following table summarizes the alternative policies and their probable consequences.

Policy	Savings in Energy Expenditures
Program X	$20M savings, with certainty
Program Y	30% chance of saving $30M, 20% chance of no savings

Imagine you were faced with the decision of adopting program X or program Y. Which would you select? [program X, 74%; program Y, 26%]

The same respondents who received problem 13 also received the following problem. Order of presenting the two problems was counterbalanced across booklets.

Problem 14 (N = 88): The state of Gamma is also interested in developing clean and safe alternative sources of energy. Its Department of Natural Resources is considering two programs for establishing solar energy within the state. If program A is adopted, then there is a 25% chance that over the next four years the state will save $20 million ($20M) in energy expenditures and a 75% chance that because of cost overruns, the program will produce no savings in energy expenditures at all. If program B is adopted, there is a 20% chance that the state will save $30M in energy expenditures and an 80% chance that because of cost overruns, the program will produce no savings in energy expenditures at all. The following table summarizes the alternative policies and their probable consequences:

Policy	Savings in Energy Expenditures
Program A	25% chance of saving $20M, 75% chance of no savings
Program B	20% chance of saving $30M, 80% chance of no savings

Imagine you were faced with the decision of adopting program A or program B. Which would you select? [program A, 39%; program B, 61%]

Because the same respondents completed both problems 13 and 14, we can examine the number who selected each of the four possible pairs of programs:

X and *A*, *X* and *B*, *Y* and *A*, *Y* and *B*. These data are shown in below.

| | Problem 14 | |
Problem 13	Program A	Program B
Program X	27	38
Program Y	7	16

The pair most frequently selected is *X* and *B*, which corresponds to the modal choices of each problem considered individually. These modal choices pose a problem for the expected utility model. Setting $u(0) = 0$, the preference for *X* over *Y* in problem 13 implies that $u(\$20M) > (4/5)u(\$30M)$, or that $u(\$20M)/u(\$30M) > 4/5$. This inequality is inconsistent with that implied by problem 14 because the preference for *A* over *B* implies that $(1/4)u(\$20M) < (1/5)u(\$30M)$, or that $u(\$20M)/u(\$30M) < 4/5$. Note that programs *A* and *B* (in problem 14) can be obtained from programs *X* and *Y* (in problem 13), respectively, by multiplying the probability of nonnull outcomes by one-fourth. The substitution axiom of expected utility theory says that if *X* is preferred to *Y*, then a probability mixture that yields *X* with probability *p* and 0 otherwise should be preferred to a mixture that yields *Y* with probability *p* and 0 otherwise. If $p = 1/4$, this axiom implies that *X* is preferred to *Y* if and only if *A* is preferred to *B*. From the above table it is evident that more than half of our respondents (45 or 88) violated this axiom.

The modal choices, *X* and *B*, however, are consistent with prospect theory. Applying the equation of prospect theory to the modal choice of problem 13 yields $\pi(1)v(\$20M) > \pi(.8)v(\$30M)$, hence $v(\$20M)/v(\$30M) > \pi(.8)/\pi(1)$. Applied to problem 14, the equation yields $\pi(.2)/\pi(.25) > v(\$20M)/v(\$30M)$. Taken together, these inequalities imply the observed violation of the substitution axiom for those individuals for which $\pi(.8)/\pi(1) < v(\$20M)/v(\$30M) < \pi(.2)/\pi(.25)$. Recall that for any ratio of probabilities $q < 1$, the ratio of decision weights is closer to unity when the probabilities are small than when they are large. In particular, $\pi(.8)/\pi(1) < \pi(.2)/\pi(.25)$. Indeed, 38 of the 45 pairs of choices that deviate from expected utility theory fit the above pattern, $p < .001$ by sign test.

It should be noted that prospect theory does not predict that all respondents will prefer *X* to *Y* and *B* to *A*. This pattern will be found only among those respondents for whom the value ratio, $v(\$20M)/v(\$30M)$, lies between the ratios of decision weights, $\pi(.8)/\pi(1)$ and $\pi(.2)/\pi(.25)$. The theory requires only that individuals who are indifferent between *X* and *Y* will prefer *B* to *A* and those who are indifferent between *A* and *B* will prefer *X* to *Y*. For group data, the theory does predict the observed shift in modal preferences. The only pair of choices not consistent with prospect theory is *Y* and *A*, for this pair implies that $\pi(.2)/\pi(.25) < \pi(.8)/\pi(1)$. This pair was in fact selected least often.

The modal preferences exhibited in the preceding two problems illustrate a phenomenon first reported by Allais (1953) that is referred to in prospect theory as the *certainty effect:* reducing the probability of an outcome by a constant factor has a greater impact when the outcome was initially certain than when it was merely possible. The Russian roulette game discussed earlier is a variant of the certainty effect.

CAUSAL VERSUS DIAGNOSTIC CONTINGENCIES

A classical problem in the analysis of political behavior concerns the rationality of voting and abstaining. According to Downs (1957), it may not be rational for an individual to register and vote in large elections because of the very low probability that the individual would cast a decisive vote coupled with the costs of registering and going to the polls. Objections to Downs's view were raised by Riker and Ordeshook (1968), who argued that an individual may derive from voting other benefits besides the possibility of casting a decisive ballot. These additional benefits are collectively referred to as *citizen's duty,* or *D,* and they include affirming one's allegiance to the democratic system, complying with a powerful ethic, participating in a common social ritual, as well as "standing up and being counted." To these rational consequences of voting, we suggest adding a somewhat less rational component.

Elsewhere (Quattrone and Tversky 1984) we have shown that people often fail to distinguish between causal contingencies (acts that produce an outcome) and diagnostic contingencies (acts that are merely correlated with an outcome). For example, there is a widespread belief that attitudes are correlated with actions. Therefore, some people may reason that if they decide to vote, that decision would imply that others with similar political attitudes would also decide to vote. Similarly, they may reason that if they decide to abstain, others who share their political attitudes will also abstain. Because the preferred candidates can defeat the opposition only if politically like-minded citizens vote in greater numbers than do politically unlike-minded citizens, the individual may infer that he or she had better vote; that is, each citizen may regard his or her single vote as diagnostic of *millions* of votes, which would substantially inflate the subjective probability of one's vote making a difference.

To test this hypothesis, which we call the *voter's illusion,* we had a sample of 315 Stanford undergraduates read about an imaginary country named Delta. Participants were to imagine that they supported party *A,* opposed party *B,* and that there were roughly four million supporters of each party in Delta as well as four million nonaligned voters. Subjects imagined that they were deliberating over whether to vote in the upcoming presidential election, having learned that voting in Delta can be costly in time and effort. To facilitate their decision, they were to consult one of two prevailing theories concerning the group of voters who would determine the electoral outcome.

Some subjects considered the *party supporter's theory.* According to this theory, the nonaligned voters would split their vote fairly equally across the two parties. The electoral outcome would be determined by whether the supporters of party

A or party *B* became more involved in the election. The political experts were split as to whether the supporters of *A* or *B* would become more involved, but all agreed that the party whose members did become more involved would win by a margin of roughly 200 thousand to 400 thousand votes. Other subjects received the *nonaligned voter's theory*, which held that the supporters of each party would vote in equal numbers. The electoral outcome would in this account be determined by whether the nonaligned voters would swing their support primarily to party *A* or party *B*. The experts were split as to which party would capture the majority of the nonaligned voters, but all agreed that the fortunate party would win by a margin of at least 200 thousand votes.

Note that the consequences of voting included in the rational analysis are held constant across the two theories. In both, the "utility difference" between the two parties, the "probability" of casting a decisive vote, the costs of voting, and citizen's duty are the same. But according to the party supporter's theory, there is a correlation between political orientation and participation; that is, either the supporters of party *A* will vote in greater numbers than will the supporters of party *B*, or vice versa. In contrast, the nonaligned voter's theory holds that political orientation is independent of participation because party supporters will turn out in equal numbers. Therefore, only subjects presented with the former theory could infer that their decision to vote or to abstain would be diagnostic of what their politically like-minded peers would decide. If being able to make this inference is conducive to voting, then a larger "turnout" should be found among subjects presented with the party supporter's theory than among those presented with the nonaligned voter's theory. In fact, when asked, "Would you vote if the theory were true and voting in Delta were costly," significantly more subjects responded no under the party supporter's theory (16%) than under the nonaligned voter's theory (7%) ($p < .05$ by sign test).

An additional finding corroborated the analysis that this difference in turnout was attributable to the perceived diagnosticity of voting. Respondents were asked to indicate how likely it was that the supporters of party *A* would vote in greater numbers than the supporters of party *B* "given that you decided to vote" and "given that you decided to abstain." Responses to these two questions were made on nine-point scales with verbal labels ranging from "extremely likely" to "extremely unlikely." Subjects were informed that their decision to vote or abstain could not be communicated to others. Nonetheless, subjects exposed to the party supporter's theory thought that their individual choice would have a greater "effect" on what others decided to do than did subjects exposed to the nonaligned voter's theory, $F(1,313) = 35.79$ ($p < .001$). Similar effects were observed in responses to a question probing how likely party *A* was to defeat party *B* "given that you decided to vote" and "given that you decided to abstain," $F(1,313) = 40.18$ ($p < .001$). This latter difference was obtained despite subject's knowing that they could cast but one vote and that the likely margin of victory was about 200 thousand votes.

The observed differences between respondents exposed to the party supporter's and nonaligned voter's theory cannot be readily justified from a normative perspective (cf. Meehl 1977). The present analysis of causal versus diagnostic contingencies recalls the tragedy of the commons, and it applies to other phenomena in which collective action dwarfs the causal significance of a single individual's contribution. The outcomes of most wars would not have changed had one fewer draftee been inducted, and the success or failure of most charity drives do not ordinarily depend on the dollars of an individual donor. These collective actions defy a routine rational analysis for the individual because if each citizen, draftee, or donor "rationally" refrains from making his or her paltry contribution, then the outcomes would be drastically affected. For this reason, exhortations to vote, to fight, and to help those less fortunate than oneself are usually framed, "If you don't vote/fight/contribute, think of what would happen if *everyone* felt the same way." This argument is compelling. Still, just how *does* an individual's private decision materially affect the decisions made by countless other persons?

CONCLUDING REMARKS

We contrasted the rational analysis of political decision making with a psychological account based on descriptive considerations. Although there is no universally accepted definition of rationality, most social scientists agree that rational choice should conform to a few elementary requirements. Foremost among these is the criterion of invariance (or extensionality [Arrow 1982]), which holds that the preference order among prospects should not depend on how they are described. Hence, no acceptable rational theory would allow reversals of preference to come about as a consequence of whether the choice is based on rates of employment or rates of unemployment, crime commission statistics or law obedience statistics. These alternate formulations of the problems convey the same information, and the problems differ from each other in no other way. We have seen, however, that these alternate frames led to predictable reversals in preference.

Whether our studies paint a humbling or flattering picture of human intellectual performance depends on the background from which they are viewed. The proponent of the rational theory of choice may find that we have focused on human limitations and have overlooked its many accomplishments. The motivational psychologist, accustomed to finding the root of all folly in deep-seated emotional needs, may find our approach much too rational and cognitive. Many readers are no doubt familiar with the versions of these opposing viewpoints found in political science. *The Authoritarian Personality* (Adorno et al. 1950), for example, well illustrates the use of motivational assumptions to explain the appeal of a particular ideology to certain elements of the population.

The descriptive failure of normative principles, such as invariance and coherence, does not mean that people are unintelligent or irrational. The failure merely indicates that judgment and choice – like perception and memory – are prone to distortion and error. The significance of the results stems from the observation that the errors are common and systematic rather than idiosyncratic or random, hence, they cannot be dismissed as noise. Accordingly, there is little hope for a theory of choice that is both normatively acceptable and descriptively adequate. A compelling analysis of the uses and abuses of rationality in theories of political behavior has been presented by Converse (1975) who has detailed the often arbitrary and inconsistent criteria by which rationality has been defined. Our intention was not to reopen the discussion about the meaning of rationality but rather to enrich the set of concepts and principles that could be used to analyze, explain, and predict the decisions made by individuals in their private lives, in the market place, and in the political arena.

26. Conflict Resolution
A Cognitive Perspective

Daniel Kahneman and Amos Tversky

Many different disciplines deal with the resolution of conflict. Even within the single discipline of psychology, conflict can be approached from different perspectives. For example, there is an emotional aspect to interpersonal conflict, and a comprehensive psychological treatment of conflict should address the role of resentment, anger, and revenge. In addition, conflict resolution and negotiation are processes that generally extend over time, and no treatment that ignores their dynamics can be complete. In this chapter we do not attempt to develop, or even sketch, a comprehensive psychological analysis of conflict resolution. Instead, we explore some implications for conflict resolution of a particular cognitive analysis of individual decision making. We focus on three relevant phenomena: optimistic overconfidence, the certainty effect, and loss aversion. Optimistic overconfidence refers to the common tendency of people to overestimate their ability to predict and control future outcomes; the certainty effect refers to the common tendency to overweight outcomes that are certain relative to outcomes that are merely probable; and loss aversion refers to the asymmetry in the evaluation of positive and negative outcomes, in which losses loom larger than the corresponding gains. We shall illustrate these phenomena, which were observed in studies of individual judgment and choice, and discuss how these biases could hinder successful negotiation. The present discussion complements the treatment offered by Neale and Bazerman (1991).

Some preliminary remarks are in order. First, the three phenomena described above represent departures from the rational theory of judgment and decision making. The barriers to conflict resolution discussed in this chapter, therefore, would be reduced or eliminated if people were to behave in accord with the standard rational model. It would be inappropriate to conclude, however, that departures from rationality always inhibit the resolution of conflict. There are many situations in which less-than-rational agents may reach agreement while perfectly rational agents do not. The prisoner's dilemma is a classic example in which rationality may not be conducive for achieving the most desirable social solution. The present chapter focuses on the obstacles imposed by the presence of optimistic overconfidence, the certainty effect, and loss aversion. We do not wish to imply; however, that these phenomena are necessarily detrimental to conflict resolution.

I. OPTIMISTIC OVERCONFIDENCE

In this section we discuss two phenomena of judgment that have both attracted a considerable amount of research attention in recent years: overconfidence and optimism. Overconfidence in human judgment is indicated by a cluster of related findings: uncalibrated assignments of probability that are more extreme than the judge's knowledge can justify (Lichtenstein, Fischhoff, and Phillips 1982), confidence intervals that are too narrow (Alpert and Raiffa 1982), and nonregressive predictions (Kahneman and Tversky 1973). Overconfidence is prevalent but not universal, and there are different views of the main psychological processes that produce it. One source of overconfidence is the common tendency to undervalue those aspects of the situation of which the judge is relatively ignorant. A recent study by Brenner, Koehler, and Tversky (1992) illustrates this effect, which is likely to be common in situations of conflict.

Participants were presented with factual information about several court cases. In each case, the information was divided into three parts: background data, the plaintiff's argument, and the defendant's argument. Four groups of subjects participated in this study. One group received only the background data. Two other groups received the background data and the arguments for one of the two sides, selected at random. The arguments for the plaintiff or the defendant contained no new evidence; they merely elaborated the facts included in the background data. A fourth group was given all the information presented to the jury. The subjects were all asked to predict the percentage of people in the jury who would vote for the plaintiff. The responses of the people who received one-sided evidence were strongly biased in the direction of the information they had received. Although the participants knew that their evidence was one-sided, they were not able to make the proper adjustment. In most cases, those who received all the evidence were more accurate in predicting the jury vote than those who received only one side. However, the subjects in the one-sided condition were generally more confident in their prediction than those who received both sides. Thus, subjects predicted the jury's decision with greater confidence when they had only one-half, rather than all, of the evidence presented to it.

Conflicts and disputes are characterized by the presence of asymmetric information. In general, each side knows a great deal about the evidence and the arguments that support its position and much less about those that support the position of the other side. The difficulty of making proper allowance for missing information, demonstrated in the preceding experiment, entails a bias that is likely to hinder successful negotiation. Each side will tend to overestimate its chances of success, as well as its ability to impose a solution on the other side and to prevent such an attempt by an opponent. Many years ago, we suggested that participants in a conflict are susceptible to a fallacy of initiative – a tendency to attribute less initiative and less imagination to the opponent than to oneself (Tversky and Kahneman 1973). The difficulty of adopting the opponent's view of the chessboard or of the battlefield may help explain why people often discover many new moves when they switch sides in a game. A related phenomenon has been observed in the response to mock trials that are sometimes conducted when a party to a dispute considers the possibility of litigation. Observers of mock trials have noted (Hans Zeisel, personal communication) that the would-be litigators are often surprised and dismayed by the strength of the position put forth by their mock opponent. In the absence of such a vivid demonstration of their bias, disputants are likely to hold an overly optimistic assessment of their chances in court. More generally, a tendency to underestimate the strength of the opponent's position could make negotiators less likely to make concessions and thereby reduce the chances of a negotiated settlement. Neale and Bazerman (1983) illustrated this effect in the context of a final arbitration procedure, in which the parties submit final offers, one of which is selected by the arbitrator. Negotiators overestimated (by more than 15 percent, on the average) the chance that their offer would be chosen. In this situation, a more realistic appraisal would probably result in more conciliatory final offers.

Another cognitive mechanism that may contribute to overconfident optimism is the tendency to base forecasts and estimates mostly on the particular features of the case at hand, including extrapolations of current achievements and assessments of the strength of relevant causal factors. This preferred "inside approach" to prediction is contrasted with an "outside approach," which draws the prediction of an outcome from the statistics of similar cases in the past, with no attempt to divine the history of the events that will yield that outcome (Kahneman and Lovallo 1993; Kahneman and Tversky 1979a). The neglect of relevant statistical information in the inside approach to forecasting is one of many manifestations of a general tendency to represent any situation in terms of a concrete (and preferably causal) model, rather than in more abstract, statistical terms. This tendency can produce an inconsistency between people's general beliefs and their beliefs about particular cases. One example of such an inconsistency applies to the overconfidence effect: respondents who are on the average much too confident in their opinions about a series of questions are likely to be less optimistic, or even slightly pessimistic, in their guess about the total number of questions that they have answered correctly (Gigerenzer, Hoffrage, and Kleinbolting 1991; Griffin and Tversky 1992). The effect is not restricted to laboratory studies. Cooper, Woo, and Dunkelberg (1988) interviewed entrepreneurs about their chances of success, and about the base rate of success for enterprises of the same kind. Over 80 percent of the respondents perceived their chances of success as 70 percent or better, and fully 33 percent of them described their success as certain. The average chance of success that these entrepreneurs attributed to a business like theirs was only 59 percent, an estimate that is also too optimistic: the five-year survival rate for new firms is around 33 percent (Dun and Bradstreet 1967). In general, of course, the individuals who freely choose to engage in an economic activity tend to be among those who have the most favorable expectations for that activity, and for their own prospects in particular. This is a version of a statistical selection effect that is known in other contexts as the "winner's curse." It is possible in principle for an agent to anticipate this bias and to correct for it, but the data suggest that the entrepreneurs studied by Cooper et al. did not do so.

The inside approach to forecasts is not by itself sufficient to yield an optimistic bias. However, in the special case of a decision maker considering a course of action, the preference for the inside view makes it likely that the forecast will be anchored on plans and intentions and that relevant statistical considerations will be underweighted or ignored. If we plan to complete a project in a couple of months, it is natural to take this date as a starting point for the assessment of completion time, maybe adding an additional month for unforeseen factors. This mode of thinking leads us to neglect the many ways in which a plan might fail. Because plans tend to be best-case estimates, such anchoring leads to optimism. Indeed, the optimism of forecasts made in the planning context is a well-documented effect (Arnold 1986; Merrow, Phillips and Myers 1981; Davis 1985). In the context of conflict, unwarranted optimism can be a serious obstacle, especially when it is bolstered by professional authority. Optimistic overconfidence is not a desirable trait for generals recommending a war or for attorneys urging a lawsuit, even if their expressions of confidence and optimism are pleasantly reassuring to their followers or clients at the time.

There are other sources and other manifestations of optimism than those mentioned so far (Taylor and Brown 1988). For example, there is evidence that most normal people expect others to rate them more favorably than they actually do, whereas mildly depressed people tend to be more realistic (Lewinsohn, Mischel, Chaplin, and Barton 1980). Similarly, people rate themselves above the mean on most desirable qualities, from effectiveness to sense of humor (Taylor and Brown 1988). People also exaggerate their ability to control their environment (Langer 1975; Crocker 1981) and accordingly prefer to bet on their skills rather than on a matched chance event (Howell 1971; Heath and Tversky 1991).

The claim that optimistic delusions are often adaptive has recently attracted much attention (Taylor and Brown 1988; Seligman 1991). To put this claim in perspective, it is useful to consider separately the effects of optimistic overconfidence on the two main phases of any undertaking: the setting of goals and plans, and the execution of a plan. When goals are chosen and plans are set, unrealistic optimism favors excessive risk-taking. Indeed, there are indications of large biases of optimistic planning in the domain of business decisions (Davis

1985), and the daily newspaper offers many examples in the political domain. However, decision makers are also very risk averse in most situations. The conjunction of overconfident optimism and risk aversion brings about a situation in which decision makers often accept risks because they deny them (Kahneman and Lovallo 1993; March and Shapira 1987). Thus, the benefit of unrealistic optimism in the decision phase may be to prevent paralysis by countering excessive aversion to risk, but this is hardly an unequivocal blessing – especially in situations of conflict.

The main advantages of optimism may be found in increasing persistence and commitment during the phase of action toward a chosen goal, and in improving the ability to tolerate uncontrollable suffering. Taylor (1989) has reviewed the role of irrational hope in promoting the adjustment of some cancer patients, and Seligman (1991) has claimed that an optimistic explanatory style, in which one takes credit for successes but views failures as aberrations, promotes persistence in the face of difficulties in diverse activities, ranging from the sale of insurance to competitive sports. The role of optimism in sports is of particular interest for a treatment of conflict. On the one hand, optimistic overconfidence will sometimes encourage athletes to take on competitors that are too strong for them. On the other hand, confidence, short of complacency, is surely an asset once the contest begins. The hope of victory increases effort, commitment, and persistence in the face of difficulty or threat of failure, and thereby raises the chances of success. A characteristic of competitive sports is that the option of abandoning the contest is not normally available to a competitor, even if defeat is certain. Under those circumstances, stubborn perseverance against the odds can only be beneficial. The situation is more complex when leaving the field is a viable option, and continuing the struggle is costly. Under these conditions, it is rarely easy to distinguish justified perseverance from irrational escalation of commitment.

In other situations of conflict, as in sports, optimism and confidence are likely to increase effort, commitment, and persistence in the conduct of the struggle. This is particularly true in conflicts that involve severe attrition. When maximal effort is exerted by both contestants, then it would appear that optimism offers a competitive advantage. In some competitive situations, the advantages of optimism and overconfidence may stem not from the deception of self, but from the deception of the opponent. This is how intimidation works – and successful intimidation accomplishes all that could be obtained by an actual victory, usually at a much lower cost. An animal that is capable of intimidating competitors away from a desirable mate, prey, or territory would have little need for techniques of conflict resolution. It is also recognized in analyses of conflict, from the game of chicken to treatments of pariah [or "outlaw"] states, that the appearance of complete confidence often pays off. Because complete confidence may be hard to fake, a tendency to sincere overconfidence could have adaptive advantages (see Frank 1989).

II. CERTAINTY AND PSEUDOCERTAINTY

A significant aspect of conflict resolution is the presence of uncertainty not only about the nature of an agreement but also about its actual outcomes. The outcomes of agreement can be classified into three types: (1) assured or certain outcomes – exchanges that are executed immediately, or promises for future actions that are unambiguous, unconditional, and enforceable; (2) contingently certain outcomes – enforceable undertakings that are conditional on objectively observed external events; and (3) uncertain outcomes – consequences (e.g., goodwill) that are more likely in the presence of agreement than in its absence. Uncertain outcomes are often stated as intentions of the parties in the "cheap talk" that precedes or accompanies the agreement.

Sure things and definite contingencies are the stuff of explicit agreements, contracts, and treaties; but the uncertain consequences of agreements are sometimes no less important. For example, a mutually satisfactory agreement between a supplier and a customer on a particular transaction can increase the probability of long-term association between them. A peace treaty between Israel and Syria might reduce the probability that Syria would seek to build or acquire nuclear weapons, but this significant consequence is not guaranteed. As these examples illustrate, an increase in the other side's goodwill is sometimes an important outcome of agreement, albeit an uncertain one. Future goodwill differs from many other consequences in that it is not necessarily in limited supply; negotiations in which goodwill is (implicitly or explicitly) a significant factor present a sharp contrast to zero-sum games. However, the characteristics of the way people think about uncertain outcomes favor a systematic underweighting of such consequences of agreement, compared to certain and to contingently certain benefits that are assured in the formal contract. This tendency reduces, in effect, the perceived value of an agreement for both parties in a dispute.

Research on individual decision making has identified a major bias in the weights that are assigned to probabilistic advantages and to sure things, which we have called the *certainty effect* (Kahneman and Tversky, 1979b, 1984). The classic demonstration of this effect is the Allais paradox, named after the French Nobel laureate in economics who in 1952 demonstrated to an audience of famous economists (several of them future Nobel laureates) that their preferences were inconsistent with expected utility theory. More specifically, these preferences imply that the difference between probabilities of 0.99 and 1.00 looms larger than the difference between 0.10 and 0.11. The intuition that the two differences are not equally significant is compelling. Indeed, it comes as a surprise to the uninitiated that the standard analysis of rational choice (expected utility theory) requires that a probability difference of, say 1 percent, be given equal weight, regardless of whether the difference lies in the middle of the range (0.30 to 0.31) or whether it involves the transition from impossibility to possibility (zero to 0.01) or from near-certainty to certainty (0.99 to 1). Intuitively, however, the qualitative distinctions between impossibility and possibility and between probability and certainty have special significance. As a consequence, many people consider it prudent to pay more to increase the probability of a desirable outcome from .99 to 1 than from .80 to .85. Similarly, people may well pay more to reduce the probability of harm from .0005 to zero than to reduce the same risk from .0015 to .0005 (Viscusi, Magat, and Huber 1987). The certainty effect has been confirmed when the probabilities are associated with well-defined chance processes and are expressed numerically. Most decisions under uncertainty, however, involve vague contingencies and ambiguous probabilities. The evidence suggests that the certainty effect is further enhanced by vagueness and ambiguity (Hogarth and Einhorn 1990; Tversky and Fox 1994). Thus, there is good reason to believe that uncertain outcomes, such as goodwill, are underweighted when people evaluate alternative agreements.

The principle that uncertain benefits are underweighted does not apply to *contingently certain outcomes*. The payment of insurance in the event of a specified property loss or in the event of a medical need is a prime example of a contingently certain outcome. The evidence indicates that people are willing to pay disproportionately more for insurance that will certainly be provided if the relevant contingencies arise than for insurance that is merely probabilistic. There is also strong evidence for a closely related phenomenon, which has been labeled the *pseudocertainty effect* (Kahneman and Tversky 1984; Tversky and Kahneman 1986), and is illustrated using the following pair of decision problems.

Problem 1: Consider the following two-stage game. In the first stage there is a 75 percent chance to end the game without winning anything and a 25 percent chance to move into the second stage. If you reach the second stage you have a choice between

A. a sure win of $30
B. an 80 percent chance to win $45

Your choice must be made before the game starts, i.e., before the outcome of the first stage is known. Please indicate the option you prefer.

Problem 2: Which of the following options do you prefer?

C. 25 percent chance to win $30
D. 20 percent chance to win $45

Because there is one chance in four to move into the second stage of problem 1, prospect A offers a .25 probability to win $30 and prospect B offers a .25 × .80 = .20 probability to win $45. Problems 1 and 2 are therefore identical in terms of probabilities and outcomes. However, the two problems elicit different preferences, which we have observed with both real and hypothetical payoffs. A clear majority of respondents preferred A over B in problem 1, whereas the majority preferred D over C in problem 2 (Tversky and Kahneman 1986). We have attributed this phenomenon to the combination of the certainty effect and the tendency to focus on the outcomes that are directly relevant to the decision at hand. Because the failure to reach the second stage of the game yields the same outcome (i.e., no gain) regardless of whether the decision maker chooses A or B, people compare these prospects as if they had reached the second stage. In this case, they face a choice between a sure gain of $30 and a .80 chance to win $45. The tendency to overweight sure things relative to uncertain outcomes (the certainty effect) favors the former option in the sequential version. Because an uncertain event (reaching the second stage of the game) is weighted as if it were certain, we called the phenomenon the pseudocertainty effect.

A study by Viscusi, Magat, and Huber (1987) provides compelling examples of both the certainty and the pseudocertainty effects. Participants in that study were exposed to a container of insecticide that was allegedly available for a stated price. After reading the warning label, they were asked to state their willingness to pay more for a product that would be safer in various ways. Two risks were mentioned (inhalation and child poisoning), each with a .0015 probability. The average willingness to pay to reduce both risks from .0015 to .0005 was $2.38 (in families with children), but the respondents were willing to pay an additional $5.71 to eliminate the last .0005 chance of harm. This large difference illustrates the certainty effect. The same respondents were also willing to pay $2.69 or $4.29, respectively, to eliminate the risk of inhalation or of child poisoning, without reducing the other risk. However, they were only willing to pay $1.84 to reduce both risks to .0005. This is an instance of a pseudocertainty effect. The respondents were willing to pay for the comfort of completely eliminating an identified risk, but the certainty they wished to purchase was illusory: the pesticide they would buy would still be associated with some danger, and in any event the amount paid to eliminate the risk of toxic inhalation or child poisoning would only reduce the overall risk of such harms, which can also occur in many other ways.

Contingently certain outcomes are important in many negotiations, in at least two ways. First, there are penalties and insurance provisions that are intended to protect one party against a failure of the other to comply with the agreement. The present analysis suggests that these provisions will loom large in the parties' view – but of course only to the extent that they are fully enforceable, and therefore contingently certain. Second, contingent certainty is involved in a less obvious way in negotiations about assets that will be significant if conflict breaks out between the parties. The negotiations between Israel and its neighbors provide many examples. Strategic assets, such as the Mitla Pass in the Sinai, or the Golan Heights near the Syrian border, provide contingently certain benefits to Israel in case of war. However, the retention of such assets raises tensions and surely increases the probability of armed conflict. An Israeli leader intent on minimizing the probability of catastrophic defeat should consider the probability that war will occur, multiplied by the probability of defeat given a war – separately for the case of withdrawal and nonwithdrawal. We do not presume to assess these probabilities; we merely suggest that the side that argues for retaining the strategic asset is likely to have the upper hand in a political debate – because of the superiority of contingent certainty over mere probability. Thus, the definite advantage of a strategic asset in case of war is likely to offset the uncertain reduction in the probability of war that might be brought about by a strategic or territorial concession.

The tendency to undervalue uncertain benefits sometimes leads to the *pseudo-dominance effect*. If it is advantageous to hold strategic assets both in war and in peace, territorial concession appears to be dominated by the strategy of holding on to key strategic positions. The fallacy in this argument is that it does not take into account the possibility that an agreement based on territorial concessions can decrease the chances of war. Even if holding to the strategic positions in question is in a country's best interest both in war and in peace, it could still make sense to give them up if this act could greatly reduce the probability of war. Since this outcome is uncertain, and its probability is in some sense unknowable, both politicians and citizens are likely to undervalue or neglect its contribution. The present discussion, of course, does not imply that strategic concessions should always be made. It only points out that the perception of dominance in such cases is often illusory.

III. LOSS AVERSION*

Loss aversion refers to the observation that losses generally loom larger than the corresponding gains. This notion may be captured by a value function that is steeper in the negative than in the positive domain. In decisions under risk, loss aversion entails a reluctance to accept even-chance gambles, unless the payoffs are very favorable. For example, many people will accept such a gamble only if the gain is at least twice as large as the loss. In decisions under certainty, loss aversion entails a systematic discrepancy in the assessments of advantages and disadvantages (Tversky and Kahneman 1991; Kahneman, Knetsch, and Thaler 1991). The general principle is quite simple: When an option is compared to the reference point, the comparison is coded in terms of the advantages and disadvantages of that option. A particularly important case of loss aversion arises when the reference point is the status quo, and when the retention of the status quo is an option. Because the disadvantages of any alternative to the status quo are weighted more heavily than its advantages, a strong bias in favor of the status quo is observed (Samuelson and Zeckhauser 1988). The argument has been extended to the context of international conflict and negotiation. Jervis (1992) notes: "If loss aversion is widespread, states defending the status quo should have a big bargaining advantage. That is, a state will be willing to pay a higher price and run higher risks if it is facing losses than if it is seeking to make gains" (p. 162).

---

* Section III is borrowed from Kahneman 1992.

The location of the reference point also affects the evaluation of *differences* between other pairs of options. Differences between disadvantages will generally have greater weight than corresponding differences between advantages because disadvantages are evaluated on a steeper limb of the value function. For example, the difference between salary offers of $40,000 and $45,000 will be viewed as a difference between two gains by someone whose current income is now $35,000, and as a difference between two losses if current income is $50,000. The psychological differences between the alternatives is likely to be greater in the latter case, reflecting the steeper slope of the value function in the domain of losses. Acceptance of the lower salary will be experienced as an increased loss if the reference point is high and as a foregone gain if it is low. It will be more painful in the former case.

The following classroom demonstration illustrates the principle of loss aversion (Kahneman, Knetsch, and Thaler 1990; see also Knetsch and Sinden 1984). An attractive object (e.g., a decorated mug) is distributed to one-third of the students. The students who have been given mugs are *sellers* – perhaps better described as owners. They are informed that there will be an opportunity to exchange the mug for a predetermined amount of money. The subjects state what their choice will be for different amounts, and thereby indicate the minimal amount for which they are willing to give up their mug. Another one-third of the students are *choosers*. They are told that they will have a choice between a mug like the one in the hands of their neighbor and an amount of cash; they indicate their choices for different amounts. The remaining students are *buyers*: they indicate whether they would pay each of the different amounts to acquire a mug. In a representative experiment, the median price set by sellers was $7.12, the median cash equivalent set by the choosers was $3.12, and the median buyer was willing to pay $2.88 for the mug.

The difference between the valuations of owners and choosers occurs in spite of the fact that both groups face the same choice: go home with a mug or with a prespecified sum of money. Subjectively, however, the choosers and owners are in different states: the former evaluate the mug as a gain, the latter as something to be given up. Because of loss aversion, more cash is required to persuade the owners to give up the mug than to match the attractiveness of the mug to the choosers. In the same vein, Thaler (1980) tells of a wine lover who will neither sell a bottle that has gained value in his cellar nor buy another bottle at the current price. The experimental studies of the discrepant valuation of owners, choosers, and buyers demonstrate that loss aversion can be induced instantaneously; it does not depend on a progressive attachment to objects in one's possession. Unlike the differences between buyers and sellers observed in some bargaining experiments (Neale, Huber, and Northcraft 1987), the above effect does not depend on the labels attached to the roles.

The market experiments conducted by Kahneman, Knetsch, and Thaler (1990) demonstrated a significant consequence of the discrepancy between the valuations of owners and buyers: far fewer transactions take place than economic theory would predict. Consider an experiment in which half the subjects are given mugs, and a market is set up where these subjects can sell their mugs to potential buyers. Economic theory predicts that when all market changes are completed, the mugs will be in the hands of the subjects who value them most. Because the initial allocation was random, half the mugs initially allocated should change hands. In an extended series of experiments, however, the observed volume of trade was about one-fourth, that is, only half the number predicted. The same result was obtained when owners and potential buyers had an opportunity to bargain directly over a possible price.

Concession Aversion

Loss aversion, we argue, could have a significant impact on conflict resolution. Imagine two countries negotiating the number of missiles that they will keep and aim at each other. Each country derives security from its own missiles and is threatened by those of the other side. Thus, missiles eliminated by the other side are evaluated as gains, and missiles one must give up are evaluated as losses, relative to the status quo. If losses have twice the impact of gains, then each side will require its opponent to eliminate twice as many missiles as it eliminates – not a promising start for the achievement of an agreement. The symmetry of the positions might help negotiators reframe the problem to trade missiles at par, but in most negotiations the sacrifices made by the two sides are not easily compared. In labor negotiations, for example, a union may be asked to give up a third pilot in the cockpit, and might be offered improved benefits or a more generous retirement plan in return. These are the circumstances under which we expect to find *concession aversion*, a systematically different evaluation of concessions made and of concessions received.

Concession aversion appears similar to the phenomenon of *reactive devaluation*, a negotiator's tendency to value a possible concession less if it is made by the opponent than by one's own side, as discussed in the previous chapter. However, the processes are quite different: reactive devaluation reflects a change in the evaluation of a proposal in response to an offer by an opponent, while concession aversion reflects the asymmetric valuation of gains and losses. Both processes could operate together to make agreement difficult.

Loss aversion does not affect all transactions: it applies to goods held for use, not goods held for exchange. Three categories of exchange goods are money held for spending, goods held specifically for sale, and "bargaining chips," goods that are valued only because they can be traded. The significance of missiles, for example, is substantially reduced when they are treated not as strategic assets but as bargaining chips. Concession aversion, we suggest, will only inhibit agreement in the latter case. Loss aversion plays little role in routine economic transactions, in which a seller and a buyer exchange a good and money, both of which were held for that purpose. In contrast, many of the objects of bargaining in labor negotiations (e.g., job security, benefits, grievance procedures) are "use goods" rather than exchange goods. Labor negotiations in which both sides seek to modify an existing contract to their advantage therefore provide the paradigm case of concession aversion.

The analysis of concession aversion has an immediate prescriptive implication. It suggests that the most effective concessions you can make are those that reduce or eliminate your opponent's losses; the least effective concessions are those that improve an attribute in which the other side is already "in the gains." Reductions of losses are evaluated on the steep lower limb of the value function – and the eliminations of losses are evaluated at its steepest region. In contrast, increments to already large gains are expected to add relatively little value.

The suggestion that it is more efficient to reduce the opponent's losses than to offset them by gains is compatible with a negotiating strategy discussed by Pruitt (1983). The *cost-cutting strategy* requires a side that seeks a concession to find ways to reduce the costs of that concession to the other side – in other words, to avoid imposing losses. The cost-cutting strategy is implicitly preferred to a strategy of offering concessions that the other side will evaluate as gains. In the terms of the present analysis, the losses that the cost-cutting strategy eliminates are evaluated in the steep region of the value function, whereas the marginal value of offsetting gains is relatively slight.

Gains, Losses, and Fairness

"I only want what is fair" is a common cry in negotiations, although adversaries who make this claim are not necessarily close to agreement. In addition to their effect on the valuation of outcomes, reference points also affect negotiations by influencing judgments of what is fair or unfair. Such judgments have impact on the outcome of bargaining – perhaps because offers that are perceived as unfair as well as disadvantageous are especially likely to evoke anger and resistance. It is generally accepted, of course, that fairness does not always govern behavior, that the rules of fairness are often ambiguous, and that disputants' interpretations of these ambiguities are likely to be self-serving (Messick and Sentis 1983; Thompson and Loewenstein 1992).

The role of reference points in judgments of fairness has been studied in the context of business practices. Judgments of fairness were obtained in a series of telephone surveys, in which the respondents assessed vignettes describing actions of price or wage setting by merchants, landlords, and employers (Kahneman, Knetsch, and Thaler 1986). The judgments appeared to be governed by a small number of rules of fairness, which treated gains and losses asymmetrically. The most prominent rule of fairness is that a firm should not impose a loss on its transactors (customers, employees, or tenants) merely in order to increase its own gain. For example, people consider it extremely unfair for a hardware store to raise the price of snow shovels after a blizzard, and they also think it unacceptable for a firm to cut the wages of employees merely because they could be replaced by cheaper labor. On the other hand, the standards of fairness allow a firm to protect itself from losses by raising the price it charges its customers or by reducing the pay of its employees. Thus, a firm can fairly use its market power to protect its reference profit, but not to increase it. In a further indication of the asymmetric treatment of gains and losses, the rules of fairness do not obligate a firm to share increases in its profits with its customers or employees. We summarized these rules by a *principle of dual entitlement:* the firm is entitled to its reference profit; customers, employees, and tenants are entitled to a reference price, wage, or rent; and in case of conflict between these entitlements the firm is allowed to protect itself from a threatened loss by transferring it to its transactors. Note that the principle defends the *rights* of both parties to a reference state, without imposing a more general egalitarian norm of sharing both pain and gain.

What determines the reference transaction? The precedent of previous transactions between the firm and the same individual transactor can be important. Thus, it is unfair to reduce the wage of an employee during a period of high unemployment, although an employee who quits can be replaced at a lower wage. The previous history of transactions between the firm and its employee defines an entitlement, which does not extend to the replacement. Note also that the wage that the new employee was paid elsewhere is entirely irrelevant. Thus, it is not the task of the firm to protect new employees from a loss relative to their previous earnings, because these are not part of the relevant reference transaction. The prevailing wage is the standard reference transaction for a new contract, especially if the new employee's job is not directly comparable to that of anyone currently in the organization.

Similar principles find expression in legal practice. Cohen and Knetsch (1992) have compiled an illuminating review of the judicial impact of the distinction between losses and foregone gains. They cite a legal expert to the effect that "To deprive somebody of something which he merely expected to receive is a less serious wrong, deserving of less protection, than to deprive somebody of the expectation of continuing to hold something which he already possesses." The familiar expression that possession is nine points of the law is another manifestation of the importance of the reference point.

The asymmetric treatment of losses and gains has generally conservative implications for judgments of economic fairness as well as for individual choice. We saw earlier that loss aversion induces a bias toward the retention of the status quo; the rules of fairness exhibit a similar bias favoring the retention of the reference transaction. There are other similarities between the two domains. For example, losses are given greater weight than foregone gains in individual choice, in judicial decisions (Cohen and Knetsch 1992), and also in lay rules of fairness. A firm is (barely) allowed to deny its transactors any share of its gains but is definitely prohibited from imposing losses on them. No one would seriously suggest that these principles extend to all human interactions. There are domains in which fairness demands that gains be shared, and competitive contexts in which the imposition of losses on others is sanctioned. It appears, however, that one common principle may apply across contexts: Actions that impose losses relative to an acceptable reference standard are viewed much more severely than actions (or omissions) that merely fail to provide a gain.

The notion of rights or entitlements is associated with a more extreme form of loss aversion called *enhanced loss aversion*. Losses that are compounded by outrage are much less acceptable than losses that are caused by misfortune or by legitimate actions of others. An example is the difference between two customers who face a steep increase in price, which one of the customers regards as unfair and the other as legitimate. According to the present analysis, both customers face the same loss, but whether they perceive that a right has been violated depends on their coding of the supplier's choice. Suppose, for example, that the supplier follows others in raising the price. If the prevailing price is accepted as a legitimate reference, the option of maintaining the old price would be coded as a loss to the supplier, which the rules of fairness do not require. If the price charged by other merchants is considered irrelevant, maintaining the old price merely foregoes an illegitimate gain.

As this example illustrates, the rules of fairness are often ambiguous, and the ambiguity typically involves the selection of the specific reference standard, rather than a more general principle. Customer and supplier could agree on the general principles that prices should be fair and that arbitrary increases beyond a proper reference price are unfair, but disagree on the proper reference price for the case at hand. Another important possibility is that the reference point by which an action is evaluated may not be unique. "Seeing the other person's point of view" might make a difference even when one does not fully accept it. There is at least a possibility that a discussion of fairness may have some persuasive effect even when it does not achieve a complete conversion.

CONCLUDING REMARKS

In this chapter we have discussed three major phenomena (optimistic overconfidence, the certainty effect, and loss aversion) which have emerged from the cognitive analysis of individual judgment and decision making. These phenomena represent systematic departures from the standard rational theory in which individuals are assumed to have realistic expectations, to weight outcomes by their probabilities, and to evaluate consequences as asset positions, not as gains and losses. We have argued that these biases in the assessment of evidence and the evaluation of consequences can hinder the successful resolution of conflict. In particular, optimistic overconfidence is likely to make opponents believe that they can prevail and hence they do not have to make concessions. The certainty effect leads disputants to undervalue some outcomes, such as goodwill, because they are not certain. Finally, loss aversion is likely to reduce the range of acceptable agreements because one's own concessions are evaluated as losses and the opponent's concessions are evaluated as gains. Although these phenomena do not exhaust the psychological barriers to the successful resolution of interpersonal conflict, they represent serious obstacles that often stand in the way of successful negotiation.

An understanding of the cognitive obstacles to conflict resolution could provide insight on two levels. On the first level, a negotiator may recognize that her opponent may not behave according to the standard rules of rational behavior, that he is likely to be overconfident, to undervalue uncertain concessions, and to be loss averse. In the spirit of Raiffa's prescriptive analysis (see Bell, Raiffa, and Tversky 1988), a rational negotiator may wish to take into account the fact that her opponent may not be entirely rational. On a higher level of insight, a negotiator may realize that she, too, does not always behave in accord with the maxims of rationality, and that she also exhibits overconfidence, the certainty effect, and loss aversion. The literature on judgment and choice (see Bazerman 1994; Dawes 1988; Kahneman, Slovic, and Tversky 1982) indicates that biases and cognitive illusions are not readily eliminated by knowledge or warning. Nevertheless, knowing the opponent's biases, as well as our own, may help us understand the barriers to conflict resolution and could even suggest methods to overcome them.

27. The Construction of Preference

Paul Slovic

ABSTRACT. One of the main themes that has emerged from behavioral decision research during the past 2 decades is the view that people's preferences are often constructed in the process of elicitation. This concept is derived in part from studies demonstrating that normatively equivalent methods of elicitation often give rise to systematically different responses. These "preference reversals" violate the principle of procedure invariance that is fundamental to theories of rational choice and raise difficult questions about the nature of human values. If different elicitation procedures produce different orderings of options, how can preferences be defined and in what sense do they exist? Describing and explaining such failures of invariance will require choice models of far greater complexity than the traditional models.

The meaning of preference and the status of value may be illuminated by this well-known exchange among three baseball umpires. "I call them as I see them," said the first. "I call them as they are," claimed the second. The third disagreed, "They ain't nothing till I call them." Analogously, we can describe three different views regarding the nature of values. First, values exist – like body temperature – and people perceive and report them as best they can, possibly with bias ("I call them as I see them"). Second, people know their values and preferences directly – as they know the multiplication table ("I call them as they are"). Third, values or preferences are commonly constructed in the process of elicitation ("They ain't nothing till

Editor's note. Articles based on APA award addresses that appear in the *American Psychologist* are scholarly articles by distinguished contributors to the field. As such, they are given special consideration in the *American Psychologist's* editorial process.

This article was originally presented as part of a Distinguished Scientific Contributions award address at the 102nd Annual Convention of the American Psychological Association in Los Angeles, California, in August 1994.

Daniel Kahneman served as action editor for this article.

Author's note. I am indebted to Sarah Lichtenstein, Baruch Fischhoff, Amos Tversky, and Danny Kahneman, who made immense contributions to the research described in this article and who made the conduct of my own research in this area a truly pleasurable and exciting venture.

I call them"). The research reviewed in this article is most compatible with
the third view of preference as a constructive, context-dependent process.

(Tversky & Thaler, 1990, p. 210)

The expression of preference by means of choice and decision making is the
essence of intelligent, purposeful behavior. Although decision making has been
studied for centuries by philosophers, mathematicians, economists, and statis-
ticians, it has a relatively short history within psychology. The first extensive
review of the theory of decision making was published in the *Psychological Bulletin* by Edwards (1954), whose article introduced psychologists to the "exceed-
ingly elaborate, mathematical and voluminous" (p. 380) economic literature
on choice and reviewed the handful of relevant experimental studies then in
existence.

Edwards's (1954) review was followed by a rapid proliferation of theories
of choice and decision making, along with carefully controlled experiments
designed to test those theories. This work followed two parallel streams. One,
the *theory of riskless choice*, had its origins in the notions of utility maximization put forth by Jeremy Bentham and James Mill. The first formal economic
theories based on these notions assumed that decision makers are (a) completely
informed about the possible courses of action and their consequences, (b) in-
finitely sensitive to differences among alternatives, and (c) rational in the sense
that they can rank order the possible choices and make decisions that maximize
some subjective measure of value or welfare – usually designated by the term
utility.

The second stream, the *theory of risky choice*, deals with decisions made in
the face of uncertainty about the events that determine the outcomes of one's
actions. Maximization also plays a key role in these theories, but the quantity
to be maximized becomes, because of the uncertainty involved, *expected utility*.
Tests of the theory that individuals behave so as to maximize expected utility
have been the topic of hundreds of experiments, many of which studied reactions to well-defined manipulations of simple gambles as their basic research
paradigm.

A basic assumption of rational theories of choice is the principle of *invariance*
(Tversky & Kahneman, 1986; Tversky, Sattath, & Slovic, 1988), which states that
the relation of preference should not depend on the description of the options
(description invariance) or on the method of elicitation (procedure invariance).
Without stability across equivalent descriptions and equivalent elicitation procedures, one's preferences cannot be represented as maximization of utility.

Between 1950 and 1960 another development was taking place that was
to have a profound influence on the study of decision making. This was the
work of Simon (1956), who sharply criticized the assumption of maximization
in utility theory. Simon argued that actual decision-making behavior is better
described in terms of *bounded* rationality. A boundedly rational decision maker
attempts to attain some satisfactory, although not necessarily maximal, level

of achievement. Simon's conceptualization highlighted the role of perception, cognition, and learning in decision making and directed researchers to examine the psychological processes by which decision problems are represented and information is processed.

In recent years the information-processing view has dominated the empirical study of decision making. Both streams of research, on risky and on riskless choice, have been merged in a torrent of studies aimed at describing and understanding the mental operations associated with judgment and decision making. The result has been a far more complicated portrayal of decision making than that provided by utility maximization theory. It is now generally recognized among psychologists that utility maximization provides only limited insight into the processes by which decisions are made.

In particular, a sizable body of research shows that description invariance and procedure invariance do not hold. Preferences appear to be remarkably labile, sensitive to the way a choice problem is described or "framed" and to the mode of response used to express the preference (Fischhoff, Slovic, & Lichtenstein, 1980; Kahneman & Tversky, 1979; Tversky & Kahneman, 1981). These failures of invariance have contributed to a new conception of judgment and choice in which beliefs and preferences are often constructed – not merely revealed – in the elicitation process.

Psychologists' claims that people do not behave according to the dictates of utility theory are particularly troubling to economists, whose theories assume that people are rational in the sense of having preferences that are complete and transitive[1] and in the sense that they choose what they most prefer.

This article reviews the history of research on preference reversals, a line of information-processing theories and experiments that has demonstrated the failure of procedure invariance and has contributed to a view of preference starkly different from the view embodied in economic theories of choice.

PREFERENCE REVERSALS AMONG GAMBLES: EARLY STUDIES

The principle of procedure invariance is violated by preference reversals that are induced by changing from one mode of eliciting a preference to another, formally equivalent, mode of response.

An early demonstration of response-mode effects by Slovic and Lichtenstein (1968) used simple gambles as stimuli (e.g., .3 chance to win $16 and .7 chance to lose $4). Slovic and Lichtenstein observed that ratings of a gamble's attractiveness and choices between pairs of gambles were influenced primarily by the probabilities of winning and losing, whereas buying and selling prices (e.g.,

---

[1] Persons' preferences are complete if, for all options x and y, they prefer x to y or y to x or are indifferent between them. Their preferences are transitive if, for all options x, y, and z, if they prefer x to y and y to z, then they prefer x to z. Completeness and transitivity are fundamental to utility theories.

"What's the most you would pay for a chance to play this gamble?" or "What's the least amount for which you would sell a ticket to play it?") were primarily determined by the dollar amounts that could be won or lost. When participants found a bet attractive, their prices correlated predominantly with the amount that could be won; when they disliked a bet, their prices correlated primarily with the amount that could be lost. This pattern of correlations was explained as the result of a starting point (anchoring) and an adjustment procedure used when setting prices. Respondents setting a price on an attractive gamble appeared to start with the amount they could win and adjust it downward to account for the probabilities of winning and losing as well as for the amount that could be lost. The adjustment process was relatively imprecise, with the price response greatly influenced by the starting point payoff. Ratings and choices, on the other hand, appeared to be governed by different rules, leading to greater emphasis on probabilities.

Lichtenstein and Slovic (1971) hypothesized that if people process information differently when making choices and setting prices, it should be possible to construct pairs of gambles so that a person would choose one member of the pair but would set a higher price on the other. They demonstrated this predicted effect in several studies, including one conducted on the floor of the Four Queens Casino in Las Vegas (Lichtenstein & Slovic, 1973). A typical pair of gambles in that study (shown below) consisted of one bet with a high probability to win a modest amount (called the P bet) and one bet with a lower probability of winning a larger payoff (called the $ bet):

> P bet: 11/12 chance to win 12 chips;
>   1/12 chance to lose 24 chips;
>
> $ bet: 2/12 chance to win 79 chips;
>   10/12 chance to lose 5 chips,

where each chip was worth 25 cents. Each participant first made a choice and later indicated a minimum selling price for each bet. For this pair of gambles, the two bets were chosen about equally often across respondents. However, the $ bet received a higher selling price about 88% of the time. Of the participants who chose the P bet, 87% gave a higher selling price to the $ bet. This is no minor inconsistency. Lichtenstein and Slovic (1971) showed that persons who persisted in this pattern of preferences (and some did) could be turned into "money pumps," continuously giving money to the experimenters without ever playing the gambles.

These early studies captured the attention of a few psychologists and other decision researchers who replicated and extended the findings. Economists were introduced to the preference reversal phenomenon by Grether and Plott (1979), who clearly recognized the threat this phenomenon posed to economic theories of choice: "The inconsistency is deeper than the mere lack of transitivity .... It suggests that no optimization principles of any sort lie behind even the simplest of human choices" (p. 623). Accordingly, they carried out a series of experiments "designed to discredit the psychologists' works as applied to economics" (p. 623). Their design was based on 13 criticisms and potential artifacts that would render preference reversals irrelevant to economic theory, including the fact that the experimenters were psychologists, which might have led the participants to behave peculiarly. Their manipulations included using special incentives to heighten motivation, controlling for income and order effects, allowing indifference in the choice responses, testing the influence of strategic or bargaining biases, and having economists conduct the study. To their surprise, preference reversals remained much in evidence despite their determined effort to eradicate them.

Grether and Plott's (1979) careful experiment served only to motivate more extreme attempts by economists to make preference reversals disappear. Pommerehne, Schneider, and Zweifel (1982) attempted to increase motivation by raising the face value of the payoffs and creating differences in expected value between the P and $ bets in a pair. They too found a substantial proportion of reversals, leading them to conclude, "Even when the subjects are exposed to strong incentives for making motivated, rational decisions, the phenomenon of preference reversal does not vanish" (p. 573).

Reilly (1982) was also skeptical of the adequacy of Grether and Plott's (1979) controls. To maximize respondents' understanding of the task, he conducted a study in which the money at risk was placed on a desk in front of the respondent and the size of potential losses in the gambles was increased to enhance motivation. Although the rate of preference reversals was somewhat lower than that observed by Grether and Plott, the phenomenon persisted to a substantial extent. Reilly conceded that these results provided "further confirmation of preference reversal as a persistent behavioral phenomenon in situations where economic theory is generally applied" (p. 582). Nevertheless, he maintained the hope that further strengthening of monetary incentives and the provision of additional information to the participants would make this troublesome phenomenon disappear, thus salvaging preference theory.

Preference reversals were also observed by Knez and Smith (1987), who allowed their participants to trade bets in an experimental market, and by Berg, Dickhaut, and O'Brien (1985), who used an arbitrage procedure that turned participants whose prices and preferences were inconsistent into money pumps. Chu and Chu (1990) and Cox and Grether (1996) were finally able to eradicate preference reversals in market settings characterized by repetition, feedback, and harsh penalties for being inconsistent.

Some economists have attempted to save utility theory by arguing that preference reversals can be accommodated by eliminating less central axioms rather than by abandoning transitivity (see, e.g., Holt, 1986; Karni & Safra, 1987). Other theorists, however, proposed more radical departures from utility theory. Both Loomes and Sugden (1983) and Fishburn (1985) designed theories that abandoned the requirement of transitivity.

Slovic and Lichtenstein (1983) responded to economists' repeated attacks and defensive posture by attempting to show how preference reversals fit into a larger picture of framing and information-processing effects that, as a whole, pose a collective challenge to preference theories far exceeding the challenge from reversals alone. They urged economists not to resist these developments but, instead, to examine them for insights into how people make decisions and the ways that the practice of decision making can be improved.

Hausman (1991) was also critical of economists' refusal to take preference reversals seriously. Writing "On Dogmatism in Economics: The Case of Preference Reversals," he traced economists' reactions to their reluctance to abandon a single systematic and parsimonious theory of choice that is also a theory of rational choice, in favor of psychologists' narrower and more complex theories. Nevertheless, he concluded, economists' reactions were hard to defend, creating "unreasonable barriers to theoretical and empirical progress" (p. 223).

CAUSES OF PREFERENCE REVERSALS

Although the early studies established the robustness of the preference reversal phenomenon, its interpretation and explanation remained unclear, leading to a second wave of studies starting in the mid-1980s.

Tversky, Slovic, and Kahneman (1990) formulated the explanatory problem as follows. First, they defined a preference reversal as the following combination of responses:

$$H \succ L \quad \text{and} \quad C_L > C_H,$$

where H refers to the high-probability gamble (earlier called the P bet), L refers to the low-probability gamble (the $ bet); C_H and C_L denote, respectively, the cash equivalent (or minimum selling price) of H and L; and $\succ$ and $\approx$ denote strict preference and indifference, respectively. Note that > refers to the ordering of cash amounts and $X > Y$ implies $X \succ Y$; in other words, more money is preferred to less.

A preference reversal can be shown to imply either the intransitivity of the preference relation $\succ$, the failure of procedure invariance, or both.

If procedure invariance holds, an individual will be indifferent between his or her stated price (cash equivalent) X and the bet B; that is,

$$B \succ X \quad \text{iff } C_B > X \quad \text{and} \quad C_B = X \quad \text{iff } B \approx X.$$

Therefore, if invariance holds, preference reversal implies the following intransitive cycle:

$$C_H \approx H \succ L \approx C_L > C_H,$$

where the two inequalities follow from the preference reversal, and the two equivalences follow from procedure invariance.

But two types of discrepancies between choice and pricing (i.e., failures of invariance) could also produce preference reversals: overpricing of L and underpricing of H. Overpricing of L is said to occur if the decision maker prefers the price over the bet when offered a choice between them (i.e., $C_L \succ L$). Underpricing of H occurs when $H \succ C_H$. Overpricing and underpricing merely identify the sign of the discrepancy between pricing and choice; the labels do not imply that choice represents one's true preference and that the bias resides only in pricing.

Tversky et al. (1990) developed a procedure for diagnosing whether any observed preference reversal was due to intransitivity, overpricing of L, underpricing of H, or both overpricing of L and underpricing of H, and they used this procedure in a new study.[2] The results were clear. The experiment yielded the usual rate of preference reversal (between 40% and 50%), but only 10% of preference reversal patterns were intransitive, and the remaining 90% violated procedure invariance. By far the major source of preference reversal was the overpricing of the L bet, which accounted for nearly two thirds of the observed patterns. These conclusions were further supported in a study by Bostic, Herrnstein, and Luce (1990), who used a somewhat different methodology.

THE COMPATIBILITY HYPOTHESIS

In the earliest studies on preference reversals, two information-processing concepts were proposed to account for the dependence on payoff cues in pricing gambles. These were starting point and adjustment strategies (e.g., starting with the amount to win and adjusting it downward) and the concept of compatibility. Lichtenstein and Slovic (1973) proposed a "general hypothesis that the compatibility or commensurability between a cue dimension and the required response will affect the importance of the cue in determining the response" (p. 20).

The finding by Tversky et al. (1990) that preference reversals were due primarily to overpricing the high payoff bets led to a reexamination and more precise formulation of the compatibility hypothesis by them and by Slovic,

---

[2] In this diagnostic procedure, the original preference reversal design was extended to include, in addition to the standard H and L bets, a cash amount X that was compared with both of them. That is, participants indicated their preferences between each of the pairs in the triple {H, L, X}. Participants also produced cash equivalents, C_L and C_H for both of the bets. By focusing on standard preference reversal patterns in which the prespecified cash amount X has been set to lie between the values of C_L and C_H generated by the respondent (i.e., $H \succ L$ and $C_L > X > C_H$), it is possible to diagnose each preference reversal pattern according to whether it was produced by an intransitivity, by an overpricing of L, by an underpricing of H, or by both. For example, if respondents indicated that $L \succ X$ and that $X \succ H$, then their preferences are intransitive because the method analyzes only those cases in which $H \succ L$. Alternatively, if respondents overprice the L bet, then their pattern of responses will be $X \succ L$ and $X \succ H$. (The respondents produce a price for L that is greater than X, but when offered a choice between X and L, they choose X.) This pattern is transitive, although it is a preference reversal.

Griffin, and Tversky (1990). Slovic et al. proposed that the weight of a stimulus attribute in judgment or in choice is enhanced by its compatibility with the response mode.[3] The rationale for this *scale compatibility hypothesis* is twofold. First, if the stimulus scale and the response scale do not match, additional mental operations are needed to map the former onto the latter. This increases effort and error and may reduce the impact of the stimulus scale. Second, a response mode tends to focus attention on the compatible features of the stimulus.

The hypothesized link between compatibility and preference reversals was supported in a number of new studies reported by Slovic et al. (1990). In one of these studies, participants were presented with six pairs of H and L bets. Three pairs involved monetary payoffs, and three pairs involved nonmonetary outcomes, such as a one-week pass for all movie theaters in town, or a dinner for two at a good restaurant. If preference reversals are due primarily to the compatibility of prices and payoffs, which are both expressed in dollars, their incidence should be substantially reduced by the use of nonmonetary outcomes. This prediction was confirmed; the overall incidence of reversals decreased from 41% (monetary bets) to 24% (nonmonetary bets).

Although the compatibility hypothesis can explain preference reversals between pairs of bets, the explanation does not depend on the presence of risk. Indeed, this hypothesis implies a similar discrepancy between choice and pricing for riskless options with a monetary component, such as delayed payments. Let (X, T) be a prospect that offers a payment of $\$X$, T years from now. Consider a long-term prospect L ($2,500, 5 years from now) and a short-term prospect S ($1,600, 1.5 years from now). Suppose that respondents (a) choose between L and S and (b) price both prospects by stating the smallest immediate cash payment for which they would be willing to exchange the delayed payment. According to the compatibility hypothesis, the monetary component X would weigh more heavily in pricing than in choice. As a consequence, respondents should produce preference reversals in which the short-term option is preferred over the long-term option in a direct choice, but the latter is priced higher than the former (i.e., $S \succ L$ and $C_L > C_S$). This was precisely the pattern observed by Tversky et al. (1990). Their participants chose the short-term option 74% of the time but priced the long-term option above the short-term option 75% of the time; the rate of reversals exceeded 50%. Further analysis revealed that – as in the risky case – the major source of preference reversal was the overpricing of the long-term option, as entailed by compatibility.

---

[3] The significance of the compatibility between input and output has long been recognized by students of human performance. Engineering psychologists have discovered that responses to visual displays of information, such as an instrument panel, will be faster and more accurate if the response structure is compatible with the arrangement of the stimuli (Fitts & Seeger, 1953). For example, the response to a pair of lights will be faster and more accurate if the left light is assigned to the left key and the right light to the right key. Similarly, a square array of four burners on a stove is easier to control with a matching square array of knobs than with a linear array.

Additional support for the role of compatibility in preference reversals came from a study by Schkade and Johnson (1989). This study used "mouselab," a computer-based method for monitoring the time spent by each participant looking at probabilities and at payoffs as they priced bets, rated their attractiveness, or made choices. They found that the percentage of time spent on payoffs was significantly greater in pricing than in choice when respondents produced preference reversals, but there was little difference when respondents did not exhibit reversals. A second experiment produced a high percentage of reversals between pricing responses and attractiveness ratings, along with strong evidence demonstrating the use of anchoring and adjustment strategies. The selection of anchors (e.g., payoffs for pricing and probabilities for rating) appeared to be guided by compatibility.

Goldstein and Einhorn (1987) also found reversals between pricing and attractiveness ratings and attributed them to the way in which the subjective value of a gamble was mapped onto the response scale. Although their model can accommodate reversals of preference, it does not predict the variety of compatibility effects that other studies have observed.

CHOICE, MATCHING, AND THE PROMINENCE EFFECT

Parallel to the early work on preference reversals, what appeared at the time to be a separate line of research was investigating the difference between choice and matching responses through the use of a diverse array of two-dimensional stimuli, such as baseball players described in terms of their batting averages and number of home runs, typists described by their speed and accuracy, and so forth. The results, reported in Slovic (1975), were framed in terms of the ancient philosophical puzzle of how to choose between equally attractive alternatives. In these studies, participants first matched different pairs of options (making them equal in value), and, in a later session, chose between the matched options. Slovic found that participants did not choose randomly but rather tended to select the option that was superior on the more important dimension (e.g., batting average and typing accuracy). About a decade later, Tversky saw in this finding the seeds of a general theory of response-mode effects that had the potential to explain a wide variety of empirical findings, including preference reversals. This theory was explicated and tested by Tversky et al. (1988).

Tversky et al. (1988) noted that choice and matching operations were fundamental to measurement in both the physical and the social sciences. To determine the heavier of two objects, for example, one can place them on two sides of a pan balance and observe which side goes down. Alternatively, one can place each object separately on a sliding scale and observe the position at which the sliding scale is balanced. Similarly, to determine the preference order between options, one can use either choice or matching (where matching includes rating scales, cash equivalents, etc.). Note that the pan balance is analogous to binary

Table 27.1. Highway Safety Problem Used to Assess the Prominence Effect

Problem: About 600 people are killed each year in Israel in traffic accidents. The ministry of transportation investigates various programs to reduce the number of casualities. Consider the following two programs, described in terms of yearly costs (in millions of dollars [M]) and the number of casualties per year that is expected following the implementation of each program. Which program do you favor?

Program	Expected Number of Casualties	Cost	Percentage of Respondents Choosing
X	500	$55M	67
Y	570	$12M	33

Note: From "Contingent Weighting in Judgment and Choice" by A. Tversky, S. Sattath, and P. Slovic, 1988, Psychological Review, 95, p. 373. Copyright 1988 by the American Psychological Association.

choice, whereas the sliding scale resembles matching. In proper physical measurement, procedure invariance holds: The ordering of two objects with regard to weight is identical with either the pan balance or the sliding scale. However, as previously seen, choice and matching often disagree when used to measure preferences.

Generalizing from the results of Slovic (1975), Tversky et al. (1988) formulated the *prominence hypothesis*: The more prominent (important) attribute will weigh more heavily in choice than in matching. This hypothesis was tested and supported through a series of problems, including the highway safety problem shown in Table 27.1. Number of casualties was presumed to be the prominent dimension in this problem. When asked to choose between the two safety programs, 67% of the respondents chose X, the program that saved more lives at a higher cost per life saved. Other groups of respondents received the same problem except that one of the four values was missing. They were asked to fill in the missing value to make the two programs equally attractive. It is possible to infer a person's response to the choice task from their response to the matching task. For example, if the cost for Program X was missing and the respondent filled in a value less than $55 million to make the two programs equally attractive, one would infer that this person would choose Y over X when the cost for X was $55 million. In fact, the overwhelming number of matches favored the more economical Program Y that saves fewer lives. Only 4% of the inferred choices favored Program X. Similar responses were observed across a variety of other problems. In every case, the primary dimension was given more weight in choice than in matching. This effect gives rise to a marked discrepancy between the preferences derived from choice and from matching, thus violating procedure invariance. Because pricing a gamble or judging its cash equivalent is a matching response, one can view preference reversals among bets as a special case of the choice–matching discrepancy, in which probability of winning is the prominent dimension that receives greater weight in choice.[4]

Tversky et al. (1988) suggested that different heuristics or computational schemes appear to be used in the two kinds of tasks. Choice invokes more qualitative reasoning, such as the use of a lexicographic strategy (i.e., selecting the alternative that is ordinally superior on the most important attribute). Lexicographic reasoning is cognitively easier than making explicit tradeoffs and is also easier to justify to oneself and to others. Matching, on the other hand, requires a more quantitative assessment. Tversky et al. proposed that ordinal considerations loom larger in the ordinal procedure of choice than in the cardinal procedure of matching. The prominence effect may thus be seen as an example of a general principle that Fischer and Hawkins (1993) later labeled *strategy compatibility*.

Tversky et al. (1988) also developed a hierarchy of contingent trade-off models to accommodate the various compatibility effects observed in studies of judgment and preference. In these models, the trade-offs between attributes depend on the nature of the response.

Reliance on the prominent dimension makes a good reason for choice. Demonstration of the prominence effect thus focused attention on the importance of reasons, arguments, and justifications in choice. In earlier work, the search for good reasons to eliminate options from consideration had been shown to guide the choice strategies observed and modeled by Tversky (1969). Slovic (1975) also invoked justifiability to explain people's preferences for the option that was superior on the prominent dimension when faced with a choice among equally valued alternatives. Montgomery (1983) argued that people search for and construct dominance structures[5] in decision problems because they provide a compelling reason for choice. The axioms of utility theory may act as compelling arguments or reasons for making a particular decision when their applicability is detected or pointed out (Tversky & Kahneman, 1986).

Additional evidence for a reason-based conception of choice is provided by Tversky and Simonson (1993) and Shafir, Simonson, and Tversky (1993). Shafir et al. argued that a reason-based conception fits well with a constructive interpretation of choice. Different frames, contexts, and elicitation procedures highlight different aspects of the options and bring forth different reasons and considerations that influence the decision.

---

[4] A nice example of prominence is the finding that personal safety looms larger in choices between options that vary in both safety and cost than in the pricing of such options (Magat, Viscusi, & Huber, 1988). Safety is more prominent than money and, thus, is given greater weight in choice than in pricing.

[5] A dominance structure is a choice situation in which one option is as good or better than another on all relevant aspects.

CONSTRUCTION OF PREFERENCE

The study of preference reversals has been one of several lines of research leading to a conception of choice quite different from the classical assumption that the decision maker has a complete preference order for all options and selects the option highest in that order. This new conception applies to judgments and choices among options that are important, complex, and perhaps unfamiliar, such as gambles, jobs, careers, homes, automobiles, surgical treatments, and environments. In these decisions, preferences are not simply read off some master list but are constructed on the spot by an adaptive decision maker (Payne, Bettman, & Johnson, 1992, 1993). Construction strategies include anchoring and adjustment, relying on the prominent dimension, eliminating common elements, discarding nonessential differences, adding new attributes into the problem frame in order to bolster one alternative, or otherwise restructuring the decision problem to create dominance and thus reduce conflict and indecision. As a result of these mental gymnastics, decision making is a highly contingent form of information processing, sensitive to task complexity, time pressure, response mode, framing, reference points, and numerous other contextual factors.

Krantz (1991) portrayed this new conception of decision making as attempting to solve several distinct problems in the absence of firm trade-offs or values. He challenged the normative status of utility theory as well as its descriptive status:

> The normative assumption that individuals *should* maximize *some* quantity may be wrong. Perhaps...there exists nothing to be maximized. Ordering may be partial...because the calculations are impossible in principle: People do and should act as *problem solvers, not maximizers*, because they have many different and incommensurable...goals to achieve. (p. 34)

PRACTICAL IMPLICATIONS OF PREFERENCE CONSTRUCTION

The study of preference aims not only to understand decision making but to improve it. The constructive view has much to offer in this regard. For as Delquié (1993) has observed, prescriptive decision analysis basically concerns constructing preferences in situations in which the right choice is not readily apparent. The analysis requires a process that is transparent, logical, and free of arbitrariness. Truth ultimately resides in the process, rather than in the outcome.

Valuing the Environment

One practical application of preference construction addresses the method of contingent valuation (CV), which has been used by economists for more than 25 years to value environmental actions such as wetlands protection, water and air quality improvements, and wildlife resources. The CV method posits a hypothetical market and asks people to imagine what they would pay in this market for a proposed change in the environmental state of interest. However, valuing environmental changes is exactly the kind of complex, unfamiliar task in which one would not expect to find stable, well-articulated preferences, making it a likely candidate for constructive processes. Irwin, Slovic, Lichtenstein, and McClelland (1993) used knowledge of constructive preferences to examine and critique the CV approach. They developed a preference reversal experiment in which they asked participants to choose between improved air quality and an upgraded computer and to indicate their cash equivalents for each improvement. Irwin et al. found, as predicted by the prominence hypothesis, that participants chose improved air quality as more valuable, presumably because choice invokes reasons, and there are stronger, more noble reasons for preferring air quality over a computer upgrade. They also predicted, and found, that people placed a higher monetary value on the computer upgrade, presumably because of the strong implicit price cues associated with a better computer. Preference reversals (preference for improved air quality in choice and the computer upgrade in pricing) were observed in 41% of the respondents.

Kahneman and Ritov (1994) also hypothesized and found prominence effects leading to reversals between choices and monetary values for environmental interventions, although the specific nature of these effects was somewhat different from that observed by Irwin et al. (1993).

With the findings of Irwin et al. (1993) in mind, Gregory, Lichtenstein, and Slovic (1993) launched a critique of the CV paradigm. They argued that if monetary values are constructed during the elicitation process in a way that is strongly influenced by context, one should take a deliberate approach to value construction, in a manner designed to rationalize the process. They recommended the use of multi-attribute utility theory (von Winterfeldt & Edwards, 1986), which provides a systematic framework for eliciting and integrating the multiple dimensions of complex values. In this way, a CV survey would serve as an active process of value construction, rather than a neutral process of value discovery, and the designers of a CV study would function "not as archaeologists, carefully uncovering what is there, but as architects, working to build a defensible expression of value" (Gregory et al., 1993, p. 179).

Informed Consent

The role of preference construction as an active process was perceived in a very different way by MacLean (1991), a philosopher interested in the role of informed consent in clinical medicine. MacLean described the move away from the traditional model whereby authority is delegated by the patient to the physician toward a new model of shared decision making, in which enlightened physicians give primary responsibility to the patient. The physician thus acts as an expert advisor, providing information and counseling. The shared decision-making model thus respects the patient's autonomy in the face of decisions that are difficult and momentous. It also protects the physician against the charge of imposing an unwanted treatment on the patient.

MacLean (1991) argued that if preferences are constructed in the process of informing, framing the options, and eliciting the response, the rationale behind the shared model of consent cannot be defended. Rather, this model makes the physician's role more difficult and risky. The physician is helping to construct preferences, which he or she should do consciously yet in a way that avoids domination. MacLean offered no simple guidelines for the physician but argued that the process must be more involved and interactive than the normal approach if the value of informed consent is to be realized.

Preference Management

The fact that preferences are highly labile, which psychologists have worked so hard to demonstrate, has been known to practical philosophers for ages. If preferences are so readily manipulable, why not manage them for one's own benefit? For example, people can choose their goals and aspiration levels. Thus, the Talmud asks, "Who is it that is rich?" and answers, "One who is content with his portion."[6] People are advised by those wiser than themselves to "put things in perspective," by comparing their misfortunes with far worse troubles or by considering how unimportant some present problem will seem 10 years from now.

The constructive theory may help people do a better job of managing their preferences. Thus MacLean's patients and physicians might be advised to sift and weigh alternative reasons or justifications, to work toward developing a rationale for action. A strong rationale might buffer the patient from regret and make it easier for him or her to accept the consequences of the decision. If the patient is an intuitive decision theorist, this process could invoke utility functions and maximization rules. However, quite different justifications could be equally legitimate if they have been thoughtfully derived.

An appreciation of framing effects could also help people manage their preferences more effectively (Thaler, 1985). Suppose, for example, that a person with $5,600 in a bank account misplaces a $100 bill. Rather than isolating and dwelling on this painful loss, assimilating it into one's total account may ease the sting by exploiting the perception that $5,500 is not that different from $5,600.

The concepts of preference construction and preference management reflect the deep interplay between descriptive phenomena and normative principles. The experimental study of decision processes appears to be forging a new conception of preference, one that may require serious restructuring of normative theories and approaches toward improving decision making.

---

[6] Not being a Talmudic scholar, I am indebted to David Krantz (1991) for this example.

28. Contingent Weighting in Judgment and Choice

Amos Tversky, Shmuel Sattath, and Paul Slovic

ABSTRACT. Preference can be inferred from direct choice between options or from a matching procedure in which the decision maker adjusts one option to match another. Studies of preferences between two-dimensional options (e.g., public policies, job applicants, benefit plans) show that the more prominent dimension looms larger in choice than in matching. Thus, choice is more lexicographic than matching. This finding is viewed as an instance of a general principle of compatibility: The weighting of inputs is enhanced by their compatibility with the output. To account for such effects, we develop a hierarchy of models in which the trade-off between attributes is contingent on the nature of the response. The simplest theory of this type, called the contingent weighting model, is applied to the analysis of various compatibility effects, including the choice-matching discrepancy and the preference-reversal phenomenon. These results raise both conceptual and practical questions concerning the nature, the meaning and the assessment of preference.

The relation of preference between acts or options is the key element of decision theory that provides the basis for the measurement of utility or value. In axiomatic treatments of decision theory, the concept of preference appears as an abstract relation that is given an empirical interpretation through specific methods of elicitation, such as choice and matching. In choice the decision maker selects an option from an offered set of two or more alternatives. In matching the decision maker is required to set the value of some variable in order to achieve an equivalence between options (e.g., what chance to win $750 is as attractive as 1 chance in 10 to win $2,500?).

This work was supported by Contract N00014-84-K-0615 from the Office of Naval Research to Stanford University and by National Science Foundation Grant 5ES-8712-145 to Decision Research.

The article has benefited from discussions with Greg Fischer, Dale Griffin, Eric Johnson, Daniel Kahneman, and Lennart Sjöberg.

The standard analysis of choice assumes procedure invariance: Normatively equivalent procedures for assessing preferences should give rise to the same preference order. Indeed, theories of measurement generally require the ordering of objects to be independent of the particular method of assessment. In classical physical measurement, it is commonly assumed that each object possesses a well-defined quantity of the attribute in question (e.g., length, mass) and that different measurement procedures elicit the same ordering of objects with respect to this attribute. Analogously, the classical theory of preference assumes that each individual has a well-defined preference order (or a utility function) and that different methods of elicitation produce the same ordering of options. To determine the heavier of two objects, for example, we can place them on the two sides of a pan balance and observe which side goes down. Alternatively, we can place each object separately on a sliding scale and observe the position at which the sliding scale is balanced. Similarly, to determine the preference order between options we can use either choice or matching. Note that the pan balance is analogous to binary choice, whereas the sliding scale resembles matching.

The assumption of procedure invariance is likely to hold when people have well-articulated preferences and beliefs, as is commonly assumed in the classical theory. If one likes opera but not ballet, for example, this preference is likely to emerge regardless of whether one compares the two directly or evaluates them independently. Procedure invariance may hold even in the absence of precomputed preferences if people use a consistent algorithm. We do not immediately know the value of 7(8 + 9), but we have an algorithm for computing it that yields the same answer regardless of whether the addition is performed before or after the multiplication. Similarly, procedure invariance is likely to be satisfied if the value of each option is computed by a well-defined criterion, such as expected utility.

Studies of decision and judgment, however, indicate that the foregoing conditions for procedure invariance are not generally true and that people often do not have well-defined values and beliefs (e.g., Fischhoff, Slovic & Lichtenstein, 1980; March, 1978; Shafer & Tversky, 1985). In these situations, observed preferences are not simply read off from some master list; they are actually constructed in the elicitation process. Furthermore, choice is contingent or context sensitive: It depends on the framing of the problem and on the method of elicitation (Payne, 1982; Slovic & Lichtenstein, 1983; Tversky & Kahneman, 1986). Different elicitation procedures highlight different aspects of options and suggest alternative heuristics, which may give rise to inconsistent responses. An adequate account of choice, therefore, requires a psychological analysis of the elicitation process and its effect on the observed response.

What are the differences between choice and matching, and how do they affect people's responses? Because our understanding of the mental processes involved is limited, the analysis is necessarily sketchy and incomplete. Nevertheless, there is reason to expect that choice and matching may differ in a predictable manner. Consider the following example. Suppose Joan faces a choice between two job offers that vary in interest and salary. As a natural first step, Joan examines whether one option dominates the other (i.e., is superior in all respects). If not, she may try to reframe the problem (e.g., by representing the options in terms of higher order attributes) to produce a dominant alternative (Montgomery, 1983). If no dominance emerges, she may examine next whether one option enjoys a decisive advantage: that is, whether the advantage of one option far outweighs the advantage of the other. If neither option has a decisive advantage, the decision maker seeks a procedure for resolving the conflict. Because it is often unclear how to trade one attribute against another, a common procedure for resolving conflict in such situations is to select the option that is superior on the more important attribute. This procedure, which is essentially lexicographic, has two attractive features. First, it does not require the decision maker to assess the trade-off between the attributes, thereby reducing mental effort and cognitive strain. Second, it provides a compelling argument for choice that can be used to justify the decision to oneself as well as to others.

Consider next the matching version of the problem. Suppose Joan has to determine the salary at which the less interesting job would be as attractive as the more interesting one. The qualitative procedure described earlier cannot be used to solve the matching problem, which requires a quantitative assessment or a matching of intervals. To perform this task adequately, the decision maker should take into account both the size of the intervals (defined relative to the natural range of variation of the attributes in question) and the relative weights of these attributes. One method of matching first equates the size of the two intervals and then adjusts the constructed interval according to the relative weight of the attribute. This approach is particularly compelling when the attributes are expressed in the same units (e.g., money, percent, test scores), but it may also be applied in other situations where it is easier to compare ranges than to establish a rate of exchange. Because adjustments are generally insufficient (Tversky & Kahneman, 1974) this procedure is likely to induce a relatively flat or uniform weighting of attributes.

The preceding discussion is not meant to provide a comprehensive account of choice or of matching. It merely suggests different heuristics or computational schemes that are likely to be used in the two tasks. If people tend to choose according to the more important dimension, or if they match options by adjusting unweighed intervals, then the two procedures are likely to yield different results. In particular, choice is expected to be more lexicographic than matching: That is, the more prominent attribute will weigh more heavily in choice than in matching. This is the *prominence hypothesis* investigated in the following section.

The discrepancy between choice and matching was first observed in a study by Slovic (1975) that was motivated by the ancient philosophical puzzle of how to choose between equally attractive alternatives. In this study the respondents first matched different pairs of (two-dimensional) options and, in a later session, chose between the matched options. Slovic found that the subjects did not choose randomly but rather tended to select the option that was superior on the more important dimension. This observation supports the prominence hypothesis, but the evidence is not conclusive for two reasons. First, the participants always matched the options prior to the choice; hence, the data could be explained by the hypothesis that the more important dimension looms larger in the later trial. Second, and more important, each participant chose between matched options; hence, the results could reflect a common tie-breaking procedure rather than a genuine reversal of preferences. After all, rationality does not entail a random breaking of ties. A rational person may be indifferent between a cash amount and a gamble but always pick the cash when forced to take one of the two.

To overcome these difficulties we develop in the next section a method for testing the prominence hypothesis that is based entirely on interpersonal (between-subjects) comparisons, and we apply this method to a variety of choice problems. In the following two sections we present a conceptual and mathematical analysis of the elicitation process and apply it to several phenomena of judgment and choice. The theoretical and practical implications of the work are discussed in the final section.

TESTS OF THE PROMINENCE HYPOTHESIS

Interpersonal Tests

We illustrate the experimental procedure and the logic of the test of the prominence hypothesis in a problem involving a choice between job candidates. The participants in the first set of studies were young men and women (ages 20–30 years) who were taking a series of aptitude tests at a vocational testing institute in Tel Aviv, Israel. The problems were presented in writing, and the participants were tested in small groups. They all agreed to take part in the study knowing it had no bearing on their test scores. Some of the results were replicated with Stanford undergraduates.

> **Problem 1 (Production Engineer):** Imagine that, as an executive of a company, you have to select between two candidates for a position of a Production Engineer. The candidates were interviewed by a committee who scored them on two attributes (technical knowledge and human relations) on a scale from 100 (superb) to 40 (very weak). Both attributes are important for the position in question, but technical knowledge is more important than human relations. On the basis of the following scores, which of the two candidates would you choose?

	Technical knowledge	Human relations	$[N = 63]$
Candidate X	86	76	[65%]
Candidate Y	78	91	[35%]

The number of respondents (N) and the percentage who chose each option are given in brackets on the right side of the table. In this problem, about two thirds of the respondents selected the candidate who has a higher score on the more important attribute (technical knowledge).

Another group of respondents received the same data except that one of the four scores was missing. They were asked "to complete the missing score so that the two candidates would be equally suitable for the job." Suppose, for example, that the lower left value (78) was missing from the table. The respondent's task would then be to generate a score for Candidate Y in technical knowledge so as to match the two candidates. The participants were reminded that "Y has a higher score than X in human relations; hence, to match the two candidates Y must have a lower score than X in technical knowledge."

Assuming that higher scores are preferable to lower ones, it is possible to infer the response to the choice task from the response to the matching task. Suppose, for example, that one produces a value of 80 in the matching task (when the missing value is 78). This means that X's score profile (86,76) is judged equivalent to the profile (80,91), which in turn dominates Y's profile (78,91). Thus, a matching value of 80 indicates that X is preferable to Y. More generally, a matching response above 78 implies a preference for X; a matching response below 78 implies a preference for Y; and a matching response of 78 implies indifference between X and Y.

Formally, let (X_1, X_2) and (Y_1, Y_2) denote the values of options X and Y on Attributes 1 and 2, respectively. Let V be the value of Y_1 for which the options are matched. We show that, under the standard assumptions, X is preferred to Y if and only if $V > Y_1$. Suppose $V > Y_1$, then (X_1, X_2) is equivalent to (V, Y_2) by matching, (V, Y_2) is preferred to (Y_1, Y_2) by dominance; hence, X is preferred to Y by transitivity. The other cases are similar.

We use the subscript 1 to denote the primary, or the more important dimension, and the subscript 2 to denote the secondary, or the less important dimension – whenever they are defined. If neither option dominates the other, X denotes the option that is superior on the primary dimension and Y denotes the option that is superior on the secondary dimension. Thus, X_1 is better than Y_1 and Y_2 is better than X_2.

Let C denote the percentage of respondents who chose X over Y, and let M denote the percentage of people whose matching response favored X over Y. Thus, C and M measure the tendency to decide according to the more important dimension in the choice and in the matching tasks, respectively. Assuming random allocation of subjects, procedure invariance implies $C = M$, whereas the prominence hypothesis implies $C > M$. As was shown earlier, the two contrasting predictions can be tested by using aggregate between-subjects data.

To estimate M, we presented four different groups of about 60 respondents each with the data of Problem 1, each with a different missing value, and we asked them to match the two candidates. The following table presents the values of M derived from the matching data for each of the four missing values, which are given in parentheses.

	1. Technical knowledge	2. Human relations
Candidate X	32% (86)	33% (76)
Candidate Y	44% (78)	26% (91)

There were no significant differences among the four matching groups, although M was greater when the missing value was low rather than high ($M_L = 39 > 29 = M_H$) and when the missing value referred to the primary rather than to the secondary attribute ($M_1 = 38 > 30 = M_2$). Overall, the matching data yielded $M = 34\%$ as compared with $C = 65\%$ obtained from choice ($p < .01$). This result supports the hypothesis that the more important attribute (e.g., technical knowledge) looms larger in choice than in matching.

In Problem 1, it is reasonable to assume – as stated – that for a production engineer, technical knowledge is more important than human relations. Problem 2 had the same structure as Problem 1, except that the primary and secondary attributes were manipulated. Problem 2 dealt with the choice between candidates for the position of an advertising agent. The candidates were characterized by their scores on two dimensions: creativity and competence. One half of the participants were told that "for the position in question, creativity is more important than competence," whereas the other half of the participants were told the opposite. As in Problem 1, most participants (65%, $N = 60$) chose according to the more important attribute (whether it was creativity or competence), but only 38% ($N = 276$) of the matching responses favored X over Y. Again, M was higher for the primary than for the secondary attribute, but all four values of M were smaller than C. The next two problems involve policy choices concerning safety and the environment.

Problem 3 (Traffic Accidents): About 600 people are killed each year in Israel in traffic accidents. The ministry of transportation investigates various programs to reduce the number of casualties. Consider the following two programs, described in terms of yearly costs (in millions of dollars) and the number of casualties per year that is expected following the implementation of each program.

	Expected number of casualties	Cost	[$N = 96$]
Program X	500	$55M	[67%]
Program Y	570	$12M	[33%]

Which program do you favor?

The data on the right side of the table indicate that two thirds of the respondents chose Program X, which saves more lives at a higher cost per life saved. Two other groups matched the cost of either Program X or Program Y so as to make the two programs equally attractive. The overwhelming majority of matching responses in both groups (96%, $N = 146$) favored the more economical Program Y that saves fewer lives. Problem 3 yields a dramatic violation of invariance: $C = 68\%$ but $M = 4\%$. This pattern follows from the prominence hypothesis, assuming the number of casualties is more important than cost. There was no difference between the groups that matched the high ($55M) or the low ($12M) values.

A similar pattern of responses was observed in Problem 4, which involves an environmental issue. The participants were asked to compare two programs for the control of a polluted beach:

Problem 4:
Program X: A comprehensive program for a complete clean-up of the beach at a yearly cost of $750,000 to the taxpayers.
Program Y: A limited program for a partial clean-up of the beach (that will not make it suitable for swimming) at a yearly cost of $250,000 to the taxpayers.

Assuming the control of pollution is the primary dimension and the cost is secondary, we expect that the comprehensive program will be more popular in choice than in matching. This prediction was confirmed: $C = 48\%$ ($N = 104$) and $M = 12\%$ ($N = 170$). The matching data were obtained from two groups of respondents who assessed the cost of each program so as to match the other. As in Problem 3, these groups gave rise to practically identical values of M.

Because the choice and the matching procedures are strategically equivalent, the rational theory of choice implies $C = M$. The two procedures, however, are not informationally equivalent because the missing value in the matching task is available in the choice task. To create an informationally equivalent task we modified the matching task by asking respondents, prior to the assessment of the missing value, (a) to consider the value used in the choice problem and indicate first whether it is too high or too low, and (b) to write down the value that they consider appropriate. In Problem 3, for example, the modified procedure read as follows:

	Expected number of casualties	**Cost**
Program X	500	?
Program Y	570	$12M

You are asked to determine the cost of Program X that would make it equivalent to Program Y. (a) Is the value of $55M too high or too low? (b) What is the value you consider appropriate?

The modified matching procedure is equivalent to choice not only strategically but also informationally. Let C^* be the proportion of responses to question (a) that lead to the choice of X (e.g., "too low" in the preceding example). Let M^* be the proportion of (matching) responses to question (b) that favor option X (e.g., a value that exceeds $55M in the preceding example). Thus, we may view C^* as choice in a matching context and M^* as matching in a choice context. The values of C^* and M^* for Problems 1–4 are

Table 28.1. Percentages of Responses Favoring the Primary Dimension under Different Elicitation Procedures

	Dimensions		Choice	Information Control		Matching	
	Primary	Secondary	(C)	C*	M*	(M)	θ
Problem:							
1. Engineer	Technical	Human relations	65	57	47	34	.82
N	knowledge		63	156	151	267	
2. Agent	Competence	Creativity	65	52	41	38	.72
N			60	155	152	276	
3. Accidents	Casualities	Cost	68	50	18	4	.19
N			105	96	82	146	
4. Pollution	Health	Cost	48	32	12	12	.45
N			104	103	94	170	
5. Benefits	1 year	4 years	59			46	.86
N			56			46	
6. Coupons	Books	Travel	66			11	.57
N			58			193	
UNWEIGHTED MEAN			62	48	30	24	

C = percentage of respondents who chose X over Y; M = percentage of respondents whose matching responses favored X over Y; C^* = percentage of responses to Question a that lead to the choice of X; M^* = percentage of matching responses to Question b that favor option X.

presented in Table 28.1, which yields the ordering $C > C^* > M^* > M$. The finding $C > C^*$ shows that merely framing the question in a matching context reduces the relative weight of the primary dimension. Conversely, $M^* > M$ indicates that placing the matching task after a choice-like task increases the relative weight of the primary dimension. Finally, $C^* > M^*$ implies a within-subject and within-problem violation of invariance in which the response to Question a favors X and the response to Question b favors Y. This pattern of responses indicates a failure, on the part of some subjects, to appreciate the logical connection between Questions a and b. It is noteworthy, however, that 86% of these inconsistencies follow the pattern implied by the prominence hypothesis.

In the previous problems, the primary and the secondary attributes were controlled by the instructions, as in Problems 1 and 2, or by the intrinsic value of the attributes, as in Problems 3 and 4. (People generally agree that saving lives and eliminating pollution are more important goals than cutting public expenditures.) The next two problems involved benefit plans in which the primary and the secondary dimensions were determined by economic considerations.

Problem 5 (Benefit Plans): Imagine that, as a part of a profit-sharing program, your employer offers you a choice between the following plans. Each plan offers two payments, in one year and in four years.

	Payment in 1 year	Payment in 4 years	[N = 36]
Plan X	$2,000	$2,000	[59%]
Plan Y	$1,000	$4,000	[41%]

Which plan do you prefer?

Because people surely prefer to receive a payment sooner rather than later, we assume that the earlier payment (in 1 year) acts as the primary attribute, and the later payment (in 4 years) acts as the secondary attribute. The results support the hypothesis: $C = 59\%$ ($N = 56$) whereas $M = 46\%$ ($N = 46$).

Problem 6 resembled Problem 5 except that the employee was offered a choice between two bonus plans consisting of a different combination of coupons for books and for travel. Because the former could be used in a large chain of bookstores, whereas the latter were limited to organized tours with a particular travel agency, we assumed that the book coupons would serve as the primary dimension. Under this interpretation, the prominence effect emerged again: $C = 66\%$ ($N = 58$) and $M = 11\%$ ($N = 193$). As in previous problems, M was greater when the missing value was low rather than high ($M_L = 17 > 3 = M_H$) and when the missing value referred to the primary rather than the secondary attribute ($M_1 = 19 > 4 = M_2$). All values of M, however, were substantially smaller than C.

Intrapersonal Tests

Slovic's (1975) original demonstration of the choice-matching discrepancy was based entirely on an intrapersonal analysis. In his design, the participants first matched the relevant option and then selected between the matched options at a later date. They were also asked afterward to indicate the more important attribute in each case. The main results are summarized in Table 28.2, which presents for each choice problem the options, the primary and the secondary attributes, and the resulting values of C. In every case, the value of M is 50% by construction.

The results indicate that, in all problems, the majority of participants broke the tie between the matched options in the direction of the more important dimension as implied by the prominence hypothesis. This conclusion held regardless of whether the estimated missing value belonged to the primary or the secondary dimension, or whether it was the high value or the low value on the dimension. Note that the results of Table 28.2 alone could be explained by a shift in weight following the matching procedure (because the matching always preceded the choice) or by the application of a common tie-breaking procedure (because for each participant the two options were matched). These explanations, however, do not apply to the interpersonal data of Table 28.1.

On the other hand, Table 28.2 demonstrates the prominence effect within the data of each subject. The value of C was only slightly higher (unweighted

Table 28.2. Percentages of Respondents ($N = 101$) Who Chose between-Matched Alternatives ($M = 50\%$) according to the Primary Dimension (after Slovic, 1975)

Alternatives	Dimensions		Choice Criterion	C
	Primary	Secondary		
1. Baseball players	Batting average	Home runs	Value to team	62
2. College applicants	Motivation	English	Potential success	69
3. Gifts	Cash	Coupons	Attractiveness	85
4. Typists	Accuracy	Speed	Typing ability	84
5. Athletes	Chin-ups	Push-ups	Fitness	68
6. Routes to work	Time	Distance	Attractiveness	75
7. Auto tires	Quality	Price	Attractiveness	67
8. TV commercials	Number	Time	Annoyance	83
9. Readers	Comprehension	Speed	Reading ability	79
10. Baseball teams	% of games won against first place team	% of games won agains last place team	Standing	86
UNWEIGHTED MEAN				76

C = percentage of respondents who chose X over Y.

mean: 78) when computed relative to each subject's ordering of the importance of the dimensions (as was done in the original analysis), presumably because of the general agreement among the respondents about which dimension was primary.

THEORETICAL ANALYSIS

The data described in the previous section show that the primary dimension looms larger in choice than in matching. This effect gives rise to a marked discrepancy between choice and matching, which violates the principle of procedure invariance assumed in the rational theory of choice. The prominence effect raises three general questions. First, what are the psychological mechanisms that underlie the choice-matching discrepancy and other failures of procedure invariance? Second, what changes in the traditional theory are required in order to accommodate these effects? Third, what are the implications of the present results to the analysis of choice in general, and the elicitation of preference in particular? The remainder of this article is devoted to these questions.

The Compatibility Principle

One possible explanation of the prominence effect, introduced earlier in this article, is the tendency to select the option that is superior on the primary dimension, in situations where the other option does not have a decisive advantage on the secondary dimension. This procedure is easy to apply and justify because it resolves conflict on the basis of qualitative arguments (i.e., the prominence ordering of the dimensions) without establishing a rate of exchange. The matching task, on the other hand, cannot be resolved in the same manner. The decision maker must resort to quantitative comparisons to determine what interval on one dimension matches a given interval on the second dimension. This requires the setting of a common metric in which the attributes are likely to be weighted more equally, particularly when it is natural to match their ranges or to compute cost per unit (e.g., the amount of money spent to save a single life).

It is instructive to distinguish between qualitative and quantitative arguments for choice. Qualitative, or ordinal, arguments are based on the ordering of the levels within each dimension, or on the prominence ordering of the dimensions. Quantitative, or cardinal, arguments are based on the comparison of value differences along the primary and the secondary dimensions. Thus, dominance and a lexicographic ordering are purely qualitative decision rules, whereas most other models of multiattribute choice make essential use of quantitative considerations. The prominence effect indicates that qualitative considerations loom larger in the ordinal procedure of choice than in the cardinal procedure of matching, or equivalently, that quantitative considerations loom larger in matching than in choice. The prominence hypothesis, therefore, may be construed as an example of a more general principle of compatibility.

The choice-matching discrepancy, like other violations of procedure invariance, indicates that the weighting of the attributes is influenced by the method of elicitation. Alternative procedures appear to highlight different aspects of the options and thereby induce different weights. To interpret and predict such effects, we seek explanatory principles that relate task characteristics to the weighting of attributes and the evaluation of options. One such explanation is the compatibility principle. According to this principle, the weight of any input component is enhanced by its compatibility with the output. The rationale for this principle is that the characteristics of the task and the response scale prime the most compatible features of the stimulus. For example, the pricing of gambles is likely to emphasize payoffs more than probability because both the response and the payoffs are expressed in dollars. Furthermore, noncompatibility (in content, scale, or display) between the input and the output requires additional mental transformations, which increase effort and error, and reduce confidence and impact (Fitts & Seeger, 1953; Wickens, 1984). We shall next illustrate the compatibility principle in studies of prediction and similarity and then develop a formal theory that encompasses a variety of compatibility effects, including the choice-matching discrepancy and the preference reversal phenomenon.

A simple demonstration of scale compatibility was obtained in a study by Slovic, Griffin, and, Tversky (1988). The subjects ($N = 234$) were asked to predict the judgments of an admission committee of a small, selective college. For each of 10 applicants the subjects received two items of information: a rank on the verbal section of the Scholastic Aptitude Test (SAT) and the presence or absence of strong extracurricular activities. The subjects were told that the admission committee ranks all 500 applicants and accepts about the top fourth. Half of the subjects predicted the rank assigned to each applicant, whereas the other half predicted whether each applicant was accepted or rejected.

The compatibility principle implies that the numerical data (i.e., SAT rank) will loom larger in the numerical prediction task, whereas the categorical data (i.e., the presence or absence of extracurricular activities) will loom larger in the categotical prediction of acceptance or rejection. The results confirmed the hypothesis. For each pair of applicants, in which neither one dominates the other, the percentage of responses that favored the applicant with the higher SAT was recorded. Summing across all pairs, this value was 61.4% in the numerical prediction task and 44.6% in the categorical prediction task. The difference between the groups is highly significant. Evidently, the numerical data had more impact in the numerical task, whereas the categorical data had more impact in the categorical task. This result demonstrates the compatibility principle and reinforces the proposed interpretation of the choice-matching discrepancy in which the relative weight of qualitative arguments is larger in the qualitative method of choice than in the quantitative matching procedure.

In the previous example, compatibility was induced by the formal correspondence between the scales of the dependent and the independent variables. Compatibility effects can also be induced by semantic correspondence, as illustrated in the following example, taken from the study of similarity. In general, the similarity of objects (e.g., faces, people, letters) increases with the salience of the features they share and decreases with the salience of the features that distinguish between them. More specifically, the contrast model (Tversky, 1977) represents the similarity of objects as a linear combination of the measures of their common and their distinctive features. Thus, the similarity of a and b is monotonically related to

$$\theta f(A \cap B) - g(A \triangle B),$$

where $A \cap B$ is the set of features shared by a and b, and $A \triangle B = (A - B) \cup (B - A)$ is the set of features that belongs to one object and not to the other. The scales f and g are the measures of the respective feature sets.

The compatibility hypothesis suggests that common features loom larger in judgments of similarity than in judgments of dissimilarity, whereas distinctive features loom larger in judgments of dissimilarity than in judgments of similarity. As a consequence, the two judgments are not mirror images. A pair of objects with many common and many distinctive features could be judged as more similar, as well as more dissimilar, than another pair of objects with fewer common and fewer distinctive features. Tversky and Gati (1978) observed this pattern in the comparison of pairs of well-known countries with pairs of countries that were less well-known to the respondents. For example, most subjects in the similarity condition selected East Germany and West Germany as more similar to each other than Sri Lanka and Nepal, whereas most subjects in the dissimilarity condition selected East Germany and West Germany as more different from each other than Sri Lanka and Nepal. These observations were explained by the contrast model with the added assumption that the relative weight of the common features is greater in similarity than in disimilarity judgments (Tversky, 1977).

DISCUSSION

The extensive use of rational theories of choice (e.g., the expected utility model or the theory of revealed preference) as descriptive models (e.g., in economics, management, and political science) has stimulated the experimental investigation of the descriptive validity of the assumptions that underlie these models. Perhaps the most basic assumption of the rational theory of choice is the principle of invariance (Kahneman and Tversky, 1984) or extensionality (Arrow, 1982), which states that the relation of preference should not depend on the description of the options (description invariance) or on the method of elicitation (procedure invariance). Empirical tests of description invariance have shown that alternative framing of the same options can lead to different choices (Tversky and Kahneman, 1986). The present studies provide evidence against the assumption of procedure invariance by demonstrating a systematic discrepancy between choice and matching as well as between rating and pricing. In this section we discuss the main findings and explore their theoretical and practical implications.

In the first part of the article we showed that the more important dimension of a decision problem looms larger in choice than in matching. We addressed this phenomenon at three levels of analysis. First, we presented a heuristic account of choice and matching that led to the prominence hypothesis; second, we related this account to the general notion of input–output compatibility; and third, we developed the formal theory of contingent weighting that represents the prominence effect as well as other elicitation phenomena, such as preference reversals. The informal analysis, based on compatibility, provides a psychological explanation for the differential weighting induced by the various procedures.

Although the prominence effect was observed in a variety of settings using both intrapersonal and interpersonal comparisons, its boundaries are left to be explored. How does it extend to options that vary on a larger number of attributes? The present analysis implies that the relative weights of any pair of attributes will be less extreme (i.e., closer to unity) in matching than in choice. With three or more attributes, however, additional considerations may come into play. For example, people may select the option that is superior on most attributes (Tversky, 1969, Experiment 2). In this case, the prominence hypothesis does not always result in a lexicographic bias. Another question is whether the choice-matching discrepancy applies to other judgmental or perceptual tasks. The data on the prediction of students' performance indicate that the prominence effect is not limited to preferential choice, but it is not clear whether it applies to psychophysics. Perceived loudness, for example, depends primarily on intensity and to a lesser degree on frequency. It could be interesting to test the prominence hypothesis in such a context.

The finding that the qualitative information about the ordering of the dimensions looms larger in the ordinal method of choice than in the cardinal method of matching has been construed as an instance of the compatibility principle. This principle states that stimulus components that are compatible with the response are weighted more heavily than those that are not presumably because (a) the former are accentuated, and (b) the latter require additional mental transformations that produce error and reduce the diagnosticity of the information. This effect may be induced by the nature of the information (e.g., ordinal vs. cardinal), by the response scale (e.g., grades vs. ranks), or by the affinity between inputs and outputs (e.g., common features loom larger in similarity than in dissimilarity judgments). Compatibility, therefore, appears to provide a common explanation to many phenomena of judgment and choice.

The preceding discussion raises the intriguing normative question as to which method, choice or matching, better reflects people's "true" preferences. Put differently, do people overweigh the primary dimension in choice or do they underweigh it in matching? Without knowing the "correct" weighting, it is unclear how to answer this question, but the following study provides some relevant data. The participants in a decision-making seminar performed both choice and matching in the traffic-accident problem described earlier (Problem 3). The two critical (choice and matching) questions were embedded in a questionnaire that included similar questions with different numerical values. The majority of the respondents (21 out of 32) gave inconsistent responses that conformed to the prominence hypothesis. After the session, each participant was interviewed and confronted with his or her answers. The subjects were surprised to discover that their responses were inconsistent, and they offered a variety of explanations, some of which resemble the prominence hypothesis. One participant said, "When I have to choose between programs I go for the one that saves more lives because there is no price for human life. But when I match the programs I have to pay attention to money." When asked to reconsider their answers, all respondents modified the matching in the direction of the choice, and a few reversed the original choice in the direction of the matching. This observation suggests that choice and matching are both biased in opposite directions, but it may reflect a routine compromise rather than the result of a critical reassessment.

Real-world decisions can sometimes be framed either as a direct choice (e.g., should I buy the used car at this price?) or as a pricing decision (e.g., what is the most I should pay for that used car?). Our findings suggest that the answers to the two questions are likely to diverge. Consider, for example, a medical decision problem where the primary dimension is the probability of survival and the secondary dimension is the cost associated with treatment or diagnosis. According to the present analysis, people are likely to choose the option that offers the higher probability of survival with relatively little concern for cost. When asked to price a marginal increase in the probability of survival, however, people are expected to appear less generous. The choice-matching discrepancy may also arise in resource allocation and budgeting decisions. The prominence hypothesis suggests that the most important item in the budget (e.g., health) will tend to dominate a less important item (e.g., culture) in a direct choice between two allocations, but the less important item is expected to fare better in a matching procedure.

The lability of preferences implied by the demonstrations of framing and elicitation effects raises difficult questions concerning the assessment of preferences and values. In the classical analysis, the relation of preference is inferred from observed responses (e.g., choice, matching) and is assumed to reflect the decision maker's underlying utility or value. But if different elicitation procedures produce different orderings of options, how can preferences and values be defined? And in what sense do they exist? To be sure, people make choices, set prices, rate options and even explain their decisions to others. Preferences, therefore, exist as observed data. However, if these data do not satisfy the elementary requirements of invariance, it is unclear how to define a relation of preference that can serve as a basis for the measurement of value. In the absence of well-defined preferences, the foundations of choice theory and decision analysis are called into question.

29. Context-Dependent Preferences

Amos Tversky and Itamar Simonson

ABSTRACT. The standard theory of choice – based on value maximization – associates with each option a real value such that, given an offered set, the decision maker chooses the option with the highest value. Despite its simplicity and intuitive appeal, there is a growing body of data that is inconsistent with this theory. In particular, the relative attractiveness of x compared to y often depends on the presence or absence of a third option z, and the "market share" of an option can actually be increased by enlarging the offered set. We review recent empirical findings that are inconsistent with value maximization and present a context-dependent model that expresses the value of each option as an additive combination of two components: a contingent weighting process that captures the effect of the background context, and a binary comparison process that describes the effect of the local context. The model accounts for observed violations of the standard theory and provides a framework for analyzing context-dependent preferences.

KEY WORDS decision making; consumer choice; independence of irrelevant alternatives

The theory of rational choice assumes that preference between options does not depend on the presence or absence of other options. This principle, called *independence of irrelevant alternatives,* is essentially equivalent to the assumption that the decision maker has a complete preference order of all options, and that – given an offered set – the decision maker always selects the option that is highest in that order. Despite its simplicity and intuitive appeal, experimental evidence indicates that this principle is often violated (see Huber et al. 1982, Simonson and Tversky 1992).

This article has benefited from discussions with Shmuel Sattath, Yuval Rottenstreich, and Peter Wakker. The work was supported by Grant 89-0064 from the Air Force Office of Scientific Research and by Grant SES-910935 from the National Science Foundation to the first author.

This chapter is an abridged version of an article that first appeared in *Management Science*, 39:10, 117–85. Copyright © 1993 The Institute of Management Sciences (currently INFORMS), 901 Elkridge Landing Road, Suite 400, Linthicum, MD 21090, USA.

1. INTRODUCTION

Let $T = \{x, y, z, \ldots\}$ be a finite set that includes all options under study. To describe choice among options we use the choice function C that associates with any offered set $S \subset T$ a nonempty subset of S, denoted $C(S)$, which consists of the options chosen by the decision maker. If there are no ties, then $C(S)$ includes a single option. If ties are allowed, then $C(S)$ consists of those elements of S that are tied for first place.

A choice function C satisfies *value maximization* (VM) if there exists a function v that assigns a real value to each x in T such that

$$x \in C(S) \quad \text{iff} \quad v(x) \geq v(y) \quad \text{for all } y \in S.$$

VM implies that the ordering of options is independent of the choice set. In particular, if x is preferred to y in a binary choice, it is also preferred to y in a multiple (i.e., nonbinary) choice. Furthermore, if $x \in C(S)$ and $x \in R \subset S$ then $x \in C(R)$. In other words, a nonpreferred option cannot become preferred when new options are added to the offered set. The principle of value maximization, therefore, captures the notion of independence of irrelevant alternatives.

Although the theory refers to the choices of a single person, most of the available data are pooled across individuals. To apply the theory to aggregate data, assume for simplicity that ties are excluded, and let $P(x, S)$ be the proportion of people for whom $x \in C(S)$. We write $P(x; y)$ for $P(x, \{x, y\})$ and $P(x; y, z)$ for $P(x, \{x, y, z\})$.

It is noteworthy that the properties of the choice function C are not always reflected in the aggregate measure P. In particular, value maximization entails that an individual who prefers x over y in a binary choice cannot select y from the set $\{x, y, z\}$. But even if each individual satisfies VM we could obtain $P(x; y) > P(y; x)$ and $P(x; y, z) < P(y; x, z)$ if those who prefer x over y also prefer z over x. For example, a liberal candidate x may defeat a conservative candidate y in a two-person race, yet y may win more votes than x in a three-person race that includes another liberal candidate z. Indeed, it has been known for more than two centuries that the aggregation of different transitive preference orders can yield intransitive majority choice. This raises the question of whether VM can be tested in aggregate data. An affirmative answer is provided by the following property.

Regularity: $x \in R \subset S$ implies $P(x, R) \geq P(x, S)$.

Regularity states that the "market share" of an option cannot be increased by enlarging the choice set. Recall that under VM, $x \in C(S)$ implies $x \in C(R)$ whenever $x \in R \subset S$. If each person who selects x from S also selects x from R, then $P(x, R) \geq P(x, S)$. Thus, VM implies regularity, which is readily tested in aggregate data.

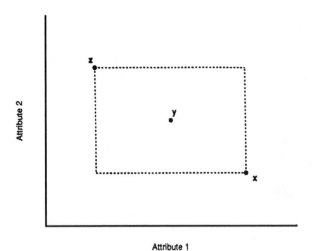

Figure 29.1. An Illustration of the betweenness relation $(x \mid y \mid z)$ in the plane.

Regularity, however, does not exhaust the testable consequences of VM. To obtain a more sensitive test of VM using aggregate data we impose additional structure on the option space. As in the standard theory of the consumer, we assume that each option x in T is represented by a vector $(x_1, \ldots, x_n)$ where x_i is the value of the option on the ith attribute. Furthermore, we assume that preference is monotonic, separately in each attribute. That is, the values of each attribute can be ordered so that, holding the values of all other attributes constant, a higher value is always preferred to a lower value. The dimensional structure allows us to define a betweenness relation among the options. We say that y lies *between* x and z, denoted $x \mid y \mid z$, if and only if for each dimension i either $x_i \leq y_i \leq z_i$ or $x_i \geq y_i \geq z_i$, $i = 1, \ldots, n$; see Figure 29.1.

To explore the implications of this relation, define

$$P_z(y; x) = \frac{P(y; x, z)}{P(y; x, z) + P(x; y, z)}.$$

This index measures the "popularity" of y relative to x inferred from the choice set $\{x, y, z\}$.

We show in the appendix (not printed here) that VM in conjunction with a highly plausible assumption, called the ranking condition, implies the following property.

Betweenness inequality: $x \mid y \mid z$ implies $P(y; x) \geq P_z(y; x)$.

The betweenness inequality states that the middle option y loses relatively more than the extreme option x from the introduction of the other extreme option z. For example, the addition of a top-of-the-line camera is expected to reduce the market share of a midline camera more than the share of a basic camera. Assuming the ranking condition, the betweenness inequality can be used, in addition to regularity, to test VM using aggregate data. Experimental tests of these properties are described in the next section.

2. DATA

In this section we introduce two psychological hypotheses, called *tradeoff contrast* and *extremeness aversion*, which give rise to a series of context effects that violate the principle of value maximization. These hypotheses are discussed in turn.

Tradeoff Contrast

Contrast effects are ubiquitous in perception and judgment. For example, the same circle appears large when surrounded by small circles and small when surrounded by large ones. Similarly, the same product may appear attractive on the background of less attractive products and unattractive on the background of more attractive products. We suggest that the effect of contrast applies not only to a single attribute, such as size or attractiveness, but also to the tradeoff between attributes. Consider, for example, products that vary on two attributes; suppose x is of higher quality but y has a better price. The decision between x and y, then, depends on whether the quality difference outweighs the price difference, or equivalently on the price/quality tradeoff. We propose that the tendency to prefer x over y will be enhanced if the decision maker encounters other choices in which a comparable improvement in quality is associated with a larger difference in price. This is the tradeoff contrast hypothesis. As illustrated below, it applies to the local context defined by the offered set as well as to the background context defined by options encountered in the past. (Throughout this article, we use the word *context* to describe the set of options under consideration.)

Background Context. Perhaps the simplest demonstration of the tradeoff contrast hypothesis involves manipulation of the background context (Simonson and Tversky 1992). Half the subjects were given a choice between options x' and y', whereas the second half chose between x'' and y'' (see Figure 29.2). Following the initial choice, all subjects were given a choice between x and y. The tradeoff contrast hypothesis implies that the tendency to prefer x over y will be stronger among subjects who first chose between x' and y' than among those who first chose between x'' and y''. Table 29.1 presents the results for two categories: tires that vary in warranty and price, and gifts consisting of a combination of cash and coupons. Each coupon could be redeemed for a regular book or compact disk at local stores. Subjects were informed that one of them, selected randomly, would actually receive the gift that he or she had selected.

Table 29.1 shows that the background influenced subsequent choice in the predicted direction. The results for tires indicate that subjects exposed to

Table 29.1. Background Contrast

Category: Tires

Warranty	Price	Background Set B' (n = 111)	Background Set B" (n = 109)
x': 55,000 miles	$85	12%	
y': 75,000 miles	$91	88%	
x": 30,000 miles	$25		84%
y": 35,000 miles	$49		16%

Warranty	Price	Target Set	Target Set
x: 40,000 miles	$60	57%	33%
y: 50,000 miles	$75	43%	67%

Category: Gifts

Cash	Coupons	Background Set B' (n = 51)	Background Set B" (n = 49)
x': $52	3	92%	
y': $22	5	8%	
x": $77	4		40%
y": $67	6		60%

Cash	Coupons	Target Set	Target Set
x: $47	5	47%	77%
y: $37	6	53%	23%

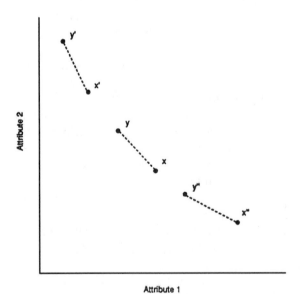

Figure 29.2. A test of background tradeoff.

Background B' in which a small difference in price ($91 versus $85) was associated with a large difference in warranty (75,000 versus 55,000 miles), were more likely to select from the target set the less expensive tire than those exposed to Background B'', in which a relatively large difference in price ($49 versus $25) was associated with a small difference in warranty (35,000 versus 30,000 miles). The same pattern was observed for gifts, as seen in the lower part of Table 29.1. Here the rate of exchange was $15 per coupon in Background B', $5 per coupon in Background B'', and $10 per coupon in the target set. The data again showed that subjects exposed to the background in which coupons were fairly expensive were significantly more likely to select from the target set the gift with more coupons than subjects exposed to the background in which coupons were relatively inexpensive.

It could be argued that the observed violations of VM can be justified in terms of the information provided by the context. We wish to make two points in response. First, regardless of whether the observed pattern of preferences can or cannot be justified on normative grounds, the data violate the principle of independence of irrelevant alternatives. If people commonly rely on the set of alternatives under consideration in order to assess the value of an option, then the standard theory should be thoroughly revised to accommodate decisions based on such inferences. Second, an account based on rational inference can explain some examples (e.g., tires) but not others (e.g., gifts). A consumer who is uncertain about the price of warranty may use the information provided by the background to evaluate whether paying $15 for 10,000 miles of warranty is a good deal or not. The background contrast effect observed in this problem, therefore, can be interpreted as rational inference based on the information provided by the context. This account, however, does not explain the background contrast effect in the choice between gifts. Suppose you are just willing to trade $10 in cash for one book coupon. Why should you change your mind after observing gifts in which the corresponding tradeoff is $5 or $15? Note that the effect of the background was no stronger for tires than for books (see Table 29.1). It appears that people's choices exhibit tradeoff contrast whether or not it is normatively justified.

Local Context. Another implication of the tradeoff contrast hypothesis is that the "market share" of x can be increased by adding to $\{x, y\}$ a third alternative z that is clearly inferior to x but not to y. Violations of regularity based on this pattern were first demonstrated by Huber et al. (1982). The following example is taken from Simonson and Tversky (1992). One group ($n = 106$) was offered a choice between $6 and an elegant Cross pen. The pen was selected by 36% of the subjects, and the remaining 64% chose the cash. A second group ($n = 115$) was given a choice among three options: $6 in cash, the same Cross pen, and a second less attractive pen. The second pen, we suggest, is dominated by the first pen but not by the cash. Indeed, only 2% of the subjects chose the less attractive pen, but its presence increased the percentage of subjects who chose the Cross pen from 36% to 46%, contrary to regularity.

In another study, subjects received descriptions and pictures of microwave ovens taken from the Best catalog. One group ($n = 60$) was asked to choose between an Emerson priced at $110 and a Panasonic priced at $180. Both items were on sale, a third off the regular price. Here, 57% chose the Emerson and 43% chose the Panasonic. A second group ($n = 60$) was presented with these options, along with a $200 Panasonic at a 10% discount. Because the two Panasonics were quite similar, the one with the lower discount appeared inferior to the other Panasonic, but it was not clearly inferior to the Emerson. Indeed, only 13% of the subjects chose the more expensive Panasonic, but its presence increased the percentage of subjects who chose the less expensive Panasonic from 43% to 60%, contrary to regularity.

As noted earlier, many violations of VM cannot be properly explained in terms of a rational inference. For example, this account does not explain the choice among the cash and the pens, or the violations of VM observed in choice among simple gambles (see, e.g., Wedell 1991) where the context provides no information about the quality of the options. We have also observed violations of regularity when the subjects reviewed all the options under study before choosing from an offered subset (Simonson and Tversky 1992). An alternative interpretation of the data in terms of range frequency theory (Parducci 1965, Birnbaum 1974) has been tested by Huber and Puto (1983) and by Wedell (1991). Both studies showed that the violations of regularity induced by the addition of an inferior option cannot be explained by the resulting extension of the attribute range, as suggested by that theory.

Extremeness Aversion

Recent work has provided a great deal of support for the principle of loss aversion, according to which losses loom larger than the corresponding gains (Kahneman et al. 1991, Tversky and Kahneman 1991). Gains and losses are defined relative to a neutral reference point that generally corresponds to the decision maker's status quo or current endowment. In some situations, however, decision makers may evaluate options in terms of their advantages and disadvantages, defined relative to each other. A natural extension of loss aversion suggests that disadvantages loom larger than the corresponding advantages. As a consequence, options with extreme values within an offered set will be relatively less attractive than options with intermediate values. This is the extremeness aversion hypothesis; it gives rise to two effects: compromise and polarization, which are discussed in turn.

Compromise. Consider two-dimensional options, x, y and z, such that y lies between x and z (see Figure 29.1). Recall that VM in conjunction with the ranking condition implies that the middle alternative y should be less popular in the context of the triple $\{x, y, z\}$ than in either one of the pairs, $\{x, y\}$ or $\{y, z\}$. That is, $P(y; x) > P_z(y; x)$ and $P(y; z) > P_x(y; z)$. Extremeness aversion, on the other hand, yields the opposite prediction. Note that y has small advantages and disadvantages with respect to x and to z, whereas both x and z have a large advantage and a large disadvantage with respect to each other. Consequently, extremeness aversion implies $P_z(y; x) > P(y; x)$ and $P_x(y; z) > P(y; z)$. This pattern is called *compromise* because the middle option y may be viewed as a compromise between the two extreme options x and z (Simonson 1989). We have observed the compromise effect in several experiments.

For example, subjects were asked to choose among 35 mm cameras varying in quality and price. One group ($n = 106$) was given a choice between a Minolta X-370 priced at \$170 and a Minolta 3000i priced at \$240. A second group ($n = 115$) was given an additional option, the Minolta 7000i priced at \$470. Subjects in the first group were split evenly between the two options, yet 57% of the subjects in the second group chose the middle option (Minolta 3000i), with the remaining divided about equally between the two extreme options. Contrary to VM, the introduction of an extreme option reduced the market share of the other extreme option, but not of the middle option. These data also illustrate the diagnostic significance of the betweenness inequality. Whereas the violation of regularity in this problem is fairly mild, $P(y; x, z) - P(y; x) = 0.57 - 0.50 = 0.07, t = 1.0$, ns, the violation of the betweenness inequality is quite pronounced:

$$P_z(y; x) - P(y; x) = 0.57/(0.57 + 0.22) - 0.50 = 0.22, \quad t = 3.2, \quad p < 0.01.$$

Polarization. Compromise refers to a symmetric form of extremeness aversion in which the popularity of the middle option is enhanced relative to both extremes. In other situations, people exhibit extremeness aversion with respect to one attribute only. If disadvantages loom larger than advantages on one dimension but not on the other, then the introduction of a third alternative would produce a bias against one of the extremes, but not against the other. We have observed this effect, called *polarization*, in several experiments involving price/quality tradeoffs. For example, we investigated choices involving three AM–FM cassette players: an inexpensive Emerson for \$40, a regular Sony for \$65, and a high-quality Sony for \$150. In all three binary choices, subjects were divided approximately equally between the options. However, in the trinary choice 9% chose the Emerson whereas 43% chose the high-quality Sony. Evidently, the option with the lower quality (and lower price) in a binary choice is less aversive than the option with the lowest quality (and lowest price) in a trinary choice. There is no extremeness aversion in binary choice because no option is more extreme than the other. For further discussion, see Simonson and Tversky (1992).

3. DISCUSSION

In contrast to the classical theory of choice that assumes stable preferences and consistent values, there is a growing body of evidence (see, e.g., Payne et al. 1992) that supports an alternative conception according to which preferences are often constructed – not merely revealed – in the elicitation process. These constructions are contingent on the framing of the problem, the method of elicitation, and the context of choice. In this article we describe how people's preferences are affected by the set of options under consideration. The findings of tradeoff contrast and extremeness aversion, which violate the assumption of value maximization, have both theoretical and practical implications. The possibility that choice among candidates, job offers, consumer products, and public policies can be manipulated by the addition or deletion of "irrelevant" alternatives presents a challenge to both theorists and practitioners.

We have developed in this article a context-dependent model that explains the observed findings in terms of two component processes: a contingent weighting model that represents the effect of the background context, and a binary comparison model that describes the effect of the local context.[1] Like other descriptive models of choice, the present account is at best approximate and incomplete. In particular, it does not address the various heuristics of choice and editing operations (e.g., eliminating common components and discarding nonessential differences) that are commonly employed to simplify the representation and the evaluation of options. We made no attempt to capture these complexities; we sought a simple mathematical model that is consistent with tradeoff contrast and extremeness aversion. The present model, however, is considerably more complicated than the standard theory of value maximization.

It may seem paradoxical that a decision process driven by an attempt to simplify choice and reduce computational complexity requires descriptive models that are considerably more complicated than the corresponding rational models. Unlike some normative models that require enormous memory and difficult computations, the principle of value maximization – as employed in the classical theory of the consumer – is extremely simple: it only requires an ordering of the relevant options with respect to preference. It is hard to conceive of a simpler model. The systematic failure of this model, we suggest, is not due to its complexity but rather to the fact that people often do not have a global preference order and, as a result, they use the context to identify the most "attractive" option.

The analysis of context effects, in perception as well as in choice, provides numerous examples in which people err by complicating rather than by simplifying the task; they often perform unnecessary computations and attend to irrelevant aspects of the situation under study. For example, in order to judge which of two circles is bigger it seems simplest to evaluate the critical figures

[1] An alternative approach to the modeling of tradeoff contrast, which does not assume additivity and expresses multiple choice probability in terms of binary advantages, has been developed by Lakshmi-Ratan et al. (1991) and Marley (1991).

and ignore the "irrelevant" circles in the background. Similarly, it appears that the easiest way to decide which of two options is preferable is to compare them directly and ignore the other options. The fact that people do not behave in this manner indicates that many departures from classical models of rational choice cannot be easily explained merely as an attempt to reduce computational complexity.

30. Ambiguity Aversion and Comparative Ignorance

Craig R. Fox and Amos Tversky

ABSTRACT. Decisions under uncertainty depend not only on the degree of uncertainty but also on its source, as illustrated by Ellsberg's observation of ambiguity aversion. In this article we propose the comparative ignorance hypothesis, according to which ambiguity aversion is produced by a comparison with less ambiguous events or with more knowledgeable individuals. This hypothesis is supported in a series of studies showing that ambiguity aversion, present in a comparative context in which a person evaluates both clear and vague prospects, seems to disappear in a noncomparative context in which a person evaluates only one of these prospects in isolation.

I. INTRODUCTION

One of the fundamental problems of modern decision theory is the analysis of decisions under ignorance or ambiguity, where the probabilities of potential outcomes are neither specified in advance nor readily assessed on the basis of the available evidence. This issue was addressed by Knight [1921], who distinguished between *measurable uncertainty* or *risk*, which can be represented by precise probabilities, and *unmeasurable uncertainty*, which cannot. Furthermore, he suggested that entrepreneurs are compensated for bearing unmeasurable uncertainty as opposed to risk. Contemporaneously, Keynes [1921] distinguished between *probability*, representing the balance of evidence in favor of a particular proposition and the *weight of evidence*, representing the quantity of evidence supporting that balance. He then asked, "If two probabilities are equal in degree, ought we, in choosing our course of action, to prefer that one which is based on a greater body of knowledge?" [p. 313]. The distinction between clear and vague probabilities has been rejected by proponents of the subjectivist school. Although Savage [1954] acknowledged that subjective probabilities are commonly vague, he argued that vagueness has no role in a rational theory of choice.

This work was supported by grants SES-9109535 and SBR-9408684 from the National Science Foundation. It has benefited from discussion with Martin Weber.

Originally published in *The Quarterly Journal of Economics*, 110:3, 585–603. Copyright © 1991 by the Presidents and Fellows of Harvard College and the Massachusetts Institute of Technology. Reprinted with permission.

Interest in the problem of decision under ignorance was revived by a series of papers and commentaries published in the early sixties in this *Journal*. The most influential of these papers, written by Ellsberg [1961], presented compelling examples in which people prefer to bet on known rather than on unknown probabilities (see also Fellner [1961]). Ellsberg's simplest example, known as the "two-color" problem, involves two urns each containing red and black balls. Urn 1 contains 50 red and 50 black balls, whereas urn 2 contains 100 red and black balls in an unknown proportion. Suppose that a ball is drawn at random from an urn and one receives $100 or nothing depending on the outcome. Most people seem indifferent between betting on red or on black for either urn, yet they prefer to bet on the 50–50 urn rather than on the urn with the unknown composition. This pattern of preferences is inconsistent with expected utility theory because it implies that the subjective probabilities of black and of red are greater in the 50–50 urn than in the unknown urn and therefore cannot sum to one for both urns.

Essentially the same problem was discussed by Keynes some 40 years earlier: "In the first case we know that the urn contains black and white balls in equal proportions; in the second case the proportion of each color is unknown, and each ball is as likely to be black as white. It is evident that in either case the probability of drawing a white ball is 1/2 but that the weight of the argument in favor of this conclusion is greater in the first case" [1921, p. 75]. In the spirit of Knight and Keynes, Ellsberg [1961] argued that people's willingness to act in the presence of uncertainty depends not only on the perceived probability of the event in question but also on its vagueness or ambiguity. Ellsberg characterized ambiguity as "a quality depending on the amount, type, and 'unanimity' of information, and giving rise to one's degree of 'confidence' in an estimate of relative likelihoods" [p. 657].

The preference for the clear over the vague bet has been demonstrated in many experiments using several variations of Ellsberg's original problems (for a comprehensive review of the literature, see Camerer and Weber [1992]). As noted above, these observations provide evidence against the descriptive validity of expected utility theory. Furthermore, many authors have attempted to justify the preference for risk over ambiguity on normative grounds, although Raiffa [1961] has argued that ambiguity can be reduced to risk by tossing a coin to decide whether to guess red or black.

Ambiguity aversion has attracted much attention because, with the notable exception of games of chance, decision makers usually do not know the precise probabilities of potential outcomes. The decisions to undertake a business venture, to go to court, or to undergo medical treatment are commonly made in the absence of a clear idea of the chances that these actions will be successful. The question arises, then, whether the ambiguity aversion demonstrated using the Ellsberg urn applies to such decisions. In other words, is the preference for clear over vague probabilities confined to the domain of chance, or does it extend to uncertain beliefs based on world knowledge?

To answer this question, Heath and Tversky [1991] conducted a series of experiments comparing people's willingness to bet on their uncertain beliefs with their willingness to bet on clear chance events. Contrary to ambiguity aversion, they found that people prefer to bet on their vague beliefs in situations where they feel especially competent or knowledgeable, although they prefer to bet on chance when they do not. In one study, subjects were asked to choose among bets based on three sources of uncertainty: the results in various states of the 1988 presidential election, the results of various professional football games, and the results of random draws from an urn with a known composition. Subjects who were preselected for their knowledge of politics and lack of knowledge of football preferred betting on political events rather than on chance events that they considered equally probable. However, these subjects preferred betting on chance events rather than on sports events that they considered equally probable. Analogously, subjects who were preselected for their knowledge of football and lack of knowledge of politics exhibited the opposite pattern, preferring football to chance and chance to politics. Another finding that is consistent with Heath and Tversky's competence hypothesis but not with ambiguity aversion is people's preference to bet on their physical skills (e.g., throwing darts) rather than on matched chance events despite the fact that the perceived probability of success is vague for skill and clear for chance [Cohen and Hansel 1959; Howell 1971].

If ambiguity aversion is driven by the feeling of incompetence, as suggested by the preceding discussion, the question arises as to what conditions produce this state of mind. We propose that people's confidence is undermined when they contrast their limited knowledge about an event with their superior knowledge about another event, or when they compare themselves with more knowledgeable individuals. Moreover, we argue that this contrast between states of knowledge is the predominant source of ambiguity aversion. When evaluating an uncertain event in isolation people attempt to assess its likelihood – as a good Bayesian would – paying relatively little attention to second-order characteristics such as vagueness or weight of evidence. However, when people compare two events about which they have different levels of knowledge, the contrast makes the less familiar bet less attractive or the more familiar bet more attractive. The main implication of this account, called the *comparative ignorance hypothesis*, is that ambiguity aversion will be present when subjects evaluate clear and vague prospects jointly, but it will greatly diminish or disappear when they evaluate each prospect in isolation.

A review of the experimental literature reveals a remarkable fact: virtually every test of ambiguity aversion to date has employed a within-subjects design in which respondents compared clear and vague bets rather than a between-subjects design in which different respondents evaluated each bet. This literature, therefore, does not answer the question of whether ambiguity aversion exists in the absence of a contrast between clear and vague bets. In the following series of studies we test the hypothesis that ambiguity aversion holds in a comparative context (or a within-subjects design) but that it is reduced or eliminated in a noncomparative context (or a between-subjects design).

II. EXPERIMENTS

Study 1

The following hypothetical problem was presented to 141 undergraduates at Stanford University. It was included in a questionnaire consisting of several unrelated items that subjects completed for class credit.

Imagine that there is a bag on the table (*Bag A*) filled with exactly 50 red poker chips and 50 black poker chips, and a second bag (*Bag B*) filled with 100 poker chips that are red and black, but you do not know their relative proportion. Suppose that you are offered a ticket to a game that is to be played as follows: First, you are to guess a color (red or black). Next, without looking, you are to draw a poker chip out of one of the bags. If the color that you draw is the same as the one you predicted, then you will win $100; otherwise you win nothing. What is the most that you would pay for a ticket to play such a game for each of the bags? ($0 – $100)

Bag A	Bag B
50 red chips	? red chips
50 black chips	? black chips
100 total chips	100 total chips

The most that I would be willing to pay for a ticket to *Bag A* (50 red; 50 black) is: ____
The most that I would be willing to pay for a ticket to *Bag B* (? red; ? black) is: ____

Approximately half the subjects performed the comparative task described above; the order in which the two bets were presented was counterbalanced. The remaining subjects performed a noncomparative task: approximately half evaluated the clear bet alone, and the remaining subjects evaluated the vague bet alone.

Mean willingness to pay for each bet is presented in Table 30.1. As in all subsequent tables, standard errors (in parentheses) and sample sizes (N) are listed below the means. The data support our hypothesis. In the comparative

Table 30.1. Results of Study 1

	Clear Bet	Vague Bet
Comparative	$24.34	$14.85
	(2.21) $N=67$	(1.80) $N=67$
Noncomparative	$17.94	$18.42
	(2.50) $N=35$	(2.87) $N=39$

condition, there is strong evidence of ambiguity aversion: subjects were willing to pay on average $9.51 more for the clear bet than for the vague bet, $t(66) = 6.00$, $p < 0.001$. However, in the noncomparative condition, there is no trace of ambiguity aversion, as subjects paid slightly less for the clear bet than for the vague bet, $t(72) = -.12$, n.s. This interaction is significant ($z = 2.42$, $p < 0.01$).

Study 2

Our next study tested the comparative ignorance hypothesis with real money at stake. Subjects were recruited via signs posted in the psychology building at Stanford University promising a chance to win up to $20 for participation in a brief study. We recruited 110 students, faculty, and staff; six subjects were excluded because of inconsistent responses.

Subjects were run individually. Participants in the comparative condition priced both the clear bet and the vague bet. Half the subjects in the noncomparative condition priced the clear bet alone; the other half priced the vague bet alone. The clear bet involved a draw from a bag containing one red Ping-Pong ball and one green Ping-Pong ball. The vague bet involved a draw from a bag containing two Ping-Pong balls, each of which could be either red or green. Subjects were first asked to guess the color of the ball to be drawn. Next, they were asked to make a series of choices between receiving $20 if their guess is correct (and nothing otherwise) or receiving $X for sure. Subjects marked their choices on a response sheet that listed the various sure amounts ($X) in descending order from $19.50 to $0.50 in steps of 50 cents. They were informed that some participants would be selected at random to play for real money. For these subjects, one choice would be selected at random, and the subjects would either receive $X or play the bet, depending on the preference they had indicated. This procedure is incentive-compatible because subjects can only make themselves worse off by misrepresenting their preferences.

Cash equivalents were estimated by the midpoint between the lowest amount of money that was preferred to the uncertain bet, and the highest amount of money for which the bet was preferred. Mean cash equivalents are listed in Table 30.2. The procedural variations introduced in this study (real bets, monetary incentive, individual administration) did not affect the pattern of results. In the comparative condition, subjects priced the clear bet $1.21 higher on average than the vague bet, $t(51) = 2.70$, $p < 0.01$. However, in the

Table 30.2. Results of Study 2

	Clear Bet	Vague Bet
Comparative	$9.74	$8.53
	(0.49) $N = 52$	(0.58) $N = 52$
Noncomparative	$7.58	$8.04
	(0.62) $N = 26$	(0.43) $N = 26$

noncomparative condition, subjects priced the vague bet slightly above the clear bet, $t(50) = -.61$, n.s. Again, the interaction is significant ($z = 1.90$, $p < 0.05$).

Two comments regarding the interpretation of studies 1 and 2 are in order. First, subjects in both the comparative and noncomparative conditions were clearly aware of the fact that they did not know the composition of the vague urn. Only in the comparative task, however, did this fact influence their prices. Hence, ambiguity aversion seems to require a direct comparison between the clear and the vague bet; an awareness of missing information is not sufficient (cf. Frisch and Baron [1988]). Second, it is noteworthy that in both Studies 1 and 2, the comparative context enhanced the attractiveness of the clear bet somewhat more than it diminished the attractiveness of the vague bet. The comparative ignorance hypothesis, however, makes no prediction about the relative magnitude of these effects.

Study 3

In addition to the two-color problem described above, Ellsberg [1961] introduced a three-color problem, depicted in Table 30.3. Consider an urn that contains ten white balls, and twenty balls that are red and blue in unknown proportion. In decision 1 subjects are asked to choose between f_1, winning on white ($p = 1/3$); or g_1, winning on red ($0 \leq p \leq 2/3$). In decision 2 subjects are asked to choose between f_2, winning on either white or blue ($1/3 \leq p \leq 1$), or g_2, winning on either red or blue ($p = 2/3$). As suggested by Ellsberg, people typically favor f_1 over g_1 in decision 1, and g_2 over f_2 in decision 2, contrary to the independence axiom of expected utility theory.

From the standpoint of the comparative ignorance hypothesis, this problem differs from the two-color problem because here the description of the bets (especially f_2) involves both clear and vague probabilities. Consequently, we expect some ambiguity aversion even in a noncomparative context in which each subject evaluates only one bet. However, we expect a stronger effect in a comparative context in which each subject evaluates both the clear and vague bets. The present study tests these predictions.

Subjects were 162 first-year law students at Willamette University who completed a short questionnaire in a classroom setting. Three subjects who violated dominance were excluded from the analysis. Subjects were informed that some people would be selected at random to be paid on the basis of their choices.

Table 30.3. Ellsberg's Three-Color Problem

		10 Balls	20 Balls	
	Bet	White	Red	Blue
Decision 1	f_1	$50	0	0
	g_1	0	$50	0
Decision 2	f_2	$50	0	$50
	g_2	0	$50	$50

The instructions included a brief description of an incentive-compatible payoff scheme (based on Becker, DeGroot, and Marschak [1964]). Subjects were asked to state their minimum selling price for the bets displayed in Table 30.3. In the comparative condition, subjects priced all four bets. In the noncomparative condition, approximately half the subjects priced the two complementary clear bets (f_1 and g_2), and the remaining subjects priced the two complementary vague bets (f_2 and g_1). The order of the bets was counterbalanced.

Let $c(f)$ be the stated price of bet f. As expected, most subjects in the comparative condition priced the clear bets above the vague bets. In particular, we observed $c(f_1) > c(g_1)$ for 28 subjects, $c(f_1) = c(g_1)$ for 17 subjects, and $c(f_1) < c(g_1)$ for 8 subjects, $p < 0.01$. Similarly, we observed $c(g_2) > c(f_2)$ for 36 subjects, $c(g_2) = c(f_2)$ for 12 subjects, and $c(g_2) < c(f_2)$ for 5 subjects, $p < 0.001$. Moreover, the pattern implied by ambiguity aversion (i.e., $c(f_1) \geq c(g_1)$ and $c(f_2) \leq c(g_2)$, where at least one inequality is strict) was exhibited by 62 percent of the subjects.

In order to contrast the comparative and the noncomparative conditions, we have added for each subject the selling prices of the two complementary clear bets (i.e., $c(f_1) + c(g_2)$) and the selling prices of the two complementary vague bets (i.e., $c(g_1) + c(f_2)$). Obviously, for subjects in the noncomparative condition, we can compute only one such sum. These sums measure the attractiveness of betting on either side of the clear and of the vague bets. The means of these sums are presented in Table 30.4. The results conform to expectation. In the comparative condition, subjects priced clear bets $10.68 higher on average than vague bets, $t(52) = 6.23$, $p < 0.001$. However, in the noncomparative condition, the difference was only $3.85, $t(104) = 0.82$, n.s. This interaction is marginally significant ($z = 1.37$, $p < 0.10$).

Inspection of the individual bets reveals that for the more probable bets, f_2 and g_2, there was a strong preference for the clear over the vague in the comparative condition ($c(g_2) = \$33.75$, $c(f_2) = \$24.66$, $t(52) = 5.85$, $p < 0.001$) and a moderate preference for the clear over the vague in the noncomparative condition ($c(g_2) = \$31.67$, $c(f_2) = \$26.71$, $t(104) = 2.05$, $p < 0.05$). However, for the less probable bets, f_1 and g_1, we found no significant differences between selling prices for clear and vague bets in either the comparative condition ($c(g_1) = \$20.26$, $c(f_1) = \$21.85$, $t(52) = 1.05$, n.s.) or the noncomparative condition ($c(g_1) = \$21.13$, $c(f_1) = \$20.02$, $t(104) = 0.43$, n.s.). The aggregate pattern displayed in Table 30.4, therefore, is driven primarily by the more probable bets.

Table 30.4. Results of Study 3

	Clear Bet	Vague Bet
Comparative	$55.60	$44.92
	(2.66) $N = 53$	(3.27) $N = 53$
Noncomparative	$51.69	$47.85
	(2.94) $N = 54$	(3.65) $N = 52$

Study 4

In the preceding three studies, uncertainty was generated using a chance device (i.e., drawing a ball from an urn with a known or an unknown composition). Our next study tests the comparative ignorance hypothesis using natural events. Specifically, we asked subjects to price hypothetical bets contingent on future temperature in a familiar city (San Francisco) and an unfamiliar city with a similar climate (Istanbul). Ambiguity aversion suggests that our subjects (who were living near San Francisco) should prefer betting on San Francisco temperature, with which they were highly familiar, to betting on Istanbul temperature, with which they were not.

Subjects were asked how much they would be willing to pay to bet on each side of a proposition that offered a fixed prize if the temperature in a given city was above or below a specified value. The exact wording was as follows.

Imagine that you have been offered a ticket that will pay you $100 if the afternoon high temperature in [San Francisco/Istanbul] is *at least* 60 degrees Fahrenheit one week from today. What is the most you would be willing to pay for such a ticket?
The most I would be willing to pay is $___

Imagine that you have been offered a ticket that will pay you $100 if the afternoon high temperature in [San Francisco/Istanbul] is *less than* 60 degrees Fahrenheit one week from today. What is the most you would be willing to pay for such a ticket?
The most I would be willing to pay is $___

In the noncomparative condition one group of subjects priced the two bets above for San Francisco, and a second group of subjects priced the same two bets for Istanbul. In the comparative condition, subjects performed both tasks, pricing all four bets. The order of the events (less than 60 degrees/at least 60 degrees) and of the cities was counterbalanced. To minimize order effects, all subjects were asked before answering the questions to consider their best guess of the afternoon high temperature in the city or cities on which they were asked to bet.

Subjects were 189 pedestrians on the University of California at Berkeley campus who completed a five-minute survey (that included a few unrelated items) in exchange for a California lottery ticket. Ten subjects who violated dominance were excluded from the analysis. There were no significant order effects. Let $c(SF \geq 60)$ denote willingness to pay for the prospect "Win $100 if the high temperature in San Francisco one week from today is at least 60 degrees," etc. As in Study 3 we added for each subject his or her willingness to pay for both sides of complementary bets. In particular, we computed $c(SF \geq 60) + c(SF < 60)$ for the San Francisco bets and $c(1st \geq 60) + c(Ist < 60)$ for the Istanbul bets. Table 30.5 presents the means of these sums. The results again support our hypothesis. In the comparative condition subjects were willing to pay on average $15.84 more to bet on familiar San Francisco temperature than on unfamiliar Istanbul temperature, $t(89) = 5.05$, $p < 0.001$. However, in the noncomparative condition subjects were willing to pay on average a scant

Table 30.5. Results of Study 4

	San Francisco Bets	Istanbul Bets
Comparative	$40.53	$24.69
	(4.27) $N=90$	(3.09) $N=90$
Noncomparative	$39.89	$38.37
	(5.06) $N=44$	(6.10) $N=45$

$1.52 more to bet on San Francisco than on Istanbul, $t(87) = 0.19$, n.s. This interaction is significant ($z = 1.68$, $p < 0.05$).

The same pattern holds for the individual bets. In the comparative condition, $c(SF \geq 60) = \$22.74$, and $c(Ist \geq 60) = \$15.21$, $t(89) = 3.13$, $p < 0.01$. Similarly, $c(SF < 60) = \$17.79$ and $c(Ist < 60) = \$9.49$, $t(89) = 4.25$, $p < 0.001$. In the noncomparative condition, however, $kc(SF \geq 60) = \$21.95$, and $c(Ist \geq 60) = \$21.07$, $t(87) = 0.17$, n.s. Similarly, $c(SF < 60) = \$17.94$, and $c(Ist < 60) = \$17.29$, $t(87) = 0.13$, n.s. Thus, subjects in the comparative condition were willing to pay significantly more for either side of the San Francisco proposition than they were willing to pay for the corresponding sides of the Istanbul proposition. However, no such pattern is evident in the noncomparative condition. Note that unlike the effect observed in Studies 1 and 2, the present effect is produced by the reduction in the attractiveness of the less familiar bet.

Study 5

We have interpreted the results of the preceding studies in terms of comparative ignorance. Alternatively, it might be argued that these results can be explained at least in part by the more general hypothesis that the difference between cash equivalents of prospects evaluated in isolation will be enhanced by a direct comparison between them. Such enhancement would apply whether or not the prospects in question involve different sources of uncertainty that vary with respect to familiarity or ambiguity.

To test this hypothesis, we recruited 129 Stanford undergraduates to answer a one-page questionnaire. Subjects were asked to state their maximum willingness to pay for hypothetical bets that offered $100 if the daytime high temperature in Palo Alto (where Stanford is located) on a particular day fell in a specified range. The two bets were described as follows:

[A] Imagine that you have been offered a ticket that will pay you $100 if the afternoon high temperature *two weeks* from today in Palo Alto is *more than* 70 degrees Fahrenheit. What is the most you would be willing to pay for such a ticket?
     The most I would be willing to pay is $___
     [B] Imagine that you have been offered a ticket that will pay you $100 if the afternoon high temperature *three weeks* from today in Palo Alto is *less than* 65 degrees Fahrenheit. What is the most you would be willing to pay for such a ticket?
     The most I would be willing to pay is $___

Table 30.6. Results of Study 5

	Bet A	Bet B
Comparative	$25.77	$6.42
	(3.68) $N = 47$	(1.84) $N = 47$
Noncomparative	$23.07	$5.32
	(3.42) $N = 42$	(1.27) $N = 40$

Subjects in the comparative condition evaluated both [A] and [B] (the order was counterbalanced). Approximately half the subjects in the noncomparative condition evaluated [A] alone, and the remaining subjects evaluated [B] alone.

Because Palo Alto temperature in the springtime (when the study was conducted) is more likely to be above 70 degrees than below 65 degrees, we expected bet [A] to be generally more attractive than bet [B]. The enhancement hypothesis, therefore, implies that the difference between $c(A)$ and $c(B)$ will be greater in the comparative than in the noncomparative condition. The mean values of $c(A)$ and $c(B)$ are presented in Table 30.6. The results do not support the enhancement hypothesis. In this study, $c(A)$ was greater than $c(B)$. However, the difference $c(A) - c(B)$ was roughly the same in the two conditions (interaction $z = 0.32$, n.s.). In fact, there were no significant differences between the comparative and noncomparative conditions in the cash equivalents of either prospect ($t(87) = 0.53$ for A; n.s.; $t(85) = 0.48$ for B, n.s.). This pattern contrasts sharply with the results of the preceding studies (see especially Table 30.5) that reveal substantially larger differences between stated prices in the comparative than in the noncomparative conditions. We conclude that the comparative ignorance effect observed in Studies 1–4 cannot be explained by the more general enhancement hypothesis.

Study 6

The comparative ignorance hypothesis attributes ambiguity aversion to the contrast between states of knowledge. In the first four studies we provided subjects with a comparison between more and less familiar events. In our final study we provided subjects with a comparison between themselves and more knowledgeable individuals.

Subjects were undergraduates at San Jose State University. The following hypothetical problem was included in a questionnaire containing several unrelated items that subjects completed for class credit.

Kaufman Broad Homes (KBH) is one of the largest home sellers in America. Their stock is traded on the New York Stock Exchange.
[1] Do you think that KBH stock will close higher or lower Monday than it did yesterday? (Circle one)
- KBH will close higher.
- KBH will close the same or lower.

[2] Which would you prefer? (Circle one)
- receive $50 for sure
- receive $150 if my prediction about KBH is correct.

Subjects in the noncomparative condition ($N = 31$) answered the questions above. Subjects in the comparative condition ($N = 32$) answered the same questions with the following additional item inserted between questions 1 and 2.

We are presenting this survey to undergraduates at San Jose State University, graduate students in economics at Stanford University, and to professional stock analysts.

Subjects were then asked to rate their knowledge of the item on a scale from 0 to 10.

The present account implies that the suggested comparison to more knowledgeable individuals (i.e., graduate students in economics and professional stock analysts) will undermine the subjects' sense of competence and consequently decrease their willingness to bet on their own judgment. The results support this prediction. The uncertain prospect of winning $150 was preferred to the sure payment of $50 by 68 percent of subjects in the noncomparative condition and by only 41 percent of subjects in the comparative condition, $\chi^2(1) = 4.66$, $p < 0.05$.

We replicated this effect using a different subject population (undergraduates at Stanford University enrolled in an introductory psychology course) and a different uncertain event. The following hypothetical problem was included in a questionnaire that contained several unrelated items that was completed for class credit.

[1] Do you think that the inflation rate in Holland over the past 12 months is greater than or less than 3.0 percent? (Circle one)
- *less than* 3.0 percent
- *at least* 3.0 percent

[2] Which of the following do you prefer? (Circle one)
- receive $50 for sure
- receive $150 if I am right about the inflation rate.

As before, subjects in the noncomparative condition ($N = 39$) evaluated the items above, and subjects in the comparative condition ($N = 37$) answered the same questions with the following additional item inserted between questions [1] and [2].

We are presenting this survey to undergraduates in Psych 1, graduate students in economics, and to professional business forecasters.

Subjects were then asked to rate their knowledge of the item on a scale from 0 to 10.

The uncertain prospect was preferred to the sure payment by 38 percent of subjects in the noncomparative condition and by only 11 percent of subjects in the comparative condition, $\chi^2(1) = 7.74$, $p < 0.01$. Thus, the tendency to bet on a vague event is reduced by a suggested comparison to more knowledgeable individuals. Note that the results of this study, obtained by the mere mention of a more expert population, should be distinguished from the finding of Curley, Yates, and Abrams [1986] that ambiguity aversion is enhanced when people anticipate that their decision will be evaluated by their peers.

Market Experiments

Before we turn to the implications of the present findings, the question arises whether the effects of ambiguity and comparative ignorance persist when decision-makers are given an opportunity to make multiple decisions in a market setting that provides incentives and immediate feedback. A positive answer to this question has been provided by Sarin and Weber [1993], who compared subjects' bids for clear and for vague bets in several experimental markets using sealed bid and double oral auctions. In one series of studies involving graduate students of business administration from Cologne University, the clear bet paid 100 Deutsche Marks (DM) if a yellow ball was drawn from an opaque urn containing ten yellow and ten white tennis balls, and nothing otherwise. The vague bet was defined similarly except that the subject did not know the proportion of yellow and white balls, which was sampled from a uniform distribution. In some studies, subjects traded both clear and vague bets in each market. In other studies, subjects traded clear bets in some markets and vague bets in other markets. Thus, all subjects evaluated both clear and vague bets. The comparative ignorance hypothesis predicts that (1) the clear bet will be generally priced above the vague bet, and (2) the discrepancy between the prices will be more pronounced when clear and vague bets are traded jointly than when they are traded separately. The data support both predictions. The difference between the average market price of the clear and the vague bets across both auction types (for the last trading period in experiments 11 through 14) was more than DM 20 in the joint markets and less than DM 5 in the separate markets. This effect was especially pronounced in the double oral auctions where there was no difference between the market price of the clear and the vague bets in the separate markets, and a substantial difference (DM 18.5) in the joint markets. Evidently, market setting is not sufficient to eliminate the effects of ambiguity and comparative ignorance.

III. DISCUSSION

The preceding studies provide support for the comparative ignorance hypothesis, according to which ambiguity aversion is driven primarily by a comparison between events or between individuals, and it is greatly reduced or eliminated in the absence of such a comparison. We hasten to add that the distinction between comparative and noncomparative assessment refers to the state of mind of the decision-maker, which we have attempted to control through the experimental context. Of course, there is no guarantee that subjects in the comparative conditions actually performed the suggested comparison, or that subjects in the noncomparative conditions did not independently generate a comparison. In Ellsberg's two-color problem, for example, people who are presented with the vague urn alone may spontaneously invoke a comparison to a 50–50 urn, especially if they have previously encountered such a problem. However, the consistent results observed in the preceding studies suggest that the experimental manipulation was successful in inducing subjects to make a comparison in one condition but not in the other.

The comparative ignorance hypothesis suggests that when people price an uncertain prospect in isolation (e.g., receive $100 if Istanbul temperature one week from today exceeds 60 degrees), they pay little or no attention to the quality or precision of their assessment of the likelihood of the event in question. However, when people are asked to price this prospect in the context of another prospect (e.g., receive $100 if San Francisco temperature one week from today exceeds 60 degrees), they become sensitive to the contrast in their knowledge regarding the two events, and as a result price the less familiar or vaguer prospect lower than the more familiar or clearer prospect (see, e.g., Heath and Tversky [1991] and Keppe and Weber [forthcoming]). Similarly, an uncertain prospect becomes less attractive when people are made aware that the same prospect will also be evaluated by more knowledgeable individuals. Thus, ambiguity aversion represents a reluctance to act on inferior knowledge, and this inferiority is brought to mind only through a comparison with superior knowledge about other domains or of other people.

Theoretical Implications

The comparative ignorance effect violates the principle of procedure invariance according to which strategically equivalent elicitation procedures should produce the same preference order (cf. Tversky, Sattath, and Slovic [1988]). In the preceding studies, the vague and clear bets were equally valued when priced in isolation, yet the latter was strictly preferred to the former when the two bets were priced jointly. Like other instances of preference reversal (see, e.g., Tversky and Thaler [1990]), a particular attribute (in this case knowledge of probabilities) looms larger in comparative than in noncomparative evaluation. However, the most noteworthy finding is not the illustration of a new variety of preference reversal, but rather the conclusion that the Ellsberg phenomenon is an inherently comparative effect.

This discrepancy between comparative and noncomparative evaluation raises the question of which preference should be considered more rational. On the one hand, it could be argued that the comparative judgment reflects people's "true" preferences, and in the absence of comparison, people fail to properly discount for their ignorance. On the other hand, it might be argued that the noncomparative judgments are more rational, and that subjects are merely intimidated by a comparison with superior knowledge. As we see it, there is no compelling argument to favor one interpretation over the other. The rational theory of choice (or more specifically, the principle of procedure invariance) requires that the comparative and noncomparative evaluations will coincide, but the theory does not provide a method for reconciling inconsistent preferences.

What are the implications of the present findings for the analysis of individual decision-making? To answer this question, it is important to distinguish two phenomena that have emerged from the descriptive study of decision under uncertainty: source preference and source sensitivity [Tversky and Fox 1995; Tversky and Wakker forthcoming]. Source preference refers to the observation that choices between prospects depend not only on the degree of uncertainty but also on the source of uncertainty (e.g., San Francisco temperature versus Istanbul temperature). Source preference is demonstrated by showing that a person prefers to bet on a proposition drawn from one source than on a proposition drawn from another source, and also prefers to bet against the first proposition than against the second (e.g., $c(SF \geq 60) > c(Ist \geq 60)$, and $c(SF < 60) > c(Ist < 60)$; see Study 4 above). We have interpreted ambiguity aversion as a special case of source preference in which risk is preferred to uncertainty, as in Ellsberg's examples.[1]

Source sensitivity refers to nonadditivity of decision weights. In particular, the descriptive analysis of decision under risk indicates that the impact of a given event on the value of a prospect is greater when it turns an impossibility into a possibility or a possibility into a certainty than when it merely makes an uncertain event more or less probable [Kahneman and Tversky 1979]. For example, increasing the probability of winning a fixed prize from 0 to 0.1 or 0.9 to 1.0 has a greater impact than increasing the probability from, say, 0.3 to 0.4. Tversky and Fox [1995] have further shown that this pattern, called bounded subadditivity, is more pronounced for uncertainty than for chance (i.e., for vague than for clear probabilities). In other words, people are less sensitive to uncertainty to chance, regardless of whether or not they prefer uncertainty than to chance. Thus, source preference and source sensitivity are logically independent.

---

[1] Some authors have interpreted as ambiguity aversion the finding that people prefer to bet on a more reliable rather than on a less reliable estimate of a given probability p (e.g., Einhorn and Hogarth [1985]). This demonstration, however, does not establish source preference because it does not also consider the complements of the events in question. Hence, the finding above can be attributed to the fact that the subjective probability associated with the less reliable estimate of p is less extreme (i.e., closer to 0.5) than that associated with the more reliable estimate of p (see Heath and Tversky [1991, Table 30.4]). More generally, the oft-cited conclusion that people are ambiguity-averse for high probabilities and ambiguity-seeking for small probabilities is questionable because the demonstrations on which it is based do not properly control for variations in subjective probability.

The present experiments show that source preference, unlike source sensitivity, is an inherently comparative phenomenon, and it does not arise in an independent evaluation of uncertain prospects. This suggests that models based on decision weights or nonadditive probabilities (e.g., Quiggin [1982]; Gilboa [1987]; Schmeidler [1989]; Tversky and Wakker [forthcoming]) can accommodate source sensitivity, but they do not provide a satisfactory account of source preference because they do not distinguish between comparative and noncomparative evaluation. One might attempt to model the comparative ignorance effect using a contingent weighting approach [Tversky, Sattath, and Slovic 1988] in which the weight associated with an event depends on whether it is evaluated in a comparative or noncomparative context. The major difficulties with this, or any other attempt to model the comparative ignorance effect, is that it requires prior specification of the decision maker's sense of his or her competence regarding the event in question and the salience of alternative states of knowledge. Although these variables can be experimentally manipulated, as we did in the preceding studies, they cannot easily be measured and incorporated into a formal model.

Despite the difficulties in modeling comparative ignorance, it could have significant economic implications. For example, an individual who is knowledgeable about the computer industry but not about the energy industry may exhibit ambiguity aversion in choosing whether to invest in a high-tech startup or an oil exploration, but not when each investment is evaluated independently. Furthermore, the present account suggests that the order in which the two investments are considered could affect their valuation. In particular, the less familiar investment might be valued more when it is considered before rather than after the more familiar investment.[2] In light of the present analysis, recent attempts to model ambiguity aversion in financial markets (e.g., Dow and Werlang [1992] and Epstein and Wang [1994]) may be incomplete because they do not distinguish between comparative and noncomparative evaluation. In particular, such models are likely to overestimate the degree of ambiguity aversion in settings in which uncertain prospects are evaluated in isolation (cf. Sarin and Weber [1993]). The role of comparative ignorance in economic transactions awaits further empirical investigation.

---

[2] Unpublished data, collected by Fox and Weber, showed that an unfamiliar prospect was priced lower when evaluated after a familiar prospect than when evaluated before that prospect.

31. Attribute Evaluability

Its Implications for Joint–Separate Evaluation Reversals and Beyond[1]

Christopher K. Hsee

ABSTRACT. The evaluability hypothesis posits that when two objects are evaluated separately, whether a given attribute of the objects can differentiate the evaluations of these objects depends on whether the attribute is easy or difficult to evaluate independently. The article discusses how the evaluability hypothesis explains joint–separate evaluation reversal, which is the phenomenon that the rank order of the evaluations of multiple objects changes depending on whether these objects are evaluated jointly or separately. The article presents empirical evidence for the evaluability hypothesis. The final section of the article discusses implications of the hypothesis for issues beyond reversals – in particular for inconsistencies between decisions and their consequences. Decisions are typically made in the joint evaluation mode, and the outcome of a decision is usually experienced (or "consumed") in the separate evaluation mode. Thus, reversals between joint and separate evaluation may manifest themselves in decision–consumption inconsistencies.

I. INTRODUCTION

All judgments and decisions are made in one (or some combination) of two basic modes: joint and separate. In the joint evaluation (JE) mode, people are exposed to multiple objects simultaneously and evaluate these objects comparatively. In the separate or single evaluation (SE) mode, people are exposed to only one object and evaluate it in isolation. For example, when shopping for a piano at a music instrument store, we are usually in the joint evaluation (JE) mode because there are typically many pianos for us to compare. On the other hand, when we debate whether to bid for a piano at an estate auction where there are no other pianos, we probably think about this particular piano alone and are therefore in the separate or single evaluation (SE) mode. Of course, our evaluations sometimes fall somewhere between the two modes. For example,

[1] This chapter incorporates new material from Hsee (1998) and Hsee et al. (1999). I thank the following people (in alphabetical order of their last names) for their comments: Scott Jeffrey, Josh Klayman, Howard Kunreuther, George Loewenstein, Cade Massey, Joe Nunes, Eldar Shafir, Paul Slovic, Jack Soll, John Wright, and George Wu.

This article is a revised version of one that appeared in *Organizational Behavior and Human Decision Processes*, 67:3, 247–57. Copyright © 1996 by Academic Press. Reprinted with permission.

when evaluating job candidates, we are partly in the JE mode and partly in the SE mode – in the JE mode to the extent that we compare one candidate with another candidate and in the SE mode to the extent that we focus on one candidate at a time. Strictly speaking, the evaluation mode is a continuum, with JE on one end and SE on the other. For the sake of simplicity, this article concerns itself mainly with the two ends of the continuum.[2]

Will a set of objects (say, two objects) be evaluated differently between JE and SE? The answer is yes. Sometimes, even the rank order of the evaluations of the two objects reverses itself between the two evaluation modes, that is, one object is favored in JE and the other object is favored in SE. This phenomenon will be referred to as joint–separate evaluation reversal or simply JE–SE reversal.

The present article is organized as follows: The next section presents evidence showing JE–SE reversals. The section that follows discusses the evaluability hypothesis, an explanation for the reversal. The succeeding section provides empirical support for that hypothesis. The last several sections of the article examine the implications of the evaluability hypothesis for issues beyond JE–SE reversals.

II. EVIDENCE FOR JOINT–SEPARATE EVALUATION REVERSALS

1. Dictionary Study

This study illustrates the JE–SE reversal effect. The study involved the evaluation of two hypothetical second-hand music dictionaries as follows:

	Dictionary A	Dictionary B
Year of publication:	1993	1993
Number of entries:	10,000	20,000
Any defects?	No, it's like new.	Yes, the cover is torn; otherwise, it's like new.

Respondents (116 students from the University of Chicago and the University of Illinois at Chicago) were assigned to one of three conditions – JE, SE–A and SE–B.[3] In each condition, participants were asked to assume that they were music majors looking for a music dictionary in a used book store and planned to spend between $10 and $50. In the JE condition, participants were told that there

---

[2] The term *separate evaluation* or *SE* refers both to (1) situations in which different objects are presented to and evaluated by different individuals so that each individual sees and evaluates only one object and to (2) situations in which different objects are presented to and evaluated by the same individuals at different times so that each individual evaluates only one object *at a given time*. The former situations are pure separate evaluation conditions. The latter situations involve some joint evaluation flavor because individuals evaluating a later object may recall the previous object(s) and make a comparison. In the studies reported in this paper, the separate evaluation conditions were like the former situations.

[3] For the sake of consistency, in all the studies discussed in this article I use the letter "A" to label the option favored in SE and the label "B" to label the other option.

Table 31.1. Mean WTP Values for the Two
Dictionaries in the Dictionary Study

Evaluation Mode	Dictionary A	Dictionary B
Joint	$19	$27
Separate	$24	$20

were two music dictionaries in the store. They were then presented with the information about both dictionaries (as listed above) and asked how much they were willing to pay for each dictionary. In each of the SE conditions, participants were told that there was only one music dictionary in the store; they were presented with the information on one of the dictionaries and asked how much they were willing to pay.

Table 31.1 summarizes the results:[4] There was a clear reversal in willingness to pay (WTP) between JE and SE. In JE, WTP values were higher for Dictionary B ($t = 7.11$, $p < .001$), but in SE, WTP values were higher for Dictionary A ($t = 1.69$, $p < 0.1$).

2. Other Evidence

Joint–separate evaluation reversals have been documented in other contexts as well. The original demonstration of JE–SE reversal was provided by Bazerman, Loewenstein and White (1992) in the context of dispute resolution. Those authors found that between an option that entailed a high payoff to oneself and looked unfair (e.g., $600 to self and $800 to the other side) and an option that entailed a lower payoff to oneself and looked fair (e.g., $500 to both sides), the former option was favored in JE and the latter option was favored in SE. Bazerman et al. (1994) replicated these results with business students in the context of hypothetical job offers. In the context of political candidate preferences, Loewenthal (1993) found that in JE people preferred a candidate who could bring 5,000 jobs to the district but had a minor conviction in the past to one who could bring only 1,000 jobs but had a clean history; in SE, the preference was reversed. Similar JE–SE reversals have been obtained by Hsee (1993) in the context of salary preferences and by Nowlis and Simonson (1994) in the context of consumer products.

Joint–separate evaluation reversals suggest that switching from one evaluation mode to the other can change the attractiveness of one object *relative* to the other object. It should be noted, however, that varying evaluation mode can also produce other types of changes. In a recent study, for example, Hsee and Leclerc (1998) showed that, under a set of predictable conditions, switching from one evaluation mode to the other increases the attractiveness of *both* objects even though their relative attractiveness stays the same. In the present

---

[4] To prevent their undue influences, willingness-to-pay values more than three standard deviations from the mean were excluded from analysis. This footnote applies to all the studies reported in this article.

article, however, I limit my discussions to changes in *relative* attractiveness of the objects – in particular to rank-order reversal.

3. Differences between JE–SE Reversal and Choice–Judgment Preference Reversals

Joint–separate evaluation reversals are not the same as the traditionally studied choice–judgment preference reversals. Of the many forms of choice-judgment reversals documented in the decision literature, the most widely studied are probably the choice-pricing reversal and the choice-matching reversal. In the choice-pricing paradigm, participants either choose between two gambles or indicate their minimum selling price for the gambles (e.g., Lichtenstein and Slovic 1971, Grether and Plott 1979). Typically, participants favor low-payoff and high-probability gambles over high-payoff and low-probability gambles in choice but demand a higher minimum selling price for the high-payoff and low-probability gambles in pricing. In the choice-matching paradigm, participants either choose between two alternatives or fill in some missing value in one of the alternatives to make the two alternatives equally attractive (e.g., Tversky, Sattath, and Slovic 1988). Typically, in choice people favor the option superior on the most prominent attribute, but in matching their responses imply more even weighting between the attributes.

In both the choice-pricing and the choice-matching paradigms, reversals occur between tasks that involve different *evaluation scales* (e.g., Goldstein and Einhorn 1987, Bazerman et al. 1992). Evaluation scale refers to the dimension on which subjects' responses are elicited, whether it is about intention to accept (acceptability), about willingness to pay, about selling price, about feelings, or about something else. In the choice-pricing paradigm, the evaluation scale for choice is acceptability and that for pricing is selling price. In the choice-matching paradigm, the evaluation scale for choice is, again, acceptability and that for matching is probability or value estimation.

Although choice and judgment reversals sometimes involve different *evaluation modes*, difference in evaluation mode is not a necessary condition for those classic preference reversals. For example, in the choice-matching reversal, a typical subclass of choice–judgment reversal, both the choice response and the matching response are elicited in the JE mode.

Unlike classic choice–judgment reversals, the critical difference between the conditions that produce JE–SE reversals is evaluation mode – whether the target objects are presented and evaluated jointly or presented and evaluated separately. Whether the two evaluation modes involve the same or different evaluation scales is not essential. A reversal can occur between JE and SE even if the evaluation scale between the two evaluation modes is held constant. In the previously described dictionary study, for instance, the reversal occurred between JE and SE, even though the evaluation scale in both conditions was invariably willingness to pay.

Joint–separate evaluation reversals cannot be easily accounted for by standard theories for choice–judgment reversals. These theories rely on difference in evaluation scale rather than difference in evaluation mode to explain preference reversals. For example, the standard explanation for choice-pricing reversals is the compatibility principle (Slovic, Griffin, and Tversky 1990). According to this principle, a given attribute will carry more weight in a response that is on the same scale as this attribute than in a response that is on a different scale. For example, monetary attributes will loom larger if the evaluation is made on a monetary scale (such as in a pricing task) than if it is made in terms of acceptability (such as in a choice task). Clearly, this principle is concerned with evaluation scales rather than with evaluation modes.

The standard explanation for choice-matching reversals is the prominence principle; it is a special case of the compatibility principle (Tversky et al. 1988; see also Fischer and Hawkins 1993). According to the prominence principle, people use a lexicographic rule when deciding which option to accept (choice) and use a trade-off analysis when judging a missing attribute value (matching). It is posited that the more prominent attribute is more compatible with a lexicographic decision task than with a value judgment task involving trade-off analyses. As a result, the more prominent attribute looms larger in choice than in matching. The prominence principle provides a compelling explanation for the standard choice-matching reversal, but it does not readily apply to the JE–SE reversal studied in the present research. As demonstrated previously, JE–SE reversals can take place even if the evaluation scale is held constant. In addition, there is no direct correspondence between matching and SE, or between choice and JE. For example, in the typical matching task, the evaluator is exposed to multiple stimulus objects and performs careful trade-off analyses (Tversky et al. 1988); in SE, on the other hand, the evaluator is presented with only one object and cannot perform trade-off analyses.

In summary, JE–SE reversals are different from traditionally studied choice–judgment preference reversals and cannot be readily explained by classic preference reversal theories.

III. THE EVALUABILITY HYPOTHESIS

In this section I discuss an explanation for JE–SE reversals called the evaluability hypothesis.[5] Unless otherwise specified, the discussion below assumes that there are two objects to be evaluated and that the two objects involve a trade-off along two attributes in the form of

	Object A	Object B
Attribute 1:	a_1	b_1
Attribute 2:	a_2	b_2

---

[5] Similar accounts of JE–SE reversals were proposed by Hsee (1993) in terms of "reference-dependency" of attribute evaluation; by Loewenstein, Blount, and Bazerman (1993) in terms of "attribute ambiguity," and by Nowlis and Simonson (1994) in terms of "context–dependency."

Assume also that decision makers care about the attributes and know which direction of the attribute is better. The two options in the dictionary study comply with these assumptions. The two dictionaries involved a trade-off along the following attributes:

	Dictionary A	Dictionary B
Number of entries:	10,000	20,000
Defects:	no	yes

According to the evaluability hypothesis, JE–SE reversals occur because one of the attributes involved in the stimulus objects is *hard to evaluate independently* and the other attribute is relatively *easy to evaluate independently*. Below I first discuss what makes an attribute easy or difficult to evaluate and then explain why it is relevant to JE–SE reversals.

1. Attribute Evaluability

To say that an attribute is hard to evaluate independently means that, even though people know which direction of the attribute is better, they do not know how good a given value on the attribute is when the value is presented alone.

Whether an attribute is hard or easy to evaluate depends on how much knowledge the decision maker has about that attribute – especially about its effective range, its neutral reference point, and its value distribution. Without such knowledge, the decision maker will not know where a given value of that attribute lies in relation to the other values of the attribute and hence will not know how to evaluate it.

To say that an attribute is hard to evaluate does not mean that the decision maker does not know the precise value on the attribute, but means that the decision maker does not know how to interpret the desirability of that value. For example, suppose that a person traveling in a foreign country is told that a particular hotel room there costs $56.78 per night. If the person is unfamiliar with the hotel rates there, then the price of that hotel, albeit precisely given, will be hard for him to evaluate independently. (For a more detailed analysis of what determines the evaluability of an attribute, see Hsee et al. 1999).

In the dictionary study, for example, the number of entries was hard to evaluate independently. Most respondents had little knowledge about the number of entries in a music dictionary. Without something to compare it with, they would not know how to judge the desirability of a dictionary with 10,000 entries (or with 20,000 entries). On the other hand, the defects attribute was relatively easy to evaluate independently. Even without a direct comparison, most people would find a defective dictionary unattractive and find a nondefective dictionary neutral or attractive.

Usually, attributes with dichotomous values (yes versus no), such as whether a dictionary is defective or not or whether an accountant has a CPA license or not, are easy to evaluate independently because people often know that these attributes have only two alternative values and know which value is good and which one is bad.[6] However, easy-to-evaluate attributes do not have to be dichotomous, as will be shown in the other studies to be reported later.

2. Explaining JE–SE Reversals

According to the evaluability hypothesis, the relative impact of the hard-to-evaluate and the easy-to-evaluate attribute changes between the SE and the JE mode. In the SE mode, the hard-to-evaluate attribute has little impact in differentiating the evaluations of the objects; the easy-to-evaluate attribute is the primary determinant. The reason is as follows: Because people do not have a clear idea of how good each value on the hard-to-evaluate attribute is, two things will happen in SE: (1) the values of the two target objects on the hard-to-evaluate attributes will cast similar impressions, and (2) these impressions will be fuzzy and involve a high variance (see Mellers, Richards, and Birnbaum 1992 for an analysis of the second point). In this circumstance, the hard-to-evaluate attribute will have little power to differentiate the evaluation of one object from the evaluation of the other object. For instance, suppose that participants in the SE conditions of the dictionary study had been asked to rate their impression of the comprehensiveness of the dictionaries on a 0–10 point scale on which increasing numbers indicated more comprehensiveness. Two things would probably have happened: (1) the mean rating given by subjects evaluating only the 10,000-entry dictionary would be similar to that by subjects evaluating only the 20,000-entry dictionary, and (2) the ratings given by either group of subjects would entail a large variance. As a consequence, the entry attribute would not contribute much to differentiating the final valuation of one dictionary from the final valuation of the other dictionary.

In contrast, the easy-to-evaluate attribute would cast different impressions in SE. For example, people evaluating the defective dictionary would have a negative impression of its appearance, and those evaluating the nondefective dictionary would have a neutral or positive impression. Thus, this attribute would discriminate the valuation of one dictionary from the valuation of the other dictionary.

In JE, people could compare one object against the other. This comparison would increase the evaluability of the otherwise hard-to-evaluate attribute and thereby increase its impact on the evaluations of the objects. For example, in the JE condition of the dictionary study, respondents could recognize, through a comparison of the two dictionaries, that the 20,000-entry dictionary

---

[6] Strictly speaking, the defect attribute in the dictionary study can also be construed as a continuous variable because there are *different degrees* of defectiveness. However, most people would probably be first concerned about whether or not a dictionary is defective before they would care about the degree of defectiveness. Therefore the defect attribute can be construed as a dichotomous variable.

was more comprehensive than the 10,000-entry dictionary. Thus, the number-of-entries attribute, which had little impact in SE, would now help differentiate the valuations of the dictionaries. Joint evaluation may also increase the impact of the easy-to-evaluate attribute. However, because the easy-to-evaluate attribute already has an impact in SE, it will not benefit as much from JE as the hard-to-evaluate attribute. In other words, the hard-to-evaluate attribute has a greater relative impact in JE than in SE, and the easy-to-evaluate attribute has a greater relative impact in SE than in JE. Indeed, the reversal found in the dictionary study supports this analysis.

The evaluability hypothesis is also consistent with the finding of the political candidate study by Lowenthal (1993). In that study, the two candidates varied on two attributes: number of jobs a candidate could bring to the district and whether or not the candidate had a prior conviction. Without a basis for comparison, it was rather difficult to know how good a candidate was if he could bring 1,000 jobs (or 5,000 jobs); in contrast, a prior conviction was obviously undesirable, and a clean history was good. According to the evaluability hypothesis, the job attribute would loom larger in JE, and the conviction attribute would loom larger in SE. The result was indeed in line with this prediction. Likewise, in the dispute resolution study by Bazerman et al. (1992), the two outcomes mentioned above can be interpreted as varying on two attributes: payoff to oneself and whether the payoffs were equal between the two parties. The payoff attribute was relatively difficult to evaluate independently, whereas the equality attribute was easy to evaluate. Again, the reversal observed in that study was consistent with the evaluability hypothesis, implying that the payoff attribute had a greater impact in JE and the equality attribute a greater impact in SE (see Bazerman, Tembrunsel, and Wade-Benzoni, 1988 for an alternative explanation of this study).

IV. EMPIRICAL SUPPORT FOR THE EVALUABILITY HYPOTHESIS

This section presents two studies that tested the evaluability hypothesis: the programmer and the CD-changer studies. The programmer study included naturally occurring, hard-to-evaluate and naturally occurring, easy-to-evaluate attributes. In the CD-changer study, whether an attribute was hard or easy to evaluate was manipulated empirically.

1. The Programmer Study

This study is a replication of the dictionary study with two extensions. First, in the dictionary study (and the other studies reviewed previously), the easy-to-evaluate attribute was always a dichotomous variable (e.g., whether the cosmetic condition of a dictionary was perfect or imperfect), and the hard-to-evaluate attribute was always a continuous variable (e.g., the number of entries in a dictionary). In the programmer study, both the easy-to-evaluate and the hard-to-evaluate attributes were continuous variables. Second, in the programmer study, a manipulation check was employed to ensure that the attribute believed to be difficult to evaluate was indeed more difficult to evaluate than the attribute believed to be easier to evaluate.

Method. This study involved the evaluations of two hypothetical job candidates for a computer programmer position. The programmer was expected to use a special language called KY. The two candidates were the following:

	Candidate A	**Candidate B**
Education:	B.S. in computer science from UIC	B.S. in computer science from UIC
GPA from UIC:	4.9	3.0
Experience with KY:	has written 10 KY programs in the last 2 years	has written 70 KY programs in the last 2 years

The abbreviation UIC stands for the University of Illinois at Chicago. The participants were students of that university and knew the abbreviation. The GPA at UIC is given on a 5-point scale.

Note that the two candidates had a trade-off between GPA and experience. Both are continuous variables. For ease of discussion later, let us simplify the descriptions of the two candidates as follows:

	Candidate A	**Candidate B**
Experience:	10 programs	70 programs
GPA:	4.9	3.0

Respondents (112 students from the University of Illinois at Chicago) were assigned to one of three conditions – JE, SE–A and SE–B. In all three conditions, participants were asked to imagine that they were the owner of a consulting firm, that they were looking for a computer programmer to use a computer language called KY, and that they planned to pay the person between $20,000 and $40,000 per year. In the JE condition, participants evaluated both candidates. In each SE condition, they evaluated only one of the candidates. The evaluation scale was constant across the three versions: willingness to pay.

To assess the evaluability of the attributes, participants in the two separate-evaluation conditions were asked the following questions after they had indicated their WTP for the candidate: (1) "Do you have any idea how good a GPA of 4.9 (3.0) from UIC is?" and (2) "If someone has written 10 (70) KY programs in the last 2 years, do you have any idea how experienced he or she is with KY?" (The numbers preceding the parentheses were for the separate-evaluation-A condition, and those in the parentheses were for the separate-evaluation-B

Table 31.2. Mean WTP Values (in $1000) for the Two Candidates in the Programmer Study

Evaluation Mode	Candidate A	Candidate B
Joint	$31.2	$33.2
Separate	$32.7	$26.8

condition.) To answer each question, participants would choose among four options ranging from (1) = I don't have any idea. to (4) = I have a clear idea. These options served as an evaluability scale on which a greater number indicated greater evaluability.

Results and Discussion. The mean evaluability score for GPA was 3.7, and that for experience was 2.1. The difference was highly significant ($t = 11.79$, $p < .001$). These results established GPA as a relatively easy-to-evaluate attribute and experience a relatively hard-to-evaluate attribute in this experiment.

According to the evaluability hypothesis, the experience attribute would have a greater impact in JE than in SE, and the GPA attribute would have a greater impact in SE than in JE. The results, summarized in Table 31.2, supported this prediction.

A clear reversal occurred between JE and SE. In JE, WTP was greater for the more experienced candidate (Candidate B) ($t = 1.65$, $p < .1$). In SE WTP was higher for the candidate with the higher GPA (Candidate A) ($t = 5.50$, $p < .001$).

2. The CD Changer Study

As mentioned earlier, the evaluability hypothesis asserts that JE–SE reversals occur because one of the attributes involved in the stimulus objects is hard to evaluate independently whereas the other attribute is relatively easy to evaluate. It implies that if both attributes are easy to evaluate independently, then there will be no reversal. If this logic is valid, then a JE–SE reversal can be turned "on" or "off" by varying the relative evaluability of the attributes.

In all of the studies discussed thus far, whether an attribute was hard or easy to evaluate independently was assumed and not manipulated empirically. In the study described below, the evaluability of an attribute was manipulated empirically. This manipulation was designed to test whether a JE–SE reversal can indeed be turned on or off as the evaluability hypothesis predicts. The study included two evaluability conditions: Hard–Easy and Easy–Easy. In the Hard–Easy condition, one of the attributes in the stimulus objects was easy to evaluate independently and the other hard to evaluate independently. In the Easy–Easy condition, both attributes were easy to evaluate independently. It was predicted that a JE–SE reversal would be more likely to exist in the Hard–Easy condition than in the Easy–Easy condition.

Method. This study involved the evaluations of two CD changers (i.e., multiple compact disc players) as follows:

	CD Changer A	**CD Changer B**
Brand:	JVC	JVC
CD capacity:	can hold 20 CDs	can hold 5 CDs
Sound quality:	THD = .01%	THD = .003%
Warranty:	1 year	1 year

The two CD changers varied on two attributes: CD-capacity and sound quality; the latter was indexed by THD. It was explained to participants in all conditions that THD stands for total harmonic distortion and that the smaller the THD, the better the sound quality. For ease of discussion, let us summarize the differences between the two CD changers as follows:

	CD Changer A	**CD Changer B**
THD:	.01%	.003%
CD capacity:	20 CDs	5 CDs

Respondents (202 students from the University of Illinois at Chicago) were assigned to one of six conditions. These six conditions constituted a 3 (evaluation mode: JE, SE–A and SE–B) × 2 (evaluability: Hard–Easy versus Easy–Easy) factorial design. In all conditions, participants were asked to assume that they were shopping for a CD changer in a department store and that the price of a CD changer would range from $150 to $300. In the joint-evaluation condition participants indicated their WTP for both CD changers; in each separate-evaluation condition, for only one of the CD changers.[7]

In the Hard–Easy condition, participants received no other information about either THD or CD-capacity than described previously. In this condition, THD was a hard-to-evaluate attribute, and CD-capacity was a relatively easy-to-evaluate attribute. Most people, although they know that less distortion is better, would not know whether a given THD rating (e.g., .01%) was good or bad, but they would have some idea of how many CDs a CD changer could hold and whether a CD changer that can hold 5 CDs (or 20 CDs) was desirable or not.

In the Easy–Easy condition, participants were provided with information about the effective range of the THD attribute. They were told, "For most CD changers on the market, THD ratings range from .002% (best) to .012% (worst)." This information was designed to make THD easier to evaluate independently. With this information, participants in the SE conditions would have some idea where the given THD rating fell in the range and hence whether the rating was good or bad.

To ensure that the evaluability manipulation was effective, participants in the two SE conditions were asked the following questions after they had indicated

---

[7] In the JE condition of this study, participants were first asked whether they were willing to pay more for A or for B and then indicated how much they were willing to pay for each. Four participants were excluded because they said that they were willing to pay more for one model but gave a higher WTP price for the other.

their WTP values: "Do you have any idea how good a THD rating of .003% (.01%) is?" and "Do you have any idea how large a CD capacity of 5 (20) CDs is?" (The numbers preceding the parentheses were for the SE–A condition, and those in the parentheses were for the SE–B condition.) As in the programmer study, answers to those questions ranged from 1 to 4, and higher numbers indicated greater evaluability.

Results and Discussion. First, the evaluability scores for the two attributes indicate that the evaluability manipulation was successful. Specifically, mean evaluability scores for THD and CD-capacity in the Hard–Easy condition were 1.98 and 3.25, respectively, and in the Easy–Easy condition were 2.53 and 3.22. A 2 (Attribute: THD versus CD-capacity) × 2 (Evaluability: Hard–Easy versus Easy–Easy) analysis of variance revealed a significant interaction effect ($F(1,135) = 9.40$, $p < .01$), indicating that the difference in evaluability between THD and CD-capacity decreased significantly from the Hard–Easy condition to the Easy–Easy condition. Planned comparisons found that evaluability scores for THD were significantly higher in the Easy–Easy condition than in the Hard–Easy condition ($t = 2.92$, $p < .01$), whereas those for CD-capacity stayed virtually the same.

Let us now turn to the main dependent variable: willingness-to-pay for the two CD changers. If the evaluability hypothesis is correct, then a JE–SE reversal was likely to exist in the Easy–Hard condition but not in the Easy–Easy condition. The results, summarized in Table 31.3, confirmed this prediction.

In the Hard–Easy condition, there was an unequivocal JE–SE reversal, and its direction was consistent with the evaluability hypothesis, implying that the hard-to-evaluate attribute (THD) lost its impact from JE to SE and the easy-to-evaluate attribute (CD capacity) gained its impact. Specifically, in JE WTP values were higher for CD Changer B than for CD Changer A ($t = 1.96$, $p < 0.1$), but in SE WTP values were higher for CD Changer A than for CD Changer B ($t = 2.70$, $p < .01$). In the Easy–Easy condition, the reversal disappeared. The WTP values were higher for CD Changer B in both JE ($t = 2.81$, $p < .01$) and SE ($t = 2.92$, $p < .01$).

That manipulating attribute evaluability could affect the existence of a JE–SE reversal lends further support to the evaluability hypothesis. It suggests that what drives this type of reversal is differential evaluability between the attributes.

Table 31.3. **Mean WTP Values for the Two CD Changers**

Evaluability	Evaluation Mode	CD Changer A	CD Changer B
Hard–Easy	Joint	$204	$228
	Separate	$256	$212
Easy–Easy	Joint	$186	$222
	Separate	$177	$222

3. Remarks

Arguably, all decisions and judgments are made either in JE or in SE or some combination of the two. The present work shows that people's responses to the same set of objects can vary drastically between JE and SE. Compared with responses in JE, responses in SE are influenced more by easy-to-evaluate attributes and less by hard-to-evaluate attributes.

Several qualifications are in order here. First, in each of the studies presented above, the dependent variable in both the JE and the SE conditions was willingness to pay. The reason to utilize such a uniform dependent variable is to demonstrate that JE–SE reversals can occur even if the evaluation scale is held constant. In reality, however, JE and SE often involve different evaluation scales. In particular, JE and SE are often naturally confounded with choice and judgment. A choice task inevitably involves JE, requiring the respondent to compare the alternative options simultaneously. On the other hand, a judgment task often entails SE or some combination of JE and SE, allowing the respondent to evaluate one object at a time. As a result, preference reversals in reality often exist between "joint choice" and "separate judgment," and these reversals can potentially be accounted for by both evaluability, and compatibility.

Second, whether an attribute is easy or difficult to evaluate is not an intrinsic characteristic of the attribute; it depends on how much knowledge decision makers have about the attribute and about its context. For example, total harmonic distortion (THD) is a hard-to-evaluate attribute for most people but would be an easy-to-evaluate attribute for an audiophile (see Coupey, Irwin, and Payne 1998 for a related argument). In addition, a given attribute can be difficult to evaluate within a certain range but easier to evaluate in another range. For example, most people would not have a good idea how desirable a music dictionary is if it has 10,000 entries but would find a music dictionary with only 50 entries clearly undesirable.

Besides the evaluability hypothesis, there are other possible explanations for JE–SE reversals. For example, in almost all of the studies demonstrating a JE–SE reversal, one can argue that the hard-to-evaluate attribute is always "more important" than the other attribute. For example, in the dictionary study, the hard-to-evaluate attribute is number of entries, and arguably it is also the more important attribute. Likewise, in the Hard–Easy condition of the CD changer study, the hard-to-evaluate attribute is sound quality (THD), and arguably it is also the more important attribute. Hence, it is tempting to speculate that it is differential attribute importance, rather than differential attribute evaluability, that drives the JE–SE reversal. However, this speculation is inconsistent with the finding of the CD changer study. In that study, increasing the evaluability of THD was able to eliminate the JE–SE reversal. This manipulation should not have affected the importance of THD. If anything, this manipulation may have only increased the importance of THD and, therefore, should have accentuated, rather than attenuated, the reversal. (One may wonder why in most studies the hard-to-evaluate attribute is also the more important attribute. This is a design feature required to induce a JE–SE reversal effect. In order to have room for a reversal, it is necessary that the hard-to-evaluate attribute be sufficiently important so that the option superior on this attribute will be favored in JE.)

Bazerman and his colleagues (1998) proposed that attributes that people *want* to consider loom large in SE and attributes that people think they *should* consider loom large in JE. Although this proposition is a possible alternative explanation for some of the JE–SE reversals (e.g., those involving trade-offs between payoffs to oneself and fairness), it does not readily apply to many other JE–SE reversals (e.g., Lowenthal's political candidate study and the CD-changer study) in which it is unclear which attribute is the "should" attribute and which is the "want" attribute. Interested in consumer behavior, Nowlis and Simonson (1997) proposed that what they call "comparative" attributes would receive more weight in purchase choices and what they call "enriched" attributes would receive more weight in purchase intention ratings, and they found evidence consistent with their proposition. However, in the studies discussed in this article, it is difficult to know a priori which attributes are comparative and which are enriched. Furthermore, purchase choice and intention ratings differ not just in evaluation mode, but also in evaluation scale.

Although the evaluability hypothesis is not the only explanation for JE–SE reversals, it is probably the most parsimonious and most consistent explanation for a wide range of JE–SE reversals.

Finally, there are also other types of JE–SE reversals than those reviewed above. For example, Irwin et al. (1993) found that in JE people were willing to pay more for improving the air quality in Denver than for improving a consumer product such as a VCR, but that in SE WTP values were higher for improving the consumer product. Kahneman and Ritov (1994) found that in JE people were willing to contribute more to programs that would save human lives (e.g., farmers with skin cancers) than to programs that would save endangered animals (e.g., dolphins), but that in SE the rank order of the two issues was reversed. Unlike the kinds of stimuli examined in the present article, the options compared in Irwin et al.'s and Kahneman and Ritov's studies were of different categories (e.g., air quality versus consumer products) and shared no common attributes. Explanations for these results require a combination of Norm Theory (Kahneman and Miller 1986) and the evaluability hypothesis and are beyond the scope of this article (see Hsee et al. 1999 for details).

V. IMPLICATIONS OF THE EVALUABILITY HYPOTHESIS BEYOND JE–SE REVERSALS

Although the evaluability hypothesis was proposed to account for JE–SE reversals, it has implications for a much broader range of issues. In this section, I discuss the following issues:

1. Why an objectively inferior option may be favored to an objectively superior option in SE,
2. Why people are often more sensitive to the proportion attribute of an object than to its actual outcome value,
3. Why people's belief about the relative importance of attributes sometimes differs from the actual influence of the attributes, and
4. Why the option people choose during the decision phase does not always yield the best experience during the consumption phase.

Let me mention here that these issues may be open to multiple explanations. My intention is not to rule out other explanations but to provide a new perspective based on the evaluability notion.

1. Less Is Better

The evaluability hypothesis suggests that when objects are evaluated in the SE mode, the rank order of these objects is determined primarily by attributes that are easy to evaluate independently, even if these attributes are not the normatively most important attributes. In the extreme case, it is possible that an objectively inferior object may be judged more favorably than an objectively superior alternative under the SE mode.

This possibility was explored in a series of studies reported in Hsee (1998). One study, for example, involved the evaluation of two hypothetical dinnerware sets in a store having a clearance sale. Set A included 24 pieces: 8 dinner plates, 8 soup bowls, and 8 dessert plates. All of the pieces were in good condition. Set B comprised 40 pieces: 8 dinner plates, 8 soup bowls, 8 dessert plates, 8 cups, and 8 saucers. All of the plates, soup bowls, and dessert plates were in good condition, but two of the cups and seven of the saucers were broken. Note that Set B contained the same 24 intact pieces as Set A, plus it also contained two intact cups and one intact saucer that were not available in Set A. Therefore, Set B should be of a greater value than Set A. However, when these two sets of dinnerware were evaluated separately, people were willing to pay significantly more for Set A, demonstrating a less-is-better effect. The valuations were reversed when the two sets of dinnerware were presented jointly.

The less-is-better effect revealed in the SE condition of the dinnerware study can be readily explained by the evaluability hypothesis. The two sets of dinnerware can be considered as varying on the following attributes:

	Dinnerware A	Dinnerware B
No. of usable pieces	24	31
Integrity of the set	complete	incomplete

In SE, it was easy to know that a complete set was good and a defective set was bad. However, for most respondents (college students), it was more difficult to determine the desirability of a set with 24 (or 31) usable pieces. Thus, the difference in valuation between the dinnerware sets in SE was determined mainly by the integrity attribute.[8]

Another study reported in Hsee (1998) involved the evaluation of two hypothetical servings of Häagen-Dazs ice cream. Serving A had 7 ounces of ice cream, and it was contained in a 5-ounce cup. Serving B had 8 ounces of ice cream, and it was contained in a 10-ounce cup. Thus, Serving A was overfilled and Serving B was underfilled. These servings were illustrated graphically as follows:

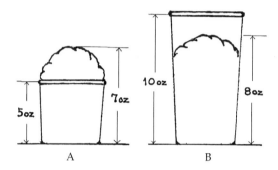

The differences between the two servings can be summarized as follows:

	Serving A	Serving B
Size of cup:	5 oz	10 oz
Amount of ice cream:	7 oz	8 oz
Filling:	overfilled	underfilled

Objectively, Serving B was more valuable because it contained more ice cream (and included a bigger cup!). However, when the two servings were evaluated separately, people were willing to pay significantly more for Serving A. The effect was reversed when the two servings were evaluated jointly.

A similar explanation to the dinnerware study applies here. Even though the amount of ice cream is what people should consider when evaluating how much they would pay for a serving, this attribute was difficult to evaluate independently. Without something to compare it with, most people would not know whether a serving with 7 ounces (or 8 ounces) of ice was desirable or not. In contrast, the filling attribute was easy to evaluate independently: People would

---

[8] In the dinnerware study, respondents may have inferred the quality of a dinnerware set based on whether it contained any broken pieces. For example, those evaluating Set B may have inferred that it must be a low-quality set because some pieces in that set were broken. Although this possibility can only explain why WTP for Set B was lower in SE, it does not explain the JE–SE reversal. If respondents had indeed made such inferences, they should have done so in both joint evaluation and separate evaluation. It should also be noted that in most of the studies demonstrating a JE–SE reversal, the attributes are entirely independent, that is, there is no reason for one to infer the desirability of one attribute from that of the other attribute. For example, in the dictionary study, whether a dictionary had a torn cover or not had nothing to do with how comprehensive the dictionary was.

consider an overfilled cup appealing and an underfilled cup unappealing. Thus, the filling attribute became the primary determinant of willingness-to-pay in SE.

2. Proportion and Base Number

Oftentimes, we need to evaluate outcome values that are expressed as proportions of some base numbers. For example, how good is an environmental protection program that can save 20% of 10,000 endangered wild birds in a certain forest? According to the evaluability hypothesis, in SE of such problems, we are often sensitive to the proportion attribute and insensitive to the base number attribute or to the actual outcome value attribute. The following example is inspired by the recent finding of Fetherstonhaugh et al. (1997) that programs expected to save a given number of lives received greater support if the number of lives at risk was smaller (see also Baron 1997 and Jenni and Loewenstein 1997). The example to be discussed below is about two environmental protection programs, each of which could save a certain number of wild birds in a given forest. In particular,

	Program A	Program B
Size of the forest:	has 5,000 birds	has 25,000 birds
Number of birds the program can save:	4,000	5,000
Percentage of birds in the forest the program can save:	80%	20%

Here, the size of the forest is a base number, number of birds the program can save is the actual outcome value, and the outcome value is a proportion of the base number. According to the evaluability hypothesis, when the two programs are evaluated separately, Program A will be favored. The reason for this prediction is simple: The proportion attribute is relatively easy to evaluate independently. It has a natural lower bound (0%) and a natural upper bound (100%), and people would know that 80% is a reasonably high number and 20% a low number. In contrast, both the base number and the outcome value are difficult to evaluate independently because most people would not know the range, distribution, or other reference information of these attributes. As a result, people's responses in SE are often dominated by the proportion attribute. The evaluability hypothesis also predicts that if either the base number or the outcome value is made easier to evaluate independently (e.g., by giving people more reference information), the relative impact of the proportion attribute will diminish (see Wright 1997 for other factors that can influence the relative impact of proportions and absolute differences).

The previous analysis can also explain why speakers are usually happier with the number of people who attend their talk if they are assigned a small room (say with 50 seats) and a high proportion of the seats (say 80%) are occupied than if they are assigned a larger room (say with 250 seats) and only a small proportion (say 20%) of the seats are occupied even though the talk is better attended in the latter scenario. The logic of this example is identical to that of the bird example.

A closer look suggests that the structure of the preceding examples is also parallel to the structure of the ice cream study discussed earlier. The size of the forest or the size of the room is like the size of the cup in the ice cream study. The number of birds the program can save or the size of the audience is like the amount of ice cream in a serving; these are the actual outcome values. The proportion attribute is like the filling attribute in the ice cream study and reflects the relationship between the base number and the outcome variable. In all of these cases, the option with the inferior outcome value is favored in SE.

3. Believed Importance versus Actual Influence[9]

When evaluating an object involving multiple attributes, we may ask ourselves about the relative importance of the attributes. For example, when evaluating a candidate, we may wonder whether his or her appearance or experience is more important. Presumably, our belief about the relative importance of the attributes should be consistent with how much influence these attributes actually have on our evaluation. However, this may not always be the case. Sometimes, we may believe that a certain attribute is more important than another (e.g., experience is more important than appearance), but the attribute believed to be more important may be hard to evaluate and therefore have little influence on our evaluation, especially when the evaluation is made in SE.

The preceding intuition was tested in a preliminary study involving the evaluation of a hypothetical job candidate for a programmer position. The study included 4 conditions, among which the candidate varied on 2 attributes: (1) experience (the candidate had written either 110 programs or 220 programs), and (2) appearance (he was either unkempt and messy or well-groomed and nicely dressed). These 2×2 conditions were presented between subjects so that the evaluation mode was always SE. Note that here, experience was more difficult to evaluate independently than appearance.

Respondents were asked three questions. The first asked what salary they would be willing to pay should the candidate be hired. The second and third questions assessed their belief about the relative influence of the attributes. The second question asked whether their salary decision in the first question was influenced more by the candidate's experience or by his appearance. The third question provided range information about the attributes and asked which of the following would make a greater difference in their salary decisions: (a) whether the candidate had written 110 or 220 programs, or (b) whether the candidate was unkempt and messy or well-groomed and nicely dressed. The reason to include both the second and the third questions was to ensure

---

[9] The idea presented in this section was inspired by discussions with Paul Slovic. The appearance–experience experiment described later is an unpublished study we designed to test the idea.

reliability. Previous research suggests that judgment of relative importance may change, depending on whether range information is given (e.g., Goldstein 1990, Goldstein and Mitzel 1992).

The results revealed a sharp inconsistency between actual influence and beliefs. In the actual WTP decisions, experience had virtually no effect, and appearance had a significant effect. People were willing to pay approximately $1,800 more for the well-groomed and nicely dressed candidate than for the messy and unkempt one. However, when asked which attribute had a greater influence on their WTP, 85% of the respondents said it was experience. Even when the ranges of the attributes were given (the last question), still the majority (84%) believed that experience would make a greater difference than appearance. These beliefs were grossly inconsistent with the actual influence of the attributes.

This study suggests that what people believe to be important for an evaluation may be at odds with what actually affects the evaluation. This inconsistency is most likely to occur if the evaluation task is made in SE and the attributes believed to be important are difficult to evaluate independently. In situations like this, the presumably important attributes will have little or no impact on the actual evaluation.[10]

4. Inconsistencies between Decision and Its Consequence

The most speculative, but also potentially the most important, implication of the present research has to do with discrepancies between people's decisions and their subsequent experience with the consequences (Kahneman and Snell 1990, 1992). Ideally, when making a decision, people ought to choose the option they will like when they use it or "consume" it later. In reality, people often fail to do so. For example, when making a decision about which piano to purchase, people may choose one model over another model, but after they purchase the piano and move it home, they may not like it. There are many possible reasons for such decision–consumption inconsistencies, and there is ample research on this topic. For example, people may not have as much information about the options at the decision phase as at the consumption phase, people may be at different arousal states (hot versus cold) during the two phases (Loewenstein 1996), or people's taste may change over time (e.g., Kahneman and Snell 1992, March 1978), to name just a few.

However, there is an important but largely neglected contributor to decision–consumption inconsistency: evaluation mode. More often than not, a decision is made in the joint evaluation mode, and the consequence of a decision is experienced or consumed in the SE mode. For example, when a person buys

---

[10] Another common reason why believed importance may differ from actual influence is that the attribute believed to be important has no variance in its values and therefore has no effect. In the study described above, however, the reason why experience had no effect was not that it had no variance in its values but that the variance in its values (i.e., 110 programs versus 220 programs) failed to generate a corresponding variance in the *evaluations* of these values because the attribute was difficult to evaluate independently.

a piano in a musical instrument store, there are typically myriad models for her to compare and choose from (JE). However, after she buys a piano and when she "consumes" it at home, that is, plays it, looks at etc., she is exposed mostly to that particular piano alone (SE). (Of course, she may also occasionally think about the forgone alternative during the consumption phase, but usually the evaluation mode in the consumption phase, though not purely SE, is much closer to SE than the evaluation mode in the decision phase.) Likewise, when we decide which candidate to vote for during a presidential election, we are in the JE mode, comparing one candidate with another. Once a candidate becomes the president and starts his or her term, we find ourselves mostly in the SE mode, facing that particular president alone. Shafir (in press) argues that the distinction between joint and separate evaluation has even wider implications. He proposes that guidelines and policies are borne out of joint evaluation of alternative scenarios, but events in the real world, to which these guidelines and policies are supposed to apply, usually present themselves one at a time.

To the extent that decisions are made in JE and consumption takes place in SE, reversals between JE and SE will manifest themselves between decision and consumption. Generally speaking, hard-to-evaluate attributes loom larger in decision making, and easy-to-evaluate attributes loom larger in consumption experience.

The analysis presented above implies that decision makers may overpredict the impact of hard-to-evaluate attributes on their consumption experience. As discussed earlier, hard-to-evaluate attributes have little discriminatory power in separate evaluation and hence make little differences to one's consumption experience in separate evaluation. However, people may not realize this when they make decisions in joint evaluation and may place too much weight on these attributes. The following story illustrates this point.

Years ago, somebody (call him Mr. S) shopping for a pair of speakers in an audio store was ushered by a salesperson to a soundproof listening room in which one could easily compare different models of speakers. After a few minutes, Mr. S narrowed his choices to two models. They had the same price, but one looked attractive and the other ugly. He then played his favorite CD on the two models, and, after careful comparisons, found the ugly-looking model sounded slightly better. Thinking that sound is important for speakers, he made the decision to buy the better-sounding model. After he took the speakers home, he was happy with them in a honeymoon sort of mood for only a few days and then became increasingly annoyed by their appearance. Before long, he relegated these speakers to the basement and has never bothered to listen to them again. Although there is no way to find out if it is true, my speculation is that he would have been happier if he had bought the other model. Chances are that, unless through direct comparisons, as in the listening room, he could not even tell the difference in sound quality between the two models. However, the model he did not buy apparently looked attractive and would have made him happier.

For most consumers, the sound quality of a speaker, at least within a certain range, is hard to evaluate independently, and the difference in sound quality between two models of speakers can only be appreciated in JE, not in SE. In contrast, the look of a speaker is much easier to evaluate independently. The moral of this story is: When making decisions, people put too much weight on hard-to-evaluate attributes and are too obsessed with differences between options that will make little difference in SE and hence little difference in consumption experience.

VI. CONCLUSION

When two objects involving a trade-off between a hard-to-evaluate attribute and an easy-to-evaluate attribute are evaluated, the evaluations of these objects may change dramatically, depending on whether the evaluations are elicited in JE or in SE. A natural question to ask here is, which evaluation mode is better, JE or SE? The answer depends on the purpose of the evaluation. If the purpose is to be consistent with the objective quality of the target objects, then JE is better. As previous examples illustrate, SE may lead to a higher valuation of an objectively inferior option. That is probably why decision experts (e.g., Janis and Mann 1977) usually advise people to compare alternatives and engage in JE when making decisions.

However, even in decision making, JE is not always better than SE. If the decision maker's purpose is to choose the option he or she will enjoy later, then SE may be better. In Mr. S's story, for instance, if his purpose was to buy the speakers that he would like after bringing them home, then he should have engaged in SE when deciding which model to purchase. In reality, however, it is impossible to engage in pure SE when faced with multiple options, but it is possible to achieve something close to SE. For instance, what Mr. S should have done was not to compare the alternatives side by side. Instead, he should have studied the two models on two separate days, focused on one model each day, imagined how he would like it at home, and written down his overall impression. He should then have bought the model with the better overall impression score.

It is clear from the current research that responses made in JE can be dramatically different from those made in SE and that the differences are predictable. But it is not clear whether JE or SE is better. In the last sections of this article, I provided evidence showing that SE can lead to preferences for objectively inferior options. At the same time, I also presented examples and speculations showing that decisions made in SE may lead to better future consumption experience. The reader is the ultimate judge about which evaluation mode is better.

32. Preferences for Sequences of Outcomes

George F. Loewenstein and Dražen Prelec

ABSTRACT. Existing models of intertemporal choice normally assume that people are impatient, preferring valuable outcomes sooner rather than later, and that preferences satisfy the formal condition of independence, or separability, which states that the value of a sequence of outcomes equals the sum of the values of its component parts. The authors present empirical results that show both of these assumptions to be false when choices are framed as being between explicitly defined sequences of outcomes. Without a proper sequential context, people may discount isolated outcomes in the conventional manner, but when the sequence context is highlighted, they claim to prefer utility levels that improve over time. The observed violations of additive separability follow, at least in part, from a desire to spread good outcomes evenly over time.

Decisions of importance have delayed consequences. The choice of education, work, spending and saving, exercise, diet, as well as the timing of life events, such as schooling, marriage, and childbearing, all produce costs and benefits that endure over time. Therefore, it is not surprising that the problem of choosing between temporally distributed outcomes has attracted attention in a variety of disciplinary settings, including behavioral psychology, social psychology, decision theory, and economics.

In spite of this disciplinary diversity, empirical research on intertemporal choice has traditionally had a narrow focus. Until a few years ago, virtually all studies of intertemporal choice were concerned with how people evaluate simple prospects consisting of a single outcome obtained at a point in time. The goal was to estimate equations that express the basic relationship between the atemporal value of an outcome and its value when delayed. Although the estimated functional forms would differ from investigation to investigation, there was general agreement on one point: that delayed outcomes are valued less. In economics, this is referred to as "positive time discounting."

This chapter is an abridged version of an article that first appeared in *Psychological Review*, 100:1, 91–108.

Although plausible at first glance, the uniform imposition of positive discounting on all of one's choices has some disturbing and counterintuitive implications. It implies, for instance, that when faced with a decision about how to schedule a set of outcomes, a person should invariably start with the best outcome, followed by the second best outcome, and so on until the worst outcome is reached at the end. Because nothing restricts the generality of this principle, one should find people preferring a declining rather than an increasing standard of living, deteriorating rather than improving health (again, holding lifetime health constant), and so on.

In the last few years, several studies have independently focused on this problem and have shown that with choices of this type, people typically exhibit *negative* time preference (i.e., they prefer an improving series of events, with all other things being equal). In this article we present results that confirm the preference for improvement but qualify it in several respects. First, we found that preference for improvement depends on whether a particular choice is viewed by the decision maker as being embedded in a sequence of outcomes. In other words, when the decision frame draws attention to the sequential nature of choice, negative time discounting typically prevails; however, when the frame draws attention to individual components of the choice, positive time preference predominates.

Second, we examined the validity of a common assumption in theoretical treatments of intertemporal choice: that preferences for outcome sequences are based on a simple aggregation of preferences for their individual components. Separable formulations, such as the discounted utility model, predict that the overall value (i.e., utility) of a sequence is equal to the summed values of its component outcomes. The findings we present challenge this prediction. In general, an individual's valuation of complex sequences cannot be extrapolated in a simple way from his or her valuation of components but responds instead to certain "gestalt" properties of the sequence.

Third, we developed and tested empirically a theoretical model of choice over outcome sequences. The model incorporates two motives that are not part of standard discounted utility formulations: a preference for improvement and a desire to spread consumption evenly over time.

In the next section, we present a series of examples of preference patterns that illustrate preference for improvement and preference for spreading good outcomes evenly over time. We then develop a theoretical model of sequential choice that incorporates these two motives. Finally, we present two studies that were designed to test the model parametrically.

BASIC MOTIVES UNDERLYING CHOICES BETWEEN SEQUENCES

A temporal sequence is a series of outcomes spaced over time. The outcomes could be specific events, such as one's activities over consecutive weekends, or they could be more abstract economic indexes (e.g., income levels over consecutive years). With a few notable exceptions (Bell, 1977; Epstein & Hynes, 1983; Gilboa, 1989; Horowitz, 1988; Meyer, 1976, 1977), most theoretical treatments of intertemporal choice have been conducted within the framework of the general discounting model, which represents the value of a sequence $X = (x_1, \ldots, x_n)$ by the weighted utility formula (Koopmans, 1960; Koopmans, Diamond, & Williamson, 1964; Samuelson, 1937):

$$V(X) = \sum_t w_t u(x_t). \tag{1}$$

The formula implies that whenever two sequences differ in only two periods, then preference between them does not depend on the common outcomes in the remaining $n = 2$ periods (separability). Economic applications normally make two additional assumptions:

1. *Impatience.* The coefficients, w_1, w_2, and so forth, are declining, which indicates that earlier periods have greater weight in determining preferences.
2. *Constant discounting.* The marginal rate of utility substitution between any two adjacent periods is the same, $w_{t+1}/w_t = \delta$. This produces the compound discounting formula,

$$V(X) = \sum_t \delta^t u(x_t).$$

In the remainder of this section, we describe simple choice patterns that are inconsistent with these properties.

Preference for Improvement and the Sequence "Frame"

A number of recent studies have shown that people typically favor sequences that improve over time. Loewenstein and Sicherman (1991) found that a majority of subjects preferred an increasing wage profile to a declining or flat one for an otherwise identical job. Varey and Kahneman (in press) studied preferences over short-term streams of discomfort, lasting from 2 to 20 min, and found that subjects strongly preferred streams of decreasing discomfort even when the overall sum of discomfort over the interval was otherwise identical. A preference for experiences that end well has also been documented by Ross and Simonson (1991). In one study, they presented subjects with a series of hypothetical choices between sequences that ended with a loss (e.g., win $85, then lose $15) or a gain (lose $15, then win $85). Subjects overwhelmingly preferred sequences that ended with a gain.

The preference for improvement appears to depend not only on the amount of improvement but the speed with which it occurs over time – its "velocity" – as Hsee and Abelson (1991) called it (see also Hsee, Abelson, & Salovey, 1991). Subjects in one of their studies played a game in which their probability of winning either decreased or increased over time at one of three rates of change. Those in conditions with increasing probabilities of winning rated the game as more satisfying than those in conditions with decreasing probabilities, and the effect of direction (increase vs. decrease) was amplified by the velocity of the change.

Preference for improvement appears to be an overdetermined phenomenon, driven in part by savoring and dread (Loewenstein, 1987), adaptation and loss aversion (Kahneman & Tversky, 1979), and recency effects (Miller & Campbell, 1959). Savoring and dread contribute to preference for improvement because, for gains, improving sequences allow decision makers to savor the best outcome until the end of the sequence. With losses, getting undesirable outcomes over with quickly eliminates dread. Although there is evidence that people sometimes like to defer desirable outcomes (Loewenstein, 1987), getting undesirable outcomes over with quickly appears to be more widespread. A number of studies have shown that people prefer immediate rather than delayed electric shocks (Barnes & Barnes, 1964; Carlsmith, 1962). A similar result has been reported by Carson, Horowitz, and Machina (1987) in the context of cigarette smoking. They found that nonsmokers, when asked how much they would need to be paid immediately to smoke a pack of cigarettes either immediately or in 1, 5, or 10 years, specified amounts that increased as a function of time delay.

Adaptation and loss aversion lead to a preference for improving sequences because people tend to adapt to ongoing stimuli over time and to evaluate new stimuli relative to their adaptation level (Helson, 1964). Loss aversion (Kahneman & Tversky, 1979) refers to the observation that people are more sensitive to a loss than to a gain of equal absolute magnitude. It is illustrated by the fact that few people will voluntarily accept a bet that provides an equal chance of winning or losing any given amount. If people adapt to the most recent level of stimuli they experience, then improving sequences will afford a continual series of positive departures (gains) from their adaptation level, whereas declining sequences provide a series of relative losses. Loss aversion implies that the latter will be especially unattractive relative to the former.

The specific psychological mechanisms underlying the adaptation and loss–aversion explanation are somewhat ambiguous. It may be that when faced with a sequence (e.g., a series of increasing or decreasing salary levels), people imagine themselves experiencing the sequence, adapting to the standard of living that each salary level implies, and reacting to negative or positive deviations from such standards. They would then recognize that upward adjustments from one's standard of living are more pleasurable than downward adjustments, leading them to prefer the increasing sequences. Alternatively, adaptation and loss aversion may not involve any explicit anticipation of future experience but may instead be a simple application of perceptual loss aversion. Just as people treat risky outcomes as gains and losses instead of absolute wealth levels, it is possible that they evaluate sequences as series of upward and downward shifts rather than as a series of levels. Loss aversion would then imply that downward shifts receive disproportionate weight. The important difference between these two accounts is that in the former case, the evaluation reflects a type of hedonic forecasting, whereas in the latter case, the preference is instead perceptually driven (i.e., based on the tendency to interpret sequences as gains and losses regardless of how they are actually experienced when they unfold).

The adaptation and loss aversion explanation is closely related to the concept of a "contrast effect" (Elster, 1985; Elster & Loewenstein, in press; Tversky & Griffin, 1991). Contrast effects refer to the effect on one's evaluation of the present of comparing the present with the past or future. If backward-looking contrast effects are more potent than forward-looking ones, as seems plausible (Prelec & Loewenstein, 1991), then the net impact of contrast effects will be to augment the preference for improvement over time. This is because inferior early experiences will create a favorable contrast that will enhance the utility of later experiences.

A final psychological mechanism that may contribute to the preference for improvement is the recency effect, which has been observed in recall, attitude formation, and belief updating (Miller & Campbell, 1959). As Ross and Simonson (1991) noted, the final outcome in a sequence is likely to be the most salient to the decision maker after the conclusion of the sequence. If decision makers naturally adopt a retrospective perspective when evaluating outcome streams, as Varey and Kahneman (in press) argued, then recency effects will cause late periods to be overweighted relative to those that occur in the middle of the sequence. Likewise, "primacy effects" would promote an overweighting of early periods.

Savoring and dread apply to single-outcome prospects as well as to outcome sequences. For this reason, they can explain why people who otherwise discount the future sometimes defer pleasurable outcomes and get unpleasant outcomes over with quickly. Neither adaptation and loss aversion, nor recency effects, on the other hand, have obvious implications for single-outcome events. Therefore, these latter effects probably do not play a major role in timing preferences for such simple prospects. Adaptation and loss aversion are, however, present as potential factors in outcome sequences. The fact that only one motive for improvement operates for simple outcomes and two operate for sequences suggests that preference for improvement will be stronger in the latter case. Our first example illustrates the preference for improvement and shows that it depends, in part, on whether a particular choice is perceived as being between individual outcomes or sequences.

Ninety-five Harvard University undergraduates were asked the following three questions and were instructed to ignore their own personal scheduling considerations (e.g., preexisting plans) in responding.

Example 1

1. *Which would you prefer if both were free?* $n = 95$
   A. Dinner at a fancy French restaurant   86%
   B. Dinner at a local Greek restaurant   14%

For those who prefer French:

2. *Which would you prefer?* $n = 82$
   C. Dinner at the French restaurant on Friday in 1 month   80%
   D. Dinner at the French restaurant on Friday in 2 months   20%

3. *Which would you prefer?* $n = 82$
    E. Dinner at the French restaurant on Friday in
       1 month and dinner at the Greek restaurant
       on Friday in 2 months   43%
    F. Dinner at the Greek restaurant on Friday in 1 month and
       dinner at the French restaurant on Friday in 2 months   57%

Because two of the three motives hypothesized to motivate the preference for improvement operate only for sequences of outcomes, we anticipated that a larger fraction of respondents would prefer to put the fancy French dinner off into the future when it was combined in a sequence with the Greek dinner than when it was expressed as a single-outcome prospect. This was indeed the pattern that we observed. Of the 86% of subjects who preferred the fancy French dinner, 80% preferred a more immediate dinner (Option C) over a more delayed dinner (Option D). Thus, only 20% preferred to delay the French dinner when it was expressed as a single, isolated item. However, when the French dinner was put into a sequence with the Greek dinner, giving subjects the option of having Greek and then French, or French and then Greek, the majority (57%) preferred to defer the French dinner. Even with single-outcome events, there was some motivation to defer the French dinner: Witness the 20% of subjects who opted for the longer delay. However, this tendency was clearly stronger for sequences than for individual items.

We observed the same pattern when we substituted "dinner at home" for the Greek dinner. Because most people eat dinner at home on most nights anyway, the mere embedding of the French dinner in an explicit binary sequence does not introduce any real modification of the problem relative to the single-outcome frame in Question 2. The only thing that happens is that the subject is reminded that the choice is "really" between complete sequences. Like other framing effects, such reminders cause preferences to shift, in this case in favor of the improving sequence.

The pattern of preferences revealed by these choices is incompatible with any discounted utility model, as defined by Equation 1. A preference for a French dinner in 1 month rather than 2 suggests that $w_1 > w_2$; however, a preference for the improving sequence indicates that $w_1 u(\text{French}) + w_2 u(\text{Greek}) < w_1 u(\text{Greek}) + w_2 u(\text{French})$, or $w_2 > w_1$, on the assumption that $u(\text{French}) > u(\text{Greek})$, which is confirmed by Question 1.

Defining a Sequence

It appears, then, that two distinct motives are relevant to time preference: impatience and a preference for improvement. Which of these two motives dominates appears to depend on whether the objects of choice are single-outcome prospects or sequences. Impatience dominates choices between single outcomes; the preference for improvement most strongly influences choices between sequences.

In many cases, however, it is not clear whether a particular prospect is properly defined as a sequence. For example, when the attributes of outcomes composing a sequence are incommensurable, or when elements in the sequence are themselves brief but separated by long delays, it seems reasonable to evaluate the elements of the sequence independently of one another. However, when outcomes are commensurable and tightly spaced, the logic for treating them as a sequence will be more compelling. In general, the greater the "integrity" of a series of outcomes, the greater should be its likelihood of being evaluated as an integral sequence.

The following examples illustrate that it is possible to vary the integrity of a sequence so as to influence preferences in a predictable manner. The following three questions were asked of 48 visitors to the Museum of Science and Industry in Chicago. Proportions of subjects giving each response are designated in brackets.

Example 2. Imagine you must schedule two weekend outings to a city where you once lived. You do not plan on visiting the city after these two outings.

You must spend one of these weekends with an irritating, abrasive aunt who is a horrendous cook. The other weekend will be spent visiting former work associates whom you like a lot. From the following pairs, please indicate your preference by checking the appropriate line.

Suppose one outing will take place this coming weekend, the other the weekend after.

This weekend	Next weekend	
A. friends	abrasive aunt	[10%] (5/48)
B. abrasive aunt	friends	[90%] (43/48)

Suppose one outing will take place this coming weekend, the other in 6 months (26 weeks).

This weekend	26 weeks from now	
A. friends	abrasive aunt	[48%] (23/48)
B. abrasive aunt	friends	[52%] (25/48)

Suppose one outing will take place in 6 months (26 weeks from now), the other the weekend after (27 weeks from now).

26 weeks from now	27 weeks from now	
A. friends	abrasive aunt	[17%] (8/48)
B. abrasive aunt	friends	[83%] (40/48)

In the first question, the series of outcomes unfold over a fairly short period (2 weeks) so that we would expect discounting to be relatively weak and the preference for improving sequences to be strong. Here, 90% of subjects opted for the improving sequence. In the second set of options, the absolute interval is much longer (26 weeks), reducing the integrity of the sequence. Here, we would expect discounting to have a greater impact relative to the preference for improvement. Indeed, a much smaller fraction of subjects (52%) chose the improving sequence given the long absolute delay. In the third pair, the sequence interval was once again reduced to 1 week, so we would anticipate a greater preference for the increasing sequences than found in the second pair. However, intuitively, we expected that the long delay prior to the beginning of the sequence would reduce its integrity to some degree. This may explain the slight reduction, relative to the first set of alternatives, in the fraction of subjects opting to get the unpleasant visit over with quickly.

It is not possible to interpret the three modal choice patterns in terms of conventional time preference. The first and third question indicates a negative rate of time preference (i.e., $w_0 < w_1$ and $w_{26} < w_{27}$) in the context of a discounted utility model (see Equation 1). It is safe to generalize that the aunt would be scheduled in the earlier of any consecutive two weekends (i.e., $w_t < w_{t+1}$). Yet, the transitive conclusion does not follow because the middle question implies that $w_0 > w_{26}$. We call this pattern the "magnet effect" because preferences for the two outcomes resemble the behavior of magnets. When distant from one another, two magnets interact only weakly; however, when brought into close proximity, they exert a force on one another, which causes them to reverse position.

Preference for Spreading

In addition to the desire for improvement over time, preferences also indicate a sensitivity to certain global or "gestalt" properties of sequences having to do with how evenly the good and bad outcomes are arranged over the total time interval. Unlike the question of positive versus negative time preference, which by now has received some attention, there have been few efforts to examine how people like to distribute outcomes over time. Important exceptions are two recent studies examining whether people like to experience two positive, negative, or mixed (positive and negative) events on the same or on different days. Applications of prospect theory imply that people should like to spread gains out across different days and to concentrate losses in a single day, and, although the first of these predictions is generally supported, the evidence for the latter is far more tenuous. Thaler and Johnson (1990) found that people generally expected to be happier when two gains (e.g., winning $25 in an office lottery and winning $50 in another) were separated by an interval but also expected to be less unhappy when two losses were separated. Thaler and Johnson argued that prior losses may sensitize people to subsequent losses, contrary to the prediction of prospect theory. Linville and Fischer (1991) likewise failed to observe a concentration of losses, although the tendency to do so was greater for small losses than for large ones. They explained this shift in terms a model of "coping capacity," which postulates that people have a limited psychological capacity to absorb losses and that they may wish to separate losses in time in order to replenish their coping resources. Thus, for both gains and losses, there does appear to be a preference for spreading outcomes out over time.

Although these results are suggestive, their applicability to the types of sequences we were concerned with is limited. First, all of the choices in these studies involved only two outcomes. This made it possible to examine whether people like to concentrate or spread out outcomes but not whether they exhibit more complex patterns of preference (e.g., for certain types of patterns of outcomes over time). Second, the choices were all between experiencing outcomes at the same or different points in time. Such a design leaves unanswered, for those who prefer to separate outcomes, the question of how much of a gap is ideal.

The central insight that we took from this research was that, when presented with more than one same-valence outcome, people generally like to spread outcomes over time rather than concentrating them. The following problem presented to 37 Yale University undergraduates (from Loewenstein, 1987) illustrates this desire for spread. Subjects were first given a choice between Options A and B then between Options C and D; they were instructed to ignore scheduling considerations. Percentages who chose each of the options are presented in the righthand column.

Example 3. *Which would you prefer?*

Option	This weekend	Next weekend	Two weekends from now	Choices
A	Fancy French	Eat at home	Eat at home	16%
B	Eat at home	Fancy French	Eat at home	84%
C	Fancy French	Eat at home	Fancy lobster	54%
D	Eat at home	Fancy French	Fancy lobster	46%

Choosing between Options A and B, the majority of subjects preferred to postpone the fancy dinner until the second weekend, consistent with the widespread preference for improvement. However, the insertion of the common lobster dinner in Options C and D caused preference to shift slightly in favor of having the French dinner right away. This pattern violates additive separability (and any model given by Equation 1). Because the third period is identical for Options A and B and for C and D, separability implies that anyone who prefers A (B) should prefer C (D).

We believe that the relative attractiveness of Options B and C stemmed in part from the fact that they "covered" the 3-week interval better than did their alternatives. Option A exposed the decision maker to a 2-week period of eating at home, whereas Option B placed the one pleasurable event at the center of the interval. Option D concentrated all of the pleasure at one extreme of the 3-week period, whereas Option C distributed the fancy dinners more evenly over time.

It is worth noting that loss aversion as traditionally conceived would not predict this type of violation. Of the four sequences in the example, only Option D was strictly increasing. It appears, therefore, that a person who strongly dislikes utility reductions across adjacent periods will have a greater tendency to prefer Option D over C than Option B over A, which is the opposite of the observed pattern of choice.

Another possibility is that people have a net liking for changes in utility between adjacent periods, as permitted in Gilboa's (1989) model. In that case, Option B has more between-period variation than Option A, and Option C more variation than Option D, in accord with the modal preferences. To rule out this explanation, and to show that preferential interactions occur between nonadjacent periods, we modified the original example by inserting additional "eat at home" weekends between the original first two weekends and between the second and third weekends (see Example 4).

Example 4. Imagine that over the next five weekends you must decide how to spend your Saturday nights. From each pair of sequences of dinners below circle the one you would prefer. "Fancy French" refers to dinner at a fancy French restaurant. "Fancy lobster" refers to an exquisite lobster dinner at a four-star restaurant. Ignore scheduling considerations (e.g., your current plans).

Option	First weekend	Second weekend	Third weekend	Fourth weekend	Fifth weekend
A	Fancy French	Eat at home	Eat at home	Eat at home	Eat at home
B	Eat at home	Eat at home	Fancy French	Eat at home	Eat at home
C	Fancy French	Eat at home	Eat at home	Eat at home	Fancy lobster
D	Eat at home	Eat at home	Fancy French	Eat at home	Fancy lobster

In this example, it is not possible to produce an independence violation solely on the basis of adjacent periods. Suppose, for example, that the utility function for sequences has a special set of functions, f_t, that register the impact of adjacent utility levels on preferences:

$$V[(x_1, \ldots, x_n)] = \sum_{t=1}^{n} u_t(x_t) + \sum_{t=1}^{n-1} f_t(x_t, x_{t+1}).$$

In that case, the difference in value between Sequences A and B still equals the difference in value between Sequences C and D because

$$\begin{aligned} V(A) - V(B) &= u_1(F) + u_3(H) + f_1(F, H) + f_2(H, H) \\ &\quad + f_3(H, H) - u_1(H) - u_3(F) - f_1(H, H) \\ &\quad - f_2(H, F) - f_3(F, H) \\ &= V(C) - V(D), \end{aligned}$$

where F, H refer to the French and home dinners. In the survey, visitors to the Museum of Science and Industry in Chicago ($N = 51$) strongly preferred Sequence B to A (88%) and just slightly preferred Sequence C to D (51%). Despite the different subject population (museum visitors vs. undergraduates), and despite the inclusion of two "filler" weekends, the preference pattern was virtually unchanged from Example 3. The violation of independence cannot therefore be attributed to particular feelings about utility changes from one period to the next.

Marking an Interval

How one distributes events over an interval clearly depends on the duration of that interval. However, in the real world the relevant interval is often ambiguous and may vary for different people and for different types of outcomes. For example, the relevant interval for a free dinner is probably shorter than for a free round-trip flight. The final example we present was constructed to test whether manipulation of the implicit interval would influence timing preferences. One hundred one visitors to Chicago's Museum of Science and Industry were asked to schedule two hypothetical free dinners at the restaurant of their choice.

Example 5. Suppose you were given two coupons for fancy dinners for two at the restaurant of your choice. The coupons are worth up to $100 each. When would you choose to use them? Please ignore considerations such as holidays, birthdays, etc.

One third of the subjects were asked to schedule the two dinners without any imposed time constraints (unconstrained group). Another one third, the "4-month constraint group," were told that they could use the coupons any time in the next 4 months. The remaining third, the 2-year constraint group, were told "You can use the coupons at any time between today and 2 years from today." Although the constraints seemingly *limited* the subjects' abilities to delay the dinners, we felt that constrained subjects would prefer to delay the dinners more than would unconstrained subjects because the default interval for unconstrained subjects was actually shorter than the explicit intervals faced by the constrained subjects. Table 32.1 presents our findings.

Medians were a more representative measure of population preferences here because they attenuated the impact of a few extremely long delays obtained in the unconstrained condition. Considering the medians, the median delay interval for the second dinner was longer under either constrained condition than the median delay in the unconstrained condition. The effect was especially prominent, however, for the 2-year delay, suggesting that the average default interval for subjects might have been close to 4 months. Overall, the effect of the two constraints on the selected delays was significant, according to a one-way analysis of variance (ANOVA), $F(2, 96) = 3.7$, $p < .03$, for the first dinner, and $F(2, 96) = 13.2$, $p < .0001$, for the second.

Table 32.1. Chosen Delay for First and Second Dinner

Condition	First Dinner	Second Dinner
Unconstrained		
M	3.3	13.1
Mdn	2.0	8.0
Four-month constraint		
M	3.0	10.4
Mdn	2.0	12.0
Two-year constraint		
M	7.7	31.1
Mdn	4.0	26.0

These results are inconsistent with the economic axiom of revealed preference, according to which the imposition of a time constraint on an initially unconstrained population should affect only the responses of that fraction of the population whose preferred delays are longer than permitted by the constraint. Therefore, the population averages should be longer in the unconstrained condition.

CONCLUSION

Understanding choice between sequences is important because planning for the future invariably requires one to choose between alternative sequences of outcomes. Taking a vacation now may forestall a future vacation; increasing one's spending in the present may force reductions in future expenditures; and dieting in the present is intended to produce delayed rewards, whereas binge eating entails delayed costs. In each of these cases, a given decision has multiple consequences that are spread out over time.

Previous empirical work on time preference has focused almost entirely on the trade-off that arises when two outcomes of different values and occurring at different times are compared. The tacit premise has been that such judgments will reveal an individual's "raw" time preference, from which one can then derive preferences over more complex objects (e.g., retirement plans, intertemporal income profiles, etc.). This view we now know is fundamentally incorrect. The empirical evidence presented in this article, in conjunction with the related work of Frank (in press), Loewenstein and Sicherman (1991), Ross and Simonson (1991), and Varey and Kahneman (in press) shows that as soon as an intertemporal tradeoff is embedded in the context of two alternative *sequences* of outcomes, the psychological perspective, or "frame," shifts, and individuals become more farsighted, often wishing to postpone the better outcome until the end. The same person who prefers a good dinner sooner rather than later, if given a choice between two explicitly formulated sequences, one consisting of a good dinner *followed* by an indifferent one, the other of the indifferent dinner *followed* by the good one, may well prefer the latter alternative. Sequences of outcomes that decline in value are greatly disliked, indicating a negative rate of time preference.

The sensitivity of intertemporal decisions to choice representation has important policy implications. Efforts to lengthen time perspectives have generally focused on material inducements. For example, attempts to increase the personal savings of Americans have typically involved tax deductions on certain types of interest income. Although not denigrating such efforts, our research suggests that there may be other, more effective and less costly methods of altering time perspective. Such methods can take the form of media and educational campaigns that express decisions as sequences rather than as individual decisions. Alternatively, policymakers could bolster and expand on the institutions that already exist that implicitly or explicitly present decision makers with choices between sequences.

The significant difference in preferences observed in intertemporal choices involving single outcomes and sequences challenges the claim often made that groups and individuals differ in their fundamental attitude toward the future. It is plausible that such variations are not attributable to any fundamental attitude toward the future but instead reflect differences in the way that options are perceived. Any factor, whether personal or situational, that causes intertemporal choices to fragment and to be perceived as a series of individual decisions will tend to induce high positive time discounting. Likewise, factors that cause such decisions to be internally "framed" as sequences will promote low and even negative time discounting.

33. Anomalies in Intertemporal Choice
Evidence and an Interpretation

George Loewenstein and Dražen Prelec

ABSTRACT. Research on decision making under uncertainty has been strongly influenced by the documentation of numerous expected utility (EU) anomalies – behaviors that violate the expected utility axioms. The relative lack of progress on the closely related topic of intertemporal choice is partly due to the absence of an analogous set of discounted utility (DU) anomalies. We enumerate a set of DU anomalies analogous to the EU anomalies and propose a model that accounts for the anomalies as well as other intertemporal choice phenomena incompatible with DU. We discuss implications for savings behavior, estimation of discount rates, and choice framing effects.

I. INTRODUCTION

Since its introduction by Samuelson in 1937, the discounted utility model (DU) has dominated economic analyses of intertemporal choice. In its most restrictive form, the model states that a sequence of consumption levels, $(c_0, \ldots, c_T)$ will be preferred to sequence $(c'_0, \ldots, c'_T)$, if and only if,

$$\sum_{t=0}^{T} \delta^t u(c_t) > \sum_{t=0}^{T} \delta^t u(c'_t), \tag{1}$$

where $u(c)$ is a concave ratio scale utility function, and δ is the discount factor for one period. DU has been applied to such diverse topics as savings behavior, labor supply, security valuation, education decisions, and crime. It has provided a simple, powerful framework for analyzing a broad range of economic decisions with delayed consequences.

We thank Wayne Ferson, Brian Gibbs, Jerry Green, Richard Herrnstein, Robin Hogarth, Mark Machina, Howard Rachlin, and, especially, Colin Camerer and Joshua Klayman for useful suggestions. The assistance of Eric Wanner, the Russell Sage Foundation, the Alfred P. Sloan Foundation, the IBM Faculty Research Fund at the University of Chicago Graduate School of Business, and the Research Division of the Harvard Business School is also gratefully acknowledged.

Originally printed in *The Quarterly Journal of Economics*, 107:2, 573–97. Copyright © 1992 by the President and Fellows of Harvard College and the Massachusetts Institute of Technology. Reprinted with permission.

Yet, in spite of its widespread use, the DU model has not received substantial scrutiny – in marked contrast to the expected utility model for choice under uncertainty, which has been extensively criticized on empirical grounds and which has subsequently spawned a great number of variant models (reviewed, for example, by Weber and Camerer [1988]).

Our first aim in this paper is to remedy this imbalance by enumerating the anomalous empirical findings on time preference that have been reported so far. Taken together, they present a challenge to normative theory that is at least as serious as that posed by the much more familiar EU anomalies. Unlike the EU violations, which in many cases can only be demonstrated with a clever arrangement of multiple choice problems (e.g., the Allais paradox), the counterexamples to DU are simple, robust, and bear directly on central aspects of economic behavior. Our second aim is to construct (in Section III) a descriptive model of intertemporal choice that predicts the anomalous preference patterns. In formal structure the model is closely related to Kahneman and Tversky's "prospect theory" [1979], but the interpretation and shape of the component functions are different. The paper concludes with a discussion of some additional implications of the model for individual behavior and market outcomes.

II. FOUR ANOMALIES

In this section we present four common preference patterns that create difficulty for the discounted utility model.

1. The Common Difference Effect

Consider an individual who is indifferent between adding x units to consumption at time t and $y > x$ units at a later time t', given a constant baseline consumption level (c) in all time periods:

$$u(c + x)\delta^t + u(c)\delta^{t'} = u(c)\delta^t + u(c + y)\delta^{t'}. \tag{2}$$

Dividing through by δ^t,

$$u(c + x) - u(c) = (u(c + y) - u(c))\delta^{t'-t} \tag{3}$$

shows that preference between the two consumption adjustments depends only on the absolute time interval separating them, or $(t' - t)$ in the example above. This is the *stationarity* property, which plays a critical role in axiomatic derivations of the DU model [Koopmans, 1960; Fishburn and Rubinstein, 1982].

In practice, preferences between two delayed outcomes often switch when both delays are incremented by a given constant amount. An example of Thaler [1981] makes the point crisply: a person might prefer one apple today to two apples tomorrow, but at the same time prefer two apples in 51 days to one apple in 50 days. We shall refer to this pattern as the *common difference effect*.[1]

The common difference effect gives rise to dynamically inconsistent behavior, as noted first by Strotz [1956], and richly elaborated in the papers of the psychologist Ainslie [1975, 1985]. It also implies that discount rates should decrease as a function of the time delay over which they are estimated which has been observed in a number of studies, including one with real money outcomes [Horowitz, 1988].[2] See Figure 33.6 for the results of Benzion et al. [1989], which are representative.

2. The Absolute Magnitude Effect

Empirical studies of time preference have also found that large dollar amounts suffer less proportional discounting than do small ones. Thaler [1981], for example, reported that subjects who were on average indifferent between receiving $15 immediately and $60 in a year were also indifferent between an immediate $250 and $350 in a year, as well as between $3000 now and $4000 in a year. Similar results were obtained by Holcomb and Nelson [1989] with real money outcomes.

3. The Gain-Loss Asymmetry

A closely related finding is that losses are discounted at a lower rate than gains are. For example, subjects in a study by Loewenstein [1988c] were, on average, indifferent between receiving $10 immediately and receiving $21 in one year, and indifferent between losing $10 immediately and losing $15 in one year. The corresponding figures for $100 were $157 for gains and $133 for losses. Even more dramatic loss-gain asymmetries were obtained by Thaler [1981], who estimated discount rates for gains that were three to ten times greater than those for losses. Several of his subjects actually exhibited negative discounting, in that they preferred an immediate loss over a delayed loss of equal value (also see Loewenstein [1987]).

The magnitude and gain–loss effects are problematic for DU in two senses. First, the predictions that DU makes are sensitive to the baseline consumption profile, since the baseline level at a given time period directly controls the marginal utility of an extra unit of consumption. Experimental subjects represent a diversity of baseline levels of consumption, yet these choice patterns are consistent over a wide range of income (and hence consumption) levels. This pattern evokes the comments of Markowitz [1952] on the Friedman–Savage explanation for simultaneous gambling and insurance purchases. Friedman and

---

[1] The common difference effect is analogous to the common ratio effect in decision making under uncertainty [Kahneman and Tversky, 1979]. For a discussion of similarities and differences between the EU and DU axioms, see Prelec and Loewenstein [1991].

[2] Horowitz [1988] used a second price-sealed bit auction to estimated discount rates for $50 "bonds" of varying maturity. Implicit discount rates were a declining function of time to bond maturity.

Savage argued that simultaneous gambling and insurance could be explained by a doubly inflected utility function defined over levels of wealth. Markowitz pointed out that no single utility function defined over levels of wealth could explain why people at vastly different levels of wealth engage in both activities; a function that predicted simultaneous gambling and insuring for people at one wealth level would make counterintuitive predictions for people at other wealth levels.

Second, even the determinate predictions that DU yields, on the assumption that the baseline consumption level is constant across time periods, are not entirely consistent with the effects just described. Note first that the present value of a consumption change at time t, from c to $c + x$, can be measured in two ways, either by assessing the *equivalent* present value $q(x, t)$ defined implicitly by

$$u(c + q) + \delta^t u(c) = u(c) + \delta^t u(c + x), \tag{4}$$

or by assessing the *compensating* present value $p(x, t)$ that would exactly balance the change at time t:

$$u(c - p) + \delta^t u(c + x) = u(c) + \delta^t u(c). \tag{5}$$

(These are also referred to as the methods of *equivalent* and *compensating* variation.)

The gain-loss asymmetry is obtained by comparing the equivalent variation ratios (q/x) for positive and negative x. Here the DU model makes the correct qualitative prediction, as the following simple calculation shows:

$$
\begin{aligned}
q(x, t) &= u^{-1}\{(1 - \delta^t)u(c) + \delta^t u(c + x)\} - c \quad \text{(solving from (4))} \\
&< (1 - \delta^t)c + \delta^t(c + x) - c \quad \text{(by concavity of } u(x)) \\
&= \delta^t x.
\end{aligned} \tag{6}
$$

Consequently, the ratio, $q(x, t)/x$, is smaller than δ^t for positive x and greater than δ^t for negative x, which is consistent with the observed greater relative discounting of gains.

The critical weakness of this explanation lies in the prediction it makes about the size of the gain-loss asymmetry at different absolute magnitudes. The normative explanation is driven by the global concavity of the utility function, which creates a gap (analogous to a risk premium) between time discounting and the pure rate of time preference. Since the utility function is approximately linear for small intervals $(c - x, c + x)$, the gain-loss asymmetry should disappear for small x. Indeed, in the limit as x goes to zero (from either side), the predicted devaluation ratio q/x will approach the discount factor δ^t, for both gains and losses. In practice, however, we observe the exact opposite, with the gain-loss asymmetry being most pronounced for small outcomes [Thaler, 1981; Benzion et al., 1989].

With regard to the magnitude effect the DU predictions hinge partly on the method of elicitation. When present values are assessed by the equivalent variation method, DU contradicts the magnitude effect. For compensating variation, DU predicts the effect when x is negative, but predicts the exact opposite (i.e., smaller discounting of *small* amounts) for positive x. We now derive this last result as an illustration; the argument in the other cases is similar.

Suppose that p is the most one would be willing to pay now in order to receive $x > 0$ at time t, as in equation (5), and consider what happens as both p and x are increased by a common factor, $\alpha > 1$:

$$\left.\frac{\partial}{\partial \alpha}\right|_{\alpha=1} \{u(c - \alpha p) + \delta^t u(c + \alpha x) - (u(c) + \delta^t u(c))\}$$
$$= -pu'(c - p) + \delta^t x u'(c + x) \quad \text{(from (5))}$$
$$> 0 \quad \text{(if the magnitude effect holds)}. \tag{7}$$

After substituting for δ^t from (5), this inequality reduces to

$$pu'(c - p)(u(c + x) - u(c)) < xu'(c + x)((u(c) - u(c - p)). \tag{8}$$

But, since $u(c)$ is concave, we have $u(c + x) - u(c) > xu'(c + x)$ and $u(c) - u(c - p)$, $< pu'(c - p)$, which are jointly incompatible with the stated inequality in (8).

4. The Delay–Speedup Asymmetry

A recent study by Loewenstein [1988a] has documented a fourth anomaly, consisting of an asymmetric preference between speeding up and delaying consumption. In general, the amount required to compensate for delaying receiving a (real) reward by a given interval, from t to $t + s$, was from two to four times greater than the amount subjects were willing to sacrifice to speed consumption up by the same interval, i.e., from $t + s$ to t. Because the two pairs of choices are actually different representations of the same underlying pair of options, the results constitute a classic framing effect, which is inconsistent with any normative theory, including DU.

III. A BEHAVIORAL MODEL OF INTERTEMPORAL CHOICE

This section presents a model of intertemporal choice that accounts for the anomalies just enumerated. Our model assumes that intertemporal choice is defined with respect to *deviations* from an anticipated status quo (or "reference") consumption plan; this is in explicit contrast to the DU assumption that people integrate new consumption alternatives with existing plans before making a choice. The objects of choice, then, are sequences of dated adjustments to consumption $\{(x_i, t_i); i = 1, \ldots, n\}$, which we shall refer to as *temporal prospects*.

As in the prospect theory for risky choice, we shall represent preference by a doubly separable formula (equation (9) below), which rests on three qualitative properties (see Appendix in Kahneman and Tversky [1979] for details).

The first property, also invoked by DU, is that preferences over prospects are intertemporally separable [Debreu, 1959] and can, therefore, be represented by an additive utility function, $\Sigma_i\, u(x_i, t_i)$. This important assumption is psychologically most questionable when the choice is perceived to be between complete alternative sequences of outcomes, e.g., savings plans, or multiyear salary contracts. In these cases, it appears that people care about global sequence properties, most notably whether the sequence improves over time [Loewenstein and Prelec, 1991; Loewenstein and Sicherman, 1991]. The present model is primarily concerned with explaining elementary types of intertemporal choices, involving no more than two or three distinct dated outcomes.

In the absence of any strong contrary evidence, we assume that x and t are separable within a single outcome, so that $u(x, t)$ equals $F(v(x)\phi(t))$, where $v(x)$ is a *value function*, $\phi(t)$ a *discount function*, and F an arbitrary monotonically increasing transformation. To eliminate F, one imposes a distributivity condition: (x, t) is indifferent to $(x, t'; x, t'')$ implies that (y, t) is indifferent to $(y, t'; y, t'')$, for any outcome y, which essentially states that the equality $\phi(t) = \phi(t') + \phi(t'')$ can be established with any one outcome [Kahneman and Tversky, 1979, p. 290]. The discount function is then uniquely specified, given the standard normalization $\phi(0) = 1$. The final model represents preference by the formula,

$$U(x_1, t_1; \ldots; x_n, t_n) = \sum_i v(x_i)\phi(t_i). \tag{9}$$

The remainder of this section specifies the properties of the two component functions and shows how the model accounts for the anomalies presented in Section II.

1. Discount Function

The common difference effect reveals that people are more sensitive to a given time delay if it occurs earlier rather than later. Specifically, if a person is indifferent between receiving $x > 0$ immediately, and $y > x$ at some later time s, then he or she will strictly prefer the better outcome if both outcomes are postponed by a common amount t:

$$v(x) = v(y)\phi(s), \quad \text{implies that } v(x)\phi(t) < v(y)\phi(t + s). \tag{10}$$

In order to maintain indifference, the later larger outcome would have to be delayed by some interval s' greater than s. To account for this phenomenon, Ainslie [1975] proposed the discount function, $\phi(t) = 1/t$, which had been found to explain a large body of data on animal time discounting. We now derive a more general functional form, by postulating that the delay that compensates for the larger outcome is a linear function of the time to the smaller, earlier outcome (holding fixed the two outcomes x and y),

$$v(x) = v(y)\phi(s), \quad \text{implies that } v(x)\phi(t) = v(y)\phi(kt + s), \tag{11}$$

for some constant k, which, of course depends on x and y. One can think of this as a more general form of stationarity, in which the "clocks" for the two outcomes being compared run at different speeds. In the normative case, the clocks are identical, and $k = 1$, which yields the exponential discount function [Fishburn and Rubinstein, 1982]. From (11) it follows that

$$v(x)\phi(t') = v(y)\phi(kt' + s), \tag{12}$$

and

$$
\begin{aligned}
v(x)\phi(\lambda t + (1 - \lambda)t') &= v(y)\phi(k(\lambda t + (1 - \lambda)t') + s) \\
&= v(y)\phi(\lambda(kt + s) + (1 - \lambda)(kt' + s)) \\
&= v(y)\phi(\lambda\phi^{-1}(v(x)\phi(t)/v(y))) \\
&\quad + (1 - \lambda)\phi^{-1}(v(x)\phi(t')/v(y)), \tag{13}
\end{aligned}
$$

after substituting for $(kt + s)$ and $(kt' + s)$ from equations (11) and (12). Letting, $r = v(x)/v(y)$, $w = \phi(t)$, $z = \phi(t')$, and $u = \phi^{-1}$, produces a functional equation,

$$ru^{-1}(\lambda u(w) + (1 - \lambda)u(z)) = u^{-1}(\lambda u(rw) + (1 - \lambda)u(rz)), \tag{14}$$

whose only solutions are the logarithmic and power functions: $u(t) = c\ln(t) + d$, $u(t) = ct^{\tau} + d$ [Aczel, 1966; p. 152, equation (18)]. As $\phi(t) = u^{-1}(t)$, the discount function must be either exponential or hyperbolic.

D1. The discount function is a generalized hyperbola:

$$\phi(t) = (1 + \alpha t)^{-\beta/\alpha}, \quad \alpha, \beta > 0. \tag{15}$$

The α-coefficient determines how much the function departs from constant discounting; the limiting case, as α goes to zero, is the exponential discount function, $\phi(t) = e^{-\beta t}$. Figure 33.1 displays the hyperbolic function for three different values of α, along with the pure exponential which is the least convex of the four lines. For each level of α a corresponding β is selected so that the discount function has value 0.3 at $t = 1$. When α is very large, the hyperbola approximates a step function, with value one at $t = 0$, and value 0.3 (in this case) at all other times. This would produce dichotomous time preferences, in which the present outcome has unit weight, and all future events are discounted by a common constant.

As noted already, equation (15) satisfies the empirical "matching law," which integrates a large body of experimental findings pertaining to animal time discounting [Chung and Herrnstein, 1967]; the special case, $(1 + \alpha t)^{-1}$, was proposed initially by Herrnstein [1981], and further investigated by Mazur [1987]; the general hyperbola was defined by Harvey [1986], and given an axiomatic derivation by Prelec [1989] along the lines presented here.

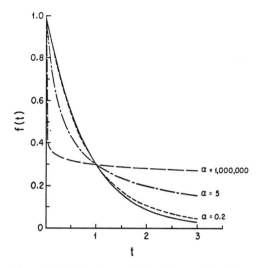

Figure 33.1. The hyperbolic discount function $\phi(t) = (1 + \alpha t)^{-\beta/\alpha}$ for three different levels of α. All βs are adjusted so that curves cross at $\phi(1) = 0.3$. The most steeply sloped curve represents conventional exponential discounting.

2. Value Function

A distinguishing feature of the current model is the replacement of the utility function with a value function with a reference point, as shown in Figure 33.2. The value function is pieced together from two independent segments, one for losses and one for gains, which connect at the reference point. Such functions have previously been applied to decision making under uncertainty [Kahneman and Tversky, 1979], consumer choice [Thaler, 1980], negotiations [Bazerman, 1984], and financial economics [Shefrin and Statman, 1984]. The shape

Figure 33.2. A value function satisfying the three conditions described in the text.

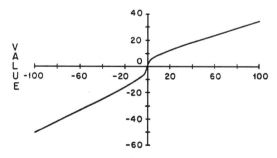

and reference point assumption reflects basic psychophysical considerations: extra attention to negative aspects of the environment, decreasing sensitivity to increments in stimuli of increasing magnitude, and cognitive limitations.

It is assumed that the reference level represents the status quo (i.e., the current level of consumption), and that new consumption alternatives are evaluated without consideration of existing plans. In certain cases, however, the reference point may deviate from the status quo to reflect psychological considerations such as social comparison [Duesenberry, 1949], or the effect of past consumption which sets a standard for the present [Ferson and Constantinides, 1988; Pollak, 1970].

The function in Figure 33.2 is representative of a class of functions that is consistent with the behavioral evidence presented earlier in Section II. The first, and most elementary assumption built into the figure is *loss aversion* [Tversky and Kahneman, 1990].

> V1. The value function for losses is steeper than the value function for gains:
>
> $$v(x) < -v(-x).$$

This means that the loss in value associated with a given monetary loss exceeds the gain in value produced by a monetary gain of the same absolute size. In this respect, our value function resembles the prospect theory value function [Kahneman and Tversky, 1979], which also places greater weight on losses.

In the context of intertemporal choice, loss aversion specifically penalizes intertemporal exchanges that are framed in compensating variation terms, i.e., as incurring a loss now in exchange for a future gain, or enjoying a current gain in return for a future loss. For instance, a person who is indifferent between receiving $+q$ now, or $+x$ at some later date, would nevertheless not be willing *to pay q* now in order to receive $+x$ at the later date, because the value of $-q$ is greater in absolute magnitude than the value of $+q$.

The remaining two constraints on $v(x)$ are geometrically more subtle and have not been explicitly discussed in the context of prospect theory. Both constraints pertain to the *elasticity* of $v(x)$:

$$\epsilon_v(x) \equiv \frac{\partial \log (v)}{\partial \log (x)} = \frac{xv'(x)}{v(x)}. \tag{15}$$

Our second assumption about the value function is behaviorally determined by the gain-loss asymmetry.

> V2. The value function for losses is more elastic than the value function for gains:
>
> $$\epsilon_v(x) < \epsilon_v(-x), \quad \text{for } x > 0.$$

Suppose that $+q$ is the equivalent present value of $+x$ at time t, so that, $v(q) = \phi(t)v(x)$. The gain–loss asymmetry then implies that one would prefer to pay $-q$ now instead of $-x$ at time t: $v(-q) > \phi(t)v(-x)$. Equating $\phi(t)$ in both of these expressions shows that

$$\frac{v(q)}{v(x)} > \frac{v(-q)}{v(-x)}, \quad \text{for all } 0 < q < x. \tag{16}$$

Consequently, $v(x)$ must "bend over" faster than $v(-x)$, in the precise sense captured by condition V2.[3]

Our third and final assumption about $v(x)$ is dictated by the magnitude effect, in equivalent variation choices. If $+q$ is the equivalent present value for x at time t, $v(q) = \phi(t)v(x)$, then the magnitude effect predicts that a proportional increase in both q and x, to αq and αx, will cause preference to tip in favor of the later positive outcome, $v(\alpha q) < \phi(t)v(\alpha x)$. As in the previous paragraph, by eliminating $\phi(t)$, we have

$$\frac{v(q)}{v(x)} < \frac{v(\alpha q)}{v(\alpha x)}, \quad \text{for all } 0 < q < x; \alpha > 1. \tag{17}$$

The value function is *subproportional*, like the probability weighting function in prospect theory. As Kahneman and Tversky remarked [1979, p. 282], such a function is convex in log–log coordinates, which for our model means that the derivative of $\log(v(x))$ with respect to $\log(x)$ is increasing, or that:

V3. The value function is more elastic for outcomes that are larger in absolute magnitude:

$$\epsilon_v(x) < \epsilon_v(y), \quad \text{for } 0 < x < y \text{ or } y < x < 0.$$

The implications of this condition can be visually assessed by comparing Figures 33.2 and 33.3. Both figures show the same value function, but plotted over a small (Figure 33.3) or a large (Figure 33.2) range of outcomes. For small outcomes the function is sharply convex, indicating that there is not much

Figure 33.3. The same value function as in Figure 33.3 but plotted over a smaller range of outcomes.

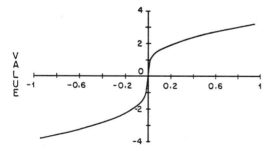

$ CHANGE RELATIVE TO STATUS QUO

---

[3] Let $u_1(x) \equiv -\ln\{v(x)\}$ and $u_2(x) \equiv -\ln\{-v(-x)\}$. Then (17) implies that $u_1(x) - u_1(q) < u_2(x) - u_2(s)$, for all $0 < q < x$, or: $u_1'(x) < u_2'(x)$, for all $x > 0$, which is equivalent to condition V2.

perceived value difference between, say, a $1 gain and a $2 gain. This property accounts for the high discount rates that apply to small outcomes (i.e., in a choice between $1 now or $2 in a year). For large outcomes, however, the function straightens out considerably (Figure 33.2) and, as a result, generates much lower discount rates.

Most probably, the elasticity of the value function does not increase indefinitely, but rather attains a maximum at some large dollar amount, and then begins to decline. When comparing large and unexpected windfalls, it may be reasonable to prefer a million dollars today to several million a few years hence – if drawing on the money in advance was completely prevented. The implausibility of this last requirement makes the interpretation of stated preference over large amounts problematic.

IV. FURTHER IMPLICATIONS OF THE MODEL

1. Aversion to Intertemporal Trade-offs

It follows from our model that a single individual will reveal not one but several discount factors for future cash outcomes, depending on how the choice is formulated. These discount factors can be geometrically derived, as in Figure 33.4. In the figure we have overlaid the positive and negative branches of the value function, so that both positive and negative outcomes can be represented

Figure 33.4. Relationship among discount factors for compensating and equivalent variation.

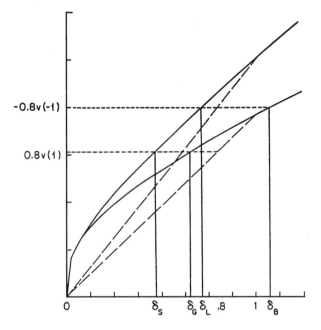

along the positive x-axis. Starting with a delayed outcome of absolute magnitude x, and a time interval yielding a discount factor *for utility* of 0.8, we can generate four distinct "present values" for x, depending on whether x is positive or negative, and whether the elicitation method is equivalent or compensating variation. Each present value, divided by x, then yields a specific discount factor.

From equivalent variation, $v(q) = \phi(t)v(x)$, we get the discount factors for gains (G) and losses (L):

$$\delta_{GL} = \frac{q}{x} = \frac{v^{-1}\{\phi(t)v(x)\}}{x} \quad (\delta_G \text{ for } x > 0, \delta_L \text{ for } x < 0). \tag{18}$$

While from compensating variation, $v(p) + \phi(t)v(x) = 0$, we have the *borrowing* (B) and *saving* (S) factors:

$$\delta_{SB} = \frac{p}{x} = \frac{v^{-1}\{-\phi(t)v(x)\}}{x} \quad (\delta_S \text{ for } x > 0, \delta_B \text{ for } x < 0). \tag{19}$$

It is apparent from the geometry of the gain and loss value functions in Figure 33.4, that these discount factors are ordered as $\delta_S < \delta_G < \delta_L < \delta_B$.

A notable aspect of the ranking is the large gap between the savings and borrowing discount factors: a person whose choices are consistent with the value functions in Figure 33.2 would require a much more favorable rate in order to borrow than he would to save. The gap between δ_B and δ_S is a measure of how averse a person is to borrowing and savings commitments generally, because it implies a range of risk-free interest rates at which a person will be unwilling to either save or borrow.

The existence of this gap was confirmed by Horowitz [1988], who elicited present and future values for real money payoffs, through a "first-rejected price" auction. According to Horowitz, "The most striking feature of [the] experiment is individuals' apparent aversion to both borrowing and lending." A substantial fraction of subjects revealed discount factors greater than one for borrowing (i.e., they refused zero-interest loans); this, too, is consistent with the model, as we can see from the fact that $\delta_B > 1$ in Figure 33.4.

2. Framing Effects

As in prospect theory [Kahneman and Tversky, 1979], we assume that the reference level is sensitive to the wording of the questions that elicit the intertemporal trade-offs. For instance, direct choices between two losses, or two gains, are presumed to be likewise encoded (or "framed") as a pair of positive or negative values. The same would be true of requests for present amounts that create subjective indifference with respect to some future amount of the same sign. In such a context we would interpret the elicited present

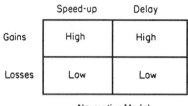

	Speed-up	Delay
Gains	High	High
Losses	Low	Low

Normative Model

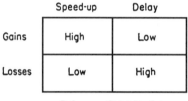

	Speed-up	Delay
Gains	High	Low
Losses	Low	High

Reference Point Model

Figure 33.5. Discount rates when expediting and speeding up gains and losses: comparison of DU and reference point model predictions.

value q for amount x at time t, according to the equivalent variation formula, $v(q) = \phi(t)v(x)$.

Questions involving delay or speedup of consumption are a clear case where the compensating variation formula is appropriate. A request, for example, for the maximum value that one would be willing to sacrifice in order to speed up some positive amount (x) from time t to the present, suggests that the baseline levels are zero now, and $+x$ at the future time. In this frame the speedup constitutes a loss of x at time t, and a gain of x minus the speedup cost at time zero. The latter value, p, would then be interpreted according to the compensating variation formula, $v(p) + \phi(t)v(x) = 0$, with $x < 0$ and $p > 0$. The same frame covers delay-of-loss judgments, because in that case there is again a positive present benefit (avoiding the immediate loss), and a future cost (absorbing the loss at the later date). The two complementary question formats – delaying a gain, and speeding up a loss – would yield present values also consistent with equation (20) but for a reversal in the sign of p and x, since there is a negative adjustment to current consumption ($p < 0$), and a positive adjustment to future consumption ($x > 0$).

Figure 33.5 compares these predictions with those of the normative model, in which the distinction between a speedup or delay is not recognized. As indicated in the top half of the figure, the discount rates estimated from expediting and delaying gains should be equal, and higher than the devaluation rates estimated from expediting and delaying losses. In contrast, the reference point model predicts that common rates will be observed for the diagonal pairs in the matrix, with the delaying gains/speeding up losses pair producing a higher estimate.

Clear support for the reference point model can be found in the data reported by Benzion et al. [1989]. Figure 33.6 displays implicit discount rates calculated from their data for each of the four elicitation methods. As predicted, discount rates are high and virtually identical for expediting a loss (white diamonds) and delaying a gain (black squares), and lower and again virtually identical for expediting a gain (black triangles) and delaying a loss (white squares).

Our second framing example is produced by the discrepancy between discounting of gains and losses. In this study 85 students in an MBA class on decision making were randomly divided into two groups which each answered one of the following two questions.

Version 1. Suppose that you bought a TV on a special installment plan. The plan calls for two payments; one this week and one in six months. You have two options for paying: (circle the one that you would choose)
  A. An initial payment of $160 and a later payment of $110.
  B. An initial payment of $115 and a later payment of $160.

Version 2. Suppose that you bought a TV on a special installment plan. The plan calls for two payments of $200; one this week and one in six months. Happily, however, the company has announced a sale which applies retroactively to your purchase. You have two options: (circle the one that you would choose)
  C. A rebate of $40 on the initial payment and a rebate of $90 on the later payment.
  D. A rebate of $85 on the initial payment and a rebate of $40 on the later payment.

Since options A and C and options B and D are the same in terms of payoffs and delivery times, DU predicts that there will be no systematic difference in responses to the two versions. Nevertheless, a higher fraction of subjects opted for the lower-discount option (the one involving greater earlier payments) when the question was framed as a loss rather than as a gain. Fifty-four percent of subjects exposed to version 1 stated a preference for A over B. However, a significantly different fraction (33 percent) preferred C over D ($X^2(1) = 3.9$, $p < 0.05$). The proposed model explains the observed pattern of responses as follows: in the first frame the large, negative outcomes suffer less discounting, which causes people to decide on the basis of total payments. In the second frame, however, the outcomes are smaller in absolute magnitude and positive. Both of these factors contribute to relatively high discounting of the delayed outcomes, leading to a preference for the second option which offers a greater initial rebate.

The choice of appropriate frame is not always unambiguous. A savings decision, for example, can be viewed as a simple choice between benefits enjoyed now or later (equation (19)) or a postponement of present consumption for the future (equation (20)). Such changes in frame will, according to our theory, affect the range of interest rates that a person considers acceptable.

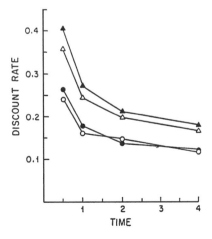

Figure 33.6. Implicit discount rates from Benzion et al. [1989]. The rates have been averaged across the four dollar amounts used in their study.

3. Effect of Prior Expectations on Choice

Consider two people waiting for an object (e.g., a computer): one has been told to expect delivery in two weeks; the other anticipates delivery in four weeks. Two weeks pass, and both are faced with a new choice: the original computer to be delivered immediately, or a superior computer to be delivered in two weeks. Who is more likely to wait? If both parties adapt their reference points to anticipated delivery times, then the reference point model predicts that the person who anticipated delivery in two weeks will be more impatient. This person frames the choice as the status quo versus a loss of a computer immediately and a gain of a slightly superior computer in two weeks. Loss aversion and discounting both mitigate against choice of the delayed, superior, model. On the other hand, the person who anticipated later delivery would frame the choice as a loss of the later computer and gain of an earlier computer. Here loss aversion discourages the choice of the earlier computer, while discounting has an opposing influence. Thus, we predict that the person anticipating two-week delivery would be more likely to accept. In effect, people who are psychologically prepared for delay are more willing to wait.

This prediction was tested in a laboratory experiment conducted with 105 suburban Chicago tenth graders [Loewenstein, 1988b]. All prizes were in the form of nontransferable gift certificates. As a result of an earlier experiment, half the students expected to obtain a $7 gift certificate at an earlier date, half at a later date. When the earlier date arrived, all subjects were given a new choice between getting the $7 certificate immediately or a larger valued certificate at a later date. As predicted, prior expectations had a significant impact on choice. Twenty-seven out of 47 subjects who anticipated getting the prize at the earlier date opted for the immediate $7; only 17 of the 57 who expected late delivery chose not to wait for the larger prize, a statistically significant difference.

4. High Discount Rates Estimated from Purchases of Consumer Durables

Several studies have estimated discount rates from purchases of consumer durables (e.g., air conditioners) [Hausman, 1979; Gately, 1980]. Such purchases typically involve an up-front charge (the purchase price) and a series of delayed charges (e.g., electricity charges). Because more expensive models are generally more energy efficient, it is possible to calculate the discount rate (or range of discount rates) implicit in a particular purchase. A second source of behavioral estimates of discount rates has been the studies of major economic decisions such as saving [Landsberger, 1971] and intertemporal labor-leisure substitution [Hotz, Kydland, and Sedlacek, 1988; Moore and Viscusi, 1988].

The estimates from these two classes of studies have differed sharply. Studies of consumer durable purchases show very high average discount rates (across different income groups), e.g., from 25 percent [Hausman, 1979] to 45–300 percent [Gately, 1980]. Research on savings behavior or labor supply has almost uniformly found much lower discount rates (typically well below 25 percent).

How can these estimates be reconciled? The proposed model predicts that the small delayed electricity charges associated with the consumer durables will be substantially devalued due to the dependence of discounting on outcome magnitude. Thus, consumer durable purchases will be insensitive to electricity charges, and discount rates estimated from those purchases will appear to be high. Discount rates estimated from major economic decisions would not be subject to such small-magnitude effects.

5. Nonmonotonic Optimal Benefit Plans

Our model makes certain predictions about the shape of the optimal intertemporal allocation of benefits under a constant market present value constraint. Assuming that consumption at a point in time, $x(t)$, is framed as a positive quantity, the value of the plan, covering the period from 0 to T, is given by the continuous version of the discounted value formula,

$$\int_0^T \phi(t) v(x(t)) \, dt. \tag{20}$$

The optimal plan $x^0(t)$, given a market interest rate r and a present value constraint,

$$\int_0^T e^{-rt} x(t) \, dt \leq I, \tag{21}$$

can be calculated by standard techniques [Yaari, 1964]. Yaari showed that if the optimal plan exists, and if the value function is concave and continuously differentiable, then the rate of change in consumption, for the optimal plan, equals [equation (21)]:

$$\frac{\partial x^0}{\partial t} = r - \left(-\frac{\phi'(t)}{\phi(t)} \right) \left(-\frac{v'(x^0(t))}{v''(x^0)} \right). \tag{22}$$

As Yaari observed, the direction of local change in consumption rate is controlled by the sign of the difference between the market interest rate and the rate of time preference $(-\phi'/\phi)$. In view of our hyperbolic discounting assumption, this allows for only three qualitatively distinct possibilities: (1) the rate of time preference is always greater than the market rate, in which case consumption is decreasing throughout the interval; (2) the rate of time preference is always lower than the market rate, in which case consumption increases over the interval; (3) the rate of time preference starts off above the market rate, but eventually drops below it and remains so, in which case consumption will decline to a minimum value (when the two rates equalize) and then increase afterwards.

Relative to normative theory, our model suggests that people may tend to prefer plans that sacrifice the medium-range future for the sake of the short and the long term. There is nothing clearly wrong with this, provided that one can commit to an entire plan at the moment of decision. However, if the optimal plan can be recalculated at later points in time, then the planned sacrifice in midrange consumption will not take effect [Strotz, 1956]. As a result, a bias in favor of the long and short runs may in practice yield behavior that is oriented only to the short run.

This discussion presupposes a concave value function, which – although not explicitly assumed in V1–V3 – is certainly true for the function in Figure 33.4. In the loss domain, however, our working assumption is that the value function is convex, at least initially, which means that the most attractive plan for intertemporal loss allocation consists of concentrating the loss at a single point in time. The (negative) value of the loss, if allowed to accumulate at the market rate to time t, equals $\phi(t)v(Ie^{rt})$, which means that it will pay to delay payment whenever $\phi'(t)v(Ie^{rt}) + rIe^{rt}\phi(t)v'(Ie^{rt}) > 0$ or, after rearranging, whenever

$$r < \frac{-\phi'(t)/\phi(t)}{\epsilon_v(Ie^{rt})}. \tag{23}$$

The product on the right is decreasing in t, since $-\phi'/\phi$ equals $\beta/(1+\alpha t)$ by Assumption D1, and $\epsilon_v(Ie^{rt})$ is increasing by Assumption V3. Hence there is a unique point in time – possibly at one or the other endpoint of the interval – at which the loss is absorbed with smallest perceived cost.

6. Other Predictions

Our model has several implications for the behavior of key economic variables during business cycles. First, it predicts that psychological factors will amplify the tendency for businesses to cut back on investment during periods of lower than anticipated profits. In high profit periods the investment project is viewed in terms of equivalent variation, as a choice between two gains: take the excess profit now, or take greater profits from investment later. But in periods of low or negative returns, an identical investment opportunity would be viewed in terms of compensating variation, i.e., as incurring a current loss in exchange for a future gain, which, as shown in the previous section, will induce a higher subjective discount rate. There may, of course, be good economic reasons for reducing investments during economic downturns; what the model suggests is that psychological factors additionally and independently contribute to the reduction.

For consumers too, an economic downturn should cause an increase in impatience and a consequent decrease in saving. Consumers are likely to frame drops in disposable income, or negative departures from expected gains, as losses, so that saving from income will be viewed in terms of compensating variation: a further loss in the present for a gain in the future.[4] Saving out of an expanding income or out of bonus income is more likely to be viewed in terms of

---

[4] The low rates of savings and negative real rates of interest in the 1970s [Mishkin, 1981] may reflect the shortfall from expectations induced by economic stagnation following the prolonged economic boom of the 1960s. At a societal level the tax cuts of the early 1980s, which entailed a transfer of income from the future to the present, can be interpreted similarly.

compensating variation, inducing lower discounting and greater saving. Consistent with this prediction, there is evidence that the marginal propensity to save income from bonuses is higher than that from normal income [Ishikawa and Ueda, 1984].

Our model is also possibly relevant to the so-called "disposition effect" in real estate [Case and Shiller, 1989] and financial markets [Shefrin and Statman, 1985; Ferris, Haugen and Makhija, 1988]. This effect refers to the fact that people tend to hold on to losing stocks and to real estate that has dropped in value, which depresses trading volume during market downturns. In such situations people have a choice between taking an immediate loss (by selling) or holding on to the asset with the potential of further loss or potential gain. Since the value function is convex in the loss domain, further losses are less than proportionately painful, while gains yield marginally increasing returns. The incentives are thus stacked in favor of holding on to the asset. The incentives are reversed on the gain side, motivating people to quickly sell assets that have gained in value.

In general, the market level implications of the model depend critically on the presence or absence of arbitrage opportunities that exist in a particular economic domain. Arbitrage opportunities are extensive in some markets, such as those for fixed rate financial assets where leveraged short sales are possible. In other markets, e.g., labor markets, arbitrage opportunities are virtually nonexistent. We would expect to see the effects of subjective time discounting manifested more clearly in the latter markets, in the specific case through labor contracts that offer large initial wage increases.

In financial markets the effects of scale and sign, produced by the curvature of the value function, will presumably be arbitraged away. If a particular market were to offer high interest rates on small investments, reflecting the magnitude effect, investors would simply borrow large sums and then invest them in small packages, driving down the rate on small investments.

Hyperbolic discounting is less easily arbitraged, even in financial markets. If most people demanded lower rates of return for long investment periods than for short ones, the yield curve would be downward sloping with no opportunities for arbitrage. Those who discounted the future at a constant rate would tend to invest in short-term securities, and might even short the long-term securities, but they could not do so without risk. Without denying that many purely economic factors influence the yield curve, our model suggests that psychological biases will independently exert pressure toward downward sloping.[5]

V. CONCLUDING REMARKS

The discounted utility model has played a dominant role in economic analyses of intertemporal choice. Although economists have experimented with alternative formulations, these efforts have typically responded to a single limitation of

---

[5] Our analysis may help to explain Fama's [1984] finding that, contrary to the liquidity preference hypothesis, the yield curve tends to drop, on average, past a certain point.

DU (e.g., increasing consumption postretirement) rather than to a more comprehensive critique. DU's basic assumptions and implications have, for the most part, not been questioned. This paper presents an integrated critique of DU, enumerating a series of intertemporal choice anomalies that run counter to the predictions of DU.

Perhaps most importantly, sensitivity to time delay is not well expressed by compound discounting. A given absolute delay looms larger if it occurs earlier rather than later; people are relatively insensitive to changes in timing for consumption objects that are already substantially delayed. Second, the marginal utility of consumption at different points in time depends not on absolute levels of consumption, but on consumption relative to some standard or point of reference. Generally, the status quo serves as reference point; people conserve on cognitive effort by evaluating new consumption alternatives in isolation, rather than by integrating them with existing plans.

Our model by no means incorporates all important psychological factors that influence intertemporal choice. For example, like any model with nonconstant discounting, it yields time-inconsistent behavior or "myopia" as Strotz [1955] called it. However, it cannot explain the high levels of conflict that such myopic behavior often evokes. Intertemporal choice often seems to involve an internal struggle for self-command [Schelling, 1984]. At the very moment of succumbing to the impulse to consume, individuals often recognize at a cognitive level that they are making a decision that is contrary to their long-term self-interest. Mathematical models of choice do not shed much light on such patterns of cognition and behavior (but see Ainslie [1985]).

Such episodes of internal conflict are not entirely random. Certain types of situations, such as when a person comes into direct sensory contact with a choice object, seem to elicit especially high rates of time discounting, while others do not. People exhibit high rates of discounting when driven by appetites such as hunger, thirst, or sexual desire. While not incompatible with the present model, these phenomena are not predicted by it.

Finally, our model does not incorporate preference interactions between periods, despite the fact that our own recent empirical research has shown such interactions to be pervasive when people choose between sequences of outcomes. Preference interactions are revealed through a strong dislike of deteriorating outcome sequences, and through a liking for evenly spreading consumption over time [Loewenstein and Prelec, 1991]. A taste for steady improvement seems to capture the preferences of most subjects, when sequences are being considered. Generally, the present model is more applicable to short-range decisions involving simple outcomes rather than long-term planning of consumption. No simple theory, however, can hope to reflect all motives that influence a particular decision. We have attempted to demonstrate that a theory with only two scaling functions can explain much of the observed deviation in preference from the normative discounted utility model.

34. Reason-Based Choice

Eldar Shafir, Itamar Simonson, and Amos Tversky

ABSTRACT. This paper considers the role of reasons and arguments in the making of decisions. It is proposed that, when faced with the need to choose, decision makers often seek and construct reasons in order to resolve the conflict and justify their choice, to themselves and to others. Experiments that explore and manipulate the role of reasons are reviewed, and other decision studies are interpreted from this perspective. The role of reasons in decision making is considered as it relates to uncertainty, conflict, context effects, and normative decision rules.

The result is that peculiar feeling of inward unrest known as *indecision*. Fortunately it is too familiar to need description, for to describe it would be impossible. As long as it lasts, with the various objects before the attention, we are said to *deliberate*; and when finally the original suggestion either prevails and makes the movement take place, or gets definitively quenched by its antagonists, we are said to *decide* . . . in favor of one or the other course. The reinforcing and inhibiting ideas meanwhile are termed the *reasons* or *motives* by which the decision is brought about.

William James (1890/1981)

My way is to divide half a sheet of paper by a line into two columns; writing over the one *Pro*, and over the other *Con*. Then, during three or four days' consideration. I put down under the different heads short hints of the different motives, that at different times occur to me for or against the measure. When I have thus got them all together in one view, I endeavor to estimate the respective weights . . . find at length where the balance lies . . . And,

This research was supported by U.S. Public Health Service Grant No. 1-R29-MH46885 from the National Institute of Mental Health, by Grant No. 89-0064 from the Air Force Office of Scientific Research and by Grant No. SES-9109535 from the National Science Foundation. The paper was partially prepared while the first author participated in a Summer Institute on Negotiation and Dispute Resolution at the Center for Advanced Study in the Behavioral Sciences, and while the second author was at the University of California, Berkeley. Funds for support of the Summer Institute were provided by the Andrew W. Mellon Foundation. We thank Robyn Dawes for helpful comments on an earlier draft.

> though the weight of reasons cannot be taken with the precision of algebraic
> quantities, yet, when each is thus considered, separately and comparatively,
> and the whole matter lies before me, I think I can judge better, and am less
> liable to make a rash step; and in fact I have found great advantage for this
> kind of equation, in what may be called *moral* or *prudential algebra*.
>
> Benjamin Franklin, 1772 (cited in Bigelow, 1887)

INTRODUCTION

The making of decisions, both big and small, is often difficult because of uncertainty and conflict. We are usually uncertain about the exact consequences of our actions, which may depend on the weather or the state of the economy, and we often experience conflict about how much of one attribute (e.g., savings) to trade off in favor of another (e.g., leisure). In order to explain how people resolve such conflict, students of decision making have traditionally employed either formal models or reason-based analyses. The formal modeling approach, which is commonly used in economics, management science, and decision research, typically associates a numerical value with each alternative, and characterizes choice as the maximization of value. Such value-based accounts include normative models, like expected utility theory (von Neumann & Morgenstern, 1947), as well as descriptive models, such as prospect theory (Kahneman & Tversky, 1979). An alternative tradition in the study of decision making, characteristic of scholarship in history and the law, and typical of political and business discourse, employs an informal, reason-based analysis. This approach identifies various reasons and arguments that are purported to enter into and influence decision, and explains choice in terms of the balance of reasons for and against the various alternatives. Examples of reason-based analyses can be found in studies of historic presidential decisions, such as those taken during the Cuban missile crisis (e.g., Allison, 1971), the Camp David accords (Telhami, 1990), or the Vietnam war (e.g., Berman, 1982; Betts & Gelb, 1979). Furthermore, reason-based analyses are commonly used to interpret "case studies" in business and law schools. Although the reasons invoked by researchers may not always correspond to those that motivated the actual decision makers, it is generally agreed that an analysis in terms of reasons may help explain decisions, especially in contexts where value-based models can be difficult to apply.

Little contact has been made between the two traditions, which have typically been applied to different domains. Reason-based analyses have been used primarily to explain non-experimental data, particularly unique historic, legal and political decisions. In contrast, value-based approaches have played a central role in experimental studies of preference and in standard economic analyses. The two approaches, of course, are not incompatible: reason-based accounts may often be translated into formal models, and formal analyses can generally be paraphrased as reason-based accounts. In the absence of a comprehensive theory of choice, both formal models and reason-based analyses may contribute to the understanding of decision making.

Both approaches have obvious strengths and limitations. The formal, value-based models have the advantage of rigor, which facilitates the derivation of testable implications. However, value-based models are difficult to apply to complex, real world decisions, and they often fail to capture significant aspects of people's deliberations. An explanation of choice based on reasons, on the other hand, is essentially qualitative in nature and typically vague. Furthermore, almost anything can be counted as a "reason," so that every decision may be rationalized after the fact. To overcome this difficulty, one could ask people to report their reasons for decision. Unfortunately, the actual reasons that guide decision may or may not correspond to those reported by the subjects. As has been amply documented (e.g., Nisbett & Wilson, 1977), subjects are sometimes unaware of the precise factors that determine their choices, and generate spurious explanations when asked to account for their decisions. Indeed, doubts about the validity of introspective reports have led many students of decision making to focus exclusively on observed choices. Although verbal reports and introspective accounts can provide valuable information, we use "reasons" in the present article to describe factors or motives that affect decision, whether or not they can be articulated or recognized by the decision maker.

Despite its limitations, a reason-based conception of choice has several attractive features. First, a focus on reasons seems closer to the way we normally think and talk about choices. When facing a difficult choice (e.g., between schools, or jobs) we try to come up with reasons for and against each option – we do not normally attempt to estimate their overall values. Second, thinking of choice as guided by reasons provides a natural way to understand the conflict that characterizes the making of decisions. From the perspective of reason-based choice, conflict arises when the decision maker has good reasons for and against each option, or conflicting reasons for competing options. Unlike numerical values, which are easy to compare, conflicting reasons may be hard to reconcile. An analysis based on reasons can also accommodate framing effects (Tversky & Kahneman, 1986) and elicitation effects (Tversky, Sattath, & Slovic, 1988), which show that preferences are sensitive to the ways in which options are described (e.g., in terms of gains or losses), and to the methods through which preferences are elicited (e.g., pricing versus choice). These findings, which are puzzling from the perspective of value maximization, are easier to interpret if we assume that different frames and elicitation procedures highlight different aspects of the options and thus bring forth different reasons to guide decision. Finally, a conception of choice based on reasons may incorporate comparative considerations (such as relative advantages, or anticipated regret) that typically remain outside the purview of value maximization.

In this article, we explore the logic of reason-based choice, and test some specific hypotheses concerning the role of reasons in decision making. The article proceeds as follows. Section 1 considers the role of reasons in choice between equally attractive options. Section 2 explores differential reliance on reasons for and against the selection of options. Section 3 investigates the interaction between high and low conflict and people's tendency to seek other alternatives, whereas section 4 considers the relation between conflict and the addition of alternatives to the choice set. Section 5 contrasts the impact of a specific reason for choice with that of a disjunction of reasons. Section 6 explores the role that irrelevant reasons can play in the making of decisions. Concluding remarks are presented in section 7.

1. CHOICE BETWEEN EQUALLY ATTRACTIVE OPTIONS

How do decision makers resolve the conflict when faced with a choice between two equally attractive options? To investigate this question, Slovic (1975) first had subjects equate pairs of alternatives, and later asked them to make choices between the equally valued alternatives in each pair. One pair, for example, were gift packages consisting of a combination of cash and coupons. For each pair, one component of one alternative was missing, as shown below, and subjects were asked to determine the value of the missing component that would render the two alternatives equally attractive. (In the following example, the value volunteered by the subject may be, say, $10).

	Gift package A	Gift package B
Cash	—	$20
Coupon book worth	$32	$18

A week later, subjects were asked to choose between the two equated alternatives. They were also asked, independently, which dimension – cash or coupons – they considered more important. Value-based theories imply that the two alternatives – explicitly equated for value – are equally likely to be selected. In contrast, in the choice between gift packages above, 88% of the subjects who had equated these alternatives for value then proceeded to choose the alternative that was higher on the dimension that the subject considered more important.

As Slovic (1975, 1990) suggests, people seem to be following a choice mechanism that is easy to explain and justify: choosing according to the more important dimension provides a better reason for choice than, say, random selection, or selection of the right-hand option. Slovic (1975) replicated the above pattern in numerous domains, including choices between college applicants, auto tires, baseball players, and routes to work. (For additional data and a discussion of elicitation procedures, see Tversky et al., 1988.) All the results were consistent with the hypothesis that people do not choose between the equated alternatives at random. Instead, they resolve the conflict by selecting the alternative that is superior on the more important dimension, which seems to provide a compelling reason for choice.

2. REASONS PRO AND CON

Consider having to choose one of two options or, alternatively, having to reject one of two options. Under the standard analysis of choice, the two tasks are interchangeable. In a binary choice situation it should not matter whether people are asked which option they prefer, or which they would reject. Because it is the options themselves that are assumed to matter, not the way in which they are described, if people prefer the first they will reject the second, and vice versa.

As suggested by Franklin's opening quote, our decision will depend partially on the weights we assign to the options' pros and cons. We propose that the positive features of options (their pros) will loom larger when choosing, whereas the negative features of options (their cons) will be weighted more heavily when rejecting. It is natural to select an option because of its positive features, and to reject an option because of its negative features. To the extent that people base their decisions on reasons for and against the options under consideration, they are likely to focus on reasons for choosing an option when deciding which to choose, and to focus on reasons for rejecting an option when deciding which to reject. This hypothesis leads to a straightforward prediction: consider two options, an *enriched* option, with more positive and more negative features, and an *impoverished* option, with fewer positive and fewer negative features. If positive features are weighted more heavily when choosing than when rejecting and negative features are weighted relatively more when rejecting than when choosing, then an enriched option could be both chosen and rejected when compared to an impoverished option. Let P_c and P_r denote, respectively, the percentage of subjects who choose and who reject a particular option. If choosing and rejecting are complementary, then the sum $P_c + P_r$ should equal 100. On the other hand, according to the above hypothesis, $P_c + P_r$ should be greater than 100 for the enriched option and less than 100 for the impoverished option. This pattern was observed by Shafir (1993). Consider, for example, the following problem which was presented to subjects in two versions that differed only in the bracketed questions. One half of the subjects received one version, the other half received the other. The enriched option appears last, although the order presented to subjects was counterbalanced.

Problem 1 ($n = 170$): Imagine that you serve on the jury of an only-child sole-custody case following a relatively messy divorce. The facts of the case are complicated by ambiguous economic, social, and emotional considerations, and you decide to base your decision entirely on the following few observations. [To which parent would you award sole custody of the child?/Which parent would you deny sole custody of the child?]

		Award	**Deny**
Parent A:	average income		
	average health		
	average working hours		
	reasonable rapport with the child		
	relatively stable social life	36%	45%

		Award	Deny
Parent B:	above average income		
	very close relationship with the child		
	extremely active social life		
	lots of work-related travel		
	minor health problems	64%	55%

Parent A, the impoverished option, is quite plain – with no striking positive or negative features. There are no particularly compelling reasons to award or deny this parent custody of the child. Parent B, the enriched option, on the other hand, has good reasons to be awarded custody (a very close relationship with the child and a good income), but also good reasons to be denied sole custody (health problems and extensive absences due to travel). To the right of the options are the percentages of subjects who chose to award and to deny custody to each of the parents. Parent B is the majority choice both for being awarded custody of the child and for being denied it. As predicted, $P_c + P_r$ for parent B ($64 + 55 = 119$) is significantly greater than 100, the value expected if choosing and rejecting were complementary ($z = 2.48$, $p < .02$). This pattern is explained by the observation that the enriched parent (parent B) provides more compelling reasons to be awarded as well as denied child custody.

The above pattern has been replicated in hypothetical choices between monetary gambles, college courses, and political candidates (Shafir, 1993). For another example, consider the following problem, presented to half the subjects in the "prefer" and to the other half in the "cancel" version.

Problem 2 ($n = 172$):

Prefer:
Imagine that you are planning a week vacation in a warm spot over spring break. You currently have two options that are reasonably priced. The travel brochure gives only a limited amount of information about the two options. Given the information available, which vacation spot would you prefer?

Cancel:
Imagine that you are planning a week vacation in a warm spot over spring break. You currently have two options that are reasonably priced, but you can no longer retain your reservation in both. The travel brochure gives only a limited amount of information about the two options. Given the information available, which reservation do you decide to cancel?

		Prefer	Cancel
Spot A:	average weather		
	average beaches		
	medium-quality hotel		
	medium-temperature water		
	average nightlife	33%	52%

		Prefer	Cancel
Spot B:	lots of sunshine		
	gorgeous beaches and coral reefs		
	ultra-modern hotel		
	very cold water		
	very strong winds		
	no nightlife	67%	48%

The information about the two spots is typical of the kind of information we have available when deciding where to take our next vacation. Because it is difficult to estimate the overall value of each spot, we are likely to seek reasons on which to base our decision. Spot A, the impoverished option, seems unremarkable yet unobjectionable on all counts. On the other hand, there are obvious reasons – gorgeous beaches, an abundance of sunshine, and an ultramodern hotel – for choosing spot B. Of course, there are also compelling reasons – cold water, winds, and a lack of nightlife – why spot B should be rejected. We suggest that the gorgeous beaches are likely to provide a more compelling reason when we choose than when we reject, and the lack of nightlife is likely to play a more central role when we reject than when we choose. Indeed, spot B's share of being preferred and rejected exceeds that of spot A ($P_c + P_r = 67 + 48 = 115$, $p < .05$). These results demonstrate that options are not simply ordered according to value, with the more attractive selected and the less attractive rejected. Instead, it appears that the relative importance of options' strengths and weaknesses varies with the nature of the task. As a result, we are significantly more likely to end up in spot B when we ask ourselves which we prefer than when we contemplate which to cancel (67% vs. 52%, $z = 2.83$, $p < .001$).

One of the most basic assumptions of the rational theory of choice is the principle of procedure invariance, which requires strategically equivalent methods of elication to yield identical preferences (see Tversky et al., 1988, for discussion). The choose–reject discrepancy represents a predictable failure of procedure invariance. This phenomenon is at variance with value maximization but is easily understood from the point of view of reason-based choice: reasons for choosing are more compelling when we choose than when we reject, and reasons for rejecting matter more when we reject than when we choose.

3. CHOICE UNDER CONFLICT: SEEKING OPTIONS

The need to choose often creates conflict: we are not sure how to trade off one attribute relative to another or, for that matter, which attributes matter to us most. It is a commonplace that we often attempt to resolve such conflict by seeking reasons for choosing one option over another. At times, the conflict between available alternatives is hard to resolve, which may lead us to seek additional options, or to maintain the status quo. Other times, the context is such that a comparison between alternatives generates compelling reasons to choose one option over another. Using reasons to resolve conflict has some non-obvious implications, which are addressed below. The present section focuses on people's decision to seek other alternatives; the next section explores some effects of adding options to the set under consideration.

In many contexts, we need to decide whether to opt for an available option or search for additional alternatives. Thus, a person who wishes to buy a used car may settle for a car that is currently available or continue searching for additional models. Seeking new alternatives usually requires additional time and effort, and may involve the risk of losing the previously available options. Conflict plays no role in the classical theory of choice. In this theory, each option x has a value $v(x)$ such that, for any offered set, the decision maker selects the option with the highest value. In particular, a person is expected to search for additional alternatives only if the expected value of searching exceeds that of the best option currently available. A reliance on reasons, on the other hand, entails that we should be more likely to opt for an available option when we have a convincing reason for its selection, and that we should be more likely to search further when a compelling reason for choice is not readily available.

To investigate this hypothesis, Tversky and Shafir (1992b) presented subjects with pairs of options, such as bets varying in probability and payoff, or student apartments varying in monthly rent and distance from campus, and had subjects choose one of the two options or, instead, request an additional option, at some cost. Subjects first reviewed the entire set of 12 options (gambles or apartments) to familiarize themselves with the available alternatives. In the study of choice between bets some subjects then received the following problem.

Conflict: Imagine that you are offered a choice between the following two gambles:

(x) *65% chance to win $15*
(y) *30% chance to win $35*

You can either select one of these gambles or you can pay $1 to add one more gamble to the choice set. The added gamble will be selected at random from the list you reviewed.

Other subjects received a similar problem except that option y was replaced by option x', to yield a choice between the following.

Dominance:

(x) *65% chance to win $15*
(x') *65% chance to win $14*

Subjects were asked to indicate whether they wanted to add another gamble or select between the available alternatives. They then chose their preferred gamble from the resulting set (with or without the added option). Subjects were instructed that the gambles they chose would be played out and that their payoff would be proportional to the amount of money they earned minus the fee they paid for the added gambles.

A parallel design presented choices between hypothetical student apartments. Some subjects received the following problem.

Conflict: Imagine that you face a choice between two apartments with the following characteristics:

(x) *$290 a month, 25 minutes from campus*
(y) *$350 a month, 7 minutes from campus*

Both have one bedroom and a kitchenette. You can choose now between the two apartments or you can continue to search for apartments (to be selected at random from the list you reviewed). In that case, there is some risk of losing one or both of the apartments you have found.

Other subjects received a similar problem except that option y was replaced by option x', to yield a choice between the following.

Dominance:

(x) *$290 a month, 25 minutes from campus*
(x') *$330 a month, 25 minutes from campus*

Note that in both pairs of problems the choice between x and y – the *conflict* condition – is non-trivial because the xs are better on one dimension and the ys are better on the other. In contrast, the choice between x and x' – the *dominance* condition – involves no conflict because the former strictly dominates the latter. Thus, while there is no obvious reason to choose one option over the other in the conflict condition, there is a decisive argument for preferring one of the two alternatives in the dominance condition.

On average, subjects requested an additional alternative 64% of the time in the conflict condition, and only 40% of the time in the dominance condition ($p < .05$). Subjects' tendency to search for additional options, in other words, was greater when the choice among alternatives was harder to rationalize than when there was a compelling reason and the decision was easy.

These data are inconsistent with the principle of value maximization. According to value maximization, a subject should search for additional alternatives if and only if the expected (subjective) value of searching exceeds that of the best alternative currently available. Because the best alternative offered in the dominance condition is also available in the conflict condition, value maximization implies that the percentage of subjects who seek an additional alternative cannot be greater in the conflict than in the dominance condition, contrary to the observed data.

It appears that the search for additional alternatives depends not only on the value of the best available option, as implied by value maximization, but also on the difficulty of choosing among the options under consideration. In situations of dominance, for example, there are clear and indisputable reasons for choosing one option over another (e.g., "This apartment is equally distant and I save $40!"). Having a compelling argument for choosing one of the options over the rest reduces the temptation to look for additional alternatives. When the choice involves conflict, on the other hand, reasons for choosing any one of the options are less immediately available and the decision is more difficult to justify (e.g., "Should I save $60 a month, or reside 18 minutes closer to campus?"). In the absence of compelling reasons for choice, there is a greater tendency to search for other alternatives.

4. CHOICE UNDER CONFLICT: ADDING OPTIONS

An analysis in terms of reasons can help explain observed violations of the principle of independence of irrelevant alternatives, according to which the preference ordering between two options should not be altered by the introduction of additional alternatives. This principle follows from the standard assumption of value maximization and has been routinely assumed in the analysis of consumer choice. Despite its intuitive appeal, there is a growing body of evidence that people's preferences depend on the context of choice, defined by the set of options under consideration. In particular, the addition and removal of options from the offered set can influence people's preferences among options that were available all along. Whereas in the previous section we considered people's tendency to seek alternatives in the context of a given set of options, in this section we illustrate phenomena that arise through the addition of options and interpret them in terms of reasons for choice.

A major testable implication of value maximization is that a non-preferred option cannot become preferred when new options are added to the offered set. In particular, a decision maker who prefers y over the option to defer the choice should not prefer to defer the choice when both y and x are available. That the "market share" of an option cannot be increased by enlarging the offered set is known as the *regularity condition* (see Tversky & Simonson, in press). Contrary to regularity, numerous experimental results indicate that the tendency to defer choice can increase with the addition of alternatives. Consider, for instance, the degree of conflict that arises when a person is presented with one attractive option (which he or she prefers to deferring the choice), compared to two competing alternatives. Choosing one out of two competing alternatives can be difficult: the mere fact that an alternative is attractive may not in itself provide a compelling reason for its selection because the other option may be equally attractive. The addition of an alternative may thus make the decision harder to justify and increase the tendency to defer the decision.

A related phenomenon was aptly described by Thomas Schelling, who tells of an occasion in which he had decided to buy an encyclopedia for his children. At the bookstore, he was presented with two attractive encyclopedias and, finding it difficult to choose between the two, ended up buying neither – this, despite the fact that had only one encyclopedia been available he would have happily bought it. More generally, there are situations in which people prefer each of the available alternatives over the status quo but do not have a compelling reason for choosing among the alternatives and, as a result, defer the decision, perhaps indefinitely.

The phenomenon described by Schelling was demonstrated by Tversky and Shafir (1992b) in the following pair of problems, which were presented to two groups of students ($n = 124$ and 121, respectively).

High Conflict: Suppose you are considering buying a compact disk (CD) player and have not yet decided what model to buy. You pass by a store that is having a 1-day clearance sale. They offer a popular SONY player for just $99, and a top-of-the-line AIWA player for just $169, both well below the list price. Do you?:

(x) buy the AIWA player.	27%
(y) buy the SONY player.	27%
(z) wait until you learn more about the various models.	46%

Low Conflict: Suppose you are considering buying a CD player and have not yet decided what model to buy. You pass by a store that is having a 1-day clearance sale. They offer a popular SONY player for just $99, well below the list price. Do you?:

(y) buy the SONY player.	66%
(z) wait until you learn more about the various models.	34%

The results indicate that people are more likely to buy a CD player in the latter, *low-conflict*, condition than in the former, *high-conflict*, situation ($p < .05$). Both models – the AIWA and the SONY – seem attractive, both are well priced, and both are on sale. The decision maker needs to determine whether she is better off with a cheaper, popular model, or with a more expensive and sophisticated one. This conflict is apparently not easy to resolve and compels many subjects to put off the purchase until they learn more about the various options. On the other hand, when the SONY alone is available, there are compelling arguments for its purchase: it is a popular player, it is very well priced, and it is on sale for 1 day only. In this situation, having good reasons to choose the offered option, a greater majority of subjects decide to opt for the CD player rather than delay the purchase.

The addition of a competing alternative in the preceding example increased the tendency to delay decision. Clearly, the level of conflict and its ease of resolution depend not only on the number of options available, but on how the options compare. Consider, for example, the following problem, in which the original AIWA player was replaced by an inferior model ($n = 62$).

Dominance: Suppose you are considering buying a CD player and have not yet decided what model to buy. You pass by a store that is having a 1-day clearance sale. They offer a popular SONY player for just $99, well below the list price, and an inferior AIWA player for the regular list price of $105. Do you?:

(x')	buy the AIWA player.	3%
(y)	buy the SONY player.	73%
(z)	wait until you learn more about the various models.	24%

In this version, contrary to the previous *high-conflict* version, the AIWA player is dominated by the SONY: it is inferior in quality and costs more. Thus, the presence of the AIWA does not detract from the reasons for buying the SONY; it actually supplements them: the SONY is well priced, it is on sale for 1 day only, *and* it is clearly better than its competitor. As a result, the SONY is chosen more often than before the inferior AIWA was added. The ability of an asymmetrically dominated or relatively inferior alternative, when added to a set, to increase the attractiveness and choice probability of the dominating option is known as the asymmetric dominance effect (Huber, Payne, & Puto, 1982). Note that in both the *high-conflict* and the *dominance* problems subjects were presented with two CD players and an option to delay choice. Subjects' tendency to delay, however, is much greater when they lack clear reasons for buying either player than when they have compelling reasons to buy one player and not the other ($p < .005$).

The above patterns violate the regularity condition, which is assumed to hold so long as the added alternatives do not provide new and relevant information. In the above scenario, one could argue that the added options (the superior player in one case and the inferior player in the other) conveyed information about the consumer's chances of finding a better deal. Recall that information considerations could not explain the search experiments of the previous section because there subjects reviewed all the potentially available options. Nevertheless, to test this interpretation further, Tversky and Shafir (1992b) devised a similar problem, involving real payoffs, in which the option to defer is not available. Students ($n = 80$) agreed to fill out a brief questionnaire for $1.50. Following the questionnaire, one half of the subjects were offered the opportunity to exchange the $1.50 (the default) for one of two prizes: a metal Zebra pen (henceforth, Zebra), or a pair of plastic Pilot pens (henceforth, Pilot). The other half of the subjects were only offered the opportunity to exchange the $1.50 for the Zebra. The prizes were shown to the subjects, who were also informed that each prize regularly costs a little over $2.00. Upon indicating their preference, subjects received their chosen option. The results were as follows. Seventy-five per cent of the subjects chose the Zebra over the payment when the Zebra was the only alternative, but only 47% chose the Zebra *or* the Pilot when both were available ($p < .05$). Faced with a tempting alternative, subjects had a compelling reason to forego the payment: the majority took advantage of the opportunity to obtain an attractive prize of greater value. The availability of competing alternatives of comparable value, on the other hand, did not present an immediate reason for choosing either alternative over the other, thus increasing the tendency to retain the default option. Similar effects in hypothetical medical decisions made by expert physicians are documented in Redelmeier and Shafir (1993).

In the above study the addition of a competing alternative was shown to increase the popularity of the default option. Recall that the popularity of an option may also be enhanced by the addition of an inferior alternative. Thus, in accord with the asymmetric dominance effect, the tendency to prefer x over y can be increased

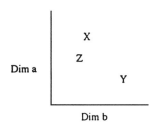

Figure 34.1. A schematic representation of asymmetric dominance. The tendency to prefer x over y can be increased by adding an alternative, z, that is clearly inferior to x but not to y.

by adding a third alternative z that is clearly inferior to x but not to y (see Figure 34.1). The phenomenon of asymmetric dominance was first demonstrated, by Huber, Payne, and Puto (1982), in choices between hypothetical options. Wedell (1991) reports similar findings using monetary gambles. The following example involving real choices is taken from Simonson and Tversky (1992). One group ($n = 106$) was offered a choice between $6 and an elegant Cross pen. The pen was selected by 36% of the subjects, and the remaining 64% chose the cash. A second group ($n = 115$) was given a choice among three options: $6 in cash, the same Cross pen, and a second pen that was distinctly less attractive. Only 2% of the subjects chose the less attractive pen, but its presence increased the percentage of subjects who chose the Cross pen from 36% to 46% ($p < .10$). This pattern again violates the regularity condition discussed earlier. Similar violations of regularity were observed in choices among other consumer goods. In one study, subjects received descriptions and pictures of microwave ovens taken from a "Best" catalogue. One group ($n = 60$) was then asked to choose between an Emerson priced at $110, and a Panasonic priced at $180. Both items were on sale, one third off the regular price. Here, 57% chose the Emerson and 43% chose the Panasonic. A second group ($n = 60$) was presented with these options along with a $200 Panasonic at a 10% discount. Only 13% of the subjects chose the more expensive Panasonic, but its presence increased the percentage of subjects who chose the less expensive Panasonic from 43% to 60% ($p < .05$).[1]

Simonson and Tversky (1992) have interpreted these observations in terms of "tradeoff contrast." They proposed that the tendency to prefer an alternative

---

[1] These effects of context on choice can naturally be used in sales tactics. For example, Williams–Sonoma, a mail-order business located in San Francisco, used to offer a bread-baking appliance priced at $279. They later added a second bread-baking appliance, similar to the first but somewhat larger, and priced at $429 – more than 50% higher than the original appliance. Not surprisingly, Williams–Sonoma did not sell many units of the new item. However, the sales of the less expensive appliance almost doubled. (To the best of our knowledge, Williams–Sonoma did not anticipate this effect.)

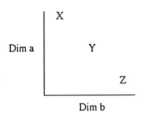

Figure 34.2. A schematic representation of extremeness aversion. Option y is relatively more popular in the trinary choice, when both x and z are available, than in either one of the binary comparisons, when either x or z are removed.

is enhanced or hindered depending on whether the tradeoffs within the set under consideration are favorable or unfavorable to that alternative. A second cluster of context effects, called *extremeness aversion*, which refers to the finding that, within an offered set, options with extreme values are relatively less attractive than options with intermediate values (Simonson, 1989). For example, consider two-dimensional options x, y, and z, such that y lies between x and z (see Figure 34.2). Considerations of value maximization imply that the middle alternative, y, should be relatively less popular in the trinary choice than in either one of the binary comparisons (y compared to x, or y compared to z). Extremeness aversion, on the other hand, yields the opposite prediction because y has small advantages and disadvantages with respect to x and to z, whereas both x and z have more extreme advantages and disadvantages with respect to each other. This pattern was observed in several experiments. For example, subjects were shown five 35 mm cameras varying in quality and price. One group ($n = 106$) was then given a choice between two cameras: a Minolta X-370 priced at $170 and a Minolta 3000i priced at $240. A second group ($n = 115$) was given an additional option, the Minolta 7000i priced at $470. Subjects in the first group were split evenly between the two options, yet 57% of the subjects in the second group chose the middle option (Minolta 3000i), with the remaining divided about equally between the two extreme options. Thus, the introduction of an extreme option reduced the "market share" of the other extreme option, but not of the middle option. Note that this effect cannot be attributed to information conveyed by the offered set because respondents had reviewed the relevant options prior to making their choice.

We suggest that both tradeoff contrast and extremeness aversion can be understood in terms of reasons. Suppose a decision maker faces a choice between two alternatives, x and y, and suppose x is of higher quality whereas y is better priced. This produces conflict if the decision maker finds it difficult to determine whether the quality difference outweighs the price difference. Suppose now that the choice set also includes a third alternative, z, that is clearly inferior to y but not to x. The presence of z, we suggest, provides an argument for choosing y over x. To the extent that the initial choice between x and y is difficult, the presence of z may help the decision maker break the tie. In the pen study, for example, the addition of the relatively unattractive pen, whose monetary value is unclear but whose inferiority to the elegant Cross pen is apparent, provides a reason for choosing the Cross pen over the cash. Similarly, in the presence of options with extreme values on the relevant dimensions, the middle option can be seen as a compromise choice that is easier to defend than either extremes. Indeed, verbal protocols show that the accounts generated by subjects while making these choices involve considerations of asymmetric advantage and compromise; furthermore, asymmetric dominance is enhanced when subjects anticipate having to justify their decisions to others (Simonson, 1989). It is noteworthy that the arguments leading to tradeoff contrast and extremeness aversion are comparative in nature; they are based on the positions of the options in the choice set; hence they cannot be readily translated into the values associated with single alternatives.

Tversky and Simonson (in press) have proposed a formal model that explains the above findings in terms of a tournament-like process in which each option is compared against other available options in terms of their relative advantages and disadvantages. This model can be viewed as a formal analog of the preceding qualitative account based on reasons for choice. Which analysis – the formal or the qualitative – proves more useful is likely to depend, among other things, on the nature of the problem and on the purpose of the investigation.

5. DEFINITE VERSUS DISJUNCTIVE REASONS

People sometimes encounter situations of uncertainty in which they eventually opt for the same course of action, but for very different reasons, depending on how the uncertainty is resolved. Thus, a student who has taken an exam may decide to take a vacation, either to reward herself in case she passes or to console herself in case she fails. However, as illustrated below, the student may be reluctant to commit to a vacation while the outcome of the exam is pending. The following problem was presented by Tversky and Shafir (1992a) to 66 undergraduate students.

> **Disjunctive version:** Imagine that you have just taken a tough qualifying examination. It is the end of the fall quarter, you feel tired and run-down, and you are not sure that you passed the exam. In case you failed you have to take the exam again in a couple of months – after the Christmas holidays. You now have an opportunity to buy a very attractive 5-day Christmas vacation package in Hawaii at an exceptionally low price. The special offer expires tomorrow, while the exam grade will not be available until the following day. Would you?:
>
> (a) buy the vacation package.   32%
> (b) not buy the vacation package.   7%
> (c) pay a $5 non-refundable fee in order to retain the rights to buy   61%
>   the vacation package at the same exceptional price the day
>   after tomorrow – after you find out whether or not you
>   passed the exam.

The percentage of subjects who chose each option appears on the right. Two additional versions, called *pass* and *fail*, were presented to two different groups of 67 students each. These two versions differed only in the expression in brackets.

> **Pass/fail versions:** Imagine that you have just taken a tough qualifying examination. It is the end of the fall quarter, you feel tired and run-down, and you find out that you [passed the exam./failed the exam. You will have to take it again in a couple of months – after the Christmas holidays.] You now have an opportunity to buy a very attractive 5-day Christmas vacation package in Hawaii at an exceptionally low price. The special offer expires tomorrow. Would you?:

	Pass	Fail
(a) buy the vacation package.	54%	57%
(b) not buy the vacation package.	16%	12%
(c) pay a $5 non-refundable fee in order to retain the rights to buy the vacation package at the same exceptional price the day after tomorrow.	30%	31%

The data show that more than half of the students chose the vacation package when they knew that they passed the exam and an even larger percentage chose the vacation when they knew that they failed. However, when they did not know whether they had passed or failed, less than one third of the students chose the vacation and 61% were willing to pay $5 to postpone the decision until the following day, when the results of the exam would be known.[2] Once the outcome of the exam is known, the student has good – albeit different – reasons for taking the trip: having passed the exam, the vacation is presumably seen as a reward following a hard but successful semester; having failed the exam, the vacation becomes a consolation and time to recuperate before a re-examination. Not knowing the outcome of the exam, however, the student lacks a definite reason for going to Hawaii. Notice that the outcome of the exam will be known long before the vacation begins. Thus, the uncertainty characterizes the actual moment of decision, not the eventual vacation.

The indeterminacy of reasons for going to Hawaii discourages many students from buying the vacation, even when both outcomes – passing or failing the exam – ultimately favor this course of action. Tversky and Shafir (1992a) call the pattern of decisions above a *disjunction effect*. Evidently, a disjunction of

---

[2] An additional group of subjects ($n = 123$) was presented with both the fail and the pass versions, and asked whether or not they would buy the vacation package in each case. Two thirds of the subjects made the same choice in the two conditions, indicating that the data for the disjunctive version cannot be explained by the hypothesis that those who like the vacation in case they pass the exam do not like it in case they fail, and vice versa. Note that while only one third of the subjects made different decisions depending on the outcome of the exam, more than 60% of the subjects chose to wait when the outcome was not known.

different reasons (reward in case of success or consolation in case of failure) is often less compelling than either definite reason alone. A significant proportion of the students above were willing to pay, in effect, for information that was ultimately not going to affect their decision – they would choose to go to Hawaii in either case – but that promised to leave them with a more definite reason for making that choice. The willingness to pay for non-instrumental information is at variance with the classical model in which the worth of information is determined only by its potential to influence decision.

People's preference for definite as opposed to disjunctive reasons has significant implications in cases where the option to defer decision is not available. Consider the following series of problems presented by Tversky and Shafir (1992a) to 98 students.

Win/lose version: Imagine that you have just played a game of chance that gave you a 50% chance to win $200 and a 50% chance to lose $100. The coin was tossed and you have [won $200/lost $100]. You are now offered a second identical gamble: 50% chance to win $200 and 50% chance to lose $100. Would you?:

	Won	Lost
(a) accept the second gamble.	69%	59%
(b) reject the second gamble.	31%	41%

The students were presented with the *win* version of the problem above, followed a week later by the *lose version*, and 10 days after that by the following version that is a disjunction of the previous two. The problems were embedded among other, similar problems so that the relation between the various versions was not transparent. Subjects were instructed to treat each decision separately.

Disjunctive version: Imagine that you have just played a game of chance that gave you a 50% chance to win $200 and a 50% chance to lose $100. Imagine that the coin has already been tossed but that you will not know whether you have won $200 or lost $100 until you make your decision concerning a second, identical gamble: 50% chance to win $200 and 50% chance to lose $100. Would you?:

(a) accept the second gamble.   36%
(b) reject the second gamble.   64%

The data show that a majority of subjects accepted the second gamble after having won the first gamble and a majority also accepted the second gamble after having lost the first gamble. However, the majority of subjects rejected the second gamble when the outcome of the first was not known. An examination of individual choices reveals that approximately 40% of the subjects accepted the second gamble both after a gain in the first and after a loss. Among these, however, 65% rejected the second gamble in the disjunctive condition, when the outcome of the first gamble was not known. Indeed, this response pattern (accepting in both conditions but rejecting in the disjunction) was the single most frequent pattern, exhibited by 27% of all subjects. This pattern, which violates Savage's (1954) sure-thing principle, cannot be attributed to unreliability (Tversky & Shafir, 1992a).

The students above were offered a gamble with a positive expected value, and an even chance of a non-trivial loss. Different reasons were likely to arise for accepting the second gamble depending on the outcome of the first. In the *win* condition, the decision maker is already up $200, so even a loss on the second gamble leaves him or her ahead overall, which makes this option quite attractive. In the *lose* condition, on the other hand, the decision maker is down $100. Playing the second gamble offers a chance to "get out of the red," which for many is more attractive than accepting a sure $100 loss. In the *disjunctive* condition, however, the decision maker does not know whether she is up $200 or down $100; she does not know, in other words, whether her reason for playing the second gamble is that it is a no-loss proposition or, instead, that it provides a chance to escape a sure loss. In the absence of a definite reason, fewer subjects accept the second gamble.

This interpretation is further supported by the following modification of the above problem in which both outcomes of the first gamble were increased by $400 so that the decision maker could not lose in either case.

> *Imagine that you have just played a game of chance that gave you a 50% chance to win $600 and a 50% chance to win $300. Imagine that the coin has already been tossed, but that you will not know whether you have won $600 or $300 until you make your decision concerning a second gamble: 50% chance to win $200 and 50% chance to lose $100.*

A total of 171 subjects were presented with this problem, equally divided into three groups. One group was told that they had won $300 on the first gamble, a second group was told that they had won $600 on the first gamble, and the third group was told that the outcome of the first gamble – $300 or $600 – was not known (the disjunctive version). In all cases, subjects had to decide whether to accept or to reject the second gamble which, as in the previous problem, consisted of an even chance to win $200 or lose $100. The percentage of subjects who accepted the second gamble in the $300, $600, and disjunctive versions, were 69%, 75%, and 73%, respectively. (Recall that the corresponding figures for the original problem were 59%, 69%, and 36%; essentially identical figures were obtained in a between-subjects replication of that problem.) In contrast to the original problem, the second gamble in this modified problem was equally popular in the disjunctive as in the non-disjunctive versions. Whereas in the original scenario the second gamble amounted to either a no-loss proposition or a chance to avoid a sure loss, in the modified scenario the second gamble amounts to a no-loss proposition regardless of the outcome of the first gamble. The increased popularity of the second gamble in the modified problem shows that it is not the disjunctive situation itself that discourages people from playing.

Rather, it is the lack of a specific reason that seems to drive the effect: when the same reason applies regardless of outcome, the disjunction no longer reduces the tendency to accept the gamble.

As illustrated above, changes in the context of decision are likely to alter the reasons that subjects bring to mind and, consequently, their choices. Elsewhere (Shafir & Tversky, 1992) we describe a disjunction effect in the context of a one-shot prisoner's dilemma game played on a computer for real payoffs. Subjects ($n = 80$) played a series of prisoner's dilemma games, without feedback, each against a different unknown player. In this setup, the rate of cooperation was 3% when subjects knew that the other player had defected, and 16% when they knew that the other had cooperated. However, when subjects did not know whether the other player had cooperated or defected (the standard version of the prisoner's dilemma game) the rate of cooperation rose to 37%. Thus, many subjects defected when they knew the other's choice – be it cooperation or defection – but cooperated when the other player's choice was not known. Shafir and Tversky (1992) attribute this pattern to the different perspectives that underlie subjects' behavior under uncertainty as opposed to when the uncertainty is resolved. In particular, we suggest that the reasons for competing are more compelling when the other player's decision is known and the payoff depends on the subject alone than when the other's chosen strategy is uncertain and the outcome of the game depends on the choices of both players.

The above "disjunctive" manipulation – which has no direct bearing from the point of view of value maximization – appears to influence the reasons for decision that people bring to mind. Another kind of manipulation that seems to alter people's reasons without bearing directly on options' values is described in what follows.

6. NON-VALUED FEATURES

Reasons for choice or rejection often refer to specific features of the options under consideration. The positive features of an option typically provide reasons for choosing that option and its negative features typically provide reasons for rejection. What happens when we add features that are neither attractive nor aversive? Can choice be influenced by features that have little or no value?

Simonson and his colleagues have conducted a number of studies on the effects of non-valued features, and tested the hypothesis that people are reluctant to choose alternatives that are supported by reasons that they do not find appealing. In one study, for example, Simonson, Nowlis, and Simonson (in press) predicted that people would be less likely to choose an alternative that was chosen by another person for a reason that does not apply to them. UC Berkeley business students ($n = 113$) were told that, because of budget cuts and in order to save paper and duplicating costs, a questionnaire that they will receive was designed for use by two respondents. Thus, when subjects had to enter a choice, they could see the choice made by the previous "respondent" and the reason given for it. The choices and reasons of the previous respondents were systematically manipulated. One problem, for example, offered a choice between attending the MBA programs at Northwestern and UCLA. In one version of the questionnaire, the previous respondent had selected Northwestern and provided the (handwritten) reason, "I have many relatives in the Chicago area." Because this reason does not apply to most subjects, it was expected to reduce their likelihood of choosing Northwestern. In a second version, no reason was given for the choice of Northwestern. As expected, those exposed to an irrelevant reason were less likely to choose Northwestern than subjects who saw the other respondent's choice but not his or her reason (23% vs. 43%, $p < .05$). It should be noted that both Northwestern and UCLA are well known to most subjects (Northwestern currently has the highest ranked MBA program; the UCLA program is ranked high and belongs to the same UC system as Berkeley). Thus, it is unlikely that subjects made inferences about the quality of Northwestern based on the fact that another respondent chose it because he or she had relatives in Chicago.

In a related study, Simonson, Carmon, and O'Curry (in press) showed that endowing an option with a feature that was intended to be positive but, in fact, has no value for the decision maker can reduce the tendency to choose that option, even when subjects realize that they are not paying for the added feature. For example, an offer to purchase a collector's plate – that most did not want – if one buys a particular brand of cake mix was shown to lower the tendency to buy that particular brand relative to a second, comparable cake mix brand (from 31% to 14%, $p < .05$). Choosing brands that offer worthless bonuses was judged (in a related study) as more difficult to justify and as more susceptible to criticism. An analysis of verbal protocols showed that a majority of those who failed to select the endowed option explicitly mentioned not needing the added feature. It should be noted that sale promotions, such as the one involving the collector's plate offer above, are currently employed by a wide range of companies and there is no evidence that they lead to any inferences about the quality of the promoted product (e.g., Blattberg & Neslin, 1990).

The above manipulations all added "positive," albeit weak or irrelevant, features, which should not diminish an option's value; yet, they apparently provide a reason against choosing the option, especially when other options are otherwise equally attractive. Evidently, the addition of a potentially attractive feature that proves useless can provide a reason to reject the option in favor of a competing alternative that has no "wasted" features.

7. CONCLUDING REMARKS

People's choices may occasionally stem from affective judgments that preclude a thorough evaluation of the options (cf. Zajonc, 1980). In such cases, an analysis of the reasons for choice may prove unwarranted and, when attempted by the decision maker, may actually result in a different, and possibly inferior, decision

(Wilson & Schooler, 1991). Other choices, furthermore, may follow standard operating procedures that involve minimal reflective effort. Many decisions, nonetheless, result from a careful evaluation of options in which people attempt to arrive at what they believe is the best choice. Having discarded the less attractive options and faced with a choice that is hard to resolve, people often search for a compelling rationale for choosing one alternative over another. In this paper, we presented an analysis of the role of reasons in decision making and considered ways in which an analysis based on reasons may contribute to the standard quantitative approach based on the maximization of value. A number of hypotheses that derive from this perspective were investigated in experimental settings.

The reasons that enter into the making of decisions are likely to be intricate and diverse. In the preceding sections we have attempted to identify a few general principles that govern the role of reasons in decision making, and thus some of the fundamental ways in which thinking about reasons is likely to contribute to our understanding of the making of decisions. A reliance on the more important dimensions – those likely to provide more compelling reasons for choice – was shown in section 1 to predict preferences between previously equated options. The notions of compatibility and salience were summoned in section 2 to account for the differential weighting of reasons in a choice versus rejection task. Reasons, it appears, lend themselves to certain framing manipulations that are harder to explain from the perspective of value maximization. In section 3, manipulating the precise relationships between competing alternatives was shown to enhance or reduce conflict, yielding decisions that were easier or more difficult to rationalize and justify. Providing a context that presents compelling reasons for choosing an option apparently increases people's tendency to opt for that option, whereas comparing alternatives that render the aforementioned reasons less compelling tends to increase people's tendency to maintain the status quo or search for other alternatives. The ability of the context of decision to generate reasons that affect choice was further discussed in section 4, where the addition and removal of competing alternatives was interpreted as generating arguments for choice based on comparative considerations of relative advantages and compromise. The relative weakness of disjunctive reasons was discussed in section 5. There, a number of studies contrasted people's willingness to reach a decision based on a definite reason for choice, with their reluctance to arrive at a decision in the presence of uncertainty about which reason is actually relevant to the case at hand. Section 6 briefly reviewed choice situations in which the addition of purported reasons for choosing an option, which subjects did not find compelling, was seen to diminish their tendency to opt for that option, even though its value had not diminished.

The nature of the reasons that guide decision, and the ways in which they interact, await further investigation. There is evidence to suggest that a wide variety of arguments play a role in decision making. We often search for a convincing rationale for the decisions that we make, whether for inter-personal purposes, so that we can explain to others the reasons for our decision, or for intra-personal motives, so that we may feel confident of having made the "right" choice. Attitudes toward risk and loss can sometimes be rationalized on the basis of common myths or clichés, and choices are sometimes made on the basis of moral or prudential principles that are used to override specific cost–benefit calculations (cf. Prelec & Herrnstein, 1991). Formal decision rules, moreover, may sometimes act as arguments in people's deliberations. Thus, when choosing between options x and z, we may realize that, sometime earlier, we had preferred x over y and y over z and that, therefore, by transitivity, we should now choose x over z. Montgomery (1983) has argued that people look for dominance structures in decision problems because they provide a compelling reason for choice. Similarly, Tversky and Shafir (1992a) have shown that detecting the applicability of the sure-thing principle to a decision situation leads people to act in accord with this principle's compelling rationale. Indeed, it has been repeatedly observed that the axioms of rational choice which are often violated in non-transparent situations are generally satisfied when their application is transparent (e.g., Tversky & Kahneman, 1986). These results suggest that the axioms of rational choice act as compelling arguments, or reasons, for making a particular decision when their applicability has been detected, not as universal laws that constrain people's choices.

In contrast to the classical theory that assumes stable values and preferences, it appears that people often do not have well-established values, and that preferences are actually constructed – not merely revealed – during their elicitation (cf. Payne, Bettman, & Johnson, 1992). A reason-based approach lends itself well to such a constructive interpretation. Decisions, according to this analysis, are often reached by focusing on reasons that justify the selection of one option over another. Different frames, contexts, and elicitation procedures highlight different aspects of the options and bring forth different reasons and considerations that influence decision.

The reliance on reasons to explain experimental findings has been the hallmark of social psychological analyses. Accounts of dissonance (Wicklund & Brehm, 1976) and self-perception (Bem, 1972), for example, focus on the reasons that people muster in an attempt to explain their counter-attitudinal behaviors. Similarly, attribution theory (Heider, 1980) centers around the reasons that people attribute to others' behavior. These studies, however, have primarily focused on postdecisional rationalization rather than predecisional conflict. Although the two processes are closely related, there are nevertheless some important differences. Much of the work in social psychology has investigated how people's decisions affect the way they think. The present paper, in contrast, has considered how the reasons that enter into people's thinking about a problem influence their decision. A number of researchers have recently begun to explore related issues. Billig (1987), for example, has adopted a rhetorical approach to understanding social psychological issues according to which "our inner deliberations are silent arguments conducted within a single self" (p. 5).

Related "explanation-based" models of decision making have been applied by Pennington and Hastie (1988, 1992) to account for judicial decisions, and the importance of social accountability in choice has been addressed by Tetlock (1992). From a philosophical perspective, a recent essay by Schick (1991) analyzes various decisions from the point of view of practical reason. An influential earlier work is Toulmin's (1950) study of the role of arguments in ethical reasoning.

In this article, we have attempted to explore some of the ways in which reasons and arguments enter into people's decisions. A reason-based analysis may come closer to capturing part of the psychology that underlies decision and thus may help shed light on a number of phenomena that remain counterintuitive from the perspective of the classical theory. It is instructive to note that many of the experimental studies described in this paper were motivated by intuitions stemming from a qualitative analysis based on reasons, not from a value-based perspective, even if they can later be interpreted in that fashion. We do not propose that accounts based on reasons replace value-based models of choice. Rather, we suggest that an analysis of reasons may illuminate some aspects of reflective choice, and generate new hypotheses for further study.

35. Value Elicitation

Is There Anything in There?

Baruch Fischhoff

ABSTRACT. Eliciting people's values is a central pursuit in many areas of
the social sciences, including survey research, attitude research, economics,
and behavior decision theory. These disciplines differ considerably in the
core assumptions they make about the nature of the values that are available
for elicitation. These assumptions lead to very different methodological concerns and interpretations, as well as to different risks of reading too much
or too little into people's responses. The analysis here characterizes these
assumptions and the research paradigms based on them. It also offers an
account of how they arise, rooted in the psychological and sociological contexts within which different researchers function.

Taken all together, how would you say things are these days – would you
say that you are very happy, pretty happy, or not too happy?

National Opinion Research Center (NORC), 1978

Think about the last time during the past month that you were tired easily.
Suppose that it had been possible to pay a sum of money to have eliminated
being tired easily immediately that *one* time. What sum of money would
you have been willing to pay?

Dickie, Gerking, McClelland, & Schulze, 1987, p. 19 (Appendix 1)

In this task, you will be asked to choose between a certain loss and a gamble
that exposes you to some chance of loss. Specifically, you must choose either:
Situation A. One chance in 4 to lose $200 (and 3 chances in 4 to lose nothing).

Preparation of this article was supported by National Science Foundation Grant No. SES-8175564
and by the Carnegie Corporation of New York, Council on Adolescent Development. The views
expressed are those of the author.

My special thanks go to Robert Abelson, who suggested the juxtaposition that is explored here,
and to Charles Turner, who has stimulated concern for nonsampling error for many years. My
thinking on these issues has benefited from discussions with many people, including Lita Furby,
Robyn Dawes, Paul Slovic, Sarah Lichtenstein, Amos Tversky, Daniel Kahneman, Alan Randall,
and Robin Gregory. I have also received valuable comments from participants in the National Research Council Panel on Survey Measure of Subjective Phenomena; the Russell Sage Foundation
Conference, "Towards a Scientific Analysis of Values"; and the U.S. Forest Service Conference
on Amenity Resource Valuation.

Or Situation B. A certain loss of $50. Of course, you'd probably prefer not to be in either of these situations, but, if forced to either play the gamble (A) or accept the certain loss (B), which would you prefer to do?

Fischhoff, Slovic, & Lichtenstein, 1980, p. 127

600 people are ill from a serious disease. Physicians face the following choice among treatments: Treatment A will save 200 lives. Treatment B has 1 chance in 3 to save all 600 lives and 2 chances in 3 to save 0 lives. Which treatment would you choose, A or B?

Tversky & Kahneman, 1981, p. 454

PROBLEMATIC PREFERENCES

A Continuum of Philosophies

A critical tenet for many students of other people's values is that "If we've got questions, then they've got answers." Perhaps the most ardent subscribers to this belief are experimental psychologists, survey researchers, and economists. Psychologists expect their "subjects" to behave reasonably with any clearly described task, even if it has been torturously contrived in order to probe esoteric theoretical points. Survey researchers expect their "participants" to provide meaningful answers to items on any topic intriguing them (or their clients), assuming that the questions have been put into good English. Economists expect "actors" to pursue their own best interests, thereby making choices that reveal their values, in whatever decisions the marketplace poses (and economists choose to study).

This article examines this *philosophy of articulated values* both in its own right and by positioning it on a continuum of philosophies toward value formation and measurement. At the other end of this continuum lies what might be called the *philosophy of basic values*. It holds that people lack well-differentiated values for all but the most familiar of evaluation questions, about which they have had the chance, by trial, error, and rumination, to settle on stable values. In other cases, they must derive specific valuations from some basic values through an inferential process.

Perhaps the clearest example of this latter perspective might be found in the work of decision analysts (Raiffa, 1968; von Winterfeldt & Edwards, 1986; Watson & Buede, 1988). These consultants lead their clients to decompose complex evaluation problems into basic dimensions of concern, called *attributes*. Each attribute represents a reason why one might like or dislike the possible outcomes of a decision. For example, the options facing someone in the market for a car are different vehicles (including, perhaps, none at all), whose attributes might include cost, style, and reliability.

The relative attractiveness (or unattractiveness) of different amounts of each attribute is then captured in a *utility function* defined over the range of possible consequences (e.g., Just how much worse is breaking down once a month than breaking down twice a year?). After evaluating the attributes in isolation, the decision maker must consider their relative importance (e.g., Just how much money is it worth to reduce the frequency of repairs from annual to biennial?). These tradeoffs are expressed in a multiattribute utility function. Having done all of this, the consequences associated with specific actions are then evaluated by mapping them into the space spanned by that function.

Between the philosophies of articulated values and basic values lie intermediate positions. These hold that although people need not have answers to all questions, neither need they start from scratch each time an evaluative question arises. Rather, people have stable values of moderate complexity, which provide an advanced starting point for responding to questions of real-world complexity. Where a particular version of this perspective falls on the continuum defined by the two extreme philosophies depends on how well developed these partial perspectives are held to be.

Each of these philosophies directs the student of values to different sets of focal methodological concerns. For example, if people can answer any question, then an obvious concern is that they answer the right one. As a result, investigators adhering to the articulated values philosophy will worry about posing the question most germane to their theoretical interests and ensuring that it is understood as intended. On the other hand, if complex evaluations are to be derived from simple evaluative principles, then it is essential that the relevant principles be assembled and that the inferential process be conducted successfully. That process could fail if it required too much of an intellectual effort and, also, if the question were poorly formulated or inadequately understood. If people have thought some about the topic of an evaluation question, then they have less far to go in order to produce a full answer. Yet, even if people hold such partial perspectives, there is still the risk that they will miss some nuances of the question and, as a result, overestimate how completely they have understood it and their value regarding the issues that it raises.

A Choice of Paradigms

The effort to deal with these different worries in a systematic fashion has led to distinct research paradigms (Kuhn, 1962). Each such paradigm offers a set of methods for dealing with its focal worries, along with empirical tests of success in doing so. Each has evolved some theory to substantiate its approach. As paradigms, each is better suited to answering problems within its frame of reference than to challenging that frame. Thus, for example, the articulated values paradigm is better at devising additional ways to improve the understanding of questions than at determining whether understanding is possible.

This is, of course, something of a caricature. Many investigators are capable of wearing more than one hat. For example, survey researchers have extensively studied the properties of the *don't know* response (T. Smith, 1984). Still, when one is trying to get a survey (or experiment or economic analysis) out the door,

Table 35.1. Risk of Misdiagnosis

	Proper Assumption		
Assumption Made	**Articulated Values**	**Partial Perspectives**	**Basic Values**
Articulated values	—	Get incomplete values Inadvertently impose perspective	Get meaningless values Impose single perspective
Partial perspectives	Promote new perspectives Distract from sharpening	—	Impose multiple perspectives Exaggerate resolvability
Basic values	Shake confidence Distract from sharpening	Discourage Distract from reconciliation	—

Note: Above diagonal: misplaced precision, undue confidence in results, missed opportunity to help. Below diagonal: needless complication, neglect of basic methodology, induced confusion.

it is hard to address these issues at length for every question. It may be easier to take *no answer* for an answer in principle than in practice. At the other extreme, it may be unprofitable for a consulting decision analyst to deal with situations in which the answer to a complex evaluation question is there for the asking, without the rigamarole of multiattribute utility elicitation.

To the extent that studies are conducted primarily within a single paradigm, it becomes critical to choose the right one. Table 35.1 summarizes the costs of various mismatches between the assumed and actual states of people's values. Above the diagonal are cases in which more is expected of people than they are prepared to give. The risk here is misplaced precision, reading too much into poorly articulated responses and missing the opportunity to help people clarify their thinking. Below the diagonal are cases in which too little is expected of people. The risk here is misplaced imprecision, needlessly complicating the task and casting doubt on already clear thinking.

The choice of a paradigm ought to be driven by the perceived costs and likelihoods of these different mismatches. Thus, one might not hire a survey researcher to study how acutely ill individuals evaluate alternative medical procedures, nor might one hire a philosopher to lead consumers through the intricacies of evaluating alternative dentifrices. Evaluation professionals should, in turn, devote themselves to the problems most suited to their methods.

Yet, it is in the nature of paradigms that they provide clearer indications of relative than of absolute success. That is, they show which applications of the set of accepted methods work better, rather than whether the set as a whole is up to the job. After describing these paradigms in somewhat greater detail, I will consider some of the specific processes by which work within them can create an exaggerated feeling for the breadth of their applicability.

As a device for doing so, I will highlight how each paradigm might interpret several sets of potentially puzzling results, namely those produced by the studies posing the four evaluation questions opening this article. In each case, two apparently equivalent ways of formulating the question produced rather different evaluations. Assuming that the studies were competently conducted, an articulated values perspective would hold that if the answers are different, then so must the questions have been. Any inconsistency is in the eye of the beholder, rather than in the answers of the respondents.

A basic values philosophy leads to quite a different interpretation: If their responses are buffeted by superficial changes in question formulation, then people must not know what they want. As a result, none of the evaluations should be taken seriously. At best, they reflect a gut level response to some very general issue. According to the intermediate, partial perspectives philosophy, each answer says something about respondents. However, neither should be taken as fully representing their values.

A Sample of Problems

Happiness. Surveys sometimes include questions asking respondents to evaluate the overall state of their affairs. Answers to these questions might be used, for example, as barometers of public morale or as predictors of responses on other items (i.e., for statistical analyses removing individual mood as a covariate). In reviewing archival data, Turner and Krauss (1978) discovered the apparent inconsistency revealed in Figure 35.1. Two respected survey organizations, asking virtually identical happiness questions, produced substantially different proportions of respondents evaluating their situation as making them *very happy*. If the temptation of naive extrapolation is indulged, then quite different societies seem to be emerging from the two surveys (happinesswise, at least).[1]

After a series of analyses carefully examining alternative hypotheses, Turner and Krauss (1978) concluded that the most likely source of the response pattern in Figure 35.1 was differences in the items preceding the happiness question. In the NORC survey, these items concerned family life; in the Survey Research Center (SRC) survey (Campbell, Converse, & Rodgers, 1976), they were items unrelated to that aspect of personal status.[2]

If respondents have fully articulated values, then different answers imply different questions. Inadvertently, the two surveys have created somewhat different happiness questions. Perhaps Happiness$_1$ (from the NORC survey)

---

[1] The two questions did differ slightly in their introductory phrase. One began "taken all together," the other "taking all things together." Only the bravest of theoreticians would try to trace the pattern in Figure 35.1 to this difference.

[2] Subsequent research (Turner, 1984; Turner & Martin, 1984) has shown a somewhat more complicated set of affairs – which may have changed further by the time this article is printed and read. Incorporating the most recent twists in this research would change the details but not the thrust of the discussion in the text.

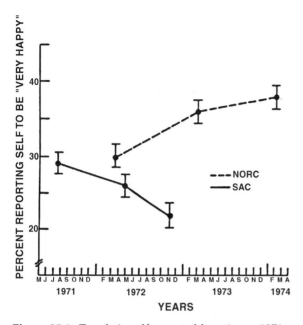

Figure 35.1. Trends in self-reported happiness, 1971–1973. (*Note.* Estimates are derived from sample surveys of noninstitutionalized population of the continental United States, aged 18 and over. Error bars demark ±1 standard error around sample estimate. NORC = National Opinion Research Center; SRC = Survey Research Center. Questions were "Taken all together, how would you say things are these days – would you say that you are very happy, pretty happy, or not too happy?" (NORC); and "Taking all things together, how would you say things are these days – would you say you're very happy, pretty happy, or not too happy these days?" (SRC). From "Why Do Surveys Disagree? Some Preliminary Hypotheses and Some Disagreeable Examples" (p. 166) by C. F. Turner, 1984, in C. F. Turner and E. Martin, *Surveying Subjective Phenomena*, New York: Russell Sage Foundation. Copyright 1984 by the Russell Sage Foundation. Reprinted by permission.)

emphasizes the role of family life, whereas Happiness$_2$ (from the SRC survey) gives respondents more freedom in weighting the different facets of their lives.

From the opposing perspective, the same data tell quite a different story. If a few marginally related questions can have so great an impact, then how meaningful can the happiness question (and the responses to it) be? Conceivably, it is possible to take all things together and assess the happiness associated with them. However, as long as assessments depend on the mood induced by immediately preceding questions, that goal has yet to be achieved.

According to the partial perspectives philosophy, the two responses might be stable. However, neither should be interpreted as a thoughtful expression of respondents' happiness. Achieving that would require helping respondents generate and evaluate alternative perspectives on the problem, not just the one perspective that happens to have been presented to them.

Headache. According to Executive Order 12291 (Bentkover, Covello, & Mumpower, 1985), cost-benefit analyses must be conducted for all significant federal actions. Where those actions affect the environment, that often requires putting price tags on goods not customarily traded in any marketplace. For regulations governing ozone levels, one such good is a change in the rate of subclinical health effects, such as headaches and shortness of breath. In order to monetize these consequences, resource economists have conducted surveys asking questions like the second example in the set of quotations at the beginning of this article (Cummings, Brookshire, & Schulze, 1986; V. K. Smith & Desvousges, 1988).

In Dickie et al.'s (1987) survey, people who reported having experienced being tired easily estimated that they would be willing to pay $17, on average, to eliminate their last day of feeling tired easily. Later in the same survey, the interviewer computed the overall monthly cost of eliminating each respondent's three most serious ozone-related health effects. This was done by multiplying how much people reported being willing to pay to eliminate the last occurrence of each effect by the number of reported episodes per month, then summing those products across symptoms. Respondents were then asked, "On a monthly basis is [__] what you would be willing to pay to eliminate these three symptoms?" (p. 20, Appendix 1). If respondents recanted, they were then asked what monthly dollar amount they would pay for the package. The markedly reduced dollar amount that most subjects provided was then prorated over the individual health effects. By this computation, respondents were now willing to pay about $2 to eliminate a day of being tired easily.

From a regulatory perspective, these strikingly different estimates indicate markedly different economic benefits from reducing ozone levels. (Indeed, the Office of Management and Budget [A. Carlin, personal communication, 1987] has seriously criticized the Dickie et al., 1987, study as a basis for revising regulations under the Clean Air Act.) From an articulated values perspective, they imply that the two questions must actually be different in some fundamental ways. For example, people might be willing to pay much more for a one-time special treatment of their last headache than for each routine treatment. From a basic values perspective, these results indicate that people know that symptomatic relief is worth something, but have little idea how much (even after an hour of talking about health effects). As a result, respondents are knocked about by ephemeral aspects of the survey, such as the highly unusual challenge to their values embodied by the request to reconsider. The investigators in this study seem to have adopted a partial perspectives philosophy. They treat respondents' values seriously, but not seriously enough to believe that respondents have gotten it right the first time. Rather, respondents need the help provided by showing them the overall implications of their initial estimates (Furby & Fischhoff, 1989).

Gamble. In samples of people shown the third example (Fischhoff et al., 1980), most people have preferred the gamble to the sure loss. However, they reverse this preference when the sure loss is described as an insurance premium, protecting them against the potentially greater loss associated with the gamble (Fischhoff et al., 1980; Hershey & Schoemaker, 1980). This difference is sufficiently powerful that it can often be evoked within subject, in successively presented problems.

From an articulated values perspective, the appearance of equivalence in these two versions of the problem must be illusory. Observers who see inconsistency in these responses must simply have failed to realize the differences. Perhaps, as a matter of principle, people refuse both to accept sure losses and to decline insurance against downside risks. In that case, these seemingly superficial differences in description evoke meaningful differences in how people judge themselves and one another. People want both to preserve a fighting chance and to show due caution. How they would respond to a real-world analog of this problem would depend on how it was presented.[3]

From a basic values perspective, these results show that people know that they dislike losing money, but that is about it. They cannot make the sort of precise trade offs depicted in such analytical problems. As a result, they cling to superficial cues as ways to get through the task.

In this case, some subsidiary evidence seemingly supports the intermediate perspective. When both versions are presented to the same person, there is an asymmetrical transfer effect (Poulton, 1968, 1989). Specifically, there are fewer reversals of preference when the insurance version comes first than when it comes second. This suggests that viewing the sure loss as an insurance premium is a relevant perspective, but not one that is immediately available. By contrast, respondents do realize, at some level, that premiums are sure losses. Studies of insurance behavior show, in fact, some reluctance to accept that perspective. For example, people prefer policies with low deductibles, even though they are financially unattractive. Apparently, people like the higher probability of getting some reimbursement so that their premium does not have to be viewed as a sure loss (Kunreuther et al., 1978).

Disease. About two thirds of the subjects responding to the fourth problem (Tversky & Kahneman, 1981) have been found to prefer Treatment A, with its sure saving of 200 lives. On the other hand, about the same portion prefer the second treatment when the two alternatives are described in terms of the number of lives that will be lost. In this version, Treatment A now provides a sure loss of 400 lives, whereas Treatment B gives a chance of no lives lost at all.

---

[3] Thus, these results would lead one to expect lower renewal rates on insurance policies were subscribers to receive periodic bills for sure losses, rather than for premiums.

Applying the alternative philosophies to interpreting these results is straightforward. One difference in this case is that there is not only some independent evidence but also some theory to direct such interpretations. The discrepancies associated with the three previous problems were discovered, more or less fortuitously, by comparing responses to questions that happened to have been posed in slightly different ways. In this case, the discrepancies were generated deliberately. Kahneman and Tversky (1979) produced the alternative wordings as demonstrations of their *prospect theory*, which predicts systematic differences in choices as a function of how options are described, or *framed*. The shift from gains (i.e., lives saved) to losses is one such framing difference.

Prospect theory embodies a partial perspectives philosophy. It views these differing preferences as representing stable derivations of intermediate complexity from a set of basic human values identified by the theory. The sources of these differences seem ephemeral, however, in the sense that people would be uncomfortable living with them. Adopting an articulated values philosophy here would require arguing that people regard the different frames as meaningfully different questions – and would continue to do so even after thoughtful reflection.

In the absence of a theoretical account (such as prospect theory) or converging evidence (such as the asymmetrical transfer effect with the sure-loss–premium questions), one's accounting of seemingly inconsistent preferences becomes a matter of opinion. Those opinions might reflect both the particulars of individual problems and the general orientation of a paradigm. The next section describes these paradigms. The following section considers how they could sustain such different views on the general state of human values.

THE PARADIGMS

However the notion of *paradigm* is conceptualized (Lakatos & Musgrave, 1970), it is likely to involve (a) a focal set of methodological worries, (b) a corresponding set of accepted treatments, (c) a theoretical basis for justifying these treatments and directing their application, and (d) criteria for determining whether problems have been satisfactorily addressed. Table 35.2 characterizes the three paradigms in these terms. This section elaborates on some representative entries in that table.

Philosophy of Articulated Values

Investigators working within this paradigm have enormous respect for people's ability to articulate and express values on the most diverse topics. Indeed, so great is this respect that investigators' worrying often focuses on ensuring that evaluative questions are formulated and understood exactly as intended. Any slip could evoke a precise, thoughtful answer to the wrong question (Fischhoff & Furby, 1988; Mitchell & Carson, 1989; Sudman & Bradburn, 1982).

A hard-won lesson in this struggle involves recognizing the powerful influence that social pressures can exert on respondents (DeMaio, 1984). As a result,

Table 35.2. Three Paradigms for Eliciting Values

Worry	Treatment	Theoretical base	Test of success
Assumption: People know what they want about all possible questions (to some degree of precision)			
Inappropriate default assumptions (for unstated part of question)	Examine interpretation, specify more, manipulate expectations	Nonverbal communication, experimenter–interviewer effects, psycholinguistics	Full specification, empathy with subjects
Inappropriate interpretation of stated question	Use good English, consensual terms	Survey technique, linguistics	Sensible answers, consensual interpretation of terms
Difficulty in expressing values	Choose correct response mode	Psychometrics, measurement theory	Consistency (reliability of representation)
Strategic response	Proper incentives, neutral context	Microeconomics, demand characteristics	Sensible answers, nonresponse to "irrelevant" changes
Assumption: People have stable but incoherent perspectives, causing divergent responses to formally equivalent forms			
Deep consistency in methods across studies (failing to reveal problem)	"Looking for trouble": multiple methods in different studies; "asking for trouble": open-ended questions	Framing theory, new psychophysics, multiple disciplines, anthropology	Nonresponse to irrelevant, changes
Eliciting values incompletely (within study)	Multiple methods within study, open ended	Same as above, counseling skills	Inability to elicit more
Inability to reconcile perspectives	Talking through implications	Normative analysis, counseling skills	Unpressured consistent response to new perspectives
Assumption: People lack articulated values on specific topic (but have pertinent basic values)			
Pressure to respond	Measure intensity, allow no response, alternative modes of expression	Survey research, social psychology	Satisfaction, stability among remainder
Instability over time	Accelerate experience	Attitude formation, behavioral decision theory	Stable convergence
Inability to relate	Client-centered process	Normative (re)analysis	Full characterization
Undetected insensitivity	Ask formally different questions	Normative analysis	Proper sensitivity

investigators take great pains to insulate the question–answerer relationship from any extraneous influences, lest those become part of the question. To prevent such complications, interviewers and experimenters stick to tight scripts, which they try to administer impassively in settings protected from prying eyes and ears. Lacking the opportunity to impose such control, economists must argue that marketplace transactions fortuitously have these desirable properties, in order to justify interpreting purchase decisions as reflecting just the value of the good and not the influences, say, of advertising or peer pressure.

At first blush, this protectiveness might seem somewhat paradoxical. After all, if people have such well-articulated preferences, why do they need to be shielded so completely from stray influences? The answer is that the investigator cannot tell just which stray influence will trigger one of those preferences. Indeed, the more deeply rooted are individuals' values, the more sensitive they should be to the nuances of how an evaluation problem is posed.

For example, it is considered bad form if the demeanor of an interviewer (or the wording of a question) suggests what the investigator expects (or wants) to hear. Respondents might move in that direction (or the opposite) because they aim to please (or to frustrate). Or, they might be unmoved by such a hint because they are indifferent to the information or social pressure that it conveys. Because a hint becomes part of the evaluation question, its influence is confounded with that of the issues that interested the investigator in the first place.

Unfortunately, the logical consistency of this position can border on tautology, inferring that a change is significant from respondents' sensitivity to it and inferring that respondents have articulated values from their responses to changes in questions now known to be significant. Conversely, responding the same way to two versions of a task means that the differences between them are not irrelevant and that people know their own minds well enough not to be swayed by meaningless variations.

The potential circularity of such claims can be disrupted either by data or by argument. At the one extreme, investigators can demonstrate empirically that people have well-founded beliefs on the specific questions that they receive. At the other extreme, they can offer theoretical reasons why such beliefs ought to be in place (bolstered, perhaps, by empirical demonstrations in other investigations). Developing these data and arguments in their general form has helped to stimulate basic research into nonverbal communication, interviewer effects, and even the psycholinguistics of question interpretations (e.g., Jabine, Straf, Tanur, & Tourangeau, 1984; Rosenthal & Rosnow, 1969; Turner & Martin, 1984).

Within this paradigm, the test of success is getting the question specified exactly the way that one wants and verifying that it has been so understood. A vital service that professional survey houses offer is being able to render the questions of diverse clients into good English using consensual terms. This very diversity, however, ensures that there cannot be specific theory and data for every question that they ask. As a result, the test of success is often an intuitive appeal to how sensible answers seem to be. The risks of circularity here, too, are obvious.[4]

Assuming that respondents have understood the question, they still need to be able to express their (ready) answer in terms acceptable to the investigator. The great edifice of psychometric theory has evolved to manage potential problems here by providing elicitation methods compatible with respondents' thought processes and investigators' needs (Coombs, 1964; Nunnally, 1968). The associated tests of success are, in part, external – the ability to predict responses to other tasks – and, in part, internal – the consistency of responses to related stimuli. The risk in the former case is that the theoretical tie between measures is flawed. The risk in the latter case is that respondents have found some internally consistent way to respond to questions asked within a common format and varying in obvious ways (Poulton, 1989).

Perhaps surprisingly, the main concern of early contingent valuation investigators was not that respondents would have difficulty expressing their values in dollar terms. On the contrary, they feared that subjects would be able to use the response mode all too well. Knowing just what they want (and how to get it), subjects might engage in strategic behavior, misrepresenting their values in order to shift to others the burden of paying for goods that they value (Samuelson, 1954). In response, investigators developed sophisticated tasks and statistical analyses. Applications of these methods seem to have allayed the fears of many practitioners (Brookshire, Ives, & Schulze, 1976).[5]

Philosophy of Basic Values

From the perspective of the philosophy of basic values, people's time is very limited, whereas the set of possible evaluative questions is very, very large. As a result, people cannot be expected to have articulated opinions on more than a small set of issues of immediate concern. Indeed, some theorists have argued that one way to control people is by forcing them to consider an impossibly diverse range of issues (e.g., through the nightly news). People who think that they can have some opinion on every issue find that they do not have thoughtful opinions on any issues (Ellul, 1963). The only way to have informed opinions on complex issues is by deriving them carefully from deeply held values on more general and fundamental issues (Rokeach, 1973).

Taking the headache question as an example, a meaningful answer is much more plausible from someone who has invested time and money in seeking symptomatic relief, which can serve as a firm point of reference for evaluating that special treatment. (Economists sometimes call these *averting behaviors*

---

[4] One is reminded of the finding that undetected computational errors tend to favor investigators' hypotheses. A nonmotivational explanation of this trend is that one is more likely to double-check all aspects of procedure, including calculations, when results are surprising (Rosenthal & Rosnow, 1969).

[5] The processes by which these fears were allayed might be usefully compared with the processes by which psychology convinced itself that it knew how to manage the effects of experimenter expectations (Rosenthal, 1967).

[Dickie et al., 1987].) Otherwise, the question seems patently unanswerable – and the wild discrepancies found in the research provide clear evidence of respondents' grasping at straws.

From the perspective of this paradigm, the existence of such documented discrepancies means that not all responses can be taken seriously. As a result, investigators adhering to it worry about any aspects of their methodology that might pressure respondents to produce unthoughtful evaluations. In this regard, an inherent difficulty with most surveys and experiments is that there is little cost for misrepresenting one's values, including pretending that one has them. By contrast, offering no response may seem like an admission of incompetence. Why would a question have been posed if the (prestigious?) individuals who created it did not believe that one ought to have an answer? With surveys, silence may carry the additional burden of disenfranchising oneself by not contributing a vote to public opinion. With psychological experiments, it may be awkward to get out, or to get payment, until one has responded in a way that is acceptable to the experimenter.

One indication of the level of perfunctory responses in surveys may be seen in the repeated finding (Schuman & Presser, 1981) that explicitly offering a *don't know* option greatly increases the likelihood of subjects offering no opinion (e.g., from 5% to 25%). Yet, even that option is a rather crude measure. Respondents must determine how intense a degree of ignorance or indifference *don't know* implies (e.g., Does it mean absolutely, positively having no idea?). Investigators must, then, guess at how respondents have interpreted the option.

Hoping to say something more about the intensity of reported beliefs, survey researchers have conducted a lively debate over alternative statistical analyses of seemingly inconsistent attitudes (e.g., Achen, 1975; Converse, 1964). Its resolution is complicated by the difficulty of simultaneously evaluating questions and answers (Schuman & Presser, 1981; T. Smith, 1984). For example, one potential measure of value articulation is the stability of responses over time. When people say different things at different times, they might just be responding randomly. However, they might also have changed their underlying beliefs or settled on different interpretations of poorly worded questions. Changes in underlying opinions may themselves reflect exogenous changes in the issues addressed by the question (e.g., "My headaches are worse now than the last time I was asked") or endogenous changes in one's thinking (e.g., "I finally came to realize that it's crazy to be squirreling money away in the bank rather than using it to make myself less miserable").

A striking aspect of many contingent valuation studies is the high rate of refusals to provide acceptable responses among individuals who have already agreed to participate in the study (Cummings et al., 1986; Mitchell & Carson, 1989; Tolley et al., 1986). These protest responses take several forms: simply refusing to answer the evaluation question, offering to pay $0 for a good that one has admitted to be worth something, and offering to pay what seems to be an unreasonably high amount (e.g., more than 10% of disposable income for relieving a headache). For investigators under contract to monetize environmental goods, these responses are quite troublesome.[6] For investigators who have the leisure to entertain alternative perspectives, these responses provide some insight into how respondents having only basic values cope with pressure to produce more. It is perhaps a testimony to the coerciveness of interview situations how rarely participants say *don't know,* much less try to bolt (as they have in these contingent valuation studies).

The term *protest response* implies hostility toward the investigator. Some of that emotion may constitute displaced frustration with one's own lack of articulated values. The investigator's "crime" is forcing one to confront not knowing exactly what an important good is worth. Perhaps a more legitimate complaint is that investigators force that confrontation without providing any help in its resolution.

As mentioned, investigators within the articulated values paradigm provide no help as a matter of principle. Elicited values are intended to be entirely those of the respondent, without any hint from the questioner. This stance might also be appropriate to investigators in the basic values paradigm in cases in which they want to know what is in there to begin with when an issue is first raised. However, basic values investigators might also be interested in prompting the inferential process of deriving specific values from general ones. That might be done nondirectively by leaving respondents to their own devices after posing an evaluative question and promising to come back later for an answer. In the interim, respondents can do whatever they usually do, such as ruminate, ask friends, listen to music, review Scripture, or experiment. Such surveys might be thought of as accelerating natural experiences, guided by descriptive research into how people do converge on values in their everyday life.

Alternatively, investigators can adopt a multiply directive approach. They can suggest alternative positions, helping respondents to think through how those positions might or might not be consistent with their basic values. Doing so requires a normative analysis of alternative positions that might merit adoption. That might require adding professions like economics or philosophy to the research team. Surveys that present multiple perspectives are, in effect, respondent centered, more akin to decision analysis than to traditional question-centered social research, with its impassive interviewers bouncing stimuli off objectified respondents. Studies that propose alternative perspectives incur a greater risk of sins of commission, in the sense of inadvertently pushing subjects in one of the suggested directions, and a reduced risk of sins of omission, in the sense of letting respondents mislead themselves by incompletely understanding the implications of the questions that they answer.

As shown in the discussion of the questions opening this article, a clear hint that people have only basic values to offer is when they show undue sensitivity to changes in irrelevant features of a question. It can also be suggested by undue *in*sensitivity to relevant features. Figure 35.2 shows the proportion of

---

[6] In actual studies, investigators sometimes just throw out protest responses. At times, they adjust them to more reasonable values (e.g., reducing high values to 10% of disposable income).

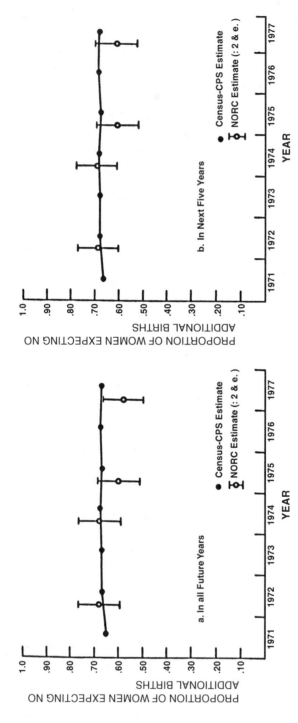

Figure 35.2. Estimates of fertility expectations of American women: proportion of women expecting no further children in (a) all future years, and (b) the next five years. (*Note:* Samples included only married women aged 18–39; sample sizes in each year were approximately 4,000 (Census-CPS) and 220 (NORC). CPS = Current Population Survey; NORC = National Opinion Research Center. From "Why Do Surveys Disagree? Some Preliminary Hypotheses and Some Disagreeable Examples" (p. 192) by C.F. Turner, 1984, in C. F. Turner and E. Martin, *Surveying Subjective Phenomena*, New York: Russell Sage Foundation. Copyright 1984 by the Russell Sage Foundation. Reprinted by permission.)

women who reported that they expect no additional births, either in all future years (left side) or in the next five years (right side).[7] In each panel, there was considerable agreement between responses elicited by two respected survey houses. So, here is a case in which all of the irrelevant differences in procedures (e.g., interviewers, sampling, preceding questions) had no aggregate effect on responses. Across panels, however, there is a disturbing lack of difference. If there are women who intend to give birth after the next five years, then the curves should be lower in the left panel than in the right one. Although the investigators took care to specify time period, respondents either did not notice or could not make use of that critical detail.

An analogous result in contingent valuation research was Tolley et al.'s (1986) finding that people were willing to pay as much for 10 days' worth as for 180 days' worth of a fixed improvement in atmospheric visibility. Even more dramatic is Kahneman and Knetsch's (Kahneman, 1986) finding that respondents to a phone survey were willing to pay equal amounts to preserve the fisheries in one Ontario lake, in several Ontario lakes, and in all of the lakes in Ontario. These results could, of course, reflect articulated values based on utility functions that flattened out abruptly after 10 days and one lake. More likely, they reflect a vague willingness to pay a little money for a little good.

Philosophy of Partial Perspectives

By adopting an intermediate position, individuals working within the partial perspectives paradigm must worry about the problems concerning both extremes. On the one hand, they face the risk of inadequately formulated and understood questions, preventing respondents from accessing those partially articulated perspectives that they do have. On the other hand, investigators must worry about reading too much into expressions of value produced under pressure to say something.

These worries may, however, take on a somewhat different face. In particular, the existence of partial perspectives may give a deceptive robustness to expressions of value. Thus, investigators using a single method may routinely elicit similar responses without realizing the extent to which their success depends on the method's ability to evoke a common perspective. That fact may be obscured further when a family of related methods produces similar consistency. It takes considerable self-reflection for investigators to discern the structural commonalities in methods that seem to them rather different. Speculative examples might include a tendency for surveys to emphasize hedonic rather than social values by asking respondents for their personal opinions, or for experimental gambles to encourage risk taking because participants cannot leave with less

---

[7] This is a question of prediction, rather than of evaluation, except in the sense that intentions to have children reflect the perceived value of having them.

than they went in with,[8] or to discourage emotional involvement because the scientific setting seems to call for a particularly calculating approach. Discovering the perspectives that it inadvertently imposes on itself is part of the continuing renewal process for any scientific discipline. In the social sciences, these perspectives may also be imposed on the people being studied, whose unruly behavior may, in turn, serve as a clue to disciplinary blinders (e.g., Furby, 1986; Gergen, 1973; Gilligan, 1982; Wagenaar, 1989).

Research methods may create consistent response sets, as well as evoke existing ones (Tune, 1964). When asked a series of obviously related questions on a common topic, respondents may devise a response strategy to cope with the experiment. The resulting responses may be consistent with one another, but not with responses in other settings. Indeed, those investigations most concerned about testing for consistency may also be the most vulnerable to generating what they are seeking. Think, for example, of an experiment eliciting evaluations for stimuli representing all cells of a factorial design in which each factor is a different outcome attribute. Why not come up with some simple rule for getting through the task?

For example, Poulton (1968, 1989) has conducted detailed secondary analyses of the quantitative estimates elicited in psychophysics experiments in an effort to capture the subjective intensity of physical stimuli (e.g., sweetness, loudness). He argued that the remarkable internal consistency of estimates across stimulus dimensions (Stevens, 1975) reflects the stability of investigators' conventions in setting up the details of their experiments. Although subjects have no fixed orientation to such unfamiliar forms of evaluation, they do respond similarly to structuring cues such as the kind of numbers to be used (e.g., integers vs. decimals) and the place of the standard stimulus in the range of possibilities.[9] The (nontrivial) antidotes are what might be called *looking for trouble* and *asking for trouble* – eliciting values in significantly different ways and using sufficiently open-ended methods to allow latent incoherence to emerge.

Economists hope to reduce these problems by discerning people's values from the preferences revealed in market behavior. Such actions ought to be relatively free of pressures to respond. After all, you don't have to buy. Or do you? Even if choices are voluntary, they can only be made between options that are on offer and with whatever information respondents happen to have. For example, you may hate ranch style homes but have little choice other than to choose one that makes the best of a bad situation in some locales. In that case, the preferences thereby revealed are highly conditional. Furthermore, even if

---

[8] The need to protect human subjects poses this constraint. Even without it, there would be problems getting people to risk their own money in a gamble contrived by some, possibly mistrusted, scientist.

[9] Many contingent valuation studies have elicited values by asking subjects questions such as "Would you pay $1, $2, $3, . . . ?"until they say no. One might compare the implicit structuring of this series of questions with that achieved by "Would you pay $10, $20, $30, . . . ?" or by moving down from $100 in $1 increments.

the choice sets are relatively open and well understood, they may be presented in ways that evoke only a limited subset of people's values. By some accounts, evoking partial perspectives is the main mission of advertising (by other accounts, it is just to provide information). Some critics have argued that some perspectives (e.g., the value of possessing material goods) are emphasized so effectively that they change from being imposed perspectives to becoming endorsed ones.[10]

If one wants to predict how people will behave in situations presenting a particular perspective, then one should elicit their values in ways evoking that perspective.[11] If one wants to get at all their potentially relevant perspectives, then more diverse probing is needed. This is the work of many counselors and consultants. Although some try to construct their clients' subjective problem representation from basic values (along the lines of decision analysis), others try to match clients with general diagnostic categories. Each category then carries prognoses and recommendations. As mentioned, the counselor stance is unusual in social research. Like any direct interaction, it carries the risk of suggesting and imposing the counselor's favored perspective. Presumably, there is a limit to how quickly people can absorb new outlooks. At some point, they may lose cognitive control of the issue, wondering perhaps, "Whose problem is it, anyway?"

HOW COULD THEY THINK THIS WAY?

Described in its own right, any paradigm sounds like something of a caricature. Could proponents really believe that one size fits all when it comes to methodology? Surely, decision analysts realize that some values are already so well articulated that their decomposition procedures will only induce confusion. Surely, survey researchers realize that some value issues are so important and so unfamiliar in their details that respondents will be unable to resist giving uninformed answers to poorly understood questions. Surely they do. Yet, equally surely, there is strong temptation to stretch the envelope of applications for one's favored tools.

Some reasons for exaggerating the applicability of one's own discipline are common to all disciplines. Anyone can exaggerate the extent to which they are ready for a challenge. Each discipline has an intact critique of its competitors. People who ask questions know what they mean and also know how they would answer. What might be called anthropology's great truth is that we underestimate how and by how much others see the world differently than we

---

[10] This is just the tip of the iceberg regarding the methodological difficulties of inferring values from observed market behavior (Campen, 1986; Fischhoff & Cox, 1985; Peterson, Driver, & Gregory, 1988). In many cases, technical difficulties make inferring values from behavior an engaging fiction.

[11] Fischhoff (1983) considered some of the difficulties of predicting which frames are evoked by naturally occurring situations.

do. Paradigms train one to soldier on and solve problems, rather than to reflect on the whole enterprise.

The inconsistent responses opening this article present an interesting challenge for that soldiering. As shown in the discussion of those results, each paradigm has a way to accommodate them. Yet, investigators in the basic values paradigm seem much more comfortable with such accommodation. They seem more ready to accept them as real (i.e., produced from sound, replicable studies) and much more ready to see them as common. Basic values investigators sometimes seem to revel in such discrepancies (e.g., Hogarth, 1982; Nisbett & Ross, 1980), whereas articulated values investigators seem to view them as bona fide, but still sporadic, problems (e.g., Schuman & Presser, 1981).[12] Insight into these discrepant views about discrepancies can be gained by examining the institutional and methodological practices of these paradigms.

Interest in Discrepancies

Basic values investigators would like to believe that there are many robust discrepancies "out there in the world" because they serve a vital purpose for this kind of science. Discovering a peculiar pattern of unexpected results has been the starting point for many theories (Kahneman & Tversky, 1982). McGuire (1969) has gone so far as to describe the history of experimental psychology as the history of turning artifacts into main effects. For example, increased awareness of experimenter effects (Rosenthal, 1967) stimulated studies of nonverbal communication (e.g., Ekman, 1985). In fact, some critics have argued that psychology is so much driven by anomalies that it tends to exaggerate their importance and generality (Berkeley & Humphreys, 1982). Anomalies make such a good story that it is hard to keep them in focus, relative to the sometimes unquirky processes that produce them (Fischhoff, 1988).

Interest in Order

On the other hand, articulated values investigators are more interested in *what* people think than in *how* they think. For those purposes, all these quirks are a major headache. They mean that every question may require a substantial development effort before it can be asked responsibly with elaborate pretesting of alternative presentations. The possibility of anomalies also raises the risk that respondents cannot answer the questions that interest the investigators – at least without the sort of interactive or directive elicitation that is an anathema within this paradigm.

Of course, investigators in this paradigm are concerned about these issues. Some of the most careful studies of artifacts have come from survey researchers (e.g., Schuman & Presser, 1981). Classic examples of the effort needed to tie

---

[12] This observation was sharply drawn by Professor Robert Abelson at a meeting of the National Research Council Panel on Survey Measure of Subjective Phenomena (Turner & Martin, 1981). This section of my article is, in large part, an attempt to work up the pattern that he highlighted.

down the subjective interpretation of even seemingly simple questions may be found in the U.S. Department of Commerce studies of how to ask about employment status (Bailar & Rothwell, 1984). However, every research program with resource constraints is limited in its ability to pursue methodological nuances. When those nuances could represent fatal problems, then it is natural to want to believe that they are rare.

For survey research houses, these constraints are magnified by the commercial pressures to keep the shop open and running at a reasonable price. To some extent, clients go to quality and will pay for it. However, there is a limit to the methodological skepticism that even sophisticated clients will tolerate. They need assurance that investigators have the general skill needed to create workable items out of their questions. Clients might know, at some level, that "different questions might have produced different answers" (according to the strange wording that quality newspapers sometimes append to survey results). However, they still need some fiction of tractability.

Ability to Experiment

A further constraint on articulated values scientists is their theoretical commitment to representative sampling. The expense of such samples means that very few tests of alternative wording can be conducted. Conversely, it means that many discrepancies (like the happiness questions) are only discovered in secondary analyses of studies conducted for other purposes. As a result, there are typically confounding differences in method that blur the comparison between questions.

By contrast, basic values scientists are typically willing to work with convenience samples of subjects. As a result, they can run many tightly controlled experiments, increasing their chances of finding discrepancies. Multiple testing also increases the chances of finding differences by chance. If they are conscientious, these scientists should be able to deal with this risk through replications (which are, in turn, relatively easy to conduct). This indifference to sampling might reflect a self-serving and cavalier attitude. On the other hand, it may be the case that *how* people think might be relatively invariant with respect to demographic features that are known to make a big difference in *what* they think.

Precision of Search

The theories that basic values scientists derive to account for discrepancies are not always correct. When they are, however, they allow investigators to produce inconsistent responses almost at will. Much of experimental psychology is directed at determining the precise operation of known effects. For example, at the core of prospect theory is a set of framing operations designed to produce inconsistencies. The prevalence of phenomena under laboratory conditions has, of course, no necessary relationship to their prevalence elsewhere. Some extrapolation of prevalence rates from the lab to the world would, however, be only natural (Tversky & Kahneman, 1973). Furthermore, continuing absorption with a phenomenon should sharpen one's eagerness and ability to spot examples. Investigators who want and expect to see a phenomenon are likely to find it more often than investigators who do not. It would be only natural if the confirmation offered by such anecdotal evidence were overestimated (Chapman & Chapman, 1969).

The theoretical tools for seeking nuisance effects in an articulated values study would likely be more poorly defined. For example, the question might be posed as generally as "How common are order effects?" Given the enormous diversity of questions whose order might be reversed, the answer is, doubtless, "very low" in the domain of all possible questions. However, with questions of related content, order effects might be much more common (Poulton & Freeman, 1966). Moreover, questions are more likely to appear in surveys with somewhat related ones, rather than with completely related ones – even in amalgam surveys pooling items from different customers. Without a theory of relatedness, researchers are in a bind. Failure to find an order effect can just be taken as proof that the items were not related.[13]

Criterion of Interest

Surveys are often conducted in order to resolve practical questions, such as which candidate to support in an election or which product to introduce on the market. As a result, the magnitude of an effect provides the critical test of whether it is worthy of notice. Unless it can be shown to make a difference, who cares? Laboratory results come from out of this world. If they cannot be mapped clearly onto practical problems, then they are likely to seem like curiosities. The psychologists' criterion of statistical significance carries little weight here. Survey researchers, with their large samples, know that even small absolute differences can reach statistical significance.

On the other hand, not all survey questions have that direct a relationship to action. One can assess the effects of being off by 5% in a preelection poll or a product evaluation as a result of phrasing differences. However, in many other cases, surveys solicit general attitudes and beliefs. These are widely known to be weak predictors of behavior (Ajzen & Fishbein, 1980). As a result, it may be relatively easy to shrug off occasional anomalies as tolerable. Discrepancies should become more important and, perhaps, seem more common as the questions driving research become sharper. The discrepancies associated with contingent valuation studies have come under great scrutiny recently because

---

[13] A related example – for which I have unfortunately misplaced the reference and must rely on memory – is the finding that people respond more consistently to items on a common topic when those are grouped in a survey than when the questions are scattered. An (expensive) attempt to replicate this finding took as its common topic attitudes toward shop stewards, and found nothing. That could mean that the first result was a fluke or that *shop stewards* is not a meaningful concept of the sort that could induce consistent attitudes when brought to people's attention.

Table 35.3. Conditions Favorable to Articulated Values

Personally familiar (time to think)
Personally consequential (motivation to think)
Publicly discussed (opportunity to hear, share views)
Uncontroversial (stable tastes, no need to justify)

Few consequences (simplicity)
Similar consequences (commensurability)
Experienced consequences (meaningfulness)
Certain consequences (comprehensibility)

Single or compatible roles (absence of conflict)
Diverse appearances (multiple perspectives)
Direct relation to action (concreteness)
Unbundled topic (considered in isolation)

Familiar formulation

of their enormous economic consequences. Changes in wording can, in principle, mean the difference between success and failure for entire companies or industries.

Thinking about Lability

How common are artifacts? is an ill-formed question, insofar as there is no clear universe over which the relative frequency of instances can be defined. Nonetheless, investigators' intuitive feeling for overall frequency must determine their commitment to their paradigms and their ability to soldier on in the absence of definitive data. Understanding the nature and source of one's own disciplinary prejudices is essential for paradigms to be used wisely and to evolve. Understanding other disciplines' (more and less legitimate) prejudices is necessary for collaboration. Implicit assumptions about the nature of human values seem to create a substantial divide among the social sciences. If they were to work together, the focal question might shift from how well articulated are values to where are they well articulated. Table 35.3 offers one possible set of conditions favorable to articulated values. Turner (1981) offered another. It might be informative to review the evidentiary record of discrepancies and nondiscrepancies in the light of such schemes.

36. Economic Preferences or Attitude Expressions?
An Analysis of Dollar Responses to Public Issues

Daniel Kahneman, Ilana Ritov, and David Schkade

ABSTRACT. Participants in contingent valuation surveys and jurors setting punitive damages in civil trials provide answers denominated in dollars. These answers are better understood as expressions of attitudes than as
indications of economic preference. Well-established characteristics of attitudes and of the core process of affective valuation explain several robust
features of dollar responses: high correlations with other measures of attractiveness or aversiveness, insensitivity to scope, preference reversals, and the
high variability of dollar responses relative to other measures of the same
attitude.

KEY WORDS preferences, attitudes, contingent valuation, psychology
and economics, utility assessment

JEL Classification D00, H00

INTRODUCTION

Economics and psychology offer contrasting perspectives on the question of
how people value things. The economic model of choice is concerned with a
rational agent whose preferences obey a tight web of logical rules, formalized
in consumer theory and in models of decision making under risk. The tradition
of psychology, in contrast, is not congenial to the idea that a logic of rational
choice can serve double duty as a model of actual decision behavior. Much behavioral research has been devoted to illustrations of choices that violate the
logic of the economic model. The implied claim is that people do not have preferences, in the sense in which that term is used in economic theory (Fischhoff,
1991; Slovic, 1995; Payne, Bettman and Johnson, 1992). It is therefore fair to ask:
If people do not have economic preferences, what do they have instead? Does
psychology provide theoretical notions that can account, at least in some contexts, both for apparent violations of the rational model of preference and for the
regularities of observed choices? Behavioral research has documented several

Journal of Risk and Uncertainty, 19:1–3; 203–235 (1999). Copyright © 1999 Kluwer Academic
Publishers. Manufactured in The Netherlands.

psychological processes that provide partial answers to this question, including concepts such as mental accounting, loss aversion and hyperbolic discounting. To this set of conceptual tools the present treatment adds the concept of *attitude*, which we borrow from social psychology, and the core process – we label it *affective valuation* – which determines the sign and the intensity of the emotional response to objects.

The main topic that we discuss in this paper – the valuation of environmental public goods – is far from the core of economic discourse. It is an unusual case in which some economists have proposed to use responses to hypothetical questions as a measure of economic preference. In the contingent valuation method (CVM), survey respondents are asked to indicate a stated willingness to pay (SWTP) for public goods, including goods from which they derive no personal benefit, such as the continued existence of obscure species and the maintenance of pristine lakes in inaccessible areas. The proponents of CVM have argued that properly elicited statements of WTP reveal genuine economic preferences, to which consumer theory applies (Mitchell and Carson, 1989; Hoehn and Randall, 1987; Smith, 1992).

We develop here an argument made earlier (Kahneman and Ritov, 1994) that statements of WTP are better viewed as expressions of attitudes than as indications of economic preferences. The conflicting views of the nature of SWTP lead to different interpretations of apparently anomalous features of CVM results, such as the low sensitivity to variations of scope and the discrepancy between the estimates of SWTP derived from open-ended and from referendum questions. The supporters of CVM have sometimes dismissed these anomalies as artifacts of poor technique (Carson and Mitchell, 1993; Smith, 1992), or explained them in terms of standard economic concepts, such as incentive compatibility and substitution and income effects (Hanemann, 1994; Randall and Hoehn, 1996; Smith, 1992). In contrast, the thesis of the present paper is that the anomalies of CV are inevitable manifestations of known characteristics of attitudes and attitude expressions.

To demonstrate the generality of the analysis of SWTP in terms of attitudes, we draw on an experimental study of the setting of punitive damages in product liability cases (Kahneman, Schkade and Sunstein, 1998). The tasks faced by a respondent to a CV survey and by a juror have little in common in the context of an economic analysis; consumer theory may apply to the former but surely not to the latter. In the framework that we propose, however, the two tasks are very similar. Both require the individual to express an attitude – to an environmental problem or to a defendant's actions – by using a dollar scale. The striking parallels between the findings in the two situations strongly support the attitude model.

The evidence that we present is drawn exclusively from studies of verbal answers to hypothetical questions about public issues. It is perhaps not surprising that, on this favorable terrain, the concepts of attitude and affective valuation provide a useful account of the data. It is early to say whether these concepts will prove equally useful in other domains to which the theory of economic preference is usually applied. On current evidence, it is possible to accept an attitude model for hypothetical CV responses while retaining the idea that the standard model of rational choice applies to more consequential decisions. This appears to be the position of economists who have criticized CVM (e.g., Diamond and Hausman, 1994). We believe, however, that the idea that actions are often interpretable as relatively direct expressions of an affective valuation is likely to prove useful in the analysis of many economically significant behaviors.

The paper is organized in two parts. The first part, which includes sections 1–4, introduces the concepts of attitude and affective valuation and explores some contrasts between attitudes and economic preferences, with examples from studies of contingent valuation and of punitive damages. Sections 5 and 6 apply a psychophysical analysis of dollar responses to explain both the unpredictability of jury awards and some important results of CV research. Section 7 discusses implications and section 8 concludes.

This article covers much ground and asserts many claims with relatively little documentation. To facilitate a separate assessment of the claims and of their associated evidence, we present our argument in the form of a series of propositions, with brief discussion of each proposition in turn.

1. INTRODUCTION TO VALUATION

1–1) *The concept of* **attitude** *has been defined as "a psychological tendency that is expressed by evaluating a particular entity with some degree of favor or disfavor" (Eagly and Chaiken, 1996). The core of an attitude is a* **valuation***, which assigns to the entity an* **affective value** *that can range from extremely positive to extremely negative.*[1]

1–2) *Affective values vary in sign (positive or negative) and in intensity. The intensity of valuation is relative: an attitude object considered on its own is implicitly compared to a set of objects of the same general kind.* (see section 4.)

1–3) *The concept of attitude has a considerably broader range of application than the standard concept of economic preferences.* In contrast to economic preferences, which are about commodity bundles (Varian, 1984), objects of attitudes include anything that people can like or dislike, wish to protect or to harm, want to acquire or to reject. People have attitudes toward abstract concepts, individual persons and social groups, events in their personal past and historical figures. Expressions of attitude are also diverse: they include smiles and frowns, verbal statements of approval or abuse, physical assault, charitable contributions, answers to survey questions, and many others. The valuation component of attitudes is assumed to be automatic and to facilitate a broad range of responses that

---

[1] The terms 'valuation' and 'affective value' are not standard in the attitude literature, but the position we take widely shared.

express positive or negative affect (Fazio, Sanbonmatsu, Powell, and Kardes, 1986; Pratto, 1994; Tesser and Martin, 1996).

1–4) *People's attitudes to objects and to activities that affect these objects are usually consistent.* For example, a positive affective response to dolphins is likely to be associated with a positive valuation of actions that protect members of this species. The link between attitudes and actions is often far from perfect, however (Eagly and Chaiken, 1993).

1–5) *The objects of attitudes and valuations are mental representations, not objective states of affairs. Valuations are therefore subject to framing effects and violate the logic of extensionality.* In an example much discussed by philosophy students, an individual may have different attitudes to the evening star and to the morning star, although they are the same star. People can also have different attitudes to the same packaged meat depending on whether it is described as containing 5% fat or as being 95% fat-free. The latter example is a *framing effect*, in which two descriptions evoke different valuations although they are transparently co-extensional – they refer to the same state of the world. Many large and robust framing effects have been identified by students of individual decision making (e.g., Tversky and Kahneman, 1986) and students of political attitudes (Bartels, 1998; Quattrone and Tversky, 1984; Zaller, 1992). Framing effects violate a condition of extensionality (Arrow, 1982) or invariance (Tversky and Kahneman, 1986), which is commonly taken for granted in economic analyses of preference. The psychological analysis of attitudes and valuations explicitly rejects the extensionality assumption.

1–6) *The following is a partial list of the properties of attitudes and of the ways they differ from preferences. (i) Attitudes are defined by the affective value of objects considered one at a time, not by choices. (See sections 2 and 4.) (ii) Attitudes violate extensionality. The same object may evoke different valuations depending on its description and on the context in which it is evaluated. (iii) The separate attitudes to two objects do not necessarily predict the outcome of a choice or direct comparison between them: reversals can occur when the comparison alters the relative salience of some attributes (Hsee, 1996), or when the objects belong to different categories. (See section 4.) (iv) The attitude to a set of similar objects is often determined by the affective valuation of a prototypical member of that set. The size of the set is neglected in this mode of valuation, which violates the logic of preferences. (See section 3.) (v) Alternative measures of attitudes differ in their precision, statistical efficiency and susceptibility to biasing influences. Dollar measures are inferior on all three counts. (See sections 5 and 6.)*

2. THE EVALUATION FACTOR

A central claim of the present treatment is that diverse responses to an object often express the same affective valuation. Consequently, the answers to ostensibly different questions are expected to yield similar rankings of attitude objects. The present section provides some evidence for this hypothesis. The data that we consider for each object are *averages* of attitude measures obtained from different samples of respondents. The correlations that we discuss in this section answer the following question: do different ways of probing average attitudes to a set of objects yield similar attitude orders?

2–1) *The affective value of an object is the major determinant of many responses to it, which are called* **attitude expressions***. A correlational analysis of the responses to a set of objects normally yields a strong* **evaluation factor***, which captures the commonality among diverse expressions of the same attitude.* The classic set of studies that introduced the semantic differential technique (Osgood, Suci and Tannenbaum, 1957) still provides the best illustration of this proposition. Participants in SD studies are presented with a series of objects or concepts. Their task is to rate each object in turn on a set of seven-point scales defined by bipolar adjectives, such as GOOD-BAD, KIND-CRUEL, BEAUTIFUL-UGLY, LARGE-SMALL, STRONG-WEAK, MASCULINE-FEMININE, IMPORTANT-UNIMPORTANT, and others. The range of objects to which this technique can be applied is hardly constrained: it includes particular objects, events, abstract ideas, activities, and nonsense figures. The participants are instructed to work quickly and to rate each object on every scale, regardless of whether or not it applies literally. Thus, 'wisdom' and 'Paris' could both be rated on the scales LARGE-SMALL and HOT-COLD – most people will rate wisdom as larger and colder than Paris.

For our purposes here, the most important conclusion of studies of the semantic differential is that the factorial structure of SD data is surprisingly simple. The same structure has been confirmed in many studies. The largest factor to emerge is invariably an *evaluation factor*, so labeled because the highest loadings are on scales such as GOOD-BAD, KIND-CRUEL and BEAUTIFUL-UGLY. The evaluation factor typically accounts for about 50% of the variance in scale responses. The scales that define the evaluation factor are not perfectly correlated, of course, and the differences among them are meaningful. For example, 'justice' is likely to be rated higher on the GOOD-BAD scale than on the KIND-CRUEL scale. Large discrepancies are rare, however, and the different evaluation scales generally yield similar orderings of the objects of judgment.

2–2) *Attitudes can be expressed on a scale of dollars, as well as on rating scales. Valuations expressed in dollars are highly correlated with those expressed on rating scales.* Willingness to pay for environmental goods – e.g., the maintenance of species – is one possible expression of attitudes to these goods, and to interventions that affect them. Similarly, attitudes to defendants in civil trials can be expressed by an amount of punitive damages. Studies in both domains have examined the following two hypotheses: (i) different measures of the valuation of issues are highly correlated, as in the semantic differential; (ii) dollar measures belong to the cluster of attitude measures.

Table 36.1. Rank Correlations between Mean Evaluations of 37 Issues

	SWTP	Support	Importance	Satisfaction
SWTP	(.87)			
Support	.84	(.85)		
Importance	.76	.84	(.88)	
Satisfaction	.84	.87	.85	(.90)

From Kahneman and Ritov, 1994.

Kahneman and Ritov (1994) studied the valuation of 37 topics, including a wide array of environmental problems and other public issues. The issues were presented as headlines, in which a brief description of a problem was followed by a single sentence describing a proposed intervention. An example was "THE PEREGRINE FALCON IS THREATENED BY POLLUTION. Intervention: Support special program to protect the Peregrine falcon." Several measures were used: SWTP for the proposed intervention, degree of political support for the intervention, personal satisfaction expected from making a voluntary contribution (both on a 0–4 rating scale), and a rating of the importance of the problem as a public issue, on a 0–6 rating scale. The participants in the study were visitors at the San Francisco Exploratorium. Each participant used only one of these four response scales to evaluate anywhere from 9 to 19 assigned of the problems. The total sample was 1441, and the number of respondents to any particular version of a problem was 50–115.

The 37 problems were ranked by the sample means for each of the response measures. Rank correlations between these means are shown in Table 36.1. The numbers on the diagonal represent measures of reliability, obtained by a bootstrapping procedure. Table 36.1 indicates that the rankings of the issues by the different measures were quite similar. Indeed, the correlations between orders derived from different measures were not substantially lower than the reliabilities of the individual measures.

What do ratings of importance, predictions of moral satisfaction, statements of political support and indications of willingness to pay have in common? Our answer is that these expressions share a common affective core, which is so prominent that it allows the public attitude order over objects to be measured almost interchangeably by ostensibly diverse responses.

Payne et al. (1999) observed a similar result in a study of 190 citizens who responded to five CV surveys of realistic length and detail. The topics were air quality in the Grand Canyon, oil spill prevention, and preservation of wolves, salmon, and migratory waterfowl. Each respondent expressed an evaluation of each commodity in SWTP and on four 0–10 rating scales – importance compared to other problems in society, seriousness compared to other environmental problems, use value and existence value. Respondents came for two

Table 36.2. Rank Correlations between Mean Evaluations of 28 Cases

	$ Awards	Outrage	Punishment
$ Awards (median)	(.89)		
Outrage	.80	(.96)	
Punishment	.92	.86	(.98)

From Kahneman, Schkade and Sunstein, 1998.

separate two–hour sessions, scheduled two weeks apart. In the first session a given respondent responded to all five commodities on either SWTP or the four rating scales. In the second, they again responded to all five surveys, but using the response mode(s) they did not use in the first session. The results showed rank correlation levels between response modes similar to those of Table 36.1, (ranging from .67 to 1.00), despite the many differences in stimuli and procedure from the Kahneman and Ritov study.

Our next example is drawn from a study which employed a similar design to study the psychology of punitive damages. Kahneman, Schkade, and Sunstein (1998) constructed 28 vignettes of cases in which a firm was found liable for compensatory damages in a product liability case. Each participant responded to a subset of 10 of these cases. Separate groups of respondents were asked to answer one of three questions about each scenario: "how outrageous was the defendant's behavior?" (on a 7-point scale), "how severely should the defendant be punished?" (on a 7-point scale), or "how much should the defendant be required to pay in punitive damages?" (in dollars). The respondents were 899 jury-eligible adults. An average of 107 respondents responded to each different case-question combination. The 28 cases were ranked by the mean ratings of outrage and punitive intent, and by the median dollar award. The correlations between these rankings are shown in Table 36.2.

Here again, we may ask what the three responses have in common that results in such high correlations. The outrage rating appears to be a rather direct measure of the affect evoked by cases of personal injury. The high correlations indicate that the same affective valuation also dominates ratings of punitive intent and judgments of punitive damages in dollars. The hypothesis that expressions of attitude are dominated by a shared affective reaction – in this case, by a degree of outrage – is again strongly supported.

The results shown in Tables 36.1 and 36.2 are correlations between averages of large samples, computed over objects. It is important to note that these correlations are not necessarily representative of the results that would be obtained within the data of individual respondents (Nickerson, 1995). As in the case of other summary statistics, it is possible for group results to be dominated by a few individuals who (i) produce more variance than others, and (ii) have an atypical pattern of responses. These hypotheses are readily testable (e.g., by examining the effects of standardizing the data of each individual), and we are satisfied that they did not apply to the data reported in this section.[2]

2–3) *Each expression of attitude also has its specific and distinctive determinants, but these account for less variance than the core affective value.* The example of justice being GOOD but not necessarily KIND was used earlier to show that different expressions of the evaluation factor in the semantic differential are not interchangeable. The same conclusion applies to the factor of affective valuation that could be extracted from diverse responses in the data of Tables 36.1 and 36.2. It is convenient to analyze an expression of affective valuation as the sum of three separable components:

$$X = A + S + e \tag{1}$$

where A is the shared affective valuation, S is a response-specific component, and e is an error term. The high correlations shown in the previous section indicate that the first of these components accounts for much more variance than the second. The shared affective value dominates the diverse expressions of attitudes. As the following examples illustrate, however, the specific content associated with different responses is both interesting and important.

Kahneman, Schkade and Sunstein (1998) offered an *outrage model* to account for both the similarities and the differences between the measures of outrage, punitive intent and punitive awards. They examined the differences in two experiments. The first experiment demonstrated that rated outrage was the same regardless of whether harm was severe or mild. This result is intuitively plausible: a behavior can be judged as more or less outrageous without knowing its consequences. In contrast, ratings of punitive intent and assessments of punitive damages were both sensitive to the severity of harm. Punishment involves a retributive intent, which depends on the consequences of the act that is to be punished; this is the intuition that justifies treating murder and attempted murder as distinct crimes. A second experiment showed that the size of the defendant firm had a large effect on the amount awarded in punitive damages, but no effect whatsoever on either outrage or punitive intent. This result is also plausible: a payment that constitutes 'very severe' punishment for a small firm may be quite insignificant for a larger one. As in the early studies of the semantic differential, we observe a pattern of meaningful differences among highly correlated expressions of the same affective valuation. Detailed examinations of responses to public goods also reveal systematic discrepancies between highly correlated measures (Kahneman and Knetsch, 1992). As the high correlations in these studies

---

[2] Within-subject correlations were computed in the study of Payne et al. (1999) and they were quite high: the median correlation between rating scales was .69, and the median correlation between rating scales and individual SWTP was .51. The lower value of the correlations with SWTP is due to the high degree of noise in dollar responses (see section 5).

suggest, however, the discrepancies between measures are small in magnitude, relative to the large common influence of the underlying affective valuation.

3. VALUATION BY PROTOTYPE AND THE SCOPE PROBLEM

The evidence reviewed in the preceding section confirmed the similarity between the rankings of objects by different measures of attitude, and provided suggestive evidence that the core of attitude is an affective valuation. In this section we argue that the affective valuation of a prototypical exemplar often determines the global attitude to sets of objects. We show that this process can explain an important finding of contingent valuation research: the inadequate sensitivity of SWTP to the quantitative aspects of problems and solutions.

3–1) *People hold stored prototypes of many categories. They also form prototypes or representative exemplars of new categories and sets that they encounter.* The prototypes of tables, of birds and of Harvard MBA's are widely shared among members of the relevant culture. People also form ad hoc representations of a typical day of a seaside vacation, or of a typical resident of a city they visit. These representations of prototypes are evoked in the service of thinking about concepts and classes (Barsalou, 1992).

3–2) *In **judgment by prototype**, a global judgment of a category or set is determined primarily by the relevant properties of its prototype.* The principle of judgment by prototype extends the older idea that a representativeness heuristic is involved in many intuitive judgments about uncertain events (Kahneman and Tversky, 1972, 1973; Tversky and Kahneman, 1971, 1983).

3–3) *When the size of the set is logically relevant to its valuation, judgment by prototype leads to a bias of **extension neglect**: Unless attention is specifically directed to it, the size of the set has little or no influence on its valuation. This pattern has been observed in different contexts, in which extension neglect takes different forms (Kahneman, 1995).* To illustrate the generality of the phenomenon of extension neglect, we briefly describe three examples:

(i) Intuitive statistical inferences are often made by assessing the similarity between the statistic of a sample and the parameter of a population. The sample and the population are both ensembles, but the judgment about them is based mainly on the relation between the prototypes that represent them. Intuitive inferences based on such reasoning are characterized by extreme lack of sensitivity to sample size, which is the form that extension neglect takes in this task (Griffin and Tversky, 1992; Kahneman and Tversky, 1972; Tversky and Kahneman, 1971).

(ii) In a familiar paradigm for the study of intuitive prediction, subjects judge the probability that an individual is a member of a specified social category (defined by a profession or an avocation) on the basis of a personality sketch (Kahneman and Tversky, 1973; Tversky and

Kahneman, 1982). Probability is judged by the similarity of the individual's personality to the stereotype of the target category. For example, an individual described as "argumentative, flashy, self-confident and competitive" will be judged more likely to be a lawyer than to be an engineer, because the description resembles the stereotype of the former profession more than that of the latter. In this paradigm, extension neglect takes the form of inadequate sensitivity to the base rates of outcomes (Kahneman and Tversky, 1973; see also Koehler, 1996; Novemsky and Kronzon, 1999).

(iii) Extension neglect has also been observed in a paradigm in which participants are exposed for some time to an unpleasant experience. The participants provide a continuous report of current discomfort, using an 'affect meter.' Later they provide a global judgment of the entire episode. Various experiences have been studied, including unpleasant films (e.g., of an amputation), immersion of the hand in cold water, exposure to loud noise, and painful medical procedures (see Kahneman, Wakker and Sarin (1997) for a review). For our purposes, an episode of discomfort can be construed as a set of unpleasant moments. The duration of the episode is the measure of extension. Valuation by prototype implies that participants will construct or remember a typical moment of the episode, and evaluate the episode as a whole by the level of unpleasantness associated with the prototypical moment – the duration of the episode will be neglected. The hypothesis of duration neglect has been confirmed in several experiments, with both ratings and choices as dependent variables (Kahneman, Wakker and Sarin, 1997).

In all three situations, judgment by prototype and extension neglect can cause violations of monotonicity. People commonly underestimate the strength of evidence provided by 'weak' results in a large sample, compared to stronger results in a small sample (Tversky and Kahneman, 1971). They assign a higher probability to the statement 'Linda is a bank teller and a feminist' than to the statement 'Linda is a bank teller,' if the description of Linda resembles the stereotype of a feminist but not the stereotype of a bank teller (Tversky and Kahneman, 1982). Because the prototypical moment of an episode of discomfort is strongly influenced by how the episode ends, adding a period of diminishing pain to an episode makes it less aversive, in violation of dominance (Kahneman et al., 1993).

3–4) *In some applications of contingent valuation, a problem or a solution is specified by the quantity of a homogeneous good. In such cases, extension neglect takes the form of* **insensitivity to scope***: the quantitative attribute has little weight in the valuation, which is determined mainly by the affective response to a prototypical instance of the good.* Economic theory imposes stringent constraints on the response to variations in the quantities of a good. Diamond and his colleagues (Diamond et al., 1993; Diamond, 1996) have formulated these constraints as a simple add-up test for SWTP in CV surveys: after allowing for an income effect, SWTP for the conjunction of two parts should equal the sum of SWTP for one part, plus SWTP for the second part conditional on already having the first part. It is generally agreed that adequate sensitivity to scope is essential to the acceptability of CVM (NOAA panel on Contingent Valuation, 1993).

Sensitivity to scope has been studied in several research paradigms (see section 3-6). We are concerned here with a particular variant, the *quantity design*, in which participants indicate their willingness to pay for a specified amount of a relatively homogeneous good.[3] The amount of the good is varied across groups of respondents. A well known example of this experimental design is due to Desvousges et al. (1992). The question these authors put to their respondents can be paraphrased as follows: "(2,000, or 20,000, or 200,000) migrating birds die each year by drowning in uncovered oil ponds, which the birds mistake for bodies of water. These deaths could be prevented by covering the oil ponds with nets. How much money would you be willing to pay to provide the needed nets?"

The principle of valuation by prototype applies in straightforward fashion to this example. The story constructed by Desvousges et al. probably evokes for many readers a mental representation of a prototypical incident, perhaps an image of an exhausted bird, its feathers soaked in black oil, unable to escape. The hypothesis of valuation by prototype asserts that the affective value of this image will dominate expressions of the attitude to the problem – including the willingness to pay for a solution. Valuation by prototype implies extension neglect. Although the number of birds that die in oil ponds is surely a relevant consideration, we would expect that – unless the respondents' attention is specifically directed to it – the number of bird deaths will have little effect on SWTP or on other measures of attitudes. Indeed, mean SWTP was $80, $78 and $88, respectively, for saving 2,000 birds, 20,000 birds or 200,000 birds annually (Desvousges et al., 1992).

Similar results have been obtained in other applications of the quantity design. In an early study using this design, Kahneman and Knetsch (see Kahneman, 1986) found that Toronto residents were willing to pay only a little more to clean up all the polluted lakes in Ontario than to clean up polluted lakes in a particular region of Ontario. McFadden and Leonard (1993) reported that residents in four western states were willing to pay only 28% more to protect all 57 wilderness areas in those states than to protect a single area. Jones-Lee et al. (1995) found that the SWTP of UK respondents for a program to reduce the risk of non-fatal road injuries increased by only 29% when the number of prevented injuries was increased by a factor of three. Laboratory studies show similar

---

[3] In the currently most popular variant of CVM, known as the referendum format, respondents are not required to state their maximal SWTP, but only to answer a yes-no question about their stated willingness to pay a specified amount. The distribution of SWTP is then inferred from the responses to various amounts. We discuss the referendum method in section 6.

insensitivity to the quantity of the good. Baron and Greene (1996, experiment 8), for instance, found no effect on SWTP of varying the number of lives saved by a factor of 10.

There is research in which the effects of quantitative variations appear to be larger, though certainly not enough to satisfy economic theory. For example, Carson and Mitchell (1995) describe an unpublished study of the value of reducing the risk associated with chlorination of drinking water. They report that an increase of risk from .004 to 2.43 annual deaths per 1,000 (a factor of 600) yielded an increase of SWTP from $3.78 to $15.23 (a factor of 4). This result does not contradict the general conclusion of other research in this area: the response to variations of scope is so slight that it is not explicable in the standard terms of economic analysis.

Explanations of insensitivity to scope in terms of an income effect are implausible, because the amounts are so small. Explanations in terms of substitution effects are equally unattractive. Several studies have shown that reminding subjects of substitutes or of their prior endowment does not substantially change their response (Loomis et al., 1994; Neill, 1995; Ritov, Baron and Hershey, 1993). An interpretation in terms of substitution effects, if it were taken seriously, would be potentially disastrous for the environment. It would indeed be good news for polluters if the public's demand for clean lakes in Ontario could be satisfied by cleaning up a small subset of its lakes.

Our aim in this section was not to deal with the details of the heated controversy concerning sensitivity to scope (see, for example, Carson and Mitchell, 1995; Frederick and Fischhoff, 1998). Our goal is both simpler and more ambitious: we hope to have shown that inadequate sensitivity to scope in CV surveys that employ the quantity design is *inevitable*, because this phenomenon is an instance of a broad class of similar effects that have been observed in diverse contexts and are explained by a single psychological principle.

3–5) *Extension neglect is neither universal nor absolute. When extension information is both salient and readily interpretable an* **additive extension effect** *is observed: the effects of the valuation of the prototype and of the size of the relevant set are additive. This pattern violates normative rules that require non-linear combination of the two types of information.* In the situations we have discussed, the relevance of extension may be obvious if the quantity mentioned in the problem is readily classified as high or low. Under such circumstances, responses will show some sensitivity to extension. For example, even naive respondents will appreciate that an annual death rate of .0004% from chlorinated water is very low, because of the impressively large number of leading zeros. However, there are situations in which the quantitative information is less easily interpreted: unless the two numbers are seen together, for example, the subjective difference between two large quantities such as 20,000 or 200,000 birds dying in oil ponds is not very impressive (Hsee, 1996). These are the conditions under which complete neglect of scope may be observed.

Studies of extension neglect in other domains have shown that multi-trial experiments in which extension varies from trial to trial have two effects: they draw attention to extension as a relevant feature, and they provide a standard that helps the subject assess values of the extensional attribute as high or low. Extension is not completely neglected under these conditions. Indeed, significant effects of extension have been found in within-S experiments in all the domains we have mentioned. When the base-rate of outcomes is varied from trial to trial, people pay attention to it (Novemsky and Kronzon, 1999). When the duration of episodes that are to be evaluated varies from trial to trial, duration neglect is imperfect (Schreiber and Kahneman, 2000; Varey and Kahneman, 1992). Sample size also affects judgments in within-subject experiments (Griffin and Tversky, 1992).

A remarkable regularity appears in these experiments: the valuation of the prototype and the extension of the set (base-rate or duration) contribute in strictly additive fashion to the global judgment (see also Anderson, 1996, p. 253). The participants in these experiments appear to reason as follows: "this medical procedure is quite painful, but it is short" or "this medical procedure is quite painful, and it is also long." In contrast to the logic of global evaluation, which requires multiplicative or quasi-multiplicative effects of extension, the size of the set is used as an extra feature in this reasoning.

The additive extension effect is also found in the valuation of environmental goods. Kahneman and Ritov (unpublished research) presented several groups of respondents to messages such as the following: "the population of Dolphins in a coastal preserve has declined by 50%." The species mentioned ranged widely in emotional appeal, and the population decline was also varied. Some respondents rated the importance of the problem. Others indicated, for each species, how much of a contribution of $40 to a general environmental fund they would divert to restore the population of the species in the nature preserve. Figures 36.1a and 36.1b present the results for both response measures. The striking feature of these data is that both the dollar measure and the rating of importance exhibit nearly perfect additivity of the effects of species popularity and size of population decline. Precisely the same pattern of results has been observed in studies of individual prediction (Novemsky and Kronzon, 1999), and of the global evaluation of episodes (Schreiber and Kahneman, 1999). A related result was obtained by DeKay and McClelland (1996), who found that the species attributes and the probability of survival were combined additively in people's ranking of programs to preserve endangered species.

We draw several conclusions from this research. First, some effect of extension can be obtained by a procedure, such as the within-subject experimental design, which simultaneously draws attention to the quantitative variable and provides a frame of reference for responding to it. Second, a demonstration that people can be responsive to extension and scope under some conditions is not sufficient to support the conclusion that they always use extension in

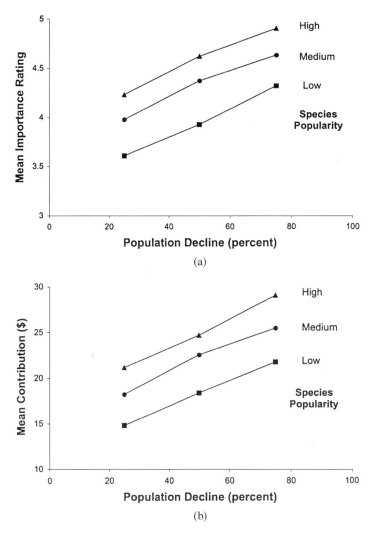

Figure 36.1. a. Mean importance ratings, by species popularity and degree of population decline. b. Mean contributions, by species popularity and degree of population decline.

accordance with the relevant logic. Third, and most important, we again find that the anomalies observed in studies of the value of public goods do not remain either puzzling or unique when they are viewed in the context of similar phenomena in other domains.

3–6) *Several different designs have been used to test sensitivity to scope. The designs are psychologically different, but the normative pattern defined by the add-up test (Diamond, 1996) is unlikely to be satisfied in any of them.* Sensitivity to scope has been examined in two designs other than the quantity design that was discussed in previous sections. (i) In the *explicit list* design, respondents in different groups value nested lists of heterogeneous goods. For example, one group may assess the value of saving both the birds and the fish in a region, while other groups value the birds or the fish in isolation. (ii) In the *embedding* design, SWTP for a good (e.g., saving dolphins) is obtained in two ways: (a) by a direct question (b) by a sequence of questions, first eliciting SWTP for an inclusive good, then the fraction of that amount that should be allocated to a specified good (e.g., SWTP for saving marine mammals, then an allocation to dolphins).

The various tests of scope are equivalent in an economic analysis, and Diamond's add-up test is applicable to all three. In a psychological analysis, however, the designs differ in important ways. The quantity design involves a set or category of elements that are similar in essential respects (e.g., polluted lakes, or different members of the same species). In contrast, the two other designs involve heterogeneous elements, which are not readily represented by a single prototype (Rosch and Lloyd, 1978). There is some evidence that a process of *judgment by maximum* operates in the valuation of heterogeneous categories and lists (Levav, 1996). A related result was reported by Rottenstreich and Tversky (1997) in a study of judgments of frequency for explicit lists (e.g., "How many Stanford students major in either English or Geography?"). Judgment of the total frequency of an explicit disjunction were barely higher than judgments of its maximum. Judgment by maximum, of course, violates the add-up rule.

Carson et al. (1994) reported a study using an explicit list design, which they described as a demonstration of sensitivity to scope. Unfortunately, a basic flaw of their study invalidates their conclusions. The study was concerned with the valuation of the damage that deposits of DDT in the soil of LA Harbor has caused to the reproductive ability of two salient species of birds (Peregrine Falcon, American Bald Eagle) and two relatively obscure species of fish (White Croaker, Kelp Bass). The authors observed higher SWTP when the description of the problem involved all four species than when it involved only the fish. Of course, the results are equally consistent with the hypothesis that WTP to restore two important species of endangered birds is higher than WTP to restore two relatively obscure species of fish. The hypothesis of judgment by maximum suggests that the value attached to the four species would not be much higher than the value attached to the most important of these species. The results of an informal replication of the LA Harbor study, using ratings of importance, were generally consistent with this hypothesis (Levav, 1996). There is no reason to expect that the results of CV using explicit lists will satisfy the add-up test (see also Frederick and Fischhoff, 1998).

The findings obtained in the embedding design unequivocally violate the add-up rule. For example, Kemp and Maxwell (1993) found that SWTP for protection from oil spills off the coast of Alaska was $85 when the good was considered on its own, but only $0.29 when it was derived as an allocation of SWTP for a more inclusive category (environmental protection programs). Kahneman and Knetsch (1992) reported similar findings.

The central point of this section has been that inadequate sensitivity to scope is not a surprise. On the contrary, it would be a major surprise to observe measures of SWTP that reliably conform to the add-up test. This conclusion is relevant to the frequently expressed hope that the scope problem might be overcome by improved instructions, exhortation or added information. Insensitivity to scope is the inevitable result of general rules that govern human judgment. It is naive to expect broad psychological laws to be overcome by minor methodological adjustments.

4. CONTEXT-DEPENDENCE AND VALUATION REVERSALS

A preference reversal is said to exist when two strategically equivalent methods for probing the preference between objects yield conflicting results (see, e.g., Hsee, 1996; Tversky and Thaler, 1992). Preference reversals simultaneously challenge two basic tenets of the standard economic analysis of choice: the existence of a preference order, and the assumption of extensionality. One of the crucial differences between the concepts of economic preference and attitude is that preference reversals are anomalous only for the former, not for the latter. In this section we discuss preference reversals that arise from the context dependence of attitudes and affective valuations. Norm theory (Kahneman and Miller, 1986) provides the theoretical background for this discussion.

4–1) *An object that is considered in isolation evokes a comparison set of similar objects. The valuation of the object is relative to the set that it evoked. Features that are common to the evoked set play no role in relative judgments and valuations.* For an illustration of the relativity of judgment to an evoked set, consider the following two questions: "Is a subcompact car BIG or SMALL?", "Is a bald eagle BIG or SMALL?" The plausible answers are that a subcompact is small and a bald eagle is big. The categories of cars and birds are spontaneously evoked by the mere mention of their members, and these categories provide the norm for a relative judgment of size. The conventions of language allow the entire range of size adjectives, from 'tiny' to 'enormous' to be applied to cars and to birds, to countries and to bacteria.

As we show later, expressions of attitudes show a similar relativity. Furthermore, casual observation indicates that affective values – not only the words used to describe them – are themselves relative. Thus, a guest's rude behavior at a party can arouse intense outrage and anger. Murder is much worse than rudeness, of course, but murder is not part of the evoked context that determines the emotional response to a rude remark. The relativity of affective value explains why people often seem to care intensely about matters that they can also view as trivial when the context changes.

4–2) *Explicit comparison of several objects imposes a shared context for their judgment and valuation. When the objects belong to different categories, comparisons and isolated valuations can yield discrepant results. Differences between the modes of valuation are*

Table 36.3. Responses to an Ecological and a Public Health Problem, by Presentation Order

	Moral Satisfaction		Importance	
Study 1	First	Second	First	Second
Coral Reefs	3.54	3.24	3.78	3.62
Myeloma	2.84	4.18	3.24	4.26

	Moral Satisfaction		SWTP[a]	
Study 2	First	Second	First	Second
Coral Reefs	3.47	3.05	$45	$59
Myeloma	2.98	3.76	$69	$109

[a] All values of WTP in excess of $500 were adjusted to $500.

found both in dollar measures and in ratings. Table 36.3 presents preliminary tests of this hypothesis, drawn from two different studies. The same pair of issues was used in both studies: damage to coral reefs caused by cyanide fishing in Asia, and increased incidence of multiple myeloma among the elderly. We surmised that the latter issue would be perceived as a fairly minor public health problem, whereas a threat to coral reefs would appear significant in an ecological context. We also surmised that public health problems would be assigned a higher general priority than ecological problems, but that this priority would only become relevant in a direct comparison.

The procedure of the two studies was similar. The participants were first asked to evaluate one problem; they were then shown the other problem and were asked to respond to it, with an explicit instruction to consider both problems before responding. The independent variable was the order of presentation of the two problems. The participants in Study 1 were 100 visitors at the San Francisco Exploratorium. They were asked to rate the importance of each problem and the satisfaction they would expect to get from making a contribution to its solution (both on a 0–6 scale). The data for Study 2 are drawn from a larger study, in which participants were jury-eligible residents of Austin. Some participants ($N = 130$) provided ratings of satisfaction as in Study 1. Others ($N = 261$) indicated their WTP to contribute to a solution; when they encountered the second problem they were instructed to treat it as the only cause to which they would be asked to contribute.

Our hypothesis about the role of context in judgments predicts a statistical interaction effect in each of the panels of Table 36.3: the difference between the valuations of the myeloma and coral reefs problems is expected to be larger when these items appear in the second position than in the first. The rationale for this prediction is that the difference between the categories of ecological and human problems is only salient when the issues are directly compared, not when they are valued in isolation. The predicted interaction is highly significant ($p < .001$) in each of the four panels of Table 36.3.

The context effect observed in SWTP is especially noteworthy, because the linguistic convention that allows words such as 'important' or 'satisfying' to be understood in a relative sense does not apply to the dollar scale. To appreciate the difference between scales that allow relativity and scales that do not, consider the questions: "What is the size of an eagle, in meters?", "What is the size of a subcompact, in meters?" Of course, there is no reason to expect any effect of category on answers to this question. A context effect on a size judgment expressed in absolute units indicates a visual illusion – a change in the underlying perception, not in the language used to describe it. By the same logic, the finding of a context effect on a dollar measure implies that the evaluation itself, not only the expression of it, is altered by the comparison.

Kahneman, Schkade and Sunstein (unpublished data) investigated the effects of a comparison context on punitive damage awards. The study was motivated by the observation that the highest punitive awards are commonly found in cases involving large financial harm, probably because the size of the compensatory damages provides a high anchoring value. Punitive damages are generally lower in cases of personal injury, where compensatory damages are also lower. We surmised, however, that cases that result in personal injury are, as a class, more outrageous than cases in which the only losses involve money. Of course, no jury ever considers cases of the two types at the same time, but we predicted that forcing jurors to do so in an experiment would alter or reverse the usual pattern of punitive awards. A sample of 114 jury-eligible citizens provided a punitive damage assessment for a personal injury case adapted from Kahneman, Schkade and Sunstein (1998): (a child seriously hurt because of a flawed child-safety cap), a financial harm case (business fraud), or both. Participants were told that compensatory damages had already been awarded, in the amount of $500,000 for the personal injury and $10 million for the financial harm. As predicted, respondents who judged only one case assessed greater punitive damages in the financial case (median = $5 million) than in the personal injury case (median = $2 million). However, a strong majority (75%) of respondents who judged the two cases together assessed larger awards in the personal injury case, resulting in a striking reversal of median awards ($2.5 million for the personal injury; $0.5 million for the financial harm). More recent data indicate similar effects in ratings of outrage and punitive intent. The same interpretation applies to these results and to the findings summarized in Table 36.3. Cases of personal injury and of financial harm, when considered in isolation, are apparently compared to very different evoked contexts. Here again, the conclusion that the context alters the underlying emotion is justified by the finding of an effect on a dollar measure. A financial transgression that appears outrageous on its own apparently arouses much less outrage when directly compared to an action that causes a child to suffer a severe injury (Kahneman, Schkade, Ritov and Sunstein, 1999).

4–3) *Choice is a special case of comparative valuation, whereas pricing (or the setting of WTP) is normally done by considering a problem in isolation. The different*

contexts of choice and pricing explain some preference reversals between the two tasks.
The analysis of context effects in the preceding section helps explains preference reversals between choice and SWTP that were reported by Kahneman and Ritov (1994). Seven critical pairs of items were constructed, each including one ecological issue and one public health problem. The responses of two groups of respondents were compared. One group encountered both items in a questionnaire that elicited statements of WTP for interventions to alleviate each of several (12–14) problems, which the respondents were instructed to consider independently. Other respondents were asked to make a choice between two items from the same list. They were told that "It sometimes happens that budget constraints force a choice between two desirable projects. One has to be given up, at least for now, so that the other can go forward." The respondents were then asked which of the two interventions they would retain, if they had to make this choice.

Robust reversals of preference were obtained. On average, only 41% of the respondents who stated different WTP for the two items indicated greater willingness to pay for the public health problem.[4] However, 66% of responses favored the public health issues in the choice condition. The difference between the two conditions was statistically significant separately for each of the seven pairs of items. A different pattern was observed in five other pairs of issues, in which the two issues were drawn from the same category. In these control pairs, the proportions favoring one issue over another were quite similar in choice and in SWTP.

4–4) *The context dependence of valuations suggests three observations: (i) the hope of measuring preferences by SWTP is unrealistic; (ii) a suitable choice of context may help improve the rationality of elicited preferences; (iii) there is no general attitude order, but modeling context-dependent affective valuations is feasible in principle.* The finding of preference reversals between SWTP and choice implies that willingness to pay does not provide a stable measure of the position of an object in a preference order – in our view, because there is no stable preference order to be measured. Like the scope problem that was discussed in the preceding section, the context dependence of SWTP is an unavoidable consequence of basic cognitive and evaluative processes. It is not a result of defective procedures, and it will not be eliminated by improved survey methods.

The reversals of valuation that we have observed in both SWTP and punitive damages raise a significant prescriptive question: When different methods for eliciting attitudes yield conflicting results, which method should be used? In general, of course, decisions that are based on a richer set of considerations and on a broader context are more likely to be stable and to satisfy standards of rationality. This principle suggests that asking people for choices may be better than

---

[4] SWTP was the same for the two issues in about 40% of the cases – most often because both responses were zero.

asking them to consider issues in isolation. We have seen, for example, that the priority of public health over ecological concerns is effectively suppressed in the SWTP measure, and only becomes evident when respondents must compare items from the two categories. Similarly, the difference in the outrageousness of actions that cause physical or financial damage was suppressed when cases were considered in isolation, and only revealed by a direct comparison. The benefits of improved rationality are more likely to be achieved if the context of comparison is truly broad, and if it has been selected impartially. Mere exhortations to consider many possibilities (NOAA panel, 1993) are not likely to be effective.

Our findings provided further evidence for a simple negative conclusion: there is no comprehensive and coherent 'attitude order.' This is not a message of despair. The phrase "Individual I likes/dislikes to extent X the description D of object O, considered in context C" is, at least in principle, subject to measurement, verification and modeling. We already know, for example, that different measures of liking will yield similar estimates of X, and that if two objects spontaneously evoke the same context C, measurements of their relative preference by liking and by choice will probably be consistent. Attitudes do not lack structure, but their structure is vastly more complex than the structure that economic analysis attributes to human preferences.

5. THE PSYCHOPHYSICS OF VALUATION

The results of section 2 demonstrated that average dollar responses for large groups yield much the same ranking of attitude objects as do other measures of attitudes. To the proponents of contingent valuation or to the supporters of the jury system this is faint praise, because they need much more than a ranking of objects. The goal of asking survey respondents to assess a public good or of asking jurors to assess punitive damages is to obtain a dollar value that is meaningful in absolute terms, not only in relation to other objects. Can this goal of absolute measurement be realized? In this section we draw on psychophysical research to examine the measurement properties of the dollar scale, and to compare it to other measures of affective valuation.

5–1) *The attitude expressions elicited in surveys can be classified as* **category scales** *or* **magnitude scales**. These terms are borrowed from the field of psychophysics, the study of the functions that relate quantitative expressions of subjective reactions to physical variables. For example, the perceived loudness of tones that vary in amplitude can be measured on a bounded category scale (e.g., from 'not loud at all' to 'very very loud'). Loudness can also be measured on a magnitude scale by presenting the subject with a series of tones, with the instruction to assign a given number (known as the **modulus**) to a specified standard tone, and to assign numbers to other tones relative to this common modulus. The defining characteristics of a magnitude scale are that it is unbounded, has a meaningful zero, and expresses the ratios of the relevant underlying variable.

In terms of this classification of scales, the normal practice of survey research is to use category scales, such as numerical ratings on a bounded scale. However, attitudes can also be measured using magnitude scales (Lodge, 1981; Stevens, 1975). For example, Stevens (1975) reported judgments of the severity of crimes, and also of the severity of different legal punishments, using an unbounded magnitude scale.

5–2) *Studies of magnitude scaling in the context of psychophysical measurement have yielded several generalizations, which apply as well to the domain of attitude measurement (Stevens, 1975).* (i) There is a fair degree of agreement among observers on the *ratios* of the magnitudes that they assign to the sensations evoked by particular stimuli. (ii) In the absence of a designated common modulus, there are large individual differences in the mean values of judgments: some observers assign generally high numbers to all stimuli, others assign low numbers. (iii) The distribution of responses to any stimulus is positively skewed; a lognormal distribution often provides an adequate fit. (iv) The standard deviation of the judgments of different stimuli is approximately proportional to their means; this relationship holds both when the same individual judges each stimulus several times and when the judgments are contributed by different observers. In contrast, category scales are characterized by a negligible correlation between the mean and the standard deviation of judgments. (v) In general, magnitude judgments of sensory intensity are a power function of the relevant physical variable: for example, brightness is a power function of luminance and loudness is a power function of sound amplitude (both with an exponent of approximately 1/3). (vi) Magnitude scales are generally related by a power function to category scales of the same stimuli.

5–3) *The elicitation of dollar responses is a special case of magnitude scaling without a modulus.* The scale of dollars is unbounded and its zero is a meaningful response; the respondents (participants in CV surveys or jurors in civil cases) are not provided with a standard problem to which a specified dollar amount must be assigned (i.e., a modulus). The defining characteristics of scaling without a modulus are therefore satisfied. The results obtained with dollar scales are similar to the results that are observed with magnitude scales in psychophysical studies. In particular, the distribution of dollar responses is positively skewed, both within the responses of each individual and within the responses to any given problem. The distribution of the mean dollar judgments of individual respondents is also highly skewed. Finally, the high correlation between the mean and the standard deviation of individuals, which is expected for magnitude scales, was observed both by Kahneman and Ritov (1994; r = .93) and by Kahneman, Schkade and Sunstein (1998; r = .90).

5–4) *As expected for an application of magnitude scaling without a common modulus, dollar responses are statistically less efficient than category scale measures of the same attitudes.* We have seen that the averages of different attitude expressions in large samples yield similar rankings of objects (see Tables 36.1 and 36.2). However,

Table 36.4. Proportion of Variance Explained by Problems

	Raw	Ranks
Support	.08	.26
Importance	.16	.28
Satisfaction	.12	.26
SWTP	.04	.23

From Kahneman and Ritov, 1994.

dollar responses produce much lower signal-to-noise ratios than do rating scales. Tables 36.4 and 36.5 present results from separate analyses of variance for each of the response measures used in the two studies. The analysis partitions the variance of responses into three components: (i) *Object (signal):* the variance associated with differences among objects of judgments (e.g., public goods that differ in value, personal injury cases that vary in the outrageousness of the defendant's actions). (ii) *Respondents:* the variance associated with individual differences in the mean level of responses, over objects (e.g., some respondents state generally higher WTP than others, some experimental jurors are generally more severe than others). (iii) *Noise:* the residual variance, which combines the effects of individual differences in variability, idiosyncratic responses of some respondents to some objects or topics, and various sources of measurement error.

Tables 36.4 and 36.5 document a striking discrepancy in the strength of the signal (as indicated by the proportion of variance explained) between dollar measures and attitude expressions measured on standard bounded scales. The proportion of Object variance (i.e., signal) was 2 to 4 times larger for rating scales than for SWTP in Kahneman and Ritov (1994). The advantage of the rating scales was even more pronounced in responses to product liability cases, where the amount of Object variance was 5 to 8 times higher for ratings than for dollar responses (Kahneman, Schkade and Sunstein, 1998).

The low signal/noise ratio of dollar awards implies poor agreement among individuals, and even among juries. Kahneman, Schkade and Sunstein (1998) used Monte Carlo techniques to assess the average rank-correlation between

Table 36.5. Proportion of Variance Explained by Scenarios

	Raw	Ranks
Outrage	.29	.42
Punishment	.49	.58
$ Awards	.06	.51

From Kahneman Schkade and Sunstein, 1998.

dollar awards across cases for simulated "juries" of size 12: the estimated reliability (.42) appears unacceptably low.[5]

5–5) *Some transformations of dollar responses improve statistical efficiency, by reducing the effects of the skewness of magnitude scales and of the large individual differences in moduli.* For example, logarithmic and rank transformations of each individual's dollar responses both yield substantial improvements of signal/noise ratio. Transforming SWTP responses to a logarithmic scale doubled the percentage of Object variance (from 4% to 8%), to a level comparable to the other measures. Logarithmic transformation of punitive awards yielded even more dramatic improvement (Object variance increased from 6% to 42%). As shown in Tables 36.4 and 36.5, a ranking transformation also yielded a substantial increase in the relative amount of Object variance in both studies. The success of these transformations is due to the fact that the effect of individual differences in the use of the dollar scale is reduced by the logarithmic transformation and eliminated by the ranking transformation. The good performance of the transformed measures also demonstrates that the dollar response contains useful information about respondents' attitudes. If the objective of research is to rank order a set of objects, the dollar response – suitably transformed, and with a sufficiently large sample – provides as much information as other expressions of affective evaluation. Of course, the proponents of CV and of the current jury system hope for much more, since their goal is to obtain an exact dollar amount.

5–6) *Individual differences in the use of the dollar scale are large, and may be arbitrary to a substantial extent.* In psychophysical research, magnitude scaling without a common modulus yields large individual differences in the responses to stimuli, because subjects spontaneously adopt quite different moduli. If two subjects who share the same underlying psychophysical function adopt different moduli, their responses to all stimuli will differ by a constant of proportionality, which is the ratio of their individual moduli.

In the psychophysical laboratory, differences in moduli are usually considered to be entirely arbitrary, a mere source of statistical noise. Except for very unusual circumstances (e.g., deafness), there is little reason to believe that an individual who consistently assigns low numbers to the loudness of tones actually experiences less loudness than an individual who assigns higher numbers. Are the moduli that CV respondents and jurors apply in assigning dollar responses also arbitrary? A positive answer to this question would remove the rationale for any procedure in which the absolute values that people state are taken seriously, including contingent valuation and the setting of monetary punishments by juries.

There are several ways of testing whether individual differences in the use of the dollar scale are meaningful or arbitrary. (i) *Prediction of behavior.* Several studies have examined the correlation between hypothetical responses to WTP questions and actual behavior (e.g., Cummings, Harrison and Rutstrom, 1995;

---

[5] The higher value shown in Table 36.2 (.89) was obtained with "juries" of 107 members.

Foster, Bateman and Harley, 1997; Seip and Strand, 1992). The data indicate a substantial upward bias in hypothetical responses. (ii) *Search for correlated variables.* If the difference between high-SWTP and low-SWTP respondents is real, it should be correlated with other characteristics of these individuals, such as income, or other indications of involvement in environmental issues. These correlations have been examined in some studies, and are usually low or nonexistent. Kahneman, Schkade and Sunstein (1998) also failed to find significant correlations between the average size of the awards set by individual respondents and several relevant predictors, including demographic attributes and individuals' ratings of the importance that they attached to different features of the cases, such as the degree of malice or the amount of harm suffered by the plaintiff. (iii) *Susceptibility to anchoring.* The large anchoring effects that we discuss in the next section indicate that dollar responses are very labile, both in CV surveys and in punitive awards. Arbitrary numbers that are mentioned in a question have considerable influence on responses – much as arbitrary moduli do.

We do not yet have the data needed to evaluate the relative size of the arbitrary and of the meaningful components in the variability of dollar responses. The available evidence, however, hardly justifies reliance on the absolute values of judgments denominated in dollars. There is at present no reason to believe that dollar responses contain useful information that cannot be obtained more simply and accurately using other expressions of attitudes.

6. ANCHORING EFFECTS

The procedure of asking people to state their maximal WTP for a good has been largely supplanted in CV practice by a protocol in which respondents are asked how they would vote in a hypothetical referendum that would guarantee the provision of public good at a specified cost to the household. Different groups of respondents face different proposed payments, and the cumulative frequency distribution of positive responses is used to estimate the parameters of the underlying distribution of WTP. The estimates of WTP that are generated by this estimation technique are substantially higher than the estimates obtained by an open-ended question, such as "What is the maximum amount of payment for which you would still support the proposition?" (Desvousges et al., 1992; McFadden, 1994). The referendum format has been defended on grounds of its supposedly superior incentive compatibility (Hanemann, 1994; Hoehn and Randall, 1987). We do not directly debate this claim here (see Green et al., 1998). Following the broad strategy of this article, we show instead that the discrepancy between the two types of WTP questions can be parsimoniously explained by a well-understood process of anchoring, which produces similar effects in contexts to which the incentive compatibility idea does not apply.

6–1) *Tasks in which respondents indicate a judgment or an attitude by producing a number are susceptible to an **anchoring effect**: the response is strongly biased toward* *any value, even if it is arbitrary, that the respondent is induced to consider as a candidate answer.* Anchoring effects are among the most robust observations in the psychological literature. In a striking demonstration Wilson and his collaborators induced an anchoring effect by the following procedure: they required subjects to write the last four digits of their SSN, then to state whether they thought that the number of physicians and surgeons listed in the local yellow pages was higher or lower than that number. Finally, the subjects provided an open-ended estimate of the number of physicians and surgeons. The estimates that different subjects offered were strongly correlated with their social security number (Wilson et al., 1996). The necessary and apparently sufficient conditions for the emergence of anchoring effects are (i) the presence of some uncertainty about the correct or appropriate response, and (ii) a procedure that causes the individual to consider a number as a candidate answer. A vast literature has documented anchoring effects in estimation tasks (see, e.g., Strack and Mussweiler, 1997; Wilson et al., 1996), as well as in other settings, including negotiations (Ritov, 1996), and the setting of both compensatory (Chapman and Bornstein, 1996) and punitive awards (Hastie, Schkade and Payne, 1999).

Jacowitz and Kahneman (1995) proposed an index of the size of anchoring effects, which they applied to estimation tasks. They first obtained a distribution of answers to open-ended questions about quantities such as the length of the Amazon or the height of the tallest redwood, and observed the 15th and 85th percentiles of the estimates for each quantity. These values were used as anchors for two additional groups. Respondents in these anchored groups first answered a binary question such as "is the height of the tallest redwood more or less than X?", where the value of X was either the high or the low anchor for that problem. The anchoring index was defined as a ratio. The numerator is the difference between the median estimates of the anchored groups; the denominator is the difference between the high and low anchors. By this measure, the anchoring effects were very large: the median anchoring index in a set of 20 problems was .49.

6–2) *Anchors have a suggestive effect on the answers to binary questions. With scales bounded on one side (such as the dollar scale) this effect causes an upward bias in binary answers, relative to corresponding open-ended responses. In the context of CV surveys, this bias explains the discrepancy previously observed between estimates of WTP from referendum questions and from open-ended questions.* The design employed by Jacowitz and Kahneman (1995) allows a comparison between two proportions: (i) the proportion of respondents in the original group (unanchored) who spontaneously offered an estimate higher than an anchor; (ii) the proportion of respondents in the anchored group who stated that the same anchor was lower than the true value of the quantity. In the absence of bias, the two proportions should be the same. However, the results showed a pronounced bias: on average, respondents in the anchored group judged the high anchor to be lower than the true value on 27% of occasions, very significantly more than the 15% expected from the responses of the unanchored group. Furthermore, there was a pronounced asymmetry in the bias: the low anchors were judged to be too high on only 14% of occasions. The asymmetry was due to the prevalence of estimation problems in which the range of possible answers is bounded by zero, e.g., the height of the tallest redwood. The result of this bias, of course, is that the estimates inferred from the binary question were generally much higher than the estimates obtained directly from open-ended questions. The discrepancy between the two response modes is similar to the discrepancy observed in CV research between estimates of WTP derived from open-ended and from referendum questions (Desvousges et al., 1992; McFadden, 1994).

The similarity between the effects of anchors on estimates of uncertain quantities and on SWTP were explored in a study reported by Green et al. (1998). Visitors at the San Francisco Exploratorium were recruited to answer five questions, including estimates of three quantities (height of the tallest redwood in California, average monthly gasoline used by car owners, annual rainfall in wettest spot on earth) and two WTP questions (save 50,000 off-shore seabirds each year from dying in oil spills, reduce auto accidents in California by 20%). The first and the last questions in each questionnaire were WTP questions. As in the Jacowitz-Kahneman study, a calibration group provided open-ended answers to all five questions. Five anchored groups answered a binary question about each quantity before estimating it. The anchors used in the binary question were chosen to be at the percentiles 25, 50, 75, 90 and 95 of the distribution of open-ended responses.

As expected, comparison of the anchored open-ended responses to the responses of the unanchored groups revealed a large anchoring effect, in both estimation and WTP questions. For example, the mean estimate of the height of a tallest redwood ranged from 282 feet (with 180 ft as an anchor) to 844 ft (with an anchor of 1,200 ft). Similarly, mean SWTP to save 50,000 birds annually ranged from $20.30 (with a $5 anchor) to $143.12 (with a $400 anchor).

An anchoring effect was also observed in answers to binary questions, for both estimates and SWTP. On average, there were 4.3% of answers exceeded the highest anchor in the calibration group, but 21.6% of respondents in the anchoring condition judged the same anchor to be too low. The pattern for low anchors was quite different: 21.5% of unanchored answers were lower than the low anchor, but the same anchor was judged to be too high on only 15.8% of occasions. As in the earlier study, high anchors induced a much larger bias. As a consequence of this asymmetric anchoring effect, the cumulative distribution derived from binary questions stochastically dominated the distribution of open ended answers. Over the five questions, the average ratio of the mean of the distribution inferred from binary questions to the unanchored mean was 3.43 (2.97 for the three estimation questions, 4.13 for the two WTP questions).[6]

---

[6] These results are based on a parametric estimation procedure described in detail by Green et al. (1998). A non-parametric estimation procedure yielded similar ratios: 2.14 for uncertain quantities, 2.22 for SWTP.

This study again illustrates the benefits of searching for parallel phenomena across domains. The psychological analysis reveals that the tasks of estimating positive quantities and of determining a willingness to pay are deeply similar to each other, in both their open-ended and binary versions. They yield similarly skewed distributions of responses, are susceptible to similarly asymmetric anchoring effects, and therefore produce the same discrepancy between the parameters estimated from open-ended and from binary questions. In light of these observations, an explanation of the discrepancy in estimates of WTP in terms of incentive compatibility has little appeal, because it cannot be applied to the identical finding in another task.

7. APPLICATIONS

The central claim of this paper has been that people are better described as having attitudes than preferences – perhaps in every domain, but certainly in the domain of public concerns. In contrast, CVM is rooted in the assumption that conventional consumer theory applies to public goods, including non-use goods such as the continued existence of the whooping crane. At least in principle, the dollar value of such a good could be read off an individual's preference order. The assumption of an inclusive preference order appears to be widely shared among economists, including critics of CVM (e.g., Diamond and Hausman, 1994) and among rational-agent theorists in political science (see Bartels (1998) for a discussion). In this theoretical framework, the main question to be asked about contingent valuation is the accuracy of measurement that it provides.

The problem with CVM, in our view, is not imprecise measurement but an incorrect theory. If consumer theory does not capture the nature of people's value for environmental goods, there can be no more hope of measuring the economic value of the whooping crane than there is of measuring the physical properties of the ether. Of course, many people do value the whooping crane and will even pay to preserve it. We have described these people as having a positive affective valuation of whooping cranes, which induces a positive attitude to interventions that will preserve this species. These valuations can be expressed in many ways, including statements of WTP, actual payments, and votes in both simulated and real referenda. Attitude objects can be ordered reliably by sample averages of diverse expressions of valuation, including SWTP. As we have seen, however, these valuations lack some of the essential properties that economic theory requires of preferences. In particular, expressions of affective valuation are susceptible to framing effects (Bartels, 1998; Zaller, 1992), inadequately sensitive to scope and severely context dependent. Moreover, dollar measures of valuation are especially susceptible to the effects of anchors and of arbitrary moduli.

The extreme context-dependence of attitudes undermines the most compelling rationale that has been offered for the contingent valuation method.

As Hanemann (1994) pointed out, the referendum question presents the respondent with a realistic task of formulating a voting intention, and answers to such survey questions have often been found to predict voting outcomes with fair accuracy. However, the only permissible inference from this argument is that CVM results predict the outcome of a real referendum that precisely mimics the context and framing of the survey question (Payne, Bettman and Schkade, 1999). The results do not provide reliable information about the voting outcomes that would be obtained with different wording of the question, or if the target proposition were embedded in a particular list of propositions. The evidence that SWTP diminishes steadily when several causes are considered in sequence (Carson and Mitchell, 1995; Payne et al., 1999) is another illustration of context dependence and another demonstration that CVM results are not sufficiently robust to provide a basis for policy.

Our pessimism about the validity of CVM does not imply despair about the possibility of using public attitudes as an aid to policy making. The affective value that people attach to issues probably conveys useful information about their possible reactions to policy proposals or to actual outcomes. More formal approaches to the elicitation of priorities are also possible, if they are developed with adequate respect for the psychology of valuation. For example, a scale of value for environmental damage could be developed by constructing a small set of hypothetical benchmark scenarios, covering a broad range of damage magnitude and commodity importance. Two criteria for including scenarios in the scale would be: (i) high consensus in the attitudes of the public to the scenario; and (ii) a hope of achieving professional and political consensus on appropriate dollar values. Public attitudes would be one input into this process, but probably not the only one. We expect that experts would bring in relevant considerations that lay judgment is prone to neglect, such as the scope and duration of the damage. The objective of the scaling effort would be to provide a mapping from attitudes and other relevant factors to dollar values for a particular class of environmental commodities.

Once a scale is established, a real issue that arises could be valued by a survey in which respondents would explicitly compare the current problem to the benchmark scenarios. The measures of attitude used in this comparison would be chosen by psychometric criteria: measures of judged importance and political support would probably be preferred to SWTP. A dollar value would be assigned based on the rank of the target issue among the benchmark scenarios of the standard scale. One advantage of this proposal is that the difficult conceptual problems of anchoring the dollar value of public goods in the preferences and opinions of the citizenry would be addressed just once, in the process of constructing the initial scale linking monetary value to attitude. Clearly, professional and political consensus is more likely to be achieved in dealing with hypothetical questions constructed for this purpose than in evaluating real goods in the context of litigation. Rutherford, Knetsch and Brown (1998) make a similar argument and propose that damage schedules be developed to replace ad hoc valuation based on SWTP responses.

The other domain that we have discussed, the setting of punitive damages, is a descendant of an old tradition which requires a small group of citizens to express their attitudes in dollars. It is remarkable that the jury system appears designed to enhance rather than minimize the deficiencies of human judgment: juries are instructed to consider cases one at a time, using a dollar measure without a modulus. Not surprisingly, dollar awards are erratic, in spite of a high level of agreement on ratings of outrage and punitive intent. Sunstein, Kahneman and Schkade (1998) provide a detailed analysis of possible reforms of the jury's task, which would require jurors to do what they can do well, not what they can do poorly. The determination of what jurors can do well combines normative evaluations with empirical facts. For example, if a normative analysis concludes that juror's intuitions about appropriate severity of punishment are valid, but their ability to translate these intuitions into dollars is weak – a plausible conclusion in view of the data reported here – the system could be reformed by requiring jurors to provide graded verbal statements of the severity of punishment that they consider just, leaving to the judge the task of translating this intent into a dollar amount.

Taken together, the examples of CV and punitive damages show that the debate about the nature of preferences and about the rationality of agents is not merely theoretical. The procedures that lead to some significant societal decisions may take different forms, depending on whether the decisions of individual citizens are best understood as a reflection of attitudes or of standard economic preferences.

8. CONCLUDING REMARKS

The stereotyped role of the psychologist in the inter-disciplinary conversation about the nature of human choice is that of a critic, engaged in the construction of counter-examples to the economist's rational models. We have attempted to expand this role here, by focusing on the power and generality of psychological principles, rather than on the limitations of rational choice theory. Our theme has been that phenomena that appear anomalous from the perspective of standard preference models are in fact predictable – indeed, inevitable – consequences of well-established rules of judgment and valuation, which apply in domains that are beyond the reach of choice theory. The alternative to rational choice as a descriptive model is neither chaos nor an endless list of ad hoc claims. It is a manageable set of concepts and testable propositions, which often predict surprising parallels between ostensibly different behaviors in different domains.

The evidence that we have discussed in this article was restricted to hypothetical questions. However, the progression of ideas from the explanation of hypothetical questions to the understanding of economically consequential behavior has an encouraging history, albeit a brief one (much of it is collected in Thaler, 1992). An example is the notion of loss aversion (Tversky and Kahneman, 1991a), which was originally formulated in the context of hypothetical choices between gambles, further developed in market experiments with real stakes, and eventually extended to significant economic phenomena. The idea that some actions are expressions of affective valuations is, in our view, a candidate for a similar trajectory.

ACKNOWLEDGMENTS

The U.S.-Israel Binational Science Foundation, the National Science Foundation and the Environmental Protection Agency provided support for the preparation of this article. Shelley Chaiken, Jack Knetsch, Kristine Kuhn and Barbara Mellers provided valuable comments.

37. Experienced Utility and Objective Happiness
A Moment-Based Approach

Daniel Kahneman

1. INTRODUCTION

The concept of utility has carried two different meanings in its long history. As Bentham (1789) used it, utility refers to the experiences of pleasure and pain, the "sovereign masters" that "point out what we ought to do, as well as determine what we shall do." In modern decision research, however, the utility of outcomes refers to their weight in decisions: utility is inferred from observed choices and is in turn used to explain choices. To distinguish the two notions I refer to Bentham's concept as *experienced utility* and to the modern usage as *decision utility*. Experienced utility is the focus of this chapter. Contrary to the behaviorist position that led to the abandonment of Bentham's notion (Loewenstein 1992), the claim made here is that experienced utility can be usefully measured.

The chapter has three main goals: (1) to present a detailed analysis of the concept of experienced utility and of the relation between the pleasure and pain of moments and the utility of more extended episodes; (2) to argue that experienced utility is best measured by moment-based methods that assess current experience; (3) to develop a moment-based conception of an aspect of well-being that I will call "objective happiness." The chapter also introduces several unfamiliar concepts that will be used in later chapters.

Pleasure and pain are attributes of a moment of experience, but the outcomes that people value extend over time. It is therefore necessary to establish a concept of experienced utility that applies to temporally extended outcomes. Two approaches to this task will be compared here.

1. The *memory-based* approach accepts the subject's retrospective evaluations of past episodes, their *remembered utility*, as valid data.
2. The *moment-based* approach derives the experienced utility of an episode from real-time measures of the pleasure and pain (*moment utility*) that the subject experienced during that episode.

I thank Shane Frederick, Barbara Fredrickson, Laura Gibson, David Laibson, Nathan Novemsky, David Schkade, Cass Sunstein, Richard Thaler, Anne Treisman, and Peter Wakker for helpful comments. I also thank Peter Wakker for allowing me to use ideas and sentences that we had fashioned together, and Peter McGraw for extremely valuable assistance and useful suggestions.

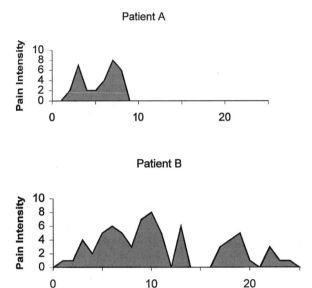

Figure 37.1. Pain intensity reported by two colonoscopy patients.

The main novelty of the treatment proposed here is that it is thoroughly moment-based. Section 2 reviews some of the evidence that raises doubts about the validity of memory-based assessments. Section 3 presents the conditions that must be satisfied to permit an assessment of the total experienced utility of episodes from the utilities of their constituent moments. Section 4 introduces a moment-based concept of objective happiness and examines the feasibility of its measurement. Section 5 exposes the ambiguity of a central idea of the well-being literature – the hedonic treadmill – and discusses how measures of objective happiness could contribute to the resolution of that ambiguity. A research agenda and some controversial issues are discussed in Section 6.

Figure 37.1 illustrates the main concepts of the present treatment. It is drawn from a study of immediate and retrospective reports of the pain of colonoscopy (Redelmeier and Kahneman 1996). Patients undergoing colonoscopy were asked every 60 seconds to report the intensity of their current pain on a scale on which 10 was "intolerable pain" and 0 was "no pain at all." These ratings were used to construct the profiles of *moment utility* illustrated in the figure. The patients later provided several measures of the *remembered utility* of the procedure as a whole. They evaluated the entire experience on a scale, and they also compared it with a set of other aversive experiences. Unlike moment utility and remembered utility, the *total utility* associated with each patient's colonoscopy is not an expression of a subjective feeling or judgment. Total utility is an objective assessment of the statistics of a utility profile, based on formal rules.

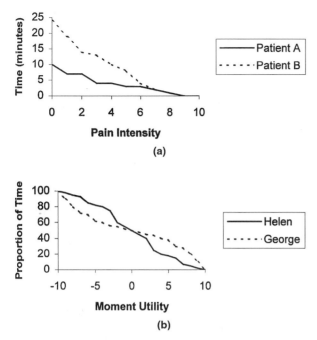

Figure 37.2. (a) Decumulative temporal function representing pain profiles of Patients A and B, and (b) fictitious decumulative functions representing the objective happiness of two individuals over a period of time.

The cases of patients A and B also illustrate the contrast between remembered utility and total utility. It is immediately apparent from inspection of Figure 37.1 that patient B had a worse experience than patient A,[1] and this impression will be confirmed by the analysis of total utility in Section 3 (see Figure 37.2). However, patient A in fact retained a worse evaluation of the procedure than patient B. In this case, as in many others, remembered utility and total utility do not coincide, and outcomes will be ranked differently depending on whether experienced utility is assessed by a memory-based or by a moment-based method.

2. MEMORY-BASED ASSESSMENT: REMEMBERED UTILITY

Anyone who has cared for an elderly relative whose memory is failing has learned that there is a crucial difference between two ostensibly similar questions. The question How are you now? may elicit a confident and cogent answer whereas the question How have you been? evokes only confusion. This distinction is rarely drawn in other settings. We normally expect people to know

---

[1] On the assumption that the two patients used the pain scale similarly. This issue is discussed further in Section 3.

how they have been as well as how they are. Memory-based evaluations of experience and reports of current pleasure and pain are treated with equal respect in routine conversations, but the respect for memory is less deserved. Studies of the psychology of remembered utility are reviewed in detail in the next chapter. The main conclusions of this research are listed below and illustrated by the colonoscopy study from which Figure 37.1 was drawn.

Duration neglect. No one would deny that it is generally better for a colonoscopy to be short than to be long. At least in principle, then, the duration of a colonoscopy is relevant to its overall utility. However, memory-based assessments do not generally conform to this principle. For example, the colonoscopies studied by Redelmeier and Kahneman (1996) varied in duration between 4 and 69 minutes, but the correlation between the duration of a procedure and the patient's subsequent evaluation of it was only .03. Furthermore, the duration of the colonoscopy had no effect on patients' hypothetical choice between a repeat colonoscopy and a barium enema. Complete or nearly complete neglect of duration has been found in other studies using a variety of different research designs. A hypothesis of "evaluation by moments" is introduced in Chapter 38 to explain these findings; it asserts that the remembered utility of an episode is determined by constructing a composite representative moment and assessing the utility of that moment.

The Peak–End rule. In contrast with the negligible effect of duration, the patients' subsequent evaluations of the procedure were predicted with relatively high accuracy ($r = .67$) from the average of the most intense level of pain reported during the procedure and the mean pain level reported over the last 3 minutes. Because the Peak–End average was higher for patient A than for patient B, this empirical rule predicts – correctly – that patient A would retain a more aversive memory of the colonoscopy than patient B. Strong support for the Peak–End rule was obtained in several other studies, reviewed in detail in Chapter 38.

Violations of dominance. The Peak–End rule implies a counterintuitive prediction: adding a period of pain to an aversive episode will actually improve its remembered utility if it lowers the Peak–End average. For example, several extra minutes at pain level 4 would be expected to improve patient A's global evaluation of the procedure. This prediction was tested in a clinical experiment with 682 patients undergoing colonoscopy. Half of the patients were randomly selected for an experimental treatment in which the examining physician left the colonoscope in place for about a minute after terminating the examination. The patients were not informed of the manipulation (Katz, Redelmeier, and Kahneman 1997).[2] The extra

---

[2] The ethical justification for the experiment was the observation of poor compliance among patients who have had a painful colonoscopy and are instructed to schedule another.

minute was distinctly uncomfortable but not very painful. The effect of the experimental treatment was to reduce the Peak–End average for patients, such as patient A, who would otherwise have experienced considerable pain in the final moments of the procedure. As predicted by the Peak–End rule, retrospective evaluations of the procedure were significantly more favorable in the group that experienced the prolonged procedure than in the group that was treated conventionally.

Similar violations of dominance were also observed in choices. In one experiment, participants were exposed in immediate succession to two unpleasant sounds of similar composition. One of them lasted for 10 seconds at 78 db; the other consisted of the same 10 seconds at 78 db followed by 8 more seconds at 66db. When given an opportunity to choose which of the two sounds would be repeated later, most participants chose the longer (Schreiber and Kahneman 2000; [ch. 38]). This choice is odd, because 8 seconds of silence are clearly preferable to 8 seconds of 66 db noise. In this simple situation, decision utility appears to be determined directly by remembered utility: people choose to repeat the sound they dislike least, and the Peak–End rule determines that.

3. MOMENT-BASED ASSESSMENT: TOTAL UTILITY

The evidence reviewed in the preceding section suggested that memory-based assessments of experienced utility should not be taken at face value. The present section introduces a moment-based alternative in which the *total utility* of an episode is derived from a temporal profile of moment utility. The same analysis extends to related episodes separated in time because utility profiles may be concatenated. For example, the total utility of a Kenya safari should include subsequent occasions of slide-showing and reminiscing.

Figure 37.2a presents the data of Figure 37.1 in the form of a decumulative function, which shows the amount of time spent at or above each pain level. If the measure of moment utility on which it is based satisfies a stringent set of conditions, total utility can be derived from the type of representation illustrated in Figure 37.2 (Kahneman, Wakker, and Sarin 1997). Six conditions are listed below. The first four impose requirements on the measure of moment utility. The last two conditions are normative; they specify the rules by which total utility is constructed from moment utilities.

Inclusiveness. The measure of moment utility should incorporate all the aspects of an experience that are relevant to its evaluation, including the residual effects of prior events (e.g., satiation, adaptation, fatigue) and the affect associated with anticipation of future events (fear, hope).

Ordinal measurement across situations. The measurement of moment utility must be ordinal or better. Experiences of different types (e.g., a stubbed toe and a humiliating rebuke) must be measured on a common scale.

Distinctive neutral point. The pain scale that was used in the colonoscopy study has a natural zero point. However, the dimension of moment utility is bipolar, ranging from intensely positive to neutral and from neutral to intensely negative. A distinctive neutral point ("neither pleasant nor unpleasant," "neither approach nor avoid") anchors the scale and permits comparisons across situations and persons.[3] As will be seen later, a stable zero is also essential for cardinal measurement of moment utility on a ratio scale.

Interpersonal comparability. The scale must permit comparisons of individuals and groups. The next section shows that this requirement may be more tractable than is commonly thought.

The next two requirements (separability and time-neutrality) are of a different nature. They are normative assumptions about the composition of total utility, which are required to justify the transformation of utility profiles (e.g., Figure 37.1) into the decumulative format (e.g., Figure 37.2). The discussion of these assumptions highlights a critical difference between the present analysis and economic models of the utility of sequences of outcomes. Economic models generally describe outcomes as physical events (see, e.g., Chapters 32 and 33). The analysis of total utility, in contrast, describes outcomes as moment utilities.

Separability. The ordering of experiences can affect the utility they confer. For example, a strenuous tennis game and a large lunch yield a better experience in one order than in the other because the enjoyment of the tennis game is sharply reduced when it follows lunch. The condition of separability, which states that the contribution of an element to the global utility of the sequence is independent of the elements that preceded and followed it, is often violated when the sequences are described in terms of physical events such as lunch and a tennis game. In a moment-based treatment of total utility, however, the elements of the sequence that is to be evaluated are not events but rather moment utilities associated with events. Because *all* the effects of the order of events are already incorporated into moment utilities, the order of these moment utilities no longer matters. Separability is necessary for the decumulative representation, which does not preserve order information. To appreciate this intuition, consider a person who receives two unexpected prizes in immediate succession, one of $500, the other of $10,000, and then promptly dies or loses her memory. In evaluating the total utility of these experiences, we recognize that it would be better for the two prizes to arrive in ascending rather than in descending order – presumably because the enjoyment of the smaller prize is greater when it comes first. Now imagine that all you know is that just before he died (or became amnesic) an individual had two pleasurable experiences

---

[3] Some authors consider valence as bivalent rather than bipolar (e.g., Cacioppo, Gardner, and Berntson 1999).

with utilities U_a and U_b, where $U_a \gg U_b$. Would we still think that their order matters? When outcomes are moment utilities, there is no compelling reason to reject separability.

Time neutrality. All moments are weighted alike in total utility. Total utility is a measure on completed outcomes and is therefore always assessed after the fact. Unlike decision making, in which the temporal distance between the moment of decision and the outcome may matter, the temporal distance between an outcome and its retrospective assessment is entirely irrelevant to its evaluation. Total utility is therefore *time neutral.* In this important respect, it is unlike decision utility and remembered utility, which both assign more weight to some parts of the sequence than to others. Outcomes that occur late in a sequence are often underweighted in decision utility and overweighted in remembered utility – a bias that is incorporated in the Peak–End rule. The normative status of both weighting schemes is dubious. Discounting of delayed outcomes in decisions favors myopic preferences for options in which the benefits are obtained quickly and the costs are delayed. The overweighting of endings may be equally unreasonable: an experience that ends very badly should still be evaluated favorably, if it has been sufficiently good for a sufficiently long time (Kahneman, Wakker, and Sarin 1997).

Measures of Total Utility

The representation of Figure 37.2 assumes that a utility profile can be rearranged at will and that all its parts are weighted equally. Separability and time neutrality are therefore necessary and, together with the assumptions of inclusiveness and ordinal measurement, sufficient for the representation of utility profiles as decumulative temporal distributions. The total utility of episodes is a measure of these distributions.

Figure 37.2 illustrates two representations of temporal distributions of utility which differ in their ordinates: time is shown in absolute units in panel (a) but in proportional units in panel (b). The representation of panel 2a is appropriate when the duration of the episode is relevant to its evaluation. Thus, it is reasonable to say that the colonoscopy of patient B was worse than that of patient A because it lasted longer. On the other hand, it does not make sense to say that Helen was happier last week than she was last Sunday because last week was longer than last Sunday. The representation of Figure 37.2b is correct when the duration of the period of evaluation is not relevant to its evaluation. It is the appropriate representation in the assessment of the well-being of individuals and groups, which is discussed in the next section.[4]

---

[4] There are situations in which both representations are relevant. The total utility (or happiness) that Alan enjoyed while he was married to Helen may depend on how long they were married before she died in an accident. On the other hand, an assessment of how happy Alan was in his marriage should not be influenced by how long it lasted.

As Figure 37.2a illustrates, the ordinal measurement of moment utility permits the detection of distributional dominance. By this simple test, patient B had a worse colonoscopy than patient A. The decumulative distribution can also be characterized by nonparametric statistics such as the median and other fractiles. Figure 37.2b presents decumulative distributions of moment utility for two individuals, George and Helen. There is no dominance in this comparison, and the medians are close. The main conclusion that can be drawn is that George experienced more extremes of affect than Helen did. As this example illustrates, distributional dominance is a blunt, but still useful measuring instrument.

Cardinal measurement of moment utility would be desirable, of course. With cardinal measurement, the most natural index of total utility could be calculated: the temporal integral of moment utility. The idea has a long history (Edgeworth discussed it in 1881), but it effectively requires a rescaling of moment-utility in terms of physical time, which is difficult to implement. This reasoning is explicit in the use of QALYs (Quality Adjusted Life Years) in medical decision making. QALYs are derived from judgments of equivalence between periods of survival that vary in duration and in level of health. For example, 2 years of survival at a QALY of 0.5 are considered equally desirable as 1 year in normal health (Broome 1993).

A formal analysis of the temporal integration rule was offered by Kahneman, Wakker, and Sarin (1997). Their treatment invoked all the assumptions that were discussed in this section, including separability and temporal neutrality. In addition, it introduced an idealized objective observer, who assesses the total utility of utility profiles, such as those of Figure 37.1. The following axioms specify the logic of this assessment.

1. The global utility of a utility profile is not affected by concatenation with a neutral utility profile.
2. Increases of moment utility do not decrease the global utility of a utility profile.
3. In a concatenation of two utility profiles, replacing one profile by another with a higher global utility will increase the global utility of the concatenation.

The following theorem can be proved: "The three axioms above hold if and only if there exists a nondecreasing ("value") transformation function of moment utility, assigning value 0 to 0, such that global utility orders utility profiles according to the integral of the value of moment utility over time." The proof is due to Peter Wakker.

The representation of total utility as a temporal integral implies a scale of moment utility monotonically related to the original scale but now calibrated by its relation to duration. For example, suppose that an idealized observer who conforms to the axioms judges that 1 minute of pain that had been rated 7 on the original scale is equivalent to 2 minutes at a rating of 6. On the transformed scale, the value that corresponds to the original rating of 7 will be double the value assigned to a rating of 6. Idealized observers are hard to find, of course, and cardinal scaling of utility is therefore a conceptual exercise rather than a practical procedure. However, the conditions identified by Kahneman, Wakker, and Sarin (1997) are sufficient to guarantee the decumulative representation which is adequate for many purposes.

4. OBJECTIVE HAPPINESS: CONCEPT AND MEASURE

Moment utility is the building block of the broader construct of experienced utility. It is also the building block for a construct of *objective happiness* with which the remainder of this chapter is concerned. Like total utility, objective happiness is derived from a distribution of moment utility (see Figure 37.2b for an example) that characterizes an individual (George or Helen), a group (Californians, Midwesterners, paraplegics), or a setting (the Washington subway, the New York subway). Like total utility, objective happiness is a moment-based concept, that is operationalized exclusively by measures of the affective state of individuals at particular moments in time. In this essential respect, objective happiness differs from standard measures of subjective well-being, which are memory-based and require the subject to report a global evaluation of the recent past. The term "objective" is used because the judgment of happiness is made according to standard rules. The ultimate data for the judgment are, of course, subjective experiences.

Continuous measures of experienced utility are, of course, impractical for the measurement of objective happiness over a period of time. Sampling techniques must be used to obtain a distribution of moment utilities that adequately represents the intended population of individuals, times, and occasions. For example, a study of the objective happiness of Californians requires a sample of observations that reflects the relative amounts of time spent on the freeway and in hot tubs. Techniques for sampling times and occasions have been developed in the context of Experience Sampling Methodology (ESM) (Csikszentmihalyi 1990; Stone, Shiffman and DeVries 1999).[5]

Reporting the sign and intensity of current hedonic and affective experience is not essentially different from the standard psychophysical tasks of reporting color or smell. The report of affect is probably intermediate in difficulty between these tasks: somewhat more difficult than labeling colors but much easier than describing smells. The worlds of affect and of color are similar in another important respect: they combine phenomenological richness with a simple underlying structure. A nonintuitive finding of color research is that the enormous variety of subjective color experience can be represented in a two-dimensional space – the color circle – with additional information provided by

---

[5] Participants in studies using ESM carry a palmtop computer that beeps at random times during the day. The palmtop computer then displays questions that elicit information about the current setting and about the subject's present affective state.

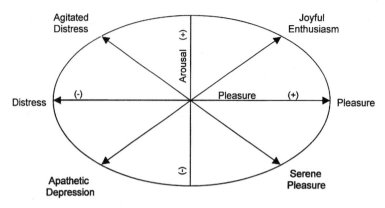

Figure 37.3. A representation of affective space.

a third dimension of luminance. A major result of research on affect is that much of the variation among affective states can be captured by specifying their positions in a space defined by the dimensions of valence (good to neutral to bad) and arousal (from frenetic to lethargic) (Plutchik and Conte 1997, Russell 1980, Russell and Carroll 1999, Stone 1995, Warr 1999). As Figure 37.3 illustrates, the two-dimensional structure permits a distinction between two forms of positive affect (exuberant joy or serene bliss) and two forms of negative affect (agitated distress or apathetic depression).

A significant limitation of the two-dimensional representation of affect is that it does not capture the nature of primary emotions such as surprise or anger. Another objection to this scheme questions the assumption that valence is a single bipolar dimension. Cacioppo, Gardner, and Berntson (1999) point out that positive and negative affective states are processed by different neural systems and may be activated concurrently. They suggest that a three-dimensional representation may be necessary, in which "good" and "bad" are independent dimensions. However, the systems are not functionally independent, and there is evidence that they inhibit each other. Lang (1995) has shown, for example, that watching pleasant pictures of food or smiling babies attenuates the startle response to a loud sound, whereas startle is actually enhanced in the presence of disgusting or horrible pictures. For the present purposes, the description of valence as a bipolar dimension can be retained as a useful approximation even if it is not perfectly correct (Russell and Carroll 1999; Tellegen, Watson, and Clark 1999). Later in this section I discuss a physiological measure that can provide convergent validation of the measurement of valence.

The simplest method for eliciting a self-report of current affective state is undoubtedly the *affect grid*: respondents describe their state by marking a single position on a grid defined by the two dimensions of valence and arousal (Russell, Wess, and Mendelsohn 1989). The affect grid appears to be applicable in all situations, for any moment of life can be characterized by the attributes of valence and arousal. The characterization is incomplete, of course, but surely relevant to an analysis of well-being. The affect grid can be used to derive a unidimensional distribution of affective values, as in Figure 37.2. Of course, finer-grain analyses that do not collapse over the arousal dimension are likely to be even more informative.

Next, I attempt to evaluate the affect grid in terms of the four criteria of adequate measurement of moment-utility that were considered in the preceding section. The purpose of this speculative discussion is to illustrate both the problems and the promise of measurement in this domain, not to endorse any particular measure.

Inclusiveness. Defining happiness by the temporal distribution of experienced affect appears very narrow, and so it is. The concept of objective happiness is not intended to stand on its own and is proposed only as a necessary element of a theory of human well-being. A comprehensive account of well-being inevitably brings in philosophical considerations (Ryff and Singer 1998) and a moral conception of "the good life" (Brock 1993, Nussbaum and Sen 1993), which are not easily reduced to experienced utility. However, good mood and enjoyment of life are not incompatible with other psychological criteria of well-being that have been proposed, such as the maintenance of personal goals, social involvement, intense absorption in activities, and a sense that life is meaningful (Argyle 1999, Cantor and Sanderson 1999, Csikszentmihalyi 1990, Fredrickson 1999). Clearly, a life that is meaningful, satisfying, and cheerful should rank higher on the scale of well-being than a life that is equally meaningful and satisfying but sad or tense. Objective happiness is only one constituent of the quality of human life, but it is a significant one.

Ordinal measurement across situations. The experiences of a stubbed toe and of a humiliating rebuke are both likely to be described on the affect grid as negative in valence and high in arousal, but can the valence and the arousal be compared? It is a familiar psychological fact that comparison along a single attribute is especially difficult if the objects compared differ in other attributes as well. For example, it is more difficult – but not impossible – to compare the loudness of sounds that differ in pitch and timbre than to compare sounds that share these attributes. The question of whether people can compare physical and emotional pain, or the thrills of food and of music, is ultimately empirical. In general, the coherence of judgments across categories is tested by examining the correspondence between ranking of objects in explicit comparisons and ratings of the same objects considered one at a time (see Chapter 36). This test is applicable to ratings and rankings of the utility of different kinds of experience, although it is complicated by the necessity of relying on memory for the comparison task.

Absolute zero point. Bipolar scales of judgment comprise scales for two qualitatively different attributes separated by a distinctive neutral point. Familiar examples include the dimensions that run from hot to cold and from red to green via red-tinged gray and green-tinged gray. The neutral point that separates the red zone from the green zone of the red–green dimension is "colorless gray or white." Similarly, "neither cold nor warm" is the natural zero of the scale of subjective temperature. The stimulus that gives rise to a neutral experience may be different in different contexts, but the neutral experience itself is constant. For example, people can completely adapt to a range of different temperatures, and within that range any temperature to which one has fully adapted will evoke the same neutral experience. The natural zero of the scale of moment utility should be "neither pleasant nor unpleasant – neither approach nor avoid." A distinctive zero permits a crude but useful assessment of well-being in terms of the amount of time spent on the positive and on the negative side of the neutral point (Diener, Sandvik and Pavot 1991; Parducci 1995). Because it is distinctive, the neutral value can be used with some confidence to match experiences, whether thermal or hedonic, across time for a given individual and even across individuals (Kahneman and Varey 1991).

Interpersonal comparability. Interpersonal comparisons of subjective experience can never be fully satisfactory, but the success of psychophysical research suggests that these comparisons do not present an intractable problem. Three illustrative lines of evidence will be mentioned in support of this conclusion:

1. There is substantial intersubject agreement on the psychophysical functions that relate reports of the intensity of subjective experience to the physical intensity of the stimulus. For example, the relation between a measure of the physical strength of labor contractions during childbirth and self-reports of pain was generally similar for different women (Algom and Lubel 1994).

2. The design of the colonoscopy study (Redelmeier and Kahneman 1996) included a group of 50 patients who were not required to report their pain every minute during the procedure. Assessments of the pain of these patients were made every 60 seconds by a minimally trained assistant on the basis of what she could see and hear of the patient's reactions. Remarkably, the Peak–End average of the observer's ratings correlated quite highly ($r = .70$) with the patients' own global evaluations of the procedure reported after its termination. The observer was evidently able to compare the experiences of different patients. Furthermore, the pattern of results implies considerable agreement among patients in the use of the response scales.

3. The high correlations between self-reports and physiological measures, which are discussed next, further support the feasibility of interpersonal comparisons.

Physiological Validation
The fundamental simplicity of affective space and the speed of developments in brain research make it likely that physiological correlates of moment utility

(affective valence) will be found. The difference between levels of electrical activity in the left and right hemispheres of the prefrontal cortex appears to meet most criteria for such a measure (Davidson 1998). Positive and negative affect are respectively associated with greater activity in the left and in the right prefrontal regions. Neurologists have long known that the misery of a stroke that affects a prefrontal area is much worse if the damage is in the left hemisphere – the happier region, where opportunities for approach appear to be calculated (Sutton and Davidson 1998). A simple measure of the difference of activity in the two regions has been validated as a measure of mood and of the response to affectively relevant stimuli. Stable individual differences in the characteristic value of this difference are highly correlated with measures of temperament and personality both in adults (Davidson and Tomarken 1989, Sutton and Davidson 1998) and in babies (Davidson and Fox 1989). Correlations with questionnaire measures of approach and avoidance tendencies and of positive and negative affect are strikingly high (Sutton and Davidson 1997, Tomarken et al. 1992). This result demonstrates, in passing, that the function that relates self-reports to brain states must be quite similar across people.

A different approach to the physiology of well-being has been adopted by investigators who study physiological markers of long-term cumulative load on coping resources (Ryff and Singer 1998, Sapolsky 1999). It is tempting to speculate that these measures of stress-induced physiological wear and tear could be correlates of long-term objective happiness. It is not science fiction to imagine that physiological measures will eventually contribute to the solution of enduring puzzles in the study of experienced utility and of well-being and provide a criterion for the validation of self-report measures.

In conclusion, the prospects are reasonably good for an index of the moment utility that will be sensitive to the many kinds of pleasure and anguish in people's lives: moods of contentment or misery, feelings of pride or regret, aesthetic thrills, experiences of "flow," worrying thoughts, and physical pleasures. However, the limits of what is claimed here should be made explicit. No one will wish to argue that the affect grid or a measure of prefrontal electrocortical asymmetry conveys all that we would wish to know about an individual's affective and hedonic experience, just as no one would argue that a measure of the pooled activity levels in the red–green and blue–yellow channels convey the experience of seeing a view. The claim made here is not that the valence of experience is all we need to know – only that we need to know the valence of experience.

5. THE AMBIGUITY OF TREADMILL EFFECTS

The fundamental surprise of well-being research is the robust finding that life circumstances make only a small contribution to the variance of happiness – far smaller than the contribution of inherited temperament or personality (Diener et al. 1999, Lykken and Tellegen 1996, Myers and Diener 1995). Although people have intense emotional reactions to major changes in their lives, these reactions appear to subside more or less completely and often quite quickly (Headey and Wearing 1992, Frederick and Loewenstein 1999). As a consequence, cross-sectional correlations between life circumstances and subjective happiness are low. Between 1958 and 1987, furthermore, real income in Japan increased five-fold, but self-reported happiness did not increase at all (Easterlin 1995). The most famous observations in this vein were made by Brickman, Coates, and Janoff-Bulman (1978), who reported that after a period of adjustment lottery winners were not much happier than a control group and paraplegics not much un-happier. In a now classic essay, Brickman and Campbell (1971) used the term *hedonic treadmill* both to describe and to interpret such observations. I will use the label *treadmill effect* to refer to the general observation while reserving hedonic treadmill to refer to a particular explanation of the effect.

Treadmill Effects

Brickman and Campbell (1971) based their conception of the hedonic tread-mill on a notion of adaptation level, which Helson (1964) had introduced earlier to explain phenomena of adaptation in perception and judgment. Anyone who has bathed in a cool pool, or in a warm sea, will recognize the basic phenomenon. As one adapts, the experience of the temperature of the water gradually drifts to-ward "neither hot nor cold," and the experience of other temperatures changes accordingly. A temperature that would be called warm in one context may feel cool in another. Brickman and Campbell proposed that a similar process of adaptation applies to the hedonic value of life circumstances.

The prevalence of treadmill effects is of psychological interest for two sepa-rate reasons: first, because of the ironic light it sheds on the pursuit of happiness, and second, because its surprise value is itself surprising, for if the treadmill effect is a common fact of life, why do people not seem to know about it? As the next chapter shows, the extent and the speed of treadmill effects in self-reported happiness are not generally anticipated. A study conducted among students in California and in the Midwest was designed to examine both the reality of regional effects in life satisfaction and beliefs about these effects (Schkade and Kahneman 1998). The results showed no trace of a difference between Californians and Midwesterners in overall life satisfaction. However, they re-vealed a widespread expectation, shared by residents of both regions, that the self-reports of Californians would indicate more happiness than the self-reports of Midwesterners.

Not everyone finds treadmill effects persuasive. Skeptics argue that the ab-sence of large effects of circumstances on self-reported happiness are due, at least in part, to differences in the use of scales of happiness and life satisfaction. If people whose circumstances differ use the scales differently, there may be less hedonic adaptation to circumstances than surveys of subjective well-being suggest. Frederick and Loewenstein (1999) present an extensive list of reasons that may cause the "true happiness" of paraplegics to be exaggerated by such studies. The main claim of this section is that these concerns are not mere quibbles and that demonstrations of treadmill effects are subject to a critical ambiguity, which can only be resolved by measuring objective happiness.

What do people mean when they assert that Californians are, in fact, happier than other people, although Californians do not report themselves as happier? The possibility that Californians have more meaningful lives than others is rarely advanced. Rather, the proposition that Californians are happier appears to mean that Californians are objectively happier: their lives are richer in pleasures and less burdened by hassles, and they are consequently in a better mood, on average, than most other people. In this view, a treadmill effect is observed because Californians use the happiness scale differently than other people. The same argument could of course be extended to the Japanese, who reported equal happiness in 1987 as in 1958 despite a large increase in standard of living. It could also apply to paraplegics. If this view is accepted, the evidence for a happiness treadmill unravels. Perhaps life circumstances do, after all, have a greater effect on well-being than surveys of subjective happiness indicate. A specific hypothesis about a mechanism that could produce spurious evidence for a hedonic treadmill is introduced next.

The Satisfaction Treadmill

Brickman and Campbell explained treadmill effects by invoking the notion of an adaptation level (Helson 1964). I propose an alternative hypothesis, called a *satisfaction treadmill*, which draws on another venerable psychological concept: the aspiration level (Irwin 1944). The aspiration level is a value on a scale of achievement or attainment that lies somewhere between realistic expectation and reasonable hope. The essential observation is that people are always satisfied when they attain their aspiration level, and they are usually quite satisfied with slightly less. The best-established finding about aspiration levels is that they are closely correlated with past attainments. Current income, for example, is the single most important determinant of the income that is considered satisfactory for one's household (Van Praag and Frijters 1999).

To illustrate the difference between a hedonic treadmill and a satisfaction treadmill, consider a former graduate student, who will be called Helen. Assume that Helen regularly eats in restaurants and that she has a well-defined ranking of experienced utility for a set of entrées, which is perfectly correlated with their price. In her graduate-student days Helen was constrained by her budget to consume mostly mediocre dishes. Now she has taken a lucrative job that allows her to consume food of higher quality. In tracking her overall satisfaction with food over the transition period, we observe that her satisfaction rises initially and then settles back to its original level. This is the standard pattern of a treadmill effect. Now consider two mechanisms that could produce this effect.

1. The hedonic treadmill hypothesis invokes the hypothesis of an *adaptation level* for palatability, which is determined by a weighted average of

the palatability experienced on recent occasions. Helen's pleasure from food rises initially because the food she consumes exceeds the adaptation level that was established in her graduate student days. As time passes, however, her adaptation level will catch up to her consumption, and her pleasure from food will return to its original level. After she has adapted to the new level of palatabilities, she will consume better entrées than she did as a graduate student but will enjoy each of them less than she had in the past. On the hypothesis of a hedonic treadmill, the temporal course of Helen's reports of subjective satisfaction correctly reflects the changes in her enjoyment of food.

2. The hypothesis of a satisfaction treadmill invokes the notion of a changing *aspiration level*, which is determined in large part by the level of pleasure recently derived from food. For the sake of an extreme example, assume now that there is no hedonic adaptation at all and that the experienced utility that Helen derives from any entrée does not change. As the quality of her entrées improves, the overall pleasure that she derives from them improves correspondingly. Suppose, however, that Helen has an aspiration level for *food pleasure*: as the pleasure that she obtains from food increases, her aspiration level gradually follows, eventually adjusting to her higher level of enjoyment. After this adjustment of aspirations, Helen reports no more *satisfaction* with food than she did when she was poorer, although she actually draws more pleasure from food now than she did earlier.

The concept of a satisfaction treadmill extends readily from food pleasure to happiness. Only one additional assumption is needed: that people require a certain balance of pleasures and pains to report themselves happy or satisfied with their lives. On this hypothesis, Californians could indeed enjoy life more than others. However, if they also require more enjoyment than others to declare themselves happy, they will not report higher subjective happiness. Californians might be happier than other people objectively but not subjectively.

The statistical test for the hypothesis of a satisfaction treadmill is straightforward: if such a treadmill exists, the regression lines that describe the relation between subjective and objective happiness will not be the same for groups in different circumstances. At any level of objective happiness, people with a higher aspiration level will report themselves less happy and less satisfied than others whose aspirations are lower. If the results for both groups fall on the same regression line, there is no satisfaction treadmill.

A satisfaction treadmill and a hedonic treadmill may co-occur, both contributing to observed treadmill effects. The critical conclusion of the analysis is that the relative contributions of the two mechanisms cannot be determined without direct measurements of experienced utility. The hypothesis of a satisfaction treadmill is both plausible and effectively untested, and the interpretation of treadmill effects observed with measures of satisfaction and subjective happiness is correspondingly indeterminate. A substantial amount of well-being research might have to be redone to resolve this ambiguity.

6. DISCUSSION

The premise of this essay was a distinction between two meanings of the term "utility," which were labeled experienced utility and decision utility. Decision utility is about wanting; experienced utility is about enjoyment. The basic dichotomy between senses of utility has been discussed elsewhere (Kahneman 1994 [Ch. 42], Kahneman, 1999). The focus of the present discussion is the further distinction between two approaches to experienced utility, which were called moment-based and memory-based.

Wanting or not wanting is not the only orientation to future outcomes. People sometimes also attempt to forecast the affective or hedonic experience – the experienced utility – that is associated with various life circumstances. These are judgments of *predicted utility* (Kahneman, Wakker, and Sarin 1997) or affective forecasting (Gilbert et al. 1998). With the inclusion of predicted utility, the number of distinct concepts of the utility of extended outcomes – bounded episodes or states of indefinite duration – rises to four. The concepts are distinguished by the operations on which they are based:

1. *Decision utility* is inferred from observed preferences.
2. *Predicted utility* is a belief about future experienced utility.
3. *Total utility* is a *moment-based* measure of experienced utility. It is derived from measurements of moment utility statistically aggregated by a formal objective rule.
4. *Remembered utility* is a *memory-based* measure of experienced utility that is based on retrospective assessments of episodes or periods of life.

Decision research and economics focus almost exclusively on decision utility whereas research on Subjective Well-Being (SWB) focuses almost exclusively on memory-based self-reports. The various concepts of utility suggest a rich and complex agenda of research; they also suggest different interpretations of utility maximization.

To extend an example already discussed, consider families that move (or might move) from California to Ohio. The *decision utility* of families that consider relocation could be studied by eliciting their global preferences as well their preferences for different attributes of the two locations. Whether or not people maximize utility is interpreted in this context as a question about the coherence of preferences: Would the choice that the family makes survive reframing or a new context? The *predicted utility* that the decision makers associate with the alternative locations could be studied by eliciting their general beliefs about the experience of living in the two places and their particular beliefs about what they might enjoy or dislike. There is considerable evidence that this task of affective forecasting is not one in which people excel (see Gilbert et al. 1998,

Kahneman 1999 [Ch. 38], Kahneman and Schkade 1999, Loewenstein and Adler 1995 [Ch. 40], Loewenstein and Schkade 1999, Schkade and Kahneman 1998). Another question of some importance is whether people even consider the uncertainty of their future tastes as part of the activity of decision making (March 1978, Simonson 1990 [Ch. 41]).

As we have seen in preceding sections, different conclusions about the outcomes of families that did move to California could be reached, depending on whether the outcomes are assessed by moment-based or memory-based techniques – by measures of total utility or objective happiness on the one hand or of remembered utility or subjective happiness on the other. Self-selection and dissonance reduction would predict high subjective happiness among people who moved voluntarily. Treadmill effects, on the other hand, predict that people who moved will eventually return to their characteristic level of subjective happiness. The argument of the preceding section was that these memory-based measures do not tell us what we would really want to know: whether people who move to California are *really* happier there than they were earlier. In the approach adopted here, this question must be answered by obtaining moment-based measures through either self-reports or physiological indices of experienced utility.

The distinctions that have been drawn between alternative concepts of utility are directly relevant to normative issues in the domain of policy, as the following list of questions illustrates:

- Does the presence of trees in a city street affect the mood of pedestrians?
- What is the contribution of an attractive subway system to the well-being of city residents?
- What are the well-being consequences of inflation, unemployment, or unreliable health insurance?

Here again, it is possible to ask what the public wants, perhaps by asking people how much they are willing to pay for the provision of some goods. It is also possible to elicit people's opinions about the welfare effects of particular public goods to obtain a measure of predicted utility. Finally, it is sometimes possible to measure the experienced utility associated with public goods. Again, this can be done either by moment-based or by memory-based methods.

Conventional economic analyses of policy recognize only one measure of the value of public goods: the aggregate willingness of the public to pay for them. There are serious doubts about the coherence of this concept and the feasibility of measuring willingness to pay (see, e.g., Kahneman, Ritov, and Schkade 1999 [Ch. 36]). A more fundamental question is whether willingness to pay should remain the only measure of value. The present analysis suggests that moment-based measures of the actual experience of consequences should be included in assessments of outcomes and as one of the criteria for the quality of decisions, both public and private.

Treadmill effects raise difficult normative questions. If there is a hedonic treadmill, then changes in circumstances will often have less long-term effects on human welfare than might be inferred from their *ex ante* desirability or from the initial hedonic response that they evoke. Should policy makers resist calls for the provision of desirable goods that convey no long-term utility benefits? A further complexity is that if there is a satisfaction treadmill, then clients of policies will never be satisfied for very long even when an improvement in their circumstances makes them objectively happier. Furthermore, people may fail to identify some circumstances that would actually make them happier. Do policy makers have a duty to provide goods that will make people truly better off, even if these goods are neither desired *ex ante* nor appreciated *ex post*? The easy answer is no, but it is perhaps too easy. Dilemmas of paternalism are raised again in Chapter 42.

The moment-based approach to experienced utility and happiness that has been presented here runs into two strong objections. The first is that there is more to human well-being than good mood. The second is that the moment-based view is based on abstract arguments and logical construction and fails to reflect the role of memory in the subjective reality of mental life. Both objections have much merit, but neither should block the judicious use of moment-based measures.

Objective happiness is not proposed as a comprehensive concept of human well-being but only as a significant constituent of it. Maximizing the time spent on the right side of the affect grid is not the most significant value in life, and adopting this criterion as a guide to life may be morally wrong and perhaps self-defeating as well. However, the proposition that the right side of the grid is a more desirable place to be is not particularly controversial. Indeed, there may be more differences among cultures and systems of thought about the optimal position on the arousal dimension – some prefer the bliss of serenity, others favor the exultation of faith or the joys of participation. Objective happiness is a common element of many conceptions of well-being. Furthermore, when it comes to comparisons of groups, such as Californians and others, or to assessments of the value of public goods such as health insurance or tree-lined streets, experienced utility and objective happiness may be the correct measure of welfare.

In a memory-centered view of life, the accumulation of memories is an end in itself. A clear statement of this position is offered by Tversky and Griffin (1991 [Ch. 39]), who speak of the stock of memories as an endowment that is enriched by storing new memories of good experiences. The moment-centered approach that has been proposed here does not deny the importance of memory in life, but it suggests a metaphor of flows rather than stocks. Without a doubt, the traveler who goes on a Kenya safari may continue to derive utility from that episode long after it ends, whether directly – by "consuming" the memories in pleasant or unpleasant reminiscing – or, perhaps more importantly, by consuming the experience of the self as it has been altered by the event (Elster and Loewenstein 1992). However, the moment-based approach raises a question that should not be dismissed too lightly: How much time will be spent in such consumption of memories relative to the duration of the original experience? The weight of memory relative to actual experience is likely to be reduced when time is taken seriously.

The memory-based and the moment-based views draw on different intuitions about what counts as real. There is an obvious sense in which present experience is real and memories are not. But memories have an attribute of permanence that lends them a weightiness that the fleeting present lacks: they endure and populate the mind. In the words of the novelist Penelope Lively (1993, p. 15), "A narrative is a sequence of present moments but the present does not exist." Because memories and stories of the past are all we ultimately get to keep, memories and stories often appear to be all that matters. These common intuitions are part of the appeal of Fredrickson's (1999) eloquent critique of the idea – central to the notion of total utility and objective happiness – that all moments of time are weighted equally. The argument for meaning is memory-based: memory certainly does not treat all moments equally, and meaningful moments must be memorable. Indeed, the statement "I will always remember this" is commonly proffered, not always correctly, at meaningful moments. Futhermore, the immense importance that most of us attach to deathbed reconciliations suggests that who does the remembering may not greatly matter in conferring meaning just as long as someone does.

The goal of this discussion has not been to reject the memory-based view, which is indeed irresistibly appealing, but to point out that intuition is strongly biased against a moment-based view. The approach proposed here is bound to be counterintuitive even if it has merit, and that was one of the reasons for proposing it. Although wholly devoid of permanence, the experiencing subject deserves a voice.

38. Evaluation by Moments
Past and Future

Daniel Kahneman

We often have the occasion to evaluate the pleasantness or awfulness of incidents in people's lives; most of us have opinions about what it is like to be old, or physically handicapped, or a resident of California. All of us spontaneously score events and situations and store evaluations of how good or bad they were, in the form of likes and dislikes. These judgments and feelings have also been produced in the laboratory, with the usual combination of artificiality and improved precision.

The goal of this chapter is to review the evidence for a unifying principle, which accounts for four conclusions of research on evaluations of outcomes. The first of these conclusions has been supported in many studies of choice.

1. *The carriers of value* in both risky and riskless choices are gains and losses. The same final state of wealth or endowment is valued differently, depending on its relation to the original state from which it has been reached (Kahneman and Tversky 1979). In studies of the endowment effect, for example, the outcomes of owning or not owning a particular decorated mug are represented, depending on the current reference point, as *getting* a mug or *giving up* a mug (Kahneman, Knetsch, and Thaler 1991; Thaler 1980; Tverksy and Kahneman 1991).

The following more recent conclusions will be documented in this chapter:

2. *Global judgments of fictitious episodes or lives* are highly sensitive to trends of improvement or deterioration and radically insensitive to duration.
3. *Retrospective evaluations of affective episodes* are strongly influenced by the affect experienced at singular moments, notably the moment at which affect was most extreme and the final moment. They show little or no sensitivity to duration.

I thank Shane Frederick, Dan Ariely, Laura Gibson, David Schkade, and Anne Treisman for helpful comments. Dan Ariely and Nathan Novemsky kindly provided data used in Figure 38.1. I thank Peter Wakker for allowing me to use ideas and sentences that we had fashioned together, Beruria Cohn for allowing me to use her undergraduate thesis data, and Peter McGraw for extremely valuable assistance and useful suggestions.

4. *Forecasts of the long-term effects of circumstances on subjective happiness* tend to neglect the likelihood of adaptation and therefore exaggerate the long-term benefits and costs of life changes.

All four findings involve the evaluation of an outcome that extends over some time: states that endure for an indefinite term [(1) and (4)] and bounded episodes, or lives [(2) and (3)]. A single psychological process, called *evaluation by moments*, will be invoked here to explain all four findings. Evaluation by moments works as follows: *when an evaluative summary of a temporally extended outcome is required, a representative moment that stands for the entire outcome is selected or constructed; the temporally extended outcome is then assigned the value of its representative moment.* The same general heuristic is applied, in slightly different forms, to the overall evaluation of past outcomes and to forecasts and decisions about future outcomes. The representative moment of a past episode is likely to be made up of a collage of impressions and affective reactions associated with salient parts of the experience – most notably its most extreme moment, or peak, and its end. The representative moment that stands for a future state is likely to be the moment of transition to that state. The temporal dimension of outcomes is neglected in both cases. Because moments are thin time slices and have no duration, the heuristic of evaluating prolonged outcomes by moments yields evaluations that are insensitive to the duration of the event and to changes of taste that occur over time.

Section 1 reviews studies of the evaluation of fictitious utility profiles and of the remembered utility of brief pleasant or unpleasant episodes. Section 2 reviews some studies of forecasts about the effect of life circumstances on well-being. Section 3 subsumes the principle of evaluation by moments under a broader judgmental heuristic called judgment by prototype.

1. EVALUATING PAST UTILITY: THE PEAK–END RULE

The research described in this chapter is part of a broader effort to explore *experienced utility,* which is a concept that restores Bentham's (1789) original definition of utility in terms of hedonic experience. The theory of experienced utility has been developed more fully elsewhere (see Chapters 37 and 42). The new terms that will be used in this section are defined below.

Moment utility: the sign and intensity of affective–hedonic experience at a given moment in time. Moment utility may be inferred from self-reports or physiological measures.
Utility profile: a verbal or graphic representation of the time course of moment utility during an episode or over a concatenation of separate episodes.[1]

---

[1] An episode is a bounded and compact interval of time defined by its content; for example, a headache or a vacation (Kahneman, Wakker, and Sarin 1997).

Evaluation of a utility profile: an observer's judgment about the overall utility of an experience described by a utility profile.

Remembered utility: a subject's own global evaluation of a past episode.

The psychological rules that govern global assessments of episodes have been studied in a diverse set of evaluations: judgments about fictitious profiles of uncomfortable experiences (Varey and Kahneman 1992) and of entire lives (Diener, Wirtz, and Oishi 1999); retrospective evaluations of the experience of pleasant or aversive plotless film clips (Fredrickson and Kahneman 1993), medical procedures (Redelmeier and Kahneman 1996), painful pressure from a vise (Ariely 1998), and annoying noises (Ariely and Zauberman 1999, Schreiber and Kahneman 2000, Expt. 2); measures of the impact of advertisements (Baumgartner, Sujan, and Padgett 1997); and choices about repeating unpleasant experiences (Kahneman et al. 1993; Schreiber and Kahneman 2000, Expt. 3).

Surprisingly, this body of research shows that the judgment of fictitious utility profiles and the remembered utility of real episodes follow similar rules and violate logic in similar ways. Another surprise is that both types of judgment are well described, at least in the case of simple affective episodes (e.g., a colonoscopy or a brief film clip of beautiful scenery), by a simple Peak–End rule: the average of the utility experienced at two singular moments of the episode quite accurately predicts subsequent global assessments.

1.1. Experimental Evidence

I first review three experiments in which the temporal profile and the duration of aversive episodes were systematically manipulated. The aim of these experiments was to identify the psychological rules that govern the global evaluation of past (or fictitious) episodes:

1. Participants in an experiment reported by Varey and Kahneman (1992, Expt. 2) used a 1–100 scale to evaluate the "total discomfort" experienced by subjects in 48 different conditions of a fictitious experiment. The information for the judgment consisted of a list of ratings of pain on a 0–10 scale allegedly reported by subjects every 5 minutes during an episode of discomfort. The lists varied in length (from 15 to 35 minutes), in overall level, in trend (ascending or descending), and in the steepness of the trends. Each participant judged 48 profiles, one at a time, after previewing the entire booklet.

2. Participants in an experiment described by Schreiber and Kahneman (2000, Expt. 2) were exposed to a series of annoying noises representing different levels of loudness and different temporal patterns. A preliminary study using continuous recordings of annoyance showed that momentary annoyance tracked sound intensity very closely. Profiles of sound intensity were therefore used as a proxy for a continuous measure of experienced

utility in subsequent experiments. The "total or overall amount of pleasantness or unpleasantness" of each noise was judged immediately after its termination. The intensity of the noise was varied within and across trials in the range of 66 to 80 db. The episodes also varied in duration (from 8 to 24 seconds) and in the shape of the temporal profile.

3. Ariely (1998, Expt. 2) reported a study in which volunteers were exposed to calibrated pressure from a vise. Several temporal profiles were used (e.g., "Up," in which pressure intensity steadily increased; "Down then Up," etc.). The duration of the trial was another experimental factor with three levels: 10, 20, and 40 seconds. Half of the participants provided a continuous record of their pain, which again closely tracked the physical measure of pressure. Subjects experienced considerable pain in this experiment: the average rating of the pain associated with the maximal pressure was about 80 on a scale of 100.

The major empirical findings of these experiments are listed below. As will be seen later, the experimental findings have been confirmed in studies that used correlational designs and choice measures.

Average Moment Utility. Other things being equal, the average level of a utility profile accurately predicts retrospective judgments. This is no surprise.

Overall Trend. A sequence of increasingly unpleasant experiences is judged much worse than the same experiences in the reverse order. In the Varey–Kahneman study of fictitious profiles, the average rating of a steeply increasing profile of discomfort was 65 on a 100-point scale; the rating of the corresponding profile of diminishing discomfort was 46. The results of Ariely's study of real (and quite severe) pain were strikingly similar: the average rating of a 40-second pattern of steadily increasing painful pressure was 75; the corresponding sequence of diminishing pressure was rated 56.

Duration Neglect. The authors of the three experimental studies concluded that the effect of duration was reliable, but small. In the study of pressure pain, for example, a change from 10 to 40 seconds in the duration of the pain increased retrospective ratings by 4.2 scale points on average – much less than the 19-point difference between the "Up" and "Down" patterns (Ariely, personal communication, July 1999). Here again, real and hypothetical results matched closely. Varey and Kahneman reported that increasing the duration of fictitious profiles from 15 to 35 seconds raised global ratings by 3.8 scale points – much less than the difference of 20 points between the "Up" and "Down" profiles.

Violations of Dominance: Better End. Adding discomfort to an episode cannot truly make it better overall. Nevertheless, adding a period of diminished discomfort to an aversive experience does improve its global evaluation. Violations of temporal dominance were first observed in judgments of fictitious utility profiles (Varey and Kahneman 1992). For example, consider the series 2–5–8 and 2–5–8–4 in which the numbers refer to reports of pain provided on a 10-point scale every 5 minutes. Although the addition of 5 extra minutes of pain can only increase total discomfort, the mean ratings were 64 for

2–5–8 and 53 for 2–5–8–4. The result was confirmed in an experiment using unpleasant noises (Schreiber and Kahneman 2000, Expt. 2). The retrospective evaluation of a loud noise was improved by adding a period of diminishing annoyance to it: the experience of 16 seconds at 78 db, for example, was rated worse overall than the same experience followed by 8 extra seconds at 66 db. Because 66 db was clearly worse than silence, the longer noise was dominated by the short one, but its remembered utility was better.

Violations of Dominance: Better Beginning. Ariely (1998) included in his experiment a "High" condition in which pressure was consistently high (and pain very severe) and an "Up" condition in which pressure was gradually increased to the same high value. The average ratings for the two conditions were not significantly different. If actual discomfort tracks physical intensity, as his results suggest, this observation also violates dominance.

Additivity of Duration Effects. The logic of evaluation implies an interaction between duration and intensity: the difference of utility between 30 seconds of pain and 40 seconds of pain should be greater if the pain is intense than if it is mild. However, analyses of duration effects in all three experiments yielded a remarkable and consistent result: the (slight) effects of duration that were observed combined in strictly additive fashion with the effects of other factors.

1.2. The Peak–End Rule

Fredrickson and Kahneman (1993) proposed a "snapshot model" of remembered utility, based primarily on the observation of duration neglect, that accounts for the first five experimental observations listed above and is readily extended to account for the last.

The snapshot model describes how evaluation by moments is applied to the evaluation of past episodes. It asserts that an episode is evaluated by constructing a representative moment, the snapshot, which may combine or pool the attributes of separate moments of the actual experience. Fredrickson and Kahneman (1993) proposed that, as a good first approximation, the affective value of the representative moment is a simple average of the most extreme affect experienced during the episode (Peak) and the affect experienced near its end (End). The affective value of that representative moment, in turn, determines the global evaluation of the entire episode. This simple predictive formula, labeled the *Peak–End rule*, has proved a good match to the data of several studies. In particular, it accounted for 94, 86, and 98% of the systematic variance in the three experiments discussed above (respectively, Varey and Kahneman 1992; Schreiber and Kahneman 2000; Ariely 1998).[2]

---

[2] The mean retrospective evaluations are predicted from the Peak and End values of physical sound intensity in the Schreiber–Kahneman study. In Ariely's experiment the predictors are Peak and End of subjective judgments; R^2 drops from .98 to .83 when a physical measure is used. The pattern of results suggests that the procedure of using physical measures as a proxy for experienced utility is unsound. However, an experimental condition in which moment utility is not elicited should also be included because the elicitation of that measure can be intrusive (Ariely 1998; Ariely and Zauberman 1999).

The Peak–End rule explains the difference between rising and falling trends: in a steadily rising trend the End is as high as the Peak, but in a falling trend the End is lower than the Peak. The Peak–End average is therefore higher in the former case than in the latter. The Peak–End rule also explains the paradoxical finding that adding a period of diminishing discomfort to an aversive episode makes it less aversive in memory. Finally, the Peak–End rule entails another paradoxical prediction, which was confirmed in the data of Varey and Kahneman (1992) and Ariely (1998): similar retrospective evaluations are assigned to an episode in which discomfort increases gradually to a high level and to an episode in which discomfort is high throughout.[3]

Two elaborations are required to improve the accuracy of the snapshot analogy. First, because the psychological present has a finite duration, the camera must be imagined as set to a moderately long exposure. No self-report of moment utility truly describes a single instant: a respondent who is asked about his or her affective state *now* will inevitably respond by evaluating a period of time that is at least a few seconds long or sometimes longer. Second, the snapshot should be imagined as including a representation of the affective trend of the experience. As Hsee, Ariely, and their colleagues have emphasized, there is an affective response to the trend of affect, which matters to global evaluations (Ariely 1998; Ariely and Carmon 1999; Hsee and Abelson 1991; Hsee, Abelson, and Salovey 1991). In the present conception, hope and fear are incorporated into moment utility. A measure of moment utility that is not sensitive to these emotions should be considered seriously flawed.

Without further elaboration, the model of evaluation by moments implies complete neglect of duration. As will be seen later this prediction has been confirmed in several studies (Diener, Wirtz, and Oishi 1999; Fredrickson and Kahneman 1993; Redelmeier and Kahneman 1996). However, everyone would endorse the principle that it is better for episodes of discomfort to be short rather than long. Duration therefore has some weight in global evaluations when the context reminds participants of this principle and makes the duration attribute easy to evaluate (Ariely and Loewenstein, (2000, in press) Varey and Kahneman 1992, Expt. 1). In particular, duration had small but reliable effects in multitrial experiments that included otherwise identical stimuli (Ariely 1998, Schreiber and Kahneman 2000, Varey and Kahneman 1992). A consistent finding of these experiments was that duration always combined additively with other determinants of global evaluation, and participants appeared to use it as a minor extra feature of each trial as if they were telling themselves, "this episode is painful and it is also rather long," or, "this episode is painful but it is short." Figure 38.1 illustrates the additive duration effect observed in two

---

[3] Ariely (1998) inferred from a regression analysis that the final slope is the most important predictor of retrospective evaluation independent of the effect predicted by the Peak–End rule. This inference is premature, however, because the magnitudes of the different factors cannot be directly compared (Ariely, personal communication, August 1999).

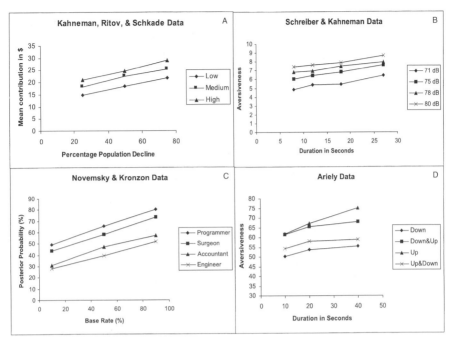

Figure 38.1. (A) Willingness to pay to restore damage to species that differ in popularity as a function of the damage they have suffered (from Kahneman, Ritov, and Schkade 2000); (B) Global evaluations of aversive sounds of different loudness as a function of duration for subjects selected for their high sensitivity to duration (from Schreiber and Kahneman 2000); (C) Ratings of probability for predictions that differ in representativeness as a function of base-rate frequency (from Novemsky and Kronzon 1999); (D) Global evaluations of episode of painful pressure that differ in temporal profile as a function of duration (from Ariely 1998).

of the experimental studies summarized above. For comparison, it also shows similar results in two other experiments: a study of the effects of variations of base-rates (Novemsky and Kronzon 1999) and a study of willingness to pay to restore the population of species that differ in popularity and in the amount of damage they have suffered in a particular habitat (Kahneman, Ritov, and Schkade 2000 [Ch. 36]). We return to this remarkably consistent pattern in Section 3.

1.3. Additional Evidence

Realistic Stimuli. The Peak–End rule was initially discovered in an experiment in which participants were exposed to short plotless film clips that varied in duration and in affective impact (e.g., an amputation, views of a coral reef, etc.). There were two versions of each film, one about three times longer than the other. Each participant saw the long version of eight film clips and the short version of eight others. The mean (computed over Ss) of the correlations (within-S) between retrospective evaluations and the Peak–End average were .78 and .69, respectively, for pleasant and unpleasant films. With the Peak–End average statistically controlled, the mean within-S correlation between the remembered utility of film clips and their duration was .06 for pleasant films and −.02 for aversive films – a striking confirmation of duration neglect. Similar results were obtained with a choice measure.

The Peak–End average also predicted the retrospective evaluation of medical procedures. In Redelmeier and Kahneman (1996) patients undergoing colonoscopy were prompted every 60 seconds to report the intensity of their current pain on a 0–10 scale. Later, the patients provided several measures of remembered utility: they evaluated the total pain they had experienced during the procedure on a numerical scale, and they also compared the procedure with other unpleasant experiences. The correlation (computed over individuals) between the Peak–End measure and the patient's global evaluation of the procedure was .67. Duration neglect was also observed. The durations of the colonoscopies ranged from 4 to 69 minutes in this study, allowing ample scope for duration to affect remembered utility. Yet the correlation between duration and the patient's subsequent global evaluation was only .03. Physicians' judgments of their patients' experience also showed duration neglect. The physicians were asked, among other questions, whether more anesthetic should have been administered at the beginning of the procedure. The correlation between answers to this question and the duration of the procedure was .05 – a discouraging finding, perhaps, for potential patients (Redelmeier and Kahneman 1996).

The colonoscopy study was followed up with a clinical experiment (Katz, Redelmeier, and Kahneman 1997). Half of a group of patients ($N = 682$) undergoing a colonoscopy were randomly assigned to a condition in which the procedure was extended by about 1 minute after the examination was complete. (The patients had given advance consent to participation in an experiment but were not informed of the possibility that the colonoscopy would be prolonged.) The colonoscope was left stationary during the added period, causing mild discomfort, but less pain than many patients had experienced just earlier. As the Peak–End rule predicts, the extension of the procedure, though distinctly unpleasant, yielded a significant improvement in the remembered utility of the procedure. A clinical application of such an intervention could be justified if it increases patients' willingness to undergo further colonoscopies when their condition requires it.

Evaluations of Lives. Diener, Wirtz, and Oishi (1999) studied duration neglect and violations of dominance in evaluations of lives. The participants in the experiment were told about a woman named Jen who had, in four basic versions of the story, either an extremely happy or an extremely unhappy life that ended in a car accident when Jen was either 30 years old or 60 years old. Jen left no descendants. Each participant saw one of the basic versions and also saw a variation in which Jen lived for 5 more years before dying in an accident. The 5 added years were described as less extreme than the preceding years, but their valence was the same: Jen became either less happy or less unhappy than she had been earlier.

Complete duration neglect was observed in answers to both the following questions: Taking Jen's life as a whole, how desirable do you think it was? and How much total happiness or unhappiness would you say that Jen experienced in her life? Merely adding 30 years to Jen's life without changing its quality did not change ratings of its desirability or of the total happiness or unhappiness that she had experienced. As in the Varey–Kahneman study of profiles of discomfort, the overall quality of Jen's life was apparently judged by a weighted average of her happiness over time. Furthermore, adding 5 moderately happy years to a very good life made it distinctly worse overall. Lest it be thought that these judgments manifest the folly of youth, a replication in a group of students' parents yielded similar results.

Violations of Temporal Dominance in Choice. The most surprising implication of the Peak–End rule is a violation of temporal dominance: adding an extra period of diminishing discomfort to an unpleasant episode improves its remembered utility by reducing the aversiveness of the Peak–End average. This hypothesis implies preferences for dominated options in choices that are guided by remembered utility. Such preferences have been observed in two experiments.

Participants in a study reported by Kahneman et al. (1993; see Kahneman 1994 [Ch. 42]) were led to expect three trials of a painful experience and actually experienced two trials labeled Short and Long. In the Short trial, the subject kept one hand immersed in water at 14 °C for 60 seconds. In the Long trial, the immersion lasted a total of 90 seconds. Water temperature was kept at 14 °C for the first 60 seconds, at which point (unbeknownst to the subject) the experimenter caused the temperature of the water to rise gradually from 14 to 15 °C over the next 30 seconds. Some time after the second trial, the subject was called in again, informed that one of the two previous procedures would be repeated exactly, and given a choice of whether the first or the second trial should be repeated. The robust result of several replications of this study was that 65% of participants chose to repeat the Long rather than the Short trial. The proportion rose to 80% when participants who did not indicate a decline of pain during the final 30 seconds of the Long trial were excluded.

Preferences for dominated experiences were also observed in an experiment using loud aversive sounds (Schreiber and Kahneman 2000, Expt. 4). Subjects heard pairs of sounds in immediate succession, were told that one of the sounds would be repeated later, and were offered a choice. In several of the pairs, one of the sounds replicated the other but with an extra period at a lower intensity (e.g., 10 seconds at 78 db might be followed by 8 seconds at 66 db). Here as well, 66% of choices favored the dominated experience. The incoherence of these preferences should be noted: if subjects had been given a button to terminate the sound as soon as they wished, they would certainly have expressed their preference for silence over more of the noise. Subjects' choice to expose themselves to extra discomfort highlights the tension between two perspectives on experience. The experiencing subject would prefer to stop the unpleasant noise as quickly as possible, but the remembering subject prefers the Long trial to the Short one. Which of these conflicting perspectives should be taken more seriously? This difficult normative question is addressed in more detail in Chapters 37 and 42.

1.4. Caveats

The Peak–End rule has only been tested and confirmed in a narrow range of situations. The participants in the studies cited here were always passive during their experience; most of the studies involved aversive experiences, but none involved a mix of positive and negative affect. Different rules could apply to other types of episodes. For example, Carmon and Kahneman (1996) suggested that an End rule applies to the evaluation of episodes associated with a goal. On this hypothesis, the affect experienced when the goal is finally achieved or given up will dominate subsequent evaluations of the entire episode. Ariely and Carmon (1999) proposed that prediction of future states is an integral part of overall evaluations. Patients' evaluations in the evening of how much they had suffered during the day appeared to be influenced by the pain they anticipated suffering in the coming night. Ariely and Zauberman (forthcoming) found that the normal preference for improving trends over deteriorating ones is substantially reduced if the same experience is composed of discrete parts. They concluded that the global evaluation of an episode that is broken up into segments is determined by the average evaluation of the separate segments. This important observation calls attention to the crucial role of the parsing of experiences in determining remembered utility: the "final score" of an episode is determined when it is known to have ended, and perhaps only then (Fredrickson 1991, 1999).

Another caveat applies specifically to studies of choice. Participants in the choice experiments reported in this section apparently let their remembered utility guide their decision. When required to choose between two unpleasant experiences, they selected the one they disliked less. There are, of course, many other strategies of choice, and people do not always make decisions simply by consulting the relative intensities of likes and dislikes. As was noted earlier, decision makers are certainly capable of performing calculations that assign a larger role to duration. Duration is not neglected, of course, in a context that resembles working for pay (Ariely and Loewenstein, 2000, in press). Informal observations suggest that more of the participants in the cold-water experiment would have elected to repeat the Short trial if they had been given a detailed description of the two trials before making their choice. When a decision is explicitly framed as a choice between a long or a short exposure to pain, people choose correctly. When they go by what they remember liking, however, their choices are governed by their evaluations of representative moments and these evaluations neglect duration.

2. FORECASTING HAPPINESS: THE TRANSITION RULE

In this section, the general hypothesis of evaluation by moments is extended to a new task: the forecasting of the effects of circumstances on well-being. The specific hypothesis that will be examined is that the representative moment used to forecast long-term well-being in a new state is the transition to that state. This hypothesis generalizes the analysis offered in prospect theory, in which the value attached to possible states (e.g., of wealth or endowment) is determined by the value that is attached to the changes – gains or losses relative to the status quo – that lead to these states. Forecasts of happiness are also made by a *transition rule*: a prediction of a person's initial reaction to a new situation, which may be quite accurate in itself, is incorrectly used as a proxy to forecast the long-term effects of that situation.

The most famous article in the literature on well-being reported that lottery winners are not particularly happy and that paraplegics are not very miserable (Brickman, Coates, and Janoff-Bulman 1978). As suggested by an earlier treatment of the *hedonic treadmill* Brickman and Campbell (1971) the effects of extreme changes in life circumstances appeared to be transient and ultimately small. The enduring appeal of the empirical study of paraplegics and lottery winners raises a puzzle of its own: If a hedonic treadmill does, in fact, fundamentally govern human well-being, why are we surprised to hear that it does? The answer to this puzzle may lie in the hypothesis that lay forecasts of happiness are made according to the transition rule. Consequently, intuitive predictions about the state of *being* a paraplegic will be dominated by thoughts about the event of *becoming* a paraplegic. Because forecasts that follow the transition rule ignore the evolution of feelings after the initial change, they are generally much too extreme. The following two studies illustrate the transition rule in forecasts of well-being.

Table 38.1 is drawn from a Princeton undergraduate thesis (Cohn 1999). The respondents (362 adults recruited by a professional survey firm) were asked to evaluate the well-being of fictitious members of various categories of people (including paraplegics and lottery winners) by answering the following question: Overall, what percentage of the time would you say that Jim is in a good mood, in a bad mood, or in a neutral mood? Half of the respondents were asked to assume that the transitional event (becoming paraplegic, winning the lottery) had occurred one month before; the other respondents were told that the event had occurred one year before. Participants also indicated whether they personally knew a paraplegic or a lottery winner, and how well. The results shown in Table 38.1 are means of the difference between estimates of the percentage of time spent in a good and in a bad mood. Negative values indicate a predominance of bad mood.

Table 38.1. Mean Mood Difference Scores (% Good Mood – % Bad Mood)

Category Knowledge	Paraplegic		Lottery winner	
	No	Yes	No	Yes
After one month	−41	−50	58	64
After one year	−37	−19	50	25

The results are clear. Respondents who were not personally acquainted with a lottery winner or a paraplegic were largely insensitive to the time variable. They attributed almost the same level of misery to paraplegics and almost the same level of joy to lottery winners whether a year or a month had passed since the event. The results support the transition rule: In the absence of direct knowledge, people forecast happiness in a long-term state by forecasting (apparently with fair accuracy) the affective impact of the transition to that state. As a consequence, the long-term effects of these life circumstances on well-being are greatly exaggerated. Considerations of adaptation apparently play little or no role in the judgments (see also Loewenstein and Frederick 1997, Loewenstein and Schkade 1999, Schkade and Kahneman 1998).

An experimental study of the lay theory of adaptation was conducted by Kahneman and Schkade (working paper). Participants were asked to consider a scenario in which a family unexpectedly had to move to a new location. Twenty-four contrasting features of the current and the new location were briefly described. For instance, the commute in the new location would be short and easy compared with the current commute, which had been long and difficult. The respondents' task was to evaluate the effect of each new feature on the well-being of the family on a scale that ranged from -5 (Extremely Negative) to 0 (Neutral) to $+5$ (Extremely Positive). The independent variable was the temporal perspective that the respondents were asked to assume. Participants in one condition of the experiment received the following instructions, which were repeated saliently on each page of the questionnaire: "For each item below, please indicate how this feature of the new location would affect Mr. and Mrs. A's well-being *during the first few months after the move* while they are still becoming familiar with the new location."

Different groups of participants evaluated the impact of the new features

1. "in anticipation of the move";
2. "in the first few months after the move";
3. "in the third year after the move";
4. "overall, for the first 5 years after the move";
5. "overall, for the first 5 years after the move," with the following additional reminder: "When you think about these features, please take a minute to imagine how their influence might change over the years."

Table 38.2 presents mean ratings of changes for the better for three pairs of features ($n = 125$ per cell) as well as the overall means for all 24 pairs. Precisely the same pattern of results was found in ratings of changes for the worse. The only difference was that ratings of impact were consistently higher for improvements than for deteriorations by about 1.2 scale points on average.[4]

---

[4] The prevailing optimistic bias is an instance of the more general effect that Cacioppo and Berntson (1994) have called a positivity offset.

Table 38.2. Estimated Impact of a Change on Well-Being

	Before	First Months	Third Year	Five Years	Five Years*
Cost of living (high to low)	3.90	3.49	3.83	3.94	3.93
Obnoxious relative (near to far)	2.92	2.89	2.64	2.69	3.01
Long winter (long to short)	2.35	2.34	2.29	2.12	2.41
Means (24 items)	2.76	2.71	2.77	2.71	2.84

Once again, the manipulation of time had no significant effect even, though the size of the sample provided ample statistical power. The respondents apparently applied a theory of well-being in which the joy of moving away from an obnoxious relative never palls and the distress of having to live without good produce never subsides. The reminder provided in condition (5) did not change the results. There was no indication that respondents were sensitive to the distinction between the short-term impact of a new circumstance and its ultimate effect on well-being.

A within-S design provides a much more sensitive test of whether people believe in a treadmill effect. We therefore included a condition in which respondents were required to evaluate (on the same line of the questionnaire) the effect of a new circumstance on well-being, both for the first few months after the move and during the third year. The results were meager. Predicted well-being effects decreased substantially (by 0.50 scale points or more) only for 4 of 48 new features: freedom from an obnoxious relative, mediocre produce, humid summers, and long, cold winters. Overall, the within-S experiment showed no evidence of a general belief in a treadmill effect: the average predicted impact of a change (disregarding sign) was exactly the same (within .02 of a scale point) for the first three months and for the third year.

Additional analyses relied on judgments provided by control groups whose members rated the well-being effect of each of the 48 separate features. The mean ratings of the separate features in each pair were used to predict the well-being effects of a change from one of these features to the other. The effect of a change from feature X to feature Y was predicted with high accuracy ($R^2 = .98$ for all temporal orientations) by the following formula:

$$V(X \rightarrow Y) = 2V(Y) - V(X),$$

where $V(X \rightarrow Y)$ is the predicted effect of the new feature, and $V(X)$ and $V(Y)$ are ratings of the separate features by the control group. The formula reflects the belief that contrast with an earlier state affects well-being in a new state, and it reasonably assigns more weight to the new feature than to the past. Thus, the equation provides a plausible representation of the utility of a *change* from one state to another.[5] The noteworthy result of the study is that the very same formula predicted the judgments for all temporal perspectives equally well. This result supports the hypothesis that respondents applied the transition rule to predict well-being in a new situation – and did so even for a situation that was no longer new. Although we had formulated the study with that hypothesis in mind, the total neglect of adaptation in our subjects' judgments was still surprising. We had expected to find at least a trend indicating an effect of time, but we found none. In the within-subjects condition, we confidently expected substantial contrasts in direct comparison of the first few months with the third year, but the differences we observed were negligible, except for a few pairs of features.

The transition rule helps explain why the Brickman et al. (1978) study of paraplegics and lottery winners is an enduring classic: its findings are counterintuitive and perennially surprising, except perhaps to those who actually know a paraplegic or a lottery winner. The present results are also relevant to a deeper puzzle: Why do people strive so eagerly to improve their circumstances when a treadmill awaits them? Our findings suggest a simple answer: This essential fact of life is not generally known, perhaps because there are no good opportunities to learn it. The emotions evoked by transitions are immediate, and often strong. They provide the feedback needed to learn the skill of forecasting affective reactions to changes – one's own and those of others. In contrast, feedback from states is always delayed and ambiguous (Loewenstein and Schkade 1999). Thus, people can learn to predict reactions to changes without ever learning to forecast the subsequent evolution of their feelings.

The hypothesis of a hedonic treadmill can also be tested in a cross-sectional design: in a steady state, categories and groups of people should not differ in happiness, if all have adapted to their circumstances. A study reported by Schkade and Kahneman (1998) applied this reasoning to a familiar question: Are people happier in California than elsewhere? The widespread belief that California is a highly desirable place to live is surely a denial of the treadmill hypothesis. Why should living in California be so desirable if it offers no greater happiness? Students at four state universities (two in California and two in the Midwest; total $N = 1070$) completed a questionnaire that probed their overall life satisfaction and their satisfaction with separate domains of life. Other participants (total $N = 890$) completed the same questionnaire with the answers that they attributed to a student at another university described by the phrase "with values and interests similar to yours." The target person was said to be located at another state university, either in the same region or in the other region.

The results tell a simple story. Students in both regions believed that Californians would report substantially higher life satisfaction, and statistical

---

[5] A different pattern was observed in a group of respondents who used the same questionnaire to predict the difference in well-being between two families that differ in the relevant feature. Unlike predictions, judgments of well-being differences assigned equal weight to the two features and were precisely symmetric around zero.

analysis traced the differential forecasts to attitudes toward climate. Participants also expected Californians to be much more satisfied with their climate. This prediction was correct: the Californians liked their climate and the Midwesterners despised theirs, but climate was not, in fact, an important determinant of overall life satisfaction. With ethnicity controlled, self-reported life satisfaction was identical among students in the two regions. The findings provide a straightforward demonstration of an illusion in the forecasting of happiness. However, an argument that adds much complexity to this simple story is presented in Chapter 37.

3. THE PRINCIPLE OF JUDGMENT BY PROTOTYPE

The principle of evaluation by moments asserts that people evaluate the utility of temporally extended outcomes by retrieving or constructing a representative moment and by evaluating the utility of that moment. This heuristic of valuation leads to violations of logic because the temporal dimension of experience is not directly included in the representations that are evaluated. Evaluation by moments provides a compact account of much of the research that has been reviewed here; it also subsumes the earlier conclusion that gains and losses are the main carriers of decision utility in choice.

Evaluation by moments is itself subsumed under a broader principle that has been labeled *judgment by prototype*. The following propositions (from Kahneman, Ritov, and Schkade 2000 [Ch. 36]) introduce this idea:

1. *People hold stored prototypes of many categories. They also form prototypes or representative exemplars for new categories and sets that they encounter.* This proposition refers to the vast separate literatures on the role of exemplars in categorization, on stereotyping, on the role of vivid examples in comprehension of abstract ideas, and on the representativeness heuristic in judgment. In the context of this chapter, the prototype is the representative moment that stands for a temporally extended outcome.

2. *In judgment by prototype, a global judgment of a category or set is determined primarily by the relevant properties of its prototype.* This proposition is central to the idea that a representativeness heuristic is applied in statistical judgment and in intuitive predictions. It is also relevant to situations in which the stereotype that represents a group in people's minds may be a small and statistically unrepresentative minority. Environmental problems, such as the deaths of numerous birds that drown in an oil spill, may be represented by one vivid image, for example, a single bird drowning in oil (see Chapter 36 for further detail). This chapter argues that global evaluations of past episodes are represented by an affectively representative moment – the Peak–End average; future states are represented by the moment of transition.

3. *When the size of the set is logically relevant to its valuation, judgment by prototype*

leads to a bias of **extension neglect:** *Unless attention is specifically directed to it, the size of the set has little or no influence on its valuation.* Extension neglect is illustrated by the neglect of sample-size information in statistical judgment (Tversky and Kahneman 1971, Tversky and Griffin 1991); by the neglect of base-rate information in some tasks of intuitive prediction (Kahneman and Tversky 1973); and by the observation that the willingness to pay for solutions to public problems is insensitive to the magnitude of the problems (Kahneman, Ritov, and Schkade 2000 [Ch. 36]). Duration neglect is, of course, a special case of extension neglect.

4. *Extension neglect is neither universal nor absolute. An* **additive extension effect** *is observed when the information about extension is both salient and readily interpretable: the effects of the valuation of the prototype and of the size of the relevant set are additive. This pattern violates normative rules that require non-linear combination of the two types of information.* Figure 38.1 illustrated the additive duration effect observed by Schreiber and Kahneman (2000) along with two figures drawn from studies in different paradigms: a study of the additive effects of representativeness and base-rate (Novemsky and Kronzon 1999) and a study of the additivity of the appeal of a species and the extent of damage to it in determining willingness to pay for restoration efforts (Kahneman, Ritov, and Schkade 2000 [Ch. 36]). The same procedure was applied in all three cases to induce sensitivity to extension: the variable was manipulated across trials in a within-subject experiment. The additive duration effect is evidently an instance of a much broader phenomenon in which people appear to add effects where they should multiply them.[6] As noted earlier, this observation implies that the extension attribute is not incorporated in the basic representation (the prototype) that is evaluated. It is added as a separate constituent of evaluation when specifically primed. Similar results have been observed in many other studies of perception and judgment (Anderson 1996).

The similarities observed in this highly diverse set of judgment tasks are too consistent to be coincidental. It is reasonable to conclude that judgment by prototype is a general-purpose heuristic that is applied to diverse cognitive tasks. Whenever possible, it seems, people tend to think in the language of prototypes and exemplars. An important advantage of this heuristic is that it achieves considerable economy of processing by retaining only the basic template or schema for a single case. Occasionally, however, judgment by prototype leads to mistakes, such as conjunction errors in judgment (Tversky and Kahneman 1983) or violations of temporal dominance in choice. In the problems that were discussed here, evaluation by moments led to economical but biased judgments of the affective past and to systematically incorrect forecasts of the affective future.

---

[6] This observation should not be misconstrued as denying people's ability to multiply. In some situations, such as negotiating for pay, people will have no difficulty multiplying an hourly rate by the time they expect to work.

39. Endowments and Contrast in Judgments of Well-Being

Amos Tversky and Dale Griffin

In a recent educational television program, an amnesic patient was asked about his childhood and high-school experiences. Verbally fluent, he was able to converse about daily events but could not remember any details about his past. Finally, the interviewer asked him how happy he was. The patient pondered this question for a few seconds before answering, "I don't know."

As Tom Schelling observed, "We consume past events that we can bring up from memory" (1984, p. 344). Thus, the memory of the past is an essential element of present well-being. As our opening anecdote suggests, the present alone may not provide enough information to define happiness without reference to the past. Yet memories have a complex effect on our current sense of well-being. They represent a direct source of happiness or unhappiness, and they also affect the criteria by which current events are evaluated. In other words, a salient hedonic event (positive or negative) influences later evaluations of well-being in two ways: through an *endowment* effect and a *contrast* effect. The endowment effect of an event represents its direct contribution to one's happiness or satisfaction. Good news and positive experiences enrich our lives and make us happier; bad news and hard times diminish our well-being. Events also exercise an indirect contrast effect on the evaluation of subsequent events. A positive experience makes us happy, but it also renders similar experiences less exciting. A negative experience makes us unhappy, but it also helps us appreciate subsequent experiences that are less bad. The hedonic impact of an event, we suggest, reflects a balance of its endowment[1] and contrast effects. This chapter explores some descriptive and prescriptive implications of this notion.

[1] Our use of this term to denote a component of hedonic experience should be distinguished from the endowment effect demonstrated by Thaler (1980), through which the acquisition of material goods influences subsequent choices.

This work was supported by a grant from the Alfred P. Sloan Foundation. It has benefited from discussions with Daniel Kahneman, Lee Ross, and Richard Zeckhauser. This is a slightly modified version of a paper that appears in *Subjective Well-being*, edited by F. Strack, M. Argyle, and N. Schwartz (1990).

A few examples illustrate the point. Consider a professor from a small Midwestern town who attends a conference in New York and enjoys having dinner at an outstanding French restaurant. This memorable event contributes to her endowment – she is happier for having had that experience – but it also gives rise to a contrast effect. A later meal in the local French restaurant becomes somewhat less satisfying by comparison with the great meal she had in New York. Similarly, exposure to great theater is enriching but makes it harder to enjoy the local repertory company. The same principle applies to accomplishments. A successful first novel contributes a great deal to the author's endowment and self-esteem, but it also reduces the satisfaction derived from future novels if they are less successful.

The effects of endowment and contrast also apply to negative events. Some people, dominated by a negative endowment, become depressed and unable to enjoy life in the aftermath of a bad experience; others are elated by the contrast between the present and the bleak past. People may vary in the degree to which their reactions are dominated by endowment or by contrast. Note that the endowment–contrast dimension of individual differences is distinct from the more familiar dimension of optimism–pessimism. Optimism-pessimism normally refers to positive or negative expectations regarding the future, whereas the endowment-contrast dimension refers to the manner in which the evaluation of the present is determined by the comparison with the past. Both endowment and contrast, of course, depend on memory. With no memory, there can be no endowment and no contrast, just immediate pleasures and pains.

There is little novelty in suggesting that well-being depends both on the nature of the experience that is being evaluated and on the standard of evaluation. Furthermore, many authors have observed that satisfaction is directly related to the quality of the experience, or its endowment, and inversely related to the evaluation standard, which serves as a contrast. Perhaps less obvious is the observation that the same (past) event makes a dual contribution to well-being – a direct contribution as endowment and an inverse contribution as contrast. Although these effects have been discussed in the well-being literature (under various names), we know of no explicit attempt to integrate them.

The distinction between endowment and contrast does not depend on the character of the event itself; any hedonic experience could affect our well-being through the endowment it generates and through the contrast to which it gives rise. The endowment depends primarily on the quality and the intensity of the event, whereas the contrast depends primarily on its similarity or relevance to subsequent events. A great meal at a French restaurant in New York will probably not reduce your ability to enjoy a Chinese meal back home; similarly, while a great theater performance may spoil your taste for the local repertory company, you will probably continue to take pleasure in concerts or even high-school plays.

Because the contrast effect depends on similarity or perceived relevance, it is susceptible to framing and other cognitive manipulations. The same sequence of events can produce varying degrees of satisfaction depending on whether an early event is viewed as similar or relevant to the evaluation of later events. Thus, happiness should be maximized by treating positive experiences as endowments and negative experiences as contrasts. To achieve this goal, one should find ways to treat the positive experiences of the past as different from the present (to avoid a sense of letdown). By the same token, one should compare present conditions to worse situations in the past (to enjoy the benefits of a positive contrast). This prescription raises some intriguing questions that lie beyond the scope of this chapter. Are people who emphasize the endowment of positive events and the contrast of negative events generally happier than those who do not? And how much freedom do people have in the framing of hedonic events?

Here we report some preliminary explorations based on experimental manipulations of endowment and contrast. In the next section we vary the quality and the relevance of past events and investigate their effects on judgments of well-being. We propose a simple method for assessing the relative contributions of endowment and contrast in these studies, and we apply this analysis to some experiments of Schwarz, Strack, and their colleagues (see Schwarz and Strack 1990), and to the study of expectation effects. In the last section of the chapter, we discuss the use of choice and of judgment for the assessment of well-being, illustrate the discrepancy between the two procedures, and relate it to the relative contribution of endowment and contrast.

STUDIES OF ENDOWMENT AND CONTRAST

The following two experiments employ the same design to study the effect of a past event on present judgments of happiness. In the first study, we use fictitious scripts to investigate the role of endowment and contrast in judgments regarding the well-being of another person. In the second study, subjects rated their own satisfaction following an actual experience.

In our first study, subjects were given a "story" – a description of two events, allegedly taken from an interview with a student – and were asked to rate the happiness of that student. In each case, the earlier event was either positive or negative, and the later event was neutral. Four types of events were used in the study: a date, a term paper, a party, and a movie. The two events presented to the subject could be of the same type (e.g., two term papers or two parties) or of different types (e.g., a date followed by a party, or vice versa). This arrangement gives rise to a 2×2 (between-subjects) design in which a neutral event is preceded by either a positive or a negative event that could be of the same type or of a different type.

Because the second event is always neutral, we can focus on the endowment and the contrast effects produced by the first event. For events of different types, we expect an endowment effect, with little or no contrast. Judged happiness, therefore, should be relatively high when the first event is positive and relatively low when the first event is negative. For events of the same type, however, both contrast and endowment effects are expected. As a consequence, a related positive event should produce less happiness than an unrelated positive event, whereas a related negative event should produce less unhappiness than an unrelated negative event. For example, an excellent paper followed by an average paper should produce less satisfaction than an excellent paper followed by an average party because the original paper makes a subsequent paper (but not a subsequent party) somewhat disappointing by contrast. On the other hand, a bad paper followed by an average paper should produce less dissatisfaction than a bad paper followed by an average party.

Sixty-four students participated in our first experiment, which was administered in a class setting in four groups of approximately sixteen students each. All subjects received the following instructions:

> On the next few pages you will find several descriptions of life events experienced by high-school students. These are everyday sorts of events that you or your friends have probably experienced some time in your high-school career.

> Your task will be to read these stories carefully and try to understand how the person felt during these episodes. Each individual narrator will present two vignettes from his or her own high-school experience. The vignettes were all gathered during the narrator's junior year in high school. After each pair of stories, you will be asked to rate the feelings of the narrator.

> Each story-teller was asked to recount two experiences. First, they were asked to describe an experience from the week before, and then they were asked to describe something that had happened that very day. These narratives were given orally, so the grammar and prose are not perfect.

> Each story is very short, so please take your time and try to imagine what the scene looked like and felt like to the narrator. Especially try to imagine how the narrator was feeling as he or she recounted the story.

The events refer to four domains: a date with a young woman, performance in a course, the planning of a party, and the reaction to an Australian movie. Three events were constructed for each domain: positive, neutral, and negative. Recall that for each story (i.e., a pair of events), the present event was always neutral and it was preceded by either a positive or a negative event that was either related or unrelated. Each respondent evaluated four stories, one in each quality/relation condition (i.e., positive/related, positive/unrelated, negative/related, and negative/unrelated). The following story describes a negative event involving class performance followed by a related neutral event; an unrelated neutral event is also given for comparison.

Tim's Story

(Past, Negative)

What happened last week? *Last week, let's see. I had a bad day. A really, really bad day. In the morning, I had a quiz in French. I was so tired and I just couldn't keep my mind on the problems. And then with about 10 minutes to go in the period, I sort of woke up and realized that I was in bad trouble. I had sort of puttered on the first page of a three-page quiz and there was no way I was going to finish. I almost broke out in a cold sweat; the quiz wasn't very important or anything, but it was like a dream where I was racing against time and my heart was pounding and there was no way I was going to get finished. So I felt bad about that all morning, not to mention embarrassed at blowing the quiz, and then in the afternoon I got a test back in Chemistry. I had almost failed it; it was a pretty hard test and everything, but it just made me want to give up. I was just stunned, not to mention tired. Good grades in Chemistry are important to me because I want to take sciences in college. So I skipped track practice that day and just went home. I didn't want to deal with anything else bad that could happen to me.*

(Present, Related)

What happened today? *I had three classes this morning, but since one of them is Civics, it wasn't too bad. In Civics, we discussed political issues that have been in the news. That was o.k., mostly a break from taking notes in other classes. First period I had Geometry, and we had a substitute teacher so we just did our homework in class. Before lunch I had French, which I am taking instead of Spanish this year. We practiced our conversations, which we have to present next week. That's pretty much it, I think.*

Story 2 (Present, Unrelated)

What happened today? *Well, I had another lunch with Susan. We had a pretty good time. We talked most of the time, about classes and some people we both know. Mostly we talked about the English class, though, and the way that exams were given. We argued some about whether the professor was fair, but we both agreed that the exams were aimed more at trivial detail than were the lectures. We ate pretty slowly, but both made it to our one o'clock classes. It was hard to get a feeling for what was going on, but I think she liked me well enough.*

The dependent variable was a rating of happiness on a scale ranging from 1 (very unhappy) to 10 (very happy). Subjects were asked "On the day that Tim answered these questions: How happy do you think he was with his life overall?" Because there were no significant differences between the responses to the different types of events, the results were pooled. Figure 39.1 displays the average rating of happiness in each of the four conditions, averaged across subjects and stories. The results confirmed our predictions. There was a significant interaction between the quality of the past event (positive or negative) and its relation (related, unrelated) to the present event, $F(1, 60) = 6.71$, $p < .02$. As expected, we observed a significant endowment effect: in both the related and unrelated conditions, judged satisfaction was higher for the positive than for the negative prior event. Furthermore, there was a significant contrast effect: for the positive prior event, satisfaction was higher in the unrelated ($M = 7.1$) than in the related condition ($M = 6.8$), whereas for the negative prior event, the pattern was reversed ($M = 4.9$ for the unrelated condition, and $M = 5.5$ for the related condition). For example, the memory of a good date last week diminished the satisfaction with a neutral date this week, but it enhanced the

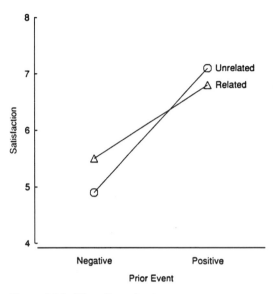

Figure 39.1. The effect of prior events.

satisfaction with a neutral movie this week. The memory of a painful date, on the other hand, enhanced the satisfaction with a neutral date this week, while it diminished the satisfaction with a neutral movie this week.

To aid in the interpretation of experimental data, we find it useful to express judgments of satisfaction as an additive combination of endowment and contrast effects. We assume that the endowment effect E_{12} is given by the sum of the endowments of the first and second events, denoted E_1 and E_2 respectively, and that the contrast effect C_{12} is expressible as the signed hedonic discrepancy between the two events d_{12}, weighted by their degree of relatedness r_{12}. Thus, we obtain the form

$$\text{Satisfaction} = \text{Endowment} + \text{Contrast}$$
$$= E_{12} + C_{12}$$
$$= E_1 + E_2 + r_{12}d_{12}.$$

To apply this scheme to the results of our first study, let S denote the rating of satisfaction. For simplicity, we suppose that the grand mean has been subtracted from all observations, so S is expressed as a deviation score. Let S^+ and S^- be respectively the responses in a condition where the first event was positive or negative, and let S_r and S_u denote the responses in a condition where the two events were related or unrelated. Let E^+ and E^- denote the endowment associated with a positive or negative event, and let C^+ and C^- denote the contrast associated with a positive or negative event, respectively. Because the second event in this study was always neutral we can neglect its endowment and set $E_2 = 0$. Naturally, the contrast associated with a prior positive event is negative, $C^+ < 0$, and the contrast associated with a prior negative event is positive, $C^- > 0$. We also assume that, for unrelated events, $r_{12} = 0$; hence the contrast term vanishes in that case. Judgments of satisfaction in the present design can be represented as:

	Negative	Positive
Unrelated	$S_u^- = E^-$	$S_u^+ = E^+$
Related	$S_r^- = E^- + C^-$	$S_r^+ = E^+ + C^+$

We use this model to estimate the effect of contrast and endowment. For the experimental results shown in Figure 39.1, the total endowment effect is

$$E = E^+ - E^- = S_u^+ - S_u^- = 7.1 - 4.9 = 2.2.$$

As we assume the unrelated events involve no contrast, the overall endowment effect is simply the difference between mean satisfaction in the cells representing positive and negative unrelated events. The contrast associated with the positive first event is

$$C^+ = S_r^+ - S_u^+ = 6.8 - 7.1 = -.3.$$

Similarly, the contrast associated with the negative first event is

$$C^- = S_r^- - S_u - S_u^- = 5.5 - 4.9 = .6.$$

Thus, the total contrast effect in this experiment is $C^- - C^+ = .9$, which is considerably smaller than the endowment effect, as can be seen in Figure 39.1.

In our second study, subjects rated their own satisfaction with actual experiences. Seventy-two subjects took part in a computer-controlled stock-market game played for real money. Subjects were given information about different stocks and were asked to construct a portfolio from these stocks. They were told that the computer would simulate the market and that their actual payoffs would depend on the performance of their portfolios. Each session included an initial game (with a payoff of $2 or $6) and a later game (with a payoff of $4) separated by a filler task involving no gains or losses. As in the first study, we manipulated two variables: (a) the payoff in the first game and (b) the similarity or relatedness of the first and the second games. In the related condition, subjects played essentially the same game with different stocks. In the unrelated condition, the games involved different markets (stocks versus commodities) and used different procedures for portfolio construction. After subjects played both games, they were asked to rate their overall satisfaction with the experience, using a ten-point scale.

This design allows us to test the following hypotheses regarding judged satisfaction. First, the difference between the low ($2) and the high ($6) payoffs will be greater in the unrelated than in the related condition. This prediction follows from the assumption that for the unrelated games, the difference reflects a pure endowment effect. In the related games, however, the positive endowment will

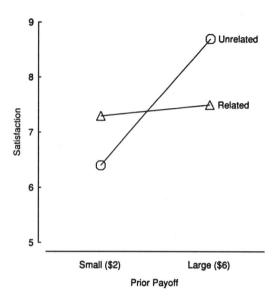

Figure 39.2. The effect of prior payoffs.

be reduced by a negative contrast, whereas the negative endowment will be reduced by a positive contrast. Second, the negative contrast effect following the high payoff (when $d_{12} > 0$) will be larger than the positive contrast effect following the low payoff (when $d_{12} < 0$), as suggested by the notion of loss aversion (Kahneman and Tversky 1984).

The pattern of results displayed in Figure 39.2 supports the endowment-contrast analysis. In the unrelated condition, where there is pure endowment and no contrast, those who received the larger payoff in the first game were considerably more satisfied ($M = 8.7$) than those who received the smaller payoff in the first game ($M = 6.4$), $t(33) = 1.95$, $p < .05$, one-tailed. However, in the related condition, where contrast and endowment worked in the opposite directions, there was essentially no difference between the satisfaction of those who received the larger reward in the first game ($M = 7.5$) and those who received the smaller reward in the first game ($M = 7.3$).

The decomposition scheme introduced in the first study is also applicable to the results of the present study. Here too, E_2 is a constant, and hence can be ignored in the analysis. To simplify matters, we also assume that the difference between the satisfaction derived from the high prior payoff and the low prior payoff in the unrelated games yields an estimate of the total endowment effect:

$$E = S_u^+ - S_u^- = 8.7 - 6.4 = 2.3.$$

The positive contrast (the increase in satisfaction caused by a low expectation) was

$$C^- = S_r^- - S_u^- = 7.3 - 6.4 = .9,$$

and the negative contrast (the decrease in satisfaction caused by a large expectation) was

$$C^+ = S_r{}^+ - S_u{}^+ = 7.5 - 8.7 = -1.2.$$

Note that the overall endowment effect was about the same in the two experiments, but the overall contrast effect, $C = C^- - C^+ = 2.1$ was doubled in the present study. As implied by loss aversion, people's disappointment with a "loss" of $2 was greater than their satisfaction with a "gain" of $2.

APPLICATIONS OF THE ENDOWMENT-CONTRAST SCHEME

Our conceptual scheme for the integration of endowment and contrast effects, described above, can be applied to two studies conducted by Schwarz, Strack, and their colleagues (see Schwarz and Strack 1990). In one experiment, Strack, Schwarz, and Geschneidinger (1985) instructed subjects in one group to recall and write down a very negative event in their lives; subjects in another group were instructed to recall and write down a very positive event in their lives. Within each group, half of the subjects were asked to recall a recent event, and half were asked to recall a past event. Subjects were then asked to rate their well-being on a ten-point scale. This procedure yields a 2×2 (between-subjects) design in which the recalled event was either positive or negative, in the present or in the past. For the events in the present, the results were hardly surprising. Recalling a positive present event made people feel good, whereas thinking about a negative present event made people feel less happy. The results for past events were more surprising: ratings of well-being were higher for those who recalled a past negative event than for those who recalled a past positive event (see Figure 39.3). We have replicated this result at Stanford.

The endowment-contrast scheme provides a natural account of these findings. For the events in the present, there is no room for contrast; hence we get a positive endowment effect for the positive event and a negative endowment effect for the negative event. The recall of past events, however, introduces a contrast with the present, which is positive for negative events and negative for positive ones. We assume here that the present is neutral. This contrast component offsets the relatively weak endowment component of past events, thereby producing the observed reversal.

Again, let S^+ and S^- refer to judged satisfaction when a positive or negative event, respectively, has been brought to mind. (As before, we first subtract the grand mean from each observation and operate on deviation scores). Let S_c and S_p refer to the judgments associated with a current and a past event, respectively. We can represent the average judgment in each cell as follows:

	Negative	Positive
Current	$S_c{}^- = E^-$	$S_c{}^+ = E^+$
Past	$S_p{}^- = E^- + C^-$	$S_p{}^+ = E^+ + C^+$

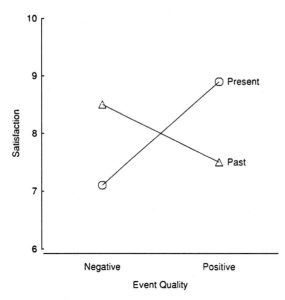

Figure 39.3. The effect of past versus present events.

The total endowment effect is

$$E = E^+ - E^- = S_c{}^+ - S_c{}^- = 8.9 - 7.1 = 1.8.$$

The contrast associated with the positive first event is

$$C^+ = S_p{}^+ - S_c{}^+ = 7.5 - 8.9 = -1.4.$$

The contrast associated with the negative first event is

$$C^- = S_p{}^- - S_c{}^- = 8.5 - 7.1 = 1.4.$$

The total contrast effect in this experiment is $C = C^- - C^+ = 2.8$. In this study, therefore, the contrast effect is considerably greater than the endowment effect.

   More generally, thinking about positive events in the past (e.g., a tour of the Greek islands, or a happy time at summer camp) calls attention to the less exciting present. This is the stuff of which nostalgia is made. On the other hand, recalling some bad times in the past (e.g., failing a test or being lonely) reminds us that the present, although imperfect, could be a great deal worse. While Strack et al. (1985) see mood as the carrier of endowment, we do not regard mood as a necessary condition for an endowment effect. We shall address this difference in emphasis at the conclusion of this section.

   In another study, Schwarz, Strack, Kommer, and Wagner (1987) required subjects to spend an hour either in an extremely pleasant room (spacious, nicely furnished, and decorated with posters and flowers) or in an extremely unpleasant room (small, dirty, smelly, noisy, and overheated). After the session, subjects were asked to assess general satisfaction as well as satisfaction with

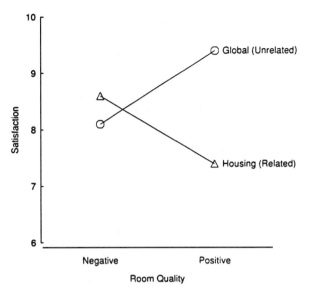

Figure 39.4. The effect of room quality.

regard to their current housing situation. The room influenced the rating of overall satisfaction; subjects who were placed in the pleasant room reported higher overall life satisfaction than those in the unpleasant room. However, subjects' rating of their normal living conditions exhibited the opposite pattern (see Figure 39.4). Those placed in the unpleasant room reported higher satisfaction with their housing than those who had been in the pleasant room. This pattern is naturally interpreted as a contrast effect. One's own room appears less attractive when compared with the pleasant room than when compared with the unpleasant room. Because contrast depends on the relevance or the similarity of the standard to the target, the contrast effect of the experimental room was confined to the evaluation of housing and did not extend to the rating of life satisfaction. A specific event, therefore, is likely to have a significant contrast effect in the domain to which it belongs, and little or no contrast effect in others.

Using the notation introduced earlier, let S^+ and S^- denote, respectively, judgments of satisfaction for the pleasant and unpleasant rooms, and let S_r and S_u denote, respectively, judgments of satisfaction for the related (housing) and unrelated (life satisfaction) domains. The analysis of these results is then identical to the analysis of the first study. In particular, the total endowment effect is

$$E = S_u{}^+ - S_u{}^- = E^+ - E^- = 9.4 - 8.1 = 1.3.$$

The contrast effect associated with the positive first event is

$$C^+ = S_r{}^+ - S_u{}^+ = 7.4 - 9.4 = -2.0.$$

The contrast effect associated with the negative first event is

$$C^- = S_r^- - S_u^- = 8.6 - 8.1 = .5.$$

As one might expect, the contrast effect produced by the room is considerably larger ($C = C^- - C^+ = 2.5$) than its endowment effect.

Although different in focus, our analysis is generally compatible with that offered by Schwarz and Strack (1990). They assume the operation of contrast effects and focus on the role of emotion or mood in generating endowment. Our account assumes the existence of endowment effects, produced through either mood or other processes, and focuses on the factors that control the relative strength of endowment and contrast.

EXPECTATIONS AS CONTRAST AND ENDOWMENT

Much psychological research on the assessment of well-being has focused on the role of expectations. It has been shown in many contexts that the same event can be perceived as more or less satisfying, depending on whether a positive or negative expectation has been induced (Feather 1966; Shrauger 1975). Whether a given test score is pleasing or disappointing will depend on whether the student was led to expect a low or a high score (Schul 1988). Expectation effects are generally interpreted as contrast. Indeed, people are commonly advised to lower their expectations in order to avoid disappointment. In line with our previous analysis, we propose that expectations produce endowment as well as contrast. We are relieved when a dreaded event does not happen, but the memory of anxiety and fear still haunts us long afterward. Imagine that you have been living two weeks with the possibility that your child has leukemia. Further tests now prove your worries unfounded. Despite your elation at this news, we suspect that you are worse off for the experience. In such circumstances, the endowment effect of a negative expectation has a strong impact on your well-being long after the specific worry has been relieved.

Much as unrealized fears can generate negative endowment, unrealized hopes can give rise to positive endowment. Consider the experience of someone who owns a lottery ticket. Because the probability of winning is very small, the failure to win does not cause much disappointment. However, the dream of becoming an over-night millionaire could produce enough pleasure to offset the mild disappointment of not winning the lottery. Indeed, it appears that many people enjoy playing the lottery even when they do not win. The contrast between prior expectations and the actual outcome is especially sensitive to the probability of winning. As the probability of winning increases, the costs of disappointment (contrast) seem to increase faster than the benefits of hope (endowment). Holding expected value constant, therefore, playing long odds should be more pleasurable than playing short odds. Losers on long odds had sweeter dreams than losers on short odds; and their disappointment was also less bitter. This analysis suggests another reason for the attractiveness of long shots in addition to the overweighting of small probabilities (Kahneman and Tversky 1979).

The present conception of well-being is guided by the observation that people derive pleasure and pain not merely from the positive and the negative events they experience but also from the memory of past events and the anticipation of future events (Elster 1985; Loewenstein 1987). Like the memories of past events, expectations of future events, we suggest, serve both as endowment and as contrast. Expectations not only control the evaluation of future events, they have a hedonic impact of their own – whether or not the event they refer to actually comes to pass. Our hedonic portfolio encompasses memories and expectations: successes and failures of the past, hopes and fears of the future. In the words of Tom Schelling, "We consume good news and bad news," (1984, p. 344).

THE ASSESSMENT OF WELL-BEING: CHOICE VERSUS JUDGMENT

The studies described here were concerned with judgments of satisfaction or happiness, which have served as a major source of data for students of well-being (Argyle 1987; Diener 1984). Another paradigm for the study of welfare focuses on choice rather than on judgment. In this paradigm, a person is said to be better off in State A than in State B if he or she chooses State A over State B. Indeed, the concept of utility has been used in economics and decision theory in two different senses: (a) experience value, the degree of pleasure or pain associated with the actual experience of an outcome, and (b) decision value, the contribution of an anticipated outcome to the overall attractiveness of an option (Kahneman and Tversky, 1984). Experience values are generally measured by judgmental methods (e.g., self-reports or judgments by observers), although physiological measures (e.g., blood pressure or heart rate) are occasionally used. Decision values are inferred from choices using an appropriate model such as expected utility theory or the theory of revealed preference. The distinction between experience and decision values is rarely made explicit because, with a few notable exceptions (e.g., March 1978; Schelling 1984; Sen 1982), it is commonly assumed that judgment and choice yield the same ordering. In many situations, however, experience values, as expressed in self-ratings, appear to diverge from decision values, as inferred from choice.

First, choice and judgment may yield different results because of moral considerations and problems of self-control. We commonly avoid certain pleasurable experiences because they are immoral, illegal, or fattening. On the other hand, there are times we cannot resist experiences that will ultimately make us unhappy because of a lack of self-control. Choice, therefore, could conceal rather than reveal one's "true preferences." Second, a choice-judgment discrepancy is likely to arise if the decision maker's prediction of the consequences of a choice is inaccurate or biased. A common bias in the prediction of utility is a tendency to overweight one's present state or mood. Some perceptive consumers have learned to avoid doing their weekly grocery shopping either when they are very hungry (because they would buy too much) or after a very large meal (because they would not buy enough). A related source of error is the failure to anticipate our remarkable ability to adapt to new states. People tend to overestimate the long-term impact of both positive events, such as winning a lottery or receiving tenure, and negative events, such as injury or personal loss (Brickman, Coates, and Janoff-Bulman 1978). The ability to predict future well-being depends largely on the nature of the experience. People generally have a reasonable idea of what it is like to lose small sums of money or to have a bad cold, but they probably do not have a clear notion of what it means to go bankrupt or to lose a limb. For illuminating discussions of the role of adaptation and the problems of predicting one's own future satisfaction, see Kahneman and Snell (1990) and Kahneman and Varey (1990).

But even if the judgment, like the choice, precedes the experience of the consequence, the two tasks can give rise to different answers because they highlight different aspects of the problem. When people are asked to assess the hedonic value of some future states (e.g., new jobs) they try to imagine what it would feel like to experience those states. But when asked to choose among these states, they tend to search for reasons or arguments to justify their choice. Consequently, the two procedures could lead to different results. For example, Tversky, Sattath, and Slovic (1988) have shown that the most important attribute of a multidimensional decision problem is weighted more heavily in choice than in judgment, presumably because it provides a convenient rationale for choice. Recall the stock-market study, presented in the first section of this chapter. Given a choice, subjects would surely elect to participate in the negative contrast condition, where they earn $10, rather than in the positive contrast condition, where they earn $6. Yet subjects who had a lower total endowment ($6) and a positive contrast were just as satisfied as subjects who had a higher total endowment ($10) and a negative contrast. It appears that the choice depends primarily on the payoffs, whereas judgments of satisfaction are more sensitive to the contrast.

To explore the choice-judgment discrepancy, we presented the following information to some sixty-six undergraduate students.

Imagine that you have just completed a graduate degree in communications and you are considering one-year jobs at two different magazines.

(A) At Magazine A, you are offered a job paying $35,000. However, the other workers who have the same training and experience as you do are making $38,000.

(B) At Magazine B, you are offered a job paying $33,000. However, the other workers who have the same training and experience as you do are making $30,000.

Approximately half the subjects were asked "Which job would you choose to take?" while the other half were asked "At which job would you be happier?"

The results confirmed our prediction that the comparison with others would loom larger in judgment, and that the salary would dominate the choice. Eighty-four percent of the subjects (27 out of 32) preferred the job with the higher absolute salary and lower relative position, while 62 percent (21 out of 34) of the subjects anticipated higher satisfaction in the job with the lower absolute salary and higher relative position ($\chi^2(1) = 14.70$, $p < .01$).

We further explored the relation between choice and judgment in the assessment of an actual experience using a within-subjects design. Thirty-eight undergraduate students participated in a study of "verbal creativity" involving two different tasks. One was described as a test of "cognitive production": the ability to come up with many words that fit a sentence. The other task was described as a test of "grammatical production": the ability to produce many words of a particular grammatical type. Subjects were told that their payoffs would depend on their performance in these tasks.

All subjects performed both tasks, each of which consisted of a practice trial followed by a payoff trial. In one task, subjects were told that their performance was below average on the practice trial and about average on the payoff trial. In the other task, subjects were told that they performed above average on the practice trial and about average on the payoff trial. Thus, the performance of each subject allegedly improved on one task and declined on the other task. The order and type of task were counterbalanced. The payoff in the declining condition ($3) was higher than the payoff in the improving condition ($1). Thus, one task paired a larger payoff with an unfavorable comparison. The other task paired a smaller payoff with a favorable comparison. After each task, subjects were asked to rate their satisfaction with their performance on a ten-point scale. Following the completion of both tasks, subjects were asked "If you could do just one task, which would you choose to do?"

As predicted, the payoffs loomed larger in choice than in judgment; or equivalently, the contrast was weighted more heavily in judgment than in choice. Of the twenty-eight subjects whose ratings were not identical on the two tasks, 75 percent chose the high-payoff task, whereas 54 percent expressed greater satisfaction with the low-payoff task. This reversal pattern is significant ($p < .05$ by a McNemar test of symmetry).

These studies show that judgments of satisfaction and choice can yield systematically different orderings. Furthermore, it appears that choice is determined primarily by the payoffs, which reflect the endowment effect, whereas the judgment is more sensitive to comparison or contrast. The salary or payoff one receives provides a more compelling reason for choice than the contrast between one's own salary and the salary of others. This contrast, however, is a very salient feature of the experience, as reflected in the judgment task. Note that the present use of *contrast* is consistent with, but considerably broader than, the concept invoked in the first part of this chapter. There the term refers to the indirect contribution of a past event to current well-being, whereas here it refers to the standard of reference by which the relevant outcomes are evaluated, which may be determined by prior experience or by other factors, such as the salary of colleagues.

The choice-judgment discrepancy raises an intriguing question: which is the correct or more appropriate measure of well-being? This question cannot be readily answered, and perhaps it cannot be answered at all, because we lack a gold standard for the measurement of happiness. We believe that both choice and judgment provide relevant data for the assessment of well-being, although neither one is entirely satisfactory. Since, as we argue below, the two methods seem to be biased in opposite directions, a compromise between them may have some merit.

Perhaps the most basic principle of welfare economics is Pareto optimality: an allocation of resources is acceptable if it improves everybody's lot. Viewed as a choice criterion, this principle is irresistible. It is hard to object to a policy that improves your lot just because it improves the lot of someone else even more. This is a pure endowment argument that neglects contrast altogether. Policies that ignore contrast effects can create widespread unhappiness, however. Consider, for example, a policy that doubles the salary of a few people in an organization and increases all other salaries by 5 percent. Even though all salaries rise, it is doubtful that this change will make most people happier. There is a great deal of evidence (e.g., Brickman 1975; Brickman and Campbell 1971; Crosby 1976) that people's reported satisfaction depends largely on their relative position, not only on their objective situation.

Both experimental and survey research on happiness have shown that judgments of well-being are highly sensitive to comparison or contrast and relatively insensitive to endowment effects. Perhaps the most dramatic illustration of this phenomenon concerns the effect of windfall gains and personal tragedies. Judged by their ratings, lottery winners are no happier than others, and quadriplegics are only slightly less happy than healthy people and no less happy than paraplegics (Brickman et al. 1978). Surveys indicate that wealthier people are slightly happier than people with less money, but substantial increases in everyone's income and standard of living do not raise the reported level of happiness (Easterlin 1974).

Do these data reflect rapid adaptation that negates the immediate impact of any endowment – as implied by the treadmill theory of happiness (Brickman and Campbell 1971)? Or do they reflect a normalization of the response scale that makes the ratings of ordinary people and paraplegics essentially incomparable? (As if the paraplegic answers the question: how do I feel relative to other paraplegics?) There is no simple answer to these questions. Obviously, everyone would choose to be healthy rather than paraplegic, and rich rather than poor. But it is not obvious how to demonstrate that the rich are actually happier than the poor if both groups report the same level of well-being. At the same time, it is clear that an adequate measure of well-being must distinguish between rich and poor, and between paraplegic and quadriplegic.

It seems that judgments of well-being are insufficiently sensitive to endowment, whereas choice is insufficiently sensitive to contrast. The exclusive reliance on either method can lead to unreasonable conclusions and unsound recommendations. Welfare policy derived from Pareto optimality could result in allocations that make most people less happy because it ignores the effect of social comparison. On the other hand, a preoccupation with judgment has led some psychologists to the view that "persons with a few ecstatic moments in their lives may be doomed to unhappiness" (Diener 1984, p. 568); hence, "if the best can come only rarely, it is better not to include it in the range of experiences at all" (Parducci 1968, p. 90). These conclusions are justified only if endowment effects are essentially ignored. A few glorious moments could sustain a lifetime of happy memories for those who can cherish the past without discounting the present.

40. A Bias in the Prediction of Tastes

George Loewenstein and Daniel Adler

ABSTRACT. Recent research has documented an 'endowment effect' whereby people become more attached to objects they receive than would be predicted from their prior desire to possess the object. In two experiments, we test whether people are aware of the effect – whether they realise that they will become attached to an object once they receive it. In both experiments, subjects without an object underestimated how much they would value the object when they received it.

Although the standard economic theory of consumer preference assumes fixed tastes, the idea that tastes change over time is not controversial. Numerous 'habit formation' models have been proposed which assume that current consumption influences future tastes (Duesenberry, 1949; Pollak, 1970; Stigler and Becker, 1977). These models have been applied to such diverse phenomena as the development of tastes for music and food, substance addiction (Becker and Murphy, 1988), and the surprisingly high rate of return on equities relative to fixed-income securities (e.g. Constantinedes, 1990).

Although it is more complicated to model than fixed tastes, there is nothing intrinsically irrational about habit formation as long as economic agents can predict without bias the effect of their current behaviour on their own future tastes. If people are aware of the effect of their actions on their own future tastes, they can adjust their consumption in a rational manner – e.g. by desisting from crack based on anticipation of future disutility from addiction.

There is some evidence, however, pointing to situations in which people systematically mispredict their own tastes. For example Ausubel (1991) noted that large numbers of credit card users expect to maintain a zero credit balance but fail to do so – apparently underestimating their own future desire for spending. This self-forecasting error can explain the downward stickiness of credit card interest rates since consumers who expect to maintain zero card balances

We thank Max Bazerman, Baruch Fischhoff, Colin Camerer, Dražen Prelec, and Shane Frederick for helpful comments and suggestions, and Tina Diekman for assistance in running the experiments. The idea for the first experiments arose in a discussion with Daniel Kahneman.

will not care about credit card interest rates. A similar pattern occurs in connection with consumer rebate programmes; consumer purchase decisions are quite sensitive to rebate offers, but very few consumers ultimately send in the forms required to obtain the rebate (Tat *et al.* 1988).

Our specific focus is on whether people are able to predict changes in their own tastes caused by the 'endowment effect' (Thaler, 1980). The endowment effect refers to the tendency for people to value an object more highly if they possess it than they would value the same object if they did not. In the typical demonstration of the endowment effect (see, e.g. Kahneman *et al.* 1990), one group of subjects (sellers) are endowed with an object and are given the option of trading it for various amounts of cash; another group (choosers) are not given the object but are given a series of choices between getting the object or getting various amounts of cash. Although the objective wealth position of the two groups is identical, as are the choices they face, endowed subjects hold out for significantly more money than those who are not endowed. As Tversky and Kahneman (1991) have shown, the endowment effect implies that indifference curves shift in a systematic manner when individuals acquire goods – increasing the valuation of the endowed good relative to all other goods. Thus, the endowment effect can be viewed as a type of endogenous taste-change.

Tversky and Kahneman analyse the effect of endowments on preferences with a 'reference-dependent preference structure' that indexes the standard preference relations ($\succ$, $\sim$, etc.) according to the individual's point of reference (typically the current asset position). For example, $x \sim_r y$ indicates that an individual with reference position r is indifferent between alternatives x and y. The selling price (s) and choice value (c) estimated in the experimental setup just described are represented in equations 1 and 2 respectively, where the first argument of each pair indicates the individual's level of wealth, the second designates possession (1) or nonpossession (0) of the object, and the preference relation is subscripted according to whether the decision maker is in possession of the object.

$$(w, 1) \sim_1 (w + s, 0) \tag{1}$$
$$(w, 1) \sim_0 (w + c, 0) \tag{2}$$

The endowment effect implies $s \gg c$.

To accommodate predictions of preferences within this framework, we generalise the notation by subscripting the preference relation by the asset position which the individual is attempting to predict, and superscripting it by the individual's current reference level. Thus, for an individual with asset position s, $\sim_r^s$ represents the indifference relations she would expect to prevail if her asset position were r instead of s.[1]

---

[1] Under the generalised notation, the conventional endowment effect can be expressed as: $(w, 1) \sim_1^1 (w + s, 0)$, and $(w, 1) \sim_0^0 (w + c, 0)$ with $s > c$.

In the experiments presented below, we asked subjects to predict their own selling price for an object they did not have – i.e. to predict a selling price, s', as defined by,

$$(w, 1) \sim_1^0 (w + s', 0) \qquad (3)$$

If subjects predict their own selling prices without bias, then, on average, $s' = s$. Our prediction is that subjects will underestimate s – i.e. $s' \ll s$.

The endowment effect has several advantages as the focus of a study of taste-change prediction. First, the effect operates very rapidly so that, unlike, for example, changes in the taste for classical music, it can be studied in a single experimental session. Second, discovery of a bias in predicting the impact of the endowment effect would have far-reaching implications for economics. The endowment effect refers to the impact on tastes of merely acquiring a good. Since many economic decisions, including most decisions involving consumer choice, involve acquisitions, documentation of a bias in the prediction of the endowment effect would call into question the rationality of a wide range of economic behaviour. Finally, we believed that there was a high likelihood of observing a prediction bias in this particular domain. This intuition is based on, first, the surprisingly long time it has taken social scientists to discover the effect, given its magnitude and robustness; second, the fact that the endowment effect disappears when people make valuation decisions on behalf of another person, as if they are not aware that others will get attached to objects in their possession (Marshall *et al.* 1986); and third, the fact that other studies have found that people tend to underestimate how quickly they will adapt to changed circumstances such as winning a lottery or becoming paraplegic (Brickman *et al.* 1978) – i.e. that they underestimate the impact of reference point shifts.

I. EXPERIMENT I

The first experiment was designed to test whether subjects without an object could predict how attached they would become if they were endowed with it. We first elicited hypothetical selling prices for an object from unendowed subjects then endowed them with the object and elicited an actual selling price.

Subjects were 27 undergraduates enrolled in a core humanities class at Carnegie Mellon University and 42 adults enrolled in two evening classes in finance at the University of Pittsburgh. In each class, the experimenter held up a mug engraved with the school logo for the students to see. A different style of mug was used at Carnegie Mellon and at the University of Pittsburgh. A form was then randomly distributed to approximately half of the students in each class. The form asked the students to imagine that they possessed the mug on display and to predict whether they would be willing to exchange the mug for various amounts of money. It was worded as follows:

We are interested in your opinion about the mug displayed at the front of the room. Imagine that we gave you a mug exactly like the one you can see, and that we gave you the opportunity to keep it or trade it for some money. Below are a series of lines marked 'Keep mug____Trade it for $ amount____.' On each line check whether you think that you would prefer to keep the mug or to trade it in for the amount of money written on the line. Check one or the other on every line.

The remainder of the page consisted of 40 lines each containing a choice between keeping the mug or trading it for an amount of money that ranged from 25 cents to 10 dollars in $0.25 increments. The experimenter waited until all subjects with a form had completed it. Next, *all* subjects were presented with a mug and given a second form which actually provided the opportunity to exchange the mug for cash. The instructions for the second form were directly analogous to those used in the prediction form, but made it clear that one of their choices would count. Subjects were told that they would receive the option they had circled on one of the lines – which line had been determined in advance by the experimenter.

The experimental design creates two groups of subjects, one that completed the prediction form prior to receiving a mug, and the other that did not. It allows us to conduct both a between- and within-subject analysis of prediction accuracy. The within-subject analysis compares the preliminary valuation predictions of the group that completed the first form with their subsequent actual valuations. The between-subject test compares those predictions with the actual valuations of the group that did *not* make initial predictions. The between-subject comparison was included in case making an initial prediction influenced subjects' subsequent choices, in which case any bias would have been attenuated in the within-subject comparison.

I.1. Results

Results for the two University of Pittsburgh classes were similar, so their data are aggregated. Three University of Pittsburgh subjects gave nonmonotonic responses to both valuation questions, rendering their data uncodable, and two provided useful predictions, but uncodable actual valuations. All five subjects are excluded from the analyses. The mean minimum selling values for the two institutions are shown in Table 40.1. For each university group, the first line shows the mean predicted and actual selling price of the prediction group. The second line shows the actual selling price for subjects who did not previously predict their own selling price.

Actual selling prices differed between the two universities, probably because different mugs were used. More interestingly, there was substantial underestimation of selling prices in both university groups, both within and between subjects. Within subjects, those who completed the first form substantially underestimated their own subsequent selling prices. For the Carnegie Mellon group, mean actual valuations were $1.67 greater than predicted valuations

Table 40.1. Predicted and Actual Valuation of the Mug

Group/Condition	Number of Subjects	Prediction of Valuation	Actual Valuation
Carnegie Mellon University			
Prediction	14	$3.73	$5.40
		(0.41)	(0.65)
No prediction	13	—	$6.46
			(0.54)
University of Pittsburgh			
Prediction	22	$3.27	$4.56
		(0.48)	(0.59)
No prediction	17	—	$4.98
			(0.53)

Std. errors in parentheses.

$(t(13) = 2.8, p < 0.02)$; for the University of Pittsburgh group they were greater by $1.17 $(t(16) = 3.2, p < 0.01)$.

Underprediction of value is also evident in the between-subjects comparison of the first group's predicted selling price and the second group's actual selling price. The mean difference between the predictions of the first group and the valuations of the second was $2.73 $(t(25) = 4.1, p < 0.0005)$ for the Carnegie Mellon group, and $1.59 $(t(35) = 2.1, p < 0.05)$ for the University of Pittsburgh group. Mug valuations of the group which did not make a prediction were higher, but not significantly so, than those of the group which did make a prediction, suggestive of a weak anchoring effect.

II. EXPERIMENT 2

A limitation of the first study is that it was not 'incentive compatible' because subjects had no incentive to provide accurate predictions of their own selling prices (although, by the same token, there was no incentive for misrepresentation). The second experiment avoided this problem by informing subjects that they had a 50% chance of getting a mug and eliciting a selling price that would apply if they got a mug. Our prediction was that subjects who only had a 50% chance of getting a mug would not feel endowed and, like the prediction subjects in the previous experiment, would underestimate the selling price that they would want to prevail if they did get a mug.

A second limitation of the first study was that it did not elicit choice prices from subjects, so it was impossible to determine where the predicted selling price lay on the continuum between choice values and actual selling prices. If subjects predict their own selling prices perfectly, then we would observe $s' = s$ (as defined in equations (1)–(3)); if they are completely unable to predict the effect of possessing the object on their preferences, then we would anticipate $s' = c$ – i.e. that predicted selling prices will correspond to choice prices. To assess where their predictions lie on this continuum, we can construct an index of prediction bias, β, defined by:

$$\beta = \frac{(s - s')}{(s - c)}. \tag{4}$$

β will equal 0 for individuals who predict their own selling prices perfectly, and 1 for those who are completely unable to predict the effect of being endowed on their valuation of the object. Note that this index reflects only the degree of prediction bias, and not the magnitude of the endowment effect which some people view as a type of bias in its own right.

II.1. Method

Two executive education classes at Northwestern University with a total of 106 students were each randomly assigned to two experimental groups which were isolated in separate rooms. In the control condition, a coin was flipped for each subject and subjects who called it correctly were given a mug emblazoned with the school logo. Selling prices were elicited from those who obtained a mug, and choice prices from those who did not, using forms that were analogous to those used to elicit selling prices in the first experiment.

For the experimental group, the identical type of mug was displayed at the front of the room, and subjects were told that there was a 50% chance of receiving one, based on whether they correctly called a coin flip. Prior to the coin flip, selling prices were elicited, which subjects were told would apply if they called the flip correctly and got a mug.[2] After providing selling prices, subjects individually called a coin toss and were given a mug if they called it correctly. Finally, those who received a mug were asked whether they would like to revise their selling price (although they were not actually allowed to do so).[3]

---

[2] The exact wording of the form was as follows: 'There is a 50% chance that you will obtain the mug displayed at the front of the room. In a moment we are going to flip a coin to determine if you receive a mug exactly like the one you can see. We are interested in how much you will value the mug if you get it. Below are a series of lines marked 'Keep mug___ Trade it for $amount___.' On each line check whether, if you do get a mug, you would prefer to keep the mug or to trade it in for the amount of money written on the line. Check one or the other on every line. Later we will announce a line number and you will get your choice on that line. Think carefully about each check mark because if you get a mug your choice on one of the lines will count.'

[3] The exact wording was as follows: 'The form you filled out earlier will determine whether you get a mug or some money. Nevertheless, we are interested in whether, if you had a chance, you would prefer to change your responses on that form. Suppose you could complete FORM 3 again; please check below how you would respond.' The subject then recompleted the form eliciting selling prices.

Table 40.2. Mean Valuation of Mugs

Group	Form	Description	Number of Subjects	Prediction of Valuation
Control	1	Selling price	24	$5.96 (0.460)
	2	Choice	29	$4.05 (0.329)
Experimental	3	Selling price contingent on getting a mug	53	$4.16 (0.293)
	4	Desired revision of selling price	34	$4.69 (0.329)

Std. errors in parentheses.

II.2. Results

The standard endowment effect is evident in the mean values presented in Table 40.2. Subjects given a mug (Form 1) valued it an average of $1.91 higher than those without the mug (Form 2) ($t(51) = 3.4$, $p < 0.002$). More importantly, the bias in prediction of selling price is again evident. Subjects with a 50% chance of receiving a mug stated a mean selling price that was $1.80 lower than that for subjects who actually possessed a mug; the mean valuation for subjects prior to flipping the coin was $4.16 compared to $5.96 for subjects already endowed with a mug ($t(75) = 3.352$, $p < 0.002$). Selling prices for those who had a 50% chance of receiving a mug were very close to the choosing prices of subjects who did not have a mug ($4.16 vs. $4.05). The prediction bias β is equal to 0.94 measured between-subjects (i.e. 94% of its plausible maximum value).

The desired price revisions of subjects who got a mug provide further evidence of a prediction bias. The mean valuation of subjects endowed with the mug after having already decided on a selling price was $4.69, which is $0.53 higher than their previous valuation, a significant difference ($t(34) = 3.3$, $p < 0.01$). If we use $4.69 as a conservative estimate of the correct selling price, then the prediction bias index, β, drops to 0.84, which is still extremely high. Three subjects indicated that they would have liked to revise their price downward, 14 did not want to revise their price, and 17 wanted to revise it upward. However, the remaining $1.27 discrepancy between the revised selling price and the mean selling price for the control condition ($t(56) = 2.3$, $p < 0.03$) indicates that the hypothetical selling prices of the experimental group were lower than they would have been if they had not 'anchored' their final valuations of the mug on their initial decisions.

III. GENERAL DISCUSSION

Despite the importance of taste prediction for rational choice, the accuracy of such predictions has only recently become a topic of systematic research and inquiry. Perhaps, as Kahneman and Snell (1990) argue, the earlier absence of such research was limited by the circularity of the revealed preference approach, in which tastes are viewed as revealed by behaviour rather than as an independent construct exerting an influence on behaviour. With tastes defined by behaviour there is, as the economists say, 'no arguing with tastes', and no possibility for tastes to be accurate or inaccurate – they simply are what they are.

While there are some prior results that are suggestive of taste-change misestimation, the current study is, to our knowledge, the first to observe a systematic bias in the prediction of taste-change. Moreover, one could argue that it is a surprising domain in which to observe such a bias. Numerous theoretical articles have focused on the process of habit formation in which tastes change as a function of past consumption. With certain important exceptions, such as, reputedly, the drug crack, such processes operate relatively slowly. The endowment effect, in contrast, leads to a much more rapid change in tastes. Our subjects predicted how their tastes would change, not over a matter of months or years, but minutes. Given how quickly the endowment effect operates, it is remarkable that people are unable to anticipate it. The failure to anticipate the endowment effect is also surprising considering the vast experience most people have had acquiring, possessing, and losing objects – experience that should provide ample opportunities for learning how tastes change following the acquisition of goods. Judging from our experiments, such learning is severely limited.

An unpublished experiment conducted by Kahneman and Loewenstein (1991) provides a possible clue as to why such learning does not occur. They found that subjects who were endowed with an object did not change their ranking of the object's desirability relative to other objects. However, when it came to exchanging the endowed object for another item, they displayed a heightened attachment to the endowed object. It thus appears that a person must be threatened with the loss of an object to appreciate his or her heightened attachment to it. Since people are rarely endowed with an object then immediately deprived of it, they may not get feedback about how attached they become to objects in their possession.

Another factor interfering with feedback is that people may forget their initial valuation of the object. Several studies have shown that people tend to forget their past attitudes – to believe that their past views were similar to those held in the present (e.g. Marcus, 1986). If the same bias applies to tastes, then people will remember their past tastes as being similar to their current tastes and erroneously conclude that their tastes have not changed. Thus, feedback about taste-change may be less plentiful than one might expect based on the accumulation of experience with possession.

Nevertheless, people probably receive more feedback about the effect of endowments than they do about a wide range of other taste changes. Their inability to predict the effect of endowment, therefore, raises the possibility that a much wider range of changes in tastes are predicted with bias. Tastes change for a variety of reasons, typically due to processes that act more slowly than the endowment effect. When hungry, can we predict how our tastes will be different when we are satiated? When unafflicted by addiction, can we accurately anticipate the agonies of addiction and withdrawal? Most changes in tastes are also less predictable and systematic than the endowment effect. Whereas most people are affected similarly by the endowment effect, other endogenous taste changes are more variable. For example, one person may learn to love classical music after repeated exposure, whereas another might grow to detest it.

The failure to predict the endowment effect suggests that hypothetical selling prices elicited from subjects who are not in possession of the relevant goods are probably biased downward. To provide a selling price for a good one does not possess requires two stages of introspection: (1) imagining one possesses the object and has adapted to ownership, and (2) imagining how one would feel about parting with it. Buying prices and choice values, in contrast, both involve one stage of introspection, and we know of no compelling evidence that estimates of either value are biased; indeed, Starmer and Sugden (1991) failed to observe a significant difference between probabilistic as compared to deterministic choices.

As a general rule, it seems likely that people will mispredict their own preferences when the superscript and subscript in equation (3) are different – i.e. when people are asked to introspect about how they would feel or behave in a situation different from their own – but not when the subscript and superscript are identical. It would be interesting to test whether people with objects overpredict the buying prices or choice values of those without such objects, as this hypothesis suggests.

The observation that individuals are unaware of the endowment effect presents a novel view of choice. It suggests that people not only become attached to what they have (as implied by the endowment effect), but do so unknowingly. People seem to be unwittingly trapped by their choices; they make choices with an unrealistic sense of their reversibility.

41. The Effect of Purchase Quantity and Timing on Variety-Seeking Behavior

Itamar Simonson

ABSTRACT. Two consumer strategies for the purchase of multiple items from a product class are contrasted. In one strategy (simultaneous choices/sequential consumption), the consumer buys several items on one shopping trip and consumes the items over several consumption occasions. In the other strategy (sequential choices/sequential consumption), the consumer buys one item at a time, just before each consumption occasion. The first strategy is posited to yield more variety seeking than the second. The greater variety seeking is attributed to forces operating in the simultaneous choices/sequential consumption strategy, including uncertainty about future preferences and a desire to simplify the decision. Evidence from three studies, two involving real products and choices, is consistent with these conjectures. The implications and limitations of the results are discussed.

Consumption of products often is separated temporally from the decision to buy those products. Hence, when making a purchase decision, consumers must predict their preferences at the time of consumption (Kahneman and Snell, in press; March 1978). The decision is complicated further if consumers want to avoid going to the store before each consumption occasion and decide to buy several items in a category for a number of occasions. For example, in one shopping trip a consumer might purchase a week's supply of yogurt. The research reported here examines the strategies consumers use when making multiple purchases in a product category for future consumption. The behavior of consumers who make multiple purchases in a product class for several consumption occasions is compared with that of consumers who purchase one item at a time before each consumption occasion.

Study 3 was conducted in collaboration with Jackie Snell. Psychology Department, UC Berkeley. The author is grateful to Jim Bettman, Pete Bucklin, Danny Kahneman, Kevin Keller, Russ Winer, the participants in the Berkeley-Stanford-Santa Clara Colloquium and the UCLA Seminar, and three anonymous *JMR* reviewers for their comments and suggestions. Financial support for the research was provided by the Institute for Business and Economic Research, University of California, Berkeley.

A comparison of these two purchase conditions suggests that making multiple purchases for several consumption occasions is a more difficult task for two main reasons. First, the mere fact that multiple decisions must be made simultaneously, rather than one decision at a time, tends to make this task more demanding, especially if no one alternative is perceived as far superior to all others. Second, this task is likely to be more difficult because of the need to predict future preferences, which often change over time (McAlister 1982). Specifically, consumers' preferences when making purchases may be poor predictors of their preferences in a future consumption period because of possible changes in state of mind (Wright and Kriewall 1980) and tastes (Rozin and Schiller 1980). For example, at one time a consumer might prefer a strawberry flavored yogurt and on the following day be in the mood for a raspberry yogurt. Similarly, for a certain period a consumer might have a strong preference for raspberry yogurt and then have a change of taste in favor of a different flavor. A question that naturally arises is: What decision strategies or heuristics do consumers use in making multiple purchases for future consumption when faced with uncertainty about future preferences and the need to make multiple decisions simultaneously?

The research proposition examined here is that consumers making multiple purchases for several consumption occasions, who are uncertain about their preferences, tend to select a greater variety of items than consumers making purchases sequentially. Variety seeking in this case reflects the uncertainty about the items that would be most preferred, diminishes the risk associated with changing preferences, and reduces the time and effort needed to reach a decision. This proposition leads to two hypotheses that were tested in three studies, two of which involved real products and choices. The findings are reported and their implications are discussed.

MAKING MULTIPLE PURCHASES FOR FUTURE CONSUMPTION AND VARIETY SEEKING

The literature on variety seeking suggests several motives for variety seeking by consumers (see McAlister and Pessemier 1982 for a review). One motive discussed by both psychologists (e.g., Driver and Streufert 1964; Fiske and Maddi 1961) and consumer researchers (e.g., Venkatesan 1973) is people's need for novelty, change, and complexity, which are inherently satisfying. A second motive for variety seeking relates to the notion of satiation, suggesting that a change from one behavior to another is attributable to the decreasing marginal value of the original behavior. For example, McAlister (1979) proposed a model that evaluates the selection of a collection at a point in time and holds that one would be unlikely to select multiple replicates of the same item. One's likely satiation with attributes in which a particular item is rich would lead to the increasing attractiveness of alternatives that offer other attributes. McAlister (1982) presents a dynamic attribute satiation model that accommodates behaviors in successive periods.

These and other motives for variety seeking discussed in the literature, however, do not allow prediction of the effect on variety seeking of simultaneously making purchases for future consumption rather than making the purchases sequentially. That is, if the consumption schedule is held constant, satiation and the desire for novelty and change should have the same effect in both situations. A closer examination of the two purchase conditions reveals two important differences between them, including a greater uncertainty about future preferences and a need to make multiple decisions simultaneously when making purchases for several consumption occasions. These differences suggest that consumers who simultaneously make purchases for several occasions would be more likely to select a variety of preferred items for three main reasons: (1) a desire for variety and change is more likely to influence purchase decisions when consumers are uncertain about their preferences, (2) given the possibility of a change in tastes, selection of variety reduces risk, and (3) in making multiple purchases, selection of the different top candidates for purchase can simplify the task and save the time and effort needed to determine which alternative is the most preferred. A discussion of each of these reasons follows.

Consumers' preference for variety. The literature on variety seeking provides much support for the notion that people generally prefer a varied experience. Less clear, however, are the conditions under which the desire for variety is most likely to influence actual purchases. For example, if consumers have a clear preference for a particular alternative, as they often do when purchasing an item for immediate consumption, that alternative is most likely to be chosen regardless of any general preference for variety. If, however, consumers are uncertain about their preferences, as they often are when making purchases for future consumption, the desire for variety is likely to have a more significant influence on the choices made. Furthermore, the degree of variety and novelty in one's selections is much more salient when multiple purchases are made simultaneously than when the purchases are temporally separated. These observations lead to the prediction that consumers making multiple purchases for future consumption would be more likely than those making one purchase at a time to select variety.

Selection of variety to reduce risk. Consumers' tastes often change over time (e.g. Rozin, Ebert, and Schull 1982; Rozin and Schiller 1980; see Kahneman and Snell, in press, for a review), though some noted economists have argued otherwise (Stigler and Becker 1977). Changes in tastes might reflect a change in hedonic preferences, such as a change in liking for a particular yogurt flavor, a type of TV program, or a vacation destination. Tastes also might be modified to reflect other factors such as changing needs (e.g., an expanding family's preference for a sedan vs. a sports car) and personal goals (e.g., going on a diet or modifying eating habits to control cholesterol level). In some product classes, including many food categories, tastes might change very frequently, whereas in other categories (e.g., cars, furniture) tastes are likely to be more enduring.

The possibility of a change in preferences poses a particular problem for consumers who want to make purchases for future consumption. Trying to anticipate taste changes (e.g., going on a diet the following week) is usually a difficult task. Kahneman and Snell (in press) present empirical evidence suggesting that people's ability to predict their future tastes is very poor. Therefore purchasing the same item for all periods is associated with a risk of disappointment in several periods should the consumer's preference for that item decrease after the purchase is made. In contrast, selection of a variety of acceptable items, such as one's current top preferences or the items preferred most often in the past, is less risky because it is very unlikely that the preferences for all selected items will decrease. For example, a person who consumes a can of soup each week and is buying a month's supply of soups may be reluctant to purchase only the most preferred kind because his or her liking for that soup might decrease. This person is similar in some respects to an investor who holds a diversified portfolio of attractive stocks rather than just the one stock with the highest expected return (Sharpe 1985). Thus, selection of variety when making multiple choices for future consumption might also be a risk-reduction strategy employed by consumers in the face of uncertainty about future tastes.

Selection of variety as a choice heuristic to save time and effort and resolve decision conflict. The preceding discussion focuses on the effect of uncertainty about future preferences when the preferences at the time of purchase are assumed to be known with certainty. However, uncertainty about future preferences might reflect uncertainty about current preferences. Indeed, consumers and other decision makers often have difficulty making a choice among perfectly familiar alternatives (March 1978; Simonson 1989a; Tversky 1988). Decision making under preference uncertainty has been described as involving discomfort, conflict, and even pain (Abelson and Levi 1985; Festinger 1957). That is, to choose one alternative, a person must forgo the other alternatives and their unique attractive aspects. Resolving that conflict and determining which of the considered options is the most preferred might require much time and cognitive effort. The literature on choice heuristics and effort-accuracy trade-offs (e.g., Beach and Mitchel 1978; Bettman 1979; Payne, Bettman, and Johnson 1988) suggests that decision makers often adopt choice heuristics that reduce cognitive effort and maintain reasonable (if not optimal) levels of decision accuracy.

In the context of buying decisions, a consumer who wants to buy several products on a shopping trip is unlikely to spend much time and effort on each decision, especially if the risk associated with the purchase is low. Hence, to simplify the task of making multiple purchases in a category, a consumer might select the top candidates for choice, thus saving the need to determine which of those options is the most preferred.

HYPOTHESES

The preceding discussion presents arguments in support of the proposition that consumers who make simultaneous purchases in a category and are uncertain about their future preferences tend to choose a variety of preferred items rather than multiple replicates of the most preferred item. This proposition can be tested by examining the effect of purchase quantity and timing, with the consumption schedule held constant, on variety-seeking behavior.

Specifically, in one condition (referred to hereafter as the sequential choices condition), a single choice from the same set is made in each period for immediate consumption. This condition is contrasted with a second one (referred to hereafter as the simultaneous choices for sequential consumption condition), in which consumers make multiple choices simultaneously, expecting to receive the selected alternatives sequentially, one in each consumption period. In both conditions, the temporal separation between consumption occasions is such that satiation with an item consumed in one period does not influence the utilities of items on subsequent consumption occasions. Despite that separation, for the reasons given in the preceding discussion, subjects in the simultaneous choices for sequential consumption condition are expected to select more variety than those in the sequential choices condition.

H_1: *Consumers who simultaneously choose multiple items in a category for sequential consumption are more likely to choose different items than consumers who sequentially make the same number of choices.*

In addition to the predicted differences in choice behavior, the relationships between consumers' preferences for the alternatives and their subsequent choices also are expected to depend on the number of items selected at one time. "Preferences" in this context refers to the overall evaluations of alternatives (Ajzen and Fishbein 1977) or the predisposition to respond to alternatives in a particular way (Bass, Pessemier, and Lehmann 1972; Blin and Dodson 1980). Preferences might be assessed by asking respondents to rate alternatives in terms of such measures as their perceived overall attractiveness and liking by the consumer. When making one selection at a time for immediate consumption, consumers are expected to select each time their most preferred item. In contrast, when making multiple purchases simultaneously for several periods, consumers are expected to select different preferred items rather than the same (most preferred) item for all periods. This expectation holds despite the fact that satiation with an item consumed in one period does not influence the utility derived from the same item on a subsequent occasion (McAlister 1982).

H_2: *Overall preferences for alternatives are stronger predictors of choice among consumers making choices sequentially than among consumers making simultaneous choices for sequential consumption. Accordingly, the choice probability of the most preferred item is greater in the former condition.*

The hypotheses were tested in three studies. In study 1, a paper-and-pencil task was used to test H_1 in several product categories. Study 2 focused on one product category, with actual products and real choices, and was designed to test both H_1 and H_2. Finally, in study 3, think-aloud protocols and an additional choice condition were used to provide greater insights into the decision processes employed by consumers in making multiple purchases for future consumption periods.

STUDY 1

Method

Subjects. The subjects were 67 undergraduate students enrolled in an introductory marketing course. Participation in the experiment was a course requirement.

Product Categories. Seven product categories were selected for study 1. In all of these categories, consumers often make multiple purchases within a short period of time. In addition, these products typically are consumed completely in one consumption occasion. The latter criterion allowed for an unconfounded test of the hypotheses. That is, if consumption of a product (e.g., a car, a box of cereal) is temporally extended (i.e., extends over several consumption periods), the difference between making multiple choices that will be received at *one* time and making multiple choices that will be received *over* time is less clear.

Procedure and Manipulation. Two conditions were used. Subjects in both conditions were told to imagine they were going to the supermarket with a shopping list that included eight items: yogurt, bread, soft drink, canned vegetable, milk, snack, fruit, and a can of soup (milk was included to test for random choice behavior, as explained subsequently). Within each category, different product alternatives such as different yogurt flavors or snacks were listed, and subjects were instructed to indicate the option(s) they would select.

In the sequential choices condition, subjects were told to assume they were going to the supermarket to do their daily shopping, and in each category they intended to buy only one item. After making choices in all categories, subjects were told to assume they had consumed the selected alternatives, and on the following day they again were going to the supermarket. The shopping list and alternatives in each category were identical to those for the first shopping day. That procedure then was repeated a third time.

In the simultaneous choices for sequential consumption condition, subjects were told to assume they were going to the supermarket to do their shopping for the next three days; in each category they intended to buy three items for the next three days such that only one item in each category would be consumed on each day. Finally, they were instructed to enter next to each item the number of units of that item (if greater than zero) that they would buy.

Because of the hypothetical nature of the choice task, a test for random choice behavior was included. One of the eight categories, milk, was selected because subjects in all conditions were expected to select the same type of milk consistently (skim, low fat, or regular). Indeed, between 94% and 97% of the subjects in all three conditions consistently selected the same type of milk. Therefore, in all conditions, subjects appear to have taken the choice task seriously, and any variety-seeking behavior observed is likely to have been intentional rather than the result of random choice behavior.

Results and Discussion

Consistent with H_1, in all seven product categories subjects who made choices sequentially were less likely to select variety than subjects who simultaneously made multiple choices for sequential consumption (see Table 41.1.) The χ^2 associated with a table of variety seeking by condition is 31.1 (2 d.f.), which is highly statistically significant ($p < .001$).

As argued before, in the simultaneous choices for sequential consumption condition, two factors underlie the tendency to select variety: the uncertainty about preferences and the fact that multiple decisions are made simultaneously rather than one at a time. In study 1 only one of these factors, making choices simultaneously, was present. That is, because subjects in the sequential choices condition made their selections only a few minutes apart without actually consuming their choices, there was no difference between conditions in uncertainty

Table 41.1. Study 1: Variety Seeking by Condition[a] (percent)

	Condition					
	Simultaneous Choices for Sequential Consumption ($n = 33$)			Sequential Choices ($n = 34$)		
Category/Variety[b]	H	M	L	H	M	L
1. Yogurt	64	24	12	44	29	27
2. Bread/bagel/rolls	76	24	0	32	45	23
3. Canned vegetable	53	41	6	35	24	41
4. Fruit	73	24	3	59	21	21
5. Snack	75	16	9	30	49	21
6. Soft drink/juice	46	30	24	29	35	35
7. Can of soup	44	44	12	38	47	15
Total	62	29	9	38	36	26

[a] χ^2 (condition * variety seeking; 2 d.f.) = 31.1 ($p < .001$).
[b] H (high) variety indicates that three different items were selected. M (medium) variety indicates that one item was chosen twice, plus an additional item. L (low) variety indicates that one item was selected three times.

about future preferences. In addition, the tendency of subjects in study 1 who made simultaneous choices to select a variety of items rather than multiple replicates of their most preferred item might be attributed, at least partially, to the fact that the choices did not have any real consequences for them. Hence, study 2 had two main objectives: (1) to replicate and extend the finding of study 1 with actual products and real choices and (2) to test both hypotheses with choice and preference data.

STUDY 2

Overview

In study 2, student subjects made selections from a choice set of snacks at the beginning of a class meeting and received their selection(s) at the end of the class. In the sequential choices condition, subjects made one choice each week for three weeks. In the simultaneous choices for sequential consumption condition, subjects made all three choices at one time, but received only one item each week. A week after making their choices/last choice, subjects were asked to rate their overall preferences for the different alternatives.

A third condition was included in study 2, referred to hereafter as the simultaneous choices for immediate consumption condition. In this condition subjects made three selections simultaneously and received all three choices at the end of the class. Though not testing any hypothesis, this condition was included to allow for a comparison of the effect of satiation on variety seeking (McAlister 1979, 1982) with that of uncertainty about future preferences. That is, whether the simultaneous choices are made for sequential or for immediate consumption, the fact that multiple choices are made simultaneously is expected to increase the tendency to select variety. The difference between the two conditions, however, is that subjects who expect to receive all items simultaneously are likely also to seek variety because of concerns about satiation whereas those who make choices for future consumption periods are expected to seek variety because of uncertainty about future preferences.

Method

Subjects. The subjects were 392 undergraduate students enrolled in 13 marketing, accounting, and organizational behavior classes in two neighboring West Coast universities. The study was conducted during regular class meetings. Subjects received snacks as part of the experiment.

Product Category and Alternative Selection. The task of study 2 involved real products and choices. Logistical and budget constraints limited the focus to one product category. Of the seven product categories included in study 1, snacks appeared most suitable for several reasons. First, most students regularly buy snacks. Second, students were expected to be receptive to an experiment in which they would receive free snacks, even if the process were repeated over a number of weeks. Third, snacks are relatively inexpensive and easy to store (by the experimenter). Fourth, snacks usually are consumed by the receiver immediately or within a short time. A product that might be stored for a long period of time, or one that has a high likelihood of not being desired by the receiver but is selected to be given as a gift, would have introduced a confound.

Another concern that arises in an experiment involving selections of products such as snacks over several occasions is that preferences might depend on the particular time of day or usage situation (Belk 1975). For example, students might prefer salty snacks for lunch and sweet snacks in the afternoon. This problem was not significant in study 2, however, because classes met at the same time and place each week. Finally, to reduce the likelihood of exploratory choice behavior, the snacks selected for the study were either "generic" products (peanuts, tortilla chips, milk chocolate with almonds, crackers and cheese), or snacks that are very familiar (Snickers bar, Oreo cookies). Information on the popularity of the different items was provided by the university vending machines operator, who later supplied the products (the same brands that were available from the vending machines). In total, there were six alternatives, three sweet and three salty snacks.

Consumers' perceptions of these six snacks were examined in a pilot study with a separate sample of 68 student subjects. Briefly, in this study, subjects were asked to assess the extent to which different pairs of snacks were good substitutes and good complements. For example, to assess substitutability, subjects were asked to assume they had chosen the first item in the pair, and then were told that it was not available but they could receive the second item as a substitute. The task was to rate how good a substitute the second item would be for the first. The results indicated that a sweet (salty) item is perceived as both a better substitute for and a better complement to another sweet (salty) item than is a salty (sweet) item. However, homogeneous pairs (sweet or salty) were rated significantly higher as substitutes than as complements, whereas mixed pairs (sweet and salty) were rated significantly higher as complements than as substitutes.

Procedure and Manipulation. At the beginning of a class meeting, students were told that they would participate in a study pertaining to snacks. The experimenter first read the instructions, and students were informed that they would receive their selection(s) from the experimenter at the end of the class. Then the six snack alternatives were taken out of their packages and shown to the students. Next, subjects received the forms, were told to reread the instructions, and indicated their choice(s). At the end of the class, the students received the item(s) they had requested. The person giving the snacks observed that most students started eating a snack as soon as they received it.

Classes were assigned randomly to one of three conditions. To minimize interference with classes' schedules and not reveal the purpose of the study, all students within each class were assigned to the same condition. Five classes with 142 students were assigned to the sequential choices condition. Students in that condition who missed one of the three choice occasions were given an additional opportunity a week later to make their third choice. However, of the 142 students, 25 did not complete three choices and were dropped from the sample. Examination of their choice behavior in the two choices that most of them did make indicates that they were similar in terms of variety seeking to the other students. Four classes with 145 students were assigned to the simultaneous choices for sequential consumption condition. Four classes with 105 students were assigned to the simultaneous choices for immediate consumption condition. The instructions given to subjects in the three conditions are summarized in the Appendix.

A week after they had made their choices/last choice, the experimenter asked the students to indicate their overall preference for the six snacks on two scales: overall liking and overall attractiveness. The ratings were on a zero to 10 scale, with zero representing "dislike very much"/"very unattractive" and 10 representing "like very much"/"very attractive," respectively.

Finally, after completion of the study but before the debriefing, individual students and a few classes as a whole were asked whether they thought they knew the purpose of the study and whether they wanted to guess its purpose. In most cases students offered no guesses. Three of four students who did try to guess thought that the study was done for a snack manufacturer or a vending machine operator.

Results and Discussion

As can be seen in Table 41.2, consistent with H_1 and the results of study 1, subjects in the sequential choices condition were significantly less likely to select different items of variety than those in the simultaneous choices for sequential

Table 41.2. Study 2: Variety Seeking by Condition[a] (percent)

	Variety		
Condition	High (3 different items)	Medium (item × 2 + item × 1)	Low (same item 3 times)
Sequential choices ($n = 117$)	9	53	38
Simultaneous choices for sequential consumption ($n = 145$)	64	21	15
Simultaneous choices for immediate consumption ($n = 105$)	81	17	2

[a] χ^2 [condition (sequential choices vs. simultaneous choices for sequential consumption) * variety] = 81.05, 2 d.f. ($p < .001$).

χ^2 [condition (sequential choices vs. simultaneous choices for immediate consumption) * variety] = 119.3, 2 d.f. ($p < .001$).

χ^2 [condition (simultaneous choices for sequential consumption vs. simultaneous choices for immediate consumption) * variety] = 14.0, 2 d.f. ($p < .005$).

consumption condition. The χ^2 associated with a table that includes these two conditions is 81.05 (2 d.f.), which is highly statistically significant ($p < .001$). Similarly, subjects in the sequential choices condition were also less likely to select variety than those who made simultaneous choices for immediate consumption ($\chi^2 = 119.3$, $p < .001$).

Another comparison of interest is between the two conditions involving three simultaneous choices. The subjects who made selections for immediate consumption were more likely to choose variety than those expecting to consume their selections sequentially ($\chi^2 = 14.0$, 2 d.f., $p < .005$). Clearly, however, subjects in the simultaneous choices for sequential consumption condition were more similar in terms of variety seeking to those who expected to receive their three selections immediately than to subjects in the sequential choices condition.

Though not hypothesized, an additional difference is noted in the choice patterns of subjects in the three conditions. In the sequential choices condition, 65% of the subjects selected three items that were all either sweet or salty and only 35% selected mixed (sweet and salty) items. In contrast, in the simultaneous choices for sequential consumption and simultaneous choices for immediate consumption conditions, only 31% and 35%, respectively, selected all sweet/salty items (the difference between the latter two conditions is not significant). In light of the pilot study's findings, these results indicate that subjects who made three separate choices tended to select substitutes whereas those who made three choices for three weeks or for the same day were more likely to select complements. The unexpected result is that subjects making simultaneous choices for three weeks were much more likely to select complements than those making choices sequentially. Note, however, that this result is confounded with the finding on the likelihood of selecting variety in the different conditions. That is, given a choice set of three salty and three sweet items, a greater tendency to select different items implies a higher likelihood of selecting both sweet and salty items and vice versa. Future research might examine whether the differences in likelihood of selecting substitutes or complements are still observed if variety-seeking level is held constant.

H_2 predicts that the overall preferences for alternatives (i.e., their ratings in terms of overall attractiveness and liking) will be a stronger predictor of choice, and the choice probability of the most preferred item will be greater, if consumers make purchases sequentially rather than simultaneously. Before H_2 was tested, however, because the preference ratings were collected after the choices, it was necessary to check for possible influences of the experimental manipulation (i.e., the choice condition) on the ratings. That is, though the ratings were collected a week after the choices/last choice, subjects may have tried to make their preference ratings consistent with their choice behavior. Considering the pattern of differences in variety seeking across conditions, a tendency for consistency would imply that subjects in the sequential choices condition would tend to rate their most preferred item significantly higher than the other alternatives. Conversely, subjects in the other conditions would tend to rate several items similarly, consistent with their tendency to select different items. The data do not show any such differences in the preferences across the three conditions. The distribution of the variance of the preference ratings within subjects (across the six items) is practically identical in the three conditions. Further, given that each subject made only three choices from the set, the difference between the most and third most preferred item also was examined. The distribution of these differences is virtually identical in all three conditions. Hence, choice condition does not appear to have significantly influenced the preference ratings taken a week after the last choice.

To test H_2, a mutinomial logit analysis was run with the choice and preference data in the sequential choices and simultaneous choices for sequential consumption conditions. Each choice of each subject served as one observation. There were nine independent variables, two of which were the preference ratings of each alternative on overall attractiveness (ATR) and overall liking (LIK). Two other variables represented the interactions between the sequential choices condition (SEQ) and the preference ratings, ATR and LIK. In addition, alternative-specific 0–1 dummy variables were included for five of the six snacks (Guadagni and Little 1983). The alternative-specific constants ensure that the average predicted choice share for each item equals the actual choice share. The estimated coefficients follow (standard errors in parentheses).

$$.36ATR + .47LIK + .39ATRSEQ + .21LIKSEQ$$
$$(.11) \qquad (.11) \qquad (.16) \qquad\qquad (.15)$$

$$-.10TORTILLA + .15CHEESE - .18PEANUTS$$
$$(.15) \qquad\qquad (.16) \qquad\qquad (.17)$$

$$+.53HERSHEY + .45SNICKERS \qquad (\chi^2 = 717)$$
$$(.13) \qquad\qquad (.13)$$

H_2 suggests that the effect of the preferences, ATR and LIK, on choice would be stronger in the sequential choices condition than in the simultaneous choices for sequential consumption condition. Consistent with this prediction, the signs of both interaction terms are positive. The coefficient of the interaction involving overall attractiveness, ATRSEQ, is statistically significant ($p < .01$) and the coefficient of LIKSEQ approaches statistical significance ($p < .10$). Hence, the overall preference ratings of alternatives are a stronger predictor of choice in the sequential choices condition.

H_2 also postulates that the share of the overall most preferred item would be greater in the sequential choices condition. Consistent with this prediction, the mean choice probability of the most preferred item is 60% in the sequential choices condition (i.e., on the average, the most preferred item was selected almost 2 of 3 times) in comparison with only 39% in the simultaneous choices for sequential consumption condition. The relationship between overall preferences and choice in the simultaneous choices for immediate consumption condition is very similar to that in the simultaneous choices for sequential consumption condition. These results indicate that subjects who made one choice at a time tended each time to select their overall most preferred item. In contrast, when subjects made multiple choices simultaneously for a number of periods, they tended to select different preferred items rather than multiple replicates of their most preferred item. They did so despite the fact that the timing of the three consumption occasions was the same in both conditions.

Though the results of studies 1 and 2 are consistent with the hypotheses, they do not afford much insight into the decision strategies actually employed by consumers in making purchases for future consumption. Therefore, though not directly testing the hypotheses, study 3 was conducted as an exploratory investigation to provide insights into the decision strategies used in the different choice conditions of study 2, with primary focus on the simultaneous choices for sequential consumption task.

STUDY 3

Overview

There were two conditions in study 3. One group started with the simultaneous choices for sequential consumption task that was used in study 2, followed by three selections for immediate consumption. In the second condition, subjects first selected one item for immediate consumption, then were informed that they would be given the same choice options in each of the following two weeks. Their task was to try to predict which item(s) they would prefer in the following two weeks. Finally, as in the other condition, they selected three items for immediate consumption.

These two conditions potentially allow observation and comparison of the decision strategies used in all three conditions of study 2. In addition, a comparison of the two conditions of study 3 might provide a better understanding of the effect on choice strategies of having to make choices for future consumption. In theory, the indicated/predicted choices should be similar in the two conditions, because choices for a future period would be based on the expected preferences at that time. However, there are two important differences between the two tasks. First, in the new condition (referred to hereafter as the prediction task), subjects were asked explicitly to predict their preferences, whereas it is not clear to what extent consumers who make purchases for future consumption actually try to predict their preferences. Second, no risk was involved in the prediction task because the predictions were not binding in any way. As suggested before, one of the motives for selecting variety when making multiple choices for the future is to reduce the risk associated with the possibility of changing tastes. Hence, subjects in the prediction task are expected to select less variety.

Think-aloud protocols (Ericsson and Simon 1980) have been used extensively by decision and marketing researchers (e.g., Bettman and Park 1980; Payne 1976) as a tool for studying decision processes. This technique appears most suitable for the purposes of study 3.

Method

The subjects were 46 undergraduate students enrolled in a psychology course. One subject who did not complete the task was dropped from the sample, leaving 22 subjects in the simultaneous choices for sequential consumption condition and 23 subjects in the prediction condition. Participation was part of a course requirement.

The experimenter first gave each subject instructions to think aloud while performing the task, followed by two practice choice problems. The snacks then were put on the table, and the subject performed either the simultaneous choices for sequential consumption task (as in study 2) or the prediction task. Next, subjects in both conditions were told that some subjects would not have to return and would receive all three selections immediately, and that they were assigned to the group that did not have to return. It was emphasized that their earlier choices did not constrain their selections for immediate consumption in any way. However, the preceding task may have influenced the choices for immediate consumption.

In the prediction condition subjects first made a single choice for immediate consumption. Then they were informed that in one week and in two weeks they again would make one selection from the same set. The task was to try to predict their preferences in the following two weeks. It was emphasized that when they returned they would be free to choose the snack they desired at that time, and their previous predictions would not constrain them in any way.

The primary focus in the protocol analysis was on the decision strategies used for (1) selecting an item for immediate consumption, (2) selecting or predicting selections for the following two weeks, and (3) selecting three items for immediate consumption. The think-aloud protocols were analyzed by two independent judges. The overall interjudge reliability was 85%. Disagreements were resolved by discussion.

Results and Discussion

Selecting an Item for Immediate Consumption. In both conditions the majority of subjects started the selection of the first item by eliminating less attractive options. Seventy-one percent of the subjects in the simultaneous choices condition and 91% in the prediction condition used an elimination strategy. In the next stage subjects usually tried to determine which of the noneliminated options they most preferred. One strategy, employed by 81% in the simultaneous choices condition and 48% in the prediction condition, was to base the final selection on the subject's current state of mind. State of mind was related to such considerations as how hungry the subject was, the food consumed earlier that day, and whether the subject was in the mood for a sweet or a salty snack. Other subjects, primarily in the prediction task, tried to determine which

Table 41.3. Study 3: Variety Seeking by Condition[a] (percent)

Condition	Variety		
	High (3 different items)	Medium (item × 2 + item × 1)	Low (same item 3 times)
Simultaneous choices for sequential consumption (n = 22)	59[b]	27	14
Prediction (n = 23)	35	44	22

[a] χ^2 (condition * variety) 2 = 2.7 d.f. ($p > .10$, not significant).
[b] The difference between conditions is statistically significant at the .05 level.

snack was their overall most preferred without referring to their current state of mind.

The protocols also suggest that the selection of a snack was more difficult for subjects in the prediction task, who believed they would receive only one item (Jecker 1964). Six of 23 subjects in the prediction task but only one subject in the other condition indicated that making a selection was a tough decision ($p < .05$). Furthermore, the average length of a protocol of the first decision was 100 words in the prediction condition and just 78 words in the other condition ($p < .05$). Hence, making a single choice from a set appears to be easier if one knows that one would make additional selections from the same set. Specially, when making multiple choices for several periods, a consumer can base the selection for immediate consumption on the current state of mind without having to determine which option is the overall most preferred.

Selections/Prediction of Selections for Later Weeks. Table 41.3 summarizes the choice data for the two conditions. As expected, these results suggest that subjects in the prediction task were significantly less likely to select three different items ($t = 1.71$, $p < .05$), though given the number of observations, the overall χ^2 associated with the table is not statistically significant.

In terms of the strategy for making selections for future consumption, strong relationship is found in the simultaneous choices for sequential consumption condition between the size of the consideration set in the first choice and later choices. In particular, subjects who identified only one acceptable snack in the first choice tended later to select that item for all weeks. Other subjects who had debated among three or more acceptable options in the first choice tended to choose for later weeks those acceptable items that were not selected for immediate consumption. In that process, most subjects did not indicate that they expected the item they chose for immediate consumption to be their most preferred in future periods. Conversely, in the prediction condition, consistent with the choice data, subjects were more likely to use their current preference for predicting future preferences. Also, 30% of the subjects in the prediction condition used anticipated changes in tastes in their predictions (e.g., "my diet wouldn't last," or "I'll probably be on a health kick") in comparison with just 9% in the other condition ($p < .05$).

In both conditions, about 25% of the subjects and 38% of those who selected three different items explicitly indicated that their selections/predictions were influenced by a desire for a varied experience. The protocols gave no indication that any of the subjects thought that after a week they still would be satiated with the item consumed the previous week.

An examination of the protocols of subjects in the simultaneous choices condition suggests that those who selected three different items had more difficulty than other subjects in making choices for later weeks. Thirty-one percent of those who selected three different items indicated that making choices for the future was difficult and/or that they were uncomfortable with the task, whereas none of the other subjects mentioned the difficulty of the task ($p < .05$). Also, the decision protocols for later weeks were, on the average, longest among subjects who selected three different items (61 words) and shortest among those who selected the same item for all three weeks (20 words) ($p < .05$). These findings are consistent with the notion that selection of variety is used as a simplifying heuristic by consumers who have difficulty determining their most preferred item.

Three Selections for Immediate Consumption. When informed that they would receive all items immediately after the task, most subjects indicated they would select the two or three items they generally most preferred. About half of the subjects mentioned that their selections were influenced by their current state of mind. Nine percent of the 45 subjects indicated that their choices were influenced by concerns about satiation and 24% mentioned considerations related to the complementarity of the selections.

DISCUSSION

Consumers often select several items in a product category for future consumption to eliminate the need to go to the store before each consumption occasion. Generally, one might expect those who make multiple choices for future consumption to select roughly the same items that would have been selected had they gone to the store before each consumption occasion. However, as previously argued, there are two important differences between these buying scenarios. First, the mere fact that multiple decisions are made simultaneously rather than one at a time might influence the selections. Second, when making purchases for multiple consumption occasions, consumers are likely to be more uncertain about preferences at the time of consumption, particularly because of possible changes in states of mind and tastes. From an analysis of the consequences of these differences, consumers who simultaneously purchase for several consumption occasions were posited to select more variety than they would if they made separate purchases in the product category. This proposition is reexamined in light of the findings of the three studies, and alternative explanations for the results are explored. The implications and limitations of the research are discussed and future research directions are suggested.

Consumers' Choice Strategies When Making Multiple Purchases for Future Consumption

Studies 1 and 2 both provide strong support for H_1, suggesting that consumers who make simultaneous purchases for sequential consumption are more likely to select variety than those making purchases sequentially. Study 1 demonstrates that merely increasing the number of decisions made simultaneously leads to more variety seeking. In studies 2 and 3, subjects made separate or simultaneous choices in the snack category, in which prediction of future preferences is often very difficult. Consistent with the notion that uncertainty about future preferences contributes to the tendency to select variety, subjects in study 3 who had greater difficulty deciding which snacks to choose for future periods were more likely to settle on variety. Furthermore, the fact that most subjects in study 3 who made choices for future consumption did not attempt to predict which item they would most prefer in future periods is an additional indicator of the difficulty in making such predictions.

The relationship between uncertainty about future preferences and variety seeking was examined further in another study not reported here (Simonson 1989b). In that study, 151 subjects performed the simultaneous choices for sequential consumption task as in study 2, and when making the choices also indicated their degree of uncertainty about their most preferred item in each period. As would be expected, subjects who selected three different snacks for the three weeks (52% of the subjects) were, on the average, significantly less confident about their most preferred item in later weeks than in the current week. Conversely, subjects who selected the same item for all weeks (20%) were only slightly less confident about their most preferred item in later weeks.

The tendency to choose variety when making multiple choices for future consumption also led to H_2 on differences in the strength of the preference–choice relationship across conditions. The assumption underlying this hypothesis is that consumers have relatively stable overall evaluations of alternatives in familiar categories (e.g., Bass, Pessemier, and Lehmann 1972; Blin and Dodson 1980; Restle 1961), which can be measured by asking respondents to indicate the overall attractiveness and liking of each alternative. As predicted, subjects in the sequential choices condition who made one selection at a time for immediate consumption tended each time to choose their overall most preferred item. In contrast, when multiple selections were made simultaneously for three weeks, preferences were a much weaker predictor of choice and there was a relatively small difference between the choice probabilities of the most preferred item and the choice probabilities of the "runners-up." These subjects tended to select a different preferred item for each week, rather than the same (overall most preferred) item for all weeks. They did so despite the fact that, with a week's separation between consumption occasions, satiation did not influence the utilities of snacks.

Though the results are consistent with H_1 and H_2, a question remains about the mechanisms by which uncertainty about future preferences and making multiple choices simultaneously lead to selection of variety. Some tentative answers to this question are provided by the think-aloud protocols of subjects in study 3. First, almost 40% of the subjects in study 3 who selected different items explicitly expressed a preference for a varied experience. This finding is consistent with those of previous work on people's preference for novelty and change (e.g., Fiske and Maddi 1961) and with the argument that the desire for variety is more likely to influence actual choices when consumers make several choices simultaneously and are uncertain about their future preferences. A second motive for selecting variety when making purchases for multiple consumption periods is to reduce the risk associated with potential changes in tastes. Specifically, selection of variety that includes several of the consumer's top preferences, rather than multiple replicates of the most preferred item, is less risky because it is very unlikely that all of the consumer's top preferences would become less attractive over the consumption period. Coombs (1964), in discussing second choices, referred to such strategy as "covering one's bets." Testing this proposition is difficult because consumers are unlikely to say explicitly that they selected variety to reduce risk. However, the lower likelihood of selecting variety among subjects in the prediction task of study 3, who did not have to make final commitments, is consistent with the notion that selection of variety is related to the risk associated with making terminal choices for future periods.

Finally, selection of variety was suggested to be a useful choice heuristic that saves the time and cognitive effort of identifying the one most preferred alternative (Bettman 1979). Consistent with this proposition, subjects who selected variety were more likely to mention explicitly the difficulty of the decision. Also, reaching a decision took significantly longer for those who chose different items.

Next, two alternative explanations are offered for the finding that consumers who simultaneously chose for sequential consumption were more likely to select variety than those making sequential choices.

Alternative Explanations. Expected utility theory holds that a person chooses consistently the alternative with the highest expected utility. However, variations of expected utility theory known as threshold theory and normal-curve theory (see Restle 1961, Ch. 4, for a review) suggest the possibility of inconsistent choices. For example, normal-curve theory, like the random utility model, posits that the utilities of alternatives, or at least their "momentarily perceived utilities," are subject to random perturbations. If someone is choosing between two alternatives that are very close in utility, one of the utilities usually will be higher than the other, but their positions sometimes will be reversed.

Though these models allow for inconsistent choices over time, they do not lead to clear predictions about the effect of temporally separating decisions on the likelihood of choosing different items. In particular, there is no reason to expect that momentarily perceived utilities of alternatives would vary more when a person is making choices simultaneously, leading to increased likelihood of selecting variety. In fact, one could argue that when choices are separated temporally there is a higher probability that decisions would be made under different states of mind or tastes – that is, alternatives would have different perceived utilities on different choice occasions. This proposition could lead to the prediction that consumers who make separate choices would be *more* likely than those making simultaneous choices to select variety. In any case, expected utility theory cannot account for the research results.

Another alternative explanation, suggested by Kahneman and Snell (in press), focuses on consumers' possible errors in making choices for future consumption. Specifically, Kahneman and Snell suggest that people have a tendency to collapse the time dimension when evaluating temporally extended outcomes. Thus, when making choices for three weeks, consumers evaluate their preferences as though the time difference between consumption occasions were much shorter than a week. If that were the case, subjects might have expected that they still would be satiated with one item when they receive their next selection. This expectation could explain why the choice patterns of these subjects, including the tendency to select complements rather than substitutes, were similar to those of subjects who expected to receive all items immediately.

The think-aloud protocols of subjects in study 3 who made selections for three weeks can be used to examine the validity of this alternative explanation. None of the subjects mentioned satiation as a reason for selecting different items. Moreover, a few of the subjects explicitly said that, with a separation of a week, one choice would be unlikely to influence the liking for that item in the following week. Indeed, one of the reasons for selecting snacks as the stimuli was the fact that most students have extensive consumption experience in that category. Their experience should enable them to estimate rather accurately the duration of satiation with a snack after consumption. As the choice behavior of subjects in the sequential choices condition indicates, satiation with snacks lasts less than a week. Hence, this alternative explanation cannot account for the results.

Theoretical Implications

The research findings have implications for several important aspects of consumer behavior, including variety-seeking behavior, attitude-behavior relationships, and consumer choice strategies in making multiple selections from a choice set.

Variety Seeking as a Choice Heuristic. McAlister and Pessemier (1982) review the causes of variety-seeking behavior by consumers. The research reported here suggests an additional motive for choosing variety, not previously explored in the literature. Specifically, selection of variety might be used by consumers as a choice heuristic to simplify purchase decisions. Such a heuristic is more likely to be employed if multiple purchases are made simultaneously, particularly in situations in which consumers are uncertain of the alternatives they most prefer.

Preferences–Choice Relationship. The relationships between overall preferences for alternatives and choice and the more general issue of attitude-behavior correspondence are among the most studied topics by both psychologists (e.g., Ajzen and Fishbein 1977) and consumer researchers (e.g., Bass, Pessemier, and Lehmann 1972). The frequently observed disagreement between preferences and choice has led some researchers to suggest that behavior is fundamentally stochastic (e.g., Bass 1974; Blin and Dodson 1980), whereas others have proposed a situational explanation for this lack of agreement (e.g., Belk 1975).

Consistent with the latter proposition, the findings suggest that one task factor moderating the preference–choice relationship is the number of choices made at one time. Specifically, if consumers make multiple choices that will be consumed over time, preferences are a rather weak predictor of choice even when satiation does not influence the utilities of alternatives (McAlister 1982). However, if consumers make separate choices before each consumption occasion, preferences are a much stronger predictor of choice. This observation is consistent with Ajzen and Fishbein's (1977) argument that stronger attitude-behavior relations are obtained under high correspondence between the two components in terms of their target, action, context, and time elements.

Consumers' Multiple Choice Strategies. Much of the work on consumers' choice strategies has pertained to selections of a single alternative from a choice set (Bettman 1979). However, consumers often choose several alternatives in a category simultaneously. A relevant question is whether the decision rules employed in making a single choice are also used in making multiple choices. The findings reported here suggest that strategies used for selecting a single alternative are modified when the consumer is making multiple selections from a choice set. In particular, consumers appear to take advantage of the additional "degrees of freedom" available to them when making multiple decisions simultaneously. For example, a common strategy observed in the research was based on an initial elimination stage, followed by selection of all of the non-eliminated alternatives. This approach is similar to a phased decision strategy often used in making a single choice (Bettman and Park 1980). However, when multiple choices are made simultaneously, a consumer can avoid the more difficult second phase of identifying which of the remaining options is most preferred. In addition to simplifying decisions, making multiple choices simultaneously enables consumers to implement, rather easily, global strategies for the different selections (e.g., choosing different preferred items to have a varied experience).

Marketing Consequences

The finding that consumers who make multiple purchases simultaneously are more likely to select different items than consumers making sequential purchases might have significant implications for marketers. A discussion of some of the marketing consequences follows.

Number of Items Purchased on a Typical Shopping Trip as a Determinant of Market Share Distribution. The findings indicate that consumers who purchase one item in a category at a time tend each time to select their overall most preferred item. Conversely, consumers who simultaneously purchase several items in a category often select a variety of preferred items. These findings suggest that whether consumers in a particular category tend to purchase one item for one period or several items for several periods influences the relative market shares of competing alternatives. Specifically, a tendency to buy just one item each time would favor the alternative that is the first preference of many consumers. Conversely, a tendency to purchase a number of items simultaneously would increase the relative shares of alternatives that are in the consideration sets but are not the first preference of many consumers. As an example, among the snacks offered in study 2, in all three conditions Snickers and Hershey bar with almonds received the highest preference rating more often than the other items. As would be predicted, the market shares of Snickers and Hershey bar were between 5 and 13% higher and the shares of the four other snacks were lower in the sequential choices condition than in the two other conditions in which multiple selections were made simultaneously.

Hence, manufacturers of products that are in the consideration set of many consumers but the first preference of a few might try to encourage consumers to expand their planning horizon and buy each time for several periods. In contrast, manufacturers of items that are the first preferences of many consumers might try to discourage selection of variety by consumers who make multiple choices simultaneously. Though manufacturers generally have only limited influence on consumers' planning horizon, the promotional schemes they employ might take that aspect in consideration. For example, if in a certain product category consumers often make purchases for several consumption periods in one shopping trip, the manufacturer of the leading brand might promote primarily the larger sizes, whereas manufacturers of second preferences might emphasize the smaller sizes.

Bundling of Items for Future Consumption. Marketers commonly offer bundles of goods, such as a package with different soaps or variety packs of different yogurt flavors. The findings suggest that preference for such bundles might reflect not only preference for a varied experience, but also situations in which consumers are uncertain which item(s) they would prefer on specific consumption occasions. The implication is that bundles of items would be more popular in product categories in which consumers are less confident about what their preferences will be at the time of consumption (i.e., categories characterized by frequent changes in states of mind or tastes). For example, in the soft drinks category, there appears to be a large segment of consumers who are uncertain when making a purchase whether they would prefer a cola or a lemon–lime carbonated drink on particular consumption occasions. The findings suggest that this segment of consumers might find a purchase of a sixpack including both cola and lemon-lime cans more appealing and an easier decision than a purchase of a sixpack with just one of the two flavors.

Using First Preference versus Top Preferences in Conjoint Measurement. In most applications of conjoint analysis, a main objective is to see what share of choices would be generated by each of several product/service profiles if they were competing with each other in the marketplace (Green and Srinivasan 1978). In estimating the share of choices, the researcher usually assumes each consumer will select that item offering him or her the highest utility. Alternatively, the researcher might also assign certain choice probabilities to profiles that do not have the highest utility. The research findings suggest that one of the factors influencing whether one should consider the runners-up in conjoint analysis is the number of selections typically made in the category on each purchase occasion. If consumers often choose more than one item at one time, an alternative that is the second choice of many consumers could have a significant market share. Hence, in such categories, share estimates can be made more accurate by assigning positive choice probabilities to the highest ranked profiles, including those that do not offer the highest overall utility.

Limitations and Future Research

The research has three limitations that suggest directions for future work. First, despite an effort to make the procedure unobtrusive and the choices as realistic as possible, the decisions were made in a class environment. Though the hypotheses probably could not be tested adequately in a much less controlled environment, one could supplement the experimental data by examining secondary data that might provide further relevant evidence. For example, scanner data might be used to examine whether consumers are more likely to seek variety when making multiple purchases simultaneously in a category than when making choices sequentially. Because of the many factors that influence actual purchases, using scanner data for that purpose would require selection of appropriate measures, product categories, and household types.

Second, consumers' observed tendency to select variety when making multiple purchases in a category is not expected to hold in all purchase situations and product categories. Specifically, if consumers have strong and stable preferences, or if they perceive only one acceptable item (e.g., a specific type of car engine oil), they will tend to purchase the same item for all periods. Similarly, the tendency to select variety is less likely in categories in which disutility is associated with switching among alternatives over time (e.g., certain types of insurance plans). Furthermore, the extent to which making multiple purchases simultaneously leads to more variety seeking may depend on how broadly the category under consideration is defined and whether the focus is on different brands of a specific product variant or different variants within a broader category. For example, the results of study 2 might have been different if only sweet snacks had been available. Future research should examine further the conditions moderating the effect of purchase quantity and timing on variety seeking.

Third, the subjects were assigned to choice conditions and were not free to decide on the number of items they selected at one time. Though this situation is similar to real-life situations in which time and other constraints affect the number of items purchased, consumers typically have more flexibility in deciding on the number of items they buy. For example, consumers could choose smaller package sizes or limit the number of items they purchase in a category if they are uncertain about their future preferences. Future research might examine the effect of uncertainty about future preferences on the quantity purchased and inventory held by consumers in different product categories. Finally, the findings suggest that in making multiple purchases for future consumption, consumers' decision strategies are not mere extensions of those used in selecting a single item. Much more research is needed to improve our understanding of the impact of temporal separation between purchase and consumption and of making multiple decisions simultaneously on consumers' purchase behavior.

APPENDIX

SUMMARY OF STUDY 2 INSTRUCTIONS BY CONDITION

Sequential Choices Condition
At the end of the class today we will be giving away to students snacks of their choice. Each student can select one item of those listed. Please mark with an X the item you wish to get. First, please enter your name so that we will know which item you should receive at the end of the class (your choice will remain totally confidential).

Simultaneous Choices for Sequential Consumption Condition
At the end of the class today, the class a week from today, and the class two weeks from today, we will be giving away to students one snack of their choice of those listed below. There is sufficient supply of all snacks. Each choice can be any one of the six items and you may select the same item more than once. Please mark with an X the item you wish to get today, the item you wish to get next week, and the item you want in two weeks. First, please enter your name.... [The choice for each week was marked on a separate column.]

Simultaneous Choices for Immediate Consumption Condition
At the end of the class today we will be giving away to students three snacks of their choice of those listed below. There is sufficient supply of all snacks. Each choice can be any one of the six items and you may select the same item more than once. Please mark your three choices below. First, please enter your name....

42. New Challenges to the Rationality Assumption

Daniel Kahneman

ABSTRACT. In contrast to logical criteria of rationality, which can be assessed entirely by reference to the system of preferences, substantive criteria of rational choice refer to an independent evaluation of the outcomes of decisions. One of these substantive criteria is the experienced hedonic utility of outcomes. Research indicates that people are myopic in their decisions, may lack skill in predicting their future tastes, and can be led to erroneous choices by fallible memory and incorrect evaluation of past experiences. Theoretical and practical implications of these challenges to the assumption of economic rationality are discussed. (JEL: A 00)

1. INTRODUCTION

The assumption that agents are rational is central to much theory in the social sciences. Its role is particularly obvious in economic analysis, where it supports the useful corollary that no significant opportunity will remain unexploited. In the domain of social policy, the rationality assumption supports the position that it is unnecessary to protect people against the consequences of their choices. The status of this assumption is therefore a matter of considerable interest. This article will argue for an enriched definition of rationality that considers the actual outcomes of decisions, and will present evidence that challenges the rationality assumption in new ways.

The criteria for using the terms "rational" or "irrational" in non-technical discourse are *substantive*: one asks whether beliefs are grossly out of kilter with available evidence, and whether decisions serve or damage the agent's interests.

Presented at the 11th International Seminar on the New Institutional Economics, Wallerfangen/ Saar, Germany, June 1993, and at the IEA Conference on Rationality and Economics, Turin, Italy, October, 1993. A different version was presented at a Political and Economic Analysis Workshop in Honor of P. Zusman, in Rehovot, Israel, June 1993. The research leading to this paper was supported by grants from Sloan Foundation, the McArthur Foundation and the National Science Foundation. I am greatly endebted to Amos Tversky for many discussions of the issue of rationality over the years, and for insightful comments on drafts of this paper. He should not be assumed to agree with all I say. Alan Schwartz provided helpful editorial assistance.

Originally published in the *Journal of Institutional and Theoretical Economics*, 150:1, 18–36,

In sharp contrast, technical discussions of rationality generally adopt a *logical* conception, in which an individual's beliefs and preferences are said to be rational if they obey a set of formal rules such as complementarity of probabilities, the sure thing principle or independence of irrelevant alternatives. In the laissez-faire spirit of modern economics and decision theory, the content of beliefs and of preferences is not a criterion of rationality – only internal coherence matters (Sen [1993]). The methodology of the debate reflects this concern for consistency: in the classic paradoxes of Allais and Ellsberg, for example, two intuitively compelling preferences are shown to be jointly incompatible with the axioms of expected utility theory, though each preference is unobjectionable on its own. Irrational preferences are diagnosed without having to observe anything that is not a preference.

Some authors have been dissatisfied with the exclusive focus on consistency as a criterion of rationality. Thus, Sen [1990, 210] has written: "Rationality may be seen as demanding something other than just consistency of choices from different subsets. It must, at least, demand cogent relations between aims and objectives actually entertained by the person and the choices that the person makes. This problem is not eliminated by the terminological procedure of describing the cardinal representation of choices as the "utility" of the person, since this does not give any independent evidence on what the person is aiming to do or trying to achieve." This article will ask whether there exists a cogent relation between a person's choices and the hedonic consequences of these choices.

In spite of occasional attempts to broaden the scope of the rationality debate in decision theory, the patterns of preference discovered by Allais and Ellsberg have been at the center of this debate for several decades. It is often implied that if these paradoxes can be resolved, then economic analysis can safely continue to assume that agents are rational. The focus on paradoxes has indirectly strengthened the rationality dogma: if subtle inconsistencies are the worst indictment of human rationality, there is indeed little to worry about. Furthermore, the preferences that Allais and Ellsberg described do not appear foolish or unreasonable, and lay people as well as many theorists believe they can be defended (Slovic and Tversky [1974]). Indeed, the ambiguous normative status of the Allais and Ellsberg patterns has inspired many attempts to reconcile observed preferences with rationality by adopting a more permissive definition of rational choice (Tversky and Kahneman [1986]).

More recent challenges to the rationality assumption do not lend themselves to such attempts at reconciliation. Numerous experiments illustrate beliefs and preferences that violate a fundamental requirement variously labeled extensionality (Arrow [1982]), consequentialism (Hammond [1985]) or invariance (Tversky and Kahneman [1986]). The same choice problem may evoke different preferences, depending on inconsequential variations in the formulation of options (Tversky and Kahneman [1986]) or in the procedure used to elicit choices (Tversky, Slovic and Kahneman [1990]). The main method of this research still involves the documentation of pairs of preferences, each acceptable on its own, which jointly violate an axiom of invariance. These inconsistencies are more difficult to rationalize than the classic paradoxes because invariance is a more compelling axiom of rational choice than cancellation or independence (Tversky and Kahneman [1986]). Some examples of this research will be presented below.

The present treatment attempts to supplement the logical analysis of preferences by introducing substantive criteria of rationality. Unlike the logical analysis, a substantive criterion is external to the system of preferences. It requires some way of assessing outcomes as they occur, not only as they are conceived at the time of decision. The substantive question on which we focus here is whether choices maximize the (expected) utility of their consequences, as these consequences will actually be experienced. Accurate prediction of future tastes and accurate evaluation of past experiences emerge as critical elements of an individual's ability to maximize the experienced quality of his outcomes. Demonstrated deficiencies in the ability to predict future experiences and to learn from the past emerge as new challenges to the assumption of rationality. More provocatively, the observed deficiencies suggest the outline of a case in favor of some paternalistic interventions, when it is plausible that the state knows more about an individual's future tastes than the individual knows presently. The basis of these developments is an analysis of the concept of utility, which is introduced in the next section.

2. MULTIPLE NOTIONS OF UTILITY

The term "utility" can be anchored either in the hedonic experience of outcomes, or in the preference or desire for that outcome. In Jeremy Bentham's usage, the utility of an object was ultimately defined in hedonic terms, by the pleasure that it produces. Others have interpreted utility as "wantability" (Fisher [1918]). Of course, the two definitions have the same extension if people generally want that which they will eventually enjoy – a common assumption in discussions of utility. Economic analysis is more congenial to wants and preferences than to hedonic experiences, and the current meaning of utility in economics and decision research is a positivistic version of wantability: utility is a theoretical construct inferred from observed choices. This definition has been thoroughly cleansed of any association with hedonistic psychology and of any reference to subjective states.

The present analysis starts with two observations. The first is that the methodological strictures against a hedonic notion of utility are a relic of an earlier period in which a behavioristic philosophy of science held sway. Subjective states are now a legitimate topic of study, and hedonic experiences such as pleasure, pain, satisfaction or discomfort are considered open to useful forms of measurement. The second observation is that it may be rash to assume as a general rule that people will later enjoy what they want now. The relation between preferences and hedonic consequences is better studied than postulated.

These considerations suggest an explicit distinction between two notions of utility. The *experienced utility* of an outcome is the measure of the hedonic experience of that outcome. This is similar to Bentham's awkward use; the first footnote of his book was properly apologetic about the poor fit of the word "utility" to pleasure and pain, but he found no better alternative. The *decision utility* of an outcome, as in modern usage, is the weight assigned to that outcome in a decision.

The distinction between experienced utility and decision utility opens new avenues for the study of rationality. In addition to the syntactic criterion of consistency, we can now hope to develop a substantive/hedonic criterion for the rationality of a decision: does it maximize the expectation of experienced utility? Of course, this criterion is not exhaustive, and its adoption implies no commitment to a hedonistic philosophy. As Sen has often pointed out (e.g., Sen [1987]), the maximization of (experienced) utility is not always "what people are trying to achieve." It is surely the case, however, that people sometimes do try to maximize pleasure and minimize pain, and it may be instructive to drop the assumption that they perform this optimization task flawlessly.

Errors in the assignment of decision utility to anticipated outcomes can arise from inaccurate forecasting of future hedonic experience. Correct prediction of future tastes is therefore one of the requirements of rational decision making (March [1978]). Kahneman and Snell [1990] defined the *predicted utility* of an outcome as the individual's beliefs about its experienced utility at some future time. Two sets of empirical questions arise: (i) How much do people know about their future tastes? Is it likely that an objective observer (or a government) could make more accurate predictions than individuals would make on their own behalf? (ii) Do people adequately consider the uncertainty of their future tastes in making decisions? Are decision utilities adequately informed by reasoned beliefs about experienced utility?

Additional issues arise because of possible disparities between memory and actual hedonic experience. Outcomes are commonly extended over time, and global evaluations of such outcomes are necessarily retrospective – and therefore subject to errors. Examples of substantial discrepancies between *retrospective utility* and *real-time utility* are discussed below.

The restoration of Bentham's notion of utility as an object of study evidently sets a large agenda for theoretical and empirical investigation. The following sections summarize highlights of what has been learned in early explorations of this agenda. Decision utility, predicted utility, and the relations between real-time and retrospective utility are discussed in turn. The final section reviews possible implications of the findings for the rationality debate.

3. SOME CHARACTERISTICS OF DECISION UTILITY

Decision utility has long been a topic of study, and much is known about it. The following discussion selectively addresses three research conclusions that are of particular relevance to the issue of rationality, as it is construed in this paper.

(i) *Carriers of utility.* The main carriers of decision utility are events, not states; in particular, utility is assigned to gains or losses relative to a reference point which is often the status quo (Kahneman and Tversky [1979]).

(ii) *Loss aversion.* Losses loom larger than corresponding gains (Kahneman and Tversky [1979]; Tversky and Kahneman [1991]).

(iii) *Framing effects.* The same objective outcomes can be evaluated as gains or as losses, depending on the framing of the reference state (Tversky and Kahneman [1986]).

An early observation that illustrates points (i) and (iii) above was labeled the isolation effect (Tversky and Kahneman [1986]).

Problem 1: Assume yourself richer by $300 than you are today. You have to choose between
a sure gain of $100
50% chance to gain $200 and 50% chance to gain nothing

Problem 2: Assume yourself richer by $500 than you are today. You have to choose between
a sure loss of $100
50% chance to lose nothing and 50% chance to lose $200.

It is easily seen that the two problems are extensionally equivalent in terms of wealth: both offer a choice between a state in which wealth is increased by $400 and a gamble with equal chances to increase current wealth by $300 or by $500. If people spontaneously evaluate options in these terms they will choose the same option in the two problems – but observed preferences favor the sure thing in Problem 1 and the gamble in Problem 2. Because the equivalence of the two problems is intuitively compelling when it is pointed out, the difference between the responses they elicit is a framing effect: an inconsequential feature of the formulation strongly affects preferences. Most important in the present context, the experiment demonstrates that people are content to assign utilities to outcomes stated as gains and losses, contrary to the standard assumption that the carriers of utility are states of wealth.

Figure 42.1 exhibits loss aversion in a schematic value function: the function is steeper in the domain of losses than in the domain of gains. The ratio of the slopes in the two domains, called the loss aversion coefficient, has been estimated as about 2:1 in several experiments involving both risky and riskless

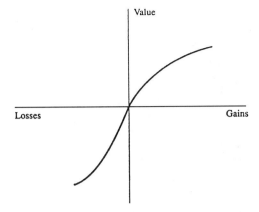

Figure 42.1. A typical value function.

options (Tversky and Kahneman [1991], [1992]). Figure 42.2 (from Kahneman, Knetsch and Thaler [1991]) illustrates the role of a reference point in the evaluation of a transaction. The choice illustrated in this figure is between a state (Point A) with more of Good Y and a state (Point D) with more of Good X. The hypotheses about the carriers of utility and about framing effects entail that the preference between A and D could differ depending on the current reference point – contrary to a substantial body of economic theory. Consider the choice between A and D from C. This is a positive choice between two gains, in Good X or in Good Y. If the reference is A, however, the two options are framed quite differently. One possibility is to retain the status quo by staying at A. The alternative is to accept a trade that involves the conjunction of a loss in Good Y and a gain in Good X. The C–A interval is evaluated as a gain in the first frame (from C), but the same interval is evaluated as a loss from A. Because of loss aversion, the impact of the C–A difference is expected to be greater in the latter

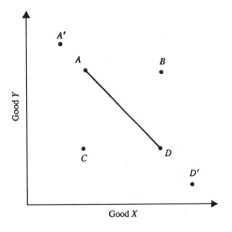

Figure 42.2. Multiple reference points for the choice between A and D.

case than in the former. We therefore predict a systematic difference between the preferences in the two frames: if people are indifferent between A and D from C, they should strictly prefer A over D from A (Tversky and Kahneman [1991]).

The predicted result, known as the endowment effect (Thaler [1980]), has been confirmed in several laboratories. Subjects in one condition of an experiment by Kahneman, Knetsch and Thaler [1990] were offered a choice between a decorated mug (worth about $6 at the University bookstore) and a sum of money; they answered a series of questions to determine the amount of money at which they were indifferent between the two options. Other subjects were first given a mug; they answered similar questions to indicate the amount of money for which they would just agree to exchange it. The subjects had no strategic incentive to conceal their true values. A critical feature of the study is that the choosers in the first group and the mug owners in the second group faced objectively identical options: they could leave the experimental situation owning a new mug, or with extra money in their pocket. The analysis of Figure 42.2 applies, however. If the mug is Good Y, the C–A interval (the difference between having a mug and not having one) is evaluated as a gain by the choosers, and as a loss by the mug owners. As predicted, the average cash value of a mug was much larger for the owners ($7.12 in one experiment) than for choosers ($3.50). A significant (but somewhat smaller) difference between owners and choosers was observed in a replication by Franciosi, Kujal, Mischelitsch and Smith [1993].

Implications of the endowment effect for various aspects of economic and legal theory have been discussed extensively elsewhere (Ellickson [1989]; Hovenkamp [1991]; Hardie, Johnson and Fader [1993]; Kahneman, Knetsch and Thaler [1991]). The effect is relevant to the present treatment because it implies that decision utilities may be extremely myopic. The subjects in the mugs experiment made a decision that was to have consequences over the relatively long term: a coffee mug is an object that one may use daily, sometimes for years. The long-term states between which the subjects had to choose – "own this mug" or "not own this mug" – were the same for all subjects. The large difference between the preferences of owners and choosers indicates that these enduring states were not the main object of evaluation. The effective carriers of utility were the transitions that distinguished the experimental treatments: "receive a mug" or "give up your mug." In this experiment, and perhaps in many other situations, people who make decisions about a long-term state appear to use their evaluation of the transition to that state as a proxy.

The results of the mugs experiment present two overlapping challenges to the assumption of rationality. The logical notion of rationality is violated by the inconsistent preferences observed in different representations of the choice between a mug and money. A substantive condition of rationality is violated if the endowment effect is viewed as a costly manifestation of extreme myopia. An agent who routinely uses transient emotions as a proxy for the utility of long-term states is manifestly handicapped in the achievement of good outcomes.

4. PREDICTED UTILITY: DO PEOPLE KNOW WHAT THEY WILL LIKE?

Although the constancy of underlying tastes is a matter of theoretical debate, the following proposition will not be controversial: the hedonic experience associated with a particular stimulus or with a particular act of consumption is susceptible to large changes over time and over varying circumstances. Some cyclical changes of experienced utility are regular and readily predictable: ingesting the same food may evoke delight in a state of hunger, disgust in satiation. At the other extreme, radical changes of circumstances produce adaptations and changes of experienced utility that violate common expectations. A well-known psychological study showed that most paraplegics adapt far better than most people would predict, and that lottery winners are generally less happy in the long run than the common fascination with lotteries might suggest (Brickman, Coates and Janoff-Bulman [1978]).

Many decisions explicitly or implicitly involve predictions of future consumption and of future utility (March [1978]). An encyclopaedia may not be worth buying if one will not use it, the premium paid for a house with a view may be wasted if the view ceases giving pleasure after a time, and a medical procedure that improves survival chances should perhaps be rejected by a patient who is likely to find life without vocal cords intolerable.

How accurately do people predict their future utility? Most of the evidence about this question is indirect. Thus, it is suggestive that some important results of hedonic research are generally considered counter-intuitive (Kahneman and Snell [1990]). The surprises include the striking increase of liking by mere exposure to initially neutral stimuli, and some effects of dissonance on tastes. A study of people's intuitions about possible ways to induce a child to like or to dislike a food showed a similar lack of collective wisdom about the dynamics of taste. Dynamic inconsistency may be another manifestation of inaccurate hedonic prediction. For example, Christensen-Szalanski [1984] documented the incidence of cases in which women in labor reversed a long-standing preference for delivery without anaesthetics. The reversals could be due to improper discounting of the pain in the initial preferences; they could also reflect an error in the initial prediction of the intensity of labor pains.

Loewenstein and Adler [1993] observed a remarkable result in a study of the endowment effect. They showed subjects a mug engraved with a decorative logo, and asked some of these subjects to "... imagine that we gave you a mug exactly like the one you can see, and that we gave you the opportunity to keep it or trade it for some money." The subjects then filled out a form indicating their preferences for a range of stated prices, following the procedure of Kahneman, Knetsch and Thaler [1990]. The mean predicted selling price was $3.73. Next, all subjects were given a mug and a second form, which actually provided an opportunity to exchange the mug for cash. The mean selling price for the subjects who had made a prediction a few minutes earlier was $4.89, significantly higher than the predicted value, and only moderately lower than the selling price of $5.62 stated by subjects who had not made a prediction. The subjects in this experiment were apparently unable to anticipate that possession of the mug would induce a reluctance to give it up.

Simonson [1990] reported a result that illustrates a failure of hedonic prediction – or perhaps a failure to make such a prediction. Simonson gave students an opportunity to select from a choice set of snacks at the beginning of a class meeting; they received their selections at the end of the class. Subjects in one experimental condition made one choice each week for three weeks. In another condition subjects made choices for all three weeks at the first session. The choices made by the two groups were strikingly different. Subjects who chose a snack on three separate occasions tended to choose the same snack or a closely similar one every time. In contrast, subjects who chose in advance for three weeks tended to pick different items for the different occasions. It is reasonable to view these variety-seeking choices as erroneous: the subjects apparently failed to realize that their current preferences would be restored after a one-week interval. A further study clarified the nature of the error. Anticipatory choices were less variable when subjects were asked, before indicating a decision, to predict the preferences they would actually have on the subsequent occasions of testing. This finding suggests that the subjects were in fact able to predict their future preferences accurately. In the absence of a special instruction, however, they did not take the trouble to generate a prediction of their future taste before making a decision about future consumption.

Kahneman and Snell [1992] reported an exploratory study of the accuracy of hedonic prediction. They examined predictions of future liking for a food item or a musical piece, under conditions that made a change of attitude likely. In an initial experiment the subjects consumed a helping of their favorite ice cream while listening to a particular piece of music, at the same hour on eight consecutive working days under identical physical conditions. Immediately after each episode they rated how much they had liked the ice cream and the music. At the end of the first session they predicted the ratings they would make on the following day, and on the final day of the experiment. This experiment was intended to test the accuracy of hedonic predictions under relatively favorable conditions. We reasoned that student subjects have not only had much experience consuming ice cream and listening to music; they have had experience with repeated consumption of these items, and could therefore be expected to anticipate the effect of frequent repetition on their tastes. Other experiments in the series used a stimulus that is less familiar and less popular than ice cream in the student population – plain low-fat yogurt.

The accuracy of hedonic predictions was generally quite poor. A comparison of the average of predictions to the average of the actual ratings revealed some shared failures to anticipate common trends in the hedonic responses. For example, most subjects predicted, after tasting one spoonful of plain low-fat yogurt, that they would assign the same rating to a 6 oz helping on the next day. In fact, the larger helping was a much worse experience. Most subjects also failed to anticipate the considerable improvement in the attitude to plain yogurt which occurred (for most of them) with further exposure to that substance. There apparently exists a lay theory of hedonic changes, of mediocre accuracy, which most of our subjects accepted. Another analysis was concerned with individual differences in predictions and in actual hedonic changes. There was substantial variability in both measures, but the correlation between them was consistently close to zero. The data provided no indication that individuals were able to predict the development of their tastes more accurately than they could predict the hedonic changes of a randomly selected stranger.

·   The results of these studies suggest two conclusions. (i) People may have little ability to forecast changes in their hedonic responses to stimuli (Kahneman and Snell [1992]; Loewenstein and Adler [1993]). (ii) Even in situations that permit accurate hedonic predictions, people may tend to make decisions about future consumption without due consideration of possible changes in their tastes (Simonson [1990]). If supported by further research, these hypotheses about the accuracy of predicted utility and about its impact on decision utility would present a significant substantive challenge to the assumption of rationality.

The properties of predicted utility have implication for other domains. Consider the issue of informed consent to an operation that will change the patient's life in some significant way. The normal procedure for consent emphasizes the provision of objective information about the effects of surgery. However, truly informed consent is only possible if patients have a reasonable conception of expected long-term developments in their hedonic responses, and if they assign appropriate weight to these expectations in the decision. A more controversial issue arises if we admit that an outsider can sometimes predict an individual's future utility far better than the individual can. Does this superior knowledge carry a warrant, or even a duty, for paternalistic intervention? It appears right for Ulysses' sailors to tie him to the mast against his will, if they believe that he is deluded about his ability to resist the fatal call of the sirens.

5. REAL-TIME AND RETROSPECTIVE UTILITY – DO PEOPLE KNOW WHAT THEY HAVE LIKED?

Retrospective evaluations of the experienced utility of past episodes are undoubtedly the most important source of predictions of the hedonic quality of future outcomes. The experiences of life leave their traces in a rich store of evaluative memories, which is consulted, apparently automatically, whenever a significant object or experience is brought to mind (Zajonc [1980]). The system of affective and evaluative memories may be independent of any ability to recall the incidents that produced an attitude. Thus, people often recognize that they like or dislike a person they have met before, without knowing why. Evaluative memories are immensely important because they contain the individual's accumulated knowledge of stimuli that are to be approached and of others that are to be avoided. Indeed, the only form of utility that people could possibly learn to maximize is the anticipated utility of future memories. Every individual has the lifelong habit of trusting memories of past episodes to guide choices among future outcomes. As we shall see, however, trusted evaluative memories are sometimes deceptive.

Although retrospective evaluations and affective memories define what is learned from the past, they are not the ultimate criterion of experienced utility. Hedonic or affective quality is an attribute of each moment of experience; the sign and intensity of the experience may vary considerably even over the course of a brief episode, such as drinking a glass of wine. The retrospective evaluation of an extended episode necessarily involves two operations: the recollection of the momentary experiences that constituted the episode, and an operation that combines the affect of these moments into a global evaluation. Because both operations are fallible, retrospective evaluations should be viewed with greater distrust than introspective reports of current experience. The effects of defective memory are sometimes painfully obvious: people who care for an elderly parent often observe that they accept their parent's immediate responses to the current situation with normal respect, even as they dismiss most retrospective evaluations as unreliable. The difficulties that arise in summarizing an episode by a global evaluation are more subtle, but no less significant.

There are strong normative intuitions about the correct way to combine the utilities of a continuous series of experiences into a global evaluation. A principle of *temporal integration* has considerable appeal: the utility of an episode extended over time is the integral of momentary hedonic value over the duration of the episode. The justification for temporal integration is the assumption that successive selves should be treated equally, an assumption so compelling that a general case for utilitarianism has been built on it (Parfit [1984]). Even more appealing than temporal integration is the principle of *temporal monotonicity*. Consider two episodes that are preceded and followed by a steady state of hedonic neutrality. Assume that the second episode is obtained by adding an unanticipated period of pain (or pleasure) to the first, prior to the return to the neutral state. The monotonicity principle asserts that the hedonic quality of the added period determines whether the longer episode has higher or lower global utility than the shorter. In other words, adding pain at the end of an episode must make it worse; adding pleasure must make it better.[1]

Several recent studies indicate that retrospective evaluations obey neither temporal integration nor temporal monotonicity. The studies conducted so far

---

[1] The temporal monotonicity principle does not apply if the addition of pain or pleasure to the episode alters hedonic after-effects, such as relief, after-glow, or the affect associated with subsequent recollection. More generally, the analysis of experienced utility becomes difficult to apply where the consumption of memories plays an important role (Elster and Loewenstein [1992]).

have dealt with episodes that were brief and uniform, both in content and in the sign of the hedonic experience, either non-negative or non-positive throughout. Several experiments involved controlled exposure to affect-inducing stimuli (films of pleasant or unpleasant content; loud unpleasant sounds; immersion of a hand in painfully cold water). Subjects used an "affect meter" to provide a continuous record of their momentary hedonic response during some of these episodes. Later they also provided retrospective global evaluations of the "overall discomfort" or "overall pleasure" of the episodes, and in some cases chose an episode to which they would be exposed again. In one non-experimental study (Redelmeier and Kahneman [1996]) patients undergoing a colonoscopy for medical reasons provided reports of pain every 60 seconds, as well as subsequent global evaluations and measures of preference for the entire episode.

The results of these studies support two empirical generalizations. (1) *"The Peak & End Rule"*: global evaluations are predicted with high accuracy by a weighted combination of the most extreme affect recorded during the episode and of the affect recorded during the terminal moments of the episode. Here again, as in the context of decision utility, the evaluation of particular moments appears to be used as a proxy for the evaluation of a more extended period of time. (2) *Duration Neglect*. The retrospective evaluation of overall or total pain (or pleasure) is not independently affected by the duration of the episode. In the colonoscopy study, for example, the duration of the procedure varied from 4 to 69 minutes in a sample of 101 patients. Surprisingly, these variations of duration had no significant effect on retrospective evaluations. The ratings of both patients and attending physicians were dominated by the intensity of pain at its worst, and by the intensity of discomfort during the last few minutes of the procedure. Duration neglect is not immutable, of course: people can judge the duration of episodes with fair accuracy and will treat this attribute as relevant when their attention is explicitly drawn to it (Varey and Kahneman [1992]). In general, however, affective peaks and endings are more salient than duration in the cognitive representation of events.

Figure 42.3 is taken from a study that examined violations of the rule of temporal monotonicity in a choice between painful episodes (Kahneman et al. [1993]). Paid volunteers expected to undergo three experiences of moderate physical pain during an experimental session. In fact they only had two trials. In the Short trial the subject held one hand in water at 14°C for 60 seconds, then immediately dried his hand with a towel. In the Long trial, the subject held the other hand in water for a total of 90 seconds. During the first 60 seconds of the Long trial the temperature of the water was 14°C, just as in the Short trial; during the extra 30 seconds the temperature of the water was gradually raised to 15°C, still unpleasant but for most subjects a clear improvement over the initial state. The order of the two trials was varied for different subjects. A few minutes after the second trial, the subjects were reminded that they were due to have another trial and were asked which of the two preceding experiences they chose to repeat.

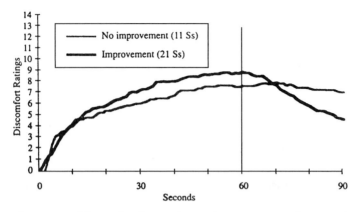

Figure 42.3. Mean of real-time discomfort measure on Long trial for 11 subjects who indicated little or no decrement of discomfort when temperature changed (thin line), and for 21 subjects who indicated decreased discomfort (thick line).

The curves shown in Figure 42.3 present average momentary ratings of discomfort for the Long trial, separately for two groups of subjects who showed different patterns of response: the majority who indicated decreasing discomfort as the temperature of the water was raised, and a minority who reported little change of discomfort. The choices of which trial to repeat were markedly different in these two groups: 17 of the 21 subjects whose discomfort diminished preferred to repeat the Long trial, in violation of temporal monotonicity; only 5 of the 11 subjects whose discomfort did not change preferred the Long trial. The results of both groups conform to the Peak & End rule and exhibit duration neglect. For the minority whose pain did not diminish, the peak and the end of the pain were at the same level (see Figure 42.3), and were the same in the Short and in the Long trials. The Peak & End rule predicts that these subjects should evaluate the two trials alike, a prediction that is confirmed by the nearly even split of preferences. For the larger group of subjects whose pain diminished at the end of the Long trial, the Peak & End rule predicts that this trial should be less aversive than the Short one, and the choice data again confirm the prediction. Overall, about 2/3 of subjects violate dominance in this situation, a robust result that has been replicated with numerous subjects under slightly different conditions.

Additional analyses clarify the mechanism that produces these violations of temporal monotonicity: most subjects erroneously believed that the coldest temperature to which they had been exposed was not the same in the two trials: their memory of the worst moment of the Long trial was mitigated by the subsequent improvement. Our evidence suggests that episodes are evaluated by a few "snapshots" rather than by a continuous film-like representation (Fredrickson and Kahneman [1993]). The snapshots are in fact montages, which may blend impressions of different parts of the experience. The overall experience is judged by a weighted average of the utility of these synthetic moments.

Other experiments showed that subjects who are only given verbal descriptions of the trials generally prefer the Short one, in accordance with the principle of temporal monotonicity. Telling these subjects that their memory of the Long trial will be more favorable does not diminish their preference for the Short trial. This observation indicates that the participants in the original experiment did not deliberately apply a policy of selecting the experience that would leave them with the most pleasant memory. However, subjects who have had personal experience of the two trials are quite reluctant to abandon their preference for the Long trial even when the nature of the two trials is carefully explained after the fact. It is evidently not easy to overcome a lifetime habit of trusting one's evaluations of personal memories as a guide to choice.

The studies reviewed in this section have documented a consistent pattern of violations of a compelling normative rule. The axiom of temporal monotonicity is a substantive principle of rationality, a variant of "more is better" formulations of dominance. The violations of this principle have been traced to basic cognitive processes that produce representations and evaluations of episodes. The requirements of substantive rationality are apparently not compatible with the psychology of memory and choice.

The results of the cold-water study illustrate an ethical dilemma that was extensively discussed by Schelling [1984]. The history of an individual through time can be described as a succession of separate selves, which may have incompatible preferences, and may make decisions that affect subsequent selves. In the cold-water experiment, for example, the experiencing subject who records momentary affect and the remembering subject who makes retrospective evaluations appear to have conflicting evaluations. Which of these selves should be granted authority over outcomes that will be experienced in the future? The principle of temporal monotonicity assigns priority to the experiencing subject. In the normal conduct of life, however, it is the remembering subject who assumes the all-important role of laying out guidelines for future actions. Is there an ethical justification for favoring one of these evaluations over the other? This question has immediate implications for the application of rules of informed consent in medical practice. Imagine a painful medical procedure that lasts a specified number of minutes and ends abruptly with pain at its peak. We have seen that the physician could probably ensure that the patient will retain a more favorable memory of the procedure by adding to it a medically superfluous period of diminishing pain. Of course, the patient would probably reject the physician's offer to provide an improved memory at the cost of more actual pain. Should the physician go ahead anyway, on behalf of the patient's future remembering self? This dilemma illustrates a class of problems of paternalism that are likely to arise in many policy debates if considerations of experienced utility are assigned the weight they deserve in these debates.

6. GENERAL DISCUSSION

The standard theory of choice provides a set of conditions for rationality that may be necessary, but are hardly sufficient: they allow many foolish decisions to be called rational. This essay has argued that it is generally useful and sometimes possible to supplement the logical analysis of decisions by substantive criteria. A substantive analysis provides a more demanding definition of rationality, which excludes some preferences that would pass a test of coherence. The core of a substantive analysis is an independent assessment of the quality of decision outcomes.

The line between logical and substantive analyses is often fuzzy. For example, the "more is better" rule of dominance is a substantive rule that has the force of a logical principle. A substantive judgment is also implicitly invoked in experimental studies of invariance, where decision makers express conflicting preferences in choice problems that are said to be "the same," "extentionally equivalent," or "not different in any consequential respect." In the mugs experiment, for example, it appears unreasonable for owners and choosers to set very different prices for the same object because the long-term consumption they will derive from it is presumably the same, and because long-term considerations carry more weight than the transient affect associated with giving up an object. A criterion of utility experienced over time is implicit in this argument.

The research reviewed in earlier sections was explicit in evaluating decisions by a criterion of experienced utility. Various proxies were used to measure this subjective variable. For example, choices made near the moment of consumption were the criterion in evaluating earlier commitments (Simonson [1990]). In other studies, the adequacy of retrospective evaluations and of the decisions they support was assessed by applying normative rules (e.g., temporal monotonicity) to real-time records of hedonic experience.

The correspondence of experienced utility and decision utility is commonly taken for granted in treatments of choice. Contrary to this optimistic assumption, two obstacles to the maximization of experienced utility have been identified here. First, preliminary findings suggest that people lack skill in the task of predicting how their tastes might change. The evidence for this conclusion is still sketchy, but its significance is clear: it is difficult to describe as rational agents who are prone to large errors in predicting what they will want or enjoy next week. Another obstacle to maximization is a tendency to use the affect associated with particular moments as a proxy for the utility of extended outcomes. This peculiarity in the cognitive treatment of time explains the importance that people attach to the emotions of transactions, and may cause other forms of myopia in decision making. The use of moments as proxies entails a neglect of duration in the evaluation of past episodes, which has been confirmed in several studies. These results illustrate one particular form of distortion in evaluative memory; there may be others. Observations of memory biases are significant because the evaluation of the past determines what is learned from it. Errors in the lessons drawn from experience will inevitably be reflected in deficient choices for the future.

The rules that govern experienced utility emerge as an important subject for empirical study. For example, research could address the question of how to maximize experienced utility under a budget constraint. Scitovsky [1976] offered an insightful analysis of this problem in his *Joyless Economy*, where he took the position that the maximization of pleasure is a difficult task, which is performed with greater success in some cultures than in others. The process of hedonic adaptation played a central role in his treatment of "comforts," which suggests that it is pointless to invest resources in objects that quickly lose their ability to give pleasure. Expenditure should be directed to goods and activities that provide recurrent pleasures when appropriately spaced over time. In this light, money may be better spent on flowers, feasts and vacations than on improved durables. A systematic empirical study of the issues that Scitovsky raised is both possible and necessary.

A deeper understanding of the dynamics of the hedonic response is needed to evaluate the welfare consequences of institutions. For example, the course of income changes over a standard academic career appears designed for a pleasure machine that responds well to gradual increments and treats any losses as highly aversive (Frank [1992]; Loewenstein and Sicherman [1991]; Kahneman and Varey [1991]). Another institution that probably delivers improving outcomes over time is the penal system: the well-being of prison inmates is likely to improve in the course of their sentence, as they gain seniority and survival skills. This arrangement is humane, but perhaps less than efficient in terms of individual deterrence. Suppose, for the sake of a provocative example, that prisoners apply a Peak & End rule in retrospective evaluations of their prison experience. The result would be a global evaluation that becomes steadily less aversive with time in prison, implying a negative correlation between sentence length and the deterrence of individual recidivism. This is surely not a socially desirable outcome. Should shorter periods of incarceration under conditions of increasing discomfort be considered? As this speculative example illustrates, detailed consideration of experienced utility can yield quite unexpected conclusions.

The hedonic criterion of experienced utility is appropriate for some decisions, but it is neither universal nor exhaustive. Rational people may have other objectives than the maximization of pleasure. As Sen has noted, the rationality of decisions is best assessed in the light of "what the person is aiming to do or trying to achieve." At least in principle, a substantive evaluation of individual decisions can be extended to other criterial objectives, such as the achievement of increased personal capabilities, or of a good reputation. As the example of experienced utility illustrates, the investigation of any proposed criterion for decision making must involve three elements: (i) a normative analysis; (ii) development of measurement tools for the evaluation of outcomes; and (iii) an analysis of ways in which decisions commonly fail, by this criterion. Experienced utility is an obvious subject for such a program, but it need not be the only one.

From the point of view of a psychologist, the notion of rationality that is routinely invoked in economic discourse is surprisingly permissive in some respects, surprisingly powerful in others. For example, economic rationality does not rule out extreme risk aversion in small gambles or radical discounting of the near term future, although these attitudes almost necessarily yield inferior aggregate outcomes. On the other hand, rationality is often taken to be synonymous with flawless intelligence. Thus, a critic of the rationality assumption faces the following well-fortified position: (i) a definition of rationality which appears to be overly permissive in some important respects; (ii) a willingness of choice theorists to make the theory even more permissive, as needed to accomodate apparent violations of its requirements; (iii) a methodological position that treats rationality as a maintained hypothesis, making it very difficult to disprove; (iv) an apparent readiness to assume that behavior that has not been proved to be irrational is highly intelligent.

In contrast to the many recent attempts to relax the definition of rational choice, the argument of this essay has been that the definition should be made more restrictive by adding substantive considerations to the logical standard of coherence. There is compelling evidence that the maintenance of coherent beliefs and preferences is too demanding a task for limited minds (Simon [1955]; Tversky and Kahneman [1986]). Maximizing the experienced utility of a stream of future outcomes can only be harder. The time has perhaps come to set aside the overly general question of whether or not people are rational, allowing research attention to be focused on more specific and more promising issues. What are the conditions under which the assumption of rationality can be retained as a useful approximation? Where the assumption of rationality must be given up, what are the most important ways in which people fail to maximize their outcomes?

References

Numbers in square brackets at the end of each entry refer to the chapter(s) in which that reference appears.

Abelson, R. P., & Levi, A. (1985). Decision making and decision theory. In G. Lindzey & E. Aronson (Eds.), *Handbook of Social Psychology* (3rd ed.,). New York: Random House. **[25, 41]**

Achen, C. H. (1975). Mass political attitudes and the survey response. *American Political Science Review, 69*, 1218–1231. **[35]**

Aczél, J. (1966). *Lectures on functional equations and their applications.* New York: Academic Press. **[2, 33]**

Adorna, T., Frenkel-Brunswik, E., Levinson, D., & Sanford, R. N. (1950). *The authoritarian personality.* New York: Harper. **[25]**

Ainslie, G. (1975). Specious reward: A behavioral theory of impulsiveness and impulse control. *Psychological Bulletin, 82*(4), 463–496. **[14, 15, 33]**

Ainslie, G. (1985). Beyond Microeconomics. Conflict among interests in a multiple self as a determinant of value. In J. Elster (Ed.), *The Multiple Self.* Cambridge: Cambridge University Press. **[33]**

Ajzen, I., & Fishbein, M. (1977). Attitude-behavior relations: A theoretical analysis and review of empirical research. *Psychological Bulletin, 84*(5), 888–918. **[41]**

Ajzen, I., & Fishbein, M. (1980). *Understanding attitudes and predicting social behavior.* Englewood Cliffs, NJ: Prentice-Hall. **[35]**

Akerlof, G. A. (1970, August). The market for "lemons": Quality uncertainty and the market mechanism. *Quarterly Journal of Economics, 84*, 488–500. **[18]**

Akerlof, G. (1979, August). The case against conservative macroeconomics: An inaugural lecture. *Economica, 46*, 219–237. **[18]**

Akerlof, G. (1980, June). A theory of social custom, of which unemployment may be one consequence. *Quarterly Journal of Economics, 94*, 749–775. **[18]**

Akerlof, G. (1982, November). Labor contracts as partial gift exchange. *Quarterly Journal of Economics, 97*, 543–569. **[18]**

Akerlof, G. A., & Yellen, J. L. (1985). Can small deviations from rationality make significant differences to economic equilibria? *American Economic Review, 75*(4), 708–720. **[12, 18, 19]**

Ali, M. (1977). Probability and utility estimates for racetrack bettors. *Journal of Political Economy, 85*, 803–815. **[16]**

Allais, M. (1953). Le comportement de l'homme rationnel devant le risque, critique des postulats et axiomes de l'école Américaine. *Econometrica, 21*, 503–546. **[1, 2, 3, 4, 5, 6, 12, 15, 25]**

Allais, M. (1979). The foundations of a positive theory of choice involving risk and a criticism of the postulates and axioms of the American School. In M. Allais and O. Hagen (Eds.), *Expected utility hypothesis and the Allais paradox*. Dordrecht: Reidel. [12]

Allais, M., & Hagen, O. E. (1979). *The expected utility hypothesis and the Allais paradox*. Dordrecht: Reidel. [1]

Allais, M., & Hagen, O. (Eds.). (1979). *Expected utility hypotheses and the Allais paradox*. Hingham, MA: D. Reidel Publishing. [1, 4]

Allen, D. W., & Lueck, D. (1995). Risk preferences and the economics of contracts. *American Economic Review, 85*, 447–451. [23]

Allison, G. T. (1971). *Essence of decision: Explaining the Cuban missile crisis*. Boston: Little Brown. [34]

Alloy, L. B., & Ahrens, A. H. (1987). Depression and pessimism for the future: Biased use of statistically relevant information in predictions for self and others. *Journal of Personality and Social Psychology, 52*, 366–378. [23]

Alpert, M., & Raiffa, H. (1982). A progress report on the training of probability assessors. In D. Kahneman, P. Slovic, & A. Tversky (Eds.), *Judgment under uncertainty: Heuristics and biases* (pp. 294–305). Cambridge, UK: Cambridge University Press. [26]

Altonji, J. G. (1986). Intertemporal substitution in labor supply: Evidence from micro data. *Journal of Political Economy, 94*, s176–s215. [20]

Anderson, N. H. (1996). *A functional theory of cognition*. Mahwah, NJ: Erlbaum. [36, 38]

Anderson, N. H., & Shanteau, J. C. (1970). Information integration in risky decision making. *Journal of Experimental Psychology, 84*, 441–451. [2]

Andreassen, P. (1987). On the social psychology of the stock market: Aggregate attributional effects and the regressiveness of prediction. *Journal of Personality and Social Psychology, 53*, 490–496. [21]

Andreassen, P. (1988). Explaining the price-volume relationship: The difference between price changes and changing prices. *Organizational Behavior and Human Decision Processes, 41*, 371–389. [21]

Andreassen, P. (1990). Judgmental extrapolation and market overreaction: On the use and disuse of news. *Journal of Behavioral Decision Making, 3*, 153–174. [21]

Andreoni, J. (1995). Warm-glow versus cold-prickle: The effects of positive and negative framing on cooperation in experiments. *Quarterly Journal of Economics, 110*, 1–21. [10]

Argyle, M. (1987). *The psychology of happiness*. London: Methuen. [39]

Ariely, D. (1998). Combining experiences over time: The effects of duration, intensity changes and on-line measurements on retrospective pain evaluations. *Journal of Behavioral Decision Making, 11*, 19–45. [38]

Ariely, D., & Carmon, Z. (2000). Gestalt characteristics of experienced profiles. *Journal of Behavioral Decision Making*, Forthcoming. [38]

Ariely, D., & Loewenstein, G. (1999). Encoding sequences and conveying information in ratings and choice: The case of sequences' characteristics and duration. Working paper, MIT. [38]

Ariely, D., & Zauberman, G. (2000). On the making of an experience: The effects of breaking and combining experiences on their overall evaluation. *Journal of Behavioral Decision Making*, Forthcoming. [38]

Arkes, H. R., & Blumer, C. (1985). The psychology of sunk cost. *Organizational Behavior and Human Decision Processes, 35.1*, 124–140. [14]

Arnold, J. III. (1986). Assessing capital risk: You can't be too conservative. *Harvard Bus. Rev., 64*, 113–121. [22, 26]

Aronson, E., & Mills, J. (1959). The effects of severity of initiation on liking for a group. *Journal of Abnormal and Social Psychology, 59*, 177–181. **[15]**

Arrow, K. J. (1963). Uncertainty and the welfare economics of medical care. *American Economic Review, 53*, 941–969. **[13]**

Arrow, K. J. (1971). *Essays in the theory of risk-bearing.* Chicago: Markham, 1971. **[2, 11]**

Arrow, K. (1973, Summer). Social responsibility and economic efficiency. *Public policy, 21*, 303–317. **[18]**

Arrow, K. J. (1982). Risk perception in psychology and economics. *Economic Inquiry, 20*, 1–9. **[3, 12, 25, 28, 36, 42]**

Arrow, K. J., Solow, R., Portney, P. R., Leamer, E. E., Radner, R., & Schuman, E. H. (1993). Report of the NOAA Panel on contingent valuation. *Federal Register, 58*, 4601–4614. **[10]**

Atiyah, P. (1971). *Consideration in contracts: A fundamental restatement.* Canberra: Australian National University Press. **[24]**

Atiyah, P. S. (1978). *Contracts, promises and the law of obligations.* **[24]**

Atiyah, P. S. (1979). *The rise and fall of freedom of contract.* Oxford: Clarendon Press. **[24]**

Ausubel, L. M. (1991). The failure of competition in the credit card market. *American Economic Review, 81*, 50–81. **[40]**

Azariadis, C. (1975, December). Implicit contracts and unemployment equilibria. *Journal of Political Economy, 83*, 1183–1202. **[18]**

Babcock, L., & Loewenstein, G. (1977). Explaining bargaining impasse: The role of self-serving biases. *Journal of Economic Perspectives, 11*, 109–126. **[23]**

Badrinath, S., & Lewellen, W. (1991). Evidence on tax-motivated securities trading behavior. *Journal of Finance, 46*, 369–382. **[21]**

Bailar, B. A., & Rothwell, N. D. (1984). Measuring employment and unemployment. In C. F. Turner & E. Martin (Eds.), *Survey measure of subjective phenomena* (pp. 129–142). New York: Russell Sage Foundation. **[35]**

Baily, M. N. (1974, January). Wages and employment under uncertain demand. *Review of Economic Studies, 41*, 37–50. **[18]**

Baldwin, J. R., Chandler, W., Le, C., & Papailiadis, T. (1994). *Strategies for success; A profile of growing small and medium-sized enterprises (GSMEs) in Canada.* Catalogue 61-523R, Ottawa: Statistics Canada. **[23]**

Baldwin, J. R., & Gorecki, P. K. (1991). Firm entry and exit in the Canadian manufacturing sector. *Canadian Journal of Economics, 24*, 300–323. **[23]**

Banford, N. D., Knetsch, J. L., & Mauser, G. A. (1980). Feasibility judgements and alternative measures of benefits and costs. *J. Bus. Admin., 11*, 25. **[24]**

Barberis, N., Hvary, M., & Santos, T. (1999). Prospect theory and asset prices. University of Chicago working paper. **[26]**

Barberis, N., Shleifer, A., & Vishny, R. (1996). A model of investor sentiment with both underreaction and overreaction. Working Paper, University of Chicago. **[21]**

Barnes, J. D., & Reinmuth, J. E. (1976). Comparing imputed and actual utility functions in a competitive bidding setting. *Decision Sciences, 7*, 801–812. **[2]**

Barnes, O., & Barnes, L. W. (1964). Choice of delay of inevitable shock. *Journal of Abnormal Social Psychology, 68*, 669–672. **[32]**

Baron, J. (1997). Confusion of relative and absolute risk in valuation. *Journal of Risk and Uncertainty, 14*, 301–309. **[31]**

Baron, J., & Greene, J. (1996). Determinants of insensitivity to quantity in valuation of public goods: Contribution, warm glow, budget constraints, availability, and prominence. *Journal of Experimental Psychology: Applied, 2*, 107–125. **[36]**

Barro, R., & Grossman, H. I. (1971). A general disequilibrium model of income and employment. *American Economic Review, 61*, 82–93. **[19]**

Barsalou, L. H. (1992). *Cognitive psychology: An overview for cognitive scientists.* Mahwah, NJ: Erlbaum. **[36]**

Bartels, L. M. (1998). Democracy with attitudes. Paper presented at the annual meeting of the American Political Science Association, Boston. **[36]**

Bass, F. M. (1974, February). The theory of stochastic preference and brand switching. *Journal of Marketing Research, 11*, 1–20. **[41]**

Bass, F. M., Pessemier, E. A., & Lehmann, R. R. (1972, November). An experimental study of relationships between attitudes, brand preference, and choice. *Behavioral Science, 17*, 532–541. **[41]**

Bateman, T. S., & Zeithaml, C. T. (1989). The psychological context of strategic decisions: A model and convergent experimental findings. *Strategic Management J., 10*, 59–74. **[22]**

Baumgartner, H., Sujan, M., & Padgett, D. (1997). Patterns of affective reactions to advertisements. The integration of moment-to-moment responses into overall judgments. *Journal of Marketing Research, 34*, 219–232. **[38]**

Bayles, M. D. (1985). Legally enforceable commitments. *L. & Phil., 4*, 311–342. **[24]**

Bazerman, M. H. (1983). Negotiator judgment. *American Behavioral Scientist, 27*, 211–228. **[25]**

Bazerman, M. (1984). The relevance of Kahneman and Tversky's concept of framing to organizational behavior. *Journal of Management, 10*, 333–343. **[33]**

Bazerman, M. H. (1985, July). Norms of distributive justice in interest arbitration. *Industrial and Labor Relations Review, 38*, 558–570. **[18]**

Bazerman, M. H. (1994). *Judgment in managerial decision making*, 3rd ed. New York: Wiley. **[26]**

Bazerman, M. & Carroll, J. S. (1987). Negotiator cognition. In B. Staw & L. L. Cummings, (Eds.). *Research in organizational behavior, 9*, Greenwich, CT: JAI Press, pp. 247–288. **[7]**

Bazerman, M. H., Loewenstein, G. F., & White, S. B. (1992). Reversals of preference in allocation decisions: Judging an alternative versus choosing among alternatives. *Administrative Science Quarterly, 37*, 220–240. **[31]**

Bazerman, M. H., & Samuelson, W. F. (1983). I won the auction but don't want the price. *J. Financial Econ., 27*, 618–634. **[22]**

Bazerman, M. H., Schroth, H. A., Shah, P. P., Diekmann, K. A., & Tenbrunsel, A. E. (1994). The inconsistent role of comparison others and procedural justice in reactions to hypothetical job descriptions: Implications for job acceptance decisions. *Organizational Behavior and Human Decision Processes, 60*, 326–352. **[31]**

Bazerman, M. H., Tembrunsel, A., & Wade-Benzoni, K. (in press). Negotiating with yourself and losing: Understanding and managing competing internal preferences. *Academy of Management Review.* **[31]**

Beach, L. R., & Mitchell, T. R. (1978). A contingency model for the selection of decision strategies. *Academy of Management Review, 3*(3), 439–449. **[41]**

Becker, G. M., DeGroot, M. H., & Marschak, J. (1963). Stochastic models of choice behavior. *Behavioral Science, 8*, 41–55. **[10]**

Becker, G. M., DeGroot, M. H., & Marschak, J. (1964). Measuring utility by a single-response sequential method. *Behavioral Science, 9*, 226–232. **[10, 30]**

Becker, G. S. (1962, February). Irrational behavior and economic theory. *Journal of Political Economy*, 1–13. **[15]**

Becker, G. S., & Murphy, K. M. (1988). A Theory of rational addiction. *Journal of Political Economy, 96*(4), 675–700. **[40]**

Becker, S., Ronen, J., & Sorter, G. (1974). Opportunity costs – An experimental approach. *Journal of Accounting Research*, 317–329. **[15]**

Belk, R. W. (1975). Situational variables and consumer behavior. *Journal of Consumer Research, 2*(2), 157–164. **[41]**

Bell, D. E. (1977). A utility function for time streams having inter-period dependencies. *Operations Research, 25*, 448–458. **[32]**

Bell, D. E. (1982). Regret in decision making under uncertainty. *Operations Research, 30*, 961–981. **[12]**

Bell, D. (1985). Disappointment in decision making under uncertainty. *Operations Research, 33*, 1–27. **[4]**

Bell, D. E., Raiffa, H., & Tversky, A. (1988). Descriptive, normative, and prescriptive interactions in decision making. In D. E. Bell, H. Raiffa, & A. Tversky (Eds.), *Decision Making: Descriptive, Normative, and Prescriptive Interactions*, 9–30. New York: Cambridge University Press. **[26]**

Bem, D. J. (1972). Self-perception theory. In L. Berkowitz (Ed.), *Advances in experimental social psychology* (Vol. 6). New York: Academic Press. **[34]**

Benartzi, S., & Thaler, R. H. (1995). Myopic loss aversion and the equity premium puzzle. *Quarterly Journal of Economics, 110*(1), 73–92. **[10, 11, 14, 16, 19, 20, 21]**

Benartzi, S., & Thaler, R. H. (1998). Illusory diversification and retirement savings. Working paper, University of Chicago and UCLA. **[14]**

Benartzi, S., & Thaler, R. H. (2000). Risk aversion or myopia: Choices in repeated gambles and retirement investments. *Management Science*, Forthcoming. **[14]**

Bentham, J. (1789). *An Introduction to the principle of morals and legislations*. Oxford, UK: (Reprinted 1948) Blackwell, UK. **[38]**

Bentkover, J., Covello, V., & Mumpower, J. (Eds.). (1985). *Benefits assessment: The state of the Art*. Amsterdam: Reidel. **[35]**

Benzion, U., Rapoport, A., & Yagil, J. (1989). Discount rates inferred from decisions: An experimental study. *Management Science, 35*, 270–284. **[33]**

Berg, E. J. (1961). Backward-sloping labor supply functions in dual economies – The Africa case, *Quarterly Journal of Economics, 75*(3), 468–492. **[20]**

Berg, J. E., Daley, L., Dickhaut, J., & O'Brien, J. (1986). Controlling preferences for gambles on units of experimental exchange. *Quarterly Journal of Economics, 101*, 281–306. **[23]**

Berg, J., Dickhaut, J., & O'Brien, J. (1985). Preference reversal and arbitrage. In V. Smith (Ed.), *Research in experimental economics* (pp. 31–72). Greenwich, CT: JAI Press. **[27]**

Berkeley, D., & Humphreys, P. (1982). Structuring decision problems and the "bias" heuristic. *Acta Psychologica, 50*, 201–250. **[35]**

Berman, L. (1982). *Planning a tragedy*. New York: Norton. **[34]**

Bernoulli, D. (1954). Exposition of a new theory on the measurement of risk. *Econometrica, 22*, 23–36. (Original work published 1738) **[1, 25]**

Bettman, J. R. (1979). *An information processing theory of consumer choice*. Reading, MA: Addison-Wesley. **[41]**

Bettman, J. R., & Park, C. W. (1980, December). Effects of prior knowledge and experience and phase of the decision process on consumer decision processes: A protocol analysis. *Journal of Consumer Research, 7*, 234–248. **[41]**

Betts, R., & Gelb, L. (1979). *The irony of Vietnam: The system worked*. Washington, DC: Brookings Institution. **[34]**

Bewley, T. F. (1994). A field study on downward wage rigidity. Unpublished manuscript, Yale University. [19]

Bigelow, J. (Ed.). (1887). *The complete works of Benjamin Franklin* (Vol. 4). New York: Putnam. [34]

Billig, M. (1987). *Arguing and thinking: A rhetorical approach to social psychology.* New York: Cambridge University Press. [34]

Bishop, R. C., & Heberlein, T. A. (1979). Measuring values of extramarket goods: Are indirect measures biased? *American Journal of Agricultural Economics, 61,* 926–930. [10, 24]

Bishop, R. C., & Heberlein, T. A. (1986). Does contingent valuation work? In R. G. Cummings, D. S. Brookshire, & W. D. Schulze (Eds.), *Valuing Environmental Goods.* Totowa, NJ: Roman & Allanheld. [24]

Biswanger, H. (1981). Attitudes toward risk: Theoretical implications of an experiment in rural India. *Economic Journal, 91,* 867–890. [14]

Black, F. (1980). The tax consequences of long-run pension policy. *Financial Analysis Journal, 36,* 21–28. [17]

Black, H. C. (Ed.). (1990). *Black's law dictionary* (6th ed.). St. Paul, MN: West Publishing. [24]

Blanchard, O. (1993). Movements in the equity premium. *Brookings Papers on Economic Activity,* 519–543. [17]

Blattberg, R. C., & Neslin, S. A. (1990). *Sales promotion: Concepts, methods, and strategies.* Englewood Cliffs, NJ: Prentice-Hall. [34]

Blin, J.-M., & Dodson, J. A. (1980). The relationship between attributes, brand preference, and choice: A stochastic view. *Management Science, 26*(6), 606–619. [41]

Borel, É. (1924). Apropos of a treatise on probability. In H. Kyburg & H. Smokler (Eds.), *Studies in subjective probability* (1st ed.), New York: John Wiley. [6]

Bostic, R., Herrnstein, R. J., & Luce, R. D. (1990). The effect on the preference-reversal phenomenon of using choice indifferences. *Journal of Economic Behavior and Organization, 13,* 193–212. [27]

Bowman, D., Minehart, D., & Rabin, M. (1999). Loss aversion in a consumption/savings model. *Journal of Economic Behavior and Organization, 38*(2), 155–178. [16, 20]

Bowman, E. (1982). Risk seeking by troubled firms. *Sloan Management Rev., 23,* 33–42. [22]

Bremer, M., & Kiyoshi, K. (1996). Trading volume for winners and losers on the Tokyo Exchange. *Journal of Financial and Quantitative Analysis, 31,* 127–142. [21]

Brenner, L., Koehler, D., & Tversky, A. (1992). On the evaluation of one-sided evidence. Working paper. Stanford: Stanford University Press. [26]

Brickman, P. (1975). Adaptation level determinants of satisfaction with equal and unequal outcome distributions in skill and chance situations. *Journal of Personality and Social Psychology, 32,* 191–198. [39]

Brickman, P., & Campbell, D. T. (1971). Hedonic relativism and planning the good society. In M. H. Apley (Ed.), *Adaptation-level theory: A symposium* (pp. 287–301). New York: Academic Press. [1, 38, 39]

Brickman, P., Coates, D., & Janoff-Bulman, R. (1978). Lottery winners and accident victims: Is happiness relative? *Journal of Personality and Social Psychology, 36,* 917–927. [38, 39, 40, 42]

Bridge, M. G. (1988). *Sale of goods.* Toronto: Butterworths. [24]

British Columbia Law Reform Commission (1992). Wrongful interference with goods. Working paper No. 67. Vancouver: British Columbia Law Reform Commission. [24]

Brock, W., Lakonishok, J., & LeBaron, B. (1992). Simple technical trading rules and the stochastic properties of stock returns. *Journal of Finance, 47,* 1731–1764. **[21]**

Bromiley, P. (1986). *Corporate capital investment: A behavioral approach.* New York: Cambridge University Press. **[22]**

Brookshire, D. S., & Coursey, D. L. (1987). Measuring the value of a public good: An empirical comparison of elicitation procedures. *American Economic Review, 77,* 554–566. **[7, 9]**

Brookshire, D. S., Ives, C. C., & Schulze, W. D. (1976). The valuation of aesthetic preferences. *Journal of Environmental Economics and Management, 3,* 325–346. **[35]**

Brookshire, D., Randall, A., & Stoll, J. R. (1980). Valuing increments and decrements in natural resource service flows. *Am. J. Agric. Econ., 62,* 478–488. **[24]**

Browning, M., Deaton, A., & Irish, M. (1985). A profitable approach to labor supply and commodity demands over the life-cycle. *Econometrica, 53,* 503–543. **[20]**

Burgstahler, D., & Dichev, I. (1997). Earnings management to avoid earnings decreases and losses. *Journal of Accounting and Economics, 24,* 99–126. **[14]**

Burrows, A. S. (1987). *Remedies for torts and breach of contract.* London: Butterworths. **[24]**

Cacioppo, J. T., & Berntson, G. G. (1994). Relationships between attitudes and evaluative space: A critical review with emphasis on the separability of positive and negative substrates. *Psychological Bulletin, 115,* 401–423. **[38]**

Cagan, P. (1979). *Persistent inflation: Historical and policy essays.* New York: *Columbia University Press.* **[18]**

Camerer, C. F. (1987). Do biases in probability judgment matter in markets? Experimental evidence. *American Economic Review, 77*(5), 981–997. **[23]**

Camerer, C. F. (1989). An experimental test of several generalized utility theories. *Journal of Risk and Uncertainty, 2*(1), 61–104. **[3, 4]**

Camerer, C. F. (1992). Recent tests of generalizations of expected utility theories. In W. Edwards (Ed.), *Utility theories: Measurement and applications.* Dordrecht: Kluwer Academic Publishers. **[3, 4]**

Camerer, C. F. (1995). Individual decision making. In J. Kagel & A. E. Roth (Eds.), *Handbook of experimental economics* (pp. 587–703). Princeton: Princeton University Press. **[6, 16, 23]**

Camerer, C., Babcock, L., Loewenstein, G., & Thaler, R. H. (1997, May). Labor supply of New York City cabdrivers: One day at a time. *Quarterly Journal of Economics, 112,* 407–442. **[14, 16, 20]**

Camerer, C. F., & Ho, T.-H. (1991). Nonlinear weighting of probabilities and violations of the betweenness axiom. Unpublished manuscript, The Wharton School, University of Pennsylvania. **[3]**

Camerer, C. F., & Ho, T.-H. (1994). Violations of the betweenness axiom and nonlinearity in probability. *Journal of Risk and Uncertainty, 8*(2), 167–196. **[4, 5, 6]**

Camerer, C. F., & Ho, T.-H. (1999). Experience-weighted attraction learning in normal-form games. *Econometrica, 67,* 827–874. **[20]**

Camerer, C. F., Johnson, E., Rymon, T., & Sen, S. (1993). Cognition and sequential bargaining over gains and losses. In K. Binmore, A. Kirman, & P. Tani (Eds.). *Frontiers of Game Theory.* Cambridge, MA: MIT Press. **[20]**

Camerer, C. F., & Kunreuther, H. C. (1989). Experimental markets for insurance. *Journal of Risk and Uncertainty, 2,* 265–300. **[13]**

Camerer, C. F., & Lovallo, D. (1999). Overconfidence and excess entry: An experimental approach. *American Economic Review, 89*(1), 306–318. **[23]**

Camerer, C. F., & Weber, M. W. (1992). Recent developments in modelling preferences: Uncertainty and ambiguity. *Journal of Risk and Uncertainty, 5*, 325–370. **[5, 6, 30]**

Campbell, A., Converse, P., & Rodgers, W. (1976). *The quality of American life: Perceptions, evaluations, and satisfaction.* New York: Russell Sage Foundation. **[35]**

Campen, J. T. (1986). *Benefit, cost, and beyond.* Cambridge, MA: Ballinger. **[35]**

Capen, E. C., Clapp, R. V., & Campbell, W. M. (1971). Competitive bidding in high-risk situations. *J. Petroleum Technology, 23*, 641–653. **[22]**

Card, D. (1983). Cost-of-living escalators in major union contracts. *Industrial and Labor Relations Review, 37*, 34–48. **[19]**

Carlsmith, J. M. (1962). Strength of expectancy: Its determinants and effects. Unpublished doctoral dissertation, Harvard University, Cambridge, MA. **[32]**

Carmon, Z., & Kahneman, D. (1996). The experienced utility of queuing: Experience profiles and retrospective evaluations of simulated queues. Working paper, Fuqua School of Business, Duke University. **[38]**

Carson, R. T., Hanemann, W. M., Kopp, R. J., Krosnick, J. A., Mitchell, R. C., Presser, S., Ruud, P. A., & Smith, V. K. (1994). *Prospective interim lost use value due to DDT and PCB contamination in the Southern California Bight.* La Jolla, CA: Natural Resource Damage Assessment. **[36]**

Carson, R. T., Horowitz, J. K., & Machina, M. J. (1987). Discounting mortality risks. Final Technical Report to the U.S. Environmental Protection Agency, UCSD Department of Economics. **[32]**

Carson, R. T., & Mitchell, R. C. (1993). The issue of scope in contingent valuation studies. *American Journal of Agricultural Economics, 75*, 1263–1267. **[36]**

Carson, R. T., & Mitchell, R. C. (1995). Sequencing and nesting in contingent valuation surveys. *Journal of Environmental Economics & Management, 28*, 155–173. **[36]**

Case, K., & Shiller, R. (1988, November/December). The behavior of home buyers in boom and post-boom markets. *New England Economic Review*, 29–46. **[21]**

Case, K. E., & Shiller, R. J. (1989, March). The efficiency of the market for single family homes. *American Economic Review, 79*, 125–137. **[33]**

Chalmers, M. D. (1905). *The Sale of Goods Act, 1889.* London: William Clowes & Sons. **[24]**

Chapman, G., & Bornstein, B. (1996). The more you ask for the more you get: Anchoring in personal injury verdicts. *Applied Cognitive Psychology, 10*, 519–540. **[36]**

Chapman, L. J., & Chapman, J. P. (1969a). Genesis of popular but erroneous psychodiagnostic observations. *Journal of Abnormal Psychology, 74*, 271–280. **[35]**

Chew, S. H. (1983). A generalization of the quasilinear mean with applications to the measurement of income inequality and decision theory resolving the Allais paradox. *Econometrica, 51*, 1065–1092. **[12]**

Chew, S.-H. (1989). An axiomatic generalization of the quasilinear mean and the gini mean with application to decision theory. Unpublished manuscript, Department of Economics, University of California at Irvine. **[3]**

Chew, S. H., & MacCrimmon, K. R. (1979). Alpha utility theory, lottery composition and the Allais paradox, Working paper, University of British Columbia Faculty of Commerce and Business Administration No. 686, Vancouver, British Columbia. **[12]**

Choquet, G. (1955). Theory of capacities. *Annales de l'Institut Fourier, 5*, 131–295. **[3]**

Christensen-Szalanski, J. J. (1984). Discount functions and the measurement of patient's values: Women's decisions during child birth. *Medical Decision Making, 4*, 47–58. **[42]**

Chu, Y. P., & Chu, R. L. (1990). The subsidence of preference reversals in simplified and market-like experimental settings: A note. *American Economic Review, 80*, 902–911. [27]

Chung, S. H., & Herrnstein, R. J. (1967). Choice and delay of reinforcement. *Journal of the Experimental Analysis of Behavior, 10*, 67–74. [33]

Churchill, N. (1982). Don't let inflation get the best of you. *Harvard Business Review*, 6–26. [19]

Cicchetti, C. J., & Dubin, J. A. (1994). A micro-econometric analysis of risk-aversion and the decision to self-insure. *Journal of Political Economy, 102*, 169–186. [16]

Clark, H. H., & Clark, E. V. (1977). *Psychology and language.* New York: Harcourt Brace Jovanovich. [1]

Clerk, J. F. (1987). *Fifth cumulative supplement to the fifteenth edition*, R. W. M. Dias (Ed.). London: Sweet and Maxwell. [24]

Clos, G. E. (1979). *Comparative law.* Littleton, CO: Fred B. Rothman. [24]

Coase, R. H. (1960). The problem of social cost. *J. L. & Econ, 3*, 1–44. [24]

Cohen, D., & Knetsch, J. (1990). Judicial choice and disparities between measures of economic values. Simon Fraser University Working Paper. [7, 8]

Cohen, D., & Knetsch, J. L. (1992). Judicial choice and disparities between measures of economic value. *Osgoode Hall Law Review, 30*, 737–770. [26]

Cohen, J., & Hansel, M. (1959). Preferences for different combinations of chance and skill in gambling. *Nature, 183*, 841–843. [30]

Cohen, M., Jaffray, J. Y., & Said, T. (1987). Experimental comparison of individual behavior under risk and under uncertainty for gains and for losses. *Organizational Behavior and Human Decision Processes, 39*, 1–22. [3, 5]

Cohn, B. (1999). *The lay theory of happiness: Illusions and biases in judging others.* Unpublished undergraduate dissertation, Princeton University. [38]

Collard, D. (1978). *Altruism and economy: A study in non-selfish economics.* Oxford: Martin Robertson. [24]

Collins, H. (1986). *The law of contract.* London: Weidenfeld & Nicolson. [24]

Combs, B., & Slovic, P. (1979). Causes of death: Biased newspaper coverage and biased judgments. *Journalism Quarterly, 56*, 837–843, 849. [13]

Committee for Economic Development. (1989). *Who shall be liable?* New York: Committee for Economic Development. [13]

The common law. (1881). Boston: Little, Brown. [24]

Constantinides, G. (1984). Optimal stock trading with personal taxes: Implications for prices and the abnormal January returns. *Journal of Financial Economics, 13*, 65–69. [21]

Constantinedes, G. M. (1990). Habit formation: A resolution of the equity premium puzzle. *Journal of Political Economy, 98*, 519–543. [17, 40]

Converse, P. E. (1964). The nature of belief systems in mass politics. In D. E. Apter (Ed.), *Ideology and discontent.* Glencoe, NY: Free Press. [35]

Converse, P. E. (1975). Public opinion and voting behavior. In *Handbook of Political Science*, Vol. 4, F. Greenstein & N. Polsby (Eds.), Reading, MA: Addison-Wesley. [25]

Cook, P. J., & Clotfelter, C. T. (1993, June). The peculiar scale economies of lotto. *American Economic Review, 83*, 634–643. [16]

Coombs, C. H. (1964). *A theory of data.* New York: Wiley. [35, 41]

Coombs, C. H. (1975). Portfolio theory and the measurement of risk. In *Human judgment and decision processes*, ed. by M. F. Kaplan & S. Schwartz. New York: Academic Press, pp. 63–85. [2]

Cooper, A., Woo, C., & Dunkelberg, W. (1988). Entrepreneurs' perceived chances for success. *J. Business Venturing*, 3, 97–108. **[22, 26]**

Cooter, R., & Ulen, T. (1988). *Law and economics*. Glenview, IL: Scott, Foresman. **[24]**

Coupey, E., Irwin, J. R., & Payne, J. W. (1998). Product category familiarity and preference construction. *Journal of Consumer Research, 24*, 459–467. **[31]**

Coursey, D. L., Hovis, J. L., & Schulze, W. D. (1987). The disparity between willingness to accept and willingness to pay measures of value. *The Quarterly Journal of Economics, 102*, 679–690. **[7, 8, 9, 10]**

Court-imposed modifications: Supplementing the all-or-nothing approach to discharge cases. (1983). *Ohio St. L. J., 44*, 1079. **[24]**

Cox, J. C., & Grether, D. M. (1996). The preference reversal phenomenon: Response mode, markets and incentives. *Economic Theory, 7*(3), 381–405. **[27]**

Crocker, J. (1981). Judgment of covariation by social perceivers. *Psychology Bulletin, 90*, 272–292. **[26]**

Crosby, F. (1976). A model of egoistical relative deprivation. *Psychological Review, 83*, 85–113. **[39]**

Cummings, R. G., Brookshire, D. S., & Schulze, W. D. (1986). *Valuing environmental goods*. Totowa, NJ: Rowman and Allenheld. **[7, 8, 9, 35]**

Cummings, R. G., Harrison, G. W., & Rutstrom, E. E. (1995). Homegrown values and hypothetical surveys: Is the dichotomous choice approach incentive-compatible? *American Economic Review, 85*, 260–266. **[36]**

Cummins, D., & Weisbart, S. (1978). *The impact of consumer services on independent insurance agency performance*. Glenmont, NY: IMA Education and Research Foundation. **[13]**

Curley, S. P., Yates, J. F., & Abrams, R. A. (1986). Psychological sources of ambiguity avoidance. *Organizational Behavior and Human Decision Processes, 38*(2), 230–256. **[22, 30]**

Dacy, D. C., & Kunreuther, H. (1969). *The economics of natural disasters*. New York: Free Press. **[18]**

Davidson, D., Suppes, P., & Siegel, S. (1957). *Decision-making: An experimental approach*. Stanford, CA: Stanford University Press. **[2]**

Davis, D. (1985). New projects: Beware of false economies. *Harvard Bus. Rev., 63*, 95–101. **[22, 26]**

Dawes, R. M. (1988). *Rational Choice in an Uncertain World*. San Francisco: Harcourt Brace Jovanovich. **[22, 25, 26]**

De Bondt, W. F. M., & Thaler, R. H. (1985). Does the stock market overreact? *Journal of Finance, 40*(3), 793–808. **[21]**

De Bondt, W. F. M., & Thaler, R. H. (1987). Further evidence on investor overreaction and stock market seasonality. *Journal of Finance, 42*(3), 557–581. **[21]**

Debreu, G. (1960). Topological methods in cardinal utility theory. *Mathematical methods in the social sciences*, ed. by K. J. Arrow, S. Karlin, & P. Suppes. Stanford CA: Stanford University Press, pp. 16–26. **[2, 7, 33]**

Degeorge, F., Patel, J., & Zeckhauser, R. J. (1999). Earnings management to exceed thresholds. *Journal of Business, 72*(1), 1–33. **[14]**

DeKay, M. L., & McClelland, G. H. (1996). Probability and utility components of endangered species preservation programs. *Journal of Experimental Psychology: Applied, 2*, 60–83. **[36]**

Delquié, P. (1993, August). *Eliciting preferences free of compatibility and prominence biases*. Unpublished manuscript, University of Texas at Austin. **[27]**

DeMaio, T. J. (1984). Social desirability and survey measurement: A review. In C. F. Turner & E. Martin (Eds.), *Survey measure of subjective phenomena* (pp. 257–282). New York: Russell Sage Foundation. **[35]**

Demsetz, H. (1972, January). When does the rule of liability matter. *Journal of Legal Studies, 28.* **[15]**

Desvousges, W., Johnson, R., Dunford, R., Boyle, K. J., Hudson, S., & Wilson, K. N. (1992). *Measuring non-use damages using contingent valuation: An experimental evaluation accuracy.* Research Triangle Institute Monograph 92-1. **[36]**

Diamond, P. (1996). Testing the internal consistency of contingent valuation surveys. *Journal of Environmental Economics and Management, 30,* 337–347. **[36]**

Diamond, P. A., & Hausman, J. A. (1994). Contingent valuation: Is some number better than no number? *Journal of Economic Perspectives, 8*(4), 45–64. **[36]**

Diamond, P. A., Hausman, J. A., Leonard, G., & Denning, M. (1993). Does contingent valuation measure preferences? Experimental evidence. In J. A. Hausman (Ed.). *Contingent Valuation: A Critical Assessment.* Amsterdam: North-Holland. **[36]**

Dias, R. W. M. (Ed.). (1982). *Clerk and Lindsell on torts* (15th ed.). Agincourt, Ont.: Carswell. **[24]**

Dickie, M., Gerking, S., McClelland, G., & Schulze, W. (1987). *Improving accuracy and reducing costs of environmental benefit assessments: Vol. 1. Valuing morbidity: An overview and state of the art assessment* (USEPA Cooperative Agreement No. CR812954-01-2). Washington, DC: U.S. Environmental Protection Agency. **[35]**

Diener, E. (1984). Subjective well-being. *Psychological Bulletin, 95*(3), 542–575. **[39]**

Diener, E., Wirtz, D., & Oishi, S. (1999). The James Dean effect: Peak–end processes in the perception of quality of life. Working paper, University of Illinois at Champaign-Urbana. **[38]**

Dionne, G., & Harrington, S. (1992). An introduction to insurance economics. In G. Dionne & S. Harrington (Eds.). *Foundations of insurance economics.* Boston: Kluwer Academic Publishers. **[13]**

Donaldson, G., & Lorsch, J. (1983). *Decision making at the top.* New York: Basic Books. **[22]**

Dow, J., & Werlang, S. R. d. C. (1992). Uncertainty aversion, risk aversion, and the optimal choice of portfolio. *Econometrica, 60*(1), 197–204. **[30]**

Downs, A. (1957). *An economic theory of democracy.* New York: Harper & Row. **[25]**

Driver, M. J., & Streufert, S. (1964). The 'general incongruity adaptation level' (GIAL) hypothesis: An analysis and integration of cognitive approaches to motivation. Paper No. 114, Institute for Research in the Behavioral, Economic and Management Sciences, Krannert Graduate School of Management, Purdue University. **[41]**

Duesenberry, J. S. (1949). *Income, saving and the theory of consumer behavior.* Cambridge, MA: Harvard University Press. **[16, 19, 20, 33, 40]**

Duhaime, I., & Schwenk, C. (1985). Conjectures on cognitive simplification in acquisition and divestment decision making. *Academy of Management Rev., 10,* 287–295. **[33]**

Dun and Bradstreet. (1967). *Patterns of success in managing a business.* New York: Dun and Bradstreet. **[22, 26]**

Dunne, T., Roberts, M. J., & Samuelson, L. (1988). Patterns of firm entry and exit in U.S. manufacturing industries. *RAND Journal of Economics, 19,* 495–515. **[23]**

Dunne, T., Roberts, M. J., & Samuelson, L. (1989a). Firm entry and post-entry performance in the U.S. chemical industries. *Journal of Law and Economics, 32,* 233–271. **[23]**

Dunne, T., Roberts, M. J., & Samuelson, L. (1989b, November). The growth and failure of U.S. manufacturing plants. *Quarterly Journal of Economics*, 671–698. **[23]**

Dunning, D., Meyerowitz, J. A., & Holzberg, A. D. (1989). Ambiguity and self-evaluation: The role of idiosyncratic trait definitions in self-serving appraisals of ability. *Journal of Personality and Social Psychology, 57*, 1082–1090. **[23]**

Dyl, E. (1977). Capital gains taxation and the year-end stock market behavior, *Journal of Finance, 32*, 165–175. **[21]**

Eagly, A., & Chaiken, S. (1993). *The psychology of attitudes.* Fort Worth. TX: Harcourt Brace. **[36]**

Eagly, A., & Chaiken, S. (1996). Attitude structure and function. In Gilbert, D., Fiske, S., & Lindzey, G. (Eds.). *The handbook of social psychology* (4th ed.). New York: McGraw-Hill. **[36]**

Easterlin, R. A. (1974). Does economic growth improve the human lot? Some empirical evidence. In P. A. David & M. W. Reder (Eds.), *Nations and Households in Economic Growth* (pp. 89–125). Academic Press. **[7, 39]**

Edwards, W. (1954). The theory of decision making. *Psychological Bulletin, 51*, 380–417. **[27]**

Edwards, W. (1962). Subjective probabilities inferred from decisions. *Psychological Review, 69*, 109–135. **[2, 5]**

Einhorn, H., & Hogarth, R. (1978). Confidence in judgment: Persistence of the illusion of validity. *Psychological Review, 85*(5), 395–416. **[12]**

Einhorn, H. J. & Hogarth, R. M. (1985). Ambiguity and uncertainty in probabilistic inference. *Psychological Review, 92*, 433–461. **[30]**

Eisenberg, M. A. (1979). Donative promises. *U. Chi. L. Rev., 47*, 1. **[24]**

Eisenberg, M. A. (1982). The principles of consideration. *Cornell L. Rev. 67*, 640. **[24]**

Eisner, R., & Strotz, R. H. (1961). Flight insurance and the theory of choice. *Journal of Political Economy, 69*, 355–368. **[13]**

Ekman, P. (1985). *Telling lies.* New York: Norton. **[35]**

Ellickson, R. (1989). Bringing culture and human frailty to rational actors: A critique of classical law and economics. *Chicago-Kent Law Review, 65*(23), 23–55. **[24, 42]**

Ellsberg, D. (1961). Risk, ambiguity and the Savage axioms. *Quarterly Journal of Economics, 75*, 643–669. **[2, 3, 5, 6, 12, 30]**

Ellul, J. (1963). *Propaganda.* New York: Knopf. **[35]**

Elster, J. (1977). Ulysses and the sirens: A theory of imperfect rationality. *Social Science Information, 16*(5), 469–526. **[15]**

Elster, J. (1985b). Weakness of the will and the free-rider problem. *Economics and Philosophy, 1*, 231–265. **[32, 39]**

Elster, J., & Loewenstein, G. (1992). Utility from memory and anticipation. In J. Elster & G. Loewenstein (Eds.), *Choice over time* (pp. 213–224). New York: Russell Sage Foundation. **[32, 42]**

Engen, E. M., Gale, W. G., & Scholz, J. K. (1996 (Fall)). The illusory effects of saving incentive programs. *Journal of Economics Perspectives, 10*, 113–138. **[14]**

Epstein, L. G. (1992). Behavior under risk: Recent developments in theory and applications. In *Advances in economic theory*. Vol. 2, J.-J. Laffont (Ed.), Cambridge, UK: Cambridge University Press, 1–63. **[11]**

Epstein, L. G., & Hynes, J. A. (1983). The rate of time preference and dynamic economic analysis. *Journal of Political Economy, 91*, 611–635. **[32]**

Epstein, L. G., & Wang, T. (1994). Intertemporal asset pricing under Knightian uncertainty. *Econometrica, 62*(2), 282–322. **[30]**

Epstein, L. G., & Zin, S. E. (1990). "First-order" risk aversion and the equity premium puzzle. *Journal of Monetary Economics, 26*(3), 387–407. **[11, 17]**

Erakar, S. E., & Sox, H. C. (1981). Assessment of patients' preferences for therapeutic outcomes. *Medical Decision Making, 1,* 29–39. **[1]**

Ericsson, K. A., & Simon, H. A. (1980). Verbal reports as data. *Psychological Review, 87*(3), 215–251. **[41]**

Fama, E. F. (1984). Term premiums in bond returns. *Journal of Financial Economics, 13,* 529–516. **[33]**

Fazio, R. H., Sanbonmatsu, D. M., Powell, M. C., & Kardes, F. R. (1986). On the automatic activation of attitudes. *Journal of Personality and Social Psychology, 50,* 229–238. **[36]**

Feather, N. T. (1966). Effects of prior success and failure on expectations of success and failure. *Journal of Personality and Social Psychology, 3,* 287–298. **[39]**

Feenberg, D., & Skinner, J. (1989). Sources of IRA saving. In L. Summers (Ed.), *Tax Policy and the Economy* (Vol. 3, pp. 25–46). Cambridge, MA: MIT Press. **[14]**

Feinberg, R. A. (1986). Credit cards as spending facilitating stimuli: A conditioning interpretation. *Journal of Consumer Research, 12,* 304–356. **[14]**

Feinman, J. M. (1984). Promissory estoppel and judicial method. *Harv. L. Rev., 97,* 86. **[24]**

Fellner, W. (1961). Distortion of subjective probabilities as a reaction to uncertainty. *Quarterly Journal of Economics, 75,* 670–694. **[2, 5, 30]**

Fellner, W. (1965). *Probability and Profit – A study of economic behavior along bayesian lines.* Homewood, IL: Richard D. Irwin. **[2]**

Ferris, S. P., Haugen, R. A., & Makhija, A. K. (1988). Predicting contemporary volume with historic volume at differential price levels: Evidence supporting the disposition effect. *Journal of Finance, 43,* 677–697. **[21, 33]**

Ferson, W. E., & Constantinides, G. M. (1988, December). Habit formation and durability in aggregate consumption: Empirical tests. Paper presented at the American Finance Association meeting. **[33]**

Ferson, W., & Constantinides, G. M. (1991). Habit persistence and durability in aggregate consumption: Empirical test. *Journal of Financial Economics, 39,* 199–240. **[17]**

Festinger, L. (1957). *A theory of cognitive dissonance.* Evanston, IL: Row, Peterson. **[41]**

Fetherstonhaugh, D., Slovic, P., Johnson, S. M., & Friedrich, J. (1997). Insensitivity to the value of human life: A study of psychophysical numbing. *Journal of Risk and Uncertainty, 14,* 283–300. **[31]**

Fiegenbaum, A. (1990). Prospect theory and the risk-return association. *J. Econ. Behavior and Organization, 14,* 187–203. **[22]**

Fiegenbaum, A., & Thomas, H. (1988). Attitudes toward risk and the risk return paradox: Prospect theory explanations. *Academy of Management J., 31,* 85–106. **[22]**

Fischer, S. (1977a). Long-term contracts, rational expectations, and the optimal money supply rule. *Journal of Political Economy, 85,* 191–206. Reprinted in S. Fischer. *Indexing, inflation, and economic policy.* Cambridge, MA: MIT Press, 1986. **[19]**

Fischer, S. (1977b). On the Nonexistence of Privately Issued Index Bonds in the U.S. Capital Market, in E. Lundberg (Ed.), *Inflation theory and anti-inflation policy.* Macmillan, pp. 502–518. Reprinted in S. Fischer, *Indexing, inflation, and economic policy.* Cambridge, MA: MIT Press, 1986. **[19]**

Fischer, S. (1982). Adapting to inflation in the United States economy. In R. E. Hall, (Ed.), *Inflation: Causes and effects.* Chicago: University of Chicago Press. **[19]**

Fischer, G., & Hawkins, S. (1993). Strategy compatibility, scale compatibility, and the prominence effect. *Journal of Experimental Psychology: Human Perception and Performance, 19,* 580–597. **[27, 31]**

Fischer, S., & Modigliani, F. Towards an understanding of the real effects and costs of inflation. *Review of World Economics (Weltwirtschaftliches Archiv),* 810–833. Reprinted in S. Fischer, *Indexing, inflation, and economic policy.* Cambridge, MA: MIT Press, 1986. **[19]**

Fischhoff, B. (1983). Predicting frames. *Journal of Experimental Psychology: Learning, Memory, and Cognition, 9,* 103–116. **[1, 35]**

Fischhoff, B. (1988). Judgment and decision making. In R. J. Sternberg & E. E. Smith (Eds.), *The psychology of human thought* (pp. 153–187). New York: Wiley. **[35]**

Fischhoff, B. (1991). Value elicitation: Is there anything in there? *American Psychologist, 46,* 835–847. **[36]**

Fischhoff, B., & Cox, L. A., Jr. (1985). Conceptual foundation for benefit assessment. In J. D. Bentkover, V. T. Covello, & J. Mumpower (Eds.), *Benefits assessment: The state of the art* (pp. 51–84). Amsterdam: Reidel. **[35]**

Fischhoff, B., & Furby, L. (1988). Measuring values: A conceptual framework for interpreting transactions with special reference to contingent valuation of visibility. *Journal of Risk and Uncertainty, 1,* 147–184. **[35]**

Fischhoff, B., Slovic, P., & Lichtenstein, S. (1978). Fault trees: Sensitivity of estimated failure probabilities to problem representation. *Journal of Experimental Psychology: Human Perception and Performance, 4,* 330–334. **[6]**

Fischhoff, B., Slovic, P., & Lichtenstein, S. (1980). Knowing what you want: Measuring labile values. In T. Wallsten (Ed.), *Cognitive processes in choice and decision behavior* (pp. 117–141). Hillsdale, NJ: Erlbaum. **[1, 27, 28, 35]**

Fishburn, P. C. (1977). Mean-risk analysis with risk associated with below-target returns, *American Economic Review, 67,* 116–126. **[2]**

Fishburn, P. C. (1982). Nontransitive measurable utility. *Journal of Mathematical Psychology, 26,* 31–67. **[12]**

Fishburn, P. C. (1983). Transitive measurable utility. *Journal of Economic Theory, 31,* 293–317. **[12]**

Fishburn, P. C. (1984). SSB utility theory and decision-making under uncertainty. *Mathematical Social Science, 8,* 253–285. **[12]**

Fishburn, P. (1985a). Nontransitive preference theory and the preference reversal phenomenon. *Rivista Internazionale di Scienze Economiche e Commerciali, 32,* 39–50. **[27]**

Fishburn, P. C. (1985b). Uncertainty aversion and separated effects in decision making under uncertainty. Working paper, AT&T Bell Labs, Murray Hill, N.J. **[12]**

Fishburn, P. C. (1988). *Nonlinear preference and utility theory*: Baltimore: The Johns Hopkins University Press. **[3]**

Fishburn, P. C., & Kochenberger, G. A. (1979). Two-piece von Neumann–Morgenstern utility functions. *Decision Sciences, 10,* 503–518. **[1, 2, 5, 22]**

Fishburn, P., & Luce, D. (1995). Joint receipt and Thaler's hedonic editing rule. *Mathematical Social Science, 29,* 33–76. **[14]**

Fishburn, P. C., & Rubinstein, A. (1982). Time preference. *International Economic Review, 23,* 677–694. **[33]**

Fisher, I. (1913). A remedy for the rising cost of living: Standardizing the dollar. *American Economic Review, 3,* 20–28. **[19]**

Fisher, I. (1918). Is 'utility' the most suitable term for the concept it is used to denote? *American Economic Review, 8,* 335–337. Reproduced in A. N. Page (Ed.) (1968). *Utility theory: A book of readings.* Wiley: New York. **[42]**

Fisher, I. (1928). *The Money Illusion.* New York: Adelphi. **[19]**

Fiske, D. W., & Maddi, S. R. (1961). *Functions of varied experience.* Homewood, IL: Dorsey Press. [41]

Fitts, P., & Seeger, C. (1953). S–R compatibility: Spatial characteristics of stimulus and response codes. *Journal of Experimental Psychology, 46,* 199–210. [27, 28]

Forrester, I. S., Goren, S. L., & Ilgen, H. M. (Trans.). (1975). *The German civil code.* South Hackensack, N.J.: Fred B. Rothman. [24]

Foster, V., Bateman, I. J., & Harley, D. (1997). Real and hypothetical willingness to pay for environmental preservation: A non-experimental comparison. *Journal of Agricultural Economics, 48,* 123–138. [36]

Fox, C. R. (1998). Subadditivity in judgment and choice: A test of the major axioms and implications of support theory. Unpublished manuscript, Duke University Fuqua School of Business, Durham, NC. [6]

Fox, C. R., Rogers, B. A., & Tversky, A. (1996). *Options Traders Exhibit Subadditive Decision Weights. Journal of Risk and Uncertainty, 13,* 5–17. [5]

Fox, C. R., & Tversky, A. (1995). Ambiguity aversion and comparative ignorance. *Quarterly Journal of Economics, 110*(3), 585–603. [5, 6]

Franciosi, R., Kujal, P., Michelitsch, R., & Smith, V. (1993). Experimental tests of the endowment effect. University of Arizona Department of Economics working paper. [42]

Frank, R. H. (1985). *Choosing the right pond; Human behavior and the quest for status.* New York: Oxford University Press. [18]

Frank, R. H. (1988). *Passions within reason: The strategic role of emotions.* New York: W.W. Norton. [26]

Frank, R. H. (1992a). Frames of reference and the intertemporal wage profile. In G. Loewenstein & J. Elster (Eds.), *Choice Over Time* (pp. 371–382). New York: Russell Sage Foundation. [32]

Frank, R. H. (1992b). The role of moral sentiments in the theory of intertemporal choice, pp. 265–286. In J. Elster & G. Loewenstein (Eds.), *Choice over time.* New York: Russel Sage Foundation. [42]

Fredrick, S., & Fischhoff, B. (1998). Scope (in)sensitivity in elicited valuations. *Risk Decision and Policy, 3,* 109–123. [36]

Fredrickson, B. L. (1991). *Anticipating endings: An explanation for selective social interaction.* Unpublished Ph.D. dissertation, Stanford University. [38]

Fredrickson, B. L. (2000). Extracting meaning from past affective experiences: The importance of peaks, ends, and specific emotions. *Cognition and emotion,* Forthcoming. [38]

Fredrickson, B. L., & Kahneman, D. (1993). Duration neglect in retrospective evaluations of affective episodes. *Journal of Personality and Social Psychology, 65*(1), 45–55. [38, 42]

Fried, C. (1981). *Contract as promise.* Cambridge, MA: Harvard University Press. [24]

Friedman, M. (1957). *A theory of consumption function.* Princeton, NJ: Princeton University Press. [14]

Friedman, M., & Savage, L. J. (1948). The utility analysis of choices involving risks, *Journal of Political Economy, 56,* 279–304. [2, 5, 15]

Frisch, D., & Baron, J. (1988). Ambiguity and rationality. *Journal of Behavioral Decision Making, 1*(3), 149–157. [5, 30]

Fuchs, V. R. (1976). From Bismark to Woodcock: The "irrational" pursuit of national health insurance. *Journal of Law and Economics, 19,* 347–359. [2]

Furby, L. (1986). Psychology and justice. In R. L. Cohen (Ed.), *Justice: Views from the social sciences* (pp. 153–203). New York: Plenum. [35]

Furby, L., & Fischhoff, B. (1989). *Specifying subjective evaluations: A critique of Dickie et al.'s interpretation of their contingent valuation results for reduced minor health symptoms* (U.S. Environmental Protection Agency Cooperative Agreement No. CR814655-01-0). Eugene, OR: Eugene Research Institute. [35]

Galanter, E., & Pliner, P. (1974). Cross-modality matching of money against other continua. In *Sensation and Measurement*. Ed. by H. R. Moskowitz et al. Dordrecht, The Netherlands: Reidel, pp. 65–76. [2]

Gately, D. (1980). Individual discount rates and the purchase and utilization of energy-using durables: Comment. *Bell Journal of Economics, 11*, 373–374. [33]

Genesove, D., & Mayer, C. (in press). Loss aversion and seller behavior: Evidence from the housing market. *Quarterly Journal of Economics.* [16]

Gerard, H. B., & Mathewson, G. C. (1966). The effects of severity of initiation on liking for a group: A replication. *Journal of Experimental Social Psychology, 2*, 278–287. [15]

Gergen, K. J. (1973). Social psychology as history. *Journal of Personality and Social Psychology, 26*, 309–320. [35]

Gertner, R. (1993). Game shows and economic behavior: Risk taking on "card sharks." *Quarterly Journal of Economics, 106*, 507–521. [14]

Gigerenzer, G., Hell, W., & Blank, H. (1988). Presentation and content: The use of base rates as a continuous variable. *Journal of Experimental Psychology, 14*(3), 513–525. [22]

Gigerenzer, G., Hoffrage, U., & Kleinbolting, H. (1991). Probabilistic mental models: A Brunswikian theory of confidence. *Psychological Review, 98*(4), 506–528. [22, 26]

Gilboa, I. (1987). Expected utility with purely subjective non-additive probabilities. *Journal of Mathematical Economics, 16*(1), 65–88. [3, 30]

Gilboa, I. (1989). Expectation and variation in multi-period decisions. *Econometrica, 57*, 1153–1169. [32]

Gilligan, C. (1982). *In a different voice: Psychological theory and women's development.* Cambridge, MA: Harvard University Press. [35]

Gneezy, U., & Potters, J. (1997). An experiment on risk taking and evaluation periods. *Quarterly Journal of Economics, 112*(May), 631–646. [11, 14, 20]

Gode, D. K., & Sunder, S. (1993). Allocative efficiency of markets with zero-intelligence traders: Market as a partial substitute for individual rationality. *Journal of Political Economy, 101*, 119–137. [20]

Goff, R., & Jones, G. (1978). *The law of restitution* (2d ed.). London: Sweet & Maxwell. [24]

Goldberg, V. P. (1985). Price adjustment in long-term contracts. *Wis. L. Rev., 3*, 527–543. [24]

Goldstein, W. M. (1990). Judgments of relative importance in decision making: Global vs. local interpretations of subjective weight. *Organizational Behavior and Human Decision Processes, 47*, 313–336. [31]

Goldstein, W., & Einhorn, H. (1987). Expression theory and the preference reversal phenomena. *Psychological Review, 94*, 236–254. [27, 31]

Goldstein, W. M., & Mitzel, H. C. (1992). The relative importance of relative importance: Inferring other people's preferences from relative importance ratings and previous decisions. *Organizational Behavior and Human Decision Processes, 51*, 382–415. [31]

Gonzalez, R., & Wu, G. (1998). On the form of the probability weighting function. Unpublished manuscript, Department of Psychology, University of Michigan, Ann Arbor, MI. [6]

Gordon, D. F. (1974, December). A neo-classical theory of Keynesian unemployment. *Economic Inquiry, 12*, 431–459. [18]

Gordon, R. J. (1983). A century of evidence on wage and price stickiness in the United States, the United Kingdom, and Japan. In J. Tobin (Ed.), *Macroeconomics, prices, and quantities*. Washington, DC: The Brookings Institution. [19]

Gourville, J. T. (1998). Pennies a day: The effect of temporal reframing on transaction evaluation. *Journal of Consumer Research, 24*, 395–408. [14]

Gourville, J. T., & Soman, D. (1998). Payment depreciation: The effects of temporally separating payments from consumption. *Journal of Consumer Research, 25*(2), 160–174. [14]

Grayson, C. J. (1960). *Decisions under uncertainty: Drilling decisions by oil and gas operators.* Cambridge, MA: Graduate School of Business, Harvard University. [2]

Green, D., Jacowitz, K. E., Kahneman, D., & McFadden, D. (1998). Referendum contingent valuation, anchoring, and willingness to pay for public goods. *Resource and Energy Economics, 20*, 85–116. [36]

Green, P. E. (1963). Risk attitudes and chemical investment decisions. *Chemical Engineering Progress, 59*, 35–40. [2]

Green, P. E., & Srinivasan, V. (1978, September). Conjoint analysis in consumer research: Issues and outlook. *Journal of Consumer Research, 5*, 103–123. [41]

Gregory, R. (1983). *Measures of consumer's surplus: Reasons for the disparity in observed values*. Unpublished manuscript, Keene State College, Keene, NH. [1]

Gregory, R., Lichtenstein, S., & Slovic, P. (1993). Valuing environmental resources: A constructive approach. *Journal of Risk and Uncertainty, 7*, 177–197. [27]

Grether, D. M. (1980). Bayes' rule as a descriptive model: The representativeness heuristic. *Quarterly Journal of Economics, 95*, 537–557. [12, 15]

Grether, D., & Plott, C. R. (1979). Economic theory of choice and the preference reversal phenomenon. *American Economic Review, 69*, 623–638. [2, 15, 27, 31]

Griffin, D., & Tversky, A. (1992). The weighing of evidence and the determinants of confidence. *Cognitive Psychology, 24*(3), 411–435. [22, 26, 36]

Guadagni, P. M., & Little, J. D. C. (1983). A logit model of brand choice. *Marketing Science, 2*(3), 203–238. [41]

Guest, A. G. (1984). *Anson's law of contract* (26th ed.). Oxford: Clarendon Press. [24]

Guth, W., Schmittberger, R., & Schwarze, B. (1982). An experimental analysis of ultimatum bargaining. *Journal of Economic Behavior and Organization, 3*, 367–388. [18]

Hagen, O. (1979). Towards a positive theory of preferences under risk. In M. Allais & O. Hagen (Eds.), *Expected utility hypotheses and the Allais paradox*. Dordrecht: Reidel. [12]

Halpern, S. W. (1987). Application of the doctrine of commercial impracticability: Searching for the "wisdom of Solomon." *U. Pa. L. Rev., 135*, 1123. [24]

Halsbury's laws of England (4th ed., Vol. 20). (1978). London: Butterworths. [24]

Halter, A. N., & Dean, G. W. (1971). *Decisions under uncertainty*. Cincinnati, OH: South Western. [2]

Haltiwanger, J., & Waldman, M. (1985). Rational expectations and the limits of rationality: An analysis of heterogeneity. *American Economic Review, 75*(3), 326–340. [12, 19]

Hammack, J., & Brown, Jr., G. M. (1974). *Waterfowl and Wetlands: Toward bioeconomic analysis*. Baltimore: Johns Hopkins University Press. [1, 9, 24]

Hammond, P. (1985). Consequential behavior in decision trees and expected utility. Institute for Mathematical Studies in the Social Sciences Working Paper no. 112. Stanford University, Stanford, CA. [12, 42]

Hanemann, M. (1994). Valuing the environment through contingent valuation. *Journal of Economic Perspectives, 8*, 19–43. **[36]**

Hanemann, W. M. (1991). Willingness to pay and willingness to accept: How much can they differ? *American Economic Review, 81*(June), 635–647. **[10]**

Hansson, B. (1975). The appropriateness of the expected utility model. *Erkenntnis, 9*, 175–194. **[2, 12]**

Hansson, B. (1988). Risk aversion as a problem of conjoint measurement. In *Decision, probability, and utility*. P. Gardenfors & N.-E. Sahlin (Eds.), New York: Cambridge University Press, 136–158. **[11]**

Hardie, B. G. S., Johnson, E. J., & Fader, P. S. (1993). Modeling loss aversion and reference dependence effects on brand choice. *Marketing Science, 12*, 378–394. **[16, 42]**

Harless, D. (1992). Actions versus prospects: The effect of problem representation on regret. *American Economic Review, 82*, 634–649. **[4]**

Harless, D. W., & Camerer, C. F. (1994). The predictive utility of generalized expected utility theories. *Econometrica, 62*(6), 1251–1289. **[11]**

Harris, L. (1988). Discussion of predicting contemporary volume with historic volume at differential price levels: Evidence supporting the disposition effect. *Journal of Finance, 43*, 698–699. **[21]**

Harrison, J. R., & March, J. G. (1984). Decision making and post-decision surprises, *Admin. Sci. Quarterly, 29*, 26–42. **[22]**

Hart, H. L. A., & Honore, A. M. (1959). In *Causation in the law*. Oxford: Clarendon Press. **[24]**

Hartman, R. S., Doane, M. J., & Woo, C.-K. (1991). Consumer rationality and the status quo. *Quarterly Journal of Economics, 106*(1), 141–162. **[8]**

Harvey, C. M. (1986). Value functions for infinite-period planning. *Management Science, 32*, 1123–1139. **[33]**

Hastie, R., Schkade, D. A., & Payne, J. W. (1999). Juror judgments in civil cases: Effects of plaintiff's request and plaintiff's identity on punitive damage awards. *Law and Human Behavior, 23*(5), 445–470. **[36]**

Hatsopoulous, G. N., Krugman, P. R., & Poterba, J. M. (1989). *Overconsumption: The challenge to U.S. economic policy*. Paper presented at the American Business Conference. **[14]**

Hausch, D. B., & Ziemba, W. T. (1995). Efficiency in sports and lottery betting markets. In R. A. Jarrow, V. Maksimovic, & W. T. Ziemba (Eds.). *Handbook of Finance*. Amsterdam: North-Holland. **[16]**

Hausch, D. B., Ziemba, W. T., & Rubenstein, M. E. (1981). Efficiency of the market for racetrack betting. *Management Science, 27*, 1435–1452. **[12]**

Hausman, D. (1991). On dogmatism in economics: The case of preference reversals. *Journal of Socio-Economics, 20*, 205–225. **[27]**

Hausman, J. (1979). Individual discount rates and the purchase and utilization of energy-using durables. *Bell Journal of Economics, 10*, 33–54. **[33]**

Heath, C. (1995). Escalation and De-escalation of commitment in response to sunk costs: The role of budgeting in mental accounting. *Organizational Behavior and Human Decision Processes, 62*, 38–54. **[14]**

Heath, C., & Soll, J. B. (1996). Mental accounting and consumer decisions. *Journal of Consumer Research, 23*, 40–52. **[14]**

Heath, C., & Tversky, A. (1991). Preference and belief: Ambiguity and competence in choice under uncertainty. *Journal of Risk and Uncertainty, 4*, 5–28. **[3, 5, 6, 26, 30]**

Heberlein, T. A., & Bishop, R. C. (1985). Assessing the validity of contingent valuation:

Three field experiments. Paper presented at the international conference on man's role in changing the global environment, Italy. [7, 9]

Heckman, J. (1979). Sample selection bias as a specification error. *Econometrica, 47,* 153–161. [20]

Heider, F. (1980). *The psychology of interpersonal relations.* New York: Wiley. [34]

Heisler, J. (1994). Loss aversion in a futures market: An empirical test. *Review of Futures Markets, 13,* 793–822. [21]

Helson, H. (1964). *Adaptation level theory: An experimental and systematic approach to behavior.* New York: Harper & Row. [2, 20, 32]

Henderson, J. M., & Quandt, R. E. (1971). *Microeconomic Theory* (2nd ed.). New York: McGraw-Hill. [9]

Henderson, P., & Peterson, R. (1992). Mental accounting and categorization. *Organizational Behavioral and Human Decision Processes, 51,* 92–117. [14]

Hendricks, W. E., & Kahn, L. M. (1985). *Wage indexation in the United States: COLA or UnCOLA.* Cambridge: Ballinger. [19]

Herrnstein, R. J. (1981). Self-control as response strength. In *Quantification of steady-state operant behavior.* C. M. Bradshaw, E. Szabadi, & C. F. Lowe (Eds.). Amsterdam: Elsevier/North-Holland. [33]

Hershey, J., Johnson, E., Meszaros, J., & Robinson, M. (1990, June). What is the right to sue worth? Wharton School, University of Pennsylvania. [8]

Hershey, J. C., Kunreuther, H. C., & Schoemaker, P. J. H. (1982, August). Sources of bias in assessment procedures for utility functions. *Management Science, 28,* 936–954. [13]

Hershey, J. C., & Schoemaker, P. (1980a). Prospect theory's reflection hypothesis: A critical examination. *Organizational Behavior and Human (Decision Processes), 25,* 395–418. [3, 5]

Hershey, J. C., & Schoemaker, P. J. H. (1980b). Risk taking and problem context in the domain of losses: An expected-utility analysis. *Journal of Risk and Insurance, 47,* 111–132. [1, 13, 35]

Hicks, J. R. (1943). The four consumer surpluses. *Review of Economic Studies, 8,* 108–116. [10]

Hicks, J. R. (1956). *A revision of demand theory.* Oxford: Clarendon Press. [10]

Hines, J., & Thaler, R. H. (1995). Anomalies: The flypaper effect. *Journal of Economics Perspectives, 9,* 217–226. [14]

Hirsch, W. Z. (1979). *Law and economics: An introductory analysis.* New York: Academic Press. [24]

Hirschberg, E. (1976). *The impact of inflation and devaluation on private legal obligations.* Ramat Gan, Israel: Bar Ilan University. [19]

Hoehn, J. P., & Randall, A. (1987). Too many proposals pass the benefit cost test. *American Economic Review, 79,* 544–551. [36]

Hoffman, E., & Spitzer, M. L. (1982, April). The Coase theorem: Some experimental tests. *Journal of Law and Economics, 25,* 73–98. [18]

Hoffman, E., & Spitzer, M. L. (1985, June). Entitlements, rights, and fairness: An experimental examination of subjects' concepts of distributive justice. *Journal of Legal Studies, 14,* 259–297. [18]

Hogarth, R. M. (Ed.). (1982). *New directions for methodology of the social sciences: Question framing and response consistency.* San Francisco: Jossey-Bass. [35]

Hogarth, R. M., & Einhorn, H. J. (1990). Venture theory: A model of decision weights. *Management Science, 36(7),* 780–803. [3, 5, 22, 26]

Holcomb, J. H., & Nelson, P. S. (1989). An experimental investigation of individual time preference University of Texas–El Paso Department of Economics. [33]

Holmes, O. W. (1897). The path of the law. *Harvard Law Review, 10*, 457–478. **[8, 24]**

Holt, C. A. (1986, June). Preference reversals and the independence axiom. *American Economic Review, 76*, 508–514. **[27]**

Horowitz, J. K. (1988). Discounting money payoffs: An experimental analysis. Working paper, Department of Agricultural and Resource Economics, University of Maryland. **[33]**

Horowitz, J. K. (1991). Discounting money payoffs: An experimental analysis. In S. Kaish & B. Gilad (Eds.), *Handbook of behavioral economics* (Vol. 2). Greenwich, CT: JAI Press. **[32]**

Hotz, V. J., Kydland, F. E., & Sedlacek, G. L. (1988). Intertemporal preferences and labor supply. *Econometrica, 56*, 335–360. **[33]**

Hovencamp, H. (1991). Legal policy and the endowment effect, *Journal of Legal Studies, 20*, 225–247. **[17, 20, 24, 42]**

Howell, W. (1971). Uncertainty from internal and external sources: A clear case of overconfidence. *Journal of Experimental Psychology, 81*, 240–243. **[26, 30]**

Howitt, P. (1986). Indexation and the adjustment to inflation in Canada. In *Postwar macro-economic developments*, Vol. 20. Toronto: University of Toronto Press, pp. 175–224. **[19]**

Howitt, P. (1987). Money illusion. In *The new palgrave: A dictionary of economics*, J. Eatwell, M. Milgate, & P. Newman (Eds.), New York: W.W. Norton. **[19]**

Hsee, C. K. (1993). When trend of monetary outcomes matters: Separate versus joint evaluation, and judgment of feelings versus choice. Unpublished manuscript, The University of Chicago. **[31]**

Hsee, C. K. (1996). The evaluability hypothesis: An explanation of preference reversals between joint and separate evaluations of alternatives. *Organizational Behavior and Human Decision Processes, 46*, 247–257. **[31, 36]**

Hsee, C. K. (1998). Less is better: When low-value options are judged more highly than high-value options. *Journal of Behavioral Decision Making, 11*, 107–121. **[31]**

Hsee, C. K., & Abelson, R. P. (1991). Velocity relation: Satisfaction as a function of the first derivative of outcome over time. *Journal of Personality and Social Psychology, 60*, 341–347. **[32, 38]**

Hsee, C. K., Abelson, R. P., & Salovey, P. (1991). The relative weighting of position and velocity in satisfaction. *Psychological Science, 2*, 263–266. **[32, 38]**

Hsee, C. K., & Leclerc, F. (1998). Will products look more attractive when evaluated jointly or when evaluated separately? *Journal of Consumer Research, 25*, 175–186. **[31]**

Hsee, C. K., Loewenstein, G., Blount, S., & Bazerman, M. H. (1999). Preference reversals between joint and separate evaluations: A review and theoretical analysis. *Psychological Bulletin, 125*(5), 576–590. **[31]**

Huber, J., Payne, J. W., & Puto, C. (1982). Adding asymmetrically dominated alternatives: Violations of regularity and the similarity hypothesis. *J. Consumer Res., 9*, 90–98. **[29, 34]**

Huber, J. J., & Puto, C. (1983). Market boundaries and product choice: Illustrating attraction and substitution effects. *J. Consumer Res., 10*, 31–44. **[29]**

Ikenberry, D., Lakonishok, J., & Vermaelen, T. (1995). Market underreaction to open market share repurchases. *Journal of Financial Economics, 39*, 181–208. **[21]**

Insurance Information Institute. (1990a). *1990 property/casualty insurance facts*. New York: Insurance Information Institute. **[13]**

Insurance Information Institute. (1990b). *No-fault auto insurance*. New York: Insurance Information Institute. **[13]**

Insurance Information Institute. (1992). *No-fault auto insurance.* New York: Insurance Information Institute. [13]

Irwin, J., Slovic, P., Lichtenstein, S., & McClelland, G. H. (1993). Preference reversals and the measurement of environmental values. *Journal of Risk and Uncertainty, 6,* 5–18. [27, 31]

Ishikawa, T., & Ueda, K. (1984). The bonus payment system and Japanese personal savings. In *The Economic Analysis of the Japanese Firm.* M. Aoki (Ed.), Amsterdam: North-Holland. [33]

Jabine, T. B., Straf, M. L., Tanur, J. M., & Tourangeau, R. (Eds.). (1984). *Cognitive aspects of survey methodology: Building a bridge between disciplines.* Washington, DC: National Academy Press. [35]

Jacowitz, K. E., & Kahneman, D. (1995). Measures of anchoring in estimation tasks. *Personality and Social Psychology Bulletin, 21,* 1161–1166. [36]

James, W. (1981). *The principles of psychology* (Vol. 2). Cambridge, MA: Harvard University Press. [34]

Janis, I. L. (1982). *Groupthink* (2nd ed.). Boston, MA: Houghton-Mifflin. [22]

Janis, I. L., & Mann, L. (1979). *Decision making: A psychological analysis of conflict, choice, and commitment.* The Free Press: New York. [31]

Jecker, J. R. (1964). The cognitive effects of conflict and dissonance. In *Conflict, decision, and dissonance.* L. Festinger (Ed.). Stanford, CA: Stanford University Press. [41]

Jegadeesh, N., & Titman, S. (1993). Returns to buying winners and selling losers: Implications for stock market efficiency. *Journal of Finance, 48,* 65–91. [21]

Jenni, K., & Loewenstein, G. (1997). Explaining the "identifiable victim effect." *Journal of Risk and Uncertainty, 14,* 235–257. [31]

Jervis, R. (1992). Political implications of loss aversion. Unpublished manuscript. New York: Columbia University. [26]

Johnson, E. J., Hershey, J., Meszaros, J., & Kunreuther, H. (1992). Framing, probability distortions, and insurance decisions. *Journal of Risk and Uncertainty, 7,* 35–51. [5, 6, 16, 19]

Jones-Lee, M. W., Hammerton, M., & Philips, P. R. (1985). The value of safety: Results of a national sample survey. *Economic Journal, 95,* 49–72. [10]

Jones-Lee, M. W., Loomes, G., & Philips, P. R. (1995). Valuing the prevention of non-fatal road injuries: Contingent valuation vs. standard gambles. *Oxford Economic Papers, 47,* 676–695. [36]

Jullien, B., & Salanié, B. (1997). Estimating preferences under risk: The case of racetrack bettors. IDEI and GREMAQ, Working paper, Toulouse University. [16]

Kachelmeier, S. J., & Shehata, M. (1992). Examining risk preferences under high monetary incentives: Experimental evidence from the People's Republic of China. *American Economic Review, 82,* 1120–1141. [3, 5, 19]

Kagel, J., & Battalio, R. (1975, March). Experimental studies of consumer behavior using laboratory animals. *Economic Inquiry,* 22–38. [15]

Kagel, J., Battalio, R., & Green, L. (1995). *Economic choice theory: An experimental analysis of animal behavior.* New York: Cambridge University Press.

Kagel, J., & Levin, D. (1986). The winner's curse and public information in common value auctions. *American Economic Review, 76,* 894–920. [22]

Kahneman, D. (1986). Comments on the contingent valuation method. In R. G. Cummings, D. S. Brookshire, & W. D. Schulze (Eds.). *Valuing environmental goods: An assessment of the contingent valuation method.* Totowa, NJ: Rowman & Allanheld. [13, 35]

Kahneman, D. (1986). Valuing environmental goods: An assessment of the contingent valuation method. In R. Cummings, D. Brookshire, & W. Schulze (Eds.). *Valuing environmental goods: An assessment of the contingent valuation method*. Totowa, NJ: Rowman & Allanheld. [36]

Kahneman, D. (1988). Experimental economics: A psychological perspective. In R. Tietz, W. Albers, & R. Selten (Eds.). *Bounded rational behavior in experimental games and markets*, Berlin: Springer–Verlag, 11–18. [23]

Kahneman, D. (1992). Reference points, anchors, norms, and mixed feelings. Special Issue: Decision processes in negotiation. *Organizational Behavior and Human Decision Processes, 51*(2), 296–312. [14]

Kahneman, D. (1994). New challenges to the rationality assumption. *Journal of Institutional and Theoretical Economics, 150*, 18–36. [14, 38]

Kahneman, D. (1995). Extension neglect and violations of monotonicity in judgment and preference: Three examples. Bartlett Lecture to the Experimental Psychology Society (UK). [36]

Kahneman, D., Fredrickson, B. L., Schreiber, C. A., & Redelmeier, D. A. (1993). When more pain is preferred to less: Adding a better end. *Psychological Science, 4*(6), 401–405. [36, 38, 42]

Kahneman, D., & Knetsch, J. L. (1992). Valuing public goods: The purchase of moral satisfaction. *Journal of Environmental Economics and Management, 22*, 57–70. [13, 36]

Kahneman, D., Knetsch, J., & Thaler, R. H. (1986). Fairness as a constraint on profit-seeking: Entitlements in the market. *American Economic Review, 76*, 728–741. [7, 8, 9, 14, 17, 19, 24, 26]

Kahneman, D., Knetsch, J. L., & Thaler, R. (1990). Experimental tests of the endowment effect and the Coase theorem. *Journal of Political Economy, 98*, 1325–1348. [7, 8, 10, 13, 16, 17, 20, 24, 26, 40, 42]

Kahneman, D., Knetsch, J. L., & Thaler, R. H. (1991). The endowment effect, loss aversion, and the status quo bias. *Journal of Economic Perspectives, 5*, 193–206. [26]

Kahneman, D., Knetsch, J., & Thaler, R. (1991, Winter). Anomalies: The Endowment effect, loss aversion, and status quo bias. *Journal of Economic Perspectives, 5*, 193–206. [22, 29, 38, 42]

Kahneman, D., Knetsch, J. L., Thaler, R. H., Kunreuther, H., Luce, R. D., & Shweder, R. A. (1986). Fairness and the assumptions of economics/comments. *Journal of Business, 59*(4), S285–S300, S329–S354. [18]

Kahneman, D., & Loewenstein, G. (1991). Explaining the endowment effect. Working Paper, Department of Social and Decision Sciences, Carnegie Mellon University. [40]

Kahneman, D., & Lovallo, D. (1993). Timid choices and bold forecasts: A cognitive perspective on risk taking. *Management Science, 39*(1), 17–31. [11, 14, 23, 26]

Kahneman, D., & Miller, D. T. (1986). Norm theory: Comparing reality with its alternatives. *Psychological Review, 93*, 136–153. [31, 36]

Kahneman, D., & Varey, C. (1991). Notes on the psychology of utility. In J. Roemer & J. Elster (Eds.), *Interpersonal comparisons of well-being* (pp. 127–163). New York: Cambridge University Press. [39, 42]

Kahneman, D., & Ritov, I. (1994). Determinants of stated willingness to pay for public goods – A study in the headline method. *Journal of Risk and Uncertainty, 9*(1), 5–38. [27, 31, 36]

Kahneman, D., Ritov, I., & Schkade, D. (1999). Economic preferences or attitude expressions? An analysis of dollar responses to public issues. *Journal of Risk and Uncertainty, 19*, 203–235. [38]

Kehneman, D., & Schkade, D. (1999). Predicting the well-being effect of new circumstances: Changes are proxies for states. Working paper, Princeton University. [38]

Kahneman, D., Schkade, D. A., & Sunstein, C. R. (1998). Shared outrage and erratic awards: The psychology of punitive damages. *Journal of Risk and Uncertainty, 16,* 49–86. [36]

Kahneman, D., Slovic, P., & Tversky, A. E. (1982). *Judgment under uncertainty: Heuristic and biases.* Cambridge University Press. [3, 25, 26]

Kahneman, D., & Snell, J. (1990). Predicting utility, In Robin Hogarth. (Ed.), *Insights in decision making* Chicago: University of Chicago Press. [7, 31, 39, 40, 41, 42]

Kahneman, D., & Snell, J. (1992). Predicting a changing taste: Do people know what they will like? *Journal of Behavioral Decision Making, 5,* 187–200. [31, 42]

Kahneman, D., & Tversky, A. (1972). Subjective probability: A judgment of representativeness. *Cognitive Psychology, 3,* 430–454. [36]

Kahneman, D., & Tversky, A. (1973). On the psychology of prediction. *Psychological Review, 80,* 237–251. [22, 26, 36, 38]

Kahneman, D., & Tversky, A. (1979a). Intuitive prediction: Biases and corrective procedures. *Management Sci., 12,* 313–327. [22, 23, 26]

Kahneman, D., & Tversky, A. (1979b). Prospect theory: An analysis of decision under risk. *Econometrica, 47,* 263–291. [1, 3, 4, 5, 6, 7, 9, 11, 12, 13, 14, 15, 17, 18, 19, 20, 21, 22, 24, 25, 26, 27, 30, 32, 33, 34, 35, 36, 38, 39, 42]

Kahneman, D., & Tversky, A. (1982). The simulation heuristic. In D. Kahneman, P. Slovic, & A. Tversky (Eds.), *Judgment under uncertainty: Heuristics and biases.* (pp. 201–208). New York: Cambridge University Press. [1]

Kahneman, D., & Tversky, A. (1982). On the study of statistical intuitions. *Cognition, 11,* 123–141. [35]

Kahneman, D., & Tversky, A. (1982). The psychology of preferences. *Scientific American, 246,* 160–173. [12]

Kahneman, D., & Tversky, A. (1984). Choices, values, and frames. *American Psychologist, 39*(4), 341–350. [3, 7, 8, 9, 13, 14, 17, 18, 25, 26, 28, 39]

Kahneman, D., & Tversky, A. (1992, October). Advances in prospect theory: Cumulative representation of uncertainty. *Journal of Risk and Uncertainty, 5,* 297–324. [16]

Kahneman, D., Wakker, P. P., & Sarin, R. (1997). Back to Bentham? Explorations of experienced utility. *Quarterly Journal of Economics, 112,* 375–405. [36]

Kalwani, M. U., Yim, C. K., Rinne, H. J., & Sugita, Y. A price expectations model of customer brand choice. *Journal of Marketing Research. 27,* 251–262. [7]

Kandel, S., & Stambaugh, R. F. (1991, February). Asset returns, investment horizons, and intertemporal preferences. *Journal of Monetary Economics,* 39–71. [11]

Karni, E., & Safra, Z. (1987). Preference reversal and the observability of preferences by experimental methods. *Econometrica, 55,* 675–685. [27]

Katz, J., Redelmeier, D. A., & Kahneman, D. (1997). *Memories of painful medical procedures.* Paper presented at the American Pain Society 15th Annual Scientific Meeting. [38]

Keeney, R. L., & Raiffa, H. (1976). *Decisions with multiple objectives: Preferences and value tradeoffs.* New York: Wiley. [2, 22]

Kemp, M. A., & Maxwell, C. (1993) Exploring a budget context for contingent valuation. In Hausman (Ed.). *Contingent valuation. A critical assessment.* Amsterdam: North-Holland. [36]

Keppe, H.-J., & Weber, M. (1995). Judged knowledge and ambiguity aversion. *Theory and Decision, 39,* 51–77. [30]

Keren, G. (1991). Additional tests of utility theory under unique and repeated conditions. *Journal of Behavioral Decision Making, 4,* 297–304. **[14]**

Keren, G., & Wagenaar, W. A. (1987). Violation of utility theory in unique and repeated gambles. *Journal of Experimental Psychology: Learning, Memory and Cognition, 13,* 387–391. **[14]**

Kessler, F., Gilmou, G., & Kronman, A. (1986). *Contracts, cases and materials* (3rd ed.). Boston: Little, Brown. **[24]**

Keynes, J. M. (1921). *A treatise on probability.* London: Macmillan. **[5, 30]**

Keynes, J. M. (1936). *The general theory of employment, interest, and money.* London: Macmillan. **[19]**

Kiewiet, D. R. (1982). The rationality of candidates who challenge incumbents in congressional elections. Social Science Working Paper no. 436, California Institute of Technology. **[25]**

Kleiman, E. (1986). Indexation in the labor market. In Y. Ben-Porath. (Ed.), *The Israeli economy.* Cambridge: Harvard University Press. **[19]**

Knetsch, J. L. (1989). The endowment effect and evidence of nonreversible indifference curves. *American Economic Review, 79,* 1277–1284. **[7, 8, 10, 24]**

Knetsch, J. L. (1990). Derived indifference curves. Working paper, Simon Fraser University. **[8]**

Knetsch, J. L., & Sinden, J. A. (1984, August). Willingness to pay and compensation demanded: Experimental evidence of an unexpected disparity in measures of value. *Quarterly Journal of Economics, 99,* 507–521. **[1, 7, 8, 9, 10, 24, 26]**

Knetsch, J. L., & Sinden, J. A. (1987). The persistence of evaluation disparities. *Quarterly Journal of Economics, 102,* 691–695. **[7, 8, 9]**

Knetsch, J. L., Thaler, R., & Kahneman, D. (1988). Experimental tests of the endowment effect and the coase theorem. Working paper, Simon Fraser University. **[9]**

Knez, M., & Smith, V. L. (1987). Hypothetical valuations and preference reversals in the context of asset trading. In A. E. Roth (Ed.), *Laboratory Experimentation in Economics: Six Points of View.* Cambridge, UK: Cambridge University Press. **[27]**

Knez, P., Smith, L., & Williams, A. W. (1985). Individual rationality, market rationality, and value estimation. *American Economic Review (Papers and Proceedings), 75,* 397–402. **[8, 12]**

Knight, F. H. (1921). *Risk, uncertainty, and profit.* New York: Houghton Mifflin. **[5, 30]**

Koehler, J. (1996). The base-rate fallacy reconsidered: Descriptive, normative, and methodological challenges. *Behavioral and Brain Sciences, 19,* 1–53. **[36]**

Koopmans, T. (1960). Stationary ordinal utility and impatience. *Econometrica, 28,* 287–309. **[32, 33]**

Koopmans, T. C., Diamond, P. A., & Williamson, R. E. (1964). Stationary utility and time perspective. *Econometrica, 46,* 82–100. **[32]**

Kooreman, P. (1997). The labeling effect of a child benefit system. Unpublished working paper, University of Groningen. **[14]**

Kramer, G. H. (1971). Short-term fluctuations in U.S. voting behavior, 1896–1964. *American Political Science Review, 65,* 131–143. **[25]**

Krantz, D. H. (1991). From indices to mappings: The representational approach to measurement. In D. Brown & J. Smith (Eds.), *Frontiers of mathematical psychology* (pp. 1–52). New York: Springer-Verlag. **[27]**

Krantz, D., Luce, R. D., Suppes, P., & Tversky, A. (1971). *Foundations of measurement, Volume 1: Additive and polynomial representations.* New York: Academic Press. **[2, 7]**

Krantz, D. H., & Tversky, A. (1975). Similarity of rectangles: An analysis of subjective dimensions. *Journal of Mathematical Psychology, 12,* 4–34. **[5]**

Kreps, D. M. (1988). Static choice in the presence of unforseen contingencies. Working Paper, Stanford Graduate School of Business, Stanford, CA. [22]

Kuhn, T. S. (1962). *The structure of scientific revolutions*. Chicago: University of Chicago Press. [35]

Kunreuther, H., Easterling, D., Desvousges, W., & Slovic, P. (1990). Public-attitudes toward siting a high-level nuclear waste repository in Nevada. *Risk Analysis, 10*, 469–484. [8]

Kunreuther, H., Ginsberg, R., Miller, L., Sagi, P., Slovic, P., Borkan, B., & Katz, N. (1978). *Disaster insurance protection: Public policy lessons*. New York: Wiley. [2, 13, 35]

Kunreuther, H., Hogarth, R., & Meszaros, J. (1993). Insurer ambiguity and market failure, *Journal of Risk and Uncertainty, 7*, 71–87. [13]

Kuran, T. (1983, June). Asymmetric price rigidity and inflationary bias. *American Economic Review, 73*, 373–382. [18]

Laisney, F., Pohlmeier, W., & Staat, M. (1992). Estimation of labor supply functions using panel data: A survey. In L. Matyas, & P. Sevestre (Eds.). *The econometrics of panel data: Handbook of theory and applications*. Boston: Kluwer. [20]

Lakatos, I., & Musgrave, A. (Eds.). (1970). *Criticism and the growth of scientific knowledge*. Cambridge, UK: Cambridge University Press. [35]

Lakonishok, J., Shleifer, A., & Vishny, R. (1992). The structure and performance of the money management industry. *Brookings Papers: Micro-economics*, 339–391. [17]

Lakonishok, J., & Smidt, S. (1986). Volume for winners and losers: Taxation and other motives for stock trading. *Journal of Finance, 41*, 951–974. [21]

Lakshmi-Ratan, R. A., Lanning, S. G., & Rotondo, J. A. (1991). An Aggregate Contextual Choice Model for Estimating Demand for New Products from a Laboratory Choice Experiment. *J. Business Res., 23*, 201–218. [29]

Landau, M., & Chisholm, D. (1990). Fault analysis, professional football, and the arrogance of optimism: An essay on the methodology of administration. Working Paper, University of California, Los Angeles. [22]

Landsberger, M. (1971). Consumer discount rate and the horizon: New evidence. *Journal of Political Economy, 79*, 1346–1359. [33]

Langer, E. J. (1975). The illusion of control. *Journal of Personality and Social Psychology, 32*, 311–328. [26]

Larkey, P., & Smith, R. (Eds.). (1984). Misrepresentation in government budgeting. *Advances in Information Processing in Organizations*. Greenwich, CT: JAI Press. 68–92. [22]

Lattimore, P. K., Baker, J. R., & Witte, A. D. (1992). The influence of probability on risky choice. *Journal of Economic Behavior and Organization, 17*, 377–400. [5]

Laughhunn, D., Payne, J., & Crum, R. (1980). Managerial risk preferences for below-target returns. *Management Sci., 26*, 1238–1249. [22]

Law Commission. (1975). Penalty clauses and forfeiture of monies paid. Working paper no. 61. London: Her Majesty's Stationery Office. [24]

Lawler, E. (1986). Control systems in organizations. *Handbook of industrial and organizational psychology*. Chicago, IL: Rand-McNally, 1247–1291. [22]

Lawler, E., & Rhode, J. (1976). *Information and control in organizations*. Pacific Palisades, CA: Goodyear. [22]

Lea, S. E. G., Tarpy, R. M., & Webley, P. (1987). *The individual in the economy*. Cambridge: Cambridge University Press. [19]

Lebow, R. N., & Stein, J. G. (1987). Beyond deterrence. *Journal of Social Issues, 43*, 5–71. [25]

Leclerc, F., Schmidt, B., & Dube, L. (1995). Decision making and waiting time: Is time like money? *Journal of Consumer Research, 22,* 110–119. **[14]**

Leibowitz, M. L., & Langetieg, T. C. (1989, January). Shortfall risks and the asset allocation decision: A simulation analysis of stock and bond risk profiles. Salomon Brothers Research Department. **[17]**

Leijonhufvud, A. (1977). Costs and consequences of inflation. In G. C. Harcourt (Ed.). *The microeconomic foundations of macroeconomics.* London: Macmillan. Reprinted in *Information and coordination.* Oxford: Oxford University Press. **[19]**

Levav, J. (1996). Questioning contingent valuation: Maximality and violations of monotonocity in willingness-to-pay for public goods. Unpublished undergraduate thesis, Princeton University. **[36]**

Lewinsohn, P. M., Mischel, W., Chaplin, W., & Barton, R. (1980). Social competence and depression: The role of illusory self-perceptions. *Journal of Abnormal Psychology, 89,* 203–212. **[26]**

Libby, R., & Fishburn, P. C. (1977). Behavioral models of risk taking in business. *Journal of Accounting Research, 15,* 272–292. **[17]**

Lichtenstein, S., Fischhoff, B., & Phillips, L. D. (1982). Calibration of probabilities: The state of the art to 1980. In D. Kahneman, T. Slovic & A. Tversky (Eds.), *Judgment under uncertainty: Heuristics and biases.* New York: Cambridge University Press. 306–334. **[22, 26]**

Lichtenstein, S., & Slovic, P. (1971). Reversals of preference between bids and choices in gambling decisions. *Journal of Experimental Psychology, 89*(1), 46–55. **[2, 27, 31]**

Lichtenstein, S., & Slovic, P. (1973). Response-induced reversals of preference in gambling: An extended replication in Las Vegas. *Journal of Experimental Psychology, 101,* 16–20. **[19, 27]**

Lichtenstein, S., Slovic, P., Fischhoff, B., Layman, M., & Combs, B. (1978). Judged frequency of lethal events. *Journal of Experimental Psychology: Human Learning and Memory, 4,* 551–578. **[13]**

Linville, P., & Fischer, G. W. (1991). Preferences for separating or combining events. *Journal of Personality and Social Psychology, 60,* 5–23. **[14, 32]**

Lodge, M. (1981). Magnitude scaling: Quantitative measurement of opinions. In J. Sullivan (Ed.). *Quantitative Applications in the Social Sciences, 25,* Beverly Hills, CA: Sage Publications. **[36]**

Loewenstein, G. (1987). Anticipation and the valuation of delayed consumption. *Economic Journal, 97,* 666–684. **[32, 33, 39]**

Loewenstein, G. (1988a). Frames of mind in intertemporal choice. *Management Science, 34,* 200–214. **[7, 33]**

Loewenstein, G. (1988b). Reference points in intertemporal choice. Working paper, Center for Decision Research, University of Chicago. **[33]**

Loewenstein, G. (1988c). The weighting of waiting: Response mode effects in intertemporal choice. Working paper, Center for Decision Research, University of Chicago. **[33]**

Loewenstein, G. (1996). Out of control: Visceral influences on behavior. *Organizational Behavior and Human Decision Processes, 65,* 2. **[31]**

Loewenstein, G., & Adler, D. (1995). A bias in the prediction of tastes. *Economic Journal, 105,* 929–937. **[10, 42]**

Loewenstein, G., Blount, S., & Bazerman, M. H. (1994). *Reversals of preference between independent and simultaneous evaluation of alternatives.* Working paper. Carnegie Mellon University. **[31]**

Loewenstein, G., & Frederick, S. (1997). Predicting reactions to environmental change.

In M. Bazerman, D. Messick, A. Tenbrunsel, & K. Wade-Benzoni (Eds.), *Environment, ethics and behavior* (pp. 52–72). San Francisco: New Lexington Press. **[38]**

Loewenstein, G., & Kahneman, D. (1991). Explaining the endowment effect. Working paper, Department of Social and Decision Sciences, Carnegie Mellon University. **[8]**

Loewenstein, G., & Prelec, D. (1991, May). Preferences over outcome sequences. *American Economic Review, Papers and Proceedings, 81,* 247–351. **[33]**

Loewenstein, G., & Schkade, D. (1999). Wouldn't it be nice: Predicting future feelings. In D. Kahneman, E. Diener, & N. Schwarz (Eds.), *Well being: The foundation of hedonic psychology* (pp. 85–108). New York: Russell Sage Foundation. **[38]**

Loewenstein, G., & Sicherman, N. (1991). Do workers prefer increasing wage profiles? *Journal of Labor Economics, 9*(1), 67–84. **[32, 33, 42]**

Loomes, G., & Segal, U. (1994). Observing different orders of risk aversion. *Journal of Risk and Uncertainty, 9*(3), 239–256. **[11]**

Loomes, G., & Sugden, R. (1982). Regret theory: An alternative theory of rational choice under uncertainty. *Economic Journal, 92*(368), 805–824. **[12]**

Loomes, C., & Sugden, R. (1983). A rationale for preference reversal. *American Economic Review, 73,* 428–432. **[27]**

Loomes, G., & Sugden, R. (1987a). Regret theory: An alternative theory of rational choice under uncertainty. *The Economic Journal, 92,* 805–824. **[3]**

Loomes, G., & Sugden, R. (1987b). Some implications of more general form of regret theory. *Journal of Economic Theory, 41*(2), 270–287. **[3]**

Loomes, G., & Sugden, R. (1995). Incorporating a stochastic element into decision theories. *European Economic Review, 39,* 641–648. **[10]**

Loomis, J., Gonzalez-Caban, A., & Gregory, R. (1994). Do reminders of substitutes and budget constraints influence contingent valuation estimates? *Land Economics, 70,* 499–506. **[36]**

Lopes, L. (1981). Decision making in the short run. *J. Experimental Psychology: Human Learning and Memory, 7,* 377–385. **[22]**

Los Angeles Times. (1996, December 31). Going after the big one. pp. F1, F8. **[23]**

Lovallo, D., & Camerer, C. F. (1996). Overconfidence and excess entry: An experimental approach, California Institute of Technology HSS, Working paper no. 975. **[23]**

Lowe, E., & Shaw, R. (1968). An analysis of managerial biasing: evidence from a company's budgeting process. *J. Management Studies, 5,* 304–315. **[22]**

Lowenthal, D. (1993). Preference reversals in candidate evaluation. Working paper, Carnegie Mellon University. **[31]**

Lucas, R., Jr., (1972). Expectations and the neutrality of money. *Journal of Economic Theory, 4,* 103–124. **[19]**

Lucas, R. E. (1989, November). The effects of monetary shocks when prices are set in advance. Unpublished manuscript, University of Chicago. **[19]**

Lucas, R. E. Jr., & Rapping, L. A. (1969). Real wages, employment, and inflation. *Journal of Political Economy, 77,* 721–754. **[20]**

Luce, R. D. (1991). Rank- and sign-dependent linear utility models for binary gambles, *Journal of Economic Theory, 53,* 75–100. **[4]**

Luce, R. D. (1998). Comment on Prelec's (1998). "The Probability Weighting Function." Working paper. University of California, Irvine. **[4]**

Luce, R. D., & Fishburn, P. C. (1991). Rank-and sign-dependent linear utility models for finite first-order gambles. *Journal of Risk and Uncertainty, 4,* 29–59. **[3, 4]**

Luce, R. D., & Krantz, D. H. (1971). Conditional expected utility. *Econometrica, 39,* 253–271. **[12]**

Luce, R. D., & Narens, L. (1985). Classification of concatenation measurement structures according to scale type. *Journal of Mathematical Psychology, 29*(1), 1–72. [12]

Lynch, J. G, & Ofir, C. (1989). Effects of cue consistency and value on base-rate utilization. *J. Personality and Social Psychology, 56*, 170–181. [22]

Lyon, J., Barber, B., & Tsai, C.-L. (1999). Improved methods for tests of long-run abnormal stock returns. *Journal of Finance, 54*, 165–201, Forthcoming. [21]

Macaulay, S. (1963). Non-contractual relations in business: A preliminary study. *Am. Soc. Rev, 28*, 55–69. [24]

Maccoby, E., & Jacklin, C. (1974). *The psychology of sex differences*. Stanford CA: Stanford University Press. [23]

MacCrimmon, K. R., & Larsson, S. (1979). Utility theory: Axioms versus paradoxes. In M. Allais & O. Hagen (Eds.), *The expected utility hypothesis and the Allais paradox* (pp. 333–409). Dordrecht: Riedel. [2]

MacCrimmon, K., & Wehrung, D. (1986). *Taking risks*. New York: Free Press. [22, 23]

Machina, M. J. (1982, March). "Expected Utility" analysis without the independence axiom. *Econometrica, 50*, 227–324. [4, 12]

Machina, M. (1987). Choice under uncertainty: Problems solved and unsolved. *Journal of Economic Perspectives, 1*, 121–154. [3, 4]

MacLean, D. (1991). A critical look at informed consent. Unpublished manuscript, University of Maryland at Baltimore County, Catonsville, MD. [27]

Macneil, I. R. (1980). *The new social contract*. New Haven: Yale University Press. [24]

Macneil, I. R. (1986). Exchange revisited: Individual utility and social solidarity" *Ethics, 96*, 567. [24]

MacPherson, C. B. (1962). *The political theory of possessive individualism*. Oxford: Clarendon Press. [24]

MaCurdy, T. E. (1981). An empirical model of labor supply in a life-cycle setting. *Journal of Political Economy, 89*, 1059–1085. [20]

MaCurdy, T., & Shoven, J. (1992, January). Accumulating pension wealth with stocks and bonds. Working paper, Stanford University. [17]

Magat, W. A., Viscusi, W. K., & Huber, J. (1988). Paired comparison and contingent valuation approaches to morbidity risk evaluation. *Journal of Experimental Economics and Management, 15*, 395–411. [27]

Maital, S. (1982). *Minds, markets, and money*. New York: Basic Books. [19]

Maital, S. & Benjamini, Y. (1980). Inflation as prisoner's dilemma. *Journal of Post Keynesian Economics, 2*, 459–481. [19]

Malinvaud, E. (1977). *The theory of unemployment reconsidered*. Oxford: Basil Blackwell. [19]

Mankiw, N. G., & Zeldes, S. (1991). The consumption of stockholders and nonstockholders. *Journal of Financial Economics, 29*(1), 97–112. [17]

Manwaring, J. A. (1987). Promissory estoppel in the supreme court of Canada. *Dalhousie L. J., 10*, 43. [24]

March, J. G. (1978). Bounded rationality, ambiguity, and the engineering of choice. *Bell Journal of Economics, 9*, 587–608. [1, 12, 28, 31, 39, 41, 42]

March, J., & Shapira, Z. (1987). Managerial perspectives on risk and risk taking. *Management Sci., 33*, 1404–1418. [22, 23, 26]

Marcus, G. B. (1986). Stability and Change in Political Attitudes: Observe, Recall, and "Explain." *Political Behavior, 8*, 21–44. [40]

Markowitz, H. (1952). The utility of wealth. *Journal of Political Economy, 60*, 151–158. [2, 5, 33]

Markowitz, H. (1959). *Portfolio selection: Efficient diversification of investments.* New York: Wiley. [2]

Marley, A. A. J. (1991). Context dependent probabilistic choice models based on measures of binary advantage. *Math. Social Sci., 21,* 201–231. [29]

Marschak, J. (1950). Rational behavior, uncertain prospects, and measurable utility. *Econometrica, 18,* 111–141. [3]

Marshall, J. D., Knetsch, J. L., & Sinden, J. A. (1986). Agents' evaluations and the disparity in measures of economic loss. *Journal of Economic Behavior and Organization, 7,* 115–127. [40]

Mazur, J. E. (1987). An adjustment procedure for studying delayed reinforcement. In M. L. Commons, J. E. Mazur, J. A. Nevins, & H. Rachlin (Eds.), *Quantitative analysis of behavior: The effect of delay and of intervening events on reinforcement value.* Hillsdale, NJ: Erlbaum. [33]

McAlister, L. (1979, December). Choosing multiple items from a product class. *Journal of Consumer Research, 6,* 213–224. [41]

McAlister, L. (1982, September). A dynamic attribute satiation model of variety seeking behavior. *Journal of Consumer Research, 9,* 141–150. [41]

McAlister, L., & Pessemier, E. (1982, December). Variety seeking behavior: An interdisciplinary review. *Journal of Consumer Research, 9,* 311–322. [41]

McFadden, D. (1994). Contingent valuation and social choice. *American Journal of Agricultural Economics, 76*(4), 689–708. [36]

McFadden, D., & Leonard, G. K. (1993). Issues in the contingent valuation of environmental goods: Methodologies for data collection and analysis. In Hausman (Ed.). *Contingent valuation. A critical assessment.* Amsterdam: North-Holland. [36]

McGlothlin, W. H. (1956). Stability of choices among uncertain alternatives. *American Journal of Psychology, 69,* 604–615. [2, 15, 16, 20]

McGuire, W. J. (1969). Suspiciousness of experimenter's intent. In R. Rosenthal & R. L. Rosnow (Eds.), *Artifact in behavioral research.* San Diego, CA: Academic Press. [35]

McKean, R. (1975). Economics of trust, altruism, and corporate responsibility. In E. S. Phelps (Ed.). *Altruism, morality and economic theory.* New York: Russell Sage Foundation. [24]

McNeil, B. J., Pauker, S. G., Sox, H. C., Jr, & Tversky, A. (1982, May 27). On the elicitation of preferences for alternative therapies. *New England Journal of Medicine, 306,* 1259–1262. [1, 19]

Mecham, P. (1926). The requirement of delivery in gifts of chattels and of choses in action evidenced by commercial instruments. *ICL. L. Rev., 21,* 341. [24]

Meehl, P. (1977). The selfish voter paradox and the thrown-away vote argument. *American Political Science Review, 71,* 11–30. [30]

Mehra, R., & Prescott, E. C. (1985). The equity premium: A puzzle. *Journal of Monetary Economics, 15,* 145–161. [14, 16, 17]

Mehra, R., & Prescott, E. C. (1988). The equity premium puzzle: A solution? *Journal of Monetary Economics, 21,* 133–136. [17]

Mellers, B. A, Richards, V., & Birnbaum, M. H. (1992). Distributional theory of impression formation. *Organizational Behavior and Human Decision Process, 51,* 313–343. [31]

Merrow, E., Phillips, K., & Myers, C. (1981). *Understanding cost growth and performance shortfalls in pioneer process plants.* Santa Barbara, CA: Rand Corporation. [22, 26]

Merton, R. (1969). Lifetime portfolio selection under uncertainty: The continuous time case. *Review of Economics and Statistics, 51,* 247–257. [17]

Messick, D. M., & Sentis, K. (1983). Fairness, preference, and fairness biases. In D. M. Messick & K. S. C. N. York (Eds.), *Equity theory: Psychological and sociological perspectives* (pp. 61–94). New York: Praeger. **[26]**

Meszaros, J., Johnson, E., Hershey, J. C., & Kunreuther, H. (1991). Framing loss aversion and insurance decisions. Working paper, Philadelphia: University of Pennsylvania Press. **[24]**

Meyer, R. F. (1976). Preferences over time. In R. L. Keeney & H. Raiffa (Eds.), *Decisions with multiple objectives: Preferences and value tradeoffs* (pp. 473–485). New York: Wiley. **[32]**

Meyer, R. F. (1977). State dependent time preference. In D. Bell, R. L. Keeney, & H. Raiffa (Eds.), *Conflicting objectives in decision* (pp. 232–244). New York: Wiley. **[32]**

Michelman, F. I. (1967). Property, utility, and fairness: Comments on the ethical foundation of just compensation law. *Harv. L. Rev., 80,* 1165–1258. **[24]**

Miller, N., & Campbell, D. T. (1959). Recency and primacy in persuasion as a function of the timing of speeches and measurements. *Journal of Abnormal and Social Psychology, 59,* 1–9. **[32]**

Mishkin, F. S. (1981). The real interest rate: An empirical investigation. *Carnegie-Rochester Conference Series on Public Policy, 15,* 151–200. **[33]**

Mitchell, R. C., & Carson, R. T. (1989). *Using surveys to value public goods: The contingent valuation method.* Washington, D.C.: Resources for the Future. **[8, 10, 35, 36]**

Modigiliani, F., & Brumberg, R. (1954). Utility analysis and the consumption function: An interpretation of cross-section data. In K. K. Kurihara (Ed.), *Post Keynesian economics.* New Brunswick, NJ: Rutgers University Press. **[14]**

Montgomery, H. (1983). Decision rules and the search for a dominance structure: Towards a process model of decision making. In P. Humphreys, O. Svenson, & A. Vari (Eds.), *Analyzing and aiding decision processes* (pp. 343–369). Amsterdam: North-Holland. **[27, 28, 34]**

Moore, M. J., & Viscusi, W. K. (1988, December). Discounting environmental health risks: New evidence and policy implications. Paper presented at the American Economic Association. **[33]**

Mosteller, F., & Nogee, P. (1951). An experimental measurement of utility. *Journal of Political Economy, 59,* 371–404. **[2]**

Myagkov, M., & Plott, C. R. (1995). Exchange economies and loss exposure: Experiments exploring prospect theory and competitive equilibria in market environments. Paper presented at the Amsterdam Workshop on Experimental Economics, University of Amsterdam. **[10]**

Nakamura, Y. (1990). Subjective expected utility with non-additive probabilities on finite state space. *Journal of Economic Theory, 51,* 346–366. **[3]**

National Opinion Research Center. (1978). *General social surveys, 1972–1978: Cumulative codebook.* Chicago: Author. **[35]**

Neale, M., & Bazerman, M. (1983). The effects of perspective-taking ability under alternate forms of arbitration on the negotiation process. *Industrial and Labor Relations Review, 36,* 378–388. **[22, 26]**

Neale, M. A., & Bazerman, M. (1991). *Cognition and rationality in negotiation.* New York: The Free Press. **[26]**

Neale, M. A., Huber, V. L., & Northcraft, G. B. (1987). The framing of negotiations: Context versus task frames. *Organizational Behavior and Human Decision Processes, 39*(2): 228–241. **[26]**

Neill, H. R. (1995). The context for substitutes in CVM studies: Some empirical observations. *Journal of Environmental Economics and Management, 29,* 393–397. **[36]**

Nelson, R. R., & Winter, S. G. (1982). *An evolutionary theory of economic change.* Cambridge MA: Harvard University Press. **[12]**

Neumann, B. R., & Friedman, L. A. (1978, Autumn). Opportunity costs: Further evidence through an experimental replication. *Journal of Accounting Research,* 400–410. **[15]**

New York Stock Exchange fact book. (1995). New York: New York Stock Exchange, Inc. **[21]**

Nickerson, C. A. E. (1995). Does willingness-to-pay reflect the purchase of moral satisfaction? A reconsideration of Kahneman & Knetsch. *Journal of Environmental Economics and Management, 28,* 126–133. **[36]**

Nisbett, R., & Ross, L. (1980). *Human Inference: Strategies and Shortcomings of Social Judgment.* Englwood Cliffs, NJ: Prentice–Hall. **[35]**

Nisbett, R. E., & Wilson, T. D. (1977). Telling more than we can know: Verbal reports on mental processes. *Psychological Review, 84*(3), 231–259. **[34]**

NOAA panel report. U.S. Department of Commerce, National Oceanic and Atmospheric Administration, Natural resource demage assessments under the Oil Pollution Act of 1990. (1993). *Federal Register, 58,* 4601–4614. **[36]**

Novemsky, N., & Kronzon, S. (1999). How are base-rates used, when they are used: A comparison of Bayesian and additive models of base-rate use. *Journal of Behavioral Decision Making, 12,* 55–69. **[36, 38]**

Nowlis, S. M., & Simonson, I. (1994). The context-dependency of attributes as a determinant of preference reversals between choices and judgments of purchase likelihood. Working paper, Stanford University. **[31]**

Nowlis, S. M., & Simonson, I. (1997). Attribute-task compatibility as a determinant of consumer preference reversals. *Journal of Marketing Research, 34,* 205–218. **[31]**

Nunnally, J. C. (1968). *Psychometric theory* (2nd ed.). New York: McGraw-Hill. **[35]**

O'Curry, S. (1997). Income source effects. Unpublished working paper, DePaul University. **[14]**

Odean, T. (1997). Do investors trade too much? Working paper, University of California, Davis. **[21]**

Odean, T. (1998, October). Are investors reluctant to realize their losses? *Journal of Finance, 53,* 1775–1798, Forthcoming. **[14, 16, 20]**

Ontario Law Reform Commission. (1979). *Report on sale of goods.* Toronto: Minister of the Attorney General. **[24]**

Okun, A. (1981). *Prices and quantities: A macroeconomic analysis.* Washington, DC: The Brookings Institution. **[7, 18]**

Olmstead, A. L., & Rhode, P. (1985). Rationing without government: The west coast gas famine of 1920. *American Economic Review, 75,* 1044–1055. **[7, 18]**

Oppe, A. S. (Ed.). (1938). *Wharton's law lexicon* (13th ed.). London: Stevens. **[24]**

Orde-Brown, G. (1946). *Labour conditions in East Africa,* London: Colonial Office, H.M.S.O. **[20]**

Osgood, C. E., Suci, G. S., & Tannenbaum, P. H. (1957). *The measurement of meaning.* Urbana: University of Illinois Press. **[36]**

Paciocco, D. (1985). Personal property security act repossession: The risk and the remedy. In M. A. Springman & E. Gertner (Eds.). *Debtor-Creditor Law: Practice and Doctrine.* Toronto: Butterworths. **[24]**

Parducci, A. (1965). Category judgment: A range-frequency model. *Psych. Rev., 72,* 407–418. **[29]**

Parducci, A. (1968). The relativism of absolute judgments. *Scientific American, 219,* 84–90. **[39]**

Parfit, D. (1984). *Reasons and persons*. Oxford University Press: Oxford. **[42]**

Pashigian, B., Schkade, L., & Menefee, G. (1966). The selection of an optimal deductible for a given insurance policy. *Journal of Business, 39*, 35–44. **[13]**

Payne, J. W. (1976). Task complexity and contingent processing in decision making: An information search and protocol analysis. *Organizational Behavior and Human Performance, 22*, 17–44. **[41]**

Payne, J. W. (1982). Contingent decision behavior. *Psychological Bulletin, 92*, 382–401. **[28]**

Payne, J. W., Bettman, J. R., & Johnson, E. J. (1988). Adaptive strategy selection in decision making. *Journal of Experimental Psychology: Learning, memory and cognition, 14*(3), 534–552. **[41]**

Payne, J. W., Bettman, J., & Johnson, E. (1992). Behavioral decision research: A constructive processing perspective. *Annual Review of Psychology, 43*, 87–131. **[27, 29, 34, 36]**

Payne, J., Bettman, J., & Johnson, E. (1993). *The adaptive decision maker*. New York: Cambridge. **[27]**

Payne, J. W., Bettman, J. R., & Schkade, D. A. (1999). Measuring constructed preferences: Toward a building code. *Journal of Risk and Uncertainty, 19*, 243–270. **[36]**

Payne, J. W., Laughhunn, D. J., & Crum, R. (1980). Translation of gambles and aspiration level effects in risky choice behavior. *Management Science, 26*, 1039–1060. **[1]**

Payne, J. W., Laughhunn, D. J., & Crum, R. (1981). Aspiration level effects in risky behavior. *Management Science, 27*, 953–958. **[5]**

Payne, J. W., Schkade, D., Desvousges, W., & Aultman, C. (1999). Valuation of multiple environmental programs: A psychological analysis. Unpublished manuscript, Duke University. **[36]**

Peloubet, S. S. (1985). *A collection of legal maxims in law and equity, with English translations*. Littleton, CO: F.B. Rothman. **[24]**

Pennington, N., & Hastie, R. (1988). Explanation-based decision making: Effects of memory structure on judgment. *Journal of Experimental Psychology: Learning, Memory, and Cognition, 14*, 521–533. **[34]**

Pennington, N., & Hastie, R. (1992). Explaining the evidence: Tests of the story model for juror decision making. *Journal of Personality and Social Psychology, 62*, 189–206. **[34]**

Peterson, G. L., Driver, B. L., & Gregory, R. (Eds.). (1988). *Amenity resource valuation: Integrating economics with other disciplines*. State College, PA: Venture. **[35]**

Pollak, R. A. (1970). Habit formation and dynamic demand functions. *Journal of Political Economy, 78*, 272–297. **[33, 40]**

Pollock, F., & Maitland, F. W. (1968). *The history of English law: Before the time of Edward I* (Vol. 2, 2nd ed.). Cambridge: Cambridge University Press. **[24]**

Pollock, F., & Wright, R. S. (1888). *An essay on possession in the common law*. Oxford: Clarendon Press. **[24]**

Pommerehne, W., Schneider, F., & Zweifel, P. (1982). Economic theory of choice and the preference reversal phenomenon: A reexamination. *American Economic Review, 72*, 569–574. **[27]**

Posner, R. (1986). *An economic analysis of law* (3rd ed.). Boston: Little, Brown. **[24]**

Posner, R. A. (1977). Gratuitous promises in economics and law. *J. Leg. Stud., 6*, 411. **[24]**

Poterba, J. (1987). How burdensome are capital gains taxes? Evidence from the United States. *Journal of Public Economics, 33*, 157–172. **[21]**

Poterba, J. M., Venti, S. F., & Wise, D. A. (1996, Fall). How retirement savings programs increase saving. *Journal of Economics Perspectives, 10*, 91–112. **[14]**

Poulton, E. C. (1989). *Bias in quantifying judgments.* London: Erlbaum. **[35]**

Poulton, E. C. (1968). The new psychophysics: Six models for magnitude estimation. *Psychological Bulletin, 69*, 1–19. **[35]**

Poulton, E. C., & Freeman, P. R. (1966). Unwanted asymmetrical transfer effects with balanced experimental designs. *Psychological Bulletin, 66*, 1–8. **[35]**

Pratt, J., Wise, D., & Zeckhauser, R. (1977). Price variations in almost competitive markets. Cambridge, MA: Harvard University, Kennedy School of Government. **[15]**

Pratt, J. W., Wise, D. A., & Zeckhauser, R. (1979). Price differences in almost competitive markets. *Quarterly Journal of Economics, 93*, 189–211. **[1]**

Pratt, J. W., & Zeckhauser, R. J. (1987). Proper risk aversion. *Econometrica, 55*, 143–154. **[17]**

Pratto, F. (1994). Consciousness and automatic evaluation. In P. M. Niedenthal & S. Kitayama (Eds.). *The heart's eye: Emotional influences in perception and attention.* San Diego, CA: Academic Press. **[36]**

Prelec, D. (1989a). Decreasing impatience: Definition and consequences. Working Paper 90-015, Harvard Business School. **[33]**

Prelec, D. (1989b). On the shape of the decision weight function. Unpublished manuscript, Harvard Graduate School of Business Administration. **[3]**

Prelec, D. (1990). A 'pseudo-endowment' effect, and its implications for some recent nonexpected utility models. *Journal of Risk and Uncertainty, 3*, 247–259. **[3, 4]**

Prelec, D. (1998). The probability weighting function. *Econometrica, 60*, 497–528. **[4, 6]**

Prelec, D., & Herrnstein, R. J. (1991). Preferences or principles: Alternative guidelines for choice. In R. J. Zeckhauser (Ed.), *Strategy and choice.* Cambridge, MA: MIT Press. **[34]**

Prelec, D., & Loewenstein, G. (1991). Decision-making over time and under uncertainty: A common approach. *Management Science, 37*, 770–786. **[32, 33]**

Prelec, D., & Loewenstein, G. (1998). The red and the black: Mental accounting of savings and debt. *Marketing Science, 17*, 4–28. **[14]**

Prelec, D., & Simester, D. (1998, March). Always leave home without it. Working paper. MIT Sloan School. **[14]**

Preston, M. G., & Baratta, P. (1948). An experimental study of the auction value of an uncertain outcome. *American Journal of Psychology, 61*, 183–193. **[5]**

Pruitt, D. G. (1983). Achieving integrative agreements. In M. H. Bazerman, & R. J. Lewicki, Eds., *Negotiating in Organizations.* Beverly Hills, CA: Sage Publications. **[26]**

Putler, D. S. (1988). Reference price effects and consumer behavior. Unpublished manuscript. Washington, DC: Economic Research Service, U.S. Department of Agriculture. **[7]**

Putler, D. (1992). Incorporating reference prize effects into a theory of consumer choice. *Marketing Science, 11*, 287–309. **[16]**

Quattrone, G .A., & Tversky, A. (1984). Causal versus diagnostic contingencies: On self-deception and on the voter's illusion. *Journal of Personality and Social Psychology, 46*, 237–248. **[25, 36]**

Quattrone, G. A., & Warren, D. (1985). The ratio-difference principle and the perception of group differences. Unpublished manuscript, Stanford University. **[25]**

Quiggin, J. (1982). A theory of anticipated utility. *Journal of Economic Behavior and Organization, 3*, 323–343. **[3, 4, 12, 30]**

Rabin, M. (1998a). Psychology and economics. *Journal of Economic Literature, 36*, 11–46. **[16]**

Rabin, M. (1998b). Risk aversion, diminishing marginal utility, and expected-utility theory: A calibration theorem. Working paper, University of California, Berkeley. **[14]**

Rabin, M. (forthcoming), Risk Aversion and expected-utility theory: A calibration theorem. *Econometrica* (in press). **[11, 16]**

Raiffa, H. (1961). Risk ambiguity and the savage axioms: Comment. *Quarterly Journal of Economics, 75*, 690–694. **[30]**

Raiffa, H. (1968). *Decision analysis: Introductory lectures on choices under uncertainty.* Reading, MA: Addison-Wesley. **[2, 12, 25, 35]**

Ramsey, F. P. (1931). Truth and probability. In R. B. Braithwaite (Ed.). *The foundations of mathematics and other logical essays by FP Ramsey.* New York: Harcourt, Brace and Co. **[6]**

Randall, A. (1987). *Resource economics.* New York: Wiley. **[24]**

Randall, A., & Stoll, J. R. (1980). Consumer's surplus in commodity space. *American Economic Review, 70*, 449–455. **[10]**

Rapoport, A. (1995). Individual strategies in a market-entry game. *Group Decision & Negotiation, 4*, 117–133. **[23]**

Rapoport, A., Seale, D. A., Ido, E., & Sundali, J. A. (1998). Equilibrium play in large group market entry games. *Management Science, 44*, 119–141. **[23]**

Read, D., & Loewenstein, G. (1995). Diversification Bias: Explaining the Discrepancy in Variety Seeking between Combined and Separated Choices. *Journal of Experimental Psychology: Applied, 1*, 34–49. **[14, 20]**

Read, D., & Loewenstein, G. (1996). Temporal bracketing of choice: Discrepancies between simultaneous and sequential choice. Working Paper, Department of Social and Decision Sciences, Carnegie Mellon University. **[20]**

Read, D., Loewenstein, G., & Rabin, M. (1999). Choice bracketing. *Journal of Risk and Uncertainty, 19*, 171–197. **[11, 14, 16]**

Redelmeier, D., & Kahneman, D. (1996). Patients' memories of painful medical treatments: Real-time and retrospective evaluations of two minimally invasive procedures. *Pain, 116*, 3–8. **[38, 42]**

Redelmeier, D. A., Koehler, D. J., Liberman, V., & Tversky, A. (1995). Probability judgment in medicine: Discounting unspecified possibilities. *Medical Decision Making, 15*, 227–230. **[6]**

Redelmeier, D., & Shafir, E. (1993). Medical decisions over multiple alternatives. Working paper, University of Toronto. **[34]**

Redelmeier, D. A., & Tversky, A. (1992). On the framing of multiple prospects. *Psychological Science, 3*(3), 191–193. **[14, 22]**

Reilly, R. (1982). Preference reversal: Further evidence and some suggested modifications in experimental design. *American Economic Review, 72*, 576–584. **[27]**

Reitz, T. (1988). The equity risk premium: A solution? *Journal of Monetary Economics, 21*, 117–132. **[17]**

Restle, F. (1961). *Psychology of judgment and choice: A theoretical essay.* New York: John Wiley. **[41]**

Rhoads, S. E. (1985). *The economist's view of the world.* Cambridge: Cambridge University Press. **[24]**

Riker, W., & Ordeshook, P. (1968). A theory of the calculus of voting. *American Political Science Review, 10*, 25–42. **[25]**

Ritov, I., Baron, J., & Hershey, J. C. (1993). Framing effects in the evaluation of multiple risk reduction. *Journal of Risk and Uncertainty, 6*, 145–159. **[36]**

Ritov, R., & Baron, J. (1992). Statusquo and Omission Biases. *Journal of Risk and Uncertainty, 5*, 49–61. **[8, 13]**

Rizzo, J. A., & Zeckhauser, R. J. (1998). Income targets and physician behavior. JFK School of Government, Harvard University working paper. **[14]**

Roell, A. (1987). Risk aversion in Quiggin and Yaari's rank-order model of choice under uncertainty. *Economic Journal, 97*, 143–159. **[4]**

Rokeach, M. (1973). *The nature of human values*. New York: Free Press. **[35]**

Roll, L. (1986). The hubris hypothesis of corporate takeovers. *J. Business, 59*, 197–218. **[22, 23]**

Romer, C. D., & Romer, D. H. (1989). Does monetary policy matter? A new test in the spirit of Friedman and Schwartz. In O. Blanchard & S. Fischer (Eds.), *NBER Macroeconomics Annuals 1989*. Cambridge: MIT Press. **[19]**

Rosch, E., & Lloyd, B. B. (1978). *Cognition and categorization*. Hillsdale, N J: Erlbaum. **[36]**

Rosenthal, R. (1967). Covert communication in the psychological experiment. *Psychological Bulletin, 67*, 356–367. **[35]**

Rosenthal, R., & Rosnow, R. L. (Eds.). (1969). *Artifact in behavioral research*. San Diego, CA: Academic Press. **[35]**

Roskies, R. (1965). A measurement axiomatization for an essentially multiplicative representation of two factors. *Journal of Mathematical Psychology, 2*, 266–276. **[2]**

Ross, L. (1986). Conflict notes. Unpublished manuscript, Stanford University. **[25]**

Ross, W. T., Jr., & Simonson, I. (1991). Evaluations of pairs of experiences: A preference for happy endings. *Journal of Behavioral Decision Making, 4*, 273–282. **[32]**

Roth, A., Molouf, M., & Murnighan, J. K. (1981, June). Sociological versus strategic factors in bargaining. *Journal of Economic Behavior and Organization, 2*, 153–177. **[18]**

Rottenstreich, Y., & Tversky, A. (1997). Unpacking, repacking, and anchoring: Advances in support theory. *Psychological Review, 2*, 406–415. **[6, 36]**

Rowe, R. D., d Arge, R. C., & Brookshire, D. S. (1980). An experiment on the economic value of visibility. *Journal of Environmental Economics and Management, 7*, 1–19. **[9, 10]**

Rozin, P., Ebert, L., & Schull, J. (1982). Some like it hot: A temporal analysis of hedonic responses to chili pepper. *Appetite, 3*, 13–22. **[41]**

Rozin, P., & Schiller, D. (1980). The nature and acquisition of a preference for chili pepper by humans. *Motivation and Emotion, 4*, 77–101. **[41]**

Ruefli, T. W. (1990). Mean-variance approaches to risk-return relationships in strategy: Paradox lost. *Management Sci., 36*, 368–380. **[22]**

Russell, T., & Thaler, R. (1985). The relevance of quasi-rationality in competitive markets. *American Economic Review, 75*, 1071–1082. **[12, 19]**

Russo, J. E. (1977). The value of unit price information. *Journal of Marketing Research, 14*, 193–201. **[19]**

Rutherford, M., Knetsch, J., & Brown, T. (1998). Assessing environmental losses: Judgments of importance and damage schedules. *Harvard Environmental Law Review, 22*, 51–101. **[36]**

Salancik, G. R., & Meindl, J. R. (1984). Corporate attributions as strategic illusions of management control. *Admin. Sci. Quarterly, 29*, 238–254. **[22]**

Samuelson, P. (1937). A note on measurement of utility. *Review of Economic Studies, 4*, 155–161. **[32]**

Samuelson, P. (1954). The pure theory of public expenditure. *Review of Economics and Statistics, 36,* 387–389. **[35]**

Samuelson, P. A. (1963). Risk and uncertainty: A fallacy of large numbers. *Scientia, 98,* 108–113. **[11, 14, 17, 22]**

Samuelson, P. A. (1969). Lifetime portfolio selection by dynamic stochastic programming. *Review of Economics and Statistics, 51,* 238–246. **[17]**

Samuelson, W., & Zeckhauser, R. (1988). Status Quo Bias in Decision Making. *Journal of Risk and Uncertainty, 1,* 7–59. **[7, 8, 10, 13, 16, 17, 20, 22, 26]**

Sarin, R. K., & Weber, M. (1993). Effects of ambiguity in market experiments. *Management Science, 39*(5), 602–615. **[30]**

Savage, L. J. (1954). *The foundations of statistics.* New York: Wiley. **[1, 2, 12, 14, 25, 30, 34]**

Schelling, T. C. (1978). Egonomics, or the art of self-management. *American Economic Review, 68*(2), 290–294. **[15]**

Schelling, T. C. (1984a). *Choice and consequence: Perspectives of an errant economics*: Cambridge, MA: Harvard University Press. **[39, 42]**

Schelling, T. (1984b). Self-command in practice, in policy, and in a theory of rational choice. *American Economic Review, 74,* 1–11. **[33]**

Schick, F. (1991). *Understanding action: An essay on reasons.* New York: Cambridge University Press. **[34]**

Schkade, D. A., & Johnson, E. J. (1989, June). Cognitive processes in preference reversals. *Organizational Behavior and Human Decision Processes, 44,* 203–231. **[27]**

Schkade, D., & Kahneman, D. (1998). Does living in California make people happy? A focusing illusion in judgments of life satisfaction. *Psychological Science, 9,* 340–346. **[38]**

Schlaifer, R. (1959). *Probability and statistics for business decisions.* New York: McGraw-Hill. **[1]**

Schlarbaum, G., Lewellen, W., & Lease, R. (1978). Realized returns on common stock investments: The experience of individual investors. *Journal of Business, 51,* 299–325. **[21]**

Schmeidler, D. (1989). Subjective probability and expected utility without additivity. *Econometrica, 57,* 571–587. **[3, 12, 30]**

Schoemaker, P. J. H., & Kunreuther, H. C. (1979). An experimental study of insurance decisions. *Journal of Risk and Insurance, 46,* 603–618. **[1]**

Schreiber, C., & Kahneman, D. (1999). Beyond the peak and end hypothesis: Exploring the relation between real-time pleasure and retrospective evaluations. Unpublished manuscript. University of California, Berkeley. **[36]**

Schreiber, C. A., & Kahneman, D. (in press). Determinants of the remembered utility of aversive sounds. *Journal of Experimental Psychology: General, 129.* **[38]**

Schul, Y. (1988). *Expectations, performance, and satisfaction.* Unpublished manuscript, The Hebrew University of Jerusalem. **[39]**

Schuman, H., & Presser, S. (1981). *Questions and answers.* San Diego, CA: Academic Press. **[35]**

Schumpeter, J. A. (1954). *History of economic analysis.* New York: Oxford University Press. **[12]**

Schwartz, A. (1983). The enforceability of security interests in consumer goods *J. L. Econ., 26,* 117. **[24]**

Schwarz, N., & Strack, F. (1990). Evaluating one's life: A judgment model of subjective well-being. In *Subjective well-being.* F. Strack, M. Argyle, & N. Schwartz (Eds.), Oxford: Pergamon Press. **[39]**

Schwarz, N., Strack, F., Kommer, D., & Wagner, D. (1987). Soccer, rooms, and the quality of your life: Mood effects on judgments of satisfaction with life in general and with specific domains. *European Journal of Social Psychology, 17*, 69–79. **[39]**

Scitovsky, T. (1976). *The joyless economy*. New York: Oxford University Press. **[15, 42]**

Scott, R. E. (1986). Error and rationality in individual decisionmaking: An essay on the relationship between cognitive illusions and the management of choices. *S. Cal. L. Rev., 59*, 329–362. **[24]**

Segal, U. (1984). Nonlinear decision weights with the independence axiom. Working Paper in Economics no. 353, University of California, Los Angeles. **[12]**

Segal, U. (1989a). Axiomatic representation of expected utility with rank-dependent probabilities. *Annals of Operations Research, 19*, 359–373. **[3]**

Segal, U., & Spivak, A. (1990). First order versus second order risk aversion. *Journal of Economic Theory, 51*(1), 111–125. **[11]**

Seip, K., & Strand, J. (1992). Willingness to pay for environmental goods in Norway: A contingent valuation study with real payment. *Environmental and Resource Economics, 2*, 91–106. **[36]**

Seligman, M. E. P. (1991). *Learned optimism*. New York: Alfred A. Knopf. **[22, 26]**

Selten, R. (1978). The equity principle in economic behavior. In H. W. Gottinger and W. Leinfellner (Eds.), *Decision theory and social ethics: Issues in social choice*. Dordrecht: D. Reidel, 289–301. **[18]**

Selten, R., Sadreih, A., & Abbink, K. (1995). Money does not induce risk neutral behavior, but binary lotteries do even worse. Discussion Paper No. B-343, University of Bonn. **[23]**

Sen, A. (1982). *Choice, welfare and measurement*. Cambridge, MA: MIT Press. **[39]**

Sen, A. (1987). *On ethics and economics*. Blackwell: Oxford. **[42]**

Sen, A. (1990). Rational behaviour. In J. Eatwell, M. Milgate, & P. Newman (Eds.), *The New Palgrave: Utility and Probability* (pp. 198–216). New York: W. W. Norton. **[42]**

Sen, A. (1993). Internal consistency of choice. *Econometrica, 61*(3), 495–521. **[42]**

Shafér, G. (1986). Savage revisited. *Statistical Science, 1*, 463–485. **[34]**

Shafer, G., & Tversky, A. (1985). Languages and designs for probability judgment. *Cognitive Science, 9*, 309–339. **[28]**

Shafir, E. (1993). Choosing versus rejecting: Why some options are both better and worse than others. *Memory and Cognition, 21* (4), 546–556. **[34]**

Shafir, E. (in press). Cognition, intuition, and policy guidelines. In R. Gowda & J. Fox (Eds.), *Judgments, Decisions and Public Policy*. New York: Cambridge University Press. **[31]**

Shafir, E., Simonson, I., & Tversky, A. (1993). Reason-based choice. Special Issue: Reasoning and decision making. *Cognition, 49* (1–2), 11–36. **[27]**

Shafir, E., & Thaler, R. (1996). Mental accounting through time. Unpublished manuscript. Princeton University. **[19]**

Shafir, E., & Thaler, R. H. (1998). Invest now, drink later, spend never: The mental accounting of advanced purchases. Working paper, Graduate School of Business, University of Chicago. **[14]**

Shafir, E., & Tversky, A. (1992). Thinking through uncertainty: Nonconsequential reasoning and choice. *Cognitive Psychology, 24*, (4), 449–474. **[34]**

Shapira, Z. (1986). Risk in managerial decision making. Working Paper, Hebrew University School of Business Administration. Jerusalem, Israel. **[22]**

Shapiro, D., & Khemani, R. S. (1987). The determinants of entry and exit reconsidered. *International Journal of Industrial Organization, 5*, 15–26. **[23]**

Sharpe, W. F. (1985). *Investments*. (3rd ed.). Englewood Cliffs, NJ: Prentice-Hall. **[41]**

Shea, J. (1995). Union contracts and the life-cycle/permanent-income hypothesis. *American Economic Review, 85*, 186–200. **[16, 20]**

Shefrin, H. M., & Statman, M. (1984). Explaining investor preference for cash dividends. *Journal of Financial Economics, 13*, 253–282. **[14, 33]**

Shefrin, H. M., & Statman, M. (1985). The disposition to sell winners too early and ride losers too long. *Journal of Finance, 40*, 777–790. **[7, 14, 16, 20, 24, 33]**

Shefrin, H. M., & Thaler, R. (1979). *Rules and discretion in intertemporal choice*. Ithaca, NY: Cornell University. **[15]**

Shefrin, H., & Thaler, R. (1988). The behavioral life-cycle hypothesis. *Economic Inquiry, 26* (October), 609–643. **[14]**

Shefrin, H. M., & Thaler, R. H. (1992). Mental accounting, saving, and self-control. In G. Loewenstein & J. Elster (Eds.), *Choice over time* (pp. 287–329). New York: Russell Sage Foundation. **[20]**

Shepsle, K. (1972). The strategy of ambiguity: Uncertainty and electoral competition. *American Political Science Review, 66*, 555–568. **[25]**

Shleifer, A., & Vishny, R. (1990). Equilibrium short horizons of investors and firms. *American Economic Review, 80*, 148–153. **[17]**

Shogren, J. F., Shin, S. Y., Hayes, D. J., & Kliebenstein, J. B. (1994). Resolving differences in willingness to pay and willingness to accept. *American Economic Review, 84*, 255–257. **[10]**

Shrauger, J. S. (1975). Responses to evaluation as a function of initial self-perception. *Psychological Bulletin, 82*, 581–596. **[39]**

Siegel, J. J. (1991). The real rate of interest from 1800–1990: A study of the U.S. and U. K. Working paper, Wharton School, University of Pennsylvania. **[17]**

Siegel, J. J. (1992). The equity premium: Stock and bond returns since 1802. *Financial Analysis Journal, 48*, 28–38. **[17]**

Siegel, J., & Thaler, R. (1997). Anomalies: The equity premium puzzle. *Journal of Economic Perspectives. 11*, 191–200. **[16]**

Simon, H. A. (1955). A behavioral model of rational choice. *Quarterly Journal of Economics, 69*, 99–118. **[12, 25]**

Simon, H. (1956). Rational choice and the structure of the environment. *Psychological Review, 63*, 129–138. **[27]**

Simon, H. (1957). *Models of man*. New York: Wiley. **[15]**

Simon, H. A. (1978). Rationality as process and as product of thought. *American Economic Review: Papers and Proceedings, 68*, 1–16. **[12, 25]**

Simon, H. (1982). *Models of bounded rationality*. MIT Press: Cambridge, Mass. **[42]**

Simonson, I. (1989a). Choice based on reasons: The case of attraction and compromise effects. *Journal of Consumer Research, 16*(2), 158–174. **[29, 34, 41]**

Simonson, I. (1989b). Consumers' choice strategies when making multiple purchases for future consumption. Working paper, Haas School of Business, University of California, Berkeley. **[41]**

Simonson, I. (1990). The effect of purchase quantity and timing on variety-seeking behavior. *Journal of Marketing Research, 17*, 150–162. **[14, 42]**

Simonson, I., Carmon, Z., & O'Curry, S. (1994). Experimental evidence on the negative effect of product features and sales promotions on brand choice. *Marketing Science, 13*(1), 23–40. **[34]**

Simonson, I., Nowlis, S. M., & Simonson, Y. (1993). The effect of irrelevant preference arguments on consumer choice. *Journal of Consumer Psychology, 2*(3), 287–306. **[34]**

Simonson, I., & Tversky, A. (1992). Choice in context: Tradeoff contrast and extremeness aversion. *Journal of Marketing Research, 29*(3), 281–295. **[29, 34]**

Sinclair, W. F. (1976). *The economic and social impact of Kemano II hydroelectric project on British Columbia's fisheries resources.* Vancouver: Fisheries and Marine Service, Department of the Environment. **[24]**

Slovic, P. (1975). Choice between equally valued alternatives. *Journal of Experimental Psychology: Human Perception and Performance, 1,* 280–287. **[27, 28, 34]**

Slovic, P. (1995). The construction of preference. *American Psychologist, 50,* 364–371. **[36]**

Slovic, P., Fischhoff, B., & Lichtenstein, S. (1977). Behavioral decision theory. *Annual Review of Psychology, 28,* 1–39. **[15]**

Slovic, P., Fischhoff, B., & Lichtenstein, S. (1982). Response mode, framing, and information-processing effects in risk assessment. In R. Hogarth (Ed.), *New directions for methodology of social and behavioral science: Question framing and response consistency* (pp. 21–36). San Francisco: Jossey-Bass. **[1, 12]**

Slovic, P., Fischhoff, B., Lichtenstein, S., Corrigan, B., & Coombs, B. (1977). Preference for insuring against probable small losses: Insurance implications, *Journal of Risk and Insurance, 44,* 237–258. **[2]**

Slovic, P., Griffin, D., & Tversky, A. (1990). Compatibility effects in judgment and choice. In R. Hogarth (Ed.), *Insights in decision making: A tribute to Hillel J. Einhorn* (pp. 5–27). Chicago: University of Chicago Press. **[27, 28, 31]**

Slovic, P., & Lichtenstein, S. (1968). The relative importance of probabilities and payoffs in risk taking. *Journal of Experimental Psychology, 78,* 1–18. **[27, 31]**

Slovic, P., & Lichtenstein, S. (1983). Preference reversals: A broader perspective. *American Economic Review, 73,* 596–605. **[10, 12, 27, 28]**

Slovic, P., & Tversky, A. (1974). Who accepts Savage's axiom? *Behavioral Science, 19,* 368–373. **[2, 12, 42]**

Smith, A. (1896). *Lectures on justice, police, revenue and arms.* E. Cannan (Ed.). Oxford: Clarendon Press. **[24]**

Smith, T. (1984). Nonattitudes: A review and evaluation. In C. F. Turner & E. Martin (Eds.), *Survey measure of subjective phenomena* (pp. 215–256). New York: Russell Sage Foundation. **[35]**

Smith, V. K. (1992). Arbitrary values, good causes, and premature verdicts. *Journal of Environmental Economics and Management, 22,* 71–89. **[36]**

Smith, V. K., & Desvousges, W. H. (1988). *Measuring water quality benefits.* Boston: Kluwer-Nijhoff. **[35]**

Smith, V. L. (1976, May). Experimental economics: Induced value theory. *American Economic Review, 66,* 274–279. **[9]**

Smith, V. L. (1985). Experimental economics: Reply. *American Economic Review, 75,* 265–272. **[12]**

Smith, V., & Walker, J. M. (1993). Monetary rewards and decision cost in experimental economics. *Economic Inquiry, 31*(2), 245–261. **[3]**

Solow, R. M. (1980, March). On theories of unemployment. *American Economic Review, 70,* 1–11. **[18]**

Soman, D. (1997). Contextual effects of payment mechanism on purchase intention: Check or charge? Unpublished working paper, University of Colorado. **[14]**

Speidel, R. E. (1981). Court imposed price adjustments under long-term supply contracts. *Nw. U. L. Rev. 76,* 369. **[24]**

Speidel, R. E. (1982). The New Spirit of Contract. *J.L. & Com., 2,* 193. **[24]**

Spence, M., & Zeckhauser, R. (1972). The effect of the timing of consumption decisions and the resolution of lotteries on the choice of lotteries. *Econometrica, 40*, 401–403. [22]

Spetzler, C. S. (1968). The development of corporate risk policy for capital investment decisions. *IEEE Transactions on Systems Science and Cybernetics*, SSC-4, 279–300. [2]

Starbuck, W., & Milliken, F. (1988). Challenger, Fine-tuning the odds until something breaks. *J. Management Studies, 25*, 319–340. [22]

Starmer, C. (1992). Testing new theories of choice under uncertainty using the common consequence effect. *Review of Economic Studies, 59*, 813–830. [4]

Starmer, C. (2000). Developments in non-expected utility theory: The hunt for a descriptive theory of choice under risk. *Journal & Economic Literature*. Forthcoming. [4]

Starmer, C., & Sugden, R. (1989c). Violations of the independence axiom in common ratio problems: An experimental test of some competing hypotheses. *Annals of Operations Research, 19*, 79–102. [3, 4]

Starmer, C., & Sugden, R. (1991). Does the random-lottery incentive system elicit true preferences? An experimental investigation. *American Economic Review, 81*, 971–978. [40]

Starr-McCluer, M. (1995). Tax losses and the stock portfolios of individual investors. Working paper, Federal Reserve Board of Governors. [21]

State Farm. (1990). *1990 State Farm year*. Bloomington, IL: State Farm. [13]

Staw, B., & Ross, J. (1989). Understanding behavior in escalation situations. *Science, 246*, 216–220. [22]

Stevens, S. S. (1975). *Psychophysics*. New York: John Wiley. [22, 35, 36]

Stigler, G. (1965). *Essays in the history of economics* Chicago: University of Chicago Press. [15]

Stigler, G. (1970). *The theory of price*. New York: Macmillan. [15]

Stigler, G. J., & Becker, G. S. (1977). De gustibus non est disputandum. *American Economic Review, 67*, 76–90. [40, 41]

Stigler, G. J., & Kindahl, J. K. (1970). *The behavior of industry prices*. New York: National Bureau of Economic Research. [18]

Strack, F., Argyle, F., & Schwartz, N. (Eds.). 1990. *Subjective well-being*, Oxford: Pergamon Press. [39]

Strack, F., & Mussweiler, T. (1997). Explaining the enigmatic anchoring effect: Mechanisms of selective accessibility. *Journal of Personality & Social Psychology, 73*, 437–446. [36]

Strack, F., Schwarz, N., & Geschneidinger, E. (1985). Happiness and reminiscing: The role of time perspective, affect, and mode of thinking. *Journal of Personality and Social Psychology, 49*(6), 1460–1469. [39]

Strotz, R. H. (1955). Myopia and inconsistency in dynamic utility maximization. *Review of Economic Studies, 23*(3), 165–180. [15, 33]

Sudman, S., & Bradburn, N. M. (1982). *Asking questions: A practical guide to questionnaire design*. San Francisco: Jossey-Bass. [35]

Sundali, J., Rapoport, A., & Seale, D. A. (1995). Coordination in market entry games with symmetric players. *Organizational Behavior and Human Decision Processes, 64*, 203–218. [23]

Sunstein, C. R., Kahneman, D., & Schkade, D. A. (1998). Assessing punitive damages. *Yale Law Journal, 107*, 2071–2153. [36]

Svenson, O. (1981). Are we all less risky and more skillful than our fellow drivers? *Acta Psychologica, 47*, 143–148. [23]

Swalm, R. O. (1966). Utility theory–Insights into risk taking. *Harvard Business Review, 44*, 123–136. [2, 17, 22]

Swan, J., & Reiter, B. J. (1985). *Contracts, cases, notes and materials* (3d ed.). Toronto: Emond Montgomery. [24]

Tat, P., Cunningham, W. A., & Babakus, E. (1988). Consumer perceptions of rebates. *Journal of Advertising Research, 28*, 45–50. [40]

Taylor, B. (1979). Estimation and control of a macroeconomic model with rational expectations. *Econometrica, 47*, 1267–1286. [19]

Taylor, S. E. (1989). *Positive illusions: Creative self-deception and the healthy mind.* New York: Basic Books. [26]

Taylor, S. E., & Brown, J. D. (1988). Illusion and well-being: A social psychological perspective on mental health. *Psychological Bulletin, 103*, 193–210. [22, 23, 26]

Teigen, K. H. (1974). Subjective sampling distributions and the additivity of estimates. *Scandinavian J. Psychology, 24*, 97–105. [6]

Telhami, S. (1990). *Power and leadership in international bargaining: The path to the Camp David accords.* New York: Columbia University Press. [34]

Tesser, A., & Martin, L. (1996). The psychology of evaluation. In E. T. Higgins, & A. Kruglanski (Eds.). *Social psychology: Handbook of Basic principles* (pp. 400–432). New York: Guilford Press. [36]

Tetlock, P. E. (1992). The impact of accountability on judgment and choice: Toward a social contingency model. In M. P. Zanna (Ed.), *Advances in experimental social psychology* (Vol. 25). New York: Academic Press. [34]

Tetlock, P. E., & Boettger, R. (1992). Accountability amplifies the status quo effect when change creates victims. Working paper, University of California at Berkeley, Berkeley, CA. [22]

Thaler, R. (1980). Toward a positive theory of consumer choice. *Journal of Economic Behavior and Organization, 39*, 36–90. [7, 8, 9, 33, 38]

Thaler, R. H. (1980). Toward a positive theory of consumer choice. *Journal of Economic Behavior and Organization, 1*, 39–60. [1, 8, 14, 18, 26, 39, 40, 42]

Thaler, R. H. (1981). Some empirical evidence of dynamic inconsistency. *Economic Letters, 81*, 201–207. [33]

Thaler, R. H. (1985). Mental accounting and consumer choice. *Marketing Science, 4*, 199–214. [13, 14, 17, 18, 21, 27]

Thaler, R. H. (1990). Saving, fungibility and mental accounts. *Journal of Economic Perspectives, 4*, 193–205. [14]

Thaler, R. (1992). *The winner's curse: Anomalies and paradoxes of economic life.* New York: Free Press. [19, 36]

Thaler, R. H. (1999). Mental accounting matters. *Journal of Behavioral Decision Making. 12*, 183–206. [16]

Thaler, R. (in press). Using mental accounting in a theory of consumer behavior. *Journal of Marketing.* [1]

Thaler, R., & Johnson, E. J. (1989). The effect of prior outcomes on risky choice. Working paper. Cornell University. [9]

Thaler, R. H., & Johnson, E. J. (1990). Gambling with the house money and trying to break even: The effects of prior outcomes on risky choice. *Management Science, 36*, 643–660. [13, 14, 17, 32]

Thaler, R. H., & Shefrin, H. M. (1981). An economic theory of self-control. *Journal of Political Economy, 89*(2), 392–406. [14, 15]

Thaler, R., & Tversky, A. (1996). Myopic loss aversion in financial investment: An experimental study. Unpublished manuscript, University of Chicago. [19]

Thaler, R. H., Tversky, A., Kahneman, D., & Schwartz, A. (1997). The effect of myopia and loss aversion on risk taking: An experimental test. *Quarterly Journal of Economics, 112,* 647–661. **[11, 14]**

Thaler, R. H., & Ziemba, W. (1988). Pari-mutual betting markets: Racetracks and lotteries. *Journal of Economic Perspectives, 2,* 161–174. **[14, 16]**

Thompson, L., & Loewenstein, G. F. (1992). Egocentric interpretations of fairness and interpersonal conflict. *Organizational Behavior and Human Decision Processes, 51* (2): 176–197. **[26]**

Tiger, L. (1979). *Optimism: The biology of hope.* New York: Simon and Schuster. **[22, 23]**

Tobin, J. (1958). Liquidity preference as behavior toward risk. *Review of Economic Studies, 25,* 65–86. **[2]**

Tolley, D. W. (1990). Fantasy baseball auctions and the price decline anomaly: An empirical analysis. Bachelor's thesis. Massachusetts Institute of Technology. **[19]**

Tolley, G. et al. (1986). *Establishing and valuing the effects of improved visibility in the eastern United Staes* (USEPA Grant No. 807768-01-0). Washington, DC: U.S. Environmental Protection Agency. **[35]**

Toulmin, S. (1950). *The place of reason in ethics.* New York: Cambridge University Press. **[34]**

Train, K. E. (1991). *Optimal regulation.* Cambridge: MIT Press. **[14]**

Tune, G. S. (1964). Response preferences: A review of some relevant literature. *Psychological Bulletin, 61,* 286–302. **[35]**

Turner, C. F. (1981). Surveys of subjective phenomena: A working paper. In D. Johnson (Ed.), *Measurement of subjective phenomena.* Washington, DC: U.S. Government Printing Office. **[35]**

Turner, C. F. (1984). Why do surveys disagree? Some preliminary hypotheses and some disagreeable examples. In C. F. Turner & E. Martin (Eds.), *Surveying subjective phenomena* (pp. 159–214). New York: Russell Sage Foundation. **[35]**

Turner, C. F., & Krauss, E. (1978). Fallible indicators of the subjective state of the nation. *American Psychologist. 33,* 456–470. **[35]**

Turner, C. F., & Martin, E. (Eds.). (1981). *Surveys of subjective phenomena.* Washington, DC: National Academy Press. **[35]**

Turner, C. F., & Martin, E. (Eds.). (1984). *Surveying subjective phenomena.* New York: Russell Sage Foundation. **[35]**

Tursky, B., Lodge, M., Foley, M. A., Reeder, R., & Foley, H. (1976). Evaluation of the cognitive component of political issues by use of classical conditioning. *Journal of Personality and Social Psychology, 34,* 865–873. **[25]**

Tversky, A. (1967). Additivity, utility and subjective probability. *Journal of Mathematical Psychology, 4,* 175–201. **[2]**

Tversky, A. (1967). Utility theory and additivity analysis of risky choices. *Journal of Experimental Psychology, 75,* 27–36. **[5, 6]**

Tversky, A. (1969). Intransitivity of preferences. *Psychological Review, 76,* 31–48. **[2, 3, 12, 27]**

Tversky, A. (1972). Elimination by aspects: A theory of choice. *Psychological Review, 79,* 281–299. **[2]**

Tversky, A. (1977a). Features of similarity. *Psychological Review, 84,* 327–352. **[28]**

Tversky, A. (1977b). On the elicitation of preferences: Descriptive and prescriptive considerations. In D. Bell, R. L. Kenney, & H. Raiffa (Eds.), *Conflicting objectives in decisions. International Series on Applied Systems Analysis* (pp. 209–222). New York: Wiley. **[1]**

Tversky, A. (1988). Context effects and argument based choice. Paper presented at Association for Consumer Research Conference, Maui, Hawaii. [41]

Tversky, A., & Bar-Hillel, M. (1983). Risk: The long Run and the short. *Journal of Experimental Psychology: Human Learning Memory and Cognition, 9*, 713–717. [14, 17, 22]

Tversky, A., & Fox, C. (1995). Weighting risk and uncertainty. *Psychological Review, 102*(2), 269–283. [4, 6, 26, 30]

Tversky, A., & Gati, I. (1978). Studies of similarity. In E. Rosch & B. Lloyd (Eds.), *Cognition and categorization* (pp. 79–98). Hillsdale, NJ: Erlbaum. [28]

Tversky, A., & Griffin, D. (1991). Endowment and contrast in judgments of well-being. In F. Strack, M. Argyle, & N. Schwarz (Eds.), *Subjective well-being* Elmsford, NY: Pergamon Press. [19, 38]

Tversky, A., & Griffin, D. (1991). Endowment and contrast in judgments of well-being. In R. J. Zeckhauser (Ed.), *Strategy and choice* (pp. 297–318). Cambridge, MA: MIT Press. [32]

Tversky, A., & Kahneman, D. (1971). Belief in the law of small numbers. *Psychological Bulletin, 76*, 105–110. [36, 38]

Tversky, A., & Kahneman, D. (1973). Availability: A heuristic for judging frequency and probability. *Cognitive Psychology, 5*(2), 207–232. [26, 35]

Tversky, A., & Kahneman, D. (1974). Judgment under uncertainty: Heuristics and biases. *Science, 185*(4157), 1124–1131. [2, 10, 15, 28]

Tversky, A, & D. Kahneman. (1981). The framing of decisions and the psychology of choice. *Science, 211*(4481), 453–458. [1, 12, 13, 14, 27, 35]

Tversky, A., & Kahneman, D. (1982a). Evidential Impact of Base Rates. In D. Kahneman, P. Slovic, & A. Tversky (Eds.), *Judgment Under Uncertainty: Heuristics and Biases* (pp. 153–160). Cambridge University Press. [36]

Tversky, A., & Kahneman, D. (1983). Extensional vs. intuitive reasoning: The conjunction fallacy in probability judgment. *Psychological Review, 90*, 293–315. [12, 13, 19, 22, 36, 38]

Tversky, A., & Kahneman, D. (1986). Rational Choice and the Framing of Decisions. *Journal of Business, 59*, S251–S278. [3, 5, 18, 19, 22, 25, 26, 27, 34, 36, 42]

Tversky, A., & Kahneman, D. (1990). Reference theory of choice and exchange. Working paper, Stanford, University. [33]

Tversky, A., & Kahneman, D. (1991a). Loss aversion in riskless choice: A reference-dependent model. *Quarterly Journal of Economics, 106*, 1039–1061. [3, 8, 10, 13, 17, 19, 20, 26, 29, 36, 38, 40, 42]

Tversky, A., & Kahneman, D. (1991b). Reference theory of choice and exchange. *Quart. J. Economics*, 1039–1061. [22]

Tversky, A., & Kahneman, D. (1992). Advances in prospect theory: Cumulative representation of uncertainty. *Journal of Risk and Uncertainty, 5*, 297–323. [4, 5, 6, 7, 14, 17, 22, 42]

Tversky, A., & Koehler, D. K. (1994). Support theory: A nonextensional representation of subjective probability. *Psychological Review, 101*, 547–567. [5, 6]

Tversky, A., Sattath, S., & Slovic, P. (1988). Contingent weighting in judgment and choice. *Psychological Review, 95*(3), 371–384. [3, 7, 10, 27, 30, 31, 34, 39]

Tversky, A., & Thaler, R. H. (1992). Preference reversals. In R. H. Thaler (Ed.). *The winner's curse: Paradoxes of economic life.* New York: The Free Press. [36]

Tversky, A., & Shafir, E. (1992). The disjunction effect in choice under uncertainty. *Psychological Science, 3*(5), 305–309. [34]

Tversky, A., & Shafir, E. (1992). Choice under conflict: The dynamics of deferred decision. *Psychological Science, 3*(6), 358–361. **[34]**

Tversky, A., & Simonson, I. (1993). Context dependent preferences: The relative advantage model. *Management Science, 39*(10), 1179–1189. **[27, 34]**

Tversky, A., Slovic, P., & Kahneman, D. (1990). The causes of preference reversal. *American Economic Review, 80,* 204–217. **[3, 10, 27, 42]**

Tversky, A., & Thaler, R. (1990). Anomalies: Preference reversals. *Journal of Economic Perspectives, 4*(2), 201–211. **[27, 30]**

Tversky, A., & Wakker, P. (1995). Risk attitudes and decision weights. *Econometrica, 63*(6), 1255–1280. **[4, 5, 6, 30]**

United Press International. (1990, September 13). The new Madrid fault and the prophecy of Iben Browning. **[13]**

United States Congress Committee on Government Operations. Teton Dam disaster. (1976, September 23). Union calendar no. 837, House Report no. 94–1667. **[15]**

United States Senate hearings before the Subcommittee on Consumer Affairs of the Committee on Banking, Housing and Urban Affairs. (1975, October 9). **[15]**

Van Dam, C. (1975, March). Another look at inconsistency in financial decision-making. Presented at the seminar on recent research in finance and monetary economics, Cergy-Pontoise, France. **[2]**

Van Praag, B. M. S. (1971). The individual welfare function of income in Belgium: An empirical investigation. *European Economic Review, 20,* 337–369. **[7]**

Van de Stadt, H., Kapteyn, A., & Van der Geer, S. (1985). The relativity of utility: Evidence from panel data. *Review of Economics and Statistics, 67,* 179–187. **[7]**

Varey, C. A., & Kahneman, D. (1992). Experiences extended across time: Evaluation of moments and episodes. *Journal of Behavioral Decision Making, 5*(3), 169–185. **[36, 38, 42]**

Varey, C., & Kahneman, D. (in press). The integration of aversive experiences over time: Normative considerations and lay intuitions. *Journal of Behavioral Decision Making.* **[32]**

Varian, H. R. (1984). *Microeconomic analysis.* New York: Norton. **[7, 36]**

Venkatesan, M. (1973). Cognitive consistency and novelty seeking. *In Consumer behavior: Theoretical sources.* S. Ward & T. S. Robertson (Eds.). Englewood Cliffs, NJ: Prentice-Hall, 355–384. **[41]**

Viscusi, W. K. (1989). Prospective reference theory: Toward an explanation of the paradoxes. *Journal of Risk and Uncertainty, 2,* 235–264. **[3, 5]**

Viscusi, W. K., Magat, W. A., & Huber, J. (1987). An investigation of the rationality of consumer valuations of multiple health risks. *RAND Journal of Economics, 18,* 465–479. **[7, 8, 10, 22, 26]**

von Neumann, J., & Morgenstern, O. (1944). *Theory of Games and Economic Behavior.* Princeton, NJ: Princeton University Press. **[1, 2, 12, 15, 25, 34]**

von Neumann, J., & Morgenstern, O. (1947). *Theory of games and economic behavior* (2nd ed.). Princeton NJ: Princeton University Press. **[1]**

von Winterfeldt, D., & Edwards, W. (1986). *Decision analysis and behavioral resarch.* New York: Cambridge. **[27, 35]**

Waddams, S. M. (1991). *The law of damages.* Toronto: Canada Law Book. **[24]**

Waddams, S. M. (1984). *The law of contracts* (2nd ed.). Toronto: Canada Law Book. **[24]**

Wagenaar, W. A. (1989). *Paradoxes of gambling behavior.* London: Erlbaum. **[35]**

Wakker, P. P. (1989a). *Additive representations of preferences: A new foundation in decision analysis.* Dordrecht, The Netherlands: Kluwer Academic Publishers. **[3, 7]**

Wakker, P. (1989b). Continuous subjective expected utility with non-additive probabilities. *Journal of Mathematical Economics, 18*(1), 1–27. **[3]**

Wakker, P. P. (1994). Separating marginal utility and probabilistic risk aversion. *Theory and Decision, 36*, 1–44. **[3, 4, 5]**

Wakker, P. P., Thaler, R. H., & Tversky, A. (1997). Probabilistic insurance. *Journal of Risk and Uncertainty, 15*, 5–26. **[16]**

Wakker, P. P., & Tversky, A. (1993). An axiomatization of cumulative prospect theory. *Journal of Risk and Uncertainty, 7*, 147–176. **[3, 5]**

Wakker, P. P., & Zank, H. (1997). A simple axiomatization of rank-dependent utility and cumulative prospect theory with constant proportional risk aversion. Working paper, Tilburg University. The Netherlands. **[4]**

Waldman, M. (1994). Systematic errors and the theory of natural selection. *American Economic Review, 84*, 482–497. **[23]**

Wales, T. J., (1973). Estimation of a labor supply curve for self-employed business proprietors. *International Economic Review, 14* (1), 69–80. **[20]**

Watson, S., & Buede, D. (1988). *Decision synthesis.* New York: Cambridge University Press. **[35]**

Weber, M., & Camerer, C. (1987). Recent developments in modeling preferences under risk. *OR Spektrum, 9*, 129–151. **[33]**

Weber, M., & Camerer, C. (1998). The disposition effect in securities trading: An experimental analysis. *Journal of Economic Behavior and Organization, 33*, 167–184. **[16, 20, 21]**

Weber, R. J. (1982). The Allais paradox, Dutch auctions, and alpha-utility theory. Working paper, Northwestern University, Evanston, IL. **[12]**

Wedell, D. H. (1991). Distinguishing among models of contextually induced preference reversals. *J. Experimental Psych: Learning, Memory, and Cognition, 17*, 767–778. **[29, 34]**

Wehrung, D. A. (1989). Risk taking over gains and losses: A study of oil executives, *Annals of Operations Research, 19*, 115–139. **[3, 5, 22]**

Weil, P. (1989). The equity premium puzzle and the risk-free rate puzzle. *Journal of Monetary Economics, 24*, 401–421. **[17]**

Weinstein, N. D. (1980). Unrealistic optimism about future life events. *Journal of Personality and Social Psychology, 39*(5), 806–820. **[23]**

Weiss, Y., Hall, A., & Dong, F. (1980). The effect of price and income in the investment in schooling: *Journal of Human Resources, 15*, 611–640. **[15]**

Wertenbroch, K. (1996). Consumption self-control via purchase rationing. Working paper, Yale University. **[14]**

Weymark, J. A. (1981). Generalized gini inequality indices. *Mathematical Social Sciences, 1*, 409–430. **[3]**

Wickens, C. D. (1984). *Engineering psychology and human performance.* Columbus, OH: Merrill. **[28]**

Wicklund, R. A., & Brehm, J. W. (1976). *Perspectives on cognitive dissonance.* Hillsdale, NJ: Erlbaum. **[34]**

Wildavsky, A. (1988). *Searching for safety.* NJ: New Brunswick, Transaction Books. **[22]**

Williams, A. C. (1966). Attitudes toward speculative risks as an indicator of attitudes toward pure risks. *Journal of Risk and Insurance, 33*, 577–586. **[2]**

Willig, R. D. (1976, September). Consumer's surplus without apology. *American Economic Review, 66*, 589–597. **[9]**

Wilson, T. D., Houston, C. E., Etling, K. M., & Brekke, N. (1996). A new look at anchoring effects: Basic anchoring and its antecedents. *Journal of Experimental Psychology: General, 125,* 387–402. **[36]**

Wilson, T. D., & Schooler, J. W. (1991). Thinking too much: Introspection can reduce the quality of preferences and decisions. *Journal of Personality and Social Psychology, 60*(2), 181–192. **[34]**

Winer, R. S. (1986). A reference price model of brand choice for frequently purchased products. *Journal of Consumer Research, 13,* 250–256. **[7]**

Winter, R. (1991). The liability insurance market. *Journal of Economic Perspectives, 5,* 115–136. **[13]**

Winter, S. (1975). Optimization and evaluation in the theory of the firm. In R. Day & T. Groves (Eds.). *Adaptive economic Models.* New York: Academic Press. **[15]**

Wolcher, L. E. (1988). The accommodation of regret in contract remedies. *Iowa L. Rev., 73,* 797. **[24]**

Wright, J. (1997). The subjective representation of monetary differences: A constructive approach. Working paper, The University of Chicago. **[31]**

Wright, P. L., & Kriewall, M. A. (1980, August). State-of-mind effects on the accuracy with which utility functions predict marketplace choice. *Journal of Marketing Research, 17,* 277–293. **[41]**

Wu, G., & Gonzalez, R. (1996b). Curvature of the probability weighting function. *Management Science, 42,* 1676–1690. **[4, 5, 6]**

Wu, G., & Gonzalez, R. (1998a). Common consequence condition in decision making under risk. *Risk and Uncertainty, 16,* 113–135. **[4, 6]**

Wu, G., & Gonzalez, R. (1998b). Dominance violations and event splitting. Unpublished manuscript, University of Chicago Graduate School of Business, Chicago, IL. **[6]**

Wu, G., & Gonzalez, R. (1998c). Nonlinearity of decision weights in decision making under uncertainty, Unpublished manuscript, University of Chicago Graduate School of Business, Chicago, IL. **[6]**

Yaari, M. E. (1964, September). On the consumer's lifetime allocation process. *International Economic Review, 5,* 304–317. **[33]**

Yaari, M. E. (1984). Risk aversion without decreasing marginal utility. Report series in theoretical economics. London: London School of Economics. **[12]**

Yaari, M. E. (1987). The dual theory of choice under risk. *Econometrica, 55,* 95–115. **[3, 17]**

Yaari, M. E., & Bar Hillel, M. (1984). On dividing justly. *Social Choice and Welfare,* I. 1–24. **[19]**

Zajac, E. E. (1978). *Fairness or efficiency: An introduction to public utility pricing.* Cambridge: Ballinger. **[18]**

Zajac, E. E. (1985). Perceived economic justice: The example of public utility regulation. In H. P. Young (Ed.). *Cost allocation: Methods, principles and applications.* Amsterdam: North-Holland. **[18]**

Zajonc, R. B. (1980). "Feeling and thinking: Preference need no inferences" *American Psychologist, 35,* 151–175. **[34, 42]**

Zaller, J. (1992). *The nature and origins of mass opinion.* Cambridge, UK: Cambridge University Press. **[36]**

Zelizer, V. A. (1994). *The social meaning of money: Pin money, paychecks, proof relief, and other currencies.* New York, Basic Books.

Author Index

Subject Index

treat their customers fairly are not motivated in each case by the anticipation of sanctions.

V. ECONOMIC CONSEQUENCES

The findings of this study suggest that many actions that are both profitable in the short run and not obviously dishonest are likely to be perceived as unfair exploitations of market power.[3] Such perceptions can have significant consequences if they find expression in legislation or regulation (Zajac, 1978; forthcoming). Further, even in the absence of government intervention, the actions of firms that wish to avoid a reputation for unfairness will depart in significant ways from the standard model of economic behavior. The survey results suggest four propositions about the effects of fairness considerations on the behavior of firms in customer markets, and a parallel set of hypotheses about labor markets.

A. Fairness in Customer Markets

Proposition 1: *When excess demand in a customer market is unaccompanied by increases in suppliers' costs, the market will fail to clear in the short run.*

Evidence supporting this propositions was described by Phillip Cagan (1979), who concluded from a review of the behavior of prices that, "Empirical studies have long found that short-run shifts in demand have small and often insignificant effects [on prices]" (p. 18). Other consistent evidence comes from studies of disasters, where prices are often maintained at their reference levels although supplies are short (Douglas Dacy and Howard Kunreuther, 1969).

A particularly well-documented illustration of the behavior predicted in proposition 1 is provided by Alan Olmstead and Paul Rhode (1985). During the spring and summer of 1920 there was a severe gasoline shortage in the U.S. West Coast where Standard Oil of California (SOCal) was the dominant supplier. There were no government-imposed price controls, nor was there any threat of such controls, yet SOCal reacted by imposing allocation and rationing schemes while maintaining prices. Prices were actually higher in the East in the absence of any shortage. Significantly, Olmstead and Rhode note that the eastern firms had to purchase crude at higher prices while SOCal, being vertically integrated, had no such excuse for raising price. They conclude from confidential SOCal documents that SOCal officers "... were clearly concerned with their public image and tried to maintain the appearance of being 'fair'" (p. 1053).

---

[3] This conclusion probably holds in social and cultural groups other than the Canadian urban samples studied here, although the detailed rules of fairness for economic transactions may vary.

Proposition 2: *When a single supplier provides a family of goods for which there is differential demand without corresponding variation of input costs, shortages of the most valued items will occur.*

There is considerable support for this proposition in the pricing of sport and entertainment events, which are characterized by marked variation of demand for goods or services for which costs are about the same (Thaler, 1985). The survey responses suggest that charging the market-clearing price for the most popular goods would be judged unfair.

Proposition 2 applies to cases such as those of resort hotels that have in-season and out-of-season rates which correspond to predictable variations of demand. To the extent that constraints of fairness are operating, the price adjustments should be insufficient, with excess demand at the peak. Because naive accounting does not properly distinguish between marginal and average costs, customers and other observers are likely to adopt offpeak prices as a reference in evaluating the fairness of the price charged to peak customers. A revenue-maximizing (low) price in the off-season may suggest that the profits achievable at the peak are unfairly high. In spite of a substantial degree of within-season price variation in resort and ski hotels, it appears to be the rule that most of these establishments face excess demand during the peak weeks. One industry explanation is: "If you gouge them at Christmas, they won't be back in March."

Proposition 3: *Price changes will be more responsive to variations of costs than to variations of demand, and more responsive to cost increases than to cost decreases.*

The high sensitivity of prices to short-run variations of costs is well documented (Cagan). The idea of asymmetric price rigidity has a history of controversy (Timur Kuran, 1983; Solow; George Stigler and James Kindahl, 1970) and the issue is still unsettled. Changes of currency values offer a potential test of the hypothesis that cost increases tend to be passed on quickly and completely, whereas cost decreases can be retained at least in part. When the rate of exchange between two currencies changes after a prolonged period of stability, the prediction from Proposition 3 is that upward adjustments of import prices in one country will occur faster than the downward adjustments expected in the other.

Proposition 4: *Price decreases will often take the form of discounts rather than reductions in the list or posted price.*

This proposition is strongly supported by the data of Stigler and Kindahl. Casual observation confirms that temporary discounts are much more common than temporary surcharges. Discounts have the important advantage that their subsequent cancellation will elicit less resistance than an increase in posted price. A temporary surcharge is especially aversive because it does not have the prospect of becoming a reference price and can only be coded as a loss.

B. Fairness in Labor Markets

A consistent finding of this study is the similarity of the rules of fairness that apply to prices, rents, and wages. The correspondence extends to the economic predictions that may be derived for the behavior of wages in labor markets and of prices in customer markets. The first proposition about prices asserted that resistance to the exploitation of short-term fluctuations of demand could prevent markets from clearing. The corresponding prediction for labor markets is that wages will be relatively insensitive to excess supply.

The existence of wage stickiness is not in doubt, and numerous explanations have been offered for it. An entitlement model of this effect invokes an implicit contract between the worker and the firm. Like other implicit contract theories, such a model predicts that wage changes in a firm will be more sensitive to recent firm profits than to local labor market conditions. However, unlike the implicit contract theories that emphasize risk shifting (Costas Azariadis, 1975; Martin Baily, 1974; Donald Gordon, 1974), explanations in terms of fairness (Akerlof, 1979, 1982; Okun; Solow) lead to predictions of wage stickiness even in occupations that offer no prospects for long-term employment and therefore provide little protection from risk. Okun noted that "Casual empiricism about the casual labor market suggests that the Keynesian wage floor nonetheless operates; the pay of car washers or stock clerks is seldom cut in a recession, even when it is well above any statutory minimum wage" (1981, p. 82), and he concluded that the employment relation is governed by an "invisible hand-shake," rather than by the invisible hand (p. 89).

The dual-entitlement model differs from a Keynesian model of sticky wages, in which nominal wage changes are always nonnegative. The survey findings suggest that nominal wage cuts by a firm that is losing money or threatened with bankruptcy do not violate community standards of fairness. This modification of the sticky nominal wage dictum is related to Proposition 3 for customer markets. Just as they may raise prices to do so, firms may also cut wages to protect a positive reference profit.

Proposition 2 for customer markets asserted that the dispersion of prices for similar goods that cost the same to produce but differ in demand will be insufficient to clear the market. An analogous case in the labor market involves positions that are similar in nominal duties but are occupied by individuals who have different values in the employment market. The prediction is that differences in income will be insufficient to eliminate the excess demand for the individuals considered most valuable, and the excess supply of those considered most dispensable. This prediction applies both within and among occupations.

Robert Frank (1985) found that the individuals in a university who already are the most highly paid in each department are also the most likely targets for raiding. Frank explains the observed behavior in terms of envy and status. An analysis of this phenomenon in terms of fairness is the same as for the seasonal pricing of resort rooms: Just as prices that clear the market at peak demand will be perceived as gouging if the resort can also afford to operate at off-peak rates, a firm that can afford to pay its most valuable employees their market value may appear to grossly underpay their less-valued colleagues. A related prediction is that variations among departments will also be insufficient to clear the market. Although salaries are higher in academic departments that compete with the private sector than in others, the ratio of job openings to applicants is still lower in classics than in accounting.

The present analysis also suggests that firms that frame a portion of their compensation package as bonuses or profit sharing will encounter relatively little resistance to reductions of compensation during slack periods. This is the equivalent of Proposition 4. The relevant psychological principle is that losses are more aversive than objectively equivalent foregone gains. The same mechanism, combined with the money illusion, supports another prediction: Adjustments of real wages will be substantially greater in inflationary periods than in periods of stable prices, because the adjustments can then be achieved without making nominal cuts – which are always perceived as losses and are therefore strongly resisted. An unequal distribution of gains is more likely to appear fair than a reallocation in which there are losers.

This discussion has illustrated several ways in which the informal entitlements of customers or employees to the terms of reference transactions could enter an economic analysis. In cases such as the pricing of resort facilities, the concern of customers for fair pricing may permanently prevent the market from clearing. In other situations, the reluctance of firms to impose terms that can be perceived as unfair acts as a friction-like factor. The process of reaching equilibrium can be slowed down if no firm wants to be seen as a leader in moving to exploit changing market conditions. In some instances an initially unfair practice (for example, charging above list price for a popular car model) may spread slowly until it evolves into a new norm – and is no longer unfair. In all these cases, perceptions of transactors' entitlements affect the substantive outcomes of exchanges, altering or preventing the equilibria predicted by an analysis that omits fairness as a factor. In addition, considerations of fairness can affect the form rather than the substance of price or wage setting. Judgments of fairness are susceptible to substantial framing effects, and the present study gives reason to believe that firms have an incentive to frame the terms of exchanges so as to make them appear "fair."